CW00503830

MANAGEMENT
INFORMATION
SYSTEMS

MANAGEMENT INFORMATION SYSTEMS

Vladimir Zwass
Fairleigh Dickinson University

 Wm. C. Brown Publishers

Book Team

Editor *Earl McPeek*
Developmental Editor *Linda M. Meehan*
Production Editor *Anne E. Scroggin*
Visuals/Design Freelance Specialist *Barbara J. Hodgson*
Photo Editor *Lori Gockel*
Permissions Editor *Mavis M. Oeth*
Visuals Processor *Jodi Wagner*
Visuals/Design Consultant *Marilyn Phelps*

Wm. C. Brown Publishers

President *G. Franklin Lewis*
Vice President, Publisher *George Wm. Bergquist*
Vice President, Operations and Production *Beverly Kolz*
National Sales Manager *Virginia S. Moffat*
Group Sales Manager *Vincent R. Di Blasi*
Vice President, Editor in Chief *Edward G. Jaffe*
Marketing Manager *Elizabeth Robbins*
Advertising Manager *Amy Schmitz*
Managing Editor, Production *Colleen A. Yonda*
Manager of Visuals and Design *Faye M. Schilling*
Production Editorial Manager *Julie A. Kennedy*
Production Editorial Manager *Ann Fuerste*
Publishing Services Manager *Karen J. Slaght*

WCB Group

President and Chief Executive Officer *Mark C. Falb*
Chairman of the Board *Wm. C. Brown*

Cover photo The Wheetley Co., Inc.

Interior design The Wheetley Co., Inc.

Illustrations rendered by The Wheetley Co., Inc.

Copyeditor Anne C. Cody

The credits section for this book begins on page 873, and is considered an extension of the copyright page.

Library of Congress Catalog Card Number: 91–70380

ISBN 0–697–01538–6

Printed in the United States of America by Wm. C. Brown Publishers, 2460 Kerper Boulevard, Dubuque, IA 52001

10 9 8 7 6 5 4 3 2 1

To my parents,
Adam and Friderika,
and to my own family—
Alicia and Joshua

BRIEF CONTENTS

C O N T E N T S

Information is now a critical corporate resource. Management information systems (MIS), which we understand broadly as information systems in organizations, make it possible to exploit this resource. It follows that an understanding of MIS is necessary for all managers and for other knowledge workers. To say it simply, today you cannot be effective in a business pursuit unless you know what information systems can—and cannot—do for your business.

Information systems are employed to rationalize business processes and increase productivity. Information systems can increase the effectiveness of managers and help change organizational structure. Finally, an information system can bring to a firm a competitive advantage in the marketplace. Indeed, these systems furnish an organization with many capabilities. Only some of them have been recognized in previous textbooks on the subject.

This book offers a comprehensive study of management information systems in the contemporary business environment. I have made an effort to ensure that both the intense changes in the organizational environment and the most recent proven technologies are discussed in their mutual interrelationship. I also provided a proper setting for information-based organizations in the information society and devoted attention to the history of ideas and technologies.

Information systems can play a strategic role in modern organizations—we all know that. However, it is not at all easy to conceptualize, plan, develop, and implement such a system. It is not easy to sustain competitive position. I have devoted particular attention to strategic information systems—both in an extensive chapter and throughout the text. A part of the general thrust of the text is teaching organizational innovation with information technology.

Here are some of the specific advantages of this text:

- Innovative use of computer and communication technologies for competitive positioning and for restructuring business processes is the principal theme of the text. A multifaceted early chapter is devoted to strategic information systems, combining analysis with numerous real applications.

- The dynamics of the current organizational environment undergird the text. Globalization, teamwork, entrepreneurship, group problem-solving processes, and other features of this environment permeate the discussion and the application examples. The chapter devoted to organizations pays specific attention to structures and processes for innovating with information technology.

- Virtually all technologies of consequence to organizational computing are discussed. Expert systems are covered in a separate chapter. Groupware, neural networks, hypertext, object-oriented programming, multimedia, digital image processing, supercomputing, and a variety of networking technologies are all discussed in the proper context and illustrated with application examples. At the same time, stress is placed on making technologies organizationally effective, rather than merely on their technical details.

- Development of information systems is the subject of a major (the last) part of the book. Planning of an enterprise-wide MIS architecture is covered broadly. Structured methodologies and varieties of prototyping are discussed at length. The vital topics of systems operation, control and maintenance, and computer-aided software engineering (CASE) are given their proper weight.

- The book relies heavily on the integration of theory with practice. Examples of successful practice are tempered with cases of failure—we do learn a lot from them. The book contains one or two extensive case studies at the conclusion of each chapter. Each of the book's five parts is concluded by a major case study. In addition, numerous vignettes in each chapter illustrate many points. *All of the cases and examples are real:* they happened in real firms, and real people are quoted. Cases were selected with extreme care: they address the central concern of the book part or of the chapter, but at the same time they illuminate major issues, such as the globalization of business, a social concern, entrepreneurship, or the role of a new technology. Altogether, the text offers hundreds of examples of how firms innovate with information technology—successfully or not. And I do believe that the cases and vignettes are interesting, to boot.

- Special care has been taken to integrate into the textbook the literature in the discipline. All of the numerous references at the ends of chapters have been referred to in the text—and have been carefully selected. They generally include the important work on the subject—both the principal sources and the very recent contributions.

The textbook has been written for junior and senior students with a variety of backgrounds and enrolled in a variety of programs, as well as for MBA students in all disciplines. The material has been thoroughly tested in several environments: as the primary graduate MIS text for MBA students; as a text for juniors who had only an introductory familiarity with computers; as a text for seniors in a computer science program; and as a text in a corporate management-education course.

Structure of the Book   The book is built in a spiral and modular fashion. Part 1 should be studied by all: it is the core of the spiral. Part 2 is devoted to the technological resources of computer systems. Part 3 presents the fundamental concepts of management and organizations, with special attention to innovation. Depending on the background of the students, these two parts may be studied selectively, or assigned as readings.

The two remaining parts of the text provide deeper understanding of management information systems, their planning, and development. Part 4 discusses, in depth, the principal types of systems for informational support, from decision support and executive information systems, through expert systems, on to the very broad category of office information systems. Part 5 teaches how to structure an MIS function and how to plan, develop, and operate information systems.

A comprehensive glossary helps those who choose a modular use of the text.

Let me now present the parts of the book in more detail.

Part 1 is the core of the text. It provides a complete orientation in the field of MIS in the context of the information society in which organizations operate today. It shows the broad array of capabilities that information systems can give an organization to help it succeed in the new economy. The overall structure of organizational information systems is discussed, and the major systems types are introduced. A discussion of transaction processing systems gives us an opportunity to both review the informational support for the functioning of a business and to lay a foundation for the discussion of the use of information systems for competitive positioning. The very extensive discussion in chapter 5 provides a broad framework for identifying opportunities for strategic information systems and offers numerous examples of actual practice by firms large and small.

Part 2 discusses the resources of computer systems: hardware, software, telecommunications networks, and databases. It also covers in detail the ever-broadening area of end-user computing. There are two principal concerns here. The first is to expose the student to the most current technological environment. The other is to show how to produce organizational results with new technologies. A thorough discussion of end-user computing at this early point will show students the extent of direct informational support a knowledge worker can have today.

Part 3 begins by imparting to the students the systems concepts that are fundamental to analyzing and designing complex entities, be they information systems or organizations. This part goes on to discuss management and organizations—with an angle. My main intent here is to discuss an *innovating* organization—the only type of organization that can succeed in the global economy in the long run. I show how, in the words of a well-known book on corporate innovation, "giants learn to dance." Global dimensions of deploying information technology are analyzed. Students go on to study the managerial roles and their informational support. Discussing the process of managerial decision making. I go beyond the techniques of rational decision making to present group decision-making processes and to introduce realistically the alternative decision-making modes.

Part 4 offers a thorough discussion of decision support systems, including their problem-solving role, their development process, and the group decision support systems (GDSS). It also discusses executive information systems as a powerful tool of management control. An entire chapter devoted to expert systems shows the role of this technology in organizational MIS, demonstrates how to build these systems, and goes on to introduce other fundamental areas of applied artificial intelligence. Learning systems based on neural networks are given special attention.

The discussion of office information systems as a vital support area for knowledge work, including a broad range of coordination tools, is all-inclusive. It covers document processing (including hypertext and hypermedia), message handling (from electronic mail to fax), conferencing (with electronic meeting systems serving a variety of purposes, from negotiation to crisis handling), and groupware which supports the teamwork vital to the performance of today's organizations.

Part 5 of the text is a comprehensive treatment of the planning, development, maintenance, and operation of information systems. It discusses the organization of an MIS function in a firm. It presents the most productive approaches to strategic planning of information systems and to valuation of alternative development projects. It tells you that internal development has become but one of several methods of acquiring a system: purchasing a package or turning to a systems integrator is increasingly common. This part does not shy away from the problems that are commonly encountered in the political environment of an organization.

Life-cycle-oriented systems development is contrasted with the prototyping methods of development. System implementation, a rock upon which many projects have foundered, is given a very thorough treatment. Techniques and tools for structured systems development—from analysis, through design, and on to testing—are discussed in depth. Computer-aided software engineering (CASE) and object-oriented programming methodology are introduced here as well.

Information systems not only bring capabilities to a firm; they also make it vulnerable. When we discuss systems operations and maintenance, we concentrate at length on the necessary controls and the auditing of information systems.

Each part is concluded with a significant *Case Study*, which places the material in the overall framework of MIS practice. In addition, you should find the glossary and the three indexes comprehensive and informative.

Chapter Structure

There are twenty chapters in the text. Each chapter has the following structure:

- A statement of *Objectives* places the chapter in the overall context of the text and states specific goals.

- A *Focus Case* or *Statement* invites the reader to focus on the subject of the chapter—with topics that are especially provocative or just interesting.

- The *Chapter Outline* lets the reader know how the discussion in the chapter will proceed.

- The *body of the chapter* follows. Glossary terms are printed in boldface. Other important items are *italicized*. High-interest *vignettes* are interspersed throughout the chapter to illustrate theoretical concepts with real-life experiences of business firms.

- The chapter *summary* helps the student to review the chapter's principal topics.

- In Parts 1 and 3, *Conclusions for MIS Practice* underscore the main points of relevance. (The themes of other parts make such sections superfluous.)

- *Key Terms and Concepts* aid students in reviewing the chapter.

- *Questions* test the student's understanding of the chapter.

- *Issues for Discussion* often introduce a new viewpoint or additional information. They may be used as vehicles for teamwork, for class discussions, and for individual research (numerous references may serve as a point of departure).

- *Problems* or *Optional Exercises* give students practice in applying concepts in chapters where this is appropriate.

- One or two *Case Studies* amplify the material with an actual application example. Frequently, these studies also complement the material (for example, the chapter where intrapreneurship is discussed contains a case study of student entrepreneurship in the field of mapping software). Principal questions are posed for each study and may serve as a point of departure for a project.

- Extensive lists of carefully *Selected References*, all of them referenced in the text, help students working on term projects or other research.

In sum, *Management Information Systems* offers what I believe is the most comprehensive study of MIS in today's business environment. I hope this is also a book to which those often-spoken but seldom-exercised words—"the joy of learning"—might apply.

INSTRUCTIONAL PACKAGE

This text is accompanied by a full complement of teaching and learning ancillaries. The following materials are included:

- *Information Systems in Context: A Casebook* by Joey George, University of Arizona.

  The casebook will give the students an opportunity to apply the concepts they learn to extensive examples of real companies' successes and failures. Epilogue sections allow students to compare their decisions with what really happened. Teaching notes for the cases are included in the *Instructor's Manual*.

- *Management Information Systems: Casebook with Applications* by J. K. Pierson, James Madison University.

  This ancillary provides numerous practical applications, featuring hands-on applications for microcomputers, along with a data disk, compatible with most commercial spreadsheet, database, and word-processing packages.

- *Instructor's Manual* by Peter Mykytyn, University of Texas at Arlington.

  This comprehensive resource includes suggested course outlines and syllabi, summaries of text chapters, classroom presentation techniques, answers to all of the chapter questions, and to the numerous case studies of the text. It also includes teaching notes by Joey George for this *Casebook*.

- *Transparency Masters*

  Over 200 masters will facilitate your lectures and classroom discussions.

- *Classroom Management Software (TestPak 3.0)*

This software includes testing, student self-quizzing, and gradebook programs, and is free to adopters. You can receive your own diskettes (available for both Macintosh and IBM microcomputers) or use the call-in/ mail-in fax service.

ACKNOWLEDGMENTS

I would like to acknowledge the students in the variety of settings where parts of this book were tested. It is my privilege to also thank the manuscript reviewers: Nabil Adams, Rutgers University; D. L. Amoroso, University of Colorado at Colorado Springs; Paul Cheney, University of South Florida; Philip Cline, Washington & Lee University; William R. Cornette, Southwest Missouri State University; Karen A. Forcht, James Madison University; Joey F. George, University of Arizona; Joan E. Hoopes, Marist College; George Jacobson, California State University, Los Angeles; Robert Klepper, Southern Illinois University at Edwardsville; Ting-Peng Liang, Purdue University; Mick L. Watterson, Drake University; Gary A. Williams, Western Carolina University.

As the book was being written, many of my colleagues, both in the academia and in industry, wittingly or unwittingly, contributed to its development during conversations with me. I would like to single out Eric Clemons of The Wharton School, Joey George of The University of Arizona, and Benn Konsynski of the Harvard Business School, as well as Roman Kadron and Patrick McGunagle of Citibank. Michael Vale and Anne Cody have vastly contributed to the readability of the text.

I would like to express appreciation to the University Seminars at Columbia University for assistance in the preparation of the manuscript for publication. Material drawn from this work was presented to the University Seminar on Computers, Man and Society on several occasions.

Last, but certainly not least, thanks go to the fine publishing professionals at Wm. C. Brown Publishers. George Wm. Bergquist, the publisher, and Edward Jaffe, the editor-in-chief, have always been very supportive. Linda Meehan valiantly led the book development team, and it was always a pleasure to work with her. I would also like to thank Earl McPeek, the book's editor, Anne Scroggin, who shepherded it through production, Mavis Oeth, who obtained all the necessary permissions, Lori Gockel, who was responsible for the photos, and Barbara Hodgson and Jodi Wagner, to whom you owe the look and feel of this text.

Finally, my gratitude will go to you if you will care to send your comments and suggestions to me through Wm. C. Brown Publishers.

MANAGEMENT INFORMATION SYSTEMS

PART ONE

Management Information Systems: Structure and Strategic Organizational Role

Management information systems support the business operations and the management of organizations. It now is virtually impossible to imagine a business or public-sector organization that would not rely on computerized information systems. Computer and telecommunications technologies have revolutionized the way organizations operate.

In broader terms, a transition to an information society has been taking place. This changing environment has produced its own demands on organizations. Much as the new technology has contributed to the creation of the new society, it has also provided a means to succeed in it.

The challenges of the information economy have created the possibility to employ information systems as competitive weapons. The use of management information systems for strategic positioning of a firm, in some cases leading to a lasting competitive advantage, is the driving force within organizational computing today.

This part of the book will introduce the structure of operational and management-oriented information systems and their role as contributors to an enterprise's competitive success.

CHAPTER 1

INTRODUCTION TO MANAGEMENT INFORMATION SYSTEMS

. . . .

I only ask for information.
Charles Dickens
David Copperfield

OBJECTIVES

This chapter will explain and illustrate what management information systems (MIS) are, adopting a broad approach to them as the "informational bloodstream" of an organization. After studying the chapter, you will appreciate that while computers and telecommunications are the enabling technologies of these systems today, technology does not in itself make for effective information systems.

We will also discuss here the essential aspects of a definition of MIS. You will learn what we mean by the terms *management, information,* and *systems* when we combine them in this definition. In later chapters, we will come back to these concepts and analyze the theoretical underpinnings of MIS in more detail.

We shall also introduce MIS as a discipline of both scholarly inquiry and professional practice.

FOCUS STATEMENT

Introducing a new editorial department called *Computers/Communications* a few years ago, a leading business magazine editorialized:

"For most of its seventy-plus years, *Forbes* has concentrated on two vital ingredients of business: people and money. But the world changes. To operate successfully in business today one must grasp the essentials of computers and communications. Not necessarily how computers work, but how to make effective use of these machines and systems that are transforming the economy and society."
Forbes, September 19, 1988, p. 8.

Today, every manager must be proficient in the use of information systems. This means that a manager must know what computers, communications, and associated technologies can contribute to the internal efficiency, managerial effectiveness, and competitive advantage of a firm.

CHAPTER OUTLINE

1.1   What are Management Information Systems?
- Definition of MIS
- A Holistic Approach to the Concept of MIS
- What Do Information Systems Do?
- Is an MIS Fully Integrated?

1.2   Computers and Telecommunications as the Enabling Technologies
- Merger of Computers and Communications
- MIS Proficiency Is Not Simply Computer Literacy

1.3   Information
- Distinctions between Data and Information
- Formal MIS and Informal Information
- Information as a Resource
- Information Resource Management

1.4   Organizations and Management
- What Are Organizations?
- An MIS Must Fit the Organization
- Management
- An MIS Must Support Managers at Their Levels and in Their Functions

1.1 WHAT ARE MANAGEMENT INFORMATION SYSTEMS?

Definition of MIS

A management information system (MIS) is an organized portfolio of formal systems for obtaining, processing, and delivering information in support of the business operations and management of an organization.

This introductory chapter will explain the concepts of this definition and—I hope—will give you an initial insight into how these systems serve organizations. Frankly, I also hope to whet your appetite for the more detailed classification and analysis to follow in later chapters.

A Holistic Approach to the Concept of MIS

In the information society that has emerged in the industrially advanced countries during the last third of the twentieth century, most people work with information rather than directly producing goods or delivering services. The management information systems (or, simply, information systems) in organizations of this society must be understood broadly. This textbook will consistently take the view that the leading practice in the field of MIS—practice which will enable an organization to thrive—must go far beyond the traditional, data-processing-oriented view of MIS. In that limited view, such a system would be used almost exclusively to keep track of things or financial events in an enterprise.

To be sure, the corporate house must be kept in order and transactions (orders, sales, payments, and so forth) must be processed. However, it is the companies that are able to use information systems for superior coordination and managerial decision making that will have the organizational foundations for success. A strong competitive position is—and will be in the future—gained by organizations that use information in a strategic fashion. Such organizations will build information into their product, make the information itself their new product, redesign their business processes, and reach their customers through information systems.

The functions of information systems have increased manyfold since the first computer was introduced into a business organization in 1954. Of course, we must not forget the weighty ledgers, sedulously kept by the bookkeepers of yore, pigeons carrying news of battles won and heralding profitable speculation opportunities for the recipient, and the clay tablets on which the Babylonians kept records as long ago as 3500 B.C.—yes, there *were* information facilities before computers. Manual calculation and nonelectronic communications have not disappeared. But would they support the complex business of today's organizations?

In the next chapter we will discuss the features of an information society. We will see what demands such a society places on organizations and what opportunities it offers them. Today's organizations have been profoundly affected by both the **technology push** created by continual innovation in information technology, and the **demand pull,** or the needs in the marketplace, arising from the growing complexity of social organizations and from the recognition of the power of information systems to solve complex problems. These two forces have led to the evolution of the MIS concept itself and have changed the nature of information systems. In turn, MIS transform organizations, the nature of work, and the products offered in the marketplace. It cannot be stressed forcefully enough that a practicing manager—or a student—at the present time must be proficient in *all* of these aspects of MIS.

A TANGIBLE EFFECT
OF INFORMATION SYSTEMS

As the economic downturn of 1991 exerted pressures on productivity, the major accounting firm of Price Waterhouse was able to reap the benefits of its advanced information systems. Owing to its extensive MIS, and particularly to Lotus Development Corporation's Notes groupware implemented throughout the firm, vast amounts of information are available to the firm's professionals and managers. Using the groupware (which we shall further discuss in chapter 16), a large firm's professionals can instantly draw on the expertise available in any office of the firm, and a manager can see the status of any project he or she is responsible for. The company can thus better serve its clients with financial advice. The use of information technology has also translated into direct benefits. The firm will need to hire fewer accountants each year: about 900 instead of 1,300.

Based on Sylvia Nasar, "Service Industry Suffers in the Economic Decline," *The New York Times*, February 3, 1991, pp. 1, 26; and on author's conversation with Sheldon Laube, National Director of Information Technology, Price Waterhouse, February 5, 1991.

What Do Information Systems Do?

The time for a more detailed discussion of MIS types will come in chapter 3, and our analysis of MIS will continue throughout the book. Already, though, we realize that in our broad interpretation of the MIS concept, these information systems include all of the following:

- Transaction processing systems for operational data processing that are needed, for example, to register customer orders and to produce invoices and payroll checks.
- Management reporting systems capable of producing reports for specific time periods, designed for managers responsible for specific functions in a firm.
- Decision support systems (DSS), expressly designed for the support of individual and collective decision making.
- Executive information systems, which support the work of senior executives and of company boards by giving them ready access to a variety of summarized company data against a background of general information on the industry and the economy at large.
- Office information systems, which support and coordinate knowledge work in an office environment by handling documents and messages in a variety of forms—text, data, image, and voice.

In a broader sense, knowledge work is also supported by computerized systems assisting professionals in nonmanagerial functions. For example, diverse professional support systems help designers, such as engineers, architects, commercial artists, or scientists who model molecular structures or study the genetic codes of living matter.

You will study the capabilities and structures of all these types of information systems in this text. Figure 1.1 visualizes the general relationships between the major categories of systems: those supporting operations, management, and knowledge work. From the organizational point of view, it is important to recognize that certain systems—of different types—are interorganizational: they integrate the organization with other firms.

In figure 1.1, operational support systems assist in the day-to-day activities of the enterprise by keeping track of its resources and commitments. Through such systems, a manufacturing company can track the inventory of finished goods, a bank can maintain the status of demand deposits for its customers, and a distributor's system can answer customer queries regarding orders. The primary function of operational support systems is thus transaction processing.

Management support systems, which will, of course, be discussed in detail in this text, assist the various levels of management in their tasks. Through such systems, managers are able to obtain summary reports on past, current, and projected activity within their areas of responsibility. Decision support systems allow managers to consider various courses of future action and see projected results in order to plan future activities. Executives are able to get an overview of the company's operations in attractive graphical form and "drill in" on any aspect they want to pursue in more detail.

Office information systems support diverse aspects of individual and group knowledge work. The range of this type of support is broad and growing. An individual may maintain his or her business calendar and communicate with co-workers through the medium of electronic mail—in some systems, also by

FIGURE 1.1

Information systems in organizations.

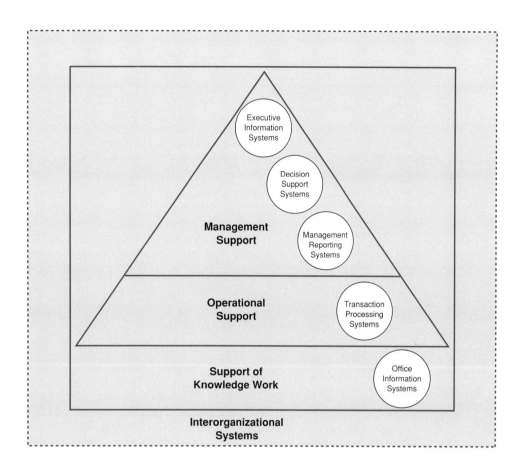

sending images. Other systems offer a variety of computerized supports for teamwork, even when the participants are widely dispersed.

In many cases, the information systems of an organization become connected to those of its suppliers and customers or to providers of information about the external environment in which the firm operates. Such interorganizational information systems speed the flow of information between companies and are frequently a source of competitive edge.

Indeed, it is increasingly common to design certain information systems to give a company a superior competitive position in the marketplace by helping it offer its customers information-related products or services that the competition will find difficult to match. An ordering system with terminals installed at thousands of client sites, or an expert system that helps to diagnose via telecommunication links how equipment installed at customer sites is operating, are prime examples of **strategic information systems.**

While they are built on a general base of MIS sophistication and supported by other information systems in the company, strategic systems often draw on leading-edge technologies. Diverse telecommunications capabilities extend computers' reach to broadly dispersed sites. Moreover, strategic systems in some cases employ **expert systems:** a software technology born in artificial intelligence laboratories and able to suggest decisions such as a diagnosis, a schedule, or an evaluation of a client's creditworthiness. An expert system bases its sug-

---

IT IS AS SIMPLE—OR AS DIFFICULT—AS THAT

"You cannot separate information technology from our business—it touches everybody and it touches every aspect of our business," says the top MIS executive at the Merchandise Group of Sears, Roebuck and Company, Robert Ferkenhoff.

Approximately $300 million, or 1 percent of the total revenue of the retailing operation, is spent annually on information systems.

Based on Michael Fitzgerald, "'When' Is Now at Sears," *Computerworld*, October 8, 1990, pp. 67, 71.

---

gestions on a stored knowledge base and the facts of a particular case. Many other technologies will be discussed later in the text.

U.S. business corporations typically spend 4 percent of their annual revenue on information systems.[1] With the increased use of these systems in line-of-business applications for strategic ends, these figures are expected to increase. Expenditures on information systems in the United States have shown a continued rapid—exponential—growth (Gurbaxani, 1990).

Financial corporations, such as banks, brokerage houses, or insurance companies are far more dependent on their information systems than manufacturing concerns. The "visible" assets of a financial company amount to bit patterns stored in computer memory, representing investments, cash on hand, or insurance premiums. Thus, small banks spend approximately 7 percent, and large banks up to 13 to 16 percent, of their budgets on information systems, with the total spending of U.S. banks on MIS surpassing ten billion dollars annually.[2]

Is an MIS Fully Integrated?

One would perhaps like to see all of the types of MIS we have discussed as subsystems of a single, fully integrated system (a supersystem, surely). In such a system, we would be able to draw on the capabilities of any of the subsystems through any other. This complete integration could be accomplished, for instance, by ensuring that all subsystems have access to the common databases and that data can flow from one system to another as desired. An ideal system with this capability, a "total system," would be designed from the outset as a single system, giving its users all the informational support they want. But a total system is a mirage, as we will presently see.

Integration of MIS is, indeed, desirable. The more integrated the portfolio (or federation) of systems is into an overall organizational information system, the better it will, in general, serve the organization. However, the term *integration* must be properly understood. An integrated system is one which conforms to a master plan supporting the overall organizational needs, assuring the requisite degree of distribution (decentralization) and communication between the subsystems. But it is *not* a single master system.

It is essential to understand that organizational information systems, particularly those in larger organizations, have not sprung to life as single entities. Rather, they have evolved over time. New systems are added to the portfolio, and older ones are more often modified and enhanced than scrapped. New hardware and software platforms are produced by vendors to offer greater functionality, frequently accompanied by lower costs as well. Moving information systems from one environment to another, and interconnecting applications that run on a variety of platforms produced by different vendors, is a daunting—and never-ending—task.

Furthermore, the highly dynamic environment created by company mergers[3] and acquisitions makes it even less realistic to expect totally integrated systems. Striving to integrate information systems (which in some organizations have accumulated over almost forty years of information processing) is an important task of MIS management. The right degree and the right kind of integration emerge only as the result of careful system planning and development. The costs of integration must be offset by the envisaged benefits. Incompatibility of equipment and software provided by various vendors is a powerful obstacle to overcome. As we shall see in chapter 7, connectivity is a technological challenge at present.

The next two vignettes illustrate the dynamics of the banking environment and the potential effects of integrating (or failing to integrate) MIS components.

ECONOMIES OF SCALE IN BANKING

As the result of deregulation in the financial services industry, banks have lost their monopoly on such financial services as savings and checking accounts. Challenged on their hallowed preserve, they have pursued all the traditional competitive strategies.

One strategy, that of cost reduction through economies of scale, has been successfully pursued by Fleet/Norstar Financial Group, Inc. Created through a merger of two financial institutions, the new "superregional" institution is consolidating all data processing into a single center, replacing four previously existing data centers. The increased efficiency arising from combining these facilities is expected to lower the annual information processing budget by 20 percent, according to Fleet/Norstar's chief information officer (CIO) Michael Zucchini.

"Fleet/Norstar was fortunate that the two banks had few incompatible systems," Zucchini says.

Note that system compatibility is an especially important consideration in proposed mergers of financial institutions, in which a large percentage of the budget goes to information processing.

Based in part on Alan Alper, "Banks Seek Higher Yield from Info Systems Investment" and Janet Mason, "Keeping Pace with Banking Race," *Computerworld*, August 15, 1988, pp. 65, 87.

First National Bank of Chicago has acquired two credit card portfolios (that is, credit-card lines of business) from Bankers Trust and Beneficial Finance. By consolidating the two lines, the bank expects to save 20 to 30 percent of the operating expenses of information systems processing. By increasing service volume while reducing cost through economies of scale, the bank expects to produce income that will help it to make further acquisitions. This will lead to further consolidation, reengineering of the bank's business processes, and even greater economies of scale.

Based on *The Business Week Newsletter for Information Executives*, August 19, 1988, p. 5.

COSTS OF FAILING TO INTEGRATE

Before 1985, various lines of business, branches, and operating units of the Bank of America had separate information systems. As a result, the Bank could not easily obtain a full customer profile from its information system. When making a decision on granting a mortgage loan, for example, it was necessary to search all the line-of-business files (checking account, savings account, and so on) to establish the extent of the total relationship between the customer and the bank. To compound the problem, each of the Bank's 950 branches operated as an independent unit, with its own reporting methods and incompatible computer systems. And finally, in international operations, there was no single database on corporate customers that would give account balances, loans outstanding, foreign exchange positions, and so forth. This information could be garnered only by accessing several information systems.

These deficiencies caused the Bank of America in 1985 to project an expenditure of $5 billion over the next five years on system development and maintenance.

Now, as the 1990s pose new demands, the Bank of America has integrated many components of its information systems. In particular, a customer information file (CIF) gives a complete picture of a customer's relationship with the bank. This information, vital to making decisions regarding the accounts, is now easy and economical to obtain.

Based in part on: Bank of America Rushes into the Information Age, *Business Week,* April 15, 1985, pp. 110–12, and Moira Johnston, *Roller Coaster: Bank of America and the Future of American Banking,* New York: Ticknor & Fields, 1990.

The following very general framework of integration presents itself. At the operational level of an enterprise, transactions are recorded and the records organized into relatively permanent databases. Once captured, the data may be processed to serve managers in their planning and control functions. The data may also be accessed for the purposes of office information systems. We will further refine this framework as we study organizational information systems.

In an influential early paper whose stimulating quality is evident from its title ("MIS Is a Mirage"), John Dearden of the Harvard Business School explored the following question, stated in the article's subtitle: "Can a single, integrated system be devised to fill all of management's information needs?" (Dearden, 1972). Many of the points Dearden raised are still valid today, and this classic article makes for rewarding reading. But let's not leave the question posed in the article's title hanging. The answer appeared in the same subtitle: "Only if Superman lends a helping hand."

As we will see later in our discussion of the systems theory, full integration of subsystems is not one of the premises of systems. The Bank of America vignette, however, demonstrates the negative consequences of failing to properly integrate subsystems: the inability to do business properly.

To ensure a directed and coherent development of their information resources, today's organizations increasingly draw up their **information system architecture:** a general model of the desired structure of the organization's information systems. We shall encounter such a model in the Case Study for this part of the text.

1.2 COMPUTERS AND TELECOMMUNICATIONS AS THE ENABLING TECHNOLOGIES

By now, it should be evident that information systems are computer-based (in fact, some authors refer to them as CBIS—computer-based information systems). A **computer** is a general-purpose information processor. Today, multiple computers are combined within information systems. They range from super-computers, costing millions of dollars and processing hundreds of millions of elementary instructions per second, to inexpensive microprocessors embedded, for example, in point-of-sale terminals. The large machines may be running elaborate economic forecasting models to position a company's products for the next two years, relying on trillions of bits of past-performance data organized into a database; the point-of-sale terminals may simply transmit the item sales data. Indeed, one of the tasks of an information system encompassing both of these computer classes is to aggregate the individual sales details into the database for long-term forecasting.

Since the late 1970s, the personal computer has been the basic tool of organizational knowledge workers: people who manipulate information (symbols) rather than handle tangible objects.

Computer programs, also called **software,** adapt general-purpose computers to the task at hand. A large application—say, an order-processing system for a manufacturer—consists of a set of programs, each with its own function within the application.

Merger of Computers and Communications

In the information systems of today, computer technology is virtually inseparable from telecommunications. Most information systems are distributed locally or geographically, and it is telecommunications technology that unifies them. Indeed, in our example, remote point-of-sale terminals are connected through a telecommunications network to a central computer that enters the transactional data into a database and processes the data as needed. This system of computers and telecommunications is a **computer network.** As we will see, it is possible to construct a variety of distributed configurations to match the structure and business goals of the organization.

The other side of the merger between computer and telecommunication technologies is the fact that modern communications equipment is itself run by computers. Both technologies are actually a package of diverse hardware and software technologies.

Thanks to local and wide area networks, the personal computer has become a true workstation. Through network infrastructure, the work of many people can be shared and coordinated.

MIS Proficiency Is Not Simply Computer Literacy

To acquire proficiency in information systems, to know what they can do for an organization, and to know how to use them to achieve those results, you must be "computer-literate." To this end, this text will analyze the technological foundations of MIS. However, we shall see that computer literacy (or, more accurately, proficiency in information technologies) is not enough to become MIS-proficient. One needs to know how to apply technology in organizational and business settings to achieve the goals of the organization.

Some of the dimensions involved in this task will become clear as we proceed to discuss various aspects of the definition of MIS. The goal of this introductory chapter is to give you an intuitive notion of the purpose and scope of information systems in organizations. Then, in the thick of the text, we shall analyze in detail the concepts, the methodologies, the tools, and the artifacts of MIS.

1.3 INFORMATION

Distinctions between Data and Information

All of us have an intuitive concept of what constitutes information. As for any intuitive notion, the ideas each of us hold about information are all probably partially correct. But how can we distinguish between *data* and *information?* Perhaps an illustration will help.

If I suddenly throw the word *five* into our discourse at this point, it obviously means nothing to you. It is a data item, but it becomes meaningful information only if it is placed within a context familiar to the intended recipient. Now, if you have just asked me, "What were the sales of the Packaged Goods division last month?" then I have provided you with information rather than data. I provided information, that is, if you already know that the sales are measured in millions of dollars.

Information, then, is an increment in knowledge—it contributes to the general framework of concepts and facts that we know. Information relies on the context (your question) and the general knowledge of the recipient for its significance. To receive really meaningful information in our example, not only would you need to know that "five" means five million dollars, but you also would need to know the previous monthly sales of the Packaged Goods division and the projections for the period under discussion.

FIGURE 1.2

An information-processing view of MIS.

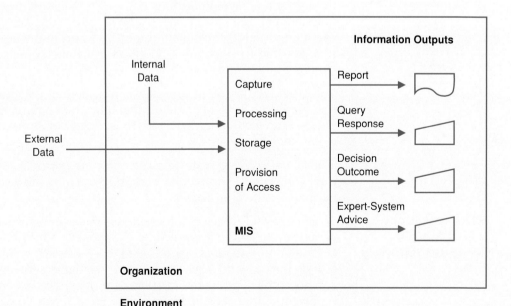

Data are only the raw material for obtaining information. Information systems use data stored in computer files and databases to provide needed information. This information-processing view of MIS is shown in figure 1.2. In the figure, MIS is shown simply as the nexus of a general set of capabilities: capture of data, various forms of processing to transform data into information, long-term storage of data, and provision of access to information.

The next chapter will permit us to broaden significantly this initial view of MIS capabilities.

Formal MIS and Informal Information

Much information flowing in an organization, and very important information at that, is informal. Indeed, any formalized information system operates within the context of informal information channels—interpersonal "networking," water-cooler gossip, or conversations with the supplier's truckers at the loading dock.

Another important point, raised in the Dearden article cited earlier, is that not all information flows require, or are capable of, computerization; in other words, "information problems do not necessarily require information systems" (Earl, 1980). Indeed, as Thomas Sowell argues, informal relationships "produce much of the background social capital without which . . . major institutions of society could not function nearly as effectively as they do."[4]

However, as I have pointed out (Zwass, 1984), the developmental axis in the field of MIS indicates that, over time, informational processes in organizations are becoming progressively formalized. The continuous functioning of an organization, its development, and, more and more frequently, its very survival, depend on formal information systems. A **formal information system** relies on procedures, established and accepted by the organizational practice, for the collecting, storing, processing, and accessing of data in order to obtain information. Formal systems do not *have* to be computerized, but those with any appreciable organizational impact usually are.

In the case of systems designed for the purpose of coordination, such as computer conferencing systems, where informality of exchange is an important goal, we will see that the system itself provides a formal structure, a framework supporting the group process of exchanging and producing information.

Information as a Resource

An organization succeeds by bringing together and managing certain **resources** in a productive way. The traditional list of resources comprises human, financial, and material resources. Only over the past two decades has information come to be recognized as another resource, one that is crucial to the management of the others and that, under certain circumstances, may be substituted for them cost-effectively.

Information shares many properties with other resources: it has value and lends itself to the process of management. Information has also its own special qualities as a resource. For example, it is not consumed or expended in the sense money is; but it does age, ungracefully, and in a different way from other resources. The data on which information is based has to be current; information must also be available in time for a decision to be rendered, and the value of information decreases as time marches on. You can certainly have too much information. As a matter of fact, one hallmark of a well-designed MIS is that it protects its users from information overload.

Most of the data collected in a company's databases and the information used by its decision makers concern the internal operations of the company. However, the importance of **external information** about the environment in which a firm operates is growing steadily. (We shall stress this repeatedly, in particular in chapter 3.) Indeed, coping and prevailing in a competitive environment requires constant opportunity-seeking through the use of information systems.

Information Resource Management

Information is a valuable resource and hence must be managed: formal information systems are a vehicle for information management. An organizational approach to information as a resource, called **information resource management** (IRM), will be discussed later in this book.

IRM is a broad approach to managing information as a corporate asset. It is possible chiefly due to our ability to organize all the data reflecting the past, present, and projected operations of an enterprise into databases, controlled by specialized software called **database management systems (DBMS).** A **database** is an organized collection of data reflecting a major aspect of a firm's activities. For example, a personnel database is the principal component of human resource management systems. DBMS include as one of their components a data dictionary facility that maintains "data about data"—a multifaceted, structured description of all the data kept in a given database.

The database environment is illustrated in figure 1.3 (pending its more detailed discussion in chapter 8). New data are entered into databases under the control of DBMS, and the needed stored data are accessed also through that system. Thus, all programs access the database through a common interface provided by DBMS—which creates the possibility of control within the IRM framework.

The organization of data into databases and the IRM approach to information form a solid foundation for the integration of information systems. As the technological capabilities of information systems develop, information bases are beginning to include nonquantitative data as well.

Managing information as a resource necessitates extensive planning of information systems on the organizational scale—a subject we shall discuss at length in chapter 17.

1.4 ORGANIZATIONS AND MANAGEMENT

What Are Organizations?

Generally speaking, **organizations** are formal social units devoted to the attainment of specific goals. Organizations use certain resources to produce outputs and thus meet their goals. For example, a business firm that produces semiconductor memory chips consumes certain resources (money, materials, labor, machinery, and information) and aims to meet certain financial objectives. A local government institution employs its resources (financed by the taxpayers) to provide a benefit for the area population—thus, a motor vehicle bureau licenses drivers and vehicles. A nonprofit hospital applies its resources to provide health care to its target population.

FIGURE 1.3

The database environment—making information resource management possible.

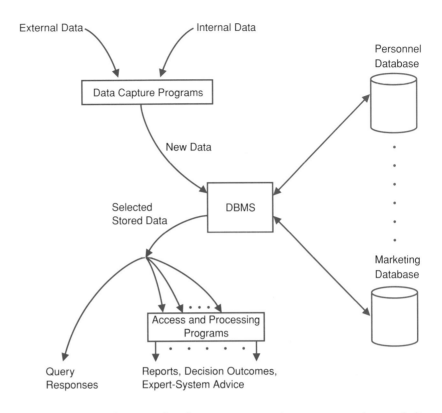

An MIS Must Fit the Organization

We will see later in the text that larger organizations are complex and diverse in the way they are managed, in their inner structures and in their relationships with the outside world. It is the goal of MIS to support both the organization as a whole and its individual business units in the achievement of their objectives.

When an information system does not fit the organizational unit it is intended to support, the system development project is likely to fail. We may observe this failure as runaway project costs, postponed deadlines, or lack of user acceptance of the completed system.

Management

Management is the process of providing an organizational environment in which individuals work and employ available resources to attain aims that contribute to the overall goals of the organization.

There are several fruitful ways to understand management. The classical way is to consider the **managerial functions:** planning, organizing, staffing, leading, and controlling. Decision making, monitoring, and coordination are information-intensive aspects of these managerial functions.

Another way to look at management is to consider the roles managers play in their work—entrepreneur and resource allocator are two examples of these roles. Detailed analyses have also been made of how managers actually spend their time; various interpersonal tasks have been found to make far greater demands on managers' time than pure decision making. However, the quality of management cannot be evaluated by measuring time allocations alone. Moreover, the information that a manager brings to bear in a meeting is often a determinant of its success.

An MIS Must Support Managers at Their Levels and in Their Functions

An MIS, obviously, is designed to support managers in as many of their functions as possible, although to different degrees. It is clear, for example, that the leadership function receives scant support from MIS, but the planning function should be extensively supported.

In our further analysis of informational support of organizations and management, we will discuss both the hierarchical and the functional support of managerial functions in the various roles managers play. Chapters 11 and 12 will be devoted to the discussion of organizations and management.

1.5 SYSTEMS

A physical **system** is a set of components (subsystems or elementary parts) that operate together to achieve a common objective (or multiple objectives). These objectives are realized in the outputs of the system. An efficient system uses its inputs economically in producing its outputs. An effective system produces the outputs that best meet the objectives of the system.

The objective of a management information system is to provide formal informational support to the members of the organization. Individual subsystems (or, in other words, portfolio components) of MIS have their own goals within this larger goal.

The general schematic view of a system is shown in figure 1.4.

The subsystems composing a system may be coupled more or less loosely. Indeed, we have already said that a wholly integrated MIS is, generally speaking, not a practical reality: components evolve over time as a system is maintained, and in that evolution they rarely congeal into a uniformly integrated system. New components are added and may not be wholly integrated into the existing structure.

The hallmark of a system, as opposed to an unrelated collection of components, is *synergy,* an effect best defined by Aristotle: "The whole is greater than the sum of its parts."

FIGURE 1.4

General schematic of a system.

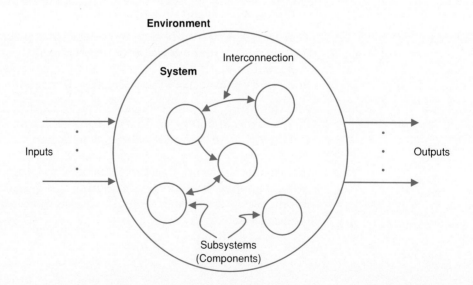

Since an organization itself may be considered a system with a well-defined place in it for MIS as a whole, and since general systems thinking has an important place in the understanding and development of MIS, we shall discuss this topic in detail in chapter 10.

1.6   WHO ACTUALLY USES INFORMATION SYSTEMS? THE ROLE OF INDIVIDUALS

Who actually uses information systems? We may answer the question in a number of ways, depending on our interpretation of the word *use:* "Well, obviously, organizations use information systems!" or "Come to think of it, it's the people who work in the organizations that use the systems."

Indeed, individuals rather than impersonal organizations work directly with information systems. Individuals interpret reports, query a database, receive electronic mail, participate in teleconferences, develop new applications for a company function, and maintain existing software. Individuals, as the word itself implies, are different. Yet, there are certain patterns in the way people exercise their **cognitive functions;** that is, in the way people acquire and handle information.

Since the impact of information depends on the recipient, it is important that systems be attuned to the cognitive functions of the individuals for whom they are intended. The well-known notion of user-friendliness is a rather superficial expression of what is needed. Chapter 13 will discuss cognitive functions as they pertain to the design of MIS.

Taken as a whole, a management information system is always a **human-machine system:** it places the computer and communications hardware, organized into a virtual "machine" by software, at the disposal of many human knowledge workers.

1.7   THE INFORMATION SYSTEM AS A SOCIOTECHNICAL PACKAGE— BRINGING IT ALL TOGETHER

The technology underlying MIS is complex and powerful. A system cannot be simply installed on its technical merits in the expectation of organizational benefits. Rather, any significant information system has to be developed to fit the present or intended structure and culture of an organization. Moreover, it must fit, or be flexible enough to accommodate, the working styles of the individuals who will use it. We can conceptualize these three aspects of system development in figure 1.5.

Technology comprises computer system hardware, telecommunications, software, and database, along with all their specific subtechnologies. The organizational aspect is expressed by the organization's structure and culture, as well as by organizational practices reflected in the already existing applications software (MIS already in place) and database contents. The people aspect includes the members of the organization and others who will work with the system or who will be affected by it. The system should match the users' level of knowledge; moreover, their psychological and, in particular, cognitive needs must be considered.

An extensive example of a financial information system which turned into a battlefield between the corporate and divisional accountants in a corporation was discussed by Lynne Markus (1984). The reason the conflict developed was not technological; rather, the system had altered the balance of power between the two groups by moving certain informational tasks from one group to the other—an effect unforeseen by the system developers. The accounting group that felt encroached upon resisted the use of the system, to the detriment of the company.

Many of us have witnessed junior banking officers using a retail-banking system in which the human-system interaction protocol did not match personnel skills. Often, repeated transactions must be entered to rectify multiple errors introduced during a somewhat complicated account manipulation.

Many a system, once developed, fell into misuse. System implementation, or the process of introducing an appropriate information system into organizational use, is of great concern. To become a successful practitioner or sophisticated user, the student has to be proficient in technological, organizational, and cognitive aspects of MIS.

FIGURE 1.5

Aspects of MIS fit.

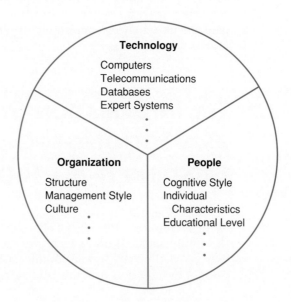

1.8 DEVELOPMENT AND MAINTENANCE OF MIS

Where Does an MIS Come From?

In this introductory chapter, we have concentrated on the nature of MIS. To meet the organizational MIS objectives, new information systems must be developed, and the existing systems must be enhanced and modified during the so-called maintenance process.

To achieve a successful fit with the organization, the overall informational support of an organization has to be planned in close alignment with overall organizational planning. Development and maintenance of individual systems is supported with software engineering techniques and extensive software tools. Large organizational MIS applications are developed by MIS professionals. Many of the tools for developing certain classes of systems have, since the early 1980s, been expressly designed for the end users. **End-user systems development** has become a very significant component in overall organizational computing. It is a part of a broader practice of **end-user computing:** end users are developing, controlling, and using directly some of the information systems they need.

Other important factors on the present scene include the availability of software packages for narrowly defined vertical markets (for example, for the determination of creditworthiness by a bank credit department) and computer-aided software engineering (CASE) tools that offer automatic assistance with various stages of software development and maintenance.

As is evident from the short vignettes we have already studied, organizational change is a way of life. MIS evolve with the organization, and their flexibility in evolving is an important measure of their quality.

In Part 5 of the text, we will discuss the development and maintenance of MIS applications.

Payoff from an MIS

As in the acquisition of any other resource, the development, modification, or purchase (usually accompanied by customization) of an information system is subject to an important question: do the projected benefits outweigh the costs?

As we will see, this question is usually easily answered for systems designed to increase the operating efficiency of an enterprise. It is more difficult to gauge the MIS payoff for systems aimed at increasing management effectiveness or gaining a competitive edge. You will appreciate, though, how important the systems in the latter category are!

We will further discuss the process of MIS cost-benefit valuation in the context of overall informational planning and MIS portfolio evaluation (chapters 17 and 18).

Alternative Usage of the Term MIS

There are alternative ways in which the term *MIS* may be used, consistent with our definition. An MIS may be

- an individual information system for a specific application within an enterprise;
- an organizational component—for example, a division—responsible for information systems;

- an area of practice (undertaken by an MIS specialist);
- an area of inquiry: MIS is an established discipline of scholarship.

Let us take a look at the latter usage—MIS as an area of inquiry.

1.9 MANAGEMENT INFORMATION SYSTEMS AS A DISCIPLINE

Management information systems is both an area of practice and a discipline of scholarly inquiry. Because of the vital role information plays in a modern organization, proficiency in MIS is virtually a prerequisite for organizational effectiveness.

In Part 5, we will discuss the fields in which MIS practitioners specialize and how MIS professionals are placed in the organizational structure.

Relationship of MIS to Reference Disciplines

As a discipline of study, MIS draws on several other established fields of scholarship to meld their results and insights into its mission: an inquiry into how organizations can make effective and efficient use of information. Modern organizations have been broadly defined as information-based (Drucker, 1988). Thus, the discipline of MIS plays a major role in contributing to the effectiveness of social organizations.

The fields of scholarship which underlie the discipline of MIS are known as its reference disciplines. MIS is influenced both by the technical fields, which contribute the knowledge of technology and algorithms for optimal use of a company's resources, and by the behavioral fields, which investigate organizations and the people in them. The discipline combines theoretical investigation with a pragmatic orientation. MIS scholars learn much from the practical tasks of constructing new types of systems, producing novel organizational solutions, and using new methodologies of systems development.

The disciplines that contribute to the field of MIS are shown in figure 1.6. Most of them were analytically reviewed in a broad study led by Fritz Machlup (1983).

The fundamental reference disciplines for MIS are computer science and the theory of organizations and management. **Computer science** is the study of automatic processing of symbolic information (Zwass, 1983). A general processor of such information is the computer. Software engineering, computer communications, database organization, and, more recently, artificial intelligence, are the fields of computer science particularly important to the field of MIS. Developments in the discipline are best followed through the *Communications of the ACM (*Association for Computing Machinery*)*. This highly dynamic discipline conveys the technological push to the field of information systems. Thus, for example, expert systems, created by artificial intelligence scholars in the early 1970s, entered the mainstream of MIS in the mid-1980s.

Organizations and their management evolve rapidly in an information society, as we will discuss in the next chapter. We already know that information technology serves organizations through their managers. The best periodicals to follow developments in the *study of organizations and management* are the *Harvard Business Review* and the *Sloan Management Review*. More demanding reading is offered in the *Administrative Science Quarterly*.

Sociological approaches help us understand the organizational behavior of people. *Cognitive science*, a new discipline incorporating the approaches of cognitive psychology and techniques aspiring to understand how mind arises from the brain, contributes to our understanding of understanding itself as it studies human information processing.

The levels of behavioral study required in the discipline of MIS are summarized in figure 1.7.

Management science, also known as operations research (OR), is a field of applied mathematics. It provides us with mathematical tools for decision making in such areas as optimal resource allocation, optimal selection of transportation routes, or optimal inventory quantities. **Systems theory** contributes approaches for dealing with complexity—that of an organization or that of a software system.

The use of computers in business began with *accounting*. MIS supports both the financial and managerial accounting functions. Financial accounting is concerned with reporting the financial position and operating results of a business

FIGURE 1.6

Disciplines contributing to the field of MIS.

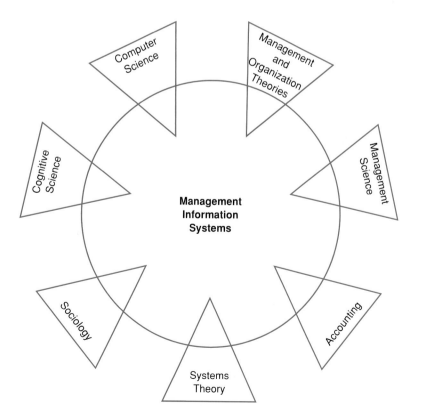

FIGURE 1.7

Levels of behavioral study in MIS.

(Adapted from Curtis, 1988)

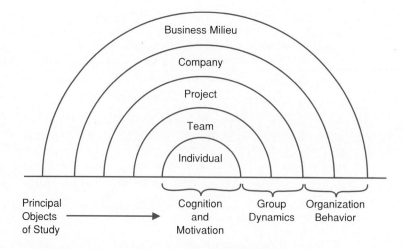

entity at the end of a specific time period, such as a quarter or a year. Financial accounting reports provide information chiefly for entities external to the company (for example, for the Securities and Exchange Commission). Managerial accounting, far more important in the company decision-making process, supplies the information needed for cost planning and control through budgeting. Auditing techniques have also been adapted from accounting practice.

Emergence of the Field of MIS

The intellectual roots of the field of management information systems go back to the study of management as a process in which the crucial aspect is decision making. The most prominent work laying the foundations for this approach was *Administrative Behavior* by Herbert Simon, an influential book that appeared in 1947. The late 1940s and early 1950s saw the development of Norbert Wiener's idea of cybernetics and Ludwig von Bertalanffy's general system theory—both searching for a general theory of control and communication in human and mechanical systems. A classical 1948 paper by Claude Shannon led to the technical conceptualization of the idea of information. The fundamental notions of decision making, information, systems, and their control have their own lives in the reference disciplines. These notions have also influenced thinking on the role of information in organizations—that is, the focus of the field of MIS.

As we have stressed, management information systems are unthinkable (well, perhaps *only* "thinkable") without computers. Technological developments related to computers and digital communication have continually driven the field in both practice and research. Many areas of research in MIS overlap with the work done by computer scientists.

The first general-purpose electronic computer, ENIAC, was completed in 1946 at the University of Pennsylvania. Developed in response to problems encountered by the military during World War II, computers were thought of at the time as devices for doing precisely what their name implies—computing. Today, the predominant tasks of computers are storing and accessing organized information and processing symbols; calculation is just one of the several functions computers perform.

Mass production of computers started in 1951 when UNIVAC I was delivered commercially as the first such machine built on an assembly line. UNIVAC I was

THE GROWING ROLE OF ORGANIZATIONAL MIS

According to a survey of large U.S. corporations conducted by the accounting firm of Coopers & Lybrand, 34 percent of the heads of corporate MIS organizations report directly to the chief executive officer (CEO) of their companies. This represents a significant increase from the 24 percent figure reported by another accounting firm, Touche Ross, five years ago. Moreover, these executives are more likely to report to the CEO that any other senior functional manager, with the exception of the executives responsible for operations, finance, and human resources. In certain information-dependent industry segments, such as insurance and financial services, this figure is much higher, with 53 percent of MIS-function heads heavily involved in top-level corporate planning.

This points up the importance of information systems—and also the fact that MIS managers are expected to be not only technicians, but generalist managers as well.

Based in part on David Freedman, "Are We There Yet?" *CIO*, January 1991, pp. 34–41.

The biggest MIS "shop" in the United States is that of American Telephone and Telegraph (AT&T). Its expenditures on information technology in 1990 were estimated to be at least $1 billion, and the employees in the Information Management Services Group of the firm numbered 7,400. In addition, many information systems specialists work in various business units of the company.

Based on "The Biggest IW 500," *InformationWeek*, September 10, 1990, pp. 100–115.

also the first computer model used for business data processing when it was installed by General Electric in 1954. However, MIS as an area of practice had a rather slow start, with only some 4,000 computers installed by the end of the 1950s (Dickson, 1981).

We will trace the evolution of the organizational role of information systems in the next chapter and the progress of computer technology in Part 2 of this book. We need to stress here, however, that the organizational computing landscape was revolutionized by the emergence of personal computers in the late 1970s. When appropriate software became available, the personal computer gave strength to end-user computing, furnishing an accessible means for users to develop their own applications and become true partners of MIS professionals in the use of technology for organizational benefit.

The development of MIS as a field of inquiry paralleled the technological developments. The first papers analyzing the role of information systems in organizations started to appear in the second half of the 1950s. The 1958 paper by Harold Leavitt and Thomas Whisler, entitled *Management in the 1980s* (Leavitt, 1958), was influential in focusing the discipline. The authors concluded that what "we shall call . . . information technology" would have "definite and far-reaching impact on managerial organization." They proceeded to set up a framework for analyzing this impact. Their forecast of reduction in the ranks of middle management due to senior managers' ability to directly control an organization with the support of information technology appears to have indeed come true (Applegate, 1988). However, as we shall further argue in the text, information technology more often bears options that may be exercised by corporate management rather than having a direct causal effect on the organization. The effects of information technology on organizations is a subject of intense study in the field of MIS (Huber, 1990). The first educational programs in the MIS field were offered by Purdue University and the University of Minnesota in 1969. The scope of the field was outlined by Gordon Davis of the latter university in the first comprehensive textbook, published in 1976.[5]

The field of MIS now has an extensive literature, some of which you will find in the references included at the end of each chapter in this book. The leading journals in the field are the *Journal of Management Information Systems* and the *MIS Quarterly,* as well as the relatively new *Information Systems Research.* Many important papers have been published in *Management Science.* Practitioners and students alike can gain much by following such monthly magazines as *Datamation* and *Infosystems,* as well as the *Computerworld* and *InformationWeek* weeklies. Several excellent personal-computer-oriented publications are also widely available.

· ·

SUMMARY

MIS are formal systems built around the hardware backbone of computer and telecommunications systems. Formal computer-based information systems are not the only informational sources in an organization. Informal information sources must be cultivated and coordinated with the use of formal sources.

The beneficial effects of an information system cannot be expected to accrue simply because a superior technology is used. Obvious benefits from a new technology are more likely to occur when a system is designed to support a firm's operations rather than its management—that is, when efficiency rather than effectiveness is the goal of the system. Indeed, efficiency is more easily achieved through computers and telecommunications than is the more elusive—and generally more weighty—goal of managerial effectiveness. Systems that have a broad organizational impact are designed not just to raise efficiency of operations, but to enhance the effectiveness of a firm in the competitive environment. To do so, the system must fit the goals of an organization or of a specific component of it, meet the needs of its users, and be introduced via a carefully designed process.

MIS is not only a field of practice, but also a discipline of scholarly inquiry, drawing in part on the findings and methodologies of several reference disciplines. Although the field of MIS originated in the late 1950s, MIS as a discipline became established a full decade later.

CONCLUSIONS FOR MIS PRACTICE

1. MIS encompasses systems supporting both the management and business operations of an enterprise.

2. It is impractical to think of an organizational MIS as a "total system." It is rather more fruitful to consider MIS an evolving portfolio of systems.

3. Integration of systems in an MIS portfolio is an important and continuing goal. However, total integration is usually impossible; in particular, it would be too costly.

4. Computers and telecommunications are the fundamental technologies of MIS.

5. An understanding of computer and communication technologies is not sufficient for MIS practice. Rather, this knowledge needs to be combined with an understanding of organizations and management, as well as cognitive and behavioral aspects of human psychology. To this end, the discipline of MIS combines contributions from several reference disciplines.

ENDNOTES

1. Robert Violino, "Tightened Belts, Heightened Productivity," *InformationWeek*, March 4, 1991, pp. 24–30.

2. G. Patrick McGunagle, "The Dangers of Expert Systems Development: Some Implications and Solutions," *Proceedings of 11th SWIFT International Banking Operations Seminar*, Vienna, Austria, 1988, pp. 37–41.

3. As an example, Shearson brokerage house, which is now known as Shearson Lehman Hutton, a business unit of American Express, underwent forty mergers in twenty-eight years.

4. Thomas Sowell, *Knowledge and Decisions*, New York: Basic Books, 1980, p. 30.

5. Gordon B. Davis, *Management Information Systems: Conceptual Foundation, Structure, and Development*. New York: McGraw-Hill, 1974. The second edition of the book was published by Davis and Margrethe H. Olson in 1985.

KEY TERMS AND CONCEPTS

Management information system (MIS)	Formal systems
	Informal information
System portfolio	Resource
Transaction processing systems	Information resource management
Management reporting systems	Internal and external information
Decision support systems	Database
Executive information systems	Database management system
Office information systems	Organization
Interorganizational systems	Management
Strategic information systems	Managerial functions
Expert systems	System
Integrated systems	Cognitive functions
Computer and telecommunication technologies	Human-machine system
	MIS development and maintenance
MIS proficiency	End-user computing
Data	Reference disciplines of MIS
Information	

QUESTIONS

1. What are management information systems? Do you believe it is fruitful to completely separate operational systems from management-oriented systems? Why or why not?

2. What did Robert Kavner, then president of AT&T Computer Systems Group, mean when he said "Modern corporations are organizing around information flow"? Relate this to the holistic approach to MIS advocated in this chapter.

3. Where do technology push and demand pull originate and what roles do they play in MIS progress?

4. Why do we stress seeking competitive advantage in our approach to MIS?

5. Should MIS be fully integrated? Should it be integrated at any cost? What criteria should be used to decide whether the level of integration in an MIS should be increased?

6. The United States Government often combines all aspects of the informational needs of one of its particular organizational units into a single procurement. It then issues a single request for proposal to potential vendors. What are the advantages and disadvantages of such an approach?

7. What is the relationship between organizational information systems and computers, telecommunications, and related technologies? What is the role of computer programs in information systems?

8. Why have computers and communications become virtually inseparable in information systems? (This prompted one of the leading scholars to coin the perhaps infelicitous term *compunications*.)

9. Is a "formal" information system the same as a "computerized" system? Give examples that illustrate your answer.

10. Distinguish between computer literacy and MIS proficiency. Which is required of managers and why?

11. Draw the distinction between data and information.

12. Why do we consider information a resource? What approach has been developed to control it as a resource? What technology makes this possible?

13. Define the terms *organization* and *management*. Do you believe an organization can exist without management? (Consider the organization's ability to attain its goals in your response.)

14. Which aspects of managerial functions are especially information-intensive? How is information used to perform these functions?

15. Why is an MIS, though not a "total system," still a system? Assume that you have decided to implement a total system—the ultimate in integration. In such a system, any input can change the state of any component; for example, a large sales transaction could immediately affect the sales plan for the next year. Consider the advantages and disadvantages of such a system in terms of costs and benefits.

16. Why are we interested in the cognitive functions of individuals in the MIS context?

17. Why has end-user computing become an important factor in organizational computing? What made this possible, and why would an end user want to be so directly involved in computing?

18. Which disciplines contribute to the field of MIS and *what* do they contribute?

19. Why do MIS evolve over time? What makes this evolution possible?

ISSUES FOR DISCUSSION

1. Who is better qualified to lead a large MIS development project—a manager or a technician?

2. What are the various aspects of fit between the organization and an MIS? Consider management style, organizational structure, and geographical dispersion of the firm. Discuss two examples of lack of fit between an organization and its MIS.

3. Do computer-based information systems obviate the need for informal information? Will all information flows ultimately be formalized and computerized? Why or why not?

4. Review the functions of organizational information systems. Which of these systems are primarily directed at efficiency ("doing things the right way"), and which are oriented at effectiveness ("doing the right thing")?

5. What do Ein-Dor and Segev mean when they offer "Proposition 13" (Ein-Dor, 1978): "MIS projects will succeed to the extent that expectations are constrained from below by motivation and from above by reality"? What would be some of the reasons for excessively high or low expectations?

6. Would you integrate a word processing program with a financial reporting program? Develop a contingency scheme for such an integration. In other words, under what circumstances would you integrate, and what would be the expected results?

CASE STUDY

EXECUTIVE USE OF INFORMATION SYSTEMS—AN EXAMPLE

This study will graphically (in more ways than one) illustrate the potential of management information systems for informing executive decision making. The case study employs an executive information system, called RESOLVE, developed by Metapraxis (of Kingston upon Thames, Great Britain, and New York) in application to a case derived from actual practice. The name of the company where the decision-making session took place has been changed.

Executive information systems (EIS), as will be further discussed in the text, are used by top corporate executives—typically chief executive officers, executive and senior vice-presidents, and top executives of principal operating units of the company, as well as by corporate boards. (You may see an EIS in a setting for a meeting in the photo

below.) The principal aim of EIS is to make all the information on the performance of a company available to the senior executives in digestible form, facilitating prompt decision making. Therefore, information is available in a highly summarized, predominantly graphic, form. However, the executive users can, if they desire, "drill down" to detailed data in pursuit of a problem. Color graphs and data are projected on a large screen or, alternatively, may be seen on a PC display.

The main objective of the EIS is to help detect exceptions in the present or projected performance of the company. Problems identified during a conference where EIS is used are resolved "off-line" by other personnel with the use of other systems, usually those for decision support.

PHOTO 1.1

An executive information system (EIS) is conveniently used in a meeting, with the reports projected onto a large screen.

(Courtesy of Metapraxis, Inc., New York)

FIGURE 1.8

An executive information system can provide a four-dimensional representation of a company's financial performance. You can see here a selection of these dimensions.

(Courtesy of Metapraxis Inc., New York)

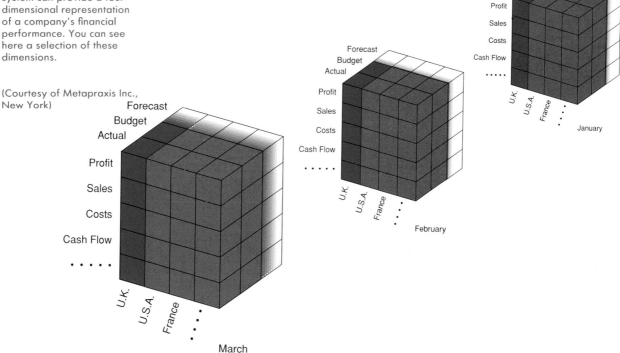

Typically, an EIS is actually a system generator: the system is customized for the environment of the specific company. RESOLVE, the particular system discussed here, runs on a personal computer. The system is able to present the performance of the company in four dimensions, as shown in figure 1.8 (RESOLVE is able to generate more complex descriptions as well). Thus, financial data, such as profits or sales, can be seen as actual results, compared to planned amounts, and projected into the future based on developing trends. The results can be shown for operating units of a company; the multinational company depicted in this case study has geographical divisions, such as the United Kingdom, the United States, and France. Selected time periods for the data are months.

The following series of reports, presented in graphical and tabular form, was obtained during an executive committee meeting of a corporation we will call Diverse Industries, meeting at the end of April 1991 (and printed out in September of that year). During the meeting, the reports were shown on a central screen. Such reports may indeed be produced during a meeting from existing company databases or, for a faster pace, prepared by the company's financial officers for the session and stored in secondary memory, such as a disk. The reports were selected to illustrate the capabilities and effectiveness of EIS without taking excessive space in the text.

FIGURE 1.9

Long-term performance of
Diverse Industries, Inc.

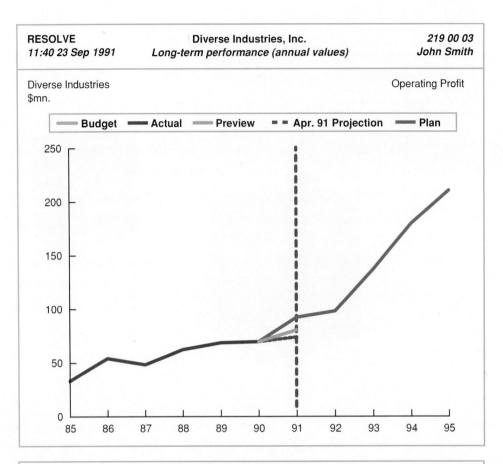

Report 1 (Figure 1.9): This figure is a summary of corporate profit performance for the last five years. The projection (made by management, which is presenting the results to the executive committee) is compared against the long-term corporate plan and against the budget (short-term plan). A problem appears: the management projection for the 1991 year end shows $73.5 million profit against the budget (annual plan) of $78.1 million. Both figures are well below the strategic (five-year) plan of $91.8 million.

In each of the following five reports, only graphs are shown; they may have also been accompanied by tables of figures in the actual presentation.

Report 2 (Figure 1.10): Monthly totals for the company reveal that the problem started in April 1991. This figure shows the capability of the system to make its own projection (preview) of the future. The negative cumulative variance shows a discrepancy between the budgeted and achieved or projected results. The management projection and the EIS forecast (preview) agree that the downturn in profitability will continue until the end of 1991.

FIGURE 1.10

Month-by-month performance of Diverse Industries, Inc.

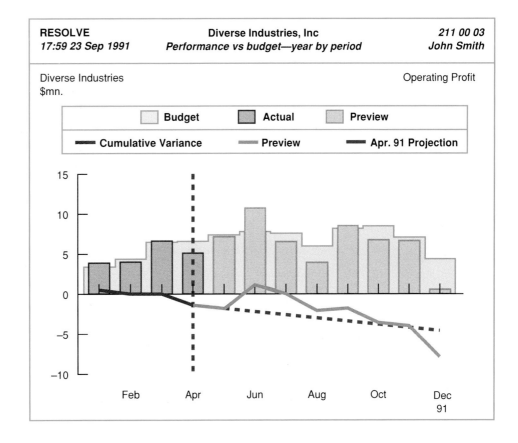

FIGURE 1.11

Quarterly performance of individual divisions of Diverse Industries, Inc.

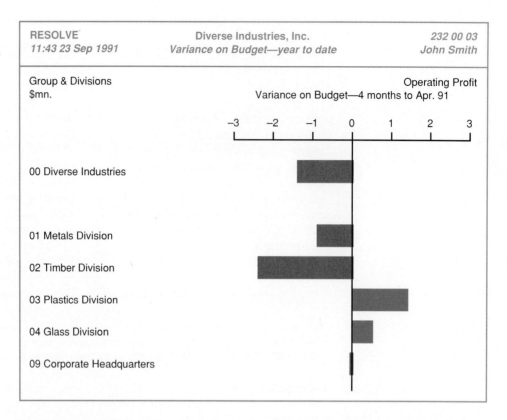

RESOLVE	Diverse Industries, Inc.	232 00 03
11:43 23 Sep 1991	*Variance on Budget—year to date*	*John Smith*

Group & Divisions $mn. — Operating Profit, Variance on Budget—4 months to Apr. 91

00 Diverse Industries
01 Metals Division
02 Timber Division
03 Plastics Division
04 Glass Division
09 Corporate Headquarters

Report 3 (Figure 1.11): An analysis of divisional results shows that the problems emerged in the Timber and Metals divisions. In fact, the other two operating divisions, Plastics and Glass, have surpassed budgeted profitability.

Report 4 (Figure 1.12): Comparison of the monthly profit figures for the four divisions shows that while the Timber division has been underperforming since the beginning of the year, the Metals division shortfall arose suddenly in April. The commentary attached to the report shows the Timber division management already has an action plan. Metals needs to be further investigated: the projection made by the management of that division is rather optimistic as compared to the projection (preview) made by the system.

FIGURE 1.12

Month-by-month
performance of individual
divisions of Diverse
Industries, Inc., with a
commentary stored in the
system.

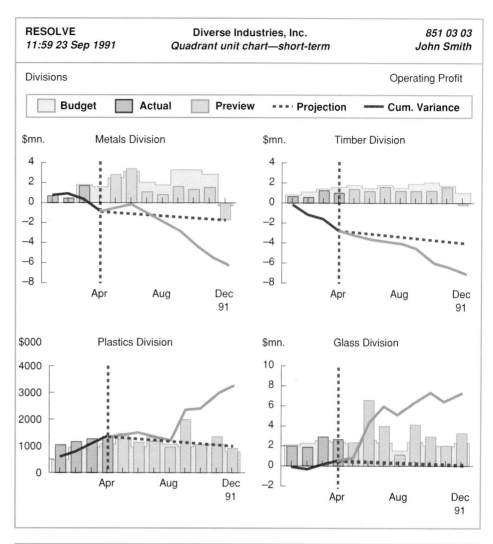

RESOLVE
12:06 23 Sep 1991

Diverse Industries, Inc.
Quadrant unit chart—short-term

851 03 03
John Smith

Commentary

The five-stage action plan agreed at the March Executive Committee meeting is currently being implemented and an improvement in results is confidently expected by the end of this quarter. The possibility of increasing marketing spending in order to win back market share from our major competitors in the sector is also being investigated.

Paul Daniels
President, Timber Division

FIGURE 1.13

Performance of the operating
companies that make up the
Metals division of Diverse
Industries, Inc.

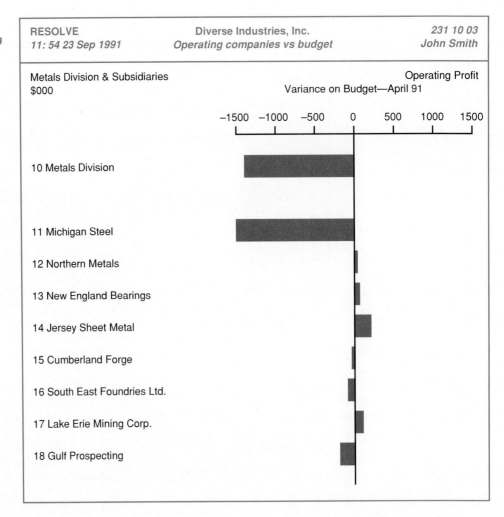

Report 5 (Figure 1.13): This figure reveals that the problem within the Metals division has been caused by the Michigan Steel Company.

Report 6 (Figure 1.14): A review of the gross profit margins (percentage of profit in sales before expenses) of Michigan Steel shows a steady decline, with a severe drop in December 1990. It also shows that the projections made by the management of that company, which indicate that the budget goals will be met in November 1991, are wildly optimistic, as compared to the forecast (preview) computed by the system.

In the actual case, the December 1990 drop in gross profit margins was the result of auditors discovering that the company was not properly costing its inventory and was using "theoretical" margins to report the division's result. Another drop, in April, was again determined by the internal auditors during their valuation of inventory.

FIGURE 1.14

A longer view of the monthly performance of Michigan Steel Company—a unit of the Metals division of Diverse Industries, Inc.

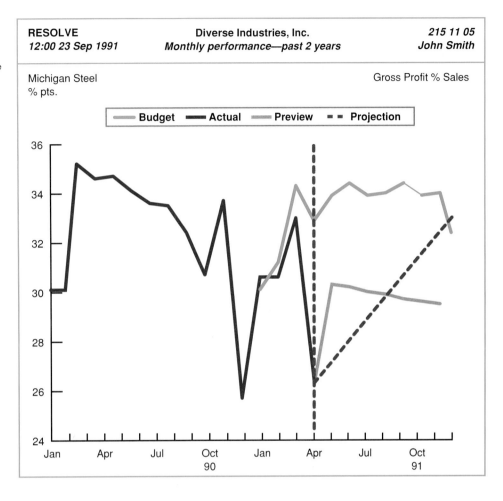

RESOLVE	Diverse Industries, Inc.	215 11 05
12:00 23 Sep 1991	*Monthly performance—past 2 years*	*John Smith*

Michigan Steel
% pts.

Gross Profit % Sales

Budget ── Actual ── Preview ─ ─ Projection

Report 7 (Figure 1.15): Is the profitability of the operating companies of the troubled Metals division increasing? Since companies operate within geographical regions, their performance is illustrated on the map of the United States. The starting year for which the data were available for each company is indicated in the last column of the table that accompanies the graph.

The graph and the table show that several companies have achieved sustained improvement in performance, and only one (Lake Erie Mining) has a severe problem with its growth.

A plan was formulated to transfer successful practices to the lagging firm.

FIGURE 1.15

Profit margins of the operating companies of the Metals division over the last several years.

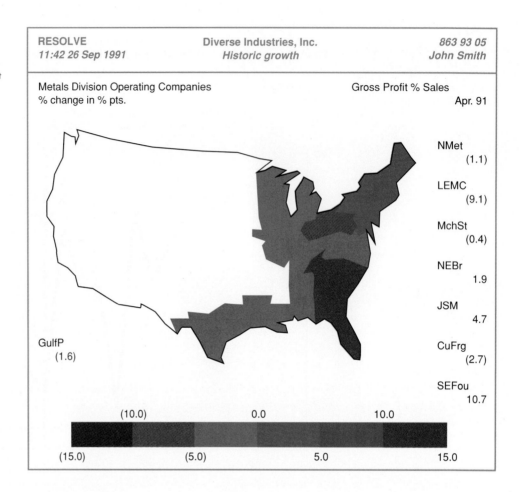

RESOLVE
11:50 26 Sep 1991

	Annual %	Current Projection		Earliest Actual	
Gulf Prospecting	(1.6)	32.3	(Apr)	35.2	(1986)
Northern Metals	(1.1)	23.7	(Apr)	24.8	(1987)
Michigan Steel	(0.4)	33.5	(Apr)	34.4	(1985)
Lake Erie Mining Corp.	(9.1)	30.5	(Apr)	37.6	(1989)
New England Bearings	1.9	34.9	(Apr)	31.1	(1985)
Jersey Sheet Metal	4.7	33.1	(Apr)	25.2	(1985)
South East Foundries Ltd.	10.7	30.0	(Apr)	27.1	(1990)
Cumberland Forge	(2.7)	34.0	(Apr)	41.3	(1985)

Case Study Questions

1. The RESOLVE system used in the case belongs to the category of executive information systems (EIS). Do you believe that only the highest level of management can profit from the use of such a system?

2. Can a small company profitably use an EIS? Why or why not? Consider the costs of gathering and maintaining the data. In chapter 11, we will introduce a personal computer program that has many EIS capabilities (and that costs below $500).

3. Which of the following do you believe is the principal cost component: the personal computer and the executive information system, or the acquisition and maintenance of the databases on which the use of the system relies?

4. Draw up two alternative scenarios for using an executive information system in a business context you are familiar with.

SELECTED REFERENCES

The thunder of several stimulating early polemical references still echoes in our approach to the field of MIS. These references include

Ackoff, Russell L. "Management Misinformation Systems." *Management Science,* 14, 4, December 1967, pp. B147–56.

Dearden, John. "Myth of Real-Time Management." *Harvard Business Review,* May–June 1966, pp. 123–32.

Dearden, John. "MIS is a Mirage." *Harvard Business Review,* January–February 1972, pp. 90–99.

Leavitt, Harold J., and Whisler, Thomas L. "Management in the 1980s." *Harvard Business Review,* November–December 1958, pp. 41–48.

These papers, along with the polemics they have prompted, have been reprinted in

Davis, Gordon B., and Everest, Gordon C., eds. *Readings in Management Information Systems.* New York: McGraw-Hill, 1976.

The first three papers have also been reprinted in

Wetherbe, James C.; Dock, V. Thomas; and Mandell, Steven L. *Readings in Informations Systems: A Managerial Perspective.* St. Paul: West, 1988.

General References

Applegate, Lynda M.; Cash, James I., Jr.; and Mills, D. Quinn. "Information Technology and Tomorrow's Manager." *Harvard Business Review,* November–December 1988, pp. 128–36.

Curtis, Bill; Krasner, Herb; and Iscoe, Neil. "A Field Study of the Software Design Process for Large Systems." *Communications of the ACM,* 31, 11, November 1988, pp. 1268–87.

Dickson, Gary W. "Management Information Systems: Evolution and Status." *Advances in Computers,* vol. 20, pp. 1–37. New York: Academic Press, 1981.

Drucker, Peter F. "The Coming of the New Organization." *Harvard Business Review,* January–February 1988, pp. 45–53.

Earl, Michael J., and Hopwood, Anthony G. "From Management Information to Information Management." In *The Information Systems Environment,* edited by Henry C. Lucas, Jr. et al., pp. 3–13. Amsterdam: North Holland, 1980.

Ein-Dor, Phillip, and Segev, Eli. "Organizational Context and the Success of Management Information Systems." *Management Science,* 24, 10, October 1978, pp. 1064–77.

El Sawy, Omar A., and Nanus, Burt. "Towards the Design of Robust Information Systems." *Journal of Management Information Systems,* 5, 4, Spring 1989, pp. 33–54.

Gurbaxani, Vijay, and Mendelson, Haim. "An Integrative Model of Information Systems Spending Growth." *Information Systems Research,* 1, 1, March 1990, pp. 23–46.

Huber, George P. "A Theory of the Effects of Advanced Information Technologies on Organizational Design, Intelligence, and Decision Making." *Academy of Management Review,* 15, 1, January 1990, pp. 47–71.

Ives, Blake; Hamilton, Scott; and Davis, Gordon B. "A Framework for Research in Computer-Based Management Information Systems." *Management Science,* 26, 9, September 1980, pp. 910–34.

Ives, Blake; and Olson, Margrethe H. "Manager or Technician? The Nature of a Systems Manager's Job." *MIS Quarterly,* 5, 4, December 1981, pp. 49–62.

McFarlan, F. Warren, ed. *The Information Systems Research Challenge.* Boston: Harvard Business School Press, 1984.

Machlup, Fritz, and Mansfield, Una, eds. *The Study of Information: Interdisciplinary Messages.* New York: Wiley-Interscience, 1983.

Markus, M. Lynne. *Systems in Organizations: Bugs and Features.* Marshfield, Mass.: Pitman, 1984.

Markus, M. Lynne, and Robey, Daniel. "Information Technology and Organizational Change: Causal Structure in Theory and Research." *Management Science* 34, 5, May 1988, pp. 583–98.

Mason, Richard O., and Mitroff, Ian I. "A Program for Research on Management Information Systems." *Management Science,* 19, 5, January 1973, pp. 475–87.

Meyer, N. Dean, and Boone, Mary E. *The Information Edge.* New York: McGraw-Hill, 1987.

Strassman, Paul. *The Information Payoff—The Transformation of Work in the Electronic Age.* New York: Free Press, 1985.

Zmud, Robert W.; Boynton, Andrew C.; and Jacobs, Gerry C. "An Examination of Managerial Strategies for Increasing Information Technology Penetration in Organizations." *Proceedings of the Eighth International Conference on Information Systems,* pp. 24–44. Pittsburgh: 1987.

Zwass, Vladimir. "The Province of Computer Science." In *The Study of Information: Interdisciplinary Messages,* edited by Fritz Machlup and Una Mansfield, pp. 151–56. New York: Wiley-Interscience, 1983.

Zwass, Vladimir. "Management Information Systems—Beyond the Current Paradigm." *Journal of Management Information Systems,* 1, 1, Summer 1984, pp. 3–10.

KNOWLEDGE WORK WITH INFORMATION SYSTEMS

In the information society, most of us do knowledge work—even if some of us do not do it all the time. Computer-based information systems play an ever more vital role in this work. The following few photographs will help you appreciate both of these facts.

PHOTO 2.1

A field engineer uses a pen-based notepad computer to complete a report right at the job site. A variety of report forms and engineering drawings stored in the highly portable computer eliminate the need for handling paper.

PHOTO 2.2

Executives increasingly work directly with information systems. Executive information systems and graphical user interfaces make this both rewarding and attractive. Ronald Compton, president of Aetna Life and Casualty Company of Hartford, Connecticut, who is shown here, believes that all executives should have hands-on experience using computers.

PHOTO 2.3

A sergeant of the Dubuque, Iowa, Police Department services the 911 emergency calls. The information systems of the emergency telephone service instantly display on the video display terminal (VDT) the caller's name, address, and telephone number, as well as information regarding the nearest police, fire, and medical facilities.

PHOTO 2.4

Seven microcomputers feed information from around the world into the trading room located at the home of this couple—investment professionals who do not need to "go to" work. The systems are programmed to alert the traders to pricing patterns that may be buy or sell cues. By giving such entrepreneurs autonomy, computers are revolutionizing the way people live and work.

PHOTO 2.5

Using a "portable office," consisting of a laptop computer, fax, cellular telephone, and a telecommunications modem, this contracting executive was able to respond to an urgent business call while on the road. He downloaded the latest competitive information from a remote database into his computer, analyzed it, and faxed an updated contract to a client.

PHOTO 2.6

Computer-aided design (CAD), supported by technical workstations, has become a necessity in many design-oriented fields. These designers are developing the circuitry of a chip.

PHOTO 2.7

Computer-aided design has dramatically cut the development time of new automobile models. You see here the designers of Chrysler Corporation working on an electronic prototype.

PHOTO 2.8

Central control room at Cadillac's Hamtramck Assembly Center. Here, production operations are monitored every six seconds via computers connected to 426 devices, which connect to 9,000 points in the plant. These screens with their "electronic text" show the status of the processes.

PHOTO 2.9

The computer-controlled welding robot shown here is one of several on the assembly line of a small manufacturer of metal doors—Karp Associates of Maspeth, New York. Robot operators program the robots with a keyboard or a joystick.

These robots increased the productivity of the firm by 400 percent. Burt Gold, the president of the company (who appears on the right), says: "It takes someone from MIS to get a handle on the issues posed by robotics"— because of the need to integrate the robots into the overall information system of the company.

PHOTO 2.10

Implemented with a touch screen, the user interface of this computer-integrated manufacturing system (CIM) is so intuitively simple that workers need very little training.

PHOTO 2.11

Workers employed at a telephone company's distribution center in Atlanta, Georgia, regularly interact with the computerized inventory management system (you can see an image scanner used for data input).

Reporting with Management Information Systems

Exception reporting with an executive information system.

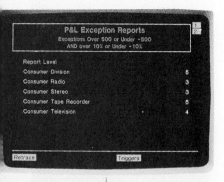

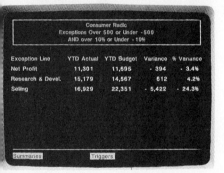

A long-term planning report.

(Courtesy of Lotus Development Corporation.)

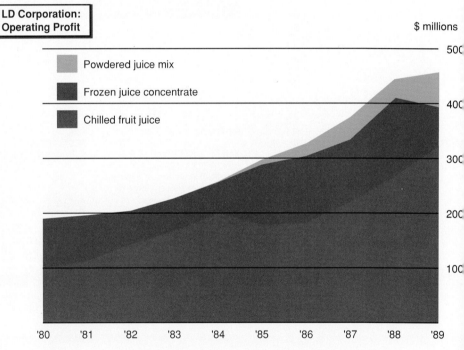

LD Corporation: Operating Profit

Frooze Pops to be introduced Q1, 1989

	Chilled fruit juice	Frozen juice concentrate	Powdered juice mix
80	99	90	—
81	111	84	—
82	142	61	—
83	166	60	—
84	198	57	1
85	177	110	9
86	182	121	23
87	220	113	41
88	266	138	71
89	321	85	88

Information Systems Architecture of American Standard

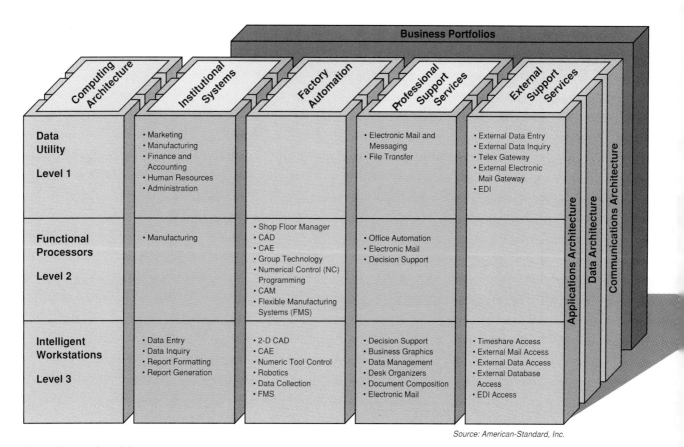

Source: American-Standard, Inc.

The architectural model developed by American Standard, one of the 200 largest U.S. corporations. Most of the original terminology employed by American Standard has been retained to expose you to some alternative nomenclature used in the field.

CHAPTER 2

INFORMATIONAL NEEDS OF ORGANIZATIONS IN AN INFORMATION SOCIETY

. . . .

Standards of living rise not because people are working harder but because they are working smarter.

Lester C. Thurow

We are constantly reminded that the past is less and less prologue to the future.

Standard & Poor's Corporation: Credit Overview

We are living in a society undergoing rapid change—an information society is coming into being. More than half of the labor force in the United States works in the information sector, and more than half of the gross national product is produced by it. The new social framework, based on information technologies, is changing the way business is conducted, the way organizations function, the products offered in the marketplace, and the way we work.

Knowledge work lends itself to effective and efficient transformation by information systems. Organizations must bring their informational activities in line with the changes taking place in the structure of the society. In this chapter, we shall discuss the outlines of an information society, the nature of knowledge work, and the demands placed on organizations by the new information-dependent economy. We shall analyze what capabilities MIS offer within this social framework. We will then examine how organizational computing is evolving to meet the challenges of the new economy.

1. Commercial fishermen use computer weather forecasts to determine the locations of warm currents in the ocean waters—because that is where the fish are. Long and costly journeys in search of promising fishing waters are no longer necessary.

2. The Atlas Door Company has grown three times faster and has earned five times more than the average for its industry. Why? Most of its competitors need four months to deliver an out-of-stock or custom-ordered industrial door, with customers waiting more than a week just to obtain a quote. Atlas has a computerized sales system integrated with its engineering, manufacturing, and shipping systems. A salesperson can offer a firm quote to the customer during the course of the initial telephone inquiry. Thanks to this integrated information system, Atlas Door has by far the fastest turnaround in the industry on special orders—and enjoys a competitive advantage.

3. In the 1970s, West Berlin appeared to be a city on the wane. Over one hundred thousand jobs had been lost in the manufacturing sector and the inhabitants were moving out of the city. In recent years, the city government has focused on international services in the financial sector, relying on computer and communication technologies. West Berlin, which is now a part of Berlin, has been revitalized by a large influx of people seeking and finding employment in the information sector.

The common denominator for these quite disparate cases is the use of information resources as a key to a thriving business in today's economic world.

2.1   The Information Society and Knowledge Work
   • What Is an Information Society?
   • Information Society at Work—Two Examples
   • What Is Knowledge Work?

2.2   Demands on Organizations in an Information Society
   • Demands of Continuing Innovation
   • Changes in the Environment of Organizations—The Informational Aspect

• •

2.1 THE INFORMATION SOCIETY AND KNOWLEDGE WORK

The technologically advanced nations of the world, the United States among them, are at present in the formative stages of the information society that is emerging from what was formerly an industrial society. Just as energy was the driving force in the industrial society, so information is the key transforming resource in this new society. The massive processing and communication of information is already placing certain demands on organizations, which will be amplified further as time goes on. These demands, in turn, define the vital informational needs of organizations. Some of the key themes of this book therefore center on how organizations can use information resources to respond to these challenges.

What Is An Information Society?

In an **information society,** which may be considered either an advanced form of industrial society, or a postindustrial society (as analyzed by Daniel Bell in 1973), most of the people active in the economy are employed in the handling of information. Similarly, most of the goods and services produced by an information society can be classified as information- (or knowledge-) related.

In a seminal work published in 1962, Fritz Machlup of Princeton University recognized and quantified the role of what he called the "production and distribution of knowledge"[1] in the total products and services produced in the United States—an advanced industrial economy. Machlup determined that in 1958, information-related activities accounted for 29 percent of gross national product (GNP) and engaged 31 percent of the labor force. A subsequent study by Marc Porat (1977), using a different approach, concluded that in 1967, close to half of the GNP and over half of labor income could be credited to information-related activities. The historical composition of the U.S. workforce shown in figure 2.1 is cogent evidence that a major societal shift has taken place.

As we can see from figure 2.1, in the late 1950s the information sector became the primary employer of the U.S. labor force. From a society in which industry employed the largest segment of the population, we have now become one in which the largest component of the workforce is employed in information-related activities. A 1981 study by the Organization for Economic Cooperation and Development (OECD, 1981) has shown that a similar development has occurred in other advanced economies.

As figure 2.1 also shows, the information sector of the economy had already started to grow in the last century. However, after World War II, the technological push of computers and telecommunications added impetus to these developments. The speed of digital data processing, the development of very high-volume storage, and the speed and capacity of transmission of an increasingly broader spectrum of information modalities—voice, data, text, and image—were made possible by innovations in microelectronics, optics, and other technologies. This staggering increase in capabilities has been accompanied by steady decreases in costs. It is estimated that the cost of information technology decreases by about

FIGURE 2.1

The U.S. civilian workforce distribution.

(From Beniger, 1986, p. 23.)

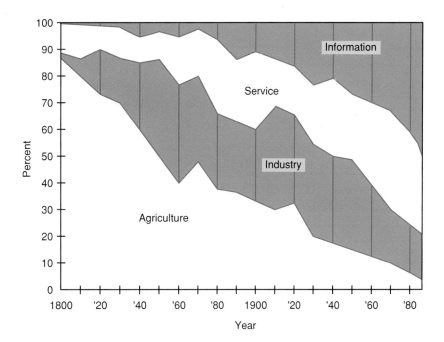

30 percent per year (Yates, 1991). However, this does not mean that we have become a society of computer programmers. Information-related activities, as broadly understood by the cited analysts, range from education to the postal service, for example.

It is extremely difficult in some cases to separate the informational and noninformational components of an activity. Hence, estimates of the dimensions of the information sector vary. Yet, the broad outlines of the information economy have been confirmed (Nass, 1987). Moreover, the growth rate is higher in these activities than in the others—therefore, the trend will last. Just as the industrial revolution transformed agriculture, which now employs somewhat less than 3 percent of the workforce, so the information revolution is transforming industry and contributing to the productivity of agribusiness as well. The number of production workers continues to decline (Roach, 1986), while both information-sector workforce and spending continue to grow. Of course, agriculture and industry do not cease to be essential to a nation's well-being. Rather, agriculture and industry have been transformed by the productive application of knowledge, which has made it possible to reduce the volume of human resources invested as direct labor in agricultural and industrial production.

What caused the shift to information society? James Beniger has advanced the argument that the origin of the information society may be found in the advancing industrialization of the late nineteenth century (Beniger, 1986). As industrial plants increased the speed with which they could process materials, they also had to devote increased resources to control manufacturing and transportation. To exercise this control, the firm had to process information ever faster. It follows that while computers and computer-based information systems did not bring about the information society, they certainly gave it its current momentum.

Peter Drucker, one of the most perceptive analysts of management, noted that the ability of a nation's economy to generate knowledge—both theory and technological know-how—and employ it through productive organizations will in the future determine that nation's success in international competition (Drucker, 1969). We may say that the ability of organizations to compete in an information economy is also based on their ability to employ what has become known as intellectual technologies. Such technologies are based on the handling of abstract information rather than of materials; work employing these technologies has been called **knowledge work.** Most of us engage in knowledge work most of the time, and information systems are a potent tool in this work. But before we look more closely at knowledge work, let's consider two examples of firms succeeding in the new marketplace.

Information Society at Work— Two Examples

Let us consider two examples of what the forces of information society can mean to large and small businesses. The first vignette will show you how information systems can contribute to restructuring of entire industries.

The Caterpillar case provides an excellent example of what some call "electronic marriage": a closer relationship between a customer and a small number of suppliers made possible by information technology. Note the savings for Caterpillar: no need for quality assurance, no need for inventories, simplified receiving and accounts payable.

A very different vignette concerns a small company that was repositioned thanks to an information system.

RESURRECTION OF THE RUST BELT

The industrial heartland of the United States has been adjusting to pressures on the "smokestack" industries. According to former Ohio Governor Richard Celeste, such industries recognize that ". . . you need a much smaller workforce to maintain your level of production." Companies are restructuring to become more effective in the new environment. This restructuring causes ripples of further restructuring in the operations of the firms' customers and suppliers.

To become a competitive manufacturer, Caterpillar, of Peoria, Illinois, reduced its labor force and began purchasing high-quality parts for its farm equipment from smaller, specialized, technologically nimble suppliers.

As an example, Wrayco of Stow, Ohio, is one of Caterpillar's certified suppliers—that is, its products are of such high quality that Caterpillar does not inspect them. An inventory control information system connects Wrayco to Caterpillar, so that shipments are dispatched just in time for their use and the client (Caterpillar) does not need to stockpile inventory.

To speed processing, Wrayco prints bar codes on its parts. The Caterpillar workers pass an electronic wand over the parts received, triggering receipt transactions in the receiving and accounting information systems. Payment to Wrayco is also processed automatically and sent over the wire.

Based on Myron Magnet, "The Resurrection of The Rust Belt," *Fortune*, August 15, 1988, pp. 40–46.

RESURRECTION OF A FAMILY FIRM

When Les, David, and Cindy Frischman inherited from their father the small business he founded in Homestead, Pennsylvania, the advice they received was to cut their losses and close the company. The firm, Commercial Textiles Inc., was selling uniforms wholesale to restaurants and hotels. Its customer base was largely local, concentrated in western Pennsylvania—and too narrow to sustain the business.

However, the family decided that the troubled business had good prospects *nationwide*. They developed a new marketing strategy based on that premise. The linchpin of the strategy was the purchase of a $30,000 computerized information system that allowed them to track on-line both widely-dispersed customers and inventories. Coupled with a toll-free telephone number and an advertising brochure sent around the country, the system produced results. The company's client list rose in just four years from 50 to over 2,000 hotels, restaurants, and country clubs.

"The computer gives us information my father would have never dreamed of," says Les Frischman. The system not only tracks payables and receivables, it helps Commercial Textiles service orders faster than many similar companies—giving the small company a vital competitive edge.

Based on Keith L. Alexander, "Second Generation Brings Modern Ways to Family Firm," *The Wall Street Journal*, July 6, 1990, p. B2.

As you can see, both a major manufacturer and a small wholesale distributor were able to turn around their businesses by recognizing the forces active in the new information-oriented marketplace and the tools available to succeed in it.

What Is Knowledge Work?

Knowledge workers deal with information (abstractions) rather than with concrete objects. Thus, knowledge work is not directly involved in the manufacturing of a physical product (such as semiconductor chips, bagged french fries, or computer paper) or in providing a physical service (for example, bagging french fries in a hamburger franchise outlet).

Someone doing knowledge work produces a plan, makes a decision, and perhaps writes software or a business letter. Obviously, the knowledge varies greatly depending on the task. It is also obvious that a physical worker may employ extensive knowledge about the production process. The main difference between physical and knowledge workers is that a knowledge worker uses not physical effort but his or her knowledge and the information appropriate for the task to produce another item of information. Knowledge workers are sometimes classified as knowledge workers proper and information workers. In these characterizations, knowledge workers produce new knowledge, or at least "add value" to the information they receive. Information workers, on the other hand, perform basically clerical tasks of processing information without significantly changing it.

Even workers directly employed in production processes deal increasingly with an "electronic text" representing these processes rather than with the processes themselves (Zuboff, 1988). Thus, a machine operator who would formerly have directly adjusted the chocolate mixture at the mixing machine, relying largely on his or her senses for the correct proportions, now monitors the control panels of a computer-driven process. It is not surprising that today's organizations keenly perceive the need for an educated and well-trained workforce.

MIS professionals are obviously knowledge workers. More important, they define the environment in which much of the knowledge work is done by others. A chief executive officer may each morning check the key indicators of the company's performance as produced by the executive information system. Later the same day, a team of financial analysts may use a group decision support system to recommend the level of prices and promotion needed to shore up a flagging product line. A company salesperson visiting a client connects her laptop computer over the telephone line with the inventory database and enters an order with a guaranteed delivery date. At the same moment, office clerks use word processing and electronic document filing, and manufacturing floor supervisors work with an expert system to reschedule production around a failed piece of equipment. All of this is knowledge work, engaged in daily in a modern organization. The broad dimensions of knowledge work with the use of information systems are illustrated in the color photos on pages 42–45.

The intellectual technology for this work, information systems, are developed and maintained by MIS specialists within organizations, increasingly with the direct participation of the end users themselves.

WILL ELECTRONIC NOTEPADS REVOLUTIONIZE KNOWLEDGE WORK?

Personal computers have transformed the way much knowledge work is done—they have truly empowered many categories of workers. However, keyboard-driven input is still a barrier for many others.

All along, another vision of personal computing has persisted: that of a truly portable, notepad-sized, powerful computer that would serve as an electronic assistant to its carrier. This was the vision of Dynabook, proposed by Alan Kay and his associates at Xerox Corporation's Palo Alto Research Center (PARC) in the 1970s.

Pen-based notepad computers have appeared within the last few years and are beginning to realize this idea. You can see such a computer in a photo on page 42. Using a pen (a special stylus, actually) to write block characters on the top surface of the pad-sized machine, an insurance adjuster can fill out a form and mark damaged parts on an exploded view diagram—completing the task right where a damaged car is; a police officer can enter a report at the scene of a crime; and an executive can simply jot down notes during a meeting.

In fact, with the electronic notepad, any form-oriented task may be simplified and completed in the field—at a construction site, during a sales call, or at the customer's location when goods are being delivered. The computer can recognize block-printed letters but will simply store notes or diagrams. You can edit a text, just as you would on a typed page, by drawing a caret under the insertion point and block-printing a new word above it. Easily connected to a network (wireless transmission modes are also emerging), notepad computers are expected to become a common briefcase accessory.

"Portable, pen-based computing will deliver the power of the computer to situations where only notebooks and the pen went before," says S. Jerrold Kaplan, the founder of Go Corporation (of Foster City, California), a leader in software development for these machines. And the effects of this will soon be seen.

Based in part on Paul Saffo, "Pen-Based Computing to Enable New Types of Tasks, Users," *InfoWorld*, January 21, 1991, p. 48; Beth Freedman, "Developers Get the Go-Ahead For PenPoint OS," *PC Week*, January 28, 1991, pp 1, 8; and Brenton R. Schlender, "Hot New PCs That Read Your Handwriting," *Fortune*, February 11, 1991, pp. 113–23.

2.2 DEMANDS ON ORGANIZATIONS IN AN INFORMATION SOCIETY

Transportation and communication networks spanning the globe have removed the protective space and time buffers shielding companies from competition. This calls for constant innovation. The operational environment of today's organization is characterized by complexity, turbulence, and a high volume of knowledge with potential impact on the company's operations.

Demands of Continuing Innovation

An **infrastructure** is the structure of facilities and services necessary for organizations and economies to function and grow. Fast and relatively inexpensive means of transportation, telecommunications networks, and global financial markets are all components of the infrastructure of the information society. These means of rapidly moving goods, information, and money have shrunk the world. They have removed the advantages provided by the remoteness of potential business competitors in the early industrial economy. By and large, firms no longer compete solely against a known handful of other companies: they must develop a general competitive capability. Runners may appreciate the analogy to the difficulty of achieving a record result running alone as compared with running against others in a race.

Not only has the space buffer that formerly shielded companies from their remote competitors been removed, but paced by computerized information systems, life cycles for product development have been shortened dramatically. With the use of CAD/CAM (computer-aided design/computer-aided engineering) technology, a new car model is developed in nine months instead of three years; financial software and global securities markets make it possible to develop and bring to the market a new financial product, such as a new type of bond, within ten days. Companies used to be able to rely on "cash cows"—products which in mature markets bring significant profits without a need for innovation. Now that time-related protection has also disappeared.

A highly dynamic information society requires constant innovation—both in marketed products and services, and in the continual restructuring of organizations to adapt to changing market demands. Moreover, successful organizations must not only react, but also proactively anticipate new developments and changes in their markets. In chapter 5, we will examine a large number of cases when the use of information technology gave a competitive edge in the marketplace to the innovating firm.

Mergers, acquisitions, and organizational restructuring have indeed been the order of the day during the past two decades. The stability and stolidity that were the hallmark of successful industrial corporations have given way to constant corporate renewal. Robert Waterman, a well-known management consultant, quotes the chief executive officer of IBM, John Akers, who "says they never reorganize except for a good business reason, but if they haven't reorganized in a while, 'that's a good business reason.' "[2] However, this dynamism has to be combined with a stable, "producing" environment. The art of balancing in corporate renewal requires that an organization ensure a sufficient degree of organizational stability to successfully carry out change. Perhaps the best way to state it is to say that an information society requires an organization to maintain a constant trait of *adaptability,* rather than adaptation; in other words, a firm must possess the capability to keep changing rather than to make a single change.

We shall further address the processes of innovation, organizational learning, and organizational change in our discussion of organizations and management in chapter 12. Information systems are a powerful tool for innovating. We will therefore describe the process of implementing large systems as an instance of organizational change.

Management information systems must be vehicles built to facilitate rather than to put the brakes on change, as unfortunately frequently occurs. The Bank of America example in the preceding chapter is an illustration of this principle.

Changes in the Environment of Organizations— The Informational Aspect

We can describe the environment in which organizations operate from the informational perspective in terms proposed by George Huber of the University of Texas (Huber, 1984). Huber has studied the organizational design required by an information society. His conclusions provide a framework for determining what is required of an organizational information system.

These, according to Huber, are the hallmarks of an information society:

1. Dramatic Increase of Available Knowledge
   Whether measured in terms of the number of scholarly journals, patents and copyrights, or in terms of the volume of corporate communications, both the production and the distribution of knowledge (to use Machlup's terms) have undergone a manifold increase.

2. Growth of Complexity
   Huber characterizes complexity in terms of numerosity, diversity, and interdependence. A growing world population and the industrial revolution combined to produce *numerosity,* or a growing number of human organizations. To succeed, people and organizations learned to specialize: they do things differently and organize themselves differently to accomplish specialized tasks. These differences lead to *diversity.*

   Two principal factors have led to increased *interdependence.* The first has been the revolution in the infrastructure of transportation and communication. The second factor is specialization in firms that make narrowly defined products, as opposed to the self-sufficiency of companies producing a complex product down to its minute elements. A company's product is typically a part of a larger system, produced with contributions from a number of interdependent firms (consider a car or a computer). Moreover, interdependence has increased on a global scale. Even the most isolated of countries participates in some way in the international division of labor.

   Organizations operating in the public sector, while rarely in a competitive situation, are still governed by the demands of society. Pressures on the public sector in democratic societies, along with the pressures conveyed from the private sector, also make the environment in which public organizations operate more complex.

3. Increased Turbulence
   The *pace of events* in an information society is set by technologies. The speeds of today's computer and communication technologies have resulted in a dramatic increase in the number of events occurring within a given time. Consider the volumes and speed of trades in the securities and currency markets. Widespread use of telefacsimile, as another example, has removed the "float"—the lag between sending and receiving—in written communications. Equally important, because of the infrastructure discussed earlier, the number of events that actually influence an organization's activities (effective events) has also grown rapidly.

   Figure 2.2 depicts some of the pressures that this new, turbulent environment exerts on organizations. Note that similar pressures make the *internal* operations of firms acquire similar characteristics.

FIGURE 2.2

Pressures exerted on
organizations in an
information society.

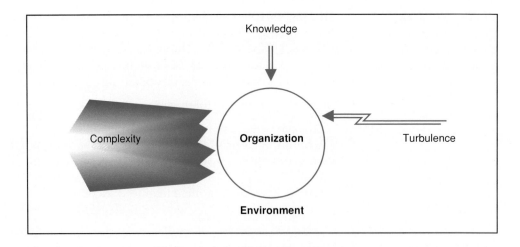

What are the events, information, and decisions that challenge organizations in an information society? They are related to the products of a company (goods and/or services) and the way the organization itself is structured and operates. The great amount of change and turbulence pressuring organizations today thus calls for rapid innovation in both product and organizational structure. To thrive, an organization must have information systems able to cope with large volumes of information in a selective fashion.

Huber concludes that these factors—an increase of available knowledge, growth of complexity, and increased turbulence—are not simply ancillary to a transition to the new societal form. Rather, they will be a permanent characteristic of the information society in the future. Moreover, we should expect that these factors will continue to expand at an accelerating rate (a positive feedback exists). Barring some catastrophic event, we expect that the rapidly changing environment will be not only "more so" but "much more so." To succeed in an information society, organizations must be compatible with this environment.

2.3 INFORMATIONAL RESPONSES TO THE NEW ENVIRONMENT

The demands of the new environment call forth a set of responses from organizations, and all of these responses have implications for information systems. Some of the requisite responses have been pointed out by George Huber and Reuben McDaniel (Huber, 1984, 1986). They proposed an organizational design based on the decision-making paradigm—that is, based on the view that decision making is a central organizing principle for current and future organizations. In this text, we consider the support of decision making as only one of the contributions MIS make to organizational functioning.

Here are the responses required of organizations in an information society:

1. Organizational design for knowledge work in general and decision making in particular

2. Continuous product and process innovation through information and information systems

3. Constant internal company renewal supported by information systems

4. Explicit mechanisms for acquisition and targeted distribution of external information

5. Protection from information overload

Let us now consider these issues in more detail. We shall return to them in the appropriate chapters of the book further on.

Organizational Design for Knowledge Work

The volume and speed of decision making in an information society continue to increase dramatically. To keep up, routine and noncritical decision making must be done by the information systems themselves, subject to human approval when appropriate.

Organizations also need to assimilate information technology for both individual and—to an increasing degree—group decision making. After all, organizations exist to leverage the work of an individual through group work; hence, support of group work is essential. Industrial organizations were built around groups of people doing physical work. An assembly line, though used only in some industrial processes, became a powerful metaphor for the industrial age.

The new, information-based organizations are expected to rely to a much greater degree on specialists—knowledge workers broadly distributed throughout an organization, rather than concentrated at its headquarters (Drucker, 1988).

The organizations of the information era have to provide both the structure and the technology not only for individual knowledge work, but also for *group knowledge work*. The size of a group depends on the task at hand. For example, a message broadcast over the company network to all managers above a certain level (perhaps a hundred of them), requesting their comments on a new budgeting policy to be implemented during the next quarter, may encompass a large group. Five corporate planners collaborating over several months on drafting a new long-range company plan form another type of group. This small, tightly collaborating group may use an electronic meeting system with a group decision support facility since the members of the group may be distributed over several company locations.

The metaphor for work in the information age is a personal **workstation**[3]; some of the facilities such a workstation can make available are shown in figure 2.3. The workstation is generally built around a personal computer, with a modem connection to the telephone network (though digital networks are being introduced on ever larger scales). A single workstation has a significant processing capability of its own; but just as important, it connects with the workstations of other workers and provides access to a number of informational services both within the company (corporate databases, for example) and outside of it (such

FIGURE 2.3

The personal workstation—
an enabling tool

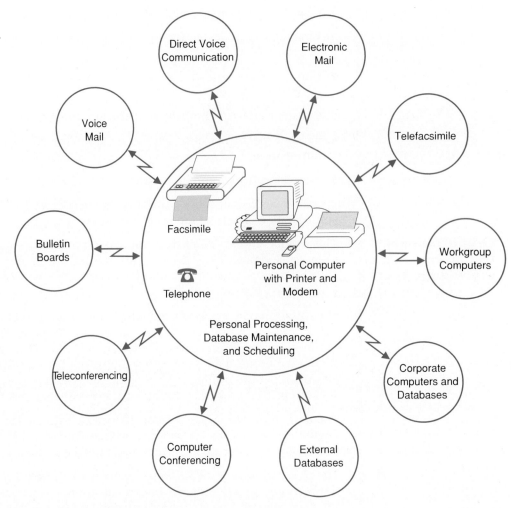

as a commercial demographic database). An isolated (nonnetworked) personal computer is not an adequate tool for most knowledge-work tasks. Massive installation of local area networks is proof of this.

Product and Process Innovation with Information Systems

Information systems have been increasingly used over the last decade to gain competitive advantage for products and services. Information systems serve to develop new products, and information itself may serve as all or a part of the product. This is called *product innovation*. But information systems also innovate in the ways products are manufactured and services are provided—this is *process innovation*. The use of information systems for competitive advantage is extensively discussed in chapter 5. The Federal Express vignette, which has become a classic example, illustrates how a company can successfully combine a product with customized service and information.

Information systems help companies add more value to their products than is possible in the manufacturing of commodity-type, standardized goods. Many U.S.

INFORMATION AS PART OF SERVICE

Federal Express is a leader in the overnight package delivery service. The high premium that its customers pay for delivery is based on an information system design that allows the company's managing director of systems engineering and design to say: "We don't just deliver packages. We deliver information with them for customer peace of mind."

Actually, the information delivery precedes the package delivery. The airbill attached to every package is bar-coded. The bar code is scanned at several points during the package's transit to its recipient. The scanned data are uploaded (sent over a telecommunication link) to a central database within two minutes. The data are then available for customer inquiries, many thousands of which are made every day. All in all, the tracking system processes 14 million on-line transactions per day.

Since the company's service is heavily dependent on the availability of transit information, its computer center is designed with extensive ("almost militaristic," according to the vice president for computer operations Ed White) availability precautions, including a complete backup facility one-half mile away from the operational center. Salary bonuses of the senior personnel are tied to system availability and response time—both of which are excellent, as you may expect.

It is in large part owing to its information systems that Federal Express was able to win in 1990 the coveted Malcolm Baldrige National Quality Award—the first service company in the United States to ever do so. Among the vital—and closely measured—factors in winning this prize are the quality of management, quality assurance of products and services, and customer satisfaction.

However, as the globalization of business progresses apace, Federal Express has encountered significant difficulties in providing the same levels of service abroad. In many countries, the necessary telecommunications infrastructure is simply not available and it is difficult to ensure proper package tracking during deliveries. The company is adding new countries to its telecommunications network at a rate of only one per quarter.

Based on David H. Freedman, "Redefining an Industry through Integrated Automation," *Infosystems*, May 1985, pp. 26–32; Elisabeth Horwitt, "Global Nets Rewrite Delivery Rules," *Computerworld*, September 17, 1990, pp. 1, 8; Bruce Caldwell, "Making It Like They Used To," *InformationWeek*, January 7, 1991, pp. 36–39; and Joanne M. Wexler, "Cosmos 2: Fedex's Next Generation," *Computerworld*, February 11, 1991, p. 29.

companies have found it advantageous in recent years to produce high-volume standardized products off the shores of the United States, where wages are lower and raw materials more accessible. However, commodity production does not bring high profits (Reich, 1988). To flourish, leading companies add more value to their products by customizing them for smaller market segments and by flexible manufacturing. Information systems are a powerful tool in these tasks, as we will see in chapter 5.

Internal Company Renewal Supported by Information Systems

Operation in the modern marketplace requires vast informational support. As we have already argued, it also requires continuing organizational adaptation through the creation of innovative organizational structures. Product- or project-oriented management structuring and company mergers are only two examples of adaptability in a changing environment. The broad goal of all such innovation is fitness in the marketplace.

SYSTEMS ARE BUILT TO ACCOMMODATE ORGANIZATIONAL CHANGE

Citicorp, a long-time leader in the use of information systems in banking, has developed a common platform called Foundation Software Architecture for developing its business applications.

In the traditional MIS environment, every time a new application system is needed—in response to an organizational change, for example—a large set of software components must be produced. These include database access software, user interfaces, software to network electronic messages to other systems, and programs that produce reports and transaction forms. The software modules are largely similar across the applications.

The common platform of Foundation Software Architecture includes these functional components, so that they do not need to be redeveloped for each application. In developing a new application, analysts and programmers use the functions provided by the platform. They can do so rapidly, inexpensively, and with predictable costs and deadlines. Moreover, application developers may not change the platform, which ensures a stable environment.

Based on G. Patrick McGunagle, "The Dangers of Expert Systems Development: Some Implications and Solutions," *Proceedings of 11th SWIFT International Banking Operations Seminar,* Vienna, Austria, 1988, pp. 37–41.

Unless organizational MIS is flexible enough to accommodate the change, the two objectives—maintaining informational support and adapting organizational structures to fit the changing environment—will contradict each other. The Citicorp vignette illustrates one way of ensuring flexibility.

We will further discuss in chapter 17 the importance of strategic planning for MIS in maintaining the fit between the evolving organization and its information system.

Mechanisms for Acquiring and Distributing External Information

As the business environment has become global, firms need explicit mechanisms for acquiring external information and distributing it to the appropriate knowledge workers.

The competitive demands of the global market lead to a certain degree of homogeneity—many can play the competitive game, regardless of their geographical locations, with a consequent increase in the number of players. Case Study One, at the end of this chapter, illustrates this point. A very large number of factors affect a company's business: no supplier is too remote and no customer too foreign. Organizations must have specialized information mechanisms as a part of **boundary spanning,** or acquiring information about their environments. Two modes for collecting information about the business environment require support:

1. Continuous *scanning* of the economic environment for opportunities and potential problems;

2. *Probing*, or making an ad hoc search for information regarding a specific problem or opportunity.

Protection from Information Overload

The vast volume of knowledge in the information society calls for coping techniques. The same information technology that helps us obtain information and make decisions also contributes to what we may call "positive informational feedback" as large numbers of knowledge workers produce an ever-increasing volume of information. If decision makers are not shielded from unneeded information, their effectiveness dwindles. The difficulty lies, of course, in determining what information is actually needed.

Software screens and filters, discussed in chapter 13 of the text, help in coping with information overload. For example, MIS users are able to define their preference profiles for incoming messages and rank them by order of importance. In the not-so-distant future, expert systems will be able to define more precisely an individual user's information-interest profile. Information systems will then be customized for the individual. A browsing mode will also be available for scanning. Thus, more complex informational tasks will be delegated to information systems.

2.4 CAPABILITIES OF INFORMATION SYSTEMS— AN ORGANIZATIONAL VIEW

Computer- and communications-based information systems offer a set of capabilities to be brought out in the development of individual systems. As we will see, some of these capabilities help to provide dynamic action, while others help to maintain operational stability even as rapid change takes place.

The principal capabilities of information systems include:

1. Fast and Accurate Data Processing, with Large-Capacity Storage and Rapid Communication between Sites
   This is the fundamental property of computers and telecommunications systems. This capability is exploited in the first order by operational-level systems, which process massive volumes of business transactions, for example, entering incoming orders or printing payroll checks. This capability is also used to derive management reports from the voluminous data stored on a semipermanent basis in secondary and archival computer memories.
   Sophisticated computer models rely on this capability for long-term planning based on a large number of factors and models for optimization of the use of resources (such as raw materials).

2. Instantaneous Access to Information
   In on-line systems, the contents of a computer database are generally available for queries in subsecond time. Through the telecommunications capability, a query may be directed to some remote site where the data are actually stored without the user's awareness (that is, in a transparent fashion). Ad-hoc (in other words, not predesigned) queries, introduced directly by end users, may in some cases produce extensive reports. Moreover, the presentation of the data may be individualized for a

particular user—with various forms of graphics, for example. A firm's databases serve as a vital part of its corporate memory—a permanent record that facilitates management.

3. Means of Coordination

Information systems have become widely accessible, primarily as a result of the proliferation of personal computers acting as workstations connected to telecommunications networks. This has made MIS a tool for coordinating organizational activities. **Coordination** brings parts of an organization together in a common effort, with the exchange of information playing a major role. In the most immediate sense, coordination is accomplished through office information systems. MIS have widened their reach to create the "portable manager"—complete with laptop and computerized home office.

In a deeper sense, the role MIS play in organizational coordination is a restatement of the fact that MIS have become crucial to management. If *coordinate* means *to harmonize in a common action or effort,* then planning with the use of appropriate information subsystems serves to establish common goals at all levels, and control aims to ensure that, once goals are established, organization members pursue them with vigor. Thus, MIS-assisted planning and control, combined with the extensive communication capabilities that information systems give to people within an enterprise, make MIS a coordination tool. Coordination activities are not limited to those that take place within an organization. Information technology is used ever more extensively to coordinate the actions of buyers and their suppliers, or to create electronic markets helping to match the needs of multiple buyers and sellers (Bakos, 1991). We shall see several examples of such coordination in chapter 5. In this regard, the coordination capability of information systems overlaps with their use for boundary spanning, which we discuss next.

4. Boundary Spanning

Aside from the internal role played by MIS *within* an organization, information systems increasingly serve to link an organization to the outside world. This may be accomplished in a variety of ways, some of which may be decisive for business success. For example, electronic data interchange (EDI) systems eliminate the exchange of paper transaction records, resulting in economy, speed, and reliability. Interorganizational systems connect suppliers with customers.

Through boundary-spanning information systems, the organization receives intelligence about the environment, which is necessary to compete successfully. Organizations also use boundary-spanning systems to provide computerized information for various external constituencies.

5. Support for Decision Making

Along with coordination, decision making is another basic aspect of management. All managerial functions, which will be further discussed later in the text, involve both coordination and decision making in varying degrees.

By informing managers and permitting them to select from among alternative courses of action, MIS support both structured and unstructured decisions. *Structured decisions* occur when courses of action under all

COORDINATION IN GLOBAL BUSINESS

The information society has brought us global interdependence—companies now must compete on a worldwide scale. To compete effectively in this environment of business globalization, larger firms must also coordinate their activities on a global scale.

"Global companies can't afford to operate as a series of independent geographic segments," says Hans Huppertz, director of corporate information systems at Dow Chemical, a large multinational corporation. "They need to operate as a single global entity."

This new approach to international business, in which overseas subsidiaries make specialized contributions and share human resources, facilities, and knowledge with corporate headquarters and other subsidiaries, has been called the *transnational organization* (Bartlett, 1989).

Dow Chemical is an excellent example of an organization that needs such an approach. Headquartered in Midland, Michigan, the company makes 50 percent of its sales outside the United States. Its manufacturing facilities are located in many countries of the Americas, Asia, and Europe. Some of them make products strictly for local needs. Others, however, deliver to global customers—including other multinational firms. A global customer such as Ford Motor Company might order products from several Dow facilities, be they located in Europe or in Latin America, and demand that the specifications for these products be the same. This obviously calls for worldwide coordination.

In the light of this new demand, many of the information systems of the foreign operations and of the central office must be integrated into a single system. Telecommunications networks, shared databases, and integrated business functions (order processing, for example) are necessary for coordination. Barriers of language, different government regulations, and differing technology standards are only some of the obstacles that must be overcome to provide this coordination.

One example of a coordinating system is Dow Chemical's worldwide order-tracking system. This system is able to track on a global scale the status of any order, from the time it is received to the time the ordered goods reach the customer. A deceptively simple problem had to be solved to implement the system: each of the organization's units involved in fulfilling an order could have previously had a different name and a different code for the item ordered—and that would make any coordination a nightmare.

Based in part on Janet Fiderio, "Information Must Conform in a World Without Borders," *Computerworld*, October 1, 1990, pp. 91–95.

possible circumstances may be programmed and thus fully automated. Management reporting systems, for example, may rely on established inventory reorder formulas to determine the quantity of supplies needed. *Unstructured decisions* require human judgment as a critical component.

Suppose that a group of managers is responsible for determining whether their firm will grant credit to another company. Granting credit to a large company involves structured, semistructured, and unstructured decisions. Various accounting ratios indicating company performance can be obtained from a management reporting system, which may also determine whether each company falls into the acceptable windows of approval—a highly structured process. Projections for the company's future—a semistructured decision—can be made for various scenarios with the use of a decision support system. But no information system can replace visiting the company and "getting the feel" of its management and operations; this is an unstructured decision. The managerial group may then employ an expert system, which would suggest a solution to the credit-granting problem based on a set of established financial criteria, on projections for the company's future, and on applying rules of thumb to the results of the on-site visit. With the expert system's suggestion and its explanation of how it arrived at its recommendation, the managers are able to make the final decision.

Remember that people remain the ultimate decision makers in any organization. However, the volume and complexity of decision making in an information society *requires* that decision makers have MIS support.

6. Formalization of Organizational Practice
Operational systems handle transactions in a specific way in every organization. Electronic mail systems and computer conferencing, both components of office information systems, provide a protocol for the interaction of people within an organization. Authorizer's Assistant—an expert system for credit card purchases developed by American Express—recommends authorization or refusal of credit for most credit card transactions, assuring high consistency of response. These are just some examples of how organizational practice may be defined through MIS.

Formalizing does not mean casting in concrete: properly designed systems should give an organization the capability to evolve as the environment changes.

7. Differentiation of Products or Services
The strategic use of information systems leads to the use of information as a part of the product or service. As will be extensively discussed in chapter 5, this capability to differentiate, customize, and individualize the product or service with the use of information in a cost-effective fashion may produce a competitive advantage.

8. Modeling
Computers are broadly used to model future economic conditions, prospective products, and environments where the products will operate. Software models are frequently substituted for the use of physical resources (other than the resource of computer time) in making these projections. Relatively inexpensive, fast, and comprehensive experimentation then becomes possible. Knowledge workers increasingly manipulate models of reality in gaining understanding, designing, and studying effects of possible changes.

9. Production Control
Computerized systems for production control are not considered a part of MIS in the strict sense. However, the line between MIS and production control systems becomes blurred and, as system integration progresses, is even likely to disappear. Flexibility and economies are the potential benefits of using computers in automated production processes. As we will see in chapter 5, it is cost-effective in computerized manufacturing to produce small lots of products, thus assuring product diversity to satisfy a variety of customer needs. Another advantage: computer-controlled

production and processing machines can immediately reject defective components and alert operators to faulty processes, leading to higher-quality output.

All nine of the capabilities we have discussed are realized through organizational information systems. However, managers who introduce such systems are not always motivated by strictly rational concerns about organizational welfare. Some managers *do* implement systems to further personal goals, such as enhancing their power, status, or credibility (Kling, 1980).

2.5 DEVELOPMENT OF ORGANIZATIONAL COMPUTING

The role played by information systems in organizations has evolved over time. This evolution has not led to wholesale discarding of the early types of systems—this would be quite expensive, and in many cases the older systems are still useful after suitable modifications. The progressive retargeting of MIS can be summarized as moving "up and out": progressive support of higher levels of management in increasingly individualized fashion, and aiming MIS at competitors to achieve strategic advantage.

The following view of MIS evolution over three eras was adapted here from the work of James I. Cash, Jr. of the Harvard Business School (Cash, 1988) and is illustrated in figures 2.4 through 2.6.[4]

FIGURE 2.4

The MIS Environment: Era I (Data Processing), mid-1950s through mid-1970s.

(John P. Gallagher, *Knowledge Systems for Business*, © 1988, pp. 7, 8. Adapted by permission of Prentice-Hall, Englewood Cliffs, New Jersey.)

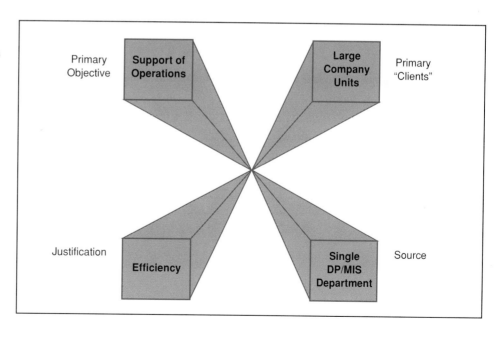

FIGURE 2.5

The MIS Environment: Era II
(Management Support), mid-
1970s through mid-1980s.

(John P. Gallagher,
*Knowledge Systems for
Business,* © 1988, pp. 7, 8.
Adapted by permission of
Prentice-Hall, Englewood
Cliffs, New Jersey.)

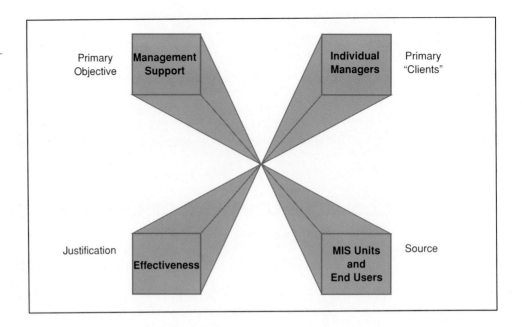

FIGURE 2.6

The MIS Environment: Era III
(Competitive Positioning),
mid-1980s through the
present.

(John P. Gallagher,
*Knowledge Systems for
Business,* © 1988, pp. 7, 8.
Adapted by permission of
Prentice-Hall, Englewood
Cliffs, New Jersey.)

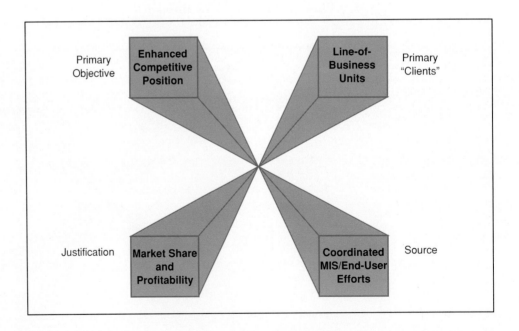

From the mid-1950s to the mid-1970s, companies generally had a single data processing department (later to be renamed MIS department). All application systems were developed within this department and largely at its discretion. Thus, end-user access to computer technology was mediated: professional computer expertise was required to obtain information from the system. The backlog of applications judged worthy of development yet having to wait for the availability of professional time ran two to three years in most organizations. Access to computing was thus severely restricted.

The primary target of data processing departments was operational support, although management support was emerging toward the end of this period in the form of voluminous reports. Raising the efficiency of company operations was the main objective of most applications.

The second era in organizational computing began in the late 1970s and was made possible by a number of technological developments spanning a decade. The development of time-sharing operating systems made it possible for a user on a terminal to access the computer directly. Specialists devised information systems directly supporting the decision-making process and organized company data in databases, making the data far more accessible and usable. Minicomputers made it not only possible but justifiable to break up the monopoly of a single MIS department. The greatest impact was made by the personal computer, which emerged on an industrial scale in 1977 as Apple II. Propelled by the broadly used spreadsheet programs (initially, VisiCalc), personal computers and end-user oriented software empowered the users themselves. End-user computing had begun: in many cases, instead of requesting that a system be developed by the MIS department, knowledge workers themselves began using a productivity software package (a database management system or a spreadsheet, for example), customizing it for their needs, and even developing systems of their own. Many information systems were brought under control of their users.

Organizations now entered a new stage in their reliance on information systems, which included extensive operational and management support systems developed during the two earlier stages. During the current, third era of MIS development, firms expect information systems to carry them beyond increased operational efficiencies and managerial effectiveness: systems are now geared to help a company to compete in the marketplace. Business functions are reengineered and extensively supported with information technology. This requires close interaction between developers and users; the sharp divide between the two groups often disappears when application systems are concerned. End users initiate and participate in the development of many systems. They also control some of the systems they use. In leading corporations, end-user computing is an important contribution to overall MIS development and maintenance. Systems integration is a vital concern.

· ·

SUMMARY

In an information society, most goods and services are related to processing of information. By recognizing the forces active in this society, and by using its tools—such as information systems—organizations can succeed; by failing to do so, they may fail.

Most people in an information society are involved in knowledge work. They have to be trained for this work and supported with appropriate tools.

The information society in which we live poses new demands on organizations. Organizations must continually innovate and be able to adapt to a complex and turbulent environment. They also need to develop a set of informational responses. In developing these responses, organizations can and should draw on the full range of capabilities offered by information systems.

In arriving at the present stage, when organizations use MIS for competitive positioning, firms have moved beyond the eras during which operational efficiency and managerial effectiveness were the sole focus of organizational computing. Today, information systems need to serve all three purposes.

CONCLUSIONS FOR MIS PRACTICE

1. Informational processes are a driving force in the information society. Most of the people in this society—and in individual organizations—are engaged in knowledge work. Information systems offer a potent leveraging tool for making this work more effective and efficient. To succeed, an MIS practitioner should have a broad understanding of the general role of information systems in his or her organization, as opposed to a narrow view limited to particular technologies or applications.

2. The information society requires organizations to engage in ongoing innovation. This, in turn, means that information systems must be flexible enough to accommodate product, process, and organizational innovations. In particular, flexibility means that systems can be modified at a reasonable cost within a limited time, with cost and time proportional to the extent of the organizational change. Such contained modifications can be achieved if systems are planned and designed in modular fashion, with their modules (software components) handling carefully selected aspects of overall functionality. This is opposed to information systems where a change in the requirements may often produce a need for extensive reprogramming.

3. Overall, organizational MIS serve multiple purposes; data processing is the basic one, however vastly insufficient it may be for supporting modern organizations. Support of decision making at various corporate levels is another fundamental role of MIS today. Among other functions, information systems in a modern organization must also support group work and facilitate coordination and connectivity. To the MIS designer, this means that a user's personal computer must be made a part of one or more computer networks, with access to coworkers and databases.

4. The expectations placed on MIS—and MIS professionals—today go beyond operations support through data processing and support of the managerial functions of decision making and coordination. Through comprehensive support of line-of-business operations, information systems are expected to boost organizational efficiency and the competitive advantage enjoyed by a company's products and services. Therefore, MIS function is evaluated increasingly in terms of its contribution to the company's bottom line. MIS professionals need to thoroughly understand the business the company is in.

5. MIS professionals must secure for the systems users extensive access to external sources of information, especially for users at higher management levels.

6. Helping users to protect themselves from information overload is an increasingly important function of MIS professionals. The study of human cognitive functions and human-system interfaces, discussed in chapter 13, will aid in this task.

ENDNOTES

1. Machlup and some of the analysts following him used the term *knowledge* in a broad sense that cannot always be differentiated from the term *information*.

2. Waterman, Robert H., Jr., *The Renewal Factor*. New York: Bantam Books, 1987, p. 10.

3. The term *workstation* (more precisely, *technical workstation*) is reserved by a segment of the literature for exceptionally powerful personal computers approximating the computing speed of mainframes and used principally for computer-aided design and engineering (see chapter 6). We use the term in a broader sense here.

4. The illustrations are designed after John P. Gallagher, *Knowledge Systems for Business*. Englewood Cliffs, N.J.: Prentice Hall, 1988.

KEY TERMS AND CONCEPTS

Information society	Workstation
Knowledge work	Information overload
Innovation	Boundary spanning
Infrastructure	Coordination
Adaptability	Decision making
Complexity	Structured decisions
Turbulence	Unstructured decisions

QUESTIONS

1. Why is the social framework of the information society important in studying MIS?

2. How is an information society distinguished from industrial society?

3. Consider this conclusion: "In the information society, industrial production is not important to the welfare of the economy." Do you agree? Why? Can you think of another possible conclusion?

4. Give five examples of knowledge work in the context of a business organization. Outline the types of support that may be offered by information systems in this work.

5. What are the relationships between MIS professionals and knowledge work?

6. What do we mean by *intellectual technology?* How is software related to it?

7. Where does the demand for continuing innovation stem from? What are the principal capabilities of information systems which may be used to respond to this challenge?

8. What do we mean when we say that the environment of an information society is more complex than that of an industrial society?

9. Which industry operates in a more complex and turbulent environment: insurance or semiconductor manufacturing? Analyze this question in terms of the ideas introduced in the chapter.

10. Which organization is, in general, better fit for knowledge work: a multilayered hierarchical company or a "California-style" firm with loosely coordinated small groups?

11. State one idea for a product innovation that would be made possible through information systems. Also, discuss one idea for a process innovation (improving the process of making a product) through the use of information systems.

12. Why has external information become increasingly important to organizations?

13. Which information system capabilities are vital to managing an organization? State the reason for the importance of each capability you name.

14. Analyze the development of organizational computing, describing the stages at which various MIS capabilities emerged.

ISSUES FOR DISCUSSION

1. Which information system capabilities are primarily derived from computer technology? Which derive primarily from telecommunications?

2. Describe point by point your ideal personal workstation.

3. As we discuss the role of information systems in organizations, we tend to stress the rationality in decision making: well-intentioned people making well-informed decisions, which will serve an organization well. What factors counteract this picture of rational decision making?

4. The Media Laboratory at MIT conducts research on the future of communication media and technologies. One of the projects the lab is working on is NewsPeek, an *individualized* electronic newspaper delivered by your personal workstation. The "newspaper" is connected to wire services and external databases. It has prodigious optical-disk memory. Ultimately, it will also know your news needs and, perhaps, your schedule (if you are attending a conference in Peoria a week from today, it will deliver some relevant news in anticipation of the event).

   How can such a system be modified for an organizational setting? How would it make knowledge work easier, and what MIS capabilities would be enhanced by it? (A fascinating description of the laboratory may be found in Stewart Brand, *The Media Lab: Inventing the Future at MIT.* New York: Viking, 1987.)

AN INDUSTRY OVERCOME BY DEMAND—AND GLOBAL INTERDEPENDENCE

Two consecutive hot summers in 1987 and 1988 left the U.S. air-conditioning industry with all its products sold out—from retailers to the factory floor.

The ability to respond to the demand was constrained by the dependence of the U.S. air-conditioning industry on the suppliers of rotary compressors, the main components of the units. Many compressors are imported from Japan, South Korea, Taiwan, Brazil, Canada, and Italy. Another level of dependence was created by the fact that these overseas suppliers also received an increased number of orders from African and Asian manufacturers. Finally, the weakness of the dollar in 1988 led to higher compressor prices for U.S. air-conditioner manufacturers and resulted in their resistance to purchasing these supplies.

Where will the industry go in the 1990s? One major manufacturer, General Electric, perceives the market as mature. On the other hand, the strategic planners at the Carrier Corporation believe future demand will grow, based on an analysis of such macroeconomic factors as gross national product, disposable income, and the rate of new household formations, as well as the greenhouse effect. The latter is the scientifically predicted increase in average temperatures by approximately 10 degrees Fahrenheit over the next 100 years, due to the rising concentrations of carbon dioxide, methane, and other gases in the atmosphere as a result of fossil-fuel use.

Based on Doron P. Levin, "An Industry Overcome by Heat," *The New York Times,* Business Day, August 19, 1988, pp. D1–D2.

Do We Have Proof of the Greenhouse Effect?

The great Swedish chemist Svante Arrhenius set forth in 1896 what we now know as the "greenhouse hypothesis." NASA's Goddard Institute for Space Studies in New York has a software simulation model (20,000 lines of FORTRAN code) that shows, according to one of the scientists involved, "without a doubt that the current warm temperatures are increasing due to the greenhouse effect." (According to the model, the hottest season between 1960 and 2010 will occur on the East Coast of the United States in June 1998.) However, these simulation results are not universally accepted.

Based in part on Kathy C. Leong, "Studying the Greenhouse Effect," *Computerworld,* August 29, 1988, p. 6; and Karen Wright, "Heating the Global Warming Debate," *The New York Times Magazine,* February 3, 1991, pp. 24–31.

An additional discussion on the business ramifications of the greenhouse effect may be found in Warren T. Brookes, "The Global Warming Panic," *Forbes,* December 25, 1989, pp. 96–102. An accessible discussion of the many open questions concerning the greenhouse effect is offered in William K. Stevens, "Global Warming: Search for the Signs," *The New York Times,* January 29, 1991, pp. C1, C4.

1. Outline, point by point, the impact of the information-society environment on the air-conditioning industry. Discuss this in terms of the concepts introduced in this chapter.

2. Outline how information systems could help Carrier Corporation to meet projected customer demand.

3. The second item in the case study describes a software simulation of the greenhouse effect. How does this tie in with our discussion of the informational environment of organizations?

CASE STUDY TWO

A PERFORMANCE-TRACKING SYSTEM

The success of an insurance company depends largely on the performance of its agents. To control this performance, the company needs to establish measurable expectations and check the agents' performance records against these expectations.

A Boston-based insurance company, The New England, has implemented a system for tracking performance of its 3,700 agents located at ninety sites around the United States. These agents sell a wide variety of financial products and services.

Robert A. Shafto, then president of The New England's Insurance and Personal Finance Division, describes the situation prior to implementation of the performance-tracking system: "We had a lot of data stored, but stored as the product of transactions. Also, a lot was stored in PCs and was not integrated—not to mention what we had on paper."

The tracking-system project was led by Shafto's executive assistant, Vincent Ficcaglia—a user himself.

The system was implemented with the user-friendly System W software produced by Comshare. The performance-tracking system includes thirteen screens displayed on Shafto's workstation. Presently, the agent data that was previously scattered is aggregated into a database on a larger computer. The database is downloaded (transferred) once a month to Shafto's personal computer. The executive can see on the screens, in graphical form, the performances of individual agents—both in absolute form and in relation to the goals that have been set.

The system also makes it possible to establish, for example, whether an agent who sells more is selling to more clients or—a simpler task—selling more to already existing clients.

"It's not that we have the information that we did not have before," said Shafto, "It's that the software organizes and communicates it. . . ."

POSTSCRIPT

The performance tracking system has become a prototype for an executive information system (EIS) that today serves Robert Shafto—now the president of The New England—and other top executives of the life insurance and financial services company. Thanks to the expanded system, the managers can track sales on a weekly and even daily basis. They can also observe the emerging trends and plan for the future. Managers of local offices are also using the system to track the performance of agents working for them.

Based on Nell Margolis, System Inspects Agents' Work, *Computerworld*, August 8, 1988, p. 25, and Susan Joslow, Case Study: Building an EIS, *Information Center Quarterly*, Winter 1991, pp. 6–9.

Case Study Two Questions

1. Which capabilities of information systems have been employed in this application? How?

2. If you were Robert Shafto, what information about the agents' work would you consider critical and want to obtain from the system?

3. Suggest additional capabilities of information systems that may be used to enhance this system.

4. What organizational effects would you expect from the new system?

5. This system appears relatively simple and generic. What other settings might you use a similar system in?

6. Who was driving this project, MIS professionals or end users?

7. When do performance-tracking systems stop being productive because the information is not timely? Do you consider, for example, the time horizon (a month) appropriate for the task at hand?

8. What role does this system play in the balance of power in the firm? Is it conceivable that a system of this type could be implemented to enhance the power of a manager?

9. What do you think of the title of the first of the two articles from which the case was drawn? Is it accurate? Why or why not?

SELECTED REFERENCES

Bakos, J. Yannis. "Information Links and Electronic Marketplaces: The Role of Interorganizational Information Systems in Vertical Markets." *Journal of Management Information Systems,* 8, 2, Fall 1991, pp. 25–47.

Bartlett, Christopher A., and Ghoshal, Sumantra. *Managing Across Borders: The Transnational Solution.* Boston: Harvard Business School Press, 1989.

Bell, Daniel. *The Coming of Post-Industrial Society.* New York: Basic Books, 1973.

Bell, Daniel. "The Information Society." In *The Computer Age: A Twenty-Year View,* edited by Michael L. Dertouzos and Joel Moses. Cambridge, Mass.: The MIT Press, 1979, pp. 163–211.

Beniger, James R. *The Control Revolution: Technological and Economic Origins of the Information Society.* Cambridge, Mass.: Harvard University Press, 1986.

Cash, James I., Jr.; McFarlan, F. Warren; McKinney, James L.; and Vitale, Michael R. *Corporate Information Systems Management: Text and Cases.* 2d. ed. Homewood, Ill.: Irwin, 1988.

Drucker, Peter F. *The Age of Discontinuity: Guidelines for Our Changing Society.* New York: Harper & Row, 1969.

Drucker, Peter F. "The Coming of the New Organization." *Harvard Business Review,* January–February 1988, pp. 45–53.

Huber, George P. "The Nature of Design of Post-Industrial Organizations." *Management Science,* 30, 8, August 1984, pp. 928–51.

Huber, George P., and McDaniel, Reuben R. "The Decision-Making Paradigm of Organizational Design." *Management Science,* 32, 5, May 1986, pp. 572–89.

Kling, Rob. "Social Analyses of Computing: Theoretical Perspectives in Recent Empirical Research." *Computing Surveys,* 12, 1, March 1980, pp. 61–110.

Machlup, Fritz. *The Production and Distribution of Knowledge in the United States.* Princeton, N.J.: Princeton University Press, 1962.

Marchand, Donald A., and Horton, Forest W., Jr. *Infotrends.* New York: Wiley, 1986.

Nass, Clifford. "Following the Money Trail: Twenty-five Years of Measuring Information Economy." *Communication Research,* 14, 6, December 1987, pp. 698–708.

Organization for Economic Cooperation and Development (OECD). *Information Activities, Electronics, and Telecommunication Technologies:Impact on Employment, Growth, and Trade.* Paris: OECD, 1981.

Porat, Marc U. *The Information Economy: Definition and Measurement.* Washington, D.C.: Office of Telecommunications, U.S. Department of Commerce, 1977.

Reich, Robert B. Keynote Address, "The Elusive Payoff in Information Technology: A Conference for Senior Executives." Proceedings of conference sponsored by *Business Week,* May 1988, pp. 52–66.

Roach, Stephen S. "The Information Economy Comes of Age." *Information Management Review,* 1, 1, Summer 1986, pp. 9–18.

Rubin, M. R., and Huber, M. T. *The Knowledge Industry in the United States, 1960–1980.* Princeton, N.J.: Princeton University Press, 1986.

Yates, Joanne, and Benjamin, Robert I. "The Past and Present as a Window of the Future." In *The Corporation of the 1990s: Information Technology and Organizational Transformation,* edited by Michael S. Scott Morton, pp. 61–92. New York: Oxford University Press, 1991.

Zuboff, Shoshana. *In the Age of the Smart Machine.* New York: Basic Books, 1988.

CHAPTER 3

STRUCTURE OF MANAGEMENT INFORMATION SYSTEMS

*Happy are those who can tie together in their thoughts
the past, the present, and the future!*

From a letter of Alexis de Tocqueville

There are as many management information systems as there are organizations: as we have said, an organization's information system to a large degree mirrors its functioning. Competitive advantage is gained by differentiating rather than by emulating the way another organization brings its products or services to the marketplace.

Yet, it is also true that all MIS consist of similar physical components, that there are only a few types of informational support systems of which MIS are composed, and that all organizations require support for similar management levels and functions. In this chapter, we will introduce MIS components and system types. We will also discuss the role of management-oriented MIS components in the informational framework of an enterprise.

FOCUS CASE

Jaguar is the pride of the British automotive industry. For a period, the company was run by a government ministry. When the government restored Jaguar to the private sector in 1984, the new management embarked on a drive to match the company's financial performance to the high performance of its products. Crucial objectives included computerizing company operations and providing management with informational support. Under chief executive officer Sir John Egan, the company increased information-systems spending to 2.5 percent of revenues.

Before privatization, the firm had been purchasing most of its information systems from its parent company, British Leyland. These and the internally developed systems were written in third-generation languages, such as PL/I and COBOL; the development and maintenance of such systems is an expensive and lengthy process. The company had several minicomputer systems, which were running in a stand-alone mode and not communicating with one another.

Modernization of Jaguar's MIS began with the creation of a network, unifying factories and offices dispersed throughout the country. A large corporate data center was also created, and a powerful mainframe computer (IBM 3090/150) introduced to support product engineering. Operational-level systems were placed on-line, so that transactions could be processed immediately. A system for distribution of management reports was created, under the control of Computer Associates CA-MANAGER software: reports are promptly distributed to forty-six user groups and automatically archived to make them available for review on-line.

A steering committee composed of representatives from Jaguar's functional divisions, such as manufacturing and finance, now controls MIS project development priorities. The MIS department, consisting of some two hundred people, uses fourth-generation languages whenever possible, which allows the programmers to specify computing tasks much more concisely than the third-generation languages do.

Having established information systems for support of operations and management, Jaguar is initiating projects aimed at introducing computer-integrated manufacturing (CIM) to the factory floor.

Based on Maggie McLening, ''Jaguar Gears up for the 90s,'' *Insight*, Summer 1988, pp. 20–22.

Integrated use of information technology is vital to the operations, management, and pursuit of the core business objectives of an enterprise. A variety of informational support systems, integrated into an enterprise-wide architecture, will ultimately furnish a corporation with an *information utility*—a platform from which each user will be able to access needed information.

CHAPTER OUTLINE

3.1 The Physical Components of MIS
- Hardware
- Software
- Database
- Personnel
- Procedures

3.2 Types of Organizational Information Systems

3.3 Information for Management
- Attributes of Quality Information
- Internal versus External Information
- Time Horizon

3.4 Management Reporting Systems
- Characteristics of MRS
- Reporting by MRS

3.5 Decision Support Systems

3.6 Executive Information Systems

3.7 The Role of Expert Systems

3.8 Informational Support of Management—A Hierarchical View

3.9 Levels of Planning and Control with MIS
- Operations Planning and Control—Information for Lower Management
- Tactical Planning and Management Control
- Long-Term (Strategic) Planning and Strategic Control

3.10 Functional Departmentation and MIS
- Functional Departmentation of Business Organizations
- Informational Support of Marketing and Sales as an Illustration of Hierarchical MIS Support

3.11 Management Support with Management-Oriented Information Systems—A Summary

Summary

Conclusions for MIS Practice

Key Terms and Concepts

Questions

Issues for Discussion

Case Study One: Chateau Rien Restaurants

Case Study Two: A Decision Support System for Delivery Routing

Selected References

• •

3.1 THE PHYSICAL COMPONENTS OF MIS

The physical components of MIS comprise the computer and communications hardware, software, database, personnel, and procedures.

A brief description of each of these components is presented in table 3.1.

Hardware

Almost all organizations employ multiple computer systems, ranging from powerful mainframe machines (sometimes including supercomputers) through minicomputers, to widely spread personal computers (also known as microcomputers). The use of multiple computers, usually interconnected into networks by means of telecommunications, is called **distributed processing.** The driving forces that have changed the information processing landscape from centralized processing, relying on single powerful mainframes, to distributed processing have been the rapidly increasing power and decreasing costs of smaller computers.

Though the packaging of hardware subsystems differs among the three categories of computers (mainframes, minicomputers, and microcomputers), all of them are similarly organized. Thus, a computer system comprises a **central processor** (though multiprocessors with several central processing units are also used), which controls all other units by executing machine instructions; a hierarchy of memories; and devices for accepting input (for example, a keyboard or a mouse) and producing output (say, a printer or a video display terminal). The **memory hierarchy** ranges from a fast primary memory from which the

TABLE 3.1	COMPONENT	DESCRIPTION
Physical Components of MIS	Hardware	Multiple computer systems: mainframes, minicomputers, personal computers
		Computer system components are: central processor(s), memory hierarchy, input and output devices
		Communications: local area networks, metropolitan area networks, and wide area networks
	Software	Systems software and applications software
	Database	Organized collection(s) of data used by applications software
	Personnel	Professional cadre of computer specialists; end users in certain aspects of their work
	Procedures	Specifications for the use and operation of computerized information systems collected in user manuals, operator manuals, and similar documents

central processor can fetch instructions for execution; through secondary memories (such as disks) where on-line databases are maintained; to the ultra high-capacity archival memories that are also employed in some cases. Chapter 6 will discuss computer system hardware in more detail.

Multiple computer systems are organized into networks in most cases. Various network configurations are possible, depending upon an organization's need. Fast **local area networks** join together machines, most frequently clusters of personal computers, at a particular organizational site such as a building or a campus. The emerging **metropolitan area networks** serve large urban communities. **Wide area networks** connect machines at remote sites, both within the company and in its environment. Through networking, personal-computer users gain access to the broad computational capabilities of large machines and to the resources maintained there, such as large databases. This connectivity converts personal computers into powerful workstations. Computer communications will be discussed further in chapter 7.

An example of the hardware organization of a distributed system is shown in figure 3.1.

Software

Computer software falls into two classes: systems software and applications software. **Systems software** manages the resources of the system and simplifies programming. **Operating systems** (UNIX, for example) control all the resources of a computer system and enable multiple users to run their programs

FIGURE 3.1

Distributed information system—hardware organization.

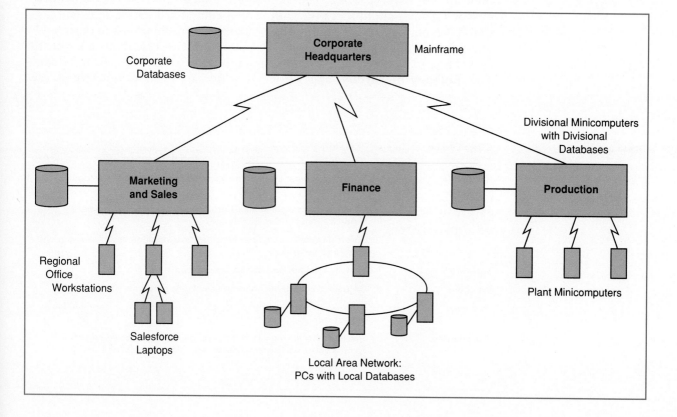

on a computer system without being aware of the complexities of resource allocation. Even if you are just using a personal computer, a complex series of actions takes place when, for example, you start the machine, check out its hardware, and call up a desired program. All of these actions fall under the control of an operating system, such as DOS or IBM OS/2. **Telecommunications monitors** manage computer communications; **database management systems** make it possible to organize vast collections of data so that they are accessible for fast and simple queries and the production of reports. Software **translators**—compilers or interpreters—make it possible to program an application in a higher-level language, such as COBOL or C. The translator converts program statements into machine instructions ready for execution by the computer's central processor.

Many categories of **applications software** are purchased as ready-to-use packages. Applications software directly assists end users in their functions. Examples include general-purpose spreadsheet or word processing programs, as well as the so-called vertical applications serving a specific industry segment (for example, manufacturing resource planning systems or accounting packages for small service businesses). The use of purchased application packages is increasing. However, the bulk of applications software used in large organizations is developed to meet a specific need. Large application systems consist of a number of programs integrated by the database. We will discuss computer software in more detail in chapter 6. The systems development process will be the subject of Part 5 of the book.

Database

To be accessible, data items must be organized so that individual records and their components can be identified and, if needed, related to one another. A simple way to organize data is to create files. A **file** is a collection of records of the same type. For example, the employee file contains employee records, each containing the same fields (for example, employee name and annual pay), albeit with different values. Multiple files may be organized into a **database,**[1] or an integrated collection of persistent data that serves a number of applications. The individual files of a database are interrelated. The way the data are organized is crucial to effective MIS; database organization will be discussed in chapter 8.

Personnel

Professional MIS personnel include development and maintenance managers, systems analysts, programmers, and operators, often with highly specialized skills. The hallmark of the present stage in organizational computing is the involvement of end users to a significant degree in the development of information systems. End-user computing will be analyzed in chapter 9 and the organization of the MIS function in chapter 17.

Procedures

Procedures to be followed in using, operating, and maintaining a computerized system are a part of the system documentation. These procedures are an important component in overall MIS operations and control, which we will discuss in chapter 20.

3.2   TYPES OF ORGANIZATIONAL INFORMATION SYSTEMS

Five types of systems may make up an organizational MIS: transaction processing systems (TPS), management reporting systems (MRS), decision support systems (DSS), executive information systems (EIS), and office information systems (OIS). An information system in a large organization would typically include multiple systems of each type, serving, for example, different functional areas within the enterprise, as discussed later in this chapter. System types differ in their processing focuses, and main objectives, as described in table 3.2.

The focus defines the mission of a system. Transaction processing systems support a company's business operations, and office information systems facilitate communication at all levels of a firm, while the remaining three system types support management functions. A hierarchical classification of MRS, DSS, and EIS users by management level is often too reductive. Thus, while many consider a DSS to be a support system for higher management, it is not; it may well support operational managers—supervisors—as well. (Such use is illustrated by Case Study Two at the end of this chapter.) In my practice, I have also encountered executive information systems successfully (that is, cost-effectively) employed by middle managers. We will further discuss management-support systems later in this chapter.

Transaction processing systems (TPS) support a firm's business operations. They also accumulate relevant data in databases for subsequent use by the management-oriented MIS components. TPS secure automation, while management-support systems aim to "informate" the organization, relying on the data accumulated through TPS, to use the term introduced by Shoshana Zuboff (Zuboff, 1988). To neglect the "informating" aspect of MIS by limiting these systems to data processing means failing to take advantage of their full potential. The informational relationship between operational-level TPS and management-oriented MIS components is shown in figure 3.2.

TABLE 3.2

Types of Organizational Information Systems

IS TYPE	WHEN APPEARED	FOCUS	MAIN OBJECTIVE
TPS	Mid-1950s	Data	Handling of routine transactions and maintenance of databases
MRS	Early 1960s	Information	Routine responsibility reporting from databases
DSS	Early 1970s	Decision	Support for decision-making sessions with analytic models and database extracts
EIS	Mid-1980s	Accessibility	Immediate access to internal and external information with stress on graphics
OIS	Late 1970s	Communication	Document and message (voice, data, text, video) handling

Office information systems (OIS) support general knowledge work in the context of a business office. The development of OIS as we know them today occurred in the late 1970s, when this field was revolutionized by the personal computer. Since then, as traditional office technology and computer and communications technologies have converged, OIS have rapidly developed towards becoming the "office of the future." The goal of OIS is to support multimedia communication within the firm and to offer gateways to the outside. Examples of activities supported by OIS include document processing, individual time scheduling and work flow coordination, project management, computer conferencing, and the exchange of messages in various formats. OIS will ultimately allow messages to be created, stored, and exchanged in any format—as documents, data sets, voice messages, holograms, still or moving images; and they will support conferencing at various levels of participants' presence—from bulletin boards to teleconferencing.

In this chapter, you will be introduced to the three management-oriented categories of information systems: management reporting systems, decision support systems, and executive information systems. You will also be introduced to the expert system—a technology that plays an important role in information systems of various categories. Office information systems will be discussed in more detail in chapter 16. Transaction processing systems will be discussed in the next chapter.

FIGURE 3.2

The informational relationship between operational and management support systems.

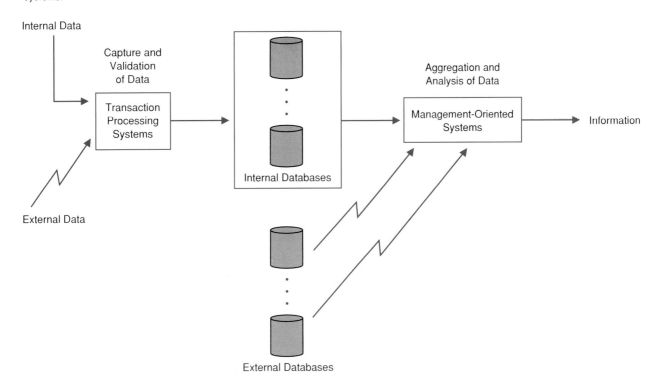

3.3 INFORMATION FOR MANAGEMENT

Attributes of Quality Information

Operational-level information systems support the conduct of business with data processing. The primary objective of management-oriented MIS components is to improve the effectiveness of managerial decision making by providing appropriate informational support. Various aspects of this broad task are discussed throughout the text. Here, we will concentrate on the general characteristics of the information needed for the task.

What do we mean when we demand *quality* information? The attributes we are talking about are summarized in table 3.3. The table is, indeed, a summary: for a detailed listing of thirty-four attributes of quality information, see Swanson (1985–86).

Many attributes of information are relative to the decision-making situation (or problem) in which the information will be used. Information should be complete, yet concise, with only relevant items brought to bear in the decision situation. Relevance provides the main protection against information overload. Determining what information is needed is the crucial aspect of the information systems planning and analysis discussed in Part 5 of this book.

Note the distinction between *accuracy* and *precision*. Suppose that, on the basis of accurate figures rounded off to the next million dollars, last year's quarterly sales were $505, $610, $408, and $456 million. If we report that average quarterly sales for the year were $494,750,000, our figure is accurate, but the precision we selected is inappropriate. The figure of $495 million better reflects the precision (degree of exactness) of the underlying data.

Many considerations influence the choice of the appropriate form in which information will be presented to a manager. Generally, the higher the management level, the less detailed—and thus more summarized—the information should be. Certain information should not be quantified (expressed in numbers); if qualitative ("soft") information is presented numerically, it may create a false impression of reliability.

TABLE 3.3

The Attributes of Information

ATTRIBUTE	DEFINITION
Timeliness	Available when needed and not outdated when made available
Accuracy	Corresponds to the reality it represents; free of errors
Precision	Offers quantitative information with a degree of exactness appropriate to the underlying data and to the decision-making situation
Completeness	Includes all the user needs to know about the situation
Conciseness	Does not include elements unneeded by the user
Relevance	Has direct bearing on the decision-making situation
Appropriateness of Form	The level of detail, tabular versus graphic display, and quantitative versus qualitative form, are selected in accordance with the situation

The "battle of the printout" is a well-known deadlock situation in a meeting where several managers offer conflicting information. Information for a decision must be obtained in a consistent fashion. Group decision support systems, discussed in chapter 14, offer a partial solution to the problem.

Internal versus External Information

Most of the data captured by TPS relates to various aspects of the organization itself. We shall further discuss in this chapter the different aspects of information on internal company operations employed by various managerial levels and stemming from various functional departments of the firm.

Increasingly, organizational advantages come from incorporating external information into the information system. Such information is partially captured by the organizational TPS, but a good part of it must be acquired from external sources. Representative examples include:

- Sales volume of a firm's primary competitor in a specific sales district
- Potential customer segments for various company product lines
- Questionnaire data regarding a projected new product, obtained via a series of focus groups
- Geographical distribution of company stockholders

Much external information is not quantitative; for example, legal, regulatory, tax, and labor union negotiations information are generally difficult to quantify.

A corporation can succeed only by adapting itself to the demands of its environment. This environment is represented by a number of groups that affect the company's ability to achieve its objectives or that are affected by it. These groups are called the **stakeholders** of a firm.[2] The internal stakeholders are, of course, a firm's employees, who may be classified in terms of their informational needs. Table 3.4 lists principal external stakeholders of organizations, along with the principal informational demands generated by their presence.

TABLE 3.4

External Stakeholders Generating Informational Requirements

STAKEHOLDER	INFORMATIONAL RELATIONSHIPS WITH THE ORGANIZATION
Customers	Marketing and sales information
Distributors	Marketing and logistics information
Competitors	Market penetration, growth trends, innovations
Suppliers	Purchasing terms and quality
Labor unions	Compensation, stability of employment
Stock- and bondholders	Company performance, performance of securities
Financial institutions	Financing terms, investment opportunities
Trade associations	Participation benefits, competitive information
Governments	Political, regulatory, and legal developments (at local, state, and federal levels, including foreign entities where necessary)
Special interest groups	Employment of disadvantaged and minority group members, contribution to communities

The boundary-spanning role of an information system consists in keeping the organization continually informed about the activities of these external stakeholders; some of them (for example, stockholders and government agencies) must also be kept informed by the organization.

The development of the information society has created an infrastructure for transmission of various types of data, such as electronic data interchange (EDI) and other value-added networks, and has made information itself an important product. Organizational MIS have become progressively embedded within these networks and markets so that now, in various areas, the distinction between external and internal data has become blurred. For example, consider:

- Inventory data maintained by your organization in behalf of a customer firm that relies on your company for all its supply needs within a certain product area (such as a hospital relying on a drug distributor)
- An information processing subsidiary of a diversified corporation handling the information of another business unit for the parent company

Time Horizon

The original data processing systems were oriented toward the past, in that they maintained accounting data about company activities. With the advent of on-line systems, it was possible to maintain up-to-date data about the present. Next, planning for the future became possible, particularly through the use of decision support systems. Continuing comparison of present and projected results is the fundamental tenet of management control.

Today, MIS maintain information about the past, present, and projected future of the company, its operating units, and the relevant aspects of its environment.

3.4 MANAGEMENT REPORTING SYSTEMS

Management reporting systems (MRS) are the most elaborate of the management-oriented MIS components. Indeed, some writers call MRS management information systems, the name we reserve for the entire area of informational support of operations and management.

The main objective of MRS is to provide lower and middle management with printed reports and inquiry capabilities to help maintain operational and management control of the enterprise.

Characteristics of MRS

MRS have the following characteristics:

1. MRS are usually designed by MIS professionals, rather than end users, over an extensive period time, with the use of life-cycle oriented development methodologies (as opposed to first building a simpler prototype system and then refining it in response to user experience). Great care is exercised in developing such systems because MRS are large and complex in terms of the number of system interfaces with various users and databases.

2. MRS are built for situations in which information requirements are reasonably well-known and are expected to remain relatively stable. Modification of such systems, like their development, is a rather elaborate process. This limits the informational flexibility of MRS but ensures a stable informational environment.

3. MRS do not *directly* support the decision-making process as a search for alternative solutions to problems. Naturally, information gained through MRS is used in the manager's decision-making process. Well-structured decision rules, such as economic order quantities for ordering inventory or accounting formulas for computing various forms of return on equity, are built into the MRS itself.

4. MRS are oriented towards reporting on the past and the present, rather than projecting the future.

5. MRS generally have limited analytical capabilities—they are not built around elaborate models, but rather rely on summarization and extraction from the database according to given criteria. Based on simple processing of the data summaries and extracts, report information is obtained and printed (or, if of limited size, displayed as a screen) in a prespecified format.

6. MRS generally report on internal company operations rather than spanning the company's boundaries by reporting external information.

Reporting by MRS

MRS may produce reports either directly from the database collected through transaction processing systems, or from databases spun off for the purpose. Separate spin-off databases may be created for several reasons, such as avoiding interference and delays in transaction processing, maintaining the security of central databases, or economizing by using local databases accessible to local managers to counter the heavy telecommunication costs of working with a central database.

MRS provide the following report forms:

1. Scheduled (Periodic) Reports

These reports are furnished on a daily, weekly, biweekly, or other basis depending on the decision making need. A weekly sales analysis report may be used by the sales manager to assess the performances of sales districts or individual salespeople. A brand manager responsible for a particular product might obtain a weekly sales report containing information useful in his or her decision making—showing regional sales and sales to various market segments, for example.

Figure 3.3 shows a fragment of a monthly accounts receivable revaluation report. It indicates as yet unrealized loss or gain on the receivables in foreign currencies (for example, since the French franc went up, any receivable amount due this company in francs also went up). This is one of the multicurrency reports produced by the International Business System of Digital Linguistics. Note that the globalization of business requires that many companies deal in several currencies: When buying in Japan, you may have to pay in yen, while you may be paid in francs when selling in France.

Austin Productions, Ltd.
Accounts Receivable Revaluation for Currency Conversion

Currency: FFR France—French Francs

Invoice Number	Pay Code	Invoice Date	Open Amount	Historical Rate	Historical Value	Current Rate	Current Value	Loss/Gain
006532		06/02/92	,784.00 FFR	6.541200	5,128.30	6.874500	5,389.61	261.31 USD
098745		06/02/92	8,796.00 FFR	6.541200	57,536.40	6.874500	60,468.10	2,931.70 USD
000099		04/25/92	1,500.00 FFR	6.000000	9,000.00	6.874500	10,311.75	1,311.75 USD

Totals: USD—U.S. Dollars $71,664.70 $76,169.46 $4,504.76 USD

Currency: HFL Benelux—Dutch Guilders

Invoice Number	Pay Code	Invoice Date	Open Amount	Historical Rate	Historical Value	Current Rate	Current Value	Loss/Gain
045632		06/02/92	66,578.50 HFL	2.654700	176,745.94	2.154700	143,456.69	−33,289.25 USD
054236		06/02/92	546.00 HFL	2.654700	1,449.47	2.154700	1,176.47	−273.00 USD
564587		06/02/92	45,000.00 HFL	2.654700	119,461.50	2.154700	96,961.50	−22,500.00 USD

Totals: USD—U.S. Dollars $297,656.91 $241,594.66 $−56,062.25 USD

Report Totals: $−51,557.49 USD

FIGURE 3.3

A monthly accounts receivable revaluation report. (Source: Digital Linguistix Corporation, Pine Brook, New Jersey)

Financial reporting systems must allow for multicurrency reporting in such cases, while the MIS in general must support the tactics a firm adopts to protect itself against unfavorable shifts in currency value. With the globalization of operations in many firms, the role of multicurrency systems is increasing.

The format and the informational content of scheduled reports is fixed in advance. However, it is crucial to identify the essential informational needs of various managers to facilitate each manager's decision making and to prevent information overload. The concept of **responsibility reporting** is generally applied: Managers receive reports within their specific areas of responsibility.

2. Exception Reports
Another means of preventing information overload is resorting to exception reports, produced only when preestablished "out-of-bounds" conditions occur and containing solely the information regarding these conditions. For example, purchasing managers may need an exception report when suppliers are a week late in deliveries. Such a report may be triggered automatically by the delay of an individual supplier, or produced on a scheduled basis—but only if there are late suppliers. The report might include a list of late suppliers, the extent to which each is late, and the supplies ordered from each. Exception reporting helps managers avoid perusal of unneeded figures.

The concept of exception reporting is illustrated by the figure on page 46.

3. Demand (Ad Hoc) Reports

The ability of a manager to request a report or screen output as needed enhances the flexibility of MRS use and gives the end user (the individual manager) the capability to request the information and format that best suit his or her needs. Query languages provided by DBMS make data accessible for demand reporting.

3.5 DECISION SUPPORT SYSTEMS

All information systems support decision making, however indirectly. Decision support systems (DSS) are a type of MIS expressly developed to support the decision-making process. DSS facilitate a dialogue between the user, who is considering alternative problem solutions, and the system, with its built-in models and access to the database. The DSS database is often an extract from the general database of the enterprise. The systems are interactive, and in a typical session, the manager using a DSS will consider a number of possible "what-if" scenarios. For example, a manager attempting to establish a price for a new product may use a marketing DSS, perhaps built with a spreadsheet. The DSS contains a model relating various factors—such as the price of the product, the cost of goods, and the promotion expense—to the projected profit (or loss) from the product sales over the first five years it is marketed. By varying the price of the product in the model, the manager can compare predicted results and then select a price.

The general structure of a DSS is shown in figure 3.4. Development of these systems will be further discussed in chapter 14.

DSS have the following characteristics:

1. DSS are developed with the participation of, and often by, individual managers or a group of managers to support a range of decisions of concern to them. Some of these systems are rather simple and may be developed with a spreadsheet package (such as Excel or Lotus 1–2–3), perhaps using prepackaged templates which customize the spreadsheet for a particular set of applications. While the maintenance of MRS is largely the province of MIS professionals, end users frequently perform DSS modifications.

2. DSS are built to be modified. The development process itself and the pattern of use of a DSS entail continuing adaptation of these systems to changing user requirements. DSS are very flexible and adaptable decision-making tools.

3. DSS *directly* support the decision-making process. Moreover, a class of these systems supports group decision making. Unlike MRS, DSS are able to support unstructured or semistructured decisions, in which some of the dependencies between factors and their consequences are expressed by models, and some parts are supplied by the manager interacting with the system. Thus, DSS offer models for the structured (programmable) parts of the problem and allow the manager to use personal judgment in formulating the final decision.

FIGURE 3.4

The structure of decision
support systems.

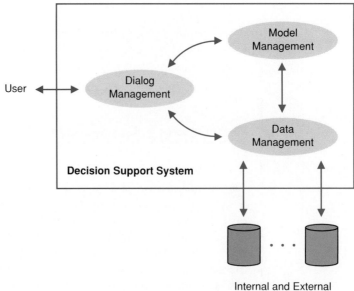

FIGURE 3.5

"What-if" analysis with a
decision support system.

(Drawn with modification from
Turban, 1990, p. 218)

```
> what if revenue increases by 3 pct sales exp increases by 5 pct -

> list by region by rep name sum (revenue) -
> sum (sales exp) as $99,999 sum (bonus) subtotal all total all -
> title effects on company bonus program   fold -
> if sales increase 3% and direct expenses increase 5%

PAGE 1
```

EFFECTS ON COMPANY BONUS PROGRAM
IF SALES INCREASE 3% AND DIRECT EXPENSES INCREASE 5%

REGION	SALESREP	SUM REVENUE	SUM EXPENSES	SUM BONUS
NORTHEAST	MARY BRENNER	$40,756	$3,432	$0
	SAM CONNERS	$117,656	$4,346	$13,084
*		$158,412	$7,778	$13,084
NORTHWEST	STAN ROBERTS	$202,995	$5,973	$31,826
	TOM FILBRITE	$83,072	$6,205	$0
*		$286,067	$12,178	$31,826
SOUTHEAST	BOB STEVENS	$83,711	$6,695	$0
	ROGER ARNESS	$37,212	$3,528	$0
*		$120,923	$10,223	$0
SOUTHWEST	CHRIS STERNMAN	$146,395	$6,953	$6,428
	JACK MILNER	$81,544	$4,129	$1,697
	PETER HANLEN	$85,665	$6,001	$0
*		$313,604	$17,083	$8,125
		$879,006	$47,263	$53,035

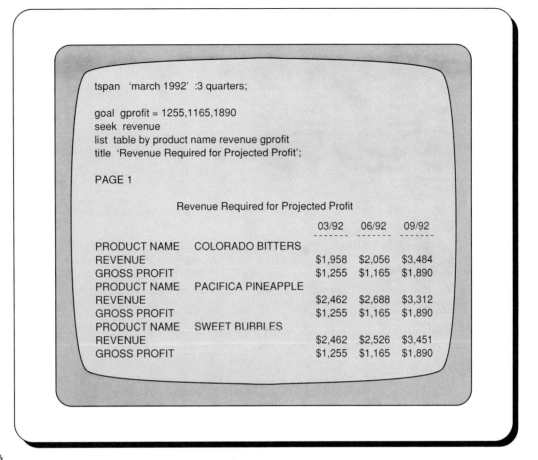

```
tspan  'march 1992'  :3 quarters;

goal  gprofit = 1255,1165,1890
seek  revenue
list  table by product name revenue gprofit
title  'Revenue Required for Projected Profit';

PAGE 1

                    Revenue Required for Projected Profit

                                          03/92    06/92    09/92

PRODUCT NAME    COLORADO BITTERS
REVENUE                                  $1,958   $2,056   $3,484
GROSS PROFIT                             $1,255   $1,165   $1,890
PRODUCT NAME    PACIFICA PINEAPPLE
REVENUE                                  $2,462   $2,688   $3,312
GROSS PROFIT                             $1,255   $1,165   $1,890
PRODUCT NAME    SWEET BUBBLES
REVENUE                                  $2,462   $2,526   $3,451
GROSS PROFIT                             $1,255   $1,165   $1,890
```

FIGURE 3.6

Goal seeking with a decision support system.

(Drawn with modification from Turban, 1990, p. 218)

The possibility of quick interaction with the system offers users a quantitative analysis literally at their fingertips. In the process, they also learn to make better decisions.

4. Projecting possible futures during a planning process is a particular strength of DSS. Two principal modes of analysis are available. In the "what-if" mode, the user considers alternative scenarios and their results. For example, "What if we increase advertising expenditures by 5 percent?" In the goal-seeking mode, the user asks, "What would it take—in terms of input factors—to achieve a particular performance?" The two modes of interaction are illustrated in figures 3.5 and 3.6, respectively. Both examples were produced with fourth-generation language NOMAD2 from MUST Software International. The language commands are shown in the upper part of each figure. The lower part shows the impact of the projections.

5. The analytical capabilities expressed in DSS models are the reason for the existence of these systems. Some of the more elaborate systems contain limited model-management capabilities, which enable the system itself to select a model appropriate to the problem—the user, relieved of this responsibility, thus does not need as thorough an understanding of models.

6. The combination of internal and external information is important in many DSS.

7. In DSS, a graphics repertoire is usually available to portray a decision situation more succinctly than it can be done with a tabular display of data.

Case Study Two at the end of this chapter offers an extensive illustration of the decision-support concept.

3.6 EXECUTIVE INFORMATION SYSTEMS

Executive information systems (EIS) provide direct support for top managers. Characteristically, senior managers employ a great variety of informal sources of information, so that computerized information systems are able to provide only limited assistance. However, the chief executive officer, senior and executive vice presidents, and the board of directors also need to be able to track the performance of their company and of its various units, assess the business environment, and develop strategic directions for the company's future. In particular, these executives need a great diversity of external information to compare their company's performance to that of its competition, and to investigate the general trends of the economies in the many countries where the company may be doing business.

Frequently, top managers equip a special "war room" with large screens onto which the EIS projects color displays. At Shearson Lehman Hutton in New York, for example, executives of the brokerage house gather in such a room to study demographic data, product lines, and corporate restructuring of their clients.

Executive information systems have these characteristics:

1. EIS provide immediate and easy access to information reflecting the key success factors of the company and of its units.

2. "User-seductive" interfaces, such as color graphics and video, allow the EIS user to grasp trends at a glance. Users' time is at a high premium here.

3. EIS provide access to a variety of databases, both internal and external, through a uniform interface—the fact that the system consults multiple databases should be transparent to the users.

4. Both current status and projections should be available from EIS. It is frequently desirable to investigate different projections; in particular, planned projections may be compared with the projections derived from actual results.

5. An EIS should allow easy tailoring to the preferences of the particular user or group of users (such as the chief executive's cabinet or the corporate board).

6. EIS should offer the capability to "drill down" into the data: It should be possible to see increasingly detailed data behind the summaries.

Executive information systems are a superior tool for exercising the control function of management. Thanks to these systems, many an executive has been able to widen his or her span of management control—in other words, to expand the number of people reporting directly to him or to her.

In a case described by John Rockart and Michael Treacy of MIT (Rockart, 1982), after six top executives of a large corporation were given access to an EIS, the chief executive officer of the company started to use the system on a daily basis. He concluded: "There is a huge advantage to the CEO to get his hands dirty in the data, because the answers to many significant questions are found in the detail. The system provides me with an improved ability to ask the right questions and to know the wrong answers."

An extensive example of the use of an EIS was presented as the Case Study in chapter 1. The figure on page 46 illustrates exception reporting with two screens obtained from an executive information system implemented with ADVANTAGE software from Pilot Executive Software. The exception report has been set to trigger on any line item in the profit-and-loss statement that is out of line with planned year-to-date results by more than 10 percent or $500,000. The first screen shows the number of exceptions in each division of the company. The second screen itemizes the three line items with exceptional variances from the plan in one of the divisions.

3.7 THE ROLE OF EXPERT SYSTEMS

Expert systems are a leading-edge technology that was successfully introduced from the research domain of artificial intelligence into MIS practice in the mid-1980s. Expert systems suggest a decision based on a computerized process resembling logical reasoning. In doing so, they rely on a **knowledge base** about the narrow domain of their application, on the facts of the case they need to decide upon, and on the built-in inferencing (reasoning) mechanism. Expert systems may be incorporated into all types of organizational information systems or used as stand-alone advisory tools. In particular, they are increasingly combined with conventional programming technologies in transaction processing and decision support systems. Expert systems are used to select the cheapest way to mail a package, to render a consumer credit decision, to diagnose equipment malfunction, to plan an investment portfolio, or to configure a complicated equipment order. Complexity of these tasks—and of the corresponding expert systems—varies widely. Most frequently these systems do not replace an expert, but rather serve as an assistant to a decision maker.

The essential component of the knowledge base is heuristics—informal, judgmental elements of knowledge within the expert system's domain. Reliance on a knowledge base is the essential distinguishing characteristic of these systems. The knowledge base is originally populated and subsequently enhanced as the system is tested on trial cases, and then further enhanced as the system is used.

FIGURE 3.7

The structure of expert
systems.

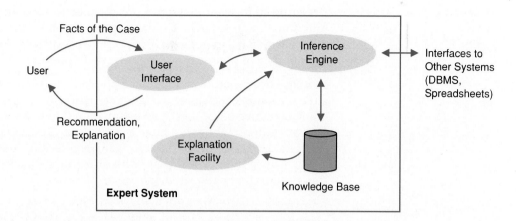

To summarize: **Expert systems** are knowledge-based programs that imitate a reasoning process to suggest a problem solution within their domain of application. The structure of an expert system from the point of view of its user (rather than that of a developer) is shown in figure 3.7.

Simpler systems are usually implemented with **expert system shells—** knowledge-based systems with empty knowledge bases. All the developer (a knowledge engineer or an end user) needs to do is populate the knowledge base with the specifics of the problem domain. There are several methods of representing knowledge, depending on the software used to implement the expert system. A very common way is to encode it in the form of "if-then" production rules.

For example, a heuristic rule in a credit evaluation system may read:

```
IF good customer
    and credit requested < $5,000
    and loan term < 1 year
THEN grant credit
```

Another rule in the same knowledge base would define a "good customer" as:

```
IF first contact > 5 years
    and default number = 0
    and business volume > $100,000
THEN good customer
```

The set of facts describing a particular situation is presented by the user to the system during a session. The **inference engine** of the expert system then acts as a reasoning mechanism and attempts to draw a conclusion by comparing the facts of the case to the knowledge base of rules. The system then gives a recommendation, with an explanation of its reasoning (presented, for example, as a sequence of rules applied). In a transaction processing system for order pro-

FIGURE 3.8

Consultation with an expert system.

(Courtesy Computer Associates International, Garden City, New York)

What type of package is it . . . Letter, Pak, Box, Tube?
= > Box

How much does the package weigh in pounds?
= > 4

Please tell me the state where you want to send this package.
= > CA

Which city? (If it's a suburb, enter the major city name.)
= > Los Angeles

What delivery service is required . . . Same day, Overnight, Two Day, Anytime?
= > Overnight

What is the combined length and girth of the package? I only need to know this if you think the sum of the length and girth exceed 84 inches. Otherwise, just press return.
= > <RETURN>

ATTN MR./MS. WARNER

After careful consideration, I have selected OTD as your best alternative, at a cost of $14.50. The selection was based on sending a 4 pound parcel with a delivery requirement of OVERNIGHT to LOS ANGELES, CA.

—Other Alternative Carriers—
EconoMail	*$26.56*
Fast Freight	*$21.00*
Overland Express	*$18.45*
Speed Shipping	*$23.00*

cessing, an expert system may determine an order price by considering the customer, order volume, and all the available promotional prices for the items ordered (because of the multiple promotions offered by companies today—with short duration, regional applicability, and other constraints—this is a nontrivial problem that an order clerk would find difficult to handle on-line). Expert systems are of particular importance in decision support, where they may be used to suggest possible decisions based on problem constraints and the available outcome range. The technology of expert systems will be further discussed in chapter 15.

Figure 3.8 shows an interactive consultation with a simple expert system that recommends shipping choices. This expert system was implemented with a rule-based shell called Application Expert from Computer Associates International. The expert system asks the questions. Note how natural the dialogue is.

Expert systems are sometimes combined with other technologies derived from artificial intelligence research, for example, limited natural language processing or limited speaker-independent speech recognition. Thus, a dialogue between the expert system and its user may resemble an interchange in simple English, as shown in figure 3.8. Certain speech-recognition systems can, for example, recognize all ten digits and yes/no answers given by any caller. Others are capable of a much broader range of recognition when they are "trained" on a particular voice.

The "MANY-PEBBLES-INTO-THE-POND" APPROACH TO INTRODUCING EXPERT SYSTEM TECHNOLOGY

Some companies have approached the assimilation of expert system technology by "casting a boulder into the pond"—that is, by developing an impressively powerful expert system that creates a big splash within the company and in the trade literature. Usually, the technology champion—an indispensable person in introducing a new technology into the rarely welcoming arms of a large corporation—is then able to muster the support of company management for the broad-scale use of technology. This road was traveled, for example, at Digital Equipment Corporation and at American Express.

Edward Mahler, who championed expert systems at E. I. Du Pont de Nemours, one of the ten largest corporations in the United States, adopted a different approach. Mahler decided to create many ripples by initiating the development of many small expert systems. The end users themselves build the systems, rather than professional knowledge engineers, by employing simple expert-system shells. The users receive a few days of training and then have personal access to internal consultants for one or two days, followed by telephone support.

There are well over two hundred operational expert systems in place at Du Pont at the present time, with hundreds more under development and thousands expected to come in this widely diversified company. The problems tackled by the systems are diagnostics, selection, and scheduling.

Diagnostic problems emerge in marketing and in after-market service. Du Pont acts mainly as a wholesaler, selling to a distributor. If the ultimate customer has problems with a product, Du Pont's technical services use an expert system to determine the cause of the malfunction.

When a sales representative is trying to sell to a customer one of perhaps six hundred kinds of synthetic rubber called neoprene, the problem is to select the one which best meets the customer's needs. An expert system is able to make this selection.

Scheduling problems usually surface in manufacturing. Maintaining very low inventory levels has now become a virtual rule in efficient manufacturing practice. Much of the work is therefore order-driven. If equipment malfunctions or suppliers make late deliveries, rescheduling must be prompt to maintain the workflow. Using expert systems to schedule the flow of work cuts down on scheduling meetings and ensures a better, more consistent quality of decision making.

Du Pont has established that an average engineer spends about one person-month on building a small expert system, while the average payback from the system is $100,000 annually. Edward Mahler reports that for every dollar Du Pont spends on expert systems, it makes back on the average $10.

Based on Edward Feigenbaum, Pamela McCorduck, and Penny Nii, *The Rise of the Expert Company*, New York: Times Books, 1988; and "Executive Summary—Artificial Intelligence," *InformationWeek*, October 29, 1990, p. 8.

3.8 INFORMATIONAL SUPPORT OF MANAGEMENT—A HIERARCHICAL VIEW

We listed the principal functions of management in chapter 1, pending a fuller analysis in chapters 11 and 12. Management-oriented MIS components directly support two of these functions: planning and controlling. The other three managerial functions—leading, organizing, and staffing (which is sometimes considered a part of organizing)—are primarily people-oriented. However, these three functions do rely increasingly on the information provided by MIS and on the coordination capability of these systems.

Figure 1.1 (in chapter 1) depicted the general framework of organizational information systems. Now let us expand the "Management Support" component of this framework: figure 3.9 diagrams the objectives of management support systems; systems of various types (EIS, DSS, or MRS) may be employed to pursue these objectives, as we shall discuss later in this chapter. This is an adaptation of the well-established "Anthony pyramid" introduced by Robert Anthony and transferred into the MIS context by Robert Head.[3] Note that, as figure 1.1 shows, this pyramid rests on a foundation of operational systems. This means that most of the underlying data are acquired by operational-level systems.

Planning is setting out measurable objectives for a period of time. **Control** is comparing the actual results of operations against planned objectives and taking action in response to deviations from the plan. Controlling without planning

FIGURE 3.9

Objectives of management
support systems.

WHAT DO WE MEASURE WHEN WE MEASURE PERFORMANCE?

Some of the leading corporations are rethinking the way they measure the performances of their subunits. Traditionally, performance measurement has been done with financial figures such as profitability or return on investment. These measures are still the bedrock of management control today.

However, as corporate strategies become based on the drive for enhanced customer service and for positioning in global markets, financial performance measures are becoming insufficient to reflect how well the firm will do in the longer term.

Realizing this, one high-technology manufacturer has added the measures of customer satisfaction, product quality, market share, and development of human resources to its management control system. Another company included a measure of innovation as well. And what is measured generally receives attention, particularly if rewards are tied to the measures.

It is expected that this broader understanding of performance measurement will lead to an expanded role for MIS in company management.

Based on Eccles, 1991.

---

would be aimless; as The Cheshire Cat observed in his immortal interchange with Alice in Wonderland, "If you do not know where you are going, it does not matter which way you go." On the other hand, planning without controls would be unproductive. "It is not enough to plan the work, you also need to work the plan," as the adage goes.

Control information falls into several categories:

- Status (or progress) information, which reflects the progress of a unit or a project toward the set goals.
- Warning information, which reflects trouble brewing and which is typically furnished in the form of exception reports.
- Comfort information, which permits the manager to see whether all is well. This type of information depends on the capability to access detailed data behind the summaries and is designed to give confidence—or to find problems—in the picture painted by the summarized information.

Concern with planning increases at the higher levels of management (as is graphically reflected in figure 3.9)—sometimes at the expense of the attention devoted to control. I believe, however, that there is a need to recognize the absolute importance of top-level control. As Tony Butler of Dee Corporation, a multibillion-dollar British operator of hyper- and supermarkets, said about the people who ignore this need, ". . . they are so obsessed with strategy that they forget they have to survive to get there."[4] Indeed, the main objective of EIS is control.[5]

We have already discussed how management-oriented MIS components rely on the databases built by transaction processing systems during operations. But not all data are accumulated as the by-product of operations. Many systems require special data-collection subsystems expressly designed for management support. In particular, boundary spanning is needed to maintain extensive information about the external environment.

3.9 LEVELS OF PLANNING AND CONTROL WITH MIS

Let us now analyze, level by level, the objectives of the management-oriented MIS components in supporting planning and control. Remember, however, that some organizations do not perform planning at all the levels we describe here.

Operations Planning and Control— Information for Lower Management

It is important to distinguish informational support for operations management (planning and control) from the automation of operations through a transaction processing system—even though the two may be integrated in a single system. The main reason for drawing this distinction is the need to equip supervisors and other line managers with informational support.

Operations-planning subsystems schedule repetitive activities performed at the transactional level, such as moving produced goods out of company warehouses, processing securities coming into a bank's back office, or assigning workers on the factory floor. Examples of operations-planning reports are plant-scheduling, transportation-scheduling, and other activity-scheduling reports.

Operational control involves examining the progress of planned activities and dealing with contingencies such as defective equipment or absent workers. Examples of reports used for control purposes include reports on defective equipment, on receivables aged over thirty days, on sold goods in transit, weekly quality control reports on defective products, and other performance reports. Exception reports include stock-outs and low-cash-position reports.

The system for delivery vehicle routing presented as Case Study Two at the end of this chapter is an example of a DSS designed for planning at this lower management level. A reporting system on uncompleted orders, supporting factory floor supervisors, is an example of an MRS designed to enhance operational control.

The detail reported for this management level is usually not far removed from the level of data handled by TPS (figure 3.3 illustrates this). The reports and screens reflect repetitive activities and deal with measurable entities. The decisions these systems serve, particularly in the area of control, are most often highly structured, since well-established and programmable control procedures exist. Time horizons are short—frequently just a day or a week.

Tactical Planning and Management Control

Tactical planning and management control are the provinces of middle management—a very broadly defined component of organizational structure that includes branch managers, staff planners, department heads, and other profit-center managers. Middle managers implement the strategic company plan (or the strategic plan for each of their business units) sent down by senior management. They do so by developing tactical plans covering a period of six months or a year and then maintaining and controlling performance within their areas of responsibility against the plans. Tactical plans expressed in financial terms are also called budgets. Budgets are often project-oriented. The objective of tactical planning is the acquisition and productive allocation of resources in the process of fulfilling long-term (strategic) plans.

Examples of tactical plans include a financing plan for a new warehouse, an operational budget for a division for the next six months, or a currency position for the next three months (including forward purchases of foreign currencies in the company's geographical domain of operations).

Management control tracks variances from the figures specified by budgets, analyzes reasons for the deviations, and adopts actions in response to them. Examples of management control include performance analysis for a sales region over a month-long period, a biweekly inventory summary, and the periodic actual-versus-budget report on department performance.

Decision support systems are most frequently deployed at this level to establish a course of action in response to a negative or positive variance (problem or opportunity) from planned performance. Exception reporting is used to pare the volume of information and avoid information overload.

Long-Term (Strategic) Planning and Strategic Control

The top management of a company is responsible for articulating the mission of the enterprise, developing concrete objectives for achieving the mission, and formulating long-term plans to achieve these objectives. Major shifts in the definition of the business the company wants to be in, organizational restructuring, diversification, and contraction of business are made at this level.

The planning horizon for top management is frequently five or more years; however, strategic plans are reviewed semiannually or annually to keep them on target—or to change the target.

Typical long-term plans include the diversification strategy, specification with total figures for the businesses the company wants to be in, marketing strategy, identification of the market segments for the company's product lines; five-year sales plans and three-year product promotion plans are examples.

To control the fulfillment of plans, management develops a set of critical performance indicators. Examples of criteria used for top-level control are overall company profitability for the last quarter, market share as of the end of the fiscal year, and quarterly sales of company operating units. The EIS reports shown in the Case Study at the end of chapter 1 illustrated this.

3.10 FUNCTIONAL DEPARTMENTATION AND MIS

To function, organizations have to be organized, or structured into subdivisions that take responsibility for their own results.

Large organizations are in many cases structured as relatively independent units called strategic business units (SBUs), which in turn may consist of smaller planning units. Each planning unit has its own strategic plan and pursues its own business goals.

Functional Departmentation of Business Organizations

Traditionally, an organization or a large business unit in a diversified enterprise has been structured along functional lines. Subdividing an organization by grouping activities in accordance with the functions of the enterprise is called **functional departmentation.** Any organization that provides goods or services has several functions to perform: marketing and sales (developing a market for the company's products and selling them); production (creating or adding value by producing goods or offering services); and financing (managing the funds of the enterprise). Figure 3.10 shows an example of a functional company organization. It is evident from the organization chart that departments in larger organizations tend to be more specialized. There is also a staff function on the higher executive level.

In some of the leading companies, functional departmentation is not the main organizing principle. Functional departmentation is not conducive to applying mixed expertise to a project; it also diffuses responsibility for the results and keeps many organizational components distant from the ultimate customer. Therefore, some organizations are structured along territorial (geographic), line-of-business, or other considerations. Structural combinations are also possible. We will discuss the alternatives in chapter 12.

FIGURE 3.10

An organization chart with functional departmentation.

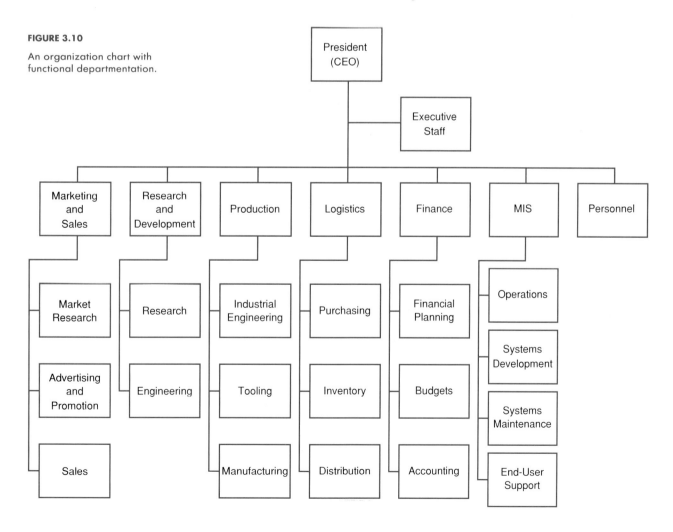

Management information systems are generally structured along the major lines of company departmental subdivision. Thus, we may have a marketing information system or a management control system for the engineering division. Systems that assist tactical and strategic planning and control tend to cross functional boundaries more often than operational-level information systems. Databases are the principal means of integration in the information resource management concept.

Now let us look at informational support of the marketing and sales function to illustrate hierarchical informational support.

Informational Support of Marketing and Sales as an Illustration of Hierarchical MIS Support

Marketing is a set of organizational activities directed toward planning, promoting, and selling goods and services to satisfy the needs of customers at a profit to the firm.

During the 1960s, leading companies moved from a production-and-sales orientation to the **marketing orientation.** This means that the driving force in these companies was redirected from selling what the companies produced to producing what the companies could profitably sell. It cannot be stressed forcefully enough that efficient production processes undergird this marketing concept. In a competitive environment, one cannot profitably sell a product or service that is not efficiently produced.

The informational support pyramid for the marketing and sales function is shown in figure 3.11.

In general, marketing information systems process data and deliver information on the marketing mix, expressed as the so-called four *P*s: *p*roduct (product lines and features), *p*lace (the way the product is distributed), *p*romotion (sales and advertising), and *p*rice (with mark-ups, discounts and other terms of sale). Of course, only some aspects of these activities can be supported by formal systems.

FIGURE 3.11

Elements of informational support for the marketing and sales function.

Marketing operations include data processing connected with sales and promotional activities, such as order processing and tracking or processing of promotional data.

Operational planning involves, for example, weekly scheduling of the salesforce and of promotion. Since the procedures for scheduling are known and fixed, the entire process may be programmed as a software subsystem (or a purchased software package may be used). The possibility of human override is desirable. Operational control reports are short-term (usually weekly) analyses of sales and promotion by salesperson, segment of the salesforce, product line, region, or customer segment. The level of operational planning and control relies chiefly on the voluminous internal database resulting from operational support.

Tactical planning involves one- or two-year sales forecasts and, based on these forecasts, salesforce plans and promotional mix plans (broadcasting, print, and other media advertising). A range of methods is available for sales forecasting; these include the judgments of managers, salesforce, or customers, and modeling of future outcomes based on current and expected facts and relationships. Various computer models are available: some of them simply extend past trends, but some tie the company's sales to one or more broad national indexes (for example, GNP or disposable income). The latter models, having established such a correlation, use nationally available index forecasts to predict sales for the next period. Any forecasting based on models has to be tempered with judgment, however, since the only "hard" data come from the past.

Management control in marketing and sales relies on the analysis of variances between planned and actual performance of the salesforce and of promotional devices over the given time period. Comparison with industry standards and competitor performance is desirable.

Strategic (long-term) planning includes five-year marketing mix plans for the company's (or business unit's) product lines and new-product introduction plans for five years. A simple strategic planning report that might have been drawn up in 1986 and that includes past and projected performance is shown in the color figure on page 46. The report is shown in both graphical and tabular forms and was produced with Lotus 1–2–3, using the Freelance Plus business graphics facility (from Lotus Development Corporation).

It must be stressed that long-range planning in an environment fraught with uncertainties is not a blueprint. It is rather a continual process through which the company integrates its activities, devises targets to focus on, and learns (improves its performance).

Strategic-level control activities include the analysis of variances and exceptions of the key indicators. For example, managers might ask, "Which division was responsible for the large negative variance in the second quarter?" or "What should be done to narrow the gap between planned sales for the current year and possible projections considering the results we have so far?"

The tactical and strategic planning levels of a marketing information system require a prodigious amount of external information on current and prospective customers and competitors, and current demographic data and projections.

An activity that straddles the strategic and tactical levels is new product development. As we have stressed, innovation is a company's main strength in a competitive environment. Activities which need informational support include: the identification of opportunity (market definition and product positioning); product development; sales forecasting; pretest market testing (modest-scale testing); full-scale test marketing; and new product introduction. Many of these activities are supported by computerized models. Simpler modeling is accomplished with spreadsheets. Marketing scientists have developed a number of models. Their use requires expertise and sophistication. One well-known model, called BRANDAID and developed by John D. C. Little of MIT, aids in product sales forecasting by considering the activities of the manufacturer, retailer, competitors, and the general business environment.

3.11 MANAGEMENT SUPPORT WITH MANAGEMENT-ORIENTED INFORMATION SYSTEMS—A SUMMARY

Table 3.5 summarizes the support offered by various types of management-oriented MIS. Expanding on table 3.2, this table shows the principal characteristics of these systems.

Note that DSS support the solution of problems characterized by a minimal structure or, in other words, problems which require the most judgment from the problem solver. It may seen surprising that this is not a characteristic of top-management support systems such as EIS. However, EIS are generally used by executives not to find a solution but to see whether a problem—or an opportunity—exists. A DSS would then typically be employed by staff analysts or middle managers to identify a solution to the problem in behalf of the senior managers.

Expert systems may be used on all levels for various tasks: They may screen the data reported by MRS to minimize output volume; they may indicate trends that require watching in EIS; and they are heavily used in conjunction with traditional DSS in the decision-making process.

A graphic summary of informational support of management is furnished in figure 3.12. We have shown in the figure that such informational needs as access to external and more highly summarized (aggregated) information grow as we progress upward in the corporate hierarchy. The higher we go in the firm, the longer the time horizon for problems people are working with, and the less structured those problems are.

TABLE 3.5

Management-Oriented MIS Components

SYSTEM TYPE	TARGET USERS	TYPICAL USE SCENARIO	DOMINANT PROBLEMS	DATA SOURCES	PREVALENT TIME HORIZON
MRS	Lower and middle management	Study of reports	Operational and management control	Largely internal	Past and present
DSS	Lower and middle management; staff analysts	Decision-making session	Planning	Internal and external	Future
EIS	Top management	Quick overview	Top-level control	Internal and external	Past-present-future time series

	PROBLEM VARIABILITY	LEVEL OF ANALYSIS	LEVEL OF DETAIL	PROBLEM STRUCTURE
MRS	Recurring problems	Very low	Very high	Very high
DSS	Ad hoc, unique problems	High or very high	Mixed	Low or very low
EIS	Similar problems	Low or medium	Aggregates, with detail available	High

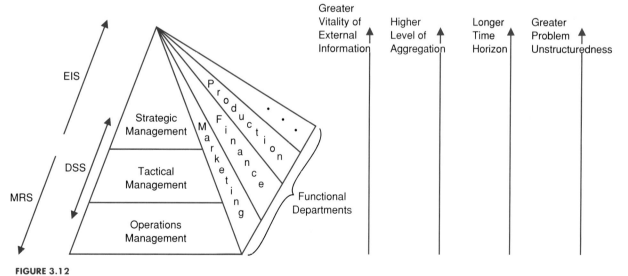

FIGURE 3.12

A summary of informational support of management.

SUMMARY

Physical components of MIS include computer and communications hardware, systems and applications software, database, personnel, and procedures.

There are five types of organizational information systems. Transaction processing systems support the business operations of an enterprise, and office information systems facilitate general knowledge work in business offices. Three MIS types support management functions. The first type, management reporting systems, furnish primarily routine and detailed reports. Decision support systems directly support the decision-making process by enabling the user to conduct a dialogue with the system and to apply a variety of models to an extract of the database in the search for a problem solution. Finally, executive information systems furnish immediate access to highly aggregated internal and external information, frequently in graphic form. Knowledge-based expert systems are more and more often employed in various types of MIS.

An MIS portfolio may also be viewed from the hierarchical and functional perspectives as furnishing information to three levels of management across the functional departments of an organization. The quality of information furnished by MIS may be evaluated with regard to a set of attributes, including timeliness, relevance, accuracy, and completeness.

CONCLUSIONS FOR MIS PRACTICE

1. Familiarity with the physical components of MIS is necessary for proficient use of technology in organizational computing.

2. Operational MIS systems are necessary to run the operations of a modern firm. They are also an indispensable source of data for management-oriented MIS components.

3. Office information systems are a rapidly evolving tool for conducting and coordinating knowledge work in organizations.

4. It is necessary to ensure that the information provided by MIS possesses the attributes of quality, such as relevance, timeliness, and accuracy.

5. A modern organization deals with a variety of external stakeholders who act as sources and recipients of information. Designers of organizational MIS need to consider with great care the provision of external information as a crucial aspect of their work.

6. Management reporting systems, decision support systems, and executive information systems deal with different, though overlapping, informational needs of management. All of these systems should be a part of the MIS portfolio and should be employed according to their capabilities.

7. Expert system technology should be a part of the tool kit in informational support of management at all levels.

8. Considering a hierarchical view of an organization, planning and control functions at all three levels—operational, tactical, and strategic—should be supported by MIS.

9. MIS should support individual units of the organization. If an organization is structured along functional lines, the functional departments should be supported by systems which they can control to a large degree. Systems should be integrated insofar as integration benefits the entire organization.

ENDNOTES

1. Note that the term *database* is used both generically, to indicate organized data stored in the secondary and archival memories of the computer over long periods of time, and as a technical term, indicating that the data are interrelated under a control of a database management system.

2. For a detailed discussion of the stakeholder role in organizations, see R. E. Freeman, *Strategic Management: A Stakeholder Approach*, Boston: Pitman, 1984.

3. The references are: Robert N. Anthony, *Planning and Control Systems: A Framework for Analysis*, Cambridge, Mass.: Harvard University Press, 1965; and Robert V. Head, "Management Information Systems: A Critical Appraisal," *Datamation*, May 1967, pp. 21–26.

4. Tony Butler, "Board Control and Information Technology—The Dee Approach," Metapraxis Ltd. Report, 1987, p. 3.

5. The problems of strategic control have been analyzed in Peter Lorange, Michael F. Scott Morton, and Sumantra Ghoshal, *Strategic Control*, St. Paul: West, 1986.

KEY TERMS AND CONCEPTS

Hardware	File
Software	Database
Database	Information attributes
Distributed processing	Stakeholders
Central processor	Responsibility reporting
Memory hierarchy	Scheduled reports
Local area network	Exception reports
Metropolitan area network	Demand (ad-hoc) reports
Wide area network	"What-if" analysis
Systems software	Goal seeking
Operating system	Expert system
Telecommunications monitor	Knowledge base
Database management system (DBMS)	Planning
	Control
Translator	Functional departmentation
Applications software	Marketing orientation

QUESTIONS

1. What are the physical components of MIS?

2. What are the hardware components of a computer system?

3. What are the systems software components of a computer system?

4. What are the main distinctions between systems software and applications software?

5. What would you consider the main criterion for the make-or-buy decision in acquiring applications software? How would a company's policy to deploy information systems as a strategic weapon influence this decision?

6. Consider the focus of each of the principal MIS types. How does the focus relate to the principal attributes of each of these systems?

7. Distinguish between the information attributes of "relevance" and the "appropriateness of form." Give examples of information that might possess one of the attributes but not the other.

8. When would graphic as opposed to tabular displays be appropriate?

9. Group the external stakeholders generating informational requirements into (1) those who are primarily sources and (2) those who are primarily consumers of company information. If it is difficult to classify a stakeholder, give major examples of that stakeholder's role as both a source and a consumer of information.

10. In a few points, compare exception reports with scheduled reports.

11. What is the principal difference between management reporting systems and decision support systems?

12. Consider the three types of organizational information systems whose primary objective is management support. List *three* characteristics which you believe distinguish each of them from the other types.

13. Give an example of a role that an expert system might play in a transaction processing system, in a management reporting system, and in a decision support system (three examples in all).

14. What is the principal difference between long-term control reports and long-term plans?

15. Sketch an informational support pyramid for the finance department of an institution, similar to that shown in figure 3.11.

ISSUES FOR DISCUSSION

1. What, in your opinion, is the rationale for distributed processing? In other words, why would an organization break up a large data center into smaller systems, placing them under the authority of the various departments the systems serve? Try to think of all the relevant factors. Does centralized processing have advantages that sometimes make it the chosen MIS configuration?

2. Report content has a great influence on how managers are evaluated. Obviously, a political play may be expected when organizational information systems are being defined. What role do you think the MIS unit should take in such a political play?

3. American Express has implemented a large expert system called Authorizer's Assistant. Since the company has no credit limit on its charge card, the charge authorization is an important step. The Authorizer's

Assistant gives advice based on the customer's charge pattern. It recommends special cases for human attention. How would you evaluate the benefits of such a system to the company? List the decisive points in order of their importance.

4. Try to conceptualize the avenues for integration of various management-support systems. Consider their complementary strengths, and sketch the possible informational flows in an integrated system supporting managerial work in a segment of the marketing and sales area of a firm.

CASE STUDY ONE # CHATEAU RIEN RESTAURANTS

Chateau Rien is a chain of five restaurants located in a major city. As is true of most restaurants today, the Chateau Rien chain is computerized.

Each restaurant contains several precheck terminals, which are modified cash registers: by pressing functional keys, the waiters enter customer orders, but no financial settlements are handled by these terminals. Attached to each terminal is a check printer that will print the customer's check for settlement. Two to five of these terminals, depending on the restaurant's size, are connected to a personal computer.

The computer stores complete data regarding each guest check as the meal progresses through aperitifs, appetizers, main dishes, wines, and dessert. A running balance for the open check, identified by a unique number, is maintained. Thanks to this unique identification, the guest may be served initially in the bar, then in the dining room, then with coffee in the lounge—all on one check. When the check is settled through a register connected with the personal computer, the open-check account is terminated and a record of the settlement manner (cash, credit card identifica-

tion, or personal check identification) is made.

The check-tracking subsystem can report at any time on each open guest check: its number, time of creation, server code, current balance, and table number. If a check has been open too long, it raises suspicion of a walkout; a check with a large outstanding balance indicates a risk of nonpayment.

Thanks to a special expansion card, the computer also serves as a network controller through which the precheck terminals communicate with remote printers located in the food and liquor areas. There are three printers in the kitchen for hot foods, cold foods, and desserts; another remote printer is in the wine cellar (a properly conditioned back room, actually). Remote printers print out orders identified by the guest check and server code numbers. The computer, acting as a network controller queues up the requests for food and wine coming from precheck terminals and routes them to the appropriate remote printer.

The Chateau Rien inventory database is maintained on another personal computer. The restaurant manager also uses this computer to process payroll for the restaurant's staff and to run simple spreadsheet applications, such as employee scheduling and tracking the performance of captains and waiters. A local area network connects the two personal computers with the third; all three are the IBM PS/2 model 50, running a disk operating system (MS/DOS). The third computer is used by the sommelier, who is in charge of the wine cellar. Chateau Rien restaurants pride themselves on their extensive wine lists, and a weekly list is printed on the laser printer in the wine cellar from the inventory file.

On the completion of service every night, the closed-check data for the day is transmitted to the headquarters minicomputer. Here all the back-office work, other than the restaurant payroll, is done for the entire chain. This includes the general ledger and financial statements as well as purchasing applications. The Chateau Rien's team of one systems analyst and three programmers have also implemented what the food consultants to the chain have proudly called "menu engineering." This application helps the menu analyst who works for the chain to answer questions such as, What is the best price for a menu item? What is the food cost for the given menu item? What is the best menu mix? The system

maintains recipes for menu items, ingredient cost files, and counts of menu items sold over various time periods for this purpose. Actually, the menu analyst, a nutritionist, learned how to access the database with her spreadsheet program and has been producing a variety of reports comparing customer preferences at the chain's restaurants. After taking a two-day course on programming in the nonprocedural language offered by the vendor of the database management system running on the minicomputer, the menu analyst even started to use the system for planning purposes.

The entire database is maintained on a minicomputer (IBM's AS/400). A local area network of ten personal computers (a variety of PS/2 models) is maintained at headquarters and connected to the minicomputer. Every manager in the company receives scheduled reports within her or his area of responsibility; all of them, including the president, outline their own correspondence and communicate with electronic mail on their personal computers.

In a more recent development, the chain receives daily price lists from major vendors and sends back purchase orders over the telephone lines using an electronic data interchange (EDI) package.

Case Study One Questions

1. Identify the physical components of the restaurant chain's information system.

2. Is the system distributed? If it is centralized, should it be distributed, considering the needs of the business? If it is distributed, can you suggest a different way the informational functions might be distributed? What would be the advantages and disadvantages of your method of distribution?

3. Sketch the Chateau Rien information system hardware in a fashion similar to figure 3.1.

4. List the management-oriented elements of the Chateau Rien's informational support system, and classify each of them into the three levels of planning and control. List the elements missing from this support system and give examples of how they could be incorporated. We will return to this case in the next chapter of the book.

A DECISION SUPPORT SYSTEM FOR DELIVERY ROUTING

The Southland Corporation is the largest U.S. operator and franchiser of convenience stores (known as the 7-Eleven stores). The corporation keeps over 7,000 stores well stocked by frequently delivering small quantities of goods, often in lots of less than a case. Over 2,500 products are distributed to the stores by four regional centers.

A principal component in the information system of a distributor is logistical: The vehicle fleet must be assigned to routes covering the stores. Southland's logistics systems had been running on a mainframe. It processed store orders, prepared a picking list for the warehouse, and formulated a set of routes to deliver the merchandise. Proper routing is the key to efficient logistics.

Optimal routing through a number of points with return to the point of origin is the famous "traveling salesman" problem of computer science. The only known algorithm for an optimal solution relies on the "try-all-possibilities" principle and is, therefore, highly demanding on central processor time.

In addition, routing practice must take into account a variety of conditions familiar to traffic managers but not lending themselves easily to an algorithmic implementation. These include rush-hour traffic congestion, local road conditions, separation of stores by rivers or controlled-access highways, and time windows during which individual stores accept deliveries.

Southland decided to move the routing function from the mainframe onto personal computers to be used by traffic managers. This makes it possible to combine algorithmic support with the experience of traffic managers in a person-machine system—a DSS. The system was developed originally for Southland's Orlando distribution center. It runs on an IBM PC/XT and uses three output devices: a twenty-five-inch color monitor, a standard monochrome monitor, and a printer.

The system is geographically oriented (the use of maps is a feature of one category of DSSs, since these systems are often used for routing). The map displays are driven by two categories of data. The fixed geography, such as bodies of water or roads, are stored as line segments. The variable data—routes and store locations—are plotted from the store file, which includes the coordinates of the convenience stores.

The main menu of the system offers four programs:

1. Input Delivery Requirements and Routes

2. Build Routes

3. Maintain Store File

4. Sort on Selected Fields

Programs 1 and 3 serve housekeeping purposes. Through the Input Delivery Requirements and Routes program, the traffic manager can originate or modify a set of routes and supply information about the individual routes, such as total weight and volume of a delivery or the vehicle type. Option 3 maintains the Store File by adding or deleting store records or updating the fields of existing records. Option 4 allows the user to report from this file. The main function of decision support is effected by the Build Routes program.

The Build Routes program displays another menu. The user can build a set of routes, which is called a cycle. The original cycle, cycle 1, is established by the user via the Input Delivery Requirements and Routes. Subsequent cycles are created and saved (up to four most recent cycles may be thus saved) as the user interacts with the system to improve the original set of routes. A

report may be printed describing all the routes in the current cycle.

The user modifies routes by selecting the Change Route(s) in Current Cycle option. A split-screen feature allows the user to request that any two routes be displayed on the screen, as shown in figure 3.13. By shuffling stores between the two routes, the manager can immediately see the effects of changes on the weight, volume, duration (time), and distance of each route. In order to make more complex changes, the traffic manager may move stores to or from a "dummy" route containing stores not currently assigned to any route. The process is complete when the dummy route is empty.

Another feature that considerably assists a manager familiar with the locale are map displays, obtained on the color monitor by selecting the Graphics option of Build Routes. A map that fits any selected group of routes may be displayed, such as the one shown in figure 3.14. Through the menu displayed at the bottom of the map, the user may choose a new map, zoom in on a part of the current one, or save the map.

If the user selects Z(oom), the corners and center (+) of a rectangle appear on the screen and can

FIGURE 3.13

A split-screen display for the routing DSS.

ROUTE SUMMARY REPORT FOR CYCLE #1								
ROUTE # 1				ROUTE # 2				
#	STORE #	WGHT	VOL	DEL.WINDOW	#	STORE #	WGHT	VOL	DEL.WINDOW
1	10479	250	600	M 2100T 0700	1	60306	200	300	W 1200W 2300
2	10480	250	500	M 2100T 0700	2	61861	300	200	M 2400M 1200
3	10481	250	700	T 2100W 0700	3	10037	100	400	M 2100T 0700
4	10485	250	100	M 2100T 0700					
WEIGHT	1000	RTE. TIME	4.75	WEIGHT	600	RTE. TIME	8.12
VOLUME	1900	RTE. DIST	222.77	VOLUME	900	RTE. DIST	400.85
1) PAGE BACK	2) PAGE FORWARD	3) CHANGE	4)SAVE RT	5) NEW RT	6)GRAPHICS	7) MENU		

be adjusted by the user to cover the desired area. That part of the map within the outline is then displayed, as shown in figure 3.15.

By using the split screen, route adjustment, and maps, the user may rapidly change the route sets to account for any new circumstances.

Once it was implemented, the system found rapid acceptance with the traffic managers. It was found that use of the system reduced the number of routes scheduled daily in the Orlando distribution center by one, resulting in savings of thousands of dollars per day.

Based on Salvatore Belardo, Peter Duchessi, and J. Peter Seagle, "Microcomputer Graphics in Support of Vehicle Fleet Routing." *Interfaces*, November–December 1985, pp. 84–92.

Note the following:

1. The initial set of routes is generated in this PC-based DSS by the users themselves. As the authors/designers point out, the original, mainframe-based system uses a heuristic (that is, a programmed set of rules of thumb) to come up with an initial set of routes. Thus, the store furthest from the distribution center and not already placed on a route serves as the anchor point for developing the route. Stores are added to the route until a constraint, such as total weight, volume, or distance, is violated. Then the next route is formed in the same way, until every store is assigned to a route. The route-generation procedure was later transferred to the PC-based DSS, as described in the follow-up paper by the same authors:

FIGURE 3.14

A map with displayed routes and a zoom outline.

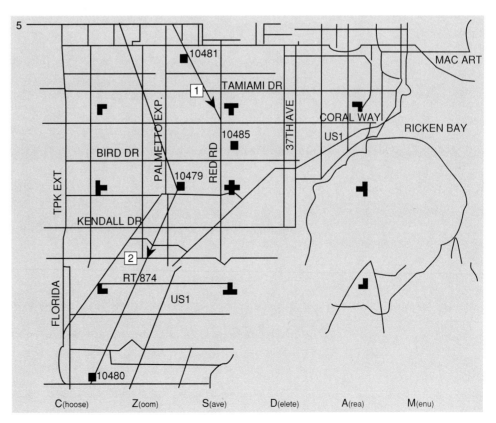

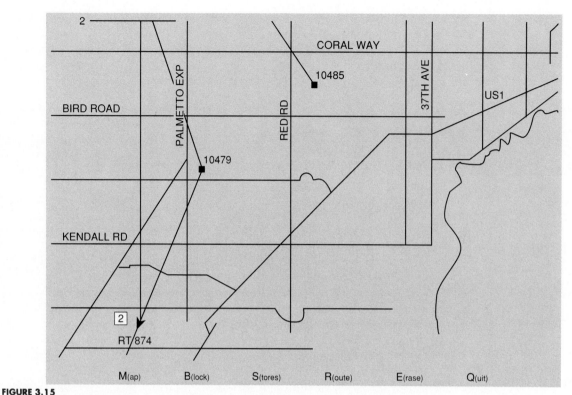

FIGURE 3.15

A zoom of a map fragment.

Peter Duchessi: Salvatore Belardo, and John P. Seagle, "Artificial Intelligence and the Management Science Practitioner: Knowledge Enhancements to a DSS for Vehicle Routing," *Interfaces*, March-April 1988, pp. 85–93.

This illustrates the fact that work can be distributed in various ways between the user and the DSS. In general, all processes that lend themselves to an algorithmic description should be allocated to the computer.

2. Note that the traffic manager relies on a number of rules in reformulating a set of routes (for example, "The delivery should be within the time window set by the store," or "You cannot use this highway if a bridge has too low an underpass"). These rules may be formulated as the contents of a knowledge base within an expert system, which would then become a part of the overall DSS. An initial design incorporating such work was also reported in the follow-up paper.

Case Study Two Questions

1. What are the advantages of moving the system from the mainframe to a personal workstation?

2. As a traffic manager, what other support would you want the DSS to offer you?

3. What role would the DSS be able to play in training new traffic managers?

4. What is in your opinion the strong point of this DSS and what is its weak point?

SELECTED REFERENCES

De Long, David W., and Rockart, John F. "Identifying the Attributes of Successful Executive Support System Implementation." In *Transactions of the Sixth Annual Conference on DSS,* edited by Jane Fedorowicz. Washington, D.C.: Institute of Management Science, 1986.

Eccles, Robert G. "The Performance Measurement Manifesto." *Harvard Business Review,* January-February 1991, pp.131–37.

Hackathorn, Richard D. "End-User Computing by Top Executives." *Data Base* 19, 1, Fall/Winter 1987/88, pp. 1–7.

Hirshheim, R. A. (ed.) *Office Automation: A Social and Organizational Perspective.* John Wiley: New York, 1985.

Holsapple, Clyde W., and Whinston, Andrew B. *Business Expert Systems.* Homewood, Ill.: Irwin, 1987.

Rockart, John F., and Treacy, Michael E. "The CEO Goes On-Line." *Harvard Business Review,* January-February 1982, pp. 82–88.

Sprague, Ralph H., Jr., and Watson, Hugh J. *Decision Support Systems: Putting Theory Into Practice.* Englewood Cliffs, N.J.: Prentice-Hall, 1986.

Swanson, E. Burton. "A Note on Information Attributes." *Journal of Management Information Systems* 2, 3, Winter 1985–86, pp. 87–91.

Turban, Efraim. *Decision Support and Expert Systems: Management Support Systems.* 2d ed. New York: Macmillan, 1990.

Zaki, Ahmed S., and Hoffman, Richard C. "Information Type and Its Impact on Information Dissemination," *Journal of Management Information Systems* 5, 2, Fall 1988, pp. 71–81.

Zuboff, Shoshana. *In the Age of the Smart Machine.* New York: Basic Books, 1988.

CHAPTER 4

TRANSACTION PROCESSING SYSTEMS

. . . .

There is no happier sound to the merchant's ear than that of a constantly ringing cash register.

F. W. Woolworth

Transaction processing systems (TPS) are the bedrock of business operations today. Using a common representational tool, system charts, we will describe two modes of transaction processing: batch and on-line. We will then discuss the activities that take place during transaction processing.

Along with its fundamental role in conducting business operations, transaction processing also secures raw data for the management-oriented components of MIS. Detailed data on internal operations are stored in the databases. At least as important, TPS are by nature boundary-spanning systems—they can be used to collect data on customers and suppliers, for example.

Another increasingly important role of these systems is to distinguish a firm's products and services to seek competitive advantage.

By familiarizing yourself with the fundamentals of transaction processing early during your study of MIS, you will be able to better understand the following chapters.

U.S. Instrument Rentals carries a line of 5,000 types of equipment. Marketing analysis has revealed that the general customer posture is price shopping: When contacted by a customer on the telephone, the order taker has about two minutes to come up with an acceptable offer, or the deal is lost.

A rental usually involves configuring several pieces of equipment from an extensive company line. The quotation would often take half an hour to produce by hand.

A configuration expert system was developed (inspired by Digital Equipment Corporation's XCON, which we will discuss at length in the case study for Part 4 of the text). This system takes from ten seconds for a simple quotation to a maximum of sixty seconds for the most complex cases—well within the acceptable time window for a telephone contact.

The final cost of the development and implementation of the expert system was $1.5 million. The system is not cost-justified merely by the savings made on salesclerks' time—rather, it is expected to pay for itself much more promptly by retaining sales the company would have otherwise lost and by proposing high-quality configurations that prevent costly problems later on.

Based on Bohdan O. Szuprowicz, "Expert Systems Use and Development Grows Rapidly." *MIS Week*, July 4, 1988, p. 34.

A sand and gravel company has developed an order entry system incorporating an expert system. Thanks to this system, inexperienced personnel may be employed taking orders at a saving to the company. The system determines the availability of the product in the current inventory and refers complex orders to experienced staff members.

Reported by John F. Rockart, Director of the Center for Information Systems Research at MIT, according to *The Business Week Newsletter for Information Executives*, July 8, 1988, p. 5.

Keeping popular items in stock is a key to superior service at a retail store. Los Angeles-based Carter Hawley Hale Stores, a chain of 115 retail stores, provides this service with an automatic reordering system driven from its point-of-sale terminals. Each time an item is purchased, its bar code is scanned and a replacement purchase order is generated. "Every time you sell a pair of socks, you are also ordering a pair," says the chief of the company's Information Systems division.

Based on Daniel Todd, "IT At Your Service." *InformationWeek*, September 10, 1990, p. 56.

All three of these cases demonstrate how a firm can seek competitive advantage through its order-processing and other transaction processing systems.

CHAPTER OUTLINE

4.1 Functions of Transaction Processing Systems
- Transaction Processing Systems Undergird Business Operations
- System Charts
- Transaction Processing Modes

4.2 Transaction Processing Subsystems in a Firm

4.3 Transaction Processing Activities
- Data Capture
- Data Validation
- Processing Steps Dependent on the Transaction and on Processing Mode
- Database Maintenance

4.4 Outputs Provided by Transaction Processing Systems
- Transaction Documents
- Query Responses and Reports

4.5 Do Not Neglect the Strategic Potential of TPS!

Summary

Conclusions for MIS Practice

Key Terms and Concepts

Questions

Issues for Discussion

Case Study One: Account Adjustment System at American Express

Case Study Two: Chateau Rien Revisited and Papa Gino's Encountered

Selected References

4.1 FUNCTIONS OF TRANSACTION PROCESSING SYSTEMS

Transaction processing systems support the operations of an enterprise by processing data that reflect its business transactions. These systems may work either in batch mode, processing accumulated transactions at a single later time, or in on-line mode, immediately processing incoming transactions. The graphic tools and processing modes introduced here are not necessarily specific to TPS; management reporting systems, for example, commonly run off certain reports in the batch mode. Indeed, the progressing integration of MIS means that some system types are beginning to blend together seamlessly.

Transaction Processing Systems Undergird Business Operations

A **transaction** is an elementary activity conducted during business operations. A merchandise sale, airline reservation, credit-card purchase, and inquiry about inventory are all transactions. TPS process data reflecting business transactions. This means, typically, that a TPS records a noninquiry transaction itself, as well as all its effects, in the database and produces documents relating to the transaction. For example, a sale transaction is accompanied by the sale record in the database, a subtraction from the inventory totals for the items purchased, and printing of a sale slip.

TPS are necessary to conduct business in almost any organization today. These systems are also a foundation on which other types of MIS rest. Accounting and payroll data processing were the first information system applications, introduced in the mid-fifties. As our three-era developmental model of MIS in chapter 2 shows, automation of business operations for the sake of efficiency was the earliest objective of computerization.

System Charts

To describe TPS, as well as other information systems, in an accessible manner, we need graphic tools. System charts are a well-established tool for such high-level representations; these charts show input sources, major processing steps, data storage, and system outputs.[1] System charts rely on a set of established graphic symbols. Figure 4.1 reproduces a useful subset of this set of symbols.

FIGURE 4.1

System chart symbols.

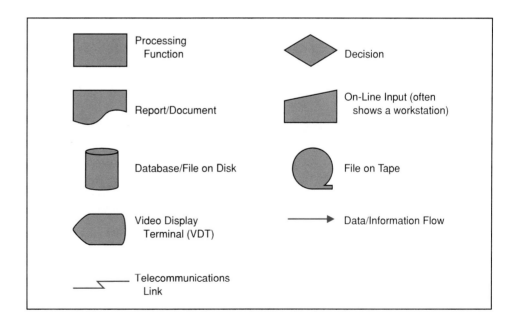

- Processing Function
- Decision
- Report/Document
- On-Line Input (often shows a workstation)
- Database/File on Disk
- File on Tape
- Video Display Terminal (VDT)
- Data/Information Flow
- Telecommunications Link

Transaction Processing Modes

Transaction processing may be accomplished in one of two modes: on-line or batch.

On-line processing means that the transaction is completely processed immediately upon entry. "Immediately" means, in turn, that processing occurs within the response time expected by the individual waiting for the transaction to be completed—in a properly designed system, most transactions should be processed within a few seconds. On-line transaction processing (with its own acronym, OLTP) is the most common mode used today—particularly in customer-driven applications, such as those supporting point-of-sale terminals, automatic teller machines, or computerized reservation systems.

FIGURE 4.2

Transaction processing— batch mode.

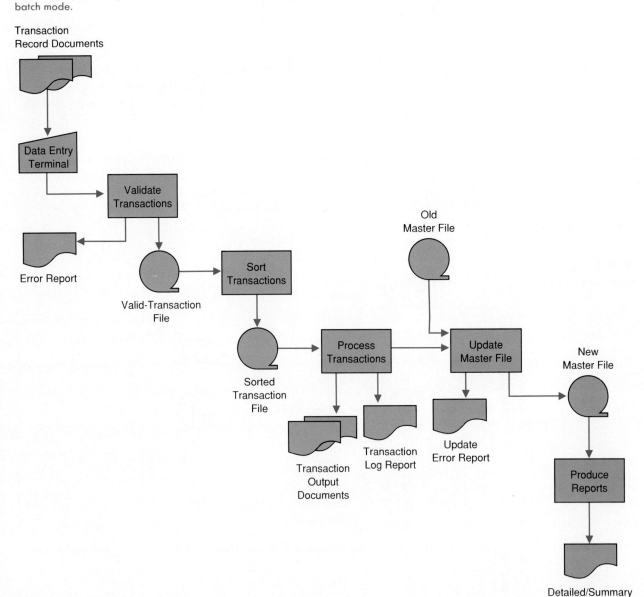

Certain kinds of transactions do not call for such an immediate and, in general, relatively costly response. The alternative processing mode, **batch processing,** relies on accumulating transaction data over a period of time and then processing the entire batch at once. Batch processing is usually cyclic—a daily, weekly, or monthly run cycle is established, depending on the nature of the transactions. Aside from the advantage of lower costs, batch processing is also easier to control than on-line processing, as we shall see in chapter 20. A typical batch application is payroll—it is run periodically and requires a special set-up for check printing, as well as calling for security precautions. Order transactions transmitted to a distributor daily over telephone lines or other media (by customers such as pharmacies or supermarkets) with hand-held bar-code readers may be processed on a daily cycle.

A system chart for batch transaction processing is shown in figure 4.2, a chart for OLTP in figure 4.3.

Note a very important distinction between these two modes: The database is always up-to-date in the case of on-line transaction processing, as opposed to batch processing. When the state government of New Hampshire wanted tight financial controls in the mid-1980s, the batch financial system was converted to OLTP. It is now possible to track revenues and expenditures in the state's $1.3 billion budget as they occur.

You will observe that we have indicated magnetic tape as the file storage medium for batch processing and magnetic disks for on-line systems. The use of a tape medium is cheaper and *can* support batch processing (though batch systems today are frequently built around disk files); on-line systems, on the other hand, *require* the use of fast secondary storage such as that offered by magnetic disks.

FIGURE 4.3

Transaction processing—on-line mode.

In batch processing, transaction files provide the means for auditing the system in order to verify the source of all data in the files and the disposition of all the

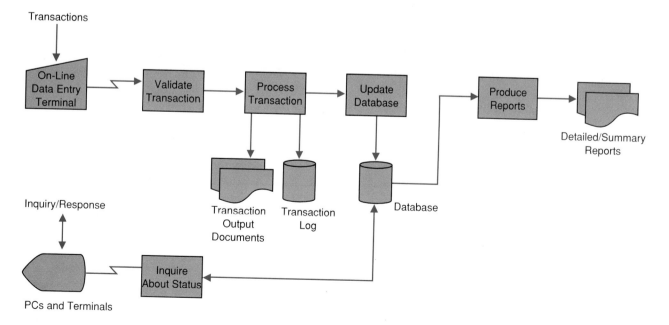

transaction data and for reconstructing files if a run failure occurs. Indeed, several generations of transaction and master files are preserved for these purposes. In on-line systems, it is necessary to log incoming transactions onto a separate log file in order to gain the same capabilities. These and other issues of MIS control are discussed in chapter 20.

Typically, invalid transactions rejected by the validation step during batch processing require either reentry by data entry clerks for some classes of errors, or more extensive manual handling based on error reports for others. In on-line systems, software validation modules request reentry or reject the transaction.

4.2 TRANSACTION PROCESSING SUBSYSTEMS IN A FIRM

It is instructive to review the principal data flows that transaction processing subsystems produce in an organization. Overall transaction processing, known also as data processing, accounts for all of the business activities of a firm. Figure 4.4 shows the principal transaction processing subsystems, which correspond to a company's principal operational units, as well as the fundamental documents that flow between them. Note that in some cases a hard-copy document may not actually be issued, with the information instead produced on a display or stored in a secondary memory.

The system chart in figure 4.4 is, of course, simplified. Each business is different to at least some degree, and of necessity a number of assumptions have been built into the chart. The general flow has been adapted, with modifications, from the text by Marvin Gore and John Stubbe (1988). To make the diagram as uncluttered as possible, we have omitted extensive detail. Also, the figure does not show databases or workstations. We have omitted any exceptions, such as back-orders for out-of-stock products or customer returns. We have also shown transaction processing exclusively, omitting the reporting usually included in these systems.

Let's briefly review the subsystems and the flows of information between them.

1. *Sales* receives a customer *order* and prepares a *sales notice* based on it, to be sent to Production and to Billing. A *shipping order* notifies Shipping about the need to send out the order.

2. *Production* bases its output levels on the *sales notices* as well as on a *sales forecast*—both furnished by Sales. Materials needed for production are requested with a *materials requisition* from Inventory.

3. *Inventory* transfers needed materials to Production, accompanied by a *materials transfer notice*. When the inventory needs replenishment, Inventory requests materials needed for Production from Purchasing with a *purchase requisition*.

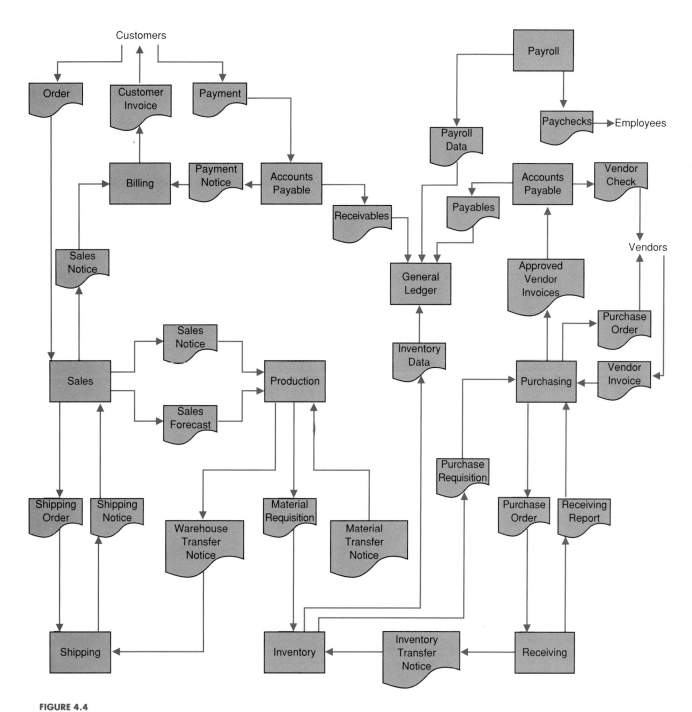

FIGURE 4.4

Transaction processing subsystems.

4. *Purchasing* sends a *purchase order* to the vendor and approves vendor invoices, which are forwarded to Accounts Payable. A copy of the *purchase order* is sent to Receiving.

5. *Shipping* receives the goods from Production, accompanied by a *warehouse transfer notice.* Shipping dispatches the products to the customer according to the *shipping order* it received from Sales and also sends a *shipping notice* to Sales.

TRANSACTION PROCESSING SYSTEMS ARE VITAL TO A BUSINESS

When a software supplier involved in a contract dispute with New York-based Revlon disabled Revlon's on-line TPS responsible for inventory management, the cosmetics company had to close two of its main distribution centers for three days. As much as $20 million in product deliveries were halted and hundreds of workers were idled.

The software supplier had planted a so-called logic bomb in the TPS code it delivered to Revlon. As we shall see in chapter 20, this method of attacking a software system involves inserting in it code that may be activated by the attacker. The code (program instructions) can cause a shutdown of the system. When Revlon failed to pay the supplier for the inventory

management system (which, according to the cosmetics giant, did not perform as promised) the supplier activated the code by accessing the system over a telephone line.

A legal action by Revlon ensued. The supplier claimed that it simply ''repossessed'' the software system; Revlon alleged that the supplier had committed ''commercial terrorism.'' Thorny legal issues, as well as technical issues of system protection, arose. The main fact, however, that this vignette demonstrates is this: The operation of many businesses today is wholly dependent on transaction processing systems.

Based on Andrew Pollack, ''Revlon Accuses a Supplier of Sabotaging Its Software,'' *The New York Times*, October 29, 1990, pp. D1, D4; and on Bruce Caldwell with John Soat, ''The Hidden Persuader,'' *Information Week*, November 19, 1990, pp. 42–47.

6. *Receiving* reports on the goods received from vendors to Purchasing.

7. *Accounts Payable* sends out *vendor checks.*

8. *Billing* sends out *invoices* to customers.

9. *Accounts Receivable* processes *customer payments* and notifies Billing with *payment notices.*

10. *Payroll* issues paychecks.

11. *General Ledger* subsystem maintains the consolidated records of all of the financial transactions of the organization. It thus receives data on such transactions from other appropriate subsystems.

When a transaction processing subsystem is developed for a business function in a firm, the development process should be considered an opportunity to rationalize the business function. To automate what is done manually or to move to a higher level of automation without a redesign of the business function itself usually means to miss that opportunity. We shall encounter numerous examples of such business reengineering (Verity, 1991) throughout the text.

Now that we have reviewed what a transaction processing system does, let's consider more analytically the activities necessary to process an individual transaction.

4.3 TRANSACTION PROCESSING ACTIVITIES

The processing of individual transactions, of course, depends to a degree on their nature. Here, however, we shall discuss the general elements of transaction processing: data capture and validation, transaction-dependent processing steps, and database maintenance.

Data Capture

Early methods of recording a transaction relied largely on manual capture; some systems still employ such techniques. They include data recorded on a hand-filled form (such as a marketing survey sheet), a document (sales order), or a marked or punched card. Computer entry from the capture medium follows: by keyboarding from the documents or by card-to-disk conversion routines for punched cards.

Today, direct entry is commonly employed. Popular examples of direct entry are summarized in table 4.1 (the alphabet soup of acronyms featured in the table has wide currency—but you do not need to remember all of these). This table depicts a major component of today's informational environment.

The proliferation of electronic data interchange (EDI), particularly in banking, transportation, and grocery retailing leads to direct transmission of transaction data from one transaction processing system to another, with no need for paperwork or repeated data entry. The electronic data interchange vignette illustrates the advantages that may be reaped with EDI; we shall encounter this technology later in the text as well.

TABLE 4.1

Sources of Direct Data Entry

TRANSACTION	DATA ENTRY DEVICE	HOW ENTERED
Inventory taking in packaged-foods warehouse	Bar-code reader (OCR scanner)	Optical character recognition (OCR) scanner reads the Universal Product Code (UPC) for the grocery product.
Order entry by sales representative	Laptop computer	Salespeople transmit orders from customer locations into headquarters' computer.
Retail sale in supermarket	POS terminal	Point-of-sale (POS) terminal registers the sale with a bar-code scanner and transmits the data to a computer.
Retail sale in department store	Touch-sensitive VDT screen	Sales clerk touches video display terminal (VDT) screen with a wand and identifies product through keyboard.
Checking account deposit	ATM	Automatic teller machine (ATM) enters the deposit; magnetic ink character recognition (MICR) unit reads in account identifications from deposit slip and checks.
Airline reservation	CRS terminal keyboard	Terminal of airline's computerized reservation system (CRS) is on-line to the computer.
Spoken inventory request	Voice recognition device	Item must be identified by numeric code (limits of speaker-independent technology today).
Gasoline purchase	"Smart-card" reader in POS terminal	POS terminal accepts credit cards or debit cards; card contains a microprocessor chip or laser-optic strip with customer information.
Insurance claim entry by adjuster	Pen-based notepad computer	Working at the damage site, the adjuster fills the form appearing on the screen with the electronic "pen" and transmits the claim to the office via cellular phone modem.

BENEFITS OF ELECTRONIC DATA INTERCHANGE (EDI)

1. U.S. railroads send 80 to 90 percent of their waybills electronically. RAILINC, a subsidiary of the Association of American Railroads, provides computer and telecommunication services to the industry and to its customers. Railroads, shippers, and private car companies exchange paperless information through the EDI services offered by RAILINC. Car location manifests, freight bills, bills of lading, and other documentation formerly delivered on paper are sent over the network. LTV Steel of Cleveland, one of the customers of Burlington Northern Railroad, for example, is able to use its computer system to verify freight bills received electronically against a database of freight rates. The company estimates savings of up to $30,000 a month in clerical costs and in avoidance of overcharges.

   The most significant present trend in the information systems employed by companies in the natural-resources sector of the U.S. economy is moving to EDI. The boom in oil and gas processing has increased the volume of shipments and the number of parties involved. Since transaction data have to be moved among the parties in a short time, EDI is the obvious method for handling these data.

   Based on Edwards, 1987; and on Thomas Hoffman, "Technology Resources." *InformationWeek*, September 10, 1990, p. 68.

2. Thanks to EDI, a supplier is able to deliver a retailer's order more quickly. Therefore, retailers can decrease their inventory levels. In apparel retailing, the merchant is also able to respond promptly to changing fashions and avoid costly overstocking. For example, having introduced EDI, Seminole Manufacturing Company has cut its delivery time on trousers to Wal-Mart Stores by 50 percent—to twenty-two days.

   Adapted from Catherine L. Harris, Dean Foust, and Matt Rothman, "An Electronic Pipeline That's Changing the Way America Does Business." *Business Week*, August 3, 1987, pp. 80–82.

Data Validation

Let us assume that a customer calls a mail order company with an order. The transaction is entered by a sales clerk through a series of VDT screens. Typical validation tests include those for missing data items, valid codes (size, alphabetic and/or numeric composition), and valid values (is the amount or the code within the proper range?). More extensive validation may entail authorization of the transaction based on the customer's record and available inventory.

Processing Steps Dependent on the Transaction and on Processing Mode

Depending on the nature of the transaction and on-line or batch mode of the system, the following processing steps may be performed.

Classification

The system classifies incoming transactions to select further processing steps. For example, transactions coming from an ATM terminal may be classified as withdrawal, deposit, or balance inquiry.

```
INQUIRY DATE: 12/31/92        TRANSACTION SYSTEM ACCOUNT INQUIRY              20-700
REQUESTING OFFICER:
                                      *--------------ACCOUNT NAME/ADDRESS----------------*
ACCOUNT NUMBER:      039 260 36      ODB   1:  KAREN ZIEGENHORN
SHORT NAME:      ZIEGENHORN  KAREN         2:  C/O  IVEYS
DATE OPENED:      6/01/75                  3:  228 EAST LAKE BLVD
O.D. LIMIT:            1                   4:  WINTER PARK, FL 32789
STATEMENT CYCLE:      020                  5:
*---------------------BALANCE DATA------------------------*
CURRENT BALANCE:                       11,209.93
AVAILABLE BALANCE:                     11,209.93   STOPS-HOLDS ACTIVE                  Y
AVAILABLE TOMORROW:                    11,209.93   DATE LAST ACTIVE             11/02/92
MEMO BALANCE:                          11,209.93   DATE LAST DEPOSIT            11/02/92
ACCOUNT TYPE:                                002   AMOUNT LAST DEPOSIT          2418.34
PROCESSED THRU                           1/04/93   CHECK CREDIT BAL          100,000.00
               *--------------------PREVIOUS STATEMENT DATA----------------------*
               LAST STATEMENT DATE                      1/05/93
               LAST STATEMENT BALANCE                   7,976.63
               CHECKS SINCE
               DEPOSITS SINCE                                 4
               SERVICE CHARGE CODE                       A 03
               STATEMENT CONTROL CODES                   D  0
               INTEREST PAID LAST YEAR                    .00
     PRESS CMD 1 FOR ANOTHER INQUIRY/CMD 2 FOR ACTIVE STOPS/CMD 3 FOR CREDIT
```

FIGURE 4.5

Status screen for checking accounts.

(Source: Citicorp Information Resources, Orlando, Florida)

Sorting

Transaction records are arranged in order of the value of the data item(s) which uniquely identifies each of them. Called the key, this value may be, for example, the identification number assigned to each transaction or the employee's Social Security number. This step is practically always included in batch systems.

Data retrieval

The purpose of an inquiry transaction is, of course, retrieval of data from the database. Other transactions may involve data retrieval as well. For example, when a product bar code is scanned by a supermarket POS scanner, the price for the product is looked up in the database: This gives great flexibility in changing prices. However, if a fast response to a transaction is needed, the number of database accesses has to be generally limited.

A screen for retrieving checking account information in the Comprehensive Banking System of Citicorp Information Resources is shown in figure 4.5. Several other screens are available to bank tellers to track deposits and withdrawals in an account.

Calculation

The calculations required depend, of course, on the nature of the transaction. A credit card authorization would entail for most cards calculating the total credit extended so far and comparing it to the customer's credit limit. An ATM withdrawal from a bank lowers the account balance in a simple calculation.

Summarization

Usually performed to obtain simple reports offered by TPS, this step computes summaries across all or some of the transactions (for example, the number of accounts over 30 days delinquent).

Database Maintenance

After transactions other than inquiries, system files or databases must be updated. The data accumulated by TPS thus serves as a source of detail for management-oriented MIS components.

Hiring a new employee may call only for the insertion of his or her record into a simple, file-oriented system. A more elaborate human resources database would be updated by also modifying the skills inventory, medical records, educational requirements file, and so forth.

The following brief review of data organization in long-term storage is based on figure 4.6. The discussion will be expanded in chapter 8.

A **record** provides data about various attributes of the real-world object it describes. The object may be tangible (for example, an employee) or intangible, such as an event (for example, a flight). Each of the object's attributes is described by a **field** of the record. Thus, as shown in figure 4.6a, a flight record in an airline management system run by an individual airline may consist of fields representing the flight code, date, origin and destination, departure time, arrival time, aircraft type, and number of seats available.

Records of the same type are aggregated into a **file.** Thus, we may have a flight file, consisting of the records of all flights offered by the airline during a certain time interval. A special field, called the **key,** identifies each record among others in the file. In our case, this would have to be a concatenated field, consisting of the flight code and the date.

FIGURE 4.6

Data organization in files and databases.

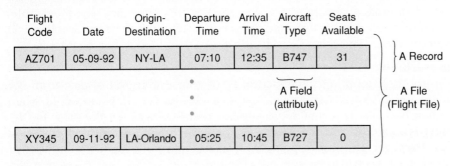

(a) A File

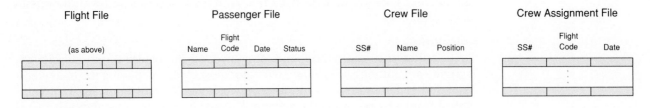

(b) A Database

Simpler systems rely on individual files. In more elaborate—though very common—systems, files are aggregated into databases. A **database** is a set of interrelated files, managed by a type of systems software called a database management system (DBMS), so that information derived from data stored in multiple files may be obtained. The database of our airline management system may, for example, also contain a passenger file and a crew file along with the flight file, as shown in figure 4.6b. The use of DBMS would allow the user to answer questions such as: When will Captain Jones arrive in Los Angeles on May 21? Who will the crew members be on the flight Mr. Flier will take? Thus, databases and the systems that manage them provide great flexibility in accessing data.

Individual transactions may result in insertions and deletions of records or updates of record fields. For example, a reservation will cause the insertion of a record into the passenger file and an update of the "seats available" field in the flight file. On completion of a flight, the flight closing transaction would cause deletion of a number of entries from the passenger file; they may be written into an archive file to be used for future marketing.

On-line transaction processing systems have to process a large number of transactions per second, with the transactions sometimes arriving from thousands of remote terminals. To measure the volume of this so-called throughput that a given system can handle, system designers can enter benchmarks (that is, standardized transactions) from multiple simulated terminals. Depending on the hardware and software platforms, some systems have a throughput of 100 or more transactions per second while maintaining a response time of less than a second.

Owing to the storage capacities, flexibility of access, and speed of processing data that database technologies offer, their use provides new business opportunities. The vignette on supermarket scanners provides examples of the flourishing practice of *database marketing:* The use of database technology to achieve marketing objectives.

Database marketing has become a source of competitive advantage for Williams-Sonoma, a direct marketer and retailer of cooking and gardening equipment. The San Francisco-based company has built its stockmarket value from $60 million in 1983 to $220 million in 1991. Relying on a database of 4.5 million customers that tracks up to 150 data items per customer, the company's two full-time statisticians can project the sales from each direct-mail catalog with 95 percent accuracy. The database also helps the company locate the most promising sites for new stores (Meeks, 1991).

Marketing databases do raise several concerns—and the cost of information is only one of them. Possible consumer resistance to what they may consider an invasion of privacy is certainly another. However, this category of applications is here to stay. We will see in the book many more examples of the strategic application of databases—a prodigious organizational memory.

FROM A SUPERMARKET SCANNER INTO A MARKETING DATABASE

When a product bearing a bar code is checked out in a supermarket or in another retail outlet, the information system the point-of-sale terminal is connected to learns something about you—you are a person who buys this sort of product.

Mammoth databases containing data about the public's buying habits and brand preferences are being assembled. Now marketers can have—at a significant cost—an actual census of people who purchase a brand. How much more reliable this is than a survey of a relatively small sample of people about their buying *intentions!* Using the data from these databases, marketers can determine the effectiveness of advertising campaigns, and their messages can be fine-tuned to the individuals who are actual or potential customers. This is obviously much more effective than simply broadcasting the message to people who would not remotely consider purchasing the product!

Citicorp has placed 2.3 million cards in the households of several major cities. When consumers use these cards at supermarkets, the purchase data are routed to Citicorp's computers. In 1990, the company projected that within five years it would be collecting and selling information about the purchases of 40 million American households. This would require processing 30 billion transactions annually incoming from 14,000 nationwide retail outlets. The information would be sold in the content and form specified by the clients: manufacturers, retailers, and advertising agencies.

Based on Martin Mayer, "Scanning the Future," *Forbes*, October 15, 1990, pp. 114–17.

4.4 OUTPUTS PROVIDED BY TRANSACTION PROCESSING SYSTEMS

The outputs provided by TPS may be classified as transaction documents, query responses, and reports.

Transaction Documents

Many TPS produce transaction documents, such as sale invoices, purchase orders, or payroll checks. The transaction documents produced by TPS may be divided into two classes: action documents and information documents.

1. Action documents

   These documents direct that an action take place. For example, an airline ticket calls for granting a flight seat, a picking slip directs a warehouse worker to pull an inventory item, and a bank has to pay against a check drawn on it. Some of these are turnaround documents, such as the portion of the credit card statement you are asked to return with the payment. Turnaround documents initiate action and are returned after its completion to the requesting agency. They therefore also serve as input documents for another transaction—in our example, payment recording.

2. Information documents

These documents confirm that a transaction has taken place or inform about one or several transactions. A voucher sent with a payment to explain it, or a list of credit card charges arriving with the bill, are examples of information documents.

Transaction documents require manual handling and, in some cases, distribution of multiple copies. The process is costly and may lead to inconsistencies if one of the copies fails to reach its destination. The advances of EDI will ultimately eliminate much of this documentation, replacing it with the electronic exchange of transaction records. Already, electronic deposits made by many employers into employee bank accounts have obviated the need for payroll checks.

Query Responses and Reports

Through the use of DBMS facilities and end-user-oriented fourth-generation languages, the users of OLTP systems may garner a wealth of information from the database. Use of query languages and report-generator facilities for ad-hoc querying and reporting will be discussed in chapter 8. Most queries produce a screenful of information. However, reports are also often produced as a result of inquiries. A range of preprogrammed screens is available in certain systems for preprogrammed queries (as shown in figure 4.5).

Unlike management reporting systems, TPS typically provide a limited range of preplanned reports. The content and format of such reports are programmed into the TPS software, and the reports are produced on schedule. The TPS reports are often quite voluminous. The status of various organizational resources—such as funds and equipment—may be specified in detail. Transactions may be tracked; for example, employee movement—into the company, within it, through educational experiences, and, perhaps, into retirement status—may be traced step by step.

The following report types are produced by TPS:

1. Transaction logs

These logs are listings of all transactions processed during a run, such as purchase order manifests or sales registers.

2. Error reports

These reports list transactions found to be in error during the processing. They identify the error and sometimes also list the corresponding master file records.

3. Detail reports

These are extracts from files that list records satisfying particular criteria. For example, a detail report would list inventory items with expiring shelf warranties or describe all copy machines in the inventory of an office equipment distributor.

4. Summary reports

Financial statements—balance sheets and profit-and-loss statements—are typically produced by TPS. A variety of other summary reports may be programmed, depending on the application.

4.5 DO NOT NEGLECT THE STRATEGIC POTENTIAL OF TPS!

Transaction processing is often written off as an efficiency-oriented area that calls for no more than, perhaps, technical ingenuity. Indeed, efficient transaction processing may be a source of competitive advantage in itself. Reengineered business functions, supported by TPS, are a source of economies in an increasing number of firms. Many companies are only now getting to the integration of their stand-alone TPS into a single-order management system, for example (Kay, 1991). However, missing other opportunities may greatly diminish the strategic potential of TPS.

Customers enter orders via order-processing TPS components; their payments are processed by accounts receivable TPS; and suppliers and subcontractors interact directly or indirectly with purchasing subsystems. A wealth of data on the environment of the firm can thus be collected by TPS. Using these data, management-oriented MIS subsystems may analyze customer behavior (who buys what, how much, and when) to identify profitable customer segments and to track supplier and subcontractor performance.

The customer-driven nature of many TPS affords some firms the opportunity to realize a competitive advantage by providing unique systems. There are many ways a customer's order can be entered and processed. Systems that provide convenience, the ability to customize or individualize a product, and prompt and flexible service are likely to bind customers to the company.

Two examples of companies that recognized these facts are discussed in the focus cases opening this chapter; many others will be examined in the next chapter.

• •

SUMMARY

Transaction processing systems (TPS) form the operational foundation of MIS. Since TPS interact, directly or indirectly, with customers, suppliers, and sometimes other stakeholders of the firm, they have high strategic potential.

If a business requires immediate transaction processing, the on-line processing mode is employed; otherwise, batch mode may be used, with greater efficiency and enhanced control. Processing of all transactions involves certain common steps, including data capture, data validation, and database maintenance. Other steps depend on the transaction and, in some cases, on the processing mode. Depending on their purpose, transactions may produce documents, and query responses, or reports.

CONCLUSIONS FOR MIS PRACTICE

1. By supporting the operations of firms, TPS ensure the level of efficiency and responsiveness demanded of a modern organization.

2. While on-line systems are increasingly prevalent, batch processing has definite advantages under certain circumstances.

3. TPS define to a large degree how a firm does business. Therefore, the development of a TPS should be viewed as an opportunity to review and rationalize business processes.

4. Data capture changes rapidly with evolving technology. Electronic data interchange has changed the way a number of industries do business.

5. Along with capturing, validating, and processing transaction data, maintenance of company databases is an important function of TPS.

6. A TPS spans the periphery of a company by interacting with customers, suppliers, and other stakeholders. Therefore, TPS can be a potent tool in forging a firm's information systems into a strategic weapon.

ENDNOTE

1. We note that system charts are not a recommended tool for system *development*, as will be discussed in chapter 19, where an alternative common representation will be introduced for development purposes.

KEY TERMS AND CONCEPTS

Transaction	Automatic teller machine (ATM)
System chart	Electronic data interchange (EDI)
On-line processing	Action document
Batch processing	Information document
Data capture	Transaction log
Optical character recognition (OCR)	Error report
	Detail report
Point-of-sale (POS) terminal	Summary report

QUESTIONS

1. What is a transaction? Give five examples of transactions other than those mentioned in the chapter.

2. In table form, list the comparative advantages and disadvantages of batch versus on-line transaction processing.

3. What roles can be played by magnetic disks and tapes in batch and on-line TPS?

4. Consider the Purchasing subsystem in figure 4.4 in more detail. Present a system chart for that subsystem alone.

5. What validation steps could you perform for a "ship order" transaction? Consider using various company databases.

6. Consider a transaction "produce vendor check," which is performed by the Purchasing subsystem in figure 4.4. What specific activities are necessary to process this transaction?

7. What is the role of sorting in batch and on-line TPS? In which is it more important, and why? Could we do without it—and at what cost?

8. Consider the database in figure 4.6b. Do you think it contains a lot of redundant data? How would you restructure the database to minimize redundancy if you assume that the same flights are offered daily by the airline?

9. What is the function of transaction logs?

10. What aspects of TPS give them strategic potential?

ISSUES FOR
DISCUSSION

1. Familiarize yourself with the operation of a small firm and represent its existing transaction processing subsystems in a manner similar to figure 4.4. What possibilities for improving these operations do you see in the firm?

2. Using the available literature, investigate the role of EDI in one of the industries.

3. Find other sources of data entry employed in today's TPS. Discuss the comparative advantages of these other techniques.

CASE STUDY ONE

ACCOUNT ADJUSTMENT SYSTEM AT AMERICAN EXPRESS

By the mid-1970s, it had become obvious that continued manual handling of American Express's credit card operations would become the limiting factor on the growth of that line of the company business. By 1984, the company had completed a multifaceted automation project in its credit card operations area. Completed several years ago, the project remains highly instructive.

One aspect of this project was the development of an Account Adjustment System—an on-line TPS for processing internally generated adjustments to cardmember accounts. Because the company is highly service-oriented, its service representatives were performing twenty-five to thirty different types of account adjustments to satisfy a variety of cardmember needs. The require-

ments of adjustment transactions vary widely. A transaction returning a credit balance to a cardmember requires printing a check. Canceling a magazine subscription by a cardmember requires sending a notification to the magazine. The main difficulty encountered in developing the adjusting system was identifying common processing steps among the transactions insofar as possible.

The company built a centralized TPS. The developers used a structured development methodology, which is discussed in Part 5 of the text.

The system was built to consist of two components: on-line and batch. The on-line component supports data entry by the clerks, validation, and writing of accepted transactions to an intermediate database. This component is available for accepting transactions twenty-four hours a day, except for a daily period of half an hour when it is taken off line. During this period, transaction records are extracted from the intermediate database and processed by the batch component. The batch subsystem updates the billing database and produces the required documents.

The main reason for the two-level system in this case was that the company controller "did not feel comfortable with direct update of the cardmember database," due to the difficulty of restoring the database in on-line systems should failure occur. Another reason was the need to ensure rapid response time in the on-line component.

The on-line component provides for ten different transactions, each with its own screen; each transaction thus performs several of the previously discussed adjustments—those with similar processing requirements. The system processed an average of 60,000 adjustments in each twenty-four-hour period during 1986. More than 1,200 employees were using the system through individual terminals. Response time was three to five seconds.

Based on Barbara Elazari, "AMEX Designs an OLTP System." *Datamation*, November 15, 1986, pp. 96–108.

Case Study One Questions

1. Construct a general system chart for the American Express Account Adjustment System.

2. Provide a more detailed system chart for the "cancel magazine subscription" transaction in the Account Adjustment System.

3. Analyze the considerations that led the company to build a batch component into the TPS. Why are these concerns absent in the system as designed?

CASE STUDY TWO — CHATEAU RIEN REVISITED AND PAPA GINO'S ENCOUNTERED

A. Consider again Case Study One in Chapter 3. Draw a system chart for the TPS component of the Chateau Rien's MIS. Can the TPS-assisted operations be rationalized in any way? List your suggestions.

B. Now let's look at another restaurant's information system. A New England pizza chain, Papa Gino's of America (of Dedham, Massachusetts), is offering a highly efficient delivery service based on personal computers.

Each store contains three or four PCs connected to the incoming telephone lines. The PCs are interconnected into a local area network, which also includes printers located in the kitchen and in the manager's office. The approximate cost of hardware is $11,000 per store.

The customer who calls in the order gives his or her phone number. If the customer made a previous order, detailed information on this customer is available in the store's database and is placed on the screen. If the caller is a first-time customer, his or her name and address are obtained. The system prints out the order on the kitchen's printer, as well as making copies for the delivery driver and the customer.

Speed of delivery is of the essence in competing with another, well-established chain. Therefore, the system plots out the destination on an on-screen locator grid to help dispatch drivers for multiple deliveries. A map of the customer's vicinity is printed out for the driver.

Thanks to the system, Papa Gino's can now accept an order within twenty seconds, make the delivery within thirty minutes, and automatically generate the daily reports at the close of the day.

Based on Richard Pastore, "Papa Gino's 'To Go' Here To Stay." *Computerworld*, October 1, 1990, p. 40.

Case Study Two Questions

1. Assuming that business considerations warrant such a move, how can a delivery service such as that at Papa Gino's be provided through the information systems at Chateau Rien's restaurants? List the modifications that would be required in the Chateau's information system. Consider that New Chateau Rien would offer a greater variety of items than Papa Gino's for delivery, but would have a comparatively low volume of delivery business.

2. What other features would be desirable in an information system for New Chateau Rien, which would now combine sit-down service with delivery service (a rapidly growing market segment)? Provide a list of the features.

SELECTED REFERENCES

Edwards, Daniel W. *Electronic Data Interchange.* Washington, D.C.: International Center for Information Technologies, 1987.

Freedman David H. "On-Line Moves Into Real-Time." *Infosystems,* November 1986, pp. 60–66.

Gore, Marvin, and Stubbe, John W. *Elements of Systems Analysis.* 4th ed. Dubuque, Iowa: Wm. C. Brown, 1988.

Kay, Emily. "Relief For Your Order-Entry Headaches." *Datamation,* July 1, 1991, pp. 51–52.

Meeks, Fleming. "Preserving the Magic." *Forbes,* February 18, 1991, pp. 60–61.

Schatz, Willie. "EDI: Putting the Muscle in Commerce and Industry." *Datamation,* March 15, 1988, pp. 56–64.

Sloan, Ken. "All Your Assets On-Line." *Computerworld,* July 11, 1988, pp. 55–58.

Verity, John W. and McWilliams, Gary. "Is It Time to Junk the Way You Use Computers?" *Business Week,* July 22, 1991, pp. 66–69.

CHAPTER 5

INFORMATION SYSTEMS FOR COMPETITIVE POSITIONING: STRATEGIC USE OF INFORMATION

. . . .

We see that victory lies
Not at some high place along the way,
But in having made the journey, stage by stage. . . .
  Gates of Repentance

The management team appreciates technology—but in
terms of serving the customer.
  Louis Gerstner
  as President of American Express

Strategic information systems are directed at improving the competitive position of an organization in the marketplace. These systems transform the way a firm does business and sometimes result from a radically new perception of the nature of this business. They change the firm's products and services, its organizational processes, and create new relationships with the firm's customers, suppliers, competitors, and partners. As you study this chapter, you will note that strategic information systems often affect related industry segments: they raise many ships. (They may also sink the ships of unprepared competitors, as was the case with the People Express airline.)

We will first explore the use of information systems in three kinds of strategic thrusts. We shall then develop a "strategic cube" of strategies and tactics designed to combat specific competing forces in the marketplace. This analysis on the macroscopic level will be followed by the study of a tool for identifying targets of opportunity in the sequence of a company's activities. This tool is called value-chain analysis.

We shall go on to consider the organizational requirements for successful implementation of strategic information systems and for gaining the ultimate in competitive positioning: sustainable competitive advantage. We will also see how the strategic use of information systems changes the structure of affected industries.

This chapter, even more than others, will rely on actual examples from leading practice: these examples, many of them in vignette form, will illustrate the very broad possibilities for ingenuity in the strategic use of information systems. The most successful systems find a way to break the mold rather than fit a framework.

Hospitals used to be considered very mildly competing organizations, if they were thought about at all in terms of competition. The economics of the health care industry—until the mid-1980s, when hospitals ceased being reimbursed on a cost-plus-investment-in-the-hospital basis—allowed the author of an influential book-length analysis of the industry to say in 1984: "The only computer services that a hospital really needs—basic financial, billing, and accounting operations—could be purchased relatively inexpensively from any service company."[1]

In April 1983, to contain the escalating costs of medical services, the U.S. government began to introduce a new reimbursement system based on diagnosis-related groups (DRGs). Under the new system, hospitals were reimbursed by Medicare and Medicaid, which cover 40 percent of the procedures a hospital performs, based on the diagnosed illness of the patient (and some related considerations). The amount received by the hospital was tied to the national and regional costs of treating the condition, rather than what the hospital spent treating the patient. Private insurers followed suit. In other words, under the new system, hospitals have been reimbursed for most of their care based on what they cure rather than on how much they spend to effect a cure.

The new system put immense pressure on the hospitals to **become competitive;** a number of hospitals closed. Information systems soon became a primary tool in the competitiveness drive. Broad strategies were needed— first to survive, and then to flourish under the new conditions.

One of the strategies hospitals developed is **cost containment,** which had to be based on precise tracking of the costs of all procedures, tests, meals, and equipment performed or used at each hospital bed. Two previously separate information flows had to be integrated: patient-care (medical) information and the financial information.

But hospitals soon found that to contain costs is not enough. Hospital beds must be marketed. They are a perishable commodity, similar to airline seats. Certain hospitals began to **differentiate** their offerings, distinguishing their products or services from those of their competitors. Some of the distinctive features are aimed at the hospital distributors—physicians, who direct ''business'' (patients) to the hospitals. (Have you ever thought of physicians as the distributors of hospital services?) Thus, for example, *High Plains Baptist Hospital* in Amarillo, Texas hoped to attract doctors from beyond its traditional local drawing area through its newly installed computer communication network, with personal computers in doctors' offices. At High Plains, doctors can order tests, review their results, and preadmit patients from the convenience of their private offices. Physicians save time. Along with drawing physicians to the hospital, the information system at High Plains helps to improve health-care quality.

Other hospitals differentiate their services to patients. They attract eminent medical specialists (either by placing them on staff or on a consulting basis through information systems, such as electronic meeting systems) and provide VIP floors with luxury-hotel amenities, including office computing facilities.

The new approach was the result of a change in strategic vision. Hospitals realized that they are information-intensive businesses. Information systems are, therefore, mission-critical (as the parlance goes) to the hospitals' core business. Hospitals found that they were spending only 2.6 percent of their total budget on information systems (according to the Healthcare MIS Society of the American Hospital Association), as compared to the 7 percent or more being spent in the banking industry.[2] This indicated a problem—but it also pointed to an opportunity: **strategic use of information systems,** designed to seek competitive advantage, could change the way a hospital serves its stakeholders and competes in the marketplace.

Once an organization embarks on the road to the strategic use of information systems, the ball keeps rolling. Once a hospital has installed a computer and telecommunications infrastructure and created integrated patient databases; formed MIS departments, frequently headed by a Chief Information Officer reporting directly to the hospital's chief executive; and introduced information systems into a hospital's culture, that hospital can build on this strength, further leveraging information technology.

One of the largest hospitals in the country, *Mount Sinai Hospital* in New York City, began in the late 1980s to install computer terminals at each of its 1,112 beds. Linked through a local area network to a IBM 3090 mainframe (as well as other computers), these terminals provide access for physicians and nurses to complete, up-to-the-minute treatment records of all patients. *Grady Memorial Hospital* in Atlanta has moved to an entirely paperless patient information system, with six and a half million records. Using bar codes for data entry, linking in diagnostic expert systems for specific medical conditions, and using laser scanners for storing radiological images are just some of the future advantages hospitals may reap from strategic information systems.

To better identify effective methods of patient care and to control their costs, hospital conclude **strategic alliances** that allow them to share relevant information. The Voluntary Hospitals of America, a national alliance of 650 hospitals and their more than 185 affiliates, has installed a Clinical/Financial Information System on an IBM 3090 mainframe at the University of Michigan. Medical and financial records from the member hospitals are extracted from their information systems and entered into a common database stored there. The appropriate comparative information is available for on-line access over a network to the planning personnel at the hospitals.

Other hospitals form **virtual partnerships** with their suppliers. *St. Luke's Episcopal Hospital* in Houston uses a stockless supply method. The hospital's supplier makes daily deliveries of all the medical supplies directly to the wards—and the hospital thus needs no warehouse. Interorganizational order processing systems are the foundation of such an arrangement. But then, St. Luke's supplier is *Baxter Healthcare,* which emerged from American Hospital Supply Company with its highly regarded ASAP computerized order-taking system. While the supplier earns fees (and increases its market share), the hospital saves money.

Based in part on Patrick Flanagan, ''Emergency Treatment for Health Care Systems,'' *Computer Decisions,* September 1988, pp. 43–49; Ellis Booker, ''Helping Hospitals Share Information,'' *Computerworld,* January 28, 1991, p. 28; and Milt Freudenheim, ''Removing the Warehouse from Cost-Conscious Hospitals,'' *The New York Times, Business Section,* March 3, 1991, p. 5.

CHAPTER OUTLINE

5.1 A Strategic Perspective on Information Systems
- Why a New Perspective?
- When Did the New Perspective Take Hold?
- Must a Change Be No Less Than Revolutionary?

5.2 Information Systems in Strategic Thrusts
- Redefining Company Business
- Creating Products and Services Based on Information Systems
- Transforming Company Products and Processes with Information Systems

5.3 Strategies, Forces, and Tactics in Competitive Markets
- Competitive Strategies
- Competitive Forces
- Tactical Moves in Pursuing a Strategy
- Strategic Cube

5.4 Value-Chain Analysis of Strategic Opportunities
- Value Chain
- Using the Value-Chain Analysis to Identify Strategic Information Systems

5.1   A Strategic Perspective on Information Systems

During the first two decades of their evolution, management information systems were oriented inward: they were directed at the internal functioning of organizations, with cost reductions as the primary objective. Initially, through efficient transaction processing, these systems reduced the amount of paperwork in the back office as business operations were automated.

Later, the thrust of MIS was targeted at improving the management process. Systems providing reports and, later, decision support for various management segments were put in place. Particularly during the latter stage, it was recognized that elaborate external information has to be brought *into* the company. Planning and control could now rest on sound and timely information about a company's activities and about conditions in the immediate marketplace and in the general business environment.

From rather humble beginnings in the mid-1970s, an entirely new perspective on the role of information systems in organizations emerged a decade later. At that time, management realized that *information systems may be designed to give a firm an enhanced ability to compete and possibly furnish the firm with a competitive advantage in the marketplace.* This outward direction in MIS has shaped our present perception of the potential role of information technology in organizations.

Why a New Perspective?

Strategic systems have become not only possible but sometimes necessary owing to the confluence of several forces:

- The dynamics of an information society, in which many sectors of industry find that much of their business consists of handling information, rather than producing tangible goods or services.
- The reduction of the costs of enabling technologies, particularly when strategic systems are added to an already existing technological base. Information resources are in many cases a cost-effective substitute for other types of resources, such as labor, materials, or energy.
- The general acculturation of people in organizations to the use of computer and communication technologies in their search for solutions to business problems.

When Did the New Perspective Take Hold?

While an early suggestion to "cross company boundaries" with information systems was made in 1966 (Kaufman, 1966), the first information systems targeted at the outside world actually appeared in the mid-seventies. Computerized airline reservation systems and automated order-taking systems introduced by distributors of pharmaceutical products led the way.

In the 1980s, leading companies realized that information systems may be used as strategic weapons to shape their competitive positions in the marketplace. Considering the importance of information processing in postindustrial society, the use of information systems for direct competition is increasing in the 1990s.

Must a Change Be No Less Than Revolutionary?

Strategic information systems vary widely in aims, scope, and complexity. Through such systems, several leading companies have managed to change the rules of the game in their industry segments. Aggressive players are followed by imitators, and the cycle sometimes repeats itself. Through the market mechanism, these systems play an extremely important role in moving entire industries into higher rates of productivity.

A strategic system significantly alters the way an organization does business. However, only a few of these systems will revolutionize an industry. In most cases, an organization takes a series of smaller steps, using information systems to improve the way the company converts input resources into products and introduces the products into the marketplace. If the system significantly lowers costs or if the targeted market segment perceives the product as significantly different, the firm is in a position to gain market share and increase its profits. Indeed, some strategic systems confer on its owner company a clear *competitive advantage* in the economist's sense of the word—higher profits or increased market share with respect to its competitors. However, such clear advantage can be attributed to information systems only in rather exceptional cases. Much more frequently, we can say that a strategic system has enabled a company to be an effective competitor in the marketplace.

Note that "rapid diffusion of technological change makes it increasingly difficult *to maintain* [emphasis added] a competitive advantage based on product features or design" (Lele, 1986). Therefore, strategic deployment of information systems has to be thought of as a dynamic capability, and not as a static attribute. This capability is produced by a combination of information systems, organizational change, and customer relationship. Together, these elements support a package of product, service, and information offered in the marketplace.

Much of the information used in strategic information systems is often obtainable through already existing transaction-processing and management-support MIS components. It is the retargeting and incorporation of some of the existing subsystems into a competitive weapon that makes the difference. Value-chain analysis, discussed in this chapter, is the tool MIS practitioners use to identify potential areas of opportunity.

5.2 INFORMATION SYSTEMS IN STRATEGIC THRUSTS

An information system is **strategic** if its objective is to improve the competitive position of the organization. A successful change means that an organization acquires the ability to attract a customer segment—profitably, and for an extended term—better than its competitors are able to do so.

Competitive positioning through the use of information technology may be achieved through a very broad spectrum of approaches. Let us first consider the principal thrusts organizations employ to position themselves in the marketplace. This will also give us an opportunity to acquaint ourselves with a few exemplars of strategic information system practice.

Redefining Company Business

The question "What business are we in?" is crucial in establishing a company's direction. A company may determine that it is actually in the information business, rather than, for example, the news or office machine business. This recognition, *if the company acts upon it,* changes the basis on which the company decides to compete. The new vision now must be channeled into contributing to the information sector of the economy by *building on existing company strengths.* This vision of the firm will define the company for years to come.

James Robinson, chairman of *American Express,* articulated this approach very clearly: "All the financial analysts keep saying that we're in the financial services business. They're wrong. American Express is in the information business. . . ."[3] Consequently, the company is now stressing the use of the most advanced technology to radically change its core business. American Express, as a leader in MIS practice, has furnished several cases and examples for this text.

Reuters Holdings PLC, a company headquartered in Great Britain and with its roots in news and currency price quotes, sees itself as a supermarket of financial information. Reuters has become the world's leading disseminator of financial data, with over 160,000 terminals in customer offices. In these days of electronic financial markets, such a market can be made by a computer network with traders at terminals. Indeed, the London Stock Exchange abandoned its trading floor in the famous Big Bang of 1986 (Clemons, 1990). Reuters has developed a computerized system that allows traders to execute deals at the prices they see on their VDT screens. The system is broadly and increasingly used for trading in currency, gold bullion, and other similar valuables.[4]

Merrill Lynch has leveraged its information systems to vastly broaden its business from stock brokerage to financial services. In 1977, it devised the cash management account (CMA), a financial product that allowed retail customers to move money between various financial instruments: stocks, bonds, and money market accounts. Customers could also write checks against their money market accounts. Why would a customer then need a retail bank? In this way, the brokerage firm entered the electronic fund transfer system (EFTS)—a specialized electronic data interchange network which until then had been an exclusive preserve of the banks.

Through this move, Merrill Lynch transformed both the banking and brokerage industries, as some of the other major brokerage firms followed suit—and the banks retaliated by broadening their own offerings. Major retailers, such as *Sears, Roebuck,* later also realized that the capability of moving financial information (or call it money) over the networks is not specific to financial companies. These retailers also entered in force the field of financial services.

To obtain the back-office services it needed for its burgeoning cash management accounts, Merrill Lynch formed a long-term alliance with *Banc One* of Columbus, Ohio, which undertook to do check and credit-card charge processing. That bank, in turn, leveraged its transaction-processing capabilities and is now processing all transactions for 1,500 credit unions across the country.[5] By using information systems strategically, Banc One, a local bank in the early 1970s, transformed itself into one of the top-performing banks in the United States. Many banks, indeed, realize that they are in the information-processing business.

Companies that have developed a broad understanding of the role of information, such as *Dun & Bradstreet* or *Dow Jones,* have become giants by consolidating their offerings in publishing, business information services, broadcasting, and marketing services.

Creating Products and Services Based on Information Systems

In an information society, companies are increasingly conscious of the know-how they accumulate during their operations. A construction company develops superior ways of managing construction projects, while a bank may use an ingenious technique for managing a total relationship with its retail customers by analyzing the customers' account dynamics over time. Unless the company prefers to exploit its know-how internally and therefore proprietary considerations prevail, the firm may decide that this know-how may be packaged as software.

The company may sell the software as a product, run it for a one-time charge, or establish an ongoing service business with it. An independent business unit may even be spun off to do this. Thus, companies in various industries distinct from the information business itself enter that field by marketing their expertise to others.

Several firms in the financial-service sector, which is closely related to information processing, have taken this route. For example, *Citicorp,* a long-time leader in information systems use for banking, has spawned a subsidiary, Citicorp Information Resources. This spin-off unit offers a range of financial software, including systems for running credit unions and wholesale international banking. The unit also runs several data centers providing on-line services to banks across the country and offers consulting and facilities management (that is, operating data centers) services to other banks. *Bechtel,* a company with a worldwide reputation in large-scale construction, markets its line-of-business software for construction management.

Any company that has built a comprehensive customer database or established an extensive value-added network (that is, a network which provides services beyond simple data transmission) may also choose to enter the information business.

Small companies have also found opportunities. *Procurement Technology* has launched a bidding information network that matches open government bids for products and services with business profiles of companies seeking government contracts. *Cimtek* has compiled a database of equipment in 14,000 U.S. factories; equipment suppliers subscribe to the database to identify potential customers.

Naturally, most companies will ultimately embed elements of computer technology in their products. Examples range from industrial robots to sneakers with microprocessors that measure running speed. If these applications are not a part of an information system (as the robots are likely to become, and the sneakers are not), they are peripheral to our discussion.

Transforming Company Products and Processes with Information Systems

How to Transform a Product or Process

Using information systems, a firm may convert a *product* into a *package,* combining the physical product with service and information. This distinguishes the firm's product from the offerings of competing vendors. The company may gain market share, even while profit margins also increase. Furthermore, by varying the service and information components, the company can customize the product for small segments of the target market or even individualize it for specific customers. Optional extra-charge add-ons may further increase profitability.

Federal Express was the first to realize that its customers would buy not only contracted delivery, but also the peace of mind that comes with access to information about the status of a given package in the delivery process. The firm has transformed its delivery service by enhancing it with this information, as we discussed in chapter 2. Federal Express's Cosmos delivery tracking system has brought success to the company and has been widely imitated by its competitors and by firms in other transportation industry segments. According to a top executive of *CSX,* a railroad operator: "The information component of our service

HOW ABOUT YOUR OWN ELECTRONIC SECURITIES EXCHANGE?

Computerized information systems are ideally suited to match buyers and sellers. As it happens, this is precisely what a securities exchange does. Here are brief stories of two daring entrepreneurs who saw this opportunity—and acted on it.

When Olof Stenhammar, an executive in a Swedish publishing company, wanted to set up his own business, he drew on his experience as a stockbroker in the United States and on his extensive contacts in the Swedish financial world. With a group of blue-chip backers, Stenhammar managed to establish the computer-based Stockholm Options Market. An option is a right to buy or sell stock at a certain price within a certain time period. The computerized system receives orders from sellers and buyers and automatically matches them. Fees generated from executing orders allowed the entrepreneur to break even within the first two months of the system's operation—and the volume keeps growing. Now, option markets based on the Stockholm model and bearing its corporate brand have appeared in the major financial centers of Europe; Hong Kong and Australia are on Stenhammar's list of future projects.

Even more daring is the project undertaken by Steven Wunsch—but then, he is a legend in the daring world of free rock climbing. Wunsch is taking on the New York Stock Exchange with his computerized system, which is designed to play the role of the specialists who trade shares on the floor of the exchange. The system actually sets the prices, as well as matches sellers and buyers—and that is a threat to the very core of the 200-year-old "Big Board." In other words, the system comes up with a price at which the buyers and sellers will trade their stocks. At this time, the system is designed to match the submitted buy and sell orders only three times a week; but it could hold more frequent sessions during a period of exceptional demand. As projected now, therefore, the electronic system does not act in real-time, as the stock exchange does. But transaction costs for large institutional investors—the target market—are much lower for the electronic system (a half-cent to two cents per trade as contrasted to three to seven cents on the floor). Naturally, the activation of the system is contested by the exchanges—but the era of electronic trading has begun.

Based on John Burton, "Olof Keeps His Options Open," *Scanorama*, December 1990–January 1991, pp. 79–84; and Leslie Wayne, "A Rock Climber's Reach for the Top on Wall Street," *The New York Times*, January 24, 1991, pp. D1, D10.

package is growing bigger and bigger. It's not just enough to deliver products. Customers want information. . . . We are an information-driven business."[6]

By transforming the *process* through which it converts input materials into a product reaching the customers' hands (or warehouses), a company may realize significant efficiencies. Information systems may be used to tightly control the process, avoiding excessive (or, in some cases, any) inventories, and to lower the cost of transactions with customers and suppliers.

Automated order-taking systems and computerized airline reservation systems are paradigmatic strategic information systems. The systems were initially put in place to facilitate business transactions; as they were enhanced over time, they have led to general transformation of business processes in the industry segments they affect. These systems continue to influence thinking in the strategic use of information systems as the practice spreads to other industries. Let's therefore examine them in more detail.

Automated Order-Taking Systems

Automated order-taking system ASAP of *Baxter Healthcare,* which has become a classic, was first introduced in 1976 to lower the costs of order taking (the company was then known as American Hospital Supply Company, a firm later acquired by Baxter). Baxter, which is now the nation's largest hospital distributor, provided its customers with a means of entering their supply orders directly into the firm's computers. The initial system relied on ordering via touch-tone telephone or a bar-code reading terminal. As the system evolved, hospitals were able to create standing order files and use other means of automatically triggered ordering. For special orders, hospital purchasing clerks were given on-line access to the complete product catalog. In 1983, American Hospital Supply made a computer-to-computer ordering system available to larger hospitals. In such a linkage, the hospital's software, called its material management system, would determine the need for an order and the optimal order size for the given product (the economic order quantity). It would then automatically generate the appropriate order, and American Hospital Supply would deliver promptly.[7]

As a result of this system, the hospitals are saving money: they need to keep only a minimal inventory, their purchasing staffs have been reduced, and the amount of paperwork they do has been minimized, lowering transaction costs. Hospitals are also able to purchase a variety of management reports from the distributor. The distributor has made the hospital concerns its own. The company continually modifies the system, closely following developments in the health care industry it serves. To avoid being squeezed out by a brokerage service that would match suppliers with customers in the distribution process, Baxter Healthcare customizes its interface with individual hospitals; for example, it uses the hospital's stock numbers. As a result, the distributor has achieved a lasting, sustainable competitive advantage, enjoying profit margins above industry average. Enhancing plain commodity products with superior service and information, combined with providing savings to the customer, has paid off handsomely.

An exceptionally successful computerized distribution system, McKesson's Economost, is discussed in the case study concluding this chapter.

Computerized Reservation Systems

Another classic case involves the computerized reservation systems introduced by the airlines. In the mid-1970s, *American Airlines* developed Sabre as we know it today, and *United Airlines* developed Apollo (now owned by Covia Consortium), each at a cost (by the time of this writing) of over $250 million dollars. With these systems, the two airlines have dominated the major distribution channel for airline tickets, travel agencies—accounting respectively for market shares of 35 and 23 percent of agency locations in 1988.[8]

Max Hopper, the executive creator of Sabre, gives us an idea of the extent of that enterprise (Hopper, 1990). The database of the system contains 45 million different fares, with 200,000 new fares a day loaded into it during routine periods. During the nonroutine periods (known also as "fare wars"), 1.5 million new fares are loaded daily. During peak use, the system handles 2,000 transactions per second.

Airline reservation systems handle the flights of the system owners and of other airlines as well. They confer on the owner airlines a significant source of income. American Airlines' Sabre, linking more than 60,000 terminals to six large mainframe computers, in 1986 produced almost twice the profits produced by the company's airline operations. (This has led wits to suggest that the airline should dispense with the folly of flying planes.) In 1988, Sabre contributed 17 percent of corporate profits, while accounting for only 6 percent of revenues—the system is indeed very profitable.

The potential for using and abusing competitive advantage is high. In 1984, the airline regulatory agency, then called the Civil Aeronautics Board, found that the two leaders were using their market power to thwart competition. The accusations included "carrier identity bias," that is, giving priority to the owner airlines' listings over others: it was allegedly rather difficult to find a direct flight by a nonowner airline if a connecting flight by the owner was available. Other accusations included the charge that, while the listings of the owner airlines were maintained in real time, those of the nonowners were updated one to four days later. Apollo's telecommunication link to the competing airlines' reservation systems was found inoperative about 20 percent of the time. Since the reliability and accuracy of the other airlines' data was often somewhat questionable, travel agents would be induced to recommend bookings on the owner airlines. These practices were estimated to increase the owner airlines' revenue by at least 20 percent.

Travel agents find switching to another reservation system costly. Therefore, the entrenched pioneering systems have high staying power and their owners have an upper hand in their relationships with travel agents.

Computerized reservation systems, as we can see, are a formidible, competitive weapon. Donald Burr, founder of People Express, ascribes the demise of his airline to its inability to offer flexible pricing due to the absence of requisite information systems.[9]

Consider some additional advantages the owner airlines enjoy. They possess an invaluable database that can be mined for profit. They can use this database to obtain information regarding their own flights—but also regarding those of *their competitors:* for example, they can determine which airline links enjoy the highest percentage of filled seats; which links attract business customers, who are generally less price-conscious than private travelers; and which travelers fly the most frequently at highest rates. The competitive potential of such information is immense.

Computerization of ticketing has also produced frequent flier programs, such as AAdvantage of American Airlines, which increase an airline's market share still further.

Computerized reservation systems facilitate yield management, a strategic application of information systems aimed at getting the maximum revenue out of a flight. A seat unsold perishes forever. Therefore, airlines use software programs to provide a mix of ticket prices that should yield optimal revenue over the short and long terms. Demand forecasting from annual reservation patterns stored in the database underlies yield management. The same technique is now making inroads into the hotel business. The *Days Inn Of America* yield-management software adjusts the mix of room rates based on forecast daily demand, considering major events, weather, and economic conditions in the area. It is, of course, important to consider that too wide a variation between room prices can hurt business in the long run. Certain hotels have also developed frequent traveler programs.

5.3 STRATEGIES, FORCES, AND TACTICS IN COMPETITIVE MARKETS

All successful organizations compete. This is obvious in the case of business corporations. In the climate of deregulation, many U.S. government restrictions on the way companies do business have been dropped over the recent years. As a result, transportation, telecommunication, utilities, and financial service companies are feeling increased pressure to compete. We have already stressed the global nature of competition in an information society. Much of U.S. manufacturing has been under acute pressure from abroad. A competitive environment is less obvious, but nevertheless present, in the operation of not-for-profit organizations, such as most hospitals or colleges and universities.

Several strategies are available to counteract competitive forces active in the marketplace. Companies use a variety of tactics to implement these strategies.

We will first discuss the competitive strategies, competitive forces in the marketplace, and the tactics that may be used to pursue a strategy. We shall then summarize them in a framework which we call a strategic cube.

Competitive Strategies

A leading analyst of competitive advantage, Michael Porter of the Harvard Business School, has identified four strategies a company may adopt to compete (Porter, 1985 and 1990).

The first two strategies apply to companies with a broad scope of products, with which they compete across a number of customer segments. The other two strategies apply to firms that focus on a specialized customer segment. This distinction in competitive scope is best seen when a company with a broad product line in the automobile industry, such as Ford Motor, is compared with a company that specializes in high-performance cars, such as BMW (Porter, 1990). The four strategies are shown in figure 5.1.

1. Differentiation
When a company aims to distinguish its product or service from that offered by the competition, it is pursuing the differentiation strategy. The distinguishing features may be the superior attributes of the product itself. However, the blurring of differences between product and service is one of the characteristics of the information society. Thus, ease and promptness of product acquisition, payment terms, and maintenance support may be equally important to the customer.

FIGURE 5.1

Competitive strategies.

(From Porter, 1990, p. 39)

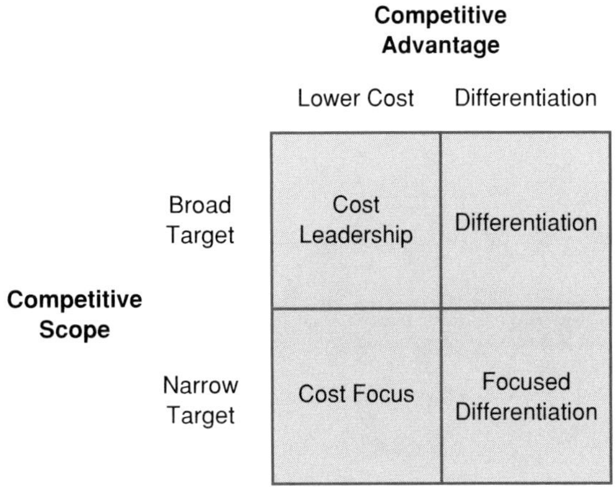

**Competitive
Advantage**

Lower Cost   Differentiation

	Lower Cost	Differentiation
Broad Target	Cost Leadership	Differentiation
Narrow Target	Cost Focus	Focused Differentiation

**Competitive
Scope**

2. Cost leadership

If a company is able to offer its product or service at a cost significantly lower than its competitors, it is exercising cost leadership. This is usually the effect of highly efficient internal operations. If based on economies of scale, this strategy is accessible to a company with a large market share. Its successful application leads to further expansion of the market share—success feeds on itself and may become self-sustaining.

3. Focused differentiation

When a company is able to identify a segment of the market (a niche) which it proceeds to serve in a superior fashion, it is engaging in focused differentiation. The firm will specialize its product or service for this niche. Information systems may be used to contribute to this goal.

The niche may be a customer segment, a narrowly defined product, or a geographical region. Information systems relying on extensive customer databases and demographic data are a potent tool in niche identification (we encountered database marketing in chapter 4).

4. Cost focus

If a company serves a narrow market segment with a product or service which it offers at a significantly lower cost than its competitors, that company is employing the cost focus strategy.

In general, strategies based on differentiation are preferable to those based on lower cost: a difference in profits is apparent.

Competitive Forces

Competitive strategies are pressed into service to combat five competitive forces identified by Porter (1985):

1. Threat of new entrants

As we discussed in chapter 2, because of the highly developed infrastructure of an information society, competition may appear from entirely unforeseen quarters. If *barriers to entry* can be built in, this threat is contained. The costs or time constraints of entering the business with an information system comparable to those of firms already in business are potent barriers. Thus, an order-taking system that costs many millions of dollars and takes several years to develop may form a formidable barrier to entry.

FIGURE 5.2

Enacting competitive forces.

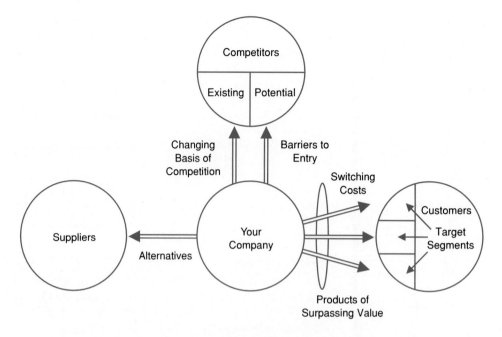

2. Intensifying rivalry among existing competitors
   A novel information system can sometimes change the *basis of competition*: if your delivery service allows the customer to track the delivery process, while your competitors' services do not, you have differentiated your offering and no longer have to compete on a price basis.

3. Pressures from potential substitute products
   A product of surpassing value, which offers substantive quality or service advantages, cannot be easily displaced by substitutes.

4. Bargaining power of customers
   Switching costs, the costs of switching to your competitor for the product or service you provide, may take bargaining power away from customers (as happened in the case of airline reservation systems).

5. Bargaining power of suppliers
   A purchasing system that maintains extensive information on available supply sources confers power on you at the expense of your suppliers.

Information systems may be used to enact or counteract these forces with respect to customers, existing and potential competitors, or suppliers. These actions are summarized in figure 5.2.

Tactical Moves in Pursuing a Strategy

Depending on its current capabilities and long-term plans, an organization may employ any of several tactics to change its products or processes through the use of strategic information systems.

The tactics, discussed by Rackoff (1985) and Wiseman (1988), include:

1. Internal innovation.

2. Internal company growth, offering the opportunity to leverage the use of information systems by spreading their use over a large volume of product (economies of scale) or over several products (economies of scope).

SHARING COSTS WITH COMPETITORS

First Boston Corporation has licensed its trading system to rival investment bank *Kidder, Peabody & Company.* The system supports sales, trading, and reporting operations of a global securities firm. Having spent $100 million to build the system, First Boston wanted to recoup a part of this investment. To protect its competitive position, the seller licensed only the parts of the system it considered nonproprietary. Thus, for example, it excluded from the sale the software that supports decisions on entering and leaving the securities market.

The attractions this system held for its purchaser were the use of relational database technology (IBM DB2) and the fact that the system was developed with a computer-aided software engineering (CASE) tool, simplifying its adaptation to the needs of the purchaser as well as its maintenance in general. The system employs a three-layer architecture, with Compaq Deskpro 386 microcomputers used by the traders, fault-tolerant Stratus minicomputers serving as on-line transaction processors, and a corporate IBM 400E mainframe running DB2, which maintains the central database with the firm's books. The system is built on the concept of cooperative processing, which means that a software application consists of several functions distributed to different computer systems (rather than parceled into several applications native to different systems). Through this technique, all transactions are immediately reflected in the databases maintained on all three levels.

Adapted from Michael Neubarth, "Investment Banks Sign Pact on Automatic Trading System," *MIS Week,* July 25, 1988, p. 11; and on Jeff Moad and Gary McWilliams, "IS Shops Form Alliances as Development Costs Rise," *Datamation,* September 1, 1988, pp. 19–21.

3. Merger with or acquisition of another company.

4. Strategic alliance (partnership) with other companies: a long-term relationship that goes beyond a joint venture. A well-known analyst of corporate strategies, Kenichi Ohmae, sees strategic alliances as vital to competing in global markets (Ohmae, 1990): these alliances enable participants to share the necessary large capital outlays.

Note that the four measures just listed are "tactics" only relative to the major strategies they support: from other points of view, mergers, for example, are strategic (rather than tactical) moves.

Because large information systems may take many millions of dollars and several years to develop, companies increasingly employ outward-directed tactics involving partnerships, mergers, or acquisitions. For example, General Motors has acquired Electronic Data Systems, a major information-processing company, instead of going through a long-term process of developing corresponding capabilities internally. Generic parts of very large systems are sometimes acquired outright, as is demonstrated by the above vignette focusing on First Boston's automatic trading system.

Benn Konsynski and Warren McFarlan of the Harvard Business School consider information partnerships, based on sharing of information systems, a potent competitive weapon (Konsynski and McFarlan, 1990). Its great advantage is economy and reciprocity of competencies. Each partner needs to contribute only a part of the requisite resources. Moreover, a partner company may contribute an organizational skill (such as development and continuing enhancement of large-scale transaction processing systems) that would be impossible to develop in a short time.

Strategic Cube

The combination of competitive strategies, their target forces, and the tactics employed to implement them gives us a framework for a company's pursuit of strategic advantage. This framework appears in figure 5.3, in a form we may call the strategic cube.

Using the strategic cube, a company may review its options in seeking strategic advantage. For example, to drive off potential new market entrants, a toy company may consider pursuing a strategy of focused differentiation by concentrating on upper-bracket toys for children up to two years of age. To do so, it may conclude an exclusive long-term agreement with a firm distributing baby milk substitutes—a firm that has access to a large database of newborns. The database permits the company to narrowly target its marketing on the desired infant sector. The two companies agree to share the marketing function. Because a potential competitor would need very large amounts of time and money to develop capabilities comparable to those of the two companies in targeting and accessing the market segment, the strategic alliance could create significant barriers to entry.

The strategic cube is a macroscopic tool—it does not tell the company exactly where it may apply information systems in its activities to gain advantage. Another tool, the value-chain approach, is designed for the detailed analysis of opportunities for competitive use of information systems.

FIGURE 5.3

Strategic cube.

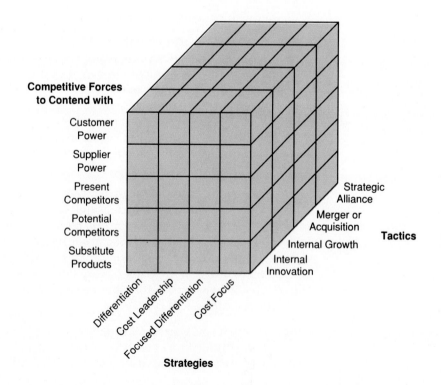

5.4 VALUE-CHAIN ANALYSIS OF STRATEGIC OPPORTUNITIES

Strategic deployment of information systems is aimed at changing both company operations and its products. To establish targets of opportunity, we need to track the chain of activities through which a company transforms its input resources, such as raw materials, into the products and services it delivers to its customers.

Value Chain

The chain of activities during which a firm adds value to its input materials is called a **value chain.** Michael Porter studied the application of the economics concept of a value-added chain to surface opportunities for seeking competitive advantage (Porter, 1985) and extended this study to information system opportunities (Porter and Millar, 1985). A value chain, showing a firm's primary activities, is presented in figure 5.4. These primary activities are assisted by support activities, such as human resource management. In the chain shown in figure 5.4, we considered the procurement of input materials to be a part of inbound logistics (Porter considers it a support activity).

The value-chain stages for a manufacturing company comprise these activities:

- Inbound logistics
  Obtaining raw materials, subassemblies, and other input products from the suppliers, warehousing them, and delivering them to the production site
- Operations
  Transformation of inputs into finished products
- Outbound logistics
  Storing products and delivering them to customers on customer orders (note that the ultimate buyer may actually receive the product from an intermediary such as a distributor)
- Marketing
  Establishing customer need for the product and assisting the customer in specifying the assortments and quantities
- Service
  After-sale service, including maintenance

While the elements of this chain were defined with a manufacturing enterprise in mind, chains for service firms are not much different. In particular, both types of businesses share the need to reconceptualize "operations" in terms of the core business of a company or business unit. Back-office processing of insurance policies, stock certificates, or charge card receipts constitutes a large part of the operations in financial services.

FIGURE 5.4

The value chain of a firm.

JUST IN TIME

The just-in-time (JIT) method of operating a plant means that the materials needed for a manufacturing operation are delivered to the proper station at the time they are to be used—"just in time." Since the suppliers are also expected to deliver just in time, warehousing is reduced or abolished. The result is minimization of a company's investment in various inventories: those of input materials, subassemblies, and work in progress.

This method is very demanding on the company's operations. The absence of safety (buffer) stock makes reliable suppliers and a smooth flow of operations absolute necessities. Often, close virtual partnerships are formed with suppliers in order to ensure cooperation (Deutsch, 1990). Quality must be monitored at each production station, rather than at the end of the process.

The necessary coordination requires extensive use of information systems. High-order economies are the reward of proper implementation of the JIT method.

The JIT technique is also known as the kanban method, from the Japanese word for billboard. On an assembly line, a worker shows a small kanban card to his or her predecessor, to indicate readiness to receive the product being assembled. At Toyota, which innovated in this area, computerized ordering systems would send each supplier a kanban which was actually a schedule of deliveries to follow over a certain period of time—but each delivery had to come just in time.

The JIT practice had been known as call-off in the United States before it came back as an advanced manufacturing system perfected in Japan.

Each of the activities in a value chain contributes value to the final product. This value is ultimately measured by what customers will pay for the good produced. A manufacturer usually adds most of the value during the operations step, a manufacturing process. A distributor firm will add most of the value in the outbound logistics and marketing.

Along with determining the discrete steps in a value chain, a company needs to analyze the linkages between them. Just-in-time deliveries into the chain by suppliers and across the chain itself prevent costly inventory build-ups and delays. For example, car manufacturer *Nissan U.S.A.* has the supplier of its car seats deliver a shipment every few hours, with the seats transferred straight to the assembly line.[10] How is that for input logistics—no inventory costs and no warehousing of bulky components!

If the value added throughout a chain exceeds the company's costs for performing the activities in the chain, the company will realize profit. If a company does this especially effectively—by lowering costs or increasing the value added more than its competitors—the firm may enjoy competitive advantage.

Using the Value-Chain Analysis to Identify Strategic Information Systems

To use information systems strategically, a company must identify the potentially information-related aspects of individual activities of its value chain and of the linkages between these activities. Figure 5.5 shows the value chain of a manufacturing firm, with some generic strategic information systems mapped onto it. The point of the analysis is to identify the stages and links where the highest-

FIGURE 5.5

A value chain with
information systems mapping.

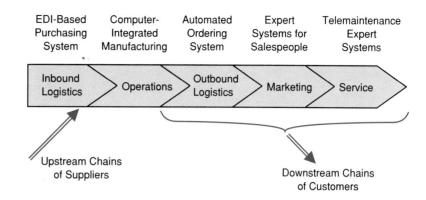

impact potential is available and creatively use information systems to bring that potential out. We will further study the techniques for doing so later in this chapter.

Today, many firms find strategic applications for information technology in redesigning crucial business processes (Sullivan-Trainor, 1990). For example, *FMC Corporation* developed a procurement tracking system that completely automated the firm's purchasing. *Hilton Hotels* developed an integrated marketing system.[11] Previously, each Hilton hotel marketed its services to corporate clients as a separate entity. With the new system, all the information concerning the relationship with each client is accessible in a database, which also contains information on future space availability in all Hilton hotels. The unified marketing function enables Hilton to match a client's needs for a meeting or travel with the total resources offered by the hotel chain. By keeping down costs and vastly increasing the effectiveness of a business function, these companies are able to increase entry barriers for new firms in their industry.

We shall again stress the importance of information in providing effective linkages, not only within the chain of a given company, but externally with the chains of its suppliers and customers. Indeed, a purchasing system will bind suppliers' (so-called upstream) value chains to a company's operations. On the outbound (also called downstream) side, an ordering system, such as Baxter's ASAP, tightly links in the customers' operations.

In performing an information-oriented value-chain analysis, companies dealing with physical products often find that the product that will enjoy marketplace advantage is actually a composite package of the physical item plus service and information. Value-chain analysis thus may lead not only to process improvement, but also enrich (differentiate) the product as well.

A value chain may be constructed for a range of products serving a particular industry segment, geographical area, or customer segment. A company with diversified products may realize synergistic efficiencies by "overlapping" certain value chains. For example, the marketing function may serve several product categories.

We will now consider the role information systems play in the value chain of business activities. Considering the marketing orientation of modern corporations, it may be wise to begin our analysis with information system contributions

FIGURE 5.6

How we shall discuss the strategic role of information systems in a value chain.

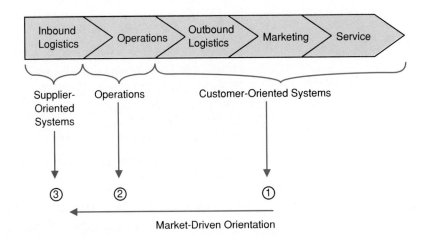

to the chain's customer-oriented components, move on to the core operations of the business, and then consider supplier-oriented systems. We will showcase several firms whose activities provide excellent sources of ideas—and, as you will see, variety abounds. Figure 5.6 gives you the road map for the next three sections.

5.5 CUSTOMER-ORIENTED STRATEGIC SYSTEMS

We shall now discuss the outbound stages of the value chain: outbound logistics, marketing and sales (as opposed to simple order taking), and service. Strategic information systems have played a particularly important role here.

We will first present a scenario showing how information systems can be used to play this role. We shall then illustrate the innovative use of information systems in the customer-directed stages. Strategic systems often cut through the individual stages of the value chain—as a matter of fact, this is one of their goals. In our discussion, we will classify each system according to its main function in the chain.

An Optimistic Scenario—The Route Traveled by Successful Companies

The Way of Success

Suppose you are a distributor of a commodity product (for example, office supplies) or a provider of commodity-level service (say, a medical laboratory). You are forced to compete on price. Your profit margins are low. Competition can come from anywhere: barriers to entry are low, too. However, you feel you have a strength you can exploit: you have maintained information systems that are technologically superior to those of your competitors.

You decide to seek competitive advantage by placing terminals on your customer sites and linking the terminals to your computer system. The speed with which you can process your customers' transactions increases. The purchaser of your office supplies can rely on your just-in-time delivery and does not need to keep inventory beyond the shelf stock. The physician obtains test results as soon as they are ready. Thus, your customers save time and money.

As a next step, you decide to eliminate paperwork, relying on electronic data interchange (EDI) of purchase orders, invoices, vouchers, and so on, between your computer and the customers' computers. The transaction costs are low as compared to handling multiple-copy transaction documents in paper form. The transaction accuracy is high.

You have established a close relationship with your customers. It is unlikely they will obtain terminals from your competitors. You are now also in a position to provide extended informational support to these customers. You may use this both to save them money (and thus lower the overall cost of your product-service-information package) and to differentiate your offering, possibly by providing additional optional information services, with a schedule of charges.

The range of MIS support you can offer begins with providing inventory and accounting information, then progresses to customized management reports for the client firms, and extends to giving customers on-line access to a decision support system for evaluating alternative supply tactics (and setting your offerings in the best light). Your information-system offerings are further extended to support the customer's line of business: you may offer the use of a drug-interaction software for physicians or an expert system for fault diagnosis or part equivalence for automobile dealerships.

To summarize, you have differentiated your offerings, you have developed a spectrum of pricing possibilities, and you have established a growth path for your company.

Whence Success?

Switching costs of the customer who wants to join your system are low: you install the terminal free of charge and provide an eight-hour consulting and training session. You also try to ensure that the costs of switching out to a potential competitor are high. Aside from long-term contractual arrangements, your staying power may be based on the money, time, and effort your customers would have to expend to switch out. You are also offering superior and responsive service, since you have "gotten close" to the customers: you intimately know each of their businesses and are able to assist them when needed.

Barriers to entry for new competitors are high: strategic ordering systems take several years to develop, and they cost—over time—millions of dollars. By offering a variety of state-of-the-art information-based options, you prevent the substitution of other products.

If you become a leader in the market segment, you have also acquired an invaluable database on your customers and their business needs. This can be a source of continuing advantage.

In the process, you have reorganized your company: no one achieves success in the strategic use of information systems through technology alone. Your salesforce acts as information consultants; you have streamlined your value chain to pare workforce and inventories.

This route has been traveled by several leaders in various market segments. Some segments are still open to this tack. In others, defenders of strategic positions need to innovate continually. Competitive advantage is not easy to gain and perhaps even more difficult to sustain. Automated teller machines (ATMs), offered first on a large scale by Citicorp so that a client could deposit or withdraw funds at any time from one of many locations, did not provide the company with a sustainable advantage: other banks followed suit; and ATMs have become a competitive necessity. In an attempt to regain an advantage, Citicorp responded by installing customer-activated service terminals that are able to provide customers with information on the status of their accounts. However, these are equally easy to emulate. Systems based on easily imitated technology do not offer sustainable advantage.

Outbound Logistics

Facilitation of customer orders provides an initial and ever-potent opportunity for the strategic use of information systems. Airline reservation systems (Sabre, Apollo) and round-the-clock order-entry systems (ASAP, Economost) are among the systems that have expanded from the support of the *ordering process.* Several firms with large retail transaction-processing capabilities have found a significant source of revenue in *facilitating payments* for goods purchased from other companies. Thus, *J.C. Penney* provides credit-card sales processing services to Gulf and Shell, while *Sears, Roebuck* offers the same services to Phillips Petroleum. An example of an alliance tactic, this provides fees to the retailer and savings to the oil companies. Major credit card companies have acquired awesome power over retailers by providing the information-system-based service demanded by the retailers' customers.[12]

Dealing with customers through ATMs has offered savings to some banks (though not to all) and, more promising, has created a mechanism for distributing other goods (tickets or coupons) in a labor-saving manner. Universities are beginning to use ATMs for dispensing information about student grades.[13]

Small companies can employ a focused strategy. *Wright Express* of Portland, Maine, has set up a charge card service at gas stations for trucking fleets. It provides fleet owners with information on their fuel, maintenance, and clerical expenses. The company also equips attendant-free gas stations with ATMs and its own credit cards. This small company has created forty jobs.[14]

Information and software are conveniently *delivered to customers over computer networks.* The gradual introduction of the Integrated Services Digital Network (ISDN), discussed in chapter 7, will so vastly broaden the communication bandwidth that movies and other image-based material will undoubtedly be distributed in this fashion.

The ability to *track a shipment* gives the customer a sense of control. *Pacific Intermountain Express,* a California-based trucker, can track the status of all shipments from origin to destination. The customer can directly access the trucker's computer. A range of reports on cost allocation is available to customers. When marketing its service to a customer, the firm' representatives discuss not only shipping, but also the customer's information needs. Thus, the firm not only sells the service-information package, but also continually learns from its marketplace and upgrades its information system.

On a different level of computer system applications, software that implements management-science optimization algorithms is used to optimize warehouse placement and trucking routes, with impressive cost economies.

Marketing and Sales

With the advent of automated ordering and reservation systems, a sales representative can be redefined as a consultant, assisted by laptop computers, portable telephones, and information systems to help customers define their needs. Though it is often difficult to draw the boundary between marketing and sales on the one hand and order taking on the other, ordering systems free the sales force for the more creative tasks of establishing new products and services and responding to changing customer needs. The salespeople can be tied in to a database that shows in detail the prospective customer's experience with the company's products.

The role of computerized telemarketing is growing—it is far more economical than traditional methods for making simple sales calls about uniform products or for developing leads. When a salesperson calls on a customer in person—with an average cost per call of hundreds of dollars—information systems should be used to garner maximum benefit from the call. If sales representatives are equipped with laptop computers tied into an information system, they can access headquarters' system, reserve stock, and place orders. They can also pick up electronic mail, receive leads from the computerized telemarketing system, and check calendars, appointment schedules, and customer lists. Salespeople can even track the order's status right in the customer's office. These types of informational support lead to increased customer satisfaction.

Information systems may be designed to play many other roles during the marketing stage, when customers establish their requirements for a product. Here are some examples of creative strategic use of information systems in the process:

- *Owens Corning Fiberglass* has developed a software system that *evaluates* insulation *requirements* for new home designs to meet energy efficiency standards. The builders, to whom the service is offered at no charge, must carry exclusively the company's insulation materials.[15] Sales representatives of the drug manufacturer *Genentech,* calling on physicians and pharmacists with their laptops, provide these customers with on-line access to proprietary clinical studies and to a staff of medical specialists who can answer highly technical questions (McKenna, 1991).
- Brokerage services have developed the ability, based on extensive databases, to *match customers' requirements with suppliers' offerings.* Examples include a computerized airline guide that displays flights matching the user's needs (but does not sell tickets) and an inventory locator service that facilitates aircraft maintenance. The service aids in finding a supplier for parts needed in maintenance and generates a request for a quotation to start the ordering process. As we have seen, the development of electronic markets is a force changing the financial marketplace.
- Expert system technology can *select and configure* complex equipment to satisfy a customer's needs. We shall discuss such a system, adopted by the Digital Equipment Corporation, in the case study for Part 4 of this book.

- Citicorp supports over 15 million credit card accounts. Using these vast databases, it offers a large variety of *marketing analyses* to a range of customers.

Service

After-sales continuation of the customer relationship is sometimes a contractual requirement and always a good business practice.

Sears, Roebuck has long recognized that being in the service business is also a way to sell replacement products. Sears makes each maintenance contract for a major appliance valid when the appliance is resold, which provides an avenue to a new customer. The company's exceptionally large customer databases are used to send reminders to customers whose service contracts are about to expire. *American Express* has a double-the-warranty program on purchases made with their card. Aside from providing a competitive edge for the card, this practice helps assemble an extensive marketing database.

Stratus Computer Corporation, whose market niche is fault-tolerant computing, employs an automatic *telemaintenance* system. This system has a database of customer computer configurations. The system periodically polls the customer installations to determine configuration changes and status of the equipment. Any detected error triggers diagnostic routines. A persistent error leads to automatic notification of Stratus's service-support facility. There, personnel use extended remote diagnostic routines and usually within an hour issue an order for a replacement part. The part is delivered overnight, together with replacement instructions, to the customer—who may even be unaware of any problem (Ives, 1988)!

Expert systems technology is increasingly used to *diagnose* malfunctions as a part of telemaintenance. *Westinghouse* has a number of expert systems running on the mainframe of its Orlando Diagnostics Center. The Center provides service to public utilities: it remotely monitors and diagnoses impending malfunctions of various parts of massive steam turbine generators owned by public utilities all over the United States. The payoff to customers is more generator up-time, thanks to an early diagnosis; each day of up-time is worth between half a million and a million dollars. The cost of service (Westinghouse's revenue) is less than one tenth of the resulting savings (Feigenbaum, 1988).

5.6 STRATEGIC SYSTEMS IN OPERATIONS

Operations depend on a firm's line of business. Let us first discuss the strategic informational support of manufacturing, which is particularly important, and then proceed to the support of service industries.

Manufacturing

Information technology has revolutionized manufacturing operations in the leading plants. The most powerful— but also most complex—development is called computer-integrated manufacturing.

Computer-integrated manufacturing (CIM) is a strategy through which a manufacturer takes control of the entire manufacturing process—from computer-aided design (CAD) and computer-aided engineering (CAE) to the factory floor, where robots and numerically controlled machinery are installed. Through the information systems supporting this strategy, the firm melds the existing "islands of automation" into a whole. A flexible factory automation system can turn out very small batches of a particular product as cost-effectively as a traditional production line can turn out millions of identical products. A full-fledged CIM is extremely difficult to implement; indeed, many firms have failed in their attempts to do so (Walton, 1989).

The CIM strategy usually incorporates a **manufacturing resource planning** system (also called MRP II or "big MRP," since it is an advanced version of material requirements planning, or MRP) as the main informational tool. This elaborate software converts the forecast demand for a factory's products into a detailed production plan (usually by quarter) and further into a master schedule of production, usually segmented into weekly periods. A simplified systems chart for MRP II, based on Cox (1984), is shown in figure 5.7.

The products listed in the master schedule are exploded into the components needed to make them. To do this, the bill of materials for each product is used; it specifies what parts go into the product. These parts have to come in on the input side of the production process. The requirements for all these components are then allocated among inventories, production, and purchasing. A capacity requirements plan is produced, using the routing file that specifies the capacities of the available production equipment. If the master schedule turns out to be unrealistic, a new master schedule is produced and the cycle repeats itself until a viable master schedule is obtained. Otherwise, a purchasing order schedule and work orders are issued.

A manufacturing resource planning system is integrated with other MIS subsystems. Thus, it receives information from the transaction processing systems that handle customer orders or the receiving of goods from suppliers. On the other hand, an MRP II delivers information to the billing and accounting systems. Through an executive information system, top managers are kept informed about the status of production at all times.

MRP II systems provide much flexibility for the modification of production schedules and produce a variety of management-oriented reports. A number of MRP II packages are available from software vendors. Competitive advantage does not come directly from the customization of such a package to the needs of a firm, but rather from creative modification of its operations, with the system used as a major tool in the process. The crucial advantage of these systems is the ability to plan future purchasing needs and to control the entire manufacturing process.

CIM integrates MRP II capabilities into an overall system, in which the assembly line is in effect driven by incoming customer orders. The two vignettes entitled "Lots of One" and "Filling an Order in Two Hours" show how, by making possible the customization of manufacturing and superior order-fulfillment speeds, CIM enables companies to compete in world markets.

FIGURE 5.7

A manufacturing resource planning system.

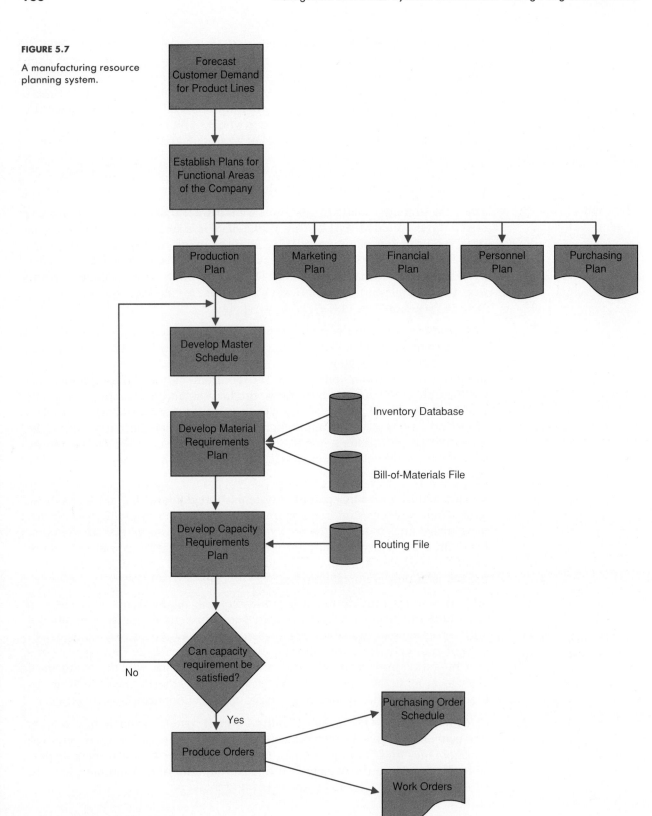

LOTS OF ONE

CIM was successfully employed for competitive positioning by a manufacturer of industrial controls, *Allen-Bradley* of Milwaukee, Wisconsin. To continue as a competitive producer of electrical relays and contactors, the company had to enter the world market with devices one-third the size and one-third the price of those used in the United States. Allen-Bradley decided against off-shore plant location, having determined that the advantages of cheap labor would be offset by lack of automation with the consequent need to employ many supporting workers. Instead, the company implemented CIM.

Allen-Bradley headquarters' mainframe computer (running MRP II software) each morning relays the day's orders to a computer that provides the schedule for the plant's fully automated assembly line.

Ingenious use of bar codes eliminates all need for human intervention. The computer running the line produces a bar-code label that is automatically affixed to the plastic casing of the future product. The label tells each station on the line which of nearly 200 different parts to install. Finished controls are packaged, sorted into customers' orders, and placed ready for shipment—all automatically. All along, computer-controlled sensors ensure quality: each product passes through 3,500 automatic inspection steps.

Here is the clincher: the system can produce different versions of the product at mass production speeds within twenty-four hours of order placement and with zero defects—*in lots of one!*

Based on Gene Bylinsky, ''A Breakthrough in Automating the Assembly Line,'' *Fortune*, May 26, 1986, pp. 64–66; with a contribution from (Walton, 1989).

FILLING AN ORDER IN TWO HOURS—AND THAT INCLUDES MANUFACTURING

Copperweld Corporation of Pittsburgh, a manufacturer of metal tubing, built a plant in Birmingham, Alabama that provides customer service extraordinary in its industry. The key is CIM.

At other plants the company owns, the process of taking a customer order, entering it into a computer system, sending it to the production-control department for scheduling, and then sending it to the factory floor takes three days. Thanks to the implemented CIM system, the same process

takes a split second in the Birmingham plant. And if the necessary parts are already in the inventory, the ordered product can be made in two hours and shipped immediately to the customer.

The start-up costs of the plant were expected to be recouped in six to eight months, as compared to a year to year-and-a-half payback time in other Copperweld plants.

Based on Peter Krass, ''Automation Turns Gold,'' *InformationWeek*, September, 1990, pp. 38–39.

HARLEY-DAVIDSON MOTOR COMPANY BECOMES COMPETITIVE

Harley-Davidson's big motorcycles, affectionately called "hogs" because of their girth and noise, attracted a cult following during the sixties and seventies. Nevertheless, at the end of 1981, the company posted a record loss and the worst market share ever. The only remaining U.S. motorcycle manufacturer was being defeated primarily by Japanese competitors. The company was saved thanks to a three-pronged strategy: zero inventories based on just-in-time deliveries, rigid quality control, and deep employee involvement. Every employee now receives forty hours of training in statistical quality control: rejection and rework are down and the number of defect-free bikes is up 165 percent.

The company has developed its own MRP II system, running on an IBM-compatible mainframe (NAS/6630) with fifty-one terminals dispersed from offices to the factory floor. The production schedule for each order is generated three days before the order goes into production. At the end of the day, the data on the units produced (identified by their bar-coded order numbers) is processed by the MRP II system to replenish the inventories of parts and subassemblies. Purchasing orders are produced automatically. The level of production is reevaluated periodically.

By 1989, Harley-Davidson's share of its market rose to 66 percent (from 28 percent in 1985), while the share of its archrival, Honda, shrunk. Harley-Davidson's management ascribes the success both to control over the manufacturing process gained through its information systems and to employee involvement based on the specialized training. Harley-Davidson did not need to differentiate: it needed to economize.

Based on Sharon Brady, "School of Hard Knocks," *Software Magazine,* April 1988, pp. 37–44; and John Holusha, "How Harley Outfoxed Japan With Exports," *The New York Times Business Section,* August 12, 1990, p. 5.

CIM is impossible without gaining full informational control of the manufacturing operation. That is why companies successfully implementing the CIM approach usually had been working for a time under an MRP II system.

Indeed, many companies do not need to go so far as to implement a full CIM to use their informational resources for competitive advantage in their manufacturing operations. This is illustrated by the Harley-Davidson vignette.

The MIS function of manufacturing companies, which was traditionally isolated from the manufacturing-support groups, is increasingly becoming involved in the core of the manufacturing business. At *Cummins Engine* of Columbus, Indiana, a leader in CIM, the mission of MIS is to integrate all the information systems, including manufacturing. Factory-floor data are stored, summarized by various MIS modules, and made available through management-level information systems.[16]

The opportunity to exercise ingenuity in using information systems in manufacturing operations is boundless. So far we have cited examples from parts manufacturing, a sector in which equipment of various types is produced. Let us now consider the other kind of manufacturing—continuous-process production. Here, the production process involves the flow of materials through several stages, which manipulate the composition of the materials by blending them, purifying

TELECOMMUNICATIONS AS A SOURCE OF COMPETITIVE ADVANTAGE

American Color of Phoenix, Arizona is a color separation company—it produces pictures for various publications—with fourteen plants around the United States. In the 1980s, the firm established, in conjunction with CONTEL ASC, a communication satellite network called COLOR/SAT for transmitting very high-quality color artwork and photographs. This extends the idea of transmitting news pages, innovated by *The Wall Street Journal* and since used widely in the news and printing industries for editorial content. Nine out of the fourteen American Color plants have transmission capability, as opposed to a single transmission site in most networks in the industry.

The company found that news is not the only time-sensitive commodity. American Color's competitive advantage comes from its capability, to change ad copy or a magazine cover at the last minute—a differentiation of service—and the ability to distribute the workload among its printing sites to lower costs. Once the network was in place, the company was ready to expand its customer base of 1,500 major accounts.

Based on Marie Kelly, "American Color Beams Itself Into 21st Century," *Printing Impressions*, September 1988, pp. 30–32.

them, or using them in a chemical reaction (oil refineries are a prime example). Porter and Millar refer to the cement industry as a prime example of a field where, despite increased information processing, opportunities for the strategic use of information systems are rather limited (Porter and Millar, 1985). However, *Raia Industries* of Hackensack, New Jersey, showed this is not necessarily so.[17] Their process-control computer system is in complete charge of concrete preparation: it produces the desired strength of concrete by dispensing the computed amounts of ingredients. It constantly adjusts the amount of moisture and cycles the mixing drum. The system then verbally notifies workers of the process completion and controls loading of the trucks. The company's productivity has increased 200 to 300 percent as compared to the traditional bag-ripping technique. As an informational side product, the computer system keeps track of materials consumed and inventory on hand in eight plants, for 300 products and 3,000 input components.

Service Industries

Service industries offer many opportunities for strategic deployment of information systems. Here, the speed and flexibility made possible by information technology may be exploited to differentiate the service or to pursue low-cost advantages by redesigning service operations around a strategic system. The American Color vignette provides just one illustration of the differentiation strategy.

In the service-oriented economies of the industrialized countries, financial services are highly information-intensive. Much of this information has historically been handled in the form of documents—sales receipts, mortgages, and other paper forms. Several technologies can be exploited to redesign document-based operations around strategic information systems. These technologies, the application of which we shall discuss more thoroughly in chapter 16, may be used to radically improve customer service, to offer service at a lower cost, or some-times even to do both. Thus, electronic data interchange (EDI) helps to dispense with much of the paperwork, particularly in relations between organizations. In the case study for chapter 16, we shall see how American Express employed the technology of digital image processing to cost-effectively provide a high level of service to its cardholders.

To obtain a total picture of their relationships with each of their customers, banks found it initially an advantage, and later a necessity, to maintain a central information file (CIF).[18] Actually a customer database in banking branch offices, it lists all of the customer's accounts and balances and makes it possible to calculate each customer's profitability to the bank. A bank can make better credit decisions and initiate targeted marketing of services based on these integrated data.

Electronic kiosks, with user-friendly terminals or "touch screens" are used in stores, banks, and other customer service centers. They direct a customer to a product—be it an appliance or a financial instrument—and can facilitate payment or dispense additional information from a database. Kiosks can process simple transactions and provide fast, accurate, and thorough information; they advise the user to request human assistance when more complex interaction is required. Newer kiosks employ a multimedia technology of interactive digital video, which gives the customer a presentation that combines full-motion video with other media such as animation and text.

5.7 SUPPLIER-ORIENTED STRATEGIC SYSTEMS

Inbound logistics is supported by information systems that deal with a company's suppliers.

Powerful suppliers possess considerable control over the cost and, in some cases, availability of the resources supplied to a smaller customer company. A low-cost producer or a producer of a highly differentiated product is able, to a degree, to absorb these increases or pass them on to customers. However, ultimately this results in shrinking profits and/or market share. A company may use information systems to increase its own power in its relationships with its suppliers.

Powerful customers are, of course, able to enforce their way of operating things on the supply side. Thus, *General Motors,* the largest U.S. automobile manufacturer, has installed computer-to-computer links with its primary suppliers. Electronic data interchange with GM through this system is a condition for doing business with the company. Suppliers have to modify their transaction processing systems to link in with the GM ordering system.

A powerful customer company may make the supplier fit its information system to the customer's need by requiring the supplier to

- maintain a just-in-time no-inventory relationship, often with the supplier connected to the customer's MRP or MRP II system;
- become a certified supplier and take responsibility for quality control;
- have a CAD/CAM system compatible with the customer's information system, to introduce engineering and other design changes into the supplier's products;
- use the customer's EDI standards for all transactions.

Companies can apply the old adage that "information is power" to increase their clout in dealings with suppliers. If you have an information system that maintains information on alternative suppliers and can evaluate their competing bids, you can get the best buy. Thus, *Equitable Life Assurance* has developed an on-line purchasing system for centralized office supply acquisitions. The system database stores information on all contracts. The company's bargaining power with respect to its suppliers is high. Smaller companies have also followed this route.

Grocery chains, using on-line retail tracking data from their computerized checkout-scanning systems, can quickly determine a product's sales and profitability. Armed with this information, supermarkets have been able to reverse the power relationship between food manufacturers and retailers in their favor: the stores demand fees (called slotting allowances) for introducing new products onto the shelves.

5.8 ORGANIZATIONAL REQUIREMENTS FOR SUCCESSFUL STRATEGIC INFORMATION SYSTEMS

A strategic thrust with the use of information systems may be the result of a perceived opportunity or a perceived threat. In some industries, such as financial services or pharmaceutical distribution, the use of certain classes of strategic information systems has become a necessity. Value-chain analysis allows a firm to identify the activities in which information systems can have the highest impact in light of general industry structure and competitive activities.

Identifying strategic opportunities is a part of the larger process of strategic planning, which we will discuss in chapter 17. The strategic cube in figure 5.3 presents the strategic and tactical alternatives for contending with various competitive forces. Management should evaluate the projected effects of the new system on the firm's financial results, at the same time assessing the degree of risk involved.

NATURALLY, STRATEGIC INFORMATION SYSTEMS CAN FAIL

Several notable failures of strategic information systems have been documented; many others have surely been swept under the carpet.

Among the documented failures is a strategic alliance of IBM and Merrill Lynch to provide microcomputer users with investment data and access to financial software over a telecommunications network. Introduced in 1984, the International Market Net (Imnet), targeted primarily at security brokers in a variety of financial institutions, failed to attract customers. In fact, the project, whose cost is estimated by some at $70 million, reached less than 1 percent of projected sales.

The reasons for Imnet's failure include a high price for services of unproven value; inappropriate user interface, placing high technological demands on brokers; resistance of potential customers (other brokerage houses) to services offered by a competitor (Merrill Lynch); and lack of clear lines of responsibility among the partners in the alliance.

Based on Wiseman, 1988, pp. 26–27.

In an AT&T-sponsored study of organizations reputed to be successful information system strategists in eleven industries, Russell Johnston and Shelley Carrico identified these preconditions for organizational success in strategic deployment of information systems (Johnston, 1988):

- Active support of senior company management (and not just of MIS management) in the discovery of strategic opportunities and in the implementation process
- Integration of planning for the strategic use of information systems into the overall company strategic planning process
- Direct reporting by those responsible for strategic use of information systems to line management in the area to be affected by the new system
- Placement of control mechanisms (budgeting and rewards, for example) in the hands of line management
- Readiness for strategic use of information systems, implying successful use of MIS already in place and organizational experience with technological innovation

Of course, there are many other reasons why strategic systems succeed or fail, as the last vignette illustrated.

Another aspect of success in the use of strategic information systems is the *sustainability* of competitive advantage, if such advantage has been gained. There have been several documented cases where, by implementing a strategic information system, a company precipitated a chain of events it did not foresee and that led to a long-term strategic disadvantage. Several such cases are discussed by Michael Vitale (1986). Thus, before moving competition onto a higher plane in its market segment or in the entire industry, the company should carry out an informed impact analysis.

David Feeny and Blake Ives offer the following three conditions of sustainability, which a firm may use to evaluate opportunities for building strategic information systems (Feeny, 1990). If all three conditions hold true, the firm has a good chance to achieve sustainable competitive advantage with a proposed system.

1. There is a strong first-move advantage and your company has it. The *lead time* you develop in launching the project first will allow you to achieve competitive advantage.

2. If your competitors attempt to copy your strategic information system, they will fail because of *unique marketplace advantages* you enjoy. For example, the International Trucks division of *Navistar* has collected a database over the years that tells them how their trucks hold up in use. This gives the firm a unique advantage with respect to fleet owners, who are offered the use of the company's database.

3. Assuming that competitors will be able to copy your strategic application, they will not succeed in exploiting it, because you have *preempted the marketplace*. This happened in the case of computerized reservation systems, for example.

Of course, no competitive advantage lasts forever; even competitive parity has to be maintained. We must stress again that a sustained commitment of resources is necessary for a sustainable competitive positioning. The leading strategic information systems discussed in this chapter are successful in the long term because they present a moving target: they are continually adapted to the changing needs of the marketplace, and they continually change with technological advances. This means continuing investment in the system.

5.9 CHANGES IN INDUSTRY STRUCTURE

Many strategic systems are **interorganizational information systems:** two or more firms share the use of such a system (Cash, 1985). Systems that cross or even blur organizational boundaries are used by a firm to solidify its relationship on the inbound or outbound side of its value chain. Usually, the system is asymmetric: it is installed by a large and technically sophisticated supplier (an airline or a distributor) to serve a large community of customers; or, vice versa, a large customer (General Motors, for example) employs such a system as a link to a multiplicity of suppliers. Since the participating firms are often widely dispersed, the telecommunication component of the system forms its main infrastructure.

Recently, organizations emerged whose business *is* to provide interorganizational systems for the use of others. In effect, these companies create an *electronic marketplace*.

An example of such an organization is Cirrus System. Cirrus is owned by five large commercial banks and offers over 10,000 ATMs to the customers of banks that participate in the service. The customers obtain the advantage of using an ATM at any participating bank (Johnston and Vitale, 1988). Similarly, a cooperatively owned international message network, SWIFT, enables over 2,000 banks worldwide to communicate with one another.

The *Centrox* service, introduced in 1991, provides on-line access to a database, combined with high-resolution color images, for art collectors, dealers, and banks that lend money against art.[19] Designed as a purely informational service for institutional subscribers (who are prepared to pay high prices for the equipment and use charges), the system contains all the catalog information and auction results on worldwide sales of major paintings and sculpture since 1989. It also lists—and shows—the artworks subscribers wish to sell.

The sponsor of an interorganizational information system that can dominate its industry has a stirring perspective of "commandeering the flow of electronic information [in their market segment] and putting a spin on it that favors one company [theirs]."[20] The Sabre airline reservation system gives an indication of such possibilities. In general, strategically deployed information systems have profound, and as yet poorly understood, effects on the distribution of power—and profits—within and among industry segments (Toffler, 1990).

Information technology lowers the costs of coordination in a marketplace by facilitating such activities as selecting suppliers, establishing prices, ordering goods, and paying bills. Market making by using information systems based on computer and communication technologies continues to offer immense business opportunities in the immediate future (Malone, 1987).

Interorganizational systems based on EDI have already significantly affected the operation of such industries as transportation, insurance, banking, drug distribution, and grocery retailing.

SUMMARY

At the present stage of organizational computing, information systems are expected not only to support business operations and management of an enterprise, but also help the firm compete in the marketplace, perhaps becoming a source of competitive advantage. Organizations use information systems to redefine the company's business, create new products or services, and transform the existing ones.

A company can choose between various strategies and tactics to grapple with the forces of the competitive marketplace. The company's value chain of activities is a vital tool for analyzing opportunities for seeking strategic advantage.

To be successful in wielding information systems as a competitive weapon, a company needs to meet certain preconditions and perform a thorough evaluation of its future actions. Companies with the most successful strategic systems transform the structure of their industry segment.

CONCLUSIONS FOR MIS PRACTICE

1. The concerns of MIS practitioners do not end with informational support of a company's operations and management. The role of information has to be raised to a higher level, as it were—that of aggressively supporting the company's lines of business in pursuit of a favorable competitive position in the marketplace.

2. To be effective, MIS managers and other practitioners need to understand thoroughly the general business their company or their business unit is in. This includes the core manufacturing or service activities of the business.

3. Strategic information systems *leverage* technology, rather than simply rely on advanced technology, to gain marketplace advantage. Advanced technology is but one component—albeit usually a necessary one—in the success of such a system. Others include the process of organizational change.

4. Favorable competitive positioning, in some cases leading to a sustainable advantage, is achieved by innovative use of technology in building on the existing strengths of the organization. This requires continual innovative modification of the strategic system and, thus, continuing investment.

5. A study of leading examples of companies who introduced strategic systems in various industries yields many insights, warnings, and rewards.

6. It is necessary to understand the range of possible strategic thrusts, as well as the forces, strategies, and tactics operative in competitive markets.

7. Value-chain analysis is a powerful tool for a systematic review of company activities with a view toward supporting them with strategic information systems. Special attention should be given to linkages with customers and suppliers and linkages between the activities of the chain.

8. A company should perform an impact analysis before it embarks on large strategic information projects. The consequences of the system introduction, including the potential responses of competitors, should be thought through.

ENDNOTES

1. Stanley Wohl. *The Medical Industrial Complex*. New York: Harmony Books, 1984, p. 150.

2. Jerry D. Scott. "Investment in Healthcare MIS Reflects Quality of Provider Group." *MIS Week*, September 12, 1988, p. 44.

3. John Diebold. "Computers are Changing the Way Your Company Competes." *Infosystems*, March 1985, p. 122.

4. Janet Guyon. "Ethereal Market." *The Wall Street Journal*, Global Finance Supplement, September 23, 1988, p. 26R.

5. Glenn Rifkin. "He Changed the Rules in Banking." *Computerworld*, April 25, 1988, pp. 1, 84–86.

6. Alvin Toffler. *Powershift: Knowledge, Wealth, and Violence at the Edge of the 21st Century*. New York: Bantam Books, 1990, p. 76.

7. Henry C. Lucas, Jr. "American Hospital Supply: The ASAP Systems." *A Casebook for Management Information Systems*. 3rd ed. New York: McGraw-Hill, 1986, pp. 3–9.

8. This subsection is based in part on: *The Business Week Newsletter for Information Executives*, September 1988, pp. 1–3; Cushman, John H., Jr., "The High-Stakes Battle for Airline Reservations," *The New York Times* Business Section, June 18, 1989, p. 2; and Jim Bartimo, "Wanted: Co-Pilots for Reservation Systems." *Business Week*, April 9, 1990, pp. 78–79.

9. "From the Founder of People Express: How Technology Can Kill." *The Business Week Newsletter for Information Executives,* December 9, 1988, pp. 6–7.

10. Sharon Brady. "School of Hard Knocks." *Software Magazine,* April 1988, pp. 37–44.

11. Janet Mason. "Meet Me at the Hilton." *Computerworld,* October 1, 1990, pp. 73–74.

12. Francine Schwadel. "Merchants Are in a Bind on Credit Cards." The *Wall Street Journal,* September 21, 1988, p. 29.

13. "Getting Your Grades At the Teller Machine." *The New York Times,* March 5, 1989, p. 51.

14. Dyan Machan. "How Gus Blythe Smelled Opportunity." *Forbes,* October 3, 1988, pp. 104–13.

15. "Business is Turning Data into a Potent Strategic Weapon." *Business Week,* August 22, 1983, pp. 92–98.

16. "MIS Ventures into CIM." *Software Magazine,* September 1988, p. 85.

17. Robert Knight. "Taking the Bull Out of Bullwork." *Software News,* September 1988, pp. 79–85.

18. Jeff M. Cohen. "Expanding Capabilities." *Financial Computing,* May/June 1985, pp. 22–26.

19. Christie Brown. "An Electronic Market for Art?" *Forbes,* March 18, 1991, p. 137.

20. Michael W. Miller and Matthew Winkler. "A Former Trader Aims to Hook Wall Street On—And To—His Data." *The Wall Street Journal,* September 22, 1988, pp. 1, 26.

KEY TERMS AND CONCEPTS

Strategic information system
Competitive advantage
Automatic order-taking system
Computerized reservation system
Competitive strategies
Differentiation
Cost leadership
Focused differentiation
Barriers to entry
Changing the basis of competition
Substitute products
Switching costs
Strategic cube
Value-chain analysis

Inbound and outbound logistics
Just-in-time operation
Telemaintenance
Computer-integrated manufacturing (CIM)
Material requirements planning (MRP)
Manufacturing resource planning (MRP II)
Electronic kiosks
Retail tracking
Sustainability of competitive advantage
Interorganizational information systems

QUESTIONS

1. What do we mean by strategic perspective?

2. Draw, point by point and in order of importance, the principal distinctions between strategic and nonstrategic information systems.

3. How does the admonition to build on existing company strengths apply to American Express?

4. How are products transformed with information systems? Relate this to the differentiation strategy.

5. What are the consequences in a company's industry segment when the company introduces a major reservation or order-taking system?

6. How can information systems be applied to achieve cost leadership?

7. Using the strategic cube, outline a plausible scenario for the use of an information system to exploit an opportunity in the Present competitors— Differentiation—Internal innovation subcube.

8. Map onto the value chain strategic systems different from those in figure 5.5. Whenever possible, try to provide two kinds of systems for a value-chain stage: one for a company pursuing the differentiation strategy, and another for a company aiming at lowest costs.

9. Why didn't ATMs offer a lasting strategic advantage to the banks that originally introduced them?

10. What other roles could strategic information systems play in the marketing and sales stage of the value chain? Try to find at least two.

11. Find a role for a strategic information system in the linkages between the three outbound stages of the value chain.

12. Relate the use of CIM to competitive strategies.

13. Find an example of a strategic information system in a service industry. To the extent that you can gain the necessary information, attempt to map the example onto the strategic cube. In other words, what strategies and tactics did the company exploit? What primary competitive forces did it contend with?

14. What are the preconditions for sustainability of competitive advantage achieved with a strategic information system?

15. What are the organizational requirements for successful deployment of a strategic information system?

16. Under what circumstances should you *not* innovate with a strategic system? Make a list of five situations and explain why strategic systems are not appropriate under these circumstances.

17. List three potential consequences of interorganizational information systems for the affected industry segment.

ISSUES FOR DISCUSSION

1. Who benefits from the strategic use of information systems by hospitals and their suppliers (as discussed in the Focus Case and Baxter's ASAP description)? Why?

2. Pepperidge Farms is equipping each truck delivering its baked goods with a Fujitsu hand-held and battery-powered computer, printer, and telecommunications interface unit. Drivers can enter orders and create invoices. At the end of the day, the data is uploaded via 9600 bps modems and through a public packet-switching network to the Pepperidge Farms computers. Drivers can also get a history of a customer's relationship with the company. (The information was obtained from "Global Communications and Computer Strategies for the 90s," a special advertising supplement in *Forbes,* September 1988.)

Considering the fact that Pepperidge Farms deals in perishable items, suggest some steps the company could take to upgrade this system to further pursue competitive advantage.

3. Suppose you are planning to start a mail-order company. You have decided that your study of strategic information systems gives *you* an advantage. How could you use strategic information systems to seek competitive advantage? How could you sustain the advantage?

AN EXEMPLAR OF STRATEGIC INFORMATION SYSTEMS: ECONOMOST OF McKESSON DRUG COMPANY

From the Boundary into the Core, or How Economost Went from an Order-Entry System to a Customer Information System

McKesson Drug of San Francisco is a large wholesale drug distributor; its primary customers are retail pharmacies. Computerized order-taking systems developed by the company, the most elaborate of which is Economost, have allowed the company to salvage its threatened marketplace and maintain its competitive position.

The Pre-Economost Situation

In the early 1970s, the wholesale drug distribution industry was highly fragmented. In 1974, 180 distributors were competing for over 50,000 customers. A typical small pharmacy would order daily from two or more distributors. Chain pharmacy stores enjoyed significant advantages over independents: they had bargaining clout when negotiating with distributors and enjoyed

economies that came with the scale of their operations and their superior management information. They also tended to cut out distributors by ordering directly from the manufacturers.

McKesson's customer base—small pharmacies—was threatened. The business of the company was threatened with it.

How It All Began

McKesson introduced a limited-capability Economost in 1970, which until 1975 was used for electronic order entry in northern California, but only for the most rapidly moving items. The initial motivation was to lower distribution costs and pass some of the savings to the customers.

The Economost System

In 1975, McKesson decided to expand the embryonic and limited Economost system from a local to a national scale. This was a vital decision for the company. Since that time, the system has evolved over the years. We'll now describe how the system currently works.

An employee of McKesson's customer—in other words, a pharmacy clerk—walks through the store, entering a complete order into a hand-held terminal. Each item of the order is entered either by waving a wand over the bar codes on the shelves or by keying in a seven-digit item identifier. Reorder points and quantities are predetermined. The retailer then transmits the complete order via a modem and telephone line to McKesson's national data center; there, the order directly enters one of the Tandem minicomputers (a fault-tolerant system). A voice synthesizer acknowledges the order. Individual orders are preprocessed, batched, and sent to the IBM 3090 mainframe computer at the data center. Minicomputers in regional distribution centers, networked with the mainframe, then access the orders directed to them. These minicomputers produce picking orders for the warehouse, as well as invoices and bar-code tags for shipments (to facilitate delivery). The system also produces price tags for the items, according to the individual customer's specifications.

Warehouse shelves are organized to correspond to pharmacy shelves; the items are delivered packed in that order as well. The result is high packing efficiency at the warehouse and unpacking efficiency on the customer's site.

Well over 90 percent of the items are delivered the day after ordering. Many pharmacies keep no inventories beyond their shelf stocks.

Economost makes a variety of management information options available to customers for a fee. The reports include order lists with prices, profitability analyses broken out by item and pharmacy department, lists of items on which promotional discounts are available from manufacturers, and monthly inventory reports. Also, credit card services and third-party claim processing (for insurance reimbursement purposes) are available.

To cut costs, McKesson has encouraged less frequent and more substantial orders with volume discounts. McKesson has realized impressive efficiencies: from 1974 to 1987, they reduced the number of order entry clerks from 700 to 15, while sales increased almost sixfold. Due to a great increase in inventory turnover, the number of warehouses has been cut in half. The salesforce has also been cut in half. The role salespeople play has changed dramatically: McKesson has transformed them from order takers into system consultants to retailers.

These impressive results have not been obtained simply because the company introduced a computerized order-taking system. They are rather the outcome of an extensive process of organizational change rationalizing all of the company operations, with Economost serving as the focus. McKesson realized that distribution itself is a commodity service, easily squeezed out of the marketplace. Adding value by providing superior service and information helps to maintain profit margins.

In 1989, the company had over 15,000 customers; more than 99 percent of orders processed in the company's forty-three regional distribution centers came from remote order entry terminals in retail pharmacies.

Analysis of the Outcome

The primary benefit to McKesson has been the preservation of its customer base. Similar systems were introduced by major competitors, such as Bergen-Brunswig. Much of the impressive productivity improvement that McKesson realized thanks to its strategic information system has been passed on to the customer in lower prices. The drug distribution industry *as a whole,* however, has kept some of the savings that resulted from the use of information systems. Thus, one measure of profitability, return on net worth, increased in that industry segment from 5 percent in 1976 to over 15 percent in 1984.

The industry has consolidated as well: out of 180 drug distributors competing in the marketplace in 1974, only 90 remained in 1986. The $20 to $30 million spent by McKesson (as well as similar amounts spent by its major competitors) on information systems since 1975 constitutes a potent barrier to entry. For example, it counteracts direct sales by manufacturers to the pharmacies.

Yet, while the profitability of the drug distribution industry has increased, no competitive advantage can be claimed for McKesson: its profit margin is no higher than the profit margins of its competitors and its market share has remained steady at 21 percent.

Competitive Position—and Strategic Systems—Must Be Maintained

Strategic information systems require continual innovation. For example, in December 1989 McKesson launched an on-line transaction processing (OLTP) system to replace batch processing of customer orders. While the batch system offered next-day order confirmation, the OLTP system is able to confirm an order within one minute.

The historical transaction data accumulated in the system are being used to hone sales forecasting and promotions management.

Based on Eric K. Clemons and Michael Row, "McKesson Drug Company: A Case Study of Economost—A Strategic Information System," *Journal of Management Information Systems, 5,* 1, Summer 1988, pp. 36–50; and David Malmberg, "Changing the Rules of the Game: A Case Study of McKesson's Economost Service." Presentation at the 21st Annual Hawaii International Conference on Systems Sciences, Kailua-Kona, Hawaii, January 7, 1988.

Certain facts were also drawn from Bruce Caldwell, "McKesson Goes On-Line," *InformationWeek,* November 6, 1989, p. 15; Janet Fiderio, "Customer Closeness at Bergen Brunswig McKesson." *Computerworld,* February 19, 1990, pp. 69, 75; and (Clemons, 1991).

Case Study One Questions

1. What are the main reasons for Economost's success?

2. Competitive position does not sustain itself—it must be sustained by continual innovation. What potential moves of all the players in this case—manufacturers, retailers, and competing distributors—had to be thwarted?

3. Can McKesson use its system to distribute other goods and thus effect economies of scope? What areas offer a target of opportunity?

4. Adapting ideas from the many examples presented in this chapter, describe the opportunities McKesson should consider in the future.

5. Eric Clemons of The Wharton School of the University of Pennsylvania is the principal originator of the term *strategic necessity.* Explain the meaning of both words in this term, using Economost as an example.

CASE STUDY TWO

LASTING COMPETITIVE ADVANTAGE AND GLOBAL SCOPE THROUGH INFORMATION TECHNOLOGY—THE CASE OF ROSENBLUTH TRAVEL

Headquartered in Philadelphia, Rosenbluth Travel (RT) is a family business—although not a typical one. Rosenbluth grew from a regional travel agency with $40 million in sales in 1980 to one of the five largest U.S. travel agencies, with sales well over $1 billion in 1990. Strategic use of information systems has been a principal vehicle for the continuing growth of the firm.

Deregulation (and Vision) as the Start
The impressive growth of RT resulted from its successful exploitation of the deregulation of the airline industry, which took place in 1978. Prior to that, the Civil Aeronautics Board (CAB), an arm of the U.S. federal government, had set airfares and assigned air routes to the airlines. Travel agencies were limited primarily to the leisure market and derived revenues from their 10 percent commission on tickets sold.

Deregulation of the airline industry changed the travel business. Now, airlines could add and delete routes almost at will and charge a variety of fares even on the same flight, exploiting computerized yield management. The complexity of the travel environment grew immensely. Few people realize that business travel is the third largest corporate expense item (after payroll and information processing). Faced with the need to control this expense in a complex environment, companies started to turn to travel agencies. In other words, the corporate travel market has come into its own.

Travel agencies could offer several vital services to add value to the plain ticketing. They had expertise in managing travel expenses. Even more important, negotiated rates and fares, which first emerged in lodging and car rentals, entered the airfare marketplace as well. A company that could identify its high-volume routes could negotiate preferential fares with an airline on a route-by-route basis. To achieve these volume efficiencies, an organization had to analyze its overall travel patterns—and this consolidation of information was more easily achieved if the organization used a single travel agency. This opened a window of opportunity for a savvy agency ready to invest in the information technology that would enable it to service large corporations and help them get the best travel deals.

RT stepped up to bat. Hal Rosenbluth, the head of the firm, says: "What did deregulation mean? We weren't sure we knew. But if all the bets were off, the company that could gather information faster and turn it into knowledge would win." Rosenbluth decided to use information systems to differentiate the services offered by the firm and exploit the economies of scale: the more business the firm handled, the more it would be able to invest in innovative information systems— and the more it would continue to grow.

Leveraging InformationTechnology for Competitive Advantage

The principal innovation introduced by RT (in 1983) was a system, called READOUT, that listed fares by price instead of by time of departure, as the airlines' computerized reservation systems (CRS) did. This apparently simple idea enabled customers to control costs far more effectively. As the system attracted clients, Rosenbluth says, "we realized we were in the information business, not just the travel business."

Other innovative information-system components followed—at a considerable investment cost. To control their travel spending, companies had to rely on the "back-office" reporting provided by the airlines' CRS—but the customer companies did not control that reporting. It could also take up to forty-five days to obtain the transac-

tion tapes. To gain control, RT introduced in 1986 a back-office system, called Vision, that trapped the records of all transactions made for clients—and that made management reports available within a day. The system has been extensively used to support negotiations with travel service suppliers; based on it, RT could guarantee lower airfares to their clients (and still earn their commission). Vision has also been linked with the clients' internal systems, such as accounting. Yet another system, UserVision, brought this information to the desktop for PC queries.

In 1988, in another of RT's series of strategic moves, the travel agency redesigned its front-end business—that is, the process of making reservations—around another major information subsystem, called Precision. This software makes available to the reservation clerk the profiles of the client company and the traveling employee. Precision also gives the clerk access to the READOUT database, with fares shown in order from the lowest to the highest, including any special negotiated fares.

Quality control—making sure that transactions are complete and accurate—is of the essence in the travel business. Another part of the software suite, UltraVision, monitors all transactions to ensure their validity.

We mentioned the results of RT's strategic deployment of information systems at the beginning of the case. By pursuing its strategy of service differentiation, RT has been able to gain a sustainable competitive advantage over its competitors. The high volume of business affords the firm, in turn, considerable economies of scale and scope. Its impressive growth over the 1980s was generally internally funded with retained profits, which were estimated to be significantly higher than the industry average.

Information Technology for Globalization of a Business

RT is going beyond its domestic success and is responding to the challenge of globalization. To succeed, it *has* to become global: as competition in foreign markets has become more important to U.S. corporations, so has global travel. A global traveler requires service at his or her destination, but RT does not possess foreign offices and cannot justify an investment in purchasing a network of travel offices around the world. Therefore, it formed a strategic alliance with foreign travel companies whose domestic markets are comparable to those RT has in the United States. The global entity is called Rosenbluth International Alliance. A Rosenbluth client now receives telephone numbers to call worldwide—and the agent will answer "Rosenbluth Travel." Rosenbluth has become a virtual global corporation.

The crucial point is that the allied travel agents all over the world have access to all the relevant information available in the traveler's home RT office. Thus, by creating a superior information technology platform, the firm enabled itself to coordinate service across borders and time zones.

Based on Eric K. Clemons and Michael C. Row, "Information Technology at Rosenbluth Travel: Competitive Advantage in a Rapidly Growing Global Service Company," *Journal of Management Information Systems*, 8, 2, Fall 1991; and Eric K. Clemons, private correspondence relating to Rosenbluth International Alliance, 1991.

Case Study Two Questions

1. How did Rosenbluth Travel make their customers' business *their* business? In other words, how did the agency develop its business strategy by identifying the concerns of its customers?

2. Relate the opportunity RT exploited to our discussion of the organizational environment of an information society in chapter 2.

3. Discuss the sequence in which RT built up its information technology platform in functional terms—that is, by stressing the function of each new subsystem.

4. Map the competitive posture of Rosenbluth Travel and of Rosenbluth International Alliance onto the strategic cube shown in figure 5.3.

5. Competitive advantage, even if sustained over an extensive period of time, is not a permanent franchise. Discuss the market forces RT will have to contend with in the future. In particular, note that the RT systems are, to a large degree, add-ons to the airlines' computerized reservation systems. Can the CRS become a threat? How?

6. Consider Rosenbluth International Alliance as a form of information partnership, based on sharing customer data. In what ways can such a partnership become a basis for differentiation? (Note: You may consult Konsynski and McFarlan (1990) for a broader view of this important development.)

SELECTED REFERENCES

Barrett, Stephanie S. "Strategic Alternatives and Interorganizational System Implementations: An Overview." *Journal of Management Information Systems,* 3, 3, Winter 1986–87, pp. 5–16.

Benjamin, Robert I., et al. "Information Technology: A Strategic Opportunity." *Sloan Management Review,* 25, 3, Spring 1984, pp. 3–9.

Cash, James I., and Konsynski, Benn R. "IS Redraws Competitive Boundaries." *Harvard Business Review,* March–April 1985, pp. 134–42.

Cash, James I., Jr., and McLeod, Poppy L. "Managing the Introduction of Information Technology in Strategically Dependent Companies." *Journal of Management Information Systems,* 1, 4, Spring 1985, pp. 5–23.

Clemons, Eric. K. "London's Big Bang: A Case Study of Information Technology, Competitive Impact, and Organizational Change." *Journal of Management Information Systems,* 6, 4, Spring 1990, pp. 41–60.

Clemons, Eric K. "Evaluation of Strategic Investments in Information Technology." *Communications of the ACM,* 34, 1, January 1991, pp. 22–36.

Cox, James F., and Clark, Steven J. "Problems in Implementing and Operating a Manufacturing Resource Planning Information System." *Journal of Management Information Systems,* 1, 1, Summer 1984, pp. 81–101.

Deutsch, Claudia H. "Just in Time: The New Partnerships." Business Section, *The New York Times,* October 28, 1990, p. 25.

Feeny, David F., and Ives, Blake. "In Search of Sustainability: Reaping Long-Term Advantage from Investments in Information Technology." *Journal of Management Information Systems,* 7, 1, Summer 1990, pp. 27–46.

Feigenbaum, Edward; McCorduck, Pamela; and Nii, H. Penny. *The Rise of the Expert Company.* New York: Times Books, 1988.

Hopper, Max D. "Rattling SABRE—New Ways to Compete on Information." *Harvard Business Review,* May–June 1990, pp. 118–25.

Ives, Blake, and Learmonth, Gerard P. "The Information System as a Competitive Weapon." *Communications of the ACM,* 27, 12, December 1984, pp. 1193–1201.

Ives, Blake, and Vitale, Michael R. "After the Sale: Leveraging Maintenance with Information Technology." *MIS Quarterly,* 12, 2, March 1988, pp. 7–21.

Johnston, H. Russell, and Carrico, Shelley R. "Developing Capabilities to Use Information Strategically." *MIS Quarterly,* 12, 2, March 1988, pp. 37–48.

Johnston, H. Russell, and Vitale, Michael R. "Creating Competitive Advantage with Interorganizational Information Systems." *MIS Quarterly,* 12, 3, June 1988, pp. 153–65.

Kaufman, Felix. "Data Systems that Cross Company Boundaries." *Harvard Business Review,* January-February 1966, pp. 51–61.

Keen, Peter G. W. *Competing in Time: Using Telecommunications for Competitive Advantage.* Cambridge, Mass.:Ballinger, 1988.

Konsynski, Benn R., and McFarlan, F. Warren, "Information Partnerships—Shared Data, Shared Scale." *Harvard Business Review,* September-October 1990, pp. 114–20.

Lele, M. M. "How Service Needs Influence Product Strategy." *Sloan Management Review,* 27, 1, Fall 1986, pp. 63–70.

McFarlan, F. Warren. "Information Technology Changes the Way You Compete." *Harvard Business Review,* May-June 1984, pp. 98–103.

McKenna, Regis. "Marketing is Everything." *Harvard Business Review,* January–February 1991, pp. 65–79.

Malone, Thomas W.; Yates, Joanne; and Benjamin, Robert I. "Electronic Markets and Electronic Hierarchies." *Communications of the ACM,* 30, 16, June 1987, pp. 484–97.

Mott, Stephen C.; Keen, Peter G. W.; and Sulser, J. David. *Electronic Information Services: Looking Ahead by Looking Back,* Washington, D.C.: International Center for Information Technologies, 1988.

Ohmae, Kenichi. *The Borderless World: Power and Strategy in the Interlinked Economy,* New York: Harper Business, 1990.

Porter, Michael E. *Competitive Advantage.* New York: Free Press, 1985.

Porter, Michael E. *The Competitive Advantage of Nations.* New York: Free Press, 1990.

Porter, Michael E., and Millar, Victor E. "How Information Gives You Competitive Advantage." *Harvard Business Review,* July-August 1985, pp. 149–60.

Rackoff, Nick; Wiseman, Charles; and Ullrich, Walter A. "Information Systems for Competitive Advantage: Implementation of a Planning Process." *MIS Quarterly,* 9, 4, December 1985, pp. 285–94.

Sullivan-Trainor, Michael L., and Maglitta, Joseph. "Competitive Advantage Fleeting." *Computerworld,* October 8, 1990, pp. 1, 4.

Synnott, William R. *The Information Weapon: Winning Customers and Markets with Technology.* New York: John Wiley, 1987.

Toffler, Alvin. *Powershift: Knowledge, Wealth, and Violence at the Edge of the 21st Century.* New York: Bantam Books, 1990.

Vitale, Michael R. "The Growing Risks of Information Systems Success." *MIS Quarterly,* 10, 4, December 1986, pp. 327–34.

Walton, Richard E. *Up and Running: Integrating Information Technology and the Organization.* Boston: Harvard Business School Press, 1989.

Wiseman, Charles. *Strategic Information Systems.* Homewood, Ill.: Irwin, 1988.

MIS ARCHITECTURE OF A LARGE ORGANIZATION

As we discussed in chapter 1, a modern MIS is not developed from ground zero. Rather, it builds on a portfolio of application systems accumulated by some companies over thirty years or more. There is rarely a line of the original code (program instructions) still existent in such a portfolio. However, some of the original subsystems survive, and new subsystems continue to be added.

To make the best use of their information systems, companies leading in MIS practice develop architectural models of their informational resources. These models serve as a vision of the informational support the company desires, as inventories of subsystems on hand, and as sources of development and integration plans for the future.

Such a conceptual framework was developed by the widely diversified manufacturing corporation American Standard of New York, one of the 200 largest U.S. corporations. Worldwide operations of the company produced about $3.6 billion in sales in 1989. The principal developer of American Standard's architectural model was Gary Biddle, the company's vice-president of MIS (who first sketched the model, as certain well-known modelers had done before, on a bar napkin). The model is shown in the color figure on page 47. Most of the original terminology employed by American Standard has been retained to expose you to some alternative nomenclature used in the field.

American Standard views its MIS as consisting of four business portfolios of applications: institutional systems (providing support to functional units of the company); factory automation (manufacturing operations support); professional support services (fundamentally, office information systems); and external support services. Notable is the inclusion of manufacturing support in the overall information systems architecture and extensive support for external connectivity, both for operations and for informational boundary spanning.

These four business portfolios are distributed over three tiers of computers: data utilities—large data centers built around mainframe computers on the corporate level; "functional processors"—minicomputers used for divisional and departmental purposes; and intelligent workstations—microcomputers, used as personal computers and for equipment control. This three-tier structure is designed to distribute processing power to departments and individual users. By processing each transaction in the functional area where it originates, the company minimizes the costs of communication with the corporate data centers.

To complete the cube-shaped model, the four portfolios are considered to consist of three architectural levels: business-oriented applications, data management, and the communications network backbone. Such structuring furthers flexibility and helps ensure that clean interfaces can be implemented between the levels. This means, for example, that only limited and predefined parts of the application programs would access the data on the data-management level. This makes it possible to change the data-management layer without affecting most of the applications code.

The company believes further advantages will come from basing its informational policies on a uniform architectural model. Spending objectives are established for each of the four portfolios, and returns on these investments can be monitored along well-defined lines. As a matter of fact, the portfolios are further broken down into subgroups of functionally related applications, so that even a finer level of control may be exercised.

The model is also considered a communication tool between MIS professionals and American Standard's general managers. This again enhances the company's ability to direct and control its MIS spending.

Notably, and consistent with the three-eras model presented in chapter 2, the functional "institutional systems" are considered comparably stable by now. Thus, MIS developers devote their attention primarily to the other three portfolios.

Based in part on Ralph E. Carlyle, "ROI in Real Time," *Datamation*, February 15, 1987, pp. 73–74; and Ralph E. Carlyle, "Managing IS at Multinationals." *Datamation*, March 1, 1988, pp. 54–66.

Case Study Questions

1. How does an architectural model, such as the one developed by American Standard, relate to the MIS integration concerns discussed in chapter 1?

2. Why are the dynamics of portfolio development at American Standard consistent with the three-era model discussed in chapter 2?

3. How are the five MIS types discussed in chapter 3 distributed among the architectural components of the American Standard model?

4. Which components of the American Standard model support management functions, as discussed in chapter 3? Which primarily support business operations, as described in chapter 4?

5. Note that there is no explicit "strategic system" level, since, as we discussed in chapter 5, strategic advantage may be achieved by exploiting any of the five MIS types. Using the strategic cube and the value-chain approach described in that chapter, outline a scenario for exploiting the potential of a component of the American Standard portfolio.

PART TWO

COMPUTER SYSTEM RESOURCES

Management information systems provide solutions to business problems: when properly developed and deployed, they raise the operational efficiency of an enterprise, enhance the effectiveness of its management, and enhance the competitive position of the firm.

Hardware and software of computer systems, telecommunications, and databases are the primary technological resources pressed into service in management information systems. A great variety of technologies may be combined in designing these systems.

To make the best use of MIS, we have to understand clearly the capabilities and the potential of these technologies.

Yet, technologies do not produce results by themselves. A technology may be viewed as a vehicle for changing the way a task is performed or the way business is done. The selection of technologies appropriate to the problem and to the organization, disciplined development of systems, and the implementation of systems so that they can reach their potential within the firm are all crucial to success. Thus, as we discuss information resources and the specific technologies deployed to create them, we have to pay unremitting attention to the methods of making them effective in an organization. In other words, we must understand how these technologies can be managed.

In this part of the book, therefore, we will continue to address the problems of information systems management. In particular, as information systems evolve from being the exclusive domain of MIS professionals to becoming the shared responsibility of end users and MIS departments, we have to understand the dimensions of end-user computing. Here, we shall discuss the tools and management techniques that enable users to become direct participants in organizational computing.

CHAPTER 6

Computer Systems: Hardware and Software

People do not want technologies, they want solutions.

Blair Pleasant
The Yankee Group, Boston

To provide computer-based solutions to business problems, or to evaluate such solutions, we need to understand the technological capabilities of the hardware and software employed in computer systems. In this chapter, we shall first discuss how a computer system is organized. We shall then review computer categories: microcomputers, minicomputers, mainframes, and supercomputers. Finally, we will discuss computer peripherals: secondary memories, as well as input and output devices. Indeed, many system capabilities derive from the proper choice of these peripherals.

In the MIS environment, the choice of hardware is driven by the applications for which we want to use the system. Applications software does not run directly on hardware: there is a layer of systems software that controls the hardware on behalf of the applications. The principal systems software is the operating system.

Today, most applications are written either in high-level languages, of which COBOL is a prime example in the business world, or in very high-level languages (also known as 4GL), which offer superior programming productivity. Keep in mind that an applications software lasts longer than the particular hardware for which it was originally developed. As you realize, much of this book is about applications software.

FOCUS STATEMENT

The technologies of computing change rapidly. The application of these technologies to business processes is no longer an option: it is often a competitive necessity.

Many authorities, such as James Cash of the Harvard Business School, therefore, propose that firms establish organizational units specifically chartered with the responsibility of tracking new computer and communications technologies and investigating their benefits in the context of that firm. "Information Systems [function] should follow the example set by the business side of a company—with one unit handling current operations and another tending to the future technology," writes Roger Wasson, another proponent of such a unit.[1] With such a structure, the pressure of daily operations will not overshadow the long-term approach that is necessary to seek out and adapt new technologies to the needs of the firm.

At Unum Life Insurance Company of Portland, Oregon, several members of an Emerging Technologies group are charged with staying abreast of high-potential technologies that are still not ready for implementation. As soon as a technology starts to look feasible, the group searches aggressively to find "customers" within the company—users who would be interested in sponsoring a project based on the technology.

The members of such an Emerging (or Advanced) Technologies group should have not only technical expertise, but also an in-depth understanding of the company's business. Moreover, they should expect resistance to change on the part of many people in the organization. Upper management's clear support for the group's operation is therefore necessary. A group of this type operates at American Express—a leader in strategic use of information technologies.

Based in part on Roger E. Wasson, "Adapting for Future Technologies." *Datamation*, April 1, 1990, pp. 93–95; and Alice LaPlante, "The Needing Edge." *Computerworld*, March 18, 1990, pp. 65–67.

6.1 ORGANIZATION OF COMPUTER SYSTEMS

Almost all computer systems have a similar, rather simple structure consisting of a processor, main memory, and peripheral devices, such as secondary memories, input, and output devices. The speeds and memory capacities of these systems have been expanding exponentially over the last decades. This translates into more and more potent business applications.

What Is the Structure of a Computer System?

As the *Encyclopaedia Britannica* tells us, computers are general-purpose processors of symbolic information (Zwass, 1988). As I write this book on my personal computer, I interact with my input device (a keyboard). Under the processor's control, the input device transmits encoded symbols, which represent letters, numbers and special characters (a "$" or a carriage return), into memory, and the output device (a monitor screen) displays them. Word processing is of course a very simple way to process information. What a computer does at any given time depends on the instructions of the program it is executing. The same machine, when controlled by an expert system program, can render advice on a complex financial deal or, running yet another software, can produce the best routes for thousands of an airline's planes.

It is rather amazing that the general organization of computer system hardware is as simple as it is (see figure 6.1). Moreover, the same organization is used whether building a microcomputer (shown in color plates 1a and b), or a mainframe (color plate 2) that costs perhaps a thousand times more. The devices actually included in these configurations, their speeds, and their processing capabilities will of course be different.

The Processor (CPU)

At the heart of the computer is its **processor.** Called also the **central processing unit (CPU)** of the computer, it executes machine instructions. These instructions are encoded in a binary form—that is, as 1s and 0s, corresponding to the operation of digital circuitry (on-off). To "execute machine instructions" means that the control unit of the CPU fetches these instructions, one by one, from the main memory; retrieves the data for each instruction from the main memory as needed; and stores the results back in the main memory. Depending on the instruction it executes, the control unit sends signals that tell all other units of the computer system what to do—it indeed controls them. A machine instruction does very detailed work; for example, it may specify:

- An arithmetic operation, such as the addition of two numbers.
- A logical operation, such as a comparison of two values, or inverting all the bits of a value: changing 0s to 1s and vice versa.
- The movement of data from one location to another, including input from or output to a peripheral device.
- The selection of which program instruction is to be executed next, depending on a certain condition. This ability to carry out sequences of instructions conditionally or repeatedly defines much of the computer's power.

FIGURE 6.1

The organization of computer systems.

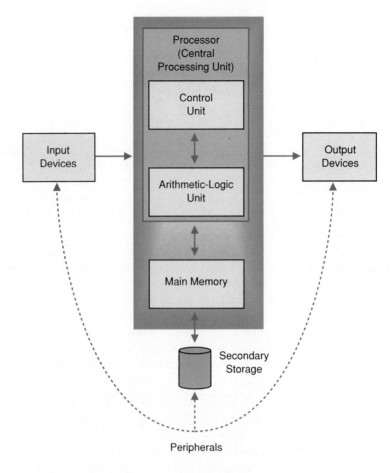

FIGURE 6.2

A schematic view of memory.

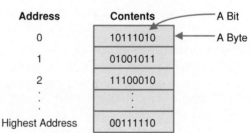

All programs are translated into the machine language for execution, as we shall further discuss in this chapter.

When arithmetic or logical operations are to be carried out, the arithmetic-logic unit (ALU) of the CPU is used: this circuitry can add or multiply operands, as well as perform logical operations (such as a comparison, AND, or OR).

Main Memory and Peripherals

To be ready for execution, the programs and the data they require must be transferred into the main memory. The main memory of the computer consists of a large number of locations, identified by their addresses, as shown in figure 6.2.

UNICODE

Have you ever thought what happens in our age of globalization when we want to write software that can interact with users in different countries? The ASCII and EBCDIC codes can represent only 256 different characters. This does not even accommodate the accented characters of French, and certainly not Chinese ideographs (which are also used in Korean and Japanese), not to mention Arabic, Bengali, or Hebrew.

To solve this problem, twelve top computer companies formed a consortium, which is developing a worldwide standard called Unicode. Using a sequence of 16 bits to represent a single character, it would allow for 65,536 representable symbols. And that is enough to give each character used in a living language its own representation (and to leave some for cuneiforms as well). Of course, new and sweeping standards are notoriously slow to be accepted—but the need is very real.

Based on Andrew Pollack, "Universal Computer Code Due." *The New York Times*, February 20, 1991, pp. D1, D5.

The elementary unit of representation is a **bit** (short for binary digit), whose value can be 0 or 1. Character representations are built out of combinations of bits, with each character represented by a sequence of eight bits, called a **byte.** Thus, each memory location, identified by its own address, can store one letter, digit, or a special symbol (say, *), encoded in the binary code used by the machine. The cell whose address is 0 in figure 6.2 stores the letter Z in the ASCII-8 code, commonly used in microcomputers and most machines other than the IBM mainframes (ASCII—pronounced "askee"—stands for American Standard Code for Information Interchange). IBM mainframes use another code called EBCDIC ("ebsedik"). Processors can generally fetch from the main memory and manipulate larger sequences of bits at one time; such an entity is called **word** (thus, a 32-bit machine has a word that equals 4 bytes).

Of course, text is only one of the data types stored in computer memories. Numerical data, for example, have a variety of representations of their own.

Today's main memories are made of semiconductor chips, which are referred to as RAM, for random-access memory, since it takes the same amount of time to access any randomly chosen memory location. A RAM chip of the current generation has a capacity of 4 megabits (more than 4 million bits!). The next generation, which is already in fabrication, will store 16 megabits per chip—the equivalent of about 1,600 pages of double-spaced typewritten text (more than the size of this book); the following generations of memory chips are in the works as well (see photo 6.1).

Even though a computer's main memory contains a number of such chips, its capacity is still limited as compared to the total requirements for the storage of data and programs. Moreover, semiconductor RAMs are volatile: when power

PHOTO 6.1

A 64-megabit memory chip (a working prototype from Hitachi, Ltd. of Japan). The narrowest circuit line on such a chip has the width of 0.25 micron, or about one-thousandth the diameter of a human hair. Manufacturers that take the lead in memory chips will gain in immense competitive advantage in semiconductor manufacturing by being able to apply their know-how and equipment to making other devices.

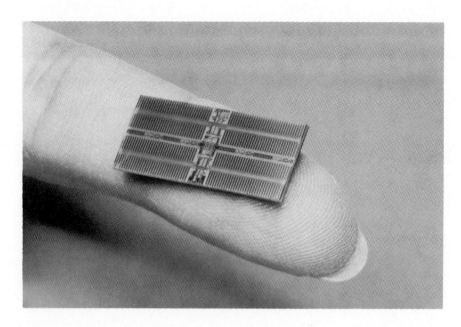

TABLE 6.1

Speeds and memory capacities in computer systems

SPEED UNIT	RELATIONSHIP TO A SECOND	ABBREVIATION	WHAT IT MEANS
Second	1	sec	Time to mount a tape in a drive: 120 sec.
Millisecond	.001	msec	Time to get a record from a disk: 20 msec.
Microsecond	.000001	μsec	IBM PS/2 Model 80 microcomputer executes four instructions in 1 μsec.
Nanosecond	.000000001	nsec	Many main memories take 200 nsec to fetch a data item.

MEMORY CAPACITY UNIT	RELATIONSHIP TO A BYTE	ABBREVIATION	WHAT IT MEANS
Byte	1	—	Stores the representation of one character (8 bits).
Kilobyte	$2^{10} = 1,024 \approx 1,000$	Kbyte (K)	The smallest realistic main memory in micro systems: 640 Kbytes.
Megabyte	$2^{20} \approx 1,000,000$	Mbyte (M)	The smallest realistic hard disk in micro systems: 30 Mbytes.
Gigabyte	$2^{30} \approx 1,000,000,000$	Gbyte (G)	Large magnetic disk units for mainframes: several Gbytes.
Terabyte	$2^{40} \approx 1,000,000,000,000$	Tbyte (T)	Optical disk "jukeboxes" for document storage: several Tbytes.

is removed, their contents disappear. To extend memory capacity in a cost-effective manner and to provide more permanent memories, secondary storage devices (mainly disks and tapes) are employed.

Input and output devices transfer programs and data between the outside world and the main memory. Together with secondary memories, these devices are called **peripherals.** They can be configured as the system's objectives require.

FROM COMPUTER HORSEPOWER TO TIME-TO-MARKET

Short product life cycles are the hallmark of today's business environment. This means that new product designs have to be developed far more rapidly than they were in the past.

While the engineers who work on the mechanical and electronic details of products have long been supported by computer-aided design (CAD) and computer-aided engineering (CAE) systems, industrial industrial product designers, who are responsible for a product's appearance, have not been so lucky. And yet, as we know full well, most people don't buy a car just for its technical prowess—for many of us, its looks are at least as important.

An industrial designer today can create a computer-generated mock-up of a product, with shapes and textures as realistic as a photograph. Software exists that can create the model's skeleton and then add the characteristics of texture (that glint of light on the car's surface)—but the software runs too slowly even on high-powered technical workstations. A single detailed image requires some 50 Mbytes of storage. To change an image in a reasonable time, a workstation must operate at speeds greater than 10 million instructions per second (MIPS). But even at this

horsepower, it may take thirty minutes to one hour to create one frame showing the product in three dimensions, including surface detail. To work efficiently, a designer needs a system that will render designs in real time, meaning that he or she can try new ideas with almost immediate results. This ability to quickly rework the design is crucial to product development.

In 1990, some experts predicted that systems capable of generating images in real time would appear on the market by 1992 at a cost of around $200,000. However, according to John Houlihan, director of industrial design at Timex Corporation, even the systems in operation in 1990 took just three days to accomplish what once took three weeks of designing.

With the powerful CAD workstations, the teamwork approach to design, known as concurrent engineering, is becoming possible. Working together on progressively refined computer models of their designs, engineers of all specialties can detect conflicts between these designs early during the product development and speed up the time-to-market.

Based on Michael Alexander, "Rendering Lifelike Images in Silicon," *Computerworld*, February 26, 1990, p. 18; and John J. Xenakis, "3-D Engineering," *InformationWeek*, February 25, 1991, pp. 22–23; and "Concurrent Engineering," Special Report, *IEEE Spectrum*, July 1991, pp. 22–37.

In a microcomputer (a micro, as we commonly call it), the processor and the main memory are packaged into the system unit, together with such peripheral equipment as disk drives. System configurations for larger computers generally include several cabinets, housing additional processors and peripherals.

Speeds and Memory Capacities in Computer Systems

Since the speeds and memory capacities of computer equipment play a vital role in understanding a system's operation and in selecting the needed system components, we have compiled table 6.1 to explain the different units of measurement.

As the previous vignette illustrates, the competitive requirements of today's firms do indeed call for very high computer speeds and memory capacities.

6.2 COMPUTER CATEGORIES: MICROCOMPUTERS, MINICOMPUTERS, MAINFRAMES, AND SUPERCOMPUTERS

Computer system hardware is now available in a spectacular variety of capabilities and costs. The relative cost of hardware as compared to software has declined no less impressively. The challenge in using information systems to increase operational efficiency and managerial effectiveness, and ultimately deploy it to competitive advantage, is to select the most appropriate technologies to meet these goals within the context of the given enterprise and its already existing MIS capabilities.

Here, we shall discuss the different categories of computers and the principal capabilities they offer a firm. Since hard-and-fast divisions between the various categories no longer exist, an appropriate selection can only be made through a careful study of a firm's needs (or an individual's needs, in the case of the microcomputer). From a micro to a supercomputer, all four computer categories find application in today's organizations.

What Are the Categories of Computers?

Computers initially emerged in the 1940s as daunting machines that filled entire rooms with equipment; today, virtually equivalent machines may be held in the palm of your hand. As we may conclude from figure 6.3, the ever-smaller machines put in their appearance when the computing field was already established.

FIGURE 6.3

How computer categories emerged.

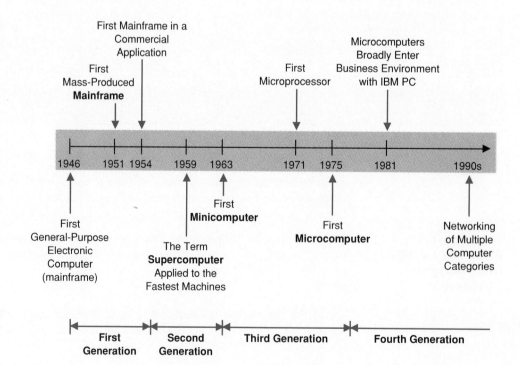

The first general-purpose electronic computer (ENIAC, shown in photo 6.2a) was completed in 1946 at the University of Pennsylvania, but the era of mass production did not dawn for computers until 1951, when UNIVAC I left the assembly line. In terms of our present categories, this was a mainframe—though it had only a fraction of the power offered by today's microcomputers. Originally used for scientific purposes, the computer was first employed in a business application by General Electric in 1954. In the late fifties, mainframes with expanded capabilities for processing numeric data acquired the name "supercomputers."

PHOTO 6.2

From a roomful to a notebook in four decades. a. The first general-purpose electronic computer, ENIAC, was quite a roomful in 1946. You can see here also its designers, J. Presper Eckert, Jr. (foreground) and John W. Mauchly (in the center).

b. Today's notebook microcomputer, with outstanding display resolution and 4.4 pounds of weight (TravelMate 2000 from Texas Instruments, Austin, Texas).

TABLE 6.2

Computer generations

GENERATION	FIRST	SECOND	THIRD	FOURTH
Years	**1946–55**	**1956–63**	**1964–77**	**1978–present**
Fundamental technology	Vacuum tubes	Transistors	Integrated circuits (small- to large-scale integration)	VLSI and microcomputers
Prominent computers	UNIVAC I and II IBM 700 series	CDC 3600 IBM 7000 series RCA 501	CDC 6600 and 7600 IBM System/360 and 370 DEC PDP-8 and PDP-11	Cray Y-MP IBM System/390 and ES/9000 DEC VAX 6000 IBM PC, PS/2 Apple Macintosh
Typical speed (instructions per second)	40,000	200,000	1–10 million	10–300 million
Typical size of main memory	2–4 Kbytes	32 Kbytes	256 Kbytes–2 Mbytes	16–512 Mbytes

The first minicomputer, a machine of more limited capabilities and lower cost than the mainframe, was produced by Digital Equipment Corporation (DEC) in 1963. Minis have been frequently dedicated to a single application, rather than being used across a range of applications as mainframes are.

Large-scale integration (LSI) resulted in 1971 in the development of the microprocessor—a processor on a chip—by Marcian "Ted" Hoff of Intel. When combined with chips for other functions, the microprocessor becomes a microcomputer—the first of which was introduced in 1975. The founders of Apple started selling their machine in 1977. But the real microcomputer revolution was launched in 1981, when IBM entered the field with its IBM PC. Capitalizing on its credibility with the business community, IBM has firmly entrenched its machines (along with the IBM-compatibles) in the business environment. At present, IBM is collaborating with Apple Computer on new software environments for microcomputers.

Throughout their development, computers have undergone several generational changes. The principal characteristic of a computer generation is the fundamental technology employed to build computer circuits. These generations are shown in table 6.2. As we can see, minicomputers emerged at the end of the second computer generation, and microcomputers in the fourth generation.

Table 6.2 shows that as new technologies were introduced, vastly enhanced performance became possible, thanks to increased speeds and memory sizes. **Very large-scale integration (VLSI)** made it feasible to initially place tens of thousands of transistors, and by now millions of transistors, on a single chip. There is presently no general agreement on what would constitute a new, fifth generation of computers—we shall discuss the Japanese "fifth generation" effort in chapter 15 of the text.

TABLE 6.3

Characteristics of computers of various categories

CATEGORY	MICROCOMPUTER	MINICOMPUTER	MAINFRAME	SUPERCOMPUTER
Computer	IBM PS/2 Model 80	DEC VAX 6000 Model 450	IBM 3090 Model 600S	Cray Y-MP Model 832
Instruction execution rate	4 MIPS	31 MIPS	102 MIPS	2.7 GFLOPS
Machine cycle time (nsec)	50	28	15	6
Main memory (Mbytes)	1–16	128–192	128–2048	256
Price (in thousands of dollars)	7–12	700	13,000	5,000–20,000

Before we discuss the four computer categories in some detail, let us look at table 6.3, which illustrates the capabilities of various computer categories in terms of data on their more prominent representatives. It is difficult to make direct speed comparisons between machines in various categories (and of different vendors). Generally, uniform benchmark programs are run on various machines to make comparisons.

Computer speed is very roughly determined by two measures: instruction execution rate and machine cycle time (the speed of the circuitry). The instruction execution rate is measured in millions of instructions per second (MIPS), but since different machines have instructions of different power, this measure can serve only as a tentative means of comparison. In supercomputers, this measure is replaced by the count of billions of floating-point operations performed per second (GFLOPS, or gigaflops). Thus, a machine whose speed is 1 GFLOP can add or multiply a billion pairs of numbers in a single second!

Machine cycle time is most frequently used to rate microcomputers. In their case, this measure is generally expressed as internal clock speed in megahertz (MHz)—an inverse of machine cycle time. Thus, a 20 MHz microcomputer has a cycle time of 50 nsec.

A graphic comparison of the speeds of various computer categories is offered in figure 6.4.

Microcomputers

Although microcomputers were the last to arrive on the computer scene, they redefined it completely, to the extent that some observers claim that at some future point microprocessor-based machines will replace all other computer classes. A **microcomputer** is built around a microprocessor—a processor on a chip. With the use of very large-scale integration (VLSI), computer designers can now place more than a million transistors on a silicon chip the size of one's fingernail, so that the chip can contain a complex CPU and even ancillary circuits.

FIGURE 6.4

Relative computing speeds
for various machine
categories.

(John W. Verity,
"Supercomputers: Brute
Strength—and a Sensitive
Issue." Reprinted from April
30, 1990 issue of *Business
Week* by special permission,
copyright © 1990 by
McGraw-Hill, Inc.)

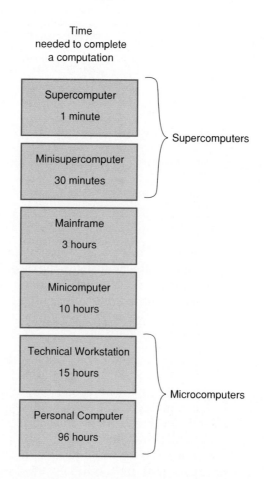

Time
needed to complete
a computation

Supercomputer
1 minute

Minisupercomputer
30 minutes

⎫ Supercomputers

Mainframe
3 hours

Minicomputer
10 hours

Technical Workstation
15 hours

Personal Computer
96 hours

⎫ Microcomputers

As the low-end computers, microcomputer systems typically cost from three to fifteen thousand dollars, depending on the processor chip and also on the peripherals configured. The most powerful microcomputers are often more costly; these **technical workstations** support technical design with high-resolution graphic processing (Sun Microsystems is a well-known vendor of such workstations).

Microcomputers are frequently called personal computers (PCs), in reference to their most common application. Indeed, unlike other machine classes, microcomputer systems are very frequently selected, configured, and installed by end users. We shall therefore return to this vital computer category in chapter 9, studying micros in the context of end-user computing.

An employee equipped with a PC can locally run productivity software—typically word processing, spreadsheets, and database management programs. The same person may also be connected to the PCs used by other members of his or her workgroup, and, further, into a computing network to access other information systems both within and outside the company (as shown in figure 2.3). In this sense, a microcomputer system becomes a personal workstation. Generally speaking, a computer **workstation** is the software-controlled hardware that enables its user to interact with a computer system; such a workstation may be a microcomputer dedicated to a single user or a video display terminal (VDT) connected to a mainframe.

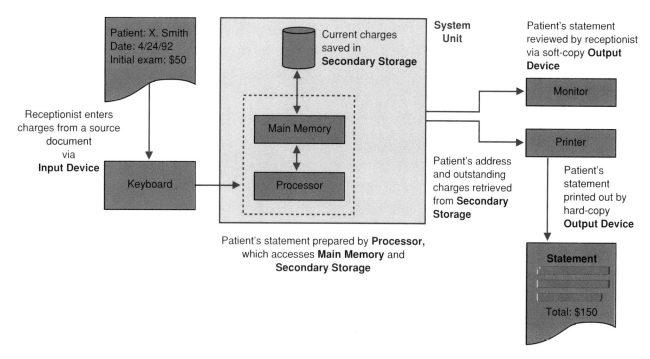

Patient: X. Smith
Date: 4/24/92
Initial exam: $50

Current charges
saved in
Secondary Storage

**System
Unit**

Patient's statement
reviewed by receptionist
via soft-copy **Output
Device**

Monitor

Receptionist enters
charges from a source
document
via
Input Device

Main Memory

Keyboard

Processor

Printer

Patient's address
and outstanding
charges retrieved
from **Secondary
Storage**

Patient's
statement
printed out by
hard-copy
Output Device

Patient's statement prepared by **Processor,**
which accesses **Main Memory** and
Secondary Storage

Statement

Total: $150

FIGURE 6.5

A microcomputer in a small business: a dental-office system handles patient billing.

On the other hand, a microcomputer is frequently a sole information processor in a small business. Figure 6.5 illustrates how a small business—in the figure, a dentist's office—may be equipped with a microcomputer system which handles all its computational needs. To review the role of various system components, we show in the figure one of the functions handled by the system—patient billing. Specialized software packages are on the market for virtually all—however small—business segments. Retailers are now specializing in some forty segments of the microcomputer market, from auto repair shops to beauty salons (Hooper, 1990).

Many microcomputers and technical workstations are now built around microprocessors called reduced instruction set computers (RISCs). In such machines, relatively few simple instructions are implemented in the microprocessor, which results in very high execution speeds. For example, a RISC microprocessor from MIPS Computer Systems, employed in various workstations, performs at about 50 MIPS (Fisher, 1991). Of course, these machines have simpler instructions than minis or mainframes they may be compared to (see table 6.3)—instruction counts are not a precise speed comparison!

The principal manufacturers of microcomputers used in the business environment are IBM, with its PC and the newer PS/2 series, and Apple Corporation (whose share is far smaller) with its Macintosh series. Companies that furnish IBM-compatible machines, such as Compaq, Leading Edge, Zenith, and many others are also a force in this market. Traditionally, the IBM microcomputers furnished a character-based interface, while machines made by Apple provided graphically oriented interfaces. With the availability of windowing software for IBM's DOS operating system (such as Windows from Microsoft) and with the

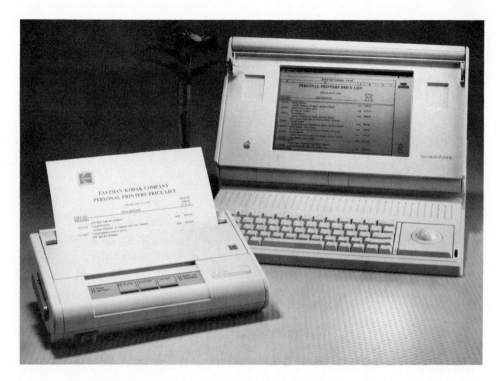

newer Presentation Manager for the IBM microcomputers running OS/2, graphical user interfaces (GUI) have come into general use. We shall discuss these interfaces further in section 9.2.

As microprocessor chips increase in power, microcomputers built around such chips are able to transcend their application as strictly personal computers and evolve toward *multiuser microcomputer systems.* Microcomputers such as IBM PS/2 Model 80 (built around the Intel 80386 chip) or Apple's Macintosh II (built around the Motorola 68020 chip) permit several users to share one system. Each user has his or her own keyboard monitor workstation, and the system is managed by an operating system such as UNIX that supports several users working concurrently. Even more powerful microcomputers are built around faster microprocessor chips—Intel 80486 and Motorola 68040. However, many elect to use the growing power of micros in a single-function application. Such applications include the use of micros as technical workstations for design applications and as so-called servers in local area networks (see chapter 7) that manage databases, support desktop publishing, or perform image processing.

Our general view of microcomputers is still that of desktop machines (even though in some cases the system unit goes under the desk, as in the IBM PS/2 Model 80). However, the needs of organizations have given rise to several far more portable machines—for example, laptops, notebook computers, and handheld computers.

Laptop computers combine all computer components, including peripherals other than the printer, in a single package that generally weighs ten to fifteen pounds. Because they are battery-powered, laptops can operate for extensive periods of time without external power sources. By moving processing power out

PALMTOPS IN THE HANDS OF NINTENDO SALES REPS

Nintendo of America, known for its skillful merchandising of video games, has equipped its 130 sales representatives with handheld computers—Data Partners from Panasonic. The sales reps monitor the company's products in retail stores by entering into the palmtops fourteen items of sales data, including sales floor and warehouse inventories, prices, and shelf space. They also use the palmtops to conduct on-site consumer surveys and keep track of their own work hours and expenses. By connecting a palmtop unit to a telephone via a modem, reps are able to transfer the data to the minicomputer located at corporate headquarters in Redmond, Washington, over the Tymnet network offered by McDonnell Douglas. This host computer processes the data overnight and makes management reports available the following morning.

Each rep tracks the stock of 160 game titles in 15 to 110 stores. Under the old manual system, reps had to fill out multipart forms with all this information. The forms were mailed to headquarters, where the data were keyboarded into the minicomputer. The lapse between the store visit and the time the processed information was made available to management was often as long as thirty to sixty days. The untimely information was almost worthless.

The new system provides the twenty-four-hour information turnaround necessary to compete in the toy industry, with its fickle consumers. The advantage of prompt information combines to produce a significant competitive edge with overall Nintendo merchandising strategy, which avoids saturating the market with products and attempts to heighten consumers' desire for the games by delivering to the stores just enough of them to create a demand for another delivery.

The low accuracy of data entry from handwritten figures has been replaced by an accuracy rate approaching 99 percent. The reps are also free to spend more time with customers and retailers, which results in enhanced service.

The eighteen-ounce handheld units are configured with 256 Kbytes of main memory (expandable to 1.5 Mbytes) and run under the MS-DOS operating system. They run a communications program that permits them to receive memos, product information updates, and instructions from the host minicomputer.

Based in part on Richard Pastore, "Handheld PCs Aid Nintendo Sales Reps." *Computerworld*, August 7, 1989, p. 39.

of the office and at the same time enabling the laptop carrier to communicate with the office via the telephone, laptops offer competitive advantage to many a company that uses them to support its salespeople in the field (Depke, 1991). Field-force automation has also changed corporate business processes; for example, Citibank conducts its internal field auditing with the help of laptops (Otte, 1990). However, simply equipping the salesforce with laptops is an action quite easily imitated by competitors. To seek sustainable advantage, companies have to incorporate this technology into a larger system which builds on a lasting business strength and which keeps evolving. Among the well-known vendors of laptops are GRiD Systems and Toshiba. Small printers for these systems are also available, for example from Kodak (see photo 6.3).

Even smaller than laptops are *notebook computers,* which weigh about five pounds (see photo 6.2b). This market is dominated by Compaq's LTE series. Some laptop and notebook computers are now providing processing power equal to that of midrange desktops.

Palmtop (or handheld) computers weigh around one pound. Along with general-purpose machines (which, however, do not use disks), these computers also include specialized devices for data collection. Handheld computers may show only an eight-line display, but they can be used to a great advantage in retail shops or in warehouses to store data about available products; data that can then be transmitted over telephone lines to a company's mini or mainframe.

In chapter 2, we introduced pen-based notepad computers. This special kind of highly portable machine has a liquid crystal display (LCD) screen built into its top panel. Instead of a keyboard or a mouse, the user employs a penlike stylus to fill out a form that appears on the screen, to edit text, to enter or modify a drawing, or to take notes. We shall encounter these very promising machines again in section 4 of the present chapter.

Minicomputers

Before microcomputers entered the scene, the smallest category of computers had been the **minicomputers (minis).** They entered the business scene from scientific and engineering applications, and they are still often used as dedicated processors for computer-assisted design (CAD) or on-line transaction processing (OLTP), where real-time demands of fast response have to be met. They are also employed as corporate machines in midsized organizations or as departmental computers in larger firms, where they communicate with personal computers on the one hand and with the corporate mainframe on the other (see figure 3.1 for such a three-tier system). The price of minis typically ranges from $100,000 to $700,000. The principal vendors are DEC, IBM, Hewlett-Packard, Data General and Wang. A midrange system is shown in photo 6.4.

PHOTO 6.4

A midrange departmental computer supports a number of users in a networked environment. The DPS 6000 model from Bull NH Information Systems (of Waltham, Massachusetts), shown here in the background, is available in a great variety of configurations and costs and can support up to 300 users.

In recent years, a perceptible squeeze has been occurring in this midrange market, with microcomputers connected into local area networks and technical workstations taking over its lower end, and with other applications migrating to mainframes. The skillful introduction by IBM of its Application System/400 series of minis has given a certain boost to this computing domain.

Mainframes

Although it is difficult at this time to say where the mini category ends and mainframes begin, the largest computers in general use are considered **mainframes.** Located in specially designed data centers (see color plate 2), mainframes require extensive professional support. The cost of building and equipping a data center whose mainframe (IBM 3090 Model 200S) costs only $5 million may run to some $24 million, not including personnel or other running costs (Connolly, 1988). This is the reason many corporations are consolidating their mainframes in as few data centers as possible, or even outsourcing them to outside vendors (see chapter 17).

Mainframe costs range from $2 million to $12 million and more. These systems are often leased, at a cost of $100,000 to $250,000 a month. Here, IBM is the undisputed world leader, with its System/390 and the newer ES/9000 series. Unisys, Control Data, Amdahl, and DEC are its major U.S. competitors, while Fujitsu and Hitachi are becoming important Japanese contenders.

Many powerful peripherals may be managed by a mainframe or, actually, by dedicated input/output processors called channels. Mainframe systems may include thousands of on-line terminals which access an organizational database of many billions of bytes. Major organizational applications, such as transaction processing or management reporting systems, are often run on a mainframe, which then acts to integrate organizational information processing. Thus, in many organizations a mainframe plays the role of the central server of information processing services in a large network (Moad, 1990).

An example of a mainframe-based configuration is shown in figure 6.6. This configuration is the central computer of a midsized distributor company with $200 million in sales.

FIGURE 6.6

A mainframe configuration.

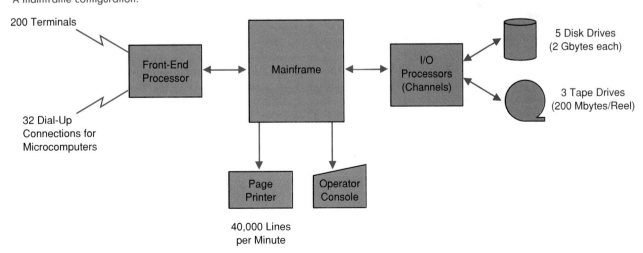

WHY MANY APPLICATIONS ARE DOWNSCALED

Shearson Lehman Hutton, the financial securities arm of American Express, implements its equity-trading systems on microcomputers, including IBM's RISC-based workstation, RS/6000. Here is the simple cost calculation behind Shearson Lehman Hutton's move. One of the firm's applications, requiring a total of 2,000 MIPS can be delivered by microcomputers at about $1,000 per million instructions per second of performance. "Were we to mount the same application on one of our IBM 3090 mainframes—even assuming that we could—it would cost us some $150,000 per CPU MIPS alone," says the firm's MIS manager. (But don't forget, the MIPS are not *quite* the same.)

Based on Leila Davis, "Where Open Systems Are Making Headway." *Datamation,* May 1, 1990, p. 58.

In the present computing environment, many applications are being "down-scaled"; or moved from mainframes to smaller machines—often microcomputers. The above vignette explains why.

Mainframes are sometimes configured with two or more central processors sharing the same memory in a so-called **multiprocessor** configuration. For example, the IBM 3090 model 600S system listed in table 6.3 is a multiprocessor that includes six processors. Aside from the obvious advantage of higher processing speed, the machine offers the additional benefit of higher reliability: should one of the processors fail, the others keep running.

Supercomputers

The most powerful computers, which are able to carry out billions of arithmetic operations per second, are called **supercomputers.** Supercomputers exploit several design approaches, all based on **parallel processing** at some level of computer design. In this type of processing, impressive speeds are achieved by carrying out a large number of operations simultaneously. Thus, many pairs of operands may be processed in parallel in a vector processor that contains a pipe-lined arithmetic-logic unit, which is broken down into segments that are all capable of working on pairs of operands at the same time. Some machines contain an array of multiple arithmetic-logic units, all applying the same operation to a different operand pair. Yet other designs comprise a large number of processors carrying out their tasks in parallel.

Supercomputers may be used to model any phenomenon that can be described by a set of equations. These machines have traditionally been used to solve mathematical problems in physics, to forecast weather, and to design rockets. More recently, with the availability of new software and with the increased sophistication of organizational computing, supercomputers have moved from the scientific laboratories into business organizations (Abbott, 1991). Some firms use them in a more traditional fashion—to help design cars or telecommunications networks—while others extend their use to determine the degree of risk in an investment or to find a trading opportunity.

SUPERCOMPUTING FOR COMPETITIVE ADVANTAGE

The investment firm of Goldman, Sachs & Co. of New York sells mortgage-backed securities: they combine outstanding mortgages into a pool and offer investors shares in it. As the mortgages are paid off, the investors receive the principal and interest payments. However, if interest rates fall, many mortgages are paid off prematurely and the yield on the investment goes down.

Goldman, Sachs has developed a mathematical model that predicts the prepayment rate depending on a number of variables, such as interest rates and the age of the mortgages. Based on this model, the firm decides to include or not include a particular mortgage in an investment pool. When the model was run on DEC VAXcluster minicomputers, it took two days—and the firm had to forego many investment opportunities because decisions could not be made fast enough. Now, a more sophisticated model is run by buying time on a Cray II supercomputer at the Minnesota Supercomputing Center in Minneapolis (one of several such machines run by consortia of major universities). Goldman, Sachs obtains the answer within an hour—and the timely information is now a useful competitive tool.

Based on James Daly, "Step Closer to Home." *Computerworld*, January 9, 1989, pp. 23, 26.

Large supercomputers range in price from $5 million to $25 million; Cray Research is the best known company in the field, although Fujitsu of Japan has also been competing very aggressively.

Minisupercomputers, which also excel in making fast computations, although they are increasingly put to such tasks as database searching, typically cost between $100,000 and $1 million. Among the vendors of these machines are Convex Computer and Alliant Computer Systems. Like the more powerful supercomputers, minisupercomputers are still plagued by lack of software, particularly software based on technologies accessible in a corporate (rather than laboratory) setting.

Minisupercomputers are most often built on the principle of parallel processing with a large number of microprocessors. This is in contrast to the large supercomputers, which are built as an extension of the mainframe concept, with a single processor, or perhaps two or four extremely powerful processors, possessing specialized circuitry for parallel arithmetic on many pairs of numbers (as we previously discussed).

Recently, this traditional supercomputing concept has been challenged by systems that lash together dozens or even thousands of microprocessors. The idea is rather simple from the economic point of view: if a thousand microprocessors costing $50 each can be put together to work in parallel, the processor obtained would be both much cheaper and much faster than a traditional supercomputer. For this to be feasible, a program must be broken down into many tasks, each of them running on a different processor. This presents many problems to solve, including dividing the work among the processors (many classes of programs are difficult to make parallel), ensuring efficient communication among parallel processors, and building up a software base for this new technology.

However, despite the problems, there is an inexorable trend toward parallel processing with multiple micros. These machines are often used to search large databases. The Internal Revenue Service employs a parallel system made by Sequent Computer Systems (which can link up to thirty microprocessors), running an Oracle database management system, to respond to taxpayers' questions. Teradata Corporation offers a specialized **database machine** (also called a back-end computer) for fast database searching. The machine, which may include up to 286 processors, has been installed by Citibank, K Mart, and AT&T, among other corporations.

Another important application of these machines is on-line transaction processing (OLTP), where they offer the advantage of scalability: system performance improves roughly in proportion to the number of processors added. Computer Language Research of Carrolton, Texas, which supplies tax-processing services to large accounting firms and corporate clients, is the largest on-line tax service in the United States. The firm believes that a parallel processor offers the advantage of adding processors only at peak times, which are a characteristic of this business segment. This flexibility gives the company substantial savings (Leibs, 1990).

The most challenging approach in supercomputing is the development of *massively parallel processing,* which is generally considered to involve a system employing over 128 processors (see color plate 3). Particularly well known, and currently the fastest (Markoff, 1991), is the Connection Machine developed by Thinking Machines of Cambridge, Massachusetts. This machine may include up to 65,096 specially designed 1-bit processors. Two such machines were installed by Dow Jones & Company to provide an on-line information retrieval service that lets a user unskilled in this task access information from the business press. Parallel machines are indeed an excellent vehicle for complex queries. The future importance of supercomputing via massively parallel processing is underscored by the fact that Japan has launched a national research and development program in this area, similar to its fifth generation program for the development of artificial intelligence, which we will discuss in chapter 15.

6.3 SECONDARY STORAGE

The existing variety of memory technologies, combined with the fact that only a small fraction of the programs and data stored in memory are actually used by the processor within an immediate time frame, make it possible to organize computer memories into a hierarchy. Secondary memories provide the high-capacity and relatively inexpensive back end of this hierarchy. Programs and data stored in these memories are brought into the main memory as required by the processor. Magnetic technologies (disks and tapes) are now being challenged by optical disks.

Memory Hierarchy

Throughout the history of computers, the demand for memory has grown steadily. A variety of memory technologies offers a trade-off between fast speed on the one hand and low cost and high capacity on the other. Computer memories are therefore organized into a hierarchy. At the top of this hierarchy, the fastest memory units are actually registers included in the CPU, where data are brought in to be manipulated by the arithmetic-logic unit. Many machines also include a fast semiconductor **cache memory** in their processors, where data and instructions may be transferred from the main memory prior to their use by the processor. As we know, semiconductor main memory is used to store the programs currently being processed (or their active parts), as well as the data they currently need or produce. All these memories are electronic and therefore fast. Since they contain no moving parts they are highly reliable. But electronic memories are volatile: their contents are lost when power is turned off.

Secondary storage devices and the media associated with them form the lower stages of the memory hierarchy. These devices offer nonvolatile, permanent means of storing large volumes of programs and data. To be used by the processor, these programs and data items must first be transferred to the main memory. The principal device for on-line storage today is the magnetic disk. The medium used for archival storage (and thus, in a sense, tertiary rather than secondary memory) is magnetic tape. Optical disks suffer from the disadvantage of slower speeds, but their higher storage capacities make them a competitor of the magnetic media as a means for secondary storage.

The memory hierarchy is illustrated in figure 6.7.

FIGURE 6.7

The memory hierarchy.

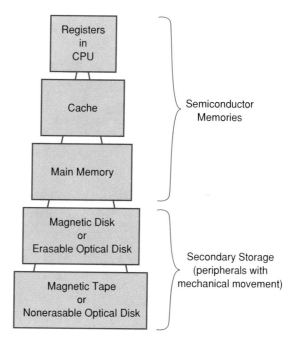

FIGURE 6.8

The design of a magnetic disk.

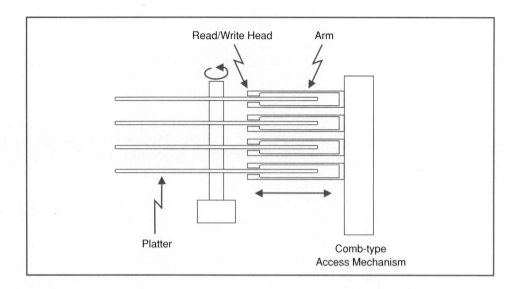

FIGURE 6.8

The design of a magnetic disk.

Magnetic Disks

Generally, secondary memories store data records, be they records of customer orders, a firm's employees, or airline flights. We shall further discuss the organization of records into files and databases in chapter 8. Magnetic disks afford the capability of both direct (random) and sequential access to records. **Sequential access** means that all records must be accessed in the sequence in which they are stored until the desired record is reached. **Direct access** to a record means that the record can be accessed by its disk address, without the need to access any intermediate records. It is this capability of direct access that has made the magnetic disk (known as the DASD—for direct-access storage device) a ubiquitous secondary storage device.

The principal varieties of magnetic disk are hard disks, which are employed in computers of all categories, and diskettes and microdisks, which are employed in microcomputers.

The design of a hard disk is shown in figure 6.8. The disk pack, which is the storage medium, consists of a stack of platters and spins continually. The platters are coated with a thin film, and data are stored in concentric circles, called tracks, on each of the two surfaces of the platter. Data are accessed by a comblike assembly of read/write heads, one of which flies over or under each surface without touching it (unless a "disk crash" occurs).

Read/write heads move together as a group horizontally, as shown in figure 6.8. Thus, the same track on each surface can be accessed when the read/write heads move to a given position. Such a set of tracks is called a **cylinder.** For faster access, consecutive records are laid out "vertically" in cylinders (rather than across a platter's surface); when a cylinder is filled, the next records are placed on the next cylinder.

To access a particular disk address, the disk unit:

1. Electronically selects the head which flies over or under the appropriate surface (this takes place in a negligible amount of time).

2. Moves the access mechanism to the desired track (this seek time may take, for example, 20 msec).

3. Continues rotational delay until the proper address is under the head and the data can be accessed (this may take some 8 msec).

Thus, hard-disk access time is typically 10 to 30 milliseconds. As soon as a disk address has been accessed, data are transferred from the disk at a very fast rate of up to 10 Mbytes per second. Disk capacity ranges from 100 Mbytes to 2 Gbytes. For example, a 100-Mbyte drive may consist of 11 platters, which provide 20 surfaces (the top and bottom surfaces are generally not used for storage), 400 tracks, and 12,500 bytes per track.

Many disks, in particular the hard disks used in microcomputers, are sectored. Each surface is then divided into pie-shaped sectors (which typically contain 256 bytes). These sectors are the smallest individually addressable elements in such disks.

Larger systems most often use hard disks with interchangeable media: a disk pack may be removed and stored off-line. On the other hand, in microcomputers (and sometimes in larger systems), nonremovable and hermetically sealed Winchester disks are employed. Their capacities commonly range from 10 to 115 Mbytes. In microcomputers, these devices are usually internal: they are packaged into the system unit.

In microcomputer systems, the most popular secondary storage media are diskettes and microdisks, which are placed in internal drives for access. Since these drives are not in permanent rotation, as hard disks are, access to the data stored on these media is much slower. The older, flexible diskette (floppy disk) has a diameter of 5 1/4 inches, while the newer microdisks are rigid disks 3 1/2 inches in diameter. Storage capacity of these devices ranges from 320 Kbytes to 1.4 Mbytes. They provide a convenient medium for distributing programs and data.

Magnetic Tape

Magnetic tape has an obvious limitation: it permits only sequential access. However, it is the least expensive of the commonly used storage media and is broadly used as a backup medium, though it may be used for on-line secondary storage in batch systems.

Systems other than microcomputers generally use detachable tape reels (see photo 6.5). The tape is coated with a magnetizable film, across which data bytes are stored in nine tracks: 8 bits plus 1 parity bit added for error detection, so that the number of 1's in all nine tracks is odd (see figure 6.9). A typical 2,400-foot reel stores 50 Mbytes of data, which may be transferred to the main memory at a rate of some 2 Mbytes per second. As the tape moves from the supply reel to the take-up reel in a tape drive, the read/write head of the drive reads or writes the consecutive bytes, as desired.

Tape cartridges, commonly used to back up hard disks in microcomputer systems, are now also used in larger systems. They are much easier to handle than detachable reels. Cartridge capacity is over 200 Mbytes in some cases, with a data transfer rate of 3 Mbytes per second. Recently developed digital data storage (DAT) cartridges, which are intended only for backup purposes, are able to back up 1.3 Gbytes of data on a single cartridge. Since this equals some twenty-six

PHOTO 6.5

Libraries of magnetic tape
reels remain in the data
archives of most
organizations.

PHOTO 6.5

Libraries of magnetic tape reels remain in the data archives of most organizations.

FIGURE 6.9

A fragment of magnetic tape.

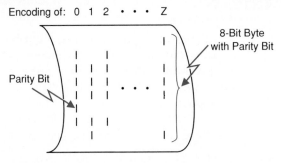

Encoding of: 0 1 2 • • • Z

Parity Bit

8-Bit Byte
with Parity Bit

reels of tape, this high-density technology may enable MIS managers to place unattended minicomputers at user sites without fear that they will neglect to back up their data.

To facilitate the management of large numbers of reels or cartridges at mainframe sites, automated tape libraries are available (Hamilton, 1990). However, some of the large installations are moving away from the conventional tape technologies, as illustrated by the Boston University vignette.

Optical Disks

Optical technologies, which offer far higher storage densities and thus far higher capacities than magnetic devices, promise to revolutionize secondary storage. The most exciting prospect is that of expanding computer capabilities in the direction of multimedia: data, text, audio, and video information may be cost-effectively stored on optical disks. Like magnetic disks, these devices offer random access to information. The information is written with high-intensity laser beams and read with lower-intensity beams. Precise beam focusing by the laser makes high storage-density possible. The main disadvantage at present is slower access as compared to magnetic disks.

BOSTON UNIVERSITY ERASES TAPE

The administrative data center of Boston University has fully phased out the use of conventional reel-to-reel and cartridge tape drives. The main motivation was to avoid the need for human intervention and to ensure faster access to archival data. The move is a part of a broader plant of going to unattended operation of the data center in the future.

The 16,000-volume tape library was replaced by two mass-storage devices manufactured by Masstor Systems Corporation of Santa Clara, California. Such a device stores data in tiny bullet-shaped tape cartridges, located in honeycomb-type cells and automatically mounted in the drive by a robotic arm. The installed units have the capacities of 220 Gbytes and 440 Gbytes. Six jobs, involving maintaining the tape library and mounting the tapes, were eliminated in the process.

Based on Rosemary Hamilton, "University Erases Tape from Computer Center." *Computerworld,* January 21, 1991, p. 29.

CD-ROM and Videodisks

The most common type of optical disk is **CD-ROM** (for Compact Disk-Read Only Memory). Such disks are used to distribute factory-recorded information. A CD-ROM disk is read by an optical disk unit—a computer peripheral, with an access time of 300 to 400 msec. Some microcomputers, for example, those made by HeadStart Technologies and by Tandy, come with built-in CD-ROM drives. A single 5 1/4-inch CD-ROM disk has a capacity of at least 550 Mbytes and may thus hold (Laub, 1986):

- The text of 150,000 printed pages (that is, enough text to fill 250 "big" books)
- Sharp images of 15,000 pages of business documents (enough to fill two tall filing cabinets)
- The contents of 760 5 1/4-inch diskettes of 720 Kbyte capacity
- A crisp color picture and ten seconds of narration for each of 3,000 segments of an educational or training program (almost eight hours of content)
- Any multimedia information that can be represented digitally

As an example, a single CD-ROM disk stores the text of twenty-one volumes of *The New Groiler Electronic Encyclopedia,* with 33,000 articles and a total of nine million words. CD-ROMs on the market now contain manuals for automobile repair and full-color guides to hotels and restaurants.

By applying techniques of image compression, the DVI Technology from Intel makes it possible to store on a single CD-ROM disk seventy-two minutes of motion video—which can be played at thirty frames per second for a full-motion effect.

This potential of CD-ROM in electronic multimedia publishing—in data, text, graphics, audio, and video information—is only beginning to be tapped. The possible uses for CD-ROM in corporate communications, just-in-time training, and new product development are numerous and varied.

PHOTO 6.6

A "jukebox" of write-once-read-many times (WORM) optical disks may be used to store very high volumes of data. You see here the RV64 Optical Jukebox from Digital Equipment Corporation (DEC), with its robotic arm for handling the disks and with a slot that permits the operator to insert another disk without interrupting the operation. With 64 optical disks installed at a time, this device can store up to 128 gigabites of data.

CD-ROM technology was originally developed on the basis of the larger (8-inch) *videodisks,* which were invented as a medium for video games but have since been widely used by retailers such as Sears or Florsheim to help customers select from a wide array of products. In a similar fashion, videodisks are used by realtors and automobile manufacturers. Lack of standardization has prevented videodisks from entering the market as a computer peripheral; standardized CD-ROM memory is, on the other hand, supported by a variety of software.

WORM Optical Disks

WORM (write-once-read-many-times) optical disk systems enable users to write on blank disks. However, the information written on the disk cannot be altered afterwards. WORM disks have advanced from the province of microcomputers to larger machines. A typical disk has 150 to 250 msec access time and 262 Kbytes per second data transfer time. A single larger disk may have capacity of 2 Gbytes, and this medium is now cheaper than most tapes.

WORM systems play a major role in office information systems, since they are used as a document storage medium. Particularly useful in this regard are WORM "jukeboxes," which may contain 16 to 2,000 optical disk platters (see photo 6.6). An addressed platter is loaded into the drive and spun to speed. This makes terabytes of storage available for access in as short a time as 10 seconds.

The Department of Motor Vehicles of the State of California uses a WORM-based system for storing the pictures, signatures, and fingerprints of the holders of driver's licenses. The Veterans Administration employs a similar system to handle benefit claims, with large savings over paper-based systems. We will further discuss this issue in chapter 16.

Erasable Optical Disks

Both the CD-ROM and WORM disks suffer from a significant limitation: the information cannot be changed once it has been written on a disk.

Erasable optical (or, actually, magneto-optical) disks are full-fledged competitors of magnetic disks. Their access time is slower (48 msec for fast ones, with

a 1 Mbyte-per-second transfer rate) because of their large read/write heads, which contain both a laser and a magnetic coil, but their capacities are high for a microcomputer configuration (250 Mbytes to 1 Gbyte). Both the drives and the 5 1/4-inch cartridges (see photo 6.7) are expensive. An attempt to use an erasable optical disk as the secondary memory in the NeXT microcomputer failed due to the slowness of the device. However, erasable optical disks show great promise: together with the high capacity of an individual cartridge, this device would offer in effect an infinite capacity, because the cartridge is removable (as opposed to the fixed Winchester-type magnetic disks). The removable cartridge may also be securely stored.

6.4 INPUT DEVICES

T he traditional input device—the keyboard—is not an efficient means to enter large amounts of data. Also, in some countries, much more so than in the United States, managers and professionals resist using it. Cursor-control devices, such as a mouse, are a partial solution to the second problem. A large and growing number of technologies have been developed to avoid keyboarding data. We shall review various technologies for direct data entry.

Keyboards

The keyboard is the principal input device in virtually all microcomputers. It is also a component of the video display terminals employed for remote access to larger machines. A variety of special-purpose keyboards are used for data input in various industries, such as fast-food outlets.

When employed as a principal method of data entry, keyboarding by data entry personnel is highly inefficient. At data entry stations, keyboarded data are transcribed onto a disk volume (key-to-disk entry) or onto a tape. The disk pack or

VIRTUAL REALITY AND DATA VISUALIZATION

Continuing the research initiated at MIT's Media Lab, researchers and engineers are developing systems that can revolutionize the way we control computers—and that extend far beyond the keyboard and the mouse. For example, Paul McAvinney of Carnegie Mellon University has developed a "sensor frame" that fits over the display screen. When you reach into it, the frame's sensors detect your hand's movement and reproduce the hand on the screen. With the appropriate software, your hand is able to manipulate graphics objects represented on the screen in three dimensions—you can move them, squeeze them, and so forth. These systems are said to create artificial— or virtual—reality.

Business applications are slowly emerging. Data visualization with such systems may help in fighting information overload. A striking display of financial data, produced by Columbia University researchers with such a system, is shown in color plate 4.

Based in part on Schroeder, 1990, and Sandra K. Helsel and Judith P. Roth (editors), *Virtual Reality: Theory, Practice, and Promise.* Westport, Conn.: Meckler, 1991.

the tape is then mounted in the on-line drive when needed. Data entry clerks generally have to enter all the data twice for verification purposes, and the process is very labor-intensive and error-prone. Many corporations use cheaper off-shore labor for this function. However, the general trend is away from keyboarding and toward direct capture of data at the source—a process called source data automation, which we shall discuss below.

Cursor-Control Devices

A *mouse* is used to control in random fashion the cursor that appears on a video display. By rolling the mouse on a flat surface, we move the cursor in a corresponding manner. Various functions (for example, file opening or deleting) may be performed at the press of a button on the mouse. Graphical user interfaces are typically mouse-driven. The mouse, joystick, trackball, and a special penlike stylus applied to the screen are all examples of devices commonly employed in various graphics or multimedia applications.

Devices for Direct Data Entry

Many advantages are gained by entering data directly into a database (after an appropriate validation) from the source of its capture, avoiding the keyboard. Among the advantages of this source data administration are labor economies, timely availability of information in databases, and far greater data accuracy. We discussed the role of these devices in a variety of transaction processing systems in chapter 4.

As you know, electronic data interchange (EDI) is one way to avoid keyboarding. Frequently, the burden of data entry is shifted onto the customer, as it is, for example, with automatic teller machines (ATMs) or point-of-sale systems based on debit cards. The ATM vignette illustrates both the possible benefits and the customer resistance that such a system must contend with.

THE CHALLENGE OF NEW AUTOMATIC TELLER MACHINES

Fierce competition in the banking industry, along with the information-intensive nature of the business, make the use of computer and telecommunications technologies for strategic positioning mandatory. Standard ATMs have become a strategic necessity. Global ATM networks are being created: you may insert your card into an ATM in Tokyo and withdraw cash from your account in your home bank in Denver—all in ten seconds.

Banks are presently considering the development and use of ATMs that would be more than cash dispensers. These machines would be rather self-service tools for a variety of banking services, such as cashing paychecks, shopping for loans, and obtaining statement printouts. The new ATMs are expected to give the banks that use them two principal advantages:

1. They would differentiate a bank's offerings and thus become a tool for seeking strategic advantage in the financial services marketplace.

2. They would further shift data entry to the customer, thus freeing bank tellers from this duty. Bankers perceive the need to free more of their staffs for marketing their products, since a lack of staff selling time places them at a competitive disadvantage with other types of financial institutions. These other institutions have, in fact, taken a share of the market from banks in recent years.

The main problem in employing the expanded ATMs is customer resistance to dealing with machines. A possible solution is to make the interface attractive, perhaps using videos based on optical disks and, as, some bankers put it only half-jokingly, hiring designers from Disney.

Based on John Mahnke, "Banking MIS Challenged to Develop Next-Generation Self-Service ATMs." *MIS Week,* May 14, 1990, pp. 13, 17; and Edmund L. Andrews, "The Internationalization of the Cash Machine." *The New York Times,* Business Section, September 9, 1990, p. 9.

PHOTO 6.8

This image scanner also has the capabilities for storing and editing images (ScanStation 4000 from Regent Peripherals of Renton, Washington).

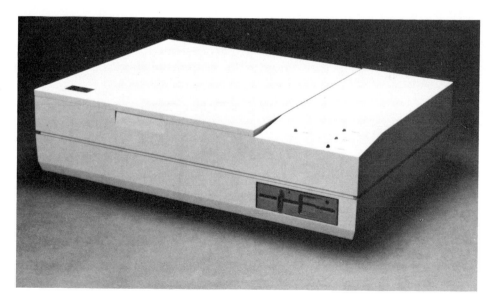

Let us review the more important technologies for direct data entry.

Image scanners are used to digitize and enter into computer memory figures,
photographs, and signed documents (see photo 6.8). As we will see, these scanners may be combined with optical character recognition software that recognizes text or codes. Thus, for example, both the illustrations and the text of a
book can be entered into a computer system, ready for modification. As we know
from part 1 of the text, image processing is a broad area of computer application.

Optical character recognition (OCR) scanners can recognize printed or typed
text and various codes and enter the corresponding characters into computer
memory. An inexpensive image scanner configured in a microcomputer system
can be combined with OCR software to read a book into a word processing or
electronic publishing file for subsequent modification. Scanners are used in larger
systems as well—for example, to enter documents, which may then be stored
on an optical disk. Bar-code scanners or wands that read bar codes have been
put to significant use in a variety of systems that give firms competitive advantage, as discussed in chapter 5. Among the many bar codes, the best known is
the universal product code (UPC) read by supermarket point-of-sale scanners.
In banking, the characteristic fonts for magnetic character recognition (MICR)
that appear on the bottoms of checks are also read by optical scanners. Photo
6.9 shows a compact bar code reader.

Smart cards, which may carry voluminous data on chips, or on laser-optic or
magnetic strips, serve as a key to many services (Kobielus, 1987).

Voice-data entry devices are able to enter limited kinds of data, such as spoken
digits or letters. If we combine such a device with one that produces spoken
output, we obtain systems which enable users—telephone users, for example—
to access databases without the need for a conventional terminal. An example
of such a system for telephone-intensive dispersal of information is DECvoice
from DEC, shown graphically in figure 6.10.

Several technologies are employed in the system. Speech (or voice) recognition
of a limited number of words (digits and "yes" and "no") uttered by any speaker
is done by an input device. Input may also be received from a touch-tone phone.
The system may respond either through a voice synthesizer that transforms a text

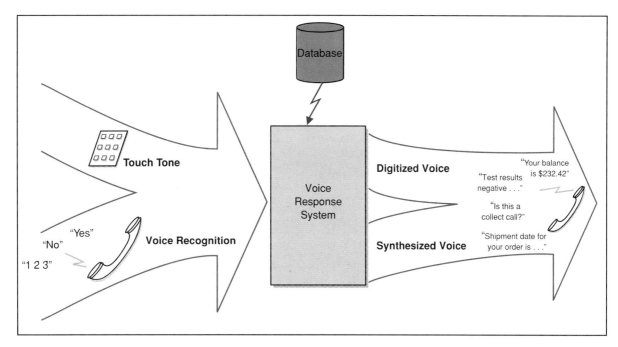

FIGURE 6.10

A voice response system makes voice-oriented database access possible.

(Adapted from Badgett, 1988, p. 39T)

represented in a character code (such as ASCII) into a spoken utterance, or with a voice digitizer that retrieves prestored speech fragments and other sounds. The entire system offers the user easy access to information.

The regional tourist agency of the French Riviera installed a system that allows callers speaking English or French to browse verbally through a database of options for booking a hotel, renting a car, or making dining reservations (Johnson, 1990). The keyword-driven system is expected to make the Riviera more accessible—and thus (combined with the well-known advantages it already enjoys) give it a competitive advantage over other destinations.

Voice-data entry is particularly advantageous in manufacturing environments, where workers' hands and eyes are busy—this technology permits them to continue what they are doing while interacting with the system.

Touch-tone telephone entry is increasingly employed to provide access to a bank account or insurance claim information (see photo 6.10)—sometimes in a rather annoying fashion. It does push a large part of the inquiry cost onto the consumer, but a lack of user acceptance is perceived as the main obstacle to the use of this technology (Leinfuss, 1989).

Handwritten characters (block-printed only) may be entered with a "pen" through a special screen located on top of notepad-size microcomputers made by such firms as GRiD Systems (see photo 6.11) or Sony (the latter recognizes Kanji characters of Japanese writing). As the vignette illustrates, some firms pursue competitive advantage by equipping their blue-collar or other workers with these palmtop computers. Devices that recognize cursive writing are not foreseeable in the near future.

THE FAMILIAR FORM OF INPUT

Since virtually all workers are familiar with handwriting, and only some with the keyboard, a number of companies are trying to derive competitive advantage from using the recently developed handheld computers that recognize block-printed handwritten characters. A user can simply "X" the screen text out or scroll the text by flicking the pen.

Best Foods Baking Group equipped its 1,500 contract truck drivers with the GridPad made by GRiD Systems in order to track deliveries of baked goods. The technology was adopted after a systems analyst performed a simple test for adequacy: he left a small machine on the counter in the

drivers' depot and disappeared. When he came back, he found drivers using the tool without any training. The company estimates that the GridPad saves $1.5 million a year in reduced billing errors, increases cash flow—and results in fewer stale bread loaves.

In the same fashion, by filling in numbers and checking off boxes on a screen, the rail workers of Southern Pacific Transportation Company do their knowledge work: tracking freight deliveries.

Based on Barbara Buell, "The Pen: Computing's Next Big Leap." *Business Week,* May 14, 1990, pp. 128–29; and Andrew Pollack, "A Battle in Pen-Based Computers." *The New York Times,* January 22, 1991, pp. D1, D5.

PHOTO 6.10

The system shown here, called RobotOperator (from Intervoice, Inc. of Richardson, Texas), replaces a human telephone operator.

Let us say you have a shipment in transit. Concerned about the status of the shipment, you call the shipping company's information line, serviced by this automatic operator device, which asks you to enter the number of your shipment document with the pushbuttons of your telephone. Speaking in the language of your choice, the RobotOperator informs you when your shipment embarked, and gives you its most recent port-of-call and its expected time of arrival.

PHOTO 6.11

A microcomputer with pen and display for entering handwritten, block-printed characters to fill forms and for activating a variety of other applications (GriDPAD from GriD Systems Corporation of Fremont, California). It weighs 4.5 pounds with its battery; lighter computer notepads are emerging as well.

6.5 OUTPUT DEVICES

The principal output devices are video displays for soft-copy and printers for hard-copy output. As we already know, devices that produce voice (speech) output are also entering the market. In chapter 16, we will also discuss computer-output microfilm (COM) technology, used to record documents on microform.

Video Displays

Computer displays have become one of the most common artifacts of our age. They display computer output on a screen and serve as the monitors in microcomputer systems and, when combined with a keyboard, as the video display terminals (VDTs) that connect users to a shared system. Much of the soft-copy output in transaction processing, decision support, and executive information systems is never printed. Progress in this area has been driven by the development of ever more sophisticated monitors, particularly for technical workstations.

PHOTO 6.12

A high-resolution display with 1664*1200 pixels (from Princeton Graphic Systems of Roswell, Georgia).

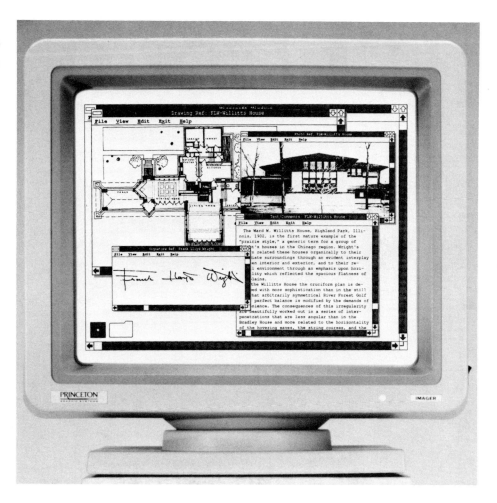

THREE-DIMENSIONAL GRAPHICS AS A COMPETITIVE WEAPON

The use of three-dimensional (3D) representations on graphics displays has enabled Chrysler Motor to reduce the time needed to develop a new automobile by 20 percent, according to a study of competitive benefits of 3D modeling done by the KPMG Peat Marwick accounting firm.

The manufacturer can use the system to view, for example, a variety of fabric and color combinations. More important, by relying on this technology, Chrysler has reorganized the way it does business with its subcontractors. Chrysler provides subcontractors with pretested 3D designs of parts and subassemblies. Those firms then use the designs to develop the parts in close correspondence with Chrysler's specs.

The use of graphic models permits firms to eliminate product prototypes and instead use a high-quality image as they refine the product. Thus, Hitachi takes its customers on "walkthroughs" of screens that represent its power plant designs. Using technical workstations in this fashion, Hitachi eliminates 30 to 75 percent of pipe cutting, welding, testing, and maintenance at the power plants. This is because most problems are removed while working with the computer model.

The Peat Marwick study recommends that firms integrate CAD modeling on technical workstations with their overall MIS efforts. If they do so, the design data obtained at the workstations can feed project management systems, costing systems, and a variety of other management information systems, including manufacturing requirements planning.

The next major advance in CAD modeling is expected to come from digital high-definition television (HDTV), currently being developed by U.S. researchers and engineers. At present, to project a workstation-generated image onto a large screen while maintaining high resolution, the image has to be placed on film—but then it cannot be manipulated by computer. Digital HDTV will make it possible to screen, transmit, and manipulate realistic, computer-generated renderings of automobiles or other products and to combine computational and real images. For example, a computer-generated car image may be seen driving through a selected real landscape.

Based on Emily Leinfuss, "3D Graphics Are Moving to MIS." *MIS Week*, May 1, 1989; and Neil Gross, "Japan's HDTV: What's Wrong with This Picture." *Business Week*, April 1, 1991, pp. 80–81.

A great variety of monochrome and color monitors is available. While monochrome monitors are sometimes preferred for pure word-processing applications, color monitors have also become very popular in the business environment. Experts expect the cathode ray tube (CRT) monitor to be gradually replaced by flat-panel displays. Today, these displays, typically based on liquid-crystal technology, may be seen in laptop, notebook, and pen-based computers: they take much less space and consume much less energy than CRTs.

Simpler monitors can display only alphanumeric characters: they typically display twenty-four lines of sixty characters each. More sophisticated are graphics monitors, which may display any image. Images are formed from tiny dots called **pixels** (for "picture element"). The smaller the dots, the greater the screen resolution and the sharper the image. The displays of graphics monitors are bit-mapped, which means that each dot can be individually controlled as to intensity and color. Images often resemble a fine photograph. For example, an advanced standard for displays, called VGA (video graphics array), has in its graphics

COMPUTERS, INFORMATION SYSTEMS, AND THEIR USE IN MANAGEMENT

COLORPLATE 1

Powerful microcomputer systems with high-resolution graphics displays. (Both systems are built around the Intel 80486 microprocessor.) (a) A desktop configuration (IBM PS/2 Model 90 XP486). (b) A configuration with the tower (floor-standing) processor (IBM PS/2 Model 95 CP486).

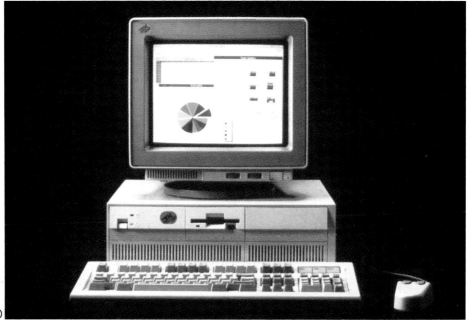

(a)

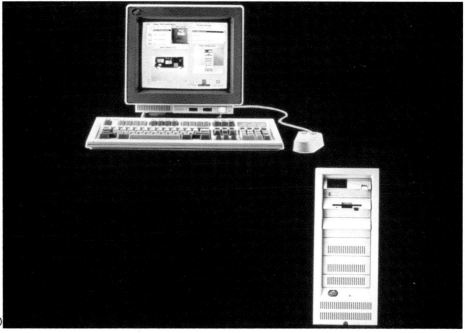

(b)

COLORPLATE 2

A mainframe-based data center. In the middle of the photograph you can see IBMs Model 900, the largest mainframe in the company's newest series Enterprise System/9000 (ES/9000). Operator's console, memory units, and other peripherals surround the mainframe (which is actually a multiprocessor, comprising up to six CPUs).

COLORPLATE 3

A supercomputer based on the concept of massively parallel processing. This machine, manufactured by nCUBE Corporation (of Beaverton, Oregon), may contain up to 8,192 processors! Supercomputer designs of this type are expected to be the fastest computers in the future. (The bold design of the outer shell is by frogdesign of Menlo Park, California, a leading industrial design firm.)

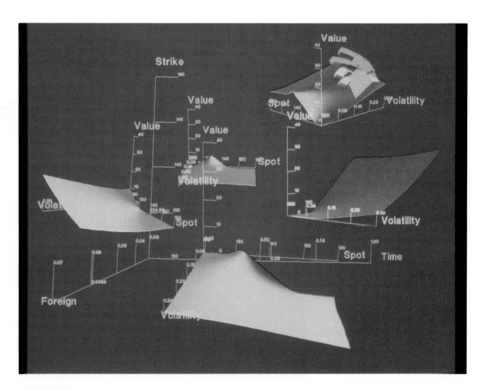

COLORPLATE 4

A display produced by an experimental system for the visualization of financial data. The user (perhaps a securities trader) explores a three-dimensional "virtual world" of geometric surfaces that represent the value of financial instruments, such as stocks or bonds, as he or she searches for the best trading strategies. A special glove detects the position of the user's hand (reproduced on the upper right), allowing the user to pick up surfaces and to move, rotate, or scale them. By doing so, the user actually manipulates variables of the securities market (for example, the interest rate) and observes the effects of these changes. Such data visualization systems will make it possible to perform "what-if" analyses on large volumes of data in MIS. (Courtesy of Clifford Beshers and Steven Feiner, Columbia University, 1991)

COLORPLATE 5

The transportation industry has been transformed by the move to electronic data interchange (EDI). Here, you can see flour being transferred from a covered hopper car on the right to the truck on the left in a center for intermodal distribution that belongs to CSX Corporation and is located near Chester, Pennsylvania. The former railroad has become a global firm that offers many modes of transportation. A major enabling factor in this transformation is CSX's EDI installation, which is one of the largest private installations of this type in the United States.

COLORPLATE 6

The very high data transmission capacities offered by fiber optics are revolutionizing computer networking. This will be the fundamental terrestrial communications medium of the coming fully digital global networks.

COLORPLATE 7

This earth station located at MCI, Yacolt, Washington, was supplied by Satellite Transmission Systems of Hauppauge, New York.

COLORPLATE 8

This very small aperture terminal (VSAT) for satellite telecommunications is used by Volkswagen of America in its network connecting 786 U.S. dealers to the data center in Warren, Michigan. The newly installed network broadcasts messages to dealers, performs credit card processing and check authorization, provides access to a database to obtain price information, and supports inventory, parts, and warranty processing. The network has replaced terrestrial telecommunications lines leased from a common carrier, at considerable savings.

COLORPLATE 9

This Network Operations Center in Bedminster, New Jersey, controls the AT&T Worldwide Intelligent Network, the most advanced telecommunications network in the world. Under control of computers located in the center, voice, data, and images flow over 2.3 billion circuit miles worldwide, with more than 75 million calls being handled a day. The video screen you see here, two stories high and 60 feet across, continuously monitors AT&T customer requirements.

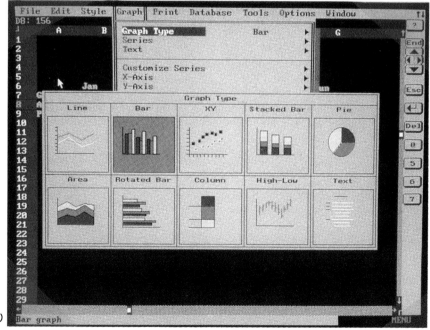

(a)

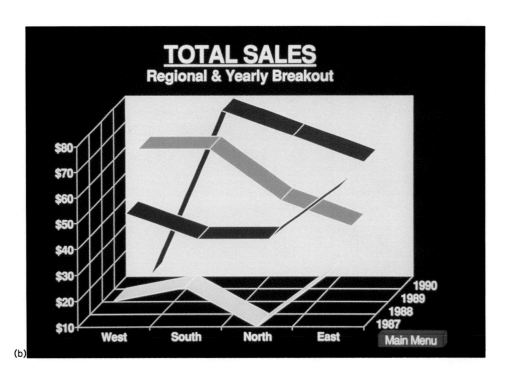

(b)

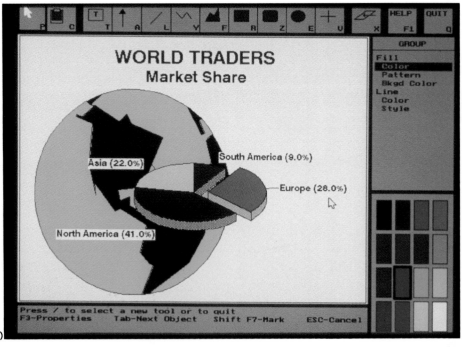

(c)

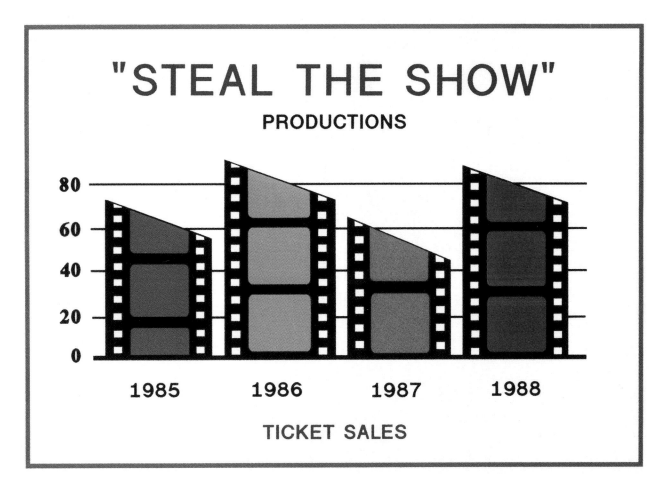

COLORPLATE 12

Reproduction of a transparency produced with the use of presentation software (Graphics Gallery by Hewlett-Packard).

COLORPLATE 13

Geographic information systems (GIS) make it possible to link map images on a VDT screen with databases for a variety of analyses. In the case shown in this photograph, a microcomputer-based GIS package was used to combine a parcel map (created with a computer-aided design software) with a tax database in order to produce a color-coded map of appraised values. This geographical visualization of data helps the decision maker, such as the tax assessor, to analyze the situation in a holistic manner. (The GIS package is MapInfo from MapInfo, Inc. of Troy, New York.)

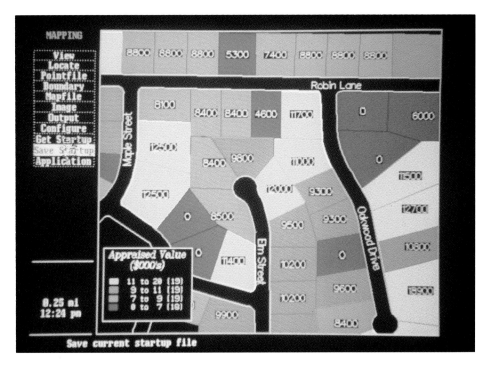

COLORPLATE 14

This machine vision system from Allen-Bradley (of Milwaukee, Wisconsin) performs quality control at CBS Records.

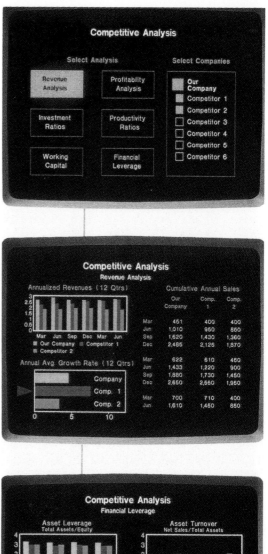

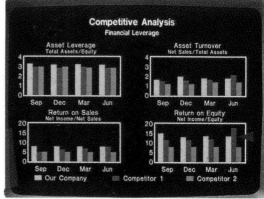

COLORPLATE 15

Competitive revenue analysis produced with an executive information system (EIS). Starting with the first screen, the decision maker "drills down" to obtain an increasingly detailed picture. We can see from the second screen that Competitor 1 has almost closed in on our company, and we can obtain the third screen to compare four financial ratios for our company and its two leading competitors in order to analyze the situation further. (The screens were obtained with Pilot EIS of Pilot Executive Software of Boston, Massachusetts.)

COLORPLATE 16

Management information systems have to work in network environments that integrate a variety of hardware and software platforms. With emerging standards, such connectivity is increasingly available. This executive information system (Commander EIS from Comshare, Inc. of Ann Arbor, Michigan) makes it possible for some of its users to work under one of the two principal operating systems used on the IBM microcomputers (DOS and OS/2), while others work on Macintosh machines (from Apple Computer). Note the graphical menu of information provided by the system.

COLORPLATE 17

A meeting room for the use of an electronic meeting system at the University of Arizona in Tucson. Such installations are provided by Ventana Corporation of Tucson, Arizona.

(a)

COLORPLATE 18

(a) With its paper-based "system" of filing ticket receipts, Northwest Airlines accumulated stacks seven feet tall and covering an area the size of a basketball court. It also kept 590 clerks busy. (b) After changing to electronic document management, the airline employs digital image processing technology to store the incoming receipts (300,000 a day) on optical disks. (c) Computer-assisted retrieval of documents is changing the office landscape at the airline. When the new document management system becomes integrated into the overall MIS of the company, a variety of management information will be easily obtainable.

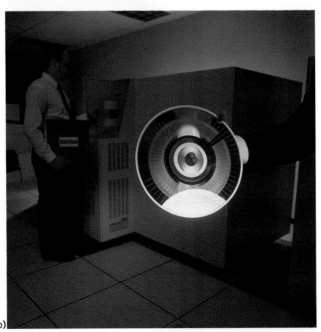

(b)

(c)

COLORPLATE 19

Computer-aided software engineering (CASE) tools are available on the desktop. Shown here is a screen with a magnified view of a data flow diagram, as well as a printed document (obtained with Excelerator of Index Technologies, Cambridge, Massachusetts).

COLORPLATE 20

Project management software assists managers in project scheduling and tracking. Shown here are two charts produced withViewpoint of Computer Aided Management Inc. of Petaluma, California. (a) A PERT chart. (b) A Gantt chart.

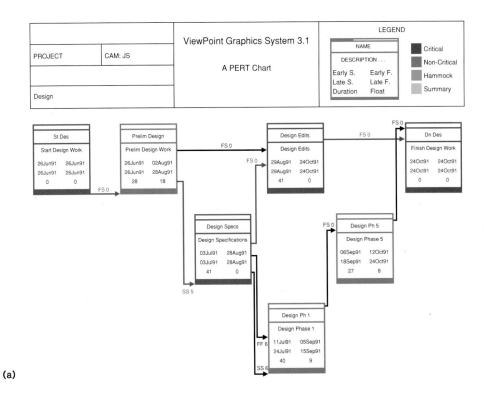

(a)

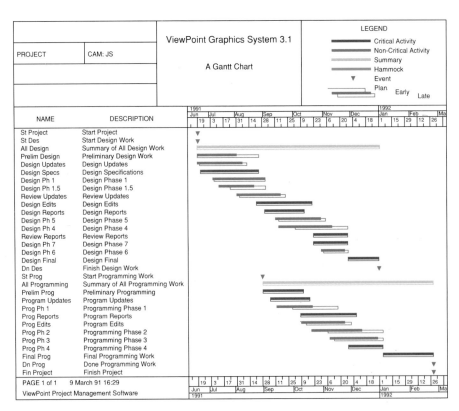

(b)

FIGURE 6.11

An X terminal displays in its windows outputs produced by applications running on a variety of computers in the network it is connected to.

(Adapted from Markoff, 1990)

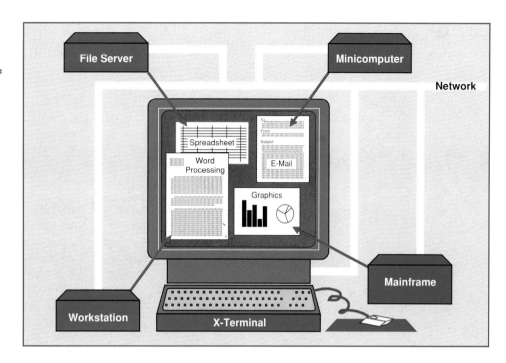

mode a resolution of 640 by 480 pixels and the ability to employ 256 colors at one time. Technical workstations offer even finer resolution and features (see photo 6.12). The use of computer-aided design (CAD) software on these workstations shortens a product's time to market and enhances a firm's competitive posture, as the vignette on three-dimensional graphics illustrates.

The proliferation of micros has made monitors the primary type of video display. What about VDTs that give users access to a larger machine? VDTs have indeed recently aroused renewed interest with the appearance of the so-called X terminals. An X terminal, which has a local processing capability thanks to a built-in microprocessor, and which includes a keyboard and a mouse but no disk drive, gives its user a window-type interface (figure 6.11). An X terminal displays outputs from several programs in different windows, just as a microcomputer monitor does. However, in the terminal's case, the actual programs that "run in the windows" are executed on other processors in the network to which the X terminal is connected (Socarras, 1991). When compared to personal computers, this terminal is often a cost-effective vehicle for the delivery of computing power to a certain class of users, since an X terminal itself costs less than a typical microcomputer used in business.

Printers and Other Hard-Copy Output Devices

A variety of technologies has been pressed into printing service—no, a paperless environment is definitely not in the cards for now.

Microcomputer systems generally include dot-matrix printers which can produce graphics or text in either a fast, draft-quality mode or more slowly in a near-letter quality mode. In some cases, microcomputer systems employ letter-quality daisy-wheel printers, which are suitable only for printing text. In recent years, the less expensive laser printers have begun to be configured in micro systems.

Laser printers print a page at a time, their print quality approaches typesetting, and they can print text in a variety of fonts as well as offer high-resolution graphics.

Larger computer systems employ either chain or band impact printers, or very fast laser printers that also ensure high-quality output.

To obtain color output, nonimpact printers based on ink-jet technology are often used. Ink-jet technology is also employed in plotters that produce graphical output and in output devices that produce transparencies for presentations.

6.6 SOFTWARE—AN OVERVIEW

The hardware of a computer system cannot directly process payroll, produce a sales report for the last quarter, or maintain the customer database. To make hardware useful, we need **software**—that is, programs that control the operation of a computer system. The trends in information systems have in most cases shifted cost concerns from hardware to software. Indeed, most of the hardware employed in the smaller systems, while not always inexpensive, has reached a commodity status (Rappaport, 1991). Since software actually customizes the hardware for specific needs, its development and maintenance is highly labor-intensive. This is reflected in the ultimate costs of a customized package as compared to the costs of an internally developed application.

Systems software manages the resources of a computer system and enables people to program in more expressive languages than the machine language of the computer. At the heart of systems software is the operating system. Other systems software includes telecommunications monitors that manage a system's communications with remote computers and terminals (see chapter 7), of which IBM's CICS is a well-known example, as well as database management systems (see chapter 8). Other software translates programs written in programming languages into machine language for execution. Once translated, programs are moved from secondary storage to the main memory by loaders and then combined with other routines by linkers—both examples of systems software. In this chapter, we shall discuss operating systems, as well as programming languages and their translators.

Another category of systems software is utilities, which perform generalized tasks in computer systems. Examples include sort/merge programs that process data files, programs that transfer data from one peripheral device to another (for example, from disk to tape), and text editors that allow the user to create and modify text files (which contain programs and data). Utility software also includes a variety of programs that assist the user in developing other software. Among these programs are debuggers and software that helps test programs under development. The general trend is to blend operating systems with software development environments.

Applications software assists a system's end users in performing various functions, be they word processing, making decisions regarding quarterly budgets, or answering customer queries by accessing a product database. Some of this software is of a more general nature and is purchased as a package (word processing packages are an example), while other software is developed internally or externally to meet the specific needs of an organization. Applications programming can be done in a variety of languages, which we shall discuss below.

The trend in the last few years has been away from the expensive development of custom-made applications software and toward the use of packages. Two types of packages are available: vertical packages that serve a well-defined market segment (for example, records management for small service businesses or manufacturing requirements planning) and horizontal packages that can perform a certain function (such as accounting, or office automation) for a range of businesses. These packages may be customized to meet some of the specific needs of a firm. We will further discuss software development and other avenues of software acquisition in Part 5 of this book.

The relationship between computer systems hardware, systems software, and application software is illustrated in figure 6.12. This "onion-skin" model indicates that the outer layers rely on the facilities furnished by the inner ones.

A large body of software has been developed to facilitate end-user computing, which we will discuss in chapter 9. While most of this software runs on microcomputers, it is not limited to that platform.

Progress in software has been made possible by the exceptional progress made in computer systems hardware over the last half century. Impressive increases in speed, vastly larger memories, and the merger of computer and telecommunication technologies are all parts of a broad array of technological innovations that have created the possibility of direct end-user access to organizational databases via attractive interfaces, sometimes on a global scale. At the same time, end users have on their desks or in their laps powerful workstations, which not only can connect them to networks featuring a variety of computing resources, but can run multifunctional software locally.

FIGURE 6.12

The principal categories of systems and applications software.

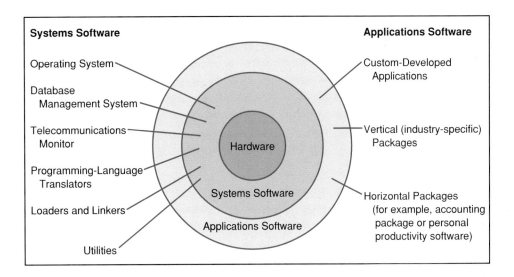

6.7 OPERATING SYSTEMS

Every computer system runs under the control of an operating system. Operating systems for computers that are shared by many users are considerably more complex than those for personal computers, since shared systems have to ensure that the programs of all users progress to completion within a reasonable time and in secure separation from one another. Operating systems can manage a computer system in various modes: batch, time-sharing, or real-time. They can also manage multiple processors in a system and ensure communication with other systems across a network. The drive toward creating open systems—systems that can employ the hardware or software of any vendor—includes a search for a standard operating system.

Principal Functions of an Operating System

The **operating system** is the software that controls all the resources of a computer system. It assigns the needed hardware to programs: it schedules programs for execution on the processor, and it allocates the memory they need as well as assigns to them the necessary input and output devices. Operating systems make translators available to the programs, so that they can be readied for execution. They also manage the data and program files stored in secondary memory, maintaining file directories and providing access to the data in the files.

We can thus view an operating system as a traffic cop in the computer system: the operating system sequences programs for the processor, giving the programs the resources they need to progress to completion. Another way to view such a system is to see it as the provider of a user-system interface. It is the operating system that makes the look and feel of a Macintosh, with its heavy graphics orientation, so different from that of the IBM and IBM-compatible micros (unless they run the software that furnishes a graphical user interface, which we will discuss in chapter 9).

Operating systems emerged in the early 1950s in response to the need to manage the complexity of input and output on behalf of the running programs. Many operating systems are among the most complex software in common use.

The operating systems of personal computers dedicated to a single user are vastly simpler than the operating systems running larger machines, to which hundreds or thousands of users may have simultaneous access. A well-known example of a single-user microcomputer system is MS-DOS. However, more complex microcomputer operating systems, such as UNIX (used on many platforms) or Operating System/2 (used on the IBM PS/2 and compatible micros), offer facilities that begin to approximate these of larger systems. One important capability an operating system can offer in a personal computing environment is **multitasking:** the ability to run several tasks at once on behalf of a user. A multitasking operating systems enables the user, for example, to run a spreadsheet program while a previously word-processed letter is being printed out.

We know that a mainframe frequently supports hundreds of users working at remote VDTs; indeed, even a micro such as IBM PS/2 Model 80 can support several users working at the same time. How can a single processor accomplish this? This capability, called **multiprogramming,** is furnished by the operating system. Because processors are much faster than input and output devices, many programs can run seemingly at the same time, although actually only one of them is using the CPU while the others are doing input- or output-related tasks or simply waiting for a needed resource for an imperceptible millisecond. After all, a 10 MIPS processor can execute 10,000 instructions in a single millisecond!

Multiprogramming requires that the active parts of the programs competing for the processor be available in main memory. To make this possible with a limited main memory size, operating systems generally have a **virtual memory** capability. They divide programs into so-called pages and keep in the main memory only those pages that appear to be needed in the immediate future. The full programs are kept on disk. As the execution of the program progresses, the pages that contain instructions to be executed or the needed data are rolled in from the disk; the unneeded pages that contain computed results are rolled out onto the secondary storage. This operating system facility vastly expands the apparent (virtual) capacity of the main memory over its physical size.

Among the well-known operating systems for larger machines are MVS and VM running on the IBM mainframes and VAX/VMS running on DEC's VAX minicomputers.

Modes of Computer System Operation

Operating systems can make the system they manage operate in various modes. In **batch processing,** the job (or program), once submitted to the system, is run without a user's interaction. The principal measure of goodness in batch processing is throughput: the number of jobs processed per unit of time. A payroll or a weekly set of reports may be run off in this mode. By contrast, **time-sharing systems** are designed to provide fast service by allowing multiple users to simultaneously interact with a program via terminals. Each terminal is allocated a time slice for the use of the processor (say, 50 milliseconds), which is generally more than necessary to handle an interaction. If not, the terminal will get another time slice after others have been served. If the processing capacity of the system is adequate, most users get the impression that a dedicated computer is working exclusively for them. The measure of goodness for such an interactive system is the response time experienced by its users. Many commercial information services are provided on time-sharing systems.

Real-time operating systems are able to handle tasks such as process control in a manufacturing plant, data collection from several pieces of equipment in a laboratory, or control of a space shuttle. In these systems, a hard constraint is imposed upon the response time of the system. If the processing of the incoming data is not completed during the allotted interval, with the system taking action as necessary, data are lost and, in some cases, considerable harm may ensue. Response time is guaranteed by ensuring high processing capacity of the hardware.

With the move toward multiprocessors, in which several (or even many) processors are configured in a single computer system, *multiprocessing operating systems* have been designed to allocate the work to the multiple processors. These systems generally do both multitasking and multiprogramming, so that the many programs and the tasks they create can compete for the processors.

As computing becomes distributed among systems included in networks, the operating system running on a given machine must support access to the variety of computer systems connected to the net. System security, an important concern of all operating systems running nondedicated computers, is of particular concern here (see the discussion of this subject in chapter 20).

WHAT ABOUT UNIX?

The UNIX operating system has become a system of record and of considerable contention. Its more advanced versions are now multiprogramming and multitasking systems. The initial version of UNIX was developed between 1969 and 1973 in a classical "bootlegging" (or "skunkworks"—see chapter 12) manner by two computer scientists, Ken Thompson and Dennis Ritchie, at Bell Laboratories. As Dennis Ritchie explained, "It began in 1969 when Ken Thompson discovered a little used PDP-7 [mini]computer and set out to fashion a computing environment that he liked."[2]

UNIX soon acquired extraordinary popularity in academic settings owing to its simple design, the great variety of facilities it offered for the development of applications, and its close connection with the increasingly popular C language, in which it was rewritten in 1973. The elegant facilities UNIX provides for systems development make it, in effect, an applications development environment. UNIX has never been known for its user-friendliness, however.

The fact that UNIX is written in a higher-level language rather than an assembly language specific to a particular machine (as most operating systems are) makes it transportable across various computer platforms. UNIX has already been moved from a variety of microprocessor platforms to larger systems—and thus across the spectrum of computer categories.

Several UNIX versions are competing for the mantle of a standard at this time (POSIX and AIX are two examples). The version developed by Santa Cruz Operation of Santa Cruz, California, is a serious contender to the open-system standard. At the microcomputer level, UNIX will have to withstand the challenge from IBM's OS/2, running on micros based on Intel 80386 and 80486 processor chips.

However, the flexibility of open systems appeals to many user companies; KMart Corporation, for example, bases its overall systems architecture on UNIX (Leibs, 1990).

It is widely expected that a successor to the current versions of UNIX will take us into the twenty-first century.

Based in part on Lawrence M. Fisher, "Small Software Maker Is Taking Giant Steps." *The New York Times*, January 4, 1991, pp.D1, D4; and Dave Trowbridge, "UNIX Evolves towards the Twenty-first Century." *Computer Technology Review*, January 1991, pp. 1, 6, 8.

The Goal of Open Systems

A drive to use **open systems** in organizational computing, so that the software and hardware of any vendor could operate with those of any other (a remote ideal at this time), calls for an operating system that would run on any hardware platform. Organizations want portability, scalability, and interoperability of applications software. A portable application can be moved from one computer system to another: if a standard operating system is used at the heart of a systems software layer (see figure 6.12), then an application in the outer layer can be easily "peeled off" and placed on a different platform as desired. A scalable application program is one that can be moved, for example, from a smaller machine to a larger one without significant reprogramming. Interoperability means that machines of various vendors and capabilities can work together to produce needed information. Altogether, the use of open systems should give an evolving organization flexible informational support. The drive to open systems is increasingly centering on the UNIX operating system as the possible universal operating system.

6.8 PROGRAMMING LANGUAGES AND THEIR TRANSLATORS

As developing the capability of computers to understand natural language remains a remote goal of artificial intelligence research, computers are programmed in programming languages designed for the purpose. Assembly languages of specific computer models are rarely used today to program applications. Most application programming is done in procedural, high-level languages, such as COBOL, C, or FORTRAN. Some of these languages are translated by compilers; others, employed to code interactive programs, are translated by interpreters. However, the fourth-generation, nonprocedural languages are now broadly employed to increase productivity in software development. Many of these languages are specifically designed for end users, which is why we shall discuss them in more detail in chapter 9.

Generations of Programming Languages

Figure 6.13 traces the generations through which the programming languages have developed, starting in the mid-1940s and with a full-fledged take-off into higher-level languages in the mid-1950s. Nonprocedural languages came into wider use during the 1970s. The third- and fourth-generation languages gave birth to important new directions in programming; with time, these new directions may evolve another language generation.

The original computers were programmed in the machine language of each specific machine. Due to the binary (on-off) nature of the computer hardware, instructions or statements in these early languages were simply strings of 0s and 1s, as shown in figure 6.14. A glance at this figure is all one needs to appreciate why machine languages are no longer used for programming.

The first real programming languages to emerge were assembly languages. Since an assembly language is also a low-level language (that is, it refers to machine resources, such as registers and memory addresses), it is also specific to a machine or a series of models. Therefore, programs written in an assembly language are not portable. As figure 6.15 indicates, an assembly language permits the use of relatively easy-to-remember operation codes and of symbolic names for memory locations (a very important facility).

An assembly language program is translated into a machine language by a simple translator called an **assembler.** Assembly languages are used today only when tight control over computer hardware resources is required—such as in certain systems programs. The advantage of efficient use of computer resources by these languages is outweighed by the high costs of systems development and lack of program portability.

Today, the bulk of programming is done in high-level programming languages. These languages are far more expressive than low-level languages: fewer instructions are needed to code a program. Moreover, the nature of these instructions permits the programmer to concentrate on the problem at hand rather than on the use of machine resources. These languages facilitate program develop-

FIGURE 6.13

Generations of programming languages.

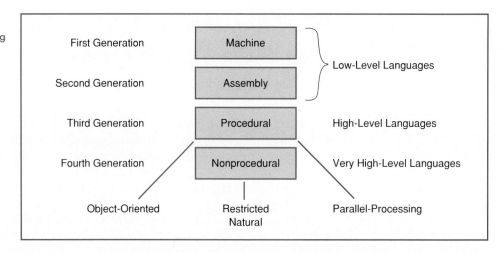

FIGURE 6.14

An instruction in a machine language.

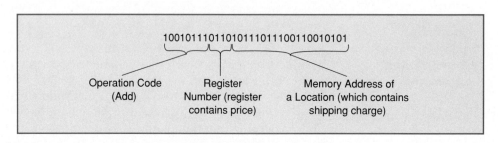

FIGURE 6.15

An instruction in an assembly language.

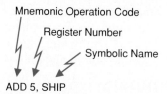

ment and maintenance, resulting in much higher productivity. Most of them support modular design and structured programming of applications (which we will discuss in chapters 18 and 19). The earliest high-level language of broad application, FORTRAN, emerged in the mid-1950s and is still widely used today in scientific and technical programming.

The language in which most business applications have been written is COBOL, developed in 1960 under the leadership of Grace Hopper. The language was specifically designed for processing large data files residing in secondary storage and for relatively easy coding. Although highly readable, COBOL programs are very lengthy. As we will further discuss in chapter 20, maintenance of a large base of COBOL programs requires a very large expenditure of effort on the part of MIS specialists.

High-Level Languages

A great variety of third-generation languages is in use. Table 6.4 summarizes the features of the high-level languages you are most likely to encounter. In particular, C and Ada are becoming more widely used.

TABLE 6.4 Important High-Level Languages	Ada	Developed as the standard language for real-time applications by the U.S. Department of Defense (for example, aircraft control), Ada is expected to be used in MIS applications as well. Its powerful facilities support parallel processing and object-oriented programming (see chapter 19).
	APL	APL is a language for very terse programming, relying on Greek characters and thus requiring a special keyboard. APL is used for scientific programming, but also in other applications where large arrays of data are to be processed—such as DSS modeling. Programs are interactive and the language is interpretive.
	Basic	Basic is a language for novice programmers, though powerful versions are available for the PC environment. Programs are interactive and the language is interpretive.
	C	C is a powerful language that combines the facilities of high-level and assembly languages. C is now widely used for systems and applications software development, particularly in the UNIX environment.
	C++	This extension of C is used for object-oriented programming (see chapter 19).
	COBOL	The preeminent language of data processing (particularly for the development of TPS and MRS), COBOL is being increasingly challenged by very high-level languages.
	FORTRAN	FORTRAN is used for scientific applications; the new versions offer facilities for developing programs for parallel-processing environments.
	LISP	The original language of artificial intelligence, LISP still dominates this area in the United States. It manipulates lists of words, numbers, sentences, or other items. The language is usually interpretive. Special-purpose hardware may be needed to ensure efficient program execution.
	Modula-2	This language is used for real-time programming, particularly for developing systems software.
	Pascal	Pascal is a good language for learning structured programming; the Turbo version is common in the PC environment.
	PL/I	PL/I is an elaborate language designed for both business and scientific computing. It is used largely in the IBM mainframe environment.
	Prolog	A contraction for "programming in logic," Prolog is used in artificial intelligence, particularly in Japan. The program is essentially a specification of facts about objects and relationships among objects, as well as rules about the "world" described by this knowledge base. The program answers questions about the "world" by inferring answers from this knowledge base.
	RPG	RPG is a report generation language. It permits the programmer to specify *what* the report should contain and *what* it should look like, rather than detailing the steps of *how* it should be produced (as in COBOL). RPG is a precursor of very high-level (4GL) languages.
	Smalltalk	This is a language used for object-oriented programming (see chapter 19).

In general, most of the third-generation languages are procedure-oriented: they specify the procedure (known as an **algorithm**) for obtaining the desired results. Detailed specification of such a procedure requires a significant effort. Since much of the processing in the MIS environment is fairly repetitive and revolves around accessing databases, many specialists and end-users moved toward very high-level, so-called fourth-generation languages. These languages permit the programmer to specify what is wanted rather than how to compute it.

Compilers and Interpreters

A program in a higher-level language must be translated into a machine language before execution. Most languages are translated by systems programs known as **compilers,** which translate the source program in its entirety into the object (binary) code (see figure 6.16).

FIGURE 6.16

How executable object code
is obtained.

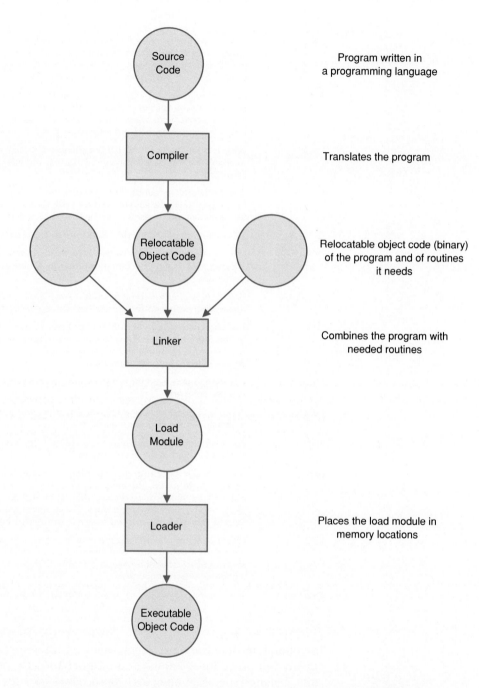

Program written in
a programming language

Translates the program

Relocatable object code (binary)
of the program and of routines
it needs

Combines the program with
needed routines

Places the load module in
memory locations

Compilers usually produce a relocatable object code for the program—that is,
a code that can be placed anywhere in the main memory. Another systems program, called a *linker,* links to this code the binary code of any routines the program needs for execution. The resulting load module is placed by a *loader*
program into the memory area assigned by the operating system. Now the object
code can be run (executed).

Some languages, such as Basic, APL, or LISP are interpretive: they are translated
statement-by-statement by a systems program called an **interpreter.** Each statement is executed immediately following its translation and no object code is

---

A FOURTH-GENERATION FAILURE

A classic example of inappropriate use of 4GL is the case of the New Jersey Motor Vehicles Division. The agency's contractor, a major accounting firm, used Applied Data Research's Ideal to develop the entire vehicle registration system, even though its vendor expressly cautions against using the 4GL for transaction processing. The system was developed and installed in 1985. Among other horrors, which included numerous incorrect registrations, the response time for on-line transactions was reaching five minutes, as opposed to the less than two seconds considered acceptable.

The critical parts of the system were ultimately reprogrammed in COBOL, at a cost of some $2 million to the consultants (who paid for the reprogramming) and a cost of $6.5 million to the agency, which had to cope with the inadequate system (and a million drivers who had problems with car registrations) during the interim period.

Based in part on Glenn Rifkin and Mitch Betts, ''Strategic Systems Plans Gone Awry.'' *Computerworld*, March 14, 1988, pp. 1, 104–5.

---

produced. Interpretive translation has the advantage when users are expected to interact with the program as it is running.

Fourth Generation and Beyond

The low productivity of programmers using high-level languages and the resulting backlogs of applications awaiting development have led to the **fourth-generation languages (4GLs),** which specify what needs to be done rather than how to do it. Unlike most of the high-level languages, which are procedure-oriented, the 4GLs are largely nonprocedural languages. The approach was derived from the RPG (report generation) language; the first general 4GL was RAMIS, which has been treated as a product (rather than a consulting vehicle) since 1975. Some of these languages are designed primarily for professional programmers, others for the end user; many languages combine end-user facilities with facilities for applications programmers. Since these languages are more and more often used by end users, we will discuss them in chapter 9, which addresses end-user computing.

Fourth-generation languages are an excellent vehicle for prototyping—that is, for developing the initial model of an application (see chapter 18). Indeed, the use of 4GLs has made prototyping a viable development methodology. When used by professionals for the development of appropriate systems, 4GLs offer a three- to fivefold increase in productivity, as reported by Green (1984–85) and Harel (1985), or even much higher in some cases. However, these systems are not appropriate when a more complex procedure for problem solving must be stated. They are also rather inefficient in their use of computer resources and should not be employed in time-critical applications, as the above vignette illustrates.

Negative experiences such as the New Jersey Motor Vehicle Division's notwithstanding, 4GLs are an appropriate tool for the development of many management information systems, and MIS specialists should always consider their use.

A number of languages could lay claim to creating a fifth generation. The following types of programming languages are likely to influence the development of such a new paradigm:

- Languages for object-oriented programming (such as Smalltalk and C++), further described in chapter 19, which are particularly apt for handling multimedia object representations, including graphics
- Languages that facilitate parallel processing in systems with a large number of processors
- Functional languages (such as LISP), based on the mathematical concept of computation as an application of functions

Progress in artificial intelligence, which we shall discuss in chapter 15, has led to the ability of computers to process limited subsets of natural languages.

• •

SUMMARY

The hardware of a computer system consists of the processor, main memory, and peripherals (secondary memories as well as input and output devices). Microcomputers, minicomputers, mainframes, and, to some degree, supercomputers are all organized in a similar manner. All of them offer specific capabilities in an organizational setting.

The on-line secondary memories in predominant use today are magnetic disks, although erasable optical disks are beginning to make inroads. Very large-capacity backing storage devices include magnetic tapes and WORM optical disks; CD-ROMs and videodisks are being used for the distribution of prerecorded information.

Devices for direct data entry, such as scanners and voice-entry devices, along with electronic data interchange, are replacing labor-intensive keyboarding. Displays give users soft-copy output, and a variety of printers provide hard-copy output when it is needed.

Computer systems are run by systems software, which is supposed to create a congenial environment for the development of as well as for running applications software. The principal systems software is the operating system, which controls all other system resources.

While most applications are programmed in high-level procedural languages, fourth-generation (4GL) languages, which offer high productivity and often lend themselves to end-user programming, are being used ever more broadly.

ENDNOTES

1. Roger E. Wasson. "Adapting for Future Technologies." *Datamation*, April 1, 1990, pp. 93–95.

2. Ritchie, Dennis M. "Reflections on Software Research" (Turing Award Lecture). *Communications of the ACM*, 27, 8, August 1984, pp. 758–63; p. 758.

KEY TERMS AND CONCEPTS

Processor or central processing
    unit (CPU)
Main memory
Bit
Byte
Word
Peripheral
MIPS (million instructions per
    second)
VLSI (very large scale integration)
Microcomputer
Technical workstation
RISC (reduced instruction set
    computer)
Laptop
Palmtop (handheld) computer
Minicomputer
Mainframe
Multiprocessor
Supercomputer
Parallel processing
Minisupercomputer
Database machine
Memory hierarchy
Cache memory
Magnetic disk

Magnetic tape
Optical disk
CD-ROM
Videodisk
WORM optical disk
Erasable (rewritable) optical disk
Image scanner
OCR scanner
Voice-data entry
Pixel
Systems software
Applications software
Operating system
Multitasking
Multiprogramming
Virtual memory
Batch processing mode
Real-time mode
Time-sharing mode
Open systems
Assembly language
High-level programming languages
Compiler
Interpreter
Fourth-generation languages (4GL)

QUESTIONS

1. What role does the processor play in a computer system?

2. What does a memory byte correspond to in meaning and size?

3. What devices are referred to as peripherals?

4. What is the ratio between tape-mounting time and the time needed to fetch a data item from the main memory?

5. Using table 6.3, compute the approximate price/performance ratios for the micro, mini, and mainframe models listed there ($/MIPS).

6. What types of microcomputers did this chapter introduce to you? List one principal advantage of each type.

7. What are the principal distinctions between minis and mainframes?

8. What applications do supercomputers handle in the business environment?

9. Why do we use a hierarchy of memories? What makes it possible?

10. Compare the uses of magnetic disks and magnetic tapes.

11. How do the three principal categories of optical disks differ in capabilities?

12. What is the difference between OCR and an image scanner?

13. Why, in your opinion, is there a greater variety of input than output peripherals?

14. What is a pixel?

15. What is the distinction between systems software and applications software?

16. What are the principal functions of an operating system?

17. What are the differences between multitasking, multiprogramming, and multiprocessing?

18. What is virtual memory?

19. Compare the objectives of batch, time-sharing, and real-time processing.

20. Describe each of the four generations of programming languages.

21. Using table 6.4, find the programming languages that support object-oriented programming.

22. What is the difference between a compiler and an interpreter?

23. What are the advantages of 4GL over the third-generation programming languages? What are their drawbacks?

ISSUES FOR DISCUSSION

1. In the Focus Statement opening this chapter, I suggested that larger firms should include a group responsible for tracking new technologies that might contribute to the firm's business objectives. What are the possible drawbacks of establishing such a separate unit? How can these drawbacks be remedied?

2. Suppose you were asked to introduce direct data entry into as many aspects of the operations of a midsized publishing company as possible. What operations could you automate, and what devices would you use?

3. Personal computer systems and, in particular, certain types of input and output devices have become great helps to the handicapped—both in everyday life and in the workplace. These devices have opened a number of professional pursuits to many people. Research several categories of such systems and discuss how they enable their users to function at work. Discuss what this means for the society at large.

4. What trends can you discern in the evolution of programming languages from the first generation onward?

5. A vignette in section 6.4 introduced you to the work on artificial reality. What other business applications of this technology can you envisage?

COMPUTER TECHNOLOGY AS A MEANS TO MANY ENDS

Prudential-Bache Securities runs a global computer system operation from a building in New York's financial district. With the high demands for speed and processing volume a retail brokerage firm such as Pru-Bache faces, the company constantly scans the technological leading edge.

The company's data center is built around a multiprocessor configuration consisting of three mainframes: two IBM 3090 Model 600s and an IBM 3084Q. Some 2,000 IBM-compatible microcomputers are scattered throughout the headquarters where the data center is located.

The data center also runs DEC's VAXcluster system, which includes the latest minicomputer model in the 6000 series. The mini configuration does heavy "number crunching": it is used for quantitative securities analysis. Since the ability to evaluate an offering quickly is of the essence, an Intel minisupercomputer, based on 32 Intel 80386 microprocessors, was recently added to the system. Reaction to new opportunities is quick: since a newer, faster Intel microprocessor (I860) has become available, the firm intends to replace eight of the 386s, thus boosting performance of the minisuper by a factor of ten.

The firm maintains 350 branch offices worldwide, equipped with Unisys minicomputers. From these offices, the firm's 6,500 brokers tap into the data center's mainframes for a daily load of at least 1.7 million transactions. There are up to 9,000 Unisys microcomputers in the branch offices, which handle some 2.5 million customer accounts around the world. The company intends to move the branch offices to a new hardware/software platform. The chosen vendor (and there are many contenders) will start a pilot project in one of the branches shortly.

Some rather esoteric technological innovations may produce important results for customer service. For example, the firm converted to the newly released IBM technique for storing backup data on tape cartridges. This technique permits Prudential-Bache to increase three- to fivefold the amount of data on cartridges for IBM 3490 tape drives. As a result, the nightly batch processing run, when backup is done, has been cut by one to two hours. This, in turn, makes it possible to transmit all updated client financial positions and account activities from the previous day to the branch offices by 4 a.m. each day.

All processing in the data center is fully automated, with the exception of tape handling; the tape pool consists of 64 cartridge drives and a library of 50,000 cartridges.

Prudential-Bache regularly serves as a beta test site: vendors make some of their newest technology available to the firm, which provides a realistic test bed for the vendors. This gives the firm a jump on its competition in assimilating new technologies. It is currently beta testing a new high-speed Siemens laser printer that also offers superior print quality (and

Prudential-Bache turns out 225 million pieces of paper a year!). Prudential-Bache is also testing the IBM's new 3390 disk drive (and the firm does store half a trillion bytes on its disks).

William Anderson, the firm's chief information officer, stresses that "genuine business requirements," rather than whizbang technology, drive Prudential-Bache to the leading edge. Anderson sees the advanced technologies as not only enablers of better customer service, but often as least-cost solutions.

Based on Maryfran Johnson, "Prudential Gets a Better Batch." *Computerworld*, April 23, 1990, p. 29.

Case Study Questions

1. What keeps the Prudential-Bache MIS operation on the leading edge of technology?

2. Imagine that you have been made responsible for the introduction of emerging technologies at Prudential-Bache. What methods would you use to facilitate this introduction?

3. Note that Prudential-Bache uses equipment from several vendors. What problems could this create?

4. What does Prudential-Bache's chief information officer mean when he says their approach to new technologies is "business-driven"? How does this approach affect the company's operation?

SELECTED REFERENCES

Abbott, Lawrence. "Supercomputers: Big Bang, Big Bucks." *Datamation*, February 15, 1991, pp. 73–77.

Badgett, Tom, and Spurgeon, Kathy. "Voice-Processing Applications: Laying the Foundation for the Technology of Tomorrow." *Digital News*, December 1988, pp. 39T–46T.

Connolly, James. "It Costs How Much?" *Computerworld*, September 19, 1988, pp. 1, 127.

Depke, Deirdre, and Gross, Neil. "Laptops Take Off." *Business Week*, March 18, 1991, pp. 118–24.

Fisher, Lawrence M. "A Giant Killer in Silicon Valley." *The New York Times*, February 8, 1991, pp. D1, D5.

Green, Jesse. "Productivity in the Fourth Generation: Six Case Studies." *Journal of Management Information Systems*, 1, 3, Winter 1984–85, pp. 49–63.

Hamilton, Rosemary. "Tape Automation Comes of Age." *Computerworld*, February 19, 1990, pp. 33, 40.

Harel, Elie C., and McLean, Ephraim R. "The Effects of Using a Nonprocedural Computer Language on Programmer Productivity." *MIS Quarterly,* 9, 2, June 1985, pp. 109–20.

Hooper, Laurence. " 'Segment' Is New Buzzword for PC Sellers," The *Wall Street Journal,* June 29, 1990, pp. B1, B4.

Johnson, Maryfran. "Voice Recognition Gives Direct Line to the Riviera." *Computerworld,* October 1, 1990, p. 29.

Kobielus, James G. *Smart Cards: A New Perspective.* Washington, D.C.: The International Center for Information Technologies, 1987.

Laub, Leonard. "What Is CD-ROM?" In *CD ROM: The New Papyrus,* edited by Steve Lambert and Suzanne Ropiequet. Redmond, Wash.: Microsoft Press, 1986, pp. 47–83.

Leibs, Scott. "Confused by a Parallel Market?" *Information Week,* February 5, 1990, pp. 34–35.

Leibs, Scott. "What UNIX Has in Store." *Information Week,* October 29, 1990, pp. 38–40.

Leinfuss, Emily. "While Voice Applications Grow, Technology Limits Still Exist." *MIS Week,* May 8, 1989, p. 14.

McMullen, John. "Rewritable Optical Still Not in Overdrive." *Datamation,* March 1, 1991, pp. 35–36.

Markoff, John. "New Rival for Personal Computer." *The New York Times,* January 3, 1990, pp. D1, D6.

Markoff, John. "Computers Said to be the Fastest." *The New York Times,* June 5, 1991, p. D1.

Moad, Jeff. "Large Systems Are Hot!" *Datamation,* May 15, 1990, pp. 24–32.

Nash, Jim. "Our Man in Cyberspace Checks out Virtual Reality." *Computerworld,* October 12, 1990, p. 109.

Otte, Peter. "Citibank." *Mobile Office,* October 1990, pp. 34–38.

Rappaport, Andrew S., and Halevi, Shmuel. "The Computerless Computer Company." *Harvard Business Review,* July–August 1991, pp. 69–80.

Schroeder, Michael, with Bluestone, Mimi. "Computers You Control with a Wave of Your Hand." *Business Week,* February 20, 1989, pp. 142–145.

Socarras, Angel E.; Cooper, Robert S.; and Stonecypher, William F. "Anatomy of an X Terminal." *IEEE Spectrum,* March 1991, pp. 52–55.

Verity, John W. "Supercomputers: Brute Strength—and a Sensitive Issue." *Business Week,* April 10, 1990, p. 83.

Zwass, Vladimir. "Computer Science." *Encyclopaedia Britannica.* Macropaedia, Vol. XVI, 1988, pp. 629–37.

CHAPTER 7

DISTRIBUTED PROCESSING SYSTEMS, TELECOMMUNICATIONS, AND COMPUTER NETWORKS

* *

The era of personal computers has ended. The 1990s will be the era of interpersonal computing.

Steven Jobs
A founder of personal computing

They that weave networks shall be confounded.

Isaiah 19:9

The electronic transmission of information over distances, which we call telecommunications, has become virtually inseparable from computers: computers and telecommunications create value together. Telecommunications enable us to bring computer processing power to the point of application. Computer networks, in which user workstations and computers are interconnected by telecommunications media, are becoming vital for integrating organizations. Indeed, it is the ability to communicate with other computers that transforms a personal computer into a true workstation.

In some cases, telecommunications provide only remote access to a shared minicomputer or mainframe. However, today's organizational information systems are generally distributed to a greater or smaller degree: they include a number of networked computers. Local area networks serve a workgroup; wide area networks serve larger organizational units. Many organizational networks are also becoming embedded in interorganizational systems. The computer has become a node in a telecommunication network—or, actually, in many networks at the same time.

MIS managers and some users are becoming telecommunications managers. The great variety of options and emerging technologies requires familiarity with the organizational capabilities offered by each alternative. This chapter will help you understand how to derive business benefits from this wide array of networking technologies.

A principal reason Walgreen enjoys profits and growth far beyond those of other drugstore chains—and this certainly defines the concept of competitive advantage—is the company's investment in on-line computer systems, which lock all its stores into a single web of information flows. Let us see a little more closely how Walgreen provides superior service with its computer network—and how the firm seeks out economies, too.

Since all 1,500 Walgreen's stores in 28 states are interconnected via the computer network, a customer can fill a prescription at a store near her home and then refill it at any other Walgreen's—near her office, or even in another state. This capability is rapidly turning Walgreen into a national drugstore chain. Moreover, the large number of Walgreen's stores enables the company to offer discounts to third-party bill payers, such as insurance companies. This should help sustain its competitive advantage.

The volume of transactions is very high: the pharmacies process 300,000 prescriptions a day, sending all the information needed to bill insurers and updating customer records to a central computer in Mount Prospect, Illinois. Furthermore, the firm saves $1 million a year by sending these data over satellite links instead of the telephone network. The firm is indeed in control of its technologies.

Based on Rick Reiff, "Convenience with Difference." *Forbes*, June 11, 1990, pp. 184–86.

As the Walgreen example shows, acquiring an understanding of the potential of telecommunications and computer networking, and gaining knowledge of technological possibilities, enables an organization to compete successfully in the marketplace.

CHAPTER OUTLINE

7.1 DISTRIBUTED PROCESSING SYSTEMS

Centralized information systems, relying on a single large processor, have largely given way to distributed computing, made possible by communication links that connect multiple computers. Local area networks and wide area networks make possible communication and coordination within a workgroup, within a company, or between multiple organizations.

In this section, we shall first contrast centralized information systems with distributed systems. We will then show you examples of business opportunities provided by distributed systems of various scope. After you gain an appreciation for these opportunities, we will go on in the remainder of this chapter to discuss the structure of distributed processing systems in a systematic manner.

When the Processing Is Not Distributed: Centralized and Dispersed Systems

Until the mid-1970s, organizational computing systems had rather simple structures. All the processing power for a company or for its major subunit was delivered by a mainframe as large as was required to meet the company's computing needs. These centralized systems were economically justified: according to the so-called Grosch's Law, valid at that time, quadrupling the processing power of a machine only doubled its cost. In that era, before personal computers or user-friendly software, virtually all access to computing resources had to be mediated by the MIS staff.

Thus, in the early years a company's computer system was *centralized,* with on-line access and sometimes remote job entry from distant terminals—the first significant element of telecommunications in computer systems (see figure 7.1). Some firms still choose to use centralized processing. For example, banks use a remote-access network with centralized processing to support automatic teller machines (ATMs), which serve as terminals. A centralized system such as that shown in figure 7.1 may also be used to provide time-sharing services.

FIGURE 7.1

A centralized system with remote terminals.

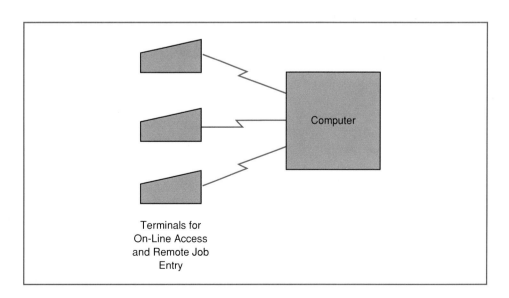

Terminals for
On-Line Access
and Remote Job
Entry

Computer

FIGURE 7.2

A local area network for
workgroup support

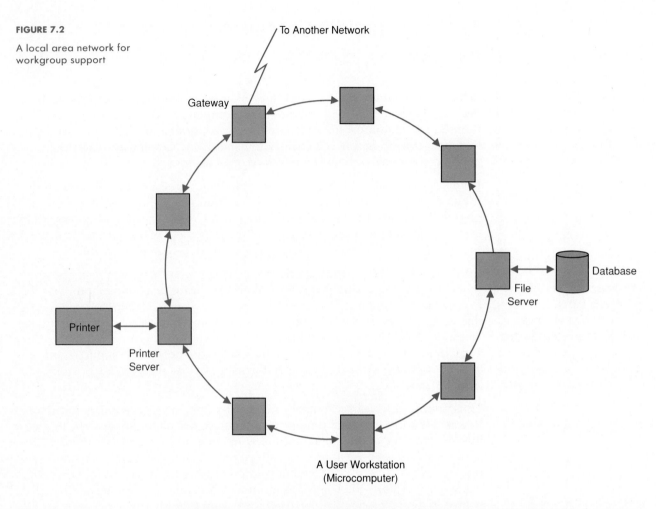

To Another Network

Gateway

Printer

Printer
Server

A User Workstation
(Microcomputer)

File
Server

Database

When in earlier days an organization would employ several machines, they were
stand-alone processors, without the ability to communicate with one another; in
other words, they were *dispersed systems*. Today, we try to bring such "islands
of automation" together through telecommunications.

As a variety of computer categories emerged, and as smaller machines became
able to offer better price/performance ratios than larger ones, it became cost-
effective to bring computing power directly to users and to ensure that these
systems were not isolated. **Distributed systems** comprise a number of processors that communicate over a telecommunications network. To better appreciate
the reasons for the great variety of such networks, let us consider three typical
organizational arrangements before we go on to discuss the principal technologies and management aspects involved.

Local Area Network for a Workgroup

Workgroup computing has become a principal means of collaboration for a team
of coworkers, as we shall further discuss in chapter 16. Located in the same
building or group of buildings, the people in a workgroup communicate over a
fast local area network (LAN) that interconnects their workstations and provides
them with shared facilities. These facilities include such items as a large-
capacity secondary storage device where database and applications software may
be maintained, and a fast printer (see figure 7.2). More and more frequently, one

LOCAL AREA NETWORK IS THE BACKBONE OF A SMALL COMPANY

We usually refer to wide area networks as backbone communication systems for larger firms. But in a small, rapidly-becoming-midsized firm, such as ETO Sterilization of Linden, New Jersey, all of the back-office work can be integrated internally by a LAN—in this case, NetWare by Novell.

ETO performs contract sterilization (batch chemical treatment) of medical and cosmetics products, as well as spices. Inventory control is the principal application: trucks come in bearing a variety of shipments and each bag or box must be accounted for as it is given an appropriate treatment and shipped to its destination.

The LAN at ETO includes seven Intel 80286–based micros used as personal computers by the office staff, with the inventory control database located on a 120 Mbyte hard disk managed by a Compaq 80386–based server. A printer server is also available to print operational documents (such as bills of lading and invoices) and various inventory reports. Thanks to the LAN, all office workers in the firm are able to share the database to answer frequent customer queries, produce documents, or analyze the firm's performance. Each knowledge worker can work independently—and yet their work is coordinated thanks to easy access to the common database.

Dr. Michael Howe, the founding president of the company, sees the LAN as the backbone of his growing firm. Indeed, ETO's LAN has been upgraded twice since its introduction, and recently a dial-up connection with the firm's out-of-state accounting offices has been instituted as well.

Source: Author

of the facilities in a LAN is a gateway—hardware and software which give the network users access to other networks.

People working in the office of a small company are an example of a workgroup. The above vignette shows how a local area network integrates such a firm.

Hierarchical Wide Area Network

Large firms rely on wide area networks for interconnecting their sometimes far-flung computer systems. The information system of an entire organization may be structured as a hierarchy—although, as we shall see further on in the chapter, other arrangements are also possible. A hierarchical system matches the structure of many organizations well: the system's architecture (that is, its overall design) looks very much like an organization chart, as you can see in figure 7.3. This type of system connects all the divisional minicomputers to the headquarters mainframe, with a variety of local microcomputers and terminals located at remote sites connected in turn to the minicomputers.

In a hierarchical system, the divisional minicomputers are generally located at geographically distant sites, meaning that wide area communication is required. Individual machines are selected according to their capacities to meet the requirements of a site.

A classic hierarchical network is the corporate network of Dow Corning Corporation. Dow's main data center is located in its Midland, Michigan, corporate headquarters, with regional processors in plants in such cities as Chicago and Elizabethtown, Kentucky, but also in area headquarters around the globe (for example, in Brussels, Sydney, and Tokyo) (Rowe, 1988).

A hierarchical network may, of course, be adapted to many organizational contexts. A retailer's use of such a network is described in the Wal-Mart vignette.

The organizational wide area network shown in figure 7.3 and workgroup LANs may be combined to obtain the type of organizational network shown before in figure 3.1. Various other network configurations are also possible, to match the structure and strategy of each organization.

Crossing Corporate Boundaries: Interorganizational Systems

By extending the reach of an information system beyond its own boundary, an organization may reap considerable strategic advantage (Cash, 1985). Indeed, many of the systems we discussed in chapter 5 were interorganizational systems that relied on telecommunications (see figure 7.4). Various forms of distributed processing are characteristic of such systems.

To take an eminent example, by providing terminals on distributor (travel agency) sites, American Airlines was able to make Sabre, its airline reservation system, a potent source of competitive advantage (and revenue). John Hancock Insurance Company opened its system to the employee-benefits managers of its client corporations (Feeny, 1990). In addition to accessing Hancock's system for insurance services, these clients use the system to communicate with one another via electronic mail. If a user switches from John Hancock to a rival insurer, the benefits manager would be cut off from a circle of his or her peers. This deterrent contributes to the insurer's sustainable competitive advantage.

Going beyond terminal access, direct interaction between the computers of two firms is a potent tool for work coordination. A growing form of interaction between organizational information systems is the use of electronic data interchange (EDI) for the transfer of business documents such as orders or invoices.

FIGURE 7.3

A hierarchical distributed system.

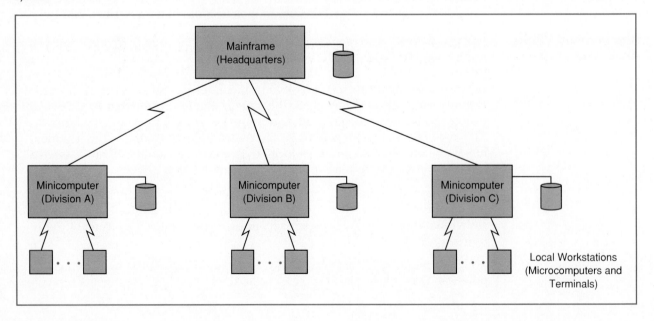

WHAT THE BEST RETAILER DOES

Wal-Mart Stores Corporation, which enjoys the reputation of being the best retailer in the United States, runs its information system from Bentonville, Arkansas. Bob Martin, senior vice-president for information services of the company, says: "Much of what we have done with technology is a large part of our ability to compete." But a service-oriented company should be aware of the fact that customers are gained and kept not by machines, but by the superior service provided by people—an opinion echoed by top service firms throughout several industries (Sellers, 1990). What, then, is the role of technology? "Our approach with technology is not trying to replace people but really supplementing what our people do and making them more effective," says Martin. In other words, technology is used to leverage human effort.

Each of the 1,550 stores of the Wal-Mart chain has an IBM Series-1 minicomputer, which monitors the store's daily sales and inventory. These data are sent to machines in Wal-Mart's seventeen regional distribution centers, which are linked in turn to the Bentonville home-office mainframe. This hierarchy of processors is interconnected with a very small aperture terminal (VSAT) satellite network, a system rapidly gaining ground in the retailing and distribution industries. Each store has such a terminal (actually, an earth station) and can send and receive data, voice, and video. This high-capacity communication channel allows the stores not only to share sales and ordering information, but also to maintain an ongoing dialogue with the company's operations, merchandising, and distribution functions. Indeed, most of the ideas for new applications come from the salespeople who have daily contact with the customers in the stores.

The firm also uses electronic data interchange (EDI) links to more than 1,800 of its 5,000 suppliers.

"If we can buy our people time to spend time with the customer or time to spend on the merchandise, that's value-added," says Martin.

Based on Ellis Booker, "IS Trailblazing Puts Retailer On Top." *Computerworld*, January 12, 1990, pp. 69, 73.

FIGURE 7.4

Systems crossing corporate boundaries.

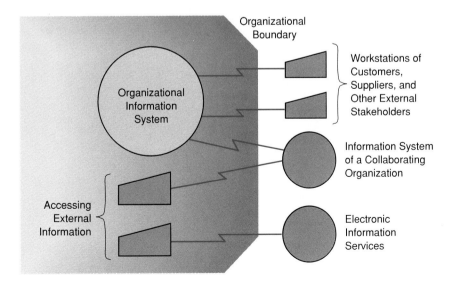

FIGURE 7.5

Interorganizational data
flows in EDI.

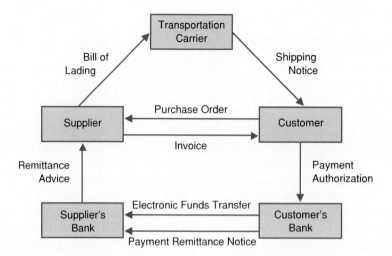

Certain industries, such as transportation (see color plate 5), have been revolutionized by EDI. Note the number of systems involved in the EDI handling of a business transaction shown in figure 7.5. One of the data flows in the figure involves electronic funds transfer (EFT), which an organization usually implements prior to EDI.

Many forms of collaboration and coordination are possible with the support of interorganizational systems, and these systems present a variety of strategic alternatives to a firm (Barrett, 1986–87). Network gateways enable a team of designers developing a product on a LAN in a customer firm to collaborate with the suppliers' designers. When the item goes into production, the customer's information system may automatically reorder needed inputs from a supplier on the just-in-time principle. In certain industries with fickle demand, such as textiles, retailers even establish telecommunications links to manufacturers for reordering (from the cash register to the factory floor): truly market-driven production is thus made possible. In this way, interorganizational information systems create virtual companies in the supplier-customer chain.

7.2 STRUCTURAL ASPECTS OF DISTRIBUTED COMPUTING

The high-level design of a distributed processing system (which is the way most organizational information processing is handled today) is known as system architecture. In this section, we will consider the structural aspects of these systems. Decisions must be made on where to locate the processing power and the databases, and how to interconnect the nodes (host computers and workstations) of the network. Finally, we will consider vital managerial aspects at the end of this chapter.

FIGURE 7.6

Possible distribution of systems in a firm.

(From Barbara C. McNurlin and Ralph H. Sprague, Jr. *Information Systems Management in Practice* 2/E, © 1989, p. 132. Reprinted by permission of Prentice-Hall, Inc., Englewood Cliffs, NJ.)

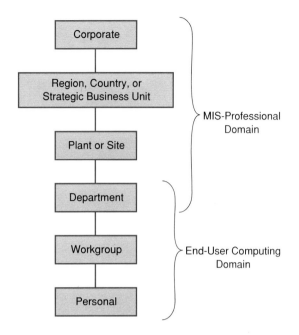

Architectural Levels of Distributed Systems

Distributed systems may extend over more than the three levels indicated in figure 7.3. In general, we may consider six levels at which processing power may be located in an organization (as shown in figure 7.6)—and at each of these levels, access to external systems may be provided as well. Naturally, the distribution of processing must be fitted to the organization's needs.

The traditional domains of computing—the top three levels in figure 7.6—have been extended over recent years to the lower levels, which used to rely on terminals to draw on the computing power located on the top three levels. At these lower levels, computing facilities are generally placed under end-user control and much of the software is *not* developed by corporate MIS professionals (see chapter 9).

Architectural Framework for Distributed Systems

There are many—very many—options in developing a distributed system for a firm. Actually, it is extremely rare to design such a system afresh. Developers work with a holdover of existing systems, which in some cases include over a dozen functioning networks. The developers need to provide a master plan for a new system architecture and an evolutionary path from the current system to this new one. The fundamental components of the architecture of distributed systems are shown in figure 7.7. According to this framework, the following concerns must be addressed in developing such systems:

1. How will the *processing power* be distributed; or, in other words, where will the computers be located, and what categories of computers will be used?

   The principal objective of distributed processing is to move processors into the user's orbit of control by distributing at least some of the computing power out of the corporate data center.

FIGURE 7.7

A framework for the
architecture of a distributed
system.

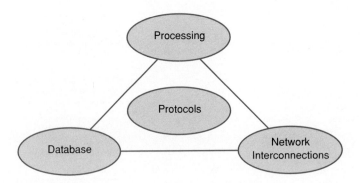

2. Where will the *database* (or databases) be located?

Broadly speaking, there are two modes of integrating the work done by the users in a distributed system, both of which are generally employed. Integration may be accomplished by having all users work with the same data, located in a database or a collection of databases. It may also be achieved by the exchange of messages over electronic mail or, beyond that, by groupware (which we will discuss in chapter 16).

The database can be maintained on a central site, with its extracts downloaded as needed to other processors. With such a centralized database, the advantages of excellent database control may be outweighed by excessive message traffic on the network due to the high volume of data accesses. Databases may also be distributed: for example, departmental processors may maintain departmental databases, which can also be accessed by other users who do not even need to know that the data are distributed. Finally, the database may be replicated: each site may contain a copy of the database or of a part of it. The last solution improves access efficiency but creates the difficult problem of maintaining all the changing data in a consistent state. We shall further discuss distributed databases in the next chapter. We need to note here that the placement of databases frequently determines the location and speed requirements of processors.

3. *Network interconnections* must be provided for user access to processors as well as for processor-to-processor communications. These interconnections include links over a variety of media as well as equipment (generally computer-based) to manage the traffic on the network. Links of appropriate capacity must be provided: the screens of workstations connected to a host computer have to be refreshed in a second or two; the average time of transaction processing should not surpass two seconds, even if the data are bounced off a satellite; and if we want a feeling of immediacy in a videoconference, high-capacity links are needed. The links must be used in an efficient manner, since telecommunications are costly: this may be accomplished by sharing the links' communication capacity with the help of the network equipment. Reliable communications require at least two paths between any two nodes in the network. Interconnections already in place are frequently modified and expanded (Zwass, 1988).

4. By their very essence, networks interconnect variety: variety of people, organizations, hardware, and software. For a network to work harmoniously (in fact, for it to work at all), rules of operation must be built into the hardware and software of the network equipment, so that all nodes may communicate and understand their respective messages. These rules are called *protocols*.

An organization may choose not to own some of the three components of the triangle in the framework shown in figure 7.7. Remote access to various external databases may be provided by information-services firms. Service bureaus may furnish processing capacity; system integrators can even run an entire firm's MIS function on its behalf—in fact, there is a significant *outsourcing* trend, which we will discuss in the following parts of this text. Wide area network interconnections are generally leased from carriers—or even from a firm that has excess communication capacity. For example, Sears, Roebuck has created a subsidiary which offers network interconnections to other firms. These firms provide their own processing; the Sears network provides only connectivity.

7.3 TELECOMMUNICATIONS LINKS

Telecommunications rely on links connecting geographically distributed nodes. A variety of media exist to implement these links. Communication channels can carry either analog or digital data. Because of its heritage as the voice-carrying medium, the contemporary telephone plant, which is the primary means of connectivity in computer networks, is still largely analog. However, in the environment of the information society, a move to digital plants is taking place. This will make possible high-capacity transmission of multimedia information.

Communication Media

Two communicating devices (network nodes) are connected by a channel—that is, a link formed by the communications medium. In figure 7.8, device 1 acts as a sender of the message and device 2 as its receiver.

Communication media are available with a variety of characteristics. The main feature of a medium is its possible transmission speed, also known as *channel capacity,* which for data transmission purposes is expressed in bits per second (bps). In general, speed over telephone lines ranges from 300 bps to 19,200 bps (although the higher speeds are difficult to achieve over the public network today), while microwave transmission speeds reach million of bits per second (Mbps).

Five principal media are employed to implement communication links. Three (twisted pair, coaxial cable, and fiber optic cable) require wiring, and the two others (terrestrial and satellite microwave transmission) do not.

FIGURE 7.8

A basic telecommunications
system.

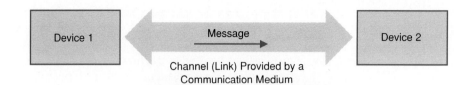

Channel (Link) Provided by a
Communication Medium

PHOTO 7.1

This device enables
microcomputers in a local
area network to communicate
with high-frequency radio
signals—without wires. The
computers and the
communication devices may
be placed a hundred feet
apart within buildings, and
they may communicate over
obstructing walls. This LAWN
(Local Area Wireless
Network) device is a product
of O'Neill Communications of
Princeton, New Jersey.

1. Twisted pair

A *twisted pair* of wires is familiar to us all—it is employed as the local
loop that connects our telephones to the central office; as they approach
the office, these wires are bunched together into cables. Each pair connects
to a single telephone or data circuit. The capacity of a twisted pair is
limited, but it may be significantly expanded by shielding the wires and
installing additional equipment.

2. Coaxial cable

A *coaxial cable,* introduced by the cable television industry, consists of
a relatively thick central conductor shielded by several layers of insulation;
several coaxes may be packed together into a very thick cable.

3. Fiber optics

A much newer medium of very high capacity is a **fiber optic cable.**
Each optical fiber in such a cable is a thin strand of pure glass with a data-
carrying core in the middle, surrounded by a reflective cladding. The total
diameter of the fiber is less than that of a human hair (see color plate 6).
Data are sent over the fiber in the form of light-beam pulses emitted by a
laser or a light-emitting diode. This medium is also quite secure: it is
virtually impossible to tap and it does not emit radiation.

4. Terrestrial microwave

Microwave radio transmission is employed for long-distance
telecommunications, and sometimes in local area networks as well (see
photo 7.1). However, these signals travel in straight lines and therefore the
transmitter and receiver must be in a direct line of sight; to extend the
distances, transmitters and receivers are placed on towers or high
buildings, ensuring a range of up to thirty miles. Companies sometimes
establish private microwave links for such limited distances. Encryption—
communicating data in a cipher—is needed for secure microwave
transmission of any kind.

FIGURE 7.9

Satellite communication.

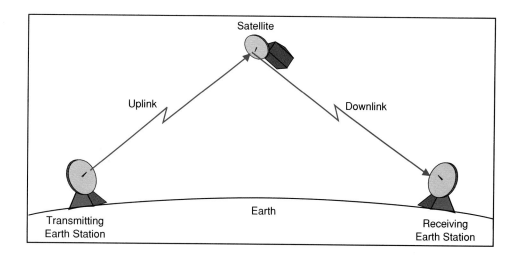

5. Satellite transmission

   Satellite transmission is a form of microwave transmission, but it can span the globe. A microwave signal is transmitted by an earth station (see color plate 7) to a satellite orbiting the earth at an altitude of 22,300 miles. The satellite appears stationary, since its speed matches that of the earth's rotation. The microwave signal is sent to the satellite on the uplink frequency, is amplified by the satellite, and is rebroadcast to the dish antenna of the receiving station (see figure 7.9). A single satellite can transmit over more than one third of the earth.

   Satellite communication is burdened by significant propagation delays. Because of the distances involved, the total delay on the uplink and the downlink is about 540 milliseconds (Martin, 1988). This delay must be taken into account in the design of on-line systems, where the average response time for many transactions should be no greater than two seconds.

At this time, relatively inexpensive and unobtrusive satellite antennas, known as very small aperture terminals (VSATs), have become widely available. A number of companies have replaced their leased-line telecommunications networks with the VSAT satellite nets (see color plate 8). The next vignette presents an example.

Table 7.1 compares the attributes of communication media. Note that the transmission speeds actually achieved in a system depend on the variety of equipment employed in the system and on how the medium's potential speed is shared among the channels using the medium.

The transmission speeds keep on rising, particularly in the fiber-optics area. A long-distance fiber optic link operating at 8.6 gigabits per second (8,600 Mbps) was reported (Gilder, 1991). As the 1990s unfold, it is becoming apparent that we are moving toward a global infrastructure of gigabit-speed fiber-optic links. In this multimedia environment, data, text, voice, images, and video will travel at speeds of billions of bits per second.

SATELLITE DISHES ARE NO BIG DEAL ANYMORE—AND COMPANIES PROFIT

Many earth stations for satellite communication are ten meters tall and cost over $100,000. But much smaller and less expensive antennas that have been developed have opened new strategic opportunities for companies involved in the distribution of goods.

Roberts Express of Akron, Ohio, is the world's largest surface expediter of "hot" freight—that is, freight that someone must have right away. Roberts dispatches 975 trucks operated by independent contractors. The firm has mounted on the cab of each truck a satellite antenna only 11 ½ inches in diameter and 6 ¾ inches high. Each cab is also equipped with a laptop computer and a communications unit which serves to pinpoint the location of the truck within 300 yards anywhere in the United States. The cost of equipment, about $4,500 per truck, is split between the company and the truckers.

A system (called Omnitracks) developed by Qualcomm of San Diego, California, enables company dispatchers to know at all times the location of any truck, its cargo, and its proximity to its destination. The dispatchers track the trucks with an on-screen mapping program (resident on Wang minicomputers) that allows them to see the vehicles moving on a map. Customers can dial in and track their shipments. The system helps avoid "dead-heading"—traveling without a cargo, because the dispatcher was unable to contact the trucker in time to make a pickup.

A message sent by a dispatcher travels by telephone lines to Qualcomm's network management facility, which bounces it off a satellite to the cab of the appropriate trucker. Truckers can either send free-form messages, which they type into their terminals, or use predefined fill-in-the-blanks message skeletons (which increases their efficiency).

Customers use Roberts Express for emergencies. Therefore, the firm competes not with other truckers, but with air-freight companies. The firm believes that the satellite-based system gives it a sustainable competitive advantage by raising entry barriers for potential entrants into its niche business; it plans to keep upgrading this system.

Based on Michael Alexander, "Satellite Communications Takes Flight." *Computerworld*, April 16, 1990, p. 22; and Agis Salpukas, "Satellite System Helps Trucks Stay In Touch." *The New York Times*, June 5, 1991, p. D7.

TABLE 7.1

Characteristics of Transmission Media. (Adapted in part from Rowe, 1988; speeds updated)

CHARACTERISTICS	TRANSMISSION MEDIUM				
	TWISTED PAIR	COAXIAL CABLE	FIBER OPTICS	MICROWAVE RADIO	SATELLITE
Potential Transmission Speed	4 Mbps	140 Mbps	10,000 Mbps	100 Mbps	100 Mbps
Ease of Installation	Easy	Moderate	Difficult	Difficult	Difficult
Cost	Low	Moderate	High	High	High
Maintenance Difficulty	Low	Moderate	Low	Low	Low

Analog and Digital Communications. Multiplexing

Most of the lines in the telephone system at present are *analog:* signals are transmitted as continuous waves. This is an excellent way to transmit voice, but digital data must be converted into an analog signal for transmission and then back into digital by interface devices called **modems** (for modulator-demodulator). Figure 7.10 shows the simple use of a modem in a terminal-computer communication. Many personal computer users, particularly those with laptops, communicate via modems. Most modems operate at speeds of 1,200 or 2,400 bps, although fast, expensive modems that operate at the maximum speed of telephone channels—19,200 bps—are also on the market (Hayes Microcomputer Products is the market leader).

Modem-based telecommunications have created a significant bottleneck in an environment where computer and peripheral speeds have increased dramatically. To give you an idea of modem speeds, 100 pages of double-spaced text may be sent from New York to San Francisco in 17.8 minutes using a 1,200 bps modem and in 1.1 minute over a 19,200 bps modem (Markoff, 1990).

As the transmission of data gained importance, a clear trend emerged toward end-to-end **digital** communications, in which signals are sent as streams of on-off pulses. Digital lines are capable of much faster communication and digital circuitry is now cheaper than analog; all the new equipment now installed in telephone networks is indeed digital. An analog line can be converted to digital by changing the circuitry. Thus, the analog/digital property is not a characteristic of the medium, but rather of the electronic equipment which ensures undistorted transmission of the signal from one end to another. (Repeaters installed in a line at certain intervals to restore the quality of the signal, which deteriorates as it is transmitted, are an example of such equipment). However, the initial costs of analog to digital conversion are weighty, and consumer resistance is expected in conversion to digital telephones (conversion of an analog voice signal into a digital one for transmission would be performed by a device called codec).

The capacities of the communication media are generally far greater than what is needed to maintain a single telephone conversation or data transmission. Many individual transmissions can share a physical channel through a variety of techniques collectively called **multiplexing.** Thanks to multiplexing, a single coaxial cable can carry up to 10,800 conversations and a fiber optic cable over 20,000.

The Move to Digital Communications

High-capacity digital telecommunications are already quite common. A digital system for telecommunications, called T1 carrier, is in wide use in parts of the telephone network. With its capacity of 1.544 Mbps, it can carry twenty-four speech channels by multiplexing. T1 facilities may also be leased by firms for high-speed data communication. Carriers of much higher speed (T2 through T4) are being introduced as well. While T1 carrier relies on the twisted-pair medium, the higher-speed versions must employ the other four higher-speed media.

FIGURE 7.10

Telecommunication over a telephone line.

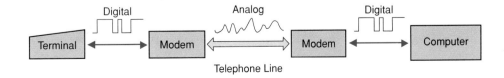

The future of world telecommunications is linked to the gradual introduction of the Integrated Service Digital Network (ISDN)—a completely digital telecommunications network standardized by an international committee (CCITT). Although these services are already available in some areas, including parts of the United States, worldwide ISDN is not expected to become operational before the year 2000. Any digital equipment conforming to ISDN standards will be able to connect directly to the network and to communicate with any appropriate device at the other end. The network will automatically furnish the channel required by a terminal, fax machine, or a telephone. The basic channel supplied by ISDN will have a speed of 64,000 bps—a significant speed-up from today's analog environment, but still not considered sufficient by many observers. Facilities offering much higher speed (broadband ISDN) will be available for computer-to-computer communications and for carrying video information. Users of broadband ISDN will be able to carry on a conversation and simultaneously exchange images and data over a single line of the telephone network.

7.4 COMPUTER NETWORKS

Computer networks differ in scope from relatively slow wide area networks, employed to transmit messages across vast geographic distances, to very fast local area networks that may connect computers located in the same building. System designers may select one of several arrangements for interconnecting network nodes, depending on an organization's requirements. Of the three principal ways to establish a connection between the sender and the receiver of a message—all three of which we shall discuss in this section—packet switching is most often used in data communications.

The Scope of Networks

Computers, terminals, equipment for communication control, and the links connecting them make up a **computer network.** Some networks extend over a wide area—a country or the entire globe—and thus are called wide area networks, or WANs. Others cover a metropolitan area (metropolitan area networks, or MANs), and still others extend no further than within a building or a campus (local area networks, or LANs).

The WAN of a transnational corporation could be global, while the WAN of a local midsized company may span just several states. Wide area networks use lines and equipment provided by common carriers, as will be discussed later in this chapter. Transmission speeds over common-carrier links usually do not surpass 9,600 bps, although much faster links may be secured from value-added carriers or through leasing.

LANs are fast networks (generally offering speeds between 1 and 10 Mbps, but sometimes reaching 100 Mbps) with equipment owned by the user firm.

Broadly speaking, WANs make the computational and data-accessing power of larger machines available to a large number of workstations. LANs, on the other hand, are generally networks of microcomputers.

The purpose of MANs, which are a recent development, is to interconnect various LANs within a metropolitan area, that is, within approximately a fifty-mile range. MANs offer speeds of 50 Mpbs (Davis, 1990).

The metaphor of a "wired society" (or at any rate, a communicating society, considering the importance of wireless satellite transmission) is slowly becoming reality as more and more of these various networks become interconnected. A variety of ownership arrangements exists today: networks may be owned by user firms (and many a small company does own a local area network), by consortia of user firms, or by firms that offer basic (connection only) or enhanced network services. The costs of networking are significant, and both the implementation decision itself and the manner in which this implementation is to take place should be subject to a rigorous economic and technological analysis.

Network Topologies

Computers and terminals interconnected by network links are collectively called *nodes:* the purpose of network control is to provide a connection between nodes that need to communicate. The arrangement of nodes and links in a network is called its **topology.** A variety of arrangements is possible, each with its own advantages and drawbacks. Network topology has to fit the structure of the organizational unit that will use the network, and it should also be adapted to the unit's communication traffic patterns and to the way the databases will be stored to facilitate access to them.

The following topologies are the most widely used:

1. Hierarchical Network

A hierarchical network with a corporate host computer (generally a mainframe or a multiprocessor), divisional minicomputers, and workgroup support via micros is shown in figure 7.3. This topology matches the organizational structure of many a firm and is frequently used for wide area networks. Failure of the host does not disable divisional processing, which is a fail-safe feature.

2. Star Network

In a star network, as shown in figure 7.11a, a central host computer or switch (such as a PBX, which we shall discuss later) interconnects a number of workstations. If the computer is located at the hub, it does most of the processing and is the site where the database is located. All communications between the workstations must go through this central node. The star network is rather easy to manage and expand—since in both cases it is largely the single central node that is affected. But this central node is also a locus of vulnerability: it may be overloaded or it may fail, disabling the entire network.

3. Ring Network

Each node in a ring network is connected to two of its neighbors, as shown in figure 7. 11b. The nodes are usually close to one another—this topology is frequently used in LANs. When one node sends a message to another, the message has to pass through each intermediate node (which also restores the signal, as it deteriorates in transmission). If a node fails, the ring is out of service, unless the ring contains two channels transmitting in opposite directions.

FIGURE 7.11

Network topologies.
a. Star; b. Ring; c. Bus.

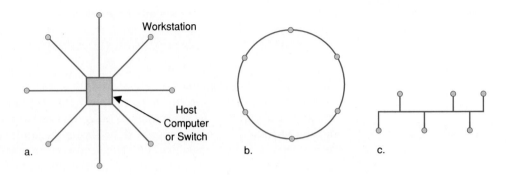

4. Bus Network

The nodes on a bus network (see figure 7.11c) are connected to a common link such as cable. As is true of the ring, this arrangement is used in LANs. A failing device does not affect the rest of the network; failure of the bus itself, of course, brings the network down.

Switching in Networks

Many users can be connected at the same time to a network of communication channels. How is the connection between two nodes established so that communication can take place? The means for establishing this interconnection is called *switching* and there are three principal techniques for doing this.

1. Circuit Switching

The circuit switching technique is employed in a telephone network. Communication links are connected to switching centers, which connect on demand one node to another; the circuit is then established for the entire duration of the communication.

2. Message Switching

In message switching, a complete message is moved through the network from its source to its destination. If a link is temporarily busy, the message is stored at an intermediate node and later forwarded to its address. Some electronic mail systems employ this technique.

3. Packet Switching

Packet switching is of particular importance for data communication owing to its speed and its superior utilization of communication links. Packet switching also offers flexibility in connecting to a network. It is used by most of the public data networks provided by value-added carriers (discussed later).

In packet switching, messages are divided at source into fixed-length packets that also include a data envelope identifying them (generally 80 to 150 characters in total). Each packet is transmitted independently, with routing determined at each node the packet passes through (as opposed to circuit and message switching, where the route is predetermined). Packet switching is illustrated in figure 7.12.

The destination node reassembles the packet into a complete message. The packet assembly and disassembly function may be handled by the communicating nodes, or, if a node is a "dumb" terminal, by an interface device. Packet switching is standardized in the CCITT Recommendation X.25. Thanks to this international standard, national public packet-switching networks may be interconnected into a global network.

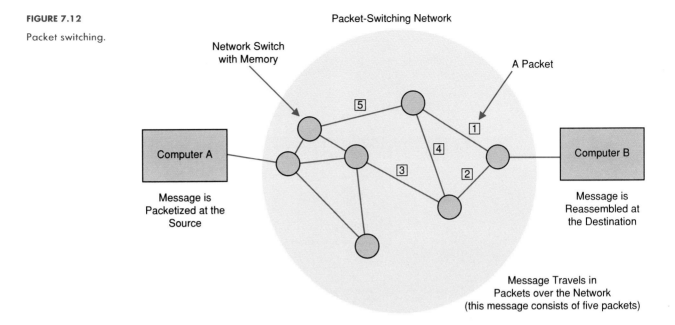

FIGURE 7.12

Packet switching.

7.5 COMMUNICATION PROTOCOLS IN COMPUTER NETWORKS

Communication rules, called protocols, enable dissimilar hardware and software to communicate over a network; internetwork communication is also a frequent requirement of businesses today.

Network Protocols   Computer networks exist to provide connectivity among a variety of computers and terminals. To ensure orderly communication over a network, all the nodes in the network must follow a set of rules called **protocol.** These rules are complex. They extend from the electric connection to the network and the format of the message all the way to the interaction between application programs that run on different nodes. As we shall see in chapter 10, a principal technique for handling complexity is to structure the complex entity into layers of abstraction. This is the technique used in network protocol design.

With the globalization of telecommunications, protocol design is best handled by international bodies. In fact, the International Standards Organization has developed the Open Systems Interconnection (OSI) model protocol—a seven-layer architecture for communicating systems. This **open-system** telecommunications architecture opens the field to a broad array of competing vendors—a situation that should benefit users, who need not be locked into the closed, proprietary architecture of a specific manufacturer. The OSI protocol gives both users and vendors much flexibility in conforming with a standard. They can select

FIGURE 7.13

The Open Systems
Interconnection (OSI) model.

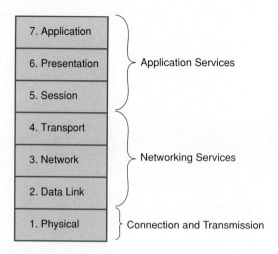

TABLE 7.2

Layers of the OSI Model
and Their Functions

LAYER	FUNCTION
1. Physical	Provides access to the telecommunications medium and ensures transmission of the bit stream over it.
2. Data link	Ensures error-free transmission of frames (blocks) of data over a network link.
3. Network	Routes message (or packets) from source to destination by selecting connecting links.
4. Transport	Provides reliable end-to-end connection between two communicating nodes. When packet switching is used (according to the X.25 standard), this layer breaks a message into packets.
5. Session	Establishes, maintains, and terminates a connection (session) between two applications running on communicating nodes. A session lasts, for example, from a log-on to a specific application to a log-off.
6. Presentation	Provides any necessary conversions of the characters being sent (encryption/decryption, compression/decompression, or character code conversions). Issues requests for establishing and terminating a session to the session layer.
7. Application	Provides services to communicating application programs; examples include file transfer, running a remote program, allocating a remote peripheral, and ensuring integrity of remote databases.

the technique a network component employs to handle a given protocol function. If a layer has to be changed, only the hardware or software implementing that layer need be modified—so long as the interfaces with the adjacent layers stay the same. The OSI standard is now being gradually implemented, and an expansive growth of open systems based on this standard is expected during the 1990s.

The OSI model protocol is illustrated in figure 7.13. A protocol layer in one node interacts with the corresponding layer in another one. It is useful to study the OSI model to understand the functions which computer networks must handle.

Table 7.2 explains the function of each of the seven layers of protocol. (It may help to start your reading with the functions of the highest, seventh, layer.)

Network architecture such as OSI involves three levels of connectivity: physical (between hardware devices and communication channels), systems (between various levels of systems programs), and applications (between application programs).

To understand how the OSI architecture operates, let us consider a user on node A who wants to send a file to a computer (node B). The application layer on both nodes would receive the user's instructions and identify the file. The presentation layer would ensure that the file, when transferred, would be in the format appropriate for node B. The session layer initiates the transfer session. The transport layer breaks up the file into packets (assuming that ours is a packet-switching net), which the network layer routes to node B. The data link layer transmits packets over individual links, checking for errors, and the physical layer makes sure that the bits reach node B.

Note that the overhead encountered in implementing the OSI model is significant. In a sending node, the "protocol stack" is descended as the message is sent, while in the receiving node, the stack is ascended as the message is received.

A widely used manufacturer's protocol, which by now has many characteristics of an open system, is IBM's Systems Network Architecture (SNA). Its functions are broken down into layers, just as in the OSI model (which SNA predates). There are five layers in SNA, basically performing the functions of the five middle OSI levels. Other vendors have their own standards—which explains why the customers' movement to the OSI model is so strong.

Interconnections among Networks

As communication needs increase, network connectivity becomes a major issue: a user at a workstation wants to be able to access a computer resource located virtually anywhere (or send a message to a remote user). To gain access to a remote resource (for example, a database or a mass storage device with a document base), the user must not only be placed on a network, but that net must be connected to the one where the resource is. The ideal is a "seamless" system, in which the user would not be aware that the resource is not directly a part of his or her system. In a multivendor environment, connectivity is difficult and costly to achieve. Gateways and bridges between networks are the solution.

Interconnection between two networks of the same type is accomplished by a relatively simple **bridge,** implemented in hardware and software. Interconnection between heterogeneous networks, for example, a LAN and a WAN, is achieved through a more complex **gateway.** A gateway is generally a computer, such as a micro, which accepts messages in the format produced by one of the networks and translates them into the format used by the other. For example, in figure 16.1, which shows networks providing an integrated environment for an office information system, gateways are available to connect the workgroup LANs to the company's backbone WAN as well as to connect this backbone to other wide area nets. Specialized software is available to control traffic in these interconnected networks (see photo 7.2).

In the future, standardization on the OSI model protocol will be the principal means of ensuring a seamless environment, which is already beginning to emerge.

PHOTO 7.2

Graphical user interface of NetWare 386 Communications Services Manager from Novell, Inc. (of Sunnyvale, California), which enables users on a central site to monitor, control, and manage telecommunications services furnished by multiple networks located anywhere in the world.

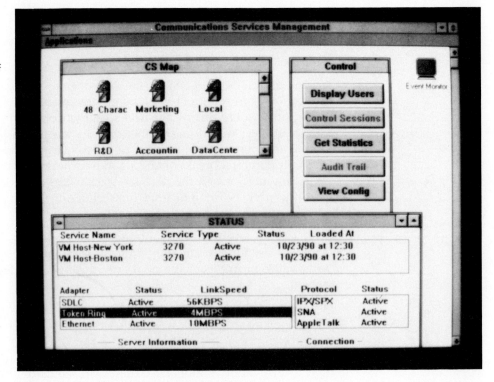

7.6 WIDE AREA NETWORKS

Long-distance communication networks employ a variety of equipment so that links may be used efficiently. The offerings of common carriers and of providers of value-added services may be combined with private networks to create an overall organizational network.

Telecommunications Equipment

Aside from telecommunication links, computer networks also include the equipment that controls message transfers and makes it possible to share the links among a number of transfers. A configuration comprised of the principal equipment is shown in figure 7.14, although a variety of topologies is, of course, possible.

The configuration in figure 7.14 includes a mainframe computer, called the *host* of the network. To relieve this machine of most of the tasks involved in network control, they are allocated to the **front-end processor** (typically a minicomputer), which handles all incoming and outgoing messages. The host runs a systems program, called a *telecommunications monitor,* which invokes the programs that process incoming messages and accepts outgoing messages from application programs in order to transmit them to their destinations. The front-end processor, under the control of its own software, handles all the remaining work. It accepts messages coming from the network, routes outgoing messages

FIGURE 7.14

Telecommunications equipment in a wide area network.

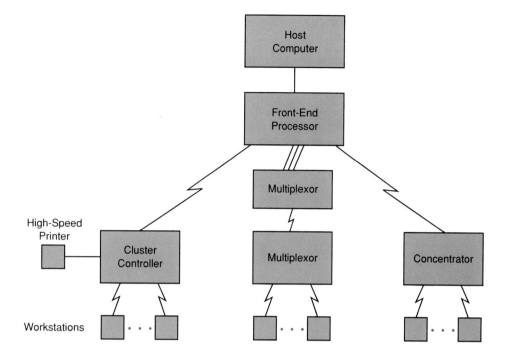

to their destinations, performs the necessary code conversions (say, from ASCII to EBCDIC), encrypts and decrypts secure messages, and performs error checking.

On remote locations of the network in figure 7.14 are three types of devices that may be used to control terminals. All of them may be implemented on minicomputers or on powerful micros. A *cluster controller* manages several terminals, connecting them to a single telecommunications link, and performs communication tasks for them, such as screen formatting, code conversion, and error checking. A cluster controller may also allow the terminals to share a high-speed printer, may handle electronic mail among the cluster terminals, or may allow the terminals to access more than one host computer (if the controller is connected to more than one telecommunications link). Such a controller may be installed, for example, in a bank's branch office for a cluster of tellers' terminals.

Multiplexors and concentrators help to utilize communication lines more efficiently—and the lines are an expensive item in network operation. A *multiplexor* combines the data that terminals send to it over local low-speed links into a single stream. This stream is then transmitted over a high-speed telecommunications channel and is split by another multiplexor on the opposite end of the channel. For example, the data from four terminals transmitting at 2,400 bps over a short cable to the local multiplexor may be combined into one transmission over a single 9,600 bps transoceanic cable, at significant savings.

A *concentrator* combines transmissions from several slower terminals that operate in a burst mode (such as data queries sent to a host) into a single transmission stream which requires a link of lower speed than the sum of the speeds of all the terminals combined. A concentrator does this by storing messages from the terminals and forwarding them when warranted—thus squeezing out idle terminal time. Concentrators produce further economies in the utilization of telecommunication links.

Another type of equipment used in computer communication networks is a switch, which is generally computer-based. A network switch establishes connections between nodes that need to communicate (since relatively few nodes are connected point-to-point); we saw such switches in the packet-switching network pictured in figure 7.12.

Network workstations include a variety of dumb terminals, which have no processing capacity, and intelligent terminals such as personal computers. When intelligent terminals are employed, some message handling tasks may be off-loaded to them.

The overall distribution of "intelligence,"—that is, processing capability—among the hosts, the various communication processors, and the workstations depends on the nature of the applications to be handled by the network and is established at the time of network design.

Where Do the Facilities of Wide Area Networks Come From?

Some network facilities are owned by user organizations; others can be leased by them, or simply used on a pay-as-you-go basis. Among the typical facilities owned by user firms are workstations, host computers, and front-end processors (although in time-sharing networks, user firms purchase both processing power and telecommunications). Local area networks, which we will discuss later in the chapter, are virtually always owned by the user organization.

The essential providers of telecommunications services are common carriers and the vendors of enhanced services on value-added networks.

1. Common Carriers

   Common carriers are companies that are licensed by the government to provide communication services to the public: the vast majority provide telephone service. These carriers offer the use of a wide-area telecommunications infrastructure, that is, facilities for the transmission of voice and data messages. Most countries of the world have a single common carrier which is owned by the government, since this service may be considered a natural monopoly. In other countries, common carriers compete. In the United States, there are thousands of common carriers, with only a few of them "major players." The best known is AT&T (see color plate 9), closely followed by seven companies that resulted from its break-up in 1983, the Regional Holding Companies. NYNEX, as one such a company, owns the operating companies that provide telephone service to Maine, Massachusetts, New Hampshire, New York, Rhode Island, and Vermont. Other larger common carriers include GTE (which operates US Sprint) and MCI Communications; most of the remaining companies are small independents. Specialized common carriers are also emerging. Of particular importance are the satellite common carriers, which operate satellites and sell communication capacities they provide. The earth stations may be owned by the user firms.

   The telecommunications links provided by common carriers are shared by their users, be it an individual making a telephone call or a retail store sending its daily operating data to corporate headquarters. Wide area corporate networks often rely on public telephone links. Linkage between communicating agents in the public telephone system is established by circuit switching.

2. Providers of Value-Added Networks

Value-added common carriers provide public data networks by leasing facilities from the common carriers and offering a variety of services to their subscribers. These services add value to the basic connectivity furnished by the common carrier. These **value-added networks (VANs)** furnish services over and above those provided by common carriers. The sophistication of the service provided varies widely. A value-added carrier may simply provide a packet-switching network: for example, Telenet (owned by GTE) offers such packet-switched communication services, as well as electronic mail. Subscribers pay for the actual number of packets transmitted, which is economical for them if they need to send moderate amounts of data over long distances.

Providers of time-shared computing services and of electronic information services, vital for acquiring information about the business environment of a firm, may also be considered value-added carriers. Another form of value-added service expanding in use is videoconferencing (Hayes, 1991). Videoconferencing enables people at different work sites not only to see and hear each other, but also to exchange data, documents, and graphics. The modern techniques of data compression have made acceptable picture quality available at lower transmission speeds, making the service far less costly than it was formerly. Highly specialized professionals and executives, who face great demands on their time, are able to use this time more productively with videoconferencing services, diminishing their need to travel. AT&T and US Sprint have introduced public videoconferencing networks (Moeller, 1990). Value-added networks which supply electronic information services will be discussed in chapter 16 in the context of office information systems.

There are many value-added networks that serve specific industries, such as the cooperatively owned SWIFT network, which connects over 2,000 banks around the globe for clearing purposes. GEISCO, a subsidiary of General Electric, is the largest "enhanced communications" supplier in the world (Keen, 1988). It uses its telecommunications infrastructure to offer a great variety of value-added services, from processing electronic payments to furnishing communications and information services for "smart buildings."

Table 7.3 lists the principal value-added services available over telecommunications networks.

The variety of services provided in telecommunications networks is constantly growing as the services themselves evolve. In the United States, audiotex is an exploding market (Keller, 1990), while videotex is growing relatively slowly, hobbled by lack of connectivity among videotex services and the complexity of a PC-based user interface as compared to the telephone.

THE ULTIMATE MAILBOX

Common carriers are always interested in providing profitable value-added services. They are now working on a complete telecommunications "mailbox." Maintained on a carrier's computer, this mailbox would receive voice messages, electronic mail sent through other computers, and faxed documents. By dialing their authorization code, customers would receive these communications in spoken form, on their computer screens, or as fax outputs— regardless of the original format of the message.

Fragments of this system are already in place. Some carriers offer fax forwarding, which delivers a faxed message anywhere the customer can get hold of a fax machine. "There are already services converting computer text to voice messages and to fax, but reversing those processes has been harder and we don't yet have fax to voice or voice to fax," says an AT&T product manager responsible for such a project.

Based on "New Kind of Mail." *The New York Times,* May 30, 1990, p. D8.

TABLE 7.3

Services Available Over Telecommunications Networks

Audiotex	Information and entertainment ("infotainment") services furnished over the telephone (800 and 900 numbers).
Videotex	Information, entertainment, and other services (such as shopping or banking) delivered via a terminal or a personal computer (for example, Prodigy—a joint venture between IBM and Sears, Roebuck).
Electronic Mail	See chapter 16 for a discussion of E-mail and related services, such as teleconferencing and special-interest networks.
Electronic Data Interchange (EDI)	The primary means of interorganizational networking to avoid paper-based communication.
Telefacsimile	Fax transmission of documents has become ubiquitous.
Transaction Processing	Banks' automatic teller machine (ATM) networks, merchants' point-of-sale (POS) services, credit verification services for credit-card companies.
Electronic Information Services	Vital for corporate environmental scanning—see the listing in chapter 16.

3. Private Lines and Private Networks

Instead of using a service that has to be shared with others, a firm may lease its own private lines or entire networks from carriers. This may have economic advantages, as well as provide for faster and more secure communications.

The U.S. common carriers, including the satellite carriers, offer a number of tariffs (services) for leased communication channels. Leasing links may result in savings for high-volume point-to-point communications. The links may also be upgraded to meet the specific requirements of a particular user firm.

7.7 LOCAL AREA NETWORKS AND PRIVATE BRANCH EXCHANGES

Organizations small and large need to interconnect local workstations and computers with fast local networks. These local networks may be configured of interconnected computers of various categories, but today they are most frequently local area networks (LANs) of personal computers—the basic workgroup tool. Instead of wiring local computers together through communication links, some firms elect to interconnect them with a private branch exchange (PBX)—an upgraded telephone switchboard.

Local Area Network—A Workplace for a Workgroup

A **local area network (LAN)** interconnects computers within a single site, such as an office building, a manufacturing plant, or a corporate or university campus. The distances covered by these nets do not surpass fifteen to twenty miles and are commonly far shorter. Communication speeds are very high, in some cases up to 100 Mbps. This makes network transmission almost transparent to the users.

Local area networks have become a vital tool in organizing workgroup activity, which we shall further discuss in chapter 16. LANs are the most common means of local connectivity. Today, they are the principal nets of smaller businesses and are used as local means of computing and communication among users in larger firms. Through LANs, personal computers—the nodes of these networks—are converted into true workstations. This is because a LAN gives users the following capabilities:

1. Users can share resources—such as a fast printer or a database.

2. Groupware that runs on a LAN helps coordinate work within a user team as well as providing a vehicle for team collaboration (which we shall further discuss in chapter 16).

3. Users can access other networks within a firm or outside of it via bridges and gateways.

LANs are owned by the organization, and, in another sense, "owned" by the workgroup that uses them. This affords flexibility and a sense of control unequaled by other arrangements in distributed computing. Indeed, LANs are the principal building blocks of today's office information systems.

There are two principal LAN designs: peer-to-peer and client/server. In peer-to-peer networks, which are generally simpler, the peripherals are located at workstations and system administration is largely left up to the users; a number of low-end LANs fall into this category. More powerful LAN architectures place shared resources at dedicated *servers:* powerful micros (and sometimes even larger machines) that manage a given resource on behalf of the *clients*—user workstations that share the resource. Thus, a network may include a file server (which manages a disk on which the database and application programs are stored), a printer server, and a gateway that connects the LAN to other dissimilar networks (see figure 7.2). An optical-disk server is shown in photo 7.3. Most of

the servers are dedicated to their task; if used as workstations, they degrade performance of the net. Client/server networks facilitate centralized administration and professional support of the net.

Two of the most frequently used LAN configurations are bus and ring topologies (Durr, 1989), shown in figure 7.11. The bus topology is used in nets based on the Ethernet system, pioneered by Xerox; in LANs that use this now standardized protocol, nodes communicate at the speed of approximately 10 Mbps. The technique is used by the DEC and Apple Computer nets. Other networks, notably IBM's PCNET, are rings. The nodes in a ring communicate by token passing: an "envelope" message, called a token, is passed from one node to the next; when a node receives the token, it may also place its message on the ring (addressing it to an appropriate receiver), or simply pass the token to the next node. The leader in the LAN market is Novell Corporation's NetWare; it offers a number of protocols and configurations.

The coaxial cable is the most frequent communication medium in LANs; twisted pair, fiber-optic cables, and even infrared wireless transmission are also used. The new standard for high-speed LANs, Fiber Distributed Data Interface (FDDI), uses the token-passing technique on optical fibers to achieve speeds of up to 100 Mbps. Even that impressive speed is considered inadequate for some applications, such as servicing technical workstations which process rotating three-dimensional graphics in industrial design (Caswell, 1990).

Local Networks Based on Private Branch Exchanges (PBXs)

A company with a number of telephones (from 50 to over 10,000) often elects to own a computer-based **private branch exchange (PBX)**—an electronic switchboard that interconnects its telephones and provides connections to the public network. A PBX gives a company control over the usage of its telephone system as well as providing the latter with a variety of additional features.

A PBX may be employed as a switch for data communications as well (figure 7.15): for example, connecting user workstations to one another, to a larger host computer, and to other equipment to be shared. Many newer PBXs are expressly designed to support data communication; they use digital technology (eliminating the need for modems) and perform conversions needed to ensure connectivity.

FIGURE 7.15

A local network based on PBX.

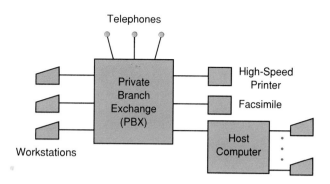

Among the advantages of PBX use for local networking is the ease of connecting a new workstation to the net: all one needs to do is plug it into a telephone outlet. However, limitations on this approach derive from differences between the demands of voice and data communication: limited transmission speeds and inefficient use of links may result.

7.8 USING TELECOMMUNICATIONS FOR RESHAPING BUSINESS PROCESSES AND FOR COMPETITIVE ADVANTAGE

The capability to move information rapidly between distant geographic locations (telecommunications), often combined with the capability to bring processing power to the point of application (distributed processing), offers a firm powerful opportunities to restructure its business processes and to capture high competitive ground in the marketplace.

A value-chain analysis of a company's activities, as discussed in chapter 5, is an excellent method for seeking these opportunities (Clemons, 1986). If one considers just some of the numerous examples presented in that chapter, it should be clear that, in most cases, telecommunications are indeed the crucial element. Many immensely successful strategic systems originated when remote terminals were placed at customer sites (as in the case of order-taking systems) or distributor sites (as in the case of airline reservations systems).

An excellent framework, which managers may use as they strive to reshape business processes and seek competitive advantage in the marketplace, is offered by Michael Hammer and Glenn Mangurian (Hammer, 1987). This framework is shown in table 7.4. The framework helps a manager seek out applications that can bring the potential impact of telecommunications to bear on the way a firm does business in order to create a value: This value might be an increase in the

	OPERATIONAL EFFICIENCY	MANAGEMENT EFFECTIVENESS	INNOVATION FOR COMPETITIVE ADVANTAGE
COMPRESSED TIME	Accelerate business process	Reduce information float	Create service excellence
GEOGRAPHY CONQUERED	Recapture scale and scope	Ensure global management control	Penetrate new markets
RESTRUCTURED RELATIONSHIPS	Bypass intermediaries	Distribute scarce knowledge	Build umbilical cords

efficiency of operations, improvement in the effectiveness of management, or innovation in the marketplace. The use of telecommunications can provide all of these values through the following impacts:

1. Time Compression

Telecommunications enable a firm to transmit raw data and information quickly and accurately between remote sites. As a consequence, any number of business processes that would otherwise rely on other media, such as mail or telephone, may be rethought and accelerated. Order filling, for example, can be done rapidly if the order is transmitted from a laptop in the field directly to the warehouse. By reducing the information float (the time it takes for a data item to reach the decision maker in the form of information), we can raise the quality of decision making. For example, as point-of-sale data become available to retailers' executives in the form of analytic reports, merchandising function is vastly improved.

The national daily newspaper *USA Today* is edited and composed at the headquarters of its publisher, Gannett Corporation in Arlington, Virginia, and transmitted over a satellite network to thirty-six printing plants in the United States, Europe, and Asia. It reaches 6 million readers each weekday in a timely fashion and offers high-quality color reproduction. Since its 1982 launch, the paper missed only one publication date because of a telecommunications failure—due to a lightning hit (Powell, 1991).

Service excellence has been recognized as the prime source of competitive advantage. By tracking deliveries and selling information as a part of service, Federal Express and its follower in that regard, United Parcel Service, raised the quality of their service and used information systems strategically.

2. Overcoming Geographical Dispersion

Telecommunications enable an organization with geographically remote sites to function (to a degree) as though these sites were a single unit. The firm can then reap benefits of scale and scope which would otherwise be unobtainable. For example, Chrysler has an inventory management system that allows it to efficiently share parts located in a number of dispersed warehouses, with huge cost savings. Back-office functions may also be performed in locales where an inexpensive labor force is available.

Consistent management is possible throughout dispersed, perhaps globally dispersed, corporate subunits. The ability to exercise effective centralized control enables corporations to decentralize decision making to local managers (Applegate, 1988).

Being close to the customers is time-hallowed business wisdom. But in the age of telecommunications, "closeness" does not require the physical presence of large corporate entity: it may mean merely a quickly established field office with a skeleton staff, supported with telecommunications links to other parts of the firm. Merrill Corporation, a financial printer, maintains only sales offices in the field, close to its clients, with its production facility located at its headquarters in St. Paul, Minnesota (Feeny, 1990). A wide area network connects sales offices to the plant in St. Paul, where an inexpensive and well-trained labor pool is on hand. This has given the firm a decisive competitive advantage over its competitors, who are saddled with high costs of multiple production facilities maintained at sales offices across the country. As the globalization of business progresses, quick-draw forms of "electronic presence" designed to penetrate new markets may be expected to proliferate. We encountered an example of a virtual global company—Rosenbluth International Alliance—in Case Study 2 of chapter 5.

3. Restructuring Business Relationships

Telecommunications make it possible to create systems which restructure the interactions of people within a firm as well as a firm's relationships with its customers. Operational efficiency may be raised by eliminating intermediaries from various business processes. Such intermediaries include people who handle paperwork now being replaced by EDI, middle managers whose primary role is providing information, and brokers whose services are no longer needed since the firm can replace them with its own telecommunications-based sales and service network.

An expert's knowledge may be distributed by providing access to him or to her via teleconferencing facilities; a locus of collective knowledge may be created by setting up a teleconference on a topic of interest (see chapter 16) or by installing a remotely accessible expert system. In more general terms, opening databases to broad remote access or establishing electronic mail links distributes knowledge throughout a firm. Some organizations move toward making all communications over corporate E-mail systems, other than administrative or otherwise classified messages, accessible to all corporate employees.

The most widely known strategic systems tie customers to a firm with telecommunications links. Once such a link is established, additional services may be provided to the customer, increasing revenue as well as raising the costs of switching to another supplier. Such links become umbilical cords, and they may be cast into many contexts. For example, a hospital may upgrade its relationship with its affiliated physicians by giving them access to its information system—and being granted access to their information bases (Osborn, 1989–90).

7.9 MANAGEMENT ASPECTS OF DISTRIBUTING INFORMATION SYSTEMS

The development of distributed systems is supported both by technology push—the lower costs of processing power delivered by smaller systems— and by demand pull—opportunities for organizational effectiveness and for greater exercise of decision-making powers within a firm's subunits. In simple words, end users increasingly demand control over their systems.

Distributed information systems, which rely on telecommunications and computer technologies, extend users' informational reach from a workstation to a workgroup LAN and on to a global organizational WAN, with connections to networks outside the organization.

Because of these opportunities, a firm's general management, as well as its MIS managers, need to create an architectural framework for corporate information systems and seek out applications that benefit the firm, as described in the preceding section. The technological options available today are daunting. Decisions in structuring an organization's computing and telecommunications should be business-driven; technologies ought to be selected to support a firm's targeted business objectives. This also means establishing business-oriented criteria of success (such as answering customer queries from anywhere within the country within two minutes), as opposed to technical criteria (such as upgrading the speed of a telecommunications link).

The architecture of organizational computing should fit the overall organizational structure, distribution of decision-making activity, corporate culture, and competitive strategy, as difficult as this fit is to achieve (Ein-Dor, 1982; Leifer, 1988). In today's fluid organizational environment, in which the internal restructuring of firms is accompanied by mergers, acquisitions, divestitures, and alliances, it is vital to maintain an overall vision of the organizational MIS (Keen, 1988). This vision must be cast into a long-term master plan, which is then implemented through lower-level plans and systems development, as we will outline in chapter 17. A path of evolution from the existing to the new environment must be provided.

As information systems cross national borders, companies develop global architectures for their distributed information systems (Karimi, 1991). We will discuss some of the considerations involved in globalization in section 12.9 of the book. In particular, legal limitations that different countries impose on **transborder data flow** must be taken into account in systems planning (Buss, 1984). Some countries indeed restrict transmission of data out of their territories, fearing loss of jobs, invasion of privacy, or even threats to national security.

Very few organizational systems are fully centralized. Companies, and even individual units of companies, display a variety of relatively centralized and relatively decentralized management forms, which we shall further discuss in chapter 12. These management structures may be supported by corresponding MIS structures. It needs to be stressed that when this support is planned, issues of effectiveness and efficiency often hide the issues of control over resources (King, 1983)—that is, political issues. The case study for Part 3 of this book will give you a chance to analyze real-life cases of centralization and decentralization of computing.

Even in environments where many aspects of management are relatively centralized, powerful forces act in favor of distributed processing. John Donovan of MIT argues that there are actually three factors in distributing computing (Donovan, 1988):

1. Distributing the processing itself, as we discussed in the framework of section 2 in this chapter. As we know, technical and organizational decisions include the distribution of computing power and databases, as well as the provision of network interconnections. Reliable and secure telecommunication links of adequate capacity must be provided. Future growth must be foreseen and accommodated (success breeds increased use).

2. Distributing applications development.

3. Distributing decision making about systems—by transferring "ownership" from MIS specialists to users.

Donovan argues that virtually every company today is moving toward distributing computing in all three directions—albeit at different paces. Under these circumstances, he further argues, the role of a company's central MIS function will be to provide the infrastructure—the backbone network which will ensure connectivity and provide global services to distributed systems. In the next vignette, Donovan offers a cautionary tale about the consequences of a lack of distributed authority over applications development.

Distributed computing supports local initiative and was associated with aggressive market posture in at least one study (Tavakolian, 1989). Today, unless other overriding considerations exist, computing is being distributed to functional units owing to the following considerations:

- Doing business effectively requires controlling the computer resources that support business processes.
- The working environment is generally improved when computing is distributed. Users equipped with their own personal computers can make up their own data processing schedules and obtain better response times than on shared machines.
- Distributed systems offer the advantages of scalability—relatively easy growth or contraction, as required, and increased fault-tolerance.

WHAT CAN HAPPEN WHEN APPLICATIONS DEVELOPMENT REMAINS CENTRALIZED

The local offices of a real estate company relied on their own customized sales and marketing information systems to track their resources: homes, condominiums, and raw land. The offices had their own computing equipment (connected to the corporate mainframe), as well as the authority to *specify* the applications they needed. However, the central MIS staff would *develop* the actual applications to these specifications to make sure that all the inventory was accounted for in the corporate database.

Applications development by the central MIS staff soon created a bottleneck. The backlog of modifications requested by local offices in response to their specific conditions kept growing. Going over the head of the chief information officer (CIO), local managers received permission to hire consultants to make the changes. Before long, information started to migrate from the corporate database on the mainframe to the personal computers in local offices, and not all updates were sent back. The company's database of property inventory became inaccurate. As users failed to back up the data that they in effect now "owned," some properties "disappeared" during hardware failures.

The CIO attempted to root out the private programs and even withheld mainframe services from the renegade offices. But the situation remained unresolved. Eventually, the company determined that a possible solution would be to allow the local offices to do their own software modifications as long as they met corporate standards of micro-to-mainframe communications aimed at database integrity.

Based on (Donovan, 1988).

7.10 FUTURE DEVELOPMENTS IN TELECOMMUNICATIONS AND ORGANIZATIONAL INFORMATION SYSTEMS ARCHITECTURE

Management information systems are increasingly called upon to support the globalization of the business environment. To compete effectively both at home and on world markets, firms need to coordinate their activities on a global scale—and at the workplace level as well. Media that demand high-capacity telecommunications, such as videoconferencing, are being used increasingly to meet these needs.

All this places growing demand for both telecommunications speed and network connectivity. Digital networks, based on the ISDN standard, are expected to gradually supplant the analog plant. In the future, high-capacity media—that is, fiber optics for terrestrial communications and microwaves for satellite communications—are expected to dominate. To ensure connectivity, vendor protocols are expected to conform to the OSI standard. Two protocols conforming to OSI standards are becoming influential. Manufacturing automation protocol (MAP), developed by General Motors, is intended to support application on the factory shop floor. The technical office protocol (TOP) of Boeing Computer Services addresses the needs of office communications.

As standards fall into place, organizations are expected to move towards enterprise-wide information systems (Targowski, 1988), a federation of functional information systems integrated by telecommunications. The Systems Application Architecture (SAA) being introduced by IBM will make it possible to develop applications with parts that run on networked micros, minis, and mainframes, drawing as needed on the capabilities of each of these computer categories (and illustrating the concept of cooperative processing).

On a national scale, a sophisticated telecommunications infrastructure is a vital factor in ensuring competitive parity or advantage in the industrial sectors. According to Michael Porter (1990), such factors have to be continually upgraded and specialized to sustain this competitiveness. Specialized telecommunications services, based on high-capacity media and conforming to international standards, would thus contribute to the general competitiveness of U.S. industries. In the absence of networks whose speed would match the processing speed of computers, this computing power cannot be properly utilized. A consortium of U.S. companies, universities, and government agencies has been set up to create a high-speed "digital highway" based on fiber optics, which will permit telecommunications at speeds above 1 gigabit per second, hundreds of times faster than is possible now on the fastest public nets.

• •

SUMMARY

In most firms, information systems are now distributed, with processing power and databases placed on user sites and often under users' control. These systems are implemented as networks of computers, terminals, communications links, and other equipment, all of which are controlled by software. Network protocols ensure connectivity of this plethora of devices. A variety of communications media, network topologies, and switching methods are available to solve a business problem and, in larger terms, to equip a firm for global competition in the information society.

Local area networks help coordinate the work of a group of knowledge workers on a single site; wide area networks provide a variety of arrangements for structuring the overall computing effort of an organization, and often cross its boundaries as well.

One of the vital functions of today's management is the creation of a distributed computing environment that will support a firm's long-term objectives in shaping its business processes and pursuing competitive advantage in the marketplace.

**KEY TERMS AND
CONCEPTS**

Distributed processing systems   Hierarchical network
Centralized systems   Star network
Dispersed systems   Bus network
Local area network   Ring network
Wide area network   Packet switching
Telecommunications   Protocol
Communication media   Open Systems Interconnection (OSI)
Twisted pair   model protocol
Coaxial cable   Bridge
Fiber optic cable   Gateway
Terrestrial microwave   Front-end processor
Satellite transmission   Cluster controller
Analog communications   Multiplexor
Digital communications   Concentrator
Modem   Telecommunications monitor
Multiplexing   Common carrier
Integrated Services Digital   Value-added common carrier
   Network (ISDN)   Private branch exchange (PBX)
Network topology   Transborder data flow

QUESTIONS

1. Define *distributed processing systems*. Contrast them with centralized and dispersed systems.

2. Present three scenarios where a local area network acts as a tool for coordinating the work of a small company or a group of knowledge workers.

3. Why is organizational computing frequently distributed in a hierarchical wide area network?

4. Give three scenarios in which information systems cross corporate boundaries (in other words, in which interorganizational systems are used).

5. What are the three principal components in the architectural framework of a distributed system?

6. Compare the respective advantages and drawbacks of satellite and fiber-optic telecommunications.

7. Assume that a book page contains 2,400 characters (each character is an 8-bit byte). How long will it take to transmit a 200-page book over each of the following:

   a. A voice-grade line at a speed of 2,400 bits per second
   b. The basic ISDN channel
   c. A T1 digital circuit (using its full capacity)

    d. An Ethernet-based LAN

    e. A very fast fiber-optic channel of 1.7 billion bits per second (which Robert Lucky of AT&T tells us is being buried for municipal networks [Lucky, 1989])

8. What prompts a company's move to digital telecommunications?

9. What is ISDN?

10. Compare the reliability of the four network topologies discussed in the chapter.

11. Why is packet switching a frequently used technique in data communications?

12. What is network protocol, and how are network bridges and gateways related to it?

13. What is the role of the OSI model protocol?

14. Consider a front-end processor, cluster controller, multiplexor, and concentrator. Which of these types of equipment are located at the site of the host computer? Which are located at a remote site?

15. What is the principal difference between a common carrier and a value-added carrier?

16. Compare and contrast peer-to-peer and client/server LAN designs.

17. Select three examples of strategic systems discussed in chapter 5 and place them in the proper cells of the framework shown in table 7.4. (You will find that some of them cover more than one cell.)

18. What three principal aspects of MIS may be distributed (according to John Donovan)?

ISSUES FOR DISCUSSION

1. Distributed systems and communications among computers and terminals span a wide territory—and not only geographically. Contrast factors that should be considered in setting up a local area network with factors the management of a transnational company would have to take into account in planning an organizational wide area net.

2. Suppose that you are considering going into business as a distributor of software packages. Your target market will be small businesses, some of them home businesses. How can you employ computers and telecommunications to efficiently organize your business processes as well as to seek advantage over existing and potential competitors?

3. Drawing on the periodicals accessible to you, find a reasonably detailed technical description of a networked computing environment in an organization. Using the information in the description, discuss the technical and organizational choices that have been made by the company's management.

BUSINESS IS RESTRUCTURED AS INFORMATION SYSTEMS ARE DISTRIBUTED

It is sometimes very instructive to observe how a system "becomes," rather than what it looks like in its final form.

The U.S. Shoe Corporation of Cincinnati started with a goal of cutting $2 million annually from its MIS budget. This project turned into a three-year project of revamping (no pun intended) the entire business of the footwear manufacturer. The principal premise from the outset was that the firm should eliminate its corporate mainframe in favor of a distributed system, which would rely on departmental computers. These machines would be connected to workgroup LANs of microcomputers.

Carol Biemel, corporate vice-president for information systems, and her staff envisaged that the new computer system would save the company as much as 40 percent in computing costs. Though technically possible, this would require that every department discard its familiar systems. As Biemel and her staff realized this, the technical project became a large business undertaking. The question of savings was superseded by a far wider consideration: "Can information technology help us be a more efficient company?"

Managers, systems analysts, and virtually all employees started a review of the entire business process (value chain, if you will), from taking orders to shipping shoes. The objective was to eliminate unnecessary steps and improve operations, thus becoming a more competitive company.

The company started a process of evolutionary change to streamlined business processes supported by distributed computing. One year into the project, after a number of operational issues had been addressed, the company had implemented a pilot system linking its factory with the suppliers of insoles and outsoles. Working on the just-in-time principle, the system eliminated the need for a warehouse and for a purchasing agent. Carol Biemel estimates that the system will save the firm as much as $500,000 a year on just these two categories of expenses. At this time, the system is being broadened to order and process materials from other suppliers.

Biemel considers the changes in business operations throughout other parts of the firm even more important than the savings resulting from the ordering system. The power of successful example is great. Thus, Biemel demonstrated the successful reshaping of the supply function to the people at the firm's home office, who take customer orders and schedule production; she hopes they will learn from the pilot system's success.

Based on Katie Crane, "Systems Must Be Engaged for Proper Handling on Turns." *Computerworld*, January 29, 1990, pp. 55–57.

Case Study Questions

1. Classify the use of telecommunications by U.S. Shoe according to the impact-value framework presented in table 7.4. What is the principal objective of the U.S. Shoe project: reshaping business processes or directly seeking strategic advantage?

2. Why do you think Carol Biemel started with a pilot project, rather than embarking on a full-scale revamping of the existing computing system at her firm? Give at least two possible reasons.

3. Do you expect that the workers at the home office welcomed Biemel's ideas with open arms (and minds)?

4. Do you believe there may be some surprises in store for the system's implementers in regard to the expected cost reductions in *information systems* operations throughout the firm? What might cause some disappointments? On the other hand, what are the financial outcomes of more efficient *business* operations likely to be?

SELECTED REFERENCES   Applegate, Lynda M.; Cash, James I., Jr.; and Mills, D. Quinn. "Information Technology and Tomorrow's Manager." *Harvard Business Review,* November-December 1988, pp. 128–36.

Barrett, Stephanie S. "Strategic Alternatives and Interorganizational System Implementation: An Overview." *Journal of Management Information Systems,* 3, 3, Winter 1986–87, pp. 5–16.

Buss, Martin D.J. "Legislative Threat to Transborder Data Flow." *Harvard Business Review,* May-June 1984, pp. 111–18.

Cash, James I., Jr., and Konsynski, Benn R. "IS Redraws Competitive Boundaries." *Harvard Business Review,* March-April 1985, pp. 134–42.

Caswell, Stephen A. "A New LAN Standard Lights the Way." *Datamation,* May 1, 1990, pp. 75–80.

Clemons, Eric, and McFarlan, F. Warren. "Telecom: Hook Up or Lose Out." *Harvard Business Review,* July-August 1986, pp. 91–97.

Davis, Leila. "The Dawn of MAN: A Promising Way to Connect LANs." *Datamation,* June 1, 1990, pp. 85–90.

Donovan, John J. "Beyond Chief Information Officer to Network Manager." *Harvard Business Review,* September-October 1988, pp. 134–40.

Durr, Michael, and Gibbs, Mark. *Networking Personal Computers.* 3rd. ed. Carmel, Ind.: Que, 1989.

Ein-Dor, Phillip, and Segev, Eli. "Organizational Context and MIS Structure: Some Empirical Evidence." *MIS Quarterly,* 6, 3, September 1982, pp. 55–63.

Feeny, David F., and Ives, Blake. "In Search of Sustainability: Reaping Long-Term Advantage from Investments in Information Technology." *Journal of Management Information Systems,* 7, 1, Summer 1990, pp. 27–46.

Gilder, George. "Into the Telecosm." *Harvard Business Review,* March-April 1991, pp. 150–61.

Hammer, Michael, and Mangurian, Glenn E. "The Changing Value of Communications Technology." *Sloan Management Review,* Winter 1987, pp. 65–71.

Hayes, Thomas C. "Doing Business Screen to Screen." *The New York Times,* February 21, 1991, pp. D1, D15.

Karimi, Jahangir, and Konsynski, Benn, R. "Globalization and Information Management Strategies." *Journal of Management Information Systems,* 7, 4, Spring 1991, pp. 7–26.

Keen, Peter G. W. *Competing in Time: Using Telecommunications for Competitive Advantage.* Cambridge, Mass.: Ballinger, 1988.

Keller, John J. "Fun and Facts Fly Across Phone Lines as the Market for 'Audiotex' Explodes." *The Wall Street Journal,* May 25, 1990, pp. B1, B4.

King, John L. "Centralized versus Decentralized Computing: Organizational Considerations and Management Options." *Computing Surveys,* December 1983, pp. 319–50.

Leifer, Richard. "Matching Computer-Based Information Systems with Organizational Structures." *MIS Quarterly,* 12, 2, March 1988, pp. 63–73.

Lucky, Robert W. *Silicon Dreams: Information, Man, and Machine.* New York: St. Martin's Press, 1989.

McNurlin, Barbara C., and Sprague, Ralph H., Jr. *Information Systems Management in Practice.* 2nd ed. Englewood Cliffs, N.J.: Prentice Hall, 1989.

Markoff, John. "Fast Modems: All Dressed Up, with Only Slow Way to Go." *The New York Times,* February 25, 1990, p. B10.

Martin, James, with Leben, Joe. *Principles of Data Communication.* Englewood Cliffs, N.J.: Prentice Hall, 1988.

Moeller, Dick. "Has Videoconferencing Found Its Niche?" *Networking Management,* March 1990, pp. 49–55.

Osborn, Charles S.; Madnick, Stuart E.; and Wang, Y. Richard. "Motivating Strategic Alliance for Composite Information Systems: The Case of a Major Regional Hospital." *Journal of Management Information Systems,* 6, 3, Winter 1989–90, pp. 99–117.

Porter, Michael E. *The Competitive Advantage of Nations.* New York: Free Press, 1990.

Powell, Dave. "Technology and Imagination Are the Stuff from which Businesses Can Be Built." *Networking Management,* March 1991, p. 20.

Rowe, Stanford H. II. *Business Telecommunications.* Chicago: SRA, 1988.

Sellers, Patricia. "What Customers Really Want." *Fortune,* June 4, 1990, pp. 58–68.

Targowski, Andrew S. "Systems Planning for the Enterprise-wide Information Management Complex: The Architectural Approach." *Journal of Management Information Systems,* 5, 2, Fall 1988, pp. 23–38.

Tavakolian, Hamid. "Linking the Information Technology Structure with Organizational Competitive Strategy: A Survey." *MIS Quarterly,* 13, 3, September 1989, pp. 309–17.

Zwass, Vladimir, and Veroy, Boris. "Capacity Expansion for Information Flow Distribution in Multi-Path Computer Communication Networks." *Journal of Management Information Systems,* 5, 2, Fall 1988, pp. 57–70.

CHAPTER 8

DATABASES

Put all your eggs in one basket and—
WATCH THAT BASKET.

Mark Twain

O f all computer systems resources, the structure of a company's data is the most permanent. The suppliers of a firm change over time, and the products they supply change as well. But the fact that a firm maintains records of its suppliers and records of products supplied by them, as well as the relationships between these suppliers and their products, will most likely stay unchanged for a long time. These records and relationships, stored in a company's databases, reflect the business the firm is in and the way it does business—they are therefore a ''mirror'' of the company.

It is precisely because of the relative permanence of a firm's databases that information resource management (IRM) rests on the management of corporate data in databases. By treating both information and the data from which this information can be obtained as a corporate resource, the firm establishes the foundations for information resource management—and is able to control its information.

The fundamental technology of database management, which today generally rests on relational principles, is not enough to guarantee this control. Organizational processes and functions are necessary to make the technology effective.

Chevron's shipping support group, located in San Francisco, has set up a database that allows the oil company to evaluate in less than an hour the safety of a tanker it wants to charter. The database is located on a minicomputer server and is managed by a relational database management system (DBMS), Oracle, from Oracle Corporation. The new responsiveness stands in stark contrast to the prior environment, when ''there were a lot of phone calls to the owner and operator of the vessel, plus to anyone who knew anything about its safety,'' according to the project supervisor.

Colgate Palmolive of New York is opening its corporate data for direct access by managers who have no background in computing. Using another relational DBMS—INGRES, from Ingres Corporation—Colgate is building a worldwide system to replace the current environment, where users request informational reports through MIS personnel. Such requests generally require at least some programming; responses are often so delayed as to render the information useless. Now end users will be able to query the database directly from remote locations around the globe.

Sears, Roebuck maintains a massive database in Menlo Park, California. This so-called Sears Household File contains data on 75 percent of the households in the United States. In fact, the database is so detailed that Sears uses it with extreme care: for example, it makes sure that unlisted telephone numbers contained in the database are not made available for any telemarketing purposes. The database is ''massaged,'' however, for a variety of marketing purposes. Database marketing makes it possible to reach a precise—and often very small—market segment.

Based on Scott Leibs, ''. . . And a Whole Lot More.'' InformationWeek, June 12, 1989, pp. 6–7; and Daniel Todd, ''Databases as Weapons.'' InformationWeek, June 18, 1990, pp. 53–56.

As we can see, database technology is a powerful tool in the quest for operational efficiency, managerial effectiveness, and competitive advantage. You shall now learn more about this technology and how to make it effective in an enterprise.

CHAPTER OUTLINE

8.2   The File-Oriented Environment
  • File Organization
  • Limitations of a File-Oriented Environment

8.3   A Database Environment and Its Advantages

8.4   Data Independence in Databases

8.5   Data Models or How to Represent Relationships between Data

8.6   Relational Databases

8.7   SQL—A Relational Query Language

8.8   Designing a Relational Database

8.9   Distributed Processing and Distributed Databases

8.10 The Data Dictionary

8.11 Organizational Factors in Information Resource Management

8.12 Data Administration and Database Administration

8.13 Beyond Relational Databases

      Summary

      Key Terms and Concepts

      Questions

      Issues for Discussion

      Optional Exercise: Database Management

      Case Study: Developing an Information Architecture for a Firm

      Selected References

• •

8.1 HIERARCHY OF DATA

Data stored in computer systems form a hierarchy extending from a single bit to a database, a major record-keeping entity of a firm. The higher rungs of this hierarchy, as shown in figure 8.1, are organized from the lower ones.

The smallest unit of data representation in a computer system is a **bit,** whose value may be 0 or 1. Bits are aggregated into **bytes** to represent characters and special symbols with the use of a character code, as we discussed in chapter 6.

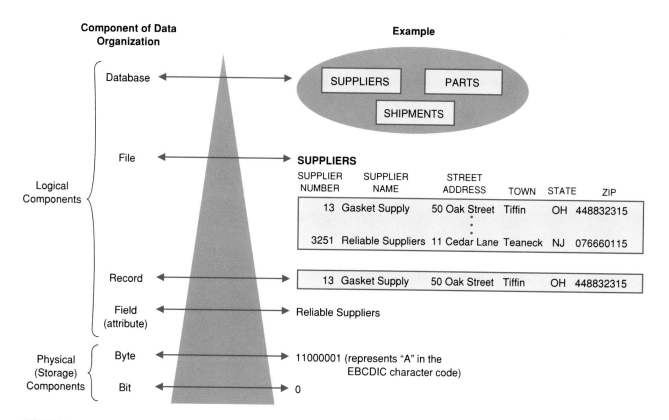

FIGURE 8.1

Hierarchy of data
organization in computer
storage.

Bits and bytes are physical units of data representation: they reflect the way computer memories are designed. The higher rungs of the data hierarchy are logical: they deal with the real-world objects the data represent.

The smallest named unit of data is a **field** (also called a data element). For example, the name of a supplier company in a supplier database is a single field, since we will never break that supplier's name down into smaller parts. On the other hand, a supplier's address may be broken down in the database into four fields: street address, town, state, and zip code. Such separation may be useful: in some applications we would like to identify all suppliers in a certain city; in others, we want to sort the suppliers by zip code. We may conclude that data organization depends on what use we want to put the data to. As we saw in chapter 6, there are many sources of organizational data, with automated data entry gaining in importance.

A **record** describes a real-world entity (an object). This object may be tangible, such as a supplier, or intangible, such as a shipment. Thus, a record consists of fields, with each field describing an attribute of the object (that is why we sometimes refer to fields as attributes). For example, the name of a supplier could be an attribute.

Records of the same type, that is, describing the same type of objects, are aggregated into a **file.** (We deal with *data* files in this chapter; a file is, of course, also a broader term for any named unit of information stored in secondary storage—thus, we may have a text file or a program file.) A supplier file would contain records of all of our suppliers. Generally, a field in the file (for example, a supplier number) identifies a record so that we may access a needed record by presenting this identifier. This field is called the **primary key** of the file. Sometimes, the key must consist of more than one field to ensure a unique identification. In certain applications, files remain the highest organizational component of persistent, that is, continually maintained, data.

As we shall discuss below, in today's MIS, files increasingly exist as parts of **databases,** managed by systems software called database management systems (DBMS). In figure 8.1, we show a database that maintains records of suppliers, the parts they supply, and parts shipments in progress. The crucial advantage of databases as compared with a collection of files is that, aside from storing the records of individual files, databases also store relationships among these records. We shall consider the broader advantages of the database environment as opposed to a file-oriented environment later in this chapter.

Files and databases are maintained in secondary storage. Traditionally, data stored in secondary storage were organized in files; many older and some new applications still rely exclusively on files. Databases managed by DBMS emerged in the late 1960s, and their sophistication has vastly increased since. Database environments rely on direct access, and databases are therefore stored on disks (with tapes often used for backup). We shall first discuss rather briefly the organization of data files and then focus on the database environment. Note that many of the concepts of file organization apply to the physical storage of data in databases.

8.2 THE FILE-ORIENTED ENVIRONMENT

The three principal methods of file organization are sequential, indexed-sequential, and direct (random); only the last two methods provide the direct access necessary in on-line systems. File management systems extend the power of a file-oriented environment by providing the capability to access records on secondary keys. The file-oriented approach may be cheaper for some applications. However, a file-oriented environment suffers from very significant limitations that make it unsuitable as an organizing principle for an enterprise's data.

File Organization

Data files are organized in a manner that facilitates access to records as well as ensuring their efficient storage. A trade-off between these two requirements generally exists: if rapid access is required, more storage must be expended to make it possible.

Access to a record for reading it (and sometimes for updating it) is the essential operation on data. As we mentioned in chapter 6 in discussing the secondary storage devices where files are kept, there are two types of access: sequential and direct. **Sequential access** is performed when records are accessed in the order they are stored. Sequential access is the main access mode only in batch systems, where files are used and updated at regular intervals—for example, every night or every week. In the interim, the contents of the master file do not reflect changes in the environment; the records that reflect these changes are kept in a transaction file, as it was shown in figure 4.2.

TABLE 8.1

File Organization Methods and Their Applications.

FILE ORGANIZATION	ACCESS METHOD	ENVIRONMENT OF APPLICATION	ADVANTAGES	DISADVANTAGES
Sequential	Sequential	Batch	Simplicity of management; efficient use of storage; may be placed on cheap storage (tape).	Insertions and updates usually impossible without creating a new file; general disadvantages of batch processing.
Indexed-sequential	Sequential or direct (random)	Batch/on-line	Relatively good storage utilization while both access modes are possible.	Space for indexes and time for their maintenance; slow direct access to large files. Periodic file reorganization is necessary.
Direct (random)	Direct (random)	On-line	Fast direct access.	Relatively poor space utilization; difficult to use when records are needed in sequence.

FIGURE 8.2

A sequential file.

SOCIAL SECURITY NUMBER	NAME	WEEKLY SALARY	DEPARTMENT
011731391	John A. Weeks	525	Manufacturing
231426182	Gilbert Lee	650	Personnel
452398651	Andrew L. Boyd	550	Manufacturing

On-line processing requires **direct access** (also called random access), in which a record can be accessed without accessing the records between it and the beginning of the file. The primary key serves to identify the needed record. A direct access storage device, such as a magnetic disk, is required.

Three methods of file organization are in predominant use and are supported by operating systems with so-called access method routines. These methods are summarized in table 8.1.

Let us briefly review these file organization methods.

1. Sequential Organization

Sequential file organization is the simplest: file records are stored in the sequence of the values of their primary keys. Thus, in figure 8.2, personnel records are stored in ascending order of employees' Social Security numbers.

Efficient use of sequential files requires that a large number of records be accessed during a run—which is typical in a batch system. All update transactions (deletions, insertions, and modifications of field values) are accumulated over a period of time, then sorted in the same primary key sequence as the master file, and finally run off against the master to create a new master file (see figure 4.2).

FIGURE 8.3

Indexes of an indexed
sequential file.

(Adapted from Zwass, 1981)

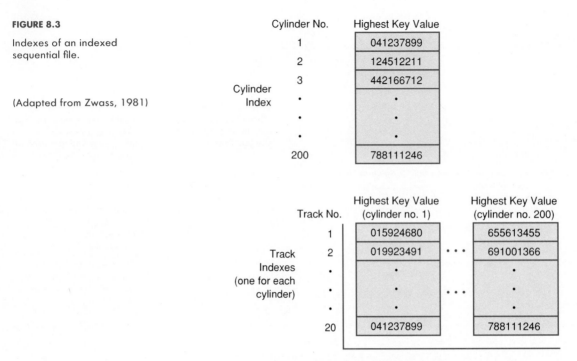

The disk has 200 cylinders and 20 surfaces (4000 tracks)

2. Indexed-Sequential Organization

In indexed-sequential files, records are also stored in their primary key sequence, which makes possible efficient sequential access. This may be needed, for example, for detailed reporting from the file. In addition, to provide direct access, indexes to the file are maintained. File *indexes* are tables (generally themselves stored as files) that show where the file records are located in secondary storage. One way to organize such indexes (as is done in IBM's ISAM access method) is shown in figure 8.3.

As we discussed in chapter 6, records are placed on a disk, cylinder by cylinder, in their key sequence. They are located on consecutive tracks of a given cylinder, that is, on consecutive disk surfaces. The index of figure 8.3 has, therefore, a hierarchical structure, with the highest values of the key on a given track or cylinder placed in the index. When a record is being accessed, first the cylinder index is used to find the record's cylinder; then the track index for that cylinder is consulted, and the track itself is searched for the record.

Insertions are usually made into a special overflow area of the disk, with a pointer to that record placed in the track where the record belongs. Periodically, the file is reorganized in order to merge the records from the overflow area into the main (prime) area of the file.

3. Direct Organization

Direct file organization provides the fastest direct access to records. No indexes are maintained in this case. Instead, the primary key of a record is transformed directly into its disk address with a so-called *hashing* algorithm. When the record is accessed in the future, the same hashing

FIGURE 8.4

A hashing procedure.

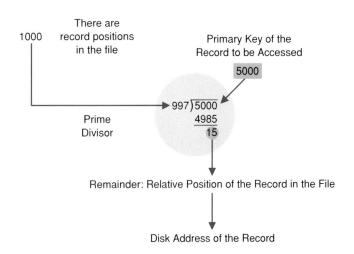

procedure will be used to find it. The idea of hashing is to spread records uniformly over the space allocated for the file.

A popular hashing procedure is the division-remainder method illustrated in figure 8.4. In this hashing technique, the key is divided by the prime number closest to (but smaller than) the number of record positions available in the file. The remainder of the division gives us the relative position of the record in the file and is simply translated into its disk address.

You may note that more than one key may hash into the same storage position on the disk (in our example, a record with the key 3006 will collide with that having the key 5000). The number of such collisions is limited, however, because significantly more space is allocated to a direct file than will actually be taken up by the records; and we must remember that hashing spreads records rather uniformly over this space. Still, we need to handle this limited number of collisions; for example, a pointer to a colliding record (placed elsewhere on the disk) may be placed in a position where it would have been found had that position not already been taken up by another record.

A number of techniques are used to improve the performance of direct files, but allocation of extra space is the prime means of insuring superior performance by avoiding collisions.

4. Providing Direct Access on Secondary Keys

What if we took the file shown in figure 8.2, equipped it for direct access with indexes on the primary key (the Social Security number) as shown in figure 8.3, but then wanted also to provide fast access to the records of employees in a specific department? To do so, we could pursue one of the two avenues.

We could create a so-called secondary index, in this case the "Department" index. The "Department" field would thus become a *secondary key,* which classifies file records into categories, rather than identifying them, as the primary key does. This index would list the departments and give the pointers (disk addresses) of the records of employees within each department.

FIGURE 8.5

A file-oriented environment.

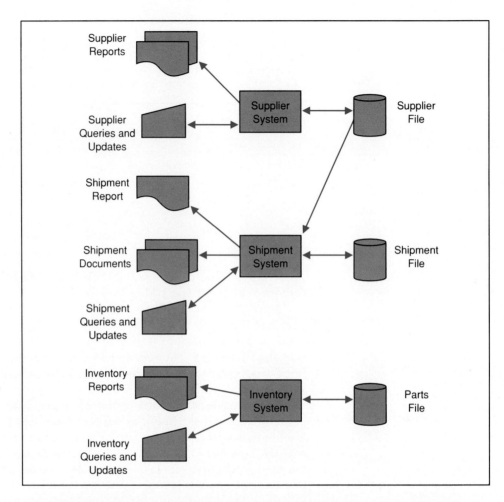

Alternatively, we could have a list of the departments, with each entry pointing to the first record of an employee in that department in the file; this record would then point to the next one, and so on, until the ring would close with the last record for the department pointing back to the index entry.

Both methods—secondary indexes and rings of pointers—enable us to classify file records into any categories we wish. We can provide any number of such chains and indexes—at a considerable cost of maintaining them as the contents change. These techniques are offered by some file management software, and they are also used as physical data organization methods by database management systems.

Limitations of a File-Oriented Environment

Let us step back and take a more general look at the file-oriented environment, illustrated by the example in figure 8.5.

As we can see, in this environment, each application program relies on its own files. In other words, files are "owned," as it were, by applications. These files are specifically designed for the needs of a given application. In a scenario that goes with our example, a supplier system was designed to maintain the file of suppliers, while the parts file is maintained by the inventory system to reflect the parts inventory stored in warehouses in various cities. The shipment system handles shipments-in-progress of parts by suppliers. Because of the sequence in which the three systems were designed, the shipment program does not have access to the parts file, although it is able to access the supplier file.

If management requests a report that would list all suppliers who are currently shipping items with inventories below a certain level, additional programming will be necessary. In particular, the shipment system will have to access the parts file. It may turn out that parts are identified in different ways in the parts file and the shipment file—which would require program and file modifications. Worse yet, it may be that although the shipment file is maintained on line, the inventory file is updated only every other day—so that the data in the two files are inconsistent. Indeed, all these programs *could* have been designed together at one time to rely on common files—but a similar problem is certain to emerge elsewhere in a file-oriented environment.

As we can see, numerous negative consequences result from the file-based approach, particularly when it is used for larger systems. Overall management of the data resource is all but impossible: there is no single locus for these data. Sharing data is, therefore, very difficult. Redundant data are maintained for various applications (the shipment file probably replicates some of the data stored in the parts file, such as current inventory levels). Beyond the high costs of redundancy, the file-based approach results in a lack of data integrity when file updates are made by one application but not by another.

Files are related to one another by programs rather than by the data themselves. For example, to answer the question, "Has a given supplier delivered all outstanding shipments?" we need to incorporate appropriate programming into either the shipment or the supplier system. Any change in the way the data are represented (for example, using a longer zip code) will call for program changes. A degree of file sharing among applications further complicates the change process. If the supplier file has to be changed because of the requirements of the supplier system, we will have to change the shipment system accordingly.

As data proliferate in applications-owned files, it becomes ever more difficult to maintain existing applications (because of the ripple effect on other systems which also need changing if data files change) and to develop new ones (because some data must be extracted from the existing files, and data redundancy problems will increase further).

These are all reasons why a database environment is necessary to gain organizational control of data.

8.3 A DATABASE ENVIRONMENT AND ITS ADVANTAGES

A **database** is an integrated collection of persistent data that serves a number of applications in an enterprise. The database stores not only the values of the attributes of various entities, but also the relationships between these entities. A database is managed by a **database management system (DBMS),** a systems software that helps organize data for effective access by a variety of users with

FIGURE 8.6

A database environment.

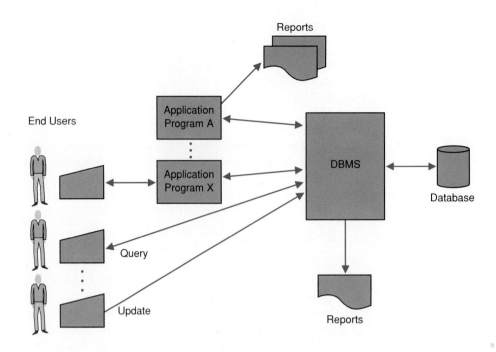

different access needs and for efficient storage. A DBMS makes it possible to create, access, maintain, and control databases. Thanks to DBMS, data can be integrated and made available on demand. Originally, these systems were developed to simplify the work of applications programmers; IDS, developed at General Electric in 1969, is considered the first full-fledged DBMS.

A database environment is illustrated in figure 8.6; contrast this illustration with figure 8.5, which showed a file-oriented environment.

Application programs access the database through the facilities provided by DBMS (which we shall discuss later). End users may access a database either through these application programs, or directly, using a query facility. To continue with our suppliers-parts-shipments example, a DBMS would control all the data that were stored in the three files and, using the relationships between the entities defined in the database itself, could provide information the individual file-based applications were unable to offer. For example, the management query regarding suppliers shipping parts with current inventories below a certain level could be answered without the need for programming if the data are managed by a DBMS.

DBMSs for larger machines permit a number of users to work simultaneously on the same database by temporarily locking records being updated by one of the users or applications. A DBMS generally relies on the access methods of an operating system to read and write actual disk records.

There are multiple advantages of integrating data into databases and controlling them with a DBMS:

1. Avoiding Uncontrolled Data Redundancy and Inconsistency

Applications share the data stored in a database, rather than owning private files that would often store redundant data. This reduces storage costs; there is no need to update multiple copies of the same data. Most important, this prevents the possibility that inconsistent data will reside in multiple files.

Even so, it is necessary to note that sometimes data redundancy is introduced in a database to ensure certain performance objectives; however, the redundant data are then known to the system and maintained in a consistent state.

2. Program-Data Independence

When the database is managed by a DBMS, programs can be written independent of the actual physical layout of the data or even of the total logical structure of the data. DBMS "knows" these structures; it thus provides the mapping from a logical view of the data in a given application to the actual physical layout of the data on the storage device, as we shall discuss later in the chapter. Should the physical layout of the data be changed, applications will remain functionally unaffected.

An applications programmer thus deals with relatively simple logical descriptions of data, without having to be concerned with their physical representations. This simplifies the development and maintenance of applications, which rely on the database; overall programming productivity is thus enhanced.

3. Flexible Access to Shared Data

The database approach has opened data for access to users and applications. Query languages enable end users to access data directly. Applications can be written to use any data stored in corporate databases, rather than to rely only on specially created files.

The "relatability" of stored data is ensured by the DBMS-managed databases themselves, rather than by special programming. A variety of relationships between entities may be rather easily defined. Thus, a variety of queries can be answered without the need for programming.

4. Advantages of Centralized Control of Data

The fact that a database may be centrally controlled with the use of a DBMS leads to several vital benefits:

- Global planning and consistent evolution of the data resource are possible.
- Security may be maintained by specifying the authorization for data access and modification to the uniform interface for all programs and users—that is, to the DBMS; these security measures may be employed to protect the privacy of individuals the stored data concern.
- Integrity constraints may be imposed to further ensure the accuracy of the data in the database. Thus, certain rules may be specified to ensure that inaccurate data cannot be entered. Examples of such data validation rules are: "No employee may work more than eighty hours a week" or "Weekly salary of an employee in Purchasing never exceeds $1,000." It is, of course, virtually impossible to make sure that no incorrect data are ever entered; moreover, existing DBMSs are generally weak in this area (Honkanen, 1989). However, just avoiding uncontrolled redundancy rids us of a major source of errors.

SEEKING COMPETITIVE ADVANTAGE WITH DATABASE MARKETING

"To know the customer better than your competition does is a very, very powerful tool," claims the head of industry consulting at Teradata, a major vendor of database machines (which we shall discuss later). To accomplish this, some companies set up sophisticated marketing databases. They integrate all the information they have about their customers and their buying patterns from operational-level systems. The firms then add to these data demographic, financial, and lifestyle information purchased from information brokers. The result is a system that helps a firm to produce very narrowly targeted direct-mail and telemarketing campaigns, customized catalogs and newsletters, and promotion programs.

The payoff can be high. By using a detailed customer database in marketing a specific kind of consumer loan, First National Bank of Chicago produced 250 loans out of 2,275 mailings—at a cost of $36 per loan. Compare this with a similar campaign from the predatabase days, when 98,000 mailings produced some 150 loans at a cost of $500 per loan. Indeed, bankers do know a lot about their customers, and marketing databases make it possible to leverage this knowledge.

A frequent objective of customer databases is to maintain an ongoing relationship with the customers. For example, some companies are introducing frequent-buyer programs (inspired, no doubt, by the success of the frequent-flier programs), which recognize customer spending by recording purchases with point-of-sale scanners.

As we mentioned before in this text, database marketing is not without problems. Privacy concerns have yet to be adequately addressed. The payoff from this major investment is often slow, and it will not be forthcoming if such a database is used for a single application only. Organizational problems of wresting the data from the control of parochial corporate interests have to be overcome. The chasm between marketing and MIS departments has to be bridged. Many experts consider involving the MIS department in the database marketing project critical to the project's success—and this means involvement from the very beginning.

Adapted from Mitch Betts, "Romancing the Segment of One." Computerworld, March 5, 1990, pp. 63–65; and Terence P. Pare, "Banks Discover the Consumer." Fortune, February 12, 1990, pp. 96–104; and (Lazos, 1991).

- Corporate-wide standards can be enforced in naming and representing the data.

Databases become corporate assets, as we can see from the database marketing vignette.

Obviously, the advantages of a database environment come at a cost. While a single-user DBMS for a microcomputer may cost $400, a mainframe DBMS could cost $300,000 or more. These systems also consume extensive hardware resources; an existing system may need to be upgraded to a more powerful one to accommodate a DBMS. The process of establishing an organizational database is also costly; in particular, conversion of existing files to a database consumes significant resources.

While a small firm may maintain a single database, large organizations typically have a number of databases and even several DBMS to maintain them (sometimes because of the history of the installation and sometimes owing to the trade-offs between performance, functionality, and costs among DBMSs). In general, it is best if a single database serves a major functional aspect of company's operations.

8.4 DATA INDEPENDENCE IN DATABASES

We have seen that in a file-oriented environment, the data and the programs that use them are highly interdependent. We shall now look more closely at how a DBMS ensures independence between the simplified view of the database offered to an individual user and the actual, complex organization of the database.

A DBMS enables us to define a database on three levels, as shown in figure 8.7.

The *external level* defines various views that particular applications, individual users, or groups of users may have of a database. The external view simplifies the database for a user or for a programmer developing an application. The user or the programmer does not need to know the logical structure of the entire database, which is available at the *conceptual level.* Of course, the conceptual level, which defines the total database, has to be defined so that all the necessary user views can be derived from it. Defining partial, external views of a database is also a technique for handling security and privacy in databases: an application or a user can access only that fragment of the database defined by the particular view.

Both the external and the conceptual levels of a database definition are *logical*— they define the data as the applications or the users see them, rather than describing how the data are actually stored. The physical layout of data in a secondary memory is specified independently of the logical layout (although we

FIGURE 8.7

Levels of database definition.

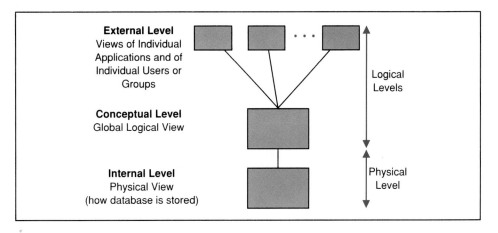

do want to ensure efficient accesses, and that calls for a certain layout optimization related to the users' views of data). Of course, the data actually exist only on the physical level—the two logical levels are the vital abstractions furnished by the DBMS.

The concept of the three levels of a database is illustrated with our suppliers-parts-shipments database (a version of that discussed by Date, [1990]) in figure 8.8.

As we can see, the conceptual view (also called the schema) defines the complete database in logical terms. Two different external views (also known as subschemas) are provided based on this conceptual view. One of the external views has been defined for an application program which processes supplier invoices for payment. The other has been defined for a user who ascertains the availability of parts in the company's warehouses. The internal view (or internal schema) of the database defines the actual layout of the files specified in the conceptual views, with all the indexes and pointers that are necessary in some types of databases to relate the data entities to one another, thereby ensuring efficient access to data.

We now realize that we actually have two levels of data independence in databases. If we change the logical representation of a database on the conceptual level, an application does not have to be changed so long as its own view of the data remains unchanged. On another level, if the physical layout of data is changed (for example, if the data are reorganized on a disk because of file growth), both logical levels remain unaffected. The mappings between the three levels are provided by the DBMS.

A DBMS provides the language, called **data definition language (DDL),** for defining the database objects on the three levels. It also provides a language for manipulating the data—**data manipulation language (DML),**—which makes it possible to access records, change values of attributes, and delete or insert records. An example of a database language that contains both a DDL for the logical levels of databases and a DML is SQL, which we shall discuss further on in this chapter.

8.5 DATA MODELS OR HOW TO REPRESENT RELATIONSHIPS BETWEEN DATA

A *data model* is a method for organizing databases on the conceptual level. The main concern in such a model is how to represent relationships among database records. There are three principal data models in use by commercially available DBMSs.

Two older models—the hierarchical and the network models—rely on explicit linking of related records. As we shall see, these two models suffer from significant disadvantages so far as the flexibility of answering ad hoc queries is concerned, but they offer superior performance in transaction processing systems.

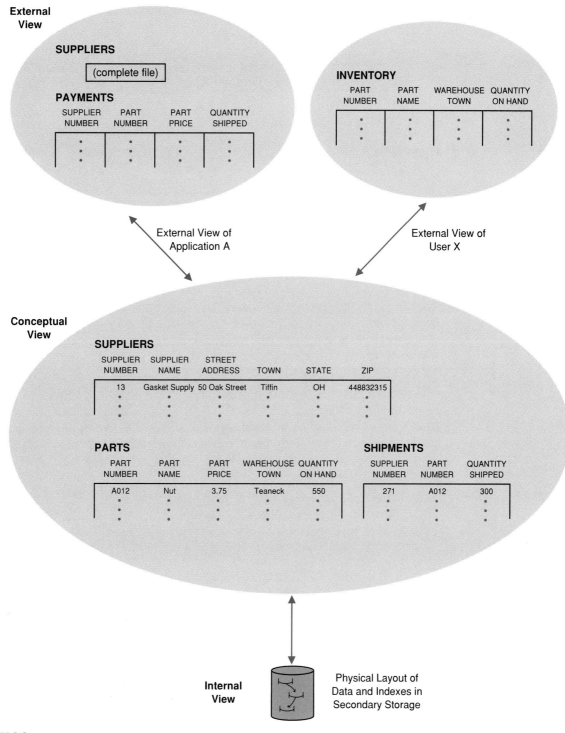

FIGURE 8.8

Three levels of definition in a suppliers-parts-shipments database.

FIGURE 8.9

A hierarchical database.

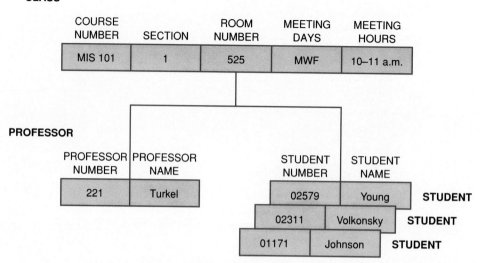

These models still remain a mainstay of the airlines' computerized reservation systems and similar operational-level systems that process routine transactions at very high rates. The internal design of a database is optimized for the specific transaction mix. Providing access paths the system was not designed for generally requires bringing the system down.

The third model, the relational, is becoming increasingly popular owing to its flexibility in relating data entities. The relationships among data entities in this model are established by field values, with no need to preestablish data access paths by linking. The relational model supports well the organization's need to provide managers and other knowledge workers with broad access to information.

1. The Hierarchical Model

Database representation with the hierarchical data model will look familiar to anyone who has seen an organization chart. Let us look at the very simple database in figure 8.9, which we shall use as a running example in this section.

To be more precise, a hierarchical database consists of a number of trees of the same kind. Each of the trees has a single top-level root record and a number of lower-level records. In our example in figure 8.9, we have a database of scheduled classes at a university, each with its professor and students. In a hierarchy, each "child" record (for example, **STUDENT**) may have only one "parent" record (here, **CLASS**). The database contains links (record addresses) to specify these parent-child relationships. An access to a "child" record begins at the root.

Since few real-world situations are strictly hierarchical, these databases require replication of records (or additional links that would depart from strict hierarchy). For example, most students take more than one course, and each professor generally teaches more than one class. Also, what happens to a student's record when the student has completed the course?

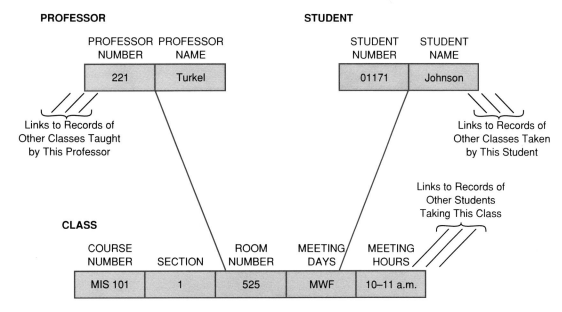

FIGURE 8.10

A network database.

We certainly do not want to delete the student's record, but it no longer has a parent to link it to. All these problems are dealt with in commercial hierarchical databases at the expense of data replication, decreased "cleanliness" of representation, and structural complexity.

However, for data that can be mapped into a treelike structure, performance is excellent. The hierarchical model is still important due to the fact that IBM's IMS database management system, introduced in 1968, remains the workhorse in many firms for transaction processing systems running on mainframes (Sehr, 1988).

2. The Network Model

The network model is more general than the hierarchical, since each record in a network can have more than one parent—and thus the records in such a database are connected by a network of links which identify relationships among them. Figure 8.10 shows a network model for our small sample database. We can see that the record replication needed with the hierarchical model can now be avoided: a professor's or a student's record can be linked to several class records.

The network model (also known as the CODASYL model, for the committee that defined it) is most prominently represented by the IDMS database management system of Computer Associates International. While they are more general than hierarchical systems, network systems are complex, and the maintenance of a large number of links (pointers) consumes hardware resources.

Hierarchical and network databases lack flexibility because the available access paths are preestablished through links at the time the database is designed. Accesses that were not provided when the database was designed usually cannot be accommodated without redesign. This is why most new databases are designed with the relational model.

3. The Relational Model

In the relational model, which we will discuss in more detail in the next section, relationships among records are established without recourse to links. Rather, these relationships emerge as correspondences between field values. Data files are represented as tables, as we can see in figure 8.11, which continues our running example.

Our database is represented by four tables (called *relations*—hence the name of the model). The relationships between students, classes, and professors, which were established with links in the other two models, are provided by the corresponding values of attributes of data entities. For example, we can establish who teaches the classes taken by a given student from the tables **CLASSES** and **ENROLLMENT:** for a given STUDENT NUMBER in the **ENROLLMENT** table, the corresponding values of the attributes COURSE NUMBER and SECTION in both tables will give us PROFESSOR NUMBER from the **CLASSES** table, which in turn allows us to look up the professor's name in the **PROFESSORS** table.

As we can see, relational databases do not need links to navigate the database. Because of the increasing importance of the relational model, we will now take a closer look at it.

FIGURE 8.11

A relational database.

CLASSES

COURSE NUMBER	SECTION	ROOM NUMBER	MEETING DAYS	MEETING HOURS	PROFESSOR NUMBER
MIS 101	1	525	MWF	10–11 a.m.	221
MIS 101	2	715	M	5–8 p.m.	413

STUDENTS

STUDENT NUMBER	STUDENT NAME
01171	Johnson
02311	Volkonsky
02579	Young

PROFESSORS

PROFESSOR NUMBER	PROFESSOR NAME
221	Turkel
315	Smythe

ENROLLMENT

COURSE NUMBER	SECTION	STUDENT NUMBER	STUDENT STATUS
MIS 101	1	01171	Auditor
MIS 101	1	02311	Regular
MIS 101	2	02579	Regular

8.6 RELATIONAL DATABASES

M ost of the databases currently being built are represented according to the relational model introduced by E. F. Codd (then of IBM) in 1970 in a paper that placed a solid mathematical foundation under the model (Codd, 1970). Since relational databases rest on a firm mathematical foundation, their properties can be studied, and their design features can be guaranteed.

Because relational databases demand more extensive processing power than the two link-based models, they have gained wide currency only since the mid-1980s, as the cost of hardware resources decreased markedly and as flexibility of access for end users became a common demand. While many organizations still maintain existing transactional databases with the hierarchical IMS database management system, its use is gradually being supplanted by the relational IBM product, DB2, which is rapidly becoming the industry standard.

The relational model represents all the database files as tables. Table rows are records for individual entities; table columns are fields of the records, which describe the attributes of the entities. Thanks to this familiar form of representation, relational databases are easy to understand. Our class database shown in figure 8.11 consisted of four tables. Another example of a relational database is the suppliers-parts-shipments database shown in figure 8.12.

FIGURE 8.12

Relational database of suppliers, parts, and shipments.

SUPPLIERS

SUPPLIERNO	SUPPLIERNAME	STREETADDRESS	TOWN	STATE	ZIP
13	Gasket Supply	50 Oak Street	Tiffin	OH	448832315
271	Parts for You	231 Market Square	Boston	MA	021153516
2274	Speedy Express	1 Shady Avenue	Tiffin	OH	448830123
3251	Reliable Suppliers	11 Cedar Lane	Teaneck	NJ	076660115

PARTS

PARTNO	PARTNAME	PARTPRICE	WHSETOWN	ONHAND
A012	Nut	3.75	Teaneck	550
D242	Pad	14.20	Boston	1200
Z971	Bolt	7.95	Columbus	325

SHIPMENTS

SUPPLIERNO	PARTNO	QUANTITY
271	A012	300
271	D242	100
3251	A012	250

FIGURE 8.13

Relational operators.

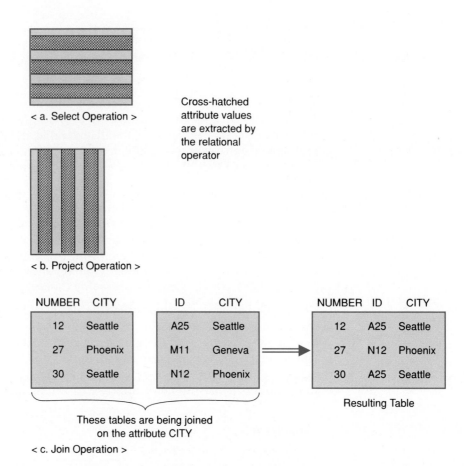

< a. Select Operation >

Cross-hatched attribute values are extracted by the relational operator

< b. Project Operation >

NUMBER	CITY
12	Seattle
27	Phoenix
30	Seattle

ID	CITY
A25	Seattle
M11	Geneva
N12	Phoenix

NUMBER	ID	CITY
12	A25	Seattle
27	N12	Phoenix
30	A25	Seattle

Resulting Table

These tables are being joined on the attribute CITY

< c. Join Operation >

The tables in figure 8.12 are actually well-defined mathematical constructs known as relations. Two tables may be interrelated by their columns, whose values are drawn from the common domain. Thus, in the suppliers-parts-shipments database of figure 8.12, we can get a list of suppliers located in the same town where parts are warehoused, since the values of the TOWN attribute in the **SUPPLIERS** table are drawn from the same domain as the values of the warehouse town (WHSETOWN) attribute in the **PARTS** table. Likewise, the relationships between the PARTS and the SHIPMENTS tables are established by the values of the PARTNO (part number) attribute. As we can see, the relationships are defined by the attribute values themselves, without any need for links.

All records in the table of a relational database must have a unique primary key, which means that all records must be distinct. A primary key may be composite; for example, the key to the **ENROLLMENT** table in figure 8.11 consists of three attributes: COURSE NUMBER, SECTION, and STUDENT NUMBER.

An access to attribute values stored in tables is composed of one or more strictly defined operations. These operations do not have to be specified by the user; their complexity may be hidden in a simpler language. Each operation produces

A RELATIONAL DATABASE AS A CORNERSTONE OF GLOBAL TRADING

Security Pacific Corporation of Los Angeles wants to get a competitive edge against other banks in its currency trading. The cornerstone of its competitive policy is setting up a relational database for all of its transaction data. The objective is to make all this data available to traders for pattern analysis and ad hoc queries.

At this time, the data are dispersed in a variety of files and in hierarchical and network databases. Information from these files and databases is displayed in separate windows of the traders' workstations. The bank believes that relational technology is necessary to ensure the desired flexibility of access. The relational DBMS of choice is DEC's RDB, running on VAX-series minis. The database controlled by this DBMS will be distributed among the company's six trading centers: Los Angeles, New York, Tokyo, London, Sydney, and Frankfurt. The round-the-clock nature of global trading crowds out the traditional overnight batch updates; "For us, the day begins in Sydney, Australia, and ends in Los Angeles," says the project manager. Trading is done on hundreds of MS-DOS-based workstations in forty currencies. Ultimately, all applications will be working off this relational database.

Based on Jean S. Bozman, "Security Pacific's New Strategy." *Computerworld*, June 18, 1990, p. 29.

a new table. Relational systems support at least three principal operations on tables, without any predefined access paths (see figure 8.13):

- *select* (don't confuse it with the SQL SELECT statement to be discussed in the next section!), which selects from a specified table the rows that satisfy a given condition;
- *project,* which selects from a given table the specified attribute values (note that select and project together can select given attributes from given rows);
- and *join,* which builds a new table from two specified tables.

The rows in that new table are all possible combinations of rows from the two original tables that satisfy a given condition. For example, in figure 8.13c, the join condition is that the values of the CITY attribute of the rows be the same.

The power of the relational model derives from the join operation. A join is actually a selective merge of records from files, which may be very large. It is precisely because records are related to one another through a join operation (rather than through pointers) that relational databases require so much processing power. A large number of time-consuming accesses to secondary memories may lie behind joining two tables. However, the join is also the reason we do not need a predefined access path. As the Security Pacific vignette illustrates, organizations are increasingly willing to pay the price for the flexibility afforded by relational databases.

The best known relational DBMSs are listed in table 8.2; a detailed performance comparison of several microcomputer relational database management systems is available in Petreley, 1990.

	PRODUCT	VENDOR
TABLE 8.2 Popular Relational Database Management Systems	**Multiuser Products**	
	DB2, SQL/DS	IBM, Armonk, New York
	INGRES	Relational Technology, Berkeley, California
	Oracle	Oracle Corporation, Belmont, California
	Microcomputer DBMS (single-user products)	
	dBase IV	Borland International, Scotts Valley, California
	Paradox	Borland International, Scotts Valley, California
	Rbase	Microrim, Redmond, Washington

8.7 SQL—A RELATIONAL QUERY LANGUAGE

A variety of language types are available for accessing a database, that is, for querying it (Vassiliou, 1984–85). Some of these languages are designed for direct access by novice users, and we shall further discuss these interfaces in the next chapter. More general query languages offer an extensive source of data definition and manipulation facilities for use primarily by MIS professionals. Foremost among the latter languages is SQL.

SQL (the acronym stands for Structured Query Language and is usually pronounced "sequel") is a data-definition-and-management language of relational databases. SQL is now an international standard and is provided by most well-known DBMS, including some nonrelational ones. SQL may be used as an independent query language to define the objects in a database, populate a database, and access the data (we have shown these direct interactions with DBMS in figure 8.6). The so-called embedded SQL is also provided for programming in procedural languages ("host" languages), such as COBOL or PL/I, in order to access a database from an applications program. In the end-user environment, SQL is generally "hidden" by more user-friendly interfaces.

Let us familiarize ourselves with the principal facilities of SQL, which will further refine our ideas about the relational data model.

1. Data Definition

To create a table of suppliers, as shown in figure 8.12, all we have to do in SQL is use the CREATE statement:

```
CREATE TABLE SUPPLIERS
    (SUPPLIERNO INTEGER NOT NULL,
     SUPPLIERNAME CHAR (20) NOT NULL,
     STREETADDRESS CHAR (20) NOT NULL,
     TOWN CHAR (10) NOT NULL,
     STATE CHAR (2) NOT NULL,
     ZIP CHAR (9) NOT NULL,
    PRIMARY KEY (SUPPLIERNO));
```

As we can see, most attributes (fields) are defined as consisting of characters, and all the attribute values must be specified when the data are loaded into the table (that is what the NOT NULL clause does). The other two tables in the database of figure 8.12 may be created in the same way.

A new database table may be created at any time with CREATE TABLE. Additional columns may be added to an existing table with the ALTER TABLE statement. An entire table may be deleted with the DROP TABLE statement. These are the three principal statements of SQL's data definition language.

SQL makes it possible to define user views with the CREATE VIEW statement, which relies on the SELECT statement we will discuss below. In this case, SELECT defines which attributes are to be included in the view—which is again a table (since in SQL a user view is a single table, several statements may be necessary to provide a complete external view, as shown in figure 8.8).

To improve access performance for often executed queries, an index may be provided for a particular attribute with the CREATE INDEX statement. An index or a view may be DROPped at any time.

2. Data Manipulation

SQL enables a user to retrieve data from a database with the SELECT statement: each retrieval produces another table (even if it consists of a single row).

Here is a query to obtain the names and full addresses of all the suppliers located in Tiffin:

```
SELECT SUPPLIERNAME, STREETADDRESS, TOWN, STATE, ZIP
FROM SUPPLIERS
WHERE TOWN = 'Tiffin';
```
As a result, we obtain this table:

SUPPLIERNAME	STREETADDRESS	TOWN	STATE	ZIP
Gasket Supply	50 Oak Street	Tiffin	OH	448832315
Speedy Express	1 Shady Avenue	Tiffin	OH	448830123

As we know, the power of the relational model derives from its capability to join tables using columns whose values are drawn from the same domain. Here is the query that gives us the numbers and names of the suppliers and the numbers and names of parts only if the supplier is located in the same town where the part is warehoused:

```
SELECT SUPPLIERNO, SUPPLIERNAME, PARTNO, PARTNAME, TOWN
FROM SUPPLIERS, PARTS
WHERE TOWN = WHSETOWN;
```

Considering the data shown in figure 8.12, we obtain the following table. (Trace it to the original tables in the figure!)

SUPPLIERNO	SUPPLIERNAME	PARTNO	PARTNAME	TOWN
271	Parts for You	D242	Pad	Boston
3251	Reliable Suppliers	A012	Nut	Teaneck

Additional features of the SELECT statement are available, including the ability to obtain a sum or an average value for all of the entries in a column.

The data manipulation language of SQL includes three statements for changing the contents of tables:

- INSERT is used to populate the table initially and to subsequently insert additional records;
- DELETE makes it possible to delete one record or a category of records from a table; and
- UPDATE makes it possible to change values of one or several attributes in one or more records in a table.

Thus, SQL furnishes the user with both data definition and data manipulation facilities.

8.8 DESIGNING A RELATIONAL DATABASE

To help you appreciate what must be done during the logical and physical design of databases, we shall now outline the process of database design.

The aim of *logical design,* also known as *data modeling,* is to form a conceptual view of the database. A relational database will consist of tables (relations), each of which describes *only* the attributes of a particular class of objects. Logical design begins with identifying the object classes to be represented in the database and establishing relationships between pairs of these objects. For example, in a database of students and classes, the relationship between the attributes is that of enrollment of a student in a class. A relationship is simply an interaction between the objects represented by the data; this relationship will be important for accessing the data. Frequently, **entity-relationship (E-R) diagrams,** introduced by Peter Chen (Chen, 1976) are used to perform data modeling. A very simple entity-relationship diagram is shown in figure 8.14.

Entity-relationship diagrams for larger systems contain scores of rectangles (entities) and diamonds (relationships between two entities). We may further refine an entity-relationship diagram to show the attributes of the entities and of the relationships (which may be considered a special type of object). We may also indicate the number of times an entity occurs. This has been done in figure 8.15.

The primary key of each entity or relationship is underlined; in some cases, this key is composite: we need several fields to identify a record. Thus, for example, the key of the ENROLLMENT relationship must consist of three fields. Our figure indicates the most general relationship: each student may take more than one class and each class may enroll more than one student, which is indicated as an N-to-M (or N:M) relationship. Such a relationship must be represented by a separate table, as shown in figure 8.11. On the other hand, the relationship between a professor and the classes he or she teaches is one-to-many (1:M) and can be

FIGURE 8.14

An entity-relationship (E-R) diagram.

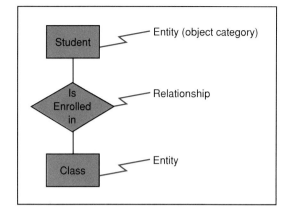

FIGURE 8.15

An E-R diagram with attributes and occurrence counts.

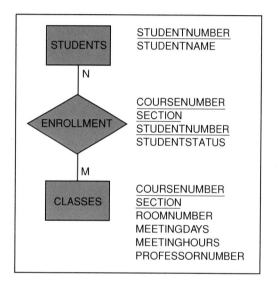

reflected by giving the professor's number in the record of each class taught. E-R data modeling proved to be an appropriate methodology for a disciplined, top-down logical design of databases by end users (Jarvenpaa, 1986).

Following the modeling with E-R diagrams, we arrive at a set of tables that represent entities and relationships between them. To complete the logical database design, this set of tables is simplified through a process known as **normalization.** Each table is normalized, which means that all its fields will contain single data elements, all its records will be distinct (we thus always have a primary key), and each table will describe only a single class of objects. The objective of normalization is to prevent replication of data, with all its negative consequences. For example, if in our table CLASSES, shown in figure 8.11, we had included the name of the course, we would have to repeat the course name for each section of the course offered. Indeed, a course name does not describe a class: it describes the course. If the database were to remain normalized when we added the name of the course, we would need to include a separate table containing course numbers and course names.

Database modeling, including normalization (which can be performed algorithmically) is assisted by computer-aided software engineering (CASE) tools, which we will discuss in chapter 19.

External views, based on the total, conceptual view of the database, are also defined during the logical design.

After logical design comes the *physical design* of the database. All fields are specified as to their length and the nature of the data (numeric, characters, and so on). A principal objective of physical design is to minimize the number of time-consuming disk accesses that will be necessary to answer typical database queries. Frequently, indexes are provided to ensure fast accesses for such queries. For example, if we know that many queries will request a printout of the utilization of particular classrooms, we may provide an index to the CLASSES table of figure 8.11 on the ROOM NUMBER attribute. Sometimes during physical design the database is denormalized to a degree by combining small tables into larger ones for greater access efficiency (Schmieder, 1988).

8.9 DISTRIBUTED PROCESSING AND DISTRIBUTED DATABASES

A powerful trend toward distributed processing has been changing information systems, as we discussed in the preceding chapter. From small firms with LANs on micros to large organizations with numbers of larger machines, organizational computing relies on multiple processors to deliver service more directly to users. The location of databases is a principal consideration in the architecture of distributed systems.

Distributed processing may rely on a single centralized database. This is frequently accomplished through **client/server** architecture, shown in figure 8.16.

FIGURE 8.16

Client/server architecture with a centralized database.

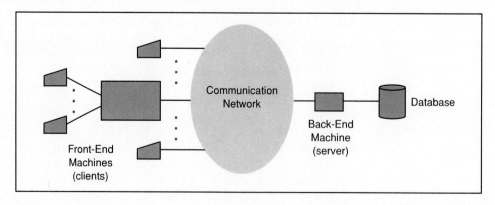

GETTING THE DATA FROM THE POINT OF SALE INTO A SPREADSHEET WITH AN SQL SERVER

"I have wanted to do this ever since I used a spreadsheet program, but no one knew how," says Robert Berger, a senior vice-president of Home Express. He is speaking about the company's newly implemented system, which draws data from databases fed by point-of-sale terminals (POS) into the spreadsheets of end users.

Home Express, a twelve-store housewares and electronics chain headquartered in Hayward, California, already had a system that downloaded sales transactions data from the stores' POS terminals into Wang VS 85 and VS 100 machines. The firm added to this system an Intel 30386-based microcomputer to host SQL Server, a relational DBMS designed to support both high-volume transaction processing and decision-support applications (developed jointly by Ashton-Tate—now a part of Borland International, Microsoft, and Sybase). The server accepts SQL queries sent in by 105 workstations (Wang terminals and PCs), tied to it by a 3Com Corporation's 3+Open local area network. The server maintains a relational database, which is accessed by specially designed software that generates SQL queries from a user-friendly interface for pulling data into spreadsheets.

The users at their workstations obtain the reports they want without a need for programming, as had been the case formerly. Perhaps a company buyer, running an Excel spreadsheet (from Microsoft), wants to see the data from precisely the angle he or she is interested in—for example, the buyer may want to obtain a ranking of individual stores by sales volume of the product for which he or she is responsible. With SQL Server, the buyer can do so.

Here is an actual example of successful business application. Home Express managers and buyers wanted to determine which products are the most effective loss leaders: these advertised items, sold at a loss or a minimal gain, are expected to attract shoppers who will then buy other merchandise as well. The system showed that when television sets were sold below cost as loss leaders, they were the only item a shopper would buy. On the other hand, bed sheets, when advertised as loss leaders, created ancillary sales of towels and other housewares, sold at a higher margin.

The system helped not only in analyzing the effectiveness of advertising, but in analyzing utility and other costs for individual stores without programming—and it would not pay to do so if programming were required.

Based on Richard Pastore, "Retail Strategy Banks on SQL." *Computerworld*, October 30, 1989, pp. 43, 48.

In a client/server system, a number of front-end machines, which may be user workstations or other computers, access the database managed by the server (back-end machine). Clients (such as user workstations) provide graphical user interfaces and run the software that facilitates user tasks. The server runs the DBMS and performs all accesses to the centralized database it controls. Variations are possible; for example, a client machine may be able to access several servers over the network. The previous vignette described how server software solves business problems.

The server of a large system may contain a **database machine**—a special-purpose computer whose hardware is designed to perform database accesses efficiently. Modern database machines are generally built to work with the relational data model: the join operation is built into their hardware, for example. The use of such machines makes relational database technology responsive enough for massive transaction processing. Database machines manufactured by such vendors as Teradata (of Los Angeles) and ShareBase (of Los Gatos, California) can manage billions of bytes of data because they are based on parallel processing technology, involving scores of microprocessors, as we discussed in chapter 6. The vast General Services Administration of the federal government uses Teradata database machines to support billing, accounting, and processing of customer service orders (Brewin, 1990).

Increasingly, **distributed databases** (as opposed to centralized databases) are being implemented as well—the data are placed where they are used most often, but the entirety of the database is available to each user, as shown in figure 8.17. Each site runs the DBMS software. The sites may be halfway across the world, connected by a WAN, or they may be in the same building and connected by a LAN.

Distributed database systems enable the structure of the database to mirror the structure of the firm (Date, 1990). The traffic on the network is minimized because local data are maintained where they are used most, but at the same time, all the organizational data are accessible to a site. Many managers of business units today insist on maintaining data on the unit's site.

Distributed database management is complex. However, this internal complexity is offset by the simplicity of the user interface. Indeed, the basic principle of distributed databases is that a distributed system ought to look to a user as though the data were *not* distributed: in other words, data distribution ought to be transparent to database users.

FIGURE 8.17

A system with a distributed database.

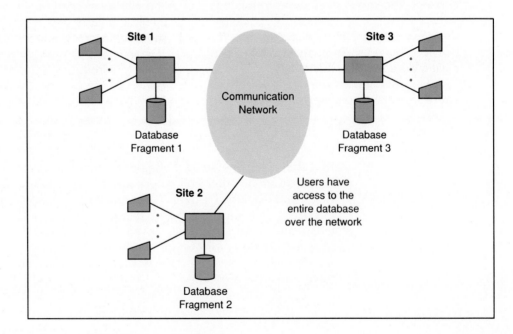

All the generalized distributed DBMS today are relational; they include DB2 Version 2 Release 2 from IBM, INGRES/STAR from Relational Technology, and SQL*STAR from Oracle Corporation.

Management of distributed databases poses several major technical problems. The primary question is how to distribute the data. Frequently, parts of the data are replicated on several sites to ensure fast access—but then an update propagation problem emerges: when data are modified, an update has to be made on all sites where the given data are stored. The other alternative is to partition the data among the sites, but then users face all the disadvantages of remote access.

The data dictionary, which describes all of the data stored in a database, must contain information on where the particular data are stored. But where is the dictionary itself stored? It may be centralized, replicated on all sites, or partly partitioned among the sites. To locate a data item, a DBMS may first have to locate the part of the data dictionary that specifies the location of the appropriate database fragment.

As networks proliferate and cross corporate boundaries, we may want to include multiple—and different—DBMSs running on different machines into a single distributed database system (Madnick, 1988), which adds an additional level of complexity.

8.10 THE DATA DICTIONARY

We gain control of data with database systems. A principal tool for maintaining this control is the data dictionary (also known as data directory or catalog). DBMSs themselves can control databases with this tool as well. A **data dictionary** contains "data about data"—it is a sophisticated inventory of the database contents. (Both the tool and the actual collection of data are referred to as the data dictionary.) Data dictionaries describe the enormous number of data elements whose values are stored in a database. Therefore, they lie at the heart of information resource management.

Data dictionaries store the following information about the data maintained in databases:

- External, conceptual, and internal views—and, thus, what entities are represented in the databases, what their attributes are, and how the entities are interrelated.
- Which applications and users may retrieve the data and which applications and users are able to modify the data; this information is used to establish security and privacy controls (as we will further discuss in chapter 20).
- Cross-reference information, such as which programs use which data and which users receive which reports; this information is necessary to assess the impact of any envisaged system modifications.

- Where individual data elements originate, and who is responsible for maintaining the data.
- What the standard naming conventions are for database objects.
- What the integrity rules are for the data (for example, a salary field cannot contain a negative value or a value over 100,000).
- Where the data are stored in distributed databases.

Thus, a data dictionary contains all the data definitions, and the information necessary to identify data ownership and to ensure security and privacy of the data, as well as the information used during the development and maintenance of applications which rely on the database (Wertz, 1989).

Larger DBMSs include active data dictionaries, which directly interact with the operation of the DBMS and ensure that all the rules regarding the data are enforced as the contents of the database are being defined and used. In contrast, passive data dictionaries play only an informational role and lack the ability to enforce the rules they store.

As we can see, a data dictionary actually maintains a database—made up of data definitions. Data dictionaries make it possible to produce these data definitions automatically for specific DBMSs. Users may also query this database and obtain reports from it—just as from the database itself. Thus, data dictionaries are a powerful auditing tool, too.

As we shall further discuss in chapter 19, many data dictionaries store not only data about data, but also a variety of information about systems under development and, in general, about the firm's information systems. Data dictionaries are a powerful tool on which more elaborate computer-aided software engineering (CASE) tools are based.

Because of the importance of data dictionaries for information resource management, efforts have been made to standardize them as so-called Information Resource Dictionary Systems (March, 1988–89). Within its broad Systems Application Architecture (SAA) framework for distributed information systems, IBM offers a Repository Manager—an extensive data dictionary that supports development and storage of corporate data models (Matthews, 1990).

8.11 ORGANIZATIONAL FACTORS IN INFORMATION RESOURCE MANAGEMENT

Before data and the information arising from them were recognized as the focal resource in organizational computing, data for an organization as a whole were managed as an afterthought (King, 1982). Data were often collected for the needs of specific applications, and their lifetimes in the system were tied to these applications. In the absence of an organization-wide inventory of data and of mechanisms for data control, data sharing among applications was generally accidental.

DISJOINT DATABASES MAY LOSE YOU CLIENTS

A major international bank maintains three separate systems, each with its own database: a cash management system, a loan management system, and a system for letter-of-credit processing (a letter of credit authorizes an advance of money). Suppose a client requests that $50,000 be transferred from her account to another bank. If the client's cash balance is insufficient to cover the transaction, the transfer will be rejected—even though the client may have a $1,000,000 active letter of credit! The rejection will be embarrassing to the client, and a manual operation will be necessary to enter a correction to draw on the letter-of-credit funds. Thus, lack of database integration may cause loss of clients, while also increasing processing costs.

Based on (Madnick, 1988).

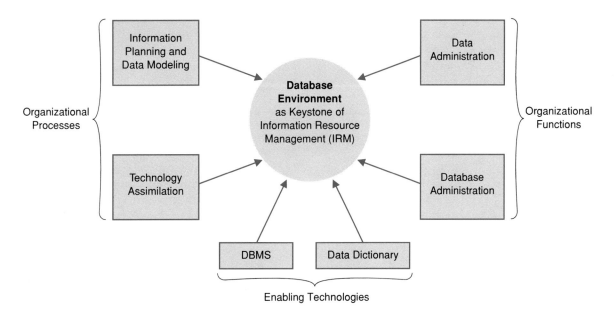

FIGURE 8.18

Organizational and technological components in information resource management.

The emergence of database technology has enabled organizations to control their data as an underpinning of information resource management (IRM). It is expected that, ultimately, firms will broadly practice enterprise-wide planning of the information resource. However, as with any technology, databases do not automatically produce desired organizational results. Databases themselves may suffer from lack of integration: a proliferation of databases may occur, to a degree resembling the proliferation of files we discussed earlier in the chapter.

Database technology is an enabling technology for managing data and information as an organizational resource. But the availability of this technology by no means automatically ensures that an organization will gain control of its data. The principal components in information resource management with the database approach are shown in figure 8.18.

GAINING CONTROL OF CORPORATE DATA IS NOT EASY

"Lack of information [or] lack of access to it is a critical problem for executives today," says Ross Brownridge, director of business planning at Pratt & Whitney, Canada. Line managers have deeply seated feelings of ownership toward their local databases. They do not want data about the functioning of their units accessible within a larger system. Brownridge says that hard-copy reports are still the primary informational tools of his company's management—and these reports are provided at the will of the functional units, not by a senior manager's request. Moreover, the reports often contain contradictory information.

In this environment, managers often ignore reports until something goes wrong—a classical case of management-by-crisis that prevents proactive decision making. Brownridge has created an on-line system for accessing the reports (note how distant this is from a central database!). However, line managers resist making the reports available on-line and thus visible to senior management. Indeed, the chief executive of the company made placing all operating reports on-line a company objective this year.

William Durell, president of a consulting firm in the field of data administration, generalizes: "The single biggest challenge to sharable data is the profit center mentality. Every profit center wants to hoard their own information. They want to get access to everyone else's information but don't want to share their own."

Based on Michael L. Sullivan-Trainor, "Ending Time-Wasting Games of Information Hide-and-Seek." *Computerworld*, June 25, 1990, pp. 77–79.

A DBMS and a data dictionary are the vital technologies in this approach. However, as with any sophisticated technology, their proper use poses vast demands on the organization. This is especially obvious in the case of data dictionaries; some firms treat them in a rather perfunctory fashion—after all, they do not contain the real, "working" data—which may lead the firm to lose control of the data resource.

Planning of the information resource is a key component of organizational strategic MIS planning. A planning methodology known as enterprise analysis aims to establish the principal business processes, the classes of data these processes require, and the individual data entities within these broad classes. We will discuss Business Systems Planning (BSP), a principal enterprise analysis methodology, in chapter 17; you will find a detailed illustration of its application in establishing an information architecture for a specific firm in the Case Study at the end of the present chapter. After the MIS planners identify the principal data classes and entities for an enterprise or one of its units during the planning process, they do data modeling. The primary objective is to establish relationships between data entities. Data modeling is often based on the entity-relationship approach previously outlined. (This modeling approach was also used by the firm in the Case Study.)

Introducing a database environment or making major changes in data ownership subsequent to such introduction is a process of organizational change that requires carefully planned implementation; these processes are described further in chapter 18. Data ownership is often jealously guarded and defended through political play. Conflicts among organizational actors, stemming from data integration in databases, must often be resolved during database implementation.

The policy-making function of data administration, with its top-level access to corporate management, aims to ensure corporate control of an organization's data. In the decentralized environment of many modern organizations, particularly with the growing practice of end-user computing, private databases may easily proliferate. It becomes vital to maintain a central view over the corporate data, to plan their evolution, and to maintain the data so as to avoid inconsistencies that would lead to "battles of the printouts" (whose data are right?).

On the technical level, in support of the often complicated DBMS technologies, the database administration function provides the necessary expertise to establish and maintain the organizational databases. We will now discuss the responsibilities of the data administrator and the database administrator.

8.12 DATA ADMINISTRATION AND DATABASE ADMINISTRATION

The use of a DBMS makes it possible for an organization to control its data as a corporate resource. The person who has the central responsibility for an organization's data is the **data administrator (DA).** Data administration is a policy-making function. The DA should thus have access to senior corporate management (see figure 8.19).

The data administrator decides what data will be stored in the database (that is, he or she plans the database) and establishes policies for accessing and maintaining the database. To be more specific, the data administrator establishes the policies and specific procedures for collecting, validating, sharing, and inventorying data to be stored in databases and for making information accessible to the members of the organization and, possibly, to persons outside of it.

The data administrator should be a manager with a keen understanding of the capabilities (but not necessarily technicalities) of databases and IRM. Effective IRM policies hinge on the effectiveness of the data administrator.

In contrast, the **database administrator (DBA)** is a database professional who creates the database and carries out the policies laid down by the data administrator. The management skills of a DA are thus combined with the technical skills of a DBA. The DBA generally belongs to the MIS department of a firm or of its subunit (see figure 8.19). In a larger organization, the DBA function is actually performed by a group of professionals. In a small firm, a programmer/analyst may perform the DBA function, while one of the managers acts as the DA.

FIGURE 8.19

Effective organizational placement of the data administrator (DA) and database administrator (DBA) functions.

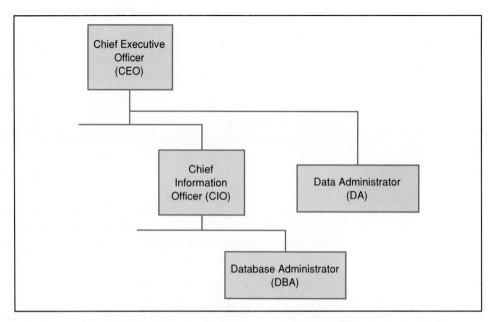

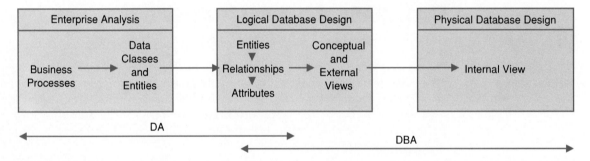

FIGURE 8.20

Developing organizational data resource.

It is vital to a firm, small or large, instituting information resource management that both the DA and the DBA roles be clearly defined and assigned to specific individuals. Central planning and data control by the DA and DBA do not, of course, necessarily imply a single centralized database for the firm; these roles may be applied to a variety of distributed database arrangements. The DA and DBA functions give an organization the capability to maintain a global perspective on its data resource.

The DA and DBA have their own responsibilities in the planning and design of organizational databases, as shown in figure 8.20.

The DA is a key person (or unit) involved in the strategic planning of the data resource, a task which may be accomplished through an enterprise analysis. In this analysis (which we shall return to in chapter 17), the DA establishes the principal business processes and often identifies the data entities needed to carry out these processes. The DA often goes on to define the principal data entities, their attributes, and the relationships among them.

The actual conceptual and external views of the database are most often defined in the data definition language of the specific DBMS by the DBA, who has the requisite technical knowledge. The DBA goes on to define the internal layout of the database, with a view towards optimizing system performance for the expected pattern of database usage. A variety of utilities furnished by DBMSs support the work of the DBA. It must be stressed that only some organizations perform enterprise analysis; logical and physical database design, on the other hand, is a must for all firms.

In addition to their responsibilities during the development of databases, the DA and the DBA, respectively, determine policies and implement these policies for the following aspects of database operation:

- Maintaining the data dictionary.
- Standardizing names and other aspects of data definition (for example, zip-code lengths).
- Providing backup: making sure that duplicates exist of the data stored in a database and that these duplicates can be entered into the database if all or a portion of it is damaged. (We shall further discuss this in chapter 20.)
- Providing security for the data stored in a database and, further, for privacy based on this security (see also chapter 20).

The main responsibilities of the DA and the DBA are summarized in figure 8.21.

Several frameworks have been proposed to describe the evolution of the DBA function as an organizational DBMS is installed (Weldon, 1981; Nolan, 1982). Most of these models include the following steps in the development and operation of the DBA function:

- Selection of the DBMS and planning of the database
- Installation of the DBMS and of the initial database
- Gaining control of the data in conjunction with data administration
- Enterprise-wide management of the data resource (so far claimed by few organizations)

Beverly Kahn has determined (Kahn, 1984; 1985) that, regrettably, in many organizations a DBMS is installed before a DBA function is established, so that installation of a data dictionary often trails the establishment of a database. It is hoped that most organizations will take a more proactive stance, as the technology has now reached a great degree of maturity.

8.13 BEYOND RELATIONAL DATABASES

The flexibility offered by relational databases has opened the appropriate organizational data to broad access by knowledge workers in organizations. Virtually all new systems are now relational. Among other factors, the support offered to relational concepts by IBM's DB2 and SQL/DS systems and, more broadly, by IBM's Systems Applications Architecture ensures that relational databases will dominate the field over the foreseeable future.

FIGURE 8.21

The responsibilities of the data administrator (DA) and the database administrator (DBA).

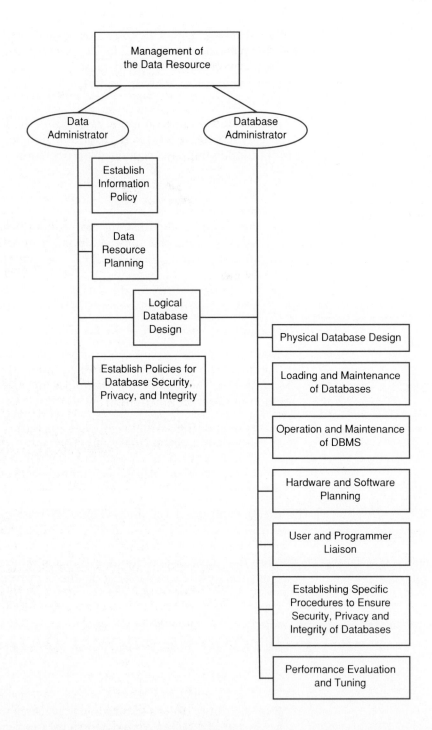

However, a drive toward postrelational systems has emerged, which is in the main an attempt to broaden the applicability of the relational model (although some argue for rejecting it). The principal need spurring this drive is to accommodate multimedia data, rather than only numerical values and short strings of characters, as the record-based relational model does. Along with the alphanumeric data stored in the fields of relational databases, we might also like to store general, unstructured text, graphics and other images (such as documents or photographs), video (images in motion), and sound. We may also want to integrate into a database objects that mix these media—for example, voice-annotated text.

The primary approach taken in postrelational database design is object orientation (McLeod, 1991), adapted from software systems development (see chapter 19). Object-oriented databases have begun to appear (Hazzah, 1990), for the present focusing primarily on the needs of the computer-aided design (CAD) and publishing markets, with their need to store a variety of graphics objects. An object-oriented database is a collection of objects that belong to various classes. The goal of postrelational DBMSs is to build into the database itself a richer set of meanings than just those of entities, their attributes, and the relationships among them (Kim, 1990). While the major relational databases, such as Oracle and INGRES, are being extended to handle complex objects, smaller database vendors are releasing DBMSs that were designed as object-oriented from the outset (for example, ObjectStore, from Object Design of Burlington, Massachusetts).

. . . .

SUMMARY

Data stored in secondary memories over extended periods of time are organized into files or databases. Data files may be organized as sequential files, which permit only batch processing, or as indexed-sequential or direct files, which allow direct access and thus support on-line processing. The file-oriented approach to data suffers from severe limitations. Redundant data are stored in files that belong to different applications, which leads to inconsistencies; and data sharing among applications is difficult to achieve.

It is common today to organize data into databases. A database serves a major aspect of a firm's operations, and its data may be shared among many users and applications. A database management system (DBMS), the systems software that manages databases, affords broad and controlled access to data. To simplify applications development and maintenance, DBMSs provide two levels of data independence: separate views of a database for individual applications, and separation of the logical definition of data from the way the data are physically stored.

While hierarchical and network data models remain in use for high-volume transaction processing, most of the new databases are implemented with relational DBMSs. A relational database is a collection of tables. Such a database is relatively easy for end users to understand and affords flexibility of access. Structured Query Language (SQL) has become a standard access language for defining and manipulating data in databases. Databases are also increasingly distributed among several sites, to better support distributed processing in organizations. All the data definitions are stored in a data dictionary, which like a DBMS, is a major tool for controlling organizational data.

The use of database technology does not automatically produce organizational control of data. Rather, the organizational processes of data planning and technology implementation, and the organizational functions of data and database administration, are necessary for effective information resource management.

While relational databases will dominate the field for years to come, object-oriented systems, which support the management of objects that do not fit a record format, have begun to emerge.

KEY TERMS AND CONCEPTS

Field (attribute)
Record
File
Database
Primary key
Sequential file
Indexed-sequential file
Direct (random) file
Hashing
Secondary key
Database management system (DBMS)
External view
Conceptual view
Internal view
Logical level of database definition

Physical level of database definition
Data definition language (DDL)
Data manipulation language (DML)
Data model
Hierarchical data model
Network data model
Relational data model
SQL
Entity-relationship data modeling
Normalization
Client/server system architecture
Database machine
Distributed database
Data dictionary
Data administrator (DA)
Database administrator (DBA)
Object-oriented database

QUESTIONS

1. What is the relationship between a field, a record, and a file? Give an example including all three.

2. What file organization methods support on-line processing, and what is the basic distinction between these methods?

3. List, point by point, the limitations of a file-oriented environment.

4. What is a database?

5. How does the database approach overcome the specific limitations of a file-oriented environment?

6. What are the two levels of data independence provided by DBMS? Why are they desirable?

7. What is logical data organization? What is physical organization? Which kind of organization is more easily understood by an end user?

8. Compare and contrast the hierarchical and network data models.

9. What advantages does the relational data model have over the other two kinds?

10. What is DB2 and how is it related to SQL?

11. a. Using SQL, define the **SHIPMENTS** and **PARTS** tables of figure 8.12.
b. Using SQL, query the database of figure 8.12 for all the towns where bolts are warehoused.
c. Using SQL, query the database of figure 8.12 for the names of all suppliers who have shipments on the way, together with the numbers of parts and quantities being shipped.

12. For what can we use entity-relationship diagrams?

13. What is normalization? What are its advantages and disadvantages?

14. How does client/server architecture provide access to a database?

15. What is the relationship between distributed databases and distributed processing?

16. What is stored in a data dictionary? Give five examples of this kind of information.

17. What is the relationship between data planning and database technology?

18. Draw three distinctions between the functions of a data administrator and a database administrator.

ISSUES FOR DISCUSSION

1. Suppose that your town library, an institution of modest resources, has asked you to investigate the feasibility of instituting a database of books and patrons. Outline how you would approach the problem, and take this feasibility study as far as you can.

2. Imagine that you have been hired by a midsized company as a database administrator. The company has not yet assigned the function of data administrator—as a matter of fact, they are not aware of the need for such a function. What difficulties do you expect to encounter, and how do you plan to handle them?

3. Acquire technical information on two different relational microcomputer systems, and compare their features. You may use comparisons done by others, such as Petreley (1990), in your investigation, but you should deal with recent product releases.

OPTIONAL EXERCISE: DATABASE MANAGEMENT

Using a DBMS available to you, define in SQL the four tables of the classes-students databases shown in figure 8.11. You may use your own class section to populate the **STUDENTS** table with some twenty records; populate **CLASSES, PROFESSORS,** and **ENROLLMENT** tables with about seven records each.

Add the column "OFFICE" to the **PROFESSORS** table and enter office numbers in it.

Write a SQL query to list the course numbers and the sections of all classes meeting in a specific room.

Write a SQL query to list all professors who teach in a specific room; include their office numbers in the list.

Make sure that each query produces at least two records!

DEVELOPING AN INFORMATION ARCHITECTURE FOR A FIRM

As organizational information processing has matured in many firms, they have come to recognize the need to plan a common base for applications. This common base is organizational data. If a firm's specific business functions can be analyzed to yield their demand for data, and if a common map of organizational data can be created and documented, we can obtain a solid foundation for managing the information resource of the organization. In other words, we can create the firm's information architecture. This effort is broad in scope, and it is good to learn from organizations that have already traveled the path. The U.S. Foods division of Pillsbury is such an organization.

Pillsbury began using DBMS in the late 1960s, and over the following fifteen years, they created a large number of applications using DBMS. In the early 1980s, the firm put in place the transaction processing MIS backbone for efficient operations. However, when the company then took stock of its MIS operations, it found that these systems would not be able to support the firm's continuing pursuit of competitiveness. Management-level information was piecemeal: there was no single source of information on customers, products, or other basic business entities. This information was scattered among various systems, controlled by various business units.

To gain control of its data, Pillsbury initiated a major data planning effort in 1984. It should be stressed that the work done by the firm at that early date still stands ahead of most firms.

Pillsbury engaged a consulting firm with experience in what is sometimes called information engineering to develop a long-term plan for the company's information architecture as a part of the total strategic MIS plan. The strategic plan was to consist of three parts:

1. A baseline study to determine what was on hand: what systems were available and how well they served the organization,

2. A target MIS architecture: where the firm should be five to seven years hence with respect to all of its MIS resources, and

3. A transition plan: how to get from where the company was to where it wanted to be.

About midway through the overall planning process, from February to August 1985, the firm's data administration group, working with the consultants, created the component of the plan that is of interest to us here—the information architecture; that is, the data side of the long-term plan. It is worth mentioning that the firm's data administration group had the advantage of extensive experience in the ongoing MIS planning process at Pillsbury U.S. Foods.

The data administration group used three principal inputs in planning the information architecture:

1. They identified the *business functions* of the firm.

2. They mapped the *organizational structure* onto these business functions; in other words, they identified the managers responsible for or having a major stake in a function to see what information the managers needed to manage the function.

3. They mapped the information provided by *existing systems* onto the business functions to see what was already there and what remained to be done.

Work on the long-range information plan yielded three principal components of the future information architecture.

The DA group obtained a table (called the business function model), showing which business functions used which data, through the Business Systems Planning (BSP) technique, which we will further describe in chapter 17. (Such a table is shown in figure 17.4.) This information was determined through a series of group interviews with managers responsible for the functions and subfunctions; textbooks on the food industry were consulted to make sure that no functions were omitted.

Thus, Pillsbury's data administration group identified 200 subfunctions, basic activities performed by the U.S. Food division, within 12 functions (for example, Sales was a function and Ordering was one of its subfunctions). Based on these, 20 major classes of data, consisting of 150 data entities, were identified (thus, Sales Data was a class, and Credit Data was an entity within that class). Owing to the extensive documentation the DA group had maintained throughout its prior planning processes, development of the business function model took only two months, with two people working on it less than half-time. Another factor in making the effort reasonable was that no attempt was made to achieve 100 percent completeness and accuracy, which could have eventually led to the abandonment of a protracted planning process.

Next, data administrators employed a technique resembling entity-relationship modeling to produce a conceptual data model for the entire firm. The relationships between the 150 data entities of the business function model were established, and a graphical model (resembling the model in figure 8.14, but with many entities) was produced. Again, to make the amount of work reasonable, only the more important relationships were mapped.

Finally, each data entity was described in more detail in three ways: what application was responsible for creating and updating the data entity, who was the primary user responsible for furnishing the data, and which MIS group was responsible for developing and maintaining the application that would create and update the data. Again, planners avoided excessive detail to cut down on the planning time.

Thus, the planning process yielded a business function model, a global entity-relationship model of the organizational data, and a description of the principal data entities.

Many an architectural plan is produced and then abandoned by a firm, frequently because it is too complex. At Pillsbury U.S. Foods, care was taken to provide an immediate linkage between the plan and its implementation. Several applications were identified for implementation in the next twelve to eighteen months. The documentation necessary for these projects was broken out of the larger documents produced for the entire organization. This downsizing of the overall plan documents for specific systems produced models that were manageable and focused enough to be really useful to systems development teams.

Seven key systems projects were identified through the strategic planning process, which the planning of information architecture was a part of. For example, the project with top priority was an application that would maintain corporate customer profiles. As we said, an appropriate fragment of the entity-relationship data model was produced for each of these.

Based on these fragments of the global data model, the teams implementing individual projects performed a more detailed logical and physical database design. The commitment of the developers to use the models produced by the information architects was a key factor in the success of the modeling effort. This commitment stemmed not only from the support given by top corporate management. The developers were also motivated by their experience: they had previously worked in an environment lacking an integrated approach to data and found it highly frustrating. The company also provided education in data modeling to the developers.

Based on James C. Brancheau, Larry Schuster, and Salvatore T. March, "Building and Implementing Information Architecture." *Data Base*, 20, 2, Summer 1989, pp. 9–17.

Case Study Questions

1. We said that database technology does not in itself produce organizational control of data. Illustrate this point with the experience of Pillsbury U.S. Foods prior to the development of its information architecture.

2. Specify the three basic inputs to the process of developing information architecture.

3. Outline in graphical form the three steps in producing information architecture at Pillsbury U.S. Foods. Specify the outputs (documents) produced at each step.

4. Many architectural planning processes turn into useless exercises that consume much time and effort and produce outputs that go unused. At Pillsbury, the planning process resulted in actual system development projects. What specific measures were taken to ensure that goal?

SELECTED REFERENCES

Brewin, Bob. "Data Base Machines." *Federal Computer Week,* February 19, 1990, pp. 22–24.

Chen, Peter. "The Entity-Relationship Model—Toward a Unified View of Data." *ACM Transactions on Database Systems,* 1,1, March 1976, pp. 9–36.

Codd, E. F. "A Relational Model of Data for Large Shared Data Banks." *Communications of the ACM,* 13,6, June 1970, pp. 377–87.

Date, C. J. *An Introduction to Database Systems.* 5th ed. Reading, Mass.: Addison-Wesley, 1990.

Hazzah, Ali. "Objects Are Taking Shape in Flat Relational World." *Software,* June 1990, pp. 32–42.

Honkanen, Pentti A. "The Integrity Problem, and What Can Be Done About It Using Today's DBMSs." *Data Base,* 20,3, Fall 1989, pp. 21–27.

Jarvenpaa, Sirkka L., and Machesky, Jefry J. "End-User Learning Behavior in Data Analysis and Data Modeling Tools." *Proceedings of the Seventh International Conference on Information Systems,* San Diego, Calif.: 1986, pp. 152–67.

Kahn, Beverly K. "Some Realities of Data Administration." *Communications of the ACM,* 26,10, October 1983, pp. 794–99.

Kahn, Beverly K., and Garceau, Linda R. "A Developmental Model of the Database Administration Function." *Journal of Management Information Systems,* 1,4, Spring 1985, pp. 87–101.

Kim, Won. *Introduction to Object-Oriented Databases.* Cambridge, Mass.: MIT Press, 1990.

King, Stephen J., and Nehyba, Susanne J. "Data Resource Management." In *Managing the Data Resource Function,* edited by Richard L. Nolan. 2d ed. St. Paul: West, 1982, pp. 185–209.

Lazos, James N. "Unleashing the Power of Your Marketing Database," *The Bankers Magazine*, March/April 1991, pp. 21–28.

McLeod, Dennis. "Perspective on Object Databases." *Information and Software Technology,* 33, 1, January-February 1991, pp. 13–21.

Madnick, Stuart E., and Wang, Richard Y. "Evolution towards Strategic Applications of Databases through Composite Information Systems." *Journal of Management Information Systems,* 5, 2, Fall 1988, pp. 5–22.

March, Salvatore T., and Kim, Young-Gul. "Information Resource Management: A Metadata Perspective." *Journal of Management Information Systems,* 5, 3, Winter 1988–89, pp. 5–18.

Matthews, Robert W., and McGee, William C. "Data Modeling for Software Development." *IBM Systems Journal,* 29, 2, 1990, pp. 228–35.

Nolan, Richard L. "Data Administration." In *Managing the Data Resource Function,* edited by Richard L. Nolan. 2d ed. St. Paul: West, 1982, pp. 286–96.

Petreley, Nicholas; Duncan, Judy; with Slovick, Linda; and Banapour, Zoreh. "Analyzing Relational Databases, Parts I and II." *Infoworld,* January 8, 1990, pp. 51–68; and June 25, 1990, pp. 55–69.

Schmieder, Thomas A. "Braving the Pitfalls of Full DB2 Implementation." *Database Programming and Design,* October 1988, pp. 50–60.

Sehr, Barbara. "Hierarchical Model Keeps Loyal Following." *Computerworld,* March 14, 1988, p. S3.

Vassiliou, Yannis. "On the Interactive Use of Databases: Query Languages." *Journal of Management Information Systems,* 1, 3, Winter 1984–85, pp. 33–48.

Weldon, Jay-Louise. *Data Base Administration.* New York: Plenum Press, 1981.

Wertz, Charles J. *The Data Dictionary: Concepts and Uses.* 2d ed. Wellesley, Mass: Q.E.D. Information Sciences, 1989.

Zwass, Vladimir. *Introduction to Computer Science.* New York: Barnes & Noble/Harper & Row, 1981.

CHAPTER 9

END-USER COMPUTING AND ITS TOOLS

. . . .

End-user computing is the future of information systems.
Raymond Panko

Personal computers and productivity software offer end users independence and autonomy they could not have had before. With technical tools such as fourth-generation languages on hand, users are now in a position to develop many of their own information systems. End-user computing is rapidly taking over many responsibilities previously discharged by MIS departments. Yet, one should not expect end-user computing to replace all MIS-unit activity in organizations.

This chapter will discuss the rapidly growing end-user computing phenomenon. We will also examine the personal computing environment built around microcomputers. End-user computing is not limited to this environment—however, it is with microcomputer systems and with personal productivity software that most end users do their work.

As we keep stressing, technologies do not automatically produce organizational results. How do we take advantage of end-user technologies? How do we avoid the risks that accompany end-user systems development and operation? How do we manage and support end-user computing? These are some of the questions we will address in this chapter.

When new and complex technologies entered the scene of human affairs, it appeared that virtually all of us would sooner or later have to become technologists in their service. When automobiles were invented, many pundits thought that those of us who could not be riders would have to become chauffeurs. When the telephone industry blossomed before World War I, in the days of manual call switching, many were pessimistic about the industry's prospects. If most offices and homes were to have a telephone, they reasoned, the country's entire workforce would have to be drafted to switch the calls!

Most of us did not become either professional drivers or telephone operators. To repeat the pattern, other prognosticators believed in the 1960s that the spread of organizational computing would be limited by the number of people available to become analysts and programmers. But once again, technology provided its own solution: direct user access.

9.1 End-User Computing and Its Benefits
   - What Is End-User Computing?
   - What Led to End-User Computing?
   - Benefits of End-User Computing
   - Who Are the End Users?

9.2 The Personal Computer as the End-User's Workstation
   - The Organization of a Microcomputer System
   - User Interface
   - Micro-to-Mainframe Links

9.3 Personal Productivity Software
   - Functions of Personal Productivity Software
   - Spreadsheet Software
   - Database Management
   - Personal Information Management
   - Word Processing

. . . .

9.1. END-USER COMPUTING AND ITS BENEFITS

End-user computing has three dimensions: a sophisticated level of computer technology use by end users, end-user development of applications, and end-user control of systems. All three aspects of this phenomenon can bring significant organizational benefits. Not all end users are created equal: there are several categories of people in organizations who may be characterized by different levels of sophistication in end-user computing.

What Is End-User Computing?

An **end user,** or simply user, employs the information produced by an MIS application in doing his or her work. Traditionally, until about the mid-1970s, a rather sharp separation existed between end users and MIS professionals. MIS specialists developd applications, and end users were furnished with the outputs, typically reports, produced by these applications. The MIS unit of an organization was in control of virtually all of its computing activities.

The computing environment of organizations has since changed dramatically. Transaction processing systems continue to be developed largely by MIS professionals. However, end users are now themselves satisfying many of their own informational requirements. This is the burgeoning phenomenon of **end-user computing:** the practice of users' developing, using directly, and controlling their own information systems.

In this new environment, many end users work directly with applications to produce the information they need. Thus, a manager will work out the plan for the next quarter by directly using spreadsheet software on her microcomputer. A secretary may use an elaborate word processing software to produce customized group mailings. An executive starts each working day by reviewing the key performance indicators for his or her division and drilling down into the data to root out the causes of any trouble. All these people access information systems themselves, without an MIS professional to act as an intermediary.

Direct and increasingly sophisticated use of information systems is only one aspect of end-user computing. End-user development of these systems has become increasingly frequent. However, the central issues in end-user computing are organizational proximity and control (Emory, 1987). End-user computing can be contrasted with a computing environment fully controlled by an MIS department, with its monopoly on the acquisition and operation of MIS resources. Today, end-user computing has severely limited MIS department control of these functions. As is only to be expected, not all firms have been able to cope successfully with the political tensions arising from this transition.

To expand our definition of end-user computing, let us say that this environment has the following characteristics:

1. Reasonably advanced *use* of information systems directly by end users. Typing a simple letter with a word processing package, using an electronic-mail system, or entering a customer's selection in a fast-food emporium are *not* considered examples of such advanced use. Advanced use deals more directly with the capabilities of the technology and generally includes the operation of the system.

2. *Development* of applications by the end users themselves, perhaps with assistance by MIS professionals.

3. *Control* of information resources—that is, the decision-making authority to acquire and operate information systems. This includes the authority to purchase computer systems resources and to plan and carry out development projects.

These three aspects of end-user computing—use, development, and control (see figure 9.1)—are exercised to different degrees in various firms, and even in their subunits. These aspects of end-user computing have been identified by Gordon Davis of the University of Minnesota (Davis, 1982). Indeed, one may categorize end users who are active in this environment by the degree to which they perform these three functions (Cotterman, 1989).

The fact that end-user computing will completely change the way information delivery is done in organizations was recognized early by Robert Benjamin of Xerox Corporation (Benjamin, 1982). Benjamin computed that in 1980 (before

FIGURE 9.1

Three dimensions of end-user computing.

(Modified from Cotterman, 1989)

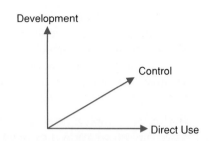

the arrival of microcomputers!), 40 percent of hardware power was already under end-user control in one of his company's strategic business units. He forecast that by the end of the 1980s, end-user computing would dominate organizational information delivery in that unit. This forecast turned out to be right—and moreover, right across a very broad area, not limited to a particular business unit. By the end of the 1980s, many companies were spending 60 percent of their MIS budgets on end-user computing activities, and some of them were even spending as much as 80 percent (Guimaraes, 1987).

What Led to End-User Computing?

The emergence and continuing growth of end-user computing is the outcome of several forces. The principal factors which precipitated this phenomenon include:

1. Technological Factors.

Fourth-generation languages were introduced, many of them sufficiently user-friendly for end users to be able to develop their own applications. Another major technological factor was the arrival of the personal computer—now a primary vehicle for information service delivery to users. Personal productivity software has accompanied the arrival of personal computers.

2. Organizational Factors.

The deployment of information systems significantly affects the managerial effectiveness and strategic posture of organizational units. A manager whose unit is able to use information systems effectively often has superior operating results to show for it. By contrast, centralized MIS units have often been unresponsive to users' requirements.

Also, the ability to respond promptly to marketplace demands calls for proximity of MIS resources to acting units and for control by those who are "in the trenches." The fact that superior competitive posture can be gained through end-user computing was recognized early by Ephraim McLean (McLean, 1979).

Combined with the general decentralization trend in many companies, these factors led to a shift in computing control to the operational units.

3. Personnel Capabilities.

Computers and computer-based systems have become part of everyday experience, curricular learning, and on-the-job training for many knowledge workers. This acculturation to computer-related technologies has enabled these workers to participate in end-user computing activities.

All of these factors are now expanding the reach of end-user computing.

Benefits of End-User Computing

End-user computing is not, of course, a total alternative to professional systems development and support. Very few predict or advocate a total dissolution of the corporate MIS function (Dearden, 1987). We shall discuss the limitations of end-user computing and the risks connected with it later in this chapter. Here, we want to see why this form of computing has rapidly become dominant in many firms. These are the vital benefits of end-user computing:

1. End-user *development* can place systems into the users' hands more quickly than an MIS department can. By developing their own systems, end users avoid the two-to-four year backlogs of systems development projects in most firms, as these projects await the attention of MIS units. This visible backlog is overshadowed by the larger, invisible backlog of applications which are not even requested by users because they are aware of the long waits (Alloway, 1983). A more responsive development process leads to increased managerial effectiveness, based on more informed decision making.

   A combination of the functional expertise possessed by end users and the technological competence of MIS specialists, who often assist end users during systems development, may result in superior systems. The communication gap between the user and the developer ceases to exist.

2. The proper unmediated (direct) *use* of information systems by end users enhances their work performance and gives them a sense of control over their working environment (resulting in what is often called empowerment). If users directly participate in computing activities, their information-systems competence grows and they become ever more effective in end-user computing.

3. *Control* over the informational environment enables users to set priorities and employ resources in the fashion that best satisfies their perceived needs. Of course, end users are also subject to overall budgetary limitations.

Who Are the End Users?

End users differ in the extent to which they control, develop, and use their information systems. In a classic paper on this subject, John Rockart and Lauren Flannery identified six categories of people who are end users or who use end-user oriented facilities (Rockart, 1983). Table 9.1 lists these categories. The classification in table 9.1 includes three categories of end users who play a primary role in end-user computing: command-level users, end-user programmers, and functional support personnel. Sophistication in the use of end-user facilities grows as we go down this list.

We should note that this classification predates the broad use of microcomputers in organizations. However, end-user computing is now virtually inseparable from these machines, which are used as personal computers. We shall now discuss the personal computer environment.

TABLE 9.1

Categories of People
Who Employ End-User
Facilities

From John F. Rockart and
Lauren S. Flannery, "The
Management of End-User
Computing" in
Communications of the ACM,
26, 10, 1983. Copyright
© 1983 Association of
Computing Machinery, New
York. Reprinted with
permission.

CATEGORY	ACTIVITY
Nonprogramming Users	Access the system through a limited and highly structured interface to perform a limited menu of functions.
Command-Level Users	Access the system through a simple query language, and are able to use a simple report generator or a similar command-driven system.
End-User Programmers	Use a 4GL to develop their own applications, some of which may be deployed by other users.
Functional Support Personnel	Non-MIS professionals who develop applications for other users in their functional area (delegated end-user development).
End-User Support Personnel	MIS professionals (such as information center personnel) who specialize in supporting end-user computing.
MIS Developers in End-User-Oriented Languages	MIS professionals who develop systems with 4GL facilities.

9.2 THE PERSONAL COMPUTER AS THE END-USER'S WORKSTATION

The most common end-user workstation in organizations is a microcomputer. Its hardware organization provides a simple way to include in a system a variety of devices a user needs. The software used for personal computing has now moved to a great extent from character-based interaction with the user to graphical user interfaces. Aside from its role as a local information processor, a personal computer is an entryway to a larger system; three principal types of links to such a system may be provided.

The Organization of a Microcomputer System

As we said in chapter 6, a user's workstation does not have to be a microcomputer. However, in practice, a microcomputer, used as a personal computer and now frequently included in a network, is the usual vehicle for end-user computing.

Let us enlarge on the discussion of microcomputers in chapter 6. The hardware of a microcomputer is generally built around a single bus—a set of lines that interconnect all the other hardware components (see figure 9.2). Input and output devices communicate with the microprocessor (CPU) and the main memory via this bus, which they share with other devices. The microprocessor chip, a part of the main memory (RAM) chips, and the read-only memory (ROM) chips are placed directly on the system (mother) board of the machine. The ROM contains a number of unalterable service routines. The vital one is the bootstrap program, which is activated when you turn on the computer: this program performs the diagnostics to check out the machine's circuitry and then loads the operating system (actually, its memory-resident part) from a disk into RAM. Now you can run an application by specifying its name to the operating system.

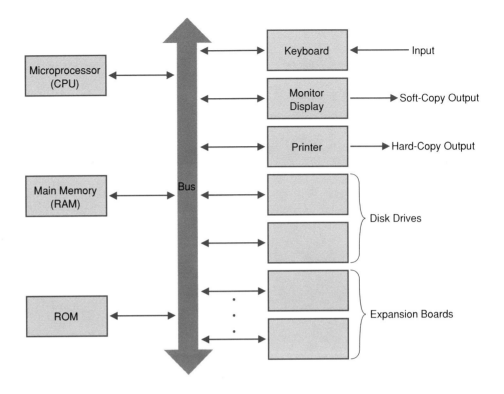

FIGURE 9.2

How a microcomputer is organized.

The input and output devices, as well as secondary memories, are connected to the bus with adapter circuits—which makes it possible to connect a variety of peripherals made by different vendors. In addition, expansion boards may be placed in the slots of the system board to enhance the performance of the microcomputer or to connect any needed devices. Table 9.2 will give you an idea of the variety of such devices and enhancements. In particular, we must stress the necessity of providing a tape backup device to periodically copy the hard disk contents. The need for a local area network must be considered as well. Multifunction boards are available: by handling several functions, these boards maximize the use of expansion slots.

Over 10 million microcomputers were shipped in 1990. The dominant microcomputers in the business environment are the IBM personal computers, currently represented by the IBM Personal System/2 (PS/2) models series, as well as the older PC, PC-XT and PC-AT models, and IBM-compatible machines offered by many vendors. MS-DOS (known also as PC-DOS) is the primary operating system for these machines, with OS/2 available for machines based on the Intel 80286 microprocessor or on its successors. Management of file directories and backup support are only some of the operating-system facilities that are directly invoked by end users.

The IBM microcomputers have been challenged for some time by the Macintosh series of the Apple Corporation, running under Macintosh System Software. Its graphical user interface offered a radically different "look and feel" from the traditional command-driven IBM environment (until the latter was changed by

TABLE 9.2

Popular Expansion Boards
for Microprocessors

BOARD	FUNCTION
Accelerator	Boosts the processing speed; often used to upgrade an older machine.
Adapter	Connects a peripheral to the system. Disk adapter boards may actually contain a hard disk. Mouse, display, or backup tape adapters connect specific devices.
Coprocessor	Contains an additional special-purpose processor. Arithmetic coprocessor speeds up numeric computations; graphics coprocessor handles high-resolution displays.
Emulator	Enables the microcomputer to operate as a terminal connected to a larger host computer; emulators for IBM 3270 terminals are common.
Local Area Network (LAN)	Connects the microcomputer to a LAN.
Memory	Provides expanded RAM capacity.
Modem	For telecommunications purposes; provides an internal modem on the board itself or connects to an external modem.

new software). The most interesting new challenger is the NeXT computer, a brainchild of Steven Jobs (an acclaimed founder of Apple) and a product of NeXT Incorporated. Its design is oriented toward a multimedia environment.

User Interface

User interface is a combination of means by which a user interacts with the computer system.

As the business world came to be dominated by IBM-compatible personal computers, we all became used to command-driven, character-based user interfaces: we simply keyboarded an instruction to the ubiquitous MS-DOS in response to a C> prompt. Obviously, not everyone considered this environment "simple." When Macintosh introduced into the wider world a graphical user interface (based in many respects on work done at the Xerox Palo Alto Research Center), many users found it both simpler and more attractive to use. The initial Macintosh screen (see figure 9.3) imitates a desktop environment, with icons representing objects or actions (for example, a trash bin icon represents discarding a file) and with menus helping to select an action. A mouse is generally used to navigate this environment. Figure 9.3 names (in five boxes) the components of this screen.

In a **graphical user interface (GUI),** verbal commands are replaced by the action of pointing an arrow (guided by a mouse, trackball, or a similar cursor-control device) at icons and menu selections. Several windows on the screen enable the user to work with several programs, either simultaneously (in a multitasking system) or by suspending all but one (see color plate 10).

A graphical user interface may be implemented in a DOS environment with a Windows utility program from Microsoft. The Presentation Manager in OS/2 also

FIGURE 9.3

Initial screen on a Macintosh microcomputer, with explanation of its components in five boxes.

(Adapted from Panko, 1988, p. 331)

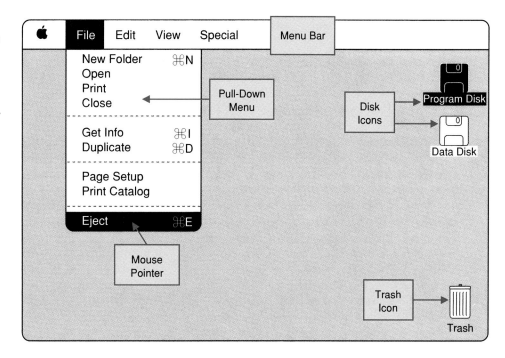

offers a graphical user interface (GUI), with windows, icons, and menus. Other GUIs include Open Look (AT&T), GEM (Digital Research), NewWave (a package from Hewlett-Packard that expands the capabilities offered by Windows), NeXTStep (NeXT), and Motif (backed by Open Software Foundation and used worldwide). These interfaces are easy to use, but they call for relatively powerful microcomputers with extensive main memories. Some windowing software, such as Windows, offer dynamic data links: if a number is changed in a spreadsheet running in one of the windows, the change will be automatically reflected in a word-processing file where the spreadsheet is used.

Today, all microcomputer operating systems are expected to offer GUIs either as a part of the system itself or as a package that runs on it. The current preference for graphical user interfaces is illustrated by the next vignette.

A radically new user interface is emerging for the pen-based notepad computers, which we discussed in chapters 2 and 6 (Miller, 1991). The interface is indeed designed to imitate pen-and-notepad operation: no keyboard or mouse is used here. The user writes with a styluslike pen on the screen on the top of the light-weight computer. When run under control of the PenPoint operating system (by Go Corporation), the virtual notepad displays a table of contents with index tabs and recognizes eleven "gestures"—strokes of the pen. The user taps the pen to activate an application, crosses out what he or she wants deleted, and circles anything that needs to be modified. These interfaces are particularly apt for form-oriented applications, but may be used to take notes or produce a drawing as well.

MOVE TO GRAPHICAL USER INTERFACES

Broad, convincing research that decisively demonstrates the superiority of GUIs is still lacking. A study by Temple, Barker & Sloane, Inc., a research company in Lexington, Massachusetts, found that experienced GUI users worked 35 percent faster and made 17 percent fewer errors than experienced users of character-based interfaces. Other studies have shown that GUIs are easier to learn, more enjoyable to use (we could have guessed that), and give users more confidence. Broad studies that show surpassing effectiveness of these interfaces are still not available.

However, a few years ago, an easy-to-use interface that minimizes training costs was just what agencies of the U.S. federal government were looking for. When the Federal Aviation Administration received 43,000 AT&T microcomputers in March

1990, they were all equipped with Microsoft Windows. Other procurements, such as the Defense Department purchase of 250,000 Unisys micros, also included Windows.

"Once a user has learned a GUI, all the applications will look the same," says a product manager for the Open Look GUI. "There will no longer be a different way to do features like leaving, cutting, copying."

The biggest hurdle preventing wider acceptance of GUI technology is that most agencies already own micros that are not powerful enough for effective use of GUIs. GUIs require a machine built around an Intel 80286SX processor or higher, with at least 2 Mbytes of RAM.

Based on Charles Von Simson, "Graphical Upstart Quelled," *Computerworld*, June 25, 1990, pp. 39, 55; and Carolyn D. Marsan, "Graphical User Interfaces: Many Federal Users Are Choosing GUIs Over Command-Driven Systems," *Federal Computer Week*, March 5, 1990, pp. 14–16, 27.

Micro-to-Mainframe Links

Microcomputers are frequently employed not only for local processing or for communication within a local area network, but as an entryway to a mainframe or another larger machine (called a host). Three types of interaction are possible:

1. Terminal Emulation.

The microcomputer is used as a dumb terminal: it serves as an input and output device, with all the processing done on the larger machine. In this case, micros frequently run the emulation software for the IBM 3270 terminal—the most common terminal in use. If all a personal computer does is work in a terminal emulation mode, the environment is very limited and hardly provides satisfactory support for end-user computing.

2. Local Processing.

Processing is done on the microcomputer, with data downloaded to it from the host, and, much less frequently, results or other data uploaded to the larger machine. Specialized communications programs are available to facilitate this task (such as NOW! from Attachmate of Bellevue, Washington). The host frequently acts as a database server, with the microcomputer as its client, sending database queries.

3. Cooperative Processing.

Some newer applications are split into tasks running on the micro (such as user interface software) and tasks running on the host (such as database management, for example). Much effort is now being directed toward this new form of processing. System architectures that encompass machines of all categories from micros to mainframes, of which IBM's Systems Applications Architecture (SAA) is a leading example, are expected to facilitate cooperative processing.

We must stress that an attempt to implement intermachine links usually brings many problems to the surface. Some of them stem from lack of compatibility between the hardware and software of different vendors. Others relate to the fact that transferring files across links may prove to be time-consuming and costly. Organizational issues, such as who controls data distribution procedures, are frequently daunting if effective data administration is lacking.

9.3 PERSONAL PRODUCTIVITY SOFTWARE

Several categories of software run on personal computers. Each of them can enhance a user's productivity in a certain range of tasks. A user's selection of equipment and software should be derived from the nature of these tasks.

Functions of Personal Productivity Software

Personal productivity software enhances end users' performance on tasks. Managers using spreadsheets are able to make higher-quality decisions by performing data analyses; secretaries are more effective with word processing, spreadsheets, and other programs; corporate communications specialists produce better work with desktop publishing systems. Obviously, some categories of software, such as personal information systems, are broadly applicable. Others are limited to a more narrow class of users; but this software often plays a vital role in the professional activity of the users who can employ it.

Software packages which enhance users' personal productivity brought microcomputers into the business environment in the first place. The invention of the first electronic spreadsheet program—VisiCalc for Apple II—turned microcomputers into business tools. Indeed, the growing hardware requirements for personal productivity software sell new generations of personal computers.

Several functional categories of personal productivity software have emerged. Figure 9.4 shows the general functions supported by the software: data management and analysis, authoring and presentation, and activity and notes tracking. The figure also shows particular categories of software to support these functions. Also included is groupware—software for computer-supported cooperative work in teams, which we will discuss in chapter 16.

Note that the capabilities of individual software packages vary widely, and a thorough selection process is necessary to ensure proper support to the functions of an individual user or of a group of users. At the same time, firms must standardize much of the personal productivity software used by their workers. Extensive capabilities come at the price of extensive hardware requirements, longer learning time, and the need to maintain the acquired proficiency. A casual end user who must once in a while prepare several slides for a business presentation

FIGURE 9.4

Functions and categories of
personal productivity
software.

Groupware

Cooperative Work

Database Management

Data Management and Analysis

Personal Productivity Software

Activity and Notes Tracking

Personal Information Management

Spreadsheet Software

Authoring and Presentation

Word Processing

Desktop Publishing

Presentation Software

Multimedia Authoring

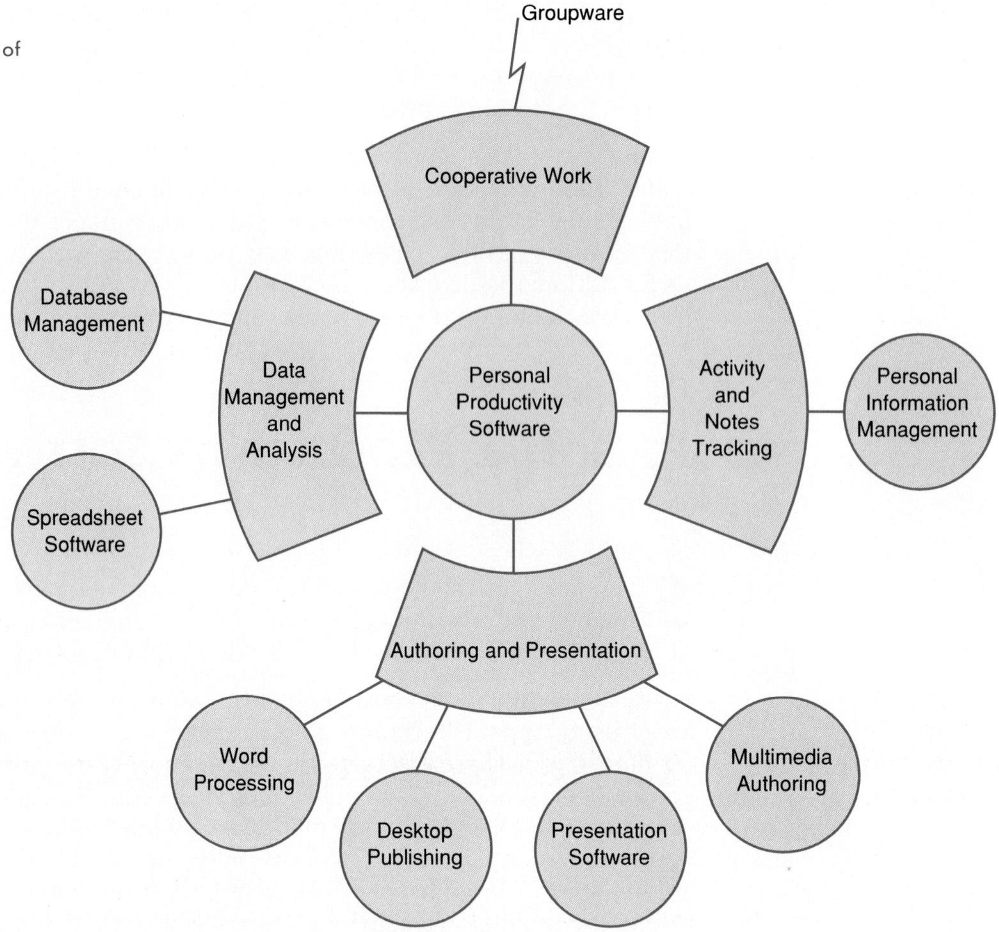

will be well served by a rudimentary presentation software; on the other hand, a specialist in developing computer-based training courseware should investigate the new field of multimedia authoring packages.

Several general trends are currently discernible. Many personal productivity packages are expanded to a LAN version and thus support the functioning of a workgroup; they may be used as part of a groupware package, or they may work with such a package. Most of the leading packages have moved toward graphical user interfaces; for example, vendors often provide a Windows version of the product.

Another trend is blurring the lines between these offerings. The functionalities of various packages overlap ever more: database management packages offer the analytical capabilities of spreadsheets, as well as data presentation capabilities; word processing and desktop publishing are sharing more functions. At the same time, a user who wants several packages to work together will encounter many difficulties and should very carefully investigate all aspects of their compatibility.

We will now review the principal categories of personal productivity software, paying particular attention to the newer technologies.

FIGURE 9.5

A worksheet displayed by a
spreadsheet program.

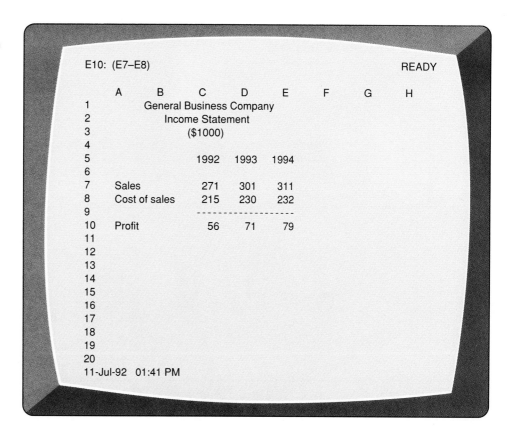

FIGURE 9.5

A worksheet displayed by a
spreadsheet program.

Spreadsheet Software

Running a spreadsheet program is the most common business use of a personal computer. Spreadsheet programs enable the user to manipulate any data that can be represented in rows and columns: the data may be sorted, summarized, and aggregated into categories. The principal advantages of spreadsheets (a term that, in the vernacular, refers to both the programs and the worksheets they produce) lie in manipulating numerical data for financial analysis—indeed, the idea came from accountants' worksheets. Spreadsheet programs are most commonly used as a planning tool relying on rather simple business models. As spreadsheet programs become more sophisticated, more complex modeling is possible, approaching the power of decision support system (DSS) generators, which we shall discuss in more detail in chapter 14.

An extremely simple worksheet displayed on a screen by a spreadsheet program is shown in figure 9.5.

The contents of a *cell,* the intersection of a numbered row and a column identified by letters, may be represented as a ready number (for example, cell C7 in figure 9.5 contains 271). However, the power of spreadsheets derives from the fact that a cell's contents may also be given as a formula. For example, in our worksheet, the contents of cell E10 were computed as E7–E8, which is indicated at the top of the display. Should the contents of any cell change, the contents of all the cells whose values depend on that first cell are automatically recomputed. This feature permits the user to consider various "what-if" alternatives—one of the analytical modes of decision support, as seen in chapter 3. The ease of spreadsheet use fosters an analytical approach to managerial decision making.

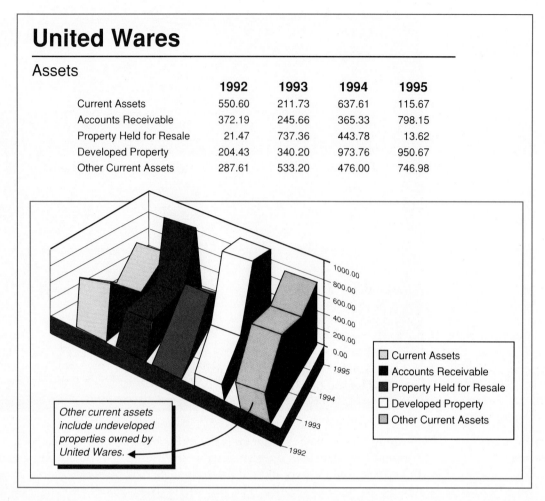

United Wares

Assets

	1992	1993	1994	1995
Current Assets	550.60	211.73	637.61	115.67
Accounts Receivable	372.19	245.66	365.33	798.15
Property Held for Resale	21.47	737.36	443.78	13.62
Developed Property	204.43	340.20	973.76	950.67
Other Current Assets	287.61	533.20	476.00	746.98

☐ Current Assets
■ Accounts Receivable
■ Property Held for Resale
☐ Developed Property
▨ Other Current Assets

Other current assets include undeveloped properties owned by United Wares.

FIGURE 9.6

Output provided by a spreadsheet package with presentation graphics capability (Wingz by Informix Software).

(Reprinted with permission of Informix Software, Lenexa, Kansas.)

A number of mathematical, statistical, financial (such as the present value of a series of cash flows), text-handling, and other functions are available in spreadsheet programs. Sets of commands may be stored as macros and reused. Templates are available from independent vendors for various business situations. A template contains only the description of a worksheet and its formulas; the data are supplied by the user.

Spreadsheet programs can handle thousands of rows and columns, which may be scrolled on the monitor screen. Leading packages handle three- and multidimensional worksheets. Many of them also offer graphical user interfaces and excellent presentation-quality output, including graphics (see figure 9.6 and color plate 11).

In general, spreadsheets suffer from disadvantages as compared to DSS generators: for example, spreadsheets have limited modeling capabilities; "programs" (formulas) and data are intertwined, which makes modifications difficult. Auditing of worksheets is also difficult because of the lack of an audit trail. However, some spreadsheet programs (Javelin Plus, for example) offer outstanding modeling capabilities. And many organizations enforce spreadsheet use standards to counteract, at least in part, the other disadvantages.

	PRODUCT	VENDOR
TABLE 9.3		
A Selection of Spreadsheet Software	Microsoft Excel	Microsoft
	Javelin Plus	Javelin Products Group
	Multiplan	Microsoft
	Lotus 1–2–3	Lotus Development
	PFS: Professional Plan	Software Publishing
	Quattro Pro	Borland International
	SuperCalc	Computer Associates International
	TM/1	Sinper
	VP-Planner	Paperback Software International
	Informix Wingz	Informix Software

A number of popular spreadsheets are listed in table 9.3; Lotus 1–2–3 has led the field for a long time.

Database Management

Database management systems for personal computers are a powerful tool for managing record-oriented, predominantly numeric data. As we discussed in the preceding chapter, most modern DBMSs employ relational technology, with data represented as tables. Microcomputer DBMSs include among their basic capabilities the ability to:

- create and maintain a database;
- query a database with a query language (see the discussion of these languages in the next section); and
- prepare formatted hard-copy reports.

In addition, many packages offer security features, network connectivity, and the ability to present graphical output, as well as to perform spreadsheet-type computations.

Database management is the foundation of many business information systems. That is why DBMS packages generally offer fourth-generation languages (4GLs) for accessing data and developing systems. We shall discuss 4GLs in the next section of this chapter.

A number of full-featured DBMS packages are listed in table 9.4. These packages are relational, and our discussion of relational systems in chapter 8 applies to them.

Multimedia databases, containing interlinked informational items represented in a variety of media, are slowly emerging. They are built with the use of hypermedia technology, which we will discuss in the section on authoring technology.

TABLE 9.4

A Selection of Database
Management Systems for
Personal Computers

PRODUCT	VENDOR
Clarion Professional Developer	Clarion Software
DataEase	DataEase International
Dataflex	Data Access
dBase IV	Borland International
Foxpro	Fox Software
Paradox	Borland International
Rbase	Microrim

Personal Information Management

In the course of their daily activities, knowledge workers deal only occasionally with data that may be represented as database records. When we discuss in chapter 13 the way managers spend their time, you will see that analytical work with such data occupies a relatively small fraction of this time. People need to organize such scraps of information as names of business contacts, reminders, telephone messages, ideas, or other short textual items. They need access to this information to track projects, write memos, or develop financial projections.

Personal information management (PIM) packages are tools that help knowledge workers track tasks, people, projects, and ideas. These packages assist users in several ways, including:

- Allowing users to enter short notes and assign them to categories they define (for example, "Accomplishments for this Quarter"). These categories may also be organized into a hierarchy (for example, a higher-level category might be "Accomplishments for the Next Performance Appraisal").
- Letting users browse through the categories and the items they contain, enabling the user to examine the information from several points of view.
- Supporting time management in scheduling events, for example, by discovering time conflicts, maintaining a "tickler" file to remind the user about "things to do," and showing time commitments in graphical form.
- Providing packages that handle various chores, such as automatic telephone dialing.

Some of these packages are listed in table 9.5.

In particular, Lotus Agenda supports a sophisticated concept of a view (Kaplan, 1990), which is equivalent to a report in this environment. The user constructs views from selected categories of notes, and the views' contents change automatically as the information in the system changes. By looking at such a view, the user accesses all the information on a particular topic (for example, "What can I discuss with Steve during our meetings in January?"). Some of these products (such as Primetime Personal) have a small program size and are easy to use, and are thus an excellent tool for laptop users.

TABLE 9.5

A Selection of Packages for Personal Information Management

PRODUCT	VENDOR
Act!	Conductor Software
Agenda	Lotus Development
Primetime Personal	Primetime Software
Totall Manager	Bartel Software
Who-What-When	Chronos Software

TABLE 9.6

A Selection of Word Processing Software

PRODUCT	VENDOR
Ami, Ami Professional	Samna
DeScribe	DeScribe
DisplayWrite	IBM
MultiMate Advantage	Borland International
Word	Microsoft
WordPerfect	WordPerfect
WordStar 2000, WordStar Professional	WordStar International
XyWrite	XyQuest

In general, PIMs are tools for controlling the complexity of the contemporary organizational environment and, in particular, for battling information overload. When similar information has to be managed for a team of knowledge workers whose workstations are interconnected via a LAN, groupware should be employed (see chapter 16).

Word Processing

Word processing packages facilitate text entry, storage, manipulation, and printing. Memos, letters, internal reports, and product documentation can be created using a word processing package with an ease that has made typewriters all but obsolete.

General capabilities of word processing include text editing with moving, deleting, or replacing blocks of text, and formatting a text on printed pages. Some advanced features are indexing and preparation of a table of contents, and use of a spelling checker or a thesaurus of word synonyms. Some packages are integrated with database management systems (which helps to produce a mailing, for example) or spreadsheet programs (which helps, say, to include a table).

The mail-merge feature of a word processing package enables the user to store a boilerplate letter and then customize it, for example, with names and addresses from a clients' file. This significantly enhances productivity (but leads one to suspect that many undesirable letters were made possible by the facility of this operation).

Some of the popular word processing packages are listed in table 9.6.

To enhance the quality of produced documents, one may use text-revision software which proofreads them for potential hitches in writing style or word usage. These packages point out faulty grammar, wordy expressions, use of slang, weak paragraphs, and similar failings. Examples include Grammatik of Reference Software International and PC Proof of Lexpertise Linguistic Software.

As a general trend, word processing software is increasingly acquiring some of the features of desktop publishing systems—our next topic of discussion.

Desktop Publishing

When instead of writing an internal memo, we have to produce a report for a customer, a catalog, or a business newsletter, we can turn to desktop publishing. The cost of the hardware necessary for these systems has become rather modest: a high-resolution display, a laser printer, and perhaps a scanner may be configured to create a functional desktop-publishing system. Simpler software (such as PFS: First Publisher from Software Publishing, or Publish It! from Timeworks) costs under $300. All this has made desktop publishing accessible to even small businesses. At the same time, sophisticated desktop publishing may require expensive hardware and software, as well as considerable skill on the part of the user—this image-processing technology is very powerful at its high end (and rather hideous designs are easy to come by).

Here is a typical example of the steps required to publish a document on a desktop:

1. *Prepare text and illustrations.* The text copy is produced with a word-processing program, or with the word-processing component of a publishing package, or scanned in with an optical character recognition (OCR) scanner. Line art may be created with a graphics program and imported into the publishing package, or clip art (prepackaged sets of images) may be used. Alternatively, artwork (including photographs) may be imported with an image scanner.

2. *Format pages.* A page-format template is created, together with a style sheet that specifies the typefaces for all of the components of the page, such as headers, captions, or borders (see figure 9.7 for a rather expensive double-page screen that facilitates this work). The appearance of the document can then be changed by simply modifying the style sheet. Scalable fonts (provided, for example, by Adobe Systems' Postscript facility) permit you to select the precise type you desire for all segments of the page.

3. *Place illustrations in the text.* Text and illustrations are placed on the appropriate pages; the system automatically "flows" the text through the publication, laying it out in columns and wrapping it around illustrations. Illustrations may be scaled to fit the allotted space. What-you-see-is-what-you-get (WYSIWYG) graphics software and monitors enable you to see the output in its final form.

4. *Print the document.* The inspected pages may be printed with a laser printer (a printer with the resolution of at least 300 dots per inch is needed). The output of such a printer is camera-ready copy. This means that it may now be reproduced in a variety of ways: by running off multiple

FIGURE 9.7

Screen display for developing page layout.

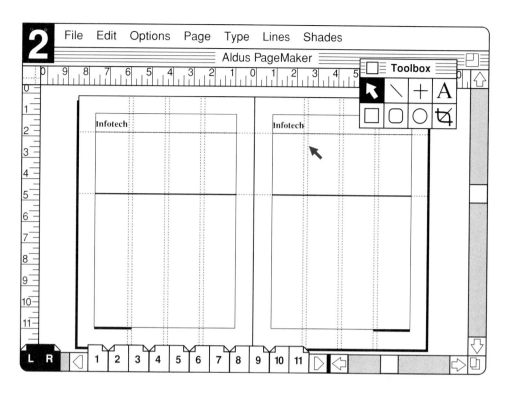

TABLE 9.7

A Selection of Desktop Publishing Packages

PRODUCT	VENDOR
Interleaf Publisher	Interleaf
Aldus PageMaker	Aldus
Quark Xpress	Quark
Ready, Set, Go	Letraset USA
Xerox Ventura Publisher	Xerox Desktop Software

copies on the laser printer, by duplicating the original on copy machines, or by photographing the copy to produce traditional printing plates. Many systems also support slide- and transparency-makers for presentation purposes.

Figure 9.8 shows a page produced with a combination of desktop publishing tools.

Some of the well-known desktop publishing packages are listed in table 9.7.

These publishing packages enable the user to print word-processed text in a great variety of typefaces (for example, Times Roman) and fonts (sets of characters in a particular size and style in the typeface, for example, 12-point Times Roman Italic), combining the text with line artwork (such as the figures in this book) and photographs. Color may be used if the appropriate equipment is available.

Talks Signal New Era for World Traders

Japan Starts Talking Europe's Language

"The importance of increased trade between Western Europe and Japan cannot be underestimated," he says through a translator. "Our regions share much in common as world traders. We both export manufactured products to many regions, while importing that most necessary of all commodities: fuel."

Takeshita is on an 11-day European tour to meet with the leaders of West Germany, France, England, Spain, Italy, Ireland, and The Netherlands. On his agenda are the trade issues so vital to the livelihood of both regions.

The trade practices of Japan and Western Europe do have strong commonality. Both regions export their manufactured products not only to the United States, Canada, and other major importing countries, but also to South Asia and West Africa. Additionally, Western Europe sends a small percentage of its products to South America, Central and Southern Africa, and Eastern Europe. Both Japan and Western Europe import the fuel they require to stay in business.

What Western European leaders would like to see is the trade ties between their countries and Japan strengthened. And they are pleased to hear Takeshita call for exactly that. At the present time Japan exports a relatively small amount of products to Western Europe, while importing almost no European goods. Until now, Japanese trade barriers have stood in the way of increased trade between Japan and Western Europe.

A recent report published by the European Executive Commission projects that the dropping of those trade barriers by the Japanese government would result in a 4.5 percent increase in European economic growth, a 6 percent drop in prices, and 1.8 million new jobs over the next five years.

A more progressive plan calls for the creation of a genuine common market between the two regions as early as 1992. However, expectations for that plan's acceptance in Tokyo are hopeful.

Whatever the final outcome, Western European leaders are extremely pleased to have this opportunity for face-to-face discussions on trade policies between Prime Minister Takeshita and themselves. To many, these discussions signal a new era that could become one of the most productive economic relationships in many generations.

Both Japan and Western Europe export to the major world importers and to South Asia and Africa.

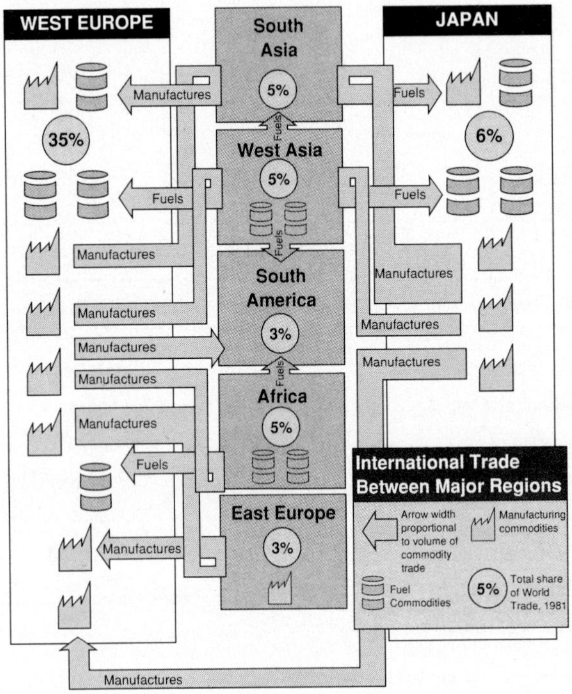

Both countries import the fuel they require to stay in business.

23 Newsmakers

FIGURE 9.8

A page produced with desktop publishing tools, including Adobe Illustrator, which assisted in the artwork.

DESKTOP PUBLISHING PROPONENTS BATTLE IT OUT WITH MIS SPECIALISTS

Desktop publishing is a natural for a public relations department. Marlene Goldsmith, publications editor in the PR department at Volkswagen of America (of Troy, Michigan), had to go to battle three years ago with the office automation specialists of the corporate MIS unit when she was told she could not have the Macintoshes she requested for desktop publishing. Wanting to enforce corporate standards, the MIS specialists suggested that she use a DEC VAX minicomputer instead—hardly an appropriate platform for her ends.

Marlene Goldsmith won her argument. Three Macintosh systems, equipped for desktop publishing, were eventually installed. They almost entirely paid for themselves with first-year savings on the cost of producing two monthly newsletters for Volkswagen (*Weathervane*) and Audi dealers. Desktop publishing made it possible to upgrade *Weathervane* from black-and-white to color without an increase in cost (only the color is produced by a service bureau—the rest of the production is done on the firm's desktops).

Desktop publishing gave the company firmer control over its publications: changes can be made right up to press time (which is often necessary, since all stories are screened by five staffers, including those in the legal department). It also provided responsiveness: when a new car model is unveiled to the press at a desirable destination, Goldsmith takes along her Macs so that maps of road rallies and the statistics of the model's performance can be published at the last minute.

Some people had to make an adjustment. The associate editor of *Weathervane* now had to get involved in end-user computing as a typesetter; this did not come naturally.

Buoyed by the success of desktop publishing, Volkswagen is initiating corporate electronic publishing, such as in-house production of car manuals. The MIS department has recognized success: the Macintoshes will be connected to the organization's LAN.

Goldsmith says: "Perhaps the moral of this whole story is that you shouldn't rely on the MIS department to make decisions for you, or without you. . . . Work with them; even if you think you know what you want, they can enhance it with things you might not have known about."

Based on James A. Martin, "Driving Force." *Publish*, June 1990, pp. 61–63.

Advanced next is a complex technology that requires extensive training. This technology is as yet rather alien to MIS professionals, and an effort is required to integrate it into the informational environment of an organization, as the last vignette illustrated.

Presentation Software

The availability of high-quality presentation software has significantly raised the expectations of an organization for a professional presentation (see color plate 12). Desktop presentation packages emphasize full-color images, rather than the text that desktop publishing concentrates on. Desktop presentation software will help users to:

- create graphs automatically from a database or from a spreadsheet;
- produce their own graphics, edit scanned-in images, or edit images from a library of clip art;
- include text in a variety of typefaces and formats (for example, bulleted text).

TABLE 9.8	PRODUCT	VENDOR
A Selection of Presentation Software	Applause II	Borland International
	Draw Perfect	WordPerfect
	Freelance Plus	Lotus Development
	Harvard Graphics	Software Publishing
	Micrografx Graph Plus	Micrografx
	Pixie	Zenographics
	PowerPoint	Microsoft

TABLE 9.9	PRODUCT	VENDOR
A Selection of Multimedia Authoring Systems	Guide	OWL International
	IconAuthor	AimTech
	Instant Replay Professional	Nostradamus
	Quest	Allen Communication
	TIE	Global Information Systems Technology

Produced output may be included in paper-based reports, but the most frequent use of presentation software is in the production of transparencies or slides. Most presentation packages include arrangements with service bureaus to generate slides or photos from the produced files, which may be transferred to the service bureaus via a modem. Some products also have the capability to run a slide show from the desktop.

Popular presentation packages are listed in table 9.8.

Multimedia Authoring Systems

The extension of presentation software into the world of multimedia is becoming possible with multimedia authoring systems. Using these systems, one may develop attractive computer-based training (CBT) courseware, customer presentations, and other interactive business presentations (Raskin, 1990). This technology, or, rather, conglomerate of technologies, is intended to deliver what is often called infotainment: superior graphic imagery, computer animation, and motion video may be combined with high-fidelity sound as well as with good old text. This software helps its user to collect pieces of the presentation from a variety of equipment (voice recorders, scanners, videotape and videodisk players, and other sources) to produce a CD-ROM disk, which may serve as a master for duplication. Still in a state of relative infancy, multimedia packages include these shown in table 9.9.

Some of the packages listed in table 9.9 (such as Guide) support the hypermedia method of information delivery, in which multiple linkages may be established among various entities in a large multimedia document. These linkages enable the user to move from one topic directly to a related one, instead of scanning the information sequentially (see chapter 16 for further discussion and illustration of hypertext and hypermedia).

Hypermedia databases may include graphics, video, voice messages, or other units of information (say, a worksheet). Imagine how you could create a complete history of your management of a customer account, including product specifications, scanned-in photos of your contacts and handwritten notes from the customer, electronic-mail messages, and voice memos. A law-enforcement database might include witness sketches, fingerprints, voice recordings, and photos. Indeed, these systems blur the distinction between a database and a maintainable document. The technology was launched into personal computing with the Macintosh HyperCard. Some of the packages that specifically support the hypermedia concept are Hyperties form Cognetics and PLUS from Spinnaker Software.

A powerful interactive digital video technology is available for PCs in Intel's DVI Technology. Based on a specialized expansion board and relying on optical storage, this technology makes possible the authoring and presentation of interactive applications with various media, including full-motion video. An authoring package is available as well—Authology MultiMedia from CEIT Systems. A variety of training and educational applications have been developed with DVI technology in several industries.

Integrated Packages

Integrated packages offer two or more facilities provided by individual packages. For example, database management, spreadsheet functions, presentation graphics, and word processing are available in several integrated packages, which also offer a communications function for linking your personal computer through a modem to another computer system. Often, you can work in several windows on different aspects of your problem by using different functions of such a package.

There is a trade-off, however. The obvious advantages of multifunctional packages may be outweighed by such drawbacks as complexity, extensive requirements for computer resources, and weakness of certain functions (generally those that were added to the original function of the package).

Among the integrated packages are Framework from Borland International, Smartware II from Informix Software, and Symphony from Lotus Development.

9.4 FOURTH-GENERATION LANGUAGES AS TOOLS FOR END-USER DEVELOPMENT

Fourth-generation languages (4GLs) permit severalfold increases in productivity in information systems development. Some of these tools, such as query languages, actually make it possible to avoid developing applications: these languages enable end users to access databases directly. Others, such as report generators, simplify the arduous tasks of output presentation. The most powerful of the 4GL tools, application generators, permit substitution of a single, relatively simple instruction for the ten or more instructions necessary in a procedural language such as COBOL.

Not all 4GLs are end-user tools; many application generators, for example, require the expertise of MIS professionals.

The Role and the Categories of Fourth-Generation Languages

Much of business information processing consists of accessing data in databases, relatively routine data processing (such as sorting, classification, and summarization), and presenting information on a monitor screen or in a report. In response to the needs of this environment, fourth-generation languages (4GL) provide direct access to the database or make it possible to develop applications without specifying copious processing details. Since details vary only to a limited degree across a range of applications, they can be built into a system that supports a fourth-generation language.

In chapter 6, we introduced the 4GLs as tools for developing applications that do not require high processing efficiency or the complex logic specifications furnished by procedural languages such as COBOL. The distinguishing feature of 4GLs is that they specify *what is to be done* rather than *how to do it.* In other words, the languages are nonprocedural: the details of the task are filled in by the code available in the tool itself. The code developed in 4GL is terse as compared to procedural language code: generally, about one tenth of the number of instructions are required. An application may therefore be developed much more rapidly. The languages are easier to learn, and the resulting programs are easier to maintain than in procedural languages. All in all, high levels of productivity result from the appropriate use of a 4GL.

Some of the packages providing these languages are specifically designed for end users; others contain end-user facilities together with the procedural facilities to be used by professional developers.

4GLs are frequently used for prototyping; that is, for developing an initial working model of an application in order to establish the requirements of its users, with the final system then often developed in a procedural language (see chapter 18).

The principal categories of 4GLs are query languages, report generators, and application generators, many of which include screen generators (Martin, 1982, 1985–86). The 4GLs, in their essence, facilitate access to corporate databases (see figure 9.9): query languages and report generators make it unnecessary to develop certain applications by providing direct access to a database, while application generators make it relatively easy to specify in nonprocedural terms a system for such access. Therefore, many 4GLs are provided as a part of a DBMS package.

One may also include among 4GLs decision support and executive information systems generators, which we will discuss in chapter 14; some 4GLs are therefore also provided by spreadsheet packages, which support decision making.

Query Languages

Query languages are employed to retrieve data from databases. They are typically used on-line, and they support ad-hoc queries (that is, the queries are not predefined). Interaction is usually simple, only very simple computations are involved, and the result is generally not formatted (it is displayed in a default format). Database updating is also possible with many query languages.

FIGURE 9.9

Categories of fourth-
generation languages.

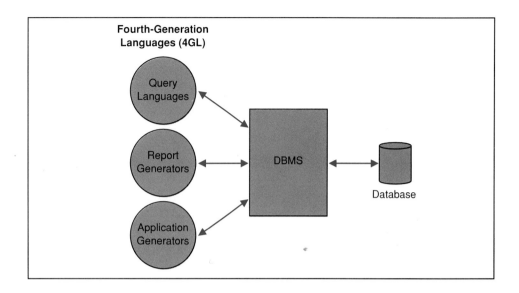

Ben Shneiderman, a noted specialist in the design of human-system interfaces, distinguishes five primary styles available for querying the system (Shneiderman, 1987). These styles include:

- form fill-in, in which the user enters the query by filling in fields on the display screen;
- menu selection, that is, choosing from a set of options displayed on the screen (a hierarchy of menus is often employed in graphical user interfaces);
- a command-type query language, such as SQL, which we discussed in chapter 8;
- direct manipulation by moving the cursor on the screen to manipulate the representation of an object or an action; and
- restricted natural language.

All of these languages, with the notable exception of SQL, a powerful and standardized query language, may be appropriate for direct access to data by end users (Vassiliou, 1984–85). SQL queries are frequently "hidden" from end users by more user-friendly interfaces.

Very simple query languages, based on a system prompting the user or on the user selecting an option from a limited menu, are appropriate for such applications as banks' automatic teller machines or electronic kiosks; but they do not have sufficient power (and may be quite annoying) for more advanced users in an organizational setting.

A query language that is available commercially as an interface to a number of systems is Query-by-Example (QBE), invented by Moshe Zloof (Zloof, 1977). This query style may be considered command-oriented, but most end users find it much simpler than SQL. Figure 9.10 shows the formulation of a reasonably complex query: "List all salespeople who sell sheets in District 3."

SALESPEOPLE	NAME	DISTRICT	SALESTARGET
	P.	<u>3</u>	

PRODUCTS	PRODUCTNAME	DISTRICT	SALESVOLUME
	SHEETS	<u>3</u>	

Assuming that we have a SALESPEOPLE table and a PRODUCTS table that lists our products in our database, the figure shows the names of the fields (attributes) displayed by the system. The user then gives the system an example of what he or she wants by underlining the "3" (district numbers have to match). The "P." specifies the field that is to be printed (or displayed): A form of QBE is the query language of such relational DBMSs for microcomputers as dBase IV and Paradox.

Direct manipulation query languages enable the user to manipulate the objects that represent what the user wants. Advanced prototypes of such systems are multimedia systems that allow the user to issue multimedia commands with voice, gesture, and even eye movement (research is being done on these systems at the Media Lab at MIT, for example).

Restricted natural languages may also be used to formulate a query such as:

REPORT SALES AND COMMISSIONS, BROKEN DOWN BY REGION, FOR
SALESPEOPLE IN CALIFORNIA, TEXAS, AND UTAH

These systems rely on a lexicon of words likely to be used in queries, including the terminology of the subject area. Some of these systems engage in dialog with the user to clarify an ambiguity; others restate the query and respond. The power of these systems is also somewhat limited: novices do not have the knowledge to state a query properly, while experienced users often prefer more concise and less ambiguous statements. These interfaces have been found superior to the command-type query languages in some studies (Napier, 1989), but not in others (Small, 1983). Natural language queries may be used in voice-input systems and are expected to become common in the future.

Many systems that support query languages contain graphics generators, which permit specification of a graphical output to a query.

Report Generators   A **report generator** enables an end user or an MIS professional to produce a report without detailing all the necessary steps. A report generator offers users greater control over the content and appearance of the output than a query language. Thus, specified data may be retrieved from specified files or databases, grouped, ordered, and summarized in a specified way, and formatted for printing as desired. The report title, headings, and other text may be included. A sample report, produced with fewer than twenty lines of nonprocedural code, is shown in figure 9.11. A program to produce this report in a procedural language would be far longer, and the detailed specification would be far more subject to error.

Report across Cities

NOVEMBER SALARY PAYMENTS

CITY		NEW YORK		LOS ANGELES	
PAY_DATE	DEPARTMENT	SOC_SEC	GROSS	SOC_SEC	GROSS
92/11/30	MIS	047-49-6523	$2,400.36	212-43-2319	$2,343.20
		113-50-3420	$2,101.30	350-88-6500	$2,450.00
		351-78-1183	$1,904.22	360-91-4301	$2,451.10
		376-11-3213	$2,001.00	400-19-6520	$3,000.21
		661-44-3210	$2,450.22	512-69-1234	$1,891.50
		961-31-5632	$2,600.00	.	.
		990-32-1290	$2,913.50	.	.
MIS DEPT. TOTAL			$16,360.60		$12,136.01
	MARKETING	042-41-6733	$1,341.94	061-21-4922	$1,530.20
		047-91-5420	$2,010.45	101-45-6720	$1,872.40
		050-79-1234	$2,179.60	212-55-3401	$2,781.00
		111-56-8721	$2,594.00	.	.
		661-32-5981	$2,439.10	.	.
		990-44-4982	$3,020.50	.	.
MARKETING DEPT. TOTAL			$13,585.59		$6,183.60
	SALES	002-34-1529	$2,789.00	150-31-5762	$2,451.10
		050-78-4987	$2,569.20	152-66-8271	$2,872.50
		350-10-3962	$2,884.50	251-10-6341	$3,001.50
		350-29-4500	$3,253.66	350-10-8727	$2,910.00
		410-30-6590	$2,520.10	410-20-7621	$2,391.50
		555-91-1001	$2,580.00	501-31-6290	$3,001.00
		.	.	678-33-5525	$3,909.44
		.	.	679-40-1101	$2,594.20
		.	.	990-30-1290	$3,103.10
		.	.	991-73-2690	$2,104.42
SALES DEPT. TOTAL			$16,596.46		$28,338.76
TOTALS BY CITY 92/11/30			$46,542.65		$46,658.37
			---------		---------
TOTAL PAY DATE 92/11/30			$93,201.02		

Total by Department — MARKETING DEPT. TOTAL

Embedded Parameters

Total across Cities

FIGURE 9.11

A report produced with the use of a report generator.

(Information Builders, Inc.)

If more complex processing is needed, many report generators permit the inclusion of a procedural code (say, in COBOL); this is generally done by an MIS professional. Indeed, some report generators (including the RPG III report-generation language) are designed to be used by these professionals.

Application Generators

An **application generator** makes it possible to specify an entire application, consisting of several programs, at a high level of abstraction. Based on this specification, most generators produce code in a procedural language, which may then be modified (or supplemented by additional routines) to meet the precise needs of the application.

Generators targeted toward end users produce a code mostly from a specification of the structure of files and databases and from the given layouts of screens and reports. The requisite processing is specified in terms natural to the end users.

Screen-oriented user interfaces are particularly important in systems developed by end users. A screen-painting facility makes it possible to specify the layout of display screens to be employed for user-system interaction, including the location of data entry fields, output fields, labels, and color or highlighting.

There are special systems available for building attractive user interfaces. For example, EASEL (by Interactive Images) is a development environment for rapid building of graphical user interfaces. It runs on microcomputers and permits the creation of colorful, windowed interfaces for executive information systems, shop floors, or information kiosks.

Application generators for use by MIS professionals most frequently run on mainframes and minicomputers. Some of the tools may be considered very high-level languages which permit a very concise procedural specification of the task. End-user 4GLs are generally targeted to a limited application domain, while those for MIS professionals are general-purpose tools. Application generators are increasingly integrated into computer-aided software engineering (CASE) environments, as we shall discuss in chapter 19.

Summary of Fourth-Generation Languages

I included a discussion of 4GLs in the chapter on end-user computing because I feel that this computing domain will be increasingly affected by the growing power of these tools. A good illustration of this power is furnished by a comparison of a procedural (COBOL) code with an equivalent 4GL code, shown in figure 9.12.

However, the demands that 4GL tools, and particularly applications generators, impose on the skills of the people who use them differ significantly. If end-user development is desired, both ease of use and the power of the tool to accomplish the task should be carefully evaluated. Table 9.10 lists some popular 4GL tools. Of these, application generators such as IDEAL, MANTIS, and Natural should be considered tools for MIS professionals rather than for end users. The Heatilator vignette provides just one example how the use of 4GLs can lead to economies and rapid applications development.

FIGURE 9.12

A comparison of codes in a procedural language and in 4GL to accomplish the same task.

COBOL PROGRAM TO LIST EMPLOYEES OF DEPARTMENT B BY NAME

```
IDENTIFICATION DIVISION.
PROGRAM-ID.
        EMPLOYEE-LIST.
AUTHOR.
      TOM SMITH.
ENVIRONMENT DIVISION.
CONFIGURATION SECTION.
SOURCE-COMPUTER.
      VAX-750.
OBJECT-COMPUTER.
      VAX-750.
INPUT-OUTPUT SECTION.
FILE-CONTROL.
        SELECT EMPLOYEE-FILE ASSIGN TO ''EMPLOYEE.INP''.
        SELECT PRT-FILE          ASSIGN TO ''EMPLOYEE.DAT''.
DATA DIVISION.
FILE SECTION.
FD EMPLOYEE-FILE
        RECORD CONTAINS 50 CHARACTERS
        LABEL RECORDS ARE STANDARD
        DATA RECORD IS EMP-REC.
01      EMP-REC.
        02      DEPT-CODE           PIC     X.
        02      EMP-NAME            PIC     X(20).
        02      EMP-ADDRESS         PIC     X(20).
        02      FILLER              PIC     X(9).
FD      PRT-FILE.
        RECORD CONTAINS 132 CHARACTERS
        LABEL RECORDS ARE OMITTED
        DATA RECORD IS PRT-REC.
01      PRT-REC.
        02      FILLER              PIC     X(20).
        02      PRT-EMP-NAME        PIC     X(20).
        02      FILLER              PIC     X(20).
        02      PRT-EMP-ADDRESS     PIC     X(20).
        02      FILLER              PIC     X(52).
WORKING-STORAGE SECTION.
01          NO-MORE-DATA            PIC     X(1) VALUE 'N'.
PROCEDURE DIVISION.
        OPEN INPUT EMPLOYEE-FILE
            OUTPUT PRT-FILE.
        PERFORM READ-EMPLOYEE.
        PERFORM PROCESS-EMPLOYEE UNTIL NO-MORE-DATA = 'Y'.
        CLOSE    EMPLOYEE-FILE PRT-FILE.
        STOP RUN.
READ-EMPLOYEE.
        READ EMPLOYEE-FILE AT END MOVE 'Y' TO NO-MORE-DATA.
PROCESS-EMPLOYEE.
        IF DEPT-CODE = 'B'
            MOVE EMP-NAME       TO PRT-EMP-NAME
            MOVE EMP-ADDRESS TO PRT-EMP-ADDRESS
            WRITE PRT-REC.
        PERFORM READ-EMPLOYEE.
```

4GL PROGRAM TO ACCOMPLISH THE SAME TASK:

```
        DATABASE EMPLOYEES
        LIST
            BY EMPLOYEE__NAME EMPLOYEE__ADDRESS
            IF DEPARTMENT__CODE = 'B'
```

SOFTWARE PACKAGE USE PLUS 4GLS YIELD HIGH PRODUCTIVITY

Heatilator is a manufacturing firm primarily engaged in making office furniture. The MIS manager of the firm, David Mayes, reduced his staff by 80 percent while increasing user satisfaction by introducing a 4GL environment built around a relational database. He also replaced custom-made software with a package purchased from a specialized software vendor.

When Mayes took over the operation, three applications programmers in what was then a COBOL shop were spending 60 to 70 percent of their time maintaining existing applications. The MIS manager found himself under pressure both to cut costs *and* to increase the responsiveness of his department to users' requests for management-level information.

Mayes purchased a Prime minicomputer, on which he installed a manufacturing resource planning (MRP) package. He also purchased a relational DBMS and INFORM, a query and report-generation package—both from Prime. The entire environment was built around a data dictionary, which simplifies control of data.

A user-manager was placed in charge of the analysis for the conversion process. A team of users simulated their business activities with the MRP package: they simulated entering orders, obtaining credit approval, manufacturing the orders, and shipping them. The users learned how to use the package—but they also learned how their business operates. The MRP package became to a large degree the "property" of the end users, supported by only two analysts/programmers.

Heatilator reports no applications development backlog at this time. Users develop 95 percent of their applications in INFORM. It is now possible to generate a complicated report in one hour, according to Mayes. When an application is developed by MIS professionals, they use INFOBASIC, a very high-level language that is an extension of BASIC. The code length in this language is about one-fifth of that in COBOL—which is no longer used at the shop. Maintenance drudgery has been reduced to the point where Mayes speaks of its virtual elimination.

Based on (Green, 1984–85).

TABLE 9.10	CATEGORY	PRODUCT	VENDOR
Popular 4GL Tools			
	Query languages	SQL	IBM and many others
		Query-by-Example	IBM and others
		INTELLECT	AICorp (licensed to many others)
	Report generators	Easytrieve Plus	Pansophic Systems
		Datatrieve	Digital Equipment Corporation
		Mark V	Answer Systems
	Application generators	FOCUS	Information Builders
		IDEAL	Applied Data Research
		MANTIS	Cincom Systems
		MAPPER	Unisys
		Natural	Software AG
		NOMAD2	MUST Software International
		Ramis II	On-Line Software
	Generators of decision support and executive information systems		See chapter 14

9.5 LIMITATIONS AND RISKS OF END-USER DEVELOPMENT

End-user applications development has definite benefits, as we discussed at the beginning of this chapter. However, this form of applications development coexists with, rather than replaces, systems development by MIS professionals. Applications that best lend themselves to end-user development have the characteristics listed in table 9.11. Obviously, many of these traits are interrelated; equally obviously, systems development by MIS professionals should be considered if an application does not possess one or more of the listed features. A broad model that identifies the factors leading to effective end-user development was proposed by Donald Amoroso and Paul Cheney (Amoroso, 1991).

As end-user systems development proliferates, end-user capabilities increase, more powerful tools for end-user development are being created, and more applications may fall into the category of end-user development.

However, distinct risks have been associated with end-user development, and it is vital to develop methods for managing these risks (Davis, 1982; Alavi, 1985–86). We can counteract these risks to a large extent by recognizing them and putting appropriate controls in place. The following organizational risks should thus be considered:

1. Ineffective Use of Financial Resources

Personal computers and limited-size user-developed systems tend to "creep up" on the organization. At the same time, we know that total spending on end-user computing in many firms surpasses one half of their MIS budgets. While many firms may choose to encourage the proliferation of end-user computing through rather loose financial controls at early stages, ultimately, cost-benefit justification of end-user development projects is necessary.

TABLE 9.11

Characteristics of Applications That Are Most Suitable for End-User Development

1. Application is of limited size and complexity with respect to computer technologies (as opposed to the demands it may make on the functional expertise of end users).

2. A fourth-generation language may be used to develop the application.

3. Expertise of end users is important to understand the application.

4. The requirements specification may be developed rapidly, generally by prototyping: developing and refining an initial version of the system (see chapter 18).

5. The application will be for personal use, or for the use of a limited group, as opposed to organization-wide use. There are no extensive documentation demands.

6. No high security, privacy, or data integrity demands are present.

7. The application has a management support rather than transaction-processing orientation.

---

2. Inappropriate Selection of Hardware and Software

Organizational benefit is achieved through the appropriate selection of compatible personal productivity software and 4GLs. It is usually counterproductive, for example, if three different microcomputer DBMSs are used in various units of a firm. The move toward a networking environment places further demands on the interoperability of hardware and software. Personal computing should be an integrating rather than divisive medium; we shall see in chapter 16 that groupware, along with other productivity software, can integrate effectively. Furthermore, quantity discounts should be sought in volume purchasing.

Enterprise-wide standards should be established for hardware and software acquisition and deployment. When it is necessary to depart from a standard (as was the case at Volkswagen of America in the earlier vignette), appropriate reasons should be provided.

3. Threats to Data Integrity, Security, and Privacy

Policies for providing end-user access to corporate databases, downloading snapshots (extracts) from these databases to end-user workstations, and uploading data from end-user workstations (which is generally undesirable) must be established. Inconsistent policies for data extraction from organizational databases and for refreshing these extracts may lead to various groups of end users obtaining conflicting information based on these data (Inmon, 1986). End users who use corporate data for their management-oriented systems should be made aware of changes in the central data. Rigid backup procedures should be instituted.

4. Errors in Systems Analysis

End users, unaided by systems analysts, can make errors of several kinds, including:

- solving the wrong problem;
- applying an inappropriate analytical method to the right problem;
- overanalysis in a time-consuming search for perfection; and
- applying the wrong software tool.

Training and consulting by information center analysts (which we will soon describe) are the primary methods of preventing these risks.

5. Lack of Quality Assurance in Systems Development and Operation

Many user-developed systems are poorly constructed, insufficiently tested, do not provide for data validation and audit trails, and are accompanied by virtually no documentation.

Operational systems arouse concerns about access to data and about the quality of that data, as we just described. Also, user ability to modify systems at will may lead to an unstable informational environment.

Many of the methods and controls applicable to professionally developed systems (which we will discuss in Part 5 of this text) have to be adapted for end-user developed systems.

6. Proliferation of Private Systems

Private systems, which can conceal information from others instead of contributing to the overall information environment of an organization, may be outright harmful. They may contain suspect data and lead to contentious discussions about whose information is right. Information resource management objectives are hampered by the presence of uncatalogued and perhaps redundant data.

7. Undesirable Information-Related Behavior

There are a variety of behaviors in the end-user development environment which may be counterproductive to an organization's goals. Users may develop systems to keep information "just in case," or for its symbolic value, related to prestige or to gaining a reputation as a rational manager; they may even collect information to put their their own spins on issues (sometimes to the extent of verging on misrepresentation). This work may also detract users from their primary tasks. As one member of senior management said in regard to the money managers in an investment firm: "We pay these people a great deal of money to make good investment decisions, not to write programs in Lotus."[1]

Many of these exposures are caused by the absence of checks and balances associated with traditional, professional systems development. Obviously, some of those checks and balances are needed here as well. As we know full well, the risks just listed do not discourage organizations from seeking increased productivity, higher managerial effectiveness, and competitive advantage in end-user computing. However, if a firm fails to create an environment in which end-user computing can succeed, the firm may shackle further development of end-user computing—to its own detriment (Cheney, 1986). Let us consider how end-user computing can be managed so as to develop its full potential.

9.6 MANAGEMENT OF END-USER COMPUTING

The management and support of end-user computing consistently rate among the top issues of concern to information systems managers. The growth of this phenomenon is still very rapid. The dividing lines between what can best be controlled and developed by MIS professionals and what is best left to end users are still evolving and are not at all clear. Since control of vital resources is involved, the evolution of end-user computing in an organization has clear political ramifications as well.

Some approaches to the management of end-user computing foster its expansion, while others seek further control over it (Munro, 1987– 88). Six major approaches have been identified (Alavi, 1987–88). Let us first consider these strategies, and then later see how they may be employed to promote end-user computing in the way that best brings out a firm's capabilities. We shall see that as end-user computing matures in a given organization, different approaches to its management become appropriate.

The following end-user management approaches have been distinguished:

1. **Laissez-faire Strategy**

    This "let-them-do-what-they-want" approach allows end users to acquire and use whatever computing resources they desire within existing budgetary constraints. There are no central control mechanisms or guidelines, and there is no support. Users are free to experiment and learn. While it is obvious that some end users will feel encouraged by this freedom, chaos may result. Organizational exposure to the risks of end-user computing is very high. This "hands-off" posture, if initially adopted, should be replaced by a more proactive management approach.

2. **Monopolist Strategy**

    The opposite of the laissez-faire approach, this strategy attempts to consolidate all control over computing resources in a monopoly—usually in the hands of the MIS function. We can see that this strategy essentially denies one of the principal advantages of end-user computing—decentralized control. In the modern computing environment, with savvy users and end-user oriented tools, this strategy is as unstable as the laissez-faire strategy. (This was stressed by Thomas Gerrity and John Rockart [Gerrity, 1986], who first identified the two strategies.)

3. **Acceleration Strategy**

    Even more directly opposite the monopolist strategy is an approach that actively supports expansion of end-user computing. The most frequently used form of support is the information center, which we will discuss in the following section. Users are offered the benefits of training and technical support. However, in this case, information centers simply react to the needs of end users as they express them; firms that adopt this strategy provide no mechanism for shaping the direction of end-user computing activities. For this strategy to succeed, extensive investment in end-user computing and support is necessary.

4. **Marketing Strategy**

    This is a strategy aimed at the directed growth of end-user computing. End users are encouraged to use certain tools and services through free-market mechanisms, such as training, support, or lower cost achieved through volume purchases. This strategy is best fostered by a central support group for end-user computing, which in turn supports departmental groups—essentially, information centers. The policies and guidelines developed by the central support group shape the end-user computing activities, but the end users retain their choice prerogative.

5. **Containment Strategy**

    This is a transition strategy aimed at introducing the organizational checks and balances to ensure that investments in end-user computing pay off. The primary objective is to put in place budgetary and data administration controls. It is vital to avoid squelching fruitful end-user initiatives by overcontrol.

6. Operations Strategy

This strategy focuses on the ongoing management of resources, with the main objective being efficient use. Explicit procedures, technological standards, cost-benefit analyses, and formal planning processes are the hallmarks of operations strategy. Integration of hardware and software is another principal objective. An effective organizational support structure may resemble that established in the marketing approach.

The principal characteristics of these six approaches to managing end-user computing are summarized in table 9.12.

Considering these principal features, Maryam Alavi and her colleagues suggest that the organization adopt consecutive phases in deploying end-user computing strategies, as shown in figure 9.13. In emerging from a period when no coherent strategy is being followed, an organization enters a primary, unstable strategy (laissez-faire or monopolist). It then encourages and supports wide end-user experimentation and gradually gains organizational control over end-user computing, resulting in an integrated and supported operation. In chapter 12, we shall see that the four phases of assimilating end-user computing into an organization correspond to the phases of the general process of technology assimilation.

Many organizations find it difficult to leave the prestrategy phase of figure 9.13, let alone undertake a full-fledged, planned assimilation of this mode of computing. To quote an MIS director: "I don't know whether I should take the lead with a strong personal computing strategy, follow the users' personal computer purchases with enough support to keep them out of trouble, or just get out of their way and simply monitor what's going on."[2]

TABLE 9.12

Principal Strategies for Managing End-User Computing

STRATEGY	PRINCIPAL FEATURE
Laissez-faire	Uncontrolled and unsupported growth of end-user computing.
Monopolist	Firm control over end-user computing by the MIS unit.
Acceleration	Undirected expansion of end-user computing, supported by information centers.
Marketing	Guidance of end-user computing through free-market incentives, together with technical support.
Containment	Introduction of budgetary and data administration controls to obtain payoff from investments.
Operations	Uniform procedures, standards, and planning tools directed at an efficient, integrated operation. These mechanisms are introduced during a containment period.

FIGURE 9.13

Recommended phases in managing end-user computing.

(Adapted from Alavi, 1987–88)

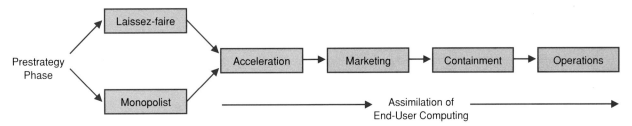

9.7 INFORMATION CENTERS

As we have just discussed, end-computing requires support to contribute to organizational goals. This support is lent most commonly by an **information center,** an organizational unit that provides end-user support services (Wetherbe, 1985). The information center concept was formalized by IBM Canada in 1974 and has since been adapted to the needs of various organizations. It evolved as microcomputers appeared and as end-user computing has matured (Carr, 1987). Indeed, as end-user computing matures in a firm, the task of the information center evolves from training novices and assisting them with acquiring microcomputers and software to assisting sophisticated users with developing, controlling, and integrating their systems.

In general, the information center's role is to train and assist end users in acquiring (perhaps developing), using, and controlling their computer resources. Thus, the information center is a concept: that of supporting end-user computing; it is also a functional unit, generally a part of the corporate MIS function. But the information center is also a physical place, where end-user computing facilities and consultants are available and where training courses are offered. Information center specialists are generally systems analysts, with extensive knowledge of the personal computing environment and with outstanding communications skills. Some of these professionals specialize in certain product categories, in functional areas (for example, in marketing), or in training.

Several functions are performed by information centers. Specifically, information centers:

1. Assist end users in evaluating, selecting, installing, and maintaining microcomputer hardware and software packages.

2. Lend assistance to end users in accessing the data resource. Typical examples include the development of procedures for downloading snapshots of databases: read-only copies of selected portions of the database, which are used, for example, in decision support applications. (As we already noted, uploading of data from end-user workstations to corporate databases is generally prohibited, unless subject to rigid limitations and standards.)

3. Lend assistance to end-user systems development. The charters of information centers differ widely on this point. "No development, assistance only" is a common policy. Many centers will assist end users in developing a working prototype (initial version) of an application with the use of a 4GL. However, some centers do develop complete applications with end-user oriented facilities.

4. Support installed applications and applications maintenance.

5. Act as an information clearinghouse on end-user development methods and tools.

A VICTIM OF ITS OWN SUCCESS

"At the Quaker Oats Company, we recently celebrated our information center's third anniversary in an unusual way. We began tearing it down," says Ronald Brzezinski, corporate vice-president of information systems at the firm.

The center's success in supporting its 2,000 users (or clients, as they were called) surpassed all expectations. The center's charter was to act as an MIS unit dedicated to providing technical support and services to the company's staff as they acquired and began using personal computers. In three years, over 1,200 PCs and over 3,000 software packages were installed on the staff's desktops. Personal productivity software was standardized. Many "power users" were developed, and other were trained to be proficient. Several hundred computerized business solutions, many of them networked, were developed by the clients and are thus now supported and "owned" by them.

As the clients matured into skilled end users, the information center entered the operations phase, assisting with applications maintenance and control through administrative procedures. The information center had now started to duplicate the procedures of the MIS department. Clients were also overwhelming the center with requests for maintenance-oriented services which the clients were now able to handle themselves.

A phase-out plan for the information center was established. Some of the information center analysts were transferred to the firm's business subunits, assisting them in assimilating new technologies (such as handheld computers for sales representatives). Others temporarily remained in the center, as its purposes shifted to the support of corporate information resource management, before it finally closed.

Based on Ronald Brzezinski, "When It's Time to Tear Down the Info Center." *Datamation*, November 1, 1987, pp. 73–82.

6. Provide hotline or help-desk assistance to users. As corporations downsize their information centers, help-desk software is increasingly used to assist the remaining specialists. This software assists in logging and tracking requests for help and managing hardware and software dispersed throughout the firm and in some cases offers simple expert systems for troubleshooting (Kador, 1991). A leading example of help-desk software is SupportMagic of Magic Solutions (Mahwah, New Jersey).

7. Assist in controlling end-user computing, and thus help set standards, support internal auditors in auditing the end-user computing environment, perform quality assurance, and certify end-user developed applications.

8. Train end users. Last but not least, information centers train end users in information technologies as part of the extensive training offered by today's corporations to their employees. Training ranges from narrowly targeted, brief sessions (for example, how to use Lotus 1–2–3 to develop quarterly budgets) to educational programs (for instance, in information resource management).

Studies of end-user training emphasize the importance of teaching users how to solve problems within their own domains with the use of end-user oriented technologies, rather than simply teaching them how to use the tools. It is also important to create a supportive social setting for user learning, in which users communicate with one another and with the information-center specialists, as well as learn from the "power users" in their own areas (Sein, 1987). One investigation showed a 24 percent increase in end-user productivity as a result of a training program based on these principles (Cronan, 1990).

As we can see, the general forms of assistance information centers give to end users involve training, consulting, participation in end-user development, and performing some of the development and maintenance functions in the end-user area.

As users become proficient with information systems and as organizations learn how to control end-user computing, information centers may become superfluous. The Quaker Oats vignette provided an example.

Some argue that to maintain its relevance as an organizational unit, an information center should broaden its traditional orientation as facilitator and become project oriented, carving out a meaningful niche in developing and maintaining end-user oriented applications (Christoff, 1990). Such an approach also helps develop career paths for information center employees.

· ·

SUMMARY

End users today develop, use, and control many of their own information systems. The phenomenon of end-user computing is fueled by technological and organizational factors, as well as by the growing MIS proficiency of people in organizations. Multiple benefits are garnered by firms that are able to properly channel the creativity of users, who are generally best qualified to judge their own computational needs.

Personal computers have become a ubiquitous user's workstation. Simplified user-system interfaces and links with larger machines, which offer extended computational capabilities, further empower end users.

Several categories of personal productivity software have evolved. They facilitate data management and analysis, authoring and presentation, and activity and notes tracking—directly by end users themselves. Fourth-generation languages (4GLs) have enabled users to access organizational databases without the need for programming and have provided powerful tools simple enough to use in developing their own applications. Query languages, report generators, and application generators are the principal categories of 4GLs.

End-user systems development cannot replace professional development by MIS specialists for many types of organizational applications. Various risks associated with end-user systems development must be recognized and counteracted.

Many companies now commit extensive organizational resources to end-user computing. It is obvious, therefore, that end-user computing must be managed. Several management strategies are available; a sequence of these strategies, leading to assimilation of this mode of computing into a firm, has been suggested. The functions of the information center—a vehicle for organizational support of end users—are also important to end-user computing. Although information centers may become superfluous as end users become more proficient, some argue that information centers should broaden their profile to become more project-oriented in actively helping users develop and maintain applications.

ENDNOTES

1. Pyburn, 1985–6, p. 50.
2. Pyburn, 1985–6, p. 51.

KEY TERMS AND CONCEPTS

End-user computing
End-user development
User interface
Graphical user interface (GUI)
Micro-to-host links
Terminal emulation
Personal productivity software
Spreadsheet software
Personal information management
Desktop publishing

Presentation software
Multimedia authoring systems
Integrated packages
Fourth-generation languages
Query languages
Report generators
Application generators
Downloading and uploading of data
Database snapshots (extracts)
Information center

QUESTIONS

1. Define end-user computing.

2. What are the benefits of direct *use* of information systems by end users?

3. What are the benefits of letting end users develop their own systems?

4. What are the advantages of having end users control their own systems?

5. Name and define the categories of end users (as opposed to people who may use end-user oriented tools).

6. What advantages may one expect from a graphical user interface?

7. What are the three types of links between a microcomputer and a host machine?

8. Specify the principal functions of personal productivity software and the categories of packages that perform these broad functions. Define in a sentence what each of these categories does.

9. What are the comparative strengths of spreadsheet and database management software?

10. How do packages for personal information management compare with database management packages? Give scenarios in which each would be used.

11. Give three specific examples of the use of desktop publishing in an organizational setting.

12. What are the three categories of 4GLs, and how does each of them contribute to end-user computing?

13. What type of an application is *unsuitable* for end-user computing? What characteristics make it unsuitable? Specify as many characteristics as you can and be specific!

14. What risks of end-user computing are related to end-user *control* of their own systems, and how are they related?

15. What strategies for managing end-user computing would you select if you desired to *expand* this practice? What are the principal differences between the strategies you selected?

16. Which strategies for managing end-user computing did the MIS director quoted at the end of section 9.6 consider?

17. What role do information centers play in helping end users *develop* their systems? Be specific!

ISSUES FOR DISCUSSION

1. Discuss this proposition: "End-user computing, including the use of packages, will ultimately obviate the need for having MIS units in organizations."

2. Select a category of personal productivity software, and study the capabilities of representative systems (using trade literature, vendors' brochures and manuals, and other sources). Discuss the capabilities, the hardware requirements, and the costs of the low-end and high-end systems in this category.

3. Suppose that you have been asked to evaluate the effectiveness and the potential for a continuing role of the information center in your organization, with a view toward possibly phasing it out. You are supposed to discuss the continuation as well as the termination option. You may assume that you find that end-user computing in your firm is mature and that your firm is at present following the Operations strategy.

OPTIONAL EXERCISE: SPREADSHEETS

Produce a worksheet of financial performance for your company, Diverse Interests, Inc., for the next five years.

Assume that your sales will start at $100,000 annually and grow 20 percent a year. Your expenses include both production and nonproduction costs. Production costs consist of the cost of materials (starting at $30,000 a year), the cost of labor (starting at $15,000), and your overhead runs 40 percent of these two costs. Labor and material costs grow 15 percent a year. The nonproduction costs (R&D, engineering, marketing, and administration) make up 30 percent of sales. Your profit is your sales minus your expenses.

Your firm also has to pay 40 percent tax on its profits. You need to compute the profit after taxes for each of the five years and the profit-to-sales ratio based on this net profit.

Print a spreadsheet with the appropriate headings. The items in the spreadsheet should be sales, production expenses (individual items and the subtotal), nonproduction expenses, total expenses, profit, taxes, profit after taxes, and profit/sales ratio for each of the five years.

Produce a bar graph of your profit/sales ratio.

What if the tax goes up 10 percent in the second year of operation? Produce the corresponding worksheet.

END USERS AND MIS PROFESSIONALS USE A FOURTH-GENERATION TOOL

Several years ago, the MIS department at The Bank of New England found itself unable to satisfy end-user requests for single-use reports. The department was too busy developing large mainframe-based transaction processing systems. At that point, the MIS department realized that end users would have to do some of their own computing.

To select an end-user development system, the bank turned to several firms offering 4GLs with a request to develop a sample application. After an evaluation of the results, the bank selected FOCUS, an end-user-oriented 4GL offering query, report-generation, and application-generation facilities. The system works in all types of environments: on mainframes, on minis, and on microcomputers, as well as on local area networks.

The FOCUS system was acquired for a three-month trial and turned over to one of the user departments for exploratory use. The end users, supported by MIS specialists, quickly started producing their own reports. The applications development cycle was becoming

shorter as experience was accumulated. "Months have turned into weeks, and weeks into days," said Ben Sloboda, vice-president for information systems. Many people actually became attracted to using personal computers as they learned to use PC/FOCUS.

Thus, FOCUS's career at the bank started as that of a tool for developing management reporting applications for end users. Then the bank installed an information center. The center's charter was to provide users with tools, education, and access to data, but it was not supposed to actually develop applications for them. Over the years, the information center has softened its stance in that regard. In the case of more complex applications, end users and the center's staff work jointly, with a FOCUS expert on the center's staff providing *well-defined* development assistance. However, the users are expected to be the owners of the developed systems.

Having gained experience, the MIS professionals at the bank started to use PC/FOCUS for system development as well. Even when an application is expected to reside on an IBM 3090 mainframe, the MIS department encourages development on a microcomputer both to reduce the load on the mainframe, where production jobs are run, and to provide system developers with better system response times. Applications to be used by one or two people are frequently developed by end users and remain on a PC. When several people in a department need to use an application and have to share data and other resources, the application is placed on a multiuser system, such as a local area network or a minicomputer.

Reporting from large mainframe databases is performed on PCs whenever possible by extracting data from these databases. In fact, 95 percent of the data processed by FOCUS to produce management information is extracted from the production files and databases.

Thus, FOCUS users at The Bank of New England represent all levels of proficiency: they range form MIS professionals to managers to clerks. As Danielle Barr, vice-president of corporate planning saw it: "The advantage of using FOCUS is that it gives the users a system they can tweak and customize as needed." End users thus have a sense of control over their informational environment.

Based on *Profiles in PC/Focus*. New York: Information Builders, Inc., 1988, pp. 2–4.

Case Study Questions

1. What needs brought end-user computing to The Bank of New England? Who initiated the move? Do you think this is a typical way end-user computing is initiated in a firm? Why or why not?

2. Relate the stages of end-user computing in this firm to the phase model described in the chapter and shown in figure 9.13. What phases are actually discernible in this case?

3. How did the role of the information center evolve at this company?

4. What are the advantages of a 4GL tool that can be used in a variety of environments—from a microcomputer to a mainframe?

SELECTED REFERENCES

Alavi, Maryam; Nelson, R. Ryan; and Weiss, Ira R. "Strategies for End-User Computing: An Integrative Framework." *Journal of Management Information Systems,* 4, 3, Winter 1987–1988, pp. 28–49.

Alloway, Robert M., and Quillard, Judith A. "User Managers' Systems Needs." *MIS Quarterly,* 7, 2, June 1983, pp. 27–41.

Amoroso, Donald L., and Cheney, Paul H. "Testing a Causal Model of End-User Application Effectiveness." *Journal of Management Information Systems,* 8, 1, Summer 1991, pp. 63–89.

Benjamin, Robert I. "Information Technology in the 1990s: A Long-Range Planning Scenario." *MIS Quarterly*, 6, 2, June 1982, pp. 11– 31.

Carr, Houston H. "Information Centers: The IBM Model vs. Practice." *MIS Quarterly*, 11, 3, September 1987, pp. 325–38.

Cheney, Paul H.; Mann, Robert I.; and Amoroso, Donald L. "Organizational Factors Affecting the Success of End-User Computing." *Journal of Management Information Systems*, 3, 1, Summer 1986, pp. 65–80.

Christoff, Kurt A. *Managing the Information Center*. Glenview, Ill.: Scott, Foresman/Little Brown, 1990.

Cotterman, William W., and Kumar, Kuldeep. "User Cube: A Taxonomy of End Users." *Communications of the ACM*, 32, 11, November 1989, pp. 1313–20.

Cronan, Timothy P., and Douglas, David E. "End-User Training and Computing Effectiveness in Public Agencies: An Empirical Study." *Journal of Management Information Systems*, 6, 4, Spring 1990, pp. 21–39.

Davis, Gordon B. "Caution: User-Developed Systems Can Be Dangerous to Your Organization." MISRC-WP-82–04, MIS Research Center, University of Minnesota, 1982. Also in *End-User Computing: Concepts, Issues, and Applications*, edited by R. Ryan Nelson. New York: John Wiley, 1989, pp. 209–28.

Dearden, John. "The Withering Away of the IS Organization." *Sloan Management Review*, 28, 4, Summer 1987, pp. 87–91.

Emery, James C. *Management Information Systems: The Critical Strategic Resource*. New York: Oxford University Press, 1987.

Gerrity, Thomas P., and Rockart John F. "End-User Computing: Are You a Leader or a Laggard?" *Sloan Management Review*, 27, 4, Summer 1986, pp. 25–34.

Green, Jesse. "Productivity in the Fourth Generation: Six Case Studies." *Journal of Management Information Systems*, 1, 3, Winter 1984–85, pp. 49–63.

Guimaraes, T., and Gupta, A. "Personal Computing and Support Services." *OMEGA*, 15, 6, 1987, pp. 467–75.

Inmon, William H. *Managing End-User Computing in Information Organizations*. Homewood, Ill.: Dow Jones-Irwin, 1986.

Kador, John. "Help Desks Take the Initiative." *Information Center Quarterly*, Summer 1991, pp. 29–34.

Kaplan, S. Jerrold; Kapor, Mitchell D.; and others. "Agenda: A Personal Information Manager." *Communications of the ACM*, 33, 17, July 1990, pp. 105–16.

McLean, Ephraim R. "End Users as Application Developers." *MIS Quarterly,* 3, 4, December 1979, pp. 37–46.

Martin, James. *Applications Development without Programmers.* Englewood Cliffs, N.J.: Prentice-Hall, 1982.

Martin, James. *Fourth-Generation Languages,* Vols. I-III. Englewood Cliffs, N.J.: Prentice-Hall, 1985–86.

Miller, Michael J. "Go's Per Point OS Lends Itself to a Variety of Applications, Especially Focus-Based Ones." *InfoWorld,* February 11, 1991, p. 76.

Munro, Malcolm C.; Huff, Sid L.; and Moore, Gary. "Expansion and Control of End-User Computing." *Journal of Management Information Systems,* 4, 3, Winter 1987–88, pp. 5–27.

Napier, H. Albert, and others. "Impact of a Restricted Natural Language Interface on Ease of Learning and Productivity." *Communications of the ACM,* 32, 10, October 1989, pp. 1190–98.

Panko, Raymond. *End-User Computing: Management, Applications, and Technology.* New York: John Wiley, 1988.

Pyburn, Philip J. "Managing Personal Computer Use: The Role of Corporate Management Information Systems." *Journal of Management Information Systems,* 3, 3, Winter 1986–87, pp. 49–70.

Raskin, Robin. "Multimedia: The Next Frontier for Business." *PC Magazine,* July 1990, pp. 151–92.

Rockart, John F., and Flannery, Lauren S. "The Management of End-User Computing." *Communications of the ACM,* 26, 10, October 1983, pp. 776–784.

Sein, Maung K.; Bostrom, Robert P.; and Olfman, Lorne. "Training End Users to Compute: Cognitive, Motivational, and Social Issues." *INFOR,* 25, 3, August 1987, pp. 236–55.

Shneiderman, Ben. *Designing End-User Interface: Strategies for Effective Human-Computer Interaction,* Reading, Mass.: Addison-Wesley, 1987.

Small, Duane W., and Weldon, Linda J. "An Experimental Comparison of Natural and Structured Query Languages." *Human Factors* 25, 2, March 1983, pp. 253–63.

Vassiliou, Yannis. "On the Interactive Use of Databases: Query Languages." *Journal of Management Information Systems,* 1, 3, Winter 1984–85, pp.33–48.

Wetherbe, James C., and Leitheiser, Robert L. "Information Centers: A Survey of Services, Decisions, Problems, and Successes." *Journal of Information Systems Management,* 2, 3, Summer 1985, pp. 3–10.

Zloof, Moshe M. "Query By Example: A Data Base Language." *IBM Systems Journal,* 16, 4, 1977, pp. 324–43.

EXPLOITING INFORMATION TECHNOLOGY IN A GLOBAL CORPORATION

When one looks for a global corporation, a firm that is a world-class competitor in many product markets and many nations, the name of E. I. Du Pont de Nemours & Co. of Wilmington, Delaware, comes to mind easily enough. A leader in the U.S. markets for many chemicals and related products, the company derives 40 percent of its revenues from outside the United States. And, perhaps unsurprisingly, this is also an organization well known for its superior use of information technology for competitive advantage.

Here are major fragments (condensed at times) of an interview with Raymond E. Cairns, Jr., who at the time of the interview was vice-president of information systems at Du Pont.

Question: What are Du Pont's corporate goals? And how might information technology help achieve them?

Answer: Our objective is to really be a great global company, in the sense that we're dealing with markets and opportunities around the world.

The main aspect of this globalization for us in information systems is to build wide area networks and run computers anywhere in the world.

Business managers now want to have information from around the world. They want it for scheduling the plants worldwide, to know where their inventories are, and where the orders are being placed. They want to be able to interface with customers around the world. And they need to communicate throughout their own organization, irrespective of location—on a worldwide basis.

Q: How is the global focus changing the information systems strategies you are pursuing?

A: We have four major strategies.

The first strategy is to have a worldwide, functionally sufficient, reliable, and secure information systems infrastructure [computer network] that we run at lower cost than our competitors. The reliability requirements are increasing every day. The network has to be secure because we're putting our customers around the world on our networks and into our computer.

The second strategy is to stimulate and enable our businesses to use information technology. So it's an education process and it's a marketing process.

The third is to introduce appropriate new technology faster than the competition. An example is our involvement with artificial intelligence. [As we shall see in chapter 15, Du Pont has introduced expert systems into diverse aspects of its operations.]

And the last strategy involves stewardship. Although I report to our upper management on the totality of the activity and define the strategy, I only have directly reporting to me 20 percent of the information systems resources. But I have to manage across those activities.

Q: How do you manage such diverse interests?

A: We decided to limit the technology base. We use only specific models of host machines all around the world: specific IBM mainframes, and specific DEC and Hewlett Packard minis. By doing that, we have been able to leverage our resources. Here is an example. Our data center outside of Frankfurt, West Germany is a clone of the major data center at the Wilmington headquarters. We operate the West German center with no systems programmers. All systems programming is done at the headquarters center and we download the program tapes electronically to Frankfurt. Thus, limiting the technology and supporting it remotely results in economies.

We are going to consolidate our four U.S. centers to two. This will give Du Pont four data centers worldwide: one in Delaware, one in Oklahoma, one in Europe, and one in Singapore. It doesn't matter where your computer is. We have a financial application where the terminal is in Korea and the application is being run in Germany.

We would like to have an open architecture, so that we can have a single operating system and a single telecommunications protocol around the world. We would define open systems in terms of UNIX.

Q: Have you also reined in the types of desktop systems that can be used at Du Pont?

A: Our PCs are limited to those running MS-DOS and to Macintoshes. We have not guidelined OS/2 yet.

Q: Earlier, you mentioned that Du Pont's chief information systems thrust in recent years has been in building up the network infrastructure. Please amplify that point.

A: We have a layered network design. The bottom layer is the basic telecommunications transport—just wires and circuits. We're pursuing every way we can to get our line costs down in the United States, such as cotransmitting voice and data using our own multiplexors. We're on the [transoceanic] fiber-optic cable to Europe. We have satellite circuits to the Far East, where we want to be on the fiber-optic cable as soon as it's in place.

Sitting on top of this layer are what we call the basic networks. Today we run three data networks, a voice network, and a video network. On top of that are three operating systems—for IBM, DEC, and HP. On top of them are some basic utility programs, such as electronic mail. That's what we call our network architecture.

Q: How much of the network management function resides within Du Pont? How much of it rests with your network suppliers?

A: It's shared. We have outsourced some of that activity, but not to the extent where network service providers have complete control.

We have to monitor how our networks are run. We have 800 companies up on our electronic data interchange. Thousands of people—our customers—are directly tied to our computers. The providers of network services don't know your computing environment, so you don't want them to manage the data network. You want them to manage the transport.

Q: How does information technology help Du Pont to compete?

A: Appropriate technology is a factor in competition. That doesn't mean all technology, but just what's appropriate for us.

We were the first chemical company with a Cray supercomputer. . . . Another example is in our initiatives in artificial intelligence. We did it differently than most other people. We did it with some very small systems. We have 800 systems out there in artificial intelligence. They're based on PC platforms. We are able to train end users to build them themselves.

Q: If only 20 percent of Du Pont's information systems resources report directly to you, who manages the other 80 percent?

A: Du Pont is organized into nine major departments [business groups]. Our strategy has been to locate information systems resources within these organizations—for two reasons.

Part of it is that we want them to be responsive to end users. By information systems' being in their organization, the users can control the amount of resources, they can control the allocation of resources, and they can control priorities without going to some central organization. We tell them only: you have to do this within these standard platforms and networks.

Second, by having that responsibility, management is more involved in information systems. It becomes part of your profit-and-loss statement.

Q: How many managers and other professionals at Du Pont have desktop systems?

A: I would say 75 to 85 percent of the 46,000 professionals have desktops. You are starting to find that they have one on their desks, one in their labs, and one at home.

Q: How many information systems professionals are there at Du Pont?

A: There are nearly 5,000 information systems people worldwide.

The trick is to combine the best of centralization and decentrilization. We only want to centralize what we can get advantage from, from our company size.

Q: How do you coordinate the information systems activities throughout the company—how do you provide stewardship?

A: The information systems heads in the nine business groups report to the departmental presidents and to me [this is matrix management]. I meet with these people probably weekly.

Q: How are most of Du Pont's departmental presidents measuring the value of information systems?

A: What's important to look at is: What value can information systems add to the business? Where do they see their competition getting competitive advantage through these systems? Where do *they* think they are getting such advantage?

Information systems would either be a facilitator or an inhibitor of globalization.

Q: How are tackling the white-collar productivity issue?

A: We have a study team right now. Roles have to change. It's not a technology problem. It's an organization/learning problem. My secretary now does spreadsheets and graph presentation, graphics, and things like that. But her role is different today than it was eight years ago.

I think my role will be different ten years from now. I'll have much greater span of control [manage more people directly].

Q: Do you have an executive information system right now?

A: Yes. It's a Comshare package. We have one with 150 people on it right now; but there will be 400 people on it. We have a situation today where the head of Du Pont in Europe is on the executive information system, which resides here in Wilmington. We download certain encrypted information every day to his PC, so that when he gets on that system to talk to somebody in the United States, whether it's the chairman or the vice-chairman or members of the executive committee, it's the same information. The same is true in Tokyo, in Brazil.

The chairman says he can't do without it.

Q: The company's annual report and other corporate messages emphasize electronic links between Du Pont and its customers and suppliers. How widespread is this activity at Du Pont?

A: We started this five years ago and we think we were a leader in this activity. We now have 800 companies that electronically deal with Du Pont. We have been much more aggressive at doing so with our customers than our suppliers.

They have access in a limited way to our databases. They are on electronic mail systems. It all has to do with the cost of switching incurred by a customer in switching from one supplier to another. If you're a company that we're dealing with and we have your engineers dealing with our engineers on electronic mail, and they've established a relationship and they know each other, it's different than just working through the purchasing agents. Say John [our competitor] comes in with a penny-a-pound decrease in the price of nickel. The cost for you to switch to him in the past would have been negligible. Now you have to switch your engineers. Who are they going to contact? How is the relationship going to be developed? How are the partnerships going to be enhanced? Because we're really talking about greater partnerships

between companies these days. And so, by doing that, switching costs will increase.

Q: How do you effect such linkage?

A: There are really two levels of links. One is electronic data interchange, which is basic. Costs of doing business in purchasing will decrease if we can do it electronically. The second aspect is setting up communications between professionals. It's going to fuzz up the boundaries between companies.

Q: Is the intercompany computing phenomenon occurring throughout the world?

A: It's being led in the United States. It's closely followed in Europe. And the professional-to-professional connection is lagging in the Far East. There are still some cultural problems there about managers and professionals having PCs on their desks.

And you have the language barrier, too. That's the thing that's going to be important in the future—the ability to communicate in various languages. You can do that today in the Romance and Germanic languages, but it's very difficult to do in the Asiatic languages. But that's the pressure globally that we are going to see—the multilingual, multicultural capability.

Q: Where do you see the major source of innovation coming from in the use of information technology?

A: The innovation continues to come from the user interface. I don't see much of it coming from the information systems function. A lot of ideas come from end users, and then information systems professionals work with them. It's important for us to champion these ideas. It's important for us to experiment.

Based on Tim Mead, "The IS Innovator at DuPont." *Datamation*, April 15, 1990, pp. 61–68.

Postscript

A few months after this interview, Raymond Cairns was promoted to senior vice-president and made member of the twenty-three-person executive operating group at Du Pont. This has been interpreted as a clear signal that the corporation considers MIS vital to its operations.

Based on Peter Krass, ''IS Becomes More
Integral to Du Pont.'' *InformationWeek*,
October 22, 1990, pp. 14–15.

Case Study Questions

1. Globalization of its business is the primary concern at Du Pont. Following Michael E. Porter, we may define global strategy as "one in which a firm sells its product in many nations and employs an integrated worldwide approach to doing so."[1] In this context, discuss the following questions.
   a. How do Du Pont's information technologies assist the company in this major business strategy? Which are the primary technologies employed in this respect? What other technologies can further assist the firm in its worldwide drive, and how?
   b. Raymond Cairns tells us that information systems may be inhibitors in a globalization drive. Describe such a scenario.

2. What functions do end users play with respect to information systems at Du Pont? Classify them according to our discussion in chapter 9, and offer specific examples from the interview.

3. What are the functions of the central MIS unit run by Raymond Cairns? What does he mean when he says that the unit "limits the technology base" of the company? What are the advantages of this strategy?

4. How is layered network architecture organized at Du Pont?

5. How does the firm tie its customers to itself with information systems in pursuit of competitive advantage? Why does the firm believe that this advantage is sustainable?

ENDNOTE

1. Porter, Michael E. *The Competitive Advantage of Nations*. New York: Free Press, 1990, p. 54.

PART THREE

MANAGEMENT AND ORGANIZATION: FUNDAMENTAL CONCEPTS FOR MIS

To understand what informational support is needed to manage an organization, we must study the fundamental concepts concerning organizations and their management. As we do so, we shall identify mutual influences and relationships between organizations and their management on the one hand, and the information systems they rely on on the other.

We shall start by discussing systems concepts: we will see that there are general principles of organization that apply to any complex entities, be they human organizations, information systems, or even just software programs. Learning these principles will help us understand our options in structuring and controlling organizations, as well as in creating systems for their informational support.

We shall then consider principal aspects of management theory and analyze the functions of management. We shall see the fundamental role MIS play in supporting the managerial functions of planning and control—the system-theoretic feedback loop vital to keeping an enterprise on track. We will familiarize ourselves with the tools of planning and control, implemented with information systems.

Organizations are both the arena of management and are themselves shaped by it. We shall discuss options in structuring organizations and their subunits, such as the MIS function itself. In particular, we want to see which organizational structures support innovation. We shall be especially interested in the organizational processes of technology assimilation and change, through which information technologies and specific systems can achieve their full, perhaps strategic, impact. The fourth function of management, along with organizing, planning, and controlling, is leadership. A leader furnishes the vision and motivation—people, indeed, should be led, not managed.

People, rather than organizations, actually work with information systems. These systems support decision making and communication between individuals in a workgroup and in larger organizational arenas. We shall see the variety of managerial actions and the multidimensional support this work requires, in particular in view of the variety of individual cognitive styles. We shall also see the severe limitations of the "rational decision-maker" model (though this model does offer some very useful tools). Supporting creativity in individual and group decision making is vital to innovative organizations.

In keeping with our approach to information systems as vehicles of change, our concern throughout this part of the book is with the management and organizational structures that support innovation and continuing adaptability to the dynamic environment of an information society.

CHAPTER 10

Systems Concepts

Observe how system into system runs,
What other planets circle other suns.
Alexander Pope

We need an organized set of concepts that enable us to cope with the complexity and turbulence of an information society, that help us to structure its organizations and to create its complex technological artifacts—such as computerized information systems. This conceptual framework is offered by systems theory. Using the systems approach based on this theory, we are better able to see, create, and manage a clear structure rather than become lost in a jungle of many interrelated details.

The application of systems-theoretic concepts will help us

- see the options available for structuring organizations;
- understand the role of MIS in an organization; and
- analyze and design information systems.

In general, the systems approach helps us analyze and develop complex entities, such as information systems, with a clear understanding of their purpose, structure, and total relationship with their environment. For example, telecommunications protocols that manage telecommunications networks are organized to conform with this approach. Systems development methodologies, which we shall discuss in Part 5 of this text, are also based on it.

FOCUS CASE

In a lawn-equipment company, the executive in charge of information systems allowed its two major plants to develop their own management information systems for tracking work orders and inventory. Even though both factories used the same minicomputer model, each system was customized to the operation of the individual plant and the programs were incompatible. When the chief executive of the company subsequently requested regular consolidated reports on shipments and inventory, the central MIS staff had to combine the information from the two plants by hand.

Based on John J. Donovan, "Beyond Chief Information Officer to Network Manager." *Harvard Business Review*, September-October 1988, pp. 134–40.

After our study of the concepts presented in this chapter, we shall be able to put a name to what happened at this lawn-equipment manufacturer: suboptimization. Much more than that, we will acquire a set of concepts that will help us avoid developing suboptimal systems.

CHAPTER OUTLINE

10.1   What Are Systems?

10.2   Systems Approach

10.3   Classification of Systems
- Natural and Artificial Systems
- Deterministic and Probabilistic Systems
- Closed and Open Systems

10.4   Structuring of Systems
- Decomposition
- Cohesion of Subsystems

10.5   Decoupling

10.1 WHAT ARE SYSTEMS?

A system is a collection of components that constitute a whole.[1] *Physical systems,* such as an information system, and *social systems,* such as an organization, are organized to achieve predefined objectives. A manager organizing the work of her or his unit is creating a system—which then becomes a *subsystem* of the broader organization. The developer of a new personal computer creates a system consisting of hardware and software components. These personal computers can, with the appropriate specialized software, become subsystems of an electronic meeting system designed to meet the objectives of a specific organization or the generalized demands of a specific market. In addition to physical and social systems, there are also *abstract systems* of concepts and ideas. (One such abstract system is systems theory itself.) An abstract system can also be of a procedural nature—such as a systems development life cycle, a system for developing software systems!

A system operates in its *environment,* from which the system is delimited by its *boundary.* Delimiting a system from its environment gives us a "black-box" view of the system: When we take this view, we do not care what is inside of the black box (see figure 10.1).

FIGURE 10.1

The "black-box" view of a system.

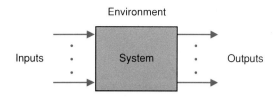

FIGURE 10.2

A system and its descriptors.

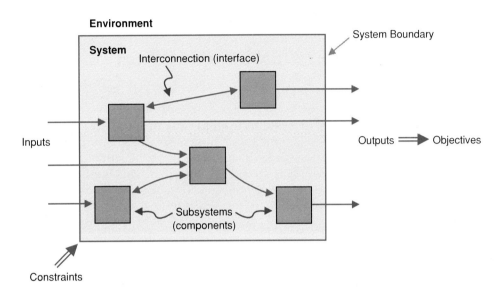

A further analysis of the system will progressively identify its subsystems and then, recursively, their own components in increasing detail. Necessary *interconnections* between these components (their individual inputs and outputs) will also be identified. A general description of systems is shown in figure 10.2.

The identification of a system's boundary is often a nontrivial task. This is where the black-box approach gives us a good start: we are able to ignore the details and concentrate on establishing the principal outline of the system. Let us say that you, as a systems analyst, have been charged with the task of analyzing and designing an on-line system for processing securities (stocks and bonds) held by your bank. One of your first tasks will be to determine exactly what should be included in the system and thus what its boundary will be. If you make the assumption that the new system should replicate what people in the bank's Securities Processing department are doing, and therefore should be delimited by the department's boundaries, you are almost guaranteed to produce an inferior system. The entire system must be rethought in the light of its *objectives* (such as the types of transactions it will need to support) and *constraints* (such as processing time, pertinent government regulations, and interactions with existing systems). This boundary delineation will, in turn, lead to identification of the *inputs* to and *outputs* from the system.

A disciplined technique for systems analysis applied to information systems, called structured analysis, will be discussed in Part 5 of this book.

A business firm or a government organization may be fruitfully considered a system. Proper identification of the system's objectives is necessary to establish measurable criteria for their achievement; this is done in the planning process.

Setting measurable objectives is also a prerequisite for controlling the system by measuring the level of plan fulfillment. Organizing—establishing the organizational structure of a company—is one of the principal functions of management. An example of such a structure was shown in figure 3.10. The company shown in that figure is organized into seven subsystems (departments) which are, in turn, built from lower-level subsystems.

10.2 SYSTEMS APPROACH

The **systems approach** is an approach to problem solving—the problem, for example, being how to structure an organization or analyze an information system—in which the entity being studied (an organization or an information system) is considered a system. This implies that we must establish the objectives of the system, consider the totality of its relationships with its environment, and identify in ever greater detail its components and their interactions.

The importance of applying the systems approach to an organization's informational problems is often best illustrated by examples of cases where such an approach was *not* used. Some of the following examples, therefore, illustrate the systems approach with such situations:

1. An organization initiates two independent information systems development projects. One of them, sponsored by the Personnel department, aims to create an inventory of personnel skills in the organization. The other, sponsored by the Office of the President of the company, is a decision support system (DSS) that will assist in the process of managerial promotions. The systems approach argues for developing a system that includes the two as subsystems. If other organizational considerations prevail, a conscious (and probably costly) decision to develop separate systems—with established linkages— should be made explicitly.

   In the Focus Case for this chapter, we encountered a similar situation. If the systems developers in this case also chose to develop two separate systems, both cases would demonstrate systems developed in a **suboptimal** fashion: while serving parts of the organization effectively, they do not serve the total firm well.

2. In a small brokerage house, each broker maintains his or her jealously guarded customer list; there is no centralized client database. The effectiveness of marketing new products to customers is sacrificed to each brokers' exclusive access to individual clients.

3. An organization's systems developers have designed a transaction processing system (TPS) with excessively long response times. The designers have failed to recognize that TPS is a *human-machine system*. Specifications for many such systems require a response time below two seconds for 90 percent of transactions and below ten seconds for the

remaining 10 percent. More sophisticated designs recognize that an acceptable response time is a function of the transaction. Users are willing to wait longer for a response to a complex query, but they expect an almost instantaneous completion and acknowledgment of a simple database update. Long response times significantly lower the performance of the total human-machine system.

4. A university sets financial performance criteria to measure its success. Planners have failed to realize that the objective of a system should be kept in clear view. Thus, a university is a normative organization: its general objective, namely, the generation and dissemination of knowledge, is nonmonetary. It would be wrong, therefore, to apply to a university the same performance criteria as are applied to a utilitarian organization such as a business enterprise.

5. An organization develops a marketing plan model in its decision support system without considering demographic changes in its targeted customer population. Ignoring an important environmental factor imperils the performance of a system designed to function in a given environment. When developing a planning model to be included in a decision support system (DSS) which is to support marketing of a consumer product, we need to consider demographic factors, such as changing age and gender distribution in the targeted consumer sector.

10.3 CLASSIFICATION OF SYSTEMS

Several aspects of systems allow us to classify and thus to characterize them. As we have said, we are primarily concerned here with physical and social systems. We shall continue to concentrate on the characteristics relevant to organizational information systems.

Natural and Artificial Systems

Natural systems occur in nature without human intervention. Each of us may be considered such a system; our alimentary (digestive) system is, for example, a subsystem of the human system.

In this book, we are concerned with *artificial systems* developed expressly to support certain objectives. A business organization has to generate surplus, such as profit. It may also pursue other objectives, such as providing employment or contributing to its community in other ways. The principal objective of a DSS is supporting a certain user community in making a certain range of decisions. The objective of one of the programs included in this DSS may be producing an extract database from the company's database and thus contributing to the overall objective of the DSS.

We use effectiveness and efficiency criteria to measure the value of an artificial system. *Effectiveness* measures the extent to which a system achieves its objectives. *Efficiency* is a measure of the consumption of input resources in producing given system outputs. In a management information system, the variety and volume of transactions processed, or user satisfaction with the system, are measures of effectiveness. These measures can be evaluated and compared with those achieved by alternative systems. Thus, a questionnaire used to establish user information satisfaction has been developed and validated (see Baroudi, 1988). The use of computer system resources (such as computer processing power measured in millions of instruction per second (MIPS) or the capacity of system memories, or the cost of operating a data center) for achieving a given level of effectiveness is a measure of system efficiency.

If the mission of a firm's MIS function is aligned with the overall mission of the enterprise, we are able to accurately gauge the effectiveness of the firm's MIS. Thus, revenue growth or market share expansion attributable to the adoption of a customer-oriented strategic system measures the system's effectiveness in the context of corporate goals.

Deterministic and Probabilistic Systems

The operation of a *deterministic system* is completely predictable. The present state and the inputs of such a system fully determine its outputs and its next state. A microprocessor chip or a correct software package are examples of such a system.

The outputs of a *probabilistic system* can be predicted only in terms of the probability distribution of their values or of some aggregate measure such as their average value. There is always uncertainty as to their actual value at any given time. Both organizations and information systems are probabilistic; their behavior is, therefore, more difficult to characterize than that of a digital hardware unit, such as a computer's central processor.

Closed and Open Systems

Systems may be fruitfully classified as open, relatively closed, or closed, as shown in figure 10.3.

A *closed system* does not exchange resources with its environment (see figure 10.3a). Since this implies that the system has no inputs and no outputs relating it to this environment, we may consider the system as having no environment in the systems-theoretic sense. A battery-run and timer-controlled system of light signals placed temporarily on the road during repairs could be considered a closed system, if we ignore the informational output provided by the color of the light. A closed system will ultimately run down (in our example, the battery will be exhausted), or its purposeful organization will cease (in the example, the light controller or timer might break down). In terms of systems theory, the *entropy* (disorder) of closed systems increases until they cease to fulfill their objectives.

Open systems, shown schematically in figure 10.3c, exchange resources with their environment via inputs and outputs, some of which are ill-defined or even unknown. Informational inputs and outputs are the category important to us. Some of these inputs serve the purpose of adaptation: as its environment changes, the system perceives the change via appropriate inputs and changes its operation. An organization is an open system. The complexity of its environment in the information society, which we analyzed in chapter 2, requires extensive boundary spanning: the organization needs various informational inputs regarding the environment. By injecting *negative entropy* into its operation (that is, by maintaining its order), an open system is able to adapt continually to its environment. As figure 10.3c shows, open systems are subject to the influence of a variety of inputs, some of which are not known when the system is developed.

FIGURE 10.3

Closed, relatively closed, and
open systems.

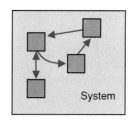

a. A closed system.

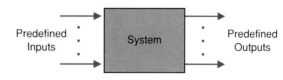

b. A relatively closed system.

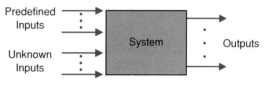

c. An open system.

Between the two extremes of closed and open systems are *relatively closed systems,* as shown in figure 10.3b. These systems exchange resources with their environment only through well-defined inputs and outputs. Their inputs and outputs are defined when the system is designed, and the inputs are controlled to conform to this predefined form. For example, if the manufacturing resource planning system (MRP II), discussed in chapter 5, is incorporated into a larger human-machine system which controls all the disturbances on the input side, then the MRP II system itself becomes a relatively closed system.

10.4 STRUCTURING OF SYSTEMS

The concepts of systems theory assist us in understanding and developing systems—organizations, information systems, and computer programs.

Systems are designed (or analyzed) by progressive decomposition. In the process of decomposition, we progressively factor (break down) a system into its subsystems, which are in turn factored, until we reach the elements we consider primitive for the purposes of our design. This gives us a powerful handle on the complexity of systems. Other things being equal, the goodness of a system's structure depends on the degree to which the subsystems are autonomous. Relatively autonomous (that is, relatively independent) subsystems display a high degree of functional cohesion: each performs a well-defined function fully. Relatively autonomous subsystems are also loosely coupled with other subsystems; that is, relatively few interfaces exist between the subsystems, and these interfaces are relatively simple. Decoupling techniques, which may be used to make subsystems relatively independent from one another by simplifying their interfaces, are discussed in the next main section of the chapter.

Decomposition

The process of decomposition involves factoring (breaking down) the system into subsystems. These subsystems are defined so that together they provide the functionality of the complete system. This process of progressive refinement continues: subsystems are decomposed into their components on the same principle. The process stops when we reach components we do not choose to decompose further; the nature of these primitive components depends on the task at hand. For example, in structuring an organization, decomposition stops when we reach units that are simple enough to manage as a whole.

This decomposition process is applicable to the structuring of organizations (further discussed in chapter 12) and to the analysis and design of information systems (further discussed in Part 5). A structure chart showing the design of a simple information system for processing accounts receivable is shown in figure 10.4.

In this figure, the overall functionality of the system was decomposed into four subsystems (modules), and some of these were broken down in finer detail. The main software module (called Accounts Receivable System) calls four other modules as needed to perform certain aspects of the overall task. Thus, for example, each order is processed by the Process Order module, which in turn calls one of three lower-level modules to perform different parts of order processing.

Interfaces must be provided between the interacting subsystems. Departures from strict hierarchy (which is an inverted treelike structure, as in figure 10.4) will often result. Thus, lateral interfaces between structure components on the same level are often desired in an organizational structure, as shown in figure 10.5a.

FIGURE 10.4

Structure of an Accounts Receivable information system.

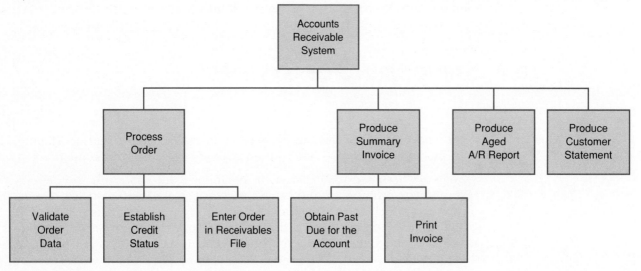

Some subsystems share resources. In the structure chart of a software system, as well as in an organization's structure, resource sharing is reflected by two or more higher-level subsystems interfacing with the same lower-level subsystem (the shared resource). For example, in a larger program, several higher-level modules may call the same report-printing module. Examples of these interfaces are shown in figure 10.5b.

The process of system decomposition is iterative: the goodness of the resultant breakdown is continually evaluated, and we may need to consider alternative ways of structuring the system. The principal measure of goodness of decomposition[2] in a software system is the relative autonomy of its modules. This, in turn, is evaluated by how functionally cohesive the subsystems are and how loosely they are coupled with the remaining subsystems.

Cohesion of Subsystems

A well-chosen subsystem displays a high degree of cohesion: it performs a well-defined function completely. What a subsystem's function is depends on the decomposition level on which the subsystem occurs. Thus, an executive responsible for the Marketing and Sales function (a subsystem) in figure 3.11 relies on the Market Research unit (a lower-level subsystem) for the performance of its subfunction, rather than doing this work himself or herself. Likewise, in a structure chart that shows the modules of a software system, a higher-level module may call several lower-level modules to perform various aspects of its task, as shown in figure 10.4.

FIGURE 10.5

Lateral interfaces and resource sharing.

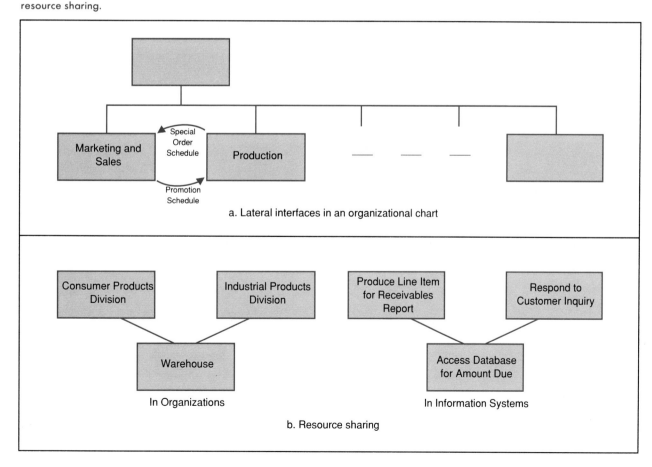

a. Lateral interfaces in an organizational chart

b. Resource sharing

A SHARED RESOURCE—AND POTENTIAL LOSS OF CONTROL

As the business downturn of the early 1990s exerted pressures for cost cutting in major brokerage houses on Wall Street, two firms considered merging and sharing their back offices. The back office of a large securities brokerage is a huge and costly operation that moves stocks, bonds, and other financial instruments to the purchaser's account and transfers the payment to the seller. Data centers with powerful mainframes are a significant component of back-office costs.

Two firms merging their back offices can save from 20 to 40 percent of the fixed costs involved—such is the power of economies of scale. In spite of the potential savings, the firms were loath to merge their offices: they feared that the loss of control might hamper their operations when special processing demands—such as a business upturn—presented themselves. Negotiations between Goldman, Sachs and Morgan Stanley broke off when it turned out that each industry giant wanted to control the shared resource and keep the other firm as a customer.

Based on Kurt Eichenwald, "Wringing More Costs Out of Wall St. Firms," *The New York Times*, April 4, 1991, pp. D1, D5.

A high degree of subsystem cohesion is usually indicated by relatively few interfaces among the subsystems. Interfaces include the necessary communications between organizational units or software modules.

When there is a large number of interfaces between subsystems, it is sometimes possible to simplify by *clustering* some of the subsystems. Functions are defined that incorporate some of the modules as subfunctions, and a single interface then joins the clusters (see figure 10.6). It is usually possible to define such a cluster in functional terms.

The remaining interfaces between subsystems can often be loosened by a process known as decoupling.

10.5 DECOUPLING

Interactions between subsystems contribute greatly to a system's complexity. These interactions make systems more difficult to organize in the first place: a software system with multiple interfaces between modules is more difficult to code and test. The interfaces also make systems more difficult to manage: the task of coordinating the work of an organizational unit with the work of other units it has to interact with grows rapidly as the number and intensity of these interactions increase. Interactions also make system modifications more difficult, since a change in one subsystem may require a change in other subsystems it interacts with—and thus the change ripples through a large part of the system. This ripple effect is the main reason a software modification is such a daunting task.

FIGURE 10.6

Simplification of
interconnections by clustering
subsystems.

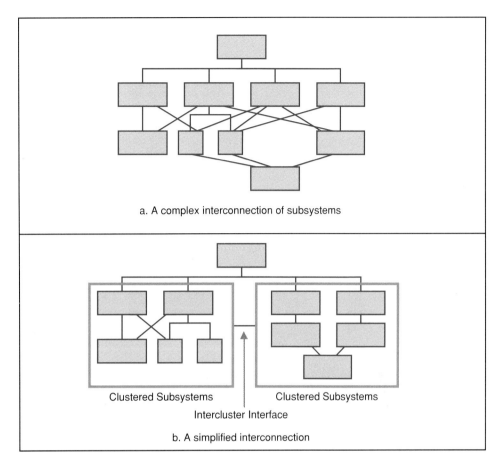

a. A complex interconnection of subsystems

Clustered Subsystems   Clustered Subsystems

Intercluster Interface

b. A simplified interconnection

Depending on the nature of the system and the trade-offs preferred, various decoupling techniques may be adopted. **Decoupling** aims at reducing the intensity of interactions between subsystems. Thus, although an interconnection between two subsystems may be necessary, we can often loosen it and thus decrease the need for coordination. But, as we shall see, decoupling has its costs as well. We may choose to forego expensive decoupling in an organizational structure by providing MIS-based coordination. As in many other organizational situations, this is a question of trade-offs and balance.

The following means of decoupling, shown in figure 10.7, are available in appropriate cases:

1. Inventories or Buffers

The Outbound Logistics subsystem, which delivers a firm's products to their distributors, may be decoupled from the Production subsystem by interposing an inventory of materials between the two (see figure 10.7a). This makes the Outbound Logistics subsystem less dependent on the vagaries of Production. Buffers are commonly used in computer hardware and software design to make parallel operation of various subsystems possible. For example, the input from a user's keyboard goes into a buffer area in memory during the slow typing process, so that the central processor can at the same time be executing another program at a far faster

FIGURE 10.7

Means of decoupling.

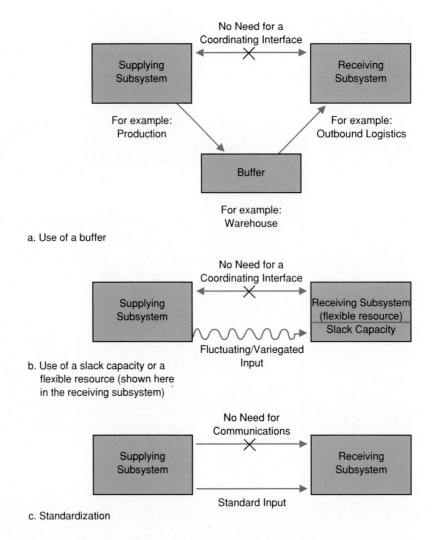

a. Use of a buffer

b. Use of a slack capacity or a
   flexible resource (shown here
   in the receiving subsystem)

c. Standardization

rate, processing the buffer contents periodically. In this human-machine system, the slow speed of the human is combined with the far greater computer speed without pacing the fast unit by the slow one.

The supplying subsystem has to wait for the receiving subsystem when the inventory warehouse or the memory buffer is full. The receiving subsystem has to wait when the warehouse or the memory buffer is empty. The greater the inventory or buffer size, the less frequently interaction between the two subsystems actually occurs.

2. Slack Capacity

If a subsystem contains a slack capacity for processing an input, the rate of input supply can be temporarily increased without the need for additional coordination or some other adjustment. Thus, if a transaction processing system which processes orders at a mail-order house has a slack capacity, it will be able to handle the November-December holiday order volumes without providing additional processing capacities or incurring delays.

Likewise, slack capacity in a supplying subsystem may ensure the smooth operation of the receiving system if it should temporarily require a greater rate of supply. For example, if the ties between supplier and customer companies become tight enough, they may be considered together as a "virtual company." If the customer company receives a surge of orders, the supplier can ensure delivery of needed materials with extra production capacity.

3. Flexible Resources

If a subsystem can easily fulfill various roles on demand from another subsystem that interacts with it, little adjustment is needed to satisfy the change in the nature of the request. Thus, flexible manufacturing systems can easily accommodate a change in the nature of orders. Training personnel for several jobs may help a company respond faster to a change in market demands. Benetton clothing company has developed a system that can respond readily to a change of colors in fashion by producing undyed goods and coloring them just before a shipment—according to demand, which is promptly identified by information systems connected to the leading stores.

The provisions of a slack capacity or a flexible resource are graphically illustrated in figure 10.7b.

4. Standardization

If the output of the supplying subsystem is standardized, the receiving subsystem, "knowing" what to expect, needs little adjustment and may be more simply structured. Standards reduce the need for communication (as shown graphically in figure 10.7c). For example, if the corporate MIS department follows a standard systems-development methodology, the need for communication among the organizational subsystems involved in development is reduced. In a similar fashion, the use of uniform end-user software tools throughout a company simplifies its operation. In general, as products become more complex, they are also becoming parts of a system's products, and standardization is needed for effective and efficient operation. Thus, standards for computer hardware and software are evolving—in spite of major difficulties related to the vested interests of their producers.

10.6 ORGANIZATIONAL DESIGN: INTEGRATION OR INDEPENDENCE?

As we now know, we can make subsystems relatively independent of one another by decoupling. However, decoupling carries resource costs in the design of an organization. If, on the other hand, we forego decoupling and tightly integrate subsystems, the complexity of the integrated unit increases, and it becomes more difficult to manage. We are faced with a trade-off. Information systems facilitate coordination and thus make the management of integrated organizational subsystems feasible. In this way, MIS offer options in the design of organizations and in the way they function. Taking an information-processing

TABLE 10.1	FORM OF DECOUPLING	COST
Costs of Decoupling.	Inventory	Resources (materials, products, warehouses) tied up in holding the inventory
	Slack Capacity	Productive resources (people, equipment) underemployed to provide the slack
	Flexible Resources	Higher costs of a flexible resource
	Standardization	Poor use of resources in certain cases in order to maintain uniformity

approach to organizational design, Jay Galbraith noted that organizations in many situations have a choice between increasing their capabilities for information processing and reducing performance levels through costly decoupling (Galbraith, 1977). Modern information technology considerably lowers the costs of coordination (Yates, 1991).

Costs of Independence through Decoupling

Decoupling subsystems makes them more independent—but at a price. In the design of software programs, we generally opt for as loose a coupling as possible, since this contributes to easier system maintenance—an overriding concern.

In designing the functioning of an organizational unit more or less loosely, the system developer—that is, the manager who is structuring the unit—has to consider the costs and benefits of decoupling. The costs of decoupling are summarized in table 10.1.

The vignette on just-in-time systems illustrates how enhancing performance may require that we forego decoupling or choose to employ only some of the available decoupling methods.

The costs of decoupling may actually be higher than just the cost of a decoupling mechanism. If each of the relatively independent subsystems created by decoupling pursues its own ends without regard for overall optimality, we then must add the costs of suboptimization to the costs of decoupling. For example, an MIS department may find it best to schedule its work six months in advance. A request from the marketing department to perform maintenance on a marketing analysis program may be refused to protect this schedule—to the overall detriment of the company.

Costs of Integration

An alternative to a loose coupling of subsystems is tight integration. When subsystems are integrated, their operation needs to be closely coordinated: inputs and outputs have to be scheduled in accord with the operation of both subsystems, and the operation of any subsystem depends on the operation of the others it is connected with. A large volume of information must be exchanged. Integration is accomplished by giving communicating systems a fair amount of knowledge about each other's operations and by regulating their work accord-

JUST-IN-TIME SYSTEMS—FOREGOING DECOUPLING

As we discussed in chapter 5, increased levels of performance in industrial activity have been achieved by reducing or entirely giving up inventories. These just-in-time systems tightly bind suppliers and customers and, when used internally within a company, tightly couple its subsystems. Very considerable economies achieved through this system design have in many cases become a necessity for competing in the marketplace.

Tight coupling in these systems has been made possible by enhanced information processing: planning production processes with MRP II, coordinating suppliers' activities with those of the customer, and controlling activities within the firm.

While the supplier-customer interface is tightened in terms of stringent timing and higher frequency of deliveries, it is frequently loosened by standardization. Thus, customers often demand that the supplier be responsible for the quality control of deliveries. Standardized supplies from certified suppliers simplify the design of the customer's production system.

ingly or by having another subsystem regulate their work. The advantage of close integration is that it avoids the inefficiencies of decoupling.

The disadvantages of integration resemble the system features we were trying to avoid when we decomposed a system into subsystems. Closely integrated subsystems in effect become a single and more complex larger subsystem. This larger virtual subsystem is more difficult to manage, and a failure anywhere within it has a far greater impact than it would have had if the subsystems were not tightly integrated. Fragmentation into subsystems limits the risk of failure to one subsystem and also limits corrective measures in scope and cost.

Trade-offs and the Role of MIS

We may conclude that a trade-off exists between the relative advantages and disadvantages of integration and interdependence; this trade-off is summarized in figure 10.8.

As we argued in chapter 2, information systems serve, in addition to their other roles, as a means of coordination. Thus, MIS make possible a tighter integration of organizational subsystems by facilitating organizational planning and control and by helping exchange information between the subsystems. Information systems make it possible to select one point in the spectrum from tight integration to independence that benefits the overall organizational objectives—information systems are a bearer of options.

Some of these conclusions apply also to entire industries. Thomas Malone and his colleagues at MIT argue that by lowering coordination costs—or, in some cases, by merely making coordination possible—information systems lead to the expansion of options in both integration- and market-oriented organizational activities (Malone, 1987). Thus, thanks to interorganizational information systems, companies are able to rely on external suppliers rather than attempting to produce many of the components contained in their products themselves.

FIGURE 10.8

Trade-offs between
integration and
independence.

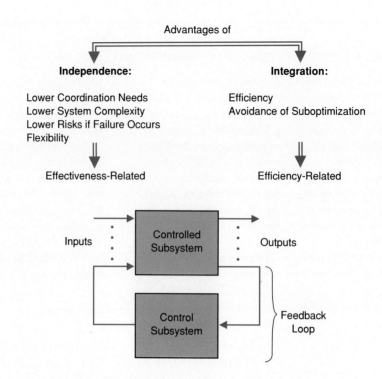

FIGURE 10.9

A closed-loop system.

10.7 CLOSED-LOOP SYSTEMS—MIS IN ORGANIZATIONAL CONTROL

A major role that a management information system plays in the organization is in the control feedback loop. MIS are used to work out plans, which are then used as the control standard, and to exercise continuing control against these standards. The broader and the more timely informational support is for the various situations that arise in an organization—for example, the sudden need to change a plan or a crisis in a company merger—the more useful MIS is to that organization.

**Closed-Loop
Systems**

Very few systems operate so that their inputs are totally independent of their outputs; such systems are so-called *open-loop systems.* Organizations, on the other hand, are *closed-loop systems.* A closed-loop system contains a subsystem that performs the control function. The general idea of **control** (of which managerial control is an example) consists in comparing the system's outputs with the desired values for these outputs and generating corrective inputs to the system as necessary. The control subsystem thus acts in a **feedback loop** that regulates the controlled subsystem, as shown in figure 10.9.

INTRODUCING A FAST FEEDBACK LOOP

Companies marketing packaged goods have recently been using up-to-the-day information fed back to them and based on product scanning in supermarkets. Prompt marketing decisions can be made on the basis of this information.

In pursuit of competitive advantage, other industries are also trying to introduce fast loops for information feedback. For example, Nissan Motor Corporation USA determined that customers who are not satisfied with their cars do not complain— they simply do not come back. Therefore, it is necessary to institute a feedback loop to ensure prompt attention to customer

problems. Using a central database, Nissan will make calls to all of the 660,000 people who buy their product each year as well as to the customers using the warranty service. Any problem discovered in these conversations, which are initiated by the manufacturer, will be forwarded to local dealers within twenty-four hours.

"We are out there in real time, turning around information so that it can lead to action," says Howard Tullman, president of the firm that conducts the survey in Nissan's behalf.

Based on Dan Koeppel, "Nissan: Calling All Car Buyers."
Adweek's Marketing Week, March 6, 1989, p. 3.

**Control via
Negative Feedback
and Feedforward**

When *positive feedback* is desired, the feedback loop inputs reinforce the divergence determined in the comparison to standards. Organizational control is based on the principle of *negative feedback*: divergences of a system's outputs from the standards they are compared to are reduced by the inputs generated in the controlling subsystem. Thus, undesirable variances from a plan (standard) are translated into the corrective actions necessary to improve the performance of a business unit. By introducing a desired order into the operations of a controlled system, feedback control reduces the entropy of the system.

The feedback-loop control process applies both to the entire organization and to its subunits. The general view of organizational control with the use of MIS, based on the feedback principle, is shown in figure 10.10. Based on the information produced by management information systems (regarded as a firm's subsystem), management introduces corrective actions to bring company operations in line with previously formulated plans, budgets, quotas, and so on. Thus, the MIS helps identify deviations from planned performance. Information systems are also used by management to formulate needed corrective actions.

As we noted in chapter 3, along with financial performance measures such as profitability or return on investment, companies are beginning to include in the feedback loop nonfinancial measures reflecting the quality of their products and services and their competitive performance. Thus, measures such as customer satisfaction, innovation, and market share are being included by some firms in the management control loop (Bertodo, 1990; Eccles, 1991). This "widening" of the feedback loop leads to a broader role for MIS in organizations.

A feedback loop does not act instantaneously: a time lag exists between the time the data are available and the time corrective actions are taken. Responsiveness of the information systems and timeliness of the information are of the essence.

FIGURE 10.10

Organizational control via
feedback loop.

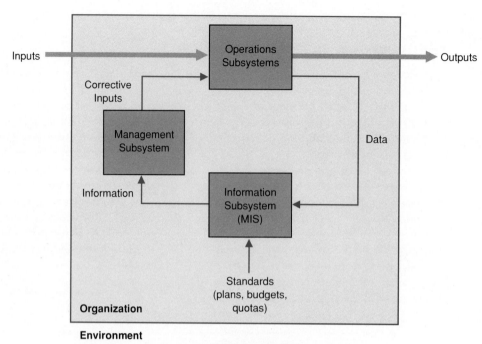

FIGURE 10.11

Feedforward in
organizational control.

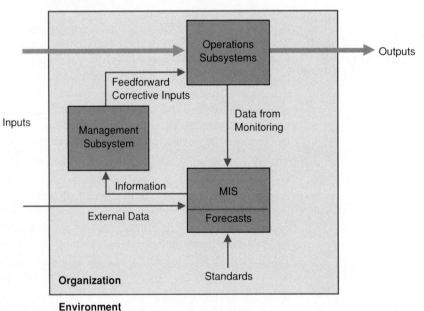

Management can also act proactively on the **feedforward** principle. In this case, information systems may be employed to forecast the projected performance of an organizational unit on the basis of current internal data and of certain system inputs, such as external information. Corrective action can then be generated ahead of time, to ensure timely fulfillment of the plan. Feedforward operation is shown in figure 10.11.

When we discussed the use of an executive information system (EIS) in chapter 1, we saw its users act in the feedforward mode. They compared the performance projections generated by the system with planned performance and took proactive measures before problems became more severe. In general, the use of EIS has increased the role of feedforward control. Instead of waiting for the end of a reporting period and then introducing an adjustment, management can use these systems to anticipate problems and introduce needed adjustments beforehand.

Are the standards a firm's performance is compared to immutable? Obviously not. The process of continuous planning adjusts these standards as time marches on, in order to respond both to encountered problems and to discovered opportunities. Another feedback loop can be used to adjust the standards themselves. Chris Argyris evolved the concept of *double-loop learning* for the broader process in which an organization questions and adjusts its objectives and the corresponding plans (Argyris, 1977). Through this process of organizational learning, a firm is able to continually improve its performance levels.

The Law of Requisite Variety

To control each possible state of a controlled subsystem, the control subsystem must have a corresponding variety of states to provide control responses—this is the **law of requisite variety.**

In simpler terms, information systems must be designed to assist management in all situations that may arise. This does not imply that the computerized system will be able to handle all the possible contingencies. But a human-machine system should be designed to take maximum advantage of computer capabilities. American Express's Authorizers' Assistant expert system handles approximately 80 percent of authorizations for a credit purchase automatically. The system is also able to determine when the help of a human expert is required and present the facts of the case to the expert.

The complexity of an overall human-MIS system is kept manageable by

- grouping and classifying various inputs and outputs to limit the requisite number of responses;
- defining normal states and acceptable variances—with the information system alerting people to exceptions only;
- placing a human in the feedback loop, when necessary, to exercise judgment.

The scope of support computerized information systems offer to managers is constantly growing, with ever larger parts of the decision-making process being handled by the machine as opposed to the human part of the overall information system. Management of organizational crises is an excellent example of this. A well-received case study, published several years ago, of an organization coping with the crisis of having been acquired showed how the company successfully handled the crises by ignoring formal information systems (Hurst, 1984). Now, the situation is changing. In a recent paper, Jay Nunamaker and his coworkers at the University of Arizona (Nunamaker, 1989) present the design of a formal, computer-supported crisis-management system, which we will further discuss as the case study for chapter 13. The inclusion of formalized informational support for unusual circumstances provides the requisite variety in MIS to control a far broader range of situations than was possible a few years ago.

10.8 SYSTEMS ANALYSIS

Information systems are developed through a process that draws on the principles of systems theory. The total development process is discussed in detail in Part 5 of the text. Systems analysis, an initial phase of the development process, is a good illustration of the systems approach to problem solving. It is carried out by professionals called, unsurprisingly, systems analysts. These analysts aim to develop systems that are relatively easy to modify as required. The principal steps in systems analysis are:

1. Problem Definition
    The problem to be solved by the system is set in the context of the environment the system will interact with.

2. Statement of System Objectives
    General objectives and specific criteria of system effectiveness are established and stated.

3. Establishing System Boundaries
    The boundaries between the future system and its environment are precisely outlined. System interfaces (inputs and outputs) are specified.

4. Establishing Constraints on the System
    The constraints on the system and on its development process (such as the cost and the time frame for system development) are specified.

5. System Decomposition
    The system is progressively decomposed into subsystems, using the concepts presented in this chapter. Strongly cohesive subsystems, loosely coupled with their environment, are preferred. Interfaces among the subsystems are identified. Thus, a systems analyst looks at the system in progressively greater detail. Only the subsystems obtained at the lowest level of decomposition will actually be designed and become parts of the implemented system. Higher levels of abstraction are simply a way of getting there—a technique for managing the complexity of the analysis process.

10.9 SYSTEMS SYNTHESIS

A system is created in a process called systems synthesis. In developing information systems, this synthesis (called systems design) follows systems analysis, when we tore apart a whole in order to understand it. Now we are building a new system. What guidance do we receive from systems theory in this design? How will it help us handle the complexity of the system during its design and during future modifications?

The following are the two principal qualities we desire in systems (Zwass, 1984):

1. Functional Modularity

Systems should be built of modules, which in the case of software systems are short code segments. Each module will perform a well-defined function in the overall system; in performing this function, the system may call upon lower-level modules. Properly implemented modules are, indeed, strongly cohesive subsystems, loosely coupled with other modules.

Functional modularity helps not only in coping with a system's complexity during its synthesis. As the functions of the system will have to be changed in the future, only the modules affected by the change will have to be modified. The rest of the system will be unaffected by the modification.

2. Hierarchical Structure

If we consider a single program to be a system, then the modules of that system should be organized into a hierarchy. This hierarchy will correspond to the one identified during the system decomposition step in systems analysis.

Thus, we shall have a single module that provides overall control at the top of the hierarchy, and then progressively lower-level modules. The lower the level of the module, the more detailed the function it handles in the overall system. Unsurprisingly, we arrive at a structure resembling an organization chart. Hierarchical structure is a powerful method for organizing complex entities.

We shall return to these concepts and see how they are implemented in the systems development process in chapter 19.

- -

SUMMARY

Understanding systems concepts gives us an understanding of our options in structuring organizations and software systems. By decomposing systems into cohesive subsystems, we are able to both analyze and synthesize (develop) complex systems. Through decoupling techniques, we are able to make the operation of subsystems relatively independent. However, in the case of organizational design, this may lead to a loss of performance. The alternative is increased integration, with the use of information systems as a means of coordination.

If we consider an organization to be a closed-loop system, management information systems serve both to establish standards of performance (plans) and to control the organization against these standards.

By applying the systems approach, we are able to perform disciplined systems analysis as an initial phase in the development of management information systems. We are also able to design the new system in a manner that helps us to cope with its complexity both in design and in future modifications.

CONCLUSIONS FOR MIS PRACTICE

1. An organization and a management information system have common properties, since they both can fruitfully be considered systems. The systems approach will help us understand both.

2. From the point of view of systems theory, a management information system is a part of the negative feedback loop controlling the performance of an organization.

3. A system should always be considered in the context of its environment, without ignoring any significant environmental factors.

4. A system's objectives should be clearly stated and quantified insofar as possible; to prevent suboptimization, the objectives of subsystems should conform to these system objectives.

5. Information systems lower the costs of coordination, which makes it possible to increase efficiency levels by foregoing decoupling.

6. The systems approach is an essential tool in systems analysis. By identifying the system's boundary and interfaces, and by progressively identifying subsystems and their interfaces, we come to understand the operation of the whole system.

7. The systems approach indicates that systems should be built of functional modules organized into a hierarchical structure.

8. The use of decoupling in systems design leads to relatively autonomous software modules, and thus to systems that are easier to develop and maintain.

9. Organizational computing is becoming increasingly decentralized. The principles of systems theory should guide MIS professionals in preserving the desirable system properties of the overall informational portfolio. Standardized interfaces merit particular attention.

ENDNOTES

1. The founders of systems theory, from which the concepts presented here are drawn, were Alexander Bogdanov (major work published in 1913) and, in its present form, Ludwig von Bertalanffy (oral presentations in the 1930s and major works published in 1945 and 1950). The fundamental work by the latter is: Ludwig von Bertalanffy, *General System Theory: Foundations, Development, Applications*, New York:Braziller, 1968. The quest of these thinkers was for holistic principles of organization, particularly in living and social systems. Similar ideas offered in the context of the processes of communication and control were proposed in the late 1940s by Norbert Wiener under the name of cybernetics.

2. Efforts have been made to express the goodness of a system decomposition in formal terms, in order to be able to compare alternative decompositions (see, for example, Wand, 1990).

KEY TERMS AND
CONCEPTS

System
Subsystem
Physical system
Social system
Abstract system
System environment, boundary,
    inputs, outputs, objectives, and
    constraints
Systems approach
Suboptimization
Human-machine system
Natural system
Artificial system
Effectiveness
Efficiency

Deterministic system
Probabilistic system
Closed system
Relatively closed system
Open system
Negative entropy
Cohesion of subsystems
Decoupling
Open-loop system
Closed-loop system
Negative feedback
Feedforward
Double-loop learning
Law of requisite variety
Systems analysis

QUESTIONS

1. Define *system* and *subsystem.*

2. Differentiate between physical, social, and abstract systems. Give two examples of each.

3. What is the difference between the objectives of a system and the constraints on it?

4. What is the objective of the "black-box" approach to systems?

5. Determine the objectives of the following systems:

   a. A town library
   b. An accounts payable system
   c. The operating system of a computer

   What effectiveness and efficiency measures could be used to evaluate the performance of each system?

6. Define the boundaries of the following systems in terms of their interfaces with their environment (that is, their inputs and outputs):

   a. A student registration system for a university
   b. An information system for a police patrol car
   c. A project scheduling system

7. How are the systems approach and systems concepts used (or not used) in the following cases?
   a. The newly appointed head of a Human Resources department claims that all aspects of personnel information should be contained in a single large database under her control.

    b. The personal secretaries of middle managers in a certain corporation are being replaced by a word-processing pool.

    c. A manufacturing company requires that each of its workers develop at least three different skills; likewise, Lechmere, a Sarasota, Florida retail-store chain, offers its workers raises based on the number of jobs they learn to perform.

    d. Information systems professionals in many companies are expected to use a standard systems development and maintenance process.

    e. The standard systems development process requires that all applications systems be highly modular.

    f. A company creates a highly computerized (and expensive) warehouse management system, while at the same time moving to just-in-time production aiming at zero inventories.

8. Advertising revenues of television networks are to a large degree based on measurement of a network's share of the audience by Nielsen Media Research. "People meters" are installed in sample households to determine what programs people watch. Recently, Nielsen has demonstrated a computerized device that uses image recognition techniques and is able to determine precisely which members of the family watch a particular show.

    What principle is employed in this system which determines network revenues?

9. A simple Accounts Payable system enters vendor invoices into a pending-invoice file. In a daily run, it also issues checks against vendor invoices with the date preceding the cutoff date specified for the run. A voucher explaining the payment is included with each check. Show the structure of this system. (In other words, how would you decompose this system into modules?)

10. How can decoupling techniques be applied to a procedural system such as the development process for applications software?

11. Define *feedback loop* and *closed-loop systems.* Why is *negative* feedback important in our understanding of the role of management information systems?

12. What is the relationship between planning and control in an organization considered a closed-loop system?

13. What are the advantages and drawbacks of feedforward control as compared to feedback?

14. What does double-loop learning accomplish in an organization?

15. How would you keep the demands of the law of requisite variety to a minimum in a human-machine system for evaluating the progress of students in a university?

16. What are the advantages of progressive system decomposition during systems analysis? Compare these with the advantages of producing a hierarchical structure during systems design.

**ISSUES FOR
DISCUSSION**

1. Relate as many systems-theoretic concepts as you can to an organization such as a university.

2. What decoupling methods are used or can be used in the following?

    a. An electronic mail system as compared to a telephone communication system

    b. A computer-supported system for cooperative work (for developing a product design, for instance) as compared to the people physically working together on the same project

    c. A small start-up company that relies on meager human and financial resources

3. Your company has a single corporate MIS department. Heads of the company's subunits are clamoring for its dispersion into these subunits. *You* have to make a decision. Discuss the trade-offs in terms of integration and independence.

• •

**CASE
STUDY**

SERVICE BUREAUS AND LIGHTS-OUT DATA CENTERS

Recently, several large corporations have come back to the service-bureau concept used widely in the 1960s and 1970s. These companies aim to reduce their information processing expenses by using mainframes in data centers (erstwhile computer centers) run by specialized vendors of computer services. The movement is one facet of "outsourcing"—going to outside firms for information services previously furnished by the in-house MIS departments. The large databases of user companies are kept on the service vendors' computer systems. However, user companies continue to develop and maintain their own applications, which are run on the service vendors' machines and accessed remotely. Some firms go even further in their move to outsourcing by almost entirely dispensing with their own MIS personnel.

Outsourcing is widely used by companies in transition (involved in mergers, acquisitions, or buy-outs) or by those aiming to cut costs. For example, some of the companies sold by parent firms have turned to external providers of information services, instead of opening their own data centers.

Here are some explanations of this trend: "It's expensive to keep and maintain competent systems programmers," "We [information systems professionals employed by user companies] now spend all our time and energy on things that help bring profits to the bottom line, not just the day-to-day things to keep the data center alive," "[We want to] build more capital instead of sinking these resources into computers." Terry Babbit, vice-president of information systems for San Diego-based Foodmaker, a large operator of restaurant chains, explained the firm's use of Litton Computer Services for information processing by saying: "We consider Litton the computer experts, while we're the restaurant application experts." "Opportunities to get services delivered differently through strategic partnerships" with outsourcing vendors are stressed by Katherine Hudson of Eastman Kodak.

Some of the companies explain their move to outsourcing as a way to use application packages that run on large mainframes without acquiring these mainframes.

Surprisingly, in some firms, chief information officers are the leading proponents of buying information services outside the corporation. These managers do not see their role as primarily technological, they see information systems as a means to achieving the strategic objectives of the firm. Placing the business goals of the company above protecting their own bailiwick, these executives support layoffs of corporate data center employees. Other managers of corporate MIS attempt to compete with departmental computing by selling data-center services to corporate divisions on a competitive basis.

Companies that do not subscribe to the outsourcing concept also attempt to cut costs. This is done with software that automates data-center chores (such as job-scheduling systems or tape library systems) and helps increase the efficiency of operations. The latter is accomplished through performance monitors, which help optimize the use of hardware, and chargeback systems, through which MIS groups can accurately bill users for computer resources. In some companies this is considered a prelude to lights-out operation—the fully automated data centers of the future. Indeed, IBM's own MIS department has twelve lights-out data centers which are managed remotely over the company's worldwide SNA-based network.

Based in part on Clinton Wilder, "Back Rooms Moving out of IS House." *Computerworld,* May 29, 1989, pp. 1, 4; "More Companies Are Chucking Their Computers." *Business Week,* June 19, 1989, pp. 72–74. Also based on Bruce Caldwell, "Is Outsourcing a Good Move?" *MIS Week,* September 25, 1989, pp. 42–47; Patricia Cinelli, "Data Centers: Dropping Walls and Building New Identities." *Computerworld,* January 23, 1989, pp. 65–66; Katherine Hudson in "Conference Call." *CIO,* February 1991, p. 84; and Peter Krauss, "CIOs: New Breeds and Diehards." *InformationWeek,* March 25, 1991, p. 20.

Case Study Questions

1. Explain the outsourcing trend in systems-theoretic terms.

2. How does outsourcing relate to the pursuit of competitive advantage by user companies?

3. What choice in the integration-independence spectrum was made by the companies using service bureaus with respect to their information systems?

4. What are the possible risks of outsourcing? Consider, for example, what could happen to the core competencies of the corporations—the fundamental skills that lead to their competitiveness in the marketplace (Prahalad, 1990).

5. Using the terms of systems theory, compare two alternative cost-saving strategies: outsourcing and the automation of an in-house data center.

SELECTED REFERENCES

Ackoff, Russell L. "Towards a System of Systems Concepts." *Management Science,* 17, 11, July 1971, pp. 661–71.

Argyris, Chris. "Double-Loop Learning in Organizations." *Harvard Business Review,* September-October 1977, p. 115–25.

Baroudi, Jack J., and Orlikowski, Wanda, J. "A Short-Form Measure of User Information Satisfaction." *Journal of Management Information Systems,* 4, 4, Spring 1988, pp. 44–59.

Bertodo, R. "Implementing a Strategic Vision." *Long-Range Planning,* 23, 5, October 1990, pp. 22–30.

Churchman, C. West. *The Systems Approach.* Revised and updated ed. New York: Dell, 1979.

Eccles, Robert G. "The Performance Measurement Manifesto." *Harvard Business Review,* January-February 1991, pp. 131–37.

Galbraith, Jay R. *Organizational Design.* Reading, Mass.:Addison-Wesley, 1977.

Hurst, David K. "Of Boxes, Bubbles, and Effective Management." *Harvard Business Review,* 62, 3, May-June 1984, pp. 78–88.

Malone, Thomas W.; Yates, Joanne; and Benjamin, Robert I. "Electronic Markets and Electronic Hierarchies." *Communications of the ACM,* 30, 6, June 1987, pp. 484–504.

Nunamaker, Jay F., Jr., and others. "Crisis Planning Systems: Tools for Intelligent Action." *Journal of Management Information Systems,* 5, 4, Spring 1989, pp. 7–32.

Prahalad, C. K., and Hamel, Gary. "The Core Competences of the Corporation." *Harvard Business Review,* May-June 1990, pp. 79–91.

Wand, Yair, and Weber, Ron. "An Ontological Model of an Information System." *IEEE Transactions on Software Engineering,* 16, 11, November 1990, pp. 1282–92.

Weinberg, Gerald M. *An Introduction to General Systems Thinking.* New York: John Wiley & Sons, 1975.

Yates, Joanne, and Benjamin, Robert I. "The Past and Present as a Window on the Future." In *The Corporation of the 1990s: Information Technology and Organizational Transformation.* Edited by Michael S. Scott Morton. New York: Oxford University Press, 1991, pp. 61–92.

Zwass, Vladimir. "Software Engineering." In *The Handbook of Computers and Computing,* edited by Arthur H. Seidman and Ivan Flores. New York: Van Nostrand Reinhold, 1984, pp. 552–67.

CHAPTER 11

MANAGEMENT CONCEPTS. PLANNING AND CONTROLLING

If we could first know where we are,
and whither we are tending,
we could better judge what to do,
and how to do it.
  Abraham Lincoln

You can predict things only after they've happened.
  Eugene Ionesco

We know that management information systems support the management of organizations. Therefore, in order to understand what these systems actually need to accomplish, we have to analyze the functions of management. In this chapter, after introducing the various aspects of management theory, we shall concentrate on the management functions of planning and controlling, which today are to a large extent based on the use of MIS. In the next chapter, we shall see how two people-oriented functions of management—leading and organizing—shape organizations and can foster a dynamic, innovative environment.

FOCUS CASE

Air Products & Chemicals, a leading manufacturer of chemical products, dispersed their corporate MIS function to the company's business units after a long planning process. Budgetary control of the decentralized information system subunits was turned over to the heads of these business units.

This move closely mirrors the recent actions of many firms. They move major components of information systems out of the corporate headquarters and place them directly under end-user control, close to customers and products.

Based in part on Clinton Wilder, "Gaining Control by Dispersing IT." *Computerworld*, May 8, 1989. p. 80.

Management information systems are not only *tools* of organizational planning and control. As a major corporate function, MIS itself has to be planned and controlled, just as marketing or product development does.

What do people actually do when they "manage"? What are the managerial functions of planning and control? How do managers actually plan? How do they exercise control? These are the issues we will tackle in the present chapter.

CHAPTER OUTLINE

11.1 Management Theory

11.2 Management Functions

11.3 Concepts of Planning

11.4 Strategic Planning

11.5 Tactical and Operational Planning

11.6 How Do We Plan?

11.7 The Role of Information Systems in the Planning Process
- Plan Modeling
- Forecasting—Qualitative Techniques
- Forecasting—Quantitative Techniques

11.8 The Controlling Function of Management

11.9 Control through Performance Reports

11.10 Break-Even Analysis

. . . .

11.1 MANAGEMENT THEORY

We have defined **management** as the process of providing an organizational environment in which individuals work to contribute to the overall goals of the organization. The effective and efficient transformation of resources such as capital, labor, and information into profitably marketable products is the main objective of management in a business organization. But we should never forget that "management" mainly concerns people.

The systematic study of management has undergone a long evolution since the beginning of the twentieth century when it was initiated by the classical work of Frederick W. Taylor. The father of management theory was the French executive Henri Fayol, who in 1916 was the first to recognize what is known today as the fundamental principle of the *universality of management:* the idea that the same general management process applies to all kinds of organizations and to all levels within them. Far from being dogmatic, Fayol's early analysis allowed room within its general framework for the subsequent *contingency approach* to management problems: the idea of adopting solutions appropriate to particular situations as they arise in the practice of management. Several schools of management thought have emerged since. The most important contributions are briefly summarized in table 11.1.

Taylor's treatment of organizations as production systems (to use a more recent term) originated with his famous time-and-motion studies applied to physical tasks in steel mills. Performance standards, originally developed for physical jobs, have been generalized and broadly applied to the performance of company units—and thus to management performance. If you can measure it, then you can plan it and control it. The widespread use of measurable performance indicators in management lies at the foundation of using information systems for

TABLE 11.1

The Emergence of Management Thought

SCHOOL OF THOUGHT	NAMES OF CONTRIBUTORS AND PRINCIPAL DATES	CONTRIBUTION TO MANAGEMENT THEORY
Scientific Management	Frederick W. Taylor (1911) Henry L. Gantt Frank and Lillian Gilbreth	How to maximize productivity through efficient work by setting and controlling measurable performance standards. Understanding lower-level (supervisory) management.
Administrative Management	Henri Fayol (1916)	Recognition of management as a systematic discipline. Formulation of fourteen principles of management, such as division of work according to specialization, direct relationship of responsibility to authority, degree of centralization of authority based on the organizational contingency, and chain of authority within the organization. Enterprise activities classified into six functions; management is the one Fayol analyzed in depth.
Behavioral and Social System Approaches	Hugo Münsterberg (1913) Elton Mayo and Fritz Roethlisberger (1933) Chester Barnard (1938)	Recognition that organizational behavior of people must be studied using sociological (people in groups) and psychological (satisfaction of needs) approaches. An organization seen as a social system. Management perceived as maintenance of this cooperative social system, in which organizational objectives are achieved through interaction of motives, ideas, and actions of individuals.
Decision-Making Approach	Herbert Simon (1960)	Decision making as the fundamental managerial activity. Use of quantitative models to support decision making. Recognition that, in general, an individual makes decisions with bounded (limited) rationality; organizations should compensate for these individual limitations. Organizations should be structured to facilitate the decision-making process.

planning (setting goals to be achieved in some future period) and control (measuring the performance indicators actually achieved). However, as the case study for this chapter illustrates, this should not be interpreted to mean that if you can measure it, you *should* measure it.

"Management by figures" is not enough: planning and control are only two of several managerial functions. Fayol regarded management as consisting of five functions: planning, organizing, commanding, coordinating, and controlling. It is generally recognized today that coordination is an underlying characteristic of all management, so that management is now most often analyzed as the process of carrying out four functions: planning, controlling, leading (Fayol's "directing"), and organizing.

The view of organizations as pure production systems, in which human motivations and needs are of no major concern, was resoundingly refuted by the famous Hawthorne experiments, conducted by Elton Mayo and Fritz Roethlisberger from 1927 to 1932 at a Western Electric Company plant. In their attempts to establish a relationship between lighting (and other working conditions) and productivity, these researchers uncovered a puzzling effect: productivity went up whether the lighting was increased, decreased, or left unchanged. The workers responded in accordance with what is now known as the *Hawthorne effect*—they improved their performance because they were given attention. These studies led to the realization that successful management must rely not only on procedures and techniques, but on an understanding of individual motives and of social behavior in groups.

The sociotechnical approach to information system development, an endeavor to match information technology to the human needs of the workers affected, is a direct result of this early work.

As we discussed in chapter 2, the environment of the information society has led some theorists to consider decision making the pivotal organizational activity. Thus, Herbert Simon wrote, with the particular emphasis characteristic of that school of thought: "In the postindustrial society, the central problem is not how to organize to produce efficiently (although this will remain an important consideration), but how to organize to make decisions. . . ."[1]

We can now see that the apparently divergent approaches of theoreticians and practitioners have contributed to our understanding of the multiple facets of management and organizational design (though the influence of the various schools of thought may have ebbed and waned).

11.2 MANAGEMENT FUNCTIONS

The fundamental functions of management are planning, controlling, leading, and organizing. Here are brief descriptions of each of these functions:

Planning refers to establishing general goals and specific objectives for an enterprise or one of its units and selecting the actions the organization must take to achieve them. There is a hierarchy of planning levels, distinguished by the organizational level on which the plan is drawn up, the scope of the plan, its level of detail, and the planning horizon (time frame).

Controlling means measuring performance against established objectives and initiating corrective action in cases of divergence.

Leading is accomplished by inducing personnel throughout the organization to contribute to the goals of the enterprise.

Organizing involves establishing an organizational structure for performing the activities of an enterprise. The people responsible for carrying out planned activities must be provided with the necessary resources and authority and must understand how their efforts fit into the overall activities of the organization. Positions in the organizational structure must be filled, and human resources must be developed to ensure that the positions will continue to be filled effectively in the future as well. (These tasks, called *staffing*, are often treated as a separate managerial function.)

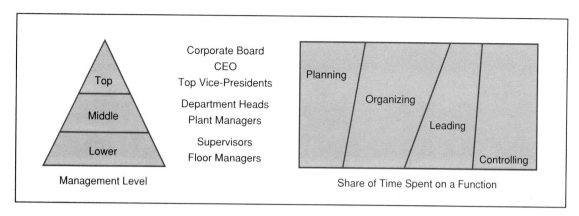

FIGURE 11.1

Relative time spent carrying out managerial functions.

(Right-hand side adapted from Mahoney, 1965)

The functions of planning and controlling, which receive the broadest and best established support from MIS, are discussed in the present chapter. Remember from the preceding chapter that these two functions implement the feedback control of an organization, considered as a closed-loop system. The leading and organizing functions of management will be discussed in the following chapter, where we shall concern ourselves with the functioning and structuring of organizations.

The relative time devoted to various managerial functions on each of the three levels of organizational structure is shown in figure 11.1. As you can see, the higher levels of management devote more attention to planning and organizing, while middle and lower managers spend more time leading and controlling.

Our analysis of the management process is based on the consideration of managerial functions—a well-established approach stemming from Fayol's work. Certain scholars, on the other hand, have studied what managers actually do by following in detail their daily activities. These researchers have interpreted these daily activities as the manager's intermittent assumption of one of several roles. The study of managerial roles, further discussed in chapter 13, is important because we concentrate on the manager as an individual: we are concerned with properly supporting managers with information systems for their work. However, I believe that there is no fundamental contradiction between the function and the role approaches to management: as managers take on various roles, they perform the organizational functions of planning, controlling, leading, and organizing. Let us now discuss the planning and controlling functions in greater detail.

11.3 CONCEPTS OF PLANNING

Planning is the primary management function: it is the process of setting objectives for the future and laying out actions necessary to reach these objectives. As we know from the preceding chapter, plans make the standards that underlie the function of managerial control. Through planning and control, an organization attempts to reduce uncertainty in its response to future events. The future always has the potential to surprise; the flexibility of MIS-based planning

FIGURE 11.2

Intent of a plan.

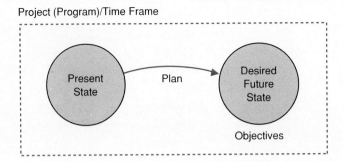

and control enables an organization to respond promptly to surprises by quickly detecting the need for a change and planning a response.

Management information systems today are broadly used to plan; the MIS function itself is planned in accordance with the concepts presented here. Moreover, MIS plans have to be aligned with the overall plans of an enterprise: information systems have to support organizational objectives. Particularly if they play a strategic role, information systems may be key to achieving these objectives.

A **plan** is a specific statement of objectives and of the means by which a firm aims to achieve them. The process of planning is arduous but very important in itself for coordinating the activities of an enterprise. As we plan, we learn what resources we already have, what goals we are reaching for, and what additional resources and actions we will need to reach these goals. This is why some consider the planning process to be even more important than the plans themselves. As figure 11.2 shows, a plan is a bridge between the current state of affairs and a desired future state.

Note that a statement such as: "The Global Universal Corporation is committed to providing exceptional service to all clients at all times" is a *mission statement* rather than a specific objective. It is a broad statement of purpose for the organization, important for leadership purposes as a focus for the employees' activities. When a mission statement is made more specific, for example, "The Global Universal Corporation shall ensure that customer orders and queries will be handled within two minutes around the clock," it becomes a specific statement of objectives. But is still does not specify how this level of service will be reached or maintained—it is still not a plan.

Specific statements of objectives for corporate information systems are especially important as information technologies help enterprises gain a competitive position in the marketplace (Davenport, 1989). For example, a statement such as "Computing software and hardware should facilitate global consistency of information throughout the company" may in turn facilitate the globalization of the company's business activities by making it possible to penetrate new markets and control activities in various parts of the globe.

Many plans are financial: they lay out the expenditures necessary to bring about a desired end. However, businesses also form personnel plans dealing with human resources, production plans specifying the output of an enterprise in physical terms, and other types of plans.

TABLE 11.2 Levels of Planning Activities	MANAGEMENT LEVEL	PLANNING SCOPE	TIME HORIZON	PLANNING ACTIVITIES
	Top (corporate board, CEO, top vice-presidents)	Strategic (entire organization or business unit)	Long-term (three years or more; sometimes ten or more years)	Overall business directions set. Market segments and competitive strategies identified.
	Middle (department or plant managers)	Tactical (subsystem of business unit)	Medium-term (one to three years)	Acquisition and allocation of resources for projects furthering the objectives stated in strategic plans. Capital expenditures and resources planned through budgets.
	Lower (supervisors)	Operational (work unit)	Short-term (one to twelve months)	Allocation of resources within the available facilities (production scheduling, cash-on-hand planning, and so forth). Detailed budgets and schedules.

All managers plan—some explicitly, others less so. The degree to which planning is formalized is an element of the organizational culture. A formal plan, stated in measurable terms, provides a blueprint for future activities and serves as a benchmark against which outcomes can be compared.

The levels of planning are summarized in table 11.2, which shows, of course, the most common practices; thus, for example, flexible management may frequently deviate from the time frames shown.

In addition to plans, organizations employ *standing-use policies,* which are guidelines for decision making and action under a variety of circumstances. For example, as the result of a well-known emergency situation in the mid-1980s, the White House has a Contingency Plan for the Transfer of Presidential Authority.

11.4 STRATEGIC PLANNING

Business organizations in the United States are often faulted for not taking a long view of their goals and of the means required to accomplish them. The purpose of **strategic planning** is to develop such long-term objectives for the entire organization and for its major business units, and to specify general strategies for the acquisition of the resources needed to accomplish these objectives. It has been stressed (Hamel, 1989) that to succeed in a globally competitive marketplace, a company has to enunciate a "strategic intent"—a focused and challenging long-term objective to which all its plans and actions will conform.

Strategic planning establishes broad, long-term objectives for an enterprise and assesses the company's current position relative to these objectives, considering, in particular, the opportunities and threats presented by the environment. It then proceeds to consider alternative strategies for reaching the objectives in the foreseen competitive environment, building on the comparative advantages the firm enjoys. Finally, strategic planning outlines the organizational structure and total resources needed to implement the plan, and plans for the implementation process.

Strategies for seeking competitive advantage through information technology (which we presented in Section 5.3 and summarized as the strategic cube in figure 5.3) represent some of the options available in the strategic planning process. The means to accomplish these strategic objectives are then identified through an analysis of the company's value chain, also discussed in chapter 5.

Obviously, strategic planning can not be done in a vacuum; it must include careful consideration of the competitive environment. *Environmental scanning* (or boundary spanning) is vital to the planning process. The crucial aspect of this scanning is monitoring the competition. Much information regarding a company's competitors is contained in the publicly available reports the firms file with various government agencies, such as the Securities and Exchange Commission (SEC), in the annual reports to stockholders, and in press reports. However, a much broader array of targeted information is available through information brokers.

One of the largest electronic information services, Dialog (from Dialog Information Services of Palo Alto, California) offers computerized access to a variety of competitive intelligence databases, including extracts from SEC filings, annual reports, patent information, and even extensive profiles of top executives. Using Dialog, you can obtain information from such business reference sources as Dun & Bradstreet, Standard & Poor's, and Moody's without selecting a database—the system does this automatically, according to the type of information the user requests. Hundreds of databases can also be accessed from such electronic information services as CompuServe Information Service, The Source, and Dow Jones News/Retrieval. A list of electronic information services appears in chapter 16.

Other providers of business information include firms such as Find/SVP (of New York), which undertakes the study of business topics (again, largely through access to a variety of databases), or from firms specializing in the analysis of various industry and market segments. A. C. Nielsen Co. provides its subscribers with a variety of retail-level data that can be used to spot a trend or assess a potential market share for a projected product. Chase Econometrics offers extensive databases as well as the use of planning software.

Your company's sales force and your customers are an immensely important source of competitive information. A study of product innovations in one industry (Pascale, 1981) found that 80 percent of the innovations were initiated due to customer inquiries and complaints. Information from all these sources needs to be integrated and made available on-line to the corporate planners. Text, data, and images may have to be included. Corporate MIS have a vital role to play in the process of gathering information on a firm's competitors, as the vignette on competitor-intelligence units demonstrates.

MIS SUPPORT FOR COMPETITOR-INTELLIGENCE UNITS

Global competition in the information society requires constant scanning of the external environment of an organization. In plain words: what you don't know *can* hurt you. Several companies have gradually created sophisticated, MIS-based competitor-intelligence units that continually watch their markets.

Successful competitor-intelligence systems usually evolve from a small prototype residing on a personal workstation; they are moved to larger systems as they grow.

For example, Motorola has a database of competitive information located on a mainframe and constantly maintained from a variety of sources. Keyword-based retrieval is done with the Inquire/Text text management system (from Infodata Systems). The database is accessible to 5,000 users worldwide over an electronic mail network.

AT&T issues a newsletter of competitor intelligence over its electronic mail system. Commentary from the company's in-house experts—who can be identified through an extensive computerized directory—is appended to the newsletter.

An innovative approach to environmental scanning is offered by Gregg Elofson of the University of Miami and Benn Konsynski of Harvard University. They have developed a prototype of an artificial-intelligence-based system called Knowledge Cache (Elofson, 1991). Relying on expert system technology, this system includes a number of software "apprentices," each of which "specializes" in a particular area (say, a chip manufacturing technique or the political situation in the European Community). As events relevant to the company's competitive position develop, an intelligence analyst enters them into the apprentice's knowledge base and the apprentice gathers (via electronic mail) assessments of this information by area specialists into its knowledge base as well. Ultimately, the organizational memory embodied in the knowledge bases of the various apprentices would make it possible to apply to a problem or opportunity a variety of experience and expertise accumulated over time.

Since management information systems have become strategic weapons wielded by many a firm, an analysis of a competitor's *information system* may lead to broader conclusions about that company's business strategy. This has been borne out by my own experience: in recent years, the organizations which I served as a consultant or with which I am familiar through other professional contacts have become extremely careful about releasing information regarding their information systems.

Based in part on Mitch Betts, "Snoopers see MIS as Dr. No." *Computerworld*, February 20, 1989, pp. 1, 113; Mark Robichaux, " 'Competitor Intelligence': a Grapevine to Rivals' Secrets." *The Wall Street Journal*, April 12, 1989, p. B2; and (Elofson, 1991).

The MIS unit of an organization should have its own strategic plan aligned with the overall company plan. The MIS-unit plan, a formal document, should be drawn up for several years ahead and should include, as described in part by Ephram McLean and John Soden (McLean, 1977):

1. A statement of objectives

2. Projection of the future MIS environment

3. Projection of the future user environment

4. Projection of the future industry environment

5. Definition and evaluation of strategic alternatives in relationship to the organization's strategic plan and selection of the preferred alternative

6. A general MIS portfolio plan

7. Infrastructure (computer and telecommunications) plan

8. A personnel plan

9. A plan for organizational structure of MIS department

10. A financial plan

11. A plan for the implementation of the strategic plan

According to a survey of 1,200 companies by The Eastern Management Group,[2] 67 percent of the companies develop MIS plans for two to four years into the future, 30 percent for five to ten years, and those remaining plan only one year ahead. We shall return to the topic of strategic planning for MIS in chapter 17.

To coordinate (or align) MIS plans with corporate strategic plans, one needs to identify and prioritize information projects that support the organizational objectives and develop these projects within the time and financial constraints set down by tactical and organizational corporate plans (Lederer, 1989).

Preservation of flexibility—the ability to change the plan in response to a changing environment—is an important concern in strategic planning, in which horizons often extend far into the future. Frequent corporate restructuring and rapidly advancing technology demand this flexibility. This is illustrated in the case study for this part of the book.

11.5 TACTICAL AND OPERATIONAL PLANNING

As we made clear earlier, long-term strategic plans are broken down into medium-term tactical plans, which, in turn, are refined into short-term operational plans. A longer-term plan establishes the end or, as some call it, the action framework, within which shorter-term plans are drawn up. This expansion of longer-term plans into more detailed, shorter-term objectives is known as the *cascade effect* in the planning process. Precise horizons for tactical and operational planning differ from one organization to another. As we said, the propensity to plan is one of the significant attributes of an organizational culture. Annual tactical-level plans, subject to review every quarter, are quite common. Several types of tactical and operational plans may be developed, depending on the number of management levels in the organization.

Let us continue our example of MIS planning. During the tactical planning process for MIS, acquisition of hardware and telecommunications equipment and services and acquisition and/or development of the software portfolio components are prioritized and laid out in detail. Detailed scheduling and budgeting are done on the level of operational planning. We shall further discuss specific techniques of MIS planning in Part 5.

FIGURE 11.3

A flexible budget produced
with a spreadsheet program.

General Development Corporation			
Monthly Sales Volume for March 1995 (in thousands of dollars)			
$100	$120	$140	$160
Expense Items			
Materials	$40	$48	$56	$62
Labor	$15	$18	$21	$24
Overhead	$8	$9	$10	$11
Production Costs	$63	$75	$87	$97
Research and Development	$5	$5	$5	$5
Engineering	$1	$1	$1	$1
Marketing and Sales	$15	$16	$18	$20
Administration	$10	$10	$10	$10
Nonproduction Costs	$31	$32	$34	$36
Total Costs	$94	$107	$121	$133
Profit	$6	$13	$19	$27
Profit/Sales Ratio	6.0%	10.8%	13.6%	16.9%

Budgets are a powerful means of expressing plans on tactical and operational levels. A **budget** specifies the resources committed to a plan for a given project or time period. For example, a tactical-level sales budget would specify expected revenues from sales for the year ahead, as well as the expenditures needed to make the sales. A budget is usually stated in monetary terms (a "dollarized" plan), though sometimes budgeting is expressed in other numerical terms such as units of product or labor-hours.

Budgets provide a powerful means of control. In the systems-theoretic view, they serve as the standard, presented in figure 10.10, we can compare the actual results against by using MIS.

Fixed budgets are independent of the level of activity of the unit for which the budget is drawn up. *Flexible budgets* commit resources depending on the level of activity: for example, the sales activity envisaged by a plan may be classified into three categories, depending on the success of the product; and, contingent on this activity, three budget levels may be drawn up.

Spreadsheet programs are the main budgeting tool—and budgeting is what made spreadsheets the leading end-user software tools they are today. An example of a flexible budget for a small company, obtained with a popular spreadsheet program is shown in figure 11.3. Here, costs are budgeted for four possible levels of sales.

New budgets have traditionally been drawn up on the basis of similar budgets for the preceding time period, with necessary changes introduced. This is an efficient technique for areas and projects which change little from one time period to the next. In contrast, *zero-based budgeting* is a technique particularly useful for an area that undergoes rapid change. Under this scheme, all activities within the area compete anew for the resources to be allocated under the plan—nothing is taken for granted simply because "we have always done it this way." With the zero-based technique, promising new projects have a greater chance to be funded.

11.6 HOW DO WE PLAN?

Planning is a problem-solving activity—perhaps the most challenging among the management functions. The steps of the planning process are shown in figure 11.4. As we shall see in the next chapter, the planning process is an expansion of a general scheme for problem solving (or decision making).

We shall see in chapter 14 that decision support systems (DSS) are the most appropriate type of MIS for planning. As a matter of fact, it is since the development of systems of this type (most of which are implemented with spreadsheets) that MIS have extended their orientation from the past and present to include planning for the future.

FIGURE 11.4

Steps of the planning process.

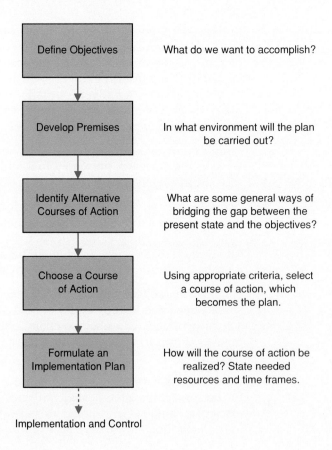

| Define Objectives | What do we want to accomplish? |

| Develop Premises | In what environment will the plan be carried out? |

| Identify Alternative Courses of Action | What are some general ways of bridging the gap between the present state and the objectives? |

| Choose a Course of Action | Using appropriate criteria, select a course of action, which becomes the plan. |

| Formulate an Implementation Plan | How will the course of action be realized? State needed resources and time frames. |

Implementation and Control

What are the mechanics of planning in organizational terms? Where does the process begin? In *top-down planning*, the planning process starts with senior management (or their planning staffs) and then extends to ever lower levels of management, which plan within the frameworks passed down to them: plans "cascade downward." *Bottom-up planning* starts with operational (line) management and plans are progressively consolidated as they move upward to the top.

Top-down planning risks missing or ignoring what's really going on in the trenches. Pure bottom-up planning, while accompanied by a strong sense of commitment on the part of the line managers who actually draw up the budgets, may ultimately lead to a plan that is not aligned with the strategic objectives of the business unit. A middle ground is needed. The planning process must begin with clear objectives set out by top management and then consider independent input from other levels of management—in particular, from operational managers.

The widespread use of personal computers now permits several iterations during a budget development cycle. As a consequence, budgets can be refined on the basis of input from managers at various levels of an organization.

11.7 THE ROLE OF INFORMATION SYSTEMS IN THE PLANNING PROCESS

Management information systems make internal and external data available to those involved in the planning process. In particular, transaction processing systems create extensive databases of corporate data. Earlier in this chapter, we discussed how the process of environmental scanning is supported by access to external databases, often combined with the company's own databases on its business environment.

In conceptual terms, information systems support two principal parts of the planning process. The first is the development of plan premises ("premising") through forecasting of sales and other planning factors (for example, costs). The other is the identification and comparison of alternative courses of action through the development and use of planning models; we call this process "plan modeling." These nodal areas of MIS support are shown in figure 11.5.

A variety of software tools support the planning process. They include specific DSS and DSS generators (for example, IFPS), which serve to develop a specific DSS. A spreadsheet program frequently serves as a tool for developing a specific DSS, instead of a more elaborate DSS generator. We shall further discuss these tools in chapter 14.

We will now consider modeling and see how it generates the need to forecast. We shall then discuss qualitative and quantitative forecasting techniques.

FIGURE 11.5

Principal areas of MIS
support of planning.

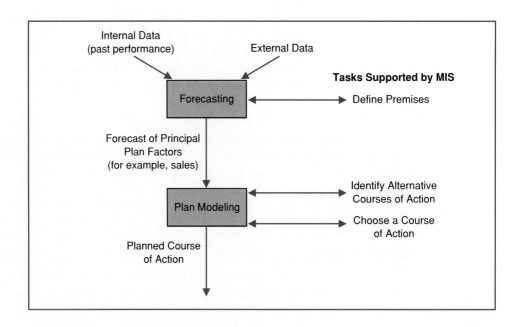

Plan Modeling

A **model** is a representation of something else, developed for a specific purpose. It is usually an abstraction or a simplification of the phenomenon being modeled.

Financial plans rely on *planning models,* which show the dependence of projected financial results on the values of input variables. These planned financial results generally represent such measures of performance as profit and market share, expressed through a variety of indicators. A typical input variable projected by forecasting is sales volume.

Financial plans obtained with these models include a statement of projected profit or loss for a given time period (which is called an income statement) and a projection of company assets and liabilities at the end of that period (called a balance sheet). These projections are prepared in the same fashion as accounting reports on actual performance; the projections are called *pro forma statements* to distinguish them from actual results.

A rather simple planning model, close to what you would actually specify using one of the DSS generators, follows. This is a model for obtaining a pro forma annual income statement.

sales volume = input variable
selling price = 1.10 * previous year selling price
sales = sales volume * selling price
unit cost = 0.50 * selling price
variable cost = sales volume * unit cost
overhead = 0.20 * variable cost
cost of goods sold = variable cost + overhead
gross margin = sales − cost of goods sold
operating expense = 0.25 * sales
net income before tax = gross margin − operating expense
tax = 0.42 * net income before tax
net income = net income before tax − tax

The following pro forma income statement was obtained with this model under the assumption that the sales volume will be 100,000 units (the selling price during the previous year was $10).

CONSOLIDATED SMALL COMPANY PRO FORMA INCOME STATEMENT FOR YEAR 1995

Sales	$1,100,000
Cost of goods sold	$660,000
Gross margin	$440,000
Operating expense	$275,000
Net income before tax	$165,000
Tax	$69,300
Net income	$95,700

As we can see, a model is built using a variety of assumptions (premises) about the dependence between its variables. By considering various alternatives ("what ifs"), we can vary these premises and compare the outcomes. For example, what if we choose a higher selling price? What if the tax rate increases?

Pro forma statements are only one example of what we may want to produce with a planning model. Such models also produce a variety of projected indicators of performance (financial ratios) that will help assess how well the company plan is being executed. Since this assessment is the essence of the controlling process, we will present the best known of these ratios—return on investment—and a model used to obtain it later in the chapter, when we discuss controlling.

Note that, typically, sales volume is an input variable. Where does this value come from? This is where forecasting comes in.

Forecasting— Qualitative Techniques

In our context, **forecasting** is the process of predicting future outcomes to serve as inputs in the development of plans. Indeed, the sales forecast—the prediction of expected sales, most often the product of sales volume times price—usually drives the planning process.

Forecasting—because its very nature involves looking into the future—is an area where any quantitative methods employed must be tempered with human insight and experience.

The external data used in forecasting are precisely the environmental data gathered by scanning the environment of an organization and discussed in the vignette on competitive intelligence. A variety of commercially available databases (sometimes called data banks) may be accessed. Internal data are marshaled from the company's databases. These data are more accessible if the company has adopted the information resource management (IRM) approach to MIS.

Qualitative techniques are generally used for *environmental forecasting*: an attempt to predict the social, economic, legal, and technological environment in which the company will attempt to realize its plans. A group technique frequently used for various aspects of environmental forecasting is the **Delphi technique.** This qualitative technique, named after the ancient Greek oracle, was developed at the RAND Corporation for marshaling broad expert opinion. The use of Delphi technique usually involves the following steps (although variations abound):

1. A panel of experts is selected.

2. The empaneled experts respond anonymously to a questionnaire regarding the subject of the forecast.

3. The following steps are repeated until the opinions of the experts converge on a consensus forecast (or reasons for a lack of consensus emerge and additional information is sought):

   - The responses of all experts are analyzed and the summarized responses are distributed back to the expert members of the panel. Sometimes new questions emerge.
   - The experts are given these summaries and are invited to reconsider their opinions in the light of the opinions of others. Their responses are again anonymous.

The anonymity of the Delphi process is designed to minimize peer pressure to reach an answer quickly. Rather, it is hoped that successive runs of the process will bring new information to the surface which can be brought to bear on the problem. The entire Delphi process can be conducted promptly and efficiently through various types of electronic meeting systems, which we shall discuss in chapter 16.

Another oft-employed qualitative forecasting technique is **scenario analysis.** Each scenario in this process is a plausible future environment in which the plan will have to operate. Royal Dutch/Shell, an oil company renowned for its preparedness when unfavorable market conditions occur, works out two to four scenarios, each reflecting a plausible combination of favorable and unfavorable future circumstances (Wack, 1985). A decision that should stand up under two or three such future scenarios is favored. Decision support systems may be used to develop models for the scenarios.

Forecasting—Quantitative Techniques

Quantitative forecasting techniques are used to estimate input variables, such as future sales volume, for a planning model. The more important quantitative techniques are:

Extrapolation through Statistical Regression Analysis
   Extrapolating means extending past and present trends into the future. In some cases, a future outcome that needs to be forecast appears to be related to some earlier known fact (we then call this fact a "leading indicator"). The future outcome may then be forecast from the known value of the leading indicator. Statistical techniques of regression analysis help us establish a relationship between what we are trying to forecast and the leading indicator, based on the past experience. Let us say that our company manufactures computer games sold to younger teenagers. If we know the percentage of teenagers who buy our game now and we also

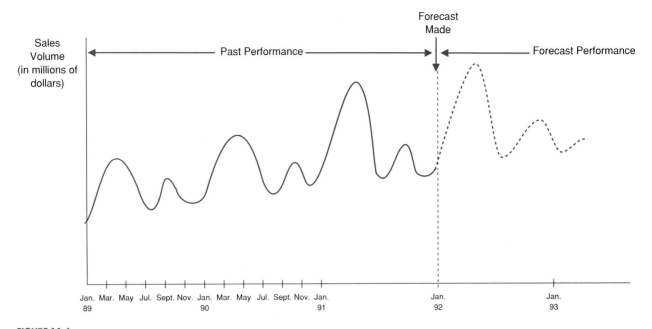

FIGURE 11.6

Sales volume forecast obtained with a time-series analysis.

know the number of children now entering first grade (the leading indicator), we can estimate our sales volume several years ahead. (This example also points out how treacherous such an estimation may be: will teenagers be interested in the same types of computer games several years from now? More likely, we shall have to innovate and introduce new products to keep our share of the market.)

If company sales can be correlated with a broad national index, such as disposable income or gross national product (GNP), then the nationally known forecasts of that indicator may be employed to forecast our sales volume.

2. Extrapolation of Trends and Cycles through a Time-Series Analysis

Many phenomena are cyclic, with the cycles repeating themselves over periods of a few years as well as seasonally. If the sales growth rate can be charted in this fashion, we can extend such a chart into the future.

Figure 11.6 shows how a computerized projection for the coming year has been made considering a time series for several years preceding. The time series for the earlier years shows both an upward trend and seasonal cycles.

3. Econometric Simulation Modeling

Forecasting may rely on the use of elaborate simulation models that express an understanding of mutual interrelationships between a number of factors. As opposed to the two prior techniques, these models actually explain the processes involved. Many large organizations have models that estimate future demand for their products or services (as well as other factors, such as costs) in relationship to several national economic indicators. These indicators may include the prime lending rate, GNP, or the volume of real estate loans. The last factor is a leading indicator of the national economy, which means that its level predicts economic activity in future periods.

11.8 THE CONTROLLING FUNCTION OF MANAGEMENT

We saw the process of managerial controlling in action in the case study for chapter 1. There, the company board was using an executive information system (EIS) to find discrepancies between planned company performance and actual current results. We also saw that the projections (forecasts) of future performance made by the EIS differed from the performance planned for these future periods.

In chapter 10, we established that MIS plays a crucial role in controlling managerial operation of an enterprise. Figure 10.10 shows that an organization may be considered a closed-loop system, in which the MIS control subsystems provide a means for comparing the standards set by the plans and the company's actual performance.

It has been established that, in accord with Harold Leavitt's and Thomas Whisler's 1958 predictions (Leavitt, 1958), MIS has given senior management the ability to control the operation of an enterprise to a great degree without the need for extensive middle-management layers. As pointed out by Lynda Applegate and her colleagues of the Harvard Business School (Applegate, 1988), this enhanced top-level control is compatible with decentralized decision making: if the top managers can easily monitor performance throughout the company, they can give line managers broader decision-making latitude.

Indeed, strategic control is vital in a decentralized firm (Goold, 1991). Top managers must monitor the progress toward the strategic objectives set out in long-term plans (such as achieving a given market share by a certain year). In doing so, some firms employ formal control processes with specific milestones for achieving certain performance targets; these processes include periodic strategy reviews for each business line, annual strategic control reporting, and tracking of strategic projects. Others—actually, a majority—rely on informal processes for developing a shared understanding of priorities.

In the following sections, we shall consider some of the principal techniques of management control. As we shall see, these tools serve a variety of control purposes. Performance reports evaluate the performances of individual managers and of their areas of responsibility. A project can be tracked with the help of break-even analysis. Financial ratios are employed to compare the performance of a business unit, or of the entire company, with the performances of other firms in the same business segment.

11.9 CONTROL THROUGH PERFORMANCE REPORTS

Budgets, which are statements of plans in financial terms, serve as the standards against which control is exercised. The manager of a work unit is responsible for carrying out planned activities without exceeding the resources allocated in the budget.

A **performance report** states the actual financial results achieved by the manager and compares them with the planned results by pointing out *variances*—differences between planned (budgeted) and actual results. A performance report should include only the items the manager can control. This is an implementation of the concept of **responsibility reporting.** Thus, a hierarchy of performance reports arises, paralleling the cascade effect in the hierarchy of plans. Figure 11.7 shows such a hierarchy: it includes the performance reports of top management, of two middle-level managers, and of a lower-level manager. Note that the hierarchy of performance reports reflects the firm's organizational structure.

Performance reports are used to monitor the plans of the corresponding level. This monitoring may be done through a management reporting system; the reports in figure 11.7 were obtained through a system of that type. Senior managers increasingly use executive information systems to monitor plans. The dynamics of plan monitoring were presented in the case study for chapter 1 of this text.

11.10 BREAK-EVEN ANALYSIS

Break-even analysis compares the revenue from the sales of a product or service with the costs incurred in producing it. This analysis may be used for a number of purposes—establishing product price, for example. When used for control purposes, break-even analysis helps managers to decide whether the project is successful or whether it should be discontinued.

The *break-even point* is the number of product or service units that must be sold for the firm to break even—in other words, to cover its costs. Total costs consist of fixed costs, which remain constant regardless of the level of production (such as lease payments, for example), and variable costs, which vary with the number

FIGURE 11.7

A hierarchy of performance reports—means of control.

(From Cushing, 1987, p. 51)

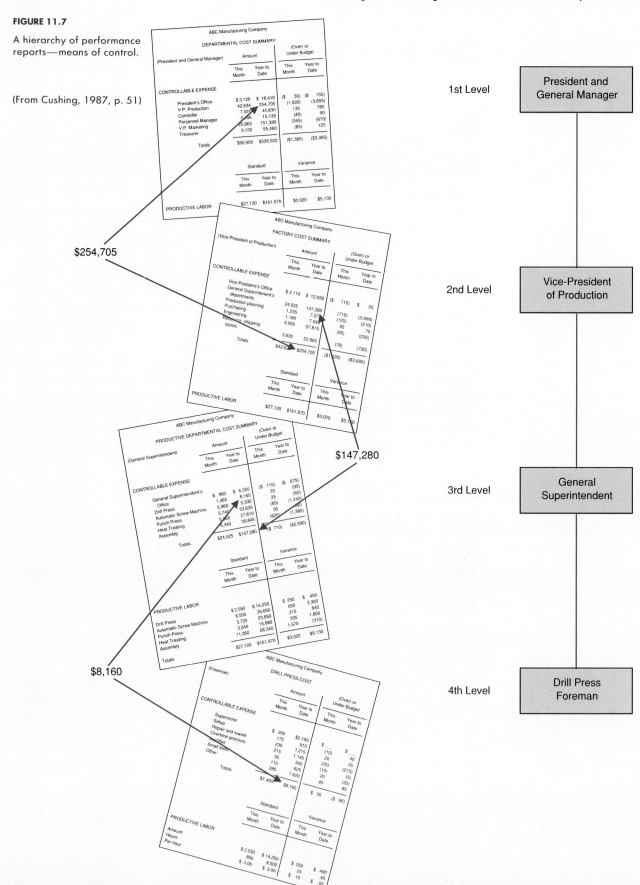

FIGURE 11.8

A chart for break-even analysis.

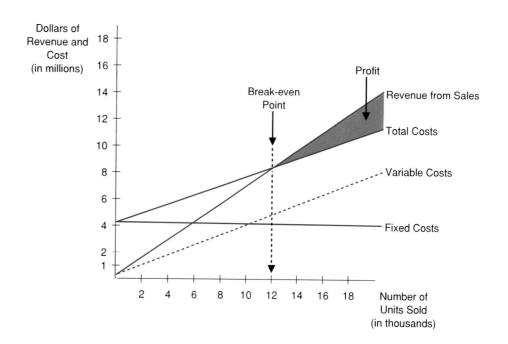

of units produced (for example, the cost of raw materials). Selling more units than the break-even point will produce profit; selling fewer units will result in a loss. The formula for the break-even point is:

$$\text{Break-Even Point (in units)} = \frac{\text{Fixed Costs}}{\text{Selling Price of Unit} - \text{Variable Cost per Unit}}$$

Break-even analysis for a product is shown graphically in figure 11.8. Straight-line variable costs have been assumed; that is, we are assuming that each additional unit of the product costs the same as any other.

In the case shown in figure 11.8, we have to sell at least 12,000 units of the product in order to break even. If sales surpassing this quantity seem unlikely, the project should be abandoned. That is, it should be abandoned unless other factors, such as product price or costs, can be changed.

Another way to conduct break-even analysis is to replace the "units" along the horizontal axis of the break-even chart with "time." We can then learn, assuming a given sales volume, how long will it take us to achieve profitability.

In the information society, speed is often the decisive factor. Because of heightened competition, products have short life cycles—there are many competing innovators and it is necessary to bring an idea to market quickly. Therefore, the break-even control approach that relies on shortening the time during which the new product or service will become profitable often takes precedence over budgetary control (making sure that projected development costs are not exceeded). The vignette discussing speed as a factor in developing competitive advantage shows how the break-even approach is often applied by a company ranked as the most admired in its industry.

SPEED AS COMPETITIVE ADVANTAGE: HALVE THE BREAK-EVEN TIME!

John Young, the chief executive officer of a leading computer manufacturer Hewlett-Packard, has articulated a mission: he wants the company to cut the break-even time for new products in half. Indeed, the company was able to cut the development time of a new type of printer, the first near-laser-quality DeskJet, to 22 months instead of the 4.5 years it used to take to develop comparable products.

Several information-system-based techniques have been employed to reach this impressive result. Using networking facilities, engineers working on a design problem send queries to the Hewlett-Packard plants around the world, assembling, as it were, an instant "invisible college" of experts to crack the problem. The same network has access to a database of parts which the company knows from its experience are reliable and cheap.

An expert system analyzes each new design and recommends changes which would make the product easier to manufacture—by using fewer, more reliable parts which can be assembled in a simpler fashion (for example, by snapping rather than screwing them together). Over a period of three years, this approach has cut the manufacturing time on thirty products by 80 percent and lowered the failure rate by 84 percent.

An organizational approach geared to speed is bringing people from various divisions of the company to work together on a project as a team. "People find speed exciting," says Young.

Based on Brian Dumaine, "How Managers Can Succeed through Speed." *Fortune*, February 13, 1989, pp. 54–59.

11.11 FINANCIAL RATIOS

Planned financial projections for a firm or its unit enable us to calculate a number of financial ratios that can be further tracked as a part of the control process. These ratios indicate performance of the business unit. A widely employed financial ratio, introduced by Du Pont in 1919, is *return on investment (ROI)*. ROI shows how well a business unit uses the resources allocated to it in the plan by relating the earnings of the business unit to its total assets. The computation of the ROI indicator is shown in figure 11.9. This computation is known as the Du Pont model.

You will find that

$$ROI = \frac{Earnings}{Total\ investment}$$

The ROI measure for a given project is compared to the minimum established by the company. It should be stressed that rigid application of the ROI measure may stifle innovation. Thus, if a company has an established floor for ROI (a

FIGURE 11.9

The DuPont model: computation of return on investment.

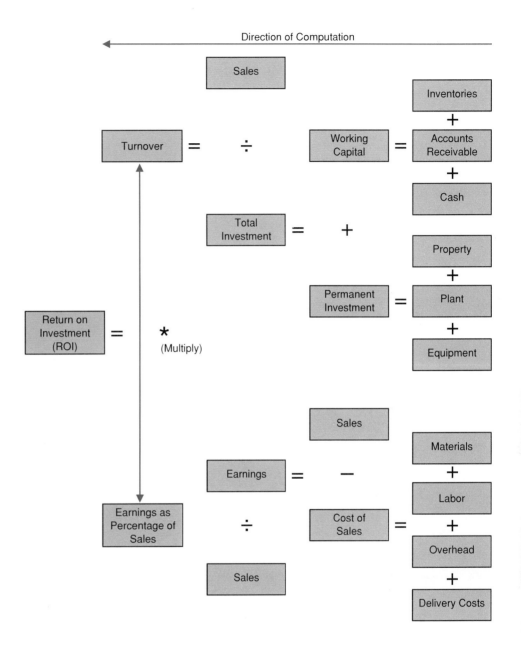

Direction of Computation

"hurdle rate") such as 20 percent, for example, it may forego developing a promising product that does not, *according to currently available information,* offer an equal or higher ROI. As discussed in the next section, innovative companies are prepared to assume more risk and suspend using the ROI indicator for a certain period with respect to a promising project.

A number of other ratios are available to establish both the current performance and the overall financial fitness of an enterprise or one of its business units. By continually monitoring a variety of ratios and performance indicators (for example, sales per employee), managers can control the operations of their units. Workstation-oriented software can assist in the task, as discussed in the next vignette.

SOFTWARE THAT HELPS YOU TO SEE THE FOREST AS WELL AS THE TREES

The Forest and Trees program (from Channel Computing, Newmarket, New Hampshire) permits the manager to define on the screen a "dashboard" of indicators based on the data stored in various databases. A cell in this dashboard (shown in figure 11. 10) may have notes or graphs associated with it. The historical value of an indicator may be stored in a file and also associated with a certain cell.

A user sets intervals at which the system automatically accesses the appropriate databases and updates the value of the indicators (such as at 5:00 p.m. daily, or on the first day of each month) for the display.

In addition, audible or visible (color) alarms may be associated with defined levels of indicators, with the system alerting the user to out-of-range values.

Such software offers users many of the control capabilities of an executive information system at a modest cost. The user is able to employ her own "vital-sign" factors, through which she may control the enterprise unit.

Based on Press/Analyst Background Information, Channel Computing, Inc., June, 1989; John Walkenbach, "Forest and Trees Makes Data Accessible to Executives." *InfoWorld*, July 2, 1990, pp. 61–64; and Michael J. Miller, "Forest and Trees Gathers Information from Numerous Sources." *InfoWorld*, January 28, 1991, p. 74.

FIGURE 11.10

Dashboard of control indicators—a screen of Forest & Trees.

(Copyright © Channel Computing, Inc., Newmarket NH, USA. Reprinted by permission.)

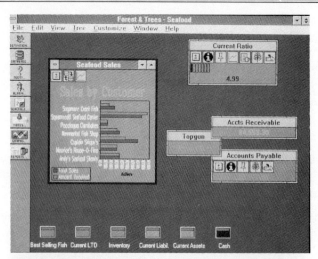

SUMMARY

Management theory was formed by the contributions of several schools of thought, each of which ascribed primary importance to a different aspect of the management process. It is fruitful to consider this process as entailing four functions: planning, controlling, leading, and organizing.

The two management functions most broadly supported by MIS are planning and controlling. Planning sets out objectives for the future and actions needed to bring them about. The three levels of planning include long-term vision for a company's future, embodied in strategic plans; tactical planning, which relies on the budgeting process within the framework of the strategic plan; and short-term planning, which takes place at the operational level and involves detailed budgeting and scheduling. Information systems make a broad contribution to planning by making internal and external data available for planning, and by offering modeling and forecasting capabilities.

Information systems are used to exercise control by comparing the actual (or currently projected) performance with the performance goals set out by the plans. Among the tools of control are performance reports, break-even analysis, and financial ratios.

CONCLUSIONS FOR MIS PRACTICE

1. Management information systems have been used for controlling purposes since their early beginnings. A wide opportunity to use these systems for planning also currently exists.

2. MIS and the planning process are related in multiple ways:
   a. Information systems, when used as strategic weapons, contribute to a firm's competitive position. Strategic deployment of information systems should be considered during the process of strategic planning.
   b. Classes of information systems represent tools to be employed in the planning process.
   c. The MIS function *itself* should be planned according to the principles outlined.

3. MIS plans should be aligned with corporate plans.

4. Databases containing internal data, as well as databases containing data on a firm's external environment (or access to such databases) are the principal sources of planning information.

5. MIS-supported modeling and quantitative forecasting techniques should be tempered with human judgment.

6. On-line information systems make possible tighter feedback loops for controlling purposes, thereby helping to enhance corporate performance.

ENDNOTES

1. Herbert A. Simon, ''Applying Information Technology to Organization Design.'' *Public Administration Review*, 33, 3, May-June 1973, pp. 268–78, p. 270.
2. *Computerworld*, February 20, 1989, p. 60.

KEY TERMS AND CONCEPTS

Management
Universality of management
Contingency approach
Planning
Controlling
Plan
Mission statement
Strategic planning
Tactical planning
Operational planning
Cascade effect
Budget
Fixed budget

Flexible budget
Zero-based budgeting
Planning model
Forecasting
Delphi technique
Scenario analysis
Econometric modeling
Performance report
Variance
Responsibility reporting
Break-even analysis
Financial ratios
Return on investment (ROI)

QUESTIONS

1. What is management?

2. What did the behavioral and social-system approaches contribute to the earlier understanding of management?

3. Why is the decision-making approach to management particularly appealing to a student of MIS? Is this approach sufficient to understand management? Why or why not?

4. What are the functions of management?

5. What is the relationship between planning and controlling in an organization?

6. Why is planning considered a primary management function?

7. Contrast the following: mission, statement of objectives, plan.

8. Explain the cascade effect, using the three-level structure of the planning process.

9. List the sources of information that can be employed in environmental scanning.

10. Prepare a pro forma annual income statement for the next five years, using the model presented in the chapter. Assume that sales volume is 10,000, and the previous year selling price was $5.00. (You may find it most convenient to use a spreadsheet program for the task.) What if the sales volume is 5,000, 20,000, or 50,000?

11. Why is anonymity an important part of in the Delphi technique?

12. What is responsibility reporting?

13. Determine the break-even point (the number of units that must be sold to break even) in the following case:
    Fixed costs are $5 million, the variable cost of each product unit to the enterprise is $10, and each unit will be sold for $20.

14. How are zero-based budgeting and the use of the ROI ratio related to corporate innovation?

1. In what ways should the use of "hard," quantitative data during the planning process be tempered with judgment? Give examples.

2. Could the availability of MIS-based control lead to harmful overcontrol? Give real or hypothetical examples of such overcontrol and discuss in what ways your examples could be harmful (or at least not helpful).

3. Recently, some companies with larger MIS departments (over 100 people) have been gaining a tighter grip on their information systems by appointing MIS controllers with financial backgrounds. Many feel this is beneficial to the controlled growth of MIS resources, which otherwise are treated simply as overhead. MIS controllers develop financial plans and control budgets, as well as evaluating lease-versus-buy decisions, contracts, and similar financial arrangements. Discuss the extent of technical versus accounting knowledge that an MIS controller should possess. Use examples to illustrate your discussion.

CASE STUDY

PERFORMANCE MONITORING SYSTEMS MAY BE A MEANS OF CONTROL AND A SOURCE OF PLANNING DATA—BUT THEY MAY COST YOU CUSTOMERS

On-line transaction processing systems make it possible to collect, analyze, and report information about the work performance of clerical workers during various computer-assisted activities. This information can then be used for planning work, budgeting, and cost reduction. It provides timely feedback to employees and can be used—as objective, factual data—in their employee evaluations. Computerized performance monitoring and control systems are now common in the banking, insurance, and airline industries. A noted expert on computer privacy, Alan Westin of Columbia University, in his work for the Office of Technology Assessment (a technology research service of the U.S. Congress) estimates that 20 to 35 percent of U.S. clerical employees are now monitored in this fashion (U.S. Congress, 1987). Systems for electronic work monitoring can measure the number of work units processed per unit of time by data entry clerks, by bank proof clerks who process checks, or by insurance claims clerks.

For example, as I use a word-processing program to write this book, my keystrokes can be captured by a monitoring program. This program could determine my typing speed and the number of errors I make while typing. If such data are available to management, they can be used for training purposes and analyzed to improve clerical performance. The data may also be used to set a high standard of performance equal to that of the best typists. But are we now talking about creating a high-performance clerical unit or an "electronic sweatshop," as some have called this arrangement?

Indeed, with all the potential advantages of computer-based work monitoring, why does it engender opposition?

The controversy centers on the allegations that computerized performance monitoring causes increased stress, raises the possibility of abuse by supervisors (who, for example, may constantly ratchet up required performance quotas), and lends itself to privacy invasion (for example, you would not necessarily want the telephone numbers you call to appear on a printout or, worse yet, to have a supervisor listen in on your conversations, as is done in some "service observation" systems).

Aetna Life & Casualty, a leading financial-service organization, has developed a code of ethics regarding electronic work monitoring (Schott, 1988). Here are some of Aetna's guidelines:

- Be sure you measure only those items that are essential for meeting your unit's business objectives.
- Make sure employees understand the business objectives supported by the monitoring program.
- Make sure employees understand how and when their work is being measured.
- Give employees access to their records.

- When analyzing electronic work-monitoring data, be careful to distinguish short-term and long-term trends.
- Don't use electronic monitoring to have a machine pacing people's work.
- Be careful about using work-monitoring statistics to inspire competition.

Computerized performance monitoring goes on in a variety of settings. Computers measure the keystroke speeds of data-entry clerks, the responses of directory-assistance operators, and the speed with which checkout clerks sweep items over the optical scanners in supermarkets. TWA's ticket reservation agents receive monthly performance ratings based on the computer's measurement of the time they spend on the telephone with customers and on the supervisor's assessments of these conversations.

In some cases, performance monitoring systems have been found to run clearly against organizational goals. It has been determined, for example, that when systems monitoring the number of telephone calls answered by order clerks are installed, customer satisfaction decreases (Grant, 1988). Obviously, the monitored clerks attempt to shorten their interactions with customers to the extent that customers' problems are not addressed, in order to increase their "productivity." In general, many simplistic performance measurement systems are rather easily "gamed": the monitored workers alter their work styles to make the numbers look good, to the detriment of organizational effectiveness.

Based on Mitch Betts, "VDT Monitoring Under Stress." *ComputerWorld*, January 21, 1991, pp. 1, 14; Rebecca A. Grant, Christopher A. Higgins, and Richard H. Irving, "Computerized Performance Monitors: Are They Costing You Customers?" *Sloan Management Review*, Spring 1988, pp. 39–45; Peter T. Kilborn, "Workers Using Computers Find a Supervisor Inside." *The New York Times*, December 23, 1990, pp. 1, 18; Fred Schott, "An Ethical Approach to Electronic Work Monitoring: The Experience of Aetna Life & Casualty." Papers from Conference on Ethics and Computerization, New Jersey Institute of Technology, November 1988; and U.S. Congress, Office of Technology Assessment, *The Electronic Supervisor: New Technology, New Tensions*, OTA-CIT-333, Washington, D.C.:U.S. Government Printing Office, September 1987.

Case Study Questions

1. Outline a planning and control system based on electronic performance monitoring of telemarketing clerks who do telephone sales.

2. Analyze the ethics guidelines of Aetna Life & Casualty and summarize their objectives.

3. How can electronic monitoring systems run against organizational objectives? (Give two instances).

4. Why, in your opinion, might employees in certain workplaces accept electronic monitoring systems quite gladly?

SELECTED REFERENCES

Anthony, Robert N. *Planning and Control Systems: A Framework for Analysis.* Cambridge, Mass.: Harvard University Press, 1965.

Applegate, Lynda M.; Cash, James I., Jr.; and Mills, D. Quinn. "Information Technology and Tomorrow's Manager." *Harvard Business Review*, November-December 1988, pp. 128–36.

Cushing, Barry E., and Romney, Marshall B. *Accounting Information Systems and Business Organizations.* 4th ed. Reading, Mass.: Addison-Wesley, 1987.

Davenport, Thomas H.; Hammer, Michael; and Metsisto, Tauno J. "How Executives Can Shape Their Company's Information Systems." *Harvard Business Review*, March-April 1989, pp. 130–34.

Elofson, Gregg, and Konsynski, Benn, R. "Delegation Technologies: Environmental Scanning with Intelligent Agents." *Journal of Management Information Systems*, 8, 1, Summer 1991, pp. 37–62.

Goold, Michael. "Strategic Control in the Decentralized Firm." *Sloan Management Review*, 32, 2, Winter 1991, pp. 69–81.

Hamel, Gary, and Prahalad, C. K. "Strategic Intent." *Harvard Business Review*, May-June 1989, pp. 63–76.

Koontz, Harold, and Weihrich, Heinz. *Management.* 9th ed. New York: McGraw-Hill, 1988.

Lederer, Albert L., and Mendelow, Aubrey L. "Coordination of Information System Plans with Business Plans." *Journal of Management Information Systems,* 6, 2, Fall 1989, pp. 5–19.

Levitt, Harold J., and Whisler, Thomas L. "Management in the 1980s." *Harvard Business Review,* November-December 1958, pp. 41–48.

McLean, Ephraim R., and Soden, John V. *Strategic Planning for MIS.* New York: John Wiley, 1977.

Mahoney, Thomas A.; Jerdee, Thomas H.; and Carroll, Stephen J. "The Job(s) of Management." *Industrial Relations,* 4, 2, February 1965, pp. 97–110.

Pascale, R. T. "Perspective on Strategy: The Real Story Behind Honda's Success." *California Management Review,* Spring 1981, pp. 70–78.

Wack, Pierre. "Scenarios: Uncharted Waters Ahead." *Harvard Business Review,* September-October 1985, pp. 73–89.

Wheelan, Thomas L., and Hunger, David J. *Strategic Management and Business Policy.* 2d ed. Reading, Mass.: Addison-Wesley, 1986.

ORGANIZATIONS: INNOVATING WITH INFORMATION TECHNOLOGY

. . . .

Nothing endures but change.
  Heraclitus

*Organizations exist to enable ordinary people to do
extraordinary things.*
  Ted Levitt

*Organizations, public and private, are not exclusively
economic production units. . . . They are also complex
arenas for people developing their career lines and
anchoring their lives in a social world outside the
family. . . .*
  Rob Kling

As we approach the twenty-first century, we realize that in modern society most people accomplish things not as individuals, but as members of organizations. Business firms, governmental agencies, voluntary associations—all extend the power of individuals to contribute to the well-being of society and to the individuals' own sense of accomplishment.

The theory of organizations is intertwined with management theory. In this chapter, we shall examine organizations as creations of the ongoing management activity of organizing. We want to know how information systems affect organizations. More than that, we want to see what makes an *innovating organization*—and we especially want to see how information technology can be a vehicle, and sometimes the product, of innovation. The information society demands that a firm be capable of rapid adaptation—or in other words, continuing innovation. Firms must innovate both by redesigning their business processes and by offering new products and services. The strategic deployment of information technology is a continuing process of innovation within the context of a firm.

Information systems provide an organization with options for internal structuring and for its pursuit of advantage in the marketplace. Simply buying a new information technology has a limited effectiveness. Organizations, after all, are collectives of people. Managed processes of technology assimilation and of organizational change are needed to bring out the potential of technology within the context of a given organization.

Business activity in the worldwide marketplace is a hallmark of today's corporations. We call this phenomenon globalization of business. Information technology may be successfully deployed to innovate internationally, reaping the benefits of scale and scope, while also addressing the needs of local markets.

When Bruce Ryan, vice-president and controller of Digital Equipment Corporation (of Maynard, Massachusetts), started a few years ago to rework the operations of the company's finance department, he did not follow the steps his company—and others—took when they were changing their business processes in the past. In earlier days, a firm usually selected an information technology and then built the business process (or even an entire organizational unit) around it. As a result, the technology dictated the way the organization functioned.

Instead, Ryan and the team he led redesigned the corporate finance function to respond to the company's business needs—and only then sought the appropriate information systems to support the function. In the process, twenty incompatible accounting systems were standardized, accounting groups were consolidated—and 450 jobs were eliminated.

I have just described an example of business reengineering: redesigning business processes to enhance productivity and competitiveness and supporting the new processes with appropriate information systems. The principal premise of this important trend is the realization that the payoff from information technology can be realized only if new forms of organization are adopted.

Examples of business reengineering keep multiplying. When Hewlett-Packard reengineered its purchasing function and furnished it with a central vendor database that is used to negotiate contracts, the results included a 150 percent improvement in on-time deliveries and a much lower cost of goods purchased. By reengineering its invoice processing, Ford Motor Company reduced the required number of employees in that area by 75 percent. Hallmark Cards (of St. Louis) has embarked on a multiyear project, dubbed The Journey, of reengineering its *entire* operations and then supporting them with new, open information systems.

Radical organizational change is not only unsettling—it threatens established positions, and even jobs. Such change requires a sense of urgency. To quote a line manager at Cigna, a Philadelphia-based financial services company, where reengineering efforts are undertaken at various organizational levels: "Technology is seen as a major enabler, [and] reengineering is seen as a necessary activity."

Indeed, Michael Hammer, a consultant active in this area, predicts (rather hopefully) that at some future time, CIO will stand not just for chief information officer, but for chief *innovation* officer.

Based on Allan E. Alter, "The Corporate Make-Over." *CIO*, December 1990, pp. 32–42; Peter Krass, "Engineering Reengineering." *InformationWeek*, February 11, 1991, pp. 25–28; Peter Krass, "Building a Better Mousetrap." *InformationWeek*, March 25, 1991, pp. 24–30; Alan J. Ryan, "Cigna Re-engineers Itself." *Computerworld*, July 8, 1991, pp. 79–81.

How do organizations open themselves to change? What organizing and leadership principles make them adaptive in a society that fosters rapid change? How do information technologies affect organizations, and how can these technologies best be exploited? These are some of the questions we shall be looking into in this chapter.

CHAPTER OUTLINE

12.1   Organizing Activity and Its MIS Support

12.2   Leading

12.3   Organizational Structure

12.4   Dimensions of Organizational Structure
   • Number of Levels in the Hierarchy and Span of Management
   • Centralization-Decentralization

12.5   Organizational Design for Dynamic Environments

12.6   Combining the Nimbleness of Smallness with the Advantages of Largeness

12.7   Assimilation of Information Technologies in an Organization

12.8   Innovation in Information Systems as a Process of Organizational Change
   • All Aspects of Organizational Life Are Affected by MIS
   • Introducing Organizational Change

• •

12.1 ORGANIZING ACTIVITY AND ITS MIS SUPPORT

An **organization** is a social unit committed to certain goals. The theory of organizations, insofar as it has evolved separately from management theory, has been primarily developed by sociologists. Indeed, a German sociologist, Max Weber, described a general model of a formal, efficiency-seeking organization in 1911. Both in the profit and the not-for-profit sectors, organizations aim to deliver products and services.

The *organizing* activity of management creates the structure of an organization, defines jobs in this structure, equips people with the resources needed for their jobs, and provides coordination among the people in the structure. A firm should be organized into a structure that facilitates the pursuit of its planned objectives. The jobs in the organizational structure are filled through the staffing process. In more general terms, staffing consists of planning, acquiring, and developing the human resources (personnel) of an enterprise. Education and training of personnel are of particular importance in the information society, where knowledge work dominates and change is the order of the day. In this regard, employers have taken over many roles played by traditional educational establishments.

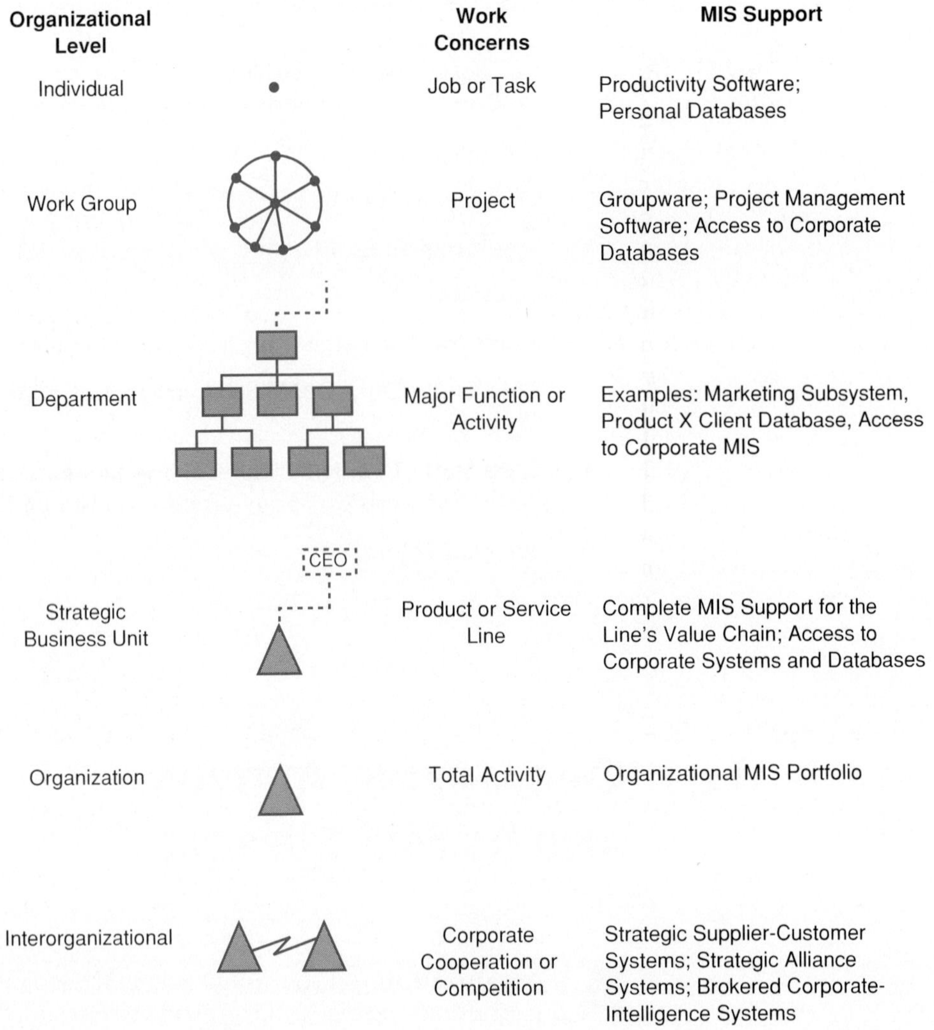

FIGURE 12.1

MIS support for various
organizational levels.

(Author; Laudon, 1988, p. 93)

Organizational Level		Work Concerns	MIS Support
Individual	●	Job or Task	Productivity Software; Personal Databases
Work Group		Project	Groupware; Project Management Software; Access to Corporate Databases
Department		Major Function or Activity	Examples: Marketing Subsystem, Product X Client Database, Access to Corporate MIS
Strategic Business Unit		Product or Service Line	Complete MIS Support for the Line's Value Chain; Access to Corporate Systems and Databases
Organization		Total Activity	Organizational MIS Portfolio
Interorganizational		Corporate Cooperation or Competition	Strategic Supplier-Customer Systems; Strategic Alliance Systems; Brokered Corporate-Intelligence Systems

Our primary concern here is with organizational designs that support continuing innovation, as demanded by the information society. Our two continuing questions are: What kinds of organizational structures are able to take advantage of information technology to achieve competitive advantage in the marketplace? What forms of support do MIS offer organizations?

Today, the various components of MIS play an important role in supporting the work of organizational subunits. These various organizational levels and the information systems that give them support are shown in figure 12.1.

The impact of information technology on organizations has been studied since the mid-1980s by the Management in the 1990s Research Program at the MIT Sloan School of Management (Scott Morton, 1991). A general theory of the effects of information technologies on organizations and decision making is only beginning to emerge (Huber, 1990).

Various types of MIS support the organizing function. Executive information systems (EIS) facilitate control from the top. The availability of such systems makes

INFORMATION SYSTEMS MEET THE CHALLENGE OF FLEXIBLE ORGANIZING

Organizations that thrive on innovations rely on informal structures of project teams and other temporary alliances rather than on formal hierarchical organizational structures. But informal structures have to be organized too! Cypress, a San Jose, California, chip maker, has developed an information system that keeps track of all of its 1,500 employees as they participate in various projects, assignments, and functions. Each employee maintains on the system a list of her or his ten to fifteen commitments and their status. The chief executive officer of the company, T. J. Rodgers, can review the goals of all the employees in about four hours—and he does that each week. Obviously, this cuts down on the number of managers.

Apple Corporation is developing a system, called Spider, that will assist managers in forming teams. The system will instantly tell a manager whether an employee is available to join a new project, what the employee's skills are, and where the employee is located in the corporation. The system combines a network of personal computers with a videoconferencing facility and relies on a database of employee records. A manager who is assembling a team can retrieve the personnel data of a candidate, see a color photo, and conduct an interview—on the computer screen.

Based on Brian Dumaine, "The Bureaucracy Busters." *Fortune*, June 17, 1991, pp. 36–50.

---

it possible to delegate decision-making authority to line management—since the way line managers exercise this authority can be checked. This decentralized decision making makes for a responsive, customer-driven organization. The use of decision support systems (DSS), including group DSS in particular, can increase the speed of decision-making at all corporate levels.

Office information systems (OIS) provide a potent tool for coordinating the activities of an organization. They assist vertical coordination along the chain of authority, but are frequently used for much broader communication. They also help in the lateral coordination of work among the various units situated across the organizational chart: for example, new product designs produced by the Engineering Department can be accessed on-line by the Marketing Department, both to provide feedback and to develop a marketing campaign. These systems also make it possible to quickly organize a work team of people from various departments to carry out some project. Such a team can be dispersed geographically; it is unified by a mix of teleconferencing, group decision support, and computer-aided design facilities. Here, information systems act both as a primary work tool and as a coordination tool.

Information systems built around organizational data and knowledge bases can furnish a potent component of organizational memory. **Organizational memory,** the memory of interpreted organizational decisions and their consequences (Walsh, 1991), can contribute to future performance by making it possible to learn from the past. As we shall further discuss in the next chapter, humans are fallible information processors (and repositories), and personnel turnover is a significant factor in "organizational forgetting." Experimental systems for growing computer-supported organizational memory are emerging (Ackerman, 1990).

Later in this chapter, we shall see that information systems are not simple tools that are easily implemented just by being developed (or purchased) and installed. There are usually several organizational options in selecting a system. The options exercised in an organization frequently reflect the organizational *culture*. Culture encompasses the *values* announced in a firm's mission and policy statements, as well as the *norms* guiding the actual behavior of organizational actors. The propensity to plan extensively or to exercise rigid forms of control over workers are examples of norms within corporate cultures. Federal Express, an air delivery company and a leader in the strategic use of information systems, provides an excellent example in expressing corporate values: "We strongly believe that information about the movement of the package is as important as the package itself."[1]

12.2 LEADING

We tend to call only outstanding managers "leaders." Such a manager uses the authority conferred by the organization as a resource that enables subordinates to contribute maximally to the goals of the organization while satisfying their own needs. Yet, leadership is an expected attribute of a manager; the manager who does not lead is abdicating his or her responsibility.

A leader inspires people with a vision, provides direction, offers support, elicits commitment to the task, and creates an environment in which the subordinates can participate in decision making, while also ensuring that the task is accomplished. More than any other managerial function, leadership summons forth a manager's personal resources, as well as the power derived from his or her position.

A number of leadership theories have evolved. The earlier theories were based on an analysis of the personal traits of a leader. More recent contingency theories focus on the match between a leader's behavior (leadership style) and the situation at hand.

Four leadership styles, shown in figure 12.2, may be distinguished. They range between two extremes: from directive style, with its overriding concern for the task to be accomplished, to the supportive style, in which concern for people overrides organizational needs. Participative leadership, which strives for a balance between the needs of people and of the organization, involves all participants in making the decisions that will affect them and encourages people to use initiative. Participative leadership inspires commitment to a common vision and offers a sense of purpose and excitement; it energizes people's creativity—and without this, there can be no significant innovation.

FIGURE 12.2

Leadership styles.

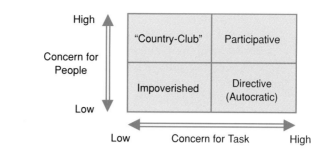

FIGURE 12.3

Maslow's hierarchy of human needs as potential motivators.

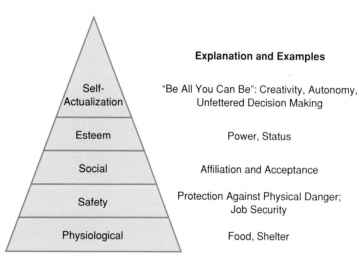

We shall see further on in this chapter how these management styles can be matched with the task the lead group or unit must perform and with its environment.

Effective communication throughout the firm is a necessary vehicle of leadership. This includes vertical communication along superior-subordinate lines, lateral communication with other units in the organization, and communication within a workgroup. We already mentioned in figure 12.1 some of the MIS support for this communication. In chapter 16, we shall further analyze how office information systems (OIS) significantly enhance the communication process.

To lead, one needs to motivate. The social systems approach to organizations, and the so-called human relations movement in particular, initiated a sophisticated analysis of motivation. A widely accepted theory of needs was developed by Abraham Maslow (1970). He grouped human needs into a hierarchy (see figure 12.3). According to Maslow, when a need is satisfied, it ceases to be a motivator—and only then does the next higher level of needs begin to be a motivator.

Further studies of what individuals need and what they seek from working have confirmed that high pay and job security motivate employees only up to a certain point (Herzberg, 1966). A broad study of a large sample of the workforce in seven developed countries showed that the dominant work goal in four of them, including the United States, was doing interesting work (Harpaz, 1990).

Human motivation has been also conceptualized in other terms. In particular, Victor Vroom's expectancy theory is of interest (Vroom, 1964). This theory argues that human motivation to carry out a certain activity is a product of three factors. The first is a person's belief that he or she can perform the activity in a satisfactory fashion (can I do it?). Second is the individual's belief that, as a result of having performed the activity, he or she will achieve a certain outcome, such as a reward (what will I get out of it?). Third is the worth of this outcome to the individual (do I really want a promotion?). The three factors in expectancy theory are subject to a multiplier effect: if any one of the factors has zero value, the person will not be motivated to carry out the activity.

The value or worth attached to outcomes varies widely among individuals (and ambition is only one of the traits that comes into play). J. Daniel Couger and Robert Zawacki found that information systems professionals have significantly higher needs for professional growth and lower social needs than other categories of workers (Couger, 1980). Couger and Scott McIntyre found that knowledge engineers have similar motivation norms (Couger, 1987–88). This gives some credence to the popular image of the "computer hacker," engrossed in his or her impersonal interaction with a computer system. It also explains why companies that consistently strive to use state-of-the-art computer infrastructure attract the best professionals. These professionals welcome the continuing change needed to maintain such a firm's competitive posture.

The use of advanced information systems generally requires commitment rather than just compliance from users: they have to use the system in a creative fashion for it to foster organizational goals (Walton, 1989). The organization must ensure both the necessary motivation and the training of these users. Optimal performance and, indeed, deep satisfaction result when the challenge of a goal-oriented activity draws on a worker's considerable skill (Csikszentmihalyi, 1990). Imparting these skills and giving employees an arena to exercise them in are vital objectives of a well-run organization.

12.3 ORGANIZATIONAL STRUCTURE

The formal structure of a company is expressed by its *organization chart*. The chart shows how work is divided, the levels of management, and authority relationships. It also shows formal vertical (superior-subordinate) communication channels. The organization chart of a company or of its subunit reflects the principle of *departmentation* adopted by the company—that is, the basis on which the company or the subunit has grouped its employees.

A complete organizational chart for a manufacturing company organized along functional lines was shown in figure 3.10. Figure 12.4 shows various departmentation principles applied to the structuring of a corporation's MIS function. Other departmentation principles are possible as well (such as regional or customer-related groupings).

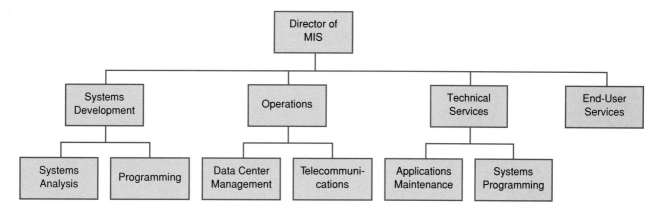

a. Functional organization

FIGURE 12.4a and b

Structuring (departmentation) of the MIS function.

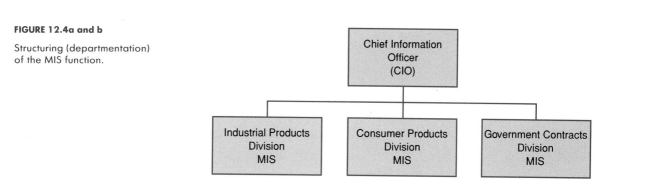

b. Divisional organization (by-product)

Functional departmentation (figure 12.4a) consists in grouping together employees performing similar activities in a company's value chain or within a particular subunit. Its main disadvantage is the diffusion of responsibility for a product or a service. If a new product is to be developed and brought to market, the multiple divisions involved in the process may engage in finger-pointing if the process is delayed. The advantages of functional departmentation lie in the ability to maintain highly specialized units, such as marketing or finance, with a high degree of economic efficiency. We discussed this type of efficiency as systemic resource sharing in chapter 10.

Divisional departmentation relies on grouping employees in a more market-oriented fashion. Divisions (which may be groups of business units in a large corporation) are formed based on product groups, geography, or customer segment—all of which aim at bringing the company closer to the customer. In figure 12.4b, we have shown direct reporting by the divisional MIS to the corporate chief information officer (CIO), usually a corporate vice-president. Alternatively, each division may operate its own MIS whose manager reports to the head of the division—the MIS function is then dispersed.

Matrix organization has been often adopted to reap the advantages of both divisional and functional structuring (although other forms of departmentation may be combined instead). In a matrix structure, functional departmentation is

FIGURE 12.4c

Structuring (departmentation)
of the MIS function.

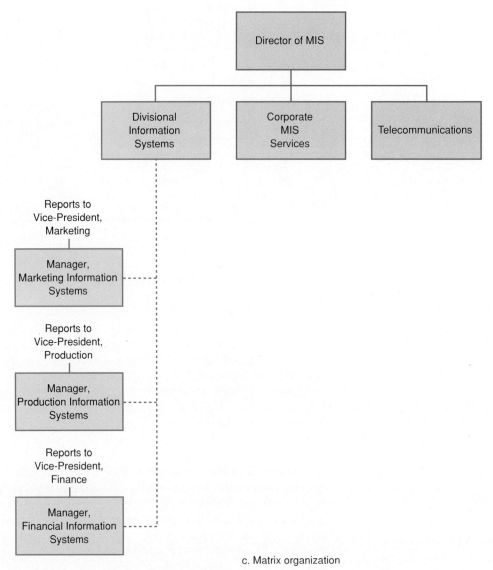

c. Matrix organization

retained. However, department members are at the same time members of project teams. A team thus includes specialists from a variety of functional areas,
such as engineering, marketing, and finance, whose efforts are brought to bear
on the project for which they are responsible at the particular time. The principle of unity of management has obviously been sacrificed here, resulting in a
greater uncertainty in the environment. A matrix structure formalizes the lateral
means of coordination often used in functional structures, such as liaison teams
and task forces.

As applied to the organization of an MIS department (see figure 12.4c), matrix
organization combines direct reporting to divisional heads with "dotted-line"
reporting to the MIS director. The MIS staff coordinates the corporate MIS effort,
technical expertise, corporate telecommunications, and standardization.

The advantages and the possible disadvantages of alternative forms of organization are summarized in table 12.1.

ORGANIZATIONAL STRUCTURE	ADVANTAGES	DISADVANTAGES
Functional	Promotes specialization and quality solution of specialized problems. Economies of scale realized in specialized functions.	Reduces responsibility for total product or service. Lack of communication across functions (at the junctions of the value chain). Narrow "specialist" perspectives lead to problems being sent up the hierarchy.
Divisional	Superior coordination of activities. Responsiveness to customers. Familiarity with the market.	Suboptimization when divisions put their interests above those of the organization. Duplication of functional services.
Matrix	Concerted effort on a project. Product or service delivery is treated as a system. Decision making at the low (project) level ensures flexibility. Maintaining functional structuring promotes specialization.	Dual authority may lead to power struggle and confusion.

The teams in a matrix structure are relatively permanent—they go from project to project. Another team-oriented way of structuring has evolved in recent years. Called *adhocracy* (Mintzberg, 1988), or *network structuring,* this approach relies on rapidly organizing a new team ad hoc, as new projects demand it. Office information systems provide the technology for work coordination. The flexibility to quickly mount a massive, multifunctional effort is available thanks to computer-supported systems for cooperative work, such as groupware (which we discuss in chapter 16). Small organizations may be entirely structured in this fashion, almost completely avoiding a management hierarchy. Large organizations, as we shall see further on, may employ such innovating units, which enjoy a high degree of independence from the other parts of the organization.

Note that an organization may maintain different organizational forms at various levels. Thus, a large company may be subdivided into several **strategic business units (SBU**s), each pursuing a distinct line of business—this is divisional departmentation by product at the top. An SBU is expected to act as a distinct business, with its own mission and strategic plan. A strategic business unit may be further subdivided along functional or divisional lines, depending on the nature of its business.

An organization's formal organizational structure only provides an approximation of what is actually going on in the company. Any functioning organization evolves a shadow, or an informal structure, based on long-term working relationships, individual expertise, political coalitions, mentor-protégé relationships, and the necessity of filling gaps in the formal structure. Informal structures are of particular importance when an organization is passing through stressful rapid change. Much of the communication in the company is lateral, rather than along the chain of command. By analyzing the volume and significance of *actual* communications between members of an organization with the aid of a computer program, Netmap International of San Francisco is able to diagnose how an organization actually functions.

A question frequently asked by practitioners and researchers alike is: Do information systems cause structural changes in organizations? In other words, is there a "technological imperative" attached to the pervasive use of these systems? According to the current research (Robey, 1981; Attewell, 1984; Markus, 1988), information systems do not directly cause structural changes in organizations: a simple search for a cause-effect relationship has so far been in vain. Indeed, by carefully analyzing the positions taken by the leading researchers, Joey George and John Leslie King have identified their common assumption: that the decision authority structures in organizations are largely the result of organizing choices made by management. Information technology is the means for implementing these choices (George, 1991).

However, what is perhaps more important, and as can be seen in this chapter, *information systems create options in organizational design.* Certain ways of organizing work that would have been impossible without information technology became possible and cost-effective with MIS.

12.4 DIMENSIONS OF ORGANIZATIONAL STRUCTURE

Two major dimensions of organizational structure are the number of levels in the organizational hierarchy and the degree to which decision-making authority is centralized.

Number of Levels in the Hierarchy and Span of Management

Each managerial position in the organizational chart has the authority and responsibility to supervise immediate subordinates. The number of these subordinates reporting directly to a particular manager is known as the **span of management** (also known as span of control) of the position.[2] There is a limit to this span, but what that limit is depends on the complexity of superior-subordinate interactions. Traditionally, the span has been higher at the lower levels of a company, where interactions are simpler owing to the number of fixed procedures in place, and lower (frequently nine) at the top executive level. Informational tools aid in managing the complexity of superior-subordinate interactions and permit expansion of the span. In the first chapter of this text, we saw how, by using an executive information system, senior managers can rapidly determine whether a company's performance is on track and discover problems and opportunities in the operation of its subunits.

The greater the span of management in an organization, the shorter the reporting line from the top to the line managers (and the smaller the number of middle managers). This larger span is associated with a company's responsiveness and flexibility in the marketplace, as well as with economies in personnel. Multiple levels in the hierarchy complicate vertical communications: overall

TOP EXECUTIVES GET ON-LINE

"Information has an immediacy to it. The person who receives information can act on it right away," says William McGowan, the chief executive of MCI Communications Corporation. McGowan used to hold breakfast meetings with his top twenty-five executives each Monday morning at 7:30. Now the meeting is held electronically. A memo called "Breakfast" is compiled on Friday afternoon by each participant—and is available through the electronic mail system on Monday morning. McGowan estimates that at present 15 percent of the chief executives in the United States get their information electronically—and virtually all will within a decade.

Based on Amanda Bennett, "The Chief Executives in Year 2000 Will Be Experienced Abroad." *The Wall Street Journal*, February 27, 1989, pp. A1, A9.

company objectives are more difficult to transmit to the "trenches," and the problems encountered in actual production or marketing do not always reach the upper levels of management.

The availability of executive information systems and other effective management information systems has increased the capability of higher management to control the operations of an organization and can thus help to flatten the management pyramid—if this is the intent of the top managers.

Centralization-Decentralization

Various aspects of management activities can be either centralized or decentralized. Entire functions in a firm, such as marketing or MIS, may be centralized as a single corporate unit, or decentralized by being largely dispersed across other company units.

In general, if decision-making authority is concentrated at the top, the company (or its subunit) is centralized. In many firms, the decision-making authority is heavily delegated to line managers—and thus decentralized. The expected advantage of centralization is avoidance of systemic suboptimization. On the other hand, in a decentralized company, the familiarity of lower-level managers with the market and with their specialized functional areas is expected to lead to higher-quality decisions.

The availability of MIS-based control techniques has made greater decentralization of decision making possible. MIS, having given the higher-level managers the ability to monitor and control overall performance throughout a company, enables them to delegate much decision making to the lower management ranks. This increases responsiveness and enhances the commitment line managers make to decisions—because those decisions are largely their own. The massive volume of decision making demanded by the information society has led many companies to decentralize decision making all the way to the factory floor. However, information technology also supports decision making at the top and reduces the costs of communicating information—and thus may be employed to support more centralized management (Gurbaxani, 1991).

DECENTRALIZING OUT—INFORMATION TECHNOLOGIES PROVIDE OPPORTUNITIES FOR SMALL COMPANIES

Small and midsized companies are creating most of the new jobs in the United States. They often act as "niche-players": their competitive positioning strategies are focused on satisfying the needs of a highly specialized market segment (niche). Many of these opportunities have arisen in specialized computer software, hardware, and services. In recent years, resounding success has propelled some of these firms, such as Apple, Microsoft, and Ashton-Tate, well into the ranks of large corporations.

But there is another role information technologies play in providing opportunities to small business. In general terms, information systems can serve as a *coordination technology*. The availability of such a technology may make vertical integration—producing input materials for the company's principal products (such as a car manufacturer producing batteries, for example)—unattractive to a large company. Instead, the company may "decentralize out" by buying many of its input materials

from a variety of smaller suppliers. Interorganizational information systems, based on telecommunications (and combined with fast transportation) provide an incentive for a large company to "stick to its knitting," or concentrate on what it does best. Small manufacturers receive orders (including just-in-time delivery schedules), send invoices, exchange quality information and general electronic mail over such information systems. Further, the engineers of a small supplier company can work with the engineers of a large customer on a computer-based product design and manufacturing specifications to ensure smooth production cycles.

In systems terms, such "virtual companies" of suppliers and customers joined by MIS form a system in which greater optimization is possible than in two individual subsystems.

Today, there are many opportunities for entrepreneurship and specialization—thanks to the information system infrastructure.

The advantages of decentralized decision making we just outlined are based on what is known as the rationalist perspective, which assumes that organizational actors aim to increase the effectiveness and efficiency of the organization's operations. The orientation of this perspective is toward "what should be" (normative). An alternative way of looking at organizations, the behavioral perspective, recognizes that people in organizations are engaged in political plays for influence over resources, and that the emerging distribution of decision-making authority is a fluid and not formally defined balance.

Notable decentralization has occurred in the MIS function itself. Thus, the central, corporate MIS function now often retains only some of its former roles and personnel. With the computer power delivered by personal workstations and departmental computers, most of the formerly centralized computing has moved to business units in many companies. Among the crucial roles of the corporate MIS function is running the network these departmental computers are connected to and ensuring their connectivity with other, external nets (Donovan, 1988). Even wider decentralization is illustrated in the vignette on that subject.

12.5 ORGANIZATIONAL DESIGN FOR DYNAMIC ENVIRONMENTS

As the information society emerges from the industrial society, organizations find themselves in an environment of increasingly rapid change and uncertainty. As we discussed in chapter 10, an organization is an open system interacting with its environment in many ways. To be effective—that is, to operate successfully and to thrive—organizations have to make themselves responsive to this environment. What organizational structures and management processes are effective in dynamic environments? How can we manage in order to employ information systems for competitive positioning? What management techniques support innovation? These are the questions we will address here.

Pioneering work on the management of organizations in environments of rapid change was carried out in the late 1950s by Tom Burns and George Stalker (Burns, 1961). They analyzed the performance of a number of firms in England and Scotland which were attempting to innovate by entering the electronics industry—a new industry at the time. The problem they faced was the general problem of innovating while maintaining efficient levels of ongoing production. We can easily appreciate the similar problems confronting today's companies, which need to maintain the volume and quality of their products and services while constantly improving and changing them—often with the use of information systems.

Burns and Stalker found two polar organizational designs that were both successful in their respective environments. In other words, they defined a contingency framework for adapting organizational management to the environment. The closer the operating and general environment of an organization is to one of these opposites, the better the firm will perform if it adopts the proper management mechanisms. **Mechanistic organizations,** characterized by centralized structures, rigid division of labor, and many standard operating procedures, proved successful in stable environments, in which rather predictable future conditions remove most uncertainty. This form of organization closely resembles what Max Weber called bureaucracy (he used this term in a positive sense, as distinguished from the arbitrary management of earlier organizations). Environments of rapid change and high uncertainty, closely associated with the transition to an information economy, have called forth a different organizational form—the **organic organization,** which is characterized by decentralized decision making, flexible division of labor, and participative management. This formation is congenial to innovation and rapid decision making. These two polarities, with their associated characteristics, are shown in figure 12.5.

Organizations may elect intermediate positions in the mechanistic-organic spectrum; as we shall see, large companies may structure various subunits differently as well. But usually there is a predominant characteristic which defines much of the company's culture. A definite shift toward organic characteristics has occurred in response to the demands of the information society.

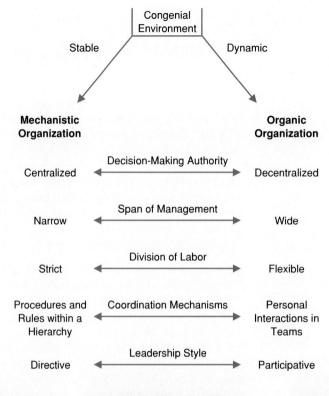

In his classical work, Alfred Chandler argued that a company's structure must support its strategy (Chandler, 1962). In our terms, a strategy for change requires organic structuring. Some researchers argue that the production technologies used by firms impose their own demands on structure, with complex technologies engendering organic structures. Innovative software firms are an excellent example of this; on the other hand, large companies providing utility-type computer services more closely resemble mechanistic structures.

Figure 12.6 shows the contingency framework for organizational design, relating the environment and a firm's strategy and technology to its decision-making and innovation needs and, in turn, to the optimal organizational forms. *Any* of the factors calling for high levels of decision making and innovation call for organic structures.

AN ORGANIC ORGANIZATION DEVELOPS AN INNOVATIVE OFFICE COMMUNICATION TOOL

Wang Laboratories was founded by one of the famed innovators in the computer industry, Dr. An Wang (who was a father of the magnetic-core memories). Although Wang has had some recent top-management problems, it has long been known as a company that innovates. The firm marketed the first calculator (in 1964) and the first word processor (in 1976).

In 1986 the company formed a team to develop another innovative product, a personal-computer-based hardware-software system that integrates all forms of office communication—data, text, image, and voice. Called Freestyle, the system enables PCs to accept handwritten notes and voice messages and integrates them with data from databases. The goal was to help people work the way they are used to working—with the equivalents of pencil (an electronic stylus with an electronic eraser on its end) and paper (a writing tablet). A supervisor may receive a sales trip request through electronic mail, pull the sales targets from the database and include them in the response, authorize the trip with his or her signature via the pad, and append a recorded voice message: "Be prepared for the customers' objections to our machine's footprint."

The project was a success. To encourage a high level of creativity, the team, which grew from three to almost sixty people, was organized along organic principles. Its leader, Stephen Levine, said, "I negotiate with people in the group the same as I negotiate with outside vendors."

All team members reported directly to the leader; coordination was informal, with the team members constantly challenging each other. To be sure, the team had a clear goal and a fixed set of product concepts to which everyone was deeply committed. It was not unusual for team members to put in sixteen-hour workdays. The team was monitored by the corporation—but faced little interference. Levine was perceived by his team as a leader rather than a manager and saw his role as marketer of the project to the corporation at large.

To test the feasibility of the concept quickly, the team developed a prototype of the system. By learning from mistakes, adding more and more functionality to the prototype, and integrating into the evolving system what was learned from its use, the project built momentum. The leader kept the common goal constantly in sight of the team members.

"If you want people to work the way these people do, you have to let them make their own decisions," concludes Levine.

The experience garnered on the project will certainly contribute to the implementation of the new strategic direction announced by Wang Laboratories in April 1991: to focus on providing systems for workgroups.

Based on David Lieberman, "Product Team Thrives in Unstructured Environment." *Computer Design News Edition,* February 13, 1989, pp. 34–37; with a contribution from Sally Cusack, "Wang to Focus on Work Groups." *Computerworld,* April 8, 1991, p. 95.

12.6 COMBINING THE NIMBLENESS OF SMALLNESS WITH THE ADVANTAGES OF LARGENESS

Growing size tends to push an organization toward a more mechanistic structure, with multiple levels of managerial hierarchy needed to integrate a variety of specialized subunits. Company size has its obvious advantages, such as economies of scale and power in a marketplace. But to counteract the disadvantages of mechanistic structures, such as lack of responsiveness and flexibility, successful organizations have evolved a variety of means to introduce features of organic management.

Paul Lawrence and Jay Lorsch (Lawrence, 1969) found that subsystems in organizations faced different environmental and internal requirements. These subsystems can, therefore, be organized along different lines over the mechanistic-organic spectrum.

As we have said, diversified corporations are often structured into strategic business units (SBUs), most frequently along product lines. Each SBU, a large operation in itself, operates to a large degree as an independent business and can be managed in accordance with its environment, the complexity of the predominant technology, and cultural traditions.

Small-scale innovating enterprises can be nurtured within large corporations. Such an independent business unit within IBM brought out the first IBM PC—an immensely successful personal computer. "Skunkworks," small and organically structured teams with challenging innovative missions, which are only very loosely controlled by the corporate hierarchy, can be given the latitude and resources to innovate. Intrapreneurs[3]—entrepreneuring individuals working within a corporation—may be given wide latitude to cultivate a business within the corporation. The highly successful Post-It business, which produces small pads of lightly adhesive note paper, was grown by Minnesota Mining and Manufacturing (3M) Corporation in this fashion. An example of intrapreneurship in the software area appears in the Du Pont vignette.

Innovation in the use of information technologies has become vital to many organizations. This innovation may be successfully performed by an organically structured team, such as an Emerging Technology group, which we introduced in chapter 6. This type of group scans the environment for information technologies that appear promising within the particular organizational context and launches them into the assimilation cycle described later in this chapter. Technologies such as expert systems, digital image processing, or neural networks can be introduced into corporations by such groups through a systematic process of assimilation and diffusion. Information centers have played this role in many companies with respect to end-user computing technologies.

For example, American Express, a company that calls information technology a key to its corporate strategy (and that spends an estimated $1 billion a year on this technology) has an Emerging Technologies group of nine people. The group

---

INTRAPRENEURSHIP GROWS A SMALL BUSINESS WITHIN A LARGE COMPANY

Du Pont not only pursues its mammoth chemical and related businesses: it also acts as a venture capitalist, providing a grubstake for enterprising employees. The SEED program of internal grants will underwrite a promising innovation in virtually any area. The successfully innovating employee winds up running a small business within the large company. The business is able to hire its own staff and purchase other resources from outside the company. It also markets the new product or service.

Matt Galas, a Du Pont employee, has assembled a staff of twenty from outside the company to develop and market his idea: software for corporate training programs. The training software is now available in several Du Pont plants. A worker who seeks advancement, say, as a computer technician, calls up the appropriate program on a personal computer. The program tells her or him about the openings the company has and administers a test. Electronic tutoring for the job follows. The software is based not only on a textbook knowledge of the field, but also on the company's training manuals and interviews with Du Pont old-timers—experts in the area. The learner is also directed to the appropriate plant library materials. Tutoring continues until the system finds a worker ready for a written and hands-on test—and subsequent promotion.

The first outside client of this intrapreneuring enterprise was Wawa Inc., a convenience-store chain interested in training their employees in properly making a hoagie sandwich.

Based on Richard Koenig, "Money from the Boss." Small Business Supplement to *The Wall Street Journal*, February 24, 1989, pp. R10–R12.

---

acts as a consulting body, with no operating responsibility (Connolly, 1988). The team evaluates new technologies and individual vendors and coordinates volume purchases among the strategic business units of the huge corporation in order to garner economies of scale.

Of course, entrepreneurial individuals, creating small businesses and growing them into innovating companies, are vital to the economy. We shall see how college students were able to create an innovative software company in Case Study Two at the end of this chapter.

12.7 ASSIMILATION OF INFORMATION TECHNOLOGIES IN AN ORGANIZATION

As information systems make increasing inroads into corporate life and often become critical to a company's performance, it is important to realize that the introduction of a major new technology is a wide-ranging and repeated process of organizational innovation. This innovation must be managed.

A stage theory for managing MIS innovation has evolved from the work of Richard Nolan, who offered a four-stage model of growth of corporate information

FIGURE 12.7

The process of information
technology assimilation.

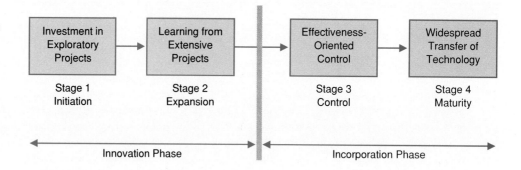

systems (Nolan, 1973). The stages he postulated were: initiation (acquisition), contagion (intense development), control (introduction of controls), and integration (user/service orientation). Nolan subsequently added two later stages—data administration and maturity—to this model (Nolan, 1979). The applicability of this model as representative of the general evolution of computing in organizations has been contested (Benbasat, 1984). However, the model has been successfully adapted to create a framework for organizational technology assimilation (diffusion). This framework, offered by Warren McFarlan and James McKenney (McFarlan, 1983), and expanded by James Cash and Poppy McLeod (Cash, 1985), is well grounded in the theory of organizational change and can guide the introduction of new information technologies into an organization. This four-stage MIS technology assimilation model is shown in figure 12.7.

The four stages of the process fall into two categories and are therefore grouped into two phases. The first phase is actual innovation in the organizational context; the approach to management here should resemble the process of guiding a research and development project. Organic principles should dominate during this phase. The stress is on nurturing pilot projects based on the technology in order to establish its effectiveness. Effectiveness criteria dominate; financial control (for example, the use of return-on-investment indicators) is relaxed, and the technology is given a chance to prove itself. Organizational learning is the primary goal: we need to learn what benefits can be drawn from the technology in *our* organization and what organizational adjustment will be needed to exploit the technology. The use of any new technology brings unexpected patterns—these are to be explored during this first phase.

If the technology proves itself in the first phase, the second phase, the incorporation of the technology, is entered. Efficiency criteria and management control are applied, and the technology is transferred to other areas of the organization. Since many firms are in the process of assimilating several major technologies at the same time, they could be on several different "assimilation curves" at the same time.

It is crucial that a new technology have both a **sponsor** and a **champion.** The sponsor is an influential high-level supporter of the effort. The champion is the person who "sells" the technology throughout the company; this frequently is

TABLE 12.2

Stages in Technology
Assimilation.

STAGE	OBJECTIVE	ACTIONS
Innovation Phase		
Initiation	Prompt exploration of technology's potential	Invest in a highly visible exploratory project of a limited size.

Causes of possible failure: Discovery that the technology is inappropriate for the firm, poor user involvement, vendor failure

Expansion	Broad experimentation with the technology; organizational learning	Initiate several pilot projects aiming at helping users develop insights about the potential of the technology for solving their problems.

Causes of possible failure: Narrow use of the technology, which leads to an inability to learn from the first applications; inability to effectively disseminate the learning in the organization

Incorporation Phase		
Control	Gaining management control over the technology	Introduce controls, first focusing on effectiveness, later on efficiency. Plan for use of the technology.

Causes of possible failure: "throttling" of the process by overcontrol: premature orientation toward efficiency as opposed to effectiveness

Maturity	Technology transfer	Introduce the use of the technology throughout the organization, based on plans and controls. Assist new users of the technology, possibly on several levels (for example, novice and advanced).

the head of the Emerging Technologies group. The technology may be found wanting during any of the stages—at least for an interim period. The organization may later return to its exploration—or to its successor technology—at a future time.

The stages of the process are described in more detail in table 12.2. The table also shows the likely causes of failure during the three initial stages (initiation, expansion, and control). Failure typically leads the company to abandon the technology for a certain period of time. The viability of this technology assimilation model was confirmed by a study of 412 companies (Raho, 1987).

The implementation of new systems during the second phase of technology assimilation is likely to encounter resistance from various organizational actors affected by the change. We shall now go on to analyze aspects of this change and discuss how the change can be managed.

12.8   INNOVATION IN INFORMATION SYSTEMS AS A PROCESS OF ORGANIZATIONAL CHANGE

Information systems affect all aspects of organizational life. Because of this, a new system will cause dislocations and pose new demands on people within the organization. Many people are naturally resistant to change, since change involves risk. As the result of a proposed change, a person may lose control over a source of information, may have to learn new skills and operate in a new environment, or may feel that his or her position in the balance of corporate power is downgraded. Many organizations cannot adjust to change: indeed, not all organizations are successful, and organizations, as well as particular projects, do fail.

Here, we shall consider how information systems affect organizational life and how the introduction of new systems can be managed.

All Aspects of Organizational Life Are Affected by MIS

Management information systems not only offer the potential to achieve competitive advantage and the ability to cope with an increasing volume of complex decision making; they also indirectly affect organizational structure: some middle-management functions related to the collection and transmission of information have become unnecessary. Many a management pyramid has been flattened by top managers exploiting this opportunity. Information systems are bearers of options in implementing management decisions to decentralize or centralize an organization or some unit of it. Distributed information systems make many organizational forms possible.

All this affects the careers and working environments of people throughout the organization. "Information is power," says an old adage. Power games are played out through *organizational politics:* competition between individuals and groups for resources and for influence over agendas and policies. New information systems very often affect the distribution of power; they are therefore resisted by some. For example, the proposed implementation of a human-resource information management (HRIM) system, an integrated database-oriented system that helps a company gain overall control over its personnel-related information, often raises many a hackle. If the system is controlled by the personnel department and includes the payroll function, which was a long-established bailiwick within the finance department, it is rather unlikely that the latter will accept the change without protest.

To go further (quoting Lynne Markus): "Designers have been known to build systems to change the balance of power among departments or other units in an organization. Because this design intention is not viewed as legitimate in most organizations, systems designed to increase one party's power and control over others are frequently masked in the language and appearance of improved efficiency or decision-making performance."[4] It should be obvious that systems are usually built at the behest of organizational actors other than the designers themselves.

Information systems deeply affect the nature of work (Zuboff, 1988). Many jobs can be enriched through the use of various systems. As we can see in the vignette on accountability and decision making, workers on factory floors, supported by

INFORMATION SYSTEMS CAN MAKE YOU ACCOUNTABLE; THEY CAN ALSO ENABLE OTHERS TO MAKE "YOUR" DECISIONS

Several years ago, Procter & Gamble built a highly computerized manufacturing plant. The plant's information systems would be able to instantaneously provide exact information on the plant's output to executives at headquarters, located 500 miles away.

Plant managers made sure that the plant's information system was not connected to headquarters. Only limited access to the plant's information was provided to higher-level executives. One may rest assured that the plant managers gave quite plausible reasons for this decision.

An expense-tracking information system was installed in a Minnesota paper manufacturing plant. The system, used by machine operators, showed them the precise costs of all the decisions they made. Using the system, the operators found cheaper chemical mixes; they also discovered that some of the equipment decisions made by managers had actually led to higher production costs. Soon after its installation, the system fell into partial disuse—at the behest of plant managers.

Based on Daniel Goleman, "Why Managers Resist Machines."
The New York Times Business Section, February 7, 1988, p. 4.

expert and other information systems, may become directly involved in decision making about production scheduling and quality control—with middle levels of supervision stripped away. Information systems can give lower-level workers information previously reserved for management or can actually distribute decision making to these workers—and clearly, not all managers like this. On the other hand, the negative potential of systems that perform such tasks as computerized performance tracking of clerical work has already been discussed in the case study for chapter 11. Jon Turner determined that the negative impact of information systems on jobs is the result of job design, rather than a direct result of the system itself (Turner, 1984). Here, again, computer systems bear options. In the words of Richard Walton, information technology has dual potentialities in organizations: its use may have either positive or negative effects (Walton 1989). Sociotechnical system design consists of selecting the technical options that address the needs of workers on their jobs, as well as the needs of the organization.

Organizations themselves do not innovate or make decisions—people do. But the organizational environment can be more or less supportive of rational decision making. Bureaucratic organizations, largely acting within the mechanistic model, evolve large bodies of standard operating procedures. These standing policies serve reliably in a stable environment (Slevin, 1990). They restrict, however, the repertoires of actions that may be taken in a new situation—which hampers innovation. By attempting to reduce uncertainty about an organization's internal environment, they may actually increase uncertainty about it when a response to an unexpected change is called for. Much as a very conservative investor who sticks to low-yield and low-risk investment instruments may deplete his or her assets in turbulent times, these firms may perish when change is demanded.

FIGURE 12.8

Lewin-Schein model of
organizational change.

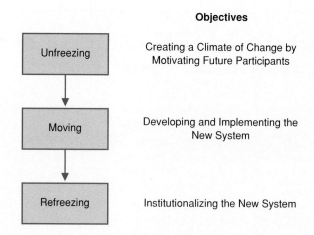

Objectives

Unfreezing — Creating a Climate of Change by
Motivating Future Participants

Moving — Developing and Implementing the
New System

Refreezing — Institutionalizing the New System

Rationality in organizational decision making is restricted by a variety of factors, which we shall discuss in the next chapter. In his thoughtful analysis of computing as a social process, Rob Kling distinguishes two basic analytical perspectives (Kling, 1980). Various rationalist perspectives, including the systems approach and management science, assume that there is a fundamental consensus among organizational actors in respect to values and goals. Another set of analytical perspectives assumes, on the contrary, that different organizational actors and groups are in conflict, with information systems playing a powerful role in this conflict. Individuals in organizations have a variety of ways to exercise power, and every organizational actor exercises some measure of it. Unpopular decisions made at the top are frequently subverted in the ranks. When long-term goals go by the wayside, short-term decisions are made so as to satisfy multiple stakeholders. Any process of organizational change has to be conducted by mustering support from possible opponents—or by neutralizing them.

**Introducing
Organizational
Change**

The implementation of a new information system is a process of organizational change going far beyond a cutover from one technological artifact (perhaps manual, perhaps an earlier form of computerization) to another. As such, the change should be managed—indeed, for that reason, this change management is called "intervention." Information systems often cut through the existing boundaries of organizational units, and thus, varying degrees of resistance are to be expected (rather than discovered with surprise). Lack of appropriate change management has led to the failure of many a technically superior system.

A widely used model of organizational change has been introduced by Kurt Lewin (1947) and refined by Ed Schein (1961). This model, shown in figure 12.8, emphasizes the necessity of first creating a climate for change, motivating the affected parties and creating a "change compact," so to speak. Evidence of senior management's commitment to the change is crucial. Only after this "unfreezing" phase should the new system be implemented (in the "moving" phase). After a change is introduced, it must be institutionalized—that is buttressed by new procedures, additional training, and, if necessary, system modifications to gain acceptance and use. Thus, the company gains a new stable ground from which the new technology may be exploited.

HOW TO UNFREEZE

Perhaps the crucial part of the organizational change model is unfreezing. Gloria Bronsema and Peter Keen show how an international bank conducted unfreezing before the introduction of a major on-line transaction processing system integrating a number of major services. A culture clash had arisen between the marketing and operations personnel, both of whom were to use the system: the marketing people felt that the use of a system of this type was beneath their dignity.

   Instead of opting simply for a training program following the implementation of the system, the bank chose to engage in a proactive educational intervention, that is, a process of educational change, based on the Lewin-Schein model. The main element in the unfreezing was a workshop. The workshop was needed to change people's attitudes and actions, rather than simply to teach them how to use the system—which many of them, most likely, would avoid doing. The workshop demonstrated the commitment of senior management to the system and used examples from the participants' world as the basis for discussions. During these discussions, workshop leaders invited the articulation of concerns. The participants planned their future individual actions with the anticipated system.

   As one of the participants stated in a postworkshop comment: "Before the workshop I was *told* I would be a part of Integrated Processing System. After the workshop I *feel* a part of it."

Based on Gloria S. Bronsema and Peter G. W. Keen, "Educational Intervention and Implementation in MIS." *Sloan Management Review*, Summer 1983, pp. 35–43.

The process of technology assimilation described earlier in the chapter involves multiple organizational change cycles, accompanying the introduction of individual information systems (Leonard-Barton, 1987).

An example of how one company accomplished the unfreezing is shown in the above vignette.

12.9 THE GLOBAL DIMENSION OF DEPLOYING INFORMATION TECHNOLOGY IN ORGANIZATIONS

A vital characteristic of the business environment of the 1990s is generally recognized to be **globalization:** the emergence of the worldwide market as the arena of corporate activities. The variety of these activities in the international domain offers organizations an opportunity to draw on the capabilities of information systems. Organizational coordination, product and service differentiation for local markets, and diffusion of innovation throughout a firm can find support from properly deployed MIS. We shall explore the four fundamental strategies pursued by multinational corporations and discuss the roles MIS can play in their support.

Globalization of Business

Over the decades since the last World War, business has become increasingly international. Relatively free flows of goods, capital, equipment, and knowledge (in the form of technological, managerial, and entrepreneurial skills) across borders, combined with the highly developed infrastructure (transportation and telecommmunications), have led to the globalization of business. When we discussed in chapter 2 the hallmarks of the environment in which today's organizations operate, we stressed that competitive pressures from this complex and turbulent environment operate on a global scale.

Virtually all large firms, and many smaller ones, acquire labor (and locate plants) where it is cost-effective, find intellectual and financial capital anywhere it is available, and pursue markets across the globe. Many products lose their nationality (Reich, 1991).

Take the midsized Hurco Companies of Indianapolis.[5] The key component of the machine tools it sells—the computerized controls—are made in the United States. Thus, the component with the highest value added is made at home; indeed, Hurco's competitive edge is in the software for these machines. The company's products are sold in Germany, Britain, Singapore—altogether in twenty-eight foreign markets, which account for about half of the firm's total revenues. But Hurco has gone well past plain exporting. Most of the machines sold in Europe are assembled in High Wycombe, England, where the controllers made in the United States are combined with the housing, fittings, and other parts from Germany, Spain, Taiwan, or wherever they can be produced most efficiently. Hurco has also established a distribution and technical-support unit in Germany, where service calls on machine tools have to be made in twenty-four hours.

Consider another example. Nearly all color TV sets sold in the United States are made locally—by seventeen foreign corporations employing 15,000 American workers[6] (but the firms do export the profits back home).

The degree of involvement in international business depends on a firm. Most firms engage only in exporting and importing, selling and buying goods and services, or trading technical and managerial skills through licensing agreements and management contracts. In a more advanced stage of involvement, a domestically based firm produces some goods or services abroad. Some of these firms expand their international operations to the extent that they value them at least as much as the domestic business. In the two latter stages, the firm is generally considered to have joined the ranks of multinational corporations.

Indeed, multinational companies have become a principal driving force of business globalization as they have grown rapidly in size and number since World War II (although some firms were already involved in similar activities during the Industrial Revolution). A *multinational corporation* owns and operates companies in more than one country. Multinational corporations generally locate their headquarters in a parent country and their subsidiaries (or subunits) in various host countries. These companies employ a variety of departmentation methods. As some of the multinationals lose ties to a domestic market, and as the host countries develop their own industrial bases, the relationships between multinational organizations and the nations where they are headquartered and

---

INTERNATIONAL MARKETS ARE NOT ONLY FOR LARGE CORPORATIONS

Small and midsized U.S. firms often ignore international markets, wrongly assuming that they are accessible only to the big players. The fact that this is not so is best proven by the many small firms in Europe and Japan, many of whom are major exporters.

To help small firms look for global opportunities, GateWaze Inc. of Manchester, Massachusetts has developed a microcomputer software package, called World Trader, whose database is updated quarterly. The package includes a primer on international trade, details on fifty foreign markets (including types of imports and distribution channels), as well as information on organizations facilitating international trade and statistics on 125 countries.

From "Software for Little Guys with Big Horizons." *Business Week*, March 18, 1991, p. 101.

---

where they do business becomes complicated. However, of primary interest to us here is how information systems can support the variety of global organizational business arrangements.

The complexity of the multinational organizational environment is engendered by the wide diversity of sociopolitical and economic conditions in the countries concerned, different ways of doing business, language and currency differences, and differences in infrastructure development (Hofstede, 1980). The great diversity of stakeholders demands a corresponding variety of requisite organizational responses. The higher risks have to be matched by benefits, such as access to a rapidly growing market or to resources superior in well-defined respects.

These problems are mirrored by the difficulties encountered by the MIS function (Buss, 1982). Staffing problems are combined with the need to coordinate across disparate infrastructures and standards. Of major concern to MIS practitioners are the limitations various countries impose on **transborder data flow,** the transmission of data across (primarily out over) their boundaries. This data export control aims in general to stimulate local business and address security and privacy concerns.

Corporate Strategies in Worldwide Business and the Roles of MIS

Difficulties notwithstanding, MIS have an important role to play in a multinational corporation. To perform and innovate successfully in a global marketplace, organizations need to develop superior coordination skills. "Coordination involves sharing information, allocating responsibility, and aligning efforts," says Michael Porter.[7] The coordination capability of information technology, with the lowered costs of coordination it provides (Malone, 1987), is of vital importance. Worldwide corporations also need to diffuse innovations internationally. A technological or managerial innovation in one location should be leveraged across the organization. Organizational designs and the use of information technology should facilitate the processes of coordinating and innovating.

In general, the potential of computer and telecommunications technologies to enhance productivity and enable pursuit of competitive advantage in the distributed environment of a multinational firm is apparent. Our discussion in section 7.8 of creating organizational values with MIS in this environment applies directly here.

TABLE 12.3

Corporate Strategies and Roles of MIS in the Global Business Environment

BUSINESS STRATEGY (AND STRUCTURE)	PRINCIPAL CHARACTERISTIC	DECISION-MAKING CHARACTERISTICS	MIS ROLE	MIS STRUCTURE
Multinational (decentralized federation)	Foreign operations regarded as a portfolio of relatively independent businesses	Decision making decentralized to subsidiaries; informal relationships between headquarters and subsidiaries	Financial reporting by subsidiaries to headquarters for control purposes	Decentralized: primarily stand-alone systems and dispersed databases
International (coordinated federation)	Foreign operations regarded as appendages to domestic corporation, where core competencies are honed	More vital decisions and knowledge in general developed at headquarters and transferred to subsidiaries	Formal planning and control systems coordinate the entire operation	Largely centralized planning and control systems implemented on a variety of hardware architectures that ensure links among units
Global (centralized federation)	Foreign operations regarded as pipelines for delivery of goods and services to a unified global market, in search of economies of scale and scope	Decisions made at the center; knowledge developed and retained at the center	Tight central control of subsidiaries through centralized planning, control, and general decision making	Centralized systems and databases
Transnational (integrated network)	Differentiated contributions by all units to integrated worldwide operations	Decision making and knowledge generation distributed among units	Vital coordination role at many levels: knowledge work, group decision making, planning and control	Integrated architecture with distributed systems and databases, supporting management and knowledge work across the organization

In their influential framework, Christopher Bartlett and Sumantra Ghoshal have identified three forces that shape the competitive posture of multinational corporations: the need for global integration—to achieve efficiency; the need for local differentiation—to respond to the requirement of local markets; and the need for worldwide innovation—to develop and diffuse technological and organizational innovations on a global scale (Bartlett, 1989). If we review the information technology capabilities discussed in chapter 2, we shall see that information systems may contribute to harnessing all three of these forces.

Bartlett and Ghoshal have also identified four models of worldwide organizations; each of them balance these four forces differently. They argue that the currently prevalent three organizational models—multinational (used in a special sense), international, and global—are evolving toward the transnational model of a firm. Jahangir Karimi and Benn Konsynski have further identified MIS strategies needed to support these organizational models (Karimi, 1991). These models and strategies are summarized in table 12.3.

Karimi and Konsynski also stress the importance of partnership-based organizations in the global area. Based on strategic alliances, each member of such a virtual organization can contribute complementary resources. We encountered such a virtual global organization—Rosenbluth International Alliance—in Case Study Two for chapter 5.

WORLDWIDE BUSINESS REQUIRES ADJUSTMENTS

The Royal Dutch/Shell Group, the second largest oil company in the world, has been run largely on the multinational model. It has a small corporate center, and most of its decision making (along with information systems) is distributed to the local operating units. For a long time, the data centers were not even networked (nor is there a data center at headquarters). This is now changing: the company has started to realize the advantages of its scale.

Take the electronic trading of petroleum. Until recently, Shell's operating companies worldwide dealt at locally set, marginally different prices—and the external arbitrage traders would profit by buying oil from one Shell unit and selling it to another. Now Shell's traders share the same information on their screens worldwide—and deal at the same price. The system also provides the traders with information on potential customers. But it is still up to the local Shell trader to make a transaction—local decision making is considered vital to the well-being of Shell.

Based on Phillip Hunter, "Tanking Up on Technology." InformationWeek, February 18, 1991, pp. 20–25.

Let us discuss the worldwide corporate strategies using the terminology of this framework. Companies operating according to the multinational model are primarily oriented toward building a strong presence in the host countries by responding to their local needs. International firms adapt the technological and managerial knowledge developed by the parent company to the local conditions of the host countries. Global companies treat the world as a single market and aim to realize efficiencies of scale and scope over this enlarged territory. The extent of central control grows as we move down this list.

Bartlett and Ghoshal find that the transnational strategy offers the greatest promise. A transnational corporation integrates its overseas components into the overall structure across several dimensions: they become a source of specialized innovation, integrated into the overall corporate web of the firm. Under this strategy, joint innovation by headquarters and by some of the overseas units leads to the development of relatively standardized and yet flexible products that can capture a number of local markets. Thus, Japan's NEC Corporation combined the hardware expertise of its central development group in Japan with the knowledge of telecommunications software at its U.S. subsidiary to develop a superior and adaptable line of digital switching equipment. Network-oriented global corporations have emerged in investment banking (Eccles, 1987) to meet the global banking needs of their clients. We should note, however, that concentrating the critical competencies of a firm, the core of its competitive position, in a narrow group of selected sites significantly lowers the risks of globalization (James, 1990).

The role of the MIS function has to be aligned with the posture of the globally competing corporation, as shown in table 12.3. Figure 12.9 summarizes the MIS aspect of the global pursuit of competitive advantage.

Of course, the strategy of a firm accommodates a variety of tactical moves—and keeps evolving, as illustrated in the above vignette.

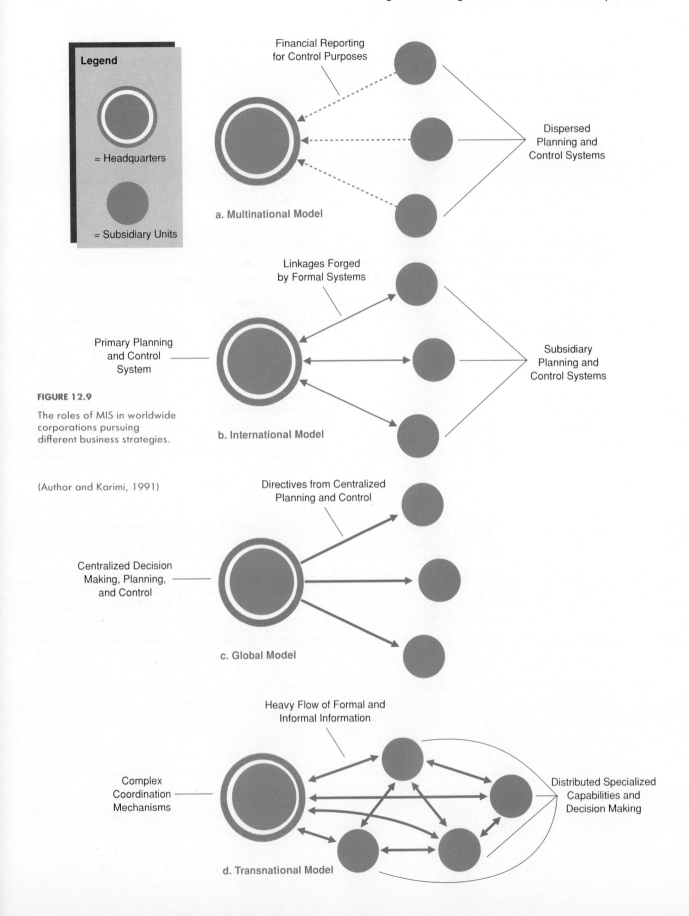

FIGURE 12.9

The roles of MIS in worldwide corporations pursuing different business strategies.

(Author and Karimi, 1991)

A broad study of the MIS functions in U.S.-based multinational corporations (Deans, 1991) offers a degree of support to the contention that, as international involvement of a firm increases, more variegated and complex organizational structures emerge. The study also showed the five issues of primary importance in the use of MIS by multinational companies: (1) educating the senior corporate managers about the potential role of MIS in the international environment; (2) data security; (3) integration of various technologies on an international scale; (4) end-user computing in an environment involving nationals of many countries; and (5) price and quality of telecommmunications.

Reaching for a global marketplace does not at all guarantee competitive advantage to a firm. But failing to reach for it may guarantee a competitive disadvantage.

. . . .

SUMMARY

Leading and organizing are the management functions directed toward the coordination of human effort in an organization. A variety of organizational structures is possible, distinguished by the way the work of an organization is subdivided into units, the number of levels in the hierarchy, and the degree to which decision making is decentralized. Environments of rapid change call for organic organizational designs, with decentralized decision making and participative leadership.

Information technologies can be a potent source of innovation. The introduction of new technologies is becoming a frequent occurrence. This calls for a managed process of technology assimilation. Since systems based on these technologies often have deep effects on people in organizations, system introduction should be conducted and managed as a process of organizational change.

Modern organizations participate ever more actively in the worldwide business arena. In this process, they can profitably draw on the capabilities of information systems to coordinate their business activities in pursuit of economies of scale and scope, to differentiate their products for a variety of local markets, and to diffuse organizational and technological innovations from wherever they have originated throughout the company.

CONCLUSIONS FOR MIS PRACTICE

1. MIS managers should understand the factors that motivate their personnel in their work. This helps develop effective leadership methods and decreases personnel turnover.

2. Various ways of structuring an MIS department in an organization are possible. In particular, dispersed and matrix management, structures that closely bind information service to the corporate functions they serve, have proven effective. MIS professionals must understand the businesses they serve.

3. To garner the full potential of MIS in continuing corporate innovation, organizations should explore organic organizational principles. Both small and large firms have the ability to employ them.

4. Businesses are introducing new information technologies with increasing frequency. An organization benefits most by doing this through a managed process of technology assimilation. This process gives the technology a chance to prove itself within the context of the given organization.

5. The technical aspect of an information system isn't everything. Systems affect power relationships in an organization and the quality of working life. These factors should be studied in the process of technology assimilation.

6. Introduction of new systems should be conducted as a process of organizational change—with the planned preparation of all involved through unfreezing.

7. As their organizations become increasingly involved in international business, MIS professionals must familiarize themselves with national and international standards, limitations on transborder data flow, limitations on telecommunications, and other constraints stemming from operating across national borders.

8. MIS managers in multinational corporations should be familiar with the principal strategy pursued by their firm and be guided by it in the MIS planning process.

ENDNOTES

1. Chris Demos, a Federal Express executive, quoted by Clinton Wilder in "Corporate Culture Key to MIS Success," *Computerworld*, May 1, 1989, p. 61.

2. The notion of span of management (or control) has a long history in the organization of military command. In the management literature, this concept has been traced to Napoleon who said, "No man can command more than five distinct bodies in the same theater of war" (as quoted in David D. Van Fleet and Arthur G. Bedeian, "A History of the Span of Management," *Academy of Management Review*, July 1977, p. 358). At this time, much as the occupants of some corporate boardrooms would consider themselves to be in theaters of war, differences in settings and in informational support have considerably increased the span of management.

3. The term was coined by Gifford Pinchot III, whose book on the subject, *Intrapreneuring: Why You Don't Have to Leave the Corporation to Become an Entrepreneur*, (New York: Harper & Row, 1985), is a fountainhead of ideas. The term *skunkworks* comes from the comic strip *Li'l Abner* by way of Lockheed Aircraft Corporation. Big Barnsmell was making the illicit liquor, Kickapoo Joy Juice, in his "Skonk Works." Lockheed first used a small "skunkworks" team to break out of the establishmentarian mode of operation.

4. M. Lynne Markus, *Systems in Organizations: Bugs and Features*. Boston: Pitman, 1984, p. 77.

5. Steve Lohr, "U.S. Industry's New Global Power." *The New York Times*, March 4, 1991, pp. D1, D3.

6. "Special Issue on Innovation." *Business Week*, June 15, 1990, p. 37.

7. Porter, 1990, p. 58.

**KEY TERMS AND
CONCEPTS**

Organization
Organizational memory
Organizational culture
Leadership styles
Maslow's hierarchy of human
  needs
Vroom's expectancy theory
Organization chart
Functional departmentation
Divisional departmentation
Matrix organization
Adhocracy

Span of management
Decentralization of decision making
Mechanistic organizations
Organic organizations
Assimilation of information technology
Sponsor
Champion
Process of organizational change
Unfreezing
Globalization
Multinational corporation
Transborder data flow

QUESTIONS

1. What are organizations, and how are they related to management?

2. What are the tasks of organizing?

3. Consider the capabilities of the information systems summarized in chapter 2. Which of these support the organizing function?

4. What are the four leadership styles?

5. What is relationship between leading and human motivation theories?

6. Present Maslow's hierarchy of human needs.

7. Show Vroom's expectancy theory of human motivation in the form of a multiplication-based equation.

8. Contrast divisional and functional organizational structures. Which advantages of each are present in the matrix structure?

9. What is the relationship between the span of management, the number of levels in an organizational hierarchy, and organizational responsiveness?

10. What advantages are generally associated with decentralized decision making?

11. Contrast mechanistic and organic organizational principles. What environments are congenial for each type of organization?

12. Give three ideas on how a large firm can build "centers of change" into its organizational structure and functioning.

13. What are the four stages of information technology assimilation? How are they grouped into two phases, and what are the differing objectives of each phase?

14. How is information technology assimilation related to the process of organizational change?

15. What are the three stages of organizational change?

16. What is the globalization of business?

17. What are the forms of corporate involvement in international business? What is a multinational corporation?

18. State three important concerns of MIS departments in the international business environment.

19. What are the three forces that influence the competitive posture of multinational corporations, according to Bartlett and Ghoshal?

20. How does the MIS role in an organization pursuing the transnational strategy differ from the MIS role in organizations pursuing the three other strategies taken together?

ISSUES FOR DISCUSSION

1. Debate this issue: "Leading and organizing are people-oriented activities, and information systems have no significant role to play in them" versus "For better or worse, MIS will increasingly play a larger role in the functions of leading and organizing." Buttress your arguments with facts.

2. Comment on this news item:

> The Environmental Protection Agency has created a database containing educational courses and career paths its workers can peruse at their personal computers.
>   According to an agency official, the system will help [the] EPA dispel the notion that personnel managers are aloof and ineffective.
> From Kimberly Taylor, "EPA Data Base Shows Staff Options." *Federal Computing Week,* February 6, 1989, p. 10.

3. The U.S. Patent and Trademark Office has recently been granting patents for algorithms and program techniques. For example, Narendra K. Karmarkar received a patent for his method (algorithm) to ensure efficient resource allocation, which is applicable to airline plane and crew scheduling and to many other problems. Quarterdeck Office Systems of Santa Monica, California, obtained a patent for the now broadly used "window" concept that allows a computer to display user interaction with several application programs in various parts of a VDT screen. This makes it possible to run scores of programs at once through Quarterdeck's Desqview package, a capability introduced a little later by Microsoft in its Windows program.

   Do you believe granting such patents stimulates innovation by protecting intellectual property or stymies it by making it difficult to accomplish anything without stumbling into someone else's claim?

4. Discuss the risks and benefits of "going global" (or just international) for a software firm that is considering setting up a software-development subsidiary in a developing country. What should the prospective parent firm consider in the search for a host country?

CASE STUDY ONE: THE MIS DEPARTMENT OF A MAJOR MULTINATIONAL CORPORATION

The MIS function at E. I. Du Pont de Nemours & Company has received wide recognition in the industry. Its chief, corporate senior vice-president Raymond E. Cairns, Jr., assumes responsibility for the corporation's networking and computer hardware standards, which are anchored in only three approved systems vendors (IBM, DEC, and HP). In 1990, for the first time, more than half of the company's revenue was derived from sales to foreign customers. Providing the information-technology infrastructure to support global operations is a daunting task. We presented an interview with Cairns in the case study for part two of this book. The annual MIS budget for Du Pont is at least $750 million.

The top level of the organization of the MIS department at Du Pont is shown in figure 12.10. Only 20 percent of Du Pont's information systems resources are under the control of managers who report directly to Cairns. The remaining 80 percent are managed by MIS heads in operating departments (business groups) of the firm. These managers report to the heads of their business groups. They report to Cairns only on the "dotted-line" principle, as shown in the figure. Cairns meets with them generally once a week to coordinate the corporate MIS activity. This reporting structure makes MIS responsive to the needs of end users. Analyze this structure in the terms introduced in the chapter in order to answer the questions which follow.

Based on Clinton Wilder and Nell Margolis, "Information on a Global Scale." *Computerworld*, May 23, 1988, pp. 1, 59–64; and Johanna Ambrosio, "Opening Systems to Span the Globe." *Computerworld*, June 24, 1991, pp. 75–78.

FIGURE 12.10

Organization chart of the MIS department at DuPont.

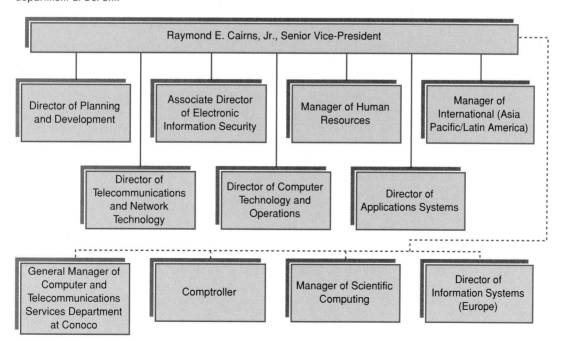

Case Study One Questions

1. Do you believe the company has a strongly centralized MIS management?

2. Which departmentation principles were employed in structuring the MIS department?

3. What is the top manager's span of management?

CASE STUDY
TWO:

How Four College Students Started a Multimillion-Dollar Software Company—and Invented an Industry Segment

Maps are one of the oldest forms of written communication between people: clay tablets with land boundary maps were used in Babylon in 2200 B.C. Electronic mapping (or digital cartography) is one of the newer applications of information systems.

Four undergraduate students brought this application to the desktop: they developed a system that allows a personal-computer user to display database information on a map and to merge in a variety of ways databases and maps of any area in the United States. While at Rensselaer Polytechnic Institute (RPI), these four students founded a company, MapInfo of Troy, New York, that markets the leading PC-based mapping package.

Sean O'Sullivan, the twenty-four-year-old president of the company, was the driving force behind the packages. He wanted to be an entrepreneur since childhood. An amateur programmer since age thirteen, O'Sullivan worked in an IBM co-op program soon after entering

college. At that time, he realized the potential of the CD-ROM technology for computerized mapping. He actively sought out a sponsor for the project at his school. He found the sponsor in a professor who was directing the college's center for interactive computer graphics. The developing project attracted five research engineers at the school. An electronic map and car-tracking system was built. It turned out to be the prototype for what later became the MapInfo system.

The young entrepreneur understood from the very beginning that technical innovation does not a business make: an organization had to be created and financed. O'Sullivan took a class on the principles of entrepreneurship, in which he developed a business plan. The plan analyzed the industry and the competition and developed a strategy, subsequently "dollarized," for the company. O'Sullivan started the company with three classmates whose ages ranged from twenty-one to twenty-three. They recruited an experienced manager, Mike Marvin, whom they also discovered at RPI. The business director of the school's center for manufacturing productivity, Marvin put up the seed money for the project and later became CEO of the firm.

O'Sullivan believes that entrepreneurship is a team effort. He quotes Andrew Carnegie in saying that his greatest achievement was to gather together people smarter than himself.

Because they wanted to keep most of the equity in the company, the partners sought very little financing beyond the $65,000 seed money. This required two years of sacrifice and work almost around the clock—particularly since the budding firm owned only a single IBM PC.

After these two initial years, the firm reached sales of about $2 million a year. Since then, the growth has been phenomenal. O'Sullivan has every reason to expect MapInfo to develop into a $50 million to $100 million company.

Geographic information systems (GIS) had been available before, but they required mainframes or minicomputers to run them. Indeed, Boise Cascade of Boise, Idaho, a leading producer of timber products in North America, has been using an advanced GIS system for managing timberlands since the early 1980s. But by making these capabilities available on an inexpensive platform, MapInfo has vastly broadened the market for these systems (see color photo 35). They are used by police departments, orange growers, cemetery planners, and scientists tracking insect populations.

Synthes, USA, a manufacturer of orthopedic instruments and implants, uses the MapInfo package to optimize its sales efforts. The program is sold with a variety of op-tional maps—with the level of detail varying from a city block to the entire globe. It even creates territorial overlays. Synthes' sales manager, Michael Ward, says: "Take, for example, hip screws, which are frequently needed by people over fifty. We can view an area, then overlay demographic census data for the area, overlay the locations of hospitals, and finally product areas. If the sales are not proportional to the percentage of people over fifty, then we know where to push."

Chase Manhattan Bank uses the mapping software to analyze the effectiveness of its automatic teller machine (ATM) program against its competitors in New York. It overlays on the area map the ATM locations and their usage frequency both for its own machines and for those of its competitors. The results form an input for ATM distribution planning.

The Office of Management and Budget of the U.S. government singled out electronic mapping in its 1989 five-year plan for federal information systems procurement as the application with the greatest growth potential. To give you an idea of the size of this market, the 1989 federal budget expenditures for information technology were $17 billion (about 2 percent of the national budget).

Sources: Michael J. Major, "The Software Entrepreneurs." *Graduating Engineer*, December 1988, pp. 18–20; "MapInfo Helps Synthes, USA, Boost Sales." MapInfo press release, April 19, 1989; Gene Bylinsky, "Managing with Electronic Maps." *Fortune*, April 24, 1989; Stephen C. Guptill and Lowell E. Starr, "Making Maps with Computers." *American Scientist*, 76, 2, March-April 1988, pp. 136–42; Leigh Riverbark, "Changes in Info Technology Buys Recommended." *Federal Computer Week*, February 6, 1989, p. 6; and David Freedman, "The Forest for the Trees." *CIO*, January 1991, pp. 25–32.

Case Study Two Questions

1. What are the components of entrepreneurial success in this case?

2. What would you have done differently if you were O'Sullivan?

3. Analyze how the college student was able to use the resources around him—his college—to succeed in building an entrepreneurial organization.

4. What are the potential applications of computerized mapping? Describe three scenarios where these systems would enjoy a particular advantage.

SELECTED REFERENCES

Ackerman, Michael A., and Malone, Thomas W. "Answer Garden: A Tool for Growing Organizational Memory." *Proceedings of ACM Conference on Office Information Systems.* Boston: MIT, 1990, pp. 31–39.

Attewell, Paul, and Rule, James. "Computing and Organizations: What We Know and What We Don't Know." *Communications of the ACM,* 27, 12, December 1984, pp. 1184–1201.

Bartlett, Christopher A., and Ghoshal, Sumantra. *Managing Across Borders: A Transnational Solution.* Boston: Harvard Business School Press, 1989.

Benbasat, Izak, and others. "A Critique of the Stage Hypothesis: Theory and Empirical Evidence." *Communications of the ACM,* 27, 5, May 1984, pp. 476–85.

Burgelman, Robert A., and Sayles, Leonard R. *Inside Corporate Innovation: Strategy, Structure, and Managerial Skills.* New York: Free Press, 1986.

Burns, Tom, and Stalker, George M. *The Management of Innovation.* London: Tavistock Publications, 1961.

Buss, Martin D. J. "Managing International Information Systems." *Harvard Business Review,* May-June 1982, pp. 111–13.

Cash, James I., Jr., and McLeod, Poppy L. "Managing the Introduction of Information Systems Technology in Strategically Dependent Companies." *Journal of Management Information Systems,* 1, 4, Spring 1985, pp. 5–23.

Chandler, Alfred D., Jr. *Strategy and Structure.* Cambridge, Mass.: MIT Press, 1962.

Connolly, James, and Horwitt, Elisabeth. "American Express Sets Its Own Limits." *Computerworld,* December 12, 1988, pp. 1, 81–86.

Couger, J. Daniel, and McIntyre, Scott C. "Motivation Norms of Knowledge Engineers Compared to Those of Software Engineers." *Journal of Management Information Systems,* 4, 3, Winter 1987–88, pp. 82–93.

Couger, J. Daniel, and Zawacki, Robert A. *Motivating and Managing Computer Personnel.* New York: Wiley, 1980.

Csikszentmihalyi, Mihaly. *Flow: The Psychology of Optimal Experience.* New York: Harper & Row, 1990.

Deans, P. Candace; Karwan, Kirk R.; Goslar, Martin D.; Ricks, David A.; and Toyne, Brian. "Identification of Key International Information Systems Issues in U.S.-Based Multinational Corporations." *Journal of Management Information Systems,* 7, 4, Spring 1991, pp. 27–50.

Donovan, John J. "Beyond Chief Information Officer to Network Manager." *Harvard Business Review,* September-October 1988, pp. 134–40.

Eccles, Robert G., and Crane, David B. "Managing through Networks in Investment Banking." *California Management Review,* 30, 1, Fall 1987, pp. 176–95.

George, Joey F., and King, John L. "Examining the Computing and Centralization Debate." *Communications of the ACM,* 34, 7, July 1991, pp. 62–72.

Gurbaxani, Vijay, and Whang, Seungjin. "The Impact of Information Systems on Organizations and Markets." *Communications of the ACM,* 34, 1, January 1991, pp. 59–73.

Harpaz, Itzhak. "The Importance of Work Goals: An International Perspective." *Journal of International Business Studies,* 21, 1, 1990, pp. 75–93.

Hertzberg, Frederick. *Work and the Nature of Man.* Cleveland: World, 1966.

Hofstede, Geert. "Motivation, Leadership, and Organization: Do American Theories Apply Abroad?" *Organizational Dynamics,* 9, 2, Summer 1980, pp. 42–63.

Huber, George P. "A Theory of the Effects of Advanced Information Technologies on Organizational Design, Intelligence, and Decision Making." *Academy of Management Review,* 15, 1, January 1990, pp. 47–71.

James, Barrie. "Reducing the Risks of Globalization." *Long Range Planning,* 23, 1, December 1990, pp. 80–88.

Karimi, Jahangir, and Konsynski, Benn R. "Globalization and Information Management Strategies." *Journal of Management Information Systems,* 7, 4, Spring 1991, pp. 7–26.

Kling, Rob. "Social Analyses of Computing: Theoretical Perspectives in Recent Empirical Research." *Computing Surveys,* 12, 1, March 1980, pp. 61–110.

Laudon, Kenneth C., and Laudon, Jane P. *Management Information Systems: A Contemporary Perspective.* New York: Macmillan, 1988.

Lawrence, Paul R., and Lorsch, Jay W. *Organization and Environment.* Homewood, Ill.: Irwin, 1969.

Leonard-Barton, Dorothy. "The Case for Integrative Innovation: An Expert System at Digital." *Sloan Management Review,* 28, 1, Fall 1987, pp. 7–19.

Lewin, Kurt. "Frontiers in Group Dynamics." *Human Relations,* Vol. 1, 1947, pp. 5–41.

McFarlan, F. Warren, and McKenney, James L. *Corporate Information Systems Management: The Issues Facing Senior Executives.* Homewood, Ill.: Irwin, 1983.

Malone, Thomas W.; Yates, Joanne; and Benjamin, Robert I. "Electronic Markets and Electronic Hierarchies." *Communications of the ACM,* 30, 6, June 1987, pp. 484–504.

Markus, M. Lynne, and Robey, Daniel. "Information Technology and Organizational Change: Causal Structure in Theory and Research." *Management Science,* 34, 5, May 1988, pp. 583–98.

Maslow, Abraham H. *Motivation and Personality.* 2d ed. New York: Harper & Row, 1970.

Mintzberg, Henry. "The Adhocracy." In *The Strategy Process,* edited by James B. Quinn, Henry Mintzberg, and Robert M. James. Englewood Cliffs, N.J.: Prentice Hall, 1988.

Nolan, Richard L. "Managing the Computer Resource: A Stage Hypothesis." *Communications of the ACM,* 16, 7, July 1973, pp. 399–405.

Nolan, Richard L. "Managing the Crises in Data Processing." *Harvard Business Review,* March-April 1979, pp. 115–26.

Porter, Michael E. *The Competitive Advantage of Nations.* New York: The Free Press, 1990.

Raho, Louis E.; Belohlav, James A.; and Fiedler, Kirk D. "Assimilating New Technology into the Organization: An Assessment of McFarlan and McKenney's Model." *MIS Quarterly,* 11, 2, June 1987, pp. 205–20.

Reich, Robert B. *The Work of Nations: Preparing Ourselves for 21st-Century Capitalism.* New York: Knopf, 1991.

Robey, Daniel. "Computer Information Systems and Organization Structure." *Communications of the ACM,* 24, 10, October 1981, pp. 679–87.

Schein, Ed. "Management Development as a Process of Influence." *Industrial Management Review,* 2, 1961, pp. 59–77.

Schermerhorn, John R., Jr., *Management for Productivity,* 2d ed., New York: John Wiley, 1986.

Scott Morton, Michael (ed.) *The Corporation of the 1990s: Information Technology and Organizational Transformation*. New York: Oxford University Press, 1991.

Slevin, Dennis P., and Covin, Jeffrey G. "Juggling Entrepreneurial Style and Organizational Structure—How to Get Your Act Together." *Sloan Management Review,* 31, 2, Winter 1990, pp. 43–53.

Turner, Jon A. "Computer-Mediated Work: The Interplay Between Technology and Structured Jobs." *Communications of the ACM,* 27, 12, December 1984, pp. 1210–17.

Vroom, Victor H. *Work and Motivation.* New York: Wiley, 1964.

Walsh, James P., and Ungson, Geraldo R. "Organizational Memory." *Academy of Management Review,* 16, 1, January 1991, pp. 57–91.

Walton, Richard E. *Up and Running: Integrating Information Technology and the Organization.* Boston: Harvard Business School Press, 1989.

Zuboff, Shoshana. *In the Age of the Smart Machine: The Future of Work and Power.* New York: Basic Books, 1988.

MANAGER AND DECISION MAKING

. . . .

*If it is obvious what you have to do, you are not getting
proper input.*

James McCormick

*Gentlemen, I take it we are all in agreement on the
decision here. Then I propose we postpone further
discussion . . . to give ourselves time to develop
disagreement and perhaps gain some understanding of
what the decision is all about.*

Alfred P. Sloan, Jr.

We have analyzed the functions of management: planning, controlling, leading, and organizing. We have also discussed organizations—the arena of management. We shall now turn our attention to people who are managers. In a sense, almost all people in organizations small and large are managers of resources. We are, therefore, concerned in general with individuals in organizations. Most of these people use information systems, and some of them also develop them.

In this chapter, we want to see what managers actually do. Information systems support individual decision making—a major component of managerial work. We shall therefore analyze the decision-making process and the tools used for rational decision making. We shall see that rational decision making is an ideal rather than a reality in most practical situations. We shall also learn what limits are imposed on rationality by the organizational setting and by human limitations. We will devote attention to creativity in decision making and, in particular, to creative problem solving in groups, where information systems support not only decision making, but also communication among individuals.

This chapter is, in a sense, a lead-in to the next, where we shall discuss decision support systems (DSS). DSS directly support the decision-making process we present here.

FOCUS STATEMENT

Suppose a general can lead his soldiers out of an ambush, in which he believes all 600 of them will be killed, by one of two routes. His advisors tell him: "If you take the first route, 200 soldiers will be saved. If you take the second, there is a one-third chance that all 600 soldiers will be saved and a two-thirds chance that none will be saved."

When faced with this choice, most people (three to one) in an experimental group chose the first route. After all, it assures that 200 lives would be saved.

But the same difficult choice could also be stated differently. Suppose the advisors told the general: "If you take the first route, 400 soldiers will die. If you take the second, there is a one-third chance that no soldiers will die and a two-thirds chance that all 600 soldiers will die."

Most of the people in another experimental group (four to one) responded to this scenario by choosing the second route. After all, they reasoned if the first route is taken, 400 lives will be lost.

Two opposite decisions were rendered by a majority in each case when faced with the same (though differently stated) problem! What implications does this hold for the relationship between information and decision making?

Drawn from the work of Daniel Kahneman and Amos Tversky, as described in Kevin McKean, "Decisions, Decisions." *Discover*, June 1985, pp. 22–31.

How do we make decisions? Is our decision-making process always rational? (It does not appear to be, considering the differing answers people proffered to the general's dilemma.) Can creative decision making be assisted? These are some of the questions we will address here in the general context of managerial work.

• •

13.1   WHAT DO MANAGERS DO?

Management information systems have evolved from offering generalized support to the controlling and, later, to the planning functions of management, to supporting the daily work of virtually every manager. Even the most computer-resistant managers are included in electronic mail networks and use reports produced by MIS. This leads us to a question: what *are* the activities of a manager? In answering this question, we will also answer another: what information-system support does a manager need?

How Managers Function

Whereas the classical model of managerial functions derived from Fayol's work provided us with a summarized view of management activities, behavioral studies of managers give us a detailed view of how these activities are actually carried out.

FIGURE 13.1

How executives spend their time.

(From Mintzberg, 1973)

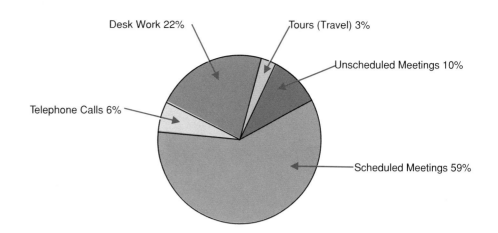

Desk Work 22%

Tours (Travel) 3%

Unscheduled Meetings 10%

Telephone Calls 6%

Scheduled Meetings 59%

A realistic behavioral picture of a modern manager has emerged from the work of Henry Mintzberg (1973). He described the daily work of a manager as hundreds of brief activities of great variety, requiring rapid shifts of attention from one issue to another, very often initiated by emerging problems. Half of the activities of chief executives last less than 9 minutes, with only 10 percent of them taking more than an hour. Confirming these findings, Blake Ives and Margrethe Olson have determined that the average activity of an information systems manager lasts 10.3 minutes (Ives, 1981).

Managers have a "bias for action" (rather than reflection). They strongly prefer verbal media, which offer flexibility and responsiveness, and they spend most of their time in face-to-face meetings, where body language and nuance of expression enhance communication. The distribution of time spent by executives is shown in figure 13.1. Ives and Olson have determined that MIS managers distribute their time in a very similar fashion.

A manager maintains a complex web of contacts, both outside and inside of the organization. A successful manager is not swamped by the onslaught of these activities: he or she maintains a personal agenda. This conclusion is confirmed by John Kotter's analysis of the work of effective managers (Kotter, 1982). Kotter described their activities as establishing personal goals and agendas, building a personal network of people at all levels of the organization, and implementing their personal agendas with the help of this network. Though personal agendas are related to organizational plans, they are separate from them—but it is through these individual agendas that organizational plans are implemented.

Effective managers carve out, as it were, their own informal structure within the corporate structure, and they use this network to keep themselves informed and to influence others. It has been observed that proactive managers make special efforts to develop a long-term view and a long-term agenda. These efforts range from quiet thinking time without telephone calls or visitors to executive retreats away from everyday concerns; through such activities, these managers attempt to develop a vision for their subunit and for the organization as a whole. Thus, actions do not preclude reflective thinking.

TABLE 13.1

Managerial Roles and
Their MIS Support

ROLE	DOMINANT	MIS SUPPORT
Interpersonal Roles	Personal Interaction	*Assistance in Communication:*
Figurehead		
Leader		Teleconferencing
Liaison		Office Information Systems
Informational Roles	Information Transfer	*Extensive:*
Monitor		Management Reporting Systems
		Executive Information Systems
Disseminator		Office Information Systems
Spokesperson		Office Information Systems
Decisional Roles	Decision Making	*Assistance in Decision Making and Communication:*
Entrepreneur		Decision Support and Executive Information Systems
Disturbance Handler		Crisis Management Systems
Resource Allocator		Decision Support Systems
Negotiator		Group DSS and Negotiation Support Systems

Managerial Roles and Their MIS Support

Henry Mintzberg classified managerial activities into ten roles falling into three categories, as shown in table 13.1. Note that Mintzberg's work was done during the first era of organizational computing (as discussed in chapter 2), when the work of an individual manager was still very poorly supported by MIS. In table 13.1, we have listed the extent of MIS support available today; some functions are, of course, supported much more broadly than others.

As a figurehead, a manager (particularly a high-level executive) represents the organization to his or her subordinates and to the outside world. As leaders, managers influence their subordinates to carry out their tasks so as to satisfy their own goals as well as the organizational goals. By developing liaisons vertically and laterally, managers build and exercise their personal networks of people. By their very nature, the function of MIS in interpersonal roles is limited, particularly in the case of figurehead and leader roles. There is just no substitute for personal contact in very many cases. However, office information systems have provided significant support for the liaison role. Certain kinds of office information systems, such as Coordinator (from Action Technologies), support a conversation (rather than a one-sided message) as a unit of social interaction in an organizational setting. Office information systems enhance communication between individuals and between various work groups. Even in roles requiring more personal contact, a busy executive can participate in a teleconference—when she or he cannot be there in person.

In their informational roles, managers receive (monitor) and disseminate information, both inside (as disseminators) and outside of the organization (as spokespersons). On-line management information systems have taken over many of these managerial roles. Reductions in the ranks of middle management, people whose work to a large degree consists in playing these roles, is due in part to this fact. Management reporting and executive support systems, complemented by office information systems, make much of the information accessible to those who need to know.

It would be misleading to assert that at the present time MIS satisfies most managers' needs in their informational roles. Particularly when facing uncertainty or equivocality, managers prefer to deal with so-called "information-rich" sources. Richard Daft and Robert Lengel (Daft, 1986) found that these preferred sources are, in order of decreasing richness: face-to-face conversations, telephone conversations, personal documents (letter or memos), impersonal documents, and numeric reports. We stress the personal and responsive nature of the "rich" media.

How Information Systems Can Help Managers Play Their Roles

All managerial roles have an element of decision making; the decisional roles are the ones where this is the crucial aspect. An entrepreneur initiates new market-oriented activities and, in the Mintzberg model, also introduces innovations in organizational activities. In this role, a manager brings together resources in a novel way. Decision support systems assist an entrepreneur in considering options, selecting one, and planning for its implementation. Handling disturbances is a part of managerial control; the emerging crisis management systems (see, for example, Nunamaker, 1989) will help here. Resource allocation is the essence of planning, and decision support systems have become indispensable in many organizations for this purpose.

The activity of any organization can be viewed as a multiplicity of negotiated conflicts; mediation between parties is a frequent role for a manager. Indeed, to implement a personal agenda, a manager in today's organization will have to negotiate: with superiors for resources, with subordinates for committed work. Using a group decision support system, or even an executive information system, may help to develop common assumptions and resolve conflicts. Another form of negotiation is dealing with customers, suppliers, and other stakeholders. Being informed of the facts—garnered to a large degree through information systems—is a basis for any negotiation. A class of systems specifically designed for the collective work of negotiating parties is presently evolving.

As you can see, the tasks of decision making and communication that underlie management activity find relatively extensive support in information systems. This support will undoubtedly increase. It is, however, up to managers to use information technology in a creative fashion.

Because of the nature of a manager's work—which is characterized by brevity, variety, and fragmentation—information systems used directly by managers need to have these characteristics:

- They should not require extensive periods of concentration.
- They should make it easy to interrupt the work and to return to it at a later time.
- They should offer the manager the capability to do various things at the same time—as is possible with a windowing environment.

AUTOMATED MESSAGE SYSTEMS HELP SCREEN TEXTUAL INFORMATION

With the spreading use of computer-mediated communication systems such as electronic mail and electronic bulletin boards, and with the rapid increase in the volume of traditional communications such as telex and financial wire service, people need assistance in coping with a plethora of information. Information overload, brought on to a large degree by computerization, can also be fought with computers.

The Chase Manhattan Bank employs a system that "reads" news reports coming from wire services, determines the subject of each report, and routes the reports to people whose profiles, stored in the system, indicate their interest in the subject. As a part of its extensive system for securities settlements, Citicorp has implemented a software component that automatically processes customer instructions (for example, regarding a sale of stock by an institution) contained in an incoming message. The system interprets the content of the message, checks it for consistency, and adds missing items by consulting databases, giving consideration to the usual practices of the given client.

The new technology goes beyond keyword-based searches of traditional textual databases, which was essentially based on pattern matching (a simple search for the keywords). Rather, it is based on partial "understanding" of natural languages. A variety of capabilities may be provided, depending on the purpose of the system. The systems determine sentence structure by parsing (much as you did in school). The system's knowledge base contains an explanation of relationships among the relevant concepts and terms. For example, one such system "knows" that in any corporate takeover, an acquirer makes an offer. The system therefore is able to "understand" a sentence such as "Hot Donuts received an offer from an investment group headed by Night Raider." By inferencing, the system can determine the degree of relevance of the message to the interests of a given user, or, in general, to a given category.

In some of these systems, users enter their profile of interest and information items that match the profile are automatically routed to them. A prototype system for such intelligent message handling, called Information Lens, has been developed at MIT (Malone, 1987). Systems can also indicate the degree of an item's presumed relevance to the user's profile.

- They should make it possible to control communication time—an electronic communication medium makes possible an asynchronous conversation, as opposed to a telephone, which requires the presence of both parties at the same time.
- Multimedia systems, including voice and imaging, can enhance communication by offering a nonverbal communication content.
- Protection from information overload is of the essence—a manager is indeed a very busy person. Systems that provide a measure of protection from overload are described in the above vignette.

Systems that help visualize data offer a significant measure of protection from information overload (see, for example, color plates 4, 11, and 13).

FIGURE 13.2

The decision-making process.

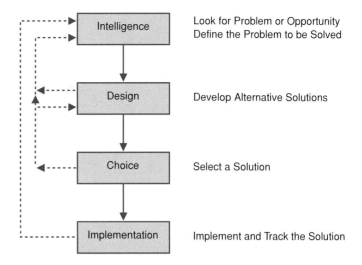

DECISION MAKING

A manager is a problem solver, and the fundamental activity in problem solving is decision making.[1] Decision making is the process of identifying a problem, developing alternative solutions, and choosing and implementing one of them. You can easily appreciate that managers do not, in general, solve logical puzzles or problems turning on the speed of two ocean liners approaching one another. Problems that require decisions are sometimes difficult to perceive, and even more difficult to define (or "frame"); often they require multiple decisions to solve.

A well-established model of the decision-making process has been proposed by Herbert Simon (1960), based on the formulation of methodical thinking by the philosopher John Dewey (though it can be traced back to Aristotle). Simon's three-step model is shown in figure 13.2; I have expanded it to include the fourth step of implementing the decision.

The process begins with a search for a problem or an opportunity—bold people do call problems "opportunities in disguise." Effective managers thus do not avoid problems—they seek them out. Innovative companies seek out customer opinions about their products. Proactive managers of information systems work closely with end users to see what problems they can solve for them. More and more, chief executives turn to their executive information systems each morning to look for first signs of developing problems or opportunities. This first stage of the decision-making process is called *intelligence,* because problem finding requires a search of the environment: problems frequently do not present themselves for some time, and opportunities do so even more rarely. Executive information systems and carefully designed management reporting systems contain built-in triggers and exceptions that help alert a manager to a problem. Systems developed to address the critical success factors (CSF) of an individual manager are likely to spotlight a problem. However, some managers feel that "God is in the detail"; they are able to find problems and opportunities in almost raw data. We shall see how the cognitive styles of individuals differ in this regard.

Once a manager finds a problem, he or she needs to formulate or "frame" it. An experienced manager often recognizes a problem as similar to one he or she has already encountered. The intuitive grasp of a problem most often relies on such an ability to establish an analogy. The systems approach to problem solving, which we discussed in chapter 10, helps to manage complexity.

The activity that Simon called *design* involves the development of alternative solutions to a problem. This is a creative, divergent (leading in many directions) process. Some of the solutions may require more intelligence—more information gathering about the problem. Solutions to the problems we are discussing are actually courses of action—there are many aspects to such a solution, and the phases of intelligence and design may be rather tightly interlocked iterations: garnering more information leads to new alternatives, which in turn call for more information.

Problem framing and development of alternatives, highly creative processes, find rather scant support from automated systems. Some decision support systems offer a certain assistance here, but most of the tools we shall discuss below rely on human ingenuity—informed by MIS.

The *choice* of an alternative often has to be made in an environment of considerable risk or uncertainty. No satisfactory solution may be found among the available alternatives, in which case the decision makers may have to go back to the design stage to develop other alternatives, or even to the intelligence stage to reformulate the problem. The what-if mode of decision support systems directly supports this phase. Expert systems begin to support it as well.

Implementation of a decision is a broad issue.[2] In general, both the quality of the decision and of its implementation are higher if the people who make the decision are also responsible for its implementation. Many implementation difficulties have been tracked to the separation of these functions (Nunamaker, 1989). Organizational change processes, which we discussed in the foregoing chapter, may need to be activated to implement more far-reaching decisions. The effects of such decisions may be tracked with management reporting and executive support systems. As in any control process, corrective actions may have to be initiated when necessary—indeed, managers may have to rethink the decision. Project management software is used to schedule human resources and to track project timelines.

Simon has also classified all decisions into two classes, now called structured and unstructured. **Structured decisions** are repetitive and can be represented as algorithms—programmable procedures. Thus, they can be relegated with ease to computer processing. **Unstructured decisions** require human judgment, while the decision-making *process* can usually profit from computerized support.

The following vignette illustrates how the same problem was solved by two very different industries.

PROBLEM: HOW TO REACH SEGMENTED CUSTOMERS?

The consumer market has become highly segmented: small groups of consumers demand different products and promotion devices. Many types of companies are faced with a problem: how to reach various segments of customers in a cost-effective fashion? Segmented markets are difficult to understand and predict, since the different segments may behave in a contradictory fashion.

Two very different industries have been dealing with this problem in a similar fashion—by using information systems to learn more about their customers. With the help of these systems, the companies are able to identify the segments and classify customers into them—and then serve each segment within the overall framework of the business.

Hundreds of casinos in the United States compete for $7 billion in annual profits. The most popular form of promotion, "shotgun perks"—indiscriminately awarding customers hotel rooms and free tickets to shows—has become too expensive to be cost-effective.

Several alternative methods for identifying customer segments have been adopted. The most advanced technique involves the use of computerized cards. At the *Claridge Hotel & Casino* in Atlantic City, players at the slot machines are offered an incentive to continually register their play on a personalized card. Before they pull the lever of the slot machine, customers insert their card into it. The machine is connected to a computer and the information is transferred directly to a database. An alternative way of collecting data is to provide discounts to customers who fill out detailed questionnaires about their life-style (including such seemingly unrelated details as pet ownership), which are also entered into the database. With these data, the customer database has been expanded from erstwhile files on a few hundred "high rollers" to detailed information on tens of thousands of customers.

Various customer segments are then drawn to the casino by targeted marketing. Slot machine players may receive an invitation to a slot tournament; big spenders receive birthday cards (along with other perks). Zip code analysis leads to focused advertising and transportation allocation. Direct mail is customized for various segments.

In a different industry, magazine publishing, the same problem manifested itself as some magazines lost advertisers to increasingly more specialized competing publications serving narrow readership segments. A solution, called computerized selective binding, has been adopted by several periodicals. New readers provide demographic data when they subscribe, and these data are entered into the publisher's database. At the printing plant, the computer system that controls the binding machine instructs it to include special sections for subscribers based on their profiles.

The innovator in selective binding, the *Farm Journal,* puts out as many as 1,000 different editions of the same monthly issue, with specialized sections bound into a core of general agricultural material. Farmers living next door to one another, but raising different crops, receive issues that differ by as much as fifty pages of editorial and advertising material.

The market-targeting strategies used by firms in both industries are continually tracked and refined. "We are asking a lot of questions, but maybe we are still not asking the right ones," says Robert Renneisen of Claridge.

Based on Warren Berger, "Casinos Leave Nothing to Chance." *Adweek's Marketing Week,* January 9, 1989 pp. 19–20; and "Knowing Which Readers Grow Wheat and Which Grow Corn." *The New York Times* Business Section, January 21, 1989, p. B5.

13.3 RATIONAL DECISION MAKING AND ITS LIMITS

The classical concept of a perfectly rational decision maker does not apply to the plethora of situations in organizational decision making. Most decision making is subject to bounded, limited rationality. Some of the limits arise from the way organizations function, some from our cognitive limitations as human individuals.

Classical Model of a Rational Decision Maker

The classical model of a decision maker was formulated in economic theory and is usually attributed to Adam Smith. This model is normative (prescriptive); that is, it describes how a person *should* make a decision. The process the model describes is known as *rational decision making*. The model makes the following very strong assumptions:

- The rational decision maker seeks to maximize the payoff from a decision (for example, profit or market share attained by a firm); in more general terms, the decision maker seeks to optimize.
- The decision maker knows all possible courses of action (alternatives).
- The decision maker knows the outcome of each course of action.

The model approximates certain real situations, and we shall discuss techniques for applying it. But with more complex, less structured decisions, it is impossible to specify all the alternatives and their outcomes, owing both to their excessive number and to lack of information. The impossibility of centralized planning of a nation's economy, even with the use of any computing power available in the foreseeable future, is just one proof that the decision-making model based on full rationality is, in general, not realistic.

The Concept of Bounded Rationality

Since full rationality, with its goal of optimizing, is an impossibility in most realistic situations, an alternative theory of decision-making behavior has evolved. In this theory, proposed by Herbert Simon (1960), the decision maker exhibits **bounded rationality.** Since a decision maker's ability to perceive all the alternatives and their outcomes is limited by cognitive abilities, financial resources, and time pressures, this model suggests that decision makers do not actually optimize when making decisions. Rather, they **satisfice** (in a word coined by Simon). That is, decision makers choose the first alternative that moves them toward their goal; the goal itself may be adjusted as incremental decisions succeed or fail.

The alternative chosen by a satisficing decision maker satisfies his or her aspiration level and risk-taking propensity. Therefore, raising the aspiration levels of managers and heightening their expectations is one technique for teaching them innovative decision making. This prevents them from settling on minimalistic departures from standard operating procedures.

If we consider the concept of bounded rationality more broadly, we should be able to identify both the organizational and individual factors that limit it.

Organizational Limits to Rational Decision Making

The rational model of organizational decision making reflects only some aspects of the decision-making environment: those that lend themselves most readily to receiving support from information systems. Other aspects include incrementalism, chance-driven choice making, political/competitive behavior, and programmed choice making. As you shall see, most of these decision-making behaviors are rooted in the divergent interests of the people involved in making a decision. Therefore, various types of group decision support systems (GDSSs) can help these groups to negotiate, foresee, and manage a crisis, or to look at a broad array of alternatives before arriving at a decision. We shall discuss such systems in chapter 16; a system supporting crisis management is presented in the case study for the present chapter.

Charles Lindblom analyzed how the decision-making process, particularly in large organizations (including governments), differs from the rational model (Lindblom, 1959). He contended that decision making in large organizations under ordinary circumstances is a process of "muddling through"—making small, *incremental changes* from existing actions and policies. The important criteria in this decision-making mode are avoiding the uncertainty of major changes and maintaining the consensus of all involved. Making a decision is not concluded by the "choice" of an alternative; it is rather a continuous process, during which any chosen course of action may be modified as it is implemented.

The more recent, and most pessimistic, so-called *garbage can* theory of organizational decision making (Cohen, 1972) is based on the premise that not all organizations are destined to succeed—many companies (even those considered excellent at some point) will fail. These firms are unable to adapt to the changing environment, and much of their decision making consists of attaching solutions to problems in a rather random manner. In one sense, "garbage-can" decision making is present to some extent in all companies: because of the difficulty in forecasting outcomes, chance does play a role in providing a solution to many an organizational problem.

Other aspects of organizational decision making are reflected by what George Huber called the *political/competitive* model (Huber, 1981). A decision process generally includes several participants, each of whom may seek to influence the decision in a direction favorable to themselves or to the unit they represent. For example, several studies of budget development clearly point to it being a political process. The need to reconcile the diverging interests of various stakeholders (for example, senior management, labor, government, and others) often leads participants to avoid making major departures from current policies—and is thus one of the reasons for incremental decision making. Another potential negative consequence is suboptimization in allocating resources within an organization (we must recognize, however, the necessity of political representation in such an allocation process).

Rational decision making in organizations is also limited by *programmed behavior.* When decision makers engage in this type of behavior, they follow standard operating procedures, which constrains their choices and prevents creative problem solving as they opt for the "safe and tried." An analysis of the results of previous choices, assisted by information systems, may help decision makers relax the constraints of programmed choice making.

Individual Limits to Rational Decision Making

Individual capability to make rational decisions is also limited. Individuals have *frames of reference* based on their experience, knowledge, and cultural backgrounds. These frames of reference act as filters, blocking out certain types of information or certain alternative courses of action—to the possible detriment of quality decision making.

Human ability to process information is limited by what Princeton University psychologist George Miller called "the magical number seven, plus or minus two" (Miller, 1956). In other words, we cannot retain in short-term memory and consider simultaneously during decision making more than five to nine "chunks" of information. A simple example is the number of digits in an international long-distance telephone number, which we usually need to dial right after being told what it is. To cope, we organize the individual digits into larger chunks (a familiar area code or country code is such a chunk—we remember it as a single unit). It is partly because of this limitation that we analyze or design information systems through a process of stepwise refinement; we are thus able to handle the system by dealing with only a few components at a time.

Human decision making is distorted by a variety of biases. Amos Tversky and Daniel Kahneman (Tversky, 1981) have established that people are highly averse to possible loss and will undergo significant risk to prevent it, even though they would not incur such a risk when seeking gain. (Note how this bias affected the decision makers in the focus statement opening this chapter.) People frequently perceive a causal relationship between two factors when there are no grounds for doing so. Vivid events that are easily recalled or events in the recent past are unjustifiably assigned higher probability and weigh more heavily in the decision (a phenomenon known as availability bias). People more readily accept information that confirms, rather than challenges, their current convictions.

Our understanding of probabilistic information is generally poor (note that we often refer to probabilistic statements as counterintuitive information). For example, unwarranted inferences are frequently drawn from small samples, with neglect of available statistical techniques for ensuring the reliability of such conclusions. This is why "lying with statistics" often encounters low resistance.

Decision makers are more likely to use only readily available information rather than transform that information into a potentially more useful form. The form in which information is displayed influences people's understanding of it. For example, items listed first or last have a greater impact than those in the middle.

All this means that people's perception of information and their decision making based on that information may be manipulated. It also points up the need to consider carefully the way information is presented in order to avoid biasing decision making. On the other hand, the skill of decision making can and must be acquired through training and reflective practice.

13.4 INDIVIDUAL DIFFERENCES AND COGNITIVE STYLES

The success of a management information system in supporting a decision maker depends heavily on certain characteristics of the individual. Some of these are differences in the attitudes of system users; others concern individual cognitive behavior.

Much of the research regarding individual differences has been summarized by Robert Zmud (1979). Individuals who tend to access information to a greater degree exhibit a low degree of dogmatism, a higher risk-taking propensity, an internal locus of control (that is, they consider themselves in control of the situation rather than at the mercy of external influences), and low tolerance for ambiguity.

It has been recognized that people do not necessarily understand their own information requirements. (This is not much different from the realization of marketers that consumers cannot always articulate their product requirements and therefore should be observed in actual situations rather than interviewed.) This underscores the need for MIS specialists to bring these requirements to light and the importance of using techniques such as prototyping of information systems, as will be discussed in Part 5 of this text.

Decision making is a cognitive activity, as are other phenomena such as learning or understanding language. In general, human cognition is human information processing. People display distinct **cognitive styles** in the ways they gather and evaluate information. In their analysis of how managers' minds work, James McKinney and Peter Keen (McKinney, 1974) have classified the information-related modes of thought along two dimensions: information gathering and information evaluation (see figure 13.3).

The information-gathering dimension focuses on perception, on the way a person organizes the verbal and visual stimuli he or she encounters. *Preceptive* individuals bring to bear concepts ("precepts") to filter incoming stimuli; from the framework of these concepts, they look for specific conformities with or deviations from the concepts they have already formed (this is related to deductive thinking—moving from the general to the specific). *Receptive* decision makers focus on details rather than on a pattern and attempt to form a general picture of the situation from these details (a characteristic of inductive thinking).

Information evaluation relates to the way an individual brings information to bear in the process of decision making. A *systematic* (or analytic) decision maker approaches a problem by structuring it and applying a well-defined method expected to lead to a solution. An *intuitive* individual applies heuristics (rules of thumb) and shortcuts and uses trial and error to find a solution; these people are more willing to go with their "gut feeling" about the problem. McKinney and Keen stress that all of these modes of thought are appropriate in certain situations, and some combinations of them are particularly fit in certain occupations (as is shown in figure 13.3).

While the importance of individual cognitive style in the design of MIS has been contested (notably, in Huber, 1983), the fact that significant differences exist among individual decision-making processes should inform the way systems are designed. In particular, developers of information systems tend to be systematic individuals and thus tend to assume that the users are (or should be) the same. End-user system development and a number of available packages have addressed the needs of intuitive (or heuristic) decision making. These systems allow the user to play out a variety of scenarios; the user is able to identify and test new alternatives. Such systems should not impose a preset processing order, but rather allow the user the freedom to set this order as he or she is working. It is desirable that the system allow an easy shift back and forth between summarized and detailed data (needed by receptive individuals). A variety of tabular and graphical output formats should also be available. Much of this wish list is now fulfilled in well-designed DSS and EIS.

In particular, information presentation modes—text, tables, and various forms of graphics with or without color—have been the subject of extensive research. This variety of interfaces is further discussed in chapter 14.

FIGURE 13.3

Cognitive styles.

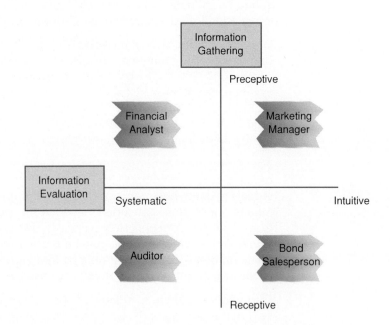

13.5 TOOLS FOR MAKING A CHOICE— THE RATIONAL MODEL

Certain structured decisions lend themselves to rational choice. We shall discuss two tools—payoff tables from the statistical decision theory, and decision trees—which can serve and support rational decision making.

Choosing an Optimal Outcome with a Payoff Table

The rational model presupposes that the decision maker should select the alternative (course of action) with the greatest payoff. The rational model can be applied in three cases. In all of them, we know the possible outcomes of each course of action (that is, of each alternative we could select). However, the cases differ as to certainty about the outcomes, as shown in table 13.2.

A rational decision maker working with *certain* knowledge about outcomes will choose the course of action that promises the outcome with the optimal payoff. Thus, if three types of personal workstations offer the same functionality, the person will select the cheapest. Obviously, the world usually does not present such clear-cut choices. However, if the problem is framed as: considering the way I intend to use my workstation, which fills my functional needs at the lowest cost?—clear solution may indeed be arrived at.

When alternative courses of action have multiple outcomes, we can employ several decision rules derived from statistical decision theory by using a tool known as a **payoff table.** A payoff table shows, in rows, the alternative strategies that a decision maker can pursue. It also shows, in columns, the possible events (contingencies, or "states of nature") that may occur in the future and affect the outcome of a strategy. The format of a payoff table is shown in figure 13.4. If the probabilities of different states of nature are known, the probabilities are stated together with the corresponding states of nature (all the probabilities should add up to 1, of course).

TABLE 13.2

Degrees of Certainty about Outcomes

KNOWLEDGE OF OUTCOMES	EXPLANATION
Certainty	There is only one outcome of each alternative, and we know the outcome.
Known Probabilities	There are multiple possible outcomes of each alternative, and we know the probabilities of their occurrence.
Unknown Probabilities	There are multiple possible outcomes of each alternative, and we do *not* know their probabilities.

FIGURE 13.4

The format of payoff table.

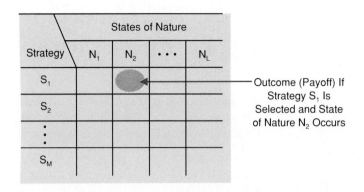

FIGURE 13.5

Payoff table for the selection
of a computerization
strategy.

Strategy	Future Company Activities		
	Significant Expansion .50	Moderate Expansion .30	No Expansion .20
Minicomputer	25	5	−5
LAN	15	10	−2
Time Sharing	5	3	0

All figures in tens of thousands of dollars

Let us consider an example. A small real estate company is considering its future computing needs. Three alternative strategies are being considered: to purchase a multiuser minicomputer system, to install a local area network of personal workstations, or to use the services of a time-sharing company. The company's executives have discussed the future of the company during a three-day retreat in a peaceful and attractive locale. They have determined that three possible states of nature could be in store for the firm:

- the company will expand significantly;
- the company will expand moderately; or
- the company will not expand.

The probabilities of each outcome and the estimated profit or loss were entered (as present values) into the payoff table shown in figure 13.5.

To optimize the decision with known (by estimation, of course) probabilities of future states, we need to select a strategy with maximum total expected value. The expected value of a given outcome is computed as follows:

Expected Value = Probability * Payoff.

The total expected value of a strategy is the sum of the expected values of all outcomes.

FIGURE 13.6

Regret table corresponding
to payoff table in figure 13.5.

Strategy	Future Company Activities			Sum of Regrets
	Significant Expansion	Moderate Expansion	No Expansion	
Minicomputer	0	5	5	10
LAN	10	0	2	12
Time Sharing	20	7	0	27

All figures in tens of thousands of dollars

Thus, in our case we have these expected values (in tens of thousands of dollars):

- Install a minicomputer: $(.50 * 25) + (.30 * 5) + (.20 * -5) = 13$
- Install a local area network: $(.50 * 15) + (.30 * 10) + (.20 * -2) = 10.1$
- Use time sharing: $(.50 * 5) + (.30 * 3) + (.20 * 0) = 3.4$

The maximum expected value is achieved with the strategy relying on the installation of a minicomputer; therefore, this alternative should be selected (unless other considerations prevail).

In many situations, probabilities of future states of nature are difficult to estimate. Then, we proceed as if the probabilities were equal, which means that we ignore them. The decision rules (criteria) that can be applied are maximin, maximax, and minimax (also known as minimization of regret). Here are these rules as applied to our situation (shown in figure 13.5)—but without probabilities.

1. Maximin

Select the strategy that offers the greatest payoff (max) if the worst state of nature occurs (min). This is, obviously, a cautious (even pessimistic) approach.

In our case, we identify "No Expansion" as the worst state of nature, and therefore select the time-sharing alternative.

2. Maximax

Select the strategy that offers the greatest payoff (max) if the best state of nature occurs (max).

In our case, this optimistic approach identifies "Significant Expansion" as the best state of nature and the installation of a minicomputer as the best alternative.

3. Minimize Regret (minimax)

This selection criterion minimizes future regrets (opportunity losses) due to the selection of a given strategy. A regret is the difference between the largest payoff for the state of nature and the payoff obtained under the given strategy. We produce a regret table (shown for our case in figure 13.6) and select the strategy with the minimum sum of regrets. The installation of a minicomputer minimizes regrets in our case.

FIGURE 13.7

Scores-and-weights method.

(Author; Gilb, 1977, p. 74)

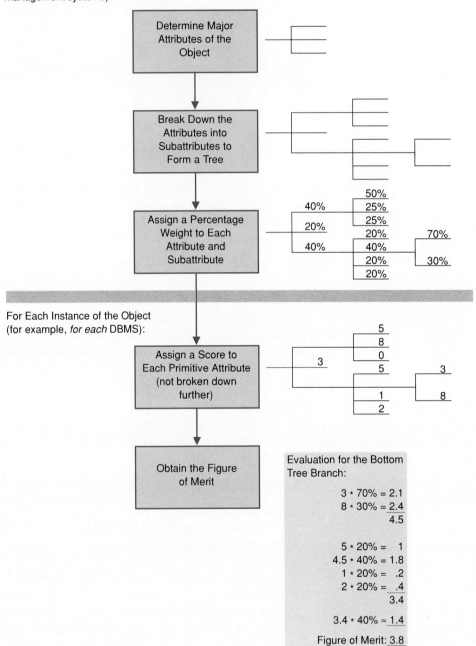

The criterion of regret minimization constitutes a compromise between optimism and pessimism about future events. Certain other decisions rules allow the decision maker to quantify the degree of optimism as a coefficient.

Selection with Decision Trees

Decision trees are a useful tool for thinking through and presenting problem analysis when a sequence of decisions is to be made (decision trees can, in general, be used in place of payoff tables). Decision trees are also useful in making a decision when a number of aspects or factors of differing importance are to be considered. We shall show their use here for the second type of decision. In the MIS environment, a decision tree may be used to select a personal workstation, an on-line information service, or any other system with multiple attributes.

The general procedure, sometimes called the scores-and-weights-method, is shown in figure 13.7.

First, all the attributes of the object under selection are analyzed and broken down into more detailed subaspects. We thus obtain a tree of object attributes (usually shown horizontally). Based on an analysis of our own needs, we establish the percentage weights by answering the question: just how important is the given aspect *to us?* These weights add up to 100 percent on each tree branching point (see figure 13.7). We now have an evaluative framework for each object (a microcomputer system, for example) we want to consider. In the process, we learn both about the object in question and about our envisaged uses for it.

For each candidate object, we score the tips of the tree—the aspects which are not further broken down—and 0 to 10 scoring is convenient. The scores should be totally independent of the weights and should also be based on our investigation of the particular product or service. While the weights are subjective (they reflect our own needs), the scores are objective (they reflect the goodness of the candidate object). In the process, we may totally eliminate from further consideration any candidates that obviously do not satisfy our major objectives (for example, those that are not compatible with our existing environment).

The total figure of merit for a candidate object is obtained by going up the tree, and multiplying scores by weights, as shown in figure 13.7.

In the process of selecting hardware, software, or telecommunications for MIS, the sources of information may be demonstrations (particularly in a similar environment), reports from information companies such as Auerbach Publishers (New York) or Datapro (Delran, New Jersey), on-line databases, user groups, or consultants. For example, *Datapro Reports on Microcomputers* offers ratings of six attributes of software packages: basic functions, documentation, advanced functions, vendor support, ease of use, and training time.

An example of applying the decision tree method in selecting a microcomputer DBMS is shown in figure 13.8.

We obtain a total rounded figure of merit for this particular DBMS of 5.9. In most situations, figures of merit are meaningful only in a comparative sense, and only significant differences between these figures point to a decision.

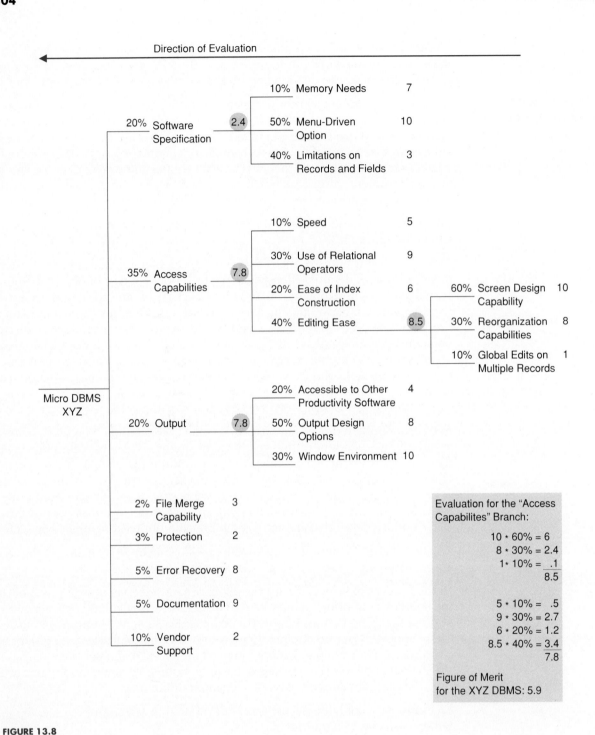

Direction of Evaluation

10% Memory Needs 7

20% Software
Specification   2.4   50% Menu-Driven 10
                                     Option

                                40% Limitations on 3
                                     Records and Fields

10% Speed 5

30% Use of Relational 9
     Operators

35% Access
Capabilities   7.8   20% Ease of Index 6   60% Screen Design 10
                                     Construction   Capability

                                40% Editing Ease   8.5   30% Reorganization 8
                                                                Capabilities

                                                           10% Global Edits on 1
                                                                Multiple Records

20% Accessible to Other 4
     Productivity Software

Micro DBMS
XYZ   20% Output   7.8   50% Output Design 8
                                              Options

                                         30% Window Environment 10

2% File Merge 3
     Capability

3% Protection 2

5% Error Recovery 8

5% Documentation 9

10% Vendor 2
     Support

Evaluation for the "Access
Capabilites" Branch:

$$10 * 60\% = 6$$
$$8 * 30\% = 2.4$$
$$1 * 10\% = \underline{.1}$$
$$8.5$$

$$5 * 10\% = .5$$
$$9 * 30\% = 2.7$$
$$6 * 20\% = 1.2$$
$$8.5 * 40\% = \underline{3.4}$$
$$7.8$$

Figure of Merit
for the XYZ DBMS: 5.9

FIGURE 13.8

Decision tree for selecting a
DBMS.

13.6 CREATIVITY IN DECISION MAKING BY INDIVIDUALS AND GROUPS

Individual creativity is the cornerstone of good decision making. Cornerstones, however, do not houses make, and organizational departures from rational decision making, as we discussed, are a frequent reason for the demise of creative problem solving.

Creative thinking offers new approaches to often ill-defined problems that are worth solving. The creative process requires cultivation, and much of it can be learned. A well-regarded approach to "creativity in business" is described in a book with that title by Michael Ray and Rochelle Myers (Ray, 1986). Ray and Myers postulate that creativity consists in learning to release the human potential present in all of us. James Adams (1979) sees the road to individual creativity as a process of overcoming the following obstacles:

- Perceptual blocks: stereotyping, preconceived notions, inability to see a problem from various viewpoints
- Emotional blocks: fear of taking risks, desire for orderliness, lack of a sense of challenge
- Cultural blocks: avoidance of fantasizing and reflection, feeling bound by tradition, fear of right-brained thinking (because we have been trained to believe that analytical thinking is superior to intuitive or qualitative judgments)
- Environmental blocks: lack of support within the organization
- Intellectual blocks: lack of information, inflexible use of problem-solving strategies, inadequate skills in expressing ideas (for example, verbally, mathematically, or visually)

As soon as we have classified obstacles in this fashion, we can identify our principal inadequacies and deal with them.

Finding new associations between ideas underlies creative thinking; the vignette on "creativity software" shows that there is some computerized support available for this process.

Recent analyses indicate that much creative decision making in organizations is performed or stimulated by groups—from a work team to the chief executive's "cabinet."

People in a group are able to bring diverse backgrounds, expertise, and cognitive styles to bear on a problem. It is sometimes said in jest that the camel is a horse designed by a committee; we may note that the committee seems to have come up with an animal that has contributed immensely to human civilization. Group work has to be carefully organized; certain individuals do not perform well in group settings.

SOFTWARE THAT ASSISTS YOUR CREATIVITY

IdeaFisher, a rather elaborate program developed by Fisher Idea Systems (Irvine, California), has the capacity to come up with new associations between ideas for you. With a knowledge base of 675,000 words and phrases and a natural-language user interface, the program helps you think through a concept.

Let us say you are preparing a marketing campaign. IdeaFisher will first guide you through a series of questions to help you clarify your goal (for example, "What symbolic meanings does the object have?" or "What is its purpose or function?"). The program can give you tens or hundreds of associations with the topic you select. For example, the category "red" will bring out, among others: crimson, Little Red Riding Hood, lobster, Red Square, communism, red alert, hot, and red sky at night. You can then cull from the list the notions you may want to use in your campaign.

Not that you did not know most of these concepts—they simply may not have sprung to your mind when you needed them. To use a term we discuss in the chapter, IdeaFisher does the *brainstorming* for you.

Probably the best known among group problem-solving techniques is **brainstorming,** originated by Alex Osborn (1953), a founder of one of the most successful U.S. advertising agencies. The goal of a brainstorming session is to generate ideas. This is of use at several stages of the decision-making process—when the group is framing the problem or identifying the pertinent information, and particularly when they are generating alternative solutions. A group of five to ten people participates, with one of the members acting as a recorder, listing ideas as they are presented. The ground rules of brainstorming are:

- No criticism—group members make no evaluation of ideas as they are freely generated.
- "Anything goes"—wild ideas are encouraged, and again, internal judgment by participants should be suspended.
- The more, the better—the more ideas the group generates, the greater the likelihood of coming up with several good alternatives.
- Build on the ideas of others—participants should feel free to combine or modify ideas generated by others and thus come up with superior ideas.

Brainstorming aims at fluency in the idea-generating process, fluency that should result in significant output. Another technique for creative problem solving, the **synectics** process (Gordon, 1961), is more selective—only the best ideas are further considered as the process progresses. Synectics encourages thinking by analogy (for example, what can your experience playing baseball teach you about the way your project team should be organized?). The **nominal group technique** addresses the needs of groups in which broad differences of goals and opinions are certain to lead to antagonism and argumentation: large parts of the sessions are spent by participants working alone, and their ideas are then circulated and evaluated. In chapter 11, we discussed the **Delphi technique**—a method for soliciting the opinions of a group of experts and arriving at a consensus among them.

COMPUTERIZED SUPPORT FOR GROUP CREATIVITY

In our discussion on how managers spend their time, we saw that most of it is spent in meetings. Many workgroups—composed of engineers, financial analysts, or quality circles of workers—produce many of their best ideas, discuss them with their peers, and coordinate their work during meetings.

Various aspects of work coordination have been addressed by software products. How about the creative aspects?

Among others, Xerox's Palo Alto Research Center (PARC) has developed an extensive environment for group work, called Colab, that includes support of creativity. Working in a small meeting room, group members using Colab are at their own desks equipped with workstations and are connected into an Ethernet local area network—and they also share a large projection screen. One of Colab's modules, called Cognoter, was developed for collaborative idea generation.

The group starts with a clean slate (though it is possible to start with previously prepared material). The users brainstorm to generate a variety of ideas, then organize them and evaluate the organized ideas. The entire process takes place in a single shared "information space" created by Colab. In this environment, individual work can be combined with the work of others. Each person's ideas are available to others through windows on their workstation screens, and, if desired, on the central projection screen. Text, numerical information, graphics, and images can be included. Users can also talk with each other.

Rich channels of communication, combined with the availability of factual information through the workstations, lead to productivity gains: users alternate between working alone with their workstations and working together through the projection screen.

Gregg Foster, the inventor of the Colab environment, says: "The problems we all work on these days are so complicated that they are very hard to deal with as an individual."

An extensive environment for electronic meetings, known as GroupSystems, is operational at the University of Arizona as an outgrowth of the PLEXSYS system. GroupSystems is actually a generator for electronic meeting systems: one can produce the environment that will be most conducive to the effectiveness of a particular meeting. Since some research has shown that individuals brainstorming alone produce a greater number of ideas (and, according to some studies, better ideas) than a group does while brainstorming, particular attention has been devoted to allowing individual group members to work alone, with their ideas being made available *anonymously* to other group members.

Based on Nunamaker, 1987, and Kelly Shea, "For Times When Two Heads Are Better Than One." *Computerworld*, March 14, 1988, p. 70.

Groups can also constrain individual creativity; some of the analytical work exploring the reasons for this is cited by Nunamaker (1987). The opposite of creative work in a group is *groupthink*, a term coined by Irving L. Janis of Yale University meaning dysfunctional decision-making behavior in a group. This drive for preservation of the group unit at the expense of grappling with the issues fosters overoptimism, the illusion of invulnerability, and collective rationalization of decisions and opinions that are not valid on rational grounds (Janis, 1977). Pressure on or the removal of dissenters from the group is a part of this behavior. The decisions surrounding the Bay of Pigs fiasco or the Challenger disaster and its aftermath are some of the more prominent examples affected by groupthink.

In a group setting, information systems serve both to support decisions and to enhance communication between group members, as described in the group creativity vignette.

A Center for Research on Creativity, particularly as applied to MIS, has been created at the University of Colorado by J. Daniel Couger (1990).

. . . .

SUMMARY

Managers play three types of roles in carrying out their functions. Interpersonal roles are mainly based on face-to-face interactions, though in some cases computerized communications media may be employed. Informational and decisional roles are supported by a variety of information systems, which make information available, assist in decision making, and serve as a means of communication.

Decision making is a fundamental managerial activity. It may be conceptualized as consisting of four stages: intelligence, design, choice, and implementation. The rational decision making model applies to a rather limited class of structured decisions. Decision rules based on payoff tables and decision trees may be employed in such cases. Rationality is limited ("bounded") by both organizational and human limitations. In their information-processing activities, people display distinct cognitive styles as well as individual differences.

Individual and group creativity underlies quality decision making. Certain techniques (for example, brainstorming) and support systems have been developed to assist creative thinking.

CONCLUSIONS FOR MIS PRACTICE

1. Information systems specialists should understand all the roles that managers have to play so that they can develop systems that provide broad support for this work. As we discussed earlier in the text, the capabilities of information systems are not limited to providing access to information or supporting decision making.

2. The rhythm of managerial work, with its brief and fragmented activities, calls for system designs that allow for interruptions, provide the capacity to perform several tasks at one time, and maintain control over the time spent communicating with others.

3. Decision support systems are built specifically to support the decision-making process.

4. Because of their training, information system specialists tend to expect that most managers will engage primarily in rational decision making. System designers should understand that the rational model applies to a rather limited set of circumstances.

5. MIS specialists should not assume that the users of the intended system know their own information requirements. The burden of establishing these requirements is on the MIS professional in performing the systems analysis process. System prototypes and other techniques help to surface these needs.

6. Systems that directly support managerial work should be built to allow for individual cognitive styles and other differences among their users. This flexibility can be achieved by providing a variety of options. In this way, an individual user will actually be able to work with the system that supports his or her way of thinking.

7. The tools of rational decision making—such as payoff tables and decision trees—may be used during the choice phase in making well-structured decisions, such as selection of equipment or software packages.

8. Both individual and group creative processes are beginning to find information system support. Information system specialists should be familiar with nonquantitative informational support, relying on textual databases and knowledge bases. Moreover, they can avail themselves of a number of creativity techniques specifically adapted to use in information systems development (Couger, 1990).

ENDNOTES

1. Many consider decision making and problem solving in the management context to be identical activities; most find that they overlap to a very large degree, with problem solving being the broader notion, involving extensive implementation, monitoring, and follow-up after a decision has been made. I do not draw a rigid distinction between the two processes here.

2. In addressing the cognitive and organizational aspects of decision making, we do not want to entirely ignore the well-known quality of decisiveness. In writing about his friend, a rather unsuccessful patent examiner, Michele Besso, Albert Einstein observed, ". . . he understands with extreme rapidity both the technical and legal aspects of each patent application, and he willingly helps his colleagues to arrive at a quick disposal of the case in question, because it is he, in a manner of speaking, who provides the illumination, and the other person will power or the *necessary spirit of decision* [my emphasis]. But when it is up to him to settle the matter, his lack of decisiveness is a great handicap." [Quoted in Jeremy Bernstein , "Besso." *The New Yorker,* February 27, 1989, p. 91]

KEY TERMS AND CONCEPTS

Managerial roles	Frames of reference
Decision making	Cognitive styles
Intelligence, design, choice, implementation (decision-making stages)	Payoff table
Rational decision-making model	Decision rules: maximin, maximax, minimization of regret
Bounded rationality	Decision tree
Satisficing	Brainstorming
	Groupthink

1. What are the ten managerial roles, as grouped into three categories?

2. Present an example of information system support for each of the ten managerial roles. (If you believe no information support is possible for a particular role, say so.)

3. List the behavioral characteristics of managerial work. In other words, specify how managers function.

4. List desirable features of information systems based on the behavioral characteristics of managerial work.

5. Present the four-stage model of the decision-making process, and briefly explain the objective of each stage.

6. How does satisficing differ from optimizing?

7. Why is rationality in organizational decision-making limited?
   a. Describe the organizational factors.
   b. List the human limitations.

8. Now that you know the nature of biases in human decision making, explain why most people give contradictory answers to the general's dilemma presented in the focus statement at the beginning of the chapter.

9. Give examples of individual characteristics that underlie differences in informational needs.

10. Explain the two dimensions of cognitive styles. Briefly outline information system features that would best support an individual in each of the four quadrants of this grid (for example, a receptive-intuitive person).

11. The following payoff table describes a decision problem with three alternative strategies and four possible states of nature.

	STATES OF NATURE WITH PROBABILITIES			
Strategy	N1 .40	N2 .30	N3 .20	N4 .10
S1	5	10	8	0
S2	10	20	−5	−5
S3	15	15	−10	10

We are not confident about the probabilities of the outcomes and thus would like to consider decisions rules that do not require probabilities along with those that do. Select the best strategy and state the payoff under each of the following rules (*you* determine when the probabilities are known):
   a. Maximum expected value
   b. Maximax
   c. Maximin
   d. Minimization of regret

12. Describe the brainstorming process.

1. Break up into groups of two or three. Identify a decision familiar to all of you, such as selecting your college or the sports team you think will win a championship. Use the four-stage decision-making model to describe how you have arrived (or could have arrived) at the decision. At each stage, state what kinds of information systems could be used to advantage.

2. Break up into groups of two or three. Each group should select any type of software, hardware, or computerized service. Determine the environment it will be used in. Then develop a decision tree of attributes, weigh them from the point of view of the intended environment, and develop scores for two or three representative objects or services. Obtain figures of merit and make a decision about using the software, hardware, or service. Discuss the results.

3. Engage in group brainstorming on the following subject. Imagine that you are the management group for a brickyard that is trying to expand its market share. You have to come up with new, and possibly very off-beat, uses for your product—the red construction brick. (This is the well-known "brick-use" test attributed by Adams [1979] to J. P. Guilford.) *Hint:* Begin by determining specific attributes bricks have and then derive uses from these attributes.

AN INFORMATION SYSTEM SUPPORTS DECISION MAKING FOR CRISIS MANAGEMENT

Productive decision making is a central concern in today's organizations as they operate in the turbulent environment of the information society. A well honed decision-making process is of particular importance in an organizational crisis, which Jay Nunamaker and his colleagues define as "a point of indecision at which the central decision group believes it must make and implement the *right* decisions if the organization is to avoid significant negative outcomes" (Nunamaker, 1989, p. 11). In other words, the people in an organization perceive a threat (even though it may be only that—a perceived, rather than a real, danger). A sudden competitive threat, new or impending government regulations striking at a core activity within an enterprise, or a company being "put in play" as an acquisition target are some of the more prominent examples of such crises. Other examples, such as a cash-flow squeeze or delay in product release, will readily convince you that crises are inevitable.

Stress caused by a crisis often leads to inferior decision making. Managers under stress may take less information into account during the decision-making process; they may invoke routine decisions that worked in the past under different circumstances; and decision groups indulge in groupthink as a defense mechanism. Low confidence in the resulting decisions, coupled with conflicting demands on resources, may cause delayed implementation of the decisions.

Information technologies can be effectively used in a group decision support setting to respond to crises—whenever possible, in a proactive fashion, before the crisis situation develops fully. Since crises are generally handled by a decision group, both the decision support and the communication aspects of these technologies are vital.

As part of its GroupSystems electronic meeting system, the Department of MIS at the University of Arizona has evolved a set of tools to support the crisis-response planning process.

These tools are best illustrated in action—when employed to handle an actual strategic planning situation for crisis management.

Federal Savings and Loan (FS&L) is a state thrift organization that faced a profits squeeze: its mortgage portfolio had been dropping due to increased competition, while its profits from deposits had been eroding due to the higher premium the firm had to pay to insure these deposits. Executive vice-president Ralph Tredwell was charged with developing a plan to handle the crisis. Together with the twelve senior managers who comprised the FS&L central decision group, he used the University of Arizona electronic meeting system facility for a one-day initial planning session, divided into four phases: goal identification, threat identification, threat analysis and problem categorization, and resource analysis (see figure 13.9).

We shall now discuss the steps of this process.

1. Goal Identification

The decision makers used networked workstations in the electronic meeting room to compile independent lists of organizational goals. The room also contained two public viewing screens. The meeting was initiated and assisted by a facilitator who was familiar with the system facilities. Interacting anonymously and at random times, the decision makers brainstormed for operative goals. They would send ideas they had generated about an issue to a file server, from which they were distributed to others for further comment and questioning. The Electronic Brainstorming module stored the resulting thirty ideas in a file. With the use of the Issue Analysis model, duplicate ideas were eliminated and similar ideas combined, to result in thirteen corporate goals. The group then used the Voting module to choose six principal goals. As prioritized with the use of the system, these goals were: profit, market niche, customer satisfaction, corporate image, efficiency, and employee satisfaction.

Thus, the decision makers surfaced corporate goals that were never before officially articulated; the newly recognized priorities would assist them in dealing with conflicting goals in the future.

2. Threat Identification

The purpose of this phase was to generate ideas about the ways each of the six identified organizational goals could be threatened. The Topic Commenter module supports

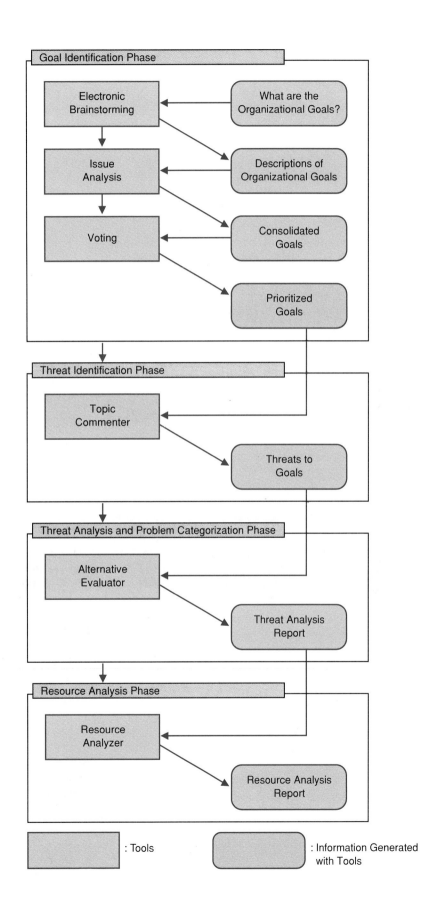

FIGURE 13.9

The process of crisis-response planning; the figure shows the tools of the electronic meeting system and the information generated with them.

Goal Identification Phase

Electronic Brainstorming

What are the Organizational Goals?

Issue Analysis

Descriptions of Organizational Goals

Voting

Consolidated Goals

Prioritized Goals

Threat Identification Phase

Topic Commenter

Threats to Goals

Threat Analysis and Problem Categorization Phase

Alternative Evaluator

Threat Analysis Report

Resource Analysis Phase

Resource Analyzer

Resource Analysis Report

: Tools

: Information Generated with Tools

more structured brainstorming: each goal was used as a topic. With the facilitator moving the individual goals to screens, the participants were able to clearly associate various threats with the organizational goals.

3. Threat Analysis and Problem Categorization

The Alternative Evaluator module helps decision makers to evaluate an alternative with respect to a set of criteria. This module was modified for the task at hand—that is, for threat analysis. For each goal, every threat was evaluated on two attributes. *Threat intensity* was an assessment of the organization's ability to counter the threat, should it materialize; *time pressure* was an assessment of the work required, should the threat occur without warning. Thus, threats were classified into four categories, with those assessed high on both criteria considered crisis points, and those assessed low on both considered as simply routine tasks.

A threat analysis report was produced, as exemplified in figure 13.10, for the profit goal and the threat of flood (affecting mortgages), with twelve decision makers evaluating the threat to the goal.

4. Resource Analysis

Using the Resource Analyzer module (a customized version of the Topic Commenter), the decision makers further explored the threats identified as crisis points. During this stage, they identified critical resources required to resist the potential threats. This included identification of key organizational actors, physical resources, communication requirements, early warning signals, and information systems that would be required to manage the crises.

In subsequent sessions, lower-level decision makers used this strategic-level information to develop detailed tactical and operational plans.

The decision group left the planning center with reports specifying goals and categorized threats as well as resources needed to counter the threats. The process itself also left them with a better understanding of basic organizational goals and of their individual assumptions and expertise.

Based on Nunamaker, 1989.

FIGURE 13.10

An excerpt from the threat analysis report.

Threat Analysis Report													
Federal Savings and Loan													
Oct. 10, 1992													
Goal: Profit													
Profit (GOAL) is threatened by: Flood (THREAT)													
Rating Scale	0	1	2	3	4	5	6	7	8	9	10	N	Mean
Threat Intensity	0	0	0	0	1	2	2	3	2	1	1	12	7
Time Pressure	0	0	0	0	0	2	3	1	3	3	0	12	7
Category: Crisis Point													

Case Study Questions

1. What are organizational crises?

2. How does the process described in the case study fit into the planning framework we discussed in chapter 11?

3. Relate the process to Simon's decision-making framework. Which stages were covered by the process, and to what extent did the information systems assist?

4. Note that the crisis-response planning process was rather thinly supported by quantitative analysis with the use of MIS. Comment on the appropriateness of this. If numbers are not analyzed during this session, when should they be analyzed?

5. What roles did information systems play in the process, and how? Refer to the discussion of their capabilities in chapter 2.

SELECTED REFERENCES

Adams, James L. *Conceptual Blockbusting: A Guide To Better Ideas.* 2d ed. New York: Norton, 1979.

Cohen, Michael; March, James; and Olsen, Johan. "A Garbage Can Model of Organizational Choice." *Administrative Science Quarterly,* 17, 1972 pp. 1–25.

Couger, J. Daniel. "Ensuring Creative Approaches in Information System Design." *Managerial and Decision Economics,* 11, 1990, pp. 281–95.

Daft, Richard L., and Lengel, Robert H. "Organizational Information Requirements, Media Richness, and Structural Design." *Management Science,* 32, 5, May 1986, pp. 554–71.

Drucker, Peter F. *Innovation and Entrepreneurship: Practice and Principles.* New York: Harper & Row, 1985.

Gilb, Tom. *Software Metrics.* Cambridge, Mass.: Winthrop, 1977.

Gordon, William J. J. *Synectics.* New York: Harper & Row, 1961.

Huber, George P. "The Nature of Organizational Decision Making and the Design of Decision Support Systems." *MIS Quarterly,* 5, 2, June 1981, pp. 1–10.

Huber, George P. "Cognitive Style as a Basis for MIS and DSS Design: Much Ado about Nothing?" *Management Science,* 29, 5, May 1983, pp. 567–97.

Ives, Blake, and Olson, Margrethe. "Manager or Technician? The Nature of Information Systems Manager's Job." *MIS Quarterly,* 5, 4, December 1981, pp. 49–62.

Janis, Irving L., and Mann, L. *Decision Making: A Psychological Analysis of Conflict, Choice, and Commitment.* New York: Free Press, 1977.

Kotter, John T. "What Effective General Managers Really Do." *Harvard Business Review,* November-December 1982, pp. 156–67.

Lindblom, Charles E. "The Science of Muddling Through." *Public Administration Review,* 19, 1959, pp. 79–88.

McKinney, James L., and Keen, Peter G. W. "How Managers' Minds Work." *Harvard Business Review,* May-June 1974, pp. 79–90.

Malone, Thomas W., and others. "Intelligent Information-Sharing Systems." *Communications of the ACM,* 30, 3, May 1987, pp. 390–402.

Miller, George A. "The Magical Number Seven, Plus or Minus Two: Some Limits on Our Capacity for Processing Information." *The Psychological Review,* 63, 2, March 1956, pp. 81–97.

Mintzberg, Henry. *The Nature of Managerial Work.* New York: Harper & Row, 1973.

Nunamaker, Jay F., Jr.; Applegate, Lynda M.; and Konsynski, Benn R. "Facilitating Group Creativity: Experience with a Group Decision Support System." *Journal of Management Information Systems,* 3, 4, Spring 1987, pp. 5–19.

Nunamaker, Jay F., Jr.; Weber, E. Sue; and Chen, Minder. "Organizational Crisis Management Systems: Planning for Intelligent Action." *Journal of Management Information Systems,* 5, 4, Spring 1989, pp. 7–32.

Osborn, Alex. *Applied Imagination.* New York: Charles Scribner's Sons, 1953.

Ray, Michael, and Myers, Rochelle. *Creativity in Business.* Garden City, New York: Doubleday, 1986.

Simon, Herbert A. *The New Science of Management Decision.* New York: Harper & Row, 1960.

Tversky, Amos, and Kahneman, Daniel. "The Framing of Decisions and the Psychology of Choice." *Science,* 211, 1981, pp. 453–58.

Zmud, Robert W. "Individual Differences and MIS Success: A Review of the Empirical Literature." *Management Science,* 23, 10, October 1979, pp. 966–79.

PART THREE
CASE STUDY

Decentralizing Management Information Systems

Flexible operation in a dynamic business environment and diseconomies of scale in computer systems have led a number of companies to disperse much of their corporate MIS function into their business units. The resulting decentralized MIS supports responsive action in the marketplace.

Why Decentralized MIS?

As corporate MIS functions grew, new applications used to be added to the others, running on mainframes in large corporate data centers. With time, many software bridges were built among these applications, and the advent of the database environment led to even greater intertwining of the applications supporting various business units. Clear architectural design of corporate systems, such as that presented in the case study for Part 1 of the book, was not the rule at all.

What happens when an organization needs to restructure? In today's highly dynamic business environment, corporate reorganizations, mergers, acquisitions and spin-offs of individual business divisions are common phenomena. Will the centralized corporate MIS be an obstacle? Very likely so.

Realization of this fact has led to a trend: decentralizing MIS operations. Departmental computing, frequently based on minicomputers, ensures the informational viability of a department or division. At the same time, corporate computing serves the entire organization with large databases and often also with mission-critical (strategic) systems.

For example, the Colonial Williamsburg Foundation of Williamsburg, Virginia, a private nonprofit organization, also runs a number of for-profit subsidiaries, such as historic eighteenth century taverns and modern motels. Financial reporting for the nonprofit and profit-oriented segments is quite different, yet the overall corporate results need to be consolidated. The foundation's 4,000 employees are employed in 800 job categories, ranging from a shepherdess or an ox-cart driver in Williamsburg's reconstructed colonial landscape to a motel manager. To manage this complex enterprise, the foundation has defined twelve major functional areas, each with its own goals and plans. The areas themselves change rapidly (particularly for an eighteenth-century environment placed into the twentieth century); a number of new businesses were recently added

to the functional groups. Properly coordinated decentralized computing is necessary to afford business flexibility to each functional area, and yet it is also necessary to obtain summarized corporate results.

Indeed, one can discern a great deal about a company's corporate strategy by following how it is decentralizing (or dispersing into divisions) its MIS operations. This is why many firms maintain a high level of confidentiality in making such a move.

We shall see here how two corporations approached the daunting task of MIS dispersal.

Decentralization at Eastman Kodak: Methodically Building in Flexibility

As has been the case with many other major corporations, Eastman Kodak has restructured from functional and regional organization into five line-of-business groups, such as, for example, Commercial and Information Systems and Eastman Chemicals. Each group includes a number of divisions. Former corporate functional divisions are gradually migrating into these groups (this means, for example, that each group will do its own marketing rather than rely on a centralized corporate marketing function). After marketing and research were decentralized in this fashion, MIS's turn came. A strategic plan was drawn up for the dispersed MIS function.

Flexibility in assimilating new technologies and adapting to a changing business environment was at the top of the goals list. MIS planners also decided that a top priority was for a group MIS to be flexible enough to allow the group to acquire or sell a business without major modification of the information system. This objective led to a long-term plan to move the information processing to microcomputers and use vertical software packages (that is, generalized packages for the specific industry rather than applications developed in-house). The role of each group's MIS department was redefined from that of a software developer to that of an integrator and educator.

The implementation of the plan was also planned: the business groups were to bring MIS functions under their own control as they became ready to do so. Thus, the company adopted a gradual decentralization process paced by the end users. To provide for a relatively painless transition, it was assumed in the plan that the load on the corporate mainframes would not diminish despite the decentralization (at a risk of maintaining excess processing capacity).

The strategic MIS plan also established the roles of the corporate MIS function. Overall corporate MIS architecture was defined. MIS managers and end users, working together, reviewed all the functions formerly performed by the corporate MIS to determine whether they should remain centralized on the corporate level or be dispersed to the appropriate divisions. Networking and interfacing are the obvious roles of the future corporate MIS. However, only some of the hardware and software requirements were subjected to corporate standards to be maintained by the corporate MIS. The rest was left up to the business groups—to allow flexible decision making.

To provide for ongoing strategic planning within each group, a position of vice-president of MIS was created in each of them. Annual reviews of strategic plans were replaced by a continuing planning process—in line with the flexibility objective.

Decentralization at Kendall Corporation: Planning to Restructure Fast

The Boston-based Kendall Corporation was restructured from a highly centralized company into five divisions, each expected to operate in an entrepreneurial fashion. As was the case with Eastman Kodak, this called for a strategic plan for MIS decentralization. Planning for decentralization started in a rather relaxed atmosphere, generally focusing on developing plans for long into the future. But four months into the planning process, Kendall's corporate parent, Colgate-Palmolive, sold Kendall and gave it only a few months to sever all ties with the parent MIS. Planning for an urgent restructuring of information processing took place.

Here are the principal elements of Kendall's strategic plan:

1. Experienced MIS managers were assigned from the corporate MIS to each division, so that they could study the needs of the division and represent it in the planning meetings. This brought the user community into the planning process.

2. The planners ranked divisions with respect to their information system needs based on present and estimated future number of products, number of customers, and annual revenue. The divisional MIS budgets were drawn up on this basis, with dispersal of the corporate MIS personnel.

3. MIS specialists established software and hardware requirements for each division in order to set company-wide standards. Setting such standards was important for two reasons. First, the much slimmer corporate MIS would find it easier to assist divisions in the presence of such standards. Second, the company could seek the advantages of volume purchasing.

Kendall made the decision to close the corporate data center equipped with an IBM 3084 mainframe. The divisional centers were standardized on the midrange IBM Application System/400 machines. The very large customer base of this computer line would ensure application software availability. The company also decided to select a single software vendor to provide packages that would satisfy the general needs of the divisions as well as customize the packages as needed.

4. Specification sheets and benchmarks were created in order to evaluate potential software vendors. A number of vendors were interviewed. One-day demonstration sessions were conducted for end users. A software developer was selected.

5. Kendall designed a short-term cutover plan (that is, a plan for replacing the old system with the new one) with simplicity in mind. Thus, a few weeks before each division was scheduled to go on-line, the new machines were installed and tested, and the databases were loaded. Subsequently, on different nights, each division was taken off the corporate system and started on its own machine (in what is known as the "cold turkey" cutover method). Time pressures caused planners to reject the less risky alternative of running the old and new systems in parallel for a period of time.

How do you keep your best technical people with a corporate reorganization impending? Ron Cipolla, Kendall's corporate MIS manager, takes his cue from company president Dale Sheratt. Sheratt says Cipolla, "hit the magic button, telling employees, 'We want you to be entrepreneurs and run your own businesses and control your own information technology resources.' "

After Decentralization

Following the decentralization of their MIS functions, both Eastman Kodak and Kendall went further—they almost entirely eliminated their centralized MIS departments. Eastman Kodak subsequently out-sourced its central MIS functions by turning them over to three external firms. Several factors contributed to the decision. Savings were needed after Eastman Kodak acquired Sterling Drug. But Katherine Hudson, Kodak's vice-president and director of corporate information systems who led the planning and implementation of outsourcing, also has this to say: "You have to look at information systems as a business within your business and then ask yourself: 'Is this a business I should be in?' "

Principal sources: John Mahnke, "Decentralizing MIS Could Mean Business Survival." *MIS Week*, April 10, 1989, pp. 2, 50; Larry Stevens, "A Good Planner Knows How to Bend." *Computerworld*, February 20, 1989, pp. 57–66; with a contribution from Peter Krass, "Chief of the Year: Kathy Hudson." *InformationWeek*, December 24/31, 1990, pp. 40–43.

Case Study Questions

1. Explain the advantages and disadvantages of the decentralization trend in systems-theoretic terms. What role do diseconomies of scale play in computer hardware?

2. Explain the organizational principles active in the decentralization trend.

3. What motivation do some employees have for welcoming decentralization? How would you motivate others?

4. How does the decentralization trend affect the distribution of decision-making authority?

5. Compare the two strategic plans for MIS decentralization: Eastman Kodak's and Kendall Corporation's. (Assume that the plans closely correspond to what I have stated here—which is only an assumption.)
   a. What were the principal objectives of the planners?
   b. What were the basic assumptions of the planners in regard to the environment each of their companies and its divisions would face?
   c. What are the respective strengths and weaknesses of the plans?
   d. What are the similarities between the two plans?
   e. What provisions were made for plan implementation?
   f. What is the principal difference between the two approaches, and what caused this difference?
   g. What were the planned responsibilities of the corporate MIS function and of the divisional MIS in each corporation?

6. How does the decision to use vertical software affect a company's ability to pursue competitive advantage with information systems?

PART FOUR

INFORMATIONAL
SUPPORT
SYSTEMS

In this part of the text, we shall study the principal types of information systems assisting a knowledge worker in a modern organization.

Decision support systems (DSS) support a decision maker during the process of arriving at a solution to an ill-structured problem—which describes much of the decision making in management. DSS are of particular importance in planning at all organizational levels. Group DSS are gaining ground in supporting group decision making in a variety of situations. Executive information systems (EIS) are, on the other hand, a powerful tool for executive control.

Expert system technology represents at this time the most important commercial contribution of artificial intelligence. An expert system assists a human decision maker by offering advice within a narrow domain of application. The system arrives at its conclusions by applying a reasoning process to its knowledge base, which describes the domain of the system's "expertise."

Office information systems (OIS) support collective knowledge work in office settings. By managing documents, handling messages, and supporting meetings, OIS facilitate communication, collaboration and coordination in small and large groups. Along with serving as an information-delivery vehicle, an OIS can also act as the glue that holds other systems together, as we suggested in figure 1.1 at the beginning of our book.

Let us see how these types of information systems provide the range of organizational capabilities we discussed in Part 1 of the book.

Decision Support Systems and Executive Information Systems

The purpose of . . . models is insight, not numbers.

Arthur Geoffrion

Decision support systems (DSS) are a type of management information system whose principal objective is to support a human decision maker during the process of arriving at a decision. The strength of DSS lies in supporting decision making in situations where both human judgment and the power of the computer are required. These systems do *not* render decisions. Rather, DSS enable their users to apply a computational model interactively to a large collection of data in a relatively easy fashion. The models generally assist DSS users in making planning decisions. We may conceptualize these systems as consisting of three components: a database, a model base, and a dialog subsystem that facilitates user access to models and data. Through the incorporation of expert system technology and by offering facilities for group decision making, DSS will in the future further enhance computerized support for organizational decision making.

While decision support systems primarily support planning at all levels—strategic, tactical, and operational—executive information systems (EIS) are a powerful control tool. A top executive using an EIS gains the ability to instantly track all aspects of the company's operation and to locate problems and opportunities. The use of an EIS can have a profound influence on organizational design by increasing the span of higher-level management.

Market analysts at Parke-Davis, a New Jersey pharmaceutical company, have been using EASYTRAC, a marketing DSS developed with EXPRESS, a DSS generator from Information Resources of Chicago. What does a decision support system actually do for these analysts?

The users of this marketing DSS want to establish consumer response to various forms of product advertising, specific promotion campaigns, and salespeople. They want to compare the product volume their own firm is shipping to various types of distribution outlets (such as drugstores, distributors, and hospitals) with the volumes shipped by competitors. Thus, they need to use both internal and external databases. By analyzing the results, they can then endeavor to plan future marketing campaigns.

Let us see how Harry Tappen, director of market research for the company, has been using EASYTRAC. During a session with the system, he requested a report on product shipments by month, broken down by type of distribution outlet. A report on one of the products led Tappen to conclude that the response of one of the consumer market segments to a recent promotion campaign had been far below projections. Tappen discovered a problem.

Using the same DSS, Tappen looked for the cause. Testing a variety of hypotheses (''what-if'' trials), Tappen searched for the factor that caused the failure of the promotion campaign. Repeated trials with the system led him to conclude that the promotion had wrongly targeted a particular consumer group.

Tappen realized that the DSS should have been used at an earlier stage to establish what induced a physician to prescribe the product (an ad in a trade journal? a salesperson's call?).

EASYTRAC's graphics module can produce, for example, a scatter plot of a product's sales from month to month correlated with various aspects of marketing tactics (such as discount percentage or amount spent on advertising). The user may then request that the system perform a regression analysis: it will find a curve and a mathematical formula that best match the points on the scatter plot. The marketer thus obtains a series of equations that show the response of various market segments (type of consumer, region, type of distribution outlet) to various promotional devices. This means that the marketer has constructed a decision model.

With the model, the marketing analyst can compare alternative decisions and select one. Using the "what-if" mode, she or he can decide, for example, the best way to spend a promotional budget of $500,000 (What if we spend $150,000 in print advertising in the northeast and $350,000 in sales calls and discounting in the southwest? What if we spend the entire sum on sales calls?). The analyst can also use the system in the goal-seeking mode: given the goal of $50 million in sales in six months, how much should we spend on print advertising?

By consolidating predictions made by the marketing department with the use of the DSS for the future sales of each product, corporate financial analysts can develop sales and profit plans for the entire company.

Based on Elisabeth Horwitt, "DSS: Effective Relief for Frustrated Management." *Business Computer Systems*, July 1984, pp. 44–58.

Note how a decision support system supports the entire process of decision making rather than just one of the stages. Note also how the *decision maker*, rather than the system, renders the decision. Using a DSS, a decision maker can both develop a decision model and apply it to a particular situation. Judgmental constraints can be introduced by the manager during the decision-making session (Our new manager in the northwest will need a boost—we have to spend at least $100,000 on discounting there over the next three months).

In this chapter, we will examine both decision support systems and executive support systems, which allow executives to track the performance of their enterprise.

CHAPTER OUTLINE

14.1   When Should You Use the Decision Support Approach?
- DSS as a Package of Capabilities
- Ill-Structured Problems
- How DSS Are Deployed
- Capabilities Offered by DSS

14.2   Components of DSS
- The Data Management Subsystem
- The Model Management Subsystem
- The Dialog Management Subsystem

14.3   Classification of DSS

14.4   Building a Decision Support System
- DSS Technology
- Who Builds a DSS?
- How DSS Are Developed

. . . .

14.1 WHEN SHOULD YOU USE THE DECISION SUPPORT APPROACH?

Decision support systems offer managers a package of capabilities for prompt and flexible access to data and to models that work with the data to produce needed information. These systems vastly expand the abilities of knowledge workers to make decisions concerning ill-structured problems. The hallmark of DSS is flexibility.

DSS as a Package of Capabilities

Decision support systems are a type of MIS that represent a distinct approach to computerized support of managerial decision making. The approach was articulated in the early 1970s by Michael Scott Morton (Scott Morton, 1971) and has since become a broad area of information system practice and research. As stressed by another pioneer in the area, Peter Keen (1980), the use of DSS in a firm that previously relied only on management reporting systems is a form of innovation, since entirely new capabilities are now available.

Decision support systems are interactive information systems that assist a decision maker in approaching ill-structured problems by offering analytical models and access to databases. The development of these systems arose from dissatisfaction with the rigidity of reporting systems that defined the early MIS environment; thus, their hallmark is (or should be) flexibility. Personal DSS should be easy to develop—end-user-oriented tools should be at hand for the purpose.

An organizational DSS, used throughout an enterprise, should be developed in a disciplined fashion. All DSS should be easy to use in the way that best supports the cognitive style of the individual decision maker.

We can therefore think of a DSS as a set of capabilities: within its area of application, such a system should give its user a way to use models and databases in an interactive session that best supports his or her way of thinking about the problem at hand. In a way, DSS steer a middle course between the severe limitations of management science models, where a number of unrealistic assumptions may have to be made, and management reporting systems, which make their user do most of the analysis and the relating of various items of information to each other.

We introduced decision support systems in section 3.5 of the text; Case Study 2 at the end of chapter 3 showed how a decision maker (a traffic manager) used a DSS to select a vehicle route. You may want to review that case, with its reliance on computerized mapping. Comparing the use of that DSS on the operational level with the marketing planning on the tactical level discussed in the focus case for this chapter, we can see that many aspects of the two DSS are different—and yet both systems directly support the decision-making process. What, then, is the essence of DSS? In what business situations should we think about using the DSS approach? We shall discuss these issues here. Later in the chapter, we shall see what tools we need to implement a DSS and how we can go about it.

Ill-Structured Problems

What type of management decisions need DSS support? Expanding Simon's categorization of problems that have to be dealt with by people in organizations, and following the work of Andrew Gorry and Michael Scott Morton (Gorry, 1971), we arrive at the categories of problems shown in table 14.1.

As we can see, the principal domain of DSS is support of decision making for semistructured problems, where parts of the *decision process itself* often require very significant computer support. This is so because a model (in some cases containing hundreds of equations) has to be applied against a database often comprising millions of data items, with human judgment injected at critical junctures.

Unstructured problems, often stemming from leading and organizing activities, are in some cases supported by DSS in minor aspects; and in certain cases, a DSS may be employed for easy access to data. Decision making to solve unstructured

TABLE 14.1

Structuredness of Problems

TYPE OF PROBLEM	EXAMPLES OF PROBLEM AREAS	CHARACTERISTICS	HOW DECISIONS ARE MADE
Structured	Order validation Inventory reorder	Availability of an algorithm (standard operating procedure)	Fully computerized (TPS or MRS)
Semistructured	Sales forecasting Budgeting Risk analysis	Programmable aspects present	Human decision maker supported by computer
Unstructured	Promotion of personnel Introducing new technology	No standard procedures or aspects available	Principally by a human, with some computer support

problems is now also supported by expert systems, but within narrow domains—such as, for example, a decision regarding loan approval. Other systems that do not support the decisional aspect of this process assist the organizational aspect by bringing the collective wisdom of a group to bear on the problem through office information systems.

In ill-structured—both semistructured and unstructured—problems, the exploration of alternative solutions cannot be completed before a choice must be made (Bonczek, 1984). Decision making in this problem environment is more typical in the work of middle and higher management; we should stress, however, that such problems occur at all three managerial levels, and therefore, the use of DSS applies to operational, tactical, and strategic organizational levels. When we say that one of a manager's principal tasks is to deal with ambiguity, we mean that he or she will be called upon to solve many ill-structured problems.

In the systems-theoretic sense, if an ill-structured problem is treated as structured and approached wholly with the aid of management science models without significant intervention from a human decision maker, then the open system being described is reduced to a closed or relatively closed system because most of the environmental factors are ignored. The use of a DSS makes it possible to include a variety of these environmental influences and thus ensures a more realistic open-system approach to problems.

To make all this more tangible to you, let us consider a few brief examples of DSS application.

How DSS Are Deployed

Let us consider five different sample arenas of DSS application. These should give us insight into what a DSS can do for us.

1. Firestone Rubber & Tire Company of Akron, Ohio built a DSS to assess the best strategy for rolling out a new brand of tires. The system permits analysts to look for relationships between past financial results and external variables, such as total car production and gross national product, and thus build sales forecasting models.

   Using the system containing these models, the Firestone analysts were able to rapidly build for the corporate vice-president of technology a database on all 200 competitive brands of tires, including data on their construction, tread, volume, and sales estimates. The executive used this database to assist him in finding a competitive strategy. The system enabled the organization to integrate the technological and financial aspects of a product decision and thus create a basis for joint decision making by the company's various functional areas (Snyders, 1984). The availability of this system conferred a competitive advantage on Firestone.

2. Houston Minerals Corporation was considering a joint venture with a petrochemicals company to build a chemical plant. Using a DSS generator—a system for building DSS—the planning staff of the company built *in a few days* a DSS projecting the risks of the venture, taking prices, supply, and demand into consideration. The results suggested that the project would have a positive outcome (Turban, 1990).

   However, the executive vice-president responsible for the decision requested an answer to the question: "What is the chance that this project will result in a disastrous outcome?" In the words of the company's chief planner: "Within twenty minutes, there in the executive boardroom, we were reviewing the results of his "what-if" questions. Those results led to the eventual dismissal of the project, which we otherwise would probably have accepted."[1]

Thus, a DSS enabled the decision maker to bring his judgment to bear on the problem; this judgment was fully supported by the the information made available by the DSS and by the insight of planners that went into the construction of the model.

3. A portfolio manager of a large pension fund is responsible for investing billions of dollars in assets. A huge variety of investment vehicles with varying degrees of risk and reward are available at all times, and the funds are at all times placed in a complex array of investments. The manager needs to make constant investment decisions consistent with the objectives of the fund, with a variety of environmental factors, and with her or his experience and informal information. Certain aspects of this work can be handled by expert systems that suggest decisions. However, overall risk analysis with the use of a DSS permits the manager to balance various forms of investment and spread the funds over a variety of investments.

4. A DSS for police-beat allocation was built for the city of San Jose, California. An officer could display a map on a VDT and call up for each zone the data showing police calls for service, service times, and activity levels. The officer could experiment with various alternatives involving the assignment of police patrols by interacting with the system. The system became a tool that helped its users to exercise their judgment. An experiment was run to compare an assignment made by an officer using the DSS with an assignment made by a linear programming model that did not rely on human judgment (a management science model). The officer-DSS team arrived at a superior solution (Sprague, 1980).

5. As the utilization of a DSS assisting the navigators of vessels on the lower Mississippi River increased, the number of accidents on this once extremely dangerous waterway decreased precipitously (Le Blanc, 1990). The system simulates the traffic of the vessels in the area by dead-reckoning: it updates the vessels' positions from their original locations by considering the direction and speed of their movement—with all the initial information radioed in by the ships' navigators. The Coast Guard personnel use the system by watching blips on their consoles, which resemble air traffic control displays. They alert navigators to developing situations of undue proximity to other vessels by radio communication, and accidents are thus prevented.

Now that we have reviewed these examples, let us consider in more general terms the capabilities offered by DSS.

Capabilities Offered by DSS

DSS have several features to offer in the general information system environment of an organization. Specifically, DSS can:

1. Support decision making in ill-structured situations—in which, precisely owing to the lack of structure, problems do not lend themselves to full computerization, and yet do require computer assistance for access to and processing of voluminous amounts of data.

PHOTO 14.1

Mary Ellen Johnson, a divisional sales manager at Frito-Lay in Southgate, Michigan, and Kenneth Hurd, one of the managers in her division, receive instruction in using the Sales Decision Support program from David Bugg, an MIS specialist.

This DSS brings all the data within Johnson's area of responsibility to her desktop and enables her to use these data to run models in order to make tactical marketing and sales decisions. This manager has available all the data on thirty-nine districts within six regions she oversees, including the data on individual accounts (for example, A&P), on brand sales broken down by store or package type, and on the performance of each of the 388 sales representatives in her territory. Soon, the data on the regional performance of the snack-food giant's competitors will also be available through this system.

2. Help to *rapidly* obtain quantitative results needed to reach a decision. We can construct a DSS model much faster than we can do modeling with other MIS components, and the model can be flexibly deployed with data as needed during the decision-making process.

3. Operate in the *ad hoc* (as needed) mode to suit the current needs of the user, as opposed to operating in a generally scheduled fashion, as management reporting systems do.

4. Support easy modification of models, which increases the organization's responsiveness to the changing environment both within and outside an organization.

5. Support various stages of the decision-making process (as presented in our discussion of Simon's model in chapter 13). As we saw in the focus case, a DSS can help to find a problem. The creative generation of alternative solutions is expected of the human decision maker. The principal strong point of DSS is their support for the consideration of alternatives ("what-if" scenarios) and for the informed choice of the preferred solution. Since the system does not actually make a decision, a manager can employ it to arrive at a decision that is organizationally desirable and that will be supported by others during the implementation stage. Decision implementation may also be facilitated by the continuing use of the model to track progress and provide visibility to the effort.

6. Foster high-quality decision making by encouraging decisions based on the integration of available information and human judgment. DSS give decision makers a degree of confidence in their decisions unavailable to the decision maker who is wholly dependent on his or her judgment.

7. Offer flexibility—as opposed to a preordained pattern of use—making it easy to accommodate the particular decision-making style of an individual. However, some systems are more restrictive than others: they may lack certain models or impose a certain sequence of operations and thus constrain the user's decision making (Silver, 1990). Restrictive systems may be simpler to use and may promote prescribed decision-making patterns.

8. Facilitate the implementation of decisions, which frequently cut across departmental boundaries. By creating and exercising common models, decision makers in the involved organizational units develop common

SHOULD WE USE A SPREADSHEET OR A DSS?

Spreadsheets are the most common personal productivity programs. Their continuing use significantly contributes to the quality of decision making. But they do have limitations.

At Zale Corporation of Dallas (a diamond importer and distributor), planners and analysts routinely use a well-known spreadsheet program—until the application runs into the limitations of spreadsheets: too much data, too many variables, or a model too complex for the spreadsheet program to handle (even though a rather cumbersome modeling language is provided with it). When this occurs, the application is rewritten with Micro W, a DSS generator from Comshare Corporation of Ann Arbor, Michigan.

"As in most companies, the amount of data and detail in financial statements keeps on escalating as we keep breaking out line items," says William Lewis, a Zale manager. Thus, the spreadsheets grow.

The biggest advantage Zale managers see in DSS is their ability to handle changes consistently. A fall in inventory levels or a change in tax regulations can be consistently reflected, respectively, in the database or model base of an organizational DSS used by all the analysts concerned. In contrast, updating your own spreadsheet is a rather wearisome task; keeping it consistent with everyone else's spreadsheets is virtually impossible.

Based on Elisabeth Horwitt, "Up From Spreadsheets." *Business Computer Systems*, June 1985, pp. 54–59; and Carol Graham and Melanie Freely, "When Spreadsheets Aren't Enough." *Datamation*, January 1, 1991, pp. 77–79.

---

assumptions and, in general, learn to communicate at a deeper level. This helps to fight the "not-invented-here" syndrome, so common in organizations, that leads to the adoption of suboptimal solutions so long as they are one's own.

9. Support group decision making, particularly through group DSS (GDSS). These systems, which we shall discuss later, permit several people with a variety of experiences and areas of expertise to bring them to bear on a decision, leading to more effective, higher-quality decision making.

10. Provide user-friendliness, a principal feature of well-designed DSS. User-friendliness can make computer-supported problem solving attractive to individuals at all levels of an organization. The user can work with the system in the style that best serves him or her (Mann, 1986). This helps managers, professionals, and other knowledge workers to perform better. It also enriches their jobs, particularly at the operational level.

11. Give managers the opportunity to gain a better understanding of their business by developing and working with models.

I must stress that DSS, particularly those that rely on complicated models, offer access to large databases, or produce high-quality graphical outputs, may require extensive computational resources. In organizations where the assimilation of DSS has reached the more mature incorporation phase, managers should adopt cost-benefit measures to ensure payoffs from larger DSS (see, for example, Keen, 1981).

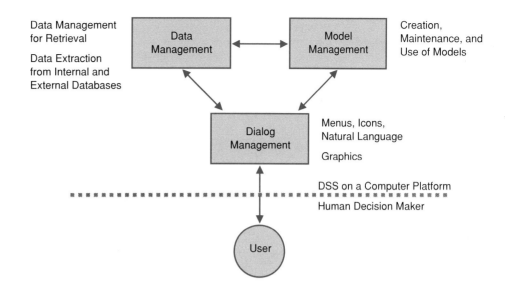

FIGURE 14.1

DSS subsystems.

14.2 COMPONENTS OF DSS

Let us expand our initial discussion of DSS components, which were introduced in chapter 3. The three principal DSS subsystems and their principal capabilities are shown in figure 14.1. Various commercial systems support DSS development and package these DSS capabilities in a variety of ways by distributing them among a series of optional modules.

Let us look more closely at the DSS subsystems.

The Data Management Subsystem

The data management subsystem of a DSS relies, in general, on a variety of internal and external databases. Indeed, we have said that the power of DSS derives from their ability to provide easy access to data. This is not to say that a simple, usually spreadsheet-based DSS for the personal use of a manager cannot rely on the manager's limited personal database. It is simply that maintaining the currency and integrity of a significant database of this kind is usually a daunting task. Proliferation of personal databases also contradicts the principles of information resource management.

On the other hand, it is usually undesirable to provide a DSS with direct access to corporate databases. The performance of the transaction processing systems that access these databases, as well as the responsiveness of the DSS, would both be degraded. Usually, therefore, the database component of DSS relies on extracts from the relevant internal and external databases. The user is able to add to these data at will. This is shown in figure 14.2.

The principles of database management we discussed in chapter 8 apply to the management of the database extract used by a DSS. The extraction procedure itself is generally specified by a specialist rather than an end user. The specialist needs to pay particular attention to data consistency across multiple decision support systems that extract data from the corporate databases. If extracts for the DSSs serving the same functional area are made at different times, the extracted databases will differ and "battles of the printout" may result.

FIGURE 14.2

The data management
subsystem of DSS.

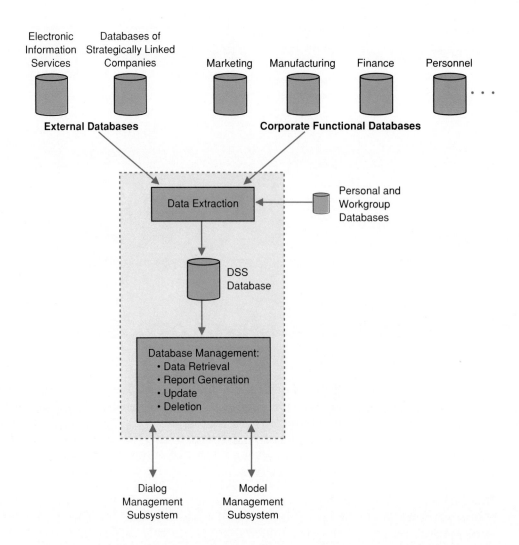

The power of DSS rests on the user's ability to apply quantitative, mathematical models to data. I introduced models to you in chapter 11, where we discussed them in the context of planning. We showed an accounting model that was used to obtain a pro forma income statement for a small company. Indeed, DSS are primarily used for planning activities of varying scope and at various corporate levels. In the following section, we shall see how the analytical sophistication of DSS varies depending on the nature of the models employed.

The Model Management Subsystem

Models have different areas of application and come from a variety of sources. Software packages for developing DSS (so-called DSS generators) contain libraries of statistical models. These models include tools for the exploratory analysis of data—tools designed to obtain summarized measures such as mean and median values, variances, scatter plots, and so forth. Other statistical models help analyze series of data and forecast future outcomes by approximating a set of data with a mathematical equation, by extending the trend of a curve by extrapolation techniques, or by providing for seasonal adjustment. We discussed the roles these models play in the planning process in section 11. 7. Other models

FIGURE 14.3

The model management
subsystem of DSS.

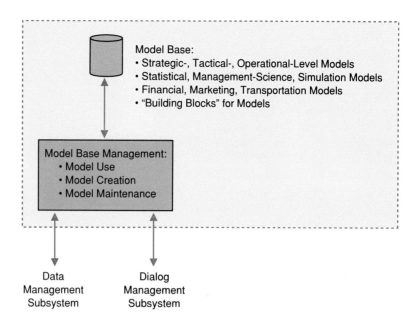

help establish (or reject) causal relationships between various factors (for example, whether the drop in sales volume is caused by the aging of our target market segment).

Market response models show how sales depend on such factors as price and promotion. Simulation models that generate input values randomly from a certain probability distribution (also called Monte Carlo models—after the city where the famous casino is, of course) are employed for waiting-line problems, such as establishing the number of operators needed for order taking or deciding on staffing levels for a service center.

Optimization models, developed by management scientists, are available for use in DSS. These models aim to allocate resources so as to maximize profit or minimize cost or time. A number of such models are based on a linear programming technique. These include models that allocate input resources (labor, materials, capital) among various products; models that assign activities to personnel or equipment; and models that determine the best shipping schedules from several points of origin to several destinations. Other models optimize inventory levels or determine optimal network configurations. Specialized model libraries are available for financial modeling, risk analysis, or marketing.

The capabilities of the model management component of DSS are summarized in figure 14.3.

A particular advantage of DSS is the decision maker's ability to use a model to explore the influence of various factors on outcomes (a process known as sensitivity analysis). Two forms of such analysis are the what-if analysis and goal seeking. We showed the results of both of these analyses in figures 3.5 and 3.6, respectively, when we first introduced you to the decision support system.

A TRULY EXPENSIVE DSS

Narendra Karmarkar of AT&T's Bell Laboratories has developed a method for solving very, very large resource allocation problems that lend themselves to the linear programming approach. This method has been made available by AT&T on a combined hardware-software platform optimized for running the large model-based DSS called Korbx. The system incorporates a mini-supercomputer and costs $9 million.

AT&T's application of the Karmarkar algorithm to the configuration of its overseas telephone network has saved the company tens of millions of dollars.

The Air Force's Military Airlift Command (MAC), responsible for hauling troops and materiel for the U.S. armed forces, was one of the first users of Korbx. MAC uses the system to find the best flight route (the command has 329 locations), with a computation for a typical mission involving tens of thousands of variables.

Other transportation companies, including Delta Air Lines, have expressed interest in the Korbx system.

Based on David Coursey, "Karmarkar Algorithm Means Better Decision Support." *MIS Week*, June 26, 1989, p. 36.

When doing *what-if* analysis, the decision maker creates multiple scenarios by assuming various realistic values for input data. Thus, the decision maker asks "What if these are the values of the inputs?" The model recomputes outputs for each case. Here are some examples of questions that can be directed toward appropriate models:

What will be the cost of goods sold *if* the cost of raw materials increases by 10 percent?

What will be the effects on the company bonus program *if* sales increase by 3 percent and direct expenses increase by 5 percent? (The result of asking this question was shown in figure 3.5.)

When *goal seeking,* the decision maker works backward from the assumed results to the needed input values. Thus, the decision maker asks "What will it take to achieve this goal?" Some examples of questions asked in this mode are:

What sales volume *will be necessary* to ensure a revenue growth of 10 percent next year?

How many service center employees *will it take* to ensure that every order is handled within three minutes?

What quarterly revenues *will we need* from each of our three products to generate the desired profits during these quarters? (This question was asked to produce the screen output shown in figure 3.6.)

The actual form in which these questions may be asked depends on the options offered by the dialog management subsystem of the DSS, which we shall discuss next.

There is significant research interest in providing a degree of automated model management. The user would be able to present the problem in a system of this kind, and the system would automatically select an appropriate model or con-

FIGURE 14.4

The dialog management subsystem of DSS.

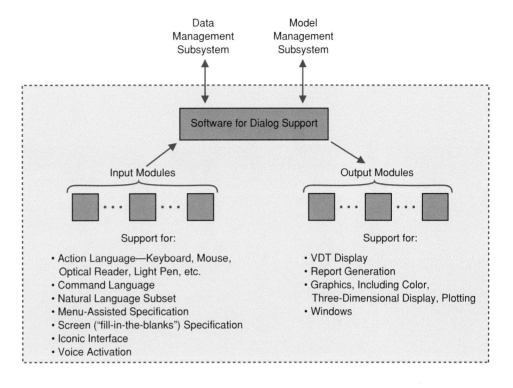

struct one from the existing models and "building blocks." Knowledge-based techniques of expert systems have been explored toward this end (as described, for example, in Applegate, 1986 or Elam, 1987).

The Dialog Management Subsystem

Along with DSS's ability to apply models to large volumes of data from a variety of sources, a single advantage of DSS is the user-friendly and flexible interface between the human decision maker and such a system. This stands in contrast to management reporting systems.

The principal components of the dialog management subsystem are shown in figure 14.4. The notable feature is support of multiple forms of input and output. By combining various input and output capabilities of a DSS, users can engage in the individual dialog styles that best support their decision-making styles.

The field of artificial intelligence has made some notable contributions to dialog management, such as the ability to specify what is wanted in a subset of natural language or to activate the system by voice. The window capability enables the user to maintain several activities at the same time, with the results displayed in screen windows (the user employs a mouse to move between the windows). A variety of help and even training-by-example capabilities may be offered.

Significant attention has been devoted by researchers to the effectiveness of computer graphics, as opposed to the tabular display of data. Gary Dickson and his colleagues (Dickson, 1986) found that, in general, one cannot claim an advantage (however intuitively appealing it may be) for graphics throughout all decision-related activities. They did find, however, that graphs outperform tables when a large amount of information must be presented and a relatively simple impression is desired. This is very often the case—and the main reason why executive information systems, discussed later in this chapter, rely heavily on graphics.

By analyzing the results of research in this area, Ali Montazemi and Shuohong Wang (Montazemi, 1988–89), concluded that line graphics have time-saving effects on decision making for more complex decision tasks only, and are less effective at providing precise information. Color graphics were found to improve decision quality, but they did not reduce the time necessary to arrive at a decision. Graphic representation of quantitative information requires considerable care to prevent distorted perception; Edward Tufte (1990) gives a thorough and exciting presentation of the subject.

Summarizing the uses of graphical presentation of business information, Richard Scovill tells us that most business graphs are designed to answer just four questions (Scovill, 1988):

1. Who is the biggest?

2. How do circumstances change over time?

3. What is typical or exceptional?

4. How well does one fact predict another?

In general, it has been established that different decision makers and tasks are best supported by different display formats. This again proves that the advantage of DSS in the area of dialog management lies in providing *a variety* of dialog styles.

14.3 CLASSIFICATION OF DSS

As we have seen from the foregoing examples, DSS can be broadly used throughout an organization. These systems can be classified by the management level they offer support to (operational, tactical, or strategic) or by the functional area they are used in (marketing, finance, and so forth). They can also be classified into personal and organizational systems.

However, to obtain a thorough view of the variety of capabilities these systems can deliver, it is best to follow Steven Alter and consider a classification based on the degree to which the outputs of a given system can determine a decision (Alter, 1980). This classification yields an entire spectrum of systems ranging from the totally data-oriented to the more powerful model-oriented systems. Clearly, a given DSS often possesses a mix of these capabilities—in which case we would classify it with respect to its most powerful capability. But the purpose of this categorization is to review the variety of capabilities offered by the DSS approach rather than to give you tags to put on a particular system.

1. Data Access Systems

These systems (which Alter calls "file-drawer systems") can provide user-friendly ad hoc access to the database. This capability is equivalent to what is offered by most DBMS through a query language. However, such systems are frequently set up to allow shop floor personnel to continuously monitor the shop floor or a particular piece of machinery; thus they fulfill operational control purposes.

BREAKING THE WALL TO MAINFRAME DATA

When one reads an orderly presentation of the capabilities of DSS, one frequently does not realize that in a particular organizational context, blood, sweat, and tears may flow before data are liberated from mainframe databases. Well, at the very least, it takes the persistent effort of a dedicated individual.

In the New York State Department of Health, Mike Zdeb is such a champion of decision support. Before direct access to data was established, the Department's users had to rely on cumbersome and inflexible reporting systems. Poring through voluminous reports was not always rewarded by finding the necessary information. Managers' decisions regarding hospital administration in the vast bureaucracy were frequently based on anecdotal evidence rather than informed consideration of alternatives. The absence of an interactive environment hindered work with data.

The superior graphics available in a personal workstation environment but lacking in mainframe peripherals was another inducement to bring the data down to PC level. "In government, the presentation of data is as important as the analysis of data," says Vito Logrill, director of information policy for the agency. Hence, it was vital to ensure that information was presented with excellent graphics. Well-presented information generates interest— and, perhaps, support for the point of view of the presenter.

Using a purchased utility package, Mike Zdeb was able to send the graphics produced on the IBM 3081 mainframe by means of SAS Graph (a graphics option of a well-known statistical software package) down to the PCs. From there, it could be presented with the Lotus Freelance graphics package on a laser printer. Well-presented data became available on demand.

Zdeb has gradually become a resource person, answering myriad questions on the newly created computing environment, acting as unofficial liaison between users and information specialists, and even offering courses on graphics and computerized mapping throughout the Department of Health.

Based on Glenn Rifkin, "User Seizes the Initiative at N.Y. Health Department." *Computerworld—Special Report on Innovative Connections,* April 10, 1989, pp. SR3–SR4.

It is easy to dismiss data access systems as offering little in terms of decision support. But, as illustrated by the above vignette, providing access to mainframe data represents a huge step forward from management reporting systems.

2. Data Analysis Systems

These systems help to analyze historical and current data, either on demand (ad hoc) or periodically. The portfolio analysis system we discussed earlier on belongs in this category. An airline uses a system of this type to compare its performance with that of its competitors. The system's database contains the data on the quarterly performances of all airlines, submitted to the Civil Aeronautics Board of the federal government (Alter, 1980).

Data analysis systems are frequently oriented toward the consolidation (aggregation) of data, such as summarizing the performances of a firm's subunits and presenting the summaries in graphs. Only very simple models are employed.

3. Forecast-Oriented Data Analysis Systems

These systems (which Alter calls "analysis information systems") generally assist in developing product plans, including market segment forecasts, sales forecasts, and analyses of competitive actions. Their operation is based on access to a variety of internal and external marketing and product databases, including series of historical data. Ad hoc use for planning purposes by a staff analyst or a marketing manager is typical. The systems in this category include only the simpler of the variety of marketing models, which show how existing trends in the marketplace will extend in the future if similar conditions prevail (DSS capabilities in marketing are discussed in Buzzell, 1985 and Clarke, 1987).

4. Systems Based on Accounting Models

These are used to consider alternative options for planning purposes, based on accounting definitions and relationships. Such systems typically produce estimated (pro forma) income statements, balance sheets, or other measures of financial performance. We saw an example of such a model in chapter 11. A system of this type accepts estimates of costs and revenues as inputs rather than forecasting them (for example, it would require a ready sales forecast). The "what-if" mode of operation is typically employed to compare alternatives.

5. Systems Based on Representational Models

These systems go beyond the use of ready standard formulas, such as those employed in systems that rely on accounting models. Rather, representational models show the dependence between a controllable variable, such as the price of a product, and an outcome, such as sales. These are frequently simulation models which yield probabilistic results.

The market analyst at Parke-Davis, introduced in the focus case for this chapter, produced a representational model of customer response to promotional devices. Another example is a risk analysis model, which considers such key factors as costs of resources (labor, raw materials, and so on) and product demand. We have seen how Houston Minerals used such a DSS to avoid exposing itself to an unacceptable degree of risk.

Staff analysts are typical developers (or customizers) and users of these DSS.

6. Systems Based on Optimization Models

Optimization models are developed by management scientists to determine optimal allocation of resources or best possible schedules. Using the techniques of linear programming, for example, one is able to establish the mix of products that must be produced to maximize an objective such as profit, subject to a variety of constraints. Using such a model, a company faced with temporary supply limitations was able to adjust the supply of raw materials it needed for its products to meet this temporary constraint.

In a DSS setting, these models are used by a human decision maker to arrive at a solution that considers environmental factors not included in the model itself.

FIGURE 14.5

Types of DSS.

(Adapted in part from Alter, 1980, p. 76)

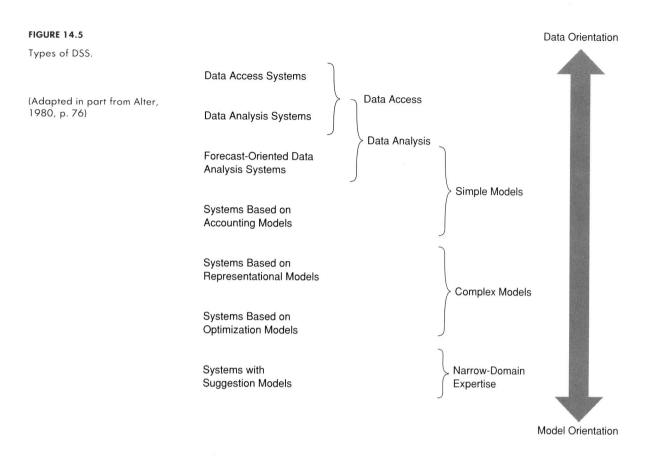

7. Systems with Suggestion Models

These systems "push the envelope" of decision support systems by actually suggesting decisions, rather than merely responding to the user's request to evaluate an alternative. Systems of this type that suggest solutions within narrow domains of knowledge are more and more frequently based on expert system technology. Such a system may suggest product price, the rate of insurance renewal, or production volume. The capabilities and limitations of expert systems will be discussed in the next chapter.

Our classification of DSS is summarized in figure 14.5. As we stressed earlier, many systems incorporate several of these capabilities.

Data-oriented DSS (or DSS components) primarily support earlier phases of the decision-making process, in particular the intelligence phase involving discovery of a problem or opportunity. The design and choice phases are supported by model-oriented DSS. The implementation of a decision is facilitated if the future implementers were involved in arriving at the decision with the use of DSS, or even in constructing a model employed in it. In general, as an organization's sophistication in DSS use grows, a shift takes place toward model-oriented DSS.

14.4 BUILDING A DECISION SUPPORT SYSTEM

How does a manager acquire a DSS? As we shall see, this depends on the technology employed and on the nature of the decision task that needs support.

DSS Technology

Three levels of DSS technology have been identified by Ralph Sprague (Sprague, 1980). We shall consider them by progressing from the level closest to the actual DSS to the one most distant from it.

1. Specific DSS

A *specific DSS* is the actual system that a manager works with during the decision process. Our examples of DSS for portfolio allocation, joint-venture evaluation, or police-beat allocation were systems of this type.

A specific DSS is constructed with the use of DSS generators or tools, which we shall later describe in more detail. There now exist a variety of specific DSS in the software marketplace; however, they require customization to the actual environment in which they are to be used. In some cases, elaborate customization may approach the complexity of using a DSS generator (which we discuss next).

As we said, a DSS usually undergoes extensive modification as it is used. Therefore, any specific DSS may be expected to evolve as time passes.

2. DSS Generators

A *DSS generator* is a software package that provides capabilities for building specific DSS rapidly and easily. Capabilities of generators vary widely. Their common characteristic is that much of the processing and data accessing functionality needed in a specific DSS is already programmed into the generator and can be combined into the context of a specific DSS without much programming.

Elaborate DSS generators, such as EXPRESS and pcEXPRESS of Information Resources (Chicago), incorporate a variety of tools for data analysis, financial modeling, and forecasting, combined with the capability of accessing multiple databases for querying and reporting; they also include comprehensive graphics packages. The first of these systems was designed for a mainframe environment, the second for personal workstations (EXPRESS, 1987). Generators based on personal workstations generally offer the same capabilities as those based on minis or mainframes but impose various limitations (for example, on the number of variables that may be used in a model). Linkage between PCs and a mainframe is available for generator products of the same family. A widely used DSS generator, oriented toward financial planning, is IFPS of Comshare.

Spreadsheet packages, such as Lotus 1–2–3 (Lotus Development Corporation) or Excel (Microsoft), offer ever increasing capabilities for generating simpler DSS. Specialized templates (prewritten models for a specific area of application) and nonprocedural languages are available to simplify the use of spreadsheets for DSS generation. Nonprocedural, fourth-generation languages of various microbased DBMS, such as FOCUS, NOMAD2, or Ramis II, provide another avenue for generating a specific

DSS. The capabilities of spreadsheets and DBMS are combined in integrated packages such as Framework (Borland International), or Symphony (Lotus Development). We discussed these software facilities in chapter 9.

The main distinction between simply using a spreadsheet and producing a DSS is that in the latter there is a clear separation of the data from the models.

3. DSS Tools

A variety of tools—such as a programming language with good capabilities for accessing arrays of data (for example, APL), a plain spreadsheet, a statistical package, or a DBMS with its query facility—may be employed as building blocks to construct a DSS generator or a specific DSS.

Sometimes personal DSS are indeed built with APL. I have observed many an actuary do so and find the experience rewarding and stimulating. On the other end of the spectrum, a company may decide to build its own DSS generator, specialized for its individual application area, from the ground up, using these tools. Such a generator may become a source of competitive advantage.

Who Builds a DSS? Both end users and MIS professionals become involved in the development of DSS. Ralph Sprague analyzed the roles in DSS development related to the technologies we just discussed (Sprague, 1982). The technologies and the roles played by organizational actors are shown in figure 14.6.

Five roles involved in exploiting the DSS technologies can be identified:

1. The *manager* is the end user of a specific DSS: this is the knowledge worker who actually employs the system to make decisions.

2. In some cases, the manager is assisted by an *intermediary*. This role may range from simply running the system in behalf of and on detailed instructions from the manager to the more substantive contribution of framing the problem for exploiting the capabilities of specific DSS and displaying the information in an appropriate fashion. Jack Hogue (1987) found that 95 percent of managers in his sample used intermediaries at least occasionally.

3. A DSS *builder* employs a DSS generator to build a specific DSS for the given end users. The builder is familiar with the business problem, as a business analyst would be, as well as with the capabilities of the generator. In some organizations, these professionals are members of a DSS group which supports the use of DSS technology throughout the enterprise.

4. The *technical support specialist* is usually a member of the information systems department who installs and maintains various modules of the generator package as they are needed. This person also ensures the linkages between the generator and other elements of the organizational computing environment, such as databases, personal workstations, and networks.

5. The *toolsmith* develops the building blocks employed by the generator (or, sometimes, directly in specific DSS). These technical experts usually work for software vendors.

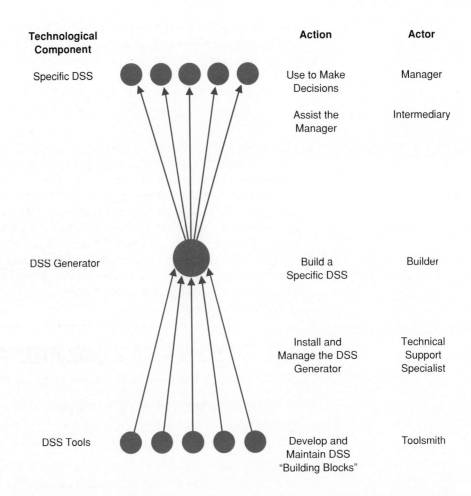

Technological Component	Action	Actor
Specific DSS	Use to Make Decisions	Manager
	Assist the Manager	Intermediary
DSS Generator	Build a Specific DSS	Builder
	Install and Manage the DSS Generator	Technical Support Specialist
DSS Tools	Develop and Maintain DSS "Building Blocks"	Toolsmith

How DSS Are Developed

By its very nature, a decision support system has a more customized orientation than a TPS or an MRS: it is a collection of capabilities that support the decision-making process of a certain individual or a relatively small group of people. As the needs of these people change, the DSS should change with them—DSS are truly built to be changed. We shall distinguish three prominent approaches to building DSS—even though a large spectrum of possibilities exists between the first two extremes (see Arinze, 1991).

1. The Quick-Hit Approach

So dubbed by Sprague (1982), the quick-hit approach is the way most DSS come into being. Indeed, most DSS are built for the personal use of a decision maker. The initiative usually comes from an individual manager, so the DSS are built either by the manager or by the builders from a more or less formal DSS group. Generally, a DSS generator is employed (frequently a spreadsheet with templates). The level of investment is very low and the payoff high.

Unless it is used as a springboard to more advanced stages of DSS assimilation into the organization, this opportunistic approach results in little organizational learning. The risks associated with end-user computing (which we discussed in chapter 9), including lack of maintainability, frequently exist in these cases.

In some organizations, however, the quick-hit approach is employed as an early stage in the process of technology assimilation, in which case it is later replaced by an orderly process of development for larger DSS.

2. Traditional Life-Cycle Development

As we shall discuss in some detail in Part 5 of the text, large software systems, such as TPS or MRS, are built in a disciplined fashion with the use of a life-cycle-oriented development methodology. This process begins with detailed system planning and analysis, progresses through the design stages followed by coding and testing, and goes on to implementation—this is the development life cycle. The process is lengthy, and there is no partial system to work with before the system is completed.

This development methodology, as we shall see later, is suitable for complex systems, in particular those which affect many users and in which informational requirements can be established early through the analysis process. This is indeed the case when a DSS generator is to be built. Therefore, a DSS generator or a very large model-based organizational DSS that affects a number of functional units in an organization may be fruitfully built using such a methodology. But in the development of a specific DSS, such usage is the exception rather than the rule.

3. Iterative Development

In DSS practice, the future user or group of users generally do not know what they want from the system. Moreover, an analysis process is not likely to surface a clear set of requirements. As in many other activities in life, we learn what we want from an activity by starting to perform it. To do so in decision making with a DSS, we need a **prototype** of the system—a simple initial version used to experiment with and learn about the desired features of the system.

Iterative (or evolutionary) development of DSS relies on the creation of such a prototype and its progressive refinement. The process begins when the future user and the DSS builder discuss the system for a few hours. They identify the most useful screens. The builder then constructs a simple version of the system, ignoring many of its aspects. To construct a DSS, all three of its components (database, model, and dialog) have to be built with the use of facilities offered by the DSS generator or with DSS tools. Particular attention is paid initially to the dialog component. Now the users have something to experiment with and react to.

The iterative, repetitive process of prototype refinement follows. End users offer suggestions for modifying the current version of the system. Builders analyze these suggestions and modify the emerging DSS. The prototype, refined over several such iterations, is tested and documented and eventually becomes the DSS.

The process of iterative development is shown in figure 14.7.

The use of the system engenders new iterations: decision problems evolve and the users' needs change. The DSS is modified to satisfy these changing requirements. These renewed iterations are shown in figure 14.7 as an adaptation loop. Each successive modification may thus be thought of as another iteration during the total evolutionary process of keeping DSS current with user needs.

FIGURE 14.7

Development and adaptation
of DSS.

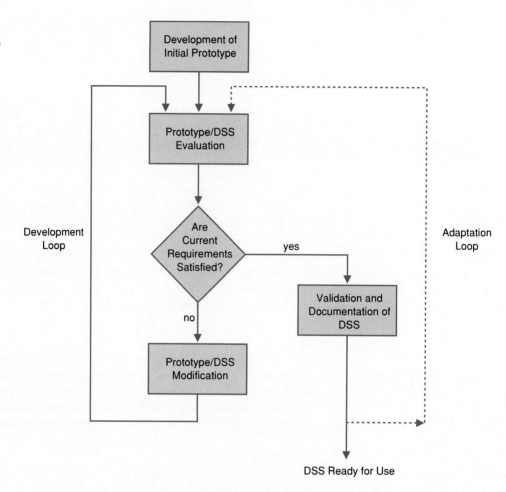

As we can see, the process of iterative development tightly binds users
and builders to ensure that the DSS satisfies actual user requirements
(rather than what the users may think they want—until they work with the
actual system).

Iterative development of DSS is an example of the general prototyping
technique broadly used in software engineering. In the version of the
technique generally used for DSS development, the prototype becomes the
actual system after an evolutionary process of refinement. By contrast, in
the engineering of large software systems, the prototype often serves to
clarify user requirements, after which it is discarded ("throwaway
prototyping").

Hogue found that DSS development time varies considerably (Hogue,
1987): from one week to four years in his sample of eighteen companies
with multiple DSS. He also found that master plans for the organizational
development of DSS were virtually nonexistent—a severe deficiency,
considering the importance of this type of MIS.

14.5 DEVELOPMENTAL TRENDS IN DSS

Lively research in the area of decision support systems continues apace. Two prominent directions this research is taking are toward the integration of expert system technology into DSS and the development of group DSS (GDSS).

Integration of Expert System Technology into DSS

We introduced you to expert system technology in section 3.7 of this book, and we shall further analyze it in the next chapter. Recall that, as opposed to DSS, which support decision making, an expert system actually suggests decisions within the narrow domain related to its knowledge base. An expert system acts as an advisor to a human on subjects within this narrow domain. Finer distinctions between DSS and expert systems will be drawn in the next chapter. At present, very few DSS are integrated with expert systems.

Here, we want to see how we can combine to best advantage the capabilities of expert systems with those of DSS. There are several major avenues of work in this area of so-called "intelligent DSS":

1. An expert system may expand the capabilities of a DSS in support of the initial phase of the decision-making process—intelligence. An expert system can assist the decision maker in retrieving information particularly relevant to the problem at hand. The system might further guide the decision maker through a session with DSS, suggesting lines of reasoning and models that would help to define the problem. A prototype system of this kind is described by Michael Goul and his colleagues (1986).

2. An expert system can assist the second ("design") phase of the decision-making process by suggesting alternative scenarios for what-if evaluation, as pointed out by Reitman (1982).

3. An expert system can assist a human in the selection of an appropriate model for the decision problem. This is an avenue of automatic model management: the user of such a system would need less knowledge about models (see, for instance, Liu, 1990).

4. An expert system can simplify model building; in particular, simulation models lend themselves to this approach.

5. Expert systems can provide an explanation of the results obtained with a DSS. This would be a new and important DSS capability.

6. Expert systems make possible friendlier user interfaces.

7. Expert systems can act as tutors (users of more sophisticated DSS welcome this facility).

In addition, expert system capabilities may be employed during DSS development; their general potential in software engineering has been recognized.

The complementary natures of DSS and of expert system technology offer many other possibilities for combining their strengths. We can expect the future blending of these two approaches to enhance organizational decision-making capabilities.

Group Decision Support Systems (GDSS)

Group decision support systems (GDSS) are expressly designed to support group communication and decision processes (some of which we discussed in section 13.6). We know from our analysis of the organizational environment in the information society that the volume of necessary decision making will continue to increase dramatically. Many decisions are complex and call for the participation of a number of experts. We also know from the previous chapter that a decision-making process may benefit significantly if people representing various political interests are explicitly brought into it. All of these factors, combined with the team orientation of the contemporary organizational design, lead us to believe that decision support systems that support group work will grow in importance.

In contrasting the capabilities of GDSS with DSS, we may use the classification of decision types and their corresponding support systems offered by Peter Keen and Richard Hackathorn (Keen, 1979) and summarized here in table 14.2.

A GDSS should support a process that brings together a group of decision makers to share information, exchange ideas, explore alternative solutions with the use of models and data, vote, and arrive at a consensus—among other possible interactions. More or less permanent groups, such as corporate boards, task forces, or teams of coworkers, increasingly form the basic work cells throughout an enterprise. When we discussed the decision-making process, we noted that dysfunctional behaviors may develop in a group's work. It is the objective of a GDSS to enable group members to bring their skills to bear on the decision process, while counteracting possible negative group dynamics. The anonymity of many GDSS interactions and the ability to work with the system rather than directly interacting with others play a role in preventing dysfunctional group behaviors. For example, interactions in a GDSS setting frequently encourage group members who would have otherwise kept their counsel, or perhaps deferred to others, to participate actively in the decision-making process.

A group working with a GDSS is actually participating in a decision-related meeting. As we shall see in chapter 16, today's computing and telecommunications technologies offer multiple options in configuring such a meeting in space and time. Settings for a GDSS session range from a face-to-face meeting for an executive planning group to a "meeting" of widely dispersed insurance company sales agents discussing possible new rates through their VDTs and a telecommunications network with the support of an electronic meeting system.

TABLE 14.2

Decision Types and Their Support

DECISION TYPE	CHARACTERISTICS	SUPPORT SYSTEM
Independent	Decision maker makes a complete decision.	Personal DSS
Sequential Interdependent	Each decision maker individually makes a part of a decision and passes the results to the next decision maker.	Organizational DSS
Pooled Interdependent	Decision makers interact and negotiate to arrive at a decision.	GDSS

Three levels of GDSS capabilities may be distinguished (DeSanctis, 1987):

Level-1 GDSS facilitate communication among group members. They provide the technology necessary to communicate: decision rooms, facilities for remote conferencing, or both. (We will discuss these settings further in chapter 16.)

Level-2 GDSS contain the communication capabilities of the Level-1 GDSS and also provide support for the decision-making process. Thus, they furnish DSS modeling capabilities and software that supports group decision processes. Level-2 GDSS thus facilitate activities involving the Delphi technique, brainstorming, and the nominal group technique (see chapter 13).

Level-3 GDSS, which at this time are still at the research stage, would formalize group interaction patterns—possibly by including expert systems that would suggest rules to be applied during a meeting. For example, Robert's Rules of Order may be automatically invoked by such a GDSS.

We have encountered a session with a GDSS already—in the case study for chapter 13, which describes a system specialized for use in crisis management.

These are the distinguishing characteristics of GDSS at their present stage of development:

1. Aside from the database, model, and dialog components of DSS, GDSS also contain a communication component. This component, which is implemented with the organization's local or wide area communication facilities, may include electronic mail, teleconferencing, or various computer conferencing facilities (discussed further in chapter 16).
   The principal settings for GDSS use are:
   a. A face-to-face session in a decision room or a similar conference room, with terminals and a large public display screen.
   b. A teleconference session taking place in several decision rooms at the same time; these are connected with video and telecommunication links.
   c. An interfaced session, in which participants work at remote terminals and do not see each other; such a session may be dispersed in time as well as place (the memories of the computers, in conjunction with the appropriate software, make asynchronous sessions possible).

2. Complete decision ("war") rooms are often provided and equipped in a fashion conducive to a group effort; a large common screen display is an essential facility.

3. GDSS should offer facilities for prompting and summarizing the votes and ideas of participants.

4. GDSS features, such as anonymity of interactions, the layout of the decision room, and the design of the dialog subsystem, should encourage both the formation of a cohesive group and the active participation of all its members.

5. GDSS expand the model base to include models supporting group decision-making processes. Models for voting, rating, and ranking should accompany other statistical models. It should be possible to run a Delphi

session (with rounds of voting, anonymous opinion sharing, and arrival at a consensus) or a brainstorming session (eliminating redundant ideas and summarizing the results).

6. It should be possible with a GDSS to obtain the protocol of a session for later analysis. A collection of such protocols from the more important decision-making sessions may be preserved as a part of organizational memory.

7. GDSS should support a facilitator to assist the orderly progress of a session; this person should be able, for example, to route individual screen contents to the large common display. Some sessions also profit from the presence of a leader.

A study of the current and expected uses of GDSS (Straub, 1988) points to a very high interest in the technology throughout both government and business organizations.

14.6 EXECUTIVE INFORMATION SYSTEMS

Executive information systems (EIS), which were introduced in section 3.6, are becoming the primary tools of top-level control in some organizations. They can be best understood by contrasting them with DSS, which they complement. You may find it useful to review table 3.5, which contrasts the principal types of management information systems in a number of respects. You may also want to refer back to our look at an EIS session in action—as the case study in chapter 1.

You are, then, already familiar with the features of EIS: access to a large variety of internal and external data, terse presentation of information with colorful graphics, the ability to "drill down" on more and more detailed data, and the ability to control the system in a very easy way. In the chapter 1 case study, this was done with a TV-like remote control device (though mice, touch screens, and even plain keyboards are also used).

Speaking tersely: while DSS are primarily used by middle- and lower-level managers to project the future, EIS primarily serve the control needs of higher-level management. They help an executive to spot a problem, an opportunity, or a trend. EIS also have forecasting capabilities that can be used in an "automatic-pilot" fashion; in addition to their other features, these capabilities make EIS a strategic planning tool. The relationship between these two types of information systems, EIS and DSS, is shown in figure 14.8.

Seen in the light of the structure of a decision-making process, EIS primarily assist top management in uncovering a problem or an opportunity. Analysts and middle managers can subsequently use a DSS to suggest a solution to the problem. More recently, EIS-type applications are coming into use by middle managers as well (Wallace, 1981).

FIGURE 14.8

Relationship between EIS and DSS.

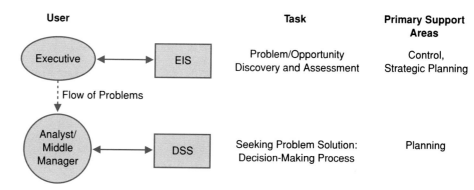

At the heart of an EIS lies access to data. EIS may work on the data extraction principle, as DSS do (see figure 14.2), or they may be given access to the actual corporate databases. The first kind of EIS can fully reside on personal workstations; EIS of the second kind need the power of minis or mainframes to access corporate data. The technical problems of EIS data access pale in comparison with the problem of potential resistance from managers below the top level. Once an EIS has been set up, its executive users are able to obtain virtually instantly any information supported by the EIS data—unfiltered by and unbeknownst to their subordinates. This is borne out by the vignette on page 552.

In the design of EIS, developers frequently rely on the **critical success factors (CSF)** methodology developed by John Rockart of MIT (Rockart, 1979). He defined CSFs as "those few critical areas where things must go right for the business to flourish." With the use of this methodology (which we shall further discuss in Part 5 of this text), executives may define just the few indicators of corporate performance they need. Many executives have already fallen into the habit of reviewing these indicators on a regular, sometimes daily, basis. With the drill-down capability, they can obtain more detailed data behind the indicators. An executive who is experienced with such a system can perceive a trend (and a problem) in seconds.

As opposed to the CSF methodology, which relies on the individual critical success factors, the strategic business objectives methodology of EIS development takes a company-wide perspective (Volonino, 1991). Following the identification of the strategic business objectives of a firm, the critical business processes are identified and prioritized, and then the information needed to support these processes is defined—to be obtained with the EIS that is being planned. This methodology avoids the frequent pitfall of aligning an EIS too closely to a particular sponsor.

In the United States, Commander EIS (by Comshare of Ann Arbor, Michigan) and Pilot EIS (by Pilot Executive Software of Boston) lead the EIS field. RESOLVE from Metapraxis (New York and of Kingston upon Thames, England) is a leader in Europe. All of these systems are actually EIS generators, which help to configure a specific EIS.

In general, organizational DSS are conceptually more complex than the rather well-structured EIS, primarily due to the model-management component of DSS.

NOW THE CEO CAN BROWSE FOR INFORMATION—WITHOUT ASSISTANCE

C. Robert Kidder, chief executive officer of the battery maker Duracell, decided one day to spend his first hour at work inspecting productivity. But he did not send his assistants scurrying far and wide for reports, and he did not have to wait two weeks to obtain the information.

Kidder simply sat down at his mouse-equipped workstation, where his EIS produced a colorful and simple table comparing the performances of the company's workforces in the United States and overseas. Within seconds, Kidder knew that the U.S. staff members were more productive—they produced more sales per employee. To narrow the problem, Kidder ''drilled down'' into detailed data. Soon he knew what the problem was overseas: the firm had too many salespeople in West Germany who made unprofitable calls on small stores.

Notice that the chief executive used the system unassisted and obtained all he needed to know during a single brief session. No unnecessary alarms were rung during this browsing process (as they would have been had the chief executive requested the information from his subordinates), and no filtering of information through the management layers took place.

As a follow-up to this EIS session, Duracell cut its German sales staff and signed up distributors to cover small accounts.

Based on Main, 1989.

Three screens from a Pilot EIS application, shown in color plate 15, bring home the principal features of EIS: use of graphics and color, crispness of presentation, strength in evaluating the competitive position of the company, and the ability to see the message at a glance (well, if you have some experience glancing). Thus, you can see from the photo that while our company's growth is good, Competitor 1 has almost closed in on us and is growing about 50 percent faster than we are. Further drill-down shows four financial ratios—both for our company and for our competitors.

Systems that combine EIS information-accessing capabilities with the decision-support capabilities of DSS are also available; they are often marketed under the name of executive support systems (an example is Executive Edge from Comshare).

14.7 ORGANIZATIONAL ASPECTS OF DSS AND EIS

Both DSS and EIS are proliferating in organizations in the private and public sectors. A single EIS is generally implemented in an organization, with more and more executives given access to it,[2] and with the system playing an integrative role. Thus, as EIS use at the Mellon Bank of Pittsburgh expands from the

INSTITUTIONALIZATION OF THE DSS APPROACH AT CONNOISSEUR FOODS

The use of the DSS approach at Connoisseur Foods, a large, multidivisional food company, was championed by top management. These executives clearly articulated the objective: they were seeking a new approach to corporate decision making, rather than continuing to make decisions based on the implementation of personal DSS by a few individuals. Senior management stated that managers would be expected to consider DSS model recommendations in making decisions. Although they did not need to slavishly follow these recommendations, in collective organizational decision making, they would be expected to argue their reasons for following or rejecting DSS recommendations. The arguments, moreover, should be based on the information provided by DSS, rather than on the good old "gut feeling."

Many brand managers responded with objections along these lines: "I just don't understand equations and that kind of stuff. I'm intuitive. I try to get a feel for the market."

This resistance was not considered surprising, but rather a predictable reaction to the impending change. Extensive training combined with fresh personnel policies led to the diffusion of DSS throughout the corporation. Assisted by DSS specialists, brand managers developed ways to more closely monitor their markets and deeply analyze their workings. They acquired the capability to monitor their brand's market position on a month-to-month basis, instead of annually as they had done earlier. DSS-based planning became routinized. A high payback was found in many cases of DSS use, which led to positive visibility within the corporation.

Based on Alter, 1980.

top corporate level down to the departmental management level, it is expected that the system will provide a shared understanding of the business throughout the management structure.[3] Multiple DSS, on the other hand, are in place in most of the medium-sized and larger firms.

The introduction of DSS, treated as a technology, lends itself to the process of technology assimilation, which we discussed in section 12.7. In analyzing a number of companies, Richard Epich concluded that a successful integration of DSS into a company's computing environment is primarily dependent on top-level commitment to the technology (as is the case with virtually all advanced information technologies) and the quality of the DSS support groups (Epich, 1986). The objective is to institutionalize the use of DSS. *Institutionalization* means that knowledge workers throughout the enterprise consider the merits of the DSS approach when appropriate and implement and use these systems, so that the DSS ultimately influence organizational processes (rather than only isolated individuals).

Resistance to change should be expected; a process of organizational change should be conducted as a part of the general implementation process, which we shall discuss in chapter 18. The refreezing phase of the organizational change is especially important: users should actually feel committed to using their DSS and allow these systems to change their work lives.

DSS groups are a resource that can play a crucial role in this change process. There are a variety of organizational arrangements for DSS groups. Most frequently, the DSS group is located either in an information center (with DSS computing considered an end-user activity) or in a staff analysis department in a functional area, such as the corporate planning department. Hugh Watson and his colleagues (Watson, 1989) analyzed how organizations actually support their DSS efforts. They found that DSS groups in most organizations include five or fewer professional members. The support offered by the DSS groups ranges from acting as builders and promoters of DSS to providing consulting services, technical support, and training.

As we have already seen, EIS have by their very nature a significant organizational impact. The organizational advantage of EIS lies in its support for a tight control from the top. This ability alone is also a potential source of resistance to EIS. A well-designed EIS can immensely increase the span of management of executives. EIS use has already made possible profound organizational changes (Applegate, 1988). Since top management can easily track the performance of virtually any company subunit, company decision making may be decentralized—and controlled with the EIS. The CEO of Lincoln National Corporation has fourteen direct reports and no executive assistant—and he attributes his ability to maintain this span of management to the EIS and electronic mail (Rockart, 1988).

EIS have weighty political aspects: they could give a top executive the capability of probing into the work of any manager without the manager's knowledge. Combined with electronic mail, EIS give top executives the capability to bypass the chain of authority. Resistance to these systems, therefore, must be expected and managed. In particular, the role of an executive sponsor is critical. George Houdeshel and Hugh Watson describe how an EIS was successfully introduced at Lockheed-Georgia thanks to an appropriate implementation process (Houdeshel, 1987), but Hugh Watson also supplies some examples of EIS failures for the vignette on that subject.

Executive information systems rely on databases, which need to be refreshed daily in many cases. EIS are no better than the data contained in their databases—and much resistance must be overcome from a variety of quarters to obtain this data on a regular basis. As analyzed by Rockart and David De Long (Rockart, 1988), resistance is to be expected not only from the staff personnel who support the executives and middle managers, but also from the executives themselves, who in some cases feel that the information will be inadequate for their needs or that the system will be difficult to use. Application of CSF methodology and a superior interface design can go a long way toward allaying these apprehensions.

Sometimes, organizational measures must be taken to ensure support for EIS. At Xerox, where the use of EIS pervades the work of high-level managers, top management has imposed a limit on drill-down depth; managers can drill down no deeper than three layers from the top.

The availability of EIS as potent tools for top-level control will shape many organizational solutions in the future.

EIS FAILURES ARE QUITE COMMON

Out of fifty firms with successful EISs that were surveyed by the University of Georgia, twenty-one indicated that they had previously experienced a failure.

In a follow-up study, researchers compiled a list of twenty-three reasons for EIS failure. The most frequent problems were inappropriate technology, lack of executive commitment, failure of the system to meet user needs, and resistance to the use of technology by executives. Let us look at some examples.

Several firms failed because they were trying to build an EIS around a DSS package. The systems were rejected by their intended users: they were not user-friendly enough for them.

An EIS developed at a large Midwestern firm, on the other hand, provided excellent graphical presentation showing which customers contributed the most to corporate revenue. The CEO's disappointment with the system was expressed as follows: "I know about these. How about the customers we lost or didn't get? Who are they? How much revenue did they represent? To whom did we lose them? Why did we lose them?" The CEO of a textile company, who obviously was not consulted heavily by the development team either, said that his EIS gave him about 1 percent of what he was looking for.

Based on Hugh Watson and Harry Glover, "Common and Avoidable Causes of EIS Failure." *Computerworld*, December 4, 1989, pp. 90–91.

WHY DID THIS EXECUTIVE INFORMATION SYSTEM FAIL?

Mutual Benefit Life Insurance Company failed in its attempt to implement an EIS. Installing a vendor's EIS package on executives' personal computers is a minor part of the project, according to June Drewry, senior vice-president of corporate planning and systems development at Mutual. The main cost is in making the appropriate company information accessible. Even though a prototype EIS was installed at Mutual, the system never caught on.

Here are the principal reasons for the failure:

- The requisite quality of information (relevance, timeliness, or form) for the executives was never identified. As a result, many numbers were available only on a monthly or even quarterly basis—which was no different from what was already being delivered by management reporting systems.
- The EIS had no committed executive sponsor.
- The project was not approached with appropriate systems development methodologies—it was thought to be an easy task.

However, the chief executive officer at Mutual wanted the system reimplemented. This CEO recognized the value of executive information systems—even after experiencing a failure.

Based on Clinton Wilder, "The *Wrong* Way to Implement an EIS." *Computerworld*, September 24, 1990, p. 69.

• •

SUMMARY

Decision support systems (DSS) are flexible interactive information systems that support managers in reaching decisions concerning ill-structured problems. Primarily applied in planning, DSS are used either directly or through intermediaries by all levels of management. They consist of three principal components that manage, respectively, data, models, and the dialog with the user. Depending on the degree to which they determine the decision, DSS may be classified into several categories, ranging from systems oriented toward data access to highly model-oriented DSS.

Specific DSS that are actually employed by users are generally developed with DSS generators, though simpler DSS tools may also be deployed. Various categories of support for DSS construction and use may be offered by the members of an organizational DSS group. While simple personal systems are frequently built through the quick-hit approach, and DSS generators are constructed through a life-cycle-oriented development process, the most apt technique for DSS building is iterative development—continual refining of an initial system prototype.

Future DSS are expected to incorporate expert system technology for various aspects of their operation. Group DSS (GDSS) expressly support group decision processes, such as the Delphi technique or brainstorming.

Executive information systems (EIS) support higher-level management control by making data regarding all aspects of corporate operations accessible in a timely and easily handled fashion. EIS give executives the capability to exercise a vast degree of control and to increase their individual spans of management. By furnishing this top-level control capability, EIS make possible a variety of novel organizational structures.

ENDNOTES

1. Turban, 1990, p. 10.
2. Thus, at Xerox, the use of EIS has spread from the initial 15 top executives to about 100 managers, with an envisioned expansion to about 500 people (Main, 1989, p. 80).
3. According to bank vice-president James Stuber (as quoted in Stan Kolodziej, "EIS Is a Prestigious 'Strategic Weapon.'" *Software*, July 1989, p. 60).

KEY TERMS AND CONCEPTS

Decision support systems (DSS)	Goal seeking
Executive information systems (EIS)	Dialog styles
Ill-structured problems	Specific DSS
Data management subsystem of DSS	DSS generator
Model management subsystem of DSS	Quick-hit development
	Life-cycle development
Dialog management subsystem of DSS	Iterative development
What-if analysis	Prototype
	Group decision support systems (GDSS)
	Critical success factors (CSF)

QUESTIONS

1. Define DSS, and list the characteristics that make them different from other information systems.

2. What is special about the DSS approach to decision making? Contrast this approach with the use of a management science algorithm on the one hand and of management reporting systems (MRS) on the other.

3. Give examples of unstructured and semistructured problems that might be encountered on each of the three organizational levels (operational, tactical, and strategic)—six examples altogether.

4. List five principal capabilities offered by DSS to their users.

5. Show the three principal DSS components, together with their basic interrelationships and their relationship to a DSS user.

6. Study and list alternative modes of input and output presentation for an actual DSS.

7. Give three examples of DSS designed for the solution of practical problems; one should be a data access system, the second a system based on an accounting model, and the third a system based on an optimization model.

8. What is the relationship between a specific DSS and a DSS generator?

9. List the five roles relevant to the exploitation of DSS technologies. Briefly describe the knowledge required to play each of these roles.

10. What are the principal *advantages* of each of the three approaches to DSS development?

11. Why is iterative development the most commonly recommended method for DSS development?

12. How can expert system technology be applied in DSS? List three possible types of applications.

13. Why is it likely that GDSS will become increasingly important in organizations?

14. What distinguishes GDSS from DSS? State and discuss three features.

15. Define EIS and contrast them with DSS.

16. What is the "drill-down" capability of EIS?

17. Why are EIS likely to encounter a significant resistance in organizations?

OPTIONAL EXERCISE: MODELING

If you have access to a DSS generator, develop a simple planning model (similar to the one in section 11.7) and obtain a printout showing your use of the model for a what-if question and a printout for a goal-seeking problem.

You may also perform this exercise with a spreadsheet program familiar to you. In this case, you would want to include several printouts and explain their interrelationship.

You may also perform *both* of the above tasks and compare the facilities of your DSS generator with those of your spreadsheet program. Comment on the ease with which you were able to perform your task in each of the two environments.

ISSUES FOR DISCUSSION

1. Discuss this contention: "All information systems support decision making. If DSS are so good at it, perhaps *all* systems for informational support of management should be built that way."

2. If you are familiar with spreadsheet programs, discuss this contention: "Using a spreadsheet, I can do what any DSS can do—why bother with a DSS?"

3. A vice-president of Kraft Inc., who is a user of EIS and whose division sells 500 products to 33,000 grocery stores, says that since he and his colleagues started to use EIS, "we conduct our work lives differently" (Gelfond, 1988). What, do you think, does he mean by that?

4. Discuss the claim made by Lynda Applegate (1988) that by offering the capability for enhanced top-level control, EIS are likely to permit decentralized decision making, since top executives can keep tabs on the company's operations at all times. Do you agree? Why or why not?

CASE STUDY ONE

SUPPORT FOR DECISION MAKING IN A BANK HOLDING COMPANY

Valley Bancorporation of Appleton, Wisconsin is a holding company which has forty subsidiary banks. It runs a DSS (Thorn EMI's FCS package) on a MicroVAX II, with an IBM PC connected to it at the site of each subsidiary. The essential DSS model employed is one that manages assets and liabilities: how the banks can profitably invest their assets (at a manageable risk) and how they can attract deposits (incur liabilities) at reasonable interest rates. The difference between what the bank pays for the deposits and what it gets from investing its assets is the bank's profit.

The DSS model Valley provides to the forty subsidiary banks includes, for example, a submodel to help decide on the rates for certificates of deposit, in order to ensure an interest rate that will entice customers to roll over their maturing certificates.

The DSS affords the corporation flexible access to a vast database. Thus, the main database represents a three-dimensional array of 5 million spreadsheet cells. Moreover, different models have to be applied to these data for various purposes. The manager of financial information systems for the holding company, Gerry Butler, says: "You could [manipulate the data in a spreadsheet], but it would be an awful lot of work."

At the time the case was described, the company was considering introducing an EIS. The primary objective was to consolidate the data from all forty business units into one set of aggregate line items for review by corporate executives.

"Top executives will be able to look at the history of the financial numbers and [at] what's planned twelve months out and longer," said Butler.

Based on Lori Valigura, "Users Gain Leverage with Decision Support." *Digital Review*, May 18, 1989, p. 70.

Case Study One Questions

1. Why does Valley Bancorporation believe it needs a DSS rather than spreadsheets for its assets and liabilities management?

2. What organizational roles does the DSS play in this case?

3. What prompted the corporation to consider using EIS?

CASE STUDY TWO

REVIEW OF DSS FOR DELIVERY ROUTING

Review the DSS for delivery routing that was presented as Case Study Two in chapter 3.

Case Study Two Questions

1. How would you place this DSS in the DSS classification presented in the current chapter? How would you classify the upgraded DSS, whose concept was transferred from a mainframe (see Note 1 to the case study)?

2. Consider the enhancement of the DSS with a knowledge base, as mentioned in Note 2 to the case study. Which avenue of DSS-ES integration was followed in this case?

SELECTED REFERENCES

Alter, Steven L. *Decision Support Systems: Current Practice and Continuing Challenges.* Reading, Mass.: Addison-Wesley, 1980.

Applegate, Lynda M.; Cash, James I., Jr.; and Mills, D. Quinn. "Information Technology and Tomorrow's Manager." *Harvard Business Review,* November–December 1988, pp. 128–36.

Applegate, Lynda M.; Konsynski, Benn R.; and Nunamaker, Jay F., Jr. "Model Management Systems: Design for Decision Support." *Decision Support Systems,* 2, 1, March 1986, pp. 81–91.

Arinze, Bay. "A Contingency Model of DSS Development Methodology." *Journal of Management Information Systems,* 8, 1, Summer 1991, pp. 149–166.

Bonczek, Robert H.; Holsapple, Clyde W.; and Whinston, Andrew B. "Developments in Decision Support Systems." In *Advances in Computers,* edited by Marshall Yovits. Vol. 23, 1984, pp. 141–75.

Buzzell, Robert D. *Marketing in an Electronic Age.* Boston: Harvard Business School Press, 1985.

Clarke, Darral G. *Marketing Analysis and Decision Making.* Redwood City, Calif.: The Scientific Press, 1987.

DeSanctis, Gerardine, and Gallupe, R. Brent. "A Foundation for the Study of Group Decision Support Systems." *Management Science,* 33, 5, May 1987, pp. 43–59.

Dickson, Gary W.; DeSanctis, Gerardine; and McBride, D. J. "Understanding the Effectiveness of Computer Graphics for Decision Support: A Cumulative Experimental Approach." *Communications of the ACM,* 29, 1, January 1986, pp. 40–47.

Elam, Joyce J., and Konsynski, Benn R. "Using Artificial Intelligence Techniques to Enhance the Capabilities of Model Management Systems." *Decision Sciences,* 18, 3, 1987, pp. 487–502.

Epich, Richard J. "Organizing for Decision Support." *Infosystems,* July 1986, pp. 91–95.

EXPRESS. *pcEXPRESS, The James Martin Productivity Series.* Marblehead, Mass.: 1987.

Gelfond, Susan M. "The Computer Age Dawns in the Corner Office." *Business Week,* June 27, 1988, pp. 84–86.

Gorry, G. Andrew, and Scott Morton, Michael. "A Framework for Management Information Systems." *Sloan Management Review,* 13, 1, Fall 1971, pp. 55–70.

Goul, Michael; Shane, Barry; and Tonge, Fred. "Using a Knowledge-Based Decision Support System in Strategic Planning Decisions: An Empirical Study." *Journal of Management Information Systems,* 2, 4, Spring 1986, pp. 70–84.

Hogue, Jack T. "A Framework for the Examination of Management Involvement in Decision Support Systems." *Journal of Management Information Systems,* 4, 1, Summer 1987, pp. 96–110.

Houdeshel, George, and Watson, Hugh J. "The Management Information and Decision Support (MIDS) System at Lockheed-Georgia." *MIS Quarterly,* 11, 2, March 1987, pp. 127–40.

Keen, Peter G. W. "Value Analysis: Justifying Decision Support Systems." *MIS Quarterly,* 5, 1, March 1981, pp. 1–16.

Keen, Peter G. W., and Hackathorn, Richard D. "Organizational Strategies for Personal Computing in Decision Support Systems." *MIS Quarterly,* 5, 3, October 1979, pp. 21–27.

Le Blanc, Louis A., and Kozar, Kenneth A. "An Empirical Investigation of the Relationship Between DSS Usage and System Performance: A Case Study of a Navigation Support System." *MIS Quarterly.* 14, 3, September 1990, pp. 263–77.

Liu, John I. C.; Yun, David Y. Y.; and Klein, Gary. "An Agent for Intelligent Model Management." *Journal of Management Information Systems,* 7, 1, Summer 1990, pp. 101–22.

Main, Jeremy. "At Last, Software CEOs Can Use." *Fortune,* March 13, 1989, pp. 77–83.

Mann, Robert I., and others. "Accommodating Cognitive Style through DSS Hardware and Software." In *Decision Support Systems: Putting Theory Into Practice,* edited by Ralph H. Sprague, Jr. and Hugh J. Watson. Englewood Cliffs, NJ: Prentice-Hall, 1986.

Montazemi, A. R., and Wang, S. "The Effects of Modes of Information Presentation on Decision Making: A Review and Meta-Analysis." *Journal of Management Information Systems,* 5, 3, Winter 1988–89, pp. 101–27.

Reitman, W. "Applying Artificial Intelligence to Decision Support." In *Decision Support Systems,* edited by Michael J. Ginzberg, W. Reitman, and Edward Stohr. Amsterdam: North Holland, 1982.

Rockart, John F. "Chief Executives Define Their Own Data Needs." *Harvard Business Review,* March–April 1979, pp. 81–93.

Rockart, John F., and De Long, David W. *Executive Support Systems: The Emergence of Top Management Computer Use.* Homewood, Ill.: Dow-Jones-Irwin, 1988.

Scott Morton, Michael S. *Management Decision Systems: Computer Based Support for Decision Making.* Cambridge, Mass.: Division of Research, Harvard University, 1971.

Scovill, Richard. "The Graphs (and How to Use Them)." *PC World,* September 1988, pp. 216–19.

Silver, Mark S. "Decision Support Systems: Directed and Nondirected Change." *Information Systems Research,* 1, 1, March 1990, pp. 47–70.

Snyders, Jan. "Decision Making Made Easier." *Infosystems,* August 1984, pp. 52–54.

Sprague, Ralph H., Jr. "A Framework for the Development of Decision Support Systems." *MIS Quarterly,* 4, 4, June 1980, pp. 1–26.

Sprague, Ralph H., Jr., and Carlson, Eric D. *Building Effective Decision Support Systems.* Englewood Cliffs, N.J.: Prentice-Hall, 1982.

Straub, Detmar W., and Beauclair, Renee A. "Current and Future Uses of Group Decision Support System Technology: Report on a Recent Empirical Study." *Journal of Management Information Systems,* 5, 1, Summer 1988, pp. 101–16.

Tufte, Edward R. *Envisioning Information.* Cheshire, Conn.: Graphics Press, 1990.

Turban, Efraim. *Decision Support and Expert Systems: Management Support Systems.* 2d ed. New York: Macmillan, 1990.

Volonino, Linda, and Watson, Hugh J. "The Strategic Business Objectives Method for Guiding Executive Information Systems Development." *Journal of Management Information Systems,* 7, 3, Winter 1990–91, pp. 27–39.

Wallace, Scott. "Everybody's System." *InformationWeek,* August 12, 1991, pp. 21–23.

Watson, Hugh J., and others. "Organizational Support for Decision Support Systems." *Journal of Management Information Systems,* 5, 4, Spring 1989, pp. 87–109.

APPLIED ARTIFICIAL INTELLIGENCE. EXPERT SYSTEMS

. . . .

. . . To follow knowledge like a sinking star
Beyond the utmost bounds of human thought.
  Alfred, Lord Tennyson

To the small part of ignorance that we arrange and
classify we give the name knowledge.
  Ambrose Bierce

OBJECTIVES

The field of artificial intelligence (AI) has been in the forefront of computer science research since the mid-1950s, with its vibrant promise of a machine with human capabilities of perceiving and reasoning. This research was for quite some time surrounded by a cloud of skepticism, due in no mean degree to the wildly optimistic overstatements of some of the scientists working in the field, but primarily owing to the awesome goals to which AI aspires.

Finally, in the early 1980s AI started to deliver—AI researchers began to commercialize the fruits of their research, and businesses began to use these applications in their daily operations. AI was no longer sheltered in laboratory environments. The principal fruits of AI research are expert systems, natural language processing, robotics, vision systems, speech recognition, and machine learning. A different research stream produced neural networks. All of these systems are significantly limited when compared with human capabilities—but they are here to stay, and development proceeds apace.

Expert systems are by far the most important product of AI research for the business environment. As vehicles for garnering, organizing, and delivering knowledge in a specific limited domain, the systems are causing profound changes in the way managers approach some cognitive aspects of business. This means that expert systems can—and frequently do—confer a competitive advantage. In an information economy, it is not surprising that a system that can bring knowledge to the point of application in a reliable and easy manner, and so provide support for rapid and consistent decision making, confers competitive advantage—this is what an information economy is all about.

We shall review the characteristics of the field of AI, concentrating primarily on expert systems (ES). We shall examine how ES are applied to important classes of problem solving, study their components, and discuss how ES work. We shall also discuss the tools and the methodology used in building expert systems, examining their organizational benefits and their limitations. We shall also review other promising fields of applied AI.

In the concluding section of the chapter, we shall describe neural networks: systems that recognize patterns after they learn about their domain during a training cycle. Through this capacity to learn, neural networks in a sense create their own knowledge—which is distributed throughout the system's structure. Because of their pattern recognition capability, neural networks can perform tasks similar to those performed by expert systems.

FOCUS CASE

One study, reported in the prestigious *New England Journal of Medicine*, compared the performance of an expert system with that of emergency room physicians at a highly regarded hospital. The problem was to establish whether a patient arriving at the emergency room with chest pain was having a heart attack. In patients who were not having a heart attack, the ES was correct 74 percent of the time, against 71 percent for the physicians; in patients who were indeed having a heart attack, ES was correct 88 percent of the time, as compared to 87.8 percent for the physicians.

The payoff from using this program has been computed as follows: by avoiding 175,000 unnecessary admissions to expensive coronary care units nationwide, decisions made by physicians *with the use of this ES* could save over $85 million annually.

Based on Cory Dean, "Computer Edges Doctors in Heart Cases." *The New York Times*, March 31, 1988, p. B13.

Most of us are well aware of the pressures that the high costs of health care exert on the productivity of U.S. industries. But expert systems are today used *directly* in many of these industries as well. Systems based on this new technology assist human decision makers in coping with an ever-growing volume of ever-more-complex decision making—and thus have a direct impact on the bottom line.

CHAPTER OUTLINE

15.1 What Is Artificial Intelligence?
- Characteristics of AI Systems
- The Field of AI
- How the AI Field Evolved

15.2 Capabilities of Expert Systems—A General View

15.3 Applications of Expert Systems
- Application Cases
- Generic Categories of ES Applications

15.4 How Expert Systems Work
- Knowledge Representation and the Knowledge Base
- Inference Engine

15.5 Expert System Technology
- Specific Expert Systems
- Expert System Shells
- Expert System Development Environments
- Higher-Level Programming Languages

15.6 Roles in Expert System Development

15.7 Development of Expert Systems

15.8 Expert Systems in Organizations: Benefits and Limitations
- Benefits of Expert Systems
- Limitations of Expert Systems

15.9 Overview of Applied Artificial Intelligence
- Natural Language Processing
- Robotics
- Computer Vision
- Computerized Speech Recognition
- Machine Learning

15.10 Neural Networks

Summary

Key Terms and Concepts

Questions

Issues for Discussion

Case Study: A Successful Start in Using Expert Systems

Selected References

15.1 WHAT IS ARTIFICIAL INTELLIGENCE?

The research field of **artificial intelligence (AI)** is concerned with, as *Encyclopaedia Britannica* tells us, "methods for developing computer programs (or software-hardware systems) that display aspects of intelligent behavior" (Zwass, 1988). Human intelligence itself remains poorly defined; in most general terms, it is associated with goal-oriented, adaptive behavior—the ability to understand a complex situation and respond to it successfully, the ability to learn, and the ability to bring knowledge and reasoning to bear in solving problems.

Characteristics of AI Systems

How do AI software systems compare with conventional software? How are they different from the technologies underlying management reporting or transaction processing systems? AI systems have two principal characteristics:

1. Symbolic (rather than numeric) Processing

In AI applications, computers process symbols[1] rather than numbers. That is, instead of obtaining numeric values through a series of database accesses and arithmetic computations, they process strings of characters that represent real-world entities or concepts. The terms *customer* and *liquidity* are examples of such strings. Symbols can be arranged in structures such as lists, hierarchies, or networks. By representing and manipulating these structures, AI techniques allow us to relate symbols to each other. Symbols can be created (or destroyed) and manipulated in symbolic expressions (somewhat analogous to arithmetic expressions); they can be inserted, deleted, replaced, or reordered. By virtue of their ability to process symbols, AI programs deal with the general domain of human thinking—we usually think in symbols, not numbers.

As we shall see, in an expert system, the knowledge base contains symbols, the facts of the case are presented as symbols, and the inference engine processes or "reasons" about symbols, drawing conclusions from the facts of the case, given the knowledge base. Quantitative processing can accompany this qualitative processing.

2. Nonalgorithmic Processing

Computer programs outside the AI domain are coded algorithms—fully specified step-by-step procedures that define the solution to the problem. The actions of a knowledge-based AI system are situationally determined to a far greater degree. An action—such as an expert system's recommendation or the movement of a robot arm—is based on knowledge about the domain, procedures for knowledge processing, and facts about the situation at hand. A well-designed system works properly in many situations that were not foreseen by its designer—though certainly not as flexibly as a human in most of these situations.

The distinctions between the information-processing approach of a system based on non-AI technologies and the knowledge-processing approach of an expert system are summarized in figure 15.1.

FIGURE 15.1

Knowledge processing
contrasted with information
processing.

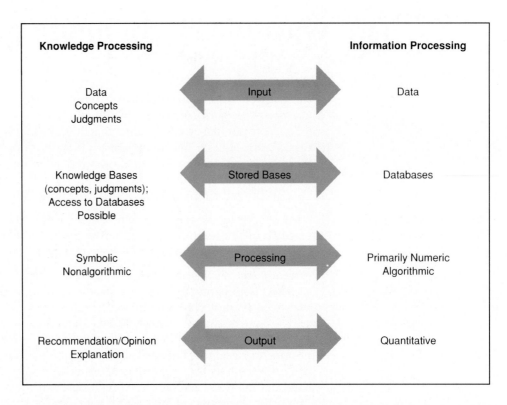

FIGURE 15.1

Knowledge processing contrasted with information processing.

The Field of AI

AI is a highly dynamic field of research, which can already point to a series of spectacular successes. A much longer path still lies ahead if AI is even to approach its stated goals. Paradoxically, the hardest, and as yet largely unsolved, problems of AI are those which we think require no particular intelligence—for example, understanding speech or comprehending a scene being viewed, or displaying common sense in an unexpected though simple situation. AI researchers are committed to pushing the envelope of computer capabilities; several problems they have solved are no longer considered a part of AI problematics. As the approaches worked out in AI labs become commercialized—and simplified, in the good sense of the word—AI researchers as often as not lose interest in them. They are aiming at a moving target.

The controversy surrounding the field AI has abated somewhat, now that it is no longer fueled by the outrageous claims of its prophets (or, perhaps, these claims have by now been widely discounted) and now, perhaps more important, that the commercial world has tasted the fruit of AI—and liked some of it. Much of the original controversy arose from hitching the field to the ill-defined concept of intelligence. We do know now that AI systems can reason about concepts—a signal feature of human intelligence. However, polemics persist over whether these systems "understand" concepts (do they really understand, or just manipulate characters according to rules?).

At this time, AI presents no clear and present danger to humans as the unique "thinking reeds." Humans can conceptualize (that is, create concepts—say, a concept of time, or the much simpler concept of a business meeting), and their thinking can be creative. Humans learn in many modes and can bring past experience to bear on a problem, while AI systems display only a very limited learning capacity. Most important, human cognitive and perceptive faculties are integrated into a whole that is greater than the sum of its parts—each of us is a very general-purpose system. We operate in multiple domains, rely on several senses, and use our faculties for perception and communication and our limbs for locomotion and a host of other activities.

An *artificial* intelligence system is narrowly focused on a specific domain, be it rendering diagnosis of a specific eye disease or recognizing a scene in a theater of war. But such a system does have its practical advantages. It is permanently housed in a computer system, where it can be accessed relatively easily from many locations. It works consistently, and it thoroughly brings to bear all it "knows." As we shall see further, expert systems, the most prominent AI offering to the business sector, have several major organizational advantages.

How the AI Field Evolved

The idea of cognition as a form of computation—or that computing machines may be made to do reasoning tasks—has its roots in the philosophical speculation of the seventeenth and eighteenth centuries. The ultimate potential of computers as intelligent machines was forecast by the brilliant British mathematician Alan Turing, who in 1950 formulated what is known as the Turing test: a machine performs intelligently if an interrogator using remote terminals cannot distinguish its responses from those of a human.

The early period of AI research culminated in the famous Dartmouth Conference of 1956. The field was given its name there by John McCarthy (the inventor of the LISP programming language for symbolic processing), and its research agenda was established by the founding fathers of AI, among them McCarthy, Marvin Minsky, Allen Newell, Claude Shannon, and Herbert Simon (who has in so many ways contributed to the foundations of MIS). The principal characteristic of this founding period was the belief in a General Problem Solver (the actual name of a major program by Newell and Simon): the search for a general problem-solving technique that would be usable across a variety of applications.

A major and extremely fruitful shift in thinking about AI occurred in the late 1960s. Researchers realized that the power of an AI system does not lie in its inferencing (reasoning) facility, but primarily in the knowledge methodically gathered, represented, and stored in its knowledge base. For roughly the next decade, techniques of knowledge-based systems were developed and perfected in research laboratories.

Then, in the late 1970s, the era of AI commercialization began. It was led by the fielding of expert systems into a variety of business environments. An organizational environment of dense and complex decision making calls for systems that can relieve humans of at least some of these tasks—and perhaps best humans in consistency and thoroughness. The declining costs of computer memories and processing power have made some systems of this type amazingly cost-effective. At this time, AI systems are being integrated into principal MIS components such as transaction processing and decision support systems.

The development of the AI field is sketched out in figure 15.2.

We shall survey the principal areas of applied AI after a thorough discussion of expert systems. Another direction in pursuing the automation of human capabilities, namely neurocomputing, which has begun to come into its own relatively recently, produced artificial neural networks as pattern recognizers. We will discuss these networks further in the last section of this chapter.

THE JAPANESE FIFTH-GENERATION PROJECT: WHAT IT'S ALL ABOUT

In 1982 (the same year that the computer was declared *Time*'s "Man of the Year"), the Japanese announced a ten-year massive national plan for moving their computer industry into the AI age (the preceding four generations of computing having been shaped by earlier technologies). Sponsored by the powerful Ministry of International Trade and Industry (MITI), the project announcement set forth dramatic aims. Computer systems hardware would be designed to draw logical inferences rather than to process simple machine instructions, with a very high level of parallelism and consequent ultra-high speed. Vast knowledge bases would be created, helping people to solve social problems. The systems would be able to translate natural languages and to learn. Ultimately, virtually all human sensing faculties would be conferred on computer systems.

A powerful bootstrapping process was envisaged. In the words of the leader of the effort, Kazuhiro Fuchi, ". . . research on artificial intelligence will provide a base on which more powerful computers can be designed. In turn, once these more powerful machines are available, research in AI will also be enhanced."[2]

The project elicited responses in the United States and in Europe. Similar projects were initiated, although they were far less trenchant in their ambitions. In the United States, a debate began on whether the government should play such an active role in industry; this controversy still continues. The fifth-generation project has brought progress to Japanese computing—in particular, it has developed a large corps of researchers—but in light of its impressive goals, it has turned out to be a disappointment: none of the goals were reached. It takes more than planning and financial backing to ensure research results.

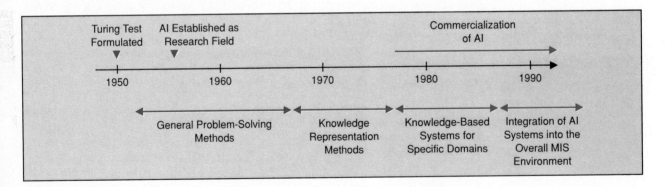

FIGURE 15.2

The development of the AI field.

THE FOUNDER

Systems acting as expert systems have been the very essence of AI research for years. But the first person to recognize expert systems as a natural class calling for a generalized approach to automation was Edward Feigenbaum of Stanford University. The first such program was DENDRAL, developed by Feigenbaum and his colleagues during the late 1960s. This system surpasses human experts at its task: given the atomic formula of a molecule (such as H_2O for water), it establishes the molecule's structure and mass spectrogram (estimated masses of the particles of the molecule).

Feigenbaum went on to codevelop MYCIN, an expert system for diagnosing blood diseases—and to cofound two leading companies in applied AI, Teknowledge and IntelliCorp. It is rare for a person to parent a major field of human endeavor to the extent that Feigenbaum did the field of expert systems.

15.2 CAPABILITIES OF EXPERT SYSTEMS— A GENERAL VIEW

Artificial intelligence research progresses as researchers build systems with ambitious goals, and then learn from their mistakes and successes. When theorists realized that the power of AI systems derives from their knowledge bases rather than from the general-purpose problem-solving technique, high-performance expert systems were born. The name of Edward Feigenbaum of Stanford University is prominently associated with their birth.

An **expert system (ES)** is a knowledge-based system: it employs knowledge about its application domain and uses an inferencing (reasoning) procedure to solve problems that would otherwise require human competence or expertise. The power of expert systems stems primarily from the specific knowledge about a narrow domain stored in the ES knowledge base.

The name *expert system* evokes a feeling of exceptional, perhaps superhuman, expertise. Indeed, the best (and the most expensive) of these systems are truly expert in their performance. Over the course of a number of consultations (advice-seeking sessions) with such a system, we obtain results surpassing the performance of experts in the field. (We encountered such a system in the focus case for this chapter.)

It would be a mistake, though, to believe that all expert systems have capacities equivalent to a human expert advisor. Some systems proffer decisions as a competent professional or semiprofessional would, within a narrow, highly focused task domain, such as diagnosing a product's quality defect or figuring out the

AN EXPERT SYSTEM FOR CREATING COMPANY PERSONNEL POLICIES

A PC-based program called Personnel Policy Expert (from KnowledgePoint of Petaluma, California) assists companies in creating a complete employee handbook. The ES covers some sixty policy subjects, ranging from safety rules and employment termination to employee benefits and immigration law compliance. It assists human-resource managers in making policy decisions based on prevailing labor laws and current practices. After briefing the user on these conditions, the system asks questions to establish which aspects of the policy are important to the company. Based on the user's responses, the ES creates a draft policy in the language of experts (stored in the knowledge base), but customized for the firm.

Maintained with an annual update, the system is used by companies employing from 10 to 100,000 people.

Based on KnowledgePoint Press Release of April 10, 1989, and Peter H. Lewis, "Laying Down Rules for Workers." *The New York Times*, Business Section, June 11, 1989, p. 12.

best mailing service for a given package. (You may want to review a consultation with this modest ES, shown in figure 3.8.) In general, these systems are assistants to decision makers and not substitutes for them.

We shall see that most expert systems today are built with shells or other tools that simplify the job considerably.

The assimilation of expert system technology in an organizational setting, as we shall discuss further on, begins with finding reasonably (but not overly) ambitious projects that require an active knowledge delivery vehicle at the point "where the rubber meets the road." If you need a system that would advise you how pertinent tax regulations would affect your company's investments, or how your existing personnel policies apply to a specific employment case, you could use an expert system. Such a system could draw on its voluminous knowledge about the domain (tax regulations or employment policies, respectively) and bring that knowledge to bear on the facts of the particular case—in a consistent fashion, with all the factors considered relevant.

The knowledge base of an expert system contains what one may call "book knowledge" about the domain; more important, it also contains *heuristic knowledge*—rules of thumb used by human experts who work in the domain. For example, a human credit manager might know that if an individual had a poor credit history over the last five years, but has been employed for the last two and had no adverse credit experiences over this period, then a credit transaction up to a certain limit should be approved. In the company's experience, known to its expert authorizers, this is a prudent policy.

Expert systems assist decision makers in the same area DSS do: with ill-structured problems. But in developing an ES, as work progresses on establishing the underlying decision process that goes toward solving the problem, the problem acquires structure—we learn more about the alternative solutions and what makes some of them better than others (Sviokla, 1986). Thus, both the process of developing an ES and the use of ES are aids in handling the complexity of organizational decision making.

15.3 APPLICATIONS OF EXPERT SYSTEMS

Let us consider several examples of successfully fielded expert systems—systems that have actually been implemented in a business environment. This will give you a feeling for the capabilities of the technology. The use of ES is expanding—an estimate of 1,500 systems worldwide at the end of 1987 (Feigenbaum, 1988) had grown to 2,500 by early 1989 (Mahnke, 1989). Let us look at some examples of ES in operation and then classify the generic areas of ES application.

Application Cases

1. Oracle Electronics Trading Company uses a Credit Advisor. The expert system identifies high-risk credit decisions based on the figures in a client company's financial statement. It also makes about 90 percent of the credit-granting decisions in these cases (which previously were determined by human decisions makers and passed on to the firm's CEO for disposition), with the remaining 10 percent passed on to a top-level decision maker. The ES presents to the decision maker the reasons why the system had its doubts. Since Credit Advisor was implemented, top executives no longer have to spend much of their time rendering credit decisions, the company's procedures manual no longer has to be consulted (and perhaps interpreted inconsistently by various people), and most credit-related decisions are made very promptly.

   The system was built with an inexpensive PC-based shell (VP-Expert) within three to four months; the total investment did not surpass $50,000.[3]

   Risk assessment is, in general, an area of ES strength. ES that assess risks are used by banks and other credit companies to make loans and by stock traders to handle portfolios. Many firms do not publicly proclaim the capabilities of these systems, since the systems are believed to give their owner companies a strategic advantage (Mahnke, 1989).

2. Expert systems are used to combine qualitative judgment with quantitative data in advertising decision making. The MORE system, developed for direct marketers by Persoft, analyzes each name on a mailing list. The system screens out unworthy names (of lucky individuals?) based on such data as the person's last direct-mail purchase, frequency of response to previous mailings, and demographic characteristics (such as address).

   Other potential advertising applications of expert system technology could serve the purposes currently covered by DSS, but also include much of the judgmental, rule-of-thumb type of knowledge. Robert Cook and John Schleede (Cook, 1988) suggest such potential ES applications as the determination of a market response curve based not only on historical databases, but also on the system's judgment of current competitor strategies and on potential competitor responses to future changes in the industry environment. Expert systems can also assist in selection of the copy (that is, the text) and layout for advertisements based on voluminous qualitative research on the subject, or in budget allocation for advertising a product brand among the different media.

Calling to mind our discussion of the role of DSS in marketing, we can appreciate that a computerized consideration of qualitative and judgmental factors using ES technology provides broader support for certain types of decisions.

3. Edward Feigenbaum and his coauthors (Feigenbaum, 1988) describe an expert system that simplifies the paperwork surrounding company-owned physical assets at IBM Endicott. The system helps people fill out the forms accompanying any acquisition, internal transfer, or disposal of machinery, electronic equipment, or other such assets. Some would consider the system an assistant to knowledge workers; others might call it a prop to unnecessary bureaucratic procedures. Given the unfortunate necessity of asset accounting, it is better to light the candle than curse the darkness (to borrow the authors' metaphor).

    Form-filling procedures are elaborate and confusing, with many of them dictated by the myriad tax laws. Until the advent of ES, these procedures were generally lodged in plentiful and cumbersome procedures manuals and in the heads of many old hands—many of whom also knew all the shortcuts.

    Here is how the ES works. At IBM Endicott: An individual needs to do something with a piece of equipment. She consults the ES for five to ten minutes, and the system tells her how to do the accompanying paperwork. During the session, the system keeps asking the person questions—but only those relevant in the light of the already established facts of the case. After the session, the person knows what forms must be filled and how to fill them, whose signatures are required, and where to send the forms. She has also received all tips, warnings, and notions pertinent to the situation.

    Did it occur to you that instead of giving our individual answers, the system might have filled out the forms and let the worker forget the entire sorry incident? This form-filling system is definitely a step toward a paperless office (a not necessarily realistic notion). Why is it then such a timid step? It is so because there are some current legal requirements that necessitate human participation. But more important is the organizational aspect: there are people in the company for whom forms are a particular fiefdom, and these people are not about to surrender all their forms to computers. As we have stressed time and time again, the availability of a technology does not obviate the need for an organizational change process.

    The expert system took one-and-a-half person-years to develop and cost less than $100,000. It will save IBM $1.5 million a year—by the most modest estimates.

4. Expert systems shine in many aspects of manufacturing—an area where we sorely need enhanced productivity and quality. The fact that much factory work has shifted to knowledge work (as was discussed in chapter 2) is underlined by Feigenbaum and his colleagues, who tell us that factory "touch" work (all the machining, assembling, and handling) accounts for only approximately a third of total costs. A full two-thirds of the manufacturing costs can be chalked up to knowledge work: design, engineering, quality assurance, sales, and management. The productivity of "touch" work can be increased by robotics; expert systems, along with other information systems, can have an even far more significant impact by reducing the other two-thirds of manufacturing costs.

An expert system implemented at Northrop Corporation, a major producer of jet fighter planes, is responsible for the planning of manufacture and assembly of up to 20,000 parts that go into an aircraft. A planner is able to enter a description of the engineering drawing of a part, and the ES will tell him what materials and processes are needed to manufacture it. The systems speeds up the actual planning work by a factor of twelve to eighteen. Considering other work saved, such as information gathering and form filling (not assisted by the ES), and time formerly spent on communication by multiple participants in the process (unneeded now), the time to task completion has been reduced from several days to about four-and-a-half hours, including a fifteen-minute session with the expert system. The payoff of the ES is easy enough to compute.

Generic Categories of ES Applications

We have discussed some illustrative cases. We can now classify the important generic areas of ES application as shown in table 15.1.

These categories of application are listed in approximate order of increasing difficulty. They should be understood broadly and creatively. Let us consider some commercially fielded (rather than research-oriented) systems.

General Electric's Metal Analyst system identifies (that is, *classifies*) common metals and alloys, based on density, color, and simple tests that can be performed by a nonmetallurgist. The knowledge base of the system contains 212 rules. To take a very different example, the U.S. Department of Energy uses an expert system to determine the security classification of documents.

Diagnosis systems, generally more complex than a simple classification (of faults for example), are widely used in industrial settings—after all, the origins of ES are connected with medical diagnosis! Canadian Pacific Railroad uses an expert system to diagnose impending failure in its diesel locomotives (with 98 percent accuracy) based on the impurities found in a sample of engine oil. The American Stock Exchange uses its Market Surveillance expert system to diagnose whether a suspected trading irregularity (such as insider trading) warrants further investigation.

Monitoring can be thought of as continuous diagnosis. Westinghouse uses and sells three expert systems for continuous on-line monitoring of steam turbines and generators. *Process control* expert systems monitor a production process and

TABLE 15.1

Generic Areas of ES Application (author; and Hayes-Roth, 1983)

APPLICATION AREA	PROBLEM ADDRESSED
Classification	Identify an object based on stated characteristics
Diagnosis	Infer malfunction or disease from observable data
Monitoring	Compare data from a continually observed system to prescribed behavior
Process Control	Control a physical process based on monitoring
Design	Configure a system according to specifications
Scheduling and Planning	Develop or modify a plan of action
Generation of Options	Generate alternative solutions to a problem

generate continuous messages to the operator aiming at optimizing operations; such real-time control is employed at one of the Nestlé Food Corporation plants.

Allen-Bradley Company employs an expert system to *design* or *configure* sophisticated computer-integrated manufacturing (CIM) cells. A CIM cell, the hallmark of modern manufacturing, is automated machining equipment that can reconfigure itself under computer control to produce a wide range of parts in lots from one to many thousands. The cell utilizes many types of sensors, controls, cutters, and other equipment (over 300 possible components). A human expert configures a cell in about a day. A 1,500–rule expert system does the job in a few minutes, based on a salesperson's specifications. Fielded worldwide, the system is strategically important to maintain Allen-Bradley's competitive position.

Stone & Webster Engineering Corporation uses an expert system to *schedule* power production; the ES makes it possible to employ not only optimization routines but also heuristics, for example, those regarding the availability of start-up and maintenance crews. The U.S. Space Command uses an expert system to *plan* satellite launches. The system plans future launch capability to match the requirements for satellite launches. The five-year launch plan is maintained on a daily basis to assess the impact of such contingencies as failures during a launch or on orbit. We should note here that general organizational planning is too broad a task for expert systems at this time.

A group at IBM Los Angeles Scientific Center has developed an expert system designed to help business managers identify competitive applications of information technology (Gongla, 1989). Using a framework similar to the strategic cube presented in chapter 5, and a knowledge base of cases of strategic information systems, the ES facilitates the *generation of options* in a search for strategic information weaponry.

15.4 HOW EXPERT SYSTEMS WORK

The strength of an ES derives from its knowledge base—an organized collection of facts and heuristics about the system's domain. An ES is built in a process known as **knowledge engineering,** during which knowledge about the domain is acquired from human experts by human knowledge engineers. The use of ES is often referred to as a consultation—which again stresses the role of the user in making the final decision. The two environments—knowledge acquisition and ES use—are shown in figure 15.3, which also shows the interaction of the principal components of ES. The isolation of knowledge in knowledge bases, from which conclusions are to be drawn by the inference engine, is the hallmark of an expert system. In this section, we shall discuss how the ES consultation environment works—in other words, how knowledge is represented and how the reasoning is done. In the following sections, we shall turn our attention to the development of ES, including knowledge engineering.

FIGURE 15.3

Structure of an expert system.

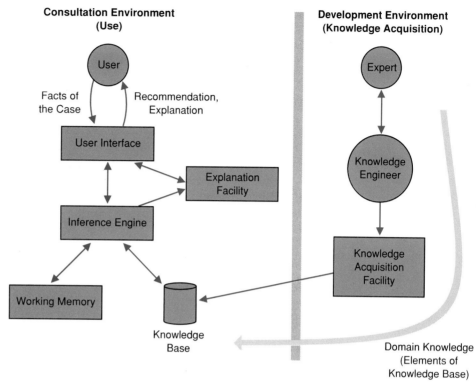

**Consultation Environment
(Use)**

**Development Environment
(Knowledge Acquisition)**

User

Facts of
the Case

Recommendation,
Explanation

User Interface

Explanation
Facility

Inference Engine

Working Memory

Knowledge
Base

Expert

Knowledge
Engineer

Knowledge
Acquisition
Facility

Domain Knowledge
(Elements of
Knowledge Base)

Knowledge Representation and the Knowledge Base

As we already know, the **knowledge base** of an ES contains both factual and heuristic knowledge. *Knowledge representation* is the method used to organize this knowledge. In contrast to knowledge bases, databases contain data of rather simple types—numbers, strings of text, or logical (true-false) values, which are organized into records that stand in quite simple relation to one another. Knowledge bases, on the other hand, must represent such notions as actions to be taken under different circumstances, causality, time dependencies, goals, and other higher-level concepts.

Several methods of knowledge representation can be drawn upon (see, for example, Rich, 1991). Among them are statements of propositional logic and predicate calculus, semantic networks, scripts, and frames. Some of these approaches, frame-based systems in particular, are employed for building powerful ES. A frame specifies the attributes of a complex object; frames for various object types have specified relationships. *Production rules* are by far the most common method of knowledge representation used in business ES. In the following discussion, therefore, we shall concentrate on **rule-based expert systems**—ES in which the knowledge is represented by such rules.

A production rule,[4] or simply a *rule,* consists of an IF part (a condition or premise) and a THEN part (an action or conclusion). We thus have this general form for rules:

IF condition THEN action (conclusion)

which is interpreted as:

IF the given condition occurs, THEN take this action (or draw this conclusion)

For example, a simple ES for selecting an advertising outlet for a product (presented in Gallagher, 1988, and modified here) may contain, among others, these rules:

```
R5:  IF product-category = toy
        or product-category = automobile
     THEN media = television.

R7:  IF product-category = toy
        or product-category = baseball-cards
     THEN target-market = children.

R12: IF media = television
        and target-market = children
     THEN advertising-outlet = "Saturday Morning Cartoon".

R15: IF media = television
        and target-market = young-adult
     THEN advertising-outlet = "Late, Late Movie".
```

Rules are also used to identify the goal: what we are trying to establish with the use of the system. For example, in our case, we may have:

```
R1: goal = advertising-outlet.
```

The rules are expressed in the language of the tool (such as a shell) used to develop the particular ES. A simple ES contains 50 to 100 such rules. During a consultation with the above system, the system will ask the user to supply the "product-category." Assuming that the user indicates "toy," the system will recommend that the "advertising-outlet" be "Saturday Morning Cartoon." Of course, the conclusions in useful systems are not usually so transparent. A description of a realistic expert system for the domain of consumer-product advertising was presented by Raymond Burke and his colleagues (1990).

Since many rules supply heuristic information, we can attach a *certainty factor* in the range from 0 (total uncertainty) to 100 (complete certainty) to them; for example:

```
R5: IF product-category = toy
       or product-category = automobile
     THEN media = television CF 90.
```

The certainty factor qualifies our confidence about the conclusion of the rule. The inference engine is able to perform a calculus of certainty factors and qualify the final recommendation by a cumulative certainty factor—which the user may then consider when acting upon the consultation.

The **explanation facility** explains how the system arrived at the recommendation. Depending on the tool used to implement the expert system, the explanation may be either in a natural language or simply a listing of rule numbers. For example, the recommendation of the advertising outlet may be explained as follows: "because of R5, R7 and R12."

The **user interface** allows a customized display format.

How are the rules of the knowledge base used to draw inferences? The rules are actually applied to the facts of the case by the inference engine of the expert system.

Inference Engine

The **inference engine** controls the order in which production rules are applied ("fired") and resolves conflicts if more than one rule is applicable at a given time. This is what "reasoning" amounts to in rule-based systems.

The facts of the given case ("toy" in our example) are entered in the *working memory,* which acts as a blackboard, accumulating the knowledge about the case at hand. The inference engine repeatedly applies the rules to the working memory, adding new information (obtained from the rules' conclusions) to it, until a goal state is produced or confirmed. In our case, once the "advertising-outlet" is defined by R12, this goal state has been reached.

The inference engine also directs the user interface to query the user for any information it needs for further inferencing.

One of several strategies can be employed by an inferencing engine to reach a conclusion (or to reason, if your will). Inferencing engines for rule-based systems generally work by either forward or backward chaining of rules (most shells supply facilities for both strategies). The two strategies are contrasted schematically in figure 15.4.

Forward chaining is a data-driven strategy: the inferencing process moves from the facts of the case to a goal (conclusion). The strategy is thus driven by the facts available in the working memory and by the premises that can be satisfied. The inference engine attempts to match the condition (IF) part of each rule in the knowledge base with the facts currently available in the working memory. If several rules match, a conflict resolution procedure is invoked—for example, the lowest-numbered rule that adds new information to the working memory is fired. The conclusion of the firing rule is added to the working memory.

In our example, if an input stating that the "product-category" is automobile has been given to the system, then rule R5 will fire, and the value of "media = television" will be added to the working memory.

The inference engine keeps iteratively (repeatedly) applying the rules of the knowledge base against the accumulating data in the working memory. In our example, if it had already been established through previous rule firings that the "target-market" is "young-adult," rule R15 will fire to reach a goal state—"Late, Late Movie" as the advertising outlet.

As we may conclude, the forward-chaining inference method consists in repeatedly answering the question: "What conclusions can be reached from the rules, given the data in the working memory?"

A **backward-chaining** inferencing strategy works in the opposite direction: from a possible goal state to the premises that would satisfy it. Here, the engine attempts to match the assumed (hypothesized) conclusion—the goal or subgoal state—with the conclusion (THEN) part of a rule. If such a rule is found, its premise becomes the new subgoal. In an ES with few possible goal states, this is a good strategy to pursue.

FIGURE 15.4

Inferencing strategies.

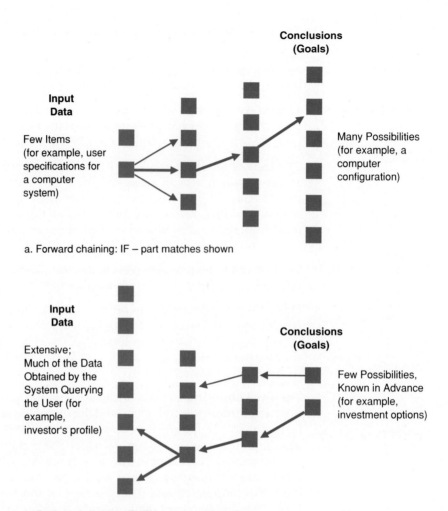

a. Forward chaining: IF – part matches shown

b. Backward chaining: THEN – part matches shown

For example, in our case the goal is to establish an ''advertising-outlet.'' The first rule we have listed that matches the goal is R12; the goal state is ''Saturday Morning Cartoon.'' The system will then back up and try to establish the validity of the two subgoals listed in the premises for this rule. If there is not enough information in the working memory to keep backing up, the system asks the user for information.

If a hypothesized goal state cannot be supported by the premises, the system will attempt to prove another goal state. Thus, possible conclusions are reviewed until a goal state that can be supported by the premises is encountered. Note that when the facts of the case are the same, both backward- and forward-chaining methods, of course, give the same results.

Backward chaining, more common in the expert systems currently developed, is best suited for applications in which the possible conclusions are limited in number and are well defined. Classification- or diagnosis-type systems, in which each of several possible conclusions can be checked to see if they are supported by the data, are typical applications. These systems are, in general, simpler to write and use; they query the user as more data are needed to prove goals or subgoals.

TRYING TO OVERCOME THE BRITTLENESS OF EXPERT SYSTEMS

Expert systems are notoriously brittle: when confronted with a situation unanticipated by its developers, an expert system is quite likely to reach a wrong conclusion. For example, a loan authorization system may approve a loan for an applicant whose "number of years at the current job" exceeds the applicant's age, or who applies for a loan from a penal institution. In these situations, a human would fall back on common sense.

A major attempt to build a knowledge base of human consensus knowledge (for example, what we mean by "buying"), intended to equip AI systems with common sense, is now under way. The project is supported by a corporate consortium, Microelectronics and Computer Technology Corporation (MCC) of Austin, Texas, and is led by Douglas Lenat. Lenat and his colleagues scan newspapers and books, seeking what is *not* explained—

since that is what readers are presumed to know and what needs to be stored in the huge knowledge base of this system.

Expert systems with access to this knowledge base (projected to include some 100 million rules) would be far less brittle. The MCC shareholder companies are beginning to use the results of this labor. Bellcore, for example, is working on an on-line expert assistant for customer advisers that would be far more flexible in "understanding" the problems faced by the telecommunication company's customers.

Started in 1984, MCC's project Cyc (for encyclopedia) is expected to be completed in the mid-1990s—with a 70 percent chance of success. The system is considered a breakthrough technology, since it could provide the United States with a competitive advantage in the global marketplace.

Based on Lenat, 1990; and on Glenn Rifkin, "Packing Some Sense Into Computers." *Computerworld*, October 15, 1990, p. 22.

Forward-chaining systems are commonly used to solve more open-ended problems of a design or planning nature, such as, for example, establishing the configuration of a complex product. The number of possible configurations is huge, and for practical reasons, not all configurations can be stated at the outset (and then chained back from). Several very powerful systems are of this nature—the most impressive of this, XCON/XSEL, is discussed in the case study for this part of the book.

15.5 EXPERT SYSTEM TECHNOLOGY

As is the case with decision support systems, there are several levels of ES technologies, ranging from a specific expert system to programming languages. Simpler tools are quite accessible to end users, who indeed have developed a large number of smaller expert systems (containing on the order of 100 rules) in various enterprises. These tools generally run on personal computers. More elaborate tools require professional knowledge engineers to develop powerful systems.

FIGURE 15.5

Expert-system technologies.

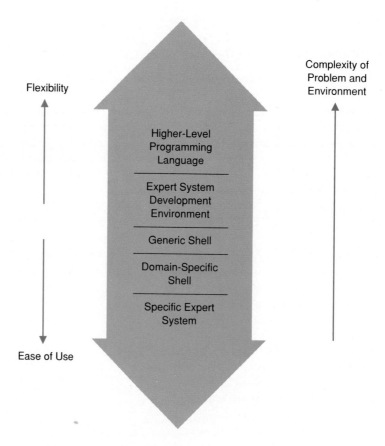

The tool selected for the project has to match the capability and sophistication of the projected ES, in particular its requirements for integration with other subsystems (such as databases and other MIS components). It also has to match the qualifications of the project team. Indeed, experts systems have been built to decide what expert system tools to use on a project (Martin, 1988). Various ES technologies are summarized in figure 15.5 and further discussed in this chapter.

Specific Expert Systems

Whenever I have referred to an expert system throughout this chapter, I had in mind a specific ES that actually provides recommendations in a specific task domain.

A specific expert system can, of course, be more general in scope, or it can be specialized to a single model of an automobile engine so that it can diagnose malfunctions in it. Many expert systems are believed by their owner companies to confer competitive edge, and their knowledge bases are thus kept confidential. Other specific ES, as we have mentioned above, are marketed by their developers.

Historically, expert systems arose within artificial intelligence research as specific systems. Thus, MYCIN was developed by Edward Shortliffe, Edward Feigenbaum, and their colleagues at Stanford University as a rule-based expert system for the diagnosis of infectious blood diseases and for treatment recommendations. At some point, the researchers recognized the generic nature of the approach—take away the knowledge base regarding blood diseases, and you are left with a shell that can inference from any appropriately represented knowledge base! They called the shell EMYCIN (for Empty MYCIN), and so expert system shells were born.

Expert System Shells

Expert system shells are the most common vehicle for the development of specific ES. A shell is an expert system without a knowledge base. If we look again at figure 15.3, we can conclude that such a shell furnishes the ES developer with the inference engine, user interface, and the explanation and knowledge acquisition facilities.

Many of the end-user-oriented shells have an induction facility: you present case examples with their conclusions, and the system automatically builds the rules.

The capability to access databases (for example, created with dBase) is important in many applications. The fixed rules in the ES knowledge base are able to make recommendations based on the changing data of the database. Consider an ES for loan evaluation. Your expert system can process a database of loan applications (built up by a TPS) once a week. Conversely, you can build an ES to decide whether an individual applicant qualifies for a loan based on a database of loan rates updated weekly.

Some shells offer a hypertext facility that allows for elaborate cross-referencing of information—of particular advantage in such applications as computerized policy manuals, on-line help facilities, or other reference systems.

A recent development is the emergence of *domain-specific shells*. As opposed to the more common generic shells, these are actually incomplete specific expert systems, which require much less effort to field an actual system. For example, Picon, a specific shell for oil-refinery applications, includes a user interface with icons useful in that environment. In an example offered by Dennis Yablonsky,[5] a Service Bay Diagnostic System, built with a domain-specific shell for constructing diagnostic systems, required only 225 rules instead of the estimated 30,000 that would have been needed with a generic shell.

Some of the popular end-user-oriented ES shells are listed in table 15.2.

Expert System Development Environments

Development environments expand the capabilities of shells in various directions. They run on engineering workstations, minicomputers, or mainframes, offer tight integration with large databases, and support the building of large expert systems. For instance, a system that runs in multiple hardware environments permits an ES to be developed on a personal computer and then ported to a mainframe for production use.

Knowledge bases can be modularized: rules can be broken down into a set of contexts, and these rule modules can be manipulated independently. Such systems allow for sophisticated handling of uncertain information, support interaction with procedural programs, permit extensive customization of user interfaces, and offer many features that ensure the robustness of a professionally developed application for production use. Procedural rules can be specified: under appropriate conditions, a course of several computational actions may be pursued.

TABLE 15.2	TOOL NAME	VENDOR
ES Shells and Development Environments	**Rule-Based ES Shells for End-User PC Applications**	
	1st-Class Fusion	1st-Class Expert Systems Wayland, Massachusetts
	VP-Expert	Paperback Software International Berkeley, California
	Personal Consultant Easy	Texas Instruments Houston, Texas
	Level5	Information Builders New York, New York
	ES Development Environments	
	Personal Consultant Plus	Texas Instruments Houston, Texas
	EXSYS Professional	EXSYS Albuquerque, New Mexico
	Guru	MDBS Lafayette, Indiana
	Aion Development System (ADS)	Aion Corporation Palo Alto, California
	KBMS	AICorp Waltham, Massachusetts
	KEE	IntelliCorp Mountain View, California

Development environments usually provide several alternative knowledge representations (for example, rules, frames, and objects) and several inferencing techniques beyond backward and forward chaining. Some of these systems are listed in table 15.2; the capabilities of these systems differ significantly, however (Loofbourrow, 1988).

Higher-Level Programming Languages

Many original expert systems were developed with LISP, an AI language designed to process lists of symbols. Indeed, LISP was also used early in the commercial environment, particularly running on Symbolics workstations, which directly interpret and execute LISP code in hardware. Later, another influential AI language, Prolog, based on predicate calculus, was also employed.

It is possible to develop an expert system with a general-purpose procedural language, and indeed, quite a few early systems were built in FORTRAN or PL/I. Actually, several environments for ES development have been rewritten from LISP into a procedural language more commonly found in the commercial environment, such as C. This simplifies the integration of expert system technology with the more traditional MIS environment.

Considering the availability of shells and environments today, such developments have become rare. They are employed only under special circumstances, in which particularly stringent performance or other special requirements that cannot be satisfied with higher-level tools are present. Even in some of these cases, custom programming in a higher-level language may augment the use of a development environment.

15.6 ROLES IN EXPERT SYSTEM DEVELOPMENT

Three fundamental roles in building expert systems are expert, knowledge engineer, and user. When elaborate systems are built using flexible lower-level tools such as development environments or using a higher-level programming language, and when integration with other systems is sought, the involvement of technical specialists conversant with these tools is essential. A wider suite of organizational roles has been identified in the case study for this part of the book.

1. Expert

The expert in the domain of a future ES is an indispensable person in its development. Much of the factual knowledge will be transferred into many a system from textbooks, manuals, policy statements, or bills of materials. However, it is the heuristic information, the problem-solving skills in the specialized domain, that will make the difference between success and failure of the system.

As Feigenbaum (1988) points out, many an expert system is called "Mike-in-the-Box" or "Geoff's Book"—since it reflects the distillation of an individual's many years of experience and application of knowledge.

Large systems generally require multiple experts. It is crucial to identify individuals who not only perform in a superior fashion, but also have the will and ability to transfer their knowledge to the system.

Acquiring knowledge from an expert is far from a trivial exercise. Any systems analyst who ever performed a user interview, which deals with far simpler and more objective questions than "What makes you think there is something wrong with the mixture in the vat?" will appreciate the difficulties involved.

Hence the need for a knowledge engineer.

2. Knowledge Engineer

The knowledge engineer has a dual task. This person should be able to elicit knowledge from the expert, gradually gaining an understanding of an area of expertise; intelligence, tact, empathy, and proficiency in specific techniques of knowledge acquisition are all required of a knowledge engineer. Knowledge-acquisition techniques include conducting interviews with varying degrees of structure, protocol analysis (in which the expert performs the task and verbalizes his or her thinking, which is recorded for subsequent analysis), observation of experts at work, and analysis of cases.

On the other hand, the knowledge engineer must be familiar with ES technology. This person should be able to select a tool appropriate for the project and use it to represent the knowledge with the application of the knowledge-acquisition facility. This facility is essentially a text editor, enhanced by error-checking.

Several corporations, such as Schlumberger or FMC, have created AI departments, whose primary objective is to support expert system efforts in the company.

3. User

Expert systems are written for different categories of users. A truly expert system is used by another expert: the ES will provide an opinion which the human expert is able to set in context and evaluate. Physicians use diagnostic systems in this mode.

A nonexpert may use an expert system as a domain consultant. A system that identifies alloys and metals for nonmetallurgists acts in this fashion. A novice entering some field of endeavor can learn from an expert system about the field. The novice would do well to use the explanation facility and analyze its output.

A user may play all three roles (expert—knowledge engineer—user) at once. As we have already said, many simpler expert systems are actually developed by end users.

Systems that might confer competitive advantage on an owner organization are generally complex. Two kinds of complexity may be present in the development of an ES (Meyer, 1991). Knowledge complexity is a characteristic of an expert system that cuts through several domains of expertise (for example, a field of medicine and the discipline of life insurance underwriting), requires deep knowledge in the domain and varied sources of information, and has to be based on uncertain information. Technological complexity emerges when the expert system has to be integrated with several other information systems, has to run on diverse hardware and software platforms, and is large in size. The selection of ES development personnel should be motivated by the nature of the complexities present in the given project.

15.7 DEVELOPMENT OF EXPERT SYSTEMS

A system developed by an end user with a simple shell, with 50 to 100 rules in its knowledge base, is built rather quickly and inexpensively. We showed the effectiveness of a company-wide application of this approach at Du Pont in chapter 3.

Larger systems are built in an organized development effort. A prototype-oriented iterative development strategy is commonly used. ES lend themselves particularly well to prototyping: a system with a few well-selected initial rules in its knowledge base can do something sensible. This brings significant psychic and organizational capital to the developers. Look at the case study for this chapter to see how a prototype played such a role.

A complete iterative process for ES development and maintenance is shown in figure 15.6.

These are the steps of the methodology:

1. Problem Identification and Feasibility Analysis

The problem has to be suitable for an expert system to solve. If you must smell the chocolate mixture in a vat to adjust the ingredients, it is unlikely that you can successfully implement an on-line ES control. James

FIGURE 15.6

Development and
maintenance of expert
systems.

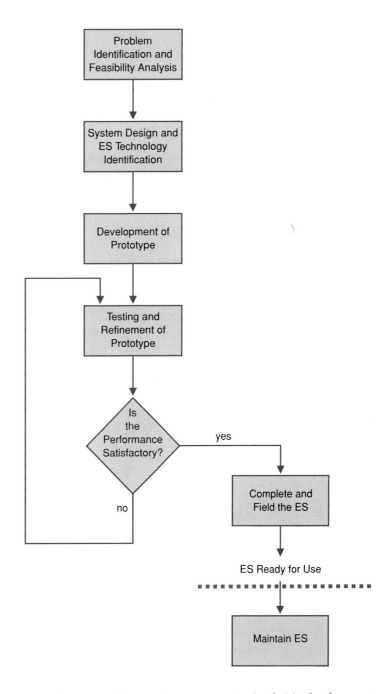

Martin, a well-known writer and consultant in the field of information systems, offers a telephone test: if you can fully describe how the problem is solved on the telephone, an expert system may be able to handle it.

Along with determining whether an ES is appropriate, system developers must find an expert (or experts who are in general agreement) who is available for the project. Also at this stage, a subset of ES functionality that will become the initial prototype of the ES should already be identified.

The cost-effectiveness of the system has to be estimated by establishing the approximate number of rules and determining the cost-per-rule in an environment similar to yours. The intangible benefits of saving the expertise of a retiring exceptional expert or the tangible benefits of rejecting fewer fundable loan applications are to be considered in determining cost-effectiveness.

2. System Design and ES Technology Identification

At this stage, the system is actually designed. In particular, the needed degree of integration with other subsystems and databases is established. Concepts that best represent the domain knowledge are worked out. The best way to represent the knowledge and to perform inferencing should be established with sample cases. The ES development tool is selected on the basis of these conclusions.

3. Development of Prototype

Using the knowledge-acquisition facility, the knowledge engineer works with the expert to place the initial kernel of knowledge in the knowledge base. The functionality of the prototype corresponds to that identified during step 1.

4. Testing and Refinement of Prototype

Using sample cases, the prototype is tested, and deficiencies in performance are noted. During the later stages of prototype refinement, end users make the best testers. The knowledge base continues to expand and be modified. To refine the knowledge base, knowledge engineers continue to work with experts, with end users ultimately testing each new release of the ES.

The refinement cycles are repeated until the system achieves satisfactory performance on a variety of test cases.

5. Complete and Field the ES

The interaction of the ES with all the elements of its environment is ensured and tested. A suite of test cases is run to validate the expert system (and kept to validate future modifications). ES is documented and user training conducted.

If the development environment differs from the actual operational environment, the ES is installed in the latter. It is integrated with the organizational environment where it will operate, with the needed organizational changes carried out.

6. Maintain the System

The system is kept current primarily by updating its knowledge base. However, with the exception of stand-alone systems, interfaces with other MIS components have to be maintained as well, as those systems evolve.

Large expert systems must be developed with maintainability in view (Prerau, 1990). The case study for this part of the book shows how extensive and frequent the maintenance can be for a large and strategically important ES.

We should note that if an innovative expert system is created, the progressive improvement of a prototype may require problem reformulation (going back to step 1) or a system redesign around a different ES development tool, with attendant redesign of the knowledge base (Hayes-Roth, 1984). Developers are accumulating lessons from the implementation of real-world expert systems—and many of these lessons are similar to those learned in developing non-AI applications (Irgon, 1990). We shall discuss the development of information systems in Part 5 of this book.

Our case study for this chapter describes a rather low-key, but organizationally very successful, initiation of an expert system project through the judicious selection of a prototype. The case study for this part of the book describes some ten years' experience with an extremely potent ES that confers a crucial competitive advantage on its owner company.

15.8 EXPERT SYSTEMS IN ORGANIZATIONS: BENEFITS AND LIMITATIONS

Expert systems offer both tangible and important intangible benefits to owner companies; these benefits should be weighed against the development and exploitation costs of an ES, which are high for large, organizationally important ES. More definite payoffs should be expected from an ES introduced at a later stage of ES technology assimilation by a firm.

The range of problems to be handled with the ES approach should be distinguished from those approached with decision support systems. Expert systems have clear limitations, and they should not be built for tasks and environments for which they are unsuitable.

Benefits of Expert Systems

Expert systems assist individual decision makers much in the way colleagues, paraprofessionals, or instructors would. ES are no substitute for a decision maker's overall performance of the problem-solving task. But they can dramatically reduce the amount of work the individual must do to solve a problem, and they do leave to people the creative and innovative aspects of problem solving.

Some of the *organizational* benefits of expert systems are:

- ES can complete their part of the task much faster than a human expert; this may mean producing an immediate response for a client asking for a credit decision or a lower downtime for an expensive piece of equipment being diagnosed.
- The error rate in successful systems is very low, often lower than the human error rate for the same tasks.
- ES maintain consistency of recommendations: given the same facts of the case, an ES will always proffer the same recommendation.

- ES are a convenient vehicle for bringing to the point of application (via networking, if needed) difficult-to-use sources of knowledge, such as voluminous procedure manuals or assembly instructions.
- An expert system can capture the scarce expertise of a uniquely qualified (and possibly retiring) expert.
- An ES can become a vehicle for building up *organizational* knowledge—as opposed to the knowledge of individuals in the organization. This makes the company more independent of human vagaries. Knowledge bases become a part of organizational memory.
- When they are used as training vehicles, ES result in a faster learning curve for novices in the domains covered by the ES.
- The company can operate an ES in environments hazardous for humans.

Both DSS and ES address the crucial problem of organizations in an information society: coping with the rapidly increasing volume of complex decision making. Let us compare the two types of systems in this regard.

Expert systems and DSS have very different origins—one grew out of AI research, the other from adapting management science and financial modeling to the needs of organizational MIS. They also offer different, though complementary, capabilities. Table 15.3 summarizes and contrasts the capabilities of DSS and ES.

It is important to manage expectations connected with a new technology (Leonard-Barton, 1988): unfounded assumptions are certain to lead to disappointment. With this in mind, let us see what the limitations of ES are.

Limitations of Expert Systems

No technology offers an easy and total solution. While systems developed by an individual user for a limited task are surprisingly inexpensive, large systems are

TABLE 15.3

Comparison of ES and DSS (author; and Turban 1990)

	ES	DSS
Objective	Replicate a human expert	Assist human decision maker
Organizational Level	Mainly operational	Mainly managerial
Who Recommends Decision?	The system	The human, assisted by the system
Major Orientation	Automating use of expertise	Support of human decision-making process
Problem Area	Narrow domain	Often a broad and complex domain
Query Direction	System queries the human	Human queries the system
Base of Support	Knowledge base of facts and heuristics (imprecise judgments)	Database of facts, largely numeric
Manipulation	Symbolic reasoning	Numeric processing
Explanation Capability	Major feature	Very limited
Decision Problems Addressed	Repetitive	Ad hoc, often unique

costly and require significant development time and computer resources. ES also have their limitations. Among the limitations of expert systems and the concerns aroused by them are:

1. Limitations of the Technology

The knowledge base of an expert system does not represent a causal model of the phenomena in its domain. The deep reasons for recommended actions are not investigated by an ES. This limits the class of applications (see table 15.1) of these systems and precludes systems that would require deeper analysis or approach creativity. The narrowness of the domain makes for brittle systems that cannot respond to situations an inexperienced user might expect them to be able to respond to. An expert system does not know what it does not know, and hence, care is required in its use.

Expert systems have no automatic learning capability. Improvement in performance has to come from system maintenance by knowledge engineers.

Good ES perform impressively—but all of them make mistakes (just as human experts do).

2. Problems with Knowledge Acquisition

Tasks for an ES implementation have to be selected to ensure that

- there is agreement on who the domain experts are;
- there is general agreement among experts in the domain on an effective approach to problem solving; and
- a domain expert, recognized for his or her performance, is available and willing to work with knowledge engineers. There are multiple disincentives for experts to cooperate—and they also have their primary jobs to do.

3. Operational Domains as the Principal Area of ES Application

Most expert systems support operational-level tasks (and will in the future probably be integrated with various TPS). Managerial decision-making produces few domains narrow enough to become domains of expert systems.

4. Maintaining Human Expertise in Organizations

Paradoxically, reliance on an expert system may lead to a long-term weakening of innovation in the performance of the tasks relegated to it. Once they have acquired basic skills, people improve their performances by actually doing diagnosis, scheduling, or loan approving. If a large part of the task is handled automatically by an expert system, many workers do not acquire a "feel" for the actual task—and they may not be creative about it. Unquestioned assumptions, cast into expert systems, lead to a hardening of the organizational decision-making arteries. Organizational measures need to be taken to prevent this from happening. When you speak to the more thoughtful executives in companies in which a strategically important system is 99 percent right, the executives express some of these rather surprising—but very real—concerns.

15.9 OVERVIEW OF APPLIED ARTIFICIAL INTELLIGENCE

As we can see in figure 15.7, expert systems are only one—albeit the most commercially prominent—of the areas of AI application.

Let us review other fields of AI research—and as yet limited, but promising, practice.

Natural Language Processing

Computers have accustomed us to giving them instructions in a variety of unnatural, computer-oriented programming languages (which we surveyed in chapter 6). The time will come, we hope, when we shall design computers that can understand to a large extent our natural language, be it English or Japanese. Research on building natural language understanding into AI systems is blooming, but the many levels of ambiguity and context dependence inherent in language make the general problem an extremely difficult one. What does "I saw a man on the hill with a telescope" mean, for example? Do I have the telescope or does the man have it? Who is actually on the hill?

However, limited-scope natural language systems do exist. Commercial translation programs can perform a rough translation in a technical field, producing an output that requires extensive human editing (Nash, 1991). The main application for a natural language system at this time is as a user interface for expert and database systems. For example, INTELLECT of AICorp (Waltham, Massachusetts) enables business users to access information from corporate databases with requests in conversational English. Based on the vocabulary of an application and its own built-in dictionary, the system maintains a lexicon of terms it understands. The system paraphrases queries, "echoing" their interpretation to the user. It also recognizes ambiguous or unclear queries: observe the user-system interaction shown in figure 15.8. After the system establishes during the first query that the user means the city, rather than the state, of New York, it is able to correctly interpret the next reference to New York in that context.

FIGURE 15.7

Applied fields of artificial intelligence.

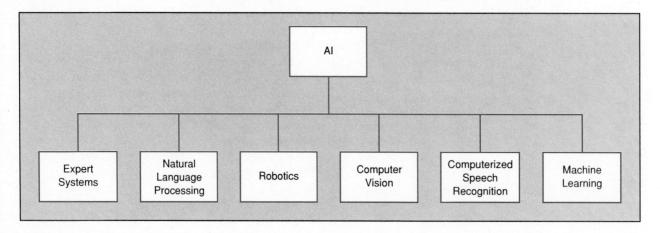

Robotics

A robot with AI capability (simpler robots do not have it!) is an electromechanical manipulator able to respond to a change in its environment based on its perception of that environment. This implies that such a robot has a sensory subsystem (usually machine vision) and is programmed to interpret what it "sees" and to act upon the interpretation. For example, an industrial robot can manufacture one of many parts in its repertoire and manipulate it to inspect it for defects, recognizing very small departures from established standards.

Robots have been used extensively in the advanced industrial countries of the world, particularly in Japan. They are reliable, consistent, accurate, insensitive to hazardous environments; and, let's face it, these "steel collars" do not do many things we wish their human counterparts would not do.

At this time, a mass advent of robots with an appreciable degree of artificial intelligence is still a vision for the future.

FIGURE 15.8

The INTELLECT natural-language query system resolving an ambiguity.

(Intersolve, Inc.)

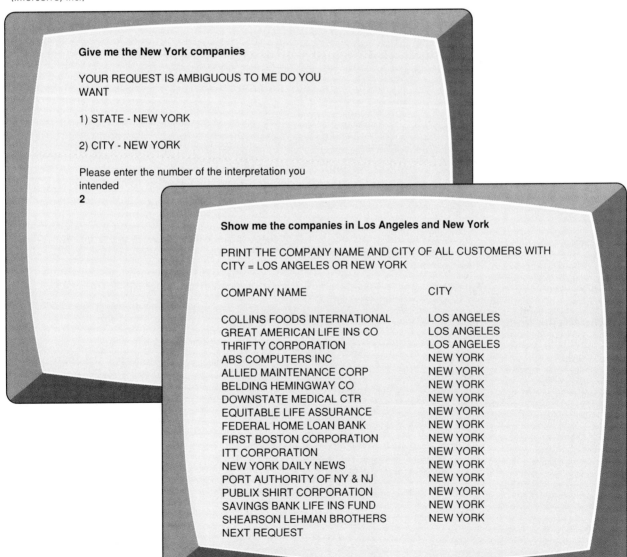

Give me the New York companies

YOUR REQUEST IS AMBIGUOUS TO ME DO YOU WANT

1) STATE - NEW YORK

2) CITY - NEW YORK

Please enter the number of the interpretation you intended
2

Show me the companies in Los Angeles and New York

PRINT THE COMPANY NAME AND CITY OF ALL CUSTOMERS WITH CITY = LOS ANGELES OR NEW YORK

COMPANY NAME	CITY
COLLINS FOODS INTERNATIONAL	LOS ANGELES
GREAT AMERICAN LIFE INS CO	LOS ANGELES
THRIFTY CORPORATION	LOS ANGELES
ABS COMPUTERS INC	NEW YORK
ALLIED MAINTENANCE CORP	NEW YORK
BELDING HEMINGWAY CO	NEW YORK
DOWNSTATE MEDICAL CTR	NEW YORK
EQUITABLE LIFE ASSURANCE	NEW YORK
FEDERAL HOME LOAN BANK	NEW YORK
FIRST BOSTON CORPORATION	NEW YORK
ITT CORPORATION	NEW YORK
NEW YORK DAILY NEWS	NEW YORK
PORT AUTHORITY OF NY & NJ	NEW YORK
PUBLIX SHIRT CORPORATION	NEW YORK
SAVINGS BANK LIFE INS FUND	NEW YORK
SHEARSON LEHMAN BROTHERS	NEW YORK

NEXT REQUEST

Computer Vision   The simulation of human senses is a principal objective of the AI field. The most advanced AI sensory system is computer vision, or visual scene recognition. The task of a vision system is to interpret the picture. These systems are employed in robots or in satellite systems, for example. Simpler vision systems are used for quality control in manufacturing (see color plate 16).

After a camera obtains the image, the vision system scans it and breaks it down into pixels (picture elements—dots with fixed positions in the image). After that, the system determines the highlights of the object in the picture. Then, the object is matched with an image in computer storage, and thus identified (or rejected as unknown). Present systems work in a narrow domain of images.

Once the image has been digitized by the scanning process, many kinds of computerized image processing are possible (for example, divorced spouses can be edited out of the picture)—but the AI component of computer vision is the actual recognition of the object—"scene understanding."

**Computerized
Speech Recognition**   Understanding spoken language is a basic human faculty. The ultimate goal of the corresponding AI area is the understanding of connected speech by an unknown speaker (as opposed to systems that recognize words or short phrases spoken one at a time, or that are trained by a specific speaker before use). Speech recognition techniques that rely on recognizing only individual words are inadequate. The best system of this sort today, SPHINX of Carnegie Mellon University, has an error rate of 29.4 percent on a vocabulary of 1,000 words (Young, 1989). Researchers are seeking further progress by incorporating higher-level knowledge sources, such as syntax, semantics, and pragmatics (knowledge of the context of the utterance) into the design of these systems. In other words, they are attempting to integrate speech recognition with natural language processing (White, 1990). The vignette on page 595 will show you future possibilities in this area.

An "intelligent typewriter" with built-in translation ability may become only one illustration of the general fact that, by combining the AI capabilities we have very briefly discussed, we may be able to create in the future any number of imaginative products. Some of them appear within our grasp—while others are well beyond it at this time.

Machine Learning   Probably the most fascinating area of AI research is the work on learning systems. What *is* learning? According to Herbert Simon, a system with learning capabilities is automatically capable of undergoing "changes that are adaptive in the sense that they enable the system to do the same task or tasks drawn from the same population more efficiently and more effectively the next time" (Simon, 1983).

The notion of learning is very broad. In the simplest interpretation of this capability, a system may "learn" by self-adjusting a few numerical parameters. A more advanced learning system is able to acquire new concepts and relate them to the knowledge already stored in its knowledge base. A learning capability can potentially be incorporated into any type of system falling into the AI domain. Because it would continually learn as it works, such a system would keep im-

A VOICE-ACTIVATED "TYPEWRITER"—AN OBVIOUS WISH

The goal of producing a speech-driven typewriter has been pursued for a number years—and finally, products have started to appear. A variety of limitations are still present: time may have to be spent to "train" the device to recognize a given speaker's voice, the vocabularies are more or less limited, a perceptible pause has to be made between spoken words, and word recognition is not error-free. But the technology is being assimilated at several sites.

Physicians at Mercy Hospital in Springfield, Massachusetts, are using four networked microcomputers equipped with the Voicemed speech-recognition system from Kurzweil Applied Intelligence of Waltham, Massachusetts. The physician dictates a patient report into a telephone-type handset, pausing between the words.

The words appear on a computer monitor and may be edited if needed, and then the report is printed—it takes two minutes to produce a standard one-page report. The system also permits the physician to use "trigger phrases"—a verbal shorthand that prompts the system to produce entire report segments. In addition, the system automatically inserts the codes required by insurers for reimbursement.

A voice-activated "typewriter" for the office—and other—markets is DragonDictate by Dragon Systems of Newton, Massachusetts, which reportedly permits experienced users to create typewritten text at a rate of thirty to over forty words per minute.

Based on Michael Alexander, "Doctors Save Time Writing without Pens." *Computerworld*, January 28, 1991; and "Tell It To Your Computer." *Microcomputer Solutions*, January-February 1991, p. 10.

---

proving its performance. For example, a vision system could more accurately recognize scenes, and a rule-based expert system could develop new rules for its knowledge base and modify the existing rules.

A number of approaches to learning are being investigated by AI researchers. One of these approaches is learning by problem solving. For example, as a rule-based expert system is applied to problems, it can accumulate "experience" about its rules in terms of their contributions to correct advice. The rules that do not contribute or those that are found to provide doubtful contributions could be automatically discarded or assigned low certainty factors. Another approach is learning by analogy (Hall, 1989). Probably the most promising learning mode is inductive learning: learning from examples. In this case, a system is able to generate its knowledge (represented as rules or as a decision tree) from a collection of training examples. One such learning system was able to infer (that is, conclude from the available evidence) a usable set of rules for granting loans (Shaw, 1988).

As we know, knowledge acquisition for larger expert systems is an expensive and time-consuming process which also presents difficulties, as we outlined earlier in this chapter. Benefits could be reaped if at least a part of knowledge acquisition could be automated by applying a learning system.

An entirely distinct AI perspective is built on the principle of learning systems—these are neural networks, which we will discuss in the next section.

15.10 NEURAL NETWORKS

The dominant symbolic approach to AI, based on logical reasoning and on the representation of knowledge with symbols, has recently been challenged by another approach known as the connectionist perspective, or neurocomputing. The AI researchers (and emerging practitioners) who work in this field are trying to imitate the behavior of the network of neuron cells in the human brain by constructing artificial neural networks.

A **neural network** is an array of interconnected processing elements, each of which can accept inputs, process them, and produce a single output. The output may be passed on through a connection to another processing element or produced to the environment of the net (see figure 15.9). The processing elements may be actual hardware components (for example, microprocessors), or their operation may be simulated by software. Over a hundred different neurocomputer designs have been built (Hecht-Nielsen, 1990), but few are available as commercial products. Most of neurocomputing today is done with software running on conventional computers. Note that while the human brain contains billions of neuron cells, neural networks with more than a thousand processing elements are rare today; the action of processing elements differs significantly from what we know about the work of neurons as well.

Actually, neural networks represent a return to the origins of AI. The original neural network was invented in 1957, under the name *perceptron,* by Frank Rosenblatt. After the "quiet years" from the mid-1960s to the mid-1980s, when the

FIGURE 15.9

A neural network.

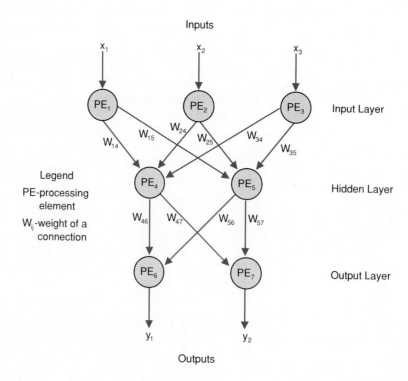

Inputs

x_1 x_2 x_3

PE$_1$ PE$_2$ PE$_3$ Input Layer

W_{14} W_{15} W_{24} W_{25} W_{34} W_{35}

Legend
PE-processing element
W_{ij}-weight of a connection

PE$_4$ PE$_5$ Hidden Layer

W_{46} W_{47} W_{56} W_{57}

PE$_6$ PE$_7$ Output Layer

y_1 y_2

Outputs

work in the field was largely stymied by a lack of funding, a resurgence of neu-rocomputing research has taken place. Immense interest in this approach has been fueled, among other reasons, by the advent of massively parallel computing (discussed in chapter 6), which promises a realistic hardware implementation of neural networks.

Our interest in neural networks is motivated by their capability for learning. The operation of a processing element depends on the number of inputs to it that are currently activated and on the weights of the inputs activated by other processing elements (see figure 15.9). Thus, knowledge is represented in a neural network by the pattern of connections among the processing elements and by the adjustable weights of these connections.

A network learns during a training process, during which it adjusts its weights in response to a collection of examples it is given. Each example contains the values of both the inputs and the outputs. In a classification task (say, the rating of loan applications), the encoded input describes the properties of sample cases (for example, income or home ownership) and the output is the specification of the category (for example, low-risk applicant). In other words, the network trains itself to recognize which attributes of applicants are most closely correlated with maintaining a good payment record and how strong that dependence is. The network strengthens, through greater weights, the appropriate connections, and weakens certain others. As soon as the network is able to perform sufficiently well on additional test cases, we can use it for new cases.

Note that the network performs its own "knowledge engineering"—as a matter of fact, there is no such thing as a knowledge base or symbolic processing here. Neural nets are an alternative to expert systems in some applications. Once the network has "learned" from data, its work will be based on the actually observable patterns, rather than on what an expert says is true through a knowledge engineer.

The strength of neural networks is in applications that require sophisticated pattern recognition. Ford Motor Company uses a neural net to spot faulty paint finish on a car and is training a net to recognize engine problems (O'Reilly, 1989). Siemens, a large West German maker of electrical equipment, checks blower motors with a neural net. Other neural networks have been trained to do quality control in a bottling plant, read handwritten zip codes (and they are working on learning signatures), and recognize a variety of patterns in financial data, such as credit-granting or stock-performance patterns.

Because of the way it works, a neural network does not furnish an explanation for its conclusions, which is a serious weakness in many potential applications. It is also a reason why neural networks may be profitably combined with expert systems (Trippi, 1989–90).

Among the more powerful microcomputer-based neural-network packages are Brainmaker from California Scientific Software (Grass Valley, California) and Neuroshell from Ward Systems Group (Frederick, Maryland).

TRAINING A NEURAL NETWORK IS A SKILL

Human care has to be exercised in supplying the factors a neural network must consider and in reviewing the conclusions it reaches. A prototype of one of these systems seemed to prefer granting credit to people with lower salaries as opposed to those with higher ones. In fact, the data on which the system was trained contained several examples of people with low salaries who happened to be excellent credit risks. The Robin-Hood system learned to associate low salary with good payment performance—ignoring many relevant factors.

In general, the technology is still in its infancy and its application to more complicated problems in organizational settings is considered premature.

Based on David Stipp, ''Computer Researchers Find 'Neural Networks' Help Mimic the Brain.'' *The Wall Street Journal*, September 29, 1988, pp. 1, 18; and Michael Alexander, ''An Inside View of Neural Technology.'' *Computerworld*, January 22, 1981, p. 17.

• •

SUMMARY

Artificial intelligence systems are designed to imitate human capabilities of cognition and perception. The field has broad promise and certain very tangible results in business applications. Practical systems work in narrow task domains. Of particular importance are expert systems: knowledge-based systems that offer recommendations to decision makers. Narrow task domains within several problem categories, such as classification, diagnosis, or monitoring, are the appropriate targets for the ES approach.

Expert systems work by applying a general inferencing (reasoning) procedure to a knowledge base specific to the task. By far the most common are rule-based systems, where the knowledge is represented as IF-THEN rules. Several levels of ES technology are available, with the tools for developing specific systems ranging from easy-to-use shells to flexible higher-level programming languages. Three principal roles in ES development are expert, knowledge engineer, and user. The process of development is generally iterative, based on continuing refinement of the initial ES prototype.

As any other, the ES technology has clear limitations that should be understood before undertaking a project.

Major areas of AI that are beginning to contribute to business information processing are natural language processing, robotics, computer vision, and computerized speech recognition. Imparting a learning ability to these systems is an active area of research.

Neurocomputing, an AI orientation that relies on artificial neural networks with learning capabilities, represents an important alternative approach to gaining for computers some of the pattern-recognition capabilities of the human brain. In certain applications, neural nets may replace expert systems; in others, they may complement them.

ENDNOTES

1. The so-called connectionist perspective on AI does not consider symbols as primitive objects of processing. Rather, it attempts to obtain artificial intelligence through a variety of hardware and software designs that resemble neuronal brain structures. We shall briefly describe neural nets, one direction this research has taken, in the last section of the chapter.

2. Kazuhiro Fuchi, "The Direction the FGCS Project Will Take." *New Generation Computing*, 1, 1, 1983, pp. 3–9.

3. This case was outlined in the *Proceedings of The Expert Systems Symposium* by Digital Consulting of Andover, Massachusetts, Fall 1988, with additional information provided during the symposium in October 1988 by Paul Harmon.

4. Production rules have a rich heritage in computer science. Introduced by Emil Post in 1936, they are a basis for a symbolic (purely conceptual) computation device, which is believed to be able to compute anything that can be computed by any computer (similar to the well-known, and also symbolic, Turing machine). Allen Newell and Herbert Simon (Newell, 1972) introduced the concept into the AI framework by using these rules to model human problem solving.

5. Dennis Yablonsky, "Domain Specific Shells—A Look at the Future of Expert Systems Technology." Presentation at the Expert Systems Symposium, Rye Brook, New York, October 1988.

KEY TERMS AND CONCEPTS

Artificial intelligence (AI)	Working memory (blackboard) of ES
Symbolic processing	Forward chaining
Knowledge-based approach to AI	Backward chaining
Expert system (ES)	ES shell
Heuristic knowledge	ES development environment
Knowledge engineering	Knowledge engineer
Knowledge representation	Natural language processing
Knowledge base	Robotics
Rule-based ES	Vision systems
Certainty factor	Speech recognition
Explanation facility	Machine learning
Inference engine	Neural networks

QUESTIONS

1. Define artificial intelligence.

2. State the reasons why businesses and other organizations should be interested in developments in AI. (Remember what you have learned about the role of new technologies!)

3. What are the two principal characteristics of AI systems?

4. Why was the shift to a knowledge-based approach in AI so important?

5. What is an expert system?

6. What is the contribution of heuristic knowledge to expert systems?

7. Consider the four application cases of expert systems presented in section 15.3. State in one sentence the importance of each system to its owner corporation.

8. Give one realistic example of an expert system for each of the generic categories of ES application listed in table 15.1.

9. What is knowledge engineering?

10. Why are rule-based ES the most common?

11. How does an inference engine relate to a knowledge base? Which of them is more general, and which is specific to a given ES?

12. Which ES applications tend to employ backward chaining, and which use forward chaining?

13. What tool is most commonly employed by end users to develop simple ES? What facilities does it offer?

14. What is the relationship between an expert and a knowledge engineer?

15. Why are ES generally developed by prototyping?

16. State five benefits an organization may derive from ES.

17. State three limitations of expert systems.

18. List five fields of AI, other than ES, that have significant potential for business application. Give an example of such an application for each of them.

19. What is the principal difference between conventional symbolic AI and neurocomputing with respect to knowledge representation?

20. State the comparative advantages and disadvantages of the expert-system and neural-network approaches to a problem (to which both are applicable).

ISSUES FOR DISCUSSION

1. In chapter 5, we discussed five competitive forces identified by Michael Porter. Expert systems are a frequently wielded competitive weapon. Give realistic examples of expert systems that could be used by a corporation to enact each of the five forces.

2. One may contend that ES will simply swallow DSS—expert systems will be developed to include all of the DSS functionality, plus their own reasoning capabilities. What are the indications that this will happen—or not happen?

3. Some contend that expert systems will replace people; others say that expert systems will "leverage" them. What do you think?

4. As a team project, define a problem-solving task in a domain familiar to you, and perform some knowledge engineering: using the techniques stated in the chapter, define twenty to thirty rules about the domain. If you have an ES shell, use its syntax for stating the rules, otherwise state them as shown in the chapter. Draw conclusions from your experience.

A Successful Start in Using Expert Systems

How do you move to a new technology, particularly one that may have inspired a degree of mistrust in your management because it was vastly oversold? And one that will, in addition, require busy end users to devote their time to cooperate with you virtually every step of the way? Here is how one Emerging Technologies team did it.

The New York Stock Exchange (NYSE), the largest exchange in the country, continually examines data provided by its approximately 700 member firms to determine their financial viability. This means that in order to protect investors, NYSE's financial analysts have to pore over immense volumes of data contained in the member corporation's balance sheets, profit-and-loss statements, and the like. These need to be tested against NYSE standards to ferret out problems or unfavorable trends.

A financial analyst's job is made even more difficult by the highly dynamic decision-making environment: the exchange's rules are often amended, the investment environment changes, new investment vehicles (such as stock indexes) are created.

Growing amounts of data to be stringently evaluated against an ever increasing and evolving set of rules threaten to overwhelm even the best financial analysts. It is not that these analysts have been poring over the data by hand; they have been accessing twenty-three different information systems to do the job. This environment cried for a solution—and when the Emerging Technolo-

gies group suggested that a mainframe-based expert system could provide it, the users were rather easy to convince.

Roles were established. Two financial analysts were selected to act as experts (and seen as potential champions in the future). A NYSE systems analyst and a consultant from an expert system "boutique" were to act as knowledge engineers—with the skills gradually being transferred into the company (the consultant was to act as in-house trainer as well).

The problem was framed as follows: The complete expert system would be expected to do a full risk assessment based on the member firms' reports and to make action recommendations. In other words, the complete ES would help establish whether a company's performance and activities conform to the rules of the stock exchange. Among the expected benefits of this future system would be the ability of the exchange to cope with increasing environmental complexity, perform a highly consistent evaluation of member firms, and ensure a faster learning curve for new analysts. The costs of developing a prototype and the future complete system (including drafting financial analysts to act as experts instead of doing their daily work), along with the projected increase in the hardware capacity needed to provide the required response time, balanced favorably against the benefits.

A carefully defined prototype was the way to begin. The complexity of the financial analyst's task in its entirety would surpass the capability of the team at hand, as well as the organizational commitment existing at the time. With a view to the future expansion of the prototype, a powerful ES development environment, ADS from Aion Corporation, was selected. ADS offers multiple ways to represent knowledge and multiple ways to inference—all to be needed some day to provide fuller support to the analyst.

The pilot project was defined. It was to cover a nontrivial subtask of a financial analyst's job, yet one that could be implemented in a prototype version in a few weeks—both to hold the users' interest and to sell the technology to management. The subtask selected for the pilot project was to identify and recommend a way to correct a problem of excessive concentration of securities. In other words, the prototype ES would establish whether a company's stock has been accumulated in certain hands. This would solve a significant problem for the users, and would not require more than six weeks of work.

Management gave their approval for the prototype. At least six three-hour sessions were held with the user experts as part of the knowledge engineering process. The process was based on an analysis of case histories. After each session,

new rules were entered into the prototype. Another form of knowledge acquisition was observation of user work by the developers.

The prototype consisted of over 100 rules. The dimensions of the complete system can be gauged by the fact that the prototype handled only three of several hundred possible problems with the report that exchange members furnish to NYSE.

The need to integrate the system with the mainframe databases has become obvious—and those databases were certainly not integrated themselves (DB2, IMS, and IDMS databases, plus VSAM and Ramis files!).

After six weeks the prototype was operational; it proved to be no "cycle hog," but ran with surprising efficiency. Now users displayed "enthusiasm at a fever pitch." They strongly advocated turning the prototype into a production system. When management came to a demonstration of the prototype, it was the users and not the developers who sold the system to them.

A funded plan for fielding the prototype and expanding its functionality has been drawn up.

Based on Jessica Keyes, "Building an Assistant. Case Study: NYSE Creates Expert System Prototype as Financial Analyst Aid." *Computerworld*, December 19, 1988, pp. 63–64.

Case Study Questions

1. What is the nature of a task selected for support by an expert system? What made the Emerging Technologies group (led by Jessica Keyes, the author of the article from which the case was drawn) to believe that ES is the technology of choice?

2. What were the goals of the overall future system?

3. Describe the projected costs and benefits of the ES.

4. What objectives were set for the prototype—both technical and organizational?

5. How were the roles defined and filled?

6. Describe what the Emerging Technologies group accomplished in the context of the ES development process shown in figure 15.6.

7. What other roles may expert systems play in regulating stock exchanges? (You may profit by consulting Freedman, 1991, before answering this question.)

SELECTED REFERENCES

Burke, Raymond; Rangaswamy, Arvind; Wind, Jerry; and Eliashberg, Jehoshua. "A Knowledge-Based System for Advertising Design." *Marketing Science,* 9, 3, Summer, 1990, pp. 212–29.

Charniak, Eugene, and McDermott, Drew. *Artificial Intelligence.* Reading, Mass.: Addison-Wesley, 1985.

Cook, Robert L., and Schleede, John M. "Application of Expert Systems to Advertising." *Journal of Advertising Research.* June/July 1988, pp. 47–56.

Dhar, Vasant, and Croker, Albert. "Knowledge-Based Decision Support in Business: Issues and a Solution." *IEEE Expert,* 3, 1, Spring 1988, pp. 53–63.

Feigenbaum, Edward; McCorduck, Pamela; and Nii, H. Penny. *The Rise of the Expert Company.* New York: Times Books, 1988.

Freedman, Roy S., "AI on Wall Street," *IEEE Expert,* 6, 2, April 1991, pp. 3–9.

Gallagher, John P. *Knowledge Systems for Business: Integrating Expert Systems and MIS.* Englewood Cliffs, N.J.: Prentice-Hall, 1988.

Gongla, Patricia, and others. "S*P*A*R*K: A Knowledge-Based System for Identifying Competitive Uses of Information Technology." *IBM Systems Journal,* 28, 4, 1989, pp. 628–45.

Hall, Rogers. "Computational Approaches to Analogical Reasoning." *Artificial Intelligence,* 39, 1, May 1989, pp. 39–120.

Hayes-Roth, Frederick. "The Knowledge-Based Expert System: A Tutorial." *Computer,* 17, 9, September 1984, pp. 11–28.

Hayes-Roth, Frederick; Waterman, Donald A.; and Lenat, Douglas B. *Building Expert Systems,* Reading, Mass.: Addison-Wesley, 1983.

Hecht-Nielsen, Robert. *Neurocomputing,* Reading, Mass.: Addison-Wesley, 1990.

Irgon, Adam, and others. "Expert System Development: A Retrospective View of Five Systems." *IEEE Expert,* 5, 3, June 1990, pp. 25–40.

Lenat, Douglas B., and others. "Cyc: Toward Programs with Common Sense." *Communications of the ACM,* 33, 8, August 1990, pp. 30–49.

Leonard-Barton, Dorothy, and Sviokla, John J. "Putting Expert Systems to Work." *Harvard Business Review,* March-April 1988, pp. 91–98f.

Loofbourrow, Tod H. *Expert Systems & AI Toolkits.* Marblehead, Mass.: The James Martin Productivity Series, 1988.

Luconi, Fred L.; Malone, Thomas W.; and Scott Morton, Michael S. "Expert Systems: The Next Challenge for Managers." *Sloan Management Review,* Summer 1986, pp. 3–14.

Mahnke, John. "Expert Systems Aid in Financial Risk Assessment." *MIS Week,* May 15, 1989, p. 24.

Martin, A., and Law, R. K. H. "Expert System for Selecting Expert System Shells." *Information and Software Technology,* 30, 10, December 1988, pp. 579–86.

Meyer, Marc H., and Curley, Kathleen F., "Putting Expert System Technology to Work," Sloan Management Review, 32, 2, Winter 1991, pp. 21–31.

Nash, Jim. "The Many Tongues of Computers." *Computerworld,* February 18, 1991, p. 20.

Newell, Allen, and Simon, Herbert A. *Human Problem Solving.* Englewood Cliffs, N.J.: Prentice-Hall, 1972.

O'Reilly, Brian. "Computers that Think Like People." *Fortune,* February 22, 1989, pp. 90–93.

Prerau, David S., and others. "Maintainability Techniques in Developing Large Expert Systems." *IEEE Expert,* 5, 3, June 1990, pp. 71–80.

Rich, Elaine, and Knight, Kevin. *Artificial Intelligence.* 2d ed. New York: McGraw-Hill, 1991.

Shaw, Michael, J., and Gentry, John. "Using an Expert System with Inductive Learning to Evaluate Business Loans." *Financial Management,* 17, 3, 1988, pp. 45–56.

Simon, Herbert A. "Why Should Machines Learn?" In *Machine Learning: An Artificial Intelligence Approach,* edited by Ryszard S. Michalski, Jaime G. Carbonell, and Tom M. Mitchell. Palo Alto, Calif.: Tioga Press, 1983.

Sviokla, John J. "Business Applications of Knowledge-Based Systems." Parts I & II. *Data Base,* 17, 4, Summer 1986, pp. 5–19; and 18, 1, Fall 1986, pp. 1–16.

Trippi, Robert, and Turban, Efraim. "The Impact of Parallel and Neural Computing on Managerial Decision Making." *Journal of Management Information Systems,* 6, 3, Winter 1989–90, pp. 85–98.

Turban, Efraim. *Decision Support and Expert Systems: Management Support Systems.* 2d ed. New York: Macmillan, 1990.

Turban, Efraim, and Watkins, Paul R. "Integrating Expert Systems and Decision Support Systems." *MIS Quarterly,* 10, 2, June 1986, pp. 121–36.

White, George M. "Natural Language Understanding and Speech Recognition." *Communications of the ACM,* 33, 8, August 1990, pp. 72–82.

Young, Sheryl R., and others. "High-Level Knowledge Sources in Usable Speech Recognition Systems." *Communications of the ACM,* 32, 2, February 1989, pp. 183–94.

Zwass, Vladimir. "Computer Science." *Encyclopaedia Britannica.* Macropaedia, Vol. XVI, 1988, pp. 629–37.

OFFICE INFORMATION SYSTEMS

Information technology offers new means for organizing office work. Automate only after you simplify.
Paul Strassman

Make a copy of everything before you throw it out.
Sam Goldwyn to his secretary, on realizing that his document files were crowding him out of his office.

Our analysis of the information society in chapter 2 showed that most jobs today may be either defined wholly as knowledge work or classified as having knowledge work as a component. The office is the primary setting for knowledge work. In industrialized countries, more people work in offices than on farms or on factory floors or in the direct delivery of services. Yet, while industrial and agricultural productivity increased by many times during this century, office productivity improved far less. Organizational change based on the use of office information systems (OIS) aims at increasing the productivity of knowledge work by providing this work with appropriate technological support.

We discussed informational support of *individual* knowledge work in chapter 9. Our model of support there was a personal workstation and productivity tools. OIS go beyond support of an individual to provide means of communication among users, which then become means of organizational coordination and integration. Our model of informational support is thus a network of workstations.

Until not very long ago, "office information systems" amounted to a telephone for one-to-one communication or a face-to-face meeting for a more general personal communication, with memos and other documents (preserved in file cabinets) serving the need for written internal and external communication. Modern OIS are the component of MIS that provides tools for communication and collaboration among knowledge workers by ensuring efficient management of documents and messages and by providing a variety of support means for electronic meetings.

OIS give us a way to control the flow of documents and support efficient access to them. Thus, electronic document management allows the user to efficiently enter, store, and retrieve documents. We shall discuss updating and electronic publishing of documents as well. Hypertext and hypermedia—a novel electronic document format—will also be presented.

We shall consider a range of possibilities in message handling and in conferencing that have emerged with the new technologies. We shall also examine the emerging groupware technology designed to support group work—recognized today as a crucial aspect of organizational effectiveness.

A decade or more ago, when Paul E. Lego, president of Westinghouse Electric, wanted to contact one of the managers in the firm's Tokyo office, he would dictate a letter to his secretary, who would take it to the telex center. There it would be retyped and telexed, taking as long as eight hours to arrive in Tokyo. Of course, Lego could have called instead: but by calling at 4:00 P.M., he would get the Tokyo manager out of bed at 5:00 A.M. local time.

Times have certainly changed. Now, Lego sends an electronic mail message to Tokyo from his PC before leaving the office and finds a response waiting for him the next morning. Globalization of business would hardly be a reality today without the changes reflected in this new mode of communication.

On a typical summer weekend, Lego gets some five hours of work done on his PC at home. A flurry of electronic mail goes from this PC to corporate managers, some of them located as far away as Australia. On the same E-mail system, Lego reads a progress report on negotiations concerning a new union contract and responds with bargaining suggestions. During his thirty-minute drive to work on Monday, Lego and the company's CEO plan the day's work; however, they do not ride together—both use cellular phones in their cars. Among the E-mail messages on his office PC, Lego finds information he requested the previous day. Now the work week begins.

Teleconferencing has significantly reduced the need to travel to meetings: now Lego may attend only those where his physical presence is actually required. But when he does go to a meeting, he does not need to leave his office, in a sense—he extends it to wherever he is. At a meeting recently in Hawaii with the company's Japanese licensing partners, Lego often used his laptop computer to stay in touch with Westinghouse's Pittsburgh headquarters.

Westinghouse is a recognized leader in white-collar productivity, with a 6 percent annual increase since the early eighties, when office information systems became available in the form we know them today. The centerpiece of Westinghouse's OIS is the PC-based E-mail network, connecting some 10,700 employees and 1,000 customers. E-mail costs approximately 90 percent less than overseas calls and overnight mail. "People are amazed at how quickly we can move information around," says a corporate vice-president. "It gives us a competitive edge."

Based on Gregory L. Miles, "At Westinghouse E-Mail Makes the World Go 'Round." *Business Week,* October 10, 1988, p. 110.

Office information systems now play a crucial role in business communications. They allow flexibility in working arrangements, in the organization of business functions, and in the way tasks are accomplished. And yes, they do bring the office home, into the car, or onto the boat—which some people like, and others may have to learn to like.

CHAPTER OUTLINE

16.1   What Are Office Information Systems?
   • Supporting Knowledge Work in the Office
   • The Functions of OIS

16.2   Document Management
   • Limiting and Controlling the Flow of Paper
   • Micrographics
   • Electronic Document Management
   • Hypertext and Hypermedia—Electronic Documents of the Future

16.3   Message Handling
   • Electronic Mail and Its Effects on Work in Organizations
   • Electronic Mail in Communication with the External Environment
   • Voice Mail
   • Facsimile

16.4   Teleconferencing and Computer Conferencing
   • Audio and Video Teleconferencing
   • Computer Conferencing

16.5   Workgroup Support and Groupware
   • The Organizational Role of Workgroups
   • Groupware and Its Functions

16.1 WHAT ARE OFFICE INFORMATION SYSTEMS?

Office information systems (OIS) support office tasks with information technology. The primary goal of these systems, which are sometimes rather threateningly called "office automation," is to increase the productivity of office work. As we noted while reviewing the objectives of this chapter, the productivity of industrial workers has been leveraged manyfold by industrial and information-age machinery, while until recently, office work has been very scantily supported by equipment.

Supporting Knowledge Work in the Office

An *office* is an environment where the management and administration of an organization take place, but it is also an arena of social action where people play out work roles, make decisions, and exchange information (Hirschheim, 1986). We know this work in the office as knowledge work. Managers, other professionals (financial analysts, engineers, or salespeople), and clerical and secretarial personnel work in an office setting. The nature of the work these categories of personnel perform varies, of course; a distinction is sometimes drawn between more creative knowledge work and clerical information work—however difficult it is to draw a line between the two. As we shall see, all these work roles are affected by OIS.

The decision-making aspects of knowledge work are supported by management reporting and decision support systems (MRS and DSS). Executive information systems (EIS) primarily facilitate executive control. Transaction processing systems (TPS) handle routine business transactions, mostly customer-driven (such as processing an order), but also internal (such as hiring a new employee). What is left to OIS? Indeed, the contours of office work have proven to be rather elusive, and OIS are only now being molded into better defined systems. It is not that we are trying to isolate OIS: remember that, rather than erecting barriers to

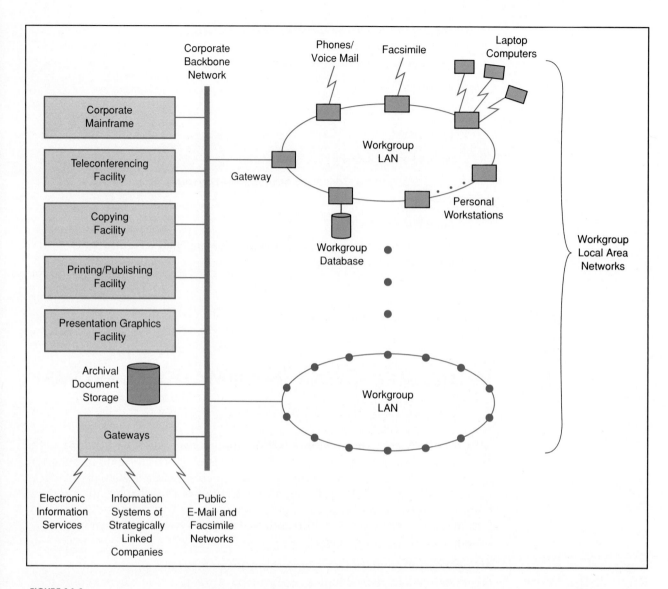

FIGURE 16.1

An integrated "office of the future."

separate various MIS components, we want them to interact seamlessly. Here, our goal is to understand how OIS can best function in such a federation of information systems.

The primary purpose of OIS is to facilitate communication between members of an organization and between the organization and its environment. An ideal (and expensive) system would allow people to communicate in the medium of their choice—data, document, image, voice (audio), or video. This ideal OIS would support the creation, storage, and transfer of such messages. Access to the system would be available anywhere in the organization. It also has become increasingly apparent that an ideal OIS should support team collaboration in working on a project. What we are talking about is known as the "office of the future." As with any futuristic concept, the contours keep evolving, but we can review the functions and facilities we see as desirable at this time. Figure 16.1 shows the connectivity and the facilities we want in an OIS at present.

This conceptual view of the "office of the future" is built around local area networks—the frequent technology of choice in today's environment. The necessary connectivity could also be provided by a hierarchical network of mainframes, minicomputers, and personal workstations, or by a private automated branch exchange (PABX), which is a computer acting as a powerful switch.

You will note that the principal OIS node is a workgroup LAN, which permits coordinated teamwork. We shall discuss informational support of group work further on. Workgroup members communicate within their local area network, as well as with other workgroups and, as needed, with the firm's environment. Communication between workgroups takes place along a high-speed "digital highway"—a backbone network. Through the gateways, the workgroup can also access the corporate mainframe (and, if needed, a divisional minicomputer), a number of facilities for office work, as well as the outside world. The diagram in the figure is meant as a conceptual blueprint; for example, certain facilities may be duplicated and connected to the local area networks of individual groups rather than to the highway—this is a matter of cost-effectiveness within each organization.

All of these facilities of the "office of the future" are available today. The problem is lack of connectivity. Because universal standards are lacking, the equipment and software made by different manufacturers and covering various aspects of office functionality are incompatible. Providing connections is often too costly because the connections require expensive conversions of information flows. Crucial functionality gaps also exist: for example, copying machines are generally made as stand-alone equipment. It is still virtually impossible to send a file from your personal workstation to a copying machine, or to create a voice message and send it to a client via a facsimile—but prototype systems for both functions are being tested.

The Functions of OIS

The present functionality of OIS is summarized in figure 16.2. This is the functionality we shall describe in this chapter.

OIS leverage personal computing; they do not replace it. As we discussed in chapter 9, end-user facilities, consisting primarily of word processing, spreadsheet programs, database access, and personal information management, are vehicles for personal knowledge work. OIS help organize work in the office by providing a smooth flow of documents and messages, assisting group work through support for meetings of various kinds, and enabling cooperative work on a project. In 1988, 15 percent of the 40.1 million personal computers in U.S. businesses were linked together; it was estimated that 47 percent of the 60.1 million PCs in use by 1992 would be networked (Brandt, 1989).

To understand OIS functions, it is a good idea to look at their heritage. Table 16.1 shows these functions and the artifacts each of them either replaces or augments. Storing documents on optical disks definitely rids us of file cabinets, but teleconferencing is a substitute for only some meetings—it augments rather than replaces this customary mode of multiperson communication.

Until the mid-1960s, the office equipment landscape consisted of telephones, typewriters, copiers, and calculators, not to mention file cabinets. Computers entered office automation with word processing in 1964. But it was in the 1980s that the personal computer changed the office landscape forever. A broad array

FIGURE 16.2

Office information systems today.

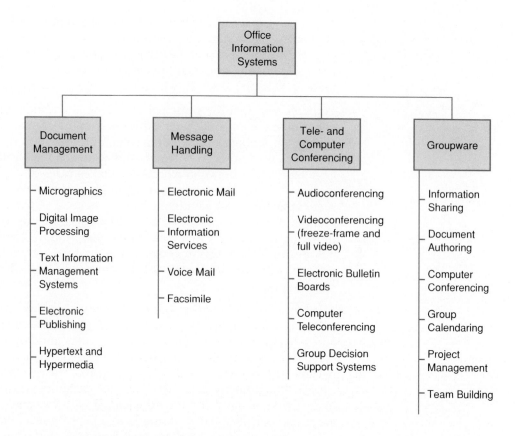

of noncomputer devices remains, of course, as part of this landscape: copiers, facsimile machines, dictation equipment, simpler forms of micrographics and, not to be forgotten, telephones and typewriters. But many of these now have microprocessors.

An exciting current development is the gradual emergence of general facilities for supporting group work. These facilities will include both the support of task-oriented meetings (such as the support offered by GDSS) and the support of group collaboration over a longer period of time (offered by groupware).

MIS designers and researchers are now undertaking a general study of **electronic meeting systems,** which are broadly defined as an "information-technology-based environment that supports group meetings, which may be distributed geographically and temporally" (Dennis, 1988). This study is expected to integrate and generalize our knowledge about support of group decision making and communication and to result in innovative organizational systems. The effectiveness of various systems depends on such factors as the facilities, the nature of the groups using them, the activities for which they are used (for example, brainstorming or negotiation), and the processes through which they are used (for example, does the group have a leader?). The variety of software tools included in the systems may address such tasks as idea generation, organizing and prioritizing of alternative ideas, or policy development and evaluation (Nunamaker, 1991). The presently available experience with various systems is partial and will be better understood in the overall framework of electronic

A TALENT AGENCY OFFICE REMADE BY INFORMATION SHARING AND EXCHANGE

The oldest and one of the largest talent brokers in the world, the William Morris Agency, headquartered (as you have guessed) in Beverly Hills, California, represents many of the leading lights of the entertainment world. "The nature of the talent business is information," says one of the agents, "that's what gives one agency the competitive edge over another; it's who has the information and who's able to disseminate it effectively to the agents."

Deals are made because agents are able to obtain on demand information on a performer's availability, credits (performance history), compensation record, and ongoing commitments—across the firm's offices in the United States and around the globe. While telephones are still the tool of record in these offices, searches of filing cabinets are a thing of the past. The agency has installed over 250 networked NeXT computers for its U.S. offices, and the agents share information using a customized version of the client-management software, Who's Calling? (from Adamation of Oakland, California).

The system is built around a client database, which may contain voice records and images along with text and numbers. The software tracks telephone calls and meetings, has an elaborate calendar function, and provides voice ticklers that remind users of scheduled events, as well as a message center for textual and voice messages, and other features for specialized office needs of the firm. Graphical user interface renders many tasks simple: you may overlay the calendars of several people to determine the next open window for a meeting, for example. NeXT's electronic mail includes a multimedia capability: voice and images can be sent now, and motion video is already available in prototype versions.

Agents see the ability to exchange critical information instantly via E-mail, combined with the sharing of stored up-to-the-minute client information, as vital changes in the contracting environment which translate into vastly improved interaction with clients—and a better ability to close a deal.

Based on Karen Balch, "Profile: The Star System." *NeXTWORLD,* March/April 1991, pp. 35–37.

TABLE 16.1	OIS FUNCTION	WHAT IT AUGMENTS/REPLACES
Augmentation or Replacement of Traditional Office Functions and Equipment by OIS	Document Management	Typewriter/Word processor File cabinet Manual typesetting/Commercial printing
	Message Handling	POTS ("plain old telephone service") Memos
	Tele- and Computer Conferencing	Travel and physical presence at meetings
	Groupware	"Sneakernet" (collaboration by exchanging diskettes) Manual scheduling and tracking of projects

meeting systems. Most studies of meetings supported by such facilities report enhanced effectiveness and efficiency as compared to meetings unsupported by the technology (Dennis, 1990–91). These studies also indicate high levels of user satisfaction.

16.2 DOCUMENT MANAGEMENT

When an office worker refers to "information," it is as likely as not that he or she has in mind a document—an insurance policy, a check, or a waybill. This is, as we know, not the way an MIS professional defines information. As Peter Keen points out (Keen, 1988), neglect of document processing is the reason why information systems have disappointed many firms. OIS must limit the flow of paper documentation within a firm, facilitate prompt access to stored document images, and make it possible to produce documents in a streamlined fashion.

Limiting and Controlling the Flow of Paper

What is a document? It may be, depending on the nature of a business, a customer's order on a paper form, a policyholder's claim against an insurance company, or a three-inch-thick user manual that accompanies a firm's equipment. Do all of these documents have to be kept on paper? In other words, is paper the necessary medium for a document, with the attendant file cabinets and "slow fires" of destruction caused by the acids contained in the paper? Most of us know the answer is no, but many of us also mistakenly believe that office automation implies a paperless office. Paper documents are not about to disappear—they are a fine presentation medium; but paper is not an appropriate medium for long-term document storage or for much office communication. Electronic data interchange (EDI) has already replaced some document flows between organizations. We shall see later on in this chapter how electronic messages have replaced many memos that used to flow within an office. Here, we want to see how to deal with the documents that remain necessary.

The document-processing functions of OIS include creation, storage, and retrieval of documents. Certain documents (such as policy manuals, for example) must also be updated as needed. Indeed, all documents are not created equal. A copy or an image of a policyholder's application has to be available, signatures and all, to the company's reviewers. Legal and regulatory requirements necessitate preservation of such documents or their images. A piece of equipment manufactured by a firm is usually accompanied by the manufacturer's documentation—but the latter is also maintained as a text file that will be updated in the future. As you may conclude from the vignette on fighting against paper at the Pentagon, paper documentation is starting to give way.

The document management function of OIS makes it possible to move documents away from paper as their primary medium: the storage, retrieval, and updating of paper information is slow and expensive and becoming unmanageable in some environments as their complexity grows (see color plates 18a and 18b). The notion of a "paperless office" has now been recognized for the myth that it has always been, particularly in communications with a firm's environment.

THE PENTAGON IS MOVING AGAINST PAPER

A 9,600-ton Navy cruiser of Ticonderoga class carries twenty-six tons of manuals on how to maintain and operate its weapons systems. If this does not exactly sink the ship, it certainly raises doubts about the possibilities of retrieving what is needed when it is needed. Working back from this volume of documentation, we can imagine what it cost the Department of Defense to approve the procurement of the cruiser in reviewing the mountains of paper generated by contractor firms during the life cycle of its development.

Now the Pentagon has mounted a $1-billion program called Computer-Aided Acquisitions and Logistics Support: all new weapons proposals, including engineering drawings, will be submitted by potential contractors in a computer-readable form. Initially, the medium will be magnetic disks and tapes, to be ultimately replaced by direct computer-to-computer transmission of documentation. Also, the Pentagon will have access to appropriate contractor databases. The Pentagon's paper files are to be converted to digital form as well. This conversion is expected to save 20 percent of the $5 billion spent annually at the Defense Department on processing technical information. (The agencies that make up the U.S. Department of Defense spend $9.6 billion a year on information technology in general—more than the three largest corporate spenders combined.)

It is widely believed that the Pentagon was prompted to move against paper by its contractors. Northrop Corporation is a good example. Its fuselage for the Hornet fighter jet is the first major aerospace product to be assembled without a paper trail—since the fall of 1988. Before conversion to the new system, workers studied instruction sheets to determine each assembly step. A ten-foot pile of documentation was necessary. Now, 1,000 assemblers, supervisors, and quality assurance personnel use 135 VDT's right on the assembly line, all linked to a fault-tolerant Tandem minicomputer system. The entire documentation is stored on thirty-six microfiche cards. Engineering changes which used to take two hours take thirty seconds. The $10 million computerization program is expected to save $20 million—and will be ported to other projects, such as the Stealth bomber program.

Based on Paul N. Pechersky, "Easing Paper Flow Could Help Slash DoD Budget," *Computerworld*, August 14, 1989, pp. 67–72; Charles Pelton, "Northrop Rolls Out Paperless Plane," *Information Week*, February 20, 1989, p. 21; Frances Seghers, "A Search-and-Destroy Mission against Paper," *Business Week*, February 6, 1989, pp. 91–95; and Jerome D. Colonna, "$18,264.84 a Minute," *InformationWeek*, March 11, 1991, p. 7.

However, the elimination of paper from many internal corporate functions means the elimination of many unreasonable and unnecessary time delays (Fisher, 1989).

Document management relies on several major technologies. Relatively inexpensive micrographic technology, over sixty years old and based on a microform storage, coexists with the new technology of digital image processing, based primarily on optical disks as the storage medium.

Micrographics

Micrographics have much to offer a smaller organization, but they are used by large firms as well. Micrographics transfer a reduced document image onto a microfilm. The use of micrographic technology is illustrated in figure 16.3 (though variations exist, of course).

FIGURE 16.3

Micrographic document
processing.

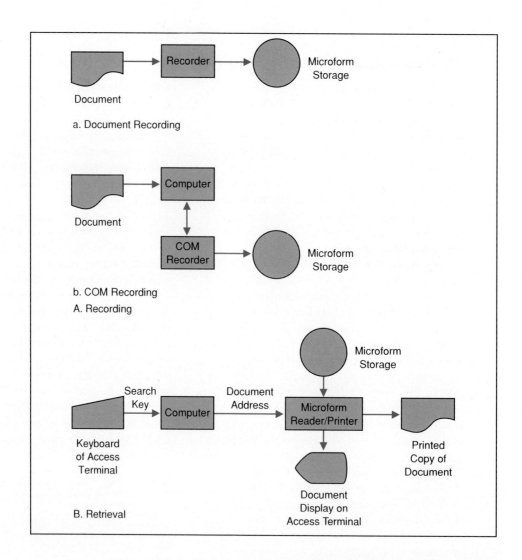

A document is copied by recorder equipment (figure 16.3a) in a vastly reduced version onto a microform, which is usually either a roll of microfilm, a microfilm cartridge, or a flat microfiche. Computer-output microfilm technology (COM) provides an alternative to computer printout on paper: a microform is produced instead. A COM recorder produces a microform directly on line under computer control (as shown in figure 16.3b) or off line from a disk or tape.

In simpler systems, a stand-alone reader device, essentially a projector with a built-in screen, may retrieve information. A printed copy may also be obtained if a reader/printer is employed. More sophisticated devices offer on-line access to documents with computer-assisted retrieval software, which maintains indexes (see figure 16.3B). The operator keys in the indexing information that is needed for access. An insurance company may use a policy number as the primary access key, but also maintain the name, address, and opening day of the policy as secondary identifiers. The primary key, which uniquely identifies the document, will bring it up on the terminal screen; a secondary key will bring up the list of matching documents.

TABLE 16.2

Elements of Electronic
Document Management

AWAY FROM PAPER	PAPERLESS			ONTO PAPER
ENTRY (INPUT)	STORAGE	RETRIEVAL	UPDATING	PRINTING/ PUBLISHING
Scanner OCR equipment Fax machine	Optical disks Magnetic disks	Computer-assisted retrieval via indexing High-resolution monitor or large-screen workstation for image viewing	Requires rewritable storage	Laser printer Color printer

Available options of micrographic technology permit the archiving of documents on a very compact microform at a low cost.

Electronic Document Management

Some documents are stored as images whose content will not be changed; others can be stored as text files that may be updated as needed. Thus, electronic document management relies on **digital image processing** technology, which stores the document image in an archival computer memory, or on managing text documents in a rewritable secondary memory.

Digital image processing, as opposed to micrographics, is more suitable for high-volume, high-speed applications. A bank may store account information on microfilmed signature cards for teller access, but if all checks are to be kept in electronic form, they will be subject to digital processing and stored on an optical disk.

The elements of electronic document management and the supporting equipment are shown in table 16.2. Note that many applications involve only the entry-storage-retrieval components of this process. An example of a system that supports this processing cycle for document images is IBM's ImagePlus (Kingman, 1990).

The use of an electronic document management system is illustrated in photo 16.1. We shall now discuss the elements of electronic document management.

1. Input

Digital image technology employs *scanners* to enter digitized images of documents, artwork, maps, and so forth into the computer—the image is preserved and may even be enhanced. The document—check or credit card receipt—is stored as an image and may be accessed within seconds. It may also be reproduced in reduced form if desired. To lower memory requirements, images are stored in a highly compressed format (a ratio of 1:15 between the respective storage requirements of compressed and original images is typical).

Optical character recognition (OCR) equipment, on the other hand, is employed as an alternative to manual entry of text or data. With OCR equipment, letters, numbers, or bar codes are converted into their equivalent representations in a computer character code (usually ASCII)

and stored as database records or records in a text management system. Most OCR units (such as CompuScan or Dest) are capable of reading in only computer-printed or typewritten text; high-end devices (such as Kurzweil Computer Products peripherals) can also read in typeset (printed) text in a variety of typefaces.

2. Storage

Documents are stored in a computer-managed archiving system. The dominant storage technology of digital image processing is optical disks, in particular, write-one-read-many-times (WORM) optical disk cartridges, which are frequently combined into high-capacity multicartridge jukeboxes. Optical disks of the WORM type, as we discussed in section 6.3, permit the user to store and retrieve but not to update a document. However, it is precisely the availability of optical disks, with their very high capacity at a reasonable cost, that has made digital image processing feasible.

Documents processed as text rather than image because they will be updated later are stored on magnetic disks or other magnetic media, which permits the current contents to be overwritten. Rewritable optical storage is only now becoming available.

Storage and retrieval of document images as opposed to textual documents are contrasted in figure 16.4.

3. Retrieval

The main advantage of computerized document management systems is that they are indexed, so that a user can retrieve a given document within seconds by employing a variety of attributes—for example, the account number or customer name, or even a topic under which the document has been filed. When a client calls an account officer at the U.S. Trust, the officer can access the original documents, memos, and even voice files regarding the bank account at a moment's notice. They are stored in a 150-gigabyte optical disk jukebox. Indeed, some document management systems permit not only storage of text, graphics, and signatures, but also of

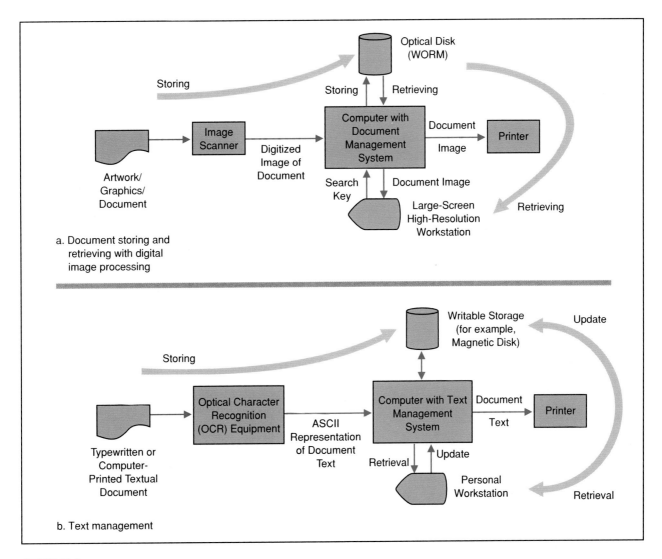

FIGURE 16.4

Document archiving and text management systems.

phone conversations or dictated memos. Such multimedia documents are an emerging trend. Systems that allow access to them with spoken commands are emerging as well (Rifkin, 1991).

Before being displayed, the compressed document image is decompressed. Large-screen workstations permit the viewing of several documents side by side. The capability for fast and accurate retrieval is a principal advantage of electronic document management, as illustrated by the next vignette.

By integrating digital image processing with the optical character recognition and expert system technologies, new retrieval capabilities may be created. Sun Microsystems relies on such an integrated system for processing of the 400 to 500 resumes the company receives daily. Both the scanned-in text and the image of the resume are stored. An expert system, containing a knowledge base of resume structures and job descriptions, assembles an abstract of the resume from the text and files it in the

COMMERCIAL LITIGATION RELIES ON A DOCUMENT RETRIEVAL SYSTEM

Members of the legal department of a leading accounting firm, Arthur Young and Company, store the immense paper flow generated by their litigation with a document management system. They employ Apple Corporation's Macintosh microcomputers with WORM optical disks and the Multi-user Archival and Retrieval System (MARS) from Micro Dynamics (of Silver Springs, Maryland).

Commercial litigation can easily run to some 500,000 pages of depositions and other documents, and a more complex trial may generate millions of pages. How do you locate a reference? Would you like to look at a specific page? The indexing capability of the document management system permits the lawyers to retrieve any document (text, graphic, or image) merely by stating a date or a keyword. Information from the opposing parties may be coded for identification and scanned (for handwritten notes and documents that must be preserved as images) or entered as text with OCR equipment.

Even more important is the benefit of being able to apply the system where the rubber meets the road. The microcomputer-based system can be brought into court, where any needed document can be instantly found and projected for all to see and may even be enlarged if needed.

Buoyed by its success, Arthur Young's legal department plans to transfer its entire filing system to the archiving system.

Based on Bart Eisenberg, "Legal Research Streamlined." *Information Center*, August 1989, p. 14.

database, ready for access by any characteristics specified by applicants. The original document's image is available for retrieval as well when a detailed study is desired (Konstadt, 1991).

4. Updating

Transaction documents and other items stored as images are not updated. We can simply add another item to a customer's "electronic file." Indeed, the entire area of document processing has traditionally concentrated on simply archiving the information in accessible form. This application still dominates.

But what if you want to enter text material with OCR equipment or simply by keyboarding, index it, and then modify it? For example, engineering documentation must not only be retrieved, but continually updated as well. Moreover, it is desirable to create a trail of such updates. Of course, you must use a rewritable form of storage. Since the content of a text document can be "understood" by software—as opposed to an image, which cannot—you can perform content-dependent queries and updates. Text information management systems are an equivalent of DBMS in the realm of words as opposed to numbers. Inquire/Text from Infodata Systems (of Falls Church, Virginia) and Stairs from IBM are some of the systems that support keyword access to and editing of text documents. Edited material is ready for printing or publishing.

PHOTO 16.2

A microcomputer-based image workstation enables its users to create, store, retrieve, edit, and print images and text for office publishing needs. Images can be captured with a scanner or created with a graphics package and then combined with text, edited, and electronically mailed to other users over the network. (You see here ONEimage Image Workstation from Bull NH Information Systems of Waltham, Massachusetts).

5. Printing and Publishing

Paradoxically, we have appended the printing/publishing capability to document management systems. This contradicts the "paperless office" notion. Remember, office automation does not imply a paperless office—it is the provision of appropriate technology for various office tasks.

Desktop publishing enables individual users to employ their personal computers for all stages of preparing a published document, as we discussed in chapter 9. Specialized workstations are also available for the purpose (as shown in photo 16.2).

Corporate electronic publishing, which is generally functionally separate from the MIS function, is growing rapidly. It is based on a mainframe or a minicomputer, since large volumes of text require the management of extensive storage. In the perception of some executives, "If you and I submit similar bids, but mine looks professionally published and yours does not—I have an advantage." Departments of a typical corporation may use electronic publishing for a variety of projects. The marketing department may produce sales brochures, the engineering department users manuals, and the finance department quarterly reports. For example at the GTE Corporation, corporate electronic publishing produces 8,000 different forms, as well as display ads, public relations material, and so on (Stevens, 1989). The latest version of a document can be printed on demand—there is no need to order and warehouse large runs from a commercial printer.

Having recognized the importance of corporate publishing, Xerox Corporation introduced in 1990 its Docutech Production Publisher. This versatile machine can change business processes related to producing bid proposals, advertising brochures, contracts, and similar documents. It integrates copying with document processing by creating an electronic image of a document to be printed (rather than a photographic image, as traditional copiers produce). This enables the Docutech "publishing machine" to manipulate the image (for example, by changing typefaces or combining several documents) and to communicate with other computers

PHOTO 16.3

DocuTech Production
Publisher from Xerox
Corporation—a vast
corporate publishing engine,
which may be used as a
server in a network.

Hypertext and Hypermedia— Electronic Documents of the Future

by sending or receiving such images (the machine is, of course, built around a powerful computer). The machine is shown in photo 16.3.

Electronic form processing, a specialized document processing function, is illustrated in the vignette on the Unum Insurance Corporation. These systems are employed primarily to automatically capture the data from forms and transfer these data into a database (Casey, 1990).

A novel form of electronic document has attracted attention. Called **hypertext,** this approach to information management stores "chunks" of information in nodes (frames) connected by meaningful links. A node may contain a unit of textual knowledge; in a broader implementation of this concept, called **hypermedia,** a node may also contain graphics, an audio message, a video image, or an executable spreadsheet. A document is built by creating nodes with information chunks and linking them to other related chunks. A user reads—or actually, navigates—the document by selecting links of interest to him or her.

Let us say I am writing a book (or a company's procedures manual). I start with a node containing a brief statement of purpose and titles of the book's parts. Each part title will be linked to the chapter outline for that part, which in turn will be linked to the chapters themselves. A hierarchy of linked nodes will result. My nodes may also contain notes to myself (for example, at some point I might insert a note saying that "a figure or drawing would help here"). Most important, I could provide links to related information. For example, in the paragraph preceding this one, I could insert a link to a discussion of spreadsheets. If you read a hypertext document, which you would generally do with a mouse, you could click the mouse to call up on the screen the node containing information about spreadsheet programs. For each node, the screen would display the "from" link

FORM PROCESSING IN AN INSURANCE COMPANY

Unum Corporation of Portland, Maine, uses information systems to innovate in both state-of-the-art marketing and the more traditional area of form processing. The insurer's databases, containing information on some 2.5 million employees in 25,000 companies, are used to segment its potential customers into homogeneous groups for which it can write highly competitive long-term disability insurance. Accurate segmentation of the customer base makes precise risk management possible. To enter the data into these databases in a cost-effective way, Unum employs electronic form processing.

As any insurance company does, Unum keeps at least five copies of every form. To manage this avalanche of forms, the firm employs the form processing software FormLink, by Access Development Corporation of Auburndale, Massachusetts. Thousands of forms come in daily from remote offices, and the data are scanned into databases. The software also helps clerks fill out forms. The system scans a form and reproduces its image on the screen. As it is filled by a clerk, each field is automatically range-checked for data validity. Forms can also be transferred to the field to be printed out on laptops—and signed by the customers.

Based on Jason Forsythe, "Unum: Divide and Conquer." *InformationWeek*, August 21, 1989, pp. 30–32.

pointing to the node you just read, and "to" links, which would lead you to related nodes, one of which you might select to read next.

Figure 16.5 presents a screen display showing node X, which has been selected from the hypertext database (whose structure is also illustrated). The node contains links to two other nodes. In a windowing environment, each window may display one node (or a part of it). A hypertext database may contain a single document, such as an extensive user's manual, with all cross-referencing done by links. On the other hand, such a database may contain the organized knowledge of an individual or a workgroup—which was Vannevar Bush's original idea of a "memex"—an "intimate supplement" to the individual's memory.[1]

An example of a hypertext screen with links to other general text passages, biographical sketches of people, and citations, is shown in figure 16.6.

When you read an electronic document, you no longer have to read a linear, booklike text. Instead, you may pursue issues of interest to you through the links—you impose your own structure on the document. This is rather similar to the way you would use an encyclopedia. The flexibility and power of hypertext, and even more so of hypermedia, are immense; the technologies, as well as the capabilities for knowledge work they offer, are the subject of intense research (summarized in Conklin, 1987; Smith, 1988; and Hall, 1990). Educational applications have led the way. Among examples of management and operational applications for hypertext are the on-line policy and maintenance manuals and the interactive task management system (for analyzing and tracking complex tasks) installed on the U.S. Navy aircraft carrier *Carl Vinson* (Akscyn, 1988). A notable hypermedia system called NoteCards has been developed recently at the Xerox Palo Alto Research Center.

FIGURE 16.5

Display of a node from a
hypertext database.

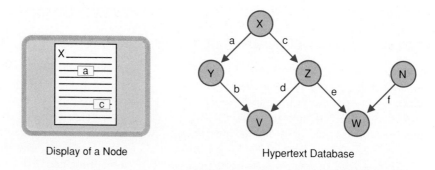

Display of a Node   Hypertext Database

FIGURE 16.6

Screen with a hypertext
document (From Lai, 1988).

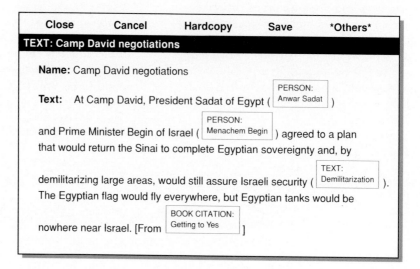

16.3 MESSAGE HANDLING

Electronic mail has brought with it immense capabilities for organizational communications. By uncoupling both the sender and the recipient of a message in time as well as in space, it offers a cost-effective medium for global communication as well as a convenient way for a telecommuter to "plug in." It also gives executives a powerful means of control.

Other messaging technologies have also become available. Thus, electronic mail enables you to communicate from your personal workstation by means of textual messages; through voice mail, you can send or receive voice messages by telephone, while a facsimile machine lets you send a handwritten message or document.

Electronic Mail and Its Effects on Work in Organizations

Electronic mail, or **E-mail,** enables knowledge workers to exchange messages over their personal workstations. A user is assigned an electronic mailbox, and the computer communication system becomes a network for sending, storing, and receiving messages. A message is frequently a memo, but it can also be a

FIGURE 16.7

An E-mail screen.

(Action Technologies,
Emeryville, California)

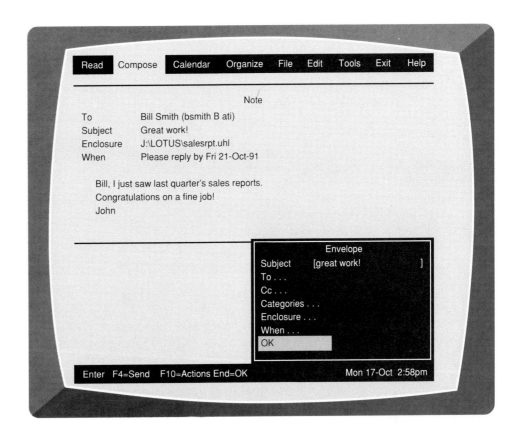

working document—such as a spreadsheet, graph, or technical proposal—sent for comment. The personal workstation may be a desktop PC, a computer terminal, or a laptop computer. The versatility and convenience of this communication medium has transformed a number of organizations.

A screen used to compose an electronic mail message in the Coordinator II system, which we shall discuss along with other groupware below, is shown in figure 16.7.

The key capability of an E-mail system is that of storing and forwarding messages. Many other E-mail capabilities derive from it. You can send your message when it is convenient to you, and the recipient can read it when it is convenient to him or her. "Telephone tag," the annoying calls back and forth to absent parties, is avoided. You get the benefit of the "VCR effect," so desirable in television viewing, of shifting time and structuring your work as you want it, rather than being at the mercy of callers. You learn how to screen out messages of no interest to you. You can work at home or sell in the field—and be always in touch via E-mail. Many systems allow you to store the incoming messages in labeled files, so that you can use the system as a private (though rather expensive) file cabinet. Some meetings can be avoided, while others may become shorter because the participants had discussed the issues over E-mail beforehand. E-mail has affected structure and corporate culture in organizations where it has become a principal means of communications, as is shown in the Mrs. Fields vignette.

MRS. FIELDS IS LEAN—AND E-MAIL IS THE RECIPE

Mrs. Fields, Inc. is a chain of over 650 cookie shops that has grown very rapidly. The firm operates with just 114 employees in its headquarters in Park City, Iowa. Its chief executive estimates that the company would need five times as many employees if not for the integrating effects of E-mail.

All the communications between headquarters and the stores, including the transfer of financial data to headquarters, is conducted over E-mail. In fact, the only paperwork is filling out the forms required by the government. Store employees send suggestions to headquarters management, skipping levels in the chain of management as necessary. This has enabled executives to expand their spans of management—and has flattened the corporate hierarchy.

Based on Richard Brandt and others, "The Personal Computer Finds Its Missing Link." *Business Week*, June 5, 1989, pp. 120–29.

A marketing manager can inform regional offices about a product promotion campaign, an executive can receive reports with key performance indicators from his or her subordinates every Monday morning, or a group of coworkers can comment on each other's work through E-mail. In fact, the last application has brought forward the very significant extensions of E-mail known as groupware, which we discuss later in this chapter. As Mrs. Fields has already shown us, E-mail has made it possible to expand the span of management (or span of control) in an organization. Philippe Kahn, founder and chief executive of Borland International, the immensely successful software company that brought us the SideKick desktop organizer and Turbo Pascal, ascribes the flattening of his organization to the way it utilizes E-mail. Kahn wants opinions from any level of his organization sent to him directly—and, as he puts it, he "cannot write louder than anyone else."[2] In fact, the chief executive of On-Line Software International, a major software company, recently announced that he plans to guide the strategic direction of the Fort Lee, New Jersey company from Washington, D.C., where he will study medicine—and he will do this via the company's E-mail system.[3] When combined with executive information systems, E-mail gives executives a powerful means of control. By electronically sending 90 percent of its internal mail in the United States, IBM shortens the business cycle for its products (Thyfault, 1991).

Some seven million North Americans now have an E-mail mailbox. About two-thirds of these are tied into an in-house system (Kleinschrod, 1989). It is estimated that in 1988, U.S. offices exchanged two billion electronic messages (Latamore, 1988). E-mail has largely replaced telex communications. Electronic mail may be implemented as a software package installed in-house, it may be purchased as a service from public E-mail vendors, or it may be implemented as part of an integrated OIS package installed on a minicomputer or on a mainframe. Large organizations generally have a variety of internal E-mail systems and integrated office packages and use public E-mail nets for intercompany communication. As we shall see further, ensuring connectivity between E-mail networks is a costly problem at this time.

The largest public E-mail providers are listed in table 16.3.

TABLE 16.3

Public E-mail Vendors[4]

VENDOR COMPANY	E-MAIL SYSTEM
CompuServe	InfoPlex
Western Union	EasyLink
Telenet/US Sprint	Telemail
GE Information Services	Quick-Comm, GEnie
Dialcom	+Mail
MCI	MCI Mail
British Telecom	Tymnet, OnTyme
AT&T	AT&T Mail

TABLE 16.4

Integrated Office Software

VENDOR COMPANY	SOFTWARE PACKAGE	HARDWARE PLATFORM
IBM	Professional Office System (PROFS)	IBM Mainframes
	Distributed Office Support System (DISOSS)	IBM Mainframes and Minis
Digital Equipment Corporation	ALL-IN-1	DEC Minis
Wang Laboratories	Office	Wang Minis

Table 16.4 shows some of the integrated office software packages available for mini and mainframe environments. These packages offer E-mail along with word processing, text management, spreadsheet programs, and other capabilities.

Among the advantages of electronic mail we have already seen are time shifting and the avoidance of telephone tag. E-mail systems can also provide greater security than many alternatives, since users have passwords for accessing their messages. Economies are possible in many uses, particularly as an alternative to overnight international mail.

Of course, some situations require the presence of both parties for meaningful communication—and some people do not like to type. The printed word is a rather dry medium of communication and it is difficult to express emotions through it. (Though not impossible: at Digital Equipment Corporation, where reliance on E-mail is a part of the corporate culture, people use a ";-" in a message to represent a wink, and a ":-" to represent a frown.) Any new communication medium relies on massive participation—if only a few users in an organization are attracted to E-mail, the system will fail.

The proliferation of E-mail brings its own problems—among others, unwanted messages. It is very easy to broadcast a message to everyone's mailbox. Information overload may result. A major research project directed at preventing this overload is briefly described in the next vignette. It illustrates a very important concept: software that acts as a user's personal agent, assisting the user with his or her information needs. Such software is known as *delegation technology*.

INFORMATION LENS—A TOOL FOR MANAGING YOUR E-MAIL

A prototype system that helps users organize the E-mail they receive and filter out unwanted messages has been developed at MIT by Thomas Malone and his colleagues (Malone, 1987). Called Information Lens, the system works on top of existing E-mail systems. It permits a user to define a set of filters which behave as automatic agents acting on the user's behalf. Such an agent can automatically screen incoming E-mail according to specified criteria. Each message has a type, such as "meeting announcement" or "request for information." Users define their own filters for handling messages with IF-THEN rules, which we know as a method of knowledge representation used in expert systems. Here is an example of such a rule:

IF Message type: Request for information
    Subject: expert systems
THEN Move to: AI

This rule assigns any E-mail in which the keyword "expert systems" is found to an electronic "folder" named "AI." Other rules may specify messages that should be deleted, that are regarded as urgent, or that come from a VIP sender (your boss). You may also move all broadcast mail into a separate central folder and have the Lens search it periodically for items of interest to you, which can then be moved into your personal files.

The principal purpose of systems such as Information Lens is to transfer control over the communication channel from the sender to the recipient. Work is also currently in progress on generalizing the Information Lens into a flexible environment for group work, called Object Lens (Lai, 1988). Object Lens incorporates hypertext, as well as many facilities we shall describe later in this chapter as groupware functions.

E-mail systems generally make available an electronic bulletin board facility, which we shall discuss later as a simpler form of a computer conferencing service.

Electronic Mail in Communication with the External Environment

Corporations are moving to extend the reach of their electronic mail systems to their customers and to their peers in the industry. To do so, they have to scale the barrier created by incompatible systems. An international standard, X.400, ratified in 1984 by the International Organization for Standards (ISO), has been adopted by a number of companies for this interenterprise E-mail. Without a standard protocol, distinct software gateways would have to be developed to link any two different E-mail systems. Managing multiple gateways presents a great burden for user organizations, many of which employ several different E-mail systems just *internally*.

As one example, Chase Manhattan Bank is adopting the X.400 gateway to communicate with its large business clients. The bank perceives the convenience of E-mail communications as a marketing tool which would bind client corporations and trust funds more closely to it. (But Chase does not use E-mail for financial transactions, which are conducted over the highly secure SWIFT international network.) The use of E-mail in pursuit of competitive advantage is seen as follows by a manager of Anchor Glass of Tampa, Florida: "By getting through the doors with E-mail, you can give customers other services" (Pelton, 1989). As a result of joint production agreements in the petroleum industry,

TABLE 16.5 Major Business Databases	DATABASE	SUBJECT	PROVIDERS	UPDATE FREQUENCY
	ABI/Inform	Business literature	BRS, Dialog, Mead	Monthly
	Business Dataline	Regional business news	BRS, Dialog, Dow Jones	Monthly
	Dun's Financial Records	Corporate financial information on U.S. businesses	Dialog	Quarterly
	Dow Jones News/ Retrieval	News and analysis	Dow Jones	Continuous
	Lexis Financial Information Service	Financial analysis of firms	Mead	Daily
	Moody's Corporate News	News on U.S. firms	Dialog	Weekly
	Nexis	Newsletters and wire services	Mead	Daily
	Standard & Poor's	Corporate information and news	CompuServe Dialog	Depends on the nature of the information

Exxon's workers are regularly communicating with their counterparts at BP America, Sun, and Texaco via E-mail. Some companies use E-mail for receiving customer orders. Nordstrom (of Seattle), a specialty retailer with an unusually large number of suppliers, finds that its business does not lend itself to electronic data interchange at this time—but the firm uses E-mail for purchase orders and invoice inquiries (McCusker, 1991).

Many public E-mail services combine E-mail facilities with access to **electronic information services.** A subscriber to such a service is connected to a variety of databases which can be accessed from a personal workstation. We saw the importance of environmental scanning for corporate planning in chapter 11. The most expensive category of these services includes databases with information on specialized subjects: patents, technical documents, legal precedents, or legislation. Another class of information services makes available a variety of general databases, such as the *Official Airline Guide,* wire service news, or financial databases for investors. Some 3,200 electronic databases are available at present. Several crucial business databases are shown in table 16.5.

The broadly marketed Prodigy information service is a joint venture between IBM and Sears. This **videotex** service, primarily aimed at consumers, hopes to emulate the success of the French Minitel, British Prestel, and West German Bildschirmtext. With a personal computer and a modem, a person can save time by banking, shopping, investing, and receiving news at home or any other place at the user's convenience.

Voice Mail

Voice mail is similar to electronic mail—but instead of a text message, a voice message is sent. The main distinction is apparent: you do not need to type in the message. Other distinctions are also present; you can convey emotions by voice, but you can send a graph via E-mail. Voice recording reflects the attitude of the sender, which enriches the message. Available since 1980, voice systems have found broader acceptance only recently.

Voice mail systems, like E-mail, are computer-based, but this fact is transparent to users, who send and retrieve messages by a telephone. A sender dictates a voice message into the recipient's phone mailbox. The voice message is digitized and stored in a secondary memory, such as a magnetic disk. When the recipient retrieves the message from the mailbox, the message is converted back to its original voice form. Voice messaging is controlled by pressing a sequence of telephone buttons. Users are guided through a sometimes elaborate sequence by a recorded voice. The message recipient can replay or skip messages or can route them to another mailbox. Messages may be circulated as voice memos, with each recipient appending an oral comment.

Voice mail can replace many real-time conversations by message-type communications. At the Travelers Companies, a Hartford, Connecticut insurance concern where 10,000 employees use voice mail, it is estimated that 60 percent of internal telephone calls do not require two-way communications (Pollack, 1988). Secretaries, receptionists, and other office workers are relieved of many chores related to handling "while you were out" slips (Travelers estimates that 75 percent of telephone calls do not reach the intended recipient).

The broadcast mode of voice mail serves to inform a large circle of people; this is cost-effective as compared to the distribution of written memos. Voice mail systems are also used to dispense information, such as airline flight schedules.

A leading supplier of voice mail systems is the Octel Communications Corporation of Milpitas, California. Prices vary, depending on the system capacity. Service bureaus rent voice mailboxes. Bell operating companies are expected to offer the service to consumers in the near future.

The development of standards for intercompany connectivity, as well as connections with E-mail systems, are emerging concerns. Already, voice synthesizers are used in some systems to convert E-mail messages into voice messages.

Facsimile

The technology that has profoundly changed the way people communicate today is facsimile—a long-distance copying technology that does not require a computer. A relatively inexpensive fax machine is used in place of a telephone to send a copy of a document or any other written message. Text, graphs, signatures, and handwritten marginalia are transmitted as they appear on the original. As shown in figure 16.8, the sender's fax machine scans the document or any handwritten message and sends the digitized image over the telephone line to the recipient's fax machine, which produces a copy of the document. A fax machine has both sending and receiving capabilities (it has a built-in modem). Some machines have a memory for storing message. Transmission speeds, copy resolution, and the available extra features depend on the sophistication—and the price—of the fax machine. Several pages can generally be sent per minute.

The fax machine is a premier tool in a portable office. Consultants rely heavily on fax transmission for client contact; lawyers use them during contract negotiations; advertising agencies exchange copies with printers before the final printing run for an ad. Even some take-out food establishments receive fax orders from nearby offices.

FIGURE 16.8

Facsimile (fax) transmission.

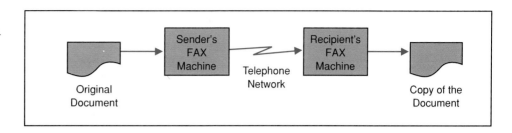

16.4 TELECONFERENCING AND COMPUTER CONFERENCING

We know from Mintzberg's analysis of managerial work (Mintzberg, 1973), which was discussed in chapter 13, that most of a manager's time is spent in meetings of various kinds. This much-maligned method for facilitating many-to-many communication has always played a crucial role in coordinating organizational work, as well in collaborating with other firms, including customers and suppliers. People develop working relationships in a meeting; they share information, negotiate common objectives, and stimulate each other's thinking. An organization's culture evolves in large measure through meetings.

The advent of computer and communication technologies has broadened the possibilities of many-to-many communications. A meeting can now be distributed in place and time, in accordance with the situation. Several technologies are combined in different ways to provide alternatives. The participants can be situated at remote locations and supported by audio, video, or computer teleconferencing facilities. Along with providing a teleconferencing capability, computer conferencing allows meetings to be distributed over time and offers support for group decision making.

Audio and Video Teleconferencing

Teleconferencing facilities enable people at remote locations to hold a meeting in which they can communicate by voice, text, or images—depending on the conferencing facility. There are three principal ways to hold a teleconference: audioconferencing, videoconferencing, and computer conferencing. We shall hold off our discussion of computer teleconferencing, since it has a broad array of capabilities of special interest to us. Audio and video teleconferencing do not require that participants use computers.

Audioconferencing is an extension of the conference call, without the need for an operator to establish the connection between remote conference sites. Typically, managers located in a conference room at one of the organization's sites hold a face-to-face meeting, and at some point they establish an audio teleconference connection with a similar meeting being held at another company site. With speaker phones installed in both conference rooms, all the participants can hear one another—but, of course, the remote participants cannot be seen. Specialized portable systems for audioconferencing are available (see photo 16.4).

Videoconferencing extends the well-established one-way closed-circuit TV concept. In a two-way video teleconference, the participants can see and hear one another at a distance. Although audio teleconferencing is less expensive, participants in a video teleconference find it reassuring to see the body language that accompanies utterances. Full-motion video is significantly more expensive than freeze-frame video, where periodic snapshots are sent over the communication channel. Freeze-frame videoconferencing limits the ability to establish eye contact but certainly makes it possible to present a graph, a report, or an image of a VDT screen. Video images are captured by one of several cameras located in the conferencing room and are seen at the remote site on a TV monitor screen, a special large-size screen (the kind we see on TV when a correspondent at a remote site is being interviewed), or on a videoconferencing workstation, as described in the next vignette.

Videoconferencing is used for instruction, to introduce a new car model to the sales force (by Ford and General Motors), or to brief brokers on new financial instruments. The result is considerable savings in travel-related expenses. Many major hotels now offer videoconferencing facilities.

The ability to produce a recording of an audio or videoconference in a business setting is limited by a variety of laws. Such a record would also be less useful than a textual record afforded by computer conferencing systems. Usually, handwritten notes must be kept by the participants.

Computer Conferencing

Computer conferencing does not necessarily imply teleconferencing, as audio and videoconferencing systems do. The latter two help bring together users distant from one another in space, though not in time: the participants use the system for a synchronous, simultaneous meeting. In audio and videoconferencing, the telecommunications media provide connectivity.

Computer conferencing systems provide not only connectivity, but also memory—the buffering capabilities of computer storage enable the participants to be spread over space and their participation to be spread over time. We shall see that decision-room computer conferencing facilities are also valuable, even though all the participants may be in the same place at the same time. In this case, computer system facilities are an aid to group decision making. The distinctions between computer conferencing and audio and videoconferencing are summarized in figure 16.9.

PHOTO 16.4

This portable audioconferencing system weighs 3.3 pounds, fits in a briefcase and may be set up in seconds. It can pick up comments from up to twenty feet away. (This is VoicePoint from NEC America, Inc.)

VIDEOCONFERENCING IN LAW ENFORCEMENT—AND ELSEWHERE

A pilot videoconferencing system was introduced by the District Attorney's (DA) office of the Manhattan borough in New York. Its purpose is to keep police officers on the street rather than tied up in red tape.

With the videoconferencing system, an assistant DA can interview arresting officers, crime victims, and witnesses right in the local station houses—by video. The DA's complaint room is linked with the police precincts, so that police personnel, victims, and witnesses need not travel to the DA's office, give their depositions, and then wait for a complaint to be typed in order to sign it—a process that could take twelve to fifteen hours. Now, an assistant DA interviews the relevant parties in a videoconference call, fills out a complaint, and sends it by fax to the arresting officer for signing. The officer returns the signed complaint by fax as well (with the original on file). Because of the videoconferencing system, police officers now spend more time on the beat, witnesses are interviewed

immediately after the arrest (they often would not show up for a meeting scheduled at a later time), and cases are built in a superior fashion.

Videoconferences are now possible in most major metropolitan areas, where the long-distance telephone companies, such as AT&T, US Sprint, and MCI, have installed fiber-optic networks. Rates for videoconference calls coast-to-coast dropped in 1991 to $30 an hour at the lowest transmission speeds. Equipment varies. At the lower end of the cost spectrum, users may employ a videoconferencing workstation (a child of the videotelephone). However, as the cost of a fully equipped videoconference room dipped below $50,000 in 1991, the use of such facilities in corporate life started to increase sharply.

Based in part on Jeanne Iida, "Teleconferencing Cuts City's Arrest Time in Half." *MIS Week,* May 8, 1989, p. 34; and Thomas C. Hayes, "Doing Business Screen to Screen." *The New York Times,* February 21, 1991, pp. D1, D15.

FIGURE 16.9

Capabilities of video and audioconferencing compared with those of computer conferencing.

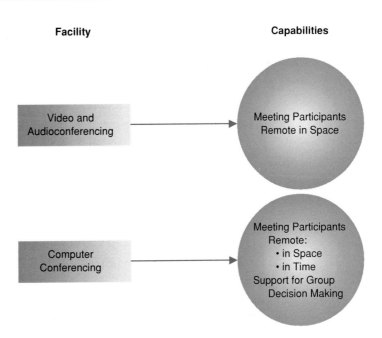

ELECTRONIC BULLETIN BOARD HELPS COORDINATE EARTHQUAKE ACTIVITIES

During the 1980s, the U.S. Geological Survey in Menlo Park, California established an electronic bulletin board to coordinate activities related to an earthquake predicted to happen in Parkfield, California within a few years. The users were several field offices, university labs, government agencies, and technicians monitoring the Parkfield site. Recent forecasts, minutes of meetings, the status of test equipment, and other notices were posted on the board.

Dr. Allan Lindh, who ran the Parkfield project, stated that he expected the real value of the bulletin board to surface when the earthquake occurred. Telephone circuits were expected to be jammed during the event, making conference calls impossible. The board would then become the primary means for coordinating the activities of the agencies involved.

Lindh's expectations were indeed confirmed during the October 1989 Bay Area earthquake, as this headline indicates: "On-Line Information Services Become Lifelines After Quake" (by Joanie M. Wexler, *Computerworld*, October 30, 1989, p. 62).

Based on Josh Brackett, "Computer Conferencing: The Right Choice for Anytime, Anyplace Meetings." *Today's Office*, November 1988, pp. 53–58.

Following are some of the modalities of computer conferencing. The boundaries between particular modalities are not always well defined, and flexibility exists in using any given service.

1. Electronic Bulletin Boards

The simplest type of computer conference, offered by most E-mail systems, is an electronic bulletin board—a rather straightforward extension of E-mail. A personal workstation is the means of access. An open mailbox is established, and users can post messages to it or scan messages posted there by others. A bulletin board may be set up where informal feedback from the company's distribution channels (distributors, wholesalers, and retailers) is posted. Internal bulletin boards are commonly used within organizations for posting company announcements. Boards for external communications may show job openings available in a company.

Bulletin board notices may be downloaded into personal files. E-mail public services levy a charge for board ownership; senders are charged for each posting, and the recipients pay for connect time.

2. Computer Teleconferencing

Electronic bulletin boards are used in a highly unstructured manner—just as their wall equivalents are. Computer teleconferencing imposes a certain degree of structure on the underlying messaging system in order to support remote and asynchronous many-to-many communications. An electronic bulletin board "meeting" takes place over an extended period of time. The conference chairperson opens the "meeting" with a statement defining its purpose and the key topics. This is then broadcast to all participants. Within the prescribed "meeting" time, perhaps a week or two,

TABLE 16.6	TELECONFERENCING MEDIUM	WHEN TO USE
When to Use Various Teleconferencing Media	Video	Do not consider it, unless you can afford it. When social presence is desirable (for example, at executive sessions or when making a sales pitch) When the task requires motion displays (for example, demonstration of TV ads or moving mechanical parts)
	Audio	When visual communication is unimportant (or too expensive)
	Computer	When computer-based resources are needed When asynchronous (distributed in time) meetings are desired When tasks are adaptable to textual and graphical communications (plus any other modes available in the system) When participants are comfortable with using keyboards

the "attendees" read the chairperson's message and the contributions of other conference participants and then broadcast their own messages. Conference members may contribute their statements at any time during the "meeting." At the prescribed completion time, or at some time deemed appropriate, the chairperson summarizes the results of the meeting, broadcasts them, and closes the meeting. The records of the meeting are available at all times in full detail.

Computer teleconferencing is supported by some of the public E-mail services. For example, The CompuServe public E-mail utility offers a service called Participate; some organizations use this system to set up internal computer conference facilities. The software package offers a branching option: a user can create a branch to any existing conference, asking some of the parent conference participants to join. A "greenhouse effect" conference may thus branch off to a "customer reaction" subconference. A well-known specialized computer teleconferencing service is the Electronic Information Exchange System (EIES) operated by the New Jersey Institute of Technology (Hiltz, 1985); others include Planet, Forum, and Com.

Managers may employ computer teleconferencing for deeper study of a topic, such as strategic perspectives for a company in the evolving marketplace. However the extreme diffusion over time sometimes makes people feel that no meeting at all is taking place (Kraemer, 1988). Groupware systems, discussed later in this chapter, try to remedy this by providing facilities for meetings that are dispersed in location but take place in real time.

A participant in a computer conference deals with "electronic text," to use the phrase of Shoshana Zuboff (Zuboff, 1988), rather than with an individual interlocutor, as in a face-to-face meeting. The fact that body language is absent and that the system acts as an equalizer creates new social dynamics which are only now being studied in depth.

Let us compare computer teleconferencing with audio and video teleconferencing. Taken in part from the recommendations of Robert Johansen and Christine Bullen (Johansen, 1984), table 16.6 shows when to use each type of system.

FIGURE 16.10

Schematic of a U-shaped
electronic meeting room
(decision room).

(From Vogel, 1989–90, p. 28)

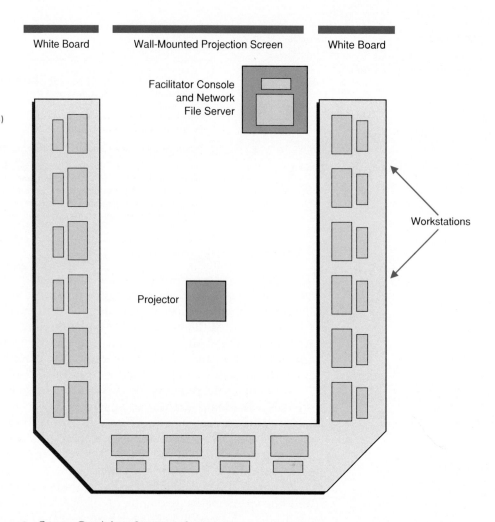

White Board   Wall-Mounted Projection Screen   White Board

Facilitator Console
and Network
File Server

Workstations

Projector

3. Group Decision Support Systems

We discussed the decision-making aspects of group decision support
systems (GDSS) when we analyzed DSS in chapter 14. We know that GDSS
assist a group of decision makers in arriving at a decision in regard to a
poorly structured problem. A GDSS has facilities which assist group
processes such as brainstorming in the search of creative ideas; reaching
consensus via voting or the Delphi method; or negotiating, which has been
defined as a form of group decision making in which the parties
communicate in an effort to resolve nonoverlapping interests (Pruitt, 1981).
Specialized techniques are available to support multiparty decision
processes. We saw how such a facility was used for crisis management in
the case study for chapter 13. A process relying on the use of GDSS
facilities for analyzing a firm's competitive position in search of competitive
advantage has been proposed and tested (Dennis, 1991).

As we know, GDSS can support all phases of Simon's decision-making
model. Typically, such a system is used in a *decision room*. The first such
room was installed at Execucom Systems Corporation (of Austin, Texas) in
1980; several decision rooms designed by the University of Arizona MIS
Department and Ventana Corporation (Tucson, Arizona) have been

installed at various industrial and academic sites. A room installed at an IBM location is shown schematically in figure 16.10; the facility at the University of Arizona is shown in color plate 17. A U-shaped table is equipped with personal workstations connected into a local area network. An additional workstation controls the central display on a large central screen. The meeting is generally conducted by a facilitator.

GDSS may be employed to conduct synchronous or asynchronous meetings. In general, there are three settings for GDSS use: decision room (face-to-face conference), videoconference supported by communicating personal workstations, and a computer teleconference (or interfaced conference) (Straub, 1988). The alternatives are illustrated in figure 16.11.

In all cases, participants have access to personal productivity software, including spreadsheet programs and database management systems, and decision models; participants may also communicate by E-mail. Specialized software tools for supporting group processes are also available. The use of personal and group decision support facilities makes GDSS a more powerful tool than plain computer teleconferencing. Among the benefits of GDSS, Kenneth Kraemer and John Leslie King list (Kraemer, 1988):

- Superior focusing of participants' attention on the major issues of a decision problem
- Rapid identification of divergences in participants' attitudes as reflected by voting, particularly since participants usually vote anonymously
- Easy resumption of debate when voting shows a lack of consensus, with new information often surfacing in the process
- Accessibility of models and databases—a decision support feature—providing a handy means for bringing facts into a debate

The principal concerns associated with the use of GDSS involve productivity losses in group processes, some of which we discussed as "groupthink" in chapter 13. As Kraemer and King tell us, "decisions that are reached quickly or with greater group consensus are not necessarily better than decisions arrived at through less expeditious and enjoyable means."[5] Group performance depends on the task (McGrath, 1984). For some tasks, such as idea generation, groups often do not perform as well as their best individual member would on her or his own. For other tasks, such as considering and selecting an alternative during the closing phases of decision making, groups often do better than individuals. It is clear that a decision-making task requiring the variety of expertise available in a group is likely to produce a result superior to an individual decision.

16.5 WORKGROUP SUPPORT AND GROUPWARE

The variety of technologies available for exchanging messages and holding meetings, combined with a recognition of the importance of teamwork, have led to the emergence of systems of a new type, whose ultimate form is currently being defined. Based on **groupware,** or software for **computer-supported cooperative work,** these systems are intended to support the collaborative efforts of a group of coworkers. Group size depends on the project and on the organization. In general, it ranges between two and forty-five members.

FIGURE 16.11

Alternative GDSS settings.

(From Detmar W. Straub, Jr. and Renee A. Beauclair, "Current and Future Uses of GDSS Technology: Report on a Recent Empirical Study" in *Hawaii International Conference on Systems Science, Vol. 3, Decisions Support and Knowledge-based Systems Track.* Copyright © 1988 IEEE. Reprinted by permission.)

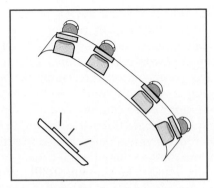

a. Decision room: all participants are in the same place at the same time

b. Videoconference with computer support: distribution in space

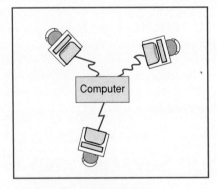

c. Computer teleconference: distribution in space and time

The Organizational Role of Workgroups

The emergence of groupware in the late 1980s (Richman, 1987) is an excellent example of how technology push and demand pull interact with one another. Just as the personal computer and productivity software equipped the individual knowledge worker, the availability of local area networks and other communication technologies created the technological base for group knowledge work.

At the same time, the realization also occurred that much of organizational effectiveness stems from the effective work of groups more than from actions of isolated individuals. Peter Drucker sees task-focused teams as the principal locus of work (Drucker, 1988), and the importance of team work both in manufacturing and in the business office has been recognized by several leading organizations (Hoerr, 1989). Back-office work, such as processing securities in a bank, lease applications in a credit corporation, or insurance policies of a certain type in an insurance company, is now increasingly assigned to a team as opposed to being fragmented into meaningless segments to be turned over to workers on an "electronic assembly line." Effective team organization and motivation result in job enrichment and a sense of responsibility; in some firms, such teams are largely self-managed. Decision makers in a chief executive's cabinet work as a team, as do marketers responsible for a product line.

The increased uncertainty of the business environment in an information society makes a cross-organizational business team a highly responsive and flexible structure in an organizational adhocracy (see section 12.3). Robert Johansen (Johansen, 1988) mentions project teams, task forces, brand teams, sales teams, account teams, new-product teams, and crisis-response teams as some of the workgroups that have come into being in organizations today. Some of these groups are relatively permanent; some are organized and disbanded ad hoc; some are homogeneous, with members doing similar jobs; and others are heterogeneous, with specialized membership. Group members may work in the same building or be separated by oceans. A work group has a functional goal, its members take on roles in the overall task set for the group, and a set of norms develops in the operation of a group.

Groupware and Its Functions

Groupware, the emergent support for a business group based on interconnected personal workstations, offers support for *communication* and *collaboration* among group members, and for *coordination* of group work. The function of groupware reaches beyond the personal productivity tools of individual members and the task-specific software the members may use to do a specific job (such as an expert system for the evaluation of creditworthiness). The principal emphasis of groupware is on the use of computers to facilitate human interaction (Ellis, 1991). Groupware runs on platforms that provide connectivity with other members of the organization and with the external world. The groupware vignette will give you an idea of what is involved in computer-supported cooperative work.

No single integrated groupware product offers all groupware functions; in fact, some of them are available through such software as database management systems or spreadsheet programs. Various groupware systems have limitations on functionality and connectivity, which should be specifically investigated. Let us discuss the principal functions of groupware.

WHAT DO WORK GROUPS DO WITH GROUPWARE?

At Healthcare Compare Corporation (of Lombard, Illinois) teams use a large network of 700 nodes to prepare proposals in response to requests for proposals (RFPs) from potential customers. In 1988, a three-person team completed 250 proposals, with each member submitting different sections and boilerplates. In a similar fashion, various departments collaborate on reports: a report is initiated and outlined by one department, and others then supplement it.

A groupware package from Broderbund Software, called For Comment, allows group members to critique and annotate a text without changing its content. The ultimate author can then incorporate appropriate comments into the main text.

Manufacturers Hanover Trust, a major New York bank, is in the forefront of workgroup computing. The bank has developed an information-sharing system for customer tracking and for developing a prospective business customer into an actual one. Bank employees at different levels and at different locales call on various customer employees. It is necessary that a bank officer making a call have all the relevant information and that no redundant calls be made.

The firm has not found an appropriate groupware product as yet. However, software developers work on groupware based on the idea of a daemon, or an active agent: when a change in the information bases occurs, this software may *automatically* cause certain action, without the need for human intervention. In the case of the customer-tracking system, all the appropriate bank officers could be alerted to an important development concerning a prospective or actual account.

Michael is a telecommuter who works at home for a small company four days a week. He has a laptop that satisfies most of his computing needs. Periodically, he needs to work at the personal Macintosh workstation of his coworker, Michelle, who works at the firm's office. She maintains most of the files pertinent to the project they are working on, as well as the appropriate software, and her workstation is connected to a laser printer. Michael can demonstrate to her what the spreadsheet model he has developed can actually do. Michelle will want to gain control of Michael's workstation from time to time, to suggest changes in the report he is writing.

With a groupware product, Timbuktu Remote (from Farallon Computing of Berkeley, California), it is possible to gain remote control of a coworker's workstation. With the software running on both machines and with a 9,600 bit-per-second modem, the collaborators can communicate over a telephone line, gain control of each other's workstations, and exchange messages. Password security is enforced.

A development team at Lotus Development Corporation, the developer of Lotus 1–2–3, prepares all its weekly meetings and keeps track of them with the help of groupware.

The groupware the team uses is Notes, a software package that they developed for the marketplace. The groupware permits team members to post and debate ideas for a meeting, print an agenda, and then write up minutes and action items to be transferred to the next week's agenda. Meetings are streamlined, since the participants are now well prepared.

Some examples are based on Katie Crane, "Sounds Good, But What Does It Really Mean." *Computerworld*, June 5, 1989, pp. 57–61; Peter H. Lewis, "Sharing a Screen—Long Distance." *The New York Times Business Section*, August 6, 1989, p. 8; Susanna Opper, "Strength in Numbers: Groupware May Revolutionize the Way We Work." *Computerworld Focus*, August 3, 1988, pp. 25–26; and Scott Leibs, "The Promise and the Pitfalls.," *InformationWeek*, February 11, 1991, pp. 38–40.

1. Information Sharing

   Group members must share data, text, and knowledge bases in order to work both in their "private" computer workspaces and in a group workspace.

   For example, Higgins workgroup software (from Higgins Group, San Leandro, California) employs an underlying relational DBMS to allow a group of users to index and share all information related to a client, date, project, or any other selected category. Any group member can assign to such an electronic folder all memos, expense reports, spreadsheets, letters, or meeting notes relating to an Acme International account, for example. We can see how this functionality could be a solution to the Manufacturers Hanover client-tracking problem discussed in the previous vignette.

   Groupware-facilitated information sharing replaces the infamous "sneakernet" of information sharing by exchanging diskettes.

2. Document Authoring

   An authoring group needs to collaborate in producing technical documentation, reports, or business proposals. Slate groupware from BBN Systems and Technologies Corporation of Cambridge, Massachusetts enables a group to produce a multimedia document, combining text, graphs, and images. Workgroup members may append text comments and voice annotations. When a loudspeaker icon appears on the screen, the reader knows that a voice comment has been appended to the text; he or she may listen to the comment by invoking the playback command. A screen containing a sample document is shown in figure 16.12.

   A variety of presentation subsystems that display the graphical information on VDT screens, transparencies, or slides may be combined with an authoring system. Hypertext and hypermedia technologies will be employed in future systems.

3. Messaging Systems

   Much of groupware software is built as an expansion of E-mail facilities. Electronic mail, with its internal and external messaging capability, is used extensively to support group communication between meetings. Management of distribution lists, notification of arriving mail, confirmation of receipts, and message history tracking are some of the available facilities.

   Certain groupware systems permit users to impose a structure on message communication. Coordinator II of Action Technologies (Emeryville, California) reflects the approach of its creator, Fernando Flores. Flores considers business communications to consist of a set of action-oriented conversations, such as requests (asking that a task be done), questions, promises (reporting on plans to perform a task), offers (proposing an idea), and so forth—seven in all (Flores, 1988). Each of the corresponding messages has a predetermined format, and certain messages impose obligations and commitments. The system automatically reminds group members about them. Some organizations do not desire that the messaging system structure their team work; they use other messaging facilities of the system. This is one example of the importance of matching groupware to an organization's culture.

FIGURE 16.12

A screen with a multimedia
document.

(Courtesy of BBN Systems
and Technologies
Corporation)

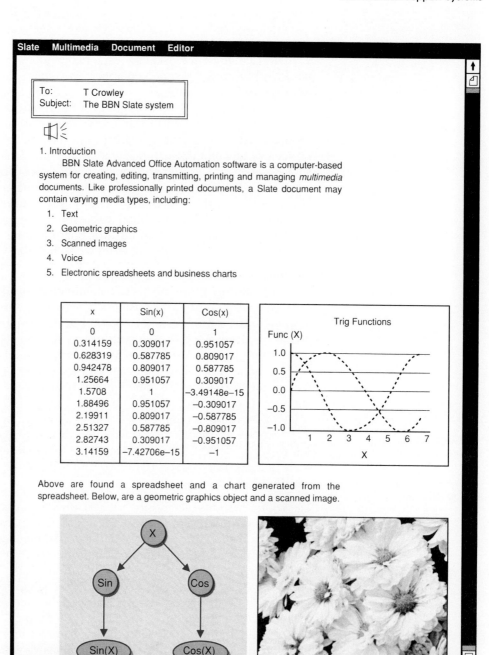

4. Computer Conferencing

Depending on the task and the makeup of a group, various computer conferencing options may be desirable.

A groupware conferencing program, such as Caucus (by Metasystems Design Group of Arlington, Virginia), assists in exchanging progress reports and "discussing" problems by exchanging messages. The complete text is saved and may be searched by any team member. As another example, Slate's multimedia teleconference facility permits several users to view the same document on their workstations and exchange messages, while the participant who has the "floor" can modify the draft in full view of everyone.

5. Group Calendaring

Groupware systems maintain individual calendars to keep track of time commitments. This simplifies the scheduling of a meeting. For example, if you were planning a meeting with OfficeWorks, a DataAccess Corporation (Miami, Florida) groupware product, you would provide the system with a list of people you want to meet, and it would scan their calendars for open time. When the system finds an open slot, it "pencils in" the meeting and requests confirmation from all parties.

6. Project Management

The progress of group projects must be tracked. Syzygy groupware by Information Research (Charlottesville, Virginia) offers such project management tools as activity lists and Gantt charts. Hierarchical activity lists define activities at three levels: objectives, projects for achieving the objectives, and tasks that make up the project (see figure 16.13a). Gantt charts, which we shall discuss among other tools for MIS project management in section 19.9, visualize workgroup activities on a project as bars and indicate the overall status of a project (completed, on schedule, overdue). Syzygy supports three levels of Gantt charts, corresponding to the activity list levels (as in figure 16.13b).

7. Support for Team Building

A team-building tool—perhaps the most original among groupware facilities—such as SuperSync of SwixTech USA (Irvine, California), "administers" questionnaires to team members to identify patterns of interpersonal communication, establish the presence of harmful alliances, and find leadership potential. A graphic output shows alignments around leaders. Since much of team work depends on good interpersonal relations, a tool of this kind assists personnel policy.

We have summarized the functions of groupware in figure 16.14 in terms of their support for coordination, communication, and collaboration. It is crucial to adapt

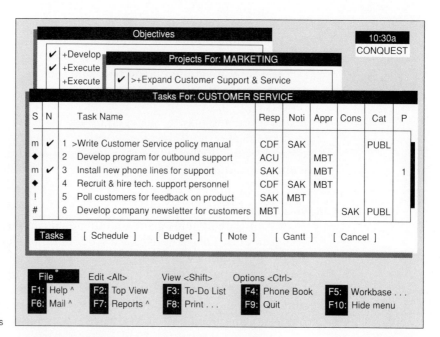

a. Hierachical activity lists

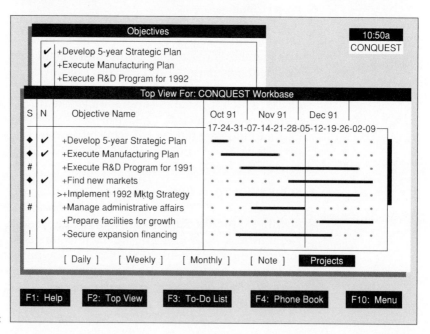

b. Gantt chart

FIGURE 16.13

Project management tools.

the capabilities of a groupware package to the needs and work styles of a specific group and the individuals within the group. New group norms emerge during groupware work; for example, members of the law department in a real estate firm cut their customary five-page memos to one page as they began to use an authoring system. The security and privacy of individual information bases should be safeguarded.

FIGURE 16.14

Workgroup support offered by groupware.

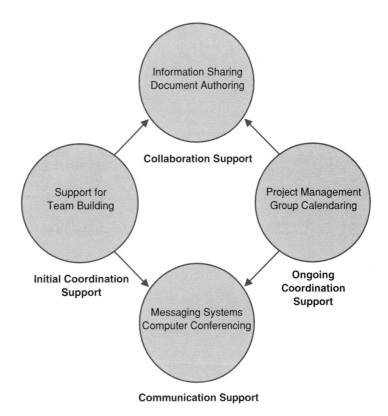

16.6 THE IMPACT OF OIS ON ORGANIZATIONS AND WORK

O ffice information systems provide new options for structuring an organization; their use affects organizational roles and the nature of knowledge work. It would be a basic fallacy to assume that because a certain technology is available and *could* bring certain organizational results, such results *will* follow if one simply purchases the technology (Hirschheim, 1985). As we have continually stressed throughout this text, organizational processes must be enacted to ensure the effective use of a technology.

Perspectives on OIS

OIS may be analyzed from various perspectives, including integration into the overall organizational MIS, support of various aspects of knowledge work and the related increase in productivity, effects of OIS on organizational structure, redefinition of the roles of knowledge workers, and organization of office information flows. Each perspective leads to a deeper understanding of OIS.

Because an OIS primarily serves the purposes of communication, it should be *integrated* with other MIS components. By their very nature, OIS are reasonably well integrated with DSS and EIS, since the equipment found in an office is the usual delivery vehicle for these systems (even though a deeper integration requires considerable effort, with GDSS being an example of OIS-DSS integration). Document management systems require integration with transaction processing systems, since paper documents result from many transactions. Management reporting systems may require integration with OIS for report archiving on computer-output microfilm or for the incorporation of environmental information obtained via videotex into the appropriate reports.

The *productivity* of the more complex forms of knowledge work has proven difficult to measure. Managerial work, as analyzed by Henry Mintzberg (Mintzberg, 1973), is 78 percent communication in various form, including meetings, telephone conversations, and travel tours. It is entirely unrealistic to expect that the electronic modes of communication offered by OIS will replace most personal communications. But the availability and advantages of OIS do cut down on the number of meetings and the amount of travel that would have been necessary in their absence. They can also make the remaining meetings more effective. The ability to promptly access a needed document, to collaborate with co-workers through groupware, or to make decisions with a GDSS are all examples of how a knowledge worker's capabilities can be augmented by OIS.

Figure 16.15 shows in a modified form how Ronald Uhlig and his colleagues (Uhlig, 1979) envision the impact of OIS on management productivity. While a savings of two hours and forty-five minutes on an eight-hour work day should be considered speculative, the nature of the productivity increase is captured nicely by this picture.

Major increases in office productivity are expected not from improving existing business processes by injecting technological innovations, but from the reengineering of office procedures by breaking away from the outdated assumptions underlying office operations—and only then selecting the appropriate technological support (Hammer, 1990). Some companies, moreover, support such overhaul with new, quality-oriented methods of evaluating office workers. In this evaluation, companies such as American Express or USAA, an insurance and investment management company, use performance indices that emphasize quality as perceived by the customer (Henkoff, 1991; Bernstein, 1991).

The communications media of OIS are able to offer managers *access to rich information:* personal, informal, and unstructured. Richard Daft and Robert Lengel (Daft, 1986) found that the information sources managers prefer are, in order of decreasing desirability and richness: face-to-face meetings, telephone, personal documents, impersonal documents, and numeric reports. We should note that OIS facilitate access to all but the last source of information.

The rapid communication afforded by OIS has enabled many organizations to change their *structures.* The principal effects include flattening of the organizational pyramid owing to executives' ability to exercise wider control, and the capability to create a flexible network organization (adhocracy) with teams as basic building blocks. Note again that these are not inherent effects of the technology, but rather of its purposeful and effective use.

The *work roles* of managerial/professional personnel versus clerical/secretarial workers are also affected by OIS. In an optimistic scenario, OIS enrich clerical work. Managers who are able to communicate with others through OIS and without the mediation of their secretaries could expect their secretaries to do

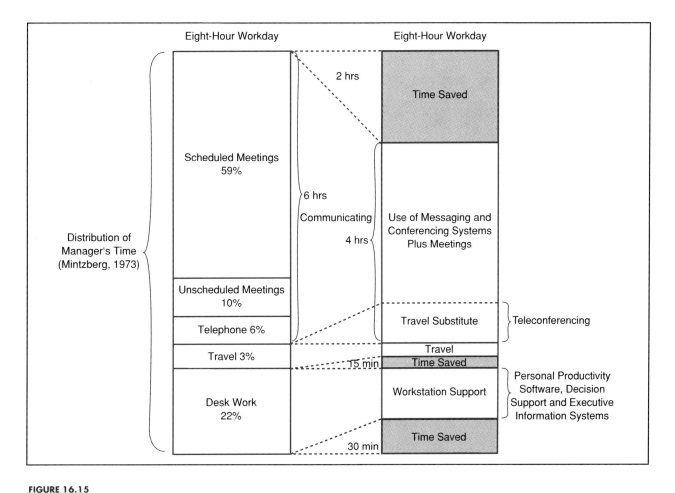

FIGURE 16.15

Potential impact of OIS on management.

(Adapted from Uhlig, 1979)

more challenging work—for example, assisting in budget development. Indeed, some job descriptions for secretarial work now call for proficiency in productivity tools, including the development of spreadsheets.

A controversy exists, however, regarding the nature of clerical work with OIS. Different theorists' perspectives range from an "electronic sweatshop," with deskilled and routinized jobs, to a self-managed group with enriched jobs and meaningful roles for each worker. Those who take the more somber views (such as Zuboff, 1988), predict that knowledge work will become polarized into challenging work done by managers and professionals and the entirely routinized work of clerks.

OIS may also impact the *distribution of power* and influence in an organization (Lee, 1991) and thus engender resistance activities that we shall introduce to you in Section 18.8 as "counterimplementation."

Office *information flows* may be affected at various levels by OIS. OIS technologies bring their own options. A study of information flows is a necessary prerequisite to the development or modification of OIS; new kinds of information flows result from the adoption of new technologies. Such studies are done as a part of corporate reengineering efforts. The notion of a "global office" means shifting office work to the areas of a country—or the world—with low labor costs, as took place earlier in manufacturing. Telecommuting, with knowledge workers working predominantly at home, often clashes with an organization's culture: you must be present to be promoted or to be plugged into the grapevine. "Portable executives" and other "portable" knowledge workers, such as brokers, have emerged—your workplace can be anywhere where you can place your laptop, fax machine, and cellular phone (certain to be packaged together soon). "Smart" buildings with digitally switched telephone communication, network readiness, and computerized building management are built to house new offices. As the Integrated Services Digital Network (ISDN), which we introduced in chapter 7, becomes the accepted medium for wide area networks, the use of OIS relying on multimedia communication is expected to increase very significantly.

As OIS evolve, they may become a repository of *organizational memory,* the knowledge of problems encountered, solutions adopted, and outcomes experienced by the organization (Schatz, 1991/92). This knowledge enables an organization to function effectively; it is today, however, largely contained in the minds of experienced managers.

Technologies Do Not Guarantee Success

OIS are built with powerful—and expensive—technologies. However, they can produce expensive failures just as they can lead to success. The most frequent reasons for failure are:

- "Technologization" of an existing work flow, instead of redesign of the structure of work to take advantage of an appropriate technology
- Lack of systems approach to OIS development: creation of unconnected "islands of automation"
- Lack of integration with other MIS systems
- Lack of relationship to clear business goals
- Lack of cost-benefit analysis (many specific OIS concerns are discussed in Strassman, 1985)
- Lack of a proper implementation process, in particular training (for a set of specific techniques, see, for example, Erlich, 1987)
- Lack of continual assessment of the way a specific technology is being used in a firm—and consequent lack of intervention when needed

Many of these issues will be further discussed in Part 5 of this book, which focuses on the development and implementation of information systems.

. . . .

SUMMARY

The primary objective of office information systems (OIS) is to support communication among knowledge workers in an office setting. Document management, message handling, electronic meeting support, and group work support are the principal functions of OIS.

Document management provides archival storage and prompt access to documents. The older and less expensive micrographic technology is being partly supplanted by digital image processing. Complete electronic management of documents includes entry, storage, retrieval, and, if needed, updating (for textual documents rather than images) as well as printing or publishing. Hypertext and hypermedia are emerging as powerful forms of electronic documents.

OIS can store and forward text messages through E-mail, voice messages via voice mail, and handwritten messages or documents with facsimile machines.

Conferencing support offered by OIS permits participants to be remote in space as well as in time. Audio and video teleconferencing facilities enable participants at multiple remote locations to communicate by voice or image and voice, respectively. Computer conferencing modes include electronic bulletin boards, computer teleconferencing, and group decision support systems.

Groupware, an emerging class of OIS software, supports collaboration, coordination, and communication in workgroups.

OIS manifestly change the landscape of organizations, and their use may have a significant impact on organizational structure and the nature of work. The OIS domain is plagued today, perhaps more than other MIS components, by the "technology archipelago" phenomenon—unconnected islands of technology that are difficult to integrate due to the absence of standards.

ENDNOTES

1. The stimulating article "As We May Think," published in 1945 by Vannevar Bush, the coordinator of the U.S. scientific effort during World War II, has been reprinted in Greif, 1988, pp. 17–34. The term *hypertext* was coined by Ted Nelson, notable for his early articulation of popular computing in the 1960s. An early implementation of hypertext was realized by Douglas Engelbart (the inventor of the computer mouse) in 1968 at the Stanford Research Institute.

2. "Management by Necessity." *Inc.*, March 1989, p. 39.

3. "Exec Prescribes Change at Firm." *Computerworld*, July 24, 1989, p. 8.

4. Based on Kleinschrod, 1989.

5. Kraemer, 1988, p. 131.

KEY TERMS AND CONCEPTS

Office information systems (OIS)
Office
Knowledge work
Electronic meeting systems
Micrographics
Computer-output microfilm
Electronic document management
Digital image processing
Text information management systems
Corporate electronic printing
Hypertext
Hypermedia
Electronic mail (E-mail)

Electronic information services
Videotex
Voice mail
Facsimile (fax)
Audio and video teleconferencing
Computer conferencing
Electronic bulletin board
Computer teleconferencing
Group decision support system (GDSS)
Decision room
Workgroup
Groupware

QUESTIONS

1. What is an office, and what are office information systems (OIS)?

2. What is the principal stumbling block still separating us from the "office of the future"?

3. Is an automated office a paperless office? Explain your answer.

4. In functional terms, contrast micrographics and electronic document management.

5. What are the principal steps in processing a document stored as an image?

6. What are the principal steps in processing a document stored as a text file?

7. What is the principal distinction between hypertext and the traditional document from the user's (reader's) point of view?

8. List the capabilities E-mail can offer to an organization and its knowledge workers.

9. What is the relationship between E-mail and electronic information services?

10. In a table, compare the advantages and drawbacks of the three messaging technologies presented in the chapter from the user's point of view (ignore financial considerations).

11. What are the different forms of teleconferencing, and what facilities do they offer? What is the role of computers in each of these?

12. List two issues which would lend themselves especially well to computer teleconferencing support and two that would be well supported by GDSS. State your reasons.

13. Describe the combination of technological opportunities and demand pull that led to the emergence of groupware.

14. Consider yourself a group manager committed to the use of groupware. List how you would employ various groupware functions, beginning with organizing your own team and continuing with work on a group project.

ISSUES FOR DISCUSSION

1. Will there ever be a fully integrated OIS? What factors facilitate integration, and what factors act against it?

2. Consider the perspective that an OIS is a system for supporting various aspects of knowledge work. How can it increase the productivity of various categories of knowledge workers?

3. Take an office function familiar to you, and specify the best way to automate it, considering interactions with other information systems and the environment. Try to establish approximate costs for the automation.

4. Trace the progress of engineering documentation from the initial "paperless" stage to a published maintenance manual.

5. Discuss this contention: "once made available, a superior technology will always have a beneficial effect on an organization."

Two Document Management Systems: A Study in Success and Failure

Digital Image Processing of Charge Card Receipts at American Express

The Travel Related Services subsidiary of American Express is committed to furnishing its cardholders with copies of charge receipts. This practice, known as country club billing, has been abandoned by other major credit card issuers as too expensive; they simply list the charges on the monthly bill. But customers do prefer country club billing for control and accounting—and this means that an opportunity for competitive edge definitely exists.

To control the cost of service differentiation, American Express has designed a system which has lowered its billing costs by 25 percent by dispensing with the actual paper charge receipts at the point of input. Digital image processing technology is employed.

Originally, the company used a micrographic system, which was abandoned in favor of digital image processing. In the former system, the incoming paper receipts were microfilmed for permanent archival storage. However, all further receipt processing was based on the actual paper copy. An OCR reader was used to read in from the paper receipt the account and invoice numbers, with only 82 percent accuracy. Charge amounts were entered from the receipt by a computer operator, who also verified the numbers read in with OCR. Receipts were coded with a printer (that is, all the numbers and charges were printed on them) and sorted. A mainframe computer printed the bill, which was attached to the receipt and mailed to the customer.

In the new system, the incoming receipts are sent through a scanner, which digitizes the image (that is, converts it to a string of bits) to be stored in the computer memory. At this point, all paper slips are discarded. Printed data, such as the account and invoice numbers, are scanned with OCR readers from the digitized image and stored. The accuracy of scanning a digitized image, as opposed to scanning a paper slip, is very high (99 percent, in fact). Handwritten charge amounts are entered by a clerk from the slip image displayed on a VDT screen. Now all the alphanumeric data are available for processing. The reduced images of receipts are printed eight to a page with a laser printer and sent to the customer. The images themselves are stored permanently on laser disks for easy retrieval later on. Some 350 million receipts are processed annually.

In the future, the company intends to employ neural network technology (discussed in chapter 15) to "recognize" the handwritten data on the slips, thus entirely eliminating clerical work from the system.

American Express stresses superior service as its competitive advantage. When a customer calls with a question about a bill, the telephone representative needs to have access to the receipts. When the older, micrographic, system was used, 300 employees were needed to retrieve records for the phone reps, and delays of several days sometimes resulted. In the new system, phone reps retrieve the receipts themselves on a VDT screen (and six people are needed to retrieve the old, micrographic records).

American Express has successfully deployed digital image processing technology to provide the missing link between paper documents and access to the data on them. It has realized immediate savings in billing costs and differentiated its service. The corporation has extensive plans for maintaining the system as a strategic weapon. By tracking charge slips, the company is able to develop very narrowly targeted marketing segments. For example, a cardholder may be identified as a frequent flier to Paris or an avid baseball player. Her monthly billing package would then contain customized advertising from a Parisian hotel or from a local sporting goods store.

American Express is experimenting with distributing image-processing equipment to merchants who accept the company's card. The equipment includes a PC—and American Express considers this a beachhead from which other services will be offered to their merchants in the future.

Success did not come suddenly to American Express. The company has an established track record and the organizational means to study emerging technologies and their applicability to its business. In 1986, the company initiated a $100-million program called Genesis to explore these technologies aggressively. The program is sponsored by top executive officers of the company, which also has an active emerging technologies group. American Express had begun actively experimenting with digital image technology several years before initiating the receipt processing project.

An Effort to Automate Patent Information at the U.S. Patent and Trademark Office

The fast pace of innovation in an information society requires the protection of rights to intellectual property through a patent system. The U.S. Patent and Trademark Office is the agency charged with reviewing patent applications and making patent records accessible to the public. A speedy process for reviewing patent claims is necessary to maintain the pace of innovation.

The agency now has a fully paper-based system. About 43 million patent documents are kept in thousands of wooden files, filling miles of shelves in three buildings in Crystal City, Virginia, a suburb of Washington, D.C. Because of the slowness and lack of discipline in the operation of a paper-based system, as many as 27 percent of patents are missing at any one time in some areas. This delays the processing of new patent applications. About a million new documents arrive each year, including 80,000 new U.S. patents which have to be cross-referenced with others and indexed, foreign patents filed at the agency, and technical journals. In the words of William Kefauver, general counsel of Bell Laboratories, the present system "is totally unacceptable. If it is working at all now, it's not likely to work much longer."

The agency initiated an automation program in 1982, with the plan calling for a totally paperless office by 1990. The system was to rely on digital image processing and optical disk storage, and was even expected to include electronic publishing. It was hoped that the system would be available for testing in 1984, made accessible to patent examiners by 1987, and to the public by 1990. In 1983, the agency awarded a $289-million eighteen-year contract for system development to a private firm. The contract guaranteed profit to the contractor even if the project significantly exceeded original cost estimates.

By 1985 the project was already a year behind schedule; the Patent Office now regards it as "not impossible" that the ultimate cost will run $600 to $800 million.

In the summer of 1988, several years behind schedule, a pilot system was tested by a small group of examiners and evaluated by outside experts. Among the problems that surfaced were: the complexity and difficulty of system use, unreliable operation (the system failed to locate some of the documents), and search speeds slower than manual search. According to Thomas P. Giammo, the new assistant commissioner of patents for information systems, who was brought in during June of 1988: "We really get no short-term increases in productivity. The real gains we're seeing now [are] a substantial improvement in the quality of the work being done."

The expert evaluators concluded that the level of skill of the Patent Office personnel who had been responsible for the project "seems to be less than that needed for a project of this scale and complexity," and that "major decisions have been delegated to the prime contractor." Moreover, the agency had not done a proper cost assessment. Critics of the computerization effort claim that the Patent Office planners did not understand the scope of the project, which will have to store for on-line access some 30 trillion bytes of text. Hundreds of users will have to be able to use the system simultaneously. Several basic system components, such as examiners' workstations and data retrieval equipment, was not specified at the outset.

Giammo has adopted a staged approach to system implementation, lauded by the experts. The present pilot system will be further tested, after which new groups of examiners will be added one at a time and assessments made after each such step. Giammo believes that modular design of the system supports this approach and will permit developers to change system components as needed in the future. It is expected that 1,500 examiners will be able to use the system by 1993, and the public will join them at a later time. The plan for a "paperless office" has been delayed indefinitely.

Concerns voiced by Congress and by interested industry groups include the following: Many express a lack of credulity as to whether the system will work at all, or whether greater productivity will be achieved even if it does work. Another concern regards public access. The current patent search room can be used free of charge. The Patent Office now plans to recoup some of the system costs by charging outside users in the future—but given the costs of the system, such charges may be prohibitive and may inhibit the process of innovation.

Based on Edmund L. Andrews, "Patent Files vs. Computer Age." *The New York Times*, September 12, 1988, pp. D1, D3; John Markoff, "American Express Goes High-Tech." *The New York Times*, Business Section, July 31, 1988, pp. 1, 6; and "The Graphics Revolution." *Business Week*, November 28, 1988, pp. 142–56.

Case Study Questions

1. How realistic were the system planners at American Express and in the U.S. Patent Office, respectively? In which case were existing organizational strengths exploited? What were these strengths? Which case exhibits the characteristics of a "grand design"?

2. Provide a block diagram of the digital image processing system used by American Express.

3. What competitive advantage has the American Express system conferred on the company? List all the aspects.

4. How can the American Express system contribute to sustaining the company's competitive advantage in the future? List all the possibilities.

5. What were the crucial deficiencies of the U.S. Patent Office's approach to the automation of document processing?

SELECTED REFERENCES

Akscyn, Robert M.; McCracken, Donald L.; and Yoder, Elise A. "KMS: A Distributed Hypermedia System for Managing Knowledge in Organizations." *Communications of the ACM,* 31, 7, July 1988, pp. 820–35.

Bernstein, Aaron. "Quality is Becoming Job One in the Office, Too." *Business Week,* April 29, 1991, pp. 52–56.

Brandt, Richard, and others. "The Personal Computer Finds Its Missing Link." *Business Week,* June 5, 1989, pp. 120–28.

Casey, Richard G., and Ferguson, David R. "Intelligent Forms Processing." *IBM Systems Journal,* 29, 3, 1990, pp. 435–50.

Conklin, E. Jeffrey. "Hypertext: An Introduction and a Survey." *Computer,* 20, 9, September 1987, pp. 17–41.

Daft, Richard L., and Lengel, Robert H. "Organizational Information Requirements, Media Richness and Structural Design." *Management Science,* 32, 5, May 1986, pp. 554–71.

Dennis, Alan R.; George, Joey F.; Jessup, L. M.; Nunamaker, Jay F., Jr.; and Vogel, Douglas R. "Information Technology to Support Electronic Meetings." *MIS Quarterly,* 12, 4, December 1988, 591–624.

Dennis, Alan R.; Nunamaker, Jay F., Jr.; and Vogel, Douglas R. "A Comparison of Laboratory and Field Research in the Study of Electronic Meeting Systems." *Journal of Management Information Systems,* 7, 3, Winter 1990/91, pp. 107–35.

Dennis, Alan R.; Nunamaker, Jay F., Jr.; and Paranka, David. "Supporting the Search for Competitive Advantage." *Journal of Management Information Systems,* 8, 1, Summer 1991, pp. 5–36.

Drucker, Peter F. "The Coming of the New Organization." *Harvard Business Review,* January-February 1988, pp. 45–53.

Ellis, Clarence; Gibbs, Simon; and Rein, Gail. "Groupware: Some Issues and Experiences." *Communications of the ACM,* 34, 1, January 1991, pp. 39–58.

Erlich, Susan F. "Strategies for Encouraging Successful Adoption of Office Communication Systems." *ACM Transactions on Office Information Systems,* 5, 4, October 1987, pp. 340–57.

Fisher, Marsha J. "Digging Out with Image Technology." *Datamation,* April 15, 1989, pp. 18–27.

Flores, Fernando, and others. "Computer Systems and the Design of Organizational Interaction." *ACM Transactions on Office Information Systems,* 6, 2, April 1988, pp. 153–72.

Greif, Irene, ed. *Computer-Supported Cooperative Work: A Book of Readings.* San Mateo, Calif.: Morgan Kaufmann, 1988.

Hall, P. A. V., and Papadopoulos, S. "Hypertext Systems and Applications." *Information and Software Technology,* 32, 7, September 1990, pp. 477–90.

Hammer, Michael. "Reeningeering Work: Don't Automate, Obliterate." *Harvard Business Review,* July-August 1990, pp. 104–12.

Henkoff, Ronald. "Make Your Office More Productive." *Fortune,* February 25, 1991, pp. 72–84.

Hiltz, Starr Roxanne, and Turoff, Murray. "Structuring Computer-Mediated Communications Systems to Avoid Information Overload." *Communications of the ACM,* 28, 7, July 1985, pp. 680–704.

Hirschheim, R. A. *Office Automation: A Social and Organizational Perspective.* Chichester, England: John Wiley, 1985.

Hirschheim, R. A. "Understanding the Office: A Social-Analytic Perspective." *ACM Transactions on Office Information Systems,* 4, 4, October 1986, pp. 331–44.

Hoerr, John. "The Payoff from Team Work." *Business Week,* July 10, 1989, pp. 56–62.

Johansen, Robert, and Bullen, Christine. "Thinking Ahead: What to Expect from Teleconferencing." *Harvard Business Review,* March-April 1984, pp. 4–10.

Johansen, Robert. *Groupware: Computer Support for Business Teams.* New York: Free Press, 1988.

Keen, Peter G. W. *Competing In Time: Using Telecommunications for Competitive Advantage.* Cambridge, Mass.: Ballinger, 1988.

Kingman, Lauren C., III; Lambert, Robert E.; and Steen, Robert P. "Operational Image Systems." *IBM Systems Journal,* 29, 3, 1990, pp. 304–12.

Kleinschrod, Walter A. "Electronic Mail Services Deliver." *Today's Office,* February 1989, pp. 34–38.

Konstadt, Paul. "The Sharper Image." *CIO,* April 1991, pp. 32–40.

Lai, Kum-Yew; Malone, Thomas W.; and Yu, Keh-Chang. "Object Lens: A 'Spreadsheet' for Cooperative Work." *ACM Transactions on Office Information Systems,* 6, 4, October 1988, pp. 332–53.

Latamore, G. Berton. "Your Choice: Public or Private Electronic Mail." *Computerworld,* April 18, 1988, pp. 87–92.

Lee, Soonchul. "Impact of Office Information Systems on Potential Power and Influence." *Journal of Management Information Systems,* 8, 2, Fall 1991.

McCusker, Tom. "The Message Is Integration." *Datamation,* August 15, 1991, pp. 31–2.

McGrath, J. E. *Groups: Interaction and Performance.* Englewood Cliffs, N.J.: Prentice Hall, 1984.

Malone, Thomas W., and others. "Intelligent Information-Sharing Systems." *Communications of the ACM,* 30, 5, May 1987, pp. 390–402.

Mintzberg, Henry. *The Nature of Managerial Work.* New York: Harper & Row, 1973.

Nunamaker, Jay F., Jr. and others. "Electronic Meeting Systems to Support Group Work." *Communications of the ACM,* 34, 7, July 1991, pp. 40–61.

Opper, Susanna. "Making the Right Moves with Groupware." *Personal Computing,* December 1988, pp. 134–40.

Pelton, Charles. "E-Mail's Message to Corporate America." *Information Week,* July 3–10, 1989, pp. 12–13.

Pollack, Andrew. "Next Office Revolution: 'Voice Mail.'" *The New York Times,* August 20, 1988, pp. 1, 35.

Pruitt, D. G. *Negotiating Behavior.* New York: Academic Press, 1981.

Richman, Louise. "Software Catches Team Spirit." *Fortune,* June 8, 1987, pp. 125–36.

Rifkin, Glenn. "Computers That Hear and Respond." *The New York Times,* August 14, 1991, pp. D1, D5.

Schatz, Bruce R. "Building an Electronic Community System." *Journal of Management Information Systems,* 8, 3, Winter 1991/92.

Smith, John B., and Weiss, Stephen F. "Hypertext." *Communications of the ACM,* 31, 7, July 1988, pp. 816–19.

Stevens, Larry. "Corporate Electronic Publishing." *Computerworld,* January 16, 1989, pp. 59–62.

Strassman, Paul A. *Information Payoff.* New York: Free Press, 1985.

Straub, Detmar W., Jr., and Beauclair, Renee A. "Current and Future Uses of GDSS Technology: Report on a Recent Empirical Study." *Journal of Management Information Systems,* 5, 1, Summer 1988, pp. 101–16.

Tapscott, Don. *Office Automation: A User-Driven Method.* New York: Plenum Press, 1985.

Thyfault, Mary E. "Spreading the Word." *Information Week,* July 15, 1991, pp. 40–42.

Uhlig, Ronald P.; Farber, David; and Bair, James H. *Office of the Future.* Amsterdam: North Holland, 1979.

Vogel, Douglas R., and others. "Electronic Meeting System Experience at IBM." *Journal of Management Information Systems,* 6, 3, Winter 1989–90, pp. 25–43.

Zuboff, Shoshana. *In the Age of the Smart Machine: The Future of Work and Power.* New York, Basic Books, 1988.

POWERFUL EXPERT SYSTEM SUITE AS A STRATEGIC RESOURCE

"**T**hese are new times. Customers demand products that suit their individual needs, and businesses have to figure out some way of delivering these customized products cost-effectively. . . . For Digital Equipment Corporation, this problem was at the heart of its minicomputer business."[1] It continues to be at the heart of the company's strategy of à la carte selling its many and varied computer system products.

If an award for the most famous business application of expert systems were granted by a pertinent academy, the XCON computer configuration system at Digital Equipment Corporation (DEC) would win hands down. XCON was the first expert system in daily industrial production use. It is today the cornerstone of a set of four expert systems deeply embedded in the value chain of the owner company. We shall look at the principal capabilities of today's XCON/XSEL ES suite and see what lessons may be drawn from organizational experience with its development and exploitation.

Why the XCON/XSEL Suite Was Developed

How did DEC become an early and immensely successful entrant in the ES arena? Its commitment to a la carte products—offering exactly what the customer needs—and its highly complex product line brought it there. Truth be told, it took committed individuals to achieve this success.

Here is the scene that Dennis O'Connor, the man who championed DEC's introduction of these systems as the 1980s dawned, saw then. The company had just successfully introduced its VAX line of minicomputers. Other product introductions were to follow. Highly complex products were being developed with increasing rates of change. Yet the key elements of the process appeared weak.

At that time, a salesperson took the customer's order, which could run to many pages. Multiple CPUs, a variety of peripheral equipment, software, interconnections, cabinets—all these had to work together and meet the customer's requirements as well as environmental constraints. Technical editors (engineers) had to check whether the order was "clean"—whether it would work. To tell the truth, if an order was complex, it was not at all likely that it would work—drawing up this highly technical material required significant engineering expertise. The embarrassment of redrawing and renegotiating an order was a frequent experience. This was the sales problem.

There was also a delivery problem at the other end of DEC's value chain. After a "clean" order was manufactured, the company had to make certain it would work when installed at the customer's site. To achieve this certainty, the order had to be assembled by field engineers at one of a number of final-assembly-and-test plants. (Order components usually came from various DEC manufacturing plants.) Then the assembled order would be tested, corrected if necessary (and owing to human error in this complex environment, this was no rare occurrence), disassembled, and shipped to the customer, to be once again assembled at the customer's site.

O'Connor saw the future doing things this way and did not like it. DEC's product line and sales were growing rapidly. The number of final-assembly-and-test plants would have to grow rapidly as well. How many highly qualified field engineers would be needed, and where would they come from? The salespeople would certainly produce fewer "clean" orders in an increasingly complex environment. Volumes and product differentiation would progress—but could the existing processes support this growth? Success could actually strangle the company—it might be forced to abandon its commitment to customized systems. Would the customers then abandon the company?

The glimmer of a solution was suggested to O'Connor by Samuel Fuller, DEC's vice-president for research: Fuller suggested the company look at the AI work done at Carnegie Mellon University, whose computer science department has always had strong ties with DEC. O'Connor earmarked a small sum from the discretionary fund of another project to engage John McDermott, a young computer science professor at Carnegie Mellon, in helping to solve DEC's problems. By April 1979, McDermott had developed a prototype expert system called, engagingly, R1. This was the beginning of XCON—the eXpert CONfigurator that would in the

future solve what originally had looked like only a delivery problem—ensuring that a customer's configuration worked correctly. Since then, XCON has permeated the very fabric of DEC.

The sales problem was addressed a few years later by the interactive XSEL expert system, which works with XCON. XSEL reduces the time a salesperson needs to configure a system from between one and three hours to just fifteen minutes. Configuration accuracy is 99 percent with the system—and 70 percent without. As one of the managers put it, "That 29 percent difference is what lets us stay in business."

The growth of the XCON/XSEL environment is shown in figure IV.1.

Functionality of the ES Suite at Digital

The functionality of the currently operational four expert systems is very extensive:

1. XCON validates the technical correctness of the customer order, configures the order, and specifies its assembly. Among other things, XCON does the following:

   - Configures hardware components, such as CPUs, memory components, power supplies, cabinets, and peripherals
   - Diagrams the complete system configuration
   - Determines full cabling
   - Generates warning messages if the order's technical validity is questionable

2. XSEL is an interactive system that assists the salespeople in selecting the actual parts that will make up each customer's order.

Thus, XSEL:

- Permits part selection by generic name
- Performs a completeness check and suggests the addition of certain parts
- Checks software compatibility
- Provides the environmental requirements for the computer room
- Is linked with the Automated Quotation System for pricing

3. XFL diagrams the computer-room floor layout for the configuration. In doing so, it:

- Provides a "minimum footprint" floor layout
- Allows the user to specify room dimension and equipment placement
- Allows for several configurations on one site

4. XCLUSTER helps to specify configurations of multiple nodes of a given equipment type.

Among the expert systems under development are:

5. XNET—for designing local area networks (component selection and validation of the configuration)

6. SIZER—a more advanced system that would perform capacity planning; that is, determine the computer resources needed for a given use in a given organization

The ES suite handles the configuration of all DEC's products: forty-two different CPU families, with supporting peripherals and software. The environment is highly dynamic: by the time a new product is announced, the expert systems have to be updated. Thus, the company provides major releases of these systems once a quarter, with at least one update in the interim.

Organizational Scope

The XCON/XSEL ES suite supports the core business of the company. The use of the expert systems spans the firm's value chain:

- The systems are the fundamental tool of the *Sales* department, which uses them to generate quotations for customers and ensure that each order is technically valid.
- *Manufacturing* employs the system to verify buildability of all incoming orders, to determine which plants are to build the order components, to guide component assembly, and to determine what diagnostic routines should be run on an order. Plant technicians use elaborate diagrams produced by XCON to put assemblies together.
- Both *Engineering* and *Manufacturing* use the systems to identify potential problems in systems level design and manufacturability; they also learn how to design better systems in the future.
- *Field Service* is supported in its need to assemble the order in the customer's individual environment, possibly integrating it with the systems already in place there. Service representatives also use the XCON-produced diagrams.

The ES suite is linked to many other information systems in DEC's worldwide operations, and many "indirect" users access them as well. The XSEL system, for example, is employed by DEC's OEM (original equipment manufacturer) customers. These firms add value to DEC's equipment by providing additional hardware and software for specialized markets and selling these as turnkey systems to their own clients.

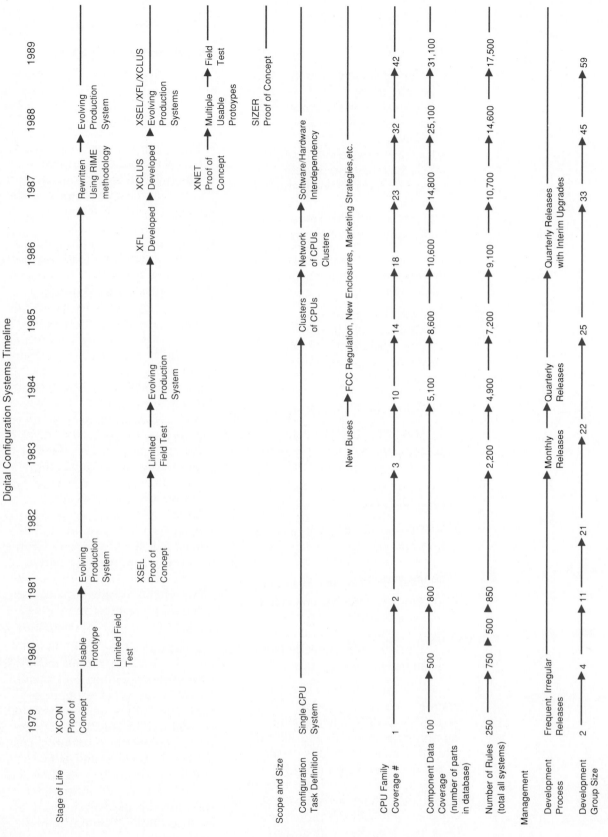

Digital Configuration Systems Timeline

FIGURE IV.1

The growth of the configuration expert systems at DEC.

DEC is a highly decentralized company—many people make decisions at all levels. The ES suite with its knowledge bases is truly the lifeblood of the firm.

A new system does not necessarily find immediate acceptance throughout its intended constituency. For example, despite its obvious advantages, many salespeople did not immediately take to XSEL. Rather the contrary—they stayed with the tried and true method, taking orders and configuring systems by hand, until they had to change. But it wasn't management that forced them to use the system—DEC's corporate culture is not stick-oriented. The fact was simply that within nine months in the early 1980s, the company's product base was almost totally modified—and the best way for a salesperson to find out what had happened was to use the expert system, which was kept fully up-to-date. With the help of XSEL, salespeople could also give a customer a few configurations to choose from and create the floor layouts with the other expert systems—in other words, they could sell more effectively. Complex (read "commission-generating") orders were won because the system could reliably configure and fully specify them in no time at all.

Benefits of the ES Suite

DEC is strategically dependent on its configuration expert systems worldwide. DEC executives feel that if XCON were turned off, the company would not be able to sell its products. Benefits accrue both in the order-processing cycle (take the order—manufacture the order—assemble the order on the customer's site) and in new product introduction.

The ability to provide a build-to-order system to customers, addressing their specialized needs within short time-lines, is considered a key competitive advantage. Customer satisfaction is also high because the configurations generated by XCON are optimal for each customer's needs. In addition, orders are configured in a consistent fashion. Since there are several ways in which an order can be configured, customer confusion was rife prior to the introduction of the expert systems. This was particularly important for the OEM firms, which order large numbers of the same system.

With the expert systems, the technical accuracy of orders entering manufacturing is high. When components configured by XCON reach the customer's site, the configuration is assured to work—and without the need to assemble and disassemble them first at a DEC site. The lag time between order entry and execution has been cut from weeks or months to days. The results are higher customer satisfaction and lower inventory-carrying costs.

All of these capabilities are achieved at a lower cost than would have been possible with other alternatives, which enables DEC to offer competitive prices.

The process of new product introduction is much simplified by the fact that the entire body of configuration information is available in one place—the expert system—in an active form (as opposed to manuals) by the time the product is introduced. This facilitates the training of field service people, as well as the manufacturing of the product itself. Realignment of manufacturing capacity is also simplified: one single source of manufacturing knowledge—again, the expert system—accessible throughout the corporation makes it possible to assign orders flexibly to plants, which ensures efficient plant utilization. The product-introduction cycle has thus been appreciably shortened—an important competitive advantage.

In 1987, the system processed some 80,000 orders. The net annual return on these systems is estimated conservatively at $40 million. The point is, however, that without this system DEC would hardly be able to do business the way it does—no dollar figure can be placed on the capability to compete effectively in the marketplace.

Technological Challenges

Here are the principal challenges the XCON/XSEL system developers face:

1. The Complexity of the Expert System Suite

The architecture of the suite is shown in figure IV.2. The importance of the overall architectural design of the system has been recognized (after some time) as paramount. Maintainability is a principal objective, considering the dynamic environment of system operation.

As we can see, the suite is considered architecturally to consist of two principal expert systems: modularized XCON, and XSEL, which includes other expert systems. XCON consisted as of September 1988 of over 10,000 rules, the three systems combined into XSEL of approximately 6,000 rules; and the proto-type of XNET was also running. Rules themselves are complex—there are many condition and action elements per rule.

The systems also include five databases. The XSEL IO database contains the questions it and the related expert systems ask the user (such as "How many of your terminals will be connected to a server?") The Component & Template database contains data on over 30,000 parts, with an average of forty attributes per part, as well as templates of their connectivity with other parts (for example, the number and size of slots). The Configuration database holds the combination of user input and system output on each order entered into the system for processing. The Output Diagram database contains over 1,200 graphical diagrams for all major part types (such as cabinets or wiring backplanes).

A large part of the overall system was programmed in procedural languages (such as Basic, C, and Pascal) to perform input/output or file processing, for example.

2. The Need for a Software Engineering Methodology and a Powerful ES Development Environment

A software development methodology and an environment for ES development (RIME) were created in-house to support ongoing development and maintenance.

The custom-made RIME simplifies the expression of rules and produces significant execution-time efficiencies (an inferencing process with many very complex rules requires huge processing power). RIME replaced the standard VAX OPS5 development environment for rule-based ES. An example of a rule, stated in the RIME language, that

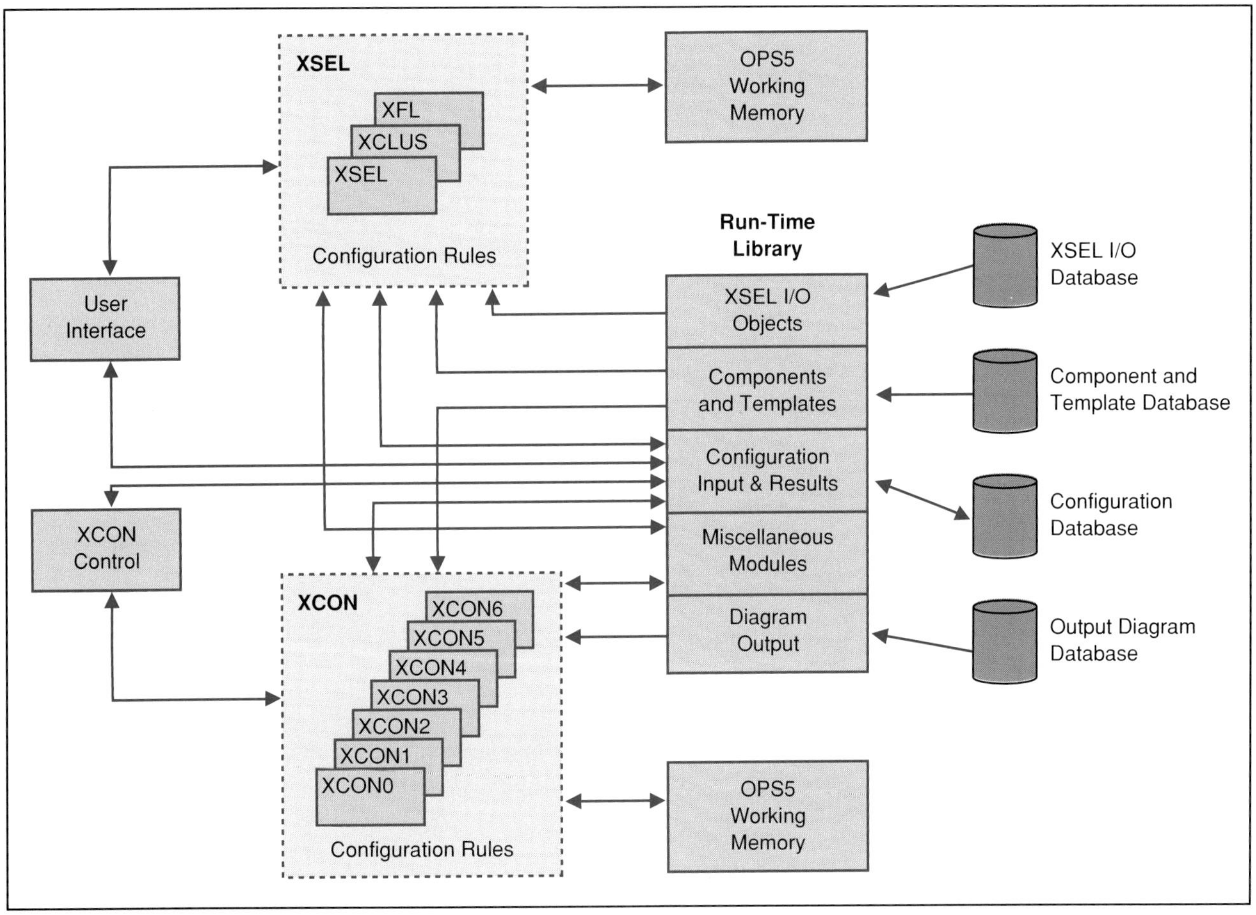

FIGURE IV.2

The architecture of the expert system suite at DEC.

has permitted immense simplification of the statements is shown in figure IV.3 (where the rule has been rendered in English for readability).

3. Volatility of the Domain

About 40 percent of the rules in the knowledge base of the ES suite are changed every year. This is due to the continuous product innovation at DEC, which releases several hundred *major* new products each year, and to the modification of existing products. It is also due to continually improved techniques of configuration and improved representation of particular knowledge aspects. Also, since the advent of distributed processing, the systems

are no longer configured in isolation; rather, they have become parts of clusters and networks.

4. Expanding Functionality

The user constituency is continually expanding, with each new group bringing its own requirements. This in turn keeps expanding the functionality of the systems. For example, when the plant technicians began to use the XCON-produced diagrams as basic blueprints for assembling computer components, specialized databases and procedural (non-ES) code had to be included for the purpose. Also, interaction with other, non-knowledge-based systems, is increasingly required.

FIGURE IV.3

An XCON rule, expressed in RIME (and simplified for presentation).

Rule Name: Configure-device:propose:500b:select-container

IF

		Comments
C1	The current step of the process of configuring devices involves proposing alternatives;	*The current activity of the system is to propose tasks that will ultimately result in the configuration of a device*
C2	and there is at least one unconfigured device that needs to be placed inside a container;	
C3	and no container has yet been chosen;	
C4	and no device in which other devices can be placed has been chosen as a container;	*There are some large tape drives that have a compartment in the bottom suitable for disk placement*
C5	and the process of selecting a container has not yet been proposed;	
C6	and there has been no problem identified concerning selecting a container;	*If there is already an identified problem with selecting a container, the task should not be proposed again until the problem has been resolved.*

THEN

A1   propose to go through the process of selecting a container.

User expectations from a system that is considered a success are high and keep rising.

Organizational Issues

A system of this strategic importance serves two purposes: to *exploit* and to *sustain* competitive advantage. The system is a "production shop" that has to operate in a timely, reliable, and accurate fashion and be maintained in the short term. In the long term, this system also serves as a testbed from which innovation flows. DEC introduced many technological innovations both in the system itself and in their products thanks to the ability to test them on the system. A balance between these two objectives—producing competitive products and creating innovations that will sustain competitive advantage—is crucial.

Key functional roles of organizational actors have been recognized and carefully maintained at DEC. The role concept is treated with the utmost seriousness: the firm periodically assesses which roles are currently filled and who fills them best. One person may play more than one role, but unfilled roles are not tolerated for any period of time.

Two roles at DEC relate to our discussion of technology assimilation in section 12.7: sponsor (a high-level management supporter who provides the funds and other resources) and champion (the manager who provides the strategic vision). Other roles are directly concerned with system development and maintenance. The program manager is a person with a business background who takes responsibility for the project and directly coordinates it. Technical specialists include both knowledge engineers and software integration engineers. The latter have a background in traditional software engineering necessary to ensure the integration of expert systems with other information systems. Experts and users are sometimes the same people, but experts need to be clearly identified. A production system of so wide a scope has many experts (hundreds in the case of XCON). The developers have also learned that initially having only a single expert on a project can be dangerous—it may skew the system toward a single perspective. An optional role is that of researcher/advanced developer, responsible for the long-term goals of a strategic system.

The group responsible for the project—now consisting of fifty-nine people—considers its principal challenge in this effort to have been maintaining a business-technology partnership. For a strategically important system, support of strategic-level management is crucial. This is because such systems create opportunities (or problems) of which tactical-level management may be unaware. Dorothy Leonard-Barton calls DEC's approach in introducing XSEL "integrative innovation":[2] the old model, in which developers "handed off" a technology to users, was replaced by a process of simultaneously altering the technology to fit the evolving organization and by changing the organizational environment to take advantage of the technology.

The development group's work is aligned with general business planning for the corporation. A steering committee, consisting of strategic-level managers from all of the system stakeholders, has been created. This provides long-term direction.

The cost of maintaining the system is very considerable. It is more than balanced, however, by the strategic role of the system and by the increased information processing capacity of the organization.[3]

The environment created at DEC, one that nurtures emerging technologies, is considered the principal reason for the company's success.

1. Feigenbaum, 1988, p. 215.
2. Dorothy Leonard-Barton, "The Case for Integrative Innovation: An Expert System at Digital." *Sloan Management Review*, Fall 1987, pp. 7–19.
3. The increased information processing capacity was computed in terms of the inputs, outputs, and task performance in John J. Sviokla, "An Examination of the Impact of Expert Systems on the Firm: The Case of XCON." *MIS Quarterly*, 14, 2, June 1990, pp. 127–40.

The case study is based primarily on

Edward Feigenbaum; Pamela McCorduck; and H. Penny Nii, *The Rise of the Expert Company*. New York: Times Books, 1988.
A. Kraft, "XCON: An Expert Configuration System," in *The AI Business*, edited by Patrick H. Winston and K. A. Prendergast, Cambridge, Mass.: MIT Press, 1984, pp. 41–49.
Dennis O'Connor and Virginia Barker, "Expert Systems for Configuration at Digital: XCON and Beyond." *Communications of the ACM*, 32, 3, March 1989, pp. 298–318.
Enid Mumford and W. Bruce McDonald, *XSEL's Progress: The Continuing Journey of an Expert System*. Chichester, England: John Wiley, 1989.

Case Study Questions

1. What characterizes the expert system suite at DEC as a system that confers strategic advantage on the company?

2. What components in the company's value chain are directly affected by the ES suite? What employee categories do the primary users come from?

3. What organizational positions are occupied by and what professional backgrounds are needed in the individuals who play the crucial organizational roles in developing and maintaining this system?

4. Relate the organizational capabilities offered by the ES suite to the technical demands on the system ("Because we needed this, we had to have that").

5. Note that, as described, the system addresses operational rather than management concerns. Could you offer three suggestions on how the system may be used, perhaps together with other MIS components, to address managerial concerns? Specify the management level and function that would be supported. (And note that DEC did experiment with expert systems for planning and scheduling and found them wanting.)

MANAGEMENT, DEVELOPMENT, AND OPERATION OF INFORMATION SYSTEMS

The MIS function of a modern organization can take on many forms, depending on the organizational objectives and on the structure of the organization itself. This function is staffed with professionals in a variety of job categories. The informational needs of an organization are also closely related to its business objectives. Information systems must be aligned with these objectives through the MIS planning process, ranging from the strategic, long-term level to an evaluation of the worth of various specific applications.

Information systems needed to satisfy organizational requirements may be acquired from a variety of sources, from purchase to in-house development. Development of a large organizational system requires a correspondingly large commitment of resources. The systems development life cycle is a method for organizing and controlling this effort. It begins with systems analysis, continues through systems design, and goes on to the programming and installation of the particular system. Structured methodologies, supported by computer-aided software engineering (CASE) tools, make it possible to develop reliable and maintainable systems.

Prototyping is an important alternative to life-cycle-based development, as well as an important technique for systems analysis during the course of such development. Decision-oriented systems are best developed with a prototyping technique. All information systems projects are best managed with the help of appropriate software tools.

The development of an operational system does not guarantee its successful implementation. To obtain user acceptance of and commitment to an information system, an implementation process must be conducted to parallel system development.

The operation of information systems is exposed to a number of hazards: human error, computer crime, natural disasters, and equipment failure are some of them. A carefully designed set of general and application controls is necessary to safeguard systems operations. An MIS audit should be performed periodically to ensure that these controls are effective.

In today's rapidly changing environment, information systems need to be changed again and again to match new requirements. This is one of the reasons that maintenance of applications over their entire lifetimes consumes a large part of MIS operations resources.

CHAPTER 17

The MIS Function and Information Systems Planning

Everyone in the information-based organization needs constantly to be thinking through what information he or she requires to do the job and make a contribution.

Peter F. Drucker

In a modern organization, virtually all employees, from line workers to the chief executive officer, are computer users. As we already know, some of them also develop systems for themselves or their workgroups. However, a coherent organizational structure of information systems emerges as the result of planned and organized development led by a specialized functional unit.

In this chapter, we shall see who builds, acquires, operates, and maintains organizational information systems. To this end, we shall discuss how the MIS function is organized and which categories of specialists are responsible for these systems.

We will then discuss how organizational MIS requirements are identified to provide support to an enterprise's business functions. We shall examine planning processes for information systems, from the long-term plans that outline how strategic information needs will be satisfied, to lower-level plans that prioritize development projects and ascertain the worth of applications to the organization.

We will explore various methods for acquiring the information systems needed to support the planned requirements and outline a process through which larger systems are developed in organizations. We shall see that there are three principal agents involved in an MIS project and that the interests of these agents do not necessarily coincide. To avoid failures, we thus need an organizational change process to implement these systems.

Sheldon Laube, the national director of information and technology for the accounting firm Price Waterhouse, has purchased 10,000 copies of the Notes groupware package by Lotus Corporation. This is reputed to be the largest purchase of PC software ever. The Notes package supports creation and sharing of indexed document databases, making document texts accessible to search by uses over a network. Through the use of the groupware, a worker encountering a problem in any of the firm's 108 U.S. offices will be able to instantly draw on expertise in any other office, with a body of experts communicating via a bulletin board where users' comments can be collected and categorized. Thus, the firm's collective expertise can be brought to bear on any client's problem.

Accounting firms are highly decentralized: they are built around major clients. To support collaboration in such a decentralized structure, major technical decisions involving information technology have to be, paradoxically, centralized—otherwise, chaos will reign. The fifty-person MIS group under Laube provides this central locus of expertise and control.

The Notes purchase required the extensive involvement of the MIS department led by Laube. The department devoted considerable effort to conceptualizing and specifying the firm's needs for communication and collaboration. The purchase was considered strategic: the MIS department showed that the use of a uniform groupware throughout the company would enable Price Waterhouse to better serve its clients.

MIS specialists made a thorough study of available software. Most of the groupware products were inadequate from the points of view of security and scalability (that is, a product might support twenty sites, but not 10,000).

Introduction of the packages is taking place gradually, with customization as necessary. The MIS specialists are studying and implementing ways to protect users from information overload.

The firm's chief executive, who is inundated with numeric information, wants no more aggregate figures. On the other hand, he has expressed a keen interest in having constant access to status reports on the firm's key projects. Such a facility is at present being established on a Notes bulletin board.

Based on the author's conversations with Sheldon Laube in March 1990 and February 1991; and on Mark Schlack, "IS Puts Notes to the Test." *Datamation*, August 1, 1991, pp. 24–26.

This case indicates that MIS specialists have a major role to play even when systems acquisition takes the route of a package purchase rather than internal software development. Let us see who these specialists are, how they develop information system requirements for the organization, and how they establish project priorities.

CHAPTER OUTLINE

17.1 Organization of the MIS Function

17.2 MIS Specialists

17.3 Establishing Organizational MIS Requirements
  • Contents of an MIS Master Plan
  • Derivation of Organizational MIS Requirements from Long-Term Organizational Objectives and Plans
  • The Strategic Cube—Value Chain Approach
  • Strategy Set Transformation
  • Enterprise Analysis with Business Systems Planning (BSP)
  • Critical Success Factors (CSF) Methodology
  • Selecting a Methodology for Establishing Organizational MIS Requirements

17.4 Evaluating the Relative Worth of MIS Applications

17.5 The MIS Steering Committee: Linking Information Systems to Organizational Goals

17.6 Cost-Benefit Analysis
  • Role of Cost-Benefit Analysis in Evaluating the Payoff from MIS
  • Cost-Benefit Analysis of an Information System

17.7 Methods of Acquiring Information Systems
  • Internal Development by MIS Professionals
  • Internal Development through End-User Computing
  • Purchase of a Package
  • External Development by a Systems Integrator
  • Comparing System Acquisition Methods

17.8 An Outline of the MIS Development Process

17.9 Agents Involved in an MIS Project
  • Principal Agents and Their Agendas
  • Who Initiates a Project?
  • Problems Encountered during Systems Development

17.1 ORGANIZATION OF THE MIS FUNCTION

The corporate *MIS unit* is the entity responsible for providing or coordinating computer-based informational services in an organization. These services include developing, operating, and maintaining organizational information systems, as well as facilitating the acquisition and adaptation of software and hardware.

Firms organize their MIS functions in very different ways. The usual name of the unit, which evolved from the Data Processing Department of yore, is the MIS Department, Information Services Department, or the like. We discussed the general principles of organizing in chapter 12 and showed in figures 12.4a–c how the MIS function may be structured along functional, divisional, and matrix lines. In practice, MIS services are usually provided by a unit that combines these designs.

Today, the central MIS department is in many firms much smaller than it was in the days preceding end-user computing. Some firms still choose to maintain an essentially centralized MIS department organized along functional lines (as shown in figure 12.4a). But in many organizations, the responsibility of the central MIS core is limited to coordinating corporate MIS efforts and providing an overall computational infrastructure. The central MIS unit is accompanied by MIS subunits located in a firm's various business units, and this is therefore known as **departmental computing.** A representative organizational structure containing the corporate (central) MIS department as well as departmental computing groups is shown in figure 17.1.

The corporate MIS department is principally responsible for the corporate information-system infrastructure, that is, for the telecommunication networks and for the corporate data center where central databases are maintained under information resource management (IRM) principles. Another common responsibility is developing and maintaining corporate MIS standards and interacting with vendors to ensure quantity discounts and other benefits of corporate scale.

FIGURE 17.1

Organization chart with
distributed MIS functions.

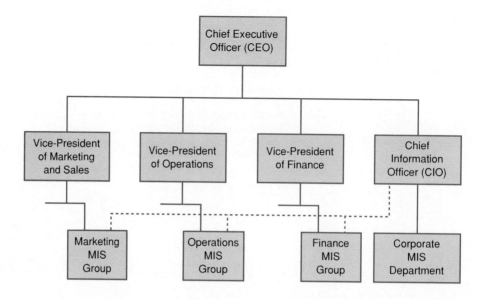

Note that this organizational structure corresponds to the tiered computer hardware configuration shown in figure 3.1, with departmental computers (often minicomputers or powerful microcomputers) linked to the corporate mainframe-based data center.

The "dotted-line" authority of the top corporate information officer (sometimes bearing the formal title of chief information officer, or CIO) with respect to departmental MIS groups ensures the coordination and uniformity of overall corporate MIS effort. However, since these groups are answerable directly to the heads of their business units, their members are familiar with the unit's business and responsive to its concerns.

Members of the MIS units, whom we may broadly call MIS specialists, possess a wide variety of skills—from the highly technical to those of generalist-managers. Owing to the vital role information technology plays in doing business, most of these people need to combine expertise in the corporate business lines they serve as well as in information technology. We shall discuss different categories of specialists in the next section.

The number of people employed by organizational MIS units depends on the size of the firm, on the role MIS plays in its business, and on the extent to which an organization chooses to secure the needed informational services internally. Companies in which MIS play a strategic role—frequently firms in the service businesses, and, particularly, in financial services (such as banks or insurance companies)—have extensive MIS units. For example, Metropolitan Life Insurance (of New York), with 42 million policyholders, employs 2,800 MIS specialists, about 8 percent of its total number of employees; MIS expenditures of $251 million in 1988 accounted for 16 percent of the total corporate expenditures for that year.[1] A small company, on the other hand, may employ a two-member MIS department consisting of programmer/analysts and heavily relying on the acquisition and customization of applications software from outside vendors.

DECENTRALIZATION AT MERRILL LYNCH

In November 1989, the MIS function of the Merrill Lynch brokerage firm was radically decentralized. Most of the functions of the formerly centralized MIS department were transferred to three MIS units that report directly to the managers of the business units they support. For example, the Field Operations and Systems Support Division, which runs systems for 480 retail offices of the firm, was assigned to Merrill Lynch's Consumer Market Group.

DuWayne Peterson, Merrill Lynch's executive vice-president for MIS, was to exercise "dotted-line" supervision of the reassigned units and be responsible for policy, strategy, and control issues.

Telecommunications and data centers also remained the responsibility of the centralized MIS function; they answer directly to Peterson (called the "million-dollar man," in reference to his annual salary). When Peterson retired in June 1991, he left to his successor, Edward Goldberg, an MIS organization highly responsive to the needs of the business units it serves.

Based on Jason Forsythe, "Million-Dollar Man." *InformationWeek*, November 6, 1989, pp. 38–44; David A. Ludlum, "Merrill Lynch Disperses IS Management." *Computerworld*, November 6, 1989, p. 8; and Peter Krass, with Bruce Caldwell and Elliott Kass, "Merrill IS: The Cautious Bull." *InformationWeek*, February 25, 1991, pp. 24–29.

17.2 MIS SPECIALISTS

Who are the MIS professionals? Let us discuss the occupational categories of MIS specialists. While two principal occupations are analyst and programmer, a variety of other specialists are also often needed.

A **systems analyst** analyzes the users' information requirements and often also designs information systems based on the specifications of these requirements. Analysts play the key role in translating business problems and opportunities into information systems. While a computerized subsystem is generally the major part of such a system today, manual procedures are also included. On another plane, analysts provide a liaison between the users and other specialists in the MIS unit. An analyst is a problem solver who can perform a variety of tasks relating to defining, developing, and exploiting information systems. He or she must possess a knowledge of both the business and the potential of technology, communicating with end users on the one hand and technical specialists (system designers or programmers) on the other. Senior systems analysts frequently become project managers.

Systems designers and programmers implement the analysts' specifications. A **systems designer** translates these specifications for what the system is expected to do into high-level specifications for the needed system components. In many cases, a systems design is produced by analysts or by experienced programmers. A **programmer** develops (codes and tests) programs that satisfy the requirements established by the analysts, using the design specifications worked up by the designer (see photo 17.1). Programmers will also maintain the programs.

DO WE REALLY NEED AN MIS FUNCTION?

That master of provocative title, John Dearden of the Harvard Business School, who authored the famous "MIS is A Mirage" paper we discussed in chapter 1, more recently wrote a paper entitled "The Withering Away of the IS Organization" (Dearden, 1987). Since Dearden previously forced the field of MIS to examine its assumptions, an examination of his arguments is always rewarding.

Dearden contends that only a user-manager can act most effectively in response to the rapidly changing business environment without being hamstrung by an MIS department, whose goals differ from those of the user. He further claims that such a total decentralization is now possible owing to technological advances, the most important of which are end-user-oriented software development tools and commercially available software packages. Dearden also believes that data inconsistencies among the various user departments can be resolved by users themselves without MIS department intervention.

In response to Dearden, Marius Janson of the University of Missouri (Janson, 1989) presents three cases where the presence of an MIS department is needed for a variety of reasons. Two of the cases show that sustainable competitive edge could not be gained by using commercially available software. Organizational systems to be implemented in-house require the presence of a central unit of MIS specialists. The third case describes the failure of an end-user effort to implement a commercial package. In this case, the cause of failure was the difference between the objectives of the users and of the *external* developers (contractors). Reliance on external contractors is a part of the outsourcing trend. Janson shows that even though the application was a run-of-the-mill system, the users did not have the requisite expertise to evaluate the system and its implementation.

As we shall see further on, implementation of a major information system is to a degree the negotiated outcome of a lengthy process, in which more parties than just the MIS developer and "user-manager" take part. We shall also see in the next section that a range of specialists is needed to provide organizational information services.

PHOTO 17.1

Programmers code and test programs based on system design specifications.

These *applications programmers* are supported by *systems programmers* who maintain systems software and have considerable technical expertise.

In many cases, the functional distinction between programmer and analyst is blurred. This is formalized in some firms in *programmer/analyst* positions, often held by senior programmers who perform both tasks.

Since MIS units, as we said, are often very large, a hierarchy of managers has evolved. The levels range from the first-level managers of programming teams and project managers, who may be responsible for several teams, to the top corporate officer responsible for MIS services. The top officer often has a vice-presidential rank and in some companies is given the formal title of **chief information officer (CIO),** analogous to a chief financial or operating officer. The CIO coordinates the entire corporate MIS effort and has primary responsibility for linking the MIS plans and implementation to the company's business plans. The growing importance of the MIS role has led to an upward movement of the rank of the top IS executive. The placement of this executive at the top reporting level is a key factor in the effective exploitation of information systems by corporations (see, for example, Benjamin, 1985, and Raghunathan, 1989). The role of the top MIS executive is to focus the attention of top corporate management on the contribution that information technology can make to the firm's business.

In addition to analysts, programmers, and managers, MIS personnel include a variety of specialists in various aspects of computer and telecommunication technologies, operations personnel responsible for running data centers, and other support personnel. The personnel supporting end-user computing are often organized into information centers (as discussed in chapter 9). However, in some cases, end-user specialists may work in a functional area but report to the MIS department. The principal functions of MIS personnel are summarized in table 17.1.

The basic workforce unit that develops and maintains information systems is a *project team.* The composition of a team, which usually includes no more than ten professional members, varies depending on the task. Large projects involve several teams. A team includes MIS professionals such as analysts and program-

PHOTO 17.2

Bill Eaton, senior vice-president and chief information officer (CIO) of Levi Strauss & Co. (as you might have guessed) of San Francisco, believes that the role of a CIO is to help set the overall goals of the company. "Information technology is so intertwined with the business plan, it has to be put up front as a shaper of strategy," says Eaton. He believes that the task of getting business processes ready to take advantage of the new information technology is the vital aspect of his corporate role (based on Melymuka, 1990).

TABLE 17.1

Principal Job Descriptions
of MIS Personnel

JOB CATEGORIES AND TITLES	JOB DESCRIPTIONS
MIS Managers	
Chief information officer (CIO) or MIS director	Responsible for the organization's MIS function
Data administrator	Manages the organization's data as a corporate resource
MIS project manager	Responsible for a project, such as the development of an information system
Team leader	Manages development or maintenance team
System Developers	
Systems analyst	In collaboration with users, determines their information requirements and designs a system that would satisfy them (though system designers may be employed for design tasks instead)
Systems designer	Designs systems based on requirements specifications provided by systems analysts
Programmer/analyst	Performs both the analyst's and the programmer's functions
Applications programmer	Codes and tests programs based on systems analyst's (or designer's) specifications
Maintenance programmer	Modifies existing programs to meet changing needs or to improve system's performance
Technical Specialists	
Systems programmer	Maintains or develops systems software
Telecommunications specialist	Designs and maintains telecommunications networks; develops telecommunications software
Database administrator (DBA)	Creates the physical design of databases and ensures their efficient operation and control
Operations Personnel	
Computer operator	Operates computers in a data center
Control clerk	Responsible for input (such as magnetic tapes to be mounted) and output (such as reports) in a data center
Data entry clerk	Enters data through a terminal
Librarian	Maintains tapes and disk volumes and delivers them to the operator
Information Center Personnel	
Director of office and group information systems	Plans and coordinates the use of OIS
Microcomputer coordinator	Develops standards and policies for the use of PCs and productivity software
Education specialist	Trains end users
MIS (or EDP) Auditors	Assess whether information systems safeguard assets, maintain data integrity, and perform in an effective and efficient fashion

mers and may at various stages of its work on the system include end users (who assist in systems analysis) and technical specialists, such as telecommunications or database experts. We shall further discuss the composition and operation of MIS teams in section 19.9.

To avoid suboptimization, the work on major MIS projects must be conducted within an overall master MIS plan. We shall now discuss how an organization's MIS requirements are identified and framed into such a strategic (long-term) plan.

17.3 ESTABLISHING ORGANIZATIONAL MIS REQUIREMENTS

To be effective competitors in the information society, companies increasingly find it vital to have models for the future of their information systems. This integrative vision (or model) establishes the general framework for the organization and management of the firm's information technology in the years to come. Such a high-level model of the firm's information system is known as the **information system architecture** of the firm. We have seen an excellent example of such a model in the case study for Part 1 of this text—the architectural model of American Standard's information system. The principal vehicle for bringing this vision into life is a long-term master MIS plan. Establishing long-term MIS requirements for an entire organization or business unit is at the heart of long-term (or strategic) MIS planning. The MIS master plan that emerges from this planning process has to be linked to a unit's long-term business plan.

We shall first discuss the principal contents of an MIS master plan (we have already discussed such a plan as an example of a product of the strategic planning process in chapter 11). We shall then present the more important methodologies for establishing the MIS requirements of an organization or one of its segments.

We shall stress that many firms, and small companies in particular, do not perform orderly long-term planning. In many firms, the development of information systems is project-driven, with priorities established by political interplay. You will encounter such a firm in the first Issue for Discussion in this chapter.

Contents of an MIS Master Plan

Management information systems are a major corporate asset, in respect to both the benefits they provide and their costs. A number of businesses have become strategically dependent on these systems. Therefore, the future of MIS in an organization has to be planned for the long term. This planning process

- helps ensure that the firm's business programs will receive the requisite informational support, and
- helps allocate information system resources in a way that benefits the corporation as a whole; the information systems most critical to the organizational objectives should receive priority.

A long-term MIS plan has to be aligned or coordinated with the corporate long-term plan. What does this mean? The coordination of MIS plans with business plans should take place in three dimensions: content, timing, and personnel involved in the planning process (Lederer, 1989). More specifically, we have evidence of the linkage if

- the corporate business plan states information needs;
- the MIS plan refers to the requirements of the business plan and is checked against the business plan;
- non-MIS managers participate in the process of MIS planning, while MIS managers are involved in corporate business planning; and
- corporate and MIS planning calendars conform with each other (Martino, 1983).

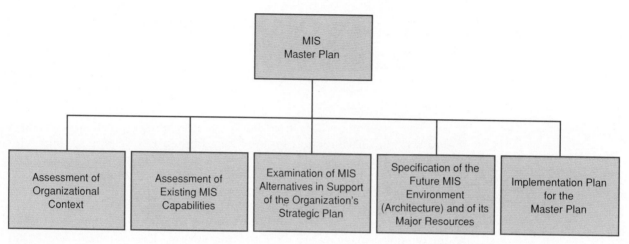

FIGURE 17.2

Contents of an MIS master plan.

As any long-term plan, the MIS master plan is reviewed both periodically and as warranted by developments. If it is not reviewed, the plan rapidly becomes invalidated by environmental changes.

Typical contents of an MIS master plan are discussed in section 11.4. Here, figure 17.2 shows these contents in conceptual terms.

In MIS planning, the strategic business directions set out in the corresponding business plans are reviewed. Planners evaluate current MIS capabilities in this light and identify the information needed to support the business objectives. They draw up specific plans for the future MIS environment and for major needed resources. A plan for the implementation of the long-term plan, possibly including detailed budgets for the coming year, is also drawn up. A detailed description of the MIS strategic planning process linked to the economic objectives of an enterprise is provided by Marilyn Parker, Edgar Trainor, and Robert Benson (Parker, 1989).

How do we establish long-term MIS requirements for an organization and thus set the course for the master plan? This question may be rephrased as follows: What do we need to support the business objectives and strategies of our organization? We shall now consider several methodologies that may be employed to answer this question: deriving MIS requirements directly from an organization's objectives and plans; the strategic cube—value chain approach; strategy set transformation; enterprise analysis with Business Systems Planning (BSP); and the critical success factors (CSF) methodology.

Derivation of Organizational MIS Requirements from Long-Term Organizational Objectives and Plans

A long-term MIS plan may be derived directly from an organization's strategic business plan (Davis, 1985). Thus, each general goal, strategy, and specific objective stated in the business plan is analyzed to derive the required MIS support. An example of such a derivation is shown in table 17.2; note that a goal often generates several strategies and a large number of specific objectives.

After all the components of the long-term business plan are analyzed in this way, the derived MIS plan components are consolidated into the MIS plan.

TABLE 17.2

Deriving MIS Plan Components from a Business Plan

	BUSINESS PLAN COMPONENT	DERIVED MIS PLAN COMPONENT
Goal	Supply exceptional quality space heaters to a narrow market segment	Provide information systems for marketing and sales to the narrow market segment Provide a quality-control information system
Strategy	Identify the market segment; ensure top quality product and after-market service	Establish customer database Establish quality-control database Establish a service information system
Objective	Run a direct-mail promotion campaign from 9/1 to 11/1/XX	Customer database system to be operational by 4/1/XX Pilot mailing to be performed by 5/15/XX

The Strategic Cube—Value Chain Approach

As we discussed in chapter 5, many organizations have recognized the strategic role played by MIS in their operations. This induces them to derive the role which MIS will play from the firm's competitive posture.

If this methodology is used, the company reviews its options for seeking strategic advantage with information systems using the strategic cube shown in figure 5.3, followed by value-chain analysis, as shown in figure 5.4. Value-chain analysis may also be conducted independently. Using the strategic cube, the planners consider the competitive forces the firm will have to contend with. Will it face, for example, increasing customer power (perhaps because of mergers, there are fewer and fewer customers who are becoming larger and larger)? Is the firm going to pursue a strategy of differentiating its product from that of its competitors by providing exceptional features and service? Does the firm have an established track record and future plans for innovation? A positive answer to these three sample questions positions the firm within a definite cell of the cube, where the capability to exploit information systems will now be sought.

The capability to exploit an information system to gain or sustain competitive advantage may be further pursued in the analysis of the company's value chain (figure 5.5). In other words, the firm's business functions are analyzed to identify the stage (or stages) of operations that may most profitably be equipped with an innovative information system. Today, this frequently turns out to be the service stage.

Let us consider an example corresponding to the situation just discussed. The International Truck division of Navistar had for a number of years been collecting a database on how the trucks the firm manufactures hold up in use (Ives, 1988). The original purpose was to use this information internally to give feedback to the company's engineers. The potential of this database as the foundation for a system that would give the firm a competitive advantage was discovered later. Decision support systems for personal computers were built for use by fleet owners—Navistar customers. These systems assist the customers in establishing maintenance staffing levels and spare parts inventories. Since only Navistar has the database, and since the information systems are important to customers, they bind customers to the firm.

Many other examples of strategically important information systems, which should be given high priority in an organization's MIS master plan, are presented in chapter 5.

Strategy Set Transformation

An approach devised by William King derives MIS requirements from the general goals and specific objectives of an organization with respect to its various stakeholders (King, 1978). First, the organizational stakeholder groups (customers, employees, suppliers, and so forth) are identified. Then, the goals, strategies, and objectives the organization plans to pursue with respect to each of these groups are outlined and validated by consulting with the appropriate corporate managers. Last, requirements for information systems needed to support these strategies are outlined.

For example, a distributor's organizational goal with respect to a key stakeholder—the customer—may be to improve service. The adopted strategy would be to differentiate distribution from that of the competition. After examining the service provided by the competitors, the goal may then be quantified as a precise objective, for example, to confirm all orders within a half hour. This would be translated into a strategic MIS requirement that the current order processing system be converted from batch to on-line. A similar consideration of the firm's goals with respect to the remaining stakeholders will produce a set of requirements for the organizational information systems.

Enterprise Analysis with Business Systems Planning (BSP)

An elaborate and comprehensive methodology for planning overall organizational MIS requirements is Business Systems Planning (BSP), developed by IBM (IBM, 1984). The methodology is well backed with training and consulting and is now partly automated.

BSP is used to develop a strategic plan for the information resource of an entire enterprise (which may be a business unit of another corporation). BSP is rooted in the information resource management (IRM) approach, which considers data to be a fundamental corporate resource. The objectives of BSP are to ensure that the data necessary to support a firm's business requirements are available and that a relatively stable information system architecture has been developed to serve the firm for years to come.

The key components of a BSP process are shown in figure 17.3. The nodal components of BSP are:

1. Defining Business Processes

   The BSP study team identifies groups of related activities and decisions required to manage the business. Such a group, called in this methodology a "business process," is the principal entity to be equipped with needed information. A business process is identified independently of the organizational unit or units that perform it. This ensures that a future organizational change will not affect the premises of this requirements analysis.

   An example of a business process in an MIS for a manufacturing firm is "Control Raw Materials Inventory," which includes the receipt, inspection, storage, and accounting of this inventory.

2. Defining Business Data

   Classes of data about each business entity are identified. Business entities include persons (for example, customers or employees), places, things (such as plants or equipment), concepts, and events.

   Next, the planners determine data usage and creation by each business process. They thus identify what data classes each process creates and what data classes it uses.

FIGURE 17.3

Key components of a BSP process.

(Reprinted by permission from *Business Systems Planning: Information Systems Planning Guide*, IBM, GE20–0527–4. Copyright © 1984 by International Business Machines Corporation.)

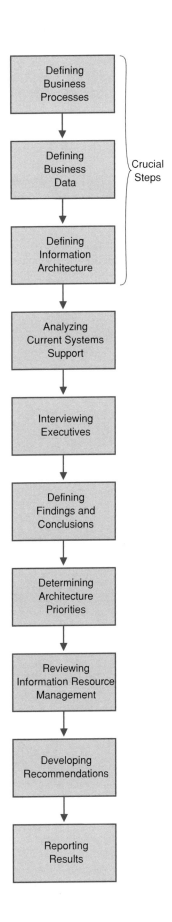

For example, the data class "Inventory Record" might include stock-keeping number, name, location, quantity in stock, lead time for restocking, and average inventory price.

3. Defining Information Architecture

The relationship between business processes and data classes is established. All processes are listed in a column and all data classes in a top row. This results initially in a process/data class matrix, shown in figure 17.4. Each data class ought to have a single creating process (denoted by a "C") that is responsible for keeping it up to date and may also have a number of using processes (denoted by "U"). Data classes are ordered in the matrix from left to right in the sequence in which the processes create these data (note the "C"s in the figure).

Process groups with similar patterns of data usage are identified as boxes in the matrix (this step requires some experience). These process groupings, based as shown on data usage patterns, are the information systems recommended for long-range implementation.

FIGURE 17.4

Process/data class matrix with process.

(Reprinted by permission from *Business Systems Planning: Information Systems Planning Guide*, IBM, GE20-0527-4. Copyright © 1984 by International Business Machines Corporation.)

Processes	Objectives	Policies & Procedures	Organization Unit Desc	Product Forecasts	Bldg & Real Estate Reqt	Equipment Requirements	Organization Unit Budget	G/L Accounts Desc & Budget	Long-Term Debt	Employee Requirements	Legal Requirements	Competitor	Marketplace	Product Description	Raw Material Description	Vendor Description	Buy Order	Product Warehouse Inventory	Shipment	Promotion	Customer Description	Customer Order	Seasonal Production Plan	Supplier Description	Purchase Order	Raw Material Inventory	Production Order	Equipment Description	Bldg & Real Estate Desc	Equipment Status	Accounts Receivable	Product Profitability	G/L Accounts Status	Accounts Payable	Employee Description	Employee Status
Establish Business Direction	C	C	C							U	U	U																					U	U		
Forecast Product Requirements	U			C																	U			U												
Determine Facility & Eqt Reqts	U		U		C	C	U																					U	U	U						
Determine & Control Fin Reqts	U		U				C	C	C																							U				
Determine Personnel Reqts		U	U		U	U	U	U		C	U																									U
Comply With Legal Reqts		U					U				C			U																					U	U
Analyze Marketplace	U											C	C								U															
Design Product	U									U	U			C	C						U															
Buy Finished Goods			U											U		C	C																		U	
Control Product Inventory														U			U	C	U						U											
Ship Product														U				U	C			U			U											
Advertise & Promote Product													U	U				U		C												U				
Market Product (Wholesale)												U	U	U						U	C	U														
Enter & Cntrl Customer Order														U					U	U	U	C									U					
Plan Seasonal Production			U											U									C					U		U					U	U
Purchase Raw Materials															U								U	C	C	U								U		
Control Raw Materials Inventory															U										U	C	U									
Schedule & Control Production														U	U								U			U	C	U							U	U
Acquire & Dispose Fac & Eqt					U	U																						C	C							
Maintain Equipment																									U			U		C						U
Manage Facilities																													U							
Manage Cash Receipts																			U		U										C					
Determine Product Profitability							U							U	U				U						U	U						C	U		U	U
Manage Accounts								U								U									U						U		C	U		U
Manage Cash Disbursements								U									U	U	U						U	U								C	U	U
Hire & Terminate Personnel		U	U			U				U	U																								C	U
Manage Personnel		U																																	U	C

The subsequent stages of the BSP process involve analysis of what is currently available vis-à-vis what has been identified as needed, setting priorities on the development or modification of individual systems, reviewing current information management policies in consideration of the new requirements, and developing an action plan for implementing the long-term master plan. We already encountered an example of BSP application in the case study for chapter 8.

Used to develop a comprehensive, long-term organizational MIS plan, BSP requires a major commitment of resources. It aids in developing an enterprise-level MIS architecture and helps to objectively identify high-priority areas (Zachman, 1982). However, unless BSP is very skillfully applied, it tends to use information systems to support existing information flows, rather than to rethink them.

Critical Success Factors (CSF) Methodology

As opposed to the massive enterprise-wide effort involved in BSP, critical success factors (CSF) methodology derives organizational information requirements from the key information needs of individual executives or managers. The CSF approach was developed by John Rockart of MIT, who defined CSFs as "those few critical areas where things must go right for the business to flourish" (Rockart, 1979). There are usually fewer than ten such factors which each executive should continually monitor.

CSFs of individual managers are identified through a series of interviews. By combining CSFs of individual managers, we can obtain factors critical to the success of the entire enterprise. These aggregated success factors are used to modify the organizational structure and to develop an organization's informational requirements. The logic of CSF methodology, as adapted to the process of establishing organizational (rather than individual) informational requirements, is shown in figure 17.5.

FIGURE 17.5

CSF methodology for establishing organizational MIS requirements.

(Adapted from Bullen, 1981 and Shank, 1985)

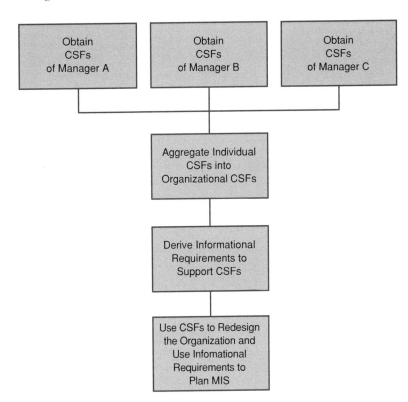

TABLE 17.3

CSFs and Derived Informational Requirements in a Healthcare Organization

CSF	KEY INFORMATION TO SUPPORT CSFs (EXAMPLES)
Access to Services	Type and number of patients referred to other institutions because of lack of resources in place
Continuous Care	Quality of the follow-up on patients as they go from one treatment to another
Adequate Response to Clients' Needs	Use rate of services offered, identification of unsatisfied needs
High-Quality Care	Compatibility between the results achieved and recognized standards
Detailed Knowledge of Population's Health Status	Epidemiological data on mortality and morbidity in the target population

There are four sources of CSFs: the industry that the firm is a part of, the enterprise itself, the business environment, and the firm's current situation (such as, for example, an excess of inventory at the present moment).

Some of the eight CSFs identified for a healthcare organization (drawn from Bergeron, 1989), along with the derived informational requirements, are shown in table 17.3 as examples.

CSF methodology is oriented toward supporting a company's strategic direction. Generally, only the CSFs of the top executives are considered during the process, which limits the amount of produced information as compared to BSP methodology, and leads to a highly (sometimes, too highly) focused approach to an organization's information needs.

By its nature, CSF methodology generally elicits only the requirements for management-oriented information systems. The methodology has been found effective for MIS planning in several well-documented cases (for example, in Shank, 1985). It has also been successfully employed to evaluate existing MIS (Bergeron, 1989). The methodology is supported by software tools such as PC Prism from Index Technology Corporation, which assists planners in identifying the critical success factors for their business and identifying the information systems that would best support these informational needs. We shall give a detailed illustration of a successful application of CSF methodology in the case study for this part of the text.

One drawback of CSF methodology is that it fosters a tendency to focus excessively on the temporary, current concerns of a few individuals (as opposed to broad organizational needs). Critical success factors are time-dependent and must therefore be reviewed periodically; informational support must also be adjusted accordingly.

Selecting a Methodology for Establishing Organizational MIS Requirements

The MIS planning method an organization selects will depend on its objectives, the resources to be committed to the planning process, and the organization's propensity for planning. Frequently, an organization devises a customized MIS planning methodology that combines several techniques for establishing

	METHODOLOGY	FEATURES
TABLE 17.4 Methodologies for Establishing Organizational MIS Requirements	Derivation from Organizational Business Plan	Explicitly links the business and MIS plans
	Strategic Cube and Value Chain	Concentrates on strategically important systems Oriented toward deploying information systems as a competitive weapon
	Strategy Set Transformation	Explicitly links corporate business objectives with MIS requirements of stakeholders Does not require availability of a corporate strategic plan
	Business Systems Planning (BSP)	Comprehensive analysis of an enterprise's information needs Very extensive resources and effort required
	Critical Success Factors (CSF)	Focused on critical information needs of top managers as representing an enterprise's critical success factors Mainly elicits requirements for management-oriented information systems

organizational MIS requirements. Thus, for example, the strategic MIS planning process at British Rail (Mainelli, 1988) consists of three major stages:

1. Understanding the business with the use of the strategic forces model (a variety of the strategic cube approach) and value chain

2. Identifying the firm's information needs, with the use of expanded CSF methodology (discussed in Henderson, 1987)

3. Ranking the opportunities presented by information technology in terms of their relative importance and the value they add to the business

The principal features of the methodologies for establishing organizational information requirements are summarized in table 17.4.

When the long-term MIS plan is being drawn up, it is vital to challenge the established assumptions and seek out new ways of doing business, rather than merely supporting old ways with information technology. This premise of business reengineering may lead to radical increases in effectiveness and efficiency of the targeted business functions of an organization (Hammer, 1990). Particular care to avoid paving the cowpaths has to be exercised when the Business Systems Planning methodology is employed.

Other methodologies for identifying the long-term MIS requirements of an organization have also been developed. Nolan's stage theory, which we briefly discussed in chapter 12, is used for planning purposes by some corporations (Abrams, 1982). A more recent approach is based on Paul Strassman's return-on-management (ROM) theory, which attempts to estimate the productivity of management (to which MIS can contribute). This method compares a corporate MIS profile against a database made up of profiles of other firms (Strassman, 1990).

17.4 EVALUATING THE RELATIVE WORTH OF MIS APPLICATIONS

What happens after long-range MIS requirements are established? Now, a master MIS plan can be drawn up. As we know, this strategic plan outlines in general terms a portfolio of the MIS systems a firm will need to support its operations and management. As we have stressed, the plan is of a rolling nature: it is typically reviewed every six months or every year, or as major developments warrant.

Based on the long-term plan and on calls for systems by various agents (whom we will identify later in this chapter), shorter-term tactical and operational plans for the MIS function may be drawn up. The planning process was discussed in detail in chapter 11. Companies vary broadly in their planning propensity; many firms, for example, do not actually draw up tactical-level plans.

As a result of tactical and operational planning:

- Projects to be implemented are identified, with the large projects being the subject of medium-term tactical planning, and the smaller ones identified on the operational level.
- Project priorities are set. Certain projects require virtually immediate implementation (for example, to satisfy a new government reporting regulation or to interface with a customer's system); others may have high priority owing to the competitive advantage the system would give the company or the high payoff the system promises.
- Resources (such as people, funds, and equipment) are allocated to projects, and project schedules are drawn up.

The approaches most often employed to identify applications worthy of implementation and to rank them in order of importance are summarized in table 17.5 (much of which is drawn from Davis, 1985).

TABLE 17.5

Methods for Evaluating the Relative Worth of Applications

METHOD	CRITERIA FOR EVALUATION
Chargeout	Are users willing to "buy" the application?
Cost-Benefit Analysis	Projects with highest payoff are given priority.
Portfolio Approach	The overall portfolio of projects should be *balanced* in terms of risk, support for the firm's strategic directions, and other identified criteria. Projects that are necessary for maintaining competitive parity also receive priority.
Contribution to the Firm's Competitive Position	Projects that promise defensible and lasting competitive advantage are favored.
Ranking by Steering Committee	Projects are selected based on negotiations of executives who represent various organizational interests.

Tools for making a choice between various alternatives, such as payoff tables and decision trees, which we discussed in chapter 13, can be employed in the decision process.

The accounting *chargeout* (or chargeback) mechanism may be employed to enable future users to express their preferences with respect to a proposed application. In this case, the firm's MIS pursues the development project only if the future users are willing to pay for the application, instead of foregoing it or acquiring it outside the company. The "payment" may in actuality be made by allocating an appropriate amount from the budget of the user subunit.

We shall further discuss the application of *cost-benefit* analysis (which we already encountered in chapter 11) to the information systems projects in this chapter. This method, with all its imperfections, is used to estimate the payoff that can be expected from a proposed system. However, many have recognized the difficulty of applying cost-benefit analysis to systems supporting knowledge work (as opposed to transaction processing). The benefits of individual systems that support managerial decision making (such as DSS, for example) or communication and coordination (such as OIS) are frequently difficult to quantify. Rational resource allocation for such projects may be done using the portfolio approach.

The **portfolio approach** was adapted for information systems evaluation from the field of securities analysis by F. Warren McFarlan (McFarlan, 1981). Applications development projects carry different degrees of risk; projects more likely to fail are those involving large systems, technology unfamiliar to the organization, or a great deal of change in the way the function is currently being performed. However, if high-risk projects promising valuable benefits are not implemented, the effectiveness of organizational MIS may suffer. The portfolio approach assesses the riskiness of each proposed project, after which it assesses the riskiness of the overall portfolio of proposed projects. An appropriate balance of risk and potential benefits for the firm should be maintained.

A tool that helps the firm to assess its information system posture is the *strategic grid,* developed by McFarlan and James McKenney (McFarlan, 1983). It characterizes the role assigned to an organization's MIS activity according to the strategic impacts of its existing applications and of the planned portfolio of development projects. As figure 17.6 demonstrates, four cells define the possible situations.

An organization in the support cell should concentrate on a portfolio of low-risk applications which principally support transaction processing. Information systems are peripheral to the firm's activities. The factory posture calls for detailed operational planning to exploit existing vital systems, but would also concentrate on implementing low-risk systems in the foreseeable future. Both the strategic and the turnaround situations necessitate the implementation of high-benefit systems and thus an inclusion of high-risk projects in the portfolio. While it is generally recognized that the development of strategic information systems carries higher degrees of risk, a detailed proactive analysis of these risks in specific cases permits the organization to contain them to some degree (Kemerer, 1991).

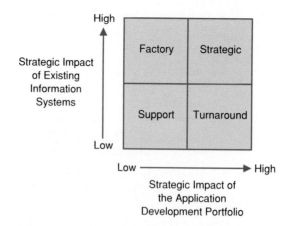

The concept of a balanced information system portfolio may be extended to other aspects, such as, for example, balancing applications for transaction processing with those for supporting managerial functions.

Even though the firm might not conduct a full portfolio analysis, the projects that credibly promise to enhance the firm's *competitive position* may be favored among the projects proposed for development. The tools for identifying the areas where competitive advantage can be sought—such as the value chain and the strategic cube—are then employed.

An important management body that coordinates the long-term MIS activities of the entire organization is its MIS *steering committee*. This committee of key managers from the user and MIS areas helps surface organizational considerations which elude economic analysis. We will now discuss the MIS steering committee further.

17.5 THE MIS STEERING COMMITTEE: LINKING INFORMATION SYSTEMS TO ORGANIZATIONAL GOALS

A close binding of the MIS function to the business needs of an organization is recognized as the major factor in the successful deployment of information resources. Earlier, we discussed what is entailed in the linkage between MIS plans and business plans. In a well-functioning firm, much of this linkage is effected through ongoing interaction between MIS managers and specialists on the one hand and line and staff workers on the other. Decentralization of the MIS function into corporate business units, liaison groups including users and developers, or information centers supporting end-user computing are some of the means an organization can deploy to enhance communication between users and developers of information systems. The work of a steering committee formalizes this communication at a high corporate level.

A **steering committee** is a high-level policy-making unit whose members are executives representing the major functions of the organization, including the MIS function. This committee combines the business expertise of the line-of-business executives with the information systems know-how of MIS managers. Collectively, this group has the ability to steer the allocation of the firm's informational resources. Negotiations during this allocation process allow for the open play of organizational politics. A steering committee also mobilizes attention for MIS-related issues at the highest organizational levels. The steering committee acts as a board of directors for MIS, which it views a corporate resource (Doll, 1987).

The primary function of a steering committee is to develop and maintain long-range MIS plans and rank the importance of major MIS projects. Thus, the committee sets the overall direction for a firm's MIS function; allocates major resources (for example, by reviewing requests for projects estimated to cost more than a given amount); monitors progress of major projects; and, last and perhaps most crucial, resolves conflicts among various claims on resources. The participation of functional executives ensures a fit between MIS and corporate strategy (Nolan, 1982). The activities of a steering committee significantly reduce the planning burden on the top MIS executive.

The committee is generally chaired by a corporate vice-president (and sometimes even the chief executive officer) and consists of five to ten members. Several organizations (24 percent in the sample studied in Drury, 1984) have found quarterly steering committee meetings adequate, though some firms hold monthly or ad hoc meetings. The duration of meetings is generally one to two hours.

17.6 COST-BENEFIT ANALYSIS

Cost-benefit analysis is a technique for estimating the payoff to be expected from an information system. Though it has many flaws, the cost-benefit approach is widely used because of its relative simplicity and the lack of consensus on a better technique.

Role of Cost-Benefit Analysis in Evaluating the Payoff from MIS

Every investment needs to be economically justifiable. So does an MIS project. **Cost-benefit analysis** helps to establish whether the benefits received from a proposed information system will outweigh its cost. As we said, this technique may be employed to establish the relative worth of applications. Such an analysis is also employed to compare how well system alternatives satisfy given user requirements. Before a system is implemented and actual costs have been incurred and benefits accrued, we are clearly dealing with *estimated* costs and benefits. When employed to evaluate an implemented system during the postimplementation audit, the development costs are of course already known, but the benefits remain largely in the future. Cost-benefit analysis is also rather commonly used as "quantitative" support in the competition for resources known as organizational politics—particularly considering that the analysis is usually done by those with a vested interest in having the proposed project approved (William King, 1978).

WHAT IS THE VALUE OF THIS SYSTEM?

A management support system that helps to make a better decision may be worth many times its cost (or, to look at it another way, its absence may cost many millions of dollars). But the value of such a system depends on whether the managers who will use the system will be called upon to make such a weighty (perhaps a bet-the-company) decision, doesn't it?

Lee Gremillion and Philip Pyburn give us an example of such a situation. The staff of a U.S. Forest Service in Montana had built a powerful decision support system (DSS) for making fire-fighting decisions. Its database contained data on the characteristics of the land within the national forest in the area, broken down by geographic location. A user-friendly query facility was included in the dialog management module. The models of the DSS could predict the expected behavior of a forest fire under the given circumstances of terrain, wind, ground cover, and so on.

A fire broke out in a wilderness area of that forest on a summer morning, and the forest supervisor had to decide whether to contain or suppress it. Current practices require that the fire be allowed to burn if the threat is limited and be attacked as quickly as possible if it may get out of control. In the absence of the DSS, the supervisor would need to fly over the area and form a judgment.

Using the DSS, the supervisor constructed likely scenarios of the fire's progress and assessed what resources would be destroyed; moreover, with the use of the database he was able to "cost out" each scenario in terms of the resources that would be damaged. The session took about two hours. Based on the DSS session, the supervisor decided to launch an all-out fire-fighting effort that cost $1.5 million.

Management were convinced that the DSS helped to make a better decision, and they incorporated the use of the DSS in the future fire analysis procedures. Clearly, the system helped to make an "expensive" decision in this instance. But what if such a high-payoff situation did not arise? And for that matter, what was the system worth in the decision situation that did come up? We would need to compare the cost of the alternative that was selected with the DSS against the cost of an alternative that would have been selected in its absence—but we do not know what that alternative would have been.

Based on Gremillion, 1985.

As we said in the preceding section, cost-benefit analysis is not the only way to evaluate the worth of an information system. Such an analysis is, however, usually an important factor in a decision concerning a proposed project. It is generally required as a part of the feasibility study performed when the desirability of a project is determined. Obviously, at that early stage of systems development, only rough estimates of most of the costs and benefits are available. These estimates may then be refined at later stages, as far firmer ground is gained only after the systems design has been completed.

I just pointed out that cost-benefit analysis should be used together with techniques that take into account the broader organizational implications of a particular system. In the case of strategic systems, an attempt to quantify financial

TABLE 17.6

Costs and Tangible Benefits in Cost-Benefit Analysis of Information Systems

SYSTEMS COSTS	TANGIBLE BENEFITS OF SYSTEMS
Fixed Costs (one-time resource acquisition)	
Hardware acquisition Software purchase and development Establishment of databases Training and hiring of personnel Establishment of new procedures	
Operating Costs (for example, annual)	*Savings* (for example, annual)
Labor (operation and maintenance) Facilities Supplies Leases	Reduced labor costs Reduced hardware costs Reduced purchasing costs Inventory reduction
	Revenue Increases
	Increased sales in existing markets Market expansion

outcomes with any precision is almost doomed to fail (Clemons, 1991). The imperfections of cost-benefit analysis as a decision-making tool were illustrated by the U.S. Forest Service vignette on page 692.

As we can see, cost-benefit analysis has many flaws. Yet, because it is detailed and remains widely used, particularly for operational-level systems, we shall now look at the technique more closely.

Cost-Benefit Analysis of an Information System

The basic stages of cost-benefit analysis as applied to information systems development are as follows:

1. Identification of the Costs of Acquisition and Operation of the Proposed System

Some of the expenses incurred will be *fixed costs,* one-time costs of acquiring systems resources (which we discussed in chapter 3), including the costs of systems development. Generally, these expenditures need to be made before the system becomes operational—and thus before any benefits may de derived from it.

Operating costs, on the other hand, will be borne on a recurring basis (say, annually) after system implementation. Table 17.6 shows the typical information systems cost categories, along with the tangible benefits such systems provide. Note that both operating costs and benefits start only following system implementation.

2. Identification of Benefits that Will Be Derived from the Use of the System

Benefits fall into two categories: **tangible benefits** that are easy to express in dollars, and **intangible benefits** that are difficult to quantify. Tangible benefits include cost savings and avoidance, and revenue increases, as shown in table 17.6. Intangible benefits, which are often of overriding importance in the case of MIS, by definition do not lend themselves easily to "dollarizing." Even though analysts may express some of them in quantitative terms, at least in part (ingenuity abounds), they may have to settle for stating many others in as precise terms as possible in the final cost-benefit statement. Some of the categories of intangible benefits are listed in table 17.7 (which is based in part on Parker, 1982).

TABLE 17.7

Important Intangible
Benefits of Information
Systems

Improved Customer Service

Achieving Specific Strategic Advantage in the Marketplace

Availability of Higher-Quality Information

Higher Utilization of Assets

Improved Work Coordination

Improved Planning

Improved Resource Control

Assimilation of Promising New Technology

Improved Working Environment

Increased Organizational Flexibility

Higher-Quality Decision Making

Streamlined Operations

Increased Reliability and Security of IS Operations

Satisfying Legal Requirements

The various aspects of information quality that may be enhanced by an information system, such as timeliness or relevance, were discussed in chapter 3. The oft-claimed benefit of higher asset utilization may be illustrated by an airline's or hotel's ability to enter reservations and cancellations more rapidly to increase the utilization of available capacity. A project may be a part of the assimilation process of new technologies—which we discussed in chapter 12—and thus, it may give the company new opportunities in the future.

In general, valuation of benefits is difficult, and it happens that while costs are generally more certain, benefits are usually more risk-prone. It is far easier to evaluate the benefits of transaction processing systems or clerically oriented office automation systems than it is to place a value on the benefits of a decision support or executive information system, which is why other evaluation techniques are frequently employed for these system types.

3. Comparison of Costs with Benefits

After the costs, tangible benefits, and those aspects of intangible benefits that can be "dollarized" are quantified, a cost-benefit evaluation technique is applied.

The time frame in which a cost is incurred or a benefit is obtained needs to be kept in mind. The *present value* of all of future money flows must be established. For example, if the organization can invest its capital at a 10 percent return, then $100 it would receive in benefits a year from now is worth only about $91 today. In other words, the value of future cash flows is discounted: multiplied by a present value factor (which is based on the discount rate used by the given organization and the number of years until the future amount will be received). Should the same $100 be coming in two years from now, it would be worth at present only about $83, at a discount rate of 10 percent (the present value factor is .826).

FIGURE 17.7

Net present value technique
of cost-benefit analysis.

It is estimated that:

- **The development time of the information system will be 18 months**
- **The system will remain in operation for 4.5 years**

After the costs and tangible benefits have been listed and quantified, the following schedule of costs and benefits is obtained:

Costs

	Fixed	Operating
Year 1:	$50,000	
Year 2:	$30,000	$10,000
Years 3–6:		$20,000

Benefits

Year 1:	0
Year 2:	$30,000
Years 3–6:	$60,000

The discount rate, as used by the finance department at the firm, is 12 percent.

The spreadsheet of the net present value computation is:

	Year Effective					
	1	2	3	4	5	6
Costs	50,000	40,000	20,000	20,000	20,000	20,000
Benefits	—	30,000	60,000	60,000	60,000	60,000
Net Values	−50,000	−10,000	40,000	40,000	40,000	40,000
Present Value Factor	1	.893	.797	.712	.636	.567
Net Present Values	−50,000	−8,930	31,880	28,480	25,440	22,680

Net present value of the system: $49,550.

A list and explanation of intangible benefits is appended.

Tables of present value factors for a variety of discount rates and periods are widely available; spreadsheet packages generally contain a function which computes the present value of a series of cash flows over a period of time.

The most commonly used cost-benefit analysis technique is the **net present value approach.** Using this method, the net present value of a system is computed by subtracting the present value of the costs from the present value of the benefits—calculated over the lifetime of the system. If a positive value is obtained, the project has merit. However, to better compare various projects, an organization may compute the ratio of the present values of benefits and costs (B/C). The organization would establish the minimum value for this ratio (known as the hurdle rate) that would make the project worthy of implementation. The net present value technique is illustrated in figure 17.7.

As an alternative cost-benefit analysis technique, some firms use the break-even method (also known as the payback technique) which we discussed in chapter 11. In that technique, the graphs for annual benefits and costs (their present values, of course) would be charted for the lifetime of the project. The point where they intersect shows when the system becomes profitable. The organization would establish a hurdle of, say, two years, to judge the merit of each project.

As management information systems play a larger and larger role in the functioning of organizations, it is, paradoxically, more and more difficult to fully gauge their benefits with a cost-benefit technique. Indeed, it may be argued that the more pervasive the impact of a system is in corporate life—as of executive information or office information systems—the more intangible become its benefits, and thus, by definition, the more difficult it will be to apply established cost-benefit analysis techniques. The valuation of the impact of information technology on organizational performance remains a "hot" research topic.

17.7 METHODS OF ACQUIRING INFORMATION SYSTEMS

In the earlier days of organizational computing, there were few alternatives to in-house development of information systems by MIS professionals. At this time, a variety of options exist for both internal systems development and for systems acquisition from external sources.

Let us review the major avenues for acquiring systems, keeping in mind that the implementation of a major system may combine several of them.

Internal Development by MIS Professionals

We shall further discuss the process and the tools of systems development in this part of the book. Here, we shall briefly outline the two principal development methods, which are:

1. Systems Development through a Systems Development Life Cycle (SDLC)

This method has become a traditional method, though it represents a significant improvement over a variety of undisciplined earlier approaches. It relies on a formally defined sequence of stages in the process of developing and maintaining an information system. Each stage has its own deliverables—work products such as documentation in the earlier stages and a system code in the later ones. This resource-intensive process helps structure the work of a number of developers over an extended period of time and produces highly maintainable systems. It is particularly advantageous when applied to large systems, such as those used for transaction processing. However, this is not a process by which an urgently needed decision support system should be developed.

2. Systems Development through Prototyping

In this method, an early pilot version of the system is built, so that future users can clarify their requirements and gain a measure of confidence in the general approach. In some cases the prototype is upgraded through several evolutions, thoroughly tested and documented, and made into the actual production system. In these cases, the prototyping process amounts to a complete evolutionary systems development. We saw (in chapters 14 and 15) that prototyping is the principal method for developing decision support and expert systems.

On the other hand, a "throwaway" prototype may serve as a tool to clarify system requirements, and later be discarded in favor of a system built through further stages of an SDLC methodology. The interest in combining the advantages of prototyping with those of SDLC-oriented development is continually growing.

Internal Development through End-User Computing

With the appropriate tools, some end users are able to develop their own systems, as was discussed in detail in chapter 9. We have seen that while there are certainly attendant risks and limitations, end-user system development is an increasing trend. It relieves bottlenecks arising from the scarcity of MIS personnel and avoids potential miscommunication between MIS developers and users.

In the case of decision-oriented systems for personal use, the users, properly supported by MIS specialists, may be the natural developers for an application.

Purchase of a Package

The organization may choose to purchase a software package which satisfies most of the relevant requirements. The software industry has blossomed since 1969, when IBM unbundled the costs of software from those of hardware (before that date, hardware manufacturers included in the price of the system hardware all programs for the system, written and supported by the manufacturer). A number of packages for so-called vertical markets (that is, for various lines of business) are available commercially from outside vendors.

The purchase of a business package is actually the purchase of a license to use the package. The customer-licensee pays a one-time charge for the right to use the product, and then continues to pay an annual sum for updates and service provided by the vendor.

This proprietary software generally has to be modified to fit the needs of a user company. Modifications may be performed by the licensee, that is, the firm that acquires the software; however, in most cases the vendor does not support modified packages. To get around this problem, the firm that acquires a package may develop additional programs which work with the package; thus, each licensee can obtain a customized system. Less frequently, a vendor may modify the package for the licensee. It should be noted that modifications are expensive; every effort should be made to avoid them, for example, by adjusting company procedures to fit the applications package.

When purchase of a proprietary software package is being considered, Requests for Proposals (RFPs) are sent to the potential package vendors, following an initial study of user requirements. An RFP outlines the requirements of the organization and asks questions as to how the vendor's systems may satisfy them. Study of independent package evaluations and interviews and visits with the vendor's clients who are currently using the package are the primary means of information gathering. The scores-and-weights method, presented in chapter 13, is an apt tool for the package selection process.

Factors that will influence the package implementation process in the context of a given firm are shown in figure 17.8.

As we can see, the package implementation process must resolve the discrepancies between the package characteristics and the informational needs of the organizational unit (Lucas, 1988). In many cases, the business operation is adjusted to fit the package. The implementation process is affected by such characteristics of the adopting unit as the structure of the work environment and the

FIGURE 17.8

Factors influencing the
success of package
implementation.

(Reprinted by special
permission from the *MIS
Quarterly*, Volume 12,
Number 4, December 1988.
Copyright 1988 by the
Society for Information
Management and the
Management Information
Systems Research Center at
the University of Minnesota.)

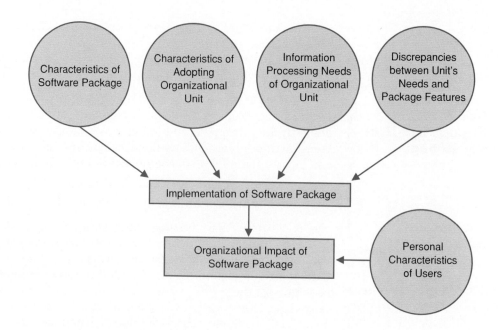

decision-making processes in the firm. The impact the package will have also
depends on the characteristics of the system users, such as their experience with
information systems and their readiness for change. As we saw in the focus case
for this chapter, acquisition of a major package (or a number of packages) is
actually a complex process.

A principal advantage of package purchase over internal development is that
purchase is generally far less expensive. Among its disadvantages is loss of flexibility in adapting the software to the evolving needs of the enterprise. A measure of control is exercised by the user firms which associate into user groups,
partly to influence the evolution of the packages they acquire.

Proprietary software purchase is now increasingly preferred to in-house development. Training is often available from the vendor or a third party. Across industry segments, the use of vertical software prevents duplication of effort and
sometimes results in very significant savings as well as avoiding the risks that
accompany in-house systems development.

External Development by a Systems Integrator

A number of firms, large and small, may be hired to develop an information system
for an organization. Known as **systems integrators,** these firms can develop
and install a turnkey (ready-to-run) system for a particular application. They also
perform other services, extending from developing a strategic plan for organizational MIS to facilities management—running a corporate data center. The term
integrator implies that to produce a needed system, such a firm has to combine
and integrate the software and hardware of various manufacturers, as well as its
own software development efforts. Smaller firms offer a variety of systems development services on a contract basis and are known as consulting companies.
Offshore systems development in countries with lower labor rates, such as India
or Ireland, has been slowly increasing.

The use of an integrator to develop a system absolves a firm from the need for
an extensive qualified MIS staff and temporarily places experienced MIS professionals at its service. In some cases, an integrator may be used to develop a system

POINTS OF VIEW ON OUTSOURCING

Let us quote two opinions published in *InformationWeek* in response to Eastman Kodak's decision to completely outsource its data centers, contracting for most of its MIS services from IBM, which would serve as systems integrator:

Subcontracting of support functions is nothing new; services such as the company cafeteria, security services, and building maintenance are farmed even by the largest of companies. But none of these is nearly as vital to the success of an enterprise as information technology. . . . Obvious[ly] . . . five to ten years from now. . . . Kodak will find that it has lost its ability to grasp possibilities inherent in information technology."
Philip H. Dorn (October 16, 1989, p. 52)

Many companies today are taking a closer look at the resources required to maintain their in-house data center operations . . . . It may make sense to some companies to outsource their DP operations to vendors whose primary business is "information management."
John Ryan (November 6, 1989, p. 2)

Here are three more opinions: Elliot McNeill, MIS manager at Southland Corporation, which had turned over the running of its data center to an integrator but has retained an in-house MIS staff of ninety-nine to develop applications and manage the relationship with the outsourcer, tells us: "Be very careful that this is what you want to do, because you can't go home again. If you don't like it, you've already given up your technical employees and software licenses, and you don't have a data center anymore."

Mario Morino of Legent Corporation (of Vienna, Virginia) stresses that "knowledge and applications systems outsourcing brings to the customer" and the critical necessity for planning and contract negotiations that do indeed provide an ability to reverse an outsourcing decision.

And, finally, Howard Anderson of Yankee Group: "Companies that don't retain the staff to do applications development are putting their future at risk."

Based on Johanna Ambrosio, "Outsourcing at Southland: Best of Times, Worst of Times." *Computerworld*, March 25, 1991, p. 61; Tom McCusker, "There Is Life After Outsourcing." *Datamation*, April 1, 1991, pp. 62–64; and David Kirkpatrick, "Why Not Farm Out Your Computing?" *Fortune*, September 23, 1991, pp. 103–112.

that would otherwise become part of the backlog facing the busy internal MIS. However, the use of integrators for developing strategically vital systems is often perceived as risking undue exposure of the firm's business.

The role of a systems integrator as a major force in systems development was originated by IBM in 1985. Integrators range from small, and often specialized, consultancies to giants such as Electronic Data Systems and Computer Sciences Corporation. Major accounting firms, notably Arthur Andersen & Co., and other firms, such as AT&T, Bechtel, and Boeing, are playing a role in this market.

The ultimate in going outside the corporation for MIS services is total **outsourcing:** hiring an integrator to maintain corporate information facilities, and in some cases even to be responsible for the entire applications development for the client firm. According to Index Group (of Cambridge, Massachusetts), applications development is the most frequently outsourced function, with 45 percent of surveyed companies using some form of outsourcing resorting to it. The most frequent motives for outsourcing are: cost cutting, gaining critical MIS skills, accelerating systems development, and relieving the firm from the burden of developing nonstrategic information systems ("Outsourcing," 1991).

TABLE 17.8

Principal Characteristics of Acquisition Methods for Information Systems

ACQUISITION METHOD	PRINCIPAL CHARACTERISTICS
Internal Development with an SDLC Methodology	System developed in stages, reflecting the analysis-design-programming cycle
	Advantageous for large organizational systems, such as TPS
	Supports project planning and control, organization of team development effort, and production of maintainable systems
	Relatively inflexible with respect to user requirements that change during the development cycle; results in voluminous documentation
Internal Development through Evolutionary Prototyping	System developed by gradually modifying an initial prototype based on feedback from users
	Relatively fast development, with early availability of a first version of the system
	Advantageous when user requirements are uncertain
	Principal technique for limited-size systems that need to evolve continually, such as DSS and expert systems
	Unless precautions are taken, may evolve into a "quick-and-dirty" system, hampering maintenance
Internal Development via End-User Computing	Relatively simple systems developed by end users, generally for their own (rather than organizational) use
	May result in faster development and does not tax MIS resources
	End-user-oriented development tools needed
	Users committed to system because they get what they believe they need
	Care required in selecting appropriate systems and controlling their impact
Purchase of Proprietary Software	Package that satisfies most user requirements acquired from external vendor
	Rapid placement into operation at a relatively low cost; cost largely known at outset
	Often need to adjust work within the organization to the package
	More reliable and better documentation than internally produced systems provide
	May need extensive modification
	May cause company to forego competitive advantage that could be realized via MIS technology
External Development by an Integrator	External developer produces system to satisfy company's requirements
	Relieves corporate MIS personnel (or the need for such personnel)
	Broad range of experience brought to bear
	May hamper organizational learning and prevent gain of competitive advantage

Comparing System Acquisition Methods

The principal features of the five methods of acquiring information systems are compared and contrasted in table 17.8.

Note that these approaches are not mutually exclusive. Thus, end-user developers generally rely on prototyping; the contribution of an integrator may be combined with the internal development of a system part (as shown in the joint development vignette); and the prototyping approach may be used just to establish user requirements during the initial phases of a life-cycle-oriented development process.

JOINT DEVELOPMENT: LEARNING FROM FAILURES

In the deregulated environment of today's financial world, where competitors may come from any quarter, banks look at many MIS development projects as strategically important. To spread costs and risks and garner both the knowledge of banking applications and MIS savvy, banks enter into joint development agreements with systems integrators.

Joint development agreements, rather common these days, benefit from lessons learned from several notable failures that occurred a few years ago. In one, for example, in the early 1980s, a developer had signed an agreement with a group of banks and produced a system that was too general to be useful to any one of them. Agreements are now very specific and involve close collaboration between bank and developer.

What do the parties to an agreement expect from one another? Coley Clark of Electronic Data Systems (EDS), an integrator

firm that develops banking software in Dallas, says: "We're not in the banking industry, and if you have the banking industry involved in this, you've got some banking expertise, some "live" input into your system." Brian Phillips, an MIS executive with Norwest Corporation of Minneapolis, a bank that entered into a joint development agreement with EDS, says: "Joint development agreements give us several things: it means that we will have immediate access to a new system developed in conjunction with a major player in the banking software industry, and it means we will have a say in how the system develops, so we will know from the start what it can do." In other words, the bank can start the process of system implementation (in a broad sense, which involves organizational change) early in the development life cycle.

Based on Robert Francis, "Joint Development Deals Lure Banks, Software Vendors." *Datamation*, October 1, 1987, pp. 28–30.

17.8 AN OUTLINE OF THE MIS DEVELOPMENT PROCESS

To summarize what we have learned in this chapter about MIS planning to satisfy an organization's informational requirements, and to introduce you to the system development process we shall discuss in the next chapter, we shall now outline the complete process of planning, developing, and operating information systems. We shall also see who is responsible for the various stages.

Figure 17.9 shows how large organizational systems come into being. The acquisition of such a system should be preceded by a broader process of strategic MIS planning, or, in other words, determining the organization's long-term informational requirements, linking them to the firm's business plans. The responsibility for the process rests with the MIS planners and, ultimately, with the

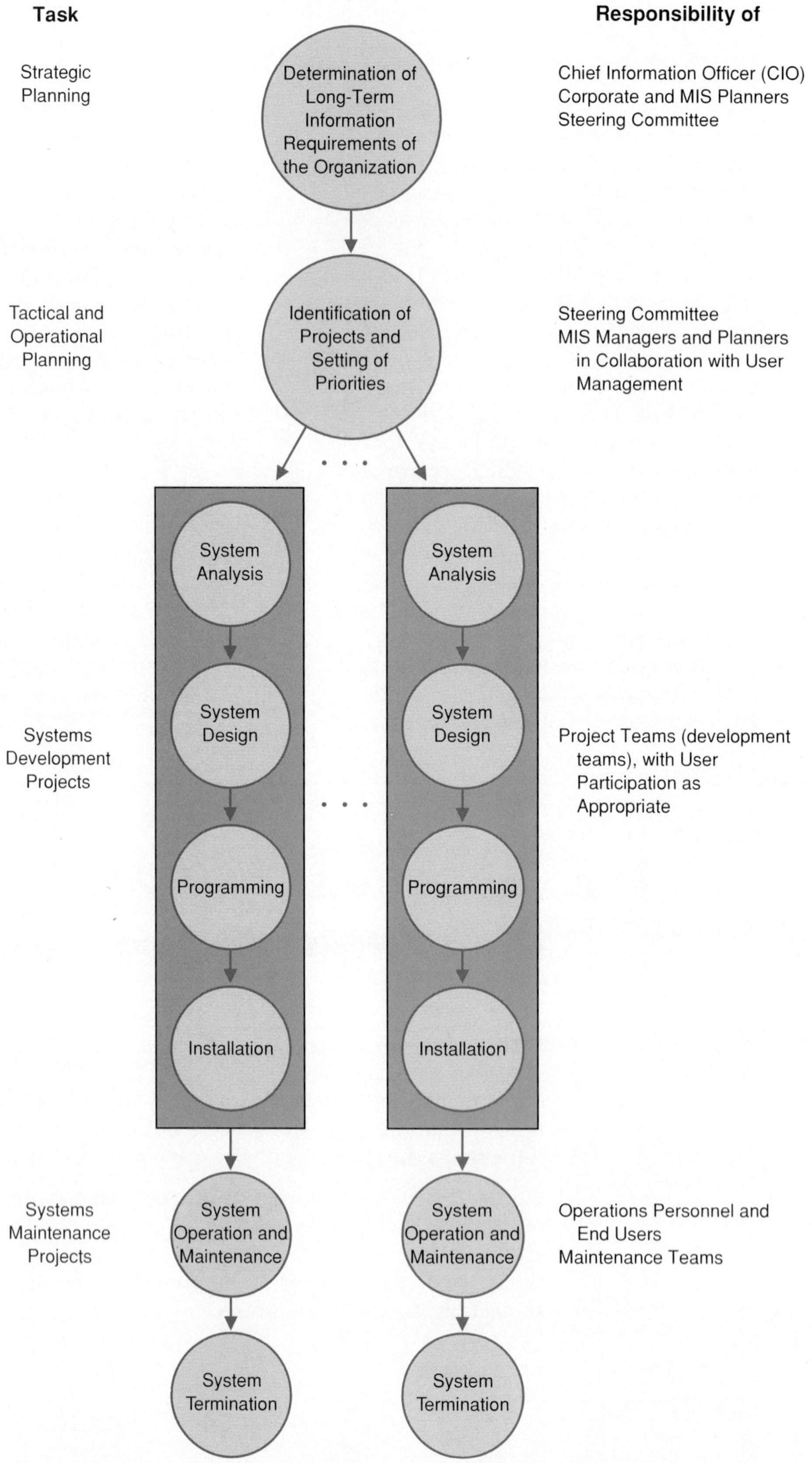

FIGURE 17.9

Planning, development, and operation of information systems—an outline of the process.

Task

Responsibility of

Strategic Planning

Determination of Long-Term Information Requirements of the Organization

Chief Information Officer (CIO) Corporate and MIS Planners Steering Committee

Tactical and Operational Planning

Identification of Projects and Setting of Priorities

Steering Committee MIS Managers and Planners in Collaboration with User Management

. . . .

Systems Development Projects

System Analysis

System Design

Programming

Installation

. . .

System Analysis

System Design

Programming

Installation

Project Teams (development teams), with User Participation as Appropriate

Systems Maintenance Projects

System Operation and Maintenance

System Termination

System Operation and Maintenance

System Termination

Operations Personnel and End Users Maintenance Teams

top MIS management of the firm. The MIS steering committee plays a significant role in channeling organizational resources towards the strategically vital or highest-payoff information systems.

Consistent with the long-term objectives of the MIS strategic plan, and in response to requests for systems, the applications to be acquired are identified and their relative priorities are established via tactical and operational planning. Based on this lower-level planning, projects may be initiated to develop individual organizational systems. As we said, this does not take place to the exclusion of alternative avenues of system acquisition, such as end-user-developed systems of limited scope, purchased systems, or systems developed by outside contractors. However, let us further consider the most arduous acquisition path for an organization—developing a system in-house via a systems development life cycle process—and discuss in a relatively informal fashion the steps involved.

A systems development project, which will be further discussed in more detail in the two following chapters, consists of four conceptually different stages: systems analysis, systems design, programming (coding and testing), and installation. The work is done by project teams, whose composition will depend on the nature of the project and will generally vary from stage to stage.

The principal objective of **systems analysis** is to provide a detailed answer to the question "*What* will the new system do?" The next stage, **systems design,** answers the question "*How* will the new system be organized?" During the **programming** stage, the individual software modules of the system are coded and tested and later integrated into an operational system as further levels of testing proceed to ensure quality control. **Installation** includes final testing of the system in the actual environment where it will be deployed, and conversion of operations to fit the new systems.

The implementation process for a major information system is a process of organizational change that involves gaining the commitment of future users, changing, as appropriate, the structure of the unit involved, and redefining work tasks.[2]

An implemented system is then handed over to the operations personnel. It will be extensively modified over its useful life in a process known as system maintenance. If the development process of a large system has taken two years and involved perhaps thirty professionals, the system will be used and maintained for some seven to ten years. The primary objective of maintenance is to adjust the system to the organization's changing informational requirements and to new hardware and software platforms on which the system will run. Another objective is, unfortunately, the removal of development errors.

After the useful life of the system comes to an end, the system should be terminated and replaced. The MIS portfolios of many organizations unfortunately contain large numbers of systems that have been in operation for ten to fifteen years, which leads to figurative and literal (for MIS managers) maintenance nightmares.

17.9 AGENTS INVOLVED IN AN MIS PROJECT

The implementation of an information system is a protracted process that requires the collaboration (and piques the political rivalry) of three principal agent groups: users, management, and developers. Each may initiate a development project, and each will play different roles during the system implementation.

Principal Agents and Their Agendas

Three groups of agents are involved in an MIS project: end users of the system to be developed, management (of the function to be served by the system as well as general corporate management), and system developers. These groups are, of course, not uniform themselves; for example, the developers include systems analysts who play the major role in planning individual systems, but who generally have different backgrounds and professional expertise from the programmers. Staff professionals, such as planners and EDP auditors, who act in behalf of corporate management, are often involved as well.

Each of the groups in the triad represents well-defined interests in initiating a project and in the continuing implementation process. This triad is shown in figure 17.10, along with the principal agendas of the participants.

The objectives, norms, and performance criteria of these agent groups do not always coincide and are sometimes in direct conflict. Much of what we call the "politics" of a project stems from these differences. Matters are further complicated by the fact that the groups of the triad are not uniform, and that other stakeholders may have an impact on various projects. A good MIS developer should clearly see his or her mission in the project as providing end users with appropriate information systems. The developer must also satisfy the financial and other objectives pursued by general management and the constraints of the business unit served by the system, whose objectives are (or should be) pursued by management. Thus, the systems developer has to understand the agendas of users and management and take action relative to those agendas.

FIGURE 17.10

Key agents in systems development and their agendas.

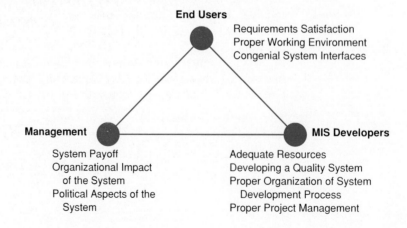

End Users
Requirements Satisfaction
Proper Working Environment
Congenial System Interfaces

Management
System Payoff
Organizational Impact
    of the System
Political Aspects of the
    System

MIS Developers
Adequate Resources
Developing a Quality System
Proper Organization of System
    Development Process
Proper Project Management

The roles of the three agent groups in the triad have been analyzed from the systems theory point of view by C. West Churchman (Churchman, 1971), and may be stated in the following terms:

- The users are interested in system performance.
- The management controls the resources to be expended in developing and operating the system.
- MIS developers implement a system that satisfies users' needs as well as the constraints and objectives of management.

Note that the roles may be collapsed. EIS and DSS are developed for users who are also managers; end-user computing merges the roles of user and developer. The ultimate merger of roles is represented by a manager who develops her own decision support system and thus plays all three roles.

The involvement of end users in systems development is considered an important factor in ensuring that the system will appropriately solve the users' problems and that it will be successfully implemented, thanks in part to user commitment. We shall further consider user involvement in systems development in the next chapter, in which system implementation is discussed at some length.

Who Initiates a Project?

Each of the three agents may be the initiator of a system development project. Most commonly, the need for a new system is first perceived by management or end users. Top management may discover the need for a major organizational system during strategic planning. A gap in the systems portfolio may be detected or a new strategic thrust may require the implementation of a new system. As sophistication in managerial use of computers grows, the management of a business unit may see the need for a system supporting the key factors of business success. An existing system often proves inflexible with respect to changing needs; for example, the need emerges to see a total relationship with a bank customer, or to track the entire employment path of an employee.

End users involved in business operations frequently recognize the deficiencies of existing transaction processing systems, which may be overwhelmed by the volume of transactions or by new transactions that are not directly supported by the existing system. End users who are managers themselves may feel the need for a more rational approach to decision making and thus for a specific DSS. Thus, projects initiated by management and end users are expressions of demand pull.

MIS professionals, and the Emerging Technologies group in particular, may keep track of the availability of new technologies appropriate to deal with certain business problems. They may perceive the inadequacy of older systems based on batch transaction processing or excessive paper handling. Their initiatives represent technology push. People who can envision what an information technology can do for a company's business are increasingly sought; the position announcement in the next vignette illustrates this.

Problems Encountered during Systems Development

Among the problems that stem from conflicting interests and miscommunication among the three agent groups and that need to be considered during the system implementation process are:

- Each of the agents may pursue their own agendas, which do not necessarily coincide with the organizational goals. A manager may want a system that enhances her organizational power; a systems analyst may want to develop a system that will give him desired credentials for a job switch, and an end user may desire an expensive and entertaining, but unwarranted, system interface.
- Users of future systems, including managers, generally do not know their requirements; the use of prototyping techniques helps significantly in solving this problem.
- Communication between business-oriented managers and users on the one hand and technology-oriented analysts on the other is a problem to contend with. Differences in the cognitive styles of analysts (who can usually be classified as systematic thinkers) and users (who are often intuitive) interfere with communication. (Cognitive styles were discussed in chapter 13.)

Indeed, a certain proportion of development projects is abandoned when well underway—and the organizational factors, such as disagreements among the agents involved in the development, loom as the principal reason (Ewusi-Mensah, 1991).

All of these problem areas point to the need to consider the implementation process as a broad organizational change rather than just the technical development of a system. The framework for the implementation of information systems is presented in the next chapter.

. . . .

SUMMARY

There are multiple ways to organize the MIS function to match the requirements, structure, and culture of an organization. Departmental computing, with decentralized MIS groups located directly within individual units of an organization, is gaining momentum. The requisite expertise is provided by a variety of MIS specialists, most of whom are analysts or programmers.

An organization may employ any of several methodologies to align its long-term MIS objectives and plans with its business objectives. With the use of one or more of these methods, a master MIS plan is developed. The worth of individual MIS projects is evaluated within the context of this plan; ranking by an MIS steering committee and cost-benefit analyses are additional evaluation tools.

There are at present several ways to acquire an information system. The most arduous road, usually taken only for large organizational systems, is that of life-cycle-based in-house development. The key agents in this process are users, management, and developers. Since their agendas and conceptual frameworks differ, system implementation requires significant attention as a process of organizational change.

ENDNOTES

1. According to Daniel J. Cavanaugh, executive vice-president for MIS for Metropolitan Life, in a speech during a session on "Case Studies: Building the Information-Driven Organization," October 10, 1989, INFO '89 Conference, New York.

2. In the software engineering community, the later stages of the development process—programming, testing, and conversion—are generally referred to as system implementation. A strictly technological orientation toward delivering quality information systems is behind this approach. It is, however, more appropriate for us to interpret the implementation process more broadly here as encompassing the insertion of the system into the life of the organization.

KEY TERMS AND CONCEPTS

Departmental computing
Systems analyst
Systems designer
Applications programmer
Systems programmer
Chief information officer (CIO)
Information system architecture
MIS master plan
Linking business and MIS
  requirements
Business System Planning (BSP)
Critical success factors (CSF)
Chargeout (chargeback)
Portfolio approach to information
  systems

Steering committee
Cost-benefit analysis
Fixed costs
Operating costs
Tangible benefits
Intangible benefits
Net present value
Systems development life cycle
  (SDLC)
Prototyping
Request for Proposal (RFP)
Systems integrator
Outsourcing

QUESTIONS

1. List the principal advantages and disadvantages of functional, divisional, and matrix organizations of the MIS function (you may have to look these up in section 12.3).

2. Why is the MIS function being distributed to individual units within organizations? Which functions generally remain in the central MIS unit?

3. List the principal functions of a systems analyst.

4. What are the principal categories of systems developers, and what do they do?

5. What is the relationship between a systems analyst and an applications programmer?

6. What are the contents of an MIS master (long-term) plan?

7. What is the difference between deriving an organization's MIS requirements from its long-term business plan and the strategy set transformation technique?

8. What are the principal distinctions between Business Systems Planning and critical success factors methodologies?

9. What do you believe are the critical success factors of a first-level sales manager? What types of information are needed to support these factors?

10. What are the advantages of the portfolio approach to project selection?

11. What are the limitations of cost-benefit analysis?

12. Perform a cost-benefit analysis for a project with these characteristics:

   - Development time: one year
   - Time system will be in operation: seven years
   - Fixed costs: $35,000
   - Operating costs: $10,000/year
   - Discount rate: 10 percent

   Use the net present value method and make a recommendation, assuming that there are no significant intangible benefits.

13. What is the principal advantage of a steering committee as compared to a cost-benefit analysis as a tool for prioritizing projects?

14. List all the methods of acquiring information systems.

15. What is outsourcing, and what are its drawbacks?

16. What are the principal steps in systems development performed with a life-cycle-oriented methodology?

17. Who are the three key agents in a systems development project?

ISSUES FOR DISCUSSION

1. Here are excerpts from an interview with two managers of relatively small MIS shops: Richard L. Norris, vice-president of information systems at Mitsubishi Motor Sales of America (MMSA of Cypress, California), and Darrall Lem, MIS director of Silicon Systems of Tustin, California. The MIS staff at MMSA grew from twenty-two in 1981 to seventy-five in 1989; the staff at Silicon Systems, a manufacturer of application-specific integrated circuits, is somewhat smaller.

Question: How do you go about planning?

Lem: Our planning is really project oriented. A user requests a project and we schedule it. We have quarterly reviews. There isn't very much hardware or network resource planning in my shop yet.

Norris: At Mitsubishi, we have a rolling five-year plan and an annual operating plan. In addition, the users are provided monthly status reports—we are very focused on dates. That's related to the type of business we're in.

Question: Do you have much top management involvement in IS in your company?

Lem: Top management is involved and supportive of IS. They recognize the need for information accuracy and accessibility. Projects are identified by top management; general direction and the approach to accomplish the projects are determined by [the] IS [department]. We currently do not have a steering committee in our company; all major capital expenditures are approved by a capital appropriations committee.

Norris: Ours is a Japanese company and so we have very few levels of management. The allocation of resources is done by a steering committee, but the budget is set by top management. . . . Top management controls IS by taking a very hard stance on headcount and by controlling major expenditures. The challenge is in building a five-year IS plan when the users have difficulty forecasting their needs for the next five years. . . .

From Robert E. Umbaugh, ''ISM Interviews Richard L. Norris and Darrall Lem On Managing a Small MIS Shop.'' *Journal of Information Systems Management, 6,* 1, Winter 1989, pp. 89–95.

Discuss the principal differences between the approaches to planning and controlling information systems in these two companies. How do you believe these differences are related to each company's business, size, and corporate culture?

2. Suppose you have been appointed to the MIS steering committee in your firm. In approximate order of importance, what methods and criteria will you apply in evaluating proposals for new systems?

3. Consider a proposed central database of student records that includes records of all past, present, and potential future students. What are the intangible benefits of a system built around such a database?

4. Imagine that you have been promoted to the position of MIS director by your employer, a midsize distributor of specialty foods. You are expected to reduce the backlog of applications awaiting development. What methods of system acquisition will you recommend? What drawbacks of these methods will you have to contend with?

5. Discuss this proposition: ''MIS proficiency will be required of *all* managers in a future organization. Therefore, we shall need neither a separate MIS function nor MIS managers.'' Do you agree or disagree? Why?

An Interview with an Information Systems Planner (or Is It a Business Analyst?)

"Individuals who know which information technology tools to use to match the products and services of their organization with the needs of their customers are fast becoming competitive necessities." So Tom McCusker of *Datamation* prefaces his interview with Michael Polosky, assistant vice-president for systems planning and technical services at Pacific Bell of San Ramon, California.

As information systems increasingly play a strategic role in organizations, more and more firms look to people such as Polosky—whose function is defined variously as strategic MIS planner, information system architect, or business analyst—to define the corporate MIS strategy within the context of their business goals.

At the time of the interview, Polosky had held his position for three years. Before that, he held twenty different positions in the company, equally divided between technical and business operations. Polosky reports to Jack Hancock, vice-president for systems technology, who in turn reports to Marty Kaplan, executive vice-president for customer services (note this!). Polosky is responsible for all information systems planning in the company; its systems include mainframes, minicomputers, and microcomputers—from a dozen manufacturers.

Let us summarize the highlights of the interview.

Question: Is it typical for a person in your position to have background in both technical and business operations?

Polosky: It's only in recent years that we have begun to recognize the need to combine both backgrounds. Before that, [systems planners] had been experts in planning or in a technical area.

Question: What is demanded of a business analyst (or a business technology planner—as you would call him or her)?

Polosky: You're involved with translating company strategies into what kind of technology infrastructure you need—and then seeing that it is being built to support the business direction.

Question: What are Pacific Bell's chief system goals?

Polosky: Over the years, we have focused on automating discrete functions in the business. Today, we need much more flexibility and interoperability (that is, hardware and software from various manufacturers have to work together). We have designed overall system architecture for the company: the environment we need to be successful in the future. We have identified the data that need to be shared across many applications.

We have realized that we must basically retool our major systems. Since we have a large investment in our information systems, we have decided to go about it step by step.

We have identified the critical systems that would receive top priority within the next three to five years. These include billing, which needs to be flexible enough to deal with the new kinds of products and services that are being offered. We needed also to simplify the customer interface: today, we have multiple interfaces between customers and the company—these need to be reduced. We have to reduce the amount of time between when a customer makes a request and when we actually provide the service. And, as said, we have to build shareable databases.

Question: With whom do you confer in performing your work?

Polosky: We work very closely with people involved with marketing and market strategy—the people who are mapping out the future products and services. We then translate this to the systems technology people to make sure that the company is putting in the right kind of processors and developing the right kind of software. In this position, you have to translate your understanding of where your business (and, in fact, the industry) is going into the terms people who will build the systems can use.

Question: Describe the makeup and operation of your team.

Polosky: I have a very small unit, which does systems planning. We are now responsible for transition planning. We translate the overall business direction into what we call strategic business objectives. We see to it that all the parts make an integrated whole. The group also manages the systems portfolio.

On a dotted-line basis, we have people within the system development units who operate what we call "strategic focus divisions." Using our transition plan, they manage the system portfolios of these units. They break down the strategic plan into more tactical steps. They worry about how to determine the user requirements, when to begin the design work, etc.

We work closely with the Integrated Task Force Group, which includes all the planners (myself among them), the marketing director, the director of technical training, and my peer on the side of network operations—we are managing planning and implementation of major components of technology.

Question: What are the career paths of technology planners?

Polosky: With a business and technological background, they could do several things. They could head one of the technical units in the organization. They could probably provide good guidance in the marketing area. They could even be well positioned to lead the entire organization—several other steps would be involved, of course. At any rate, you would be in a position to act in an advisory capacity to the key officers of the business.

Question: What other skills are required to be an effective technology planner?

Polosky: Very good listening skills. You're trying to understand the direction of various components within the organization. You also need to have the ability to compromise. As you deal with overall business direction, there's always a series of constraints, whether they are financial or human capabilities.

Based on Tom McCusker, "Why Business Analysts Are Indispensable to IS." *Datamation,* January 15, 1990, pp. 76–78.

Case Study Questions

1. Show the fragment of the Pacific Bell organization chart that includes all the components of the system planning group run by Michael Polosky.

2. What roles does the information systems planning unit play at Pacific Bell?

3. Who are the principal stakeholders in the planning unit? What are the relationships between the unit and these various stakeholders?

4. What background and skills are required of MIS planners in this firm?

SELECTED REFERENCES

Abrams, Robert I.; Foley, John J.; and Robbins, Laurence G. "The Stage Assessment." In *Managing the Data Resource Function,* edited by Richard L. Nolan. 2d ed. St.Paul: West, 1982, pp. 159–71.

Benjamin, Robert I.; Dickinson, Charles, Jr.; and Rockart, John F. "Changing Role of Corporate Information Systems Officer." *MIS Quarterly,* 9, 3, September 1985, pp. 177–88.

Bergeron, François, and Bégin, Clermont. "The Use of Critical Success Factors in Evaluation of Information Systems: A Case Study." *Journal of Management Information Systems,* 5, 4, Spring 1989, pp. 111–24.

Bullen, Christine V., and Rockart, John F. "A Primer on Critical Success Factors." CISR Working Paper No. 69, Sloan School of Management. Cambridge, Mass.: Massachusetts Institute of Technology, June 1981.

Churchman, C. West. *The Design of Inquiring Systems: Basic Concepts of Systems and Organizations.* New York: Basic Books, 1971.

Clemons, Eric K. "Evaluation of Strategic Investments in Information Technology." *Communications of the ACM,* 34, 1, January 1991, pp. 22–36.

Davis, Gordon B., and Olson, Margrethe H. *Management Information Systems: Conceptual Foundations, Structure, and Development.* 2d. ed. New York: McGraw-Hill, 1985.

Dearden, John. "The Withering Away of the IS Organization." *Sloan Management Review,* 28, 4, Summer 1987, pp. 87–91.

Doll, William J., and Torkzadeh, Golamreza. "The Relationship of MIS Steering Committees to Size of Firm and Formalization of MIS Planning." *Communications of the ACM,* 30, 11, November 1987, pp. 972–78.

Drury, D. H. "An Evaluation of Data Processing Steering Committees." *MIS Quarterly,* 8, 4, December 1984, pp. 257–65.

Ewusi-Mensah, Kweku, and Przasnyski, Zbigniew H. "On Information Systems Project Abandonment: An Exploratory Study of Organizational Practices." *MIS Quarterly,* 15, 1, March 1991, pp. 67–85.

Gremillion, Lee L., and Pyburn, Philip J. "Justifying Decision Support and Office Systems." *Journal of Management Information Systems,* 2, 1, Summer 1985, pp. 5–17.

Hammer, Michael. "Reengineering Work: Don't Automate, Obliterate." *Harvard Business Review,* July-August 1990, pp. 104–12.

Henderson, John C.; Rockart John F.; and Sifonis, John G. "Integrating Management Support Systems into Strategic Information Systems Planning." *Journal of Management Information Systems,* 4, 1, Summer 1987, pp. 5–24.

Ives, Blake, and Vitale, Michael R. "After the Sale: Leveraging Maintenance with Information Technology." *MIS Quarterly,* 12, 1, March 1988, pp. 7–21.

Janson, Marius A. "Evidence to Support the Continuing Role of the IS Department in Organizations." *Journal of Management Information Systems,* 6, 2, Fall 1989, pp. 21–31.

Kemerer, Chris F., and Sosa, G. L. "Systems Development Risks in Strategic Information Systems." *Information and Software Technology,* 33, 3, April 1991, pp. 212–23.

King, Leslie John, and Schrems, Edward L. "Cost-Benefit Analysis in Information Systems Development and Operation." *Computing Surveys,* 10, 1, March 1978, pp. 19–34.

King, William R. "Strategic Planning for Management Information Systems." *MIS Quarterly,* 2, 1, March 1978, pp. 27–37.

IBM Business Systems Planning: Information Systems Planning Guide, GE20–0527–4. 4th ed. Atlanta: IBM Corporation, 1984.

Lederer, Albert L., and Mendelow, Aubrey L. "Coordination of Information Systems Plans with Business Plans." *Journal of Management Information Systems,* 6, 2, Fall 1989, pp. 5–19.

Lucas, Henry C., Jr.; Walton, Eric J.; and Ginzberg, Michael J. "Implementing Packaged Software." *MIS Quarterly,* 12, 4, December 1988, pp. 537–49.

McFarlan, F. Warren. "Portfolio Approach to Information Systems." *Harvard Business Review,* September-October 1981, pp. 142–50.

McFarlan, F. Warren, and McKinney, James L. *Corporate Information Systems Management: The Issues Facing Senior Executives.* Homewood, Ill.: Irwin, 1983.

Mainelli, Michael R., and Miller, David R. "Strategic Planning for Information Systems at British Rail." *Long Range Planning,* 21, 4, 1988, pp. 65–76.

Martino, C. A. *Information Systems Planning to Meet Business Objectives: A Survey of Practices.* New York: Cresap, McCormick and Paget, 1983.

Melymuka, Kathleen. "Reinventing the Corporate Culture." *CIO,* November 1990. pp. 34–40.

Nolan, Richard L. "Managing Information Systems by Committee." *Harvard Business Review,* July-August 1982, pp. 72–79.

"Outsourcing." *Computerworld,* March 11, 1991, p. 94.

Parker, Marilyn M. "Enterprise Information Analysis: Cost-Benefit Analysis and the Data-Managed System." *IBM Systems Journal,* 21, 1, 1982, pp. 108–23.

Parker, Marilyn M.; Trainor, H. Edgar; and Benson, Robert J. *Information Strategy and Economics.* Englewood Cliffs, N.J.: Prentice Hall, 1989.

Raghunathan, Bhanu, and Raghunathan, T. S. "Relationship of the Rank of Information System Executive to the Organizational Role and Planning Dimensions of Information Systems." *Journal of Management Information Systems,* 6, 1, Summer 1989, pp. 111–26.

Rockart, John F. "Chief Executives Define Their Own Data Needs." *Harvard Business Review,* March-April 1979, pp. 81–93.

Shank, Michael E.; Boynton, Andrew C.; and Zmud, Robert W. "Critical Success Factor Analysis as a Methodology for MIS Planning." *MIS Quarterly,* 9, 2, June 1985, pp. 121–30.

Strassman, Paul A. *The Business Value of Computers.* New Canaan, Conn.: Information Economics Press, 1990.

Zachman, John A. "Business Systems Planning and Business Information Control Study: A Comparison." *IBM Systems Journal,* 21, 1, 1982, pp. 31–53.

CHAPTER 18

DEVELOPMENT AND IMPLEMENTATION OF INFORMATION SYSTEMS

· ·

But change is an unnatural act, particularly in successful companies; powerful forces are at work to avoid and defeat it.

Michael E. Porter

Management information systems are built and installed in a process known as systems development. There are two principal approaches to this development: the life-cycle approach and prototyping. Large organizational information systems are generally developed through a systems development life cycle (SDLC). This development method organizes the team effort into a series of stages, with each stage terminating in a demonstrable event—a milestone, during which well-defined deliverables are indeed demonstrated. An SDLC-oriented methodology aims to produce reliable systems that are thoroughly documented and that lend themselves relatively easily to maintenance during the extensive period of system operation.

SDLC-based development methodologies are increasingly being either supported or entirely supplanted by prototyping—the development of an initial pilot system that can be exercised by end users to establish their requirements and to secure their commitment to the new system. The prototype of such a system may be either refined into a final product (in a process known as evolutionary development) or discarded, having served as an excellent tool for establishing user requirements. In evolutionary development, it is possible to turn an initial version of a system over to its users quite early.

Here, we shall first discuss the entire systems development life cycle. We shall then present the prototyping technique and the two principal ways it may be used.

A system's technological superiority is no guarantee of its success. System failures caused by organizational factors abound. We shall discuss the implementation of information systems as a process of preparing the organization for a new system and establishing the system within the organization.

For some twenty years, the U.S. Army had used a systems development methodology based on a strict analysis-design-programming sequence. The methodology was based on two implicit assumptions. One was that such a linear development model is applicable to all systems, and the other that an effective system can be produced from predefined requirements specifications. While these assumptions are generally valid for transactions processing systems, they have proven inadequate for decision-oriented system types.

In the early 1980s, a new methodology involving the evolutionary development of an initial system prototype was introduced, and the life-cycle-based methodology was entirely abandoned. User representatives and developers worked together to quickly construct a working prototype. Software development tools and fourth-generation languages were employed. Productivity was high. However, pitfalls soon opened up. Systems analysis was inadequate. For example, when three systems developed in this fashion were being integrated, they proved to be incompatible. Also, users either embraced early prototypes as final system versions or would endlessly ask for new features in yet another version. Project controls were almost nonexistent.

Heeding this experience, the Army combined the advantages of both development methods into its Contemporary Life-Cycle Development Methodology. Now system design and programming begin immediately after the creation of a broad functional description of the new system, which specifies its boundary and interfaces and no more. The system documentation is continually revised during the evolutionary development of the initial version. The final definition of user requirements is documented following end-user testing of this prototype. Formal quality reviews and milestones are employed to control the process and product quality.

The new methodology has produced significant savings in effort and shorter delivery times.

Based on Mary L. Cesena and Wendell O. Jones, "Accelerated Information Systems Development in The Army." *SIM SPECTRUM*, September 1987. Also available in Andrew C. Boynton and Robert W. Zmud, *Management Information Systems: Readings and Cases, A Managerial Perspective.* Glenview, Ill.: Scott, Foresman, 1990, pp. 189–202.

As we have just seen, life-cycle-based methodologies can be creatively combined with prototyping to match the needs of an organization or of a particular system to be developed. However, such creativity requires a keen understanding of the principal development methodologies, which we shall discuss in this chapter.

CHAPTER OUTLINE

18.1 What Is Systems Development Life Cycle?
- Why Do We Need Life-Cycle-Based Development?
- What Is Structured SDLC?
- The Development Process Continues to Evolve

18.2 Systems Development Life Cycle: Systems Analysis Stages
- Objectives of Systems Analysis
- The Feasibility Study—Preliminary Survey
- Requirements Analysis

18.3 Systems Development Life Cycle: Systems Design Stages
- Objectives of Systems Design
- Conceptual (Logical) Design
- Detailed (Physical) Design

18.4 Systems Development Life Cycle: Programming

18.5 Systems Development Life Cycle: Conversion

18.6 Systems Development Life Cycle: Postimplementation Audit

18.7 Prototyping
- What Is Prototyping?
- Two Prototyping Scenarios
- Why Prototype?
- Potential Problems with Prototyping

18.8 Implementation of Information Systems
- Systems May "Work"—Yet Be Failures
- What is Implementation?
- What is Successful Implementation?
- Factors in Successful Implementation

. . . .

18.1   WHAT IS SYSTEMS DEVELOPMENT LIFE CYCLE?

The systems development life cycle (SDLC) approach gives organizations a means of controlling a development project. Structured SDLC equips each development stage with appropriate tools for producing reliable and maintainable systems. Since life-cycle-oriented development suffers from a certain lack of flexibility, many systems developers are combining it with prototyping techniques.

Why Do We Need Life-Cycle-Based Development?

Large systems development projects involve a number of people over an extensive period of time. Thus, to develop a transaction processing system, such as an on-line order processing system that supports hundreds of terminals, two project teams, consisting of ten people each, may need to work for about two years. Such a significant commitment of organizational resources has to be managed in a formal fashion.

Systems development life cycle is a method for managing this effort based on the management techniques of industrial engineering. With SDLC, the complexity of the development process is dealt with by breaking a project up into stages. Every stage is defined in terms of the activities and responsibilities of the development team members. Every stage terminates in a milestone defined in terms of the subproducts to be delivered, such as system requirements specifications or coded and tested software modules. Early versions of SDLC relied heavily on narrative descriptions of what the system was expected to do, as well as on system and program flowcharts (a variety of these early cycles have been described in Murdick, 1970). A heavy concentration on programming, rather than on the earlier stages of systems analysis and design, was the hallmark of these approaches.

In the early 1970s, SDLC emerged in the form of the waterfall model,[1] a modern version of which is shown in figure 18.1. A variety of methodologies based on the SDLC concept have been evolved by various organizations and vendors. All of them correspond in the main to what we shall describe in the present chapter.

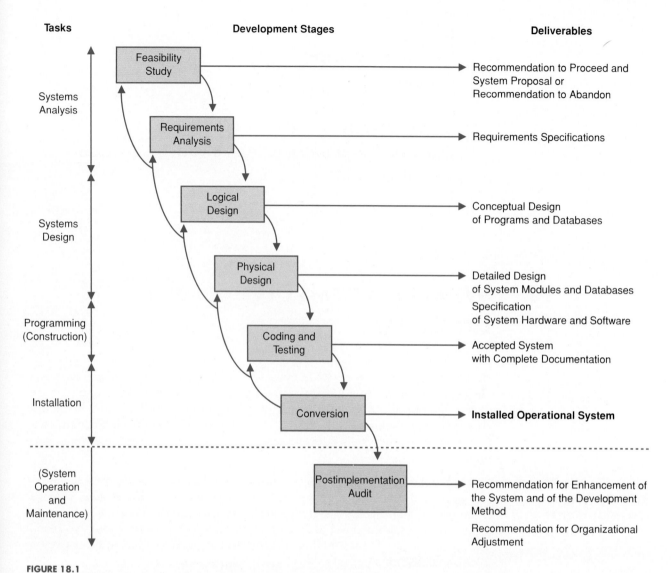

FIGURE 18.1

Systems development life cycle (the "waterfall model").

Note that the arrows in the figure point in both directions, up and down the "waterfall." This reflects the fact that the developers need to rework the deliverables produced at earlier stages in light of the experience they gain as the development effort progresses. This experience, as well as justifiable end-user requests for changes that must be accommodated during the sometimes lengthy development process, may oftentimes go back even further, requiring the reworking of several earlier stages of development.

Each stage of a life-cycle-oriented development project is terminated by a project milestone. At that time, the deliverables of that stage—such as documentation for the system, and later, its code—are signed off by all the concerned parties as an agreement to proceed. The parties are generally the three agents involved in the development (users, developers, and management), as well as whatever experts are needed in the development stage, such as MIS auditors and database administration personnel.

FIGURE 18.2

Distribution of systems development effort.

(From Marvin V. Zelkowitz, et al., *Principles of Software Engineering and Design,* © 1979, p. 3. Reprinted by permission of Prentice-Hall, Inc., Englewood Cliffs, NJ.)

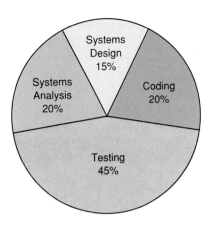

FIGURE 18.3

Effort expended during the total system life cycle.

(From Marvin V. Zelkowitz, et al., *Principles of Software Engineering and Design,* © 1979, p. 3. Reprinted by permission of Prentice-Hall, Inc., Englewood Cliffs, NJ.)

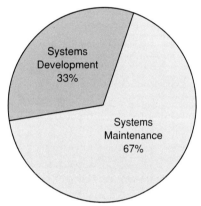

What is Structured SDLC?

In the late 1970s, a structured SDLC (or **structured systems development**) began to emerge, distinguished by the techniques and tools it uses to handle the complexity of information systems by progressively bringing detail into the system under development. Structured methods evolved from the systems approach, which we discussed in chapter 10. Both systems analysis and systems design move from the abstract level to more detailed levels through a process known as stepwise refinement. Specific tools (graphic, if possible) are employed for the analysis (data flow diagrams) and design (structure charts) stages. Narrative descriptions are avoided, as they generally prove both ambiguous and difficult to maintain as the system is maintained in the future. Effort is concentrated on these early stages, rather than on coding, in order to avoid errors in establishing user requirements (chiefly during analysis) and to produce a system that could be relatively easily modified during maintenance (the principal objective of systems design).

The distribution of effort, that is, of time spent on the principal activities in system development, is shown in figure 18.2.

The need to expend very significant effort during the stages that ensure the effectiveness, reliability, and maintainability of the system is brought home by figure 18.3. This figure shows the effort required during the total system life cycle, which includes both development and maintenance. We can see that most information systems require twice as much effort (and, correspondingly, expenditure) for maintenance as they do for development. This experience has been consistently reported by MIS managers over the last two decades. Indeed, many organizations spend 60 to 70 percent of their MIS budgets on system maintenance, which we shall further discuss in chapter 20. It pays, then, to develop systems that will be easier to maintain.

If the systems developers use the proper development techniques and tools, their SDLC effort should result in a product that

- satisfies the organization's requirements and, in particular, fits into the overall MIS plan of the enterprise;
- operates reliably;
- creates an appropriate working environment for its users;
- is maintainable; that is, because of the way in which it was developed and documented, the system is relatively easy to modify so as to adapt it to changing business requirements and to the software and hardware environments in which it will operate;
- has built-in controls to ensure security, privacy, and auditability, as required (and as described in chapter 20).

Life-cycle-based development produces the voluminous documentation necessary to operate and maintain a system. To avoid additional—and unattractive— work on developing this documentation, and to make sure that the documentation corresponds to the actual software product, it is highly desirable that it emerge as a by-product of the development process. When structured development methodologies are used, the principal tools of analysis and design become the principal system documentation.

Structured methodologies are now frequently used in systems development. In a survey of ninety-seven organizations (Necco, 1987), it was found that 69 percent used SDLC based on traditional tools (such as narratives and flowcharts) on some of their projects, and 62 percent used structured SDLC; of the firms that at the time used no disciplined SDLC, twice as many were considering using a structured SDLC in the future as were leaning toward traditional life-cycle development. Moreover, computer-aided software engineering (CASE) tools, which we shall discuss in the next chapter, are based on structured methodologies.

The Development Process Continues to Evolve

Most companies that develop large systems have their own versions of an SDLC. However, all of these versions display significant similarities, since all use the analysis-design-programming paradigm. The methodologies differ with respect to the permitted overlap between the various stages. The more traditional versions do not allow for such an overlap; some of the newer methodologies encourage partial phase overlapping. As speed expectations on the MIS department increase, overlapping becomes even more important. Moreover, methodologies differ in their use of prototyping as a systems analysis technique or as a replacement for SDLC for some system classes. One attempt to combine the advantages of both SDLC-based development and prototyping is the so-called spiral model (Boehm, 1989), which produces requirements specifications based on several early prototypes of the system.

It is necessary to build a degree of flexibility into an SDLC methodology. Since it is applied to large projects implemented over perhaps two or more years, the requirements on the system may change. There must be a process whereby legitimate changes are incorporated as early as possible into the system being developed. An example of how such a process may be organized is offered by Charles Snyder and James Cox (1985).

In this chapter, we shall present the stages of SDLC and the managerial aspects of the process. In the next, we shall discuss the techniques and tools of structured SDLC, as well as the emerging CASE toolset that automates some of the SDLC steps.

18.2 SYSTEMS DEVELOPMENT LIFE CYCLE: SYSTEMS ANALYSIS STAGES

The objective of systems analysis is to establish what the system will do in terms of a firm's business functions. In its preliminary phase, the feasibility study, planners analyze the desirability of the proposed system to the organization. Should a commitment be made to the development, a full-scale requirements analysis is made, and a detailed requirements specifications document is produced.

Objectives of Systems Analysis

The task of **systems analysis** is to establish in considerable detail *what* the proposed system will do (as opposed to *how* it will be accomplished technologically). This includes establishing the objectives of the new system, conducting an analysis of its costs and of the benefits to be derived from it, and outlining the process of system implementation, including the organizational change required. Detailed systems analysis must also establish who the system users are, what information they should get and in what form, and how this information will be obtained from the incoming data and from the databases. In other words, the flow of data into the system, data transformation and storage by the system, and the delivery of information to users are subject to a detailed analysis.

The first of the systems analysis stages of SDLC is the system feasibility study (also known as the preliminary survey), which may actually result in tabling the project, should it be found undesirable for any of the reasons examined. The main analysis stage is the extensive requirements analysis, which results in the requirements specifications for the system—a detailed statement of what users expect (and what developers will deliver).

These two stages of SDLC are performed by systems analysts, in close collaboration with the intended system users. Users are routinely consulted as information is gathered for this phase; some users may be members of a liaison team which facilitates communication between users and developers or may be active participants in the analysis process. One of the better known methods for including users in the analysis is Joint Applications Development (JAD), which we will discuss in section 18.8. User involvement is often vital to the success of a system development project, as illustrated by the vignette on the failure of such a project.

ANATOMY OF A FAILURE

Blue Cross/Blue Shield (BCBS) of Wisconsin launched a highly ambitious MIS project in 1983 that cost it millions in lost business and taught it a lot about system implementation as an organizational change process. That year, the firm signed a contract with a major integrator company for a "grand design" system that would handle all aspects of the business, including claims processing, enrollment of new customers, cost-containment analyses, and many other functions. The integrator estimated the cost at $200 million and the delivery time at eighteen months.

The deadline was indeed met—but the system worked erratically. To mention just one problem, the system sent hundreds of checks to a nonexistent Wisconsin town. All in all, in its first year of operation (yes, it was allowed to operate for quite a while), the system caused $60 million in overpayments and duplicate checks, and the insurance company lost 35,000 clients. Both

the integrator company that developed the system and the customer firm were to blame. The integrator underestimated the complexity of the system and was too optimistic in setting its contractual delivery time; it delivered an untested system.

Perhaps even more important, the client company failed to involve the future users in the systems development process. The project was sponsored at BCBS by the members of the technical staff, who were not intimately familiar with the business requirements. When BCBS analyzed the failure, they found, moreover, that the system implementation should have included an organizational restructuring. At a later time, this involved the removal of three levels of management and thus shortened significantly the management chain. At that late point, "we came to know what we were trying to achieve with the system," said a corporate vice-president.

Based on Karen Gullo, "Stopping Runaways in Their Tracks." *InformationWeek*, November 13, 1989, pp. 63–70.

The Feasibility Study— Preliminary Survey

The main objective of the feasibility study, the introductory phase of development, is to establish whether the proposed system is feasible or, to be more accurate, desirable, before resources are committed to the full-scale project. If all systems proposals were the result of careful planning, there would be a very limited need for feasibility studies. The realities are different, however. Most proposals for new systems stem from business problems and opportunities—as they are encountered—and require a preliminary evaluation.

In a feasibility study, systems analysts perform a preliminary investigation of the business problem or opportunity represented by the proposed system development project. Specifically, they undertake the following tasks:

- Define the problem or the opportunity which the system will address
- Establish the overall objectives of the new system
- Identify the users of the system
- Establish the functional scope of the system (a structured analysis tool such as a context diagram, discussed in the next chapter, may serve this purpose)

SYSTEMS ANALYSIS AS AN OPPORTUNITY TO RETHINK THE BUSINESS FUNCTION

Ford Motor Company needed a system to support the processing of invoices coming from its suppliers. Instead of simply developing another, better system for invoice processing, the analysts rethought the way its accounts payable were handled—and moved to a radically different, invoiceless processing.

Instead of continuing to receive invoices from its vendors, matching them against purchase orders and documentation confirming the receipt of goods, Ford has asked its suppliers to cease sending invoices. Now, Ford will pay simply on the receipt of goods.

This new approach called for an on-line receiving information system. Incoming goods are matched with outstanding purchase orders at the loading dock, and payment is initiated there. This new way of organizing the accounts payable function, supported by an appropriate information system, has led to a 75 percent headcount reduction in the business area. And that is just one example of business reengineering.

Based on an interview with Michael Hammer, "From Cow Paths to Data Paths." *Computerworld*, December 25, 1989, pp. 16–17.

Here is an example of an executive summary which briefly establishes a system project in these terms:

> The project will address the need for a system that presents the total relationship of our company with each customer firm. The objective of the system is to assist the marketing department in devising the appropriate promotion for the customers, as well as to enable the sales department to price orders appropriately. The users of the system will be marketing planners, and sales managers and representatives in the field. The system will interface with the present order processing system and the customer database.

In addition, the systems analysts perform the following tasks during the feasibility study:

- Propose general options or scenarios for the new system (for example, a minicomputer versus a local area network of PCs), which is necessary to size the project
- Perform make-or-buy analysis for the application
- Perform cost-benefit analysis for the selected option(s), based in part on the estimate of the development project size
- Assess the project risk
- Recommend whether to proceed with (perhaps assigning a priority rating as well) or abandon the project.

It is vital at this early stage to address the business problem the new system is expected to solve, rather than to simply automate an existing way of doing business. The above vignette offers an example of how this is done, as explained by Michael Hammer, a noted MIS consultant.

DO WE WANT THIS CHANGE?

A Swedish bank developed a transaction processing system to support its tellers on the assumption that 80 percent of them were uninterested in their jobs. Based on this premise, the system requirements were defined so as to make minimum demands on its users.

The system development was a success. However, after it had been in operation for a year, management noted an alarming change in the attitudes of the tellers, based on the suggestions they were making in the employee suggestion program. The managers also detected a deterioration in customer relations.

Before the system was installed, teller suggestions were aimed at improved customer service—tellers thought of themselves as "minibankers." After conversion to the new system, teller suggestions became oriented toward modifying the system to make it more efficient (for example, by adding new screens or forms). In a way, the tellers now thought of themselves as part of a computerized system rather than as service representatives.

Based on N. French, "DP Deprives Workers of Job Satisfaction, Europe Studies Show." *Computerworld*, August 22, 1977, pp. 1, 7.

The assessment of system feasibility may be based on a narrative system description, perhaps supported by a context diagram, or it may be supported by an initial system prototype. Thus, a system's technological, economic, and organizational feasibility (or desirability) have to be established. While this is being done, a risk assessment also needs to be performed. Prototyping, whose use in the development of DSS and expert systems was described in the earlier chapters of this text (and will be further discussed in the present chapter), is recommended when there is significant uncertainty about the project. It is, in general, more costly to develop a prototype than to use a narrative.

The *technological feasibility* study aims to answer the question: do we have the capability to develop this system? This necessitates an assessment of MIS personnel capabilities and the hardware and software environment available for development. Lack of appropriate technological capabilities and experience qualifies the project as a high-risk undertaking. In addition, certain technological solutions may lead to undesirable exposures. For example, a centralized database may be undesirable for some firms in this respect.

The *economic feasibility* of the project is evaluated by comparing its costs with the envisaged benefits. Are we going to have an economic payoff from the system; or, in other words, will the benefits the organization expects to derive from the system outweigh its costs? An initial cost-benefit analysis is performed, as we described in the preceding chapter. The initial estimate will be refined during further stages of development, when we know more about the new system.

Organizational feasibility has two aspects: the system has to be accepted by the users and by the managers of the affected units. The sociotechnical approach, for example, mandates an investigation of the impact of the system on the quality

TABLE 18.1	FEASIBILITY ASPECT	ISSUES THAT NEED EVALUATION
Aspects of a Feasibility Study	Technological	Do we have the technology and skills needed to develop and operate the system?
	Economic	Will the system result in strategic advantage or some other payoff to the enterprise?
	Organizational	Will the organizational change result in an acceptable quality of working life for those affected by the system? Will the political changes caused by the system be accepted?

of the users' working life (Bostrom, 1977). It is necessary to establish whether the organizational change that will accompany system implementation is desirable (see the previous vignette) and if so, whether it can be managed—and then to set in motion the change management process. The proposed system may also alter the power structure in the affected part of the organization, in which case a negotiation process has to take place. The many dimensions of implementation are discussed later in this chapter.

The three aspects of a feasibility study are summarized in table 18.1.

Based on the estimated size of the system, the novelty of the technology in the context of the given organization, and the extent of required organizational change, a system risk assessment may be made, to become a part of portfolio analysis (see chapter 17). An organization that places itself in the "turnaround" or "strategic" cells of the strategic grid (figure 17.6) has to undertake some risky—and potentially high-payoff—projects.

A project plan is also produced during this stage: this plan lays out the schedule and the budgets for the remaining stages of the project. The plan will be refined as the project proceeds; in particular, system developers will conduct a significant review of the plan on completion of systems analysis. We shall discuss project management later in this chapter.

Typically, a feasibility study consumes 5 to 10 percent of project resources. Among the tools that may be used at this stage, along with the cost-benefit analysis, are interviews, questionnaires, observation, and participation. Since these are the general tools of systems analysis, we shall discuss them in the next section, as we discuss the systems requirements analysis, in which they are used extensively.

The following stages of SDLC for a project are subject to management approval of a recommendation to proceed and to commit resources to the project.

Requirements Analysis

The main objective of this extensive systems analysis stage is to produce **requirements specifications** for the system. These set out in detail what the system will do (rather than how the system resources will be organized to do it). Requirements (also known as functional) specifications establish an understanding between the system developers and its future users, as well as management and other stakeholders (for example, internal auditors). This understanding may be treated as a formal contract between the parties.

Thus, the objective of this stage in the SDLC framework is to perform a *complete* analysis of the system to be implemented. We stated the objectives of systems analysis at the beginning of this section. To summarize, this stage needs to establish:

- What outputs the system will produce, what inputs will be needed, what processing steps will be necessary to transform inputs into outputs, and what data stores (files or databases) will have to be maintained by the system
- What volumes of data will be handled, what numbers of users in various categories will be supported and in what fashion, what file and database capacities the system will need to maintain, and other quantitative estimates of this type
- What control measures will be undertaken in the system (these are further discussed in chapter 20)

The next chapter will present the analysis tools offered for the phase by structured methodologies, such as data flow diagrams and entity descriptions for data dictionaries. Here, we shall concentrate on the techniques that can be used in the massive information-gathering effort that the phase entails. To describe these techniques, we will employ the framework proposed by Gordon Davis of the University of Minnesota (Davis, 1981; 1982), which groups the techniques for obtaining the requirements into four categories:

- Asking future users
- Deriving from an existing information system
- Synthesizing from the characteristics of the system which will use the information system under development (that is, from the needs of the business unit or the managers who will use the system)
- Discovering from experimentation with the information system as it evolves during development

FIGURE 18.4

Techniques for information gathering in systems analysis.

These techniques are summarized in figure 18.4. A combination of techniques is generally employed.

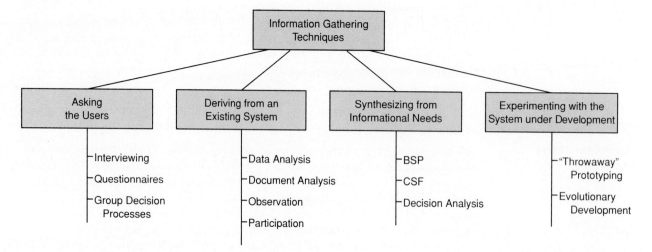

Let us discuss these techniques in order of increased uncertainty on the part of the users as to what they want from the proposed system.

1. Asking the Users

When applying these techniques, analysts assume that users have a fair understanding of what they want in the new system and that they, the analysts, will be able to compensate for a variety of cognitive and other biases exhibited by the users. The principal techniques are interviews and questionnaires, though group decision-making techniques are sometimes used as well.

Interviewing requires considerable skill and preparation. Interviews are a very rich but costly and time-consuming communication channel. Appropriate office information systems (see chapter 16) may be employed to facilitate the interviewing process. Both open ("How could order processing be done better?") and closed ("Describe the steps you perform in processing this type of security.") questions may be employed where appropriate.

The interviewing process must be planned, since it may encompass several levels within the firm, and the cooperation of management must therefore be gained. The analyst has to prepare for each interview by establishing the position, activities, and background of the interviewee. The analyst then prepares questions. During an interview, the analyst must convey a clear understanding of the purpose of the interview, ask specific questions in terms understandable to the interviewee, listen rather than anticipate answers, control the interview but be open to a sudden "information vein," and create a record (notes or recording) of what is learned. An interviewer learns how the interviewee makes decisions (frequently, the interviewee actually learns this during the interview as well). The analyst should analyze the results immediately following an interview session.

While the analyst may learn from managers what information they need to make decisions, an experienced claims clerk will be the best source of information on how insurance claims or supplier invoices are actually handled and on ideas for how they may be handled more expeditiously. Operational supervisors generally know best what volumes of various transactions the system will be expected to handle.

Questionnaires are an efficient way of asking *many* users at once, users who may also be dispersed in the field (such as insurance agents). However, questionnaires have limitations: for instance, clarification of questions or follow-up is generally impossible; and then, it is necessary to motivate an addressee to actually fill out a questionnaire. An easy-to-fill-out questionnaire with concise and closed questions is most likely to meet with success. Simple yes/no questions and checklists are preferable. Questions that aim to ascertain respondents' attitudes are usually designed with a so-called Likert scale which expresses the degree of agreement with a statement. Figure 18.5 shows an example of a question which employs a five-point Likert scale (a seven- or ten-point scale may be used for finer discrimination).

Your present customer information system permits you to answer customer queries in a
satisfactory fashion. (Circle one.)

Strongly Disagree				Strongly Agree
1	2	3	4	5

Generally, questionnaires are employed together with other, more
powerful means of eliciting user requirements.

Group decision processes, such as the Delphi method, brainstorming,
and nominal group technique, which were discussed in chapter 13, may be
used in search of creative new solutions. The Joint Application Design
(JAD) technique relies on group system-planning sessions involving users
and analysts (August, 1991). We shall return to it later in this chapter.

2. Deriving Requirements from an Existing Information System

The requirements for a proposed system may be derived from an
existing system such as:

- The system (manual or computerized) that will be replaced by the
  proposed system
- A system similar to the proposed one that has been installed elsewhere
  and is accessible to the analyst
- A proprietary package, whose functionality may be analyzed

In the approach known as data analysis (Munro, 1977), the requirements
for the proposed system are derived from the outputs of the existing system
(reports, worksheets, documents, and so forth) and inputs to it (orders,
invoices, time cards, and so on) as well as from its code and documentation
(procedure manuals, organization charts, file descriptions, operations
manuals, and so forth). Published sources, such as handbooks or technical
papers, may also be employed to see how similar systems have been
developed. Other techniques that may be employed include document
gathering and analysis, observation, and analyst participation in the work
processes. These techniques have their greatest impact in developing
transaction processing systems.

Document analysis usually accompanies the "asking" methods, since
documents are difficult to interpret independently; for example, documents
are frequently brought to an interview. By sampling the incoming
documents (orders, for example) over a period of a day, an analyst may
establish the necessary processing capacity for the proposed system. It is
important that the documents be used merely as a point of departure rather
than "frozen" into the new system (for example, the format of an order will
change radically when conversion is made to electronic data interchange).

By *observing* the work of an intended user or by actually *participating*
in the work, the analyst learns firsthand about the inadequacies of the
existing system. For example, by observing a securities processing area in a
bank, the analyst may note the job fragmentation imposed by the existing
system and the lack of responsibility users take for the results (at the same
time as he or she is also able, say, to establish the volumes of various
securities and peak processing times). The need to reengineer the business
area and integrate the fractured functions into a system that supports a
workgroup would become apparent to the analyst.

3. Synthesizing from the Characteristics of the Utilizing System

The information system we are developing will assist a manager in making decisions or make a business unit more effective in its operations. If we take this point of view, we may then use the methodologies applicable to the organization's MIS planning to derive the requirements for a particular information system as well. These methodologies were described in chapter 17.

Specifically, informational analysis of the business unit to be served by a system may be carried out with Business Systems Planning (BSP), critical success factors of individual managers may be established and supported by information based on the CSF methodology, or the business objectives of the unit may help the analyst to derive system functionality.

A tool that will help to establish the informational needs of an individual manager is *decision analysis*. As will be illustrated in the Part 5 Case Study, decision analysis consists of the following steps:

- Identifying the key decisions that a manager makes
- Defining the steps of the process whereby the manager makes these decisions
- Defining the information needed for the decision process
- Establishing what components of this information will be delivered by the information system and what data will be needed to do so

4. Experimentation with the System as It Is Developed

This is the prototyping approach: a pilot or an initial system version which embodies some of the requirements is built, and the users are able to define their requirements in an "as-compared-to-something" manner—which is much easier than defining them without such a comparison. As we will discuss later in this chapter, the prototype may be discarded after having served its purpose in establishing user requirements, or it may evolve into a production system.

As the systems analysts gather information, they may perform structured analysis by a stepwise refinement of the context diagram obtained during the feasibility study stage. We shall discuss this process in the next chapter.

18.3 SYSTEMS DEVELOPMENT LIFE CYCLE: SYSTEMS DESIGN STAGES

The objective of systems design is to produce the specifications for the system that will satisfy the requirements defined in the systems analysis. These specifications should be detailed enough to become inputs to the programming stage that follows the design. The design process is usually broken down into two parts. Conceptual (logical) design produces the general blueprint of the resources that will make up the system. Detailed (physical) design produces a complete specification of the software modules to be coded and of the databases to be maintained by the system.

Objectives of Systems Design

In systems design, a solution is devised to the problem posed by systems analysis. Whereas in the analysis stage the developers establish *what* the system will do, in the design they come up with a blueprint showing *how* the system will accomplish its task. Thus, system designers need to establish the way the physical components of information systems, which we discussed in chapter 3, will be deployed to satisfy user requirements.

Specifically, the following system aspects have to be determined and described in the appropriate documentation:

- The hardware and systems software platforms for the application system
- The programs that will constitute the application and the modules which will make up the programs
- Specification of individual software modules
- The design of the database
- The design of user interfaces
- Procedures for system use

The system may be designed by systems analysts who have an appropriate degree of technical knowledge or by specialized system designers.

The system design task is usually broken down into two stages. During the conceptual (logical) design stage, a general view of the system is developed by specifying its components and their interrelationships. This design is ultimately validated when the system development project reaches the milestone that terminates the stage. After this, the physical (detailed) design follows, in which the component details are specified. For example, in conceptual design, the system is broken down into programs, which are in turn broken down into modules. However, the modules themselves are designed in the physical design stage (to be programmed in the subsequent SDLC stage).

Conceptual (Logical) Design

Often taking the existing system as a point of departure, the developers create the system blueprint. They will devise alternative major solutions to the problem identified during the analysis phase and recommend one of these solutions.

These activities are included in logical design:

- The components of the hardware and systems software environment for the system are specified.
- System outputs and the inputs needed to produce these outputs are identified.
- **User interface,** that is, the means whereby the user interacts with the system, is specified. Attractive interfaces have become increasingly important. They are often furnished as carefully designed menu trees—hierarchies of menus that help to select the desired activity. Graphical user interfaces (GUI) are incorporated in many PC-based systems.
- The logical design of the database (see chapter 7) is developed.
- The programs that will compose the system and the modules that will make up the programs are designed. A structured methodology for this major task of conceptual design is described in the next chapter.
- The procedures to be employed in operating the system are specified.
- The controls that will be incorporated in the system (see chapter 20) are specified, with MIS auditors participating in the process.

A SAMPLE PRODUCT OF CONCEPTUAL DESIGN

Figure 18.6 shows an example of a system chart for a distributed payroll processing system. A system chart is accompanied by the following explanatory narrative. Such a design would be arrived at after its alternatives had been considered and rejected. In this case, the alternatives would include fully centralized payroll processing at headquarters and, on the other hand, distribution of all payroll changes to the individual plants.

Explanatory Narrative

1. Employee payroll data are collected as each employee inserts her or his badge into a terminal on entry to each of the three plants. The data are entered into the human resources database at each of the plants.
2. Weekly payroll processing is done on the plant minicomputers.
3. At the end of each day, each plant minicomputer transfers the work data for all three shifts to the headquarters mainframe.
4. The headquarters payroll is produced biweekly by the headquarters mainframe.
5. The headquarters mainframe produces all the tax reporting.
6. The central human-resources database, maintained at headquarters, is also used for management support systems, which are separate from the payroll system.

Individual subsystems of the payroll system may be acquired by combining several methods. Some existing systems will be modified and incorporated in the design, certain proprietary software will be purchased (for example, payroll programs are rather common), and the remaining application subsystems will be developed in-house.

System charts (also known as system flowcharts), which we introduced in chapter 4, are commonly used to show the principal physical components of a system.

The application software itself is designed with the aid of structured methodologies. We shall introduce to you a principal tool for such design—the structure chart—in the next chapter.

The above vignette illustrates a product of systems design—an order processing system—with its system chart. The application components of the system chart, such as the Weekly Plant Payroll program, for example, are designed in a structured fashion with structure charts.

Detailed (Physical) Design

The objective of detailed design is to produce a complete specification of all system modules and of interfaces between them, and to perform physical design of the database (as discussed in chapter 7). Structured design methodologies help specify module logic during this stage, as shown in the next chapter.

When detailed design is completed, the following aspects of the system will have to be specified:

- System outputs—report layouts, document designs, and screen designs.
- System inputs—data inputs and their validation procedures.
- User-system interface—exact protocols of user-system interaction (menu trees, icons for graphic interfaces, and so forth).
- Platforms—hardware and software platform(s) on which the system will run and the systems with which it will interface.

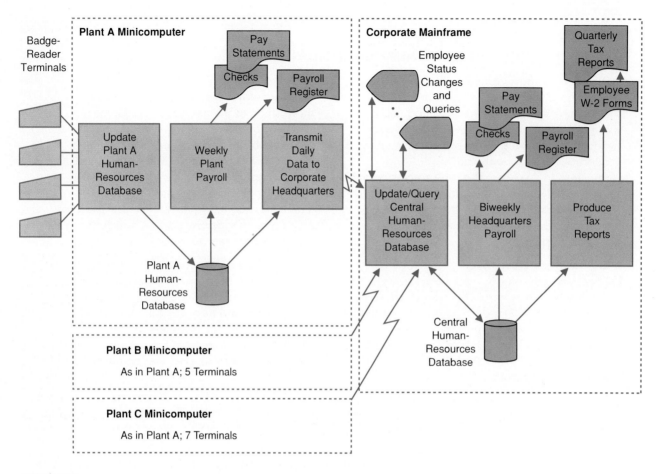

FIGURE 18.6

System chart of a payroll processing system—a product of conceptual design.

- Acquisition method—the way each component of the application will be acquired.
- Modular design of the programs that will be developed for the application, interfaces between the modules, and the specifications of the logic of individual modules. This means that the algorithms (strictly specified procedures for computer execution) to be implemented in the modules are selected (for example, a sorting routine or a routine for looking up an entry in a table).
- Test suite—a set of tests for various levels of testing to be conducted during the later stages of development.
- Database—logical and physical designs. Needed capacities of files and databases have been estimated.
- Controls—application-specific controls (discussed in chapter 20), as well as the necessary general controls.
- Documentation—a full set of documentation to be delivered with the system, including the user manual, systems and operation documentation, and maintenance documentation, as needed. The documentation items produced up to this point, notably system requirements specification and the system design documentation (system and structure charts) are updated, if necessary.
- Conversion plan—including design of any programs that may be needed for conversion (of databases, for example).

It is crucial to sustain the processes of organizational change connected with system implementation. This includes the initiation of structural changes in the affected unit, redesigning the jobs of people who will be affected by the system, and conducting user training, as we shall see further in this chapter.

18.4 SYSTEMS DEVELOPMENT LIFE CYCLE: PROGRAMMING

At this stage, the system is coded, tested, and debugged in a process that is summarily called programming. The objective of programming is to produce reliable software based on appropriate design specifications. At this point, programmers take over from system analysts or designers, unless programmer/ analysts have been developing the project and hence will continue it.

Programming is writing instructions for computer execution and testing the written code to ensure that it performs according to specifications. Programming tasks thus include:

- Coding the software module specifications produced during system design into statements that a computer can execute (after the systems software translates them into a binary form)
- Testing at several levels, beginning with testing individual modules as they are programmed and culminating in acceptance testing before the system is placed into operation

Structured programming and testing are further described in the next chapter. Problems discovered during testing are tracked down to their source in the code through a process known as *debugging*.

We can thus see that coding and testing activities are intertwined in the programming process and that the two tasks are almost never performed in strict sequence ("first we code everything, and then we test it" is not the way programming is done). As we can conclude from figure 18.2, testing is a more daunting task—by far—than coding. As a matter of fact, as we can see in the figure, testing of various system aspects is the most time-consuming task in systems development.

As we discussed in chapter 6, most applications programming is performed today in a higher-level language, or a nonprocedural, fourth-generation language (4GL). The 4GL approach exploits the fact that hardware resources are inexpensive relative to programmers' time.

Notwithstanding the existence of a variety of software tools to support the programming process, programming is to a large degree a craft, and some people are far better at it than others. Selecting superior programmers for a project often guarantees its success.

WHAT KIND OF PROGRAMMERS DOES "THE BEST PAYING SOFTWARE COMPANY" LOOK FOR?

Philip Pyburn, the founder and president of Boston-based Pyburn Systems Inc., is rumored to be the highest-paying employer of exceptionally skilled programmers.

Pyburn believes that the best programmers are brilliant analytical thinkers as well as artisans who are exceptionally proficient in applying the appropriate technology to business problems. He also believes such people "have to be nurtured in an entrepreneurial environment." Pyburn Systems' programmers receive bonuses of two to three times their annual salary of over $125,000 on completion of their projects—and this may have something to do with meeting or beating deadlines.

Pyburn Systems employs small teams, never larger than five, even on very large projects—to minimize the amount of communications, which Pyburn considers to be at the heart of programming.

The company uses so-called four-and-a-half generation languages, which permit a small group of analysts/designers to generate a system prototype, and later a complete system, directly from the requirements specifications, eliminating the design and programming steps (although a complete such generation is not possible at this time).

Based on "The Best Paying Software Company?" *Datamation*, December 1, 1989, p. 31.

18.5 SYSTEMS DEVELOPMENT LIFE CYCLE: CONVERSION

Following acceptance testing, a planned conversion to the new system is performed. The four common conversion methods are illustrated in figure 18.7.

The *parallel operation* method is the safest: the old and the new systems run simultaneously until sufficient confidence is gained in the new system. Of course, the method can be used only if there is an "old" system in place; it is also expensive to run both systems.

Direct conversion is the most risky (and thus potentially the most expensive): at a certain point the old system is completely replaced by the new one. This was the conversion technique used by Kendall Corporation, which we described in the Part 3 case study.

The two other methods involve gradual conversion and are a compromise between the first two extremes.

During a *phased conversion,* the new system is introduced in incremental stages, which are divided by function, organizational units served, the hardware on which the new system will reside, or some other factor. Eastman Kodak used this approach in decentralizing its MIS function, as we saw, again, in the Part 3 case study.

FIGURE 18.7

Conversion methods.

(From Zmud, 1984, p. 256)

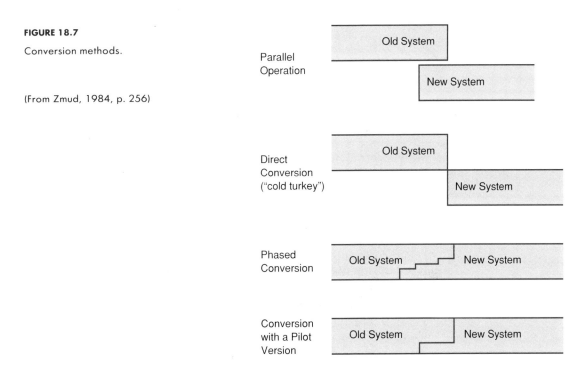

FIGURE 18.7

Conversion methods.

(From Zmud, 1984, p. 256)

The *pilot version* method relies on introducing a part of the system into one carefully delimited organizational area, learning from this experience, and then introducing the complete system. Because it is a learning tool, the pilot version is different from a system segment implemented during the phased conversion.

After full conversion to the new system has been completed, the system becomes operational. During the system's operational life, which is generally from seven to ten years, the system will need maintenance. Maintenance is the process of modifying a system to maintain its effectiveness and to meet changing needs. Major maintenance projects may be quite large and are generally also conducted in a life-cycle fashion. We shall further discuss maintenance of information systems in chapter 20.

Finally, there is a phase conducted during systems operations that concludes the development cycle. Its objective is to evaluate both the system and the development methodology, and it is an important aspect of organizational learning. This stage is called the postimplementation audit.

18.6 SYSTEMS DEVELOPMENT LIFE CYCLE: POSTIMPLEMENTATION AUDIT

Some time after the system becomes fully operational, a formal review of its operation and of its development process is conducted. This audit should take place after the system has been used for several months to allow for the "burn-in" period. However, it has been found that in many organizations, such an audit is instead performed either right before or right after the conversion

(Kumar, 1990). In such cases, the audit is employed primarily as a means of closing out the development project—it is too soon to perform a meaningful evaluation.

A properly conducted audit pursues several objectives:

- The organizational impact of the system is studied and further effort is made to ensure successful implementation (unless the system is recognized to be an outright failure, which, unfortunately does happen). The audit may trigger adjustments in organizational structure and job designs also.
- A major systems development project should be a source of organizational learning: we want to improve future system implementations based on the experience. The *process* of system implementation is accordingly reviewed and actual costs and development time are compared with the schedules and budgets developed during the systems analysis stage. Systems development methodology may be modified in the future in light of these results.
- The system's performance and controls are evaluated, with the MIS auditors participating. Requests for maintenance frequently follow this evaluation.

A major conceptual objective of the postimplementation audit is to establish whether the system has been successfully implemented: whether it has achieved its organizational goal. Later in this chapter, we shall discuss the dimensions of successful system implementation.

18.7 PROTOTYPING

Systems development life cycle has been frequently faulted for its long system development times, voluminous documentation requirements, and for failing to meet actual user requirements at the end of the long development road. Prototyping has emerged as one way to break what has become known as "the systems development bottleneck," which is described in the next vignette.

Indeed, just as in the vignette example, many companies have two-to-three year backlogs of systems development projects approved for development, and a far greater "invisible backlog." These companies seek faster development techniques for systems which lend themselves to less cumbersome approaches than life-cycle-based systems development. Prototyping is becoming increasingly important among the alternative approaches to systems acquisition, which we discussed in chapter 17. Prototyping is sometimes done within the broader context of end-user computing (which we discussed in chapter 9); together with computer-aided software engineering (CASE) tools, these are the principal development techniques that augur well for breaking the bottleneck at some future time.

THE BOTTLENECK THAT NEEDS BREAKING

Top management of a large paperboard manufacturer asked its MIS department to develop a system that would help evaluate trades the company could make with other companies in the industry. Such trades are designed to exploit a company's comparative advantage in the marketplace. In a typical trade, the firm makes and sells to a competitor one grade of paperboard in return for a different grade the other firm is able to produce more efficiently. The right trade at the right time enhances a firm's competitive position. The marketing vice-president at this particular company has this to say: "When we talked to [the] information systems [department about the project], we got quite a shock. They told us that unless we could convince the corporate systems planning group to change its priorities, we had a minimum three-year wait."

The MIS department had a long list of projects to work off. Priorities set by the MIS steering committee had already committed the department to projects that would require several dozen person-years to complete.

"Backlogs are so big that most people have stopped counting them in any meaningful fashion," comments Tom O'Flaherty, vice-president of a market research firm speaking about the information systems projects awaiting development.

Based on Gremillion, 1983; with the last quote drawn from Maryfran Johnson, "Drowning in a Sea of Code." *Computerworld*, December 25, 1989, p. 10.

What Is Prototyping?

A **prototype** is a preliminary working version of an application (or of one of its parts) that is built quickly and inexpensively, with the intention of modifying it. The capabilities of the initial prototype are limited as compared to those intended for the final system. The prototype is turned over to the users, who work with it and make suggestions for modifications. In the process, both users and developers discover what the actual user requirements will be for the system. The objective of **prototyping,** a systems development technique that relies on the development of a prototype, is to obtain "an unambiguous functional specification, serve as a vehicle for organizational learning, and (possibly) evolve ultimately into a fully implemented version"[2] of the system.

Just as a car manufacturer produces a prototype automobile, so system developers can rapidly place a system prototype before the users. An early prototype generally includes the human interface, such as screens and reports, and some of the principal system functions. The costs of producing a prototype are kept low by ignoring in this first version such aspects of the final application as nonessential functions, validation of input data, system controls, exception handling, and efficiency considerations. For example, some have reported prototyping costs of less than 10 percent of the total development cost of a system being prototyped (Gomaa, 1981). Fourth-generation programming languages (4GL) and CASE tools (discussed in the next chapter) make prototyping fast and economically attractive. Indeed, such software tools are imperative for effective prototyping.

The prototyping technique may be used in various ways. It can be employed as the complete development method for decision-oriented systems, such as DSS and expert systems, as we discussed in chapters 14 and 15. It may also be used

FIGURE 18.8

Prototyping.

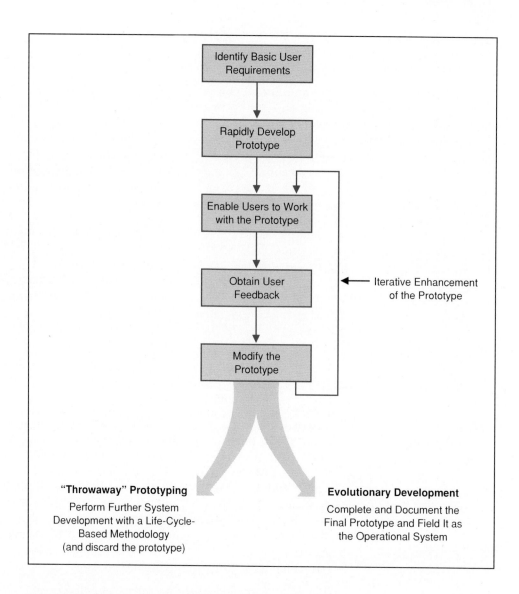

Identify Basic User Requirements

Rapidly Develop Prototype

Enable Users to Work with the Prototype

Obtain User Feedback ← Iterative Enhancement of the Prototype

Modify the Prototype

"Throwaway" Prototyping

Perform Further System Development with a Life-Cycle-Based Methodology (and discard the prototype)

Evolutionary Development

Complete and Document the Final Prototype and Field It as the Operational System

in a similar fashion for personal-use systems developed by end users, as we discussed in chapter 9. In addition, prototyping may be combined with an SDLC methodology to establish user requirements (Boar, 1984). Thus, prototyping may be used either to replace or to become a part of SDLC during the early development stages.

A general view of the prototyping process is shown in figure 18.8.

As you can see, a prototype may be used as a tool in establishing user requirements in an SDLC-based methodology. After requirements have been established, the prototype is discarded—this is "throwaway" prototyping. On the other hand, prototyping may be the principal methodology for developing certain types of systems, such as decision support and expert systems, or certain management reporting systems—this is evolutionary development. This development method results in a faster system delivery than SDLC—but it should be used only for appropriate systems. Let us consider two typical scenarios.

Two Prototyping Scenarios

Our bank's MIS department needs to develop a new on-line system for checking account inquiries. This elaborate transaction processing system will have to be developed to meet very high standards of efficiency, reliability, maintainability, and auditability. It will also have to interact with the existing parts of the bank's information systems. It will therefore be built through a complete SDLC process.

However, to establish user requirements, we build a prototype. The prototype produces data entry screens and report screens, as well as hard-copy reports. The bank officers should be able to enter the data identifying the account by various means. They need screens and reports which present basic account information, show credit history for the account, give instant statements for any past period, and show activity for the current period.

Mock-up screens, which are not derived from a database, are created by system developers with a prototyping tool, such as an application generator. The prototype is installed on user workstations. The users work (or "play") with the prototype for several days, trying to imitate practical situations. They see how easy it is to enter data, how well the screens are designed, and how many screens they have to navigate to complete a typical transaction. The users then provide feedback to the developers, who modify the prototype, perhaps repeatedly.

At this stage, a "dummy" database of customer accounts may be established and principal processing routines may be written in a simplified form (without error checking or exception handling). The users attempt to run their typical transactions on the enhanced prototype, and another series of enhancements follows until the users are satisfied with the operation. Throughout the process, the developers make it abundantly clear to the users that the prototype is *not* a working system and that it serves only to establish their needs.

After the prototype has served this purpose, the system is designed and programmed in the language of choice, such as C or COBOL. All the necessary features of so-called production systems, such as data validation, efficient database accessing, and controls are included, along with full documentation. The prototype is a "throwaway"—since it was only used to establish user requirements, it is now discarded.

Let us now consider another typical case. The information systems group of the company's human resources department is asked to develop a decision support system to help analyze alternative packages of wages and benefits. Having spent a few days with the middle-level managers who are the intended users, the developers produce an initial version of the application. The prototype is developed in the nonprocedural language of the database management system used to manage the human resources database. It is then turned over to the users, who try it to support typical decisions. They write their comments into a text file set up for the purpose. Several iterations of "enhancement (by developers)—exercising (by users)" follow, until a satisfactory DSS is produced and subsequently documented. When the next round of labor negotiations comes around, it turns out that other features were desirable. The DSS is rapidly modified to satisfy the need. This prototype has become the working system, and the prototyping process was actually the system development process. The prototyping process has replaced SDLC.

Why Prototype?   The following are the principal advantages of using the prototyping technique.

1. User Involvement

As we said earlier, involving end users in the system development process is generally recognized as a key factor in successful system implementation. Encouraging end users to work with the prototype and to influence the direction of system development is an excellent vehicle for generating user commitment to the system. Discussions leading to enhanced prototypes form an arena for communication between the agents involved in the system's development and for constructive conflict resolution.

2. Establishing Real User Requirements

Abstract, nonworking system models produced during traditional systems analysis may fail to establish true requirements, since users may find it difficult to visualize how the system functions. The ultimate system may miss the mark—and correcting mistakes of analysis, if at all possible, is very expensive after the system has been completed. Moreover, SDLC-based methodologies tend to freeze user requirements at an early stage of systems development: there is a strong tendency to oppose even well-justified modifications during the design or programming stages of the process.

Prototyping is particularly recommended in situations with high equivocality, when it is unclear what questions to ask—as opposed to uncertainty, when we know the questions, but not the answers (Kydd, 1989). Indeed, prototyping is the technique of choice for developing decision-oriented systems—executive information systems, decision support systems, and expert systems. In all of these cases, the requirements evolve as the system is used.

3. Support for Organizational Change and Learning

A prototype makes the future system more real to all involved. It is easier to determine what organizational changes are necessary for successful system implementation, and an early start in these directions can be made. Users learn as they work with the prototype—thus, training is begun early as well.

The benefits of prototyping, as seen by developers who employ the technique in a cross-section of firms, are shown in figure 18.9.

Potential Problems with Prototyping   Problems emerge when prototyping is used for unsuitable purposes or when it is used inappropriately. Let us review the typical problem areas.

1. Inappropriate Evolutionary Development via Prototyping in the Cases of Large Organizational Systems

Large systems that are to serve major organizational components and perhaps cross a number of organizational boundaries are not good candidates for evolutionary development (although certain aspects of these systems may be clarified by using "throwaway" prototypes).

To assure the quality of a complex product and to provide management control during development, a more stringent SDLC-based approach is necessary. The final product needs to be brought to the level of reliability, efficiency, and maintainability generally associated with a life-cycle-based approach.

FIGURE 18.9

Reasons for prototyping.

(From Carey, 1989)

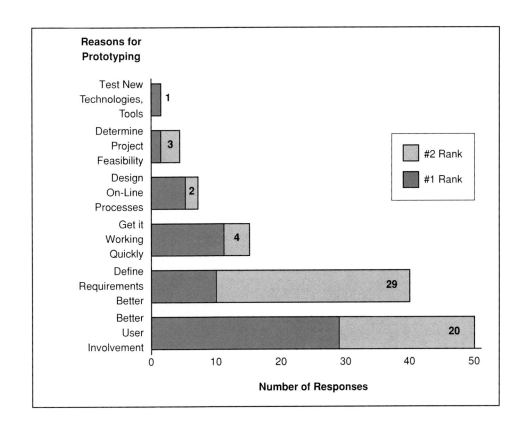

SDLC provides a project management structure absent in pure prototyping. This structure makes it possible to gain significant time and cost efficiencies in system building by teams run on organic principles (which we discussed in chapter 12). But this also makes the method unsuitable for developing large organizational systems, in which large numbers of people are involved.

2. Prototyping as a ''Quick-and-Dirty'' Development

Before SDLC was introduced, systems had been developed largely by programming and testing, with not enough attention paid to analysis and design. It is important that prototyping does not degenerate into this ''development'' mode.

3. Behavioral Problems

When the scope and purposes of prototyping are not made clear to the users, behavioral problems may emerge. In the case of ''throwaway'' prototyping, the users may want to use a prototype instead of waiting for the final system—to the detriment of the task. Users may also be dissatisfied with the system because the developers are unable to accommodate their growing appetite for improvements. Too many iterations of prototype enhancement increase costs and may sorely try users' patience—and thus should be avoided. The developers should be careful to limit the number of prototype versions. As any other systems development methodology, prototyping requires proper coordination of work within the team, sometimes across several teams, and with the organizational environment (Cooprider, 1990/91).

I must stress that just as there are a variety of possible versions of SDLC, there also is flexibility in combining life-cycle-based development with prototyping (see, for example, Dennis, 1987; and Cerveny, 1990). Thus, some developers attempt both to loosen the excessively rigid SDLC by incorporating a process for accepting changes as the system is developed (see Snyder, 1985) and to structure the prototyping process (see, for example, Pliskin, 1989). The already mentioned spiral development process proposed by Barry Boehm of TRW (Boehm, 1989) is an important effort in combining the advantages of both principal development methods.

18.8 IMPLEMENTATION OF INFORMATION SYSTEMS

The success of an information system is not at all assured by its technical qualities alone. It also depends to a large degree on a variety of organizational measures and processes which are collectively called system implementation. Here, we shall discuss what the accepted criteria of system success are and what implementation factors may lead to success.

Systems May "Work"—Yet Be Failures

Bank tellers are provided with a new system for entering account transactions. The system is complex, the tellers are given a cursory two-hour orientation, and they make multiple errors as they navigate several densely filled screens needed to open a new account or renew a certificate of deposit. As a result, the tellers make mistakes. Adjustments have to be made at a later time, which further increases the load on the system, response time goes up, and the frustration level is high. The system is judged to be a failure.

A decision support system, introduced with a great fanfare, is not used by managers, who feel that they are experienced enough that they do not need any such system. On the other hand, an expert system introduced into a major accounting firm works so well that the young accountant-trainees rely on it entirely and do not improve their expertise—they simply get answers from the system.

For lack of an executive sponsor, a project to develop a major organizational system is shelved—even though its implementation was recommended by a steering committee, and it passed a feasibility study with a high-priority rating.

These are all examples of implementation problems. Developing and fielding an information system is much more than a technical problem solved by using appropriate techniques and tools for system analysis, design, coding, and testing. It is, in fact, a broader problem that involves organizational change, which we discussed in general terms in chapter 12.

What Is Implementation?

The **implementation** of an information system is the process of preparing people in an organization for a new system and introducing the system into the organization. In other words, it is an ongoing process, which should start early during system development (or even precede actual development) and culminate in the institutionalization of the new system. An excellent example of such a system and of the process by which it was institutionalized is the XCON/XSEL expert

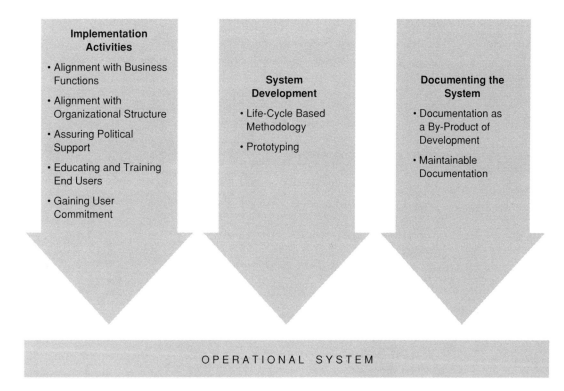

FIGURE 18.10

Implementation activities should accompany system development and documentation.

system suite (described in the Part 4 case study), which has become a major strategic resource for Digital Equipment Corporation.

A major system runs a high risk of failure without a properly planned implementation process. As was seen in one of the examples in the last several paragraphs, a worthy proposed system may be drawn into the vortex of organizational politics and never be developed in the first place. A fully developed system may become a technical success but be an organizational failure (Keen, 1981). To its developers, the system "works," but it falls into disuse because of organizational factors. The need to begin implementation activities before systems development begins, and to continue these activities as the development progresses (and as the system is documented) is illustrated in figure 18.10.

Throughout the SDLC-based development of a large organizational system, a carefully planned interaction between the developers and the two other principal agents involved in the process has to take place on a regular basis. The developers must be assured of continuing management support and must gain user commitment to the system they will be expected to work with. This interaction with future users occurs naturally during prototyping, when users and developers collaborate in development; users of management-oriented systems developed in this fashion are most often the managers themselves. In end-user development, it is frequently important to involve MIS professionals to ensure that the system does not become the private property of a handful of individuals and to prevent undesirable effects on the firm's total information processing efforts.

Before we investigate the factors that lead to the success or failure of an information system, let us attempt to determine what we mean by achieving success in system implementation—by no means an easy task.

What Is Successful Implementation?

Since information systems are artificial systems, it would appear that their implementation, successful or otherwise, could be easily gauged by checking to what degree the system fulfills the objectives stated at the outset of the development process. Nothing could be further from the truth—in fact, consensus on the definition of implementation success has eluded investigators. It is difficult to measure to what degree an increase in managerial effectiveness is attributable to a management-oriented information system. Also, as complex technology affects various aspects of organizational life, the multiple effects a system may have will be seen in different lights by various stakeholders.

The following criteria may be employed to judge the success of an information system:

1. High Level of Use

   The number of transactions processed by an on-line system is easily monitored; use of a decision support system may be observed over a period of time; and intended users may be surveyed on their use of a management reporting system.

2. Appropriate Nature of Use

   High levels of use are not always a sufficient measure of success. Michael Ginzberg has convincingly argued that in the case of more sophisticated systems, it is the nature rather than frequency of use that is important (Ginzberg, 1978). If the system permits the user to redefine his or her job for greater effectiveness, then use of the system that does not lead to such a redefinition is not adequate. It is easy to observe how such relatively simple technology as word processing is used ineffectively.

3. High Level of User Satisfaction

   It is frequently simpler to ask users whether they are satisfied with an information system or the total information service they receive than to supply more elaborate measures of use. Various questionnaires have been developed to ask users appropriate questions (Ives, 1983), though there is no standard measure. A thirteen-question short-form questionnaire, proposed by Blake Ives, Margrethe Olson, and Jack Baroudi, was presented and validated (Baroudi, 1988).

4. Accomplishment of Original Objectives

   During the initial phases of system development, notably during the feasibility study, a cost-benefit analysis of the system is performed and intangible benefits are spelled out. The success of the system may then be defined in terms of achieving the planned payoff and realizing the intangible, but crucial, benefits. The latter may include improved quality of decision making for a DSS, gaining a market share for a strategic information system, or improving the quality of working life for an office information system.

   The organizational effectiveness of a system may be judged in terms of the increase in the information processing capacity which the system brings about. Jay Galbraith (Galbraith, 1977) defines this capacity in terms of diversity of outputs (for example, products) delivered by a firm, diversity of inputs the firm handles to produce the outputs, and level of task performance (for instance, the speed at which products are delivered or

ARE USERS HAPPY WITH INFORMATION SYSTEMS SERVICES?

Nearly 40 percent of large MIS shops now regularly survey the users of information systems. When they are treated as customers, end users are more likely to understand the problems encountered by the MIS unit.

At Eastman Kodak of Rochester, New York, user satisfaction surveys were instituted as one measure of MIS effectiveness. Now that the information systems function of the company has been outsourced and will be in large part performed by IBM, it is the performance of this integrator end users will evaluate.

Kodak first identified nineteen products and services provided by the information systems unit (for example, E-mail and mainframe computing). A three-page survey was produced that asks users to rate their satisfaction with each service on a scale from 1 to 5. Users were also asked to

specify a single action that would be most productive in improving a given service. Different sets of users will be surveyed at least five times a year.

When the first survey resulted in a 60 percent satisfaction rating (instead of the expected 80 percent), swift action followed. The MIS group contacted the users and held a number of focus groups to find the sources of dissatisfaction. Ratings started to rise. Now, the results of a variety of evaluative measures are available to the corporate and MIS executives via an executive information system, which permits comparison with the ratings at competing firms. The measures correspond to four identified MIS success factors: service quality as perceived by users, management, and MIS personnel, as well as the cost-competitiveness of information service.

Based on Jeff Moad, "Asking Users to Judge IS." *Datamation*, November 1, 1989, pp. 93–100.

new products are developed). The success of implementation of an expert system for financial planning in a financial consulting firm is analyzed in these terms by John Sviokla (1989/90).

5. Indication of Institutionalization of the System

An important indicator of successful implementation is the system's role as an evolving part of the organizational landscape. Such a system is continually modified to meet new needs; new generations of users emerge, supported by ongoing training; and the organizational structures around the system evolve continually as well.

Factors in Successful Implementation

The failure of information system projects has many faces. Some examples of failures that many organizations could (but are not eager to) recount include the following situations: owing to political opposition, resources are diverted from a system development project, which is never completed; development costs and time wildly exceed original estimates; the intended users ignore the operational system; the system produces disappointing results; a system falls into disuse as soon as its original users are transferred elsewhere—and the list could go on.

A number of factors determine the success—or failure—of an information system. Proper implementation planning, the enactment of organizational change processes, and obtaining of informed commitment of all the system's stakeholders

FIGURE 18.11

Factors in successful system
implementation.

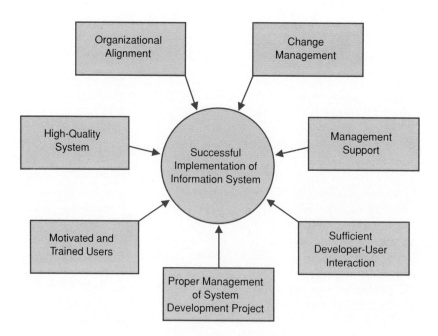

(that is, all parties affected by the system), along with the development of a technically sound system, are the key components of successful implementation.
Figure 18.11 shows the principal factors in more detail. As we shall see presently,
these factors are interdependent.

Let us now consider these factors more closely.

1. Organizational Alignment

The planning processes we outlined earlier need to ensure that the
information system's objectives are in line with organizational objectives.
Recent research shows that this alignment has begun to appear in corporate
practice (Zviran, 1990).

Introduction of a major information system requires a mutual
adjustment of four principal components: people who will work with the
system, the task to be accomplished with the use of the system, the
organizational structures surrounding the use of the system, and the system
(technology) itself (as postulated by Harold Leavitt [1965] and illustrated by
his well-known "diamond," shown in figure 18.12). One may add that an
information system must fit the corporate culture as well.

The *technology* employed in an information system has to be consistent
with the level of the company's sophistication in using information systems.
Numerous attempts to buy technology have failed, notably in
manufacturing firms that attempted to introduce manufacturing resource
planning (MRP II) systems without adequate—and extensive—preparatory
steps. In chapter 12, we discussed the process of technology assimilation
necessary to master a major technology in organizational terms.

The *structure* of an organizational unit has to be aligned with the
system that will support this unit; for example, if the unit operates in a
decentralized fashion, a highly centralized management control system is
likely to fail.

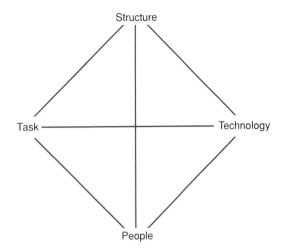

The specific *tasks* and even the entire jobs of the people who will work
with the system may have to be redefined, or the system may need to be
built to match the desired job design. For instance, if team work is to be
encouraged, a groupware system (see chapter 16) must be selected and
customized to match the pattern of work in the group. This could provide
an opportunity to define meaningful tasks for each individual, with a high
degree of autonomy and task significance. In broader terms, business
reengineering relies on the premise that the redesign of business functions
has to precede system development.

The **sociotechnical design** of systems (Mumford, 1979) emphasizes
matching the requirements of the social system formed by the people who
will work with the system with the technological requirements of the
information systems. Only those technological alternatives that provide a
work environment and task structure that will enhance the quality of
working life are selected for implementation.

The informed commitment of *people*—the stakeholders of the system
who will be affected by it—must be sought. Change processes, which we
shall discuss later, must be initiated to gain commitment from these
individuals.

2. Management Support and Support of Other Stakeholders

Absence of support at higher management levels dooms many a worthy
project. One of the principal objectives of the work of a steering committee
is to ensure that systems approved for development find such support. The
project sponsor, who can remove the organizational obstacles that are an
offshoot of political maneuvering, is vital to a project.

It is the task of management to make appropriate resources available to
the project, including qualified personnel, funds, computer resources, and
sufficient time for system development. Changes in organizational structure
and in job design likewise require management involvement. When the
management of a company or of its subunit supports continuing innovation,
as is true, for example, in such firms as 3M or Du Pont, it has a profound
effect on corporate culture and encourages innovative uses of information
technology.

WHAT ARE THE SOCIAL IMPLICATIONS OF AN INFORMATION SYSTEM?

The development of a system based on an integrated financial database at Citibank Brazil achieved only limited results. Its originators envisioned using the new database to provide a variety of new products and services—to use it to develop rapidly new financial products (to "informate" the company, rather than simply automating it, in the terms we introduced in chapter 12). However, the project succeeded only in automating some of the back-office functions of the bank. The reason was that the sponsors of the project were afraid to seek a commitment to the social implications of the full-fledged project, since they saw them as too far-reaching. Here are some of the organizational effects they had foreseen:

- Back-office managers, who were originally responsible only for processing the paperwork resulting from transactions, would come into direct contact with customers—which might be perceived as a threat by account managers in the marketing department.
- The existing separation between the operations and marketing departments would become obsolete.
- The performance of various units would become more visible.
- Fewer layers of management would be needed.
- The resulting job profiles would stress analytic skills, innovativeness, and teamwork, at the expense of routine.

Based on Walton, 1989.[3]

Stakeholders other than management may need to be committed to the project as well. For example, the commitment of labor unions is necessary to information system projects that will affect the labor force. At the General Electric dishwasher plant in Louisville, Kentucky, conversion to highly automated computer-integrated manufacturing (CIM) was effected after the labor unions had been persuaded of the competitive necessity of the conversion.

Recent research indicates that the political motives of system stakeholders are of basic importance (Cooper, 1990). What appear to be rational actions are often actually facades masking these motives. Sponsorship by top management and other political actions are vital to the project's success, particularly to ensure that the new system is used to its fullest potential. We will discuss this issue later as it applies to the principal stakeholder—the intended system users.

3. The Process of Change Management

The introduction of a new system is an organizational change. A systems analyst is a change agent. In a social system such as an organization, different groups and individuals have different objectives, expectations, and levels of power. The changes caused by the introduction of a new system arouse uncertainty among organizational members as to how these factors will be affected. As Rudy Hirschheim puts it, "the most characteristic individual and group reaction to change is resistance."[4]

To introduce change, appropriate processes must be enacted. Major new systems are introduced through a process of organizational change, as

TABLE 18.2	LEWIN/SCHEIN MODEL PHASE	KOLB/FROHMAN MODEL PHASE	OBJECTIVE
The Organizational Change Process for System Implementation	Unfreezing	1. Scouting	Developer and user become acquainted. User's needs and developer's abilities are assessed.
		2. Entry	User and developer establish a collaboration. Objectives of the project are established.
		3. Diagnosis	Information is gathered and the problem is defined.
	Moving	4. Planning and goal setting	User and developer consider alternative courses of action and develop criteria for evaluation of the system that will be built. A course of action is selected and an action plan is developed.
		5. Action	The selected problem solution (that is, the system) is developed. User and developer communicate to ensure that the action plan is modified as needed; a training program for users is instituted.
	Refreezing	6. Evaluation	User and developer assess how well the system meets the criteria set out in phase 4. If remedial action is needed, it is initiated.
		7. Termination	It is confirmed that the user is able to use and "own" the system, and the ownership is transferred accordingly.

discussed in section 12.8. There we introduced the Lewin/Schein model, relying on three phases: unfreezing, change (moving), and refreezing. A more detailed model of organizational change has been furnished by Kolb and Frohman (Kolb, 1970). It is shown in table 18.2, as adapted to the implementation of information systems, along with the corresponding stages of the Lewin/Schein model.

Note that the change process is terminated only when the system comes under user ownership and thus becomes institutionalized.

4. Sufficient Interaction between Users and Developers

The involvement of future users in systems development is considered an important factor in ensuring that the system will appropriately solve the users' problem and that it will be successfully implemented with the users' full commitment. User involvement in systems development is a form of participatory decision making and thus makes for greater commitment to a decision. MIS researchers have met with mixed success in confirming this generally accepted proposition (as discussed in Ives, 1984); a valuable confirmation under a specific set of circumstances was provided by Jack Baroudi, Margrethe Olson, and Blake Ives (Baroudi, 1986).

Cognitive differences between analytically oriented developers and future users (see chapter 13) may be a source of misunderstanding and friction. As information systems specialists become increasingly involved in specific business functions, they become more attuned to the users' frame of reference. Indeed the developers are increasingly helping users define their *problems,* rather than trying to offer them solutions (Freedman, 1991). Prototyping approaches to systems development are a form of collaboration between users and developers that can remove many a misunderstanding.

The means whereby users are involved in the SDLC-based development process cover a wide range. Among these approaches are: providing developers with feedback by means of questionnaires which users are asked to fill out during system development; conducting focus groups, with eight to ten users giving their reactions to system features (Mantei, 1989); employing formal user liaisons; having users work with the system prototypes; and assigning users to a development team. It is important that users' expectations with respect to the system and its development process be in tune with reality; systems developers are thus often advised to "manage users' expectations." The continuing involvement in the development process of several influential and MIS-proficient users addresses that need. Opportunities for this involvement depend on the context of system development: in-house or custom development offers greater opportunities for interaction than external contract development based on requirements specifications (Grudin, 1991).

Perhaps the best known technique for user participation in the development process is JAD (for Joint Application Design), originally developed by IBM in 1977. JAD and similar techniques bring end users, managers, and systems developers together in group work sessions, with developers serving as leaders, recorders, and mediators (August, 1991). The two major JAD phases are joint system planning, during which the objectives and scope of an application are defined, and detailed specification of system requirements, which describes the business processes that will be supported by the new system. More recently, CASE tools have been employed to translate user requirements into models of a future system (Kerr, 1989).

In certain cases where user resistance exists, owing to a perceived loss of power resulting from system implementation, user participation may be counterproductive, unless resistance problems are handled beforehand.

5. Motivated and Trained Users

It would be foolhardy to expect that user participation in the development process will in itself remove user resistance to a system that users perceive as a threat to their interests. They might instead embark on a variety of tactics to protect these interests and so may ultimately subvert the implementation. Such tactics, called by Peter Keen *counterimplementation* (Keen, 1981), rely on ambiguity and lack of control mechanisms. They include diverting resources from the project; deflecting the goals of the project; keeping the project complex, vaguely defined, and difficult to coordinate; and dissipating the developers' energies ("We are certainly interested and will be happy to provide some input, but . . .").

TABLE 18.3	SOURCE OF RESISTANCE	IMPLEMENTATION MEASURES
Sources of Resistance to Information Systems and What to Do About Them	People	Educate and train users Coerce Persuade Restructure incentives for users Select appropriate personnel Induce user participation to draw out commitment
	Information System	Educate users in the technology Modify system to conform with organizational practices and culture Encourage user participation to improve the system Improve the human factors of the system
	Interaction (people and information system)	Make organizational modifications before introducing the system Directly address the issues of power redistribution Use a sociotechnical design approach Restructure the user-developer relationship Make the benefits of system use greater than the benefits of avoidance

User resistance is explained in several theories, which may be classified (Markus, 1983) as:

- People-oriented: Users as individuals or as a group produce resistance.
- System-oriented: Resistance occurs because of the way the system is designed (or, to be more accurate, the way the design is perceived by users).
- Interaction-oriented: Resistance arises because of a conflict between users' interests and perceptions and the features of the future system.

Table 18.3 lists the implementation tactics needed to counteract these sources of resistance.

User training is an important factor in allaying user fears of the unknown caused by the new system. Education and training should renew the future users' sense of mastery over their working environment. New skills may be acquired through formal instruction, through self-study with a system prototype or a training system, or through a combination of both. Training should enable users not only to use the system, but to become its "owners" and thus have a hand in its evolution. Education should show the users how they can use information more effectively in their work.

6. Proper Management of a System Development Project

Information system projects are notorious for such problems as drastic cost overruns and dramatic schedule slippages (we will see an unfortunately typical example of a plagued maintenance project in Case Study 2 in chapter 20). Much of this stems from the relative immaturity of software production as an engineering discipline which nevertheless has to cope with developing complex systems in complex organizational settings.

However, many problems are due to lax, or even entirely absent, project management practices. Project management tools (described in the next chapter) should be used to control a project.

The more ambitious the scope of a project and the newer the technologies to the given organization, the more inclined the project will be to fail. As we have stressed throughout this text, it is necessary to avoid the "grand-design" syndrome: to lower project risk, a complex undertaking should be broken down into stages to be implemented progressively.

Estimating development time and cost should be a true assessment, rather than, as it frequently becomes, a political ploy, a case of overselling, or a way to motivate developers (DeMarco, 1982).

Technology assimilation processes, which we explained in chapter 12, should be followed: a complex new technology should not be introduced without an appropriate buildup of expertise in the firm. Worse yet, in some cases, attempts are made to exploit several new technologies in a complex project without such preparation—which makes the project very likely to fail.

7. System Quality

A "working" system often falls into disuse because of its low quality. Some quality problems are:

- Poor human factors: Users face long response times in on-line systems, poor screen designs, or long and confusing menu sequences.
- Poor data quality: Reliable information cannot be generated from inaccurately entered data, or from data that is not entered on a timely basis, or that is simply unavailable.
- Poor quality of information provided: Inaccurate data introduced into databases gives rise to inaccurate information. Similarly, irrelevant information hardly helps users in their decision making. Information overload may result from frequent and voluminous reports, and information provided too late for the decision is useless.
- Operation cost overruns: These overruns make it cost-beneficial to abandon a system.
- Operational problems: The system "goes down" frequently and takes a long time to repair.

As one may conclude from a study of these success (or failure) factors, many of them are interrelated, making the implementation of information systems a complex process. Multiple system failures certainly attest to this complexity.

· ·

SUMMARY

Large organizational systems are developed via a systems development life cycle (SDLC), which is designed to organize the development process when a relatively large number of people are involved and which aims to produce a reliable and maintainable system. We have devoted particular attention to the analysis of systems requirements, the vital stage in ensuring that the system will meet an organization's needs and the needs of the intended users. The objective of subsequent design stages is to produce a system blueprint to satisfy the requirements specifications. The next stage is programming, which consists of coding and extensive testing, followed by conversion and the postimplementation audit. Structured methodologies, discussed in the next chapter, provide a set of tools for producing quality software.

A major alternative to SDLC-based development is evolutionary development through prototyping. Prototyping may also be employed to establish user requirements in systems analysis. This technique is employed more and more often to make sure that the developers produce what is needed and to make possible the release of an early system version.

System development should be accompanied by an extensive effort to implement the system—that is, to ensure that it will in fact be utilized in accordance with the needs of the organization. There are several criteria by which a system's success can be measured, and there are a number of factors through which this success can be attained.

ENDNOTES

1. The waterfall model of SDLC was originally described in an early complete form in W. W. Royce, "Managing the Development of Large Software Systems: Concepts and Techniques." *Proceedings of Wescon,* August 1970; though it was foreshadowed by an Air Force methodology dating as early as 1966.

2. James C. Emery, *Management Information Systems: The Critical Strategic Resource.* New York: Oxford University Press, 1987, p. 325.

3. This case was presented in Gloria Schuck and Shoshana Zuboff, *Data Administration in Citibank Brazil (A): The Competitive Advantage.* Harvard Business School Case 9–486–109, 1986.

4. R. A. Hirschheim, *Office Automation: A Social and Organizational Perspective.* Chichester: John Wiley & Sons, 1975, p. 159.

KEY TERMS AND CONCEPTS

Systems development life cycle (SDLC)
Milestone
Deliverable
Structured SDLC
Systems analysis
Feasibility study
Requirements analysis
Functional specifications
Interviewing
Questionnaires
Document analysis
Systems design
Conceptual (logical) design

Detailed (physical) design
Programming
Coding
Testing
Debugging
System conversion
Postimplementation audit
Prototyping
Evolutionary development
Information system implementation
Sociotechnical design
Change management
Joint Application Design (JAD)
Counterimplementation

QUESTIONS

1. Define systems development life cycle (SDLC), and specify its objectives.

2. List the seven stages of SDLC. Why does the "waterfall" SDLC model show two-way arrows?

3. What is *structured* SDLC?

4. Why is system maintenance a top concern during a system's development?

5. What are the objectives of systems analysis, and why is it broken down into two stages?

6. List five principal tasks of a feasibility study.

7. What are the three aspects of system feasibility?

8. List four categories of techniques for information gathering during requirements analysis.

9. Compare and contrast interviewing and questionnaires as sources of information on user requirements.

10. Compare the objectives of the conceptual and detailed system design stages.

11. Why are coding and testing brought together into a single SDLC stage?

12. Compare and contrast four methods of system conversion. Construct a scenario for a system conversion effort that could be managed with each of these tactics.

13. What are the advantages and disadvantages of SDLC-based systems development as compared to prototyping?

14. Why use a "throwaway" prototype?

15. Why do we need system implementation? Isn't development enough?

16. List three criteria we can use to judge the success of a system. What are their drawbacks?

17. What implementation measures could be undertaken *before* system development begins? List them and describe each in one or two sentences.

PROBLEMS

1. Produce an executive summary that might be the result of a feasibility study of a development project for an information system. Use a system you are familiar with or which you can familiarize yourself with from the trade literature available to you.

2. As a student, you want to have a Student Information System available to you on-line. Consider what information would be important to you—about the functioning of the university, the community where it is located, summer employment possibilities, travel and recreation possibilities, or future employment prospects, for example.

   Carefully outline one of the aspects of such a system, give it a catchy name, and analyze it. Design a set of interviews with key people from whom you can obtain the relevant information, including other potential users of the system.

   Based on the information you obtain, produce a system chart for your system, and accompany it with a narrative description. Try to quantify the number of users, volumes of various transactions, needed storage capacity, and other system requirements as realistically as you can.

3. Produce a system chart for an information system you are familiar with. Carefully name all the entities that appear in it.

1. Discuss the roles of the three agents—users, managers, and developers—in the seven stages of SDLC.

2. Since an SDLC-based project takes a long time, organizational and user requirements often change before the system is delivered. If we ignore these changes, we shall deliver a partly (or fully) obsolete system. What can be done about this problem, considering that developers generally resist requests for change?

3. Discuss Hirschheim's proposition, cited in the chapter, that the most characteristic response to change—such as that created by a new information system—is resistance. Is resistance always unjustified from the point of view of organizational effectiveness?

4. Give several examples of counterimplementation; you could perhaps quote characteristic phrases you may hear as a developer, which would identify the speaker as a "counterimplementer." In each case, counter these with counter-counterimplementation—in other words, describe what action you would take to combat counterimplementation.

HOW WOULD YOU DIAGNOSE THIS DEVELOPMENT FAILURE?

Wang Laboratories had long suffered with a reputation for chaotic order processing and poor customer billing practices. Customers would wait for months for orders to be delivered and invoices processed. The firm had a problem with revenue tracking, which is typical for many companies—small or large—which grow very fast (as Wang did at the time).

The internal MIS department was very small, and repeated attempts to solve the problem internally failed. In 1980, Wang contracted with a small Wellesley, Massachusetts consulting firm (Computer Partners, Inc.) to develop a system that would track revenue from the time of order placement to the time a payment on invoice was collected.

The project was scheduled to be completed in eighteen months. Three years later, with no end in sight, and with annual costs estimated by some at $10 million, the consultants were dismissed.

The consultants did manage to deliver an accounts receivable system and a corporate accounts receivable database, but the key component, the order processing system, was never finished.

Analysis of the failure indicates that the project was too large and complex for the consultants. "The dynamics of system development change so fast that a project which takes three years to complete is self-defeating. Modifications start to overtake the original design," according to one of the consultants. In other words, the consultant firm was too small to provide an acceptable and realistic deadline and to manage changes.

The project also included too many applications. The interdependencies among them caused logjams. For example, subsystem X frequently needed inputs from subsystem Y—which was not yet finished (and there were many subsystem Ys). The consulting firm also had no demonstrable experience with the technology employed: a complicated database management package that was at the center of the project.

Many consultants were working on a variety of projects throughout the firm. Corporate executives did not know what they wanted from MIS and had no strong MIS staff to lean on. In an environment of widely distributed computing, a number of independent and incompatible revenue tracking systems sprung up throughout the company.

Did the users and developers live happily ever after? The project was indeed completed internally, but the system suffered quality problems for years.

Based on Glenn Rifkin and Mitch Betts, "Strategic Systems Plans Gone Awry." *Computerworld*, March 14, 1988, pp. 1, 104–5.

Case Study Questions

1. Write a concise memo that specifies, in so many points, why the development project undertaken by the consultants failed.

2. Consultants are frequently employed for computing projects (and when the projects and the consulting firms are big, we use the term *system integrators* rather than consultants). Considering this example, what can be done to ensure that the performance of consultants is satisfactory to the firm that engages them?

3. What recommendations would you give to Wang management regarding organizational matters, based on this case?

4. Why do you think there is no happy ending to this story?

SELECTED REFERENCES

August, Judy. *Joint Application Design: The Group Session Approach to System Design.* Englewood Cliffs, N.J.: Yourdon Press/Prentice Hall, 1991.

Baroudi, Jack J., Olson, Margrethe H., and Ives, Blake. "An Empirical Study of the Impact of User Involvement on System Usage and Information Satisfaction." *Communications of the ACM,* 29, 3, March 1986, pp. 232–38.

Baroudi, Jack J., and Orlikowski, Wanda J. "A Short-Form Measure of User Information Satisfaction: A Psychometric Evaluation and Notes on Use." *Journal of Management Information Systems,* 4, 4, Spring 1988, pp. 44–59.

Boar, Bernard H. *Application Prototyping: A Requirements Definition Strategy for the Eighties.* New York: John Wiley & Sons, 1984.

Boehm, Barry, and Belz, Frank. "Applying Process Programming to the Spiral Model." Proceedings of the Fourth International Software Process Workshop. *ACM SIGSOFT Software Engineering Notes,* 14, 4, June 1989, pp. 46–56.

Bostrom, Robert P., and Heinen, J. Stephen. "MIS Problems and Failures: A Socio-technical Perspective." Parts I and II. *MIS Quarterly,* 1, 3, September 1977, pp. 17–32; and 1, 4, December 1977, pp. 11–28.

Carey, J. M., and Currey, J. D. "The Prototyping Conundrum." *Datamation,* June 1, 1989, pp. 29–33.

Cerveny, Robert P.; Garrity, Edward J.; and Sanders, G. Lawrence. "The Application of Prototyping to Systems Development: A Rationale and Model." *Journal of Management Information Systems,* 3, 2, Fall 1986, pp. 52–62.

Cerveny, Robert P.; Garrity, Edward J.; and Sanders, G. Lawrence. "A Problem-Solving Perspective on Systems Development." *Journal of Management Information Systems,* 6, 4, Spring 1990, pp. 103–22.

Cooper, Randolph B., and Zmud, Robert W. "Information Technology Implementation Research: A Technological Diffusion Approach." *Management Science,* 36, 2, February 1990, pp. 123–39.

Cooprider, Jay G., and Henderson, John C. "Technology-Process Fit: Perspectives on Achieving Prototyping Effectiveness." *Journal of Management Information Systems,* 7, 3, Winter 1990/91, pp. 67–87.

Davis, Gordon B. "Information Analysis for Information Systems Development." In *Systems Analysis and Design: A Foundation for the 1980's,* edited by William W. Cotterman and others. New York: North Holland, 1981, pp. 41–57.

Davis, Gordon B. "Strategies for Information Requirements Determination." *IBM Systems Journal,* 21, 1, January 1982, pp. 4–30.

DeMarco, Tom. *Controlling Software Projects: Management, Measurement and Estimation.* Englewood Cliffs, N.J.: Yourdon Press/Prentice Hall, 1982.

Dennis, A. R.; Burns, R. N.; and Gallupe, R. B. "Phased Design: A Mixed Methodology for Application System Development." *Data Base,* 18, 4, Summer 1987, pp. 31–37.

Freedman, David. "What Do Users Really Want?" *CIO,* September 1, 1991, pp. 24-28.

Galbraith, Jay R. *Organization Design.* Reading, Mass.: Addison-Wesley, 1977.

Ginzberg, Michael J. "Redesign of Managerial Tasks: A Requisite for Successful Decision Support Systems." *MIS Quarterly,* 2, 1, March 1978, pp. 39–52.

Gomaa, Hassan, and Scott, Douglas B. H. "Prototyping as a Tool in the Specification of User Requirements." *Proceedings of the Fifth International Conference on Software Engineering,* San Diego, Calif., March 9–12, 1981, pp. 333–39.

Gremillion, Lee L., and Pyburn, Philip. "Breaking the Systems Development Bottleneck." *Harvard Business Review,* 61, 2, March-April 1983, pp. 130–37.

Grudin, Jonathan. "Interactive Systems: Bridging the Gaps Between Developers and Users." *Computer,* 24, 4, April 1991, pp. 59–69.

Ives, Blake, and Olson, Margrethe H. "User Involvement and MIS Success: A Review of Research." *Management Science,* 30, 5, May 1984, pp. 586–603.

Ives, Blake; Olson, Margrethe H.; and Baroudi, Jack J. "The Measurement of User Information Satisfaction." *Communications of the ACM,* 26, 10, October, 1983, pp. 785–93.

Keen, Peter G. W. "Information Systems and Organizational Change." *Communications of the ACM,* 24, 1, January 1981, pp. 24–33.

Kerr, James D. "Systems Design: Users in the Hot Seat." *Computerworld,* February 27, 1989, pp. 87–96.

Kolb, David A., and Frohman, Alan L. "An Organization Development Approach to Consulting." *Sloan Management Review,* 12, 1, Fall 1970, pp. 51–65.

Kumar, Kuldeep. "Post Implementation Evaluation of Computer-Based Information Systems: Current Practices." *Communications of the ACM,* 33, 2, February 1990, pp. 203–12.

Kydd, Christine. "Understanding the Information Content in MIS Management Tools." *MIS Quarterly,* 13, 3, September 1989, pp. 277–91.

Leavitt, Harold J. "Applied Organizational Change in Industry: Structural, Technological, and Humanistic Approaches." In *Handbook of Organizations,* edited by James G. March. Chicago: Rand McNally, 1965.

Lucas, Henry C., Jr. *Implementation: The Key to Successful Information Systems.* New York: Columbia University Press, 1981.

Mantei, Marilyn M., and Teorey, Toby J. "Incorporating Behavioral Techniques into the Systems Development Life Cycle." *MIS Quarterly,* 13, 3, September 1989, pp. 257–73.

Markus, M. Lynne. "Power, Politics, and MIS Implementation." *Communications of the ACM,* 26, 6, June 1983, pp. 430–44.

Mumford, Enid, and Weir, Mary. *Computer Systems in Work Design: The ETHICS Method.* New York: John Wiley & Sons, 1979.

Munro, Malcolm C., and Davis, Gordon B. "Determining Management Information Needs: A Comparison of Methods." *MIS Quarterly,* 1, 2, June 1977, pp. 55–67.

Murdick, Robert G. "MIS Development Procedures." *Journal of System Management,* 21, 12, December 1970, pp. 22–26.

Naumann, Justus D., and Jenkins, A. Milton. "Prototyping: The New Paradigm for Systems Development." *MIS Quarterly,* 6, 3, September 1982, pp. 29–44.

Necco, Charles R.; Gordon, Carl L.; and Tsai, Nancy W. "Systems Analysis and Design: Current Practices." *MIS Quarterly,* 11, 4, December 1987, pp. 461–76.

Pliskin, N., and Shoval P. "Responsibility Sharing between Sophisticated Users and Professionals in Structured Prototyping." *Information and Software Technology,* 31, 8, October 1988, pp. 438–48.

Robey, Daniel; Farrow, Dana L.; and Franz, Charles R. "Group Process and Conflict in System Development." *Management Science,* 35, 10, October 1989, pp. 1172–91.

Snyder, Charles A., and Cox, James F. "A Dynamic Systems-Development Life-Cycle Approach: A Project Management Information System." *Journal of Management Information Systems,* 2, 1, Summer 1985, pp. 61–76.

Sviokla, John J. "Expert Systems and Their Impact on the Firm: The Effects of PlanPower Use on the Information Processing Capacity of the Financial Collaborative." *Journal of Management Information Systems,* 6, 3, Winter 1989/90, pp. 65–84.

Swanson, E. Burton. *Information System Implementation.* Homewood, Ill.: Irwin, 1988.

Walton, Richard E. *Up and Running: Integrating Information Technology and the Organization.* Boston: Harvard Business School Press, 1989.

Zelkowitz, Marvin V.; Shaw, Alan C.; and Gannon, John D. *Principles of Software Engineering and Design.* Englewood Cliffs, N.J.: Prentice-Hall, 1979.

Zmud, Robert W. *Information Systems in Organizations.* Glenview, Ill.: Scott, Foresman, 1983.

Zviran, Moshe. "Relationship between Organizational and Information Systems Objectives: Some Empirical Evidence." *Journal of Management Information Systems,* 7, 1, Summer 1990, pp. 65–84.

CHAPTER 19

TECHNIQUES AND TOOLS FOR STRUCTURED SYSTEMS DEVELOPMENT

Order and simplification are the first steps toward the mastery of a subject—the actual enemy is the unknown.
Thomas Mann
The Magic Mountain

While other avenues of systems acquisition are available, most organizations continue to produce many of the applications they need. Over the last twenty years, methodologies have evolved for handling the complexity of a system under development and of the process of development itself. From what we learned about systems in chapter 10, we know that the two major approaches to handling complexity are a gradual introduction of detail into a system as it is developed, and the divide-and-conquer tactic of separating different concerns into well-chosen interacting subsystems.

Structured methodologies are procedural systems for systems development. As such, they provide techniques and tools for this process. We shall discuss here the tools and techniques of structured analysis, design, and programming employed by the most commonly used methodology.

In the past decade, software that automates various aspects of the development process, called computer-aided software engineering (CASE) tools, has been introduced. There is no cradle-to-grave tool that can generate a complete code from systems specifications. However, individual stages of the development process, as well as system prototyping, can be conducted faster and more reliably today with CASE tools.

We shall also discuss a systems development approach, known as object-oriented programming, which aims to facilitate code reusability—the creation of software components that can be used in a variety of applications. A library of such components would be akin to inventories of hardware parts.

Poor organization of software projects—both during development and during maintenance—has been behind many a failure. We shall therefore turn our attention to the organization of software development teams and the techniques and tools needed for project management.

FOCUS STATEMENT

Let us think for a moment about these figures:

These figures, offered by Capers Jones (Jones, 1989) tell us that, if we consider all the work on a system—from analysis to acceptance testing—we can expect a developer to contribute only a few lines of code a day! Moreover, the ratio between the outputs of the most and least productive developers is about eight to one. As was discovered long ago and as has since been confirmed, even experienced developers vary greatly in productivity: individual productivity among pairs of equally experienced programmers working side by side was found to differ by as much as twenty-eight to one (Sackman, 1968).

Software Productivity Ranges
(Lines of code produced per person-year, with complete systems development included)

	MAXIMUM	MEDIAN	MINIMUM
Very Large Systems	3,000	800	400
Large Systems	4,000	1,300	670
Medium-Size Systems	8,000	2,000	1,000

All this points to a continuing need to vastly improve software development processes, supplant some of them with computer-aided software engineering, and develop other measures, such as reusable software modules, to enhance productivity in software development.

19.1 QUALITY SOFTWARE

The objective of a system development process is to produce quality software to satisfy organizational needs and user requirements. Software quality assurance is the crucial concern of the development process. And just as you cannot ensure quality in a car by testing the product after it leaves the assembly line, you cannot assure that a software system is of high quality by simply testing the code. Quality applications emerge from a planned process, carried out with proper techniques and tools, with results checked continually as development proceeds.

There are many attributes of software quality (Zwass, 1984). A summary of them is provided in figure 19.1.

The primary software characteristic, *effectiveness,* is the satisfaction of user and organizational requirements as established through an analysis of these requirements, possibly including prototyping. To stress the importance of a proper user-system interface, I have defined this quality attribute as *usability.* Usability design is becoming an increasingly important aspect of systems development (Gould, 1991).

Efficient operation is reflected mainly in how economically hardware resources are used to satisfy the given effectiveness requirements. Software *reliability* refers to the probability that it will operate correctly (that is, according to specifications) over a period of time; it may also be defined as the mean time between failures. If a system must run on different hardware and/or software platforms, *portability* should be included as a desired attribute.

FIGURE 19.1

Principal attributes of software quality.

We have consistently stressed that rapidly changing organizational environments require today more than ever that software be *maintainable.* We also saw

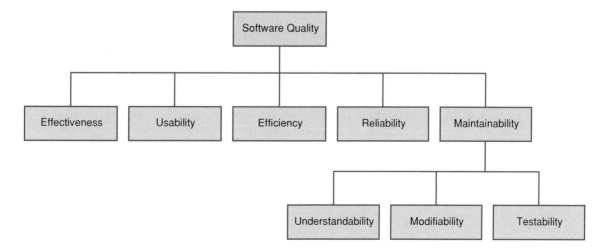

YOU CAN GET WHAT YOU WANT!

Sometimes, software attributes are in conflict. For example, a highly maintainable system may be less efficient (and the trade-off may be well worth it). A number of experiments conducted by various researchers illustrate the importance of clearly stating the priority attributes to the developers. In an experiment, Gerald Weinberg, a noted authority on systems development, gave the same task to several groups of developers, but gave each group a different priority objective, such as efficiency, reliability, or understandability. Each group achieved its priority objective— but not necessarily other characteristics of system quality.

Based on Gerald Weinberg, "The Psychology of Improved Programmer Performance." *Datamation*, November 1972, pp. 82–85.

in figure 18.3 that the cost of maintenance is the overriding component of a system's cost throughout its total life cycle. We shall further discuss maintenance in the next chapter. However, since the delivery of maintainable software is a primary objective of development, we should establish what we mean by it. Maintainable software is easy to understand, modify, and test.

Understandability means that it is relatively easy to understand what the system does and how it does it, down to the requisite level of detail. This understanding is achieved by referring to the internal documentation (extensive comments in the code and the code itself, assuming it is written in a readable manner), and external documentation (requirements specifications, system documentation, user manuals, and, sometimes, special maintenance documentation). *Modifiability* means that it is relatively easy to identify and change a part of the system without affecting its other parts. *Testability* is the ease with which we can demonstrate that a modification resulted in a quality system.

One means of assuring the production of quality software is the verification and validation process (V&V) embedded throughout development (Adrion, 1982; Deutsch, 1982; Wallace, 1989). **Verification** ensures that what was accomplished at a given stage of development corresponds to the specification obtained in the previous development stage ("we are building the system right"). For example, it must be verified that the system code produced during the programming stage corresponds to design specifications. **Validation** activities aim to establish that the system being built will satisfy user requirements ("we are building the right system"). Thus, validation requirements are a part of functional system specifications. Both V&V activities extend throughout development; the final validation of the system occurs during acceptance testing.

The principal V&V activities to be carried out in systems development are shown in figure 19.2. We shall further discuss the means used in V&V later in this chapter.

FIGURE 19.2

Principal validation and verification (V & V) activities—software quality assurance.

Quality Assurance Activities

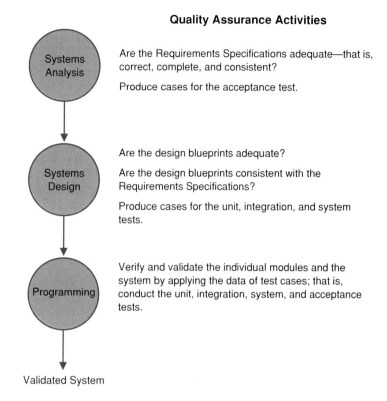

Are the Requirements Specifications adequate—that is, correct, complete, and consistent?

Produce cases for the acceptance test.

Are the design blueprints adequate?

Are the design blueprints consistent with the Requirements Specifications?

Produce cases for the unit, integration, and system tests.

Verify and validate the individual modules and the system by applying the data of test cases; that is, conduct the unit, integration, system, and acceptance tests.

19.2 WHAT IS REQUIRED OF TECHNIQUES AND TOOLS FOR STRUCTURED DEVELOPMENT

Structured methodologies[1] have emerged in response to the complexity of software-driven systems. What is it about software that makes its construction complex? Here are some of the main factors:

- Large software systems interact with complex environments in which they perform many functions—and thus, by the law of requisite variety we discussed in chapter 10, they are themselves complex.
- During its operation, a software system can assume a very large number of states (a change of value of a single bit is a new state!), which precludes exhaustive testing to ensure correctness.
- Software is meant to be changed; its modifiability is a primary rationale for casting a system into software rather than hardware. Yet, changes can easily lead to the corruption of a stable software system.

A methodology is a coherent system of general methods and more specific techniques, some of which are supported by tools, such as software packages or conceptual devices. Structured methodologies offer techniques and tools that help manage the systemic complexity of software and its development. Some of the tools serve analysis tasks, others help synthesize the new system (that is, design and program it). As we shall see later in the chapter, many of these techniques are becoming automated (or semiautomated) with CASE tools.

Here is the principal demand we pose on these techniques and tools: we should be able to visualize a system under development in levels of decreasing abstraction. In other words, we develop a system top-down, by stepwise refinement. First we see the system as a single unit, interacting with its environment—this is the most abstract view. We then progressively bring in detail by breaking the system down into its interacting components, which in turn are themselves broken down, and so forth.

An example of such a tool is the data flow diagram (DFD), which we shall discuss below. As graphical tools employed to analyze systems, DFDs are used to produce more and more detail as analysis progresses via what is called "leveling." We shall see that a similar facility is offered in the design stage by structure charts.

Here are some more detailed requirements, many of which flow from the principal demand for top-down development:

- *Graphic* tools are needed to visualize the system.
- We should be able to maintain the desired level of detail for a given time during development.
- The tools we use should also become an essential part of system documentation, which should thus emerge as a by-product of the development process.
- The representation we obtain with these tools should be easy to change. We need this requirement to be able to introduce changes both during development and during maintenance, when documentation may have to be changed to correspond to a changed code.
- The tools should help in the next development stage. Thus, the tools used for systems analysis should facilitate systems design.
- The tools should facilitate communication among the agents involved in development. For example, the system representation obtained in the analysis stage should be easy for the future system users to understand. Design blueprints should unambiguously communicate information to programmers.

Let us now consider the most commonly used techniques and tools of structured methodologies in the three principal development phases: analysis, design, and programming.

19.3 SYSTEMS ANALYSIS 1: DATA FLOW DIAGRAMS

The purpose of systems analysis is to devise a logical model of the proposed system. In other words, we wish to specify the new system in business terms, independent of its physical implementation. As we have seen in the previous chapter, to achieve this, it may be necessary to first analyze the system presently in place.

A comprehensive structured analysis method was developed in the late 1970s (Yourdon, 1989a). The objective of structured analysis is to graphically describe the system as interacting processes that transform input data into output data. These processes may then become code modules as the system is further designed and programmed.

Introduction to Data Flow Diagrams

The principal tool used in structured analysis is the **data flow diagram (DFD).** A DFD representation of a system is the vital depiction of what the system will do. This is not simply graphics: this is what will ultimately become the system itself! There are only four symbols employed by a DFD (as shown in figure 19.3).

A DFD may be designed using these symbols in a rather freestyle manner. However, since these diagrams are a communication tool, it is important that they be highly readable and show the principal data flow well (for example, from left to right, insofar as possible). Each symbol in a DFD must be appropriately labeled with a name that best and briefly describes the object represented.

Let us discuss the symbols and their meanings.

1. A *process* is shown as a circle, also called a bubble (though some analysts prefer rectangles with rounded corners).

A process transforms its inputs into outputs. For example, a *Compute discount* process will transform data about the customer and the order into a discount percentage. The name of the process very briefly explains what the process does. Since the processes are the "active" components of the system (they are likely ultimately to become modules of instructions), their

FIGURE 19.3

Symbols of data flow diagrams.

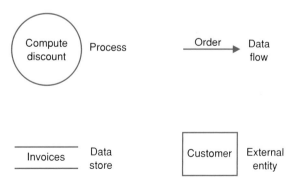

names reflect this. Therefore, the name of a process generally consists of a verb ("Compute") and an object ("discount"). All processes in a DFD are numbered.

2. A *data flow,* shown as an arrow, represents a flow of data into or out of a process. (In systems that contain noncomputerized components, these symbols may be used also to show the flow of materials). In general, data flows show the movement of data between the components of a DFD.

   While during the initial analysis we may consider physical data flows (for example, a report or an invoice), ultimate analysis will deal with their logical data content (such as customer data or order data).

3. A *data store,* shown as parallel lines (though some analysts use a rectangle open on the right), shows the repository of data maintained by the system. Such a repository may become a data file or a database component, but it may also be implemented as a table in a program or even as a file cabinet with folders—these decisions are made at a later time during the system development. Both data stores and data flows are data structures; note the similarity in the way they are named and further analyzed. Data store names are frequently in the plural (for example, *Invoices*), to distinguish them from data flows.

4. An *external entity,* represented as a square (or a rectangle) is a source from which the system draws data or a receiver of information from the system. These entities are external to the system; they are beyond the system boundary. Thus, *Customer* may present an *Order* to the system and receive an *Invoice* from it. External entities may also be other systems with which the given system interacts.

Let us first familiarize ourselves with DFDs by reviewing (walking through) the simple diagram shown in figure 19.4. The objective of our Travel Information System (other than introducing DFDs to you in their simplest form) is to respond to queries regarding flights and accommodations and log the queries into a client file that could be used for marketing purposes.

As *Clients* present a *Travel-query* to the system, the process *Obtain travel information* accesses the data stores called *Hotel-information* and *Airline-schedules,* to obtain respectively, *Accommodation-data* and *Flight-data.* Another

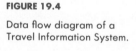

FIGURE 19.4

Data flow diagram of a Travel Information System.

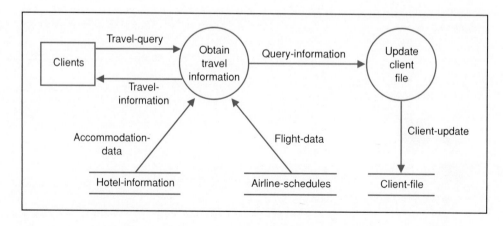

process of the system, called *Update client file,* logs summarized queries and responses into the *Client-file,* a data store that will be used for marketing purposes.

Note that this data flow diagram is expressed in logical terms: we are not committing ourselves to any physical implementation of how queries are entered or how data stores are implemented. For example, both *Hotel-information* and *Airline-schedules* may be a part of a single database. All we know is that our system does not maintain these data (note that there are no inputs to the stores from the system's processes); they are, perhaps, provided by a third-party vendor. The process of analysis must produce such *a logical DFD* for the new system—this is a logical model of the system. The implementation of this logical DFD will be decided on later, during the design stages. Systems diagrams are an apt tool for the physical design, as we learned in chapter 18 (see figure 18.6).

We shall now consider how DFDs are used to analyze larger systems.

Refining Data Flow Diagrams: From Context Diagram to Level-0

Our fundamental requirement concerning tools for systems development was that they lend themselves to a process of progressive refinement, or top-down development, of the system. That is, we want to introduce details gradually as we break the system down into progressively finer components. DFD leveling is such a process of progressive refinement.

We start structured systems analysis with a special kind of DFD called the **context diagram** of the system, which is generally the product of a feasibility study. This diagram shows only the system interfaces (inputs and outputs) flowing to or from external entities. A context diagram shows the system as a single process bearing the system's name, with its principal incoming and outgoing data flows, as they are known at this early stage of analysis. If there are too many to show, a table may be employed to show inputs and outputs in two columns. A context diagram of a simple *Order Processing System* is shown in figure 19.5.

As we can see from the context diagram, our *Order Processing System* accepts customer orders and produces the invoices sent to customers; it also prints picking labels, which are sent to the warehouse. A picking label directs warehouse pickers to the bins where the product is located, so that an order can be assembled for shipment. Instead of an invoice, a customer may receive an order-rejection notice (rejection may be for a variety of reasons, including absence of good credit standing), or an out-of-stock notice. Our simple system does not handle backorders: our warehouse is restocked periodically and all the goods that we are able to deliver to customers are there.

FIGURE 19.5

The context diagram of the *Order Processing System.*

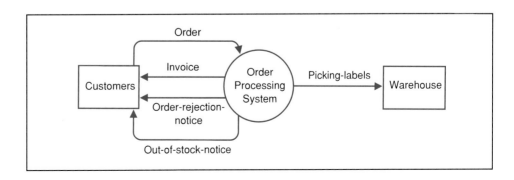

Using this context diagram, let us now produce a level-0 DFD, which shows the major functions of the system. We shall first walk you briefly through this DFD, shown in figure 19.6, and then discuss the rather simple principles of leveling (decomposition) of DFDs.

The mainline of the DFD, which shows the processing of a valid order for available products, is laid out from left to right for easy understanding of the system. The appropriate processes (1 to 5) check order validity and product availability, update the inventory file for the quantities that will be removed for the order, determine the price, and produce the invoice.

Note that we need to ensure sufficiency of data for a proper process operation. It would be a grave error, for example, if the only information passed on by the *Check order validity* process to the subsequent processes were an indication whether the order is valid or not. The process should, rather, pass on the appropriate data about the order itself. Observe that we show only a net flow from a data store. For example, we do not show that the *Check product availability* process must send a key (product identification) to the *Inventory-file* to identify the product; the objective of access is to get the *Product-quantity-on-hand*, and that is what is shown in the DFD.

Note that the external entity *Customers* is repeated for readability. Indeed, we can replicate like this any external entity or data store (but not a process or a data flow). With the exception of these repetitions, each entity must have a distinct name (even if it appears to us at this point in the analysis that certain data flows actually contain the same data items). Careful and proper naming of entities to reflect their meaning in the system is important. I did not produce this DFD on the first try, and neither should you expect that your first attempt at drawing a DFD will be correct, complete, or consistent—or that it will show what the system is supposed to do in the best way. Do not forget that DFDs are communication tools—you should be able to show them to future system users, and they should be able to comment on them.

Orders that are found invalid by the *Check order validity* process (we do not at this time have to determine exactly what criteria will be used, but we know that a credit check will be included) are placed in the *Suspense-file*. They will be further reviewed (perhaps manually?), and an *Order-rejection-notice* may have to be produced. Placing any *Suspended-order* in a data store makes it possible for the two processes that access the store to operate at different times. Likewise, an *Out-of-stock-notice* will be sent if the product is not currently available.

For an order subject to shipment, a set of *Picking-labels* for the *Warehouse* will be generated. To do so, the *Inventory-file* will be accessed to determine the *Bin-numbers* indicating where the products are located.

Leveled Data Flow Diagrams—General Principles

Going from the context diagram to the level-0 DFD, we have encountered the first instance of DFD leveling. *Leveling* is the gradual refinement of DFDs, which brings more and more detail into the picture. Let us now consider the basic principles of DFD leveling:

1. The top-level DFD is the context diagram of the system. Subsequent levels are obtained by progressively decomposing individual processes into separate DFDs.

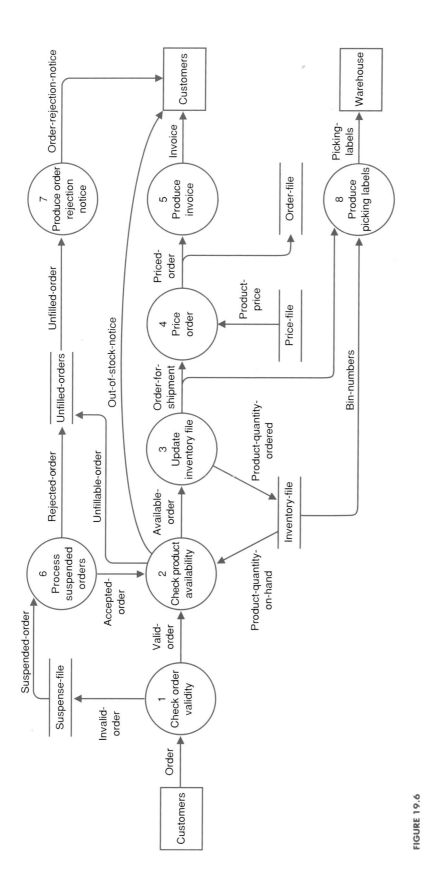

FIGURE 19.6

Level-0 DFD of the *Order Processing System*.

2. Decomposition is governed by the **balancing rule,** which ensures consistency. Thus: data flows coming into and leaving a process must correspond to those coming into and leaving the DFD which shows this process in more detail. Observe the balancing rule in action on figures 19.5 and 19.6 with respect to the *Order Processing System* process which is being decomposed: all five data flows on figure 19.5 match the appropriate flows on figure 19.6 (actually, we did not have to show the external entities in the level-0 DFD, but at that top level this is frequently done for readability's sake). Sometimes, minor data flows are added on lower levels, but do not appear at the higher level.

3. No more than ten processes should be shown on a given DFD to prevent cluttering the diagram—use leveling!

4. Not all processes have to be decomposed—only those whose complexity warrants it. Typically, you stop decomposing a process if you feel that you can describe what it does in detail in procedural terms (as you shall soon see) in about a page.

5. The leveling process is not over until it's over, to use Yogi Berra's immortal phrase. That is, as you introduce more detail into the analysis by leveling, you will note omissions in higher-level DFDs—and you will correct them.

6. The numbering rule for processes is as follows. Use 1, 2, 3, and so on in the level-0 DFD. If you decompose, say, process 3, the processes shown on process 3's level-1 DFD will be numbered 3.1, 3.2, 3.3, and so on. Therefore, if I see a process numbered 5.1.4, I know that it belongs to a level-2 DFD of process 5.

Let us now look at leveling once again on a more detailed example of the *Check order validity* process, as shown in figure 19.7.

FIGURE 19.7

Level-1 DFD for the process *Check order validity.*

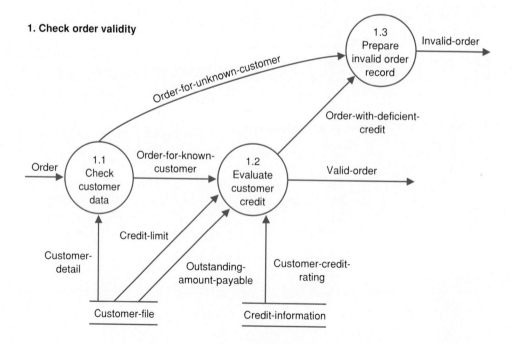

Since our system handles only known customers, an order will be rejected if *Customer-file* contains no customer record or if the *Evaluate customer credit* process comes up with a deficient credit rating, based on access to the *Credit-information* store. This data store contains a variety of "soft" data on customers' and potential customers' credit standing, as well as an overall rating of customers' creditworthiness. A separate data store for credit information is maintained due to the sometimes sensitive nature of the data contained there. Note that our system only obtains the data from both data stores but does not store the data; the data stores are maintained by another system.

We did not have to show the stores used by the *Check order validity* process on a higher-level DFD, since they are used internally, rather than being used to interface this process with others (as *Suspense-file* does, for example). Sometimes we may choose to show a data store used by a single process in order to make a DFD more readable (as we chose to show *Credit-information,* for example).

A DFD description of the system is the higher-level model in structured analysis. We still must describe the primitive processes, as well as the data structures contained in the data flows and data stores. Now let us see how this is done.

19.4 SYSTEMS ANALYSIS 2: DESCRIPTION OF ENTITIES

The entities that appear in the data flow diagrams are described in further detail in a **data dictionary.** Originally used to store only descriptions of data, data dictionaries have evolved into powerful tools as repositories of descriptions of all project entities. Such dictionaries are available as specialized software packages; a dictionary facility also lies at the heart of CASE tools.

Here, we shall see how to show the logic of the primitive DFD processes, that is, of those processes not further described via leveled DFDs. We shall then illustrate the description of data structures contained in data stores and data flows.

Description of Processes: Basic Logic Constructs

To show how the primitive DFD processes transform their inputs into outputs, we must describe their logic. The principal tool for this specification is *structured English,* which is a form of **pseudocode;** that is, a code describing the processing logic to a human rather than to a computer. Structured English is more readable and less detailed than a code expressed in a programming language for computer execution.

As any structured code, structured English relies on imperative sentences (orders for a computational action) and three fundamental programming structures expressing how these computational orders are to be applied.

FIGURE 19.8

Sequence.

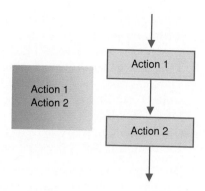

Here are some examples of orders for a computational action as they might appear in structured English:

Compute Tax = 6.25 * *Sale-total*
Read *Customer-record* from *Customer-file*
Add *Sale-amount* to *Sale-total*
Delete *Supplier-record* from *Approved-supplier-file*

Just three fundamental constructs are sufficient to express any processing logic: sequence, loop, and decision. An additional construct represents multiple choice. Each of these constructs is itself an action. This fact enables us to express any procedural logic, since the constructs may be expanded by detailing these actions, again in the same form. These constructs, along with their explanatory flowcharts, are shown in figures 19.8 through 19.11.

Let us explain and illustrate these constructs:

1. *Sequence* specifies that one action be carried out after another (figure 19.8).

For example, here is a sequence of two actions:

Read *Supplier-record* from *Approved-supplier-file*
Print *Supplier-address*

2. *Loop* specifies that certain actions be carried out repeatedly while the given condition holds (figure 19.9).

For example:

DO WHILE there are more records in *Customer-file*
    Read next *Customer-record* from *Customer-file*
    Write *Customer-address* onto *Mailing-list*
END DO

3. *Decision* specifies alternative courses of action, depending on whether a certain condition holds or not (figure 19.10). It expresses this thought: "If a given condition exists, one action (or actions) should be taken, or else the alternative action(s) should be carried out."

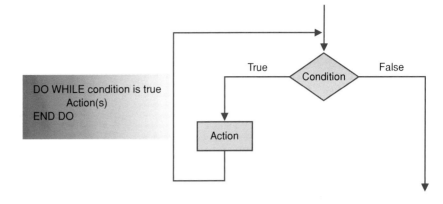

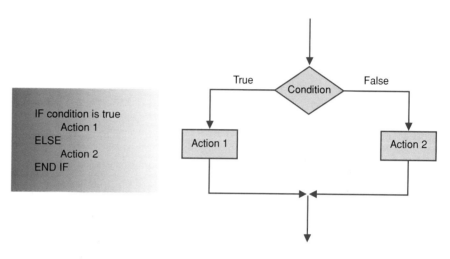

For example:

IF *Customer-credit-rating* is satisfactory
    Write *Customer-order* into *Valid-order-file*
ELSE
    Write *Customer-order* into *Suspense-file*
END IF

4. Frequently, a need arises to choose one of a set of actions, based on a condition that may have more than two outcomes. Though this situation may be expressed with nested IF constructs, it is far easier to express it with the multiple selection (CASE) construct shown in figure 19.11.

For example:

CASE OF *Customer-state*
CASE *Customer-state* = "New Jersey"
    Set *Sales-tax* to 0.0725
CASE *Customer-state* = "New York"
    Set *Sales-tax* to .0825
CASE *Customer-state* = "New Hampshire"
    Set *Sales-tax* to 0
END CASE

FIGURE 19.11

Multiple selection.

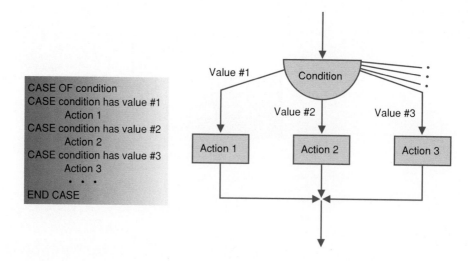

Note the following:

- The data entities referred to in the constructs must be defined in the data dictionary. They will be data flows, or their components, or records of data stores. (Data items which are local to a process, as is *Order-total* in the process *Evaluate customer credit* described next, do not have to be entered in the dictionary.)
- The scope of the structure is shown by indentation (ENDs are sometimes omitted).

As we said, an "action" in any of these structures may be any other structure. Thus, by nesting these structures within one another, we can express the needed process logic. Consider this specification of a process from the DFD shown in figure 19.7, which employs all of the above structures (and where some ends are skipped for readability):

1.2 *Evaluate customer credit*
Obtain *Customer-credit-rating*
CASE OF *Customer-credit-rating*
CASE *Customer-credit-rating* = 1
   Mark *Order-for-known-customer* as *Valid-order*
   Indicate "Credit granted" on *Valid-order*
CASE *Customer-credit-rating* = 2
   Read *Outstanding-amount-payable* from *Customer-file*
   Read *Credit-limit* from *Customer-file*
   Set *Order-total* to 0
   DO WHILE there are more *Order-items*
      Add *Item-amount* to *Order-total*
   Mark *Order-for-known-customer* as *Valid-order*
   IF *Outstanding-amount-payable* + *Order-total* < *Credit-limit*
      Mark "Credit granted" on *Valid-order*
   ELSE
      Mark "COD payment" on *Valid-order*
CASE *Customer-credit-rating* = 3
   Mark *Order-for-known-customer* as *Order-with-deficient-credit*
END CASE

FIGURE 19.12

General format of decision tables.

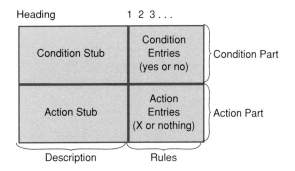

It may be noted that while the structured English could be considered rather clumsy, it is eminently readable to end users. In fact, in many cases, the end users produce these specifications themselves.

Rather frequently, a process specification requires that a complex decision, based on several factors, be specified. In those cases, a decision table or decision tree may be employed to advantage (instead of deeply nested decisions constructs). Let us discuss these tools next.

Description of Complex Decisions in Processes: Decision Tables and Trees

Decision tables and decision trees help us consider all the possible actions that need be taken under a given set of circumstances in a complete and unambiguous fashion.

A **decision table** specifies in tabular form the actions to be carried out when given conditions exist. A decision table has the general format specified in figure 19.12.

To design a decision table:

1. Specify the name of the table as its heading, and insert a reference to it at the place in the process description where the table applies.

2. List all possible conditions in the condition stub.

3. List all possible actions in the action stub.

4. Fill in the condition entries by marking the presence (Y) or absence (N) of the conditions. The number of rules, that is, entries in the righthand side of the table, equals the number of possible combinations of conditions. Thus, two conditions may have up to four rules, three conditions up to eight, etc. Impossible or unneeded conditions may be eliminated.

5. For every condition entry, mark with an X an action entry opposite the action(s) to be taken under these circumstances.

Let us apply these rules to the following example:

To compute an employee's weekly pay, apply the standard hourly rate for forty or fewer hours worked on weekdays. Apply overtime rates to the weekend work and work beyond forty hours on weekdays. Print out the names of employees who only worked overtime.

The table in figure 19.13 results from applying the above rules (you may trace how they have been applied). If the first rule is considered impossible under our circumstances, it could be eliminated.

FIGURE 19.13

Decision table for *Weekly Pay.*

Weekly Pay

	1	2	3	4
1. Worked Weekdays Up to 40 Hrs	N	N	Y	Y
2. Worked During Overtime Periods	N	Y	N	Y
1. Compute Pay at Standard Rate			X	X
2. Compute Pay at Overtime Rate		X		X
3. Compute Total Pay				X
4. Print Out Employee's Name		X		

FIGURE 19.14

Decision tree for *Weekly Pay.*

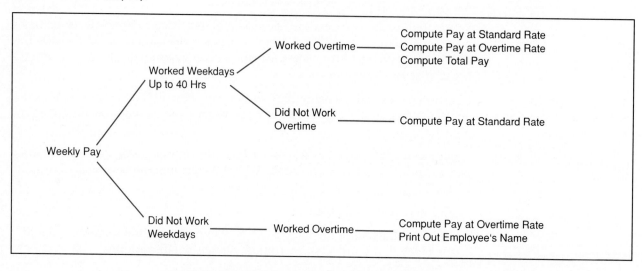

Decision trees, which we encountered earlier in chapter 13, present conditions as branches of a tree, going from left to right. The decision tree for the same sample problem is shown in figure 19.14.

Decision trees are easier to read than are decision tables, but the greater the number of conditions, the more tedious they are to draw up. Also, decision tables are better for checking the completeness of the policy represented.

Data Dictionaries and the Description of Data

Data are the crucial ingredient of information systems. As we discussed it in chapter 8, many organizations have adopted the information resource management (IRM) approach to their MIS. IRM involves extensive planning of what data and what relationships among data are stored in an organization's databases, controlling database ownership, and controlling access to the data. To be able to do this, we need to store and manage a *description* of the data in addition to the data values. The principal vehicle for managing data is a **data dictionary—** a repository of data about data. We know from chapter 8 that a data dictionary plays a crucial role in data administration and in database administration.

It is the data dictionary of our project that will explain to the user reading a data flow diagram what the analyst means by *Picking-label* or by *Unfilled-orders.* Without a data dictionary description, DFDs would remain loose sketches rather than become a part of system documentation. The composition of each data store and data flow appearing in the DFDs must be described in the dictionary. Generally, both data flows and the records in data stores are data structures, that is, they are composed of more elementary data entities.

Let us take the *Valid-order* data flow that appears in the DFD shown in figure 19.6. This data flow would be described in the data dictionary as follows:

Valid-order = *Order-number*
  + *Customer-data*
  + {*Product-data*}
  + (*Comment*)

The symbols used in the data dictionary permit the analyst to describe the composition of the data entities in rather simple terms. Thus, our data dictionary uses the following symbols:

- = means "is composed of"
- + means "and" (this is not an arithmetical symbol here!)
- { } means "several"
- ( ) means "optional"

While additional symbols are used by various data-dictionary packages which support the analysis process, the four just listed are the most typical.

We may, then, interpret our data dictionary description as follows. The data flow *Valid-order* consists of the *Order-number* and the *Customer-data,* several *Product-data* entries, and sometimes a *Comment.*

Some of the entities are elementary data items that are further described in the data dictionary as to physical makeup. Thus, *Order-number* may be described as a numeric item of a particular length (say, seven digits). Other parts of the *Valid-order* are, in turn, also structured and are described as the data flow itself was described, namely in terms of their composition—until all the elementary data items are described in physical terms.

Data dictionary software is available as a part of DBMS packages, CASE tools, or as a stand-alone facility. Frequently, data dictionaries are employed not only to store "data about data," but more broadly to store all the information about system entities that emerge during analysis (such as process descriptions) and during later development stages (such as descriptions of the system modules). This makes data dictionaries powerful tools for a systems developer. An example of a data dictionary description of an elementary data item (*Order-number*) is shown in figure 19.15.

Data dictionaries provide an analyst with the ability to automatically perform consistency and completeness checks of the system specification. They also offer a variety of listings, permitting, for example, an answer to a question such as "Which processes use the data flow named *Picking-label?*" This capability is particularly valuable in conducting impact analysis of maintenance requests arising during operation of a system. If we should want to change the data content of the *Picking-label* at any time in the future, for example, we can identify the parts of the system that would be affected by the modification.

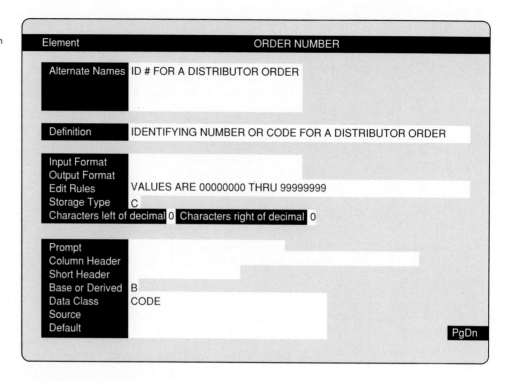

19.5 SYSTEMS DESIGN

The principal objective of *structured design* (Yourdon & Constantine, 1989) is to specify the structure of the programs in the system in such a way that the system will be relatively easy to program and modify.

The principal product of the logical design stage of structured design are the *structure charts* of the programs that need to be coded and tested. An example is shown in figure 19.16.

In the figure, I have shown the structure of the principal program of our *Order Processing System* (suspended orders are handled by another program that is run at the close of the day). Each box corresponds to a module, a named routine that is handled as a unit. The main module of the program will call six others, as shown in the figure. For two of these lower-level modules, I have also shown the next-level modules which they will in turn call to perform subtasks. Thus, the *Check order validity* module calls three other modules. We can see a close relationship between the structure chart and the DFD on which the design is based.

This design method, grounded in systems theory, which we discussed in chapter 10, rests on two basic principles:

1. Modular Structure

Programs must be constructed of **modules**—relatively short segments of code that are invoked (called) by their names during program execution. In such a call, certain data may have to be passed between the two modules. A module ought to perform completely a well-defined function in

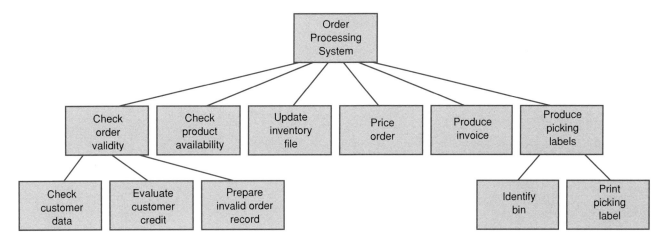

FIGURE 19.16

A structure chart.

the overall system; many processes shown in a DFD become modules in the system. A module should be short enough that its logic is relatively easy to understand—for example, a page-long description in pseudocode (such as structured English).

Modules ought to be selected with great care. We may think of a module as "hiding" from the rest of the system a certain data structure or similar design solution. A well-selected module displays a high degree of *cohesion*—it performs one well-defined operation reflected in its name; for example, the *Check order validity* module establishes whether an order is valid (and does nothing that is unrelated to this task). In performing its function, a module may call lower-level modules to perform certain subfunctions—very much as a manager would delegate responsibility for certain tasks to his or her subordinates. Thus, any action of a calling module could be a call to a lower-level one.

A cohesive module is generally connected rather loosely with others—we say that it displays loose *coupling* with other modules. In other words, such a module needs few data items to be passed to it by other modules. Those data items (called parameters) which are passed between modules are shown in the completed structure chart. A fragment of a structure chart showing these items is presented in figure 19.17. Here, the calling module, *Check order validity,* passes the *Customer-id* to the called module, which accesses the *Customer-file* to find the customer record. Having done this, the *Check customer data* module passes back *Customer-detail* or an indicator that the customer is unknown (*Unknown-customer-flag*).

Structured design entails selecting solutions which lead to cohesive and loosely coupled modules. Proper selection of modules ensures that whenever a system must be modified in the future, maintenance procedures will be localized only within the appropriate modules. Since maintenance most often concerns a needed change in the functioning of the system, then if modules reflect system functions, only the modules involved in the given function will be affected. Thus, if sometime in the future we wish to change our order validation process, we will not have to concern ourselves with modules other than those which handle that aspect of system operation.

On the other hand, if modules are selected in a rather haphazard fashion, with system functions being handled by several unrelated

FIGURE 19.17

A fragment of structure chart
with parameters shown.

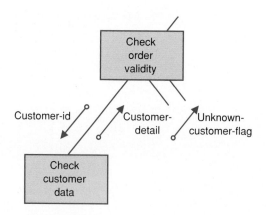

modules, we get an undesirable "ripple effect"—a change ripples through
a large number of modules.

The obvious question to ask is: what is the best size for a module?
Recent research relating error density in a code to module size indicates
that "the smaller the better" is not the way to go: too many small modules
create a problem in managing the structural complexity that ensues. A
middle road of 200 to 500 lines in the code of larger systems programmed
in languages such as Ada, C, or COBOL is suggested (Withrow, 1990).

2. Hierarchical Design

Program modules are identified top-down; thus, a hierarchical program
structure emerges. We start with the single top module which provides the
overall control. We then decompose its function into lower-level functions
and so identify the modules it must call. This stepwise decomposition,
based on the DFDs produced during the analysis, results in a structure
chart for the system. The designer thus starts with an abstract view of the
program and introduces more and more detail as the lower-level modules
are specified.

In system maintenance, the maintainer will be able to understand the
program structure by studying the structure chart and relating it to the
program code. To continue our example, if a change in order validation
procedures is limited to a new way of evaluating a customer's credit, only
the *Evaluate customer credit* module will be affected.

After the logical design stage, the processing steps to be carried out by individual modules are specified during the physical design stage. Specification is
done in a pseudocode, which we encountered earlier during our discussion of
process specification. Structured English is a form of pseudocode, though more
precise forms also exist. Many modules derive directly from their corresponding
DFD processes, and their logic is already largely specified in structured English,
including perhaps decision tables or trees.

For certain modules, algorithms (for example, an efficient table look-up or a sort)
must be selected, and these are pseudocoded at this stage. Algorithm design is
critically dependent on a careful selection of data structures employed to represent data and the dependencies between them.

The resultant structure charts for a system's programs, together with the pseudocoded module specifications, are now ready for programming.

19.6 STRUCTURED PROGRAMMING

In coding the modules of a system, the discipline of *structured programming* is essential. Structured programming relies on a small number of control constructs for organizing the logic in the program. It has been proven[2] that the three structures—sequence, decision, and loop—which we have presented in this chapter and which are shown in figures 19.8 through 19.10 are sufficient to represent all programming logic.

Structured programming postulates that program modules should be coded exclusively with these constructs and a few related constructs, such as CASE, shown in figure 19.11. All these constructs have the vital property of possessing a single entry and a single exit (which you can verify by looking at the equivalent flowcharts, shown in the figures: a single arrow leads into each construct and a single one leaves it). This makes a code which relies only on these constructs relatively easy to understand, test, and modify.

Unconditional transfers of control—that is, go-to statements—should be avoided, since their presence makes it difficult to follow the sequence in which the program statements will be executed and their effects. Organizations today are faced with the massive task of maintaining older systems produced before structured programming principles were adopted. This code, which relied heavily on go-to statements, is notably difficult to understand or modify. It has earned the nickname "spaghetti code," for its complex patterns of control transfer.

Modern programming languages generally offer the logic constructs of structured programming as actual language statements (see chapter 6). In addition to using these structures, good programming practices demand that the code be laid out in a readable fashion and thoroughly commented on.

19.7 SOFTWARE QUALITY ASSURANCE. STRUCTURED TESTING

Software quality assurance includes a variety of techniques aimed at producing a software product that satisfies stated requirements. We have discussed the attributes of quality software in the first section of this chapter, where we stressed that quality must be assured by ongoing measures throughout the development process.

The use of a disciplined system development methodology is in itself a crucial measure for producing quality software. Early detection of errors is crucial to cost-effective software quality assurance. Let us study figure 19.18, which is based

FIGURE 19.18

Dramatic increase in the cost
to fix an error or to make a
change in a software system.

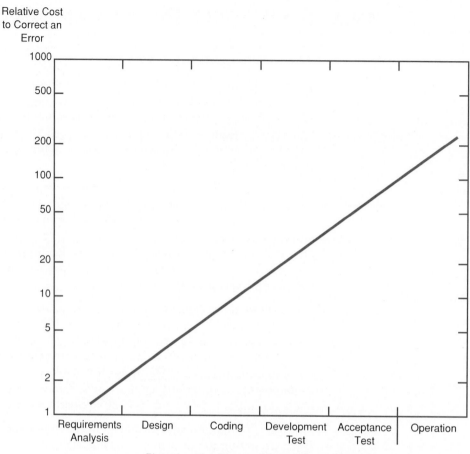

Phase in which Error was Detected and Corrected

on actual experience with several software systems presented by Barry Boehm
(1981). Note the rapidly increasing numbers on the vertical axis. The figure shows
that an error made during the early system development stage of Requirements
Analysis will cost perhaps 100 times more to fix if it is discovered during system
operation, rather than during the analysis stage itself! Indeed, if there are major
errors committed during systems analysis, the software may be entirely useless.
It "works," but it does not do what is required.

It is, therefore, crucial to discover errors made during the early development
stages—systems analysis and design. It is also important to introduce any necessary changes in requirements specifications as early as possible. During these
stages, of course, we have no program code to test. Certain CASE tools, which
we shall discuss later in the chapter, assist the developer in producing correct
system specifications during analysis and design. However, the principal means
of software quality assurance in these stages are walkthroughs and inspections.
These quality assurance techniques retain their importance in the programming
stage, but the principal means of quality assurance when the program code is
available is software testing.

Walkthroughs and Inspections

A **walkthrough** is a review by a small group of people of a product presented by its author. Walkthroughs should be scheduled frequently during systems development, so that a manageable piece of work—such as a data flow diagram, a structure chart, or code listing—can be thoroughly reviewed in one to two hours. Walkthroughs thus include (Yourdon, 1989b):

- specification walkthroughs, where the group looks for errors, omissions, and ambiguities in the data flow diagrams at various levels, in the data dictionary entries, and in other requirements specifications;
- design walkthroughs, where structure charts and the pseudocode of individual modules are inspected;
- code walkthroughs, where program listings are studied;
- test walkthroughs, to ensure that the test cases are prepared thoroughly for all testing levels we shall discuss further on.

Who participates in the walkthrough? That depends on what is being "walked." Thus, for example, during a specification walkthrough, users, analysts, a designer, and perhaps an invited expert (such as an MIS auditor) may participate, since all of them will be able to make a contribution.

A walkthrough is scheduled in advance, so that all participants can come prepared, having studied the work the author will "walk" them through. The walkthrough is generally conducted by a coordinator, who mediates any conflicts that might arise and who maintains a collegial spirit. The purpose is not to put the author on the spot; rather, everyone should understand that finding inadequacies in the "walked" item is in the common interest. To further this attitude, no error correction is performed during the walkthrough.

It is crucial for the effectiveness of walkthroughs that they be established as a quality assurance tool, as opposed to a management tool for evaluating the performance of MIS professionals. When regular walkthroughs are conducted, the intellectual integrity and uniformity of style of the ultimate product may be maintained. Since all the participants become familiar with the work of other developers, fewer problems will emerge if one of them leaves the project in midstream.

An **inspection** is similar to a walkthrough in its objectives, but it is a more formal review technique. In an inspection, a review team checks a data flow diagram or a program against a prepared list of concerns. At the heart of code inspection is the paraphrasing technique: an inspector verbally expresses the meaning of one or more lines of code at a time, with other participants striving to detect errors in this code. Inspections also include formal rework and follow-up stages. Inspections have been found highly effective by Michael Fagan, the original proponent of the technique (first used at IBM Kingston, New York, in 1972): they succeeded in finding 60 to 90 percent of all errors in the systems in whose development they were used (Fagan, 1986).

The more recently developed cleanroom software engineering technique (Mills, 1987) heavily relies on code reading, walkthroughs, and inspections, as well as on mathematical verification of correctness whenever possible—which minimizes the necessary amount of code testing. As with cleanroom hardware development, the objective is preventing errors rather than detecting them by testing and removing them by debugging.

Testing

As soon as we begin programming the system specified in the design stage, we should begin testing the resulting code. As a matter of fact, testing plans are drawn up in the earlier development stages. Ideally, there should be no need for software testing: software engineering techniques and tools should enable a programming professional to produce programs that work properly at the completion of coding. As we have explained, we are a long way from reaching this ideal. While formal techniques for proving program correctness have been studied for some time now, their power is limited. To achieve a desired level of confidence in a software system, a variety of tests are performed. In *testing,* system components, and later the entire system, are run for the purpose of finding errors, which are then removed by *debugging*—locating the source of the errors and correcting them (Araki, 1991). Note that testing cannot prove the *absence* of errors; it can only diagnose their *presence.*

As we saw in figure 18.2, the various levels of testing can consume up to half of the resources allocated to systems development. Testing levels are summarized in figure 19.19.

Before we discuss these tests in detail, let us specify the general principles of testing:

- A test plan must be prepared to specify the sequence in which the modules will be coded, individually tested, and then integrated into the program.
- Test cases must be prepared as a part of the plan. Each test case should include a specification of the data to be submitted as inputs and the conditions under which the code will be tested, as well as—and this is crucial!—a specification of the expected results of the test.
- All test results should be studied and recorded.
- Test cases should be prepared for both valid and invalid input conditions: we expect the program not to fail when improper input is submitted.
- It is desirable to have a special testing group to perform most testing activities: the members of this group would have specialized expertise and no vested interest in "proving" the absence of errors; they could also contribute their own thoughts about the code being tested.
- Software tools are available to support testing and debugging; their use significantly increases the effectiveness of the process.

The following are the principal levels of software testing:

1. Module (Unit) Testing

After a module has been coded, the code is thoroughly reviewed and then tested with predesigned test cases. A set of test cases is necessary. These must include "black-box" tests (corresponding to the black-box view of systems theory—see figure 10.1), which test the outputs produced by a module in response to given inputs. They should also include "glass-box" tests, which exercise as many execution paths through the module as possible.

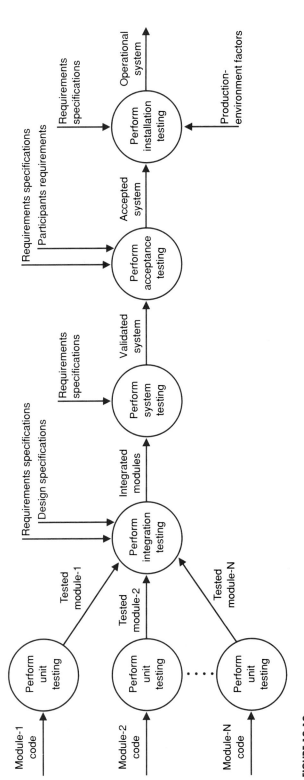

FIGURE 19.19

Testing levels.

2. Integration Testing

After individual modules are coded and unit-tested, they are integrated into the overall program. Generally, one module at a time is added to the structure and the resulting partial product is tested. If we look at a structure chart such as that in figure 19.16, an important question arises: in what order should the modules be added to the structure?

Top-down testing starts with the top module, and then consecutively adds modules of the next lower level, and so forth, until the lowest-level modules have been integrated. The as yet unavailable lower-level modules are temporarily replaced by dummy modules (called stubs). The advantage of this integration method is having a "system skeleton" available early, which provides insight into and creates confidence in the overall program operation.

In bottom-up testing, the traditional approach, the lowest-level modules are first unit-tested with dummy modules (so-called drivers) to call them. Since the lowest-level modules generally read in data from databases, print reports, or display screens, the advantage here is that we have the real "worker" modules available early.

Several methods are available to combine the advantages of both of these techniques. For example, key functional "threads" of the program—chains of modules that perform a certain function—may first be implemented, perhaps in a "sandwich" fashion, with the top and bottom first, and the middle last. The program containing these threads may even be released to users as a preliminary version. Other threads may be added later. In the example shown in figure 19.16, the main module (*Order Processing System*) may be implemented first, followed by the thread of modules that obtain the customer order (*Check customer data* and *Check order validity*), and, next, the thread that produces picking labels (*Identify bin, Print picking labels,* and *Produce picking labels*). Other modules will be added later on.

3. System Testing

Now that all the system programs have been tested, the full functionality of the system and its performance are tested next. The system is validated against its functional specifications, in an environment and under loads that resemble actual operation as closely as possible. The system is subjected to stress loads to see whether it degrades gracefully. Its compatibility with the systems it will have to interact with is established. Controls and recovery procedures are also tested. The documentation that will accompany the system is tested along with it.

Sometimes, a *beta test* of software is performed (particularly by software vendors): early copies of software are offered to end users to uncover problems in actual use.

4. Acceptance Testing

Before the system is "put into production," all parties—users, developers, future maintainers, management, and MIS auditors—must perform a set of system tests to ensure that their requirements have been satisfied.

A suite of tests validating the overall system operation is identified, documented, and preserved for maintenance purposes. These *regression tests* will be used to revalidate the system following each maintenance procedure.

5. Installation Testing

If acceptance testing was done before a system was installed in its production environment, a set of system tests is run again following installation. The system is now ready for operation.

19.8 IMPORTANT NEW METHODS OF SOFTWARE DEVELOPMENT

Although the field of software development is brimming with activity aimed at raising the productivity of the development process and enhancing the quality of the resulting product, two technologies in this field are of preeminent importance and promise.

Computer-aided software engineering (CASE) technology offers software development tools that automate important aspects of the software development process. (Do not confuse CASE technology with the CASE construct of figure 19.11!) The other technology, **object-oriented programming (OOP)** is a software development methodology that offers the all-important promise of software reusability: an ability to build up a collection of basic software components from which larger and larger systems may be constructed—just as is done in hardware manufacturing.

The two technologies—CASE and OOP—are in many respects complementary. For example, some CASE tools have been built using the OOP methodology, just as CASE tools are currently being built to support the building of applications with the use of OOP methodology. Both technologies are complex and a long way from maturity.

Computer-Aided Software Engineering (CASE)

Software developers had for a long time been in the proverbial role of the shoemaker's barefoot children. While they supported the knowledge work of others with their software tools, their own work had to rely on methodologies supported by rudimentary tools. Finally, in the mid-1980s, computer-aided software engineering (CASE) began to come into its own. An analogy has been drawn between this technology and the computer-aided design (CAD) systems used in hardware engineering.

CASE technology assists software developers in planning, analyzing, designing, programming, and maintaining systems. Indeed, a general approach to enterprise-wide system planning, development, and maintenance, relying on the ever-broader variety of CASE tools and called *information engineering,* is practiced by some corporations (Martin, 1990). The principal advantage of a CASE

FIGURE 19.20

"Front-end" and "back-end" CASE tools.

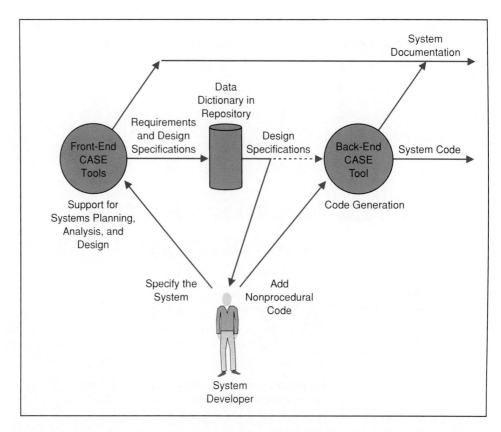

tool is that it offers an integrated package of capabilities for these tasks. Ideally, we might imagine a developer producing a set of data flow diagrams with a supporting data dictionary using a CASE system; the system will then generate the program code automatically. Though limited systems of this type have begun to appear (such as MicroSTEP of Syscorp International of Austin, Texas), general cradle-to-grave CASE support is not yet available. In other words, executable specifications (or, if you will, automatic programming) are a remote possibility.

The best-known CASE tools (among which Excelerator of Index Technologies of Cambridge, Massachusetts is the leader—see color plate 19) assist the developer in creating a complete set of user requirements specifications, with all the data flow diagrams, and with the entities defined in the data dictionary. The tool subsequently supports the development of structure charts. Alternative development methodologies (such as Warnier-Orr techniques, or Jackson design), as well as the conceptual design of databases are also supported.

Computer-aided software engineering has emerged from the confluence of several technologies:

- Structured methodologies
- Fourth-generation languages (4GLs) whose main orientation has been to support access to databases by the end users
- Powerful workstations/personal computers that can accommodate the very significant memory requirements of CASE tools, since most of these tools are PC-based.

The capabilities of CASE tools are illustrated in figure 19.20.

ANOTHER REASON TO MOVE TO CASE

Many firms are decentralizing information processing: moving from mainframes to local processors. Pacific Bell, for example, is moving to 1,800 workstations. Adhering to standards in such a widely distributed environment may become a major problem and lead to chaos. Pacific Bell decided to use a CASE tool—Maestro II of Softlab—as the vehicle for ensuring uniform systems development methodology, following in the footsteps of British Telecom of London, which had successfully done so.

Based on Martin Garvey, "A CASE for Networking." *InformationWeek*, February 12, 1990, pp. 10–11.

While most often when we refer to CASE we mean the "front-end" tools that support the earlier phases of systems development, such as analysis and design, the definition also covers what are known as code generators—software that produces a runnable code from a terse specification. As we already know, automatic code generation from a specification produced with a "front-end CASE" (or "upper CASE") is not possible. As is shown in the figure, the specifications produced by front-end CASE must be translated into a form acceptable to "back-end CASE" (or lower CASE) tools. The dotted line in the figure indicates that some of these specifications can be "picked up" by a back-end tool, but much of the work needs to be done by the developer.

Comprehensive CASE packages include both front-end and back-end tools. Today, front-end CASE systems are able to assist the developer in producing complete and consistent system specifications, which are then entered into the data dictionary (or repository) facility offered by the tool. Documentation, the preparation of which is a significant drain on resources when structured techniques are used, is generated automatically by the CASE tools. Back-end tools may be used independently of front-end tools. The general objective of these *code generators* (also known as **application generators**) is to generate code from the specifications of the database structure and from screen and report layouts. The programmer can often use a simple fill-in-the blanks interface to input this information, which the generator uses to produce executable code. This code may then be refined by the programmer.

CASE tools are an excellent vehicle for prototyping. They help to specify the hierarchy of menus for the user interface, and to specify screens and reports—all in consultation with the users. The code generator then produces the necessary code.

A CASE system may be considered a delivery vehicle for structured methodologies (Martin, 1988). Thanks to CASE, these quality-enhancing methodologies can be used more productively (a 30 to 40 percent productivity increase during analysis and design was reported in Chikofsky, 1988). Another study (Loh, 1989) points to higher productivity, improved software product quality, and better project management as benefits associated with CASE techniques.

The focal facility of a CASE tool is the *repository,* a central database for storing and managing project data dictionaries, which may contain all the information

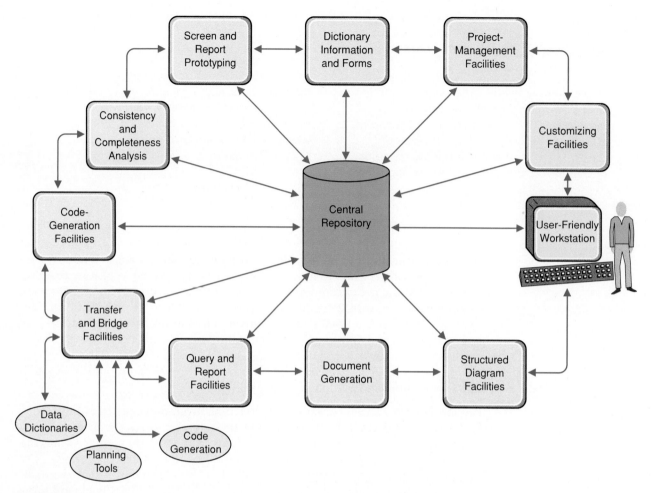

FIGURE 19.21

The key components of a
CASE tool.

about the systems being developed—from the plans through the entities that
appear in data flow diagrams, on to the code and even to project management
information. The central role of this repository is illustrated in figure 19.21, which
shows the facilities of Excelerator, a well-known front-end CASE tool.

In its endorsement of CASE technology for its sweeping Systems Application
Architecture, IBM has made a repository the bedrock of AD/Cycle, the CASE-
based systems development life cycle. A variety of CASE tools offered by different
vendors could "collaborate" by using the standard Repository Manager.

Several CASE tools (which are generally product families) with extensive front-
end capabilities are listed in table 19.1; a variety of tools are discussed by Chris
Gane (1990). Adoption of a CASE tool requires a detailed study, with close participation of the MIS professionals who will use them.

Going beyond development, CASE tools make it possible to maintain system
specifications as they are changed in maintenance. CASE tools facilitate *trace-
ability*—the ability to relate program code to the analysis and design entities it
implements.

TABLE 19.1	TOOL	VENDOR
Selected CASE Tools		
	CASE 2000	Nastec Southfield, Michigan
	Excelerator	Index Technologies Cambridge, Massachusetts
	Foundation	Arthur Andersen & Co Chicago, Illinois
	Information Engineering Workbench	KnowledgeWare Atlanta, Georgia
	Teamwork	Cadre Technologies Providence, Rhode Island

The capability to develop software faster thanks to the use of CASE technology has been recognized as one element in the formula for significantly reducing time-to-market for products and services—and thus as a component in the search for competitive advantage, in a recent MIT research program entitled *Management in the 1990s* (Arthur Young, 1989).

While there are quite a few success stories in CASE use, some of which are presented in the next vignette, this complex technology has also produced a good measure of failures as well (Bouldin, 1989). As a matter of fact, several studies showed an absence of productivity increases when CASE was used in some organizations. As any other complex technology, CASE must be brought into an organization using the technology assimilation process outlined in chapter 12.

John Henderson and Jay Cooprider tell us that in evaluating the organizational effectiveness of CASE technology, we must consider its three dimensions (Henderson, 1990). Namely, CASE is not only a software production technology, but also a technology for coordinating a team effort and an organizational technology that helps to shorten the time-to-release of software across the teams and units of a firm.

Object-Oriented Programming

The ability to build up libraries of reusable code has long had an understandable appeal. Instead of rediscovering the wheel with each new software project, the developers would be able to reach for software components that had been developed for other systems—and tested through prior use.

Object-oriented programming (OOP) aims at achieving this end by changing the way programmers think about the system being developed. Indeed, far more than just a programming technique, OOP is actually a systems *development* methodology. Instead of decomposing a system into modules that represent subfunctions of the overall system, the central principle in OOP is decomposing the system into interacting objects. If program objects represent real-world objects, we obtain a rather close correspondence between the program components and their real-world equivalents. There is a smooth transition from systems analysis to design here: both of these development tasks deal with objects (Coad, 1989; Korson, 1990).

A SOPHISTICATED NEW TECHNOLOGY REQUIRES CAREFUL ASSIMILATION—BUT PROMISES RESULTS

"The learning curve was much more difficult than what we thought it would be," says George Shackelford, director of MIS for SCI (a Houston-based operator of funeral homes) about CASE. "Training was expensive, the package was expensive, and then we found we had to spend several months to become proficient in it."
According to a development manager with Electronic Data Systems in Houston, the three most common reasons for failure of CASE projects are these: developers do not understand the underlying development methodologies, training is inadequate, and management support is lacking. The relative immaturity of the technology and lack of tool integration also create obstacles which some fail to overcome.

But there are also successes. A large software team at E. I. du Pont de Nemours estimates that 92 percent of its code is now being produced with a CASE tool, CorVision from Cortex of Waltham, Massachusetts. The group has produced seventy systems for internal Du Pont use—and ten for external clients, and outside business is picking up. The group estimates the payback time on the investment of $62,000 spent on the CASE tool to have been five-and-a-half weeks. Use of the tool is combined with prototyping, during which the evolving system is demonstrated to the user at least every two weeks. To avoid the temptation to keep developing prototypes, total development time is generally limited to 120 days.

Based on Loh, 1989; and Johanna Ambrosio, "Du Pont Brings CASE Solutions Inside—and Out." *Digital Review*, June 26, 1989, pp. 41–43.

In a human-resources information system, we may develop a program with an object called "Employee." This object would have the general attributes that describe our employees, such as education and previous experience. We would also define operations which can be meaningfully applied to this object, say Hire, Promote, Move, Fire. We then program that object by *encapsulating* employee data and operations on them together (as opposed to separating the data and instructions, as in traditional methodologies). Thus, a programmed object includes both data and instructions which describe the object's attributes and behavior. Computation is done by objects sending messages to other objects: a message tells an object what operation to apply to data.

We can reuse the object (the code, that is) in any program. We can also customize it. For example, having defined an object "Employee," we may then need an object "Retired Employee." To implement it, we use the crucial *inheritance property* of OOP, whereby new objects may inherit the properties of more general object classes and add their own special properties.

A NEW TECHNOLOGY IS NOT ALWAYS A SELLING POINT

Innovative System Techniques Inc. of Newton, Massachusetts has sold its Vision financial analysis system, built with OOP and relying on object-oriented databases, to a number of investment banks and brokerage houses. Its users are able to pull financial information from a variety of commercial databases to perform yield analysis. When the firm was first selling Vision, it never mentioned the development technology, fearing that this would be no help in the rather conservative financial market.

On the other hand, BehavHeuristic Inc. of College Park, Maryland considers OOP a selling point for its Airline Marketing Tactician. The system is designed to help airlines balance their no-shows and overbooked seats on a flight-by-flight basis. Written in Smalltalk, the program estimates the demand for a number of fare classes airlines offer. The developers feel that developing the program using more conventional methods would have taken a multimillion dollar budget and twenty people—instead of the six person-years it took the firm to develop a working prototype.

Based on David Stamps, "Taking an Objective Look." *Datamation*, May 15, 1989, pp. 45–48.

"Reusable software components tend to denote objects or classes of objects."[3] Thus, OOP offers a way of building up libraries of components that may be used in many contexts as black boxes—just as a hardware designer would use a memory chip. Ideally, we would assemble programs from prewritten objects.

I should stress that producing reusable software components is only one of the potential benefits of the object-oriented approach. The process of systems analysis and design based on object orientation is a powerful technique for gaining understanding of a business system and casting this understanding into modifiable software components (McIntyre, 1988). In particular, the technique is highly applicable to the development of graphical user interfaces, where objects such as icons are common.

The object-oriented approach may be used when programming in any procedural language; however, specialized languages (or extensions of the traditional languages) vastly facilitate the work. The original OOP language is Smalltalk; OOP is also supported by C++, Objective-C, Actor, and Metaphor, although the method is also used with more conventional languages, such as Ada.

As we discussed in chapter 8, there is also a movement toward the use of object-oriented databases, where the structuring of stored data is determined by the relationships among the objects these data represent (Gupta, 1991). These databases enable representations of a variety of objects to be stored, including images or voice, and thus can support multimedia environments.

19.9 PROJECT MANAGEMENT

Capers Jones, a recognized expert on software productivity, reports the following industry-wide experience with large software systems (those with over 64,000 lines of code):

- As many as 25 percent of development projects are canceled before completion.
- As many as 60 percent of projects will experience significant cost and schedule overruns; it is considered average for a large project to be completed over a year late and to cost almost twice as much as the initial estimate.
- Less than 1 percent of software development projects meet all user requirements and are completed on time and within budget.
- As many as 75 percent of completed systems experience quality problems, resulting in operational difficulties and excessive maintenance costs.

Based on Jones, 1989.

We have opened this section with a vignette to impress on you that severe project management problems persist in software development. It is difficult to estimate the effort needed to develop a software system, and the development process itself is difficult to manage as compared with the practices in more established engineering disciplines.

Here, we shall review three main aspects of project management in software development: estimation of the effort needed to develop a system, project planning (or scheduling), and the organization of development teams.

Estimation of System Development Effort

The effort needed to develop a system (or to perform major maintenance), from the initial planning phase through delivery, is best expressed by a snail-shaped curve showing the number of people needed to work on a project relative to its development schedule (figure 19.22). The area under the curve represents the total number of person-months needed to develop the system. As we can see, in general, projects start with a small number of people in the initial stages—feasibility study, analysis, and design. The number then increases when the coding and testing stage begins. This workforce distribution (which is approximated by a Rayleigh curve) was first proposed by Peter Norden of IBM (Norden, 1958) and has since been used in many effort estimation models.

The actual shape of the curve—that is, the staffing pattern over the project's duration—depends on a variety of factors. Thus, incremental development, achieved by releasing to users initial partial versions of the system, flattens the curve. The use of CASE tools could result in shifting more effort to the analysis and design stages and in a reduction of total effort—this will shift the "hump" to the left and reduce the area under the curve.

There are several ways to go about estimating development time and cost for a software system (DeMarco, 1982). Often estimating is done by analogy with a previously developed system. If the previous system was developed in the same environment, this rather simple technique often gives reasonable results.

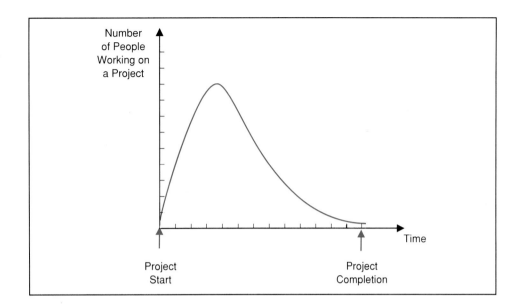

Time and costs may also be estimated by establishing a measure for the software product and by determining the relationship of this measure to the cost and time of software development. A frequent measure is the estimate count of lines of code to be delivered; when combined with the knowledge that our developers deliver on the average, say, twenty instructions of fully tested code per day (when the entire life cycle is taken into account), this measure allows us to estimate the cost and time. There are a variety of software metrics other than lines of code (Conte, 1986); the general problem with metrics based on code is that a reliable estimate of this sort is obtainable only late in the life cycle.

A sophisticated cost estimation model called COCOMO has been developed by Barry Boehm of TRW (Boehm, 1981) and placed in the public domain, where it is available as a software product. COCOMO permits consideration of a variety of factors influencing development, such as the quality of the product and the characteristics of the development environment. Another method of cost estimation, the function points technique (Albrecht, 1983) makes it possible to estimate the required effort early in development by considering the number and complexity of system inputs, outputs, inquiries, and files. As the sophistication of estimation techniques grows, efforts are made to develop methods that would establish the impact of proposed information systems on the business outcomes of a firm, such as profitability or product cycle time (Rubin, 1991).

Once the total development effort on the project has been estimated, a project schedule may be established. A schedule breaks the project up into stages, which may be further broken down into lower-level activities. Major activities terminate in a milestone, which is defined in terms of completed deliverables. A deliverable might be a development document or an operational prototype in the earlier development stages, or, during the later stages, an operational subsystem or the complete system. For example, the systems analysis stage is terminated by the delivery of requirements specifications.

Project Scheduling and Tracking—Use of Software Tools

There are hundreds of activities to be carried out as a project progresses. In scheduling these activities and controlling the project, software developers employ tools long established in project management. These are available as general project management tools or as a part of groupware, which we discussed in chapter 16.

To schedule and control project activities, project managers most frequently use the **PERT/CPM** method. This method was created by combining the Program Evaluation and Review Technique (PERT), developed in the 1950s for the Polaris missile project, with the Critical Path Method (CPM) developed for running industrial projects (Anderson, 1988).

To use the method, we first list the specific activities that make up the project and their estimated durations. Along with each activity, we list its immediate predecessors—that is, the activities that must be completed before the given one can be started.

Using the PERT/CPM method, we may then answer questions such as these:

- How much total time will be needed to complete the project?
- What are the scheduled start and finish times for each activity?
- What activities are critical and must be completed exactly as scheduled?
- How long may noncritical activities be delayed?

Let us take a simple example. For a small part of a project, we might come up with the activity list shown in table 19.2.

Note that if activities A and B are both started at the same time, activity B is *critical:* any delay in this activity will cause the entire project to be delayed. Activity C is also critical. On the other hand, a noncritical activity, such as A, may be delayed: in our case, the maximum delay possible without adversely affecting project completion is two days for activity A. This permissible delay is called *slack*.

Based on such activity lists presented by the project manager, project management packages implementing the PERT/CPM method may be used to answer the questions we listed. They also may be used to print out a PERT chart, such as that in figure 19.23, which shows the precedence relationships among the activities listed and the numbered completion events (milestones). The *critical path* (or paths), which consists only of critical activities, has been highlighted. Any delay in an activity on this path will cause project delay.

Another, simpler, tool made available by project management packages is the **Gantt chart** (also known as *time chart*): this is a bar representation of project tasks over time. An activity's duration is shown as a black bar, and its slack may

---

TABLE 19.2

An Activity List for Part of a Software Project

ACTIVITY	DESCRIPTION	DURATION (Days)	PREDECESSORS
A	Code and test module XYZ	3	—
B	Code and test module MNP	5	—
C	Integrate modules XYZ and MNP	2	A,B

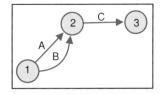

FIGURE 19.23

A PERT chart.

be shown as a white bar; critical activities are, of course, solid black (see figure 19.24). We have already seen in chapter 15 that this tool is often provided by groupware.

At the beginning of this section, we stressed that software development projects are not noted for adhering to schedules. To be of real assistance in project control, PERT and Gantt charts (such as those shown in color plates 20a and 20b) have to be constantly updated to identify new project bottlenecks. Recovering late projects by "throwing people at them" is limited by what is known as "Brooks's law": adding people to a late software project will delay it further (Brooks, 1978). The reason for this is the complexity of software development: the effort required to bring additional people up-to-date becomes greater than their potential contribution.

Software Project Teams

Most software projects, in both development and maintenance, are carried out by teams. Team composition varies depending on the development phase: initially, it may include largely systems analysts, but in the end it will consist chiefly of programmers. It is generally recognized that teams should be small (no more than ten people), since the development of a complex product such as a computerized information system calls for intense communication among team members. With n team members, the number of communication paths is $n(n - 1)/2$, which means that with nine members, for example, we have thirty-six such paths; but with ten, we have forty-five.

FIGURE 19.24

Gantt chart produced with Timeline project outliner. (Courtesy of Applitech Software, Cambridge, Massachusetts)

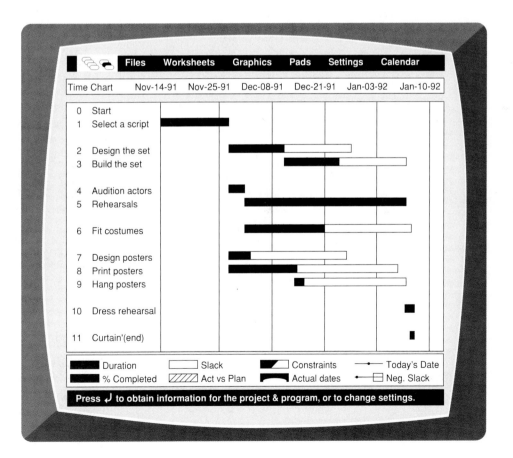

Two organizational structures for a team, representing opposite extremes, are the chief programmer team and the democratic (or egoless) team.

The **chief programmer team** is built around an outstanding software developer, the chief programmer, who personally defines systems requirements specifications and system design and programs the key modules. This professional is assisted by others, such as a back-up programmer of almost equal qualifications, an administrator responsible for managerial aspects of the project, a project librarian responsible for documentation and program versions, and several other professionals. The team is built hierarchically, with all the members answering to the chief programmer (Baker, 1972).

On the opposite end of the spectrum is the **democratic team,** which implements the idea of egoless programming proposed by Gerald Weinberg (1971). In such a structure, all the team members bear equal responsibility for the project, and the relationships between them are informal. The "egoless" approach means that the team members are generally responsive to a walkthrough of their product, since their individual egos are not on the line: the team's success is their own. The number of communication paths is far larger here than in the chief programming team, where vertical communications prevail. In a variant of the democratic team, called a structured open team, decisions are made by consensus, but team members are assigned fixed roles, which may be rotated as changing situations require (Rettig, 1990). In particular, it is vital to preserve group memory as the work on the project progresses—this role is assigned to the project librarian, who maintains all the project information in an accessible computerized form.

The two concepts of team organization clearly correspond to the mechanistic versus organic organizational designs we introduced in chapter 12. Thus, the mechanistic chief programmer team is more applicable to a large project involving a known set of technologies. The organic democratic team lends itself better to an environment of new technologies and smaller, exploratory projects, such as those developed during an early stage of technology assimilation by an organization. In practice, team structures generally reflect a compromise between the two poles (Mantei, 1981).

· ·

SUMMARY

Structured methodologies of systems development are employed to produce quality software. These methodologies are based on complexity-handling approaches of systems theory.

We have reviewed the quality attributes of software; some of these attributes define a software product's maintainability. To assure quality, verification and validation activities are conducted throughout the development process.

Data flow diagrams (DFDs) are the principal graphic tool of structured systems analysis. Through the leveling process, DFDs make possible the stepwise refinement of our view of the system being analyzed. The entities that appear in data flow diagrams are further described in a data dictionary. The logic of primitive processes is described in structured English, which is a form of pseudocode that relies on the fundamental constructs of programming logic. Decision tables or trees may be employed to describe complex decisions. The composition of the data structures that underlie data flows and data stores is also described in the data dictionary.

In conceptual (logical) system design, a structure chart is produced for each of the system's programs to show their modular structure in a hierarchical fashion. In the physical design stage, the logic of individual modules is pseudocoded.

Structured programming relies on the use of fundamental control structures and thus avoids go-to statements, so that the product will be an understandable code.

Software quality assurance is upheld throughout development by walkthroughs (or inspections), followed by several levels of testing in the programming stage, when the code becomes available.

The tools of computer-aided software engineering (CASE) automate certain aspects of the development process. Object-oriented programming methodology is aimed at developing libraries of reusable modules. Both techniques promise breakthroughs in reducing total systems development and maintenance effort.

Software development and maintenance projects must be organized, planned, and controlled. Project management software should be used in the two latter tasks. Project teams should be organized to match the task at hand—a chief programmer team is suitable for a more structured, mechanistic project, while a democratic team may be more appropriate for a project involving newer, more exploratory technology.

ENDNOTES

1. We should give credit to the developers of structured methodologies (see the references at the end of this footnote, rather than at the chapter's end). Larry Constantine and Edward Yourdon evolved the design concepts (published first in Stevens, 1974, and then in extensive form in Yourdon, 1979); Tom DeMarco (1979), Chris Gane and Trish Sarson (Gane, 1977) are the creators of structured analysis; and Edsger Dijkstra proposed structured programming (Dijkstra, 1969). As we can see, the development chronology is the reverse of that in which the methods are used—it proceeded from programming, to design, and then to analysis.

It should be stressed that alternative methodologies of structured systems development are available, among the better known the method developed by Jean-Dominique Warnier and extended by Ken Orr (Orr, 1977), and that developed by Michael Jackson (Jackson, 1975).

An early technique for representing system analysis and design documentation, which is still sometimes employed, is HIPO (IBM, 1974). Developed by IBM, HIPO (Hierarchy plus Input-Process-Output), offers assistance in decomposing a system to a certain level of detail. Its highest-level system description, called VTOC (for visual table of contents), is a rough equivalent of a structure chart, though it does not show the data through which modules communicate. The overview and detail diagrams further describe the system components shown in VTOC.

An overview of structured methodologies is available in Martin, 1988.

DeMarco, Tom. *Structured Analysis and System Specification.* Englewood Cliffs, N.J.: Prentice Hall, 1979.

Dijkstra, Edsger W. "Structured Programming." In *Software Engineering Techniques*, edited by J. N. Buxton and B. Randell. Rome: NATO Science Committee, 1969, pp. 88–93.

Gane, Chris, and Sarson, Trish. *Structured Systems Analysis: Tools and Techniques.* New York:

Improved Systems Technologies/Prentice Hall, 1977.

IBM HIPO: A Design Aid and Documentation Technique. GC20–185D. White Plains, N.Y.: IBM, 1974.

Jackson, Michael A. *Principles of Programming.* London: Academic Press, 1975.

Martin, James, and McClure, Carma. *Structured Techniques: The Basis for CASE.* rev. ed. Englewood Cliffs, N.J.: Prentice Hall, 1988.

Orr, Kenneth T. *Structured Systems Development.* New York: Yourdon Press, 1977.

Stevens, Wayne; Myers, Glenford J.; and Constantine Larry L. "Structured Design." *IBM Systems Journal,* 13, 2, May 1974, pp. 115–39.

Yourdon, Edward, and Constantine, Larry L. *Structured Design: Fundamentals of a Discipline of Computer Program and Systems Design.* Englewood Cliffs, N.J.: Prentice Hall, 1979.

2. The formal proof has been offered in C. Boehm and G. Jacopini, "Flow Diagrams, Turing Machines and Languages with Only Two Formation Rules." *Communications of the ACM,* 9, 5, May 1966, pp. 366–71.

3. Grady Booch. *Software Components with Ada: Structures, Tools, and Subsystems.* Menlo Park, Calif.: Benjamin/Cummings, 1987, p. 30.

KEY TERMS AND CONCEPTS

Software quality
Software reliability
Software portability
Software maintainability
Verification
Validation
Data flow diagram (DFD)
Context diagram
Leveled data flow diagram
Data dictionary
Structured English
Pseudocode
Decision table
Decision tree
Structure chart
Module
Cohesion of modules

Structured programming
Walkthrough
Inspection
Module testing
Integration testing
System testing
Acceptance testing
Regression test
Computer-aided software engineering (CASE)
Code generator
Object-oriented programming (OOP)
PERT chart
Critical path
Gantt chart
Chief programmer team
Democratic team

QUESTIONS

1. What are the attributes of software quality? What are the relationships among software maintainability attributes?

2. What is the difference between verification and validation in software quality assurance? Give examples of systems that fail one of these criteria but not the other.

3. Give three requirements that we impose on structured development methodologies.

4. Compare data flow diagrams with systems charts, and list three distinctions you consider principal.

5. What is accomplished by leveling a data flow diagram?

6. Which processes shown in leveled DFDs are described in a data dictionary?

7. Name the fundamental logic constructs. At which stages of development are they used, and how are they used in each of these stages?

8. What is the relationship between structured English and decision tables (or trees)?

9. Compare the use of DFDs in structured analysis with the use of structure charts in the design stage—what are the similarities?

10. Why do we seek cohesive modules, loosely coupled with others?

11. What do we mean by structured programming?

12. What is the difference between a walkthrough and an inspection?

13. List all levels of testing and state their objectives.

14. What benefits can you obtain from CASE at this time? Be specific.

15. What benefits are expected from object-oriented programming?

16. What is wrong with lines of code as an estimate of software development effort?

17. What is a critical path in a project?

18. Compare and contrast chief programmer and democratic teams.

PROBLEMS

1. Incorporate a backorder function into the Order Processing System discussed in this chapter. In order to do so, you may modify the data flow diagrams shown in figures 19.5 and 19.6.

    Assume that a system ought to order a preestablished quantity of a product as soon as its current inventory level falls below a certain (also preestablished) threshold quantity. Products are ordered from one of several distributors. State any other assumptions you need to make.

    (*Hint*: Make all the necessary modifications to the context diagram and then modify the Level-0 diagram accordingly. Check whether the two diagrams balance, and modify the context diagram again, if necessary.)

2. Develop a context diagram and a level-0 DFD for an on-line Accounts Receivable (A/R) System. If you have access to a CASE tool, such as Excelerator, you may use it for this problem.

    The A/R System maintains the records of all the invoices you have sent to your customers, both those that have been paid and those that remain to be paid. The system receives two principal inputs: invoices from the Order Processing System (such as the one discussed in the chapter) and receipt records from a Payments Acceptance System. The A/R System sends monthly statements to the customers. A statement lists all the invoices that were outstanding at the beginning of the month, all the payments that were received against these invoices during the month, as well as invoices issued during the month for which the statement is rendered. (You may study a handy monthly credit card statement as an example.)

The system maintains an Accounts-receivable master file, which contains records of all transactions for each customer (who is identified by account number)—that is, records of both invoices sent and payments received. The system also has access to the Customer-file maintained by the Order Processing System, where all the particulars about a customer are specified. When an invoice is paid, its record is deleted from the Accounts-receivable file and transferred to the Paid-invoices file (but make sure it shows up in the proper monthly statement!).

3. Modify the data flow diagrams of the Accounts Receivable System of problem 2 to include an aging function. If you used a CASE tool for problem 2, continue using it for the present problem.

The aging function places outstanding invoices into several preestablished aging categories, such as those that are less than thirty days old, those that have remained unpaid for more than thirty but less than sixty days, and those that are more than sixty but less than ninety days old. Dunning letters should be sent to the customers in the last category. Invoices that have remained unpaid ninety or more days are sent to an outside collection agency. A receipt record is then received from our Payment Acceptance System, or a copy of an instruction to write off the invoice is received from the collection agency.

4. On the basis of the transaction processing system specified in Problem 3, produce a specification for a management reporting system that supports the control of receivables. Specifically, show the data flow diagrams (two top levels) of the resulting combined system.

5. Select a process in the level-0 DFD of problem 2 and produce a level-1 DFD for that process. You may continue to use your CASE tool.

6. Select a primitive process in the level-0 DFD of problem 2 (that is, a process that would not be further decomposed into a lower-level DFD). Present a specification of the process in structured English.

7. Customers often query us on the total amount they owe us. Present a structured English specification for the process that determines the total payment a customer owes our company in the following fashion:

Produce the total amount of all outstanding invoices for a specified customer, considering the following adjustments. Customers who have done business with our company for five or more years receive a 5 percent discount on the total amount of the purchase; those of two to five years standing a 2 percent discount. No discount is offered if there is an invoice more than thirty days old. All customers pay 15 percent interest on any amount outstanding over thirty days.

Customer records, which tell us when a customer first bought our products, are available in the Customer-file. Invoices outstanding for each customer are available in the Accounts-receivable file.

8. Represent the following Sales Personnel Pay policy in a decision table and a decision tree:

The salespeople are paid monthly. The pay consists of the individual's salary and a commission. If a salesperson sells more than $50,000 worth of goods, he or she receives a commission of 5 percent of the sales amount. A salesperson who has been with the firm for more than two years and sells less than $50,000 worth of goods a month receives a commission of 3 percent; on the other hand, a salesperson who has been with the firm for two years or less receives an additional bonus of 2 percent of any amount sold over $50,000. The total monthly pay has to be determined.

Compare how easy it is to produce and understand each of the two documents.

9. Represent the data structure of a voucher that we send to our supplier with a payment.

All vouchers are numbered. The voucher identifies the supplier and states all the invoice numbers the payment is intended to cover. Sometimes we want to enclose a remark on the quality of the goods received.

10. Modify the structure chart shown in figure 19.16 to include the backorder function from problem 1.

11. Produce a structure chart for the Accounts Receivable System from problem 2. Include only the two top levels.

ISSUES FOR DISCUSSION

1. Discuss this proposition: "There is nothing special about structured methodologies. *Any* reasonable, disciplined development technique will produce comparable results."

2. Familiarize yourself with another structured methodology (see footnote 1, in particular—Martin, 1988). Compare it to the methodology described in the chapter.

Several teams may serve as advocates (or prosecutors) for a variety of methodologies.

3. Discuss the differences between data flow diagrams and system charts. Why are data flow diagrams considered an appropriate tool for systems analysis, while system charts are recommended for physical design?

4. Discuss the relationship between structured methodologies and computer-aided software engineering (CASE).

5. Why does the approach adopted in object-oriented programming evoke high hopes? Read two or three articles in the trade press to buttress your argument.

HOW STREAMLINING SYSTEMS DEVELOPMENT WITH A CASE TOOL CAN PRODUCE SAVINGS

BDM International of Kettering, Ohio, a subsidiary of Ford Aerospace and Communications Corporation, is one of the top twenty systems integrators (see chapter 17) in the United States. It reports $5 million savings over a two-year period during the development of an MIS for worldwide spare parts management for its client—the U.S. Air Force. These savings are credited to the use of CASE technology.

When completed, a material requirements planning system will manage for the Air Force an inventory of over 900,000 parts and equipment items, worth nearly $28 billion, and forecast procurement needs for some $18 billion more. Called Requirements Data Base (RDB), the system will serve 5,600 geographically dispersed users. The hardware will include seven Amdahl 5865 mainframes, to which will be linked several thousand Zenith V-248 personal computers.

The Air Force is already using some of the subsystems—the system is being produced in an incremental fashion. The released subsystems include some 1.7 million lines of documented code. When the ten-year, $220 million software-hardware contract is completed in 1994, it will include 3.3 million lines of code.

Approximately 1.2 million lines of the code delivered so far were developed using Excelerator CASE software to support analysis and design. The developers working on those stages use twenty-six copies of Excelerator, installed on relatively powerful Compaq 80386 PCs linked to an Amdahl mainframe. Joint Application Design (JAD) sessions were conducted to validate the products of analysis and design.

The results have been impressive. As compared to the early part of the project, which was not supported by CASE software, error rates in tests done by end users have declined from about 8 errors per 1,000 lines of COBOL code to fewer than 1.2 today. At the same time, project staffing has been cut from 280 to 180 professionals. However, this number now contains a higher percentage of senior designers and software engineers—as opposed to junior programmers, whose tasks have been largely automated by the CASE tool.

Mark Filteau, vice president of the information systems division at BDM, stresses that these results did not come from simply installing CASE software. "If you just drop a CASE tool in a typical chaotic MIS environment . . . it will become shelfware," he says. A far-reaching reorganization was needed to derive maximum benefits from CASE.

Filteau replaced the functionally-based organization of the MIS unit by teams responsible for a complete product. Before the reorganization, there was an analysis group, a design group, a programming group, and so on, and the groups would point fingers at one another when anything went wrong with the product. The reason for the structure was that each subsystem—a unit of development—was too large for a reasonable-sized team to handle. "You would end up with sixty-person product teams, which were much too big for effective interpersonal communication," says Filteau.

Therefore, Filteau reorganized by breaking down the sixteen subsystems of RDB into some sixty products of more manageable size. Each product is being developed by a team of no more than ten analysts, designers, programmers, and other professionals, headed by a manager who is directly responsible for the product. Filteau feels that, to maintain control of the project and of its quality, the size of individual products should be under 100,000 lines of code. A separate test group, which reports directly to Filteau, inspects each product for quality before it is turned over to the end users.

The transition to the new organizational structure is characterized by Filteau as follows: "We went through a very painful period, but morale is now higher than it's ever been."

Filteau claims that the use of CASE can mean greater productivity as well since it makes it possible to employ fewer, though more sophisticated, professionals. "Due to better documentation and cleaner software provided through CASE, projects that used to require ten to fifteen programmers can now be handled by five or six senior analysts." Also, only four programmers are needed to maintain the 1.2 million lines of code produced so far.

CASE also helps significantly with the voluminous documentation required by the Air Force (a 5,000-page manual is required for a 100,000-line software product). Document processing is organized as follows: The manuals are created with Xerox Ventura Publisher electronic publishing package, which merges graphics (data flow diagrams, structure charts, and so forth) produced by Excelerator, descriptions of database elements from Microrim R:Base DBMS, and a narrative text produced with Ami Professional word processor from Samna Corporation (a laser printer—Hewlett Packard's Laserjet—is the printer of choice). Feeding information directly from the development database to the desktop publishing system helps avoid documentation errors.

Based on Mike Feuche, "CASE Tool Saves Firm $5 Million." *MIS Week,* July 31, 1989, pp. 1, 17; and Mary Alice Hanna, "Prototyping Helps Users Get Design Satisfaction." *Software,* April 1991, pp. 43–49, 57–60.

Case Study Questions

1. List all the ways in which CASE means savings, according to the BDM experience.

2. Note that Mark Filteau stresses organizational aspects as the key to BDM's CASE success. What about training and other factors? Would the nature of BDM have anything to do with the emphasis on organizational aspects?

3. Can the positive results obtained in this case be clearly ascribed to the use of CASE tools? Or would you be rather inclined to defend the proposition that effective utilization of a major tool is always accompanied by changes in organizational structure and job design?

SELECTED REFERENCES

Adrion, W. Richards; Branstad, Martha A.; and Cherniavsky, John C. "Validation, Verification, and Testing of Computer Software." *Computing Surveys,* 14, 2, June 1982, pp. 159–92.

Albrecht, Allan J., and Gaffney, John E., Jr. "Software Function, Source Lines of Code, and Development Effort Prediction: A Software Science Validation." *IEEE Transactions on Software Engineering,* 9, 6, November 1986, pp. 639–48.

Anderson, David. R.; Sweeney, Dennis J.; and Williams, Thomas A. *An Introduction to Management Science.* 5th ed. St. Paul, Minn.: West, 1988.

Araki, Keijiro; Furukawa, Zengo; and Cheng, Jingde. "A General Framework for Debugging." *IEEE Software,* 8, 3, May 1991, pp. 14–20.

Arthur Young, Inc. *The Landmark MIT Study: Management in the 1990.* 1989.

Baker, F. T. "Chief Programmer Team Management of Production Programming." *IBM Systems Journal,* 11, 1, January 1972, pp. 56–73.

Boehm, Barry. *Software Engineering Economics.* Englewood Cliffs, N.J.: Prentice Hall, 1981.

Bouldin, Barbara. *Agents of Change.* Englewood Cliffs, N.J.: Prentice-Hall, 1989.

Brooks, Frederick P, Jr. *The Mythical Man-Month: Essays in Software Engineering.* 2nd printing. Reading, Mass.: Addison-Wesley, 1978.

Chikofsky, Elliot J., and Rubenstein, Burt L. "CASE: Reliability Engineering for Information Systems." *IEEE Software,* 5, 2, March 1988, pp. 11–16.

Coad, Peter, with Yourdon, Edward. *Object-Oriented Analysis.* Englewood Cliffs, N.J.: Yourdon Press/Prentice Hall, 1989.

Conte, S. D.; Dunsmore, H. E.; and Shen, V. Y. *Software Engineering Metrics and Models.* Menlo Park, Calif.: Benjamin/Cummings, 1986.

DeMarco, Tom. *Controlling Software Projects: Management, Measurement, & Estimation.* Englewood Cliffs, N.J.: Yourdon Press/Prentice Hall, 1982.

Deutsch, Michael S. *Software Verification and Validation: Realistic Project Approaches.* Englewood Cliffs, N.J.: Prentice Hall, 1982.

Fagan, Michael E. "Advances in Software Inspections." *IEEE Transactions on Software Engineering,* 12, 7, July 1986, pp. 744–51.

Gane, Chris. *Computer-Aided Software Engineering: The Methodologies, the Products, and the Future.* Englewood Cliffs, N.J.: Prentice Hall, 1990.

Gould, John D.; Boies, Stephen J.; and Lewis, Clayton. "Making Usable, Useful, Productivity-Enhancing Computer Applications." *Communications of the ACM,* 34, 1, January 1991, pp. 74–85.

Gupta, Rajiv, and Horowitz, Ellis (eds.). *Object-Oriented Databases with Applications to CASE, Networks, and VLSI CAD.* Englewood Cliffs, N.J.: Prentice Hall, 1991.

Henderson, John C., and Cooprider, Jay G. "Dimensions of I/S Planning and Design Aids: A Functional Model of CASE Technology." *Information Systems Research,* 1, 3, September 1990, pp. 227–54.

Jones, Capers. "Program Quality and Programmer Productivity: A Survey of the State of the Art of CASE." Presentation at the National CASECON, New York City, June 20–22, 1989.

Kim, Won. "Defining Object Databases Anew." *Datamation,* February 1, 1990, pp. 33–36.

Korson, Tim, and McGregor, John D. "Understanding the Object-Oriented: A Unifying Paradigm." *Communications of the ACM,* 33, 9, September, 1990, pp. 40–59.

Loh, Marcus, and Nelson, R. Ryan. "Reaping CASE Harvest." *Datamation,* July 1, 1989, pp. 31–34.

McIntyre, Scott C., and Higgins, Lexis F. "Object-Oriented Analysis and Design: Methodology and Application." *Journal of Management Information Systems,* 5, 1, Summer 1988, pp. 25–35.

Mantei, Marilyn. "The Effect of Programming Team Structures on Programming Tasks." *Communications of the ACM,* 24, 3, March 1981, pp. 106–13.

Martin, James, and McClure, Carma. *Structured Techniques: The Basis for CASE.* Rev. ed. Englewood Cliffs, N.J.: 1988.

Martin, James. *Information Engineering.* (Three volumes.) Englewood Cliffs, N.J.: Prentice-Hall, 1990.

Mills, Harlan D.; Dyer, Michael; and Linger, Richard C. "Cleanroom Software Engineering." *IEEE Software,* 4, 5, September 1987, pp. 19–25.

Norden, Peter V. "Curve Fitting for a Model of Applied Research and Development Scheduling." *IBM Journal of Research and Development,* 2, 3, July 1958, pp. 232–48.

Page-Jones, Meilir. *The Practical Guide to Structured Systems Design.* 2d. ed. Englewood Cliffs, N.J.: Yourdon Press/Prentice Hall, 1988.

Rettig, Marc. "Software Teams." *Communications of the ACM,* 33, 10, October 1990, pp. 23–27.

Rubin, Howard. "Measure for Measure." *Computerworld,* April 15, 1991, pp. 77–79.

Sackman, Harold J.; Ericson, W. J.; and Grant, E. E. "Exploratory Experimental Studies Comparing Online and Offline Programming Performance." *Communications of the ACM,* 11, 1, January 1968, pp. 3–11.

Wallace, Dolores R., and Fujii, Roger U. "Software Verification and Validation: An Overview." *IEEE Software,* 6, 3, May 1989, pp. 10–17.

Weinberg, Gerald M. *The Psychology of Computer Programming.* New York: Van Nostrand Reinhold, 1971.

Withrow, Carol. "Error Density and Size in Ada Software." *IEEE Software,* 7, 1, January 1990, pp. 26–30.

Yourdon, Edward. *Modern Structured Analysis.* Englewood Cliffs, N.J.: Yourdon Press/Prentice Hall, 1989(a).

Yourdon, Edward. *Structured Walkthroughs.* 4th ed. Englewood Cliffs, N.J.: Yourdon Press/Prentice Hall, 1989(b).

Yourdon, Edward, and Constantine, Larry. *Structured Design.* 2d ed. Englewood Cliffs, N.J.: Yourdon Press/Prentice Hall, 1989.

Zwass, Vladimir. "Software Engineering." In *The Handbook of Computers and Computing,* edited by Arthur R. Seidman and Ivan Flores. New York: Van Nostrand Reinhold, 1984, pp. 552–67.

Operation, Control, and Maintenance of Information Systems

. . . .

Recipe for Big Trouble:
Use remote-access distributed data systems to
electronically transfer information among separate
locations. Mix in millions of personal computers.
Sprinkle with a computer-wise generation.
  Rockwell International Corporation

The computer security specialist must think like the
enemy and be as innovative as he is.
  Donn B. Parker

Gentlemen do not read each other's mail.
  Henry L. Stimson, U.S. Secretary of State, 1929

Once successfully implemented, an information system will be used over an extensive period of time. In this chapter, we shall study the principal aspects of this process.

We shall discuss how organizational information systems are operated. We shall see that there are manifold threats to these operations, ranging from computer crime to natural disasters. Next we shall discuss what can be done about these threats: what information systems controls an organization can employ to safeguard assets and to ensure reliable operation. We will introduce the MIS audit function, responsible for evaluation of these controls. Finally, we shall see how information systems can be modified in the process of maintenance to satisfy changing user requirements.

Here are some headlines culled from recent publications:

- "Software Bug Costs Millions at Airline"
- "Burst Water Pipe Forces Extel to Suspend Financial Services"
- "Imaging System Snafu Snarls California Banks"
- "Virus Outbreaks Thwart Computer Experts"
- "Is Nothing Private? Computers Hold Lots of Data on You—and There Are Few Limits on Their Use"
- "Report Finds Fault with Emergency Medical Service Computers: A Power Failure Could Cripple Ambulances"
- "Stray Rodent Halts Nasdaq Computers"
- "Top-Secret and Vulnerable: 'Unguarded Doors' in U.S. Computers Disturb Experts"
- "Chief Improperly Uses Police Computer System to Investigate Job Applicants"

As you may see, a great variety of calamities may befall people who are in any way involved with information systems—that is, all of us.

Here are some more hopeful—though less common—headlines:

- "Managing the Virus Threat"
- "Planning Averts Disaster at L.A. Bond Trading Firm"
- "The Quest for Intruder-Proof Computer Systems"

How do we avoid headlines of the first kind and create headlines of the second, less frequent kind—that is, how do we safeguard computer and communication systems? As we shall see, this responsibility is one of the most vital aspects of MIS department operations.

We shall also see that, once implemented, information systems need to be modified—both to correct problems such as those featured in the first group of headlines, and to adjust systems to changing needs. The process of maintenance is, indeed, much more costly than the process of systems development.

CHAPTER OUTLINE
20.1 MIS Operations
- Objectives of MIS Operations and a Typical Case
- Functions of MIS Operations
- Financial Control of Operations and Emerging Trends

20.2 Threats to Security, Privacy, and Confidentiality in MIS Operations
- Vulnerabilities, Controls, and Auditing of Information Systems
- Information System Security and Threats to It
- Computer Crime and Abuse
- Risk Assessment in Safeguarding Information Systems
- Privacy and Confidentiality

20.3 Information Systems Controls. General Controls
- The Role of Information System Controls
- Types of General Controls
- Administrative Controls
- Systems Development and Maintenance Controls
- Operations Controls
- Physical Protection of Data Centers
- Controls Built into Hardware and Systems Software
- Controlling Access to Computer Systems and to Information
- Controls of Last Resort

20.4 Application Controls
- Input Controls
- Processing Controls
- Database Controls
- Communications Controls
- Output Controls

20.5 Auditing Information Systems
- What Is an MIS Audit?
- How Is an MIS Audit Conducted?

20.6 Systems Maintenance
- What Is Involved in the Maintenance of Information Systems?
- The Dynamics of Software Maintenance

Summary

Key Terms and Concepts

Questions

Problem

Issues for Discussion

Case Study One: How a Maintenance Project Failed

Case Study Two: When Disaster Recovery Planning Proves Its Worth

Selected References

Part Five Case Study: A Process for Information Systems Planning and Development to Support Specific Needs of a Business

20.1 MIS OPERATIONS

Once implemented, an information systems goes into production use—it becomes a part of MIS operations. In the terms we introduced in chapter 1, systems produce information from data. The productive life of an implemented system generally ranges from three to ten years, although some systems last much longer.

Objectives of MIS Operations and a Typical Case

The objective of *MIS operations* is to keep an information system running smoothly: to process transactions with an acceptable responsiveness, deliver reports on time, and ensure reliable and efficient operation of data centers (the physical location of larger, non-personal computers) and telecommunication networks. In face of the general trend toward distribution of the information processing function and the growth of end-user computing, corporate data centers retain their vital role as repositories of corporate databases. Like any other major corporate asset, information systems must be controllable. MIS operations are a major concern of MIS departments. This is very clearly reflected in corporate MIS budgets. A typical such budget is that of Nissan Motor Corporation, U.S.A. Its composition, which is quite instructive, was described by the MIS director of the company, William Congleton (McNurlin, 1989) and is shown in figure 20.1.

As we can see, of the total annual budget of $30 million, $10.3 million is spent on systems and programming (of which 30 percent goes to the development of new systems while 70 percent is spent on the maintenance of existing systems). The remaining $17.3 million is spent on operations. Thus, over half of the annual budget of the firm is devoted to operations—a structure comparable to the budgets of MIS departments elsewhere. In this chapter, therefore, we shall concentrate on the often neglected MIS aspects that consume most of the expenditures: MIS operations and software maintenance.

FIGURE 20.1

Annual budget of MIS department at Nissan Motor, U.S.A.

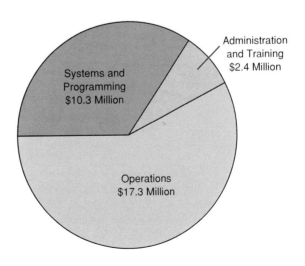

What is it that the MIS department at Nissan (or elsewhere) actually operates? The firm's operations include computer systems at sixty-four locations, including ports, parts warehouses, and sales offices—a typical situation in today's distributed computing environment. They also include the networking infrastructure that connects these locations. A large part of the budget is used up by the personnel at the data centers, where computer and network equipment must be monitored and kept operational, systems software must be installed, production jobs scheduled and run, tapes mounted in drives for the appropriate runs, and reports printed and distributed.

Functions of MIS Operations

The principal concern of MIS operations is to ensure that information services are delivered in an uninterrupted, reliable, and secure fashion. This poses a special challenge in the distributed hardware environment, with today's on-line systems. Another set of challenges is provided by the variety of possible organizational designs for the MIS function, from centralized through a variety of decentralized options, and on to partial or total outsourcing. The design must be selected to match corporate objectives—and this design must be modified as the objectives change.

These are the major functions of MIS operations:

- Data entry: introducing validated data into the system using a variety of data entry equipment (see chapter 3), preferably with automatic data capture at the source, to avoid keyboarding
- Operation of computer systems in data centers, for example, console operations
- Operational support for the equipment in the hands (or on the desks) of end users
- Maintenance of wide area telecommunication links and of local area networks
- Maintenance of databases, including periodic reorganizations for efficiency's sake
- Production control in data centers: scheduling, running, and monitoring jobs, including mounting the necessary tape and disk volumes; ensuring backup; and initiating restart and recovery in the case of operating problems
- Production support: maintenance of data libraries in archival storage volumes (tapes and disks), providing a flow of necessary supplies
- Ensuring the physical security of operations
- Controlled distribution of information output, such as reports
- Dealing with vendors and consultants
- Planning the necessary processing and telecommunication capacities

Financial Control of Operations and Emerging Trends

In administering an MIS unit (or multiple units), the principles of management we discussed in chapters 11 and 12 are applied. In particular, MIS budgets need to be developed and controlled (as discussed in chapter 11). Traditionally, the MIS function has been run as a cost center, which would have a fixed budget and would not be expected to generate revenue. Some firms treat MIS costs as a part of the general overhead. Better control of the quality of MIS services may be gained through a **chargeout** scheme, in which the cost of information services is allocated to the users, preferably in a manner based on the actual volume of use (Allen, 1987). MIS managers generally favor usage-based chargeout

WHEN CAPACITY PLANNING HELPS

Brooklyn Union Gas of New York had been running its operations efficiently with an IBM 3090E mainframe. But its customer information system, needed to track some four million people who were billed every month, was seventeen years old. It was impossible to access the database with query commands.

Finally, the firm decided to rewrite most of the system in a fourth-generation language and assigned ninety developers to the project. At this point, according to Tim Marco, director of IS planning for the utility, "we were afraid that we might not be able to get through the development effort without buying more equipment that we wouldn't need later."

Brooklyn Union Gas hired a consulting firm, SRM Associates of Halesite, New York, which specializes in capacity planning. The consultants estimated the load that would be added on the system during the development. They used Best/1 software to predict future response time based on the proposed increased workload and Crystal system to size the projected application (both from BGS Systems of Waltham, Massachusetts).

The consultants decided that the company would be able to make it through development without adding equipment if some of the analysts and programmers worked second shift until the project was completed.

Based on Marvin Bryan, "Help Is on the Way." *Datamation,* March 15, 1989, pp. 45–51.

schemes to control utilization of computing resources (Choudhury, 1986). However, particular attention must be given to ensuring that the chargeout system is perceived as fair and understandable, otherwise users will find a way to subvert it (Hufnagel, 1989).

A newer approach, preferred by some organizations, is to run the function as a profit center. As such, the function has a variable budget, which depends on the volume of services it sells to users within the organization (and, sometimes, outside of it as well). Users are free to seek alternative ways of obtaining information services, including running their own systems, purchasing packages, or using outside service bureaus or systems integrators. The profit-center approach may not be appropriate for all firms or even for all the services in the same firm, but it increases the efficiency of MIS operations when it is used appropriately.

Later in this chapter, we shall concentrate in detail on information system control aspects other than budgetary control.

Important trends in operations will influence the way this service is delivered in the future:

1. Some data centers are becoming network control centers, managing geographically distributed computing. This calls for higher levels of expertise on the part of operations personnel, while the number of employees decreases due to trends to be mentioned next (Stevens, 1989). The key concern is now broader than running a computer system, however large: now it is running a network of computers.

PHOTO 20.1

A rack-mounted model of IBM Enterprise System/9000 (ES/9000) deployed in a "lights-out" environment. The console is used for trouble-shooting; otherwise, it requires no operating personnel.

2. There is a movement toward unattended operations ("lights-out" computer rooms, such as the one shown in photo 20.1). Replicating the concept of a lights-out robotized factory, the only people who would come into this room will be service technicians. Sophisticated monitoring software, including expert systems which would take care of special situations, would run the computer system.

   One of the principal obstacles to unattended operations is the need to mount transportable media (tape and disk volumes) for archival storage or for periodic backup. Ultra-high-capacity optical media offer a prospective solution to this difficulty.

   The move to unattended operations is taking place gradually (Peterson, 1988). Today, partial automation has been achieved by some firms. For example, software such as AF Operator (from Candle Corporation of Los Angeles) is able to handle most messages, which formerly flashed on console screens to be handled by a human operator. Many technical and behavioral problems remain to be resolved before a network operations center can be run automatically.

3. As we discussed in chapter 17, some firms are resorting to outsourcing, moving some or all of the data center operations to outside contractors.

20.2 THREATS TO SECURITY, PRIVACY, AND CONFIDENTIALITY IN MIS OPERATIONS

The operation of information systems is vulnerable to a number of constant threats—from earthquakes to human error. Computer crime, one of the threats to MIS security, has summoned forth a fountainhead of ingenuity. Controls need to be instituted to counteract these threats, and periodic auditing of these controls is necessary to see that they remain effective. Privacy and confidentiality of information rely on security measures as technical safeguards.

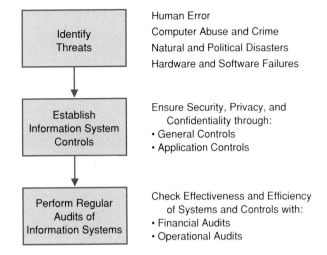

FIGURE 20.2

Threat identification, controls, and auditing in information systems.

Identify Threats

Human Error
Computer Abuse and Crime
Natural and Political Disasters
Hardware and Software Failures

Establish Information System Controls

Ensure Security, Privacy, and
  Confidentiality through:
• General Controls
• Application Controls

Perform Regular Audits of Information Systems

Check Effectiveness and Efficiency
  of Systems and Controls with:
• Financial Audits
• Operational Audits

Vulnerabilities, Controls, and Auditing of Information Systems

Most of today's organizations are dependent on the reliable operation of their information systems. It has been estimated that financial institutions could not survive a total failure of their information processing capacity for longer than a day or two. Electronic funds transfer systems (EFTS) handle immense amounts of money that exists only as a bit stream or as a minute domain on a magnetic disk. Intensive care units and air traffic control systems are dependent on computers to function reliably. When you read a software package from a diskette into a personal computer that handles sensitive correspondence, how do you know the package does not contain a surreptitious code which will send copies of your correspondence to your competitor? Vital systems may malfunction for a variety of reasons, and functioning information systems are the target of ingenuous and high-stakes crime.

It is necessary for an organization to identify the nature of possible threats to its information systems, establish a set of controls to ensure their security (and, beyond that, to also ensure the privacy and confidentiality of information stored in the systems), and then continually control the controls with the auditing process.

Figure 20.2 illustrates the conceptual relationship between threats to information systems, necessary controls, and auditing.

We know that one of the main ways organizations use MIS is as a control tool—we discussed this MIS role in terms of systems theory in section 10.7 of this text. The means of control we are discussing here control the information systems themselves—and auditing is a means of controlling these controls!

In this section, we shall concentrate on threats to information systems, after which we shall analyze the nature of possible controls, concluding with a discussion of the function of MIS (or EDP) auditing.

Information System Security and Threats to It

The **security** of information systems is maintained by measures taken to prevent threats to them, or to detect and correct the effects of damage, should it take place. Such measures include corporate policies, procedures, and technological means that safeguard both the systems themselves and the data within them.

TABLE 20.1

Threats to Information Systems

NATURE OF THREAT	EXAMPLES
Human Error	Wrong input data keyed in Errors in program development or maintenance Operator error (for example, mislabeling of tapes)
Computer Abuse or Crime	Using a system to steal Sabotaging the system Unauthorized access to or modification of data
Natural and Political Disasters	Earthquake, flood, hurricane Fire War
Failures of Hardware or Software	Failure of equipment in a data center Network failure Power failure Systems software malfunction

Information system security aims to protect corporate assets or, at least, to limit their loss (Parker, 1981). Security measures limit access to information to authorized individuals; there can be no privacy or confidentiality of data records without adequate security.

Security measures are often costly, and, moreover, are often at odds with other objectives of information systems. Obviously, the more secure the system, the less accessible it is. This is why we often hear of intruders invading university computers, where accessibility is a primary objective. Likewise, the integration of databases, which may be desirable for a particular business opportunity or for the efficient functioning of government agencies, raises valid concerns about privacy and undesirable "data surveillance" (Clarke, 1988).

Security threats have four principal sources, summarized and exemplified in table 20.1 (partly drawn from Parker, 1989).

While instances of computer crime receive the greatest attention, human error is estimated to cause far greater losses in information systems operation. This security threat should be considered particularly carefully, therefore, in setting up a system of controls.

Disasters such as earthquakes, floods, or fires are the particular concern of disaster recovery planning, which we shall discuss in the next section. One aim of such planning is, for example, to establish an answer to the question: What should be done if our data center is totally destroyed? A contingency scheme is also necessary in case of major equipment failure, such as of the corporate mainframe or of a network (or its segment) that is part of a corporate information system.

The ingenuity involved in computer crime warrants a closer look.

Computer Crime and Abuse

Computer crime is estimated to cost the U.S. economy billions of dollars annually. However, this well-publicized phenomenon still resists definition, and the legal system finds it difficult to deal with its high-technology nature and the novel issues it presents. We may define *computer crime* as any illegal act in which a computer is used as the primary tool.

Here are the more widespread security threats related to computer crime or abuse:

1. *Impersonation:* gaining access to a system by identifying oneself as another person. Having defeated the identification and authentication controls employed by the system, the impersonator enjoys the privileges of a legitimate user.

2. *Trojan horse method:* concealing within an authorized program a routine of instructions that will cause unauthorized actions.

3. *Logic bomb:* unauthorized instructions, often introduced with the Trojan horse technique, which stay dormant until a specific event occurs (or a specific time comes—the instructions may keep checking the computer's internal clock), at which time they effect an unauthorized act. The act is often malicious, for example, erasing files. A well-known case involved a programmer who placed a logic bomb in his company's personnel system; should his name ever be absent from the personnel file (indicating his dismissal), the entire file would be erased.

4. *Computer viruses:* segments of code, which, once introduced by an attacker into a "host" program, are able to gain control of the system and replicate themselves onto other programs in the system and onto floppy disks inserted into the "infected" PC. In this manner, a virus will progressively "infect" "healthy" programs. Viruses may transmit themselves across local area networks, through bulletin boards, and, obviously through shared floppies. They have become a pervasive threat in personal computing.

    Most viruses are insidious, and their presence is not obvious after the infection. In the meantime, they "infect" other programs. After a period of dormancy, the virus activates itself (on the logic-bomb principle) and may display a message on the VDT ("It's Friday the 13th!") or erase all the data files.

    Protection against viruses requires that only original diskettes be used for any program introduced into the system as well as a variety of other precautions, some of which were detailed by John McAfee (1989). Commercial "antiviral" software is available for various virus strains, of which, unfortunately, there are quite a number. The bestiary of viruses and worms (the subject of the vignette on page 824) is extensive (Hoffman, 1990).

5. *Data diddling:* changing data before or during their input, often to change the contents of a database.

6. *Salami technique:* diverting small amounts from a large number of accounts maintained by the system; these small amounts, like thin slices disappearing from a salami sausage, will not be noticed. A well-known example was provided by programmers who rounded down the interest on account balances to the nearest cent—and transferred the accumulated fractions into their own accounts.

7. *Superzapping:* using a systems program that can bypass regular system controls (such as the IBM superzap utility, which gave the technique its name) to perform unauthorized acts. Superzap utilities are provided to handle emergency situations, such as restoring system operation after a malfunction that cannot be handled with a regular recovery method.

A WORM IS A RELATIVE OF A VIRUS

The well-publicized case of a Cornell graduate student, Robert Morris, involved an experiment, conducted in 1988, which he describes thus: "I wanted to see if I could write a program that would spread as widely as possible on the Internet." A program of this type is called a worm: it races through the network, reproducing itself on sites in its way and propelling itself to further sites. However, because of a bug, Morris lost control of the worm (which is an independent program rather than a code segment hidden within a host program, as a virus is). In fact, the worm program spread itself faster than its designer had expected. Because of this programming error, the worm jammed the memories of a large number of computers in the network, bringing whole systems to a standstill.

Internet links some 2,000 data centers and 60,000 computers at national laboratories, universities, and military installations (no classified military research is performed on these systems, however).

In January 1990, Morris was convicted under the 1986 Federal Computer Abuse Act. He was sentenced in March of that year to a three-year suspended jail term and a $10,000 fine, plus 400 hours of community service. The relatively light sentence was prompted by the lack of malice or intent to defraud on the part of the student.

As years pass since the incident, the U.S. legal community is disappointed by the lack of legislation aimed specifically at computer viruses and worms (Alexander, 1991). The legal codes are even more permissive in some of the European countries. Using essentially the same technique as Morris, Dutch computer intruders were openly breaking into Internet computers over telephone lines for over six months—they even provided a television demonstration of an intrusion. Alas, in the Netherlands, there are no legal restrictions on unauthorized computer access (Markoff, 1991).

8. *Scavenging:* unauthorized access to information by searching through the residue after a job has been run on a computer. Techniques range from searching wastebaskets for printouts to scanning the contents of a computer's memory.

9. *Data leakage:* a variety of methods for obtaining the data stored in a system. The data may be encoded into an innocuous report in sophisticated ways—for example, as the number of characters per line.

10. *Wiretapping:* tapping computer communication lines to obtain information.

A top expert in the field of information systems security, Donn Parker[1] of SRI International, stresses that while other types of threats are rather predictable, and therefore can be handled if an appropriate investment is economically justifiable, computer crime and abuse draw on virtually an infinite resource of human ingenuity. As the law of requisite variety (see chapter 10) tells us, a response requires an equally sophisticated system of safeguards rather than a simple cookbook approach, which is adequate, for example, for minimizing the effects of natural disasters.

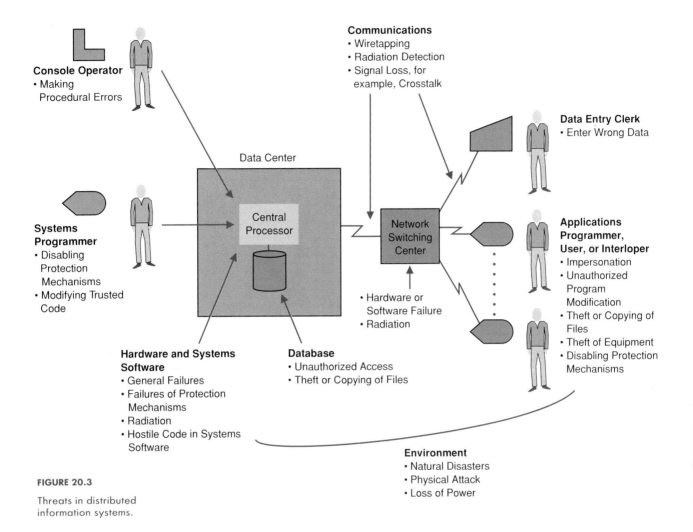

FIGURE 20.3

Threats in distributed information systems.

Risk Assessment in Safeguarding Information Systems

In a distributed systems environment, with virtually every employee of an organization having some form of access to systems, security threats are an extremely serious concern. Possible sources of threats are summarized in figure 20.3.

Once the enormity of security exposures in information systems is appreciated, it is easy to see that no system is perfectly secure and that no MIS manager can devote to this vital aspect of MIS operations the amount of resources necessary to even approach that goal. What to do?

A system of controls can be based on a *risk assessment* procedure. Risk is defined as the product of the amount that may be lost due to a security exposure and the probability (or frequency) that such a loss will occur. A variety of techniques exist for estimating this probability (Parker, 1981). Past experience and estimation by experts with the Delphi technique are some examples. A threat that could occur once a month, with a maximum loss of $100,000, is well worth counteracting with a control that costs $10,000 to develop and $5,000 a year to maintain. Another method of assessing vulnerabilities is a scenario analysis, sometimes involving simulated attacks on the system. A general risk-assessment process can rely on the combination of qualitative and quantitative techniques to estimate risks to the individual activities within the organizational value chain (Rainer, 1991).

Controls which safeguard against the greatest exposures are instituted, including last-resort methods of insurance and disaster recovery planning. The variety of controls available are described in the next section.

Privacy and Confidentiality

Privacy is an individual's right to retain certain information about himself or herself without disclosure, including the right to have any information collected about him or her protected against unauthorized access. This right is not guaranteed by The Bill of Rights in the United States; nor is it constitutionally protected in most countries of the world. Both in the United States and in many other countries, however, a number of legal acts offer varying degrees of privacy protection. In the United States, the most essential legal document at the present time is The Privacy Act of 1974, which protects individual privacy with respect to databases maintained by civilian agencies of the U.S. government; a variety of legislation of concern to business organizations exists on the federal and state levels (Laudon, 1986). Much of the legislation in this area is still being created—it is apparently difficult to keep up with the rapid progress of technology.

In an organizational context, privacy concerns have these implications:

- The right of an organization to indiscriminately collect information about individuals (say, employees or potential customers) may be legally challenged.
- Information collected may not be used for arbitrary purposes, and precautions should be taken to ensure confidentiality.
- Individuals about whom information has been collected have the right to know what information has been collected, as well as the right to review and challenge that information (information collected by credit bureaus to verify the creditworthiness of prospective borrowers is one prime example).
- The management of an organization will be held accountable for improper use of any information.

People whom you suspect of invading your privacy by collecting information about you do not need to be engaging in some kind of surveillance—they may be simply marketers, trying to cater to your tastes. As we discussed in chapter 5, data regarding a potential customer's life-style are a fundamental tool of targeted marketing. Yet, marketers should be aware that the nature of the information they collect and the way it is used may be legally challenged.

Privacy concerns are not limited to databases; electronic mail systems, for example, arouse a similar set of concerns.

We may draw some conclusions from this discussion about what the relationship between security, privacy, and confidentiality is. Comprehensive security safeguards are a prerequisite for the privacy of information stored in a system (Ware, 1984)—however, while such security is necessary, it is not sufficient. Assuring privacy of information requires an additional set of policies and procedures built on the foundation of security. One example of an area of concern is **computer**

A WOULD-BE "COMPUTER TRESPASS"

A former police chief of a major railroad in the northeastern United States was acquitted of charges that he improperly used a police computer system to investigate job applicants and people who were suing the railroad. The indictment charged the chief with "computer trespass" under a 1986 New York State law that restricts the use of confidential criminal justice records. The chief faced up to four years in prison, had the charge been proven.

Based on Ronald Sullivan, "Ex-Metro-North Police Chief Is Acquitted in Computer Case." *The New York Times*, February 23, 1990, p. B2.

---

matching: merging the data from two or more personal-information databases created for different purposes. The Computer Matching and Privacy Protection Act of 1988 offers privacy protection of a limited scope; it does not apply, for example, to computer matching done for tax or law enforcement purposes (Rothfeder, 1989).

Confidentiality is the status accorded to data, be it data about an individual or about a new product development project (Hoffman, 1977), limiting its use and dissemination. Thus, we may keep certain data confidential to enforce our privacy policies; in enforcing our policies, we must rely in part on information systems controls.

20.3 INFORMATION SYSTEMS CONTROLS. GENERAL CONTROLS

Information systems are safeguarded through a combination of general and application controls. In this section, we shall describe general controls, which apply to the entire MIS activity of an organization. We shall follow in the next section with a discussion of controls specific to given applications.

The Role of Information Systems Controls

To ensure secure operation of information systems and thus safeguard assets and the data stored in these systems, and to ensure that application systems achieve their objectives in an efficient manner, an organization needs to institute a set of policies, procedures, and technological measures collectively called **controls.** Some of these controls *prevent* an error or an attack from taking effect; for example, when data are entered into the system, they may be validated to prevent erroneous entry. Other controls help *detect* a violation: a log of all amounts payable above a certain amount will help to detect embezzlement. Yet a third category of controls will both *detect* and *correct* an exceptional situation: when a power failure is detected, an uninterruptible power source (UPS) may automatically take over to maintain operations for a period of time.

A comprehensive set of internal controls must conform with the Foreign Corrupt Practices Act (of 1977), which requires that:

- all transactions be authorized;
- all transactions be recorded;
- access to systems, including access to data stored in them, be controlled; and
- data produced by information systems be correct and verifiable.

Information systems controls are classified as **general controls,** that is, controls applying to the whole of an organization's MIS activity, or as **application controls,** which are specific to a given application such as order processing or accounts payable. The boundary line between these control types is rather flexible—particularly in such new environments as cooperative processing, where an application may be run partly on a mainframe and partly on personal computers. An effective combination of general and application controls should ensure an adequately secure processing environment.

Surveys of actual practices in organizations show significant deficiencies in what the firms actually do in terms of controls. When a development project is late or goes over its budget (or both), controls are generally the first aspect of the system to be sacrificed. General controls can help here.

In a contemporary computer environment, where systems are increasingly developed by end users, meaning that application controls cannot be relied upon, it is particularly vital to maintain a comprehensive set of general controls.

Types of General Controls

General controls cover all the systems of an organization or one of its subunits. The roles played by general controls are summarized in table 20.2.

In the remainder of this chapter, we shall discuss general controls in more detail.

Administrative Controls

This broad area aims to ensure that the entire control framework is instituted, continually supported by management, and enforced with proper procedures, including audits.

Administrative controls include:

- A *published controls policy* which makes it obvious that MIS controls are taken with utmost seriousness by an organization's top management.
- *Formal procedures,* such as a systems development life cycle itself with standards for its individual phases, operator manuals, backup and recovery procedures, and regulations for managing archival data.
- Careful *screening* of personnel during the hiring process, followed by orientation and necessary training.
- Continuing *supervision* of personnel, including paying particular attention to deviations from expected behavior (cases have been known of maintenance programmers parking their Ferraris in the corporate lot without anyone questioning their sources of income).
- *Separation of duties* as a fundamental principle of job definition, so that no single individual would have access to a complete process which could lead to abuse. User duties must be separated from those of the MIS personnel (this places obvious limitations on end-user computing), and duties must be separated within the MIS function itself. The duties of those who use a transaction processing system should be separated

TABLE 20.2

General Controls

TYPE OF CONTROL	PRINCIPAL ROLES
Administrative	Published formal control policies Published procedures and standards Screening and supervision of personnel Separation of duties in job design Disaster recovery planning
Systems Development and Maintenance	Auditing of systems development process to ensure systems controls and auditability Postimplementation audit Ensuring that only authorized maintenance is performed Documentation audits
Operations Controls	Control of access to data centers Control over operations personnel Control over equipment maintenance Control over archival storage
Physical Protection of Data Centers	Environmental controls Protection against fire and flooding Emergency power supply (for example, UPS—uninterruptible power supply) Radiation shielding
Controls Built into Hardware and Systems Software	Error detection circuitry Protection measures implemented as hardware mechanisms Fault-tolerant computer systems Operating systems and DBMS security measures
Controlling Access to the System and Information	Identification and authentication of users Encryption
Controls of Last Resort	Disaster recovery plan Insurance

from the duties of those who maintain it, and the duties of analysts and programmers should be separated from those of system operators. Duties may also be periodically rotated to prevent personnel members from becoming bored and succumbing to the temptation to tamper with the system as a challenge.

Studies of what corporations actually do about computer abuse (such as Straub and Nance, 1990) find that targeted activities to detect this abuse are carried out by relatively few companies. Proactive measures aimed at identifying irregularities and following up on them should be implemented, and the punishment should fit the crime. Indeed, studies show that when security measures are undertaken, they significantly lower the extent of computer abuse (Straub, 1990).

Instilling norms of *ethical behavior* with respect to information and information systems is an important management responsibility. Employees should be educated in morally acceptable conduct (computer ethics, in short)—beginning with the fact that software piracy is wrong (when you are copying a diskette's contents without authorization, you are stealing) and on to the concerns of privacy and confidentiality. It has long been known that the atmosphere where smaller departures from ethical behavior are tolerated breeds larger departures. The code of professional conduct of the Association for Computing Machinery (ACM) offers general guidelines for both MIS professionals for whom it was designed and for the ever more MIS-proficient users.[2]

Systems Development and Maintenance Controls

Internal MIS auditors should be a party to the entire systems development process. They should participate in major milestones and sign off on the appropriate deliverables. Their participation is crucial at the sign-off on the system requirements specifications, when they need to ensure that the system will be not only secure, but also auditable. MIS auditors should also be principal participants in the postimplementation audit. As part of their concern for the system as a corporate asset, they must check that appropriate documentation is developed and maintained.

During system maintenance, auditors need to ensure that only authorized changes are made to the system and that the appropriate version of the system goes into operation.

Operations Controls

Operations controls are the policies, procedures, and technology established to ensure that data centers are operated in a reliable fashion. Included among these controls are:

- *Controls over access to the computer room.* Access should be strictly limited to authorized personnel. Both the personnel who work there and escorted visitors should be appropriately identified. Protective measures include guarded entry, identification using badges or coded cards, sign-in/sign-out registers, and closed-circuit monitors connected to a panel monitored by security personnel.
- *Control over operations personnel.* Procedures manuals should be available, and their instructions regarding running processing jobs strictly followed. Operating logs (console logs), which record all of the system's messages and operator instructions, should be maintained (on tape, for example). An equipment log showing how processing time is utilized, perhaps including data from hardware and software monitors, should also be kept.
- *Control over maintenance of computer equipment.* System downtime due to equipment maintenance should be minimal; only authorized personnel should perform maintenance.
- *Control over archival storage.* All movement of tape and disk volumes should be logged; the volumes should be securely stored.

Physical Protection of Data Centers

Operations controls in data centers must be supplemented by a set of controls that will protect these centers from the elements and from environmental attacks.

Normal operating conditions should be ensured with environmental controls (such as air conditioning, air filtering, humidification, and dehumidification), as required by the equipment. Drains and pumps should be installed in case of fire or flood. Fire detection and extinguishing systems are necessary.

It is vital that emergency power sources be available. A battery-based *uninterruptible power supply (UPS)* should be installed to provide continuous operation in case of total or partial power failure. Depending on its capacity and cost, a UPS will be able to maintain uninterrupted operation for a few minutes to about an hour, which should be enough time to shut down the system without loss of data integrity. Systems that must be operated continuously for economic or functional reasons (such as life-support systems in hospitals) require an independent power generator.

When operating, computers emanate radio-frequency waves which can be picked up by detection equipment located at a significant distance from the data center. The equipment, the wiring, and the computer rooms themselves must therefore be shielded to contain this radiation.

Controls Built into Hardware and Systems Software

The hardware of a central processor contains circuitry for detection and, in some cases, correction of processing errors. A rudimentary example of such a measure is a *parity check:* each byte in storage contains an additional bit, called a parity bit, which helps detect an erroneous change in the value of a single bit during processing. *Echo checks* are performed, for example, when the central processor sends a message to a VDT, which then echoes it back for validation of receipt. Processor hardware usually has at least two states: a *privileged state,* in which any operation can be performed (for example, setting the internal clock), and a user state, in which only some operations can be done. Some computers contain far more elaborate hardware support for ensuring that a running program accesses only the objects (for example, a file or a directory) it is entitled to access.

Fault-tolerant computer systems are important in environments where interruption of processing has highly undesirable effects, such as in securities trading or hospital systems. These systems will continue to operate after some of their processing components fail. Fault-tolerant computer systems are built with redundant components; they generally include more than one processor (in a so-called multiprocessing configuration). If one of the processors fails, the other (or others) can provide degraded, yet effective service. Among the most frequently used fault-tolerant computers are systems produced by Tandem Computers and Stratus Computer (Churbuck, 1991); the VAXft 3000 Model 310 of the Digital Equipment Corporation is a pair of MicroVAX machines, linked by hardware and software, which recovers from a hardware failure in less than one second.

Systems software may contain a wide variety of security features. Operating systems, for example, include a number of measures to ensure controlled sharing of system resources by multiple users, starting with authentication of the user (that is, establishing whether a password belongs to a legitimate user). Database management systems log all transactions before any changes are made to a database to ensure orderly recovery from a failure.

Controlling Access to Computer Systems and to Information

A principal security measure involves controlling access to the information in a computer system. In a modern computing environment, users may access the system from many widely dispersed workstations. Yet we need to ensure that only authorized accesses take place. There are several safeguards that may be used. A variety of rather obvious physical safeguards exist to prevent users from accessing certain terminals. Once a person has gained access to a terminal, more sophisticated safeguards are necessary.

The principal means of access control include user identification and authentication, as well as cryptographic barriers to access by unauthorized users.

1. Identification and Authentication

A user first identifies himself or herself to the system, typically with a name or an account number. The system then looks up the authentication information stored for the identified user and does a double-check. It

NONSTOP ON-LINE TRANSACTION PROCESSING IS BECOMING STRATEGICALLY IMPORTANT

Since Helene Curtis Industries of Chicago redefined its mission from being a low-cost cosmetic manufacturer to being the supplier offering the best service to its retailers, the company has redefined the way it looks at its information systems. To meet the "quick response" demands of the retail industry (which cuts costs by minimizing inventories), a supplier such as Helene Curtis must consider its order processing and inventory management as strategically important systems.

On-line transaction processing (OLTP) is crucial to providing a quick response. And fault tolerance is crucial to nonstop OLTP. The company has placed its inventory management system on-line on a fault-tolerant Stratus XA2000 model 120 minicomputer. According to Tom Gildea, the company's vice-president of business information services (note how MIS is interpreted in his title!): ". . . high reliability is not fault tolerance. Our entire warehouse is dependent on this system. Any delay is intolerable to us. Some businesses can take an outage of an hour or so, but we can't."

Based on Leila Davis, "On-Line Applications Grow Up." *Datamation,* January 1, 1990, pp. 61–63.

requests the user to provide a password or another means by which he or she can be authenticated. The principal means of identification (user's knowledge) and authentication (user's possession or a personal characteristic) are summarized in table 20.3.

The most traditional scheme, using passwords, puts excessive reliance on the user's willingness to select a nonobvious password, remember it, and keep it secret. A simple defense against a person who is masquerading as a legitimate user is to limit the number of repeat trials and trigger an alarm. Many systems, such as automatic teller machines and other electronic fund transfer systems, rely on a combination of a personal identification number (PIN) with other means of identification, for example, a card with a magnetic strip.

Possessed objects may, of course, be improperly handled in a variety of ways. The use of so-called biometric access devices that rely on each user's personal characteristics is growing rapidly.

Following identification and authentication, the user's requests—for example, for accessing database records—are subject to authorization checks (yes, this is a legitimate user, but can she access an employee's medical records?).

2. Encryption

A totally different way to prohibit access to information is to keep it in a form that is not intelligible to an unauthorized user. The technique long used in the three traditional forms of international intercourse—diplomacy, war, and espionage—is encryption. **Encryption,** or scrambling data into a cipher that can only be decoded if one has the appropriate key, has also been pressed into the service of computer security.

TABLE 20.3	MEANS	IMPLEMENTATION
Means of User Identification and Authentication	User's Knowledge	Name, account number, password
	User's Possession	Card with a magnetic strip, smart card (with a microprocessor), key
	Personal Characteristic	Fingerprint, voiceprint, hand geometry, retinal scanning, signature

Encryption renders access to encoded data useless to an interloper who has managed to gain access to the system by masquerading as a legitimate user (and so has passed through the identification and authentication schemes), or to an industrial spy who can employ a rather simple receiver to pick up data sent over a satellite telecommunication link. Thus, the technique is important not only to protect the system boundary but also in the communications and database controls we shall discuss in the next section. The two most common encryption techniques are the Data Encryption Standard (DES) and public-key encryption.

DES in an encryption algorithm most often used in business and government applications that warrant this protection. The system relies on software or hardware implementation of the DES algorithm and on a user-supplied 64–bit-long key. Using the key, the DES algorithm encodes 64–bit-long blocks of data into cipher through a series of complex steps. The receiver applies the same secret key and the DES algorithm "in reverse" to restore the original data. The DES approach based on the 64–bit key has been challenged on the grounds that owners of powerful supercomputers can try all the key combinations to break the code.

A major disadvantage of cryptosystems such as DES, which rely on private (secret) keys both for encryption and for decryption, is that the keys must be distributed in a secure manner. Also, since the keys must be changed rather frequently, this represents a significant exposure. An alternative is a public-key encryption, invented by Whitfield Diffie and Martin Hellman of Stanford University (Diffie, 1976). In a public-key system, *two* keys are needed to ensure secure transmission: one is the encoding key, and the other is the decoding key. Because the secret decoding key cannot be derived from the encoding key, the encoding key can be made public. Therefore, a user can generate both keys and publicize the encoding key only, and thus be able to receive encoded messages. If the recipient wants to be able to authenticate the sender or, in other words, to obtain a "digital signature" for the message, the sender keeps the encoding key secret and makes the decoding key public. To send both secure and authenticated messages, the two techniques are combined (Rivest, 1978), with two keys per user, as shown in figure 20.4. Note that the private keys need not be distributed, and the knowledge of a public key is insufficient to break the code.

Controls of Last Resort

Notwithstanding safeguards, a disaster may strike or an attack on the system may succeed either because management has not foreseen it or because it has decided to accept the risk of this attack. Two controls of last resort—to use the terminology of Ron Weber (1988)—should be available. One of them is

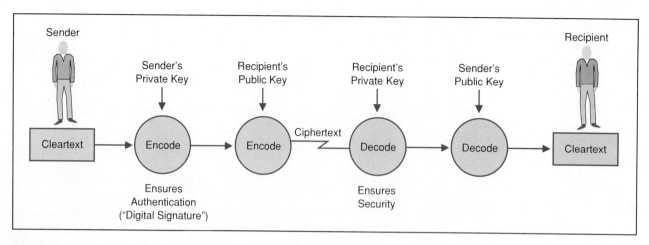

FIGURE 20.4

A public key encryption for secure transmission and for a "digital signature".

adequate insurance for the residual risk (unless the firm chooses to self-insure the risk). The other control is a necessary component of a general control system: a disaster recovery plan.

A **disaster recovery plan** specifies how a company will maintain the information services necessary for its business operations in the face of disaster. A fire or an explosion in a data center would bring the business of most financial corporations (and many other types of firms) to a standstill—information services are, in other words, vital to their operations. In addition, a disaster plan may be required by regulatory agencies or to obtain insurance. Case Study 2 for this chapter illustrates in detail how such a plan was successfully enacted.

In disaster recovery planning, the first task is to identify the necessary business functions to be supported by the plan, since covering less vital functions is, in general, too costly. According to Michael Cerullo (Cerullo, 1981), a disaster recovery plan for these functions should contain four components: an emergency plan, a backup plan, a recovery plan, and a test plan. Here are their roles:

- An *emergency plan* specifies in what situation a disaster is to be declared and what actions are to be taken by various employees.
- A *backup plan,* the principal component of a disaster recovery plan, specifies how information processing will be carried out during the emergency. It details how backup computer tapes or disks are to be maintained and specifies the facility where they can be run on very short time notice. Also, backup telecommunications facilities need to be specified. Some companies maintain a telecommunications link between their data centers and the recovery site in order to have access to the latest data if disaster strikes (Korzeniowski, 1990).
  The alternatives for a recovery site include:
  (1) A company-owned backup facility, distant geographically from the data center; in a distributed processing environment, operations may be structured so that each data center is backed up by another.
  (2) A reciprocal agreement with a company that runs a compatible computer system.

(3) A hot site or a shell (cold site) offered by a disaster recovery firm under contract. A *hot site* is a facility which operates computers compatible with the client's, who may use the site within twenty-four hours of disaster. During an August 1990 blackout, the Federal Reserve Bank of New York was able to move its processing to a hot site nearly forty miles away from the city within forty minutes after the switch was approved (Ambrosio, 1991). *Shells* are computer-ready buildings, available to accept equipment on very short notice. Two leading firms offering such services are Comdisco Disaster Recovery Services of Rosemont, Illinois, and Sungard Recovery Services of Wayne, Pennsylvania; since April 1989, IBM has offered these services as well. A disaster-recovery operations center is shown in photo 20.2.

• A *recovery plan* specifies how processing will be restored on the original site, including detailed personnel responsibilities.

• A *test plan* specifies how the other components of the disaster-recovery plan will be tested. A plan that is not periodically tested through simulated emergencies generally turns out to be useless in a real emergency. Chase Manhattan Bank, for example, follows the generally recommended procedure of testing its plan twice a year without warning.

At this time, disaster recovery planning is becoming part of a broader process of business resumption planning, which aims to ensure that all the activities of an enterprise (and not only its information processing) can be resumed after a disaster.

FIGURE 20.5

Areas covered by application
controls.

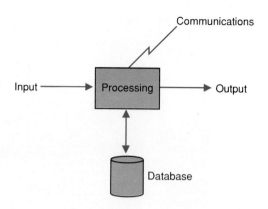

20.4 APPLICATION CONTROLS

Application controls are controls implemented specifically for a particular
information system, for example, accounts payable or an order processing
system. Both the automated, and the manual aspects of processing need to be
controlled. The principal areas of concern of application controls are summarized in figure 20.5.

We shall now describe the principal measures undertaken in application controls.

Input Controls

Data input is an area where most controls are applied, since significant exposures exist to both abuse and error. The purpose of input controls is to prevent
the entry of incomplete, erroneous, or otherwise inappropriate data into the information system. These controls must ensure the following results:

1. Accuracy of Data
   System developers should:
   a. Provide for direct data entry (as discussed in chapter 4) whenever
      possible
   b. If data are keyboarded from documents, design both the documents and
      the screens so as to minimize the number of errors which could be
      made by the data entry personnel
   c. Include in codes that identify transactions and other entities so-called
      check digits, which enable a computer to check whether a code has
      been entered correctly

2. Completeness of Input
   The main tools for checking whether all transactions have been entered
   are batch controls. In a batch processing system (see chapter 4), we
   actually have a *physical* batch of transactions. Therefore, a manual count of
   transactions to be entered may be compared against the count for the batch

FIGURE 20.6

Validation of input.

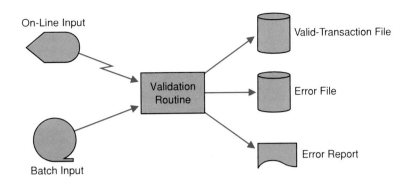

On-Line Input

Batch Input

Validation Routine

Valid-Transaction File

Error File

Error Report

produced by the computer. Alternatively, financial totals for the batch might be compared for the transaction fields that contain dollar amounts. In an on-line system, *logical* batches may be created. For example, each data entry clerk may keep the count of transactions she or he enters, while the system groups the transactions entered by each clerk into a logical batch. The two totals may then be compared.

3. Validation of Input

Input routines, known as edit routines, perform a variety of checks, such as:

a. Format checks (if a customer's name contains digits, the format is improper)

b. Reasonableness of the value (if an invoice amount is over $10,000, it may be considered suspect in the particular system)

c. Code checks, using check digits, as we just discussed. The system compares the code in the transaction with a table of valid codes.

Extensive validation which cross-references input data with the database contents may be performed, if it is feasible in terms of speed and cost.

The result of validation, as shown in figure 20.6, is an error file and an error report for human inspection.

Processing Controls An application system should be developed in such a way that processing errors are prevented from occurring in the first place. But, as we know full well, problems will occur, and controls are necessary. Processing controls include:

• Crossfooting: two independent computations of a total figure can be made and compared. For example, in a payroll program, control totals may be calculated for net pay, deductions, and gross pay of all employees. At the end of the payroll run, gross pay should equal net pay plus deductions.

• Reasonableness check: after an employee's deductions have been computed, they may be compared against a table of reasonable values.

• Rounding off: correct rounding off of financial data can avoid a possible salami-technique attack, as previously discussed.

• Functional checks: this check can make sure you are not sending off an invoice for $0.00 (as many have done)!

Database Controls   Information systems files and databases hold the very data we seek to protect from destruction and from improper access or modification. The following are the principal measures for safeguarding data stored in systems.

1. Backup and Recovery

The primary concern is, of course, to be able to recover a file or database in case of a failure. This concern is addressed by a *backup and recovery policy:* we maintain a version of the database from some prior time and a log of transactions (changes to the database) from that time on. The need to maintain backup files in personal computing cannot be overemphasized.

In a batch system, the master file, prior to the transaction file being run off against it, serves as an excellent backup file. In an on-line system, it is necessary to dump (copy to tape, for example) the database periodically to create such a backup file. To recover from the failure of the database (for example, as the result of a disk crash), logged transactions are run off against the previous version or against the dump.

The common grandfather-father-son backup policy is shown in figure 20.7. The prior master file (grandfather) and the prior transaction file were used during the previous update cycle to create an old master file (father). If a problem occurs with the current father file, the grandfather file is available as backup. After the run, the father becomes grandfather, and the new master file (son) will be the father in the next run.

It is common for organizations to maintain multiple backup versions (dumps) of their database with the corresponding transaction files, some of them in vaults on highly secure remote sites (including former salt mines in Utah). This file retention policy should be clearly stated and adhered to.

2. File Handling Controls

File handling controls aim to ensure that an appropriate storage medium (tape or disk volume) is mounted in the drive. Header and trailer records, as well as the control total stored with the file, serve this purpose.

3. Access Authorization

A certain level of security from improper access and modification is reached by enforcing general access control to the system. Beyond the identification and authentication safeguards thus furnished, database controls include an authorization system (encryption is also sometimes used).

Authorization rules, stored in the system, ensure that users have access to information strictly on a need-to-know basis. For example, as shown in figure 20.8, access privileges stored in the system for payroll clerks would permit the clerk to read the name, department location, and salary of each employee, but no more, while a personnel clerk could access the home address field as well and modify the values stored in any of these four fields.

More sophisticated authorization rules prevent access to a data item depending on its value (for example, the payroll clerk could be prevented from accessing the salary field if the value stored there exceeds $50,000). In so-called statistical databases, the purpose of which is to furnish only aggregate statistics (for example, average values), it is necessary to ensure that a snooper would not be able to get at individual values by designing a

FIGURE 20.7

Grandfather-father-son backup.

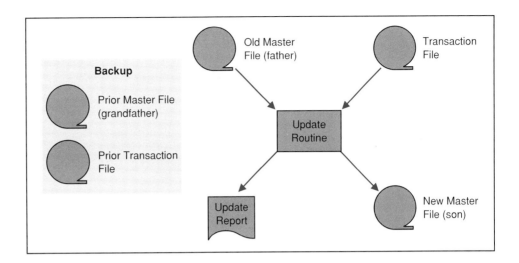

FIGURE 20.8

Access control in databases.

(From Weber, 1988, p. 516)

Personnel Database

Name	Location	Salary	Home Address	Performance Rating
Smith	Production	28000	16 Park St., Anytown	2
Jones	Accounting	22000	2 Odd St., Anytown	4
Brown	Marketing	32000	26 Small Lane, Somewhere	1
Thomas	Research	34000	84 March St., Anytown	1

Read

Payroll Clerk

Read Modify

Personnel Clerk

series of queries (Adam, 1989) and then deducing confidential information from the multiple responses.

Communications Controls

As it has often been pointed out (for example, in the classic paper by Petersen, 1973), communication lines are the most vulnerable component of information systems. An infiltrator can gain access to transmitted information by intercepting radio-frequency waves bouncing off a satellite. By tapping into a line with a terminal, he or she can perform active attacks—inserting, deleting, or modifying messages by masquerading as a genuine user who is currently connected to the system.

The principal technique for securing communications is to render any intercepted information useless to the attacker by encrypting it. Authenticity is guarded by assigning to the messages sequence numbers and authentication codes such as "digital signatures," which are, of course, also encrypted.

Output Controls

Output controls are largely manual procedures aimed at ensuring that the information presented in reports and screens is of high quality (see chapter 2 for a discussion of these attributes), complete, and available only to authorized individuals. The techniques employed include:

- Review of documents and reports by qualified individuals to confirm that output values balance back to the inputs from which they are derived, to check reasonableness of figures, and to perform a variety of spot checks on the printed information
- Making sure that all documents and reports have been produced as scheduled
- Proper report design, including a distribution list, production date, and retention time, and an indication whether special security procedures are to be followed in report handling
- Making sure that the printed output is distributed in conformity with the rules of security (for example, negotiable instruments, such as checks), privacy (for example, payroll or employee health information), and confidentiality (for example, company-confidential data on pricing).

20.5   AUDITING INFORMATION SYSTEMS

MIS auditing has evolved into both a profession and an organizational function. An audit process consists of two fundamental steps, compliance testing and substantive testing, and is supported by extensive specialized software.

What Is an MIS Audit?

The effectiveness of information systems controls is evaluated through a process known as **MIS auditing** (or EDP auditing, to remind us of an earlier name for the MIS function—electronic data processing). The process of verifying an organization's accounting records and financial statements, known as auditing, has, of course, been around for years. Today, it would be unconscionable to render an opinion on the financial state of a firm without a thorough audit of information systems, which are the primary tool for managing these records. Because the expertise required to analyze all the controls is very extensive, MIS auditing has evolved as a profession in its own right.

Information systems are audited by external auditors, who render their opinion on the veracity of corporate financial statements, and by internal auditors, who work for the organization itself. In addition to performing *financial audits* and thus rendering an opinion on the financial health of various corporate units, internal auditors perform *operational audits* to evaluate the effectiveness and efficiency of MIS operations. The requirements of the Accounting Standards Provision of the Foreign Corrupt Practices Act of 1977 have led to a significant strengthening of internal controls in organizations. At the same time, a trend has developed toward strengthening internal auditing as a means of *management* control. An independent audit department, in many cases answerable to the chief executive officer and, in any case, independent of the unit being audited, now exists in most of the country's 10,000 largest businesses (Gallegos, 1987). Such a department now often includes a group that performs information systems audits as well.

The principle behind the auditability of information systems is that every transaction must be reliably traceable to the aggregate figures it affects, and each aggregate figure must be traceable back to the transactions which gave rise to it. In other words, an **audit trail** must exist, making it possible to establish where each transaction originated and how it was processed. Transaction logs provide a basic audit trail.

As end-user computing proliferates, audits of systems developed and controlled by end users are conducted increasingly often. Lack of auditability is one of the faults generally associated with many of these systems—unless appropriate policies and controls are enacted and audited on a regular basis.

How Is an MIS Audit Conducted?

MIS auditors primarily concentrate on evaluating information system controls, on the assumption that if a system has adequate controls that are consistently applied, then the information produced by it is also reliable. They perform both scheduled and unscheduled audits.

At the beginning of the audit, auditors study the information system and its documentation, inputs, and outputs, and interview the key user and MIS personnel. They study both the general and application controls in detail.

Then, the auditors select a sample of the transactions processed by the system and trace their processing from the original documents on to the totals they affect. Auditors replicate the processing done by the system, and if the results they obtain are in compliance with those produced by the system, they gain some confidence in the controls the system is supposed to have. In other words, reasonable assurance exists that assets are being protected and that the information furnished by the system is reliable.

This so-called compliance testing is followed by substantive tests to independently validate the totals contained in the financial records. The extent of substantive testing depends on the results of compliance testing: if controls were found operative, then a limited substantive testing will be sufficient; in the areas where controls were inadequate, extensive validation of financial totals is necessary. One example of an action which may be taken during substantive testing is requesting that the company's suppliers verify that their account payables are represented properly by the audited company.

An audit is concluded by reporting the findings to the corporate management, with a detailed statement of all the control deficiencies discovered.

One would expect MIS auditors to use audit software to help them. Indeed they do. Generalized audit software is available to specify a variety of accessing, analysis, and reporting operations on databases in a higher-level language. Among these packages are Dyl-Audit from Dylakor, EDP Auditor from Cullinane, and Pan Audit from Pansophic Systems. In operational audits, software and hardware monitors are employed to gauge how efficiently MIS equipment is utilized.

20.6 SYSTEMS MAINTENANCE

What Is Involved in the Maintenance of Information Systems?

Operational information systems must be maintained—that is, they must be modified as necessary for these systems to continually satisfy organizational and user requirements. The maintenance of applications software consumes huge amounts of resources. Computer-aided software engineering tools promise to relieve some of this burden.

There is a vast difference between hardware and software maintenance in costs as well as in objectives. The purpose of maintaining computer system hardware is to keep the equipment in working order without changing its functionality. Traditionally, this aspect of system maintenance has been covered by maintenance contracts with equipment manufacturers. But user companies have been opting against this alternative as they seek to lower their maintenance costs. The reasons for this trend are the increased reliability of computer equipment and downsizing of much of the processing to the personal computer level (at which it is frequently more cost-effective to purchase a new model rather than to repair), as well as the use of fault-tolerant designs which obviate the need for an emergency service. Many firms that used to set aside 10 percent of equipment costs to cover annual maintenance now spend only 3 to 4 percent (McWilliams, 1990).

The principal effort in system maintenance is directed at maintaining the applications software. *Software maintenance* includes all modifications of a software product after it has been turned over to operations. You will remember from chapter 18 that the cost of this maintenance over the useful life of an application is typically twice the development cost. The preeminent costs of maintenance are graphically illustrated in figure 20.9, while the next vignette will give you a more precise idea about the extent of systems maintenance.

The perception of maintenance as the repair or replacement of defective parts applies only in part to software maintenance. The principal objective of software maintenance follows from the very objective of having software: to provide flexible systems in the face of changing needs. But there are other, less cheerful reasons, for such high maintenance costs.

Software maintenance actually consists of three types of activities:

- *Perfective* maintenance: enhancing and modifying the system to respond to changing user requirements and organizational needs, improving system efficiency, and enhancing documentation
- *Adaptive* maintenance: changing the system to adapt it to a new hardware or software environment, for example, to move it from a mainframe to a minicomputer, or to convert it from a file to a DBMS environment
- *Corrective* maintenance: correcting an error that has been discovered during operations

Figure 20.10 illustrates the distribution of effort that goes into these three maintenance components, as reported in the classical work by Bennet Lientz and Burton Swanson (1978).

WHAT HAS TO BE MAINTAINED—A FEW FIGURES

The worldwide investment in existing software is estimated at over $2 trillion. Three are 80 to 100 billion lines of (just!) COBOL code being maintained today across the world. It is estimated that $30 billion is spent worldwide on maintenance, one third of that amount in the United States alone.

The average age of a business system in the United States is 6½ years, with some 25 percent more than 10 years old. The average Fortune 100 company maintains 35 million lines of code and adds 3.5 million more lines a year—just as maintenance (not includng newly developed systems).

Based on Melymuka, 1991.

FIGURE 20.9

Software maintenance dominates life-cycle costs of software.

(From James Martin and Carma McClure, *Software Maintenance: The Problem and Its Solutions,* © 1983, p. 7. Reprinted by permission of Prentice-Hall, Inc., Englewood Cliffs, NJ.)

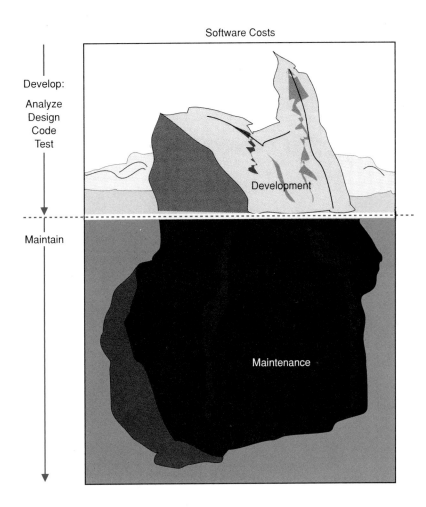

Software Costs

Develop:

Analyze
Design
Code
Test

Development

Maintain

Maintenance

FIGURE 20.10

Distribution of effort in
software maintenance.

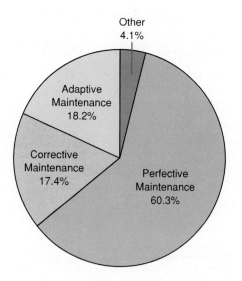

It must be stressed that classification of a maintenance activity is not always easy. In particular, if the maintainers and developers are the same people, there is a strong tendency to disguise correcting an error in systems analysis by classifying its fixing as perfective maintenance.

Even if, as figure 20.10 shows, most of the maintenance resources are expended on improving the system rather than correcting its imperfections or adapting it to new environments, the total maintenance expenditures are nevertheless very high. The effort spent on maintaining existing systems is a drain on MIS resources in an environment where large backlogs of systems are awaiting development.

The Dynamics of Software Maintenance

A maintenance procedure consists of three steps:

1. We need to *understand* the software to be modified and identify the parts targeted for maintenance. This often proves the most difficult task.

2. We must then *modify* the appropriate components of the application system without adversely affecting the rest of the system.

3. Finally, we must *test* and thus validate the modified components, as well as the entire system; in system testing, we use the regression tests we described in the preceding chapter.

If we look back at figure 19.1, we will see that software maintainability is one of the principal qualities we seek when we develop a software system—and that maintainability has three aspects (understandability, modifiability, and testability) that correlate directly with the three maintenance steps. As we stressed earlier, a primary objective of the development process should be to develop software which is easy to maintain.

The high costs of software maintenance today are in large part due to the need to maintain systems that were developed without the use of structured methodologies and that are poorly documented. These systems are difficult to understand. Because such a system lacks proper modular structure and contains

SOMETIMES, IT'S EASIER TO CHANGE LAWS THAN SOFTWARE

On November 22, 1989, the U.S. Congress repealed the Medicare Catastrophic Coverage Act. The repeal removes highly controversial charges that had been added to the premiums charged Medicare recipients.

A week later, the U.S. Social Security Administration announced that it would be unable to modify its systems in response to this repeal until the spring of the following year. The agency ordinarily takes nine months to perform their annual software maintenance, which is necessary to introduce cost-of-living and other regular adjustments to its payments.

As a result, some 27 million of 33 million Social Security recipients would continue to pay higher premiums—until the programs were modified. The total amount of excess charges was expected to top $1 billion. Of course, the agency planned to develop a program to process the refunds; however, it is not the policy of the Social Security Administration to pay interest on the amounts refunded.

Based on Ellis Booker, "Social Security Systems Can't Handle Law Repeal." *Computerworld*, December 11, 1989, p. 8.

unstructured "spaghetti" code, it is difficult to modify one part of it without affecting others, and as a consequence, it is difficult to devise an appropriate sequence of tests to validate the modified system.

In their extensive study of the dynamics of program evolution during years of operation and maintenance, Meir Lehman and Laszlo Belady (Lehman, 1985) stress that as a system is maintained over time, its structure becomes more complex; in order to facilitate future maintenance, active effort is necessary to prevent this deterioration. (In the terms of systems theory, this is a predictable increase of system entropy.) Since a system also tends to grow with each maintenance procedure, this means that the costs of maintaining a system will increase during its lifetime.

Maintenance costs are frequently increased by low morale on the part of the maintainers, with resultant low productivity. This is a consequence of the lower status accorded by many organizations to maintenance work as compared to development. The jobs of software maintainers must be designed properly: their responsibility for a meaningful unit of work and the factors that will signify their success should be clearly defined. Frito-Lay of Dallas holds annual symposia for its software maintainers, where workshops covering the developments in the field are conducted. The symposia have resulted in an establishment of a task force that facilitates sharing ideas, techniques, and tools among maintenance groups in various functional areas of the company. And the work of the task force has, in turn, resulted in changes in the corporate software maintenance procedures—and in increased efficiency of maintenance.

Computer-aided software engineering (CASE) tools are expected to contribute significantly to improved maintenance. In the first place, the use of CASE in development (discussed in the preceding chapter) means better documented systems, with essential documentation kept in a data dictionary and thus relatively easy to maintain. It is possible to trace a user's request for an enhancement from a data flow diagram to the code modules to be modified and thus determine the impact of the change.

Certain CASE tools are expressly designed for maintenance activities. These tools have evolved from the far simpler utilities that have helped programmers to *restructure* programs. Such packages automatically recast a program from a "spaghetti" code, which is difficult to understand, into a structured format that relies on single-entry, single-exit programming constructs. CASE packages are becoming available in support of **reverse engineering:** developing analysis and design specifications from the program code (Chikofsky, 1990). This approach derives from the well-known method of analyzing a competitor's product, such as a new car model. Once a design specification, for instance a structure chart, has been produced from the program with the aid of a CASE tool, the program is far easier to maintain than if the maintainers were faced only with page upon page of code printout. The use of a tool of this category, Excelerator for Design Recovery (from Index Technology), saved some 25 percent of the reverse-engineering effort at AT&T Long Distance Services in East Brunswick, New Jersey (Melymuka, 1991). And if we consider the role of maintenance in MIS budgets, we shall see that our ability to control maintenance costs is vital to the effective cost control of organizational information systems.

. . . .

SUMMARY

Systems operations consume the major part of the budget of a typical MIS unit. Their objective is to ensure uninterrupted, reliable, and secure information services throughout an organization. The possibilities available for conducting these operations, combined with the complexity of a distributed environment, make operations a challenging assignment.

As the very existence of many organizations has come to depend on their information systems, safeguarding these systems and the assets they contain in electronic form has become a major concern. System vulnerabilities should be carefully identified and the systems protected by a combination of general and application controls. The privacy and confidentiality of information rests on the foundation of security measures. No system is perfectly secure, and the appropriateness of these measures should be evaluated in a risk assessment procedure. MIS audits continually evaluate the effectiveness of controls.

Operational systems, and applications software in particular, evolve in response to changing organizational and user requirements. Maintaining an application consumes many more resources than developing it and should, therefore, be carefully organized and controlled. Maintenance projects should be approached in the same fashion as systems development, which we previously discussed in this part of the book. As new systems are developed with the CASE tools relying on structured methodologies, the continuity between development and maintenance becomes more clear.

ENDNOTES

1. Donn Parker, *Crime by Computer*, New York: Charles Scribner's Sons, 1976, fully bears out its subtitle, "Startling New Kinds of Million-Dollar Fraud, Theft, Larceny, and Embezzlement," with one qualification—many other, newer kinds of activities have since emerged. Clifford Stoll describes how a member of a spy ring invaded multiple geographically distant computers in the networked environment in *The Cuckoo's Egg*, New York: Doubleday, 1989. From a California site, the author stalked the computer hacker (who, as it turned out, operated from West Germany), giving the invader enough time—and enough rope—to hang himself (see also Stoll, 1988). The word "hacker," originally used to indicate a person highly familiar with technical intricacies of software systems (if somewhat antisocial) has itself become largely a term of opprobrium, to refer to a person who uses such technical knowledge to gain unauthorized access to information systems.

2. The ACM Code of Professional Conduct is available from the Association for Computing Machinery, 11 West 42nd Street, New York, NY 10036.

KEY TERMS AND CONCEPTS

MIS operations

Capacity planning

Chargeout

MIS security

Computer crime

Computer virus

Privacy

Confidentiality

Information systems controls

General controls

Application controls

Separation of duties

Uninterruptible power supply (UPS)

Fault-tolerant computer systems

User identification

User authentication

Encryption

Disaster recovery plan

Backup and recovery

Access authorization

MIS audit

Software maintenance

Reverse engineering

QUESTIONS

1. Define MIS operations.

2. List five principal functions of MIS operations.

3. Why is chargeout of information system services considered desirable in many organizations?

4. How are information systems controls related to system vulnerabilities and to MIS audits?

5. List the principal categories of threats to computer systems, and give two examples of each.

6. How is a computer virus related to a logic-bomb attack on a computer system?

7. Why do we need risk assessment in safeguarding information systems?

8. In what sense are privacy and confidentiality related to system security?

9. Draw a distinction between general and application controls.

10. State all the categories of general controls and give one example of each.

11. What is the relationship between administrative and operations controls?

12. What are the respective roles of uninterruptible power supplies and fault-tolerant computer systems?

13. Why do we need both identification and authentication to control access to a system? Give an example of a scheme for these from a system you are familiar with.

14. Why is encryption particularly important in a secure *distributed* environment?

15. What are the principal components of a disaster recovery plan?

16. Describe how you would adapt the grandfather-father-son recovery scheme to your work with a personal computer.

17. Why do we need access authorization even though we have implemented identification and authentication schemes? Why is access authorization classified as an application control?

18. Distinguish between the roles of financial and operational audits in MIS.

19. What are the components of software maintenance?

20. What are the three principal steps in a maintenance procedure?

21. What is reverse engineering, and how does it address various steps of maintenance?

PROBLEM

Consider the Accounts Receivable System you produced to solve problem 2 in the preceding chapter. Identify the specific security threats to that system and specify application controls you would employ.

ISSUES FOR DISCUSSION

1. Discuss the relationship between computer crime and abuse.

2. One way to learn about the security mechanisms in information systems is to "hack" a system, that is, to experiment with it for the express purpose of finding loopholes in its protection schemes. Do you believe hacking should be encouraged as a part of formal instruction? Is it legitimate for a professor to award a grade in a systems course, for example, on the basis of how clever a student is in invading a system?

3. From the sources available to you, including the daily press, collect information on an instance of computer abuse or crime. Discuss controls which could have prevented this occurrence.

4. Discuss this proposition: "As more and more systems in organizations' MIS portfolios are developed with structured methodologies, the share of maintenance expenditures in MIS budgets will go down."

HOW A MAINTENANCE PROJECT FAILED

A firm that shall remain nameless had been running for eight years an interactive system for building financial planning models (a DSS generator, in the terms we used in chapter 14). The system was called IFMS and was written in a dialect of FORTRAN. It was run on a rather outdated mainframe computer. The system was accessed directly by its end users. A maintenance project was initiated, with the objective of adding to the system a Report Generator Subsystem, which would greatly expand report editing and formatting capabilities.

The project was initiated by management with the intention of extending the use of an aging software product and at the same time limiting user retraining insofar as possible. The Systems and Programming Group estimated maintenance as an eight person-months effort, based on a similar project that had been recently completed in the same firm but in a different, newer, hardware environment. The Group warned management that the project could be adversely affected by the outdated hardware and the absence of systems documentation for the DSS generator. Support software for the project consisted only of a poor text editor and debugger.

The project was started in February and scheduled for completion in July. The maintenance team consisted of a project leader familiar with the IFMS concept and the user requirements, but not with the computer system at hand; a programmer, experienced in FORTRAN but unfamiliar with IFMS and the computer system; and a consultant, who had been a member of the team which had developed the DSS generator, and thus was also familiar with the computer system "internals," or the details of its operating system and utilities.

Although the consultant was hired to teach the computer system internals to the team, he preferred to design the Report Generator Subsystem. The project leader, who had no management training, felt his authority challenged and became passive. The programmer developed a split loyalty between the consultant, who acted as his mentor, and the project leader. As a result, each of the team members came up with his own ideas for the system's design. Design disputes dominated weekly status meetings but were never resolved. All communications were verbal and issues were frequently swept under the carpet. Project tasks were never defined in detail. System components became the "property" of the individuals who worked on them, and when problems occurred team members would not cross these "territorial boundaries."

Unsurprisingly, the project failed. External help was necessary to complete the Report Generator Subsystem. Completion was delayed until December, forcing cancellation of new product demonstrations and other losses.

Based on Carma L. McClure, *Managing Software Development and Maintenance.* New York: Van Nostrand Reinhold, 1981.

Case Study One Questions

Case Study One Questions

1. What were the technical reasons for this project's failure?

2. What failings occurred in the area of project management?

3. Was the small size of the project a plausible reason for the adoption of an informal (not to say lax) management approach?

4. What was wrong with the team?

5. What software engineering principles and techniques should have been employed—but were ignored?

6. Lay out a set of suggestions which would help a project leader to face this specific project if he or she had a chance to do it over.

CASE STUDY TWO

WHEN DISASTER RECOVERY PLANNING PROVES ITS WORTH

Fall 1989 gave MIS managers in two areas of the United States an excellent chance to prove the worth of their disaster recovery plans. The San Francisco Bay Area was shaken by a major earthquake, and the southeastern states were ravaged by hurricane Hugo. Both ranked among the most severe natural disasters of the computer age.

Heritage Trust Federal Credit Union, a medium-sized financial institution in Charleston, South Carolina, had just signed a disaster recovery contract providing a hot site on August 15, about a month before Hugo blew into town and seriously damaged most of its buildings. The contract had been signed with a firm specializing in such services, which it provided on its Atlanta, Georgia, hot site, an hour's flight from Charleston.

The MIS director at Heritage Trust, Jim McDaniel, believes that this saved the credit union from a nightmare. Soon after McDaniel had been hired by Heritage, an exten-sive MIS audit was performed, and he told the auditor that the disaster recovery plan then in place was unworkable. The auditor agreed. McDaniel investigated several hot-site vendors before settling on Sun Data, Inc. (of Norcross, Georgia), which runs the Atlanta facility.

As in most of the firms affected by Hugo and by the earthquake, Heritage's data center was not damaged, and access to it was unobstructed. But the firm faced a most common disaster—an extended power outage. After Hugo struck, the company was faced with the prospect of up to six weeks without proper electric power (though the power was actually restored in eight days) for its IBM System/38 model 700 minicomputer, which runs the headquarters information systems as well as supporting automatic teller machines (ATMs) at the main site and in five branch offices. But quarter-end reporting had to be done, and 52,000 account holders needed access to their funds to handle the extraordinary living expenses they faced in the devastated city. Regulatory agencies expressed keen interest in the credit union's being able to make the funds available promptly. The executives at Heritage declared a disaster and moved to the hot site.

In the days preceding the storm, several backups had been done so that the system and the data were on tapes. A UPS had ensured no loss of data when the system was shut down. Staff was brought in from the cities to which they had evacuated to put in sixteen-hour days to handle the emergency.

Although the on-line transaction processing system could not be used, the credit union kept its doors open. Transactions were handled manually and then keyed into the system, so that the databases were kept complete. The databases on the Atlanta hot site were maintained via dial-in communication lines from the Heritage branches that still had power. Customers could draw cash—although, without on-line verification, the union had to take a chance that some people did not have funds in their accounts.

The quarter-end processing was done on the Atlanta hot site, and then the tapes were moved back to Charleston after power was restored. There, reports were printed and the on-line system was brought up.

Learning from this experience, McDaniel is considering new options for disaster recovery. He intends to lease a diesel generator that would be available on twenty-four hours notice. Should the processor itself be damaged, Sun Data is under contract to bring in the same model on a flatbed trailer.

Some other firms in the area did not do as well. Another credit union relied on a reciprocal arrangement to use another firm's data center in the case of an emergency. Unfortunately, it found that the system was incompatible with its own. Still others found that their reciprocal agreements were with firms for whom power was also unavailable. The possible effects from such extended waiting range from damaged public relations to bankruptcy. In South Carolina, if a bank cannot process a check before a set period for the return of bad checks runs out, the bank must cover the loss. Keeping the bank closed would cause a loss of customer confidence and a loss of accounts.

In the San Francisco Bay Area, Comdisco Disaster Recovery Services had to face the greatest challenge in its existence: three banks, two manufacturing companies, and two distribution firms declared disaster on the same evening when an earthquake struck, measuring 7.1 on the Richter scale. In addition to the IBM and DEC data centers, two voice networks required immediate backup. The voice networks offer a free 800-number access to customers; when they are down, orders do not come in. One third of Comdisco's twenty-six hot sites were occupied by companies which declared disasters. To add to this, nine companies declared "disaster alerts," which indicate a probability of declaring disaster in the near future.

To relieve the pressure on its hot sites, Comdisco chartered a jet from Chicago to bring in emergency backup equipment for recovery on the customers' sites. In addition, twenty cold sites were available for the use of customers who could fly equipment to them. But, according to an expert, if the California quake had occurred during the same week as Hurricane Hugo, the capacities of the two leading disaster recovery firms, Comdisco and Sungard Recovery Services of Wayne, Pennsylvania, would have been exceeded. Sungard handled the processing for five of its Bay Area clients who had declared disasters. Within two weeks of the quake, all but one hot-site user managed to bring up their own systems.

In anticipation of a future quake, many firms in the Bay Area are moving their data centers from the most vulnerable areas, putting in satellite links to remote hot sites, and performing periodic earthquake drills to test their recovery plans.

Based on John Mahnke, "Planning Saves MIS from Disasters' Wrath." MIS Week, October 30, 1989, pp. 1, 20; Michael Putte and John Mahnke, "Disaster Recovery Firms Rescue Businesses Shaken by Quake." MIS Week, October 30, 1989, p. 18; and Jean S. Bozman, "Quake Threat Still Haunts Data Sites." Computerworld, October 15, 1990, pp. 1, 139.

Case Study Two Questions

1. Describe the components of the controls maintained by Heritage Trust that led to a reasonably reliable MIS operation after disaster struck.

2. Point out what errors some of the other firms made in their disaster recovery planning.

3. How will the described upgrade of Heritage's preparedness affect its performance in the event of a future threat?

4. In the face of a calamity of a scale surpassing the two disasters combined, some firms would be unable to use the hot sites they had contracted for: the sites would be full to capacity. What provisions could be made for such an eventuality?

SELECTED REFERENCES

Adam, Nabil, and Wortmann, John C. "Security-Control Methods for Statistical Databases: A Comparative Study." *Computing Surveys,* 21, 4, December 1989, pp. 515–56.

Alexander, Michael. "Morris Case Impact Slight." *Computerworld,* January 21, 1991, pp. 1, 4.

Allen, Brandt. "Make Information Services Pay Their Way." *Harvard Business Review,* January-February 1987, pp. 57–63.

Ambrosio, Johanna. "Planning Is Key at Reserve Bank." *Computerworld,* April 22, 1991, p. 31.

Cerullo, Michael J. "Accountants' Role in Computer Contingency Planning." *The CPA Journal,* January 1981, pp. 22–26.

Chikofsky, Elliot J., and Cross, James H., II. "Reverse Engineering and Design Recovery: A Taxonomy." *IEEE Software,* 7, 1, January 1990, pp. 13–17.

Choudhury, N.; Sircar, S.; and Rao, K. V. "Chargeout of Information Systems Services." *Journal of Systems Management,* 37, 9, September 1986, pp. 16–21.

Churbuck, David. "Fail-Safe." *Forbes,* April 1, 1991, p. 116.

Clarke, Roger A. "Information Technology and Dataveillance." *Communications of the ACM,* 31, 5, May 1988, pp. 498–512.

Diffie, Whitfield, and Hellman, Martin E. "New Directions in Cryptography." *IEEE Transactions on Information Theory,* 22, 6, November 1976, pp. 644–54.

Gallegos, Frederick; Richardson, Dana R.; and Bortnick, A. Faye. *Audit and Control of Information Systems.* Cincinnati: Southwestern, 1987.

Hoffman, Lance J. *Modern Methods for Computer Security and Privacy.* Englewood Cliffs, N.J.: Prentice Hall, 1977.

Hoffman, Lance J. *Rogue Programs.* New York: Van Nostrand Reinhold, 1990.

Hufnagel, Ellen M., and Birnberg, Jacob G. "Perceived Chargeback System Fairness in Decentralized Organizations: An Examination of Issues." *MIS Quarterly,* 13, 4, December 1989, pp. 415–29.

Korzeniowski, Paul. "How to Avoid Disaster with a Recovery Plan." *Software,* February 1990, pp. 46–55.

Laudon, Kenneth C. *Dossier Society: Value Choices in the Design of National Information Systems.* New York: Columbia University Press, 1986.

Lehman, Meir M., and Belady, Laszlo. *Program Evolution: Process of Software Change.* London: Academic Press, 1985.

Lientz, B. P.; Swanson, E. B.; and Tompkins, G. E. "Characteristics of Application Software Maintenance." *Communications of the ACM.* 21, 6, June 1978, pp. 466–71.

McAfee, John. "The Virus Cure." *Datamation,* February 15, 1989, pp. 29–40.

McNurlin, Barbara, and Sprague, Ralph H., Jr. (eds.) *Information Systems Management in Practice.* 2d ed. Englewood Cliffs, N.J.: Prentice Hall, 1989.

McWilliams, Gary. "If It Ain't Broke, Why Pay to Fix It?" *Business Week,* March 5, 1990, pp. 82–84.

Markoff, John. "Dutch Computer Rogues Infiltrate American Systems with Impunity." *The New York Times,* April 21, 1991, pp. 1, 29.

Martin, James, and McClure, Carma. *Software Maintenance: The Problem and Its Solutions.* Englewood Cliffs, N.J.: Prentice Hall, 1983.

Melymuka, Kathleen. "Managing Maintenance: The 4,000–Pound Gorilla." *CIO,* March 1991, pp. 74–82.

Parker, Charles S. *Management Information Systems: Strategy and Action.* New York: McGraw-Hill, 1989.

Parker, Donn B. *Computer Security Management.* Reston, Va.: Reston, 1981.

Petersen, H. E., and Turn, R. "System Implications of Information Privacy." In *Security and Privacy in Computer Systems,* edited by Lance J. Hoffman. Los Angeles: Melville, 1973, pp. 76–95.

Peterson, Robert O. "Data Center Depopulation." *Datamation,* December 1, 1988, pp. 49–57.

Rainer, Rex K., Jr.; Snyder, Charles A.; and Carr, Houston H. "Risk Analysis for Information Technology." *Journal of Management Information Systems,* 8, 1, Summer 1991, pp. 129–47.

Rivest, R. L.; Shamir, A.; and Adleman, L. "A Method for Obtaining Digital Signatures and Public-Key Cryptosystems." *Communications of the ACM,* February 1978, pp. 120–26.

Rothfeder, Jeffrey. "Is Nothing Private?" *Business Week,* September 4, 1989, pp. 74–82.

Stevens, Lawrence. "The Open Data Center." *Datamation,* August 1, 1989, pp. 55–56.

Stoll, Clifford. "Stalking the Wily Hacker." *Communications of the ACM,* 31, 5, May 1988, pp. 484–97.

Straub, Detmar W. "Effective IS Security: An Empirical Study." *Information Systems Research,* 1, 3, September 1990, pp. 255–76.

Straub, Detmar W., Jr., and Nance, William D. "Discovering and Disciplining Computer Abuse in Organizations: A Field Study." *MIS Quarterly,* 14, 1, March 1990, pp. 45–55.

Ware, Willis H. "Information Systems Security and Privacy." *Communications of the ACM,* 27, 4, April 1984, pp. 315–21.

Weber, Ron. *EDP Auditing: Conceptual Foundations and Practice.* 2d ed. New York: McGraw-Hill, 1988.

PART FIVE CASE STUDY

INFORMATION SYSTEMS PLANNING AND DEVELOPMENT TO SUPPORT THE SPECIFIC NEEDS OF A BUSINESS

Out of a variety of methodologies and techniques for planning and developing information systems, an organization can craft a process that suits its specific needs. An excellent example of such a customized process has been enacted at Southwestern Ohio Steel, a medium-sized company headquartered in Hamilton, Ohio.

1. The Firm and Its Objectives
   Southwestern Ohio Steel (SOS) is a steel service company employing 400 people. Such a

company purchases steel of differing quality from major steel producers and distributes it, usually after some processing, to its customers. Service orientation pervades the culture of the firm.

SOS management was prompted to review the organizational MIS function owing to the following factors:

• A significant growth of business was forecast. The traditional competitive strength of SOS, providing customized steel materials quickly to help its customers reduce costly inventories, was the decisive factor in this growth forecast, as more actual or potential SOS customers were adopting just-in-time delivery methods and thus keeping almost no inventory. Material requirements planning (MRP) and manufacturing requirements planning (MRP II) systems used by the customers increasingly called for deliveries of smaller lots, sometimes overnight.

- The existing SOS information systems base was limited to transaction processing systems supporting only the accounting function.
- The management team was changing. A need emerged to use systems to formalize organizational practices introduced over the years by key executives now going into retirement.

2. A Failed First Attempt to Solve the Problem

SOS management turned to the company's accounting firm for a solution. They received a proposal that called for the implementation of several conventional on-line transaction processing systems which would process orders, track inventory, and so forth. The estimated cost was $2.4 million over four years, with major benefits available only after the fourth year. Management wisely rejected the proposal, because of the cost, time frame, and business risk.

The main reason, however, that SOS management looked elsewhere for a solution was the absence of any linkage between the proposed information systems and the business needs at hand. To quote Thomas Heldman, the SOS chief financial officer: "I wasn't quite sure what I wanted. But I knew that there had to be a more creative approach toward assisting top management to understand its systems needs and to bring up systems more quickly, with reduced risk and costs."

The three-phase process for planning and developing information systems for SOS was subsequently developed by Index Systems, a Cambridge, Massachusetts consultancy.

3. The Process Adopted for Information Systems Planning and Development

The three-phase process begins with establishing information requirements linked to business needs and leads to systems development, as shown in figure V.1. The vital goals of the process are

- establishing the informational needs of SOS in close relationship to the firm's business needs;
- involving management in the entire process; and
- fielding the needed information systems or their components as early as possible.

During the first phase of the process, management clearly defined the business of SOS and stated its critical business functions. An initial statement concerning the information systems needed to support these functions was developed.

The second phase was aimed at ensuring that the information systems would support key decisions and create confidence in the proposed systems.

FIGURE V.1

A customized process for systems planning and development.

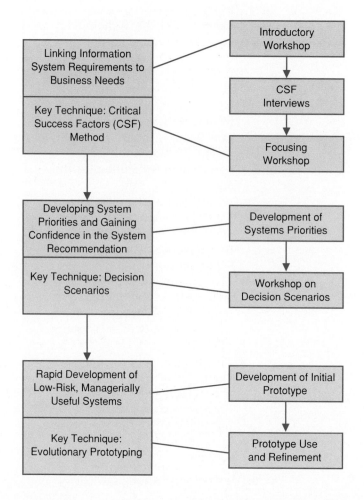

The third phase consisted in developing systems via a prototyping approach, with the explicit goal of using initial prototypes as actual applications. Aside from the obvious benefit of providing operational systems early in the process, this step raised the comfort level of management.

We shall now review how the process was conducted in more detail.

4. Phase One: Linking Information Systems Requirements to Business Needs

During the introductory workshop, the consultants presented the entire process to the five key company executives.

A managerial perspective for systems development was established, namely, deriving system requirements from the needs related to managing the vital business activities.

The key technique employed in this phase was that of critical success factors (CSFs), which was employed during a subsequent series of interviews with five key executives and ten other managers. Each manager explicitly stated what he (as it happened, they were all male) believed was critical to his own job and to the firm. The consultants acquired a keen understanding of the business and of the organizational culture.

During the focusing workshop that was held to conclude the first phase, the consultants presented a "strawman," which they had constructed, of corporate missions, objectives, and CSFs. It served as a point of departure for a heated discussion—hidden assumptions and agendas came to the surface.

Out of forty CSFs initially suggested for the company, the workshop participants crafted four:

- Maintaining excellent supplier relationships
- Maintaining or improving customer relationships
- Merchandising available inventory to its most value-added use (that is, putting the available inventory to use in a way that would enable SOS to make the most money by processing the steel)
- Utilizing available human resources, capital, and inventory effectively and efficiently

Measures for each CSF were then developed. Thus, for example, "Customer Relationships" were operationalized in terms of thirteen measures, such as volume, number of inquiries, customer turnover, on-time delivery, and so forth.

5. Phase Two: Developing System Priorities and Confidence Gaining

Based on the outcome of the first phase, the consultants identified three systems necessary to support management of the SOS business. These were:

- An inventory management system (that would also support the buying process)

- A steel marketing system
- A production scheduling system

Each of these systems significantly affected the firm's CSFs.

The phase concluded with a workshop enacting decision scenarios. In their preparation for the workshop, the consultants observed the daily activities of the key managers and noted recurring decisions these managers had to make and the questions they had to ask (the information they needed) to make the decisions. From these "decision situations," the consultants developed a set of decision scenarios.

A decision scenario lists an event requiring a managerial decision (for example, an offer from a supplier to purchase a quantity of a particular kind of steel at a certain price), and the questions the manager must ask to make that decision (for instance, "What are our inventory levels for this type of steel? What is our order volume for the products we make of this steel?") In the workshop, the managers went through these scenarios, learning which questions would be answered by the three proposed systems and which would have to be answered by other means. They affirmed the appropriateness of the systems.

During the last of the three workshop sessions, participants discussed the information technology needed to support the systems, includng the expected transaction volumes.

6. Phase Three: Systems Development via Prototyping

The right type of prototype was selected for each of the three systems.

The inventory system was prototyped with a pilot system: complete management of a separable segment of the inventory (about 15 percent) was computerized. The marketing system was implemented as a data-analysis DSS, supported by a database which in the prototype version included data on actual and potential customers, open orders, and accounts receivable. The prototype of the production scheduling system was designed to provide only some of the ultimate functionality of the full system.

The principal advantage of the prototyping approach was described by one of the executives: "Managers at all levels are also concerned about the risk in the development of a nonviable system to which the company is committed because of the expenditure. For some, it is only when they realize that they can get their hands on the prototype at an early stage and assess its utility before going forward that they can relax."

The prototypes of the three on-line systems were implemented by the SOS staff (plus one outside programmer) on a minicomputer with the use of the RPGIII programming language. The prototypes were made available quickly. Thus, the prototype of the inventory management system became available in two months. After three months, new functionality was added, and yet more was added after six months.

7. What Has Been Accomplished?

The systems are used by operational and management personnel at all levels of the company. Though some scheduled reports are furnished, most interaction with the systems occurs via menu-based query processing.

The process brought significant benefits to the firm on several levels. Among the results of the process were:

- Operational and management benefits in computerizing inventory, marketing, and production scheduling. Order status can be accessed on-line and the relationship with a customer analyzed. More accurate inventory control helps manage slow-moving items. Improved production scheduling makes it possible to foresee potential problems.
- The company management gained a better understanding of the relationships among various aspects of the company's business, of the factors critical for its success— and of the benefits to be derived from daily use of a computer workstation.
- Further development and broader use of the corporate MIS has been progressing since the consultants' intervention.

Instead of a costly proposal that was wisely rejected by the management of the medium-sized company, "we have achieved in nine months at far lower cost [and at a far less risk] what we expected would take six years under the previously proposed plan," says a company executive.

Based on John F. Rockart and Adam D. Crescenzi, "A Process for the Rapid Development of Systems in Support of Managerial Decision-Making," CISR WP #104, Center for Information Systems Research, Sloan School of Management, MIT, June 1983. See also John F. Rockart and

Adam D. Crescenzi, "Engaging Top Management in Information Systems Planning and Development: A Case Study," In *The Rise of Managerial Computing*, edited by John F. Rockart and Christine V. Bullen. Homewood, Ill.: Dow Jones-Irwin, 1986.

Cast Study Questions

1. What are the principal distinctions between the unsuccessful proposal rejected by the SOS management and the successful process they adopted?

2. The process was clearly driven by the firm's top management. Is this always possible? Is it always desirable?

3. Do you believe this process can work for other medium-sized companies? Why or why not?

4. Discuss the customized MIS planning and development process adopted by SOS in the context of the general process we presented in chapter 17 (see figure 17.9). Who were the key agents in the overall process? (Compare your answer with figure 17.10.)

5. What are the potential drawbacks of the prototyping approach adopted in the development phase? What could be done to counteract these disadvantages?

Algorithm A procedure for solving a problem.

Application controls *Controls* implemented specifically for a particular information system (contrasted with *general controls*).

Application generator A fourth-generation language that makes it possible to specify an entire application at a high level of abstraction (avoiding detailed specification of *how* the various tasks are to be done).

Applications software Programs that directly assist end users in their functions.

Architecture The information system architecture of an organization is a general model of the desired structure of the organization's information systems.

Arithmetic-logic unit The subunit of a computer's central processing unit that performs computations and logical operations (such as AND, for example).

Artificial intelligence (AI) The field of study and practice concerned with methods of developing programs (or software-hardware systems) that display aspects of intelligent behavior.

Assembler A systems program that translates programs written in the *assembly language* of a computer into its *machine language*.

Assembly language A low-level programming language that represents a simple encoding of the machine language of a computer.

Audit trail A record that makes it possible to establish where each transaction in an information system originated and how it was processed.

Authentication Double-checking that the user who has identified himself or herself to the system has the right to access the system. The principal means are a possession or a personal characteristic.

Backup In relation to data and software, maintaining copies of data and programs in order to recover from a system failure.

Backward chaining In expert systems, an inferencing (reasoning) process that moves from a possible conclusion to the premises that would satisfy it. The purpose of backward chaining is to see whether the facts of the case are such premises (contrasted with *forward chaining*).

Bar code An encoding in which vertical bars of various widths represent characters.

Batch processing Processing of programs or transactions in batches, with the interaction with a user (opposite of *on-line processing*).

Bit Short for "binary digit," this is the smallest unit of information representation, with a value of either 0 or 1.

Boundary spanning Acquiring information about the organization's environment.

Brainstorming A group problem-solving technique for generating ideas.

Break-even analysis Comparison of revenues from the sales of a product or service with the costs incurred in producing it to identify the point where revenues match costs (the break-even point).

Budget Specification of resources committed to a plan for a given project or time period.

Business reengineering Radical redesign of business processes in order to increase productivity, followed by equipping the new processes with the appropriate information technology.

Business Systems Planning (BSP) A comprehensive methodology for enterprise-wide strategic planning of the information resource.

Byte A sequence of eight bits, used to represent a character (one of a possible 256 printable or control characters available in the character set). Generally, a byte is the smallest unit that can be accessed in the main memory of a computer.

Cache memory Small and fast memory, contained in the central processing unit, which is used to speed up accesses to the main memory.

CASE See *computer-aided software engineering.*

CD-ROM Compact Disk-Read Only Memory, an optical disk used to distribute factory-recorded information. Used in multimedia publishing.

Central processing unit (CPU) The unit of the computer that controls all the other units by executing machine instructions.

Champion The person who "sells" a new technology throughout the company.

Chargeback (chargeout) Charging information system users for applications development or for the use of system resources.

Chief information officer (CIO) The title accorded to the top MIS manager in some organizations.

Chief programmer team An organization of a software development team around an outstanding performer who does most of the essential work.

Client/server networks Computer networks in which certain nodes (servers) are dedicated to performing services (such as printing or database management) in behalf of the nodes (clients) accessed by the users.

COBOL The preeminent high-level language used for business applications.

Cognition Processes of acquiring knowledge.

Cognitive styles The distinct ways in which people gather and evaluate information.

Common carrier A company licensed by the government to provide communication services to the public.

Communication medium The means by which a communication channel is implemented (for example, a twisted pair or a fiber optic cable).

Compiler A systems program which translates a program in a high-level language in its entirety into binary code ready for execution.

Computer A general-purpose processor of symbolic information.

Computer-aided software engineering (CASE) A technology that offers tools for automating important aspects of the software development process.

Computer conferencing Computer-based technology for supporting meetings.

Computer-integrated manufacturing (CIM) A very complex system that integrates the information systems supporting the design, engineering, and production processes with those supporting other business functions of the manufacturer.

Computer matching Merging the data from two or more personal-information databases which had been created for different purposes. Raises privacy concerns.

Computer network In a distributed system, computers, terminals and other equipment, as well as the communications links connecting them.

Computer-supported cooperative work Knowledge work in workgroups supported by *groupware.*

Confidentiality Status accorded to data to limit its use and dissemination.

Control In management, comparing the actual results of operations against planned objectives and taking actions based on deviations from the plan.

Controls In the area of information systems, a set of policies, procedures, and technological measures that safeguard assets and their accurate accounting, as well as safeguard the data stored in the systems.

Cooperative processing   Splitting an application into tasks that run on more than one type of computer, typically a micro and a mainframe (or a mini).

Coordination   Harmonizing people in an organization in a common action or effort; the exchange of information (communication) plays a major role in this process.

Cost-benefit analysis   Estimating and comparing the costs of a project (such as the development of an information system) and the projected benefits from it.

Cost leadership   A competitive strategy relying on a company's ability to offer its product or service at a cost significantly lower than that of its competitors.

Critical success factors (CSF) methodology   A methodology for establishing informational requirements based on the need to support critical success factors: the critical activities that an organization must perform properly to meet its objectives.

Cylinder   A set of tracks on a magnetic disk which may be accessed without moving the access mechanism. Includes all the same tracks from all the recording surfaces of a disk.

Data   A collection of values of various types (numbers, characters, and so on) that are used by information systems to produce *information*.

Data administration   An organizational function responsible for database planning and for establishing policies for accessing and maintaining databases.

Database   An integrated collection of persistent data that serves a number of applications in an enterprise.

Database administration   An organizational function responsible for the technical aspects of establishing and maintaining databases, in line with the policies laid down by the *data administration*.

Database machine   A computer designed specifically for providing fast access to large databases.

Database management system (DBMS)   A systems software that makes it possible to create, access, maintain, and control databases.

Data definition language (DDL)   A language for defining database objects; furnished by a DBMS.

Data dictionary   A tool for describing the contents of a database or, more generally, for describing the entire system under development. The actual repository of such data is also referred to as a data dictionary.

Data element   See *field*.

Data flow diagram (DFD)   A principal tool of structured systems analysis, used to show the flows of data into the system, their transformation and storage, and the flows leaving the system—on several levels of detail.

Data manipulation language (DML)   A language for manipulating data in a database, furnished by a DBMS. A DML is used to access records, change values of their attributes, and delete or insert records.

Decision support systems (DSS)   Interactive information systems that assist a decision maker in approaching ill-structured problems by offering analytical models and access to databases.

Decision table   A tabular specification of actions that are to be carried out when given conditions exist.

Decision tree   A graphical tool that assists the decision maker in making a series of decisions or evaluating several increasingly detailed aspects of a problem.

Decoupling   Reducing the intensity of interactions between subsystems and thus making them more independent.

Delphi technique   A group decision-making technique generally used for forecasting.

Demand pull   Influence of the needs of the marketplace on organizational innovation. Thus, technologies are most often adopted to solve specific problems, rather than because of their availability, as when *technology pull* prevails.

Departmental computing   Decentralized structure of an organizational MIS function in which most of the MIS activity takes place in the subunits of the firm, with the central MIS department playing a coordinating role.

Desktop publishing   Use of microcomputer-based systems to produce camera-ready, near typeset-quality copy.

Differentiation   A competitive strategy relying on distinguishing a company's product or service from that of the competition.

Digital communications   End-to-end telecommunications of digital signals—the expected future global telecommunications.

Digital image processing   Storing document images in a digital form in computer memory and manipulating them in that form.

Direct access   Accessing a record directly by its key (an identifying field value) rather than sequentially from the beginning of the file.

Direct data entry   Entering data directly into a database at the point of data capture, avoiding keyboarding.

Direct file organization   Storing file records for *direct access* (by employing a hashing technique).

Disaster recovery plan   A plan that specifies how an organization will maintain information services in the face of a disaster.

Distributed database   A database that is stored in several locations.

Distributed processing systems   Computer systems with a number of processors that communicate over a telecommunications network.

Downloading   Extracting data from a database located in a shared mainframe or minicomputer system and transferring it to a microcomputer (opposite of *uploading*).

EDP auditing   See *MIS auditing*.

Electronic data interchange (EDI)   Direct transmission of transaction data between transaction processing systems, replacing paperwork and repeated data entry.

Electronic document management   Computerized systems for entering, storing, retrieving, and possibly updating documents.

Electronic information services   Commercial services that provide access to a variety of general or specialized databases.

Electronic mail (E-mail)   A system that enables knowledge workers to exchange messages over their computer workstations.

Electronic meeting systems   An environment based on information technology to support group collaboration and meetings, which may be distributed in space and time.

Emerging Technologies group   An organizational unit charged with the task of identifying appropriate new information technologies and initiating their implementation.

Encryption   Scrambling information stored and communicated in a computer system in a cipher that can be decoded only if one has the appropriate key. A principal security measure.

End user   An individual who uses the information produced by an MIS application in his or her work.

End-user computing   The practice of having end users develop, use directly, and control their own information systems.

Enterprise analysis   Developing a strategic plan for the organizational information resource by identifying the data needs of various business processes (as in the *Business Systems Planning* methodology).

Entity-relationship diagram   A data model that shows entities represented in a database and the relationships among them.

Exception reports   Reports produced only when "out-of-bounds" conditions occur.

Executive information systems (EIS)   Information systems which provide higher-level managers with direct and easy access to aggregated information and detailed data.

Expert system   A system employing a knowledge base and an inferencing procedure to solve problems within its particular domain that would otherwise require human competence or expertise.

Expert system shell   A tool for expert system development; an expert system with an empty knowledge base.

Explanation facility   In expert systems, this facility explains how the system has arrived at its conclusion (recommendation).

Fault-tolerant computer systems   Systems that continue to operate after some of their components fail (they include redundant components).

Feasibility study   The first stage of the system development life cycle, the objective of which is to establish whether the proposed system is feasible and desirable.

Feedback   Informational inputs to the system to indicate variances from planned performance.

Feedback loop   Feeding some of the transformed system outputs back as the system's inputs to control performance. In organizational control, an information system monitors the firm's performance (outputs) by comparing it with plans; undesirable variances may be translated into corrective actions (inputs) by management—thus, the information system is in the (negative) feedback loop.

Feedforward   Informational inputs to a system to indicate projected variances from planned future performance in order to correct performance proactively.

Fiber optics   A very-high-capacity communication medium: a cable of thin strands of pure glass, over which data are sent as light-beam pulses.

Field (data element)   The smallest named unit of data.

File   (1) Data file: a collection of records of the same type. (2) A named unit of information maintained in a secondary storage, such as a text, program, or data file.

FLOPS   Floating-point operations per second: a measure of supercomputer speed; a 1 GFLOPS ("gigaflops") machine can perform a billion arithmetic operations per second.

Forecasting   Predicting future outcomes, generally for planning purposes.

Formal information system   A system relying on established procedures for collecting, storing, processing, and accessing data to obtain information.

Forward chaining   In expert systems, the process of inferencing (reasoning) that moves from the facts of the case to the conclusion (contrasted with *backward chaining*).

Fourth-generation language (4GL)   A very-high-level programming language that permits the programmer or user to specify what is wanted from the computer rather than how this result should be obtained. Many of these languages are directly employed by end users.

Front-end processor   A computer that handles all the message traffic in behalf of a larger computer (a host) in a computer network.

Functional departmentation   Subdividing an organization by grouping activities in accordance with the functions of the enterprise (for example, marketing, production, and finance).

Gantt chart   A project management tool that uses a horizontal bar chart to represent project tasks.

Gateway   An interconnection between two networks of different types (typically implemented with a microcomputer).

General controls   *Controls* that apply to the entire MIS activity of an organization (contrasted with *application controls*).

Geographic information systems (GIS)   Systems for gathering and managing geographic and spatial data, generally represented with maps.

Graphical user interface (GUI)   A user interface that relies on windows, cursor-control devices (for example, a mouse), icons, and menus instead of verbal commands.

Group decision support systems (GDSS) Information systems designed to support group communication and decision processes.

Groupware Software that supports communication and collaboration among the members of a workgroup, as well as assists them in coordinating their work.

Hardware Physical components of computer systems.

Hierarchical DBMS A database management system that organizes databases into treelike hierarchical structures. Notable example: IBM's IMS.

High-level language A programming language that permits the programmer to state the procedure for obtaining results in problem-oriented terms and in a much terser way than an *assembly language* does.

Hypermedia An extension of *hypertext* in which interlinked nodes of information may include such media as graphics, audio messages, video images, and others along with text.

Hypertext A form of electronic document in which nodes with textual information are interconnected by meaningful links to allow nonsequential access to the text.

Image scanner A device for digitizing and entering images, such as figures, photographs, or signed documents, into computer memory.

Implementation For an information system, the process of preparing people in the organization for a new system and introducing the system into the organization.

Indexed-sequential file organization Storing file records in their primary-key sequence and supplying indexes that provide for direct access.

Inference engine The component of an expert system which draws conclusions from the facts of the case and from the knowledge base.

Information An increment in knowledge. In MIS, obtained by processing *data* into a form meaningful to the users.

Information center An organizational unit that provides support for end-user computing.

Information resource management (IRM) An organizational approach to information as a resource. Implies organization-wide planning and controlling of information bases (such as databases) and of systems that derive information from them.

Information society An advanced form of industrial society (or a postindustrial society) in which most people active in the economy are employed in handling information.

Infrastructure The structure of facilities and services necessary for the functioning and growth of organizations and economies (for example, transportation or telecommunications networks).

Innovation A company's efforts in introducing new methods of production or service (process innovation) and in bringing new products or services into the marketplace (product innovation).

Intangible benefit A benefit that cannot be measured in financial terms (for example, improved customer service owing to the implementation of an information system).

Interactive system A system offering the possibility of a dialog between user and computer.

Interoperability The ability of computers of various vendors and various capabilities to work together.

Interorganizational information systems Systems whose use is shared by two or more firms.

Interpreter A systems program that translates a source program (written in a *high-level language*) into *machine language* one statement at a time. The statement is executed immediately after its translation. This translation method (in contrast to compilation) is used for interactive languages such as APL or Basic.

Iterative development Developing a software system by producing and refining its initial version, called a prototype.

Key   Generally refers to the *primary key*. A secondary key is a field that classifies file records into categories.

Knowledge-based systems   Artificial intelligence systems which contain a knowledge base about their domain of operation (for example, about granting credit).

Knowledge engineering   In building an expert system, the process of acquiring knowledge about its domain of operation and transferring it into the knowledge base.

Knowledge work   Working with information (abstractions) rather than with concrete things.

Local area network (LAN)   A fast computer network that interconnects computers (usually microcomputers) within a single site, such as a building or a campus.

Machine language   A language of binary instructions directly executable by the central processing unit of a computer.

Mainframe   The computer in the category of largest machines in general use, which can handle large numbers of peripherals and thus support many users and large databases.

Maintenance   The process of modifying an information system to meet new requirements, correct deficiencies, and incorporate new technology.

Management   The process of providing an organizational environment in which individuals work and employ available resources to contribute to the goals of the organization.

Management information system (MIS)   This term has several usages. The most general use of the term: MIS is an organized portfolio of formal systems for obtaining, processing, and delivering information in support of the business operations and management of an organization. An individual information system for a specific application in a firm is also sometimes referred to as an MIS. MIS may also be the name of an organization's department responsible for information services. As a scholarly discipline, MIS investigates the use of information processing technologies in organizations.

Management reporting systems (MRS)   A type of MIS whose main objective is to provide lower and middle management with reports and inquiry capabilities.

Management science   Application of mathematical modeling in managerial decision making.

Manufacturing resource planning (MRP II)   Information systems that convert the forecast demand for a plant's product into a detailed production plan. These systems are designed to interact with the other information systems of a firm.

Master file   A principal file of an application program, whose contents change relatively slowly.

Matrix organization   An organization structure in which two simpler forms of departmentation are combined; for example, in which management is done by functional department and by project.

Mechanistic organization   A centralized organization with rigid division of labor and many standard operating procedures (the opposite of an *organic organization*).

Megabyte   Approximately one million bytes of memory capacity.

Microcomputer   A small computer built around a microprocessor. It is frequently called a personal computer in reference to its most common use, but the category also includes powerful *technical workstations*.

Micrographic document processing   Transferring document image onto microfilm and retrieving documents stored in that form.

Microprocessor   Central processing unit on a single chip.

Minicomputer   A midrange computer whose power and price places it between a microcomputer and a mainframe. Designed for multiple uses, minicomputers are often used as departmental computers.

MIPS   Million of instructions per second—a measure of a computer's speed.

MIS auditing   Evaluation of the effectiveness of information system *controls*.

Model   A symbolic representation of a real-world system developed for a specific purpose (for example, a planning model of an enterprise).

Modem   A device (modulator-demodulator) that converts digital data into an analog signal for transmission over an analog communication medium such as a telephone line.

Module   A short segment of program code designed to be relatively independent of other similar program components.

Multimedia systems   Systems that go beyond the management and display of textual information by incorporating a variety of communications media, such as sound, graphics, computer animation, and motion video.

Multiplexing   Sharing a telecommunications channel over several (perhaps tens of thousands) simultaneous transmissions. A number of multiplexing techniques are available.

Multiprocessor   A computer system with more than one central processing unit, in which the processors share a common main memory.

Multiprogramming   A computer system's capability to run more than one program concurrently. This capability is furnished by an *operating system*.

Multitasking   A computer system's capability to run several tasks on behalf of a user at the same time. This capability is provided by an *operating system*.

Natural language processing   A branch of *artificial intelligence* that attempts to enable computers to "understand" ever larger subsets of natural languages (such as English).

Net present value approach   A common technique of *cost-benefit analysis*.

Network DBMS   A database management system that organizes database records into networks through links which identify the relationships among the records. A notable example is IDMS.

Neural networks   Artificial intelligence systems which learn from a large number of examples how to recognize patterns in data and to perform other tasks similar to those done by expert systems.

Normalization   Methodical simplification of a logical data model.

Object-oriented programming (OOP)   A methodology of system development that aims to decompose a system into interacting components that correspond to real-world objects. A principal goal is to produce reusable code.

Office information systems   Systems designed to support office tasks with information technology.

On-line processing   Processing transactions immediately upon their entry from a workstation (opposite of *batch processing*).

Open systems   Computer systems which permit the software or hardware of any vendor to be employed in them. In systems theory, an open system exchanges resources with its environment (for example, an organization is an open system).

Operating system   Software that controls all the resources of a computer system.

Operational level   In an organization, the lowest level of decision making, at which relatively routine issues are dealt with.

Optical character recognition (OCR)   Scanning of printed or coded (for example, bar-coded) text into computer memory.

Optical disk A secondary storage device relying on laser technology for storing and accessing information. Optical disks offer much higher capacities but lower speeds than magnetic disks.

Organic organization A decentralized organization with flexible division of labor and participative management (the opposite of a *mechanistic organization*).

Organization A formal social unit devoted to the attainment of specific goals. A business organization (firm) employs certain resources to meet its financial objectives. A nonprofit organization employs its resources to furnish a certain benefit (thus, a hospital furnishes health care).

OSI model protocol A standard telecommunications protocol for computer networks established by the International Standards Organization.

Outsourcing Hiring a specialized firm to provide all or a major part of information services for an organization.

Package A generalized program marketed to a certain market segment. The program may be customized to meet more specific needs.

Packet switching A form of telecommunications where the message is divided into a number of short packets of bits, which travel independently through the network and are reassembled at the destination.

Parallel processing In computer hardware design, the use of a large number of processing elements that can cooperate for increased processing speed.

Payoff table In decision making, a table that shows the alternative strategies the decision maker can pursue, as well as the possible events that may take place in the future, together with the expected gains or losses (payoffs) for each such contingency.

PBX See *private branch exchange*.

Peripherals Input and output devices and secondary memories (such as disks).

Personal information management (PIM) software Software that helps knowledge workers track tasks, people, projects and ideas by managing textual information.

PERT/CPM A method of scheduling and tracking project activities.

Pixel An elementary "picture element"—a dot—on a display screen. Graphics are created by selecting and energizing the appropriate pixels.

Plan A specific statement of objectives and of the means required to achieve them.

Planning Setting out measurable objectives for a period of time.

Portable software Software that can be easily moved from one type of computer system to another.

Portfolio approach In reference to the evaluation of prospective information systems, balancing the risks and benefits of the systems across the entire portfolio of all the proposed systems development projects.

Postimplementation audit A formal review of an information system that has recently become operational, conducted to make any modifications necessary for the system's success and to learn from the development process.

Primary key The field (or fields) whose value identifies a record among others in a data file.

Privacy An individual's right to retain certain information about himself or herself without disclosure.

Private branch exchange (PBX) An electronic switchboard that interconnects a firm's telephones and provides connections to the public network.

Processor See *central processing unit*.

Protocol In a computer network, a set of rules followed by the nodes (computers and terminals) to maintain a communication.

Prototyping A systems development technique that relies on the early development of a prototype: a preliminary working version of the system.

Pseudocode A code describing the logic of a program of a module to a human reader. Pseudocode description is further coded in a selected programming language.

Query language A fourth-generation language for retrieving data from databases.

RAM Random access memory, that is, a memory in which any location takes the same amount of time to access. Main memories, made of semiconductor chips, are random access.

Random access See *direct access.*

Random file organization See *direct file organization.*

Real-time system An operating system which can respond to incoming data within a predetermined short time interval.

Record A component of a file or a database which describes a real-world entity. A record consists of related fields.

Relational database A database established and managed with a *relational DBMS.*

Relational DBMS A database management system that represents data files as tables, with relationships among the records established as corresponding attribute values, with no need for links. A notable example is IBM's DB2.

Report generator A fourth-generation langauge for producing reports without detailed specification of the necessary steps.

Requirements specification Detailed specification of what a proposed information system will do; produced during the *systems analysis.*

Responsibility reporting Furnishing managers with reports regarding only the area for which they are responsible.

Reverse engineering In software development and maintenance, development of analysis and design specifications from the program code.

RISC Reduced instruction set computer, a microprocessor whose high speed is primarily due to the fact that its machine language contains relatively few and simple instructions.

ROM Read-only memory, which in microcomputers contains unalterable service routines such as the bootstrapping program that starts the computer running.

Rule-based expert system An expert system in which the knowledge base is specified as a set of rules of this form: IF condition—THEN action (conclusion).

Satellite telecommunications Microwave signal transmission over very long distances, but with significant signal propagation delays; obtained by rebroadcasting the signal by satellites.

Satisficing In decision making, choosing the first alternative that moves towards the goal, rather than choosing an optimal alternative (optimizing).

Scenario analysis A forecasting technique used in planning, based on developing and analyzing a range of plausible future contingencies.

Secondary memory Known also as secondary storage, this category comprises devices for long-term storage of large volumes of programs and data. Includes devices for on-line storage, such as magnetic disks, and for archival storage, such as magnetic tapes.

Security In information systems, measures taken to prevent threats to these systems (such as unauthorized access or theft) and to detect and correct the effects of damage should it take place.

Sequential access Accessing records in a data file in the order these records are stored in (contrasted with *direct access*).

Sequential file organization Storing file records in the sequence of their primary key values.

Server In a distributed system, a computer that manages a resource (for example, a disk with databases or a printer) on behalf of other computers (called clients).

Sociotechnical design Designing information systems in a manner that satisfies both the technological requirements of the organization and the needs of the people who will be affected by the system.

Software Computer programs (contrasted with *hardware*).

Span of control See *span of management*.

Span of management The number of subordinates directly reporting to a particular manager.

Speech recognition An area of artificial intelligence in which the ultimate goal is the computer's ability to "understand" connected speech by any speaker.

Sponsor A high-level supporter of the effort to assimilate a new technology in an organization.

Spreadsheet software Personal productivity software which enables the user to manipulate data that can be represented in rows and columns.

SQL Pronounced "sequel"; a language for defining and managing relational databases.

Stakeholder A person or an entity with a stake in the performance of an organization or in the outcome of a decision.

Steering committee A policy-making unit, consisting of high-level managers representing the major subunits of a firm, whose mission is to steer the allocation of resources in the MIS area.

Strategic business unit (SBU) A subdivision of a large company pursuing a distinct line of business and treated as an independent business.

Strategic cube A framework for a company's pursuit of strategic competitive advantage that combines competitive strategies and tactics and the competitive forces the company needs to counteract.

Strategic information system An information system designed to give the owner organization a strategic competitive advantage.

Strategic level In regard to an organization and its functions (such as planning), the highest level of decision making, dealing with broad and long-term issues and objectives.

Structured decision A repetitive decision that can be represented by a computer algorithm and thus easily handled by a software application.

Structured systems development Systems development that relies on specific tools for handling complexity during systems analysis, systems design, and programming. We thus speak of structured analysis, structured design, and structured programming.

Suboptimal In an organization, the performance of a unit that meets its own objectives optimally, but does not serve the overall objectives of the organization well.

Supercomputer A computer in the category of the most powerful computers available, based on parallel processing on one or more levels of its design.

System A set of components that operate together as a whole to achieve a common objective (or multiple objectives).

System chart A graphic tool for representing the sources of input, major processing steps, data storage, and outputs of an information system.

Systems analysis The initial task in the systems development process, in which the objective is to establish what the system will do (as opposed to how it will do it).

Systems analyst An MIS professional who analyzes the users' information requirements and often designs systems based on these requirements.

Systems design The task of producing the blueprint of an information system to satisfy the requirements established during systems analysis. This includes the specification of hardware, software, database, user interfaces, and procedures for system use.

Systems development life cycle (SDLC) A systems development process consisting of well-defined stages during which systems analysis, systems design, programming, and installation of the system are accomplished.

Systems integrator A firm that develops information systems for client organizations.

Systems software Programs that manage computer systems and facilitate the programming process. These programs are independent of an application area and are thus contrasted with *applications software*.

Tactical level In regard to an organization and its functions (such as planning), the middle level of decision making, dealing with medium-range issues and objectives intended to support the *strategic-level* decisions.

Technical workstation A fast microcomputer with extensive graphics capabilities, often used in design and engineering applications.

Technology push The influence of the availability of new technologies on organizational innovation; generally considered weaker than *demand pull*.

Telecommunications Electronic transmission of information over distances.

Telecommuting Using computer and telecommunications technology to work at sites remote from the workplace (such as home) and thus avoiding commuting to work.

Teleconferencing A variety of technologies that enable people at remote locations to hold meetings during which they may communicate by voice, text, or images.

Time-sharing system A multiprogramming system which enables multiple users to work concurrently at their terminals.

Topology of a computer network The arrangement of computers and terminals (collectively called nodes) in a network.

Transaction An elementary activity conducted during business operations (for example, the sale of an item or an airline reservation).

Transaction processing system (TPS) An information system which supports the operations of an enterprise by processing data reflecting business transactions.

Transborder data flow The flow of data across national borders; this flow is restricted by a number of countries.

UNIX A multiuser operating system available on a great variety of hardware platforms, with a variety of tools for software development.

Unstructured decision A nonroutine decision which requires human judgment, meaning that only a part of the decision-making process can be apportioned to a software application.

Uploading Transferring data from a personal workstation to a shared mainframe or minicomputer system (opposite of *downloading* and generally restricted in organizations).

User interface The means by which a user interacts with the computer system.

Utilities Service programs for general use, such as programs that sort and merge data files, or text editors.

Validation In software development, ensuring that the system will satisfy user requirements by answering the question: "Are we building the right system?" (contrasted with *verification*).

Value-added network (VAN) A network that offers services over and above those furnished by common carriers.

Value chain The chain of activities through which a firm adds value to its input materials.

Variance In control, a difference between the planned results and those actually achieved.

VDT   See *video display terminal.*

Verification   In software development, ensuring that the system is being built correctly by answering the question "Are we building the system right?" (contrasted with *validation*).

Very large-scale integration (VLSI) Technologies that make it possible to produce chips (VLSI circuits) with very densely packed electronic components; at present, millions of transistors may be placed on a single chip.

Video display terminal   A terminal in which information is displayed to the user on a televisionlike screen and presented to the computer through a keyboard.

Videotex   Information, entertainment, and other services (such as shopping or banking) delivered via a personal computer or a terminal.

Virtual memory   A technique for managing the main and secondary memories of a computer system so as to expand the apparent (virtual) capacity of the main memory over its physical size.

VLSI   See *very large-scale integration.*

Voice mail   A computer-based system for sending voice messages over the telephone for storage in a digital form in the recipient's electronic mailbox, to be converted back to voice on retrieval.

Walkthrough   A review of a product obtained during systems development (such as requirements specifications or program code) performed by a small group of people.

Wide area network   A network that interconnects computers in a large geographical area.

Word   A fixed-length sequence of bits (for example, 32) manipulated by a computer as a single entity. A word may hold a data item or an instruction.

Workstation   Hardware that permits the user to interact with a computer system; it may be a microcomputer or a terminal connected to a larger computer. See also *technical workstation.*

WORM optical disks   Write-once-read-many-times disks, on which users can store information that cannot be subsequently altered. Used for document storage in office information systems.

CREDITS

ILLUSTRATIONS

CHAPTER 1

Figure 1.7: From Bill Curtis, Herb Krasner, and Neil Iscoe, "A Field Study of the Software Design Process for Large Systems" in *Communications of the ACM*, 31, 11, Nov. 1988, pp. 1268–87. Copyright © 1988 Association for Computing Machinery, Inc., New York. Reprinted by permission; **Figure 1.8:** From Metapraxis, Inc., New York.

CHAPTER 2

Figure 2.1: Reprinted by permission of the publishers from *The Control Revolution: Technological and Economic Origins of the Information Society* by James R. Beniger, Cambridge, Mass.: Harvard University Press, Copyright © 1986 by the President and Fellows of Harvard College.

CHAPTER 3

Figure 3.5: Reprinted by permission of Macmillan Publishing Company from *Decision Support and Expert Systems* by Efraim Turban. Copyright © 1988 by Macmillan Publishing Company; **Figure 3.6:** Reprinted by permission of Macmillan Publishing Company from *Decision Support and Expert Systems* by Efraim Turban. Copyright © 1988 by Macmillan Publishing Company.

CHAPTER 4

Figure 4.5: Source: Citicorp Information Resources, Orlando, Florida.

CHAPTER 5

Figure 5.1: Reprinted with permission of The Free Press, a Division of Macmillan, Inc. from *The Competitive Advantage of Nations* by Michael E. Porter. Copyright © 1990 by Michael E. Porter; **Figure 5.7:** From James F. Cox and Steven J. Clark, "Problems in Implementing and Operating a Manufacturing Resource Planning Information System." Reprinted from *Journal of Management Information Systems*, Vol. 1, No. 1, 1984 by permission of M. E. Sharpe, Inc., Armon, NY.

CHAPTER 6

Figure 6.10: From Tom Badgett and Kathy Spurgeon, "Voice-Processing Applications: Laying the Foundation for the Technology of Tomorrow" in *Digital News*, December 1988, pp. 39T–46T. Copyright © Digital News, Framingham, Massachusetts. Reprinted by permission; **Figure 6.11:** From John Markoff, "New Rival for Personal Computer" in *The New York Times*, January 30, 1990. Copyright © 1990 by The New York Times Company. Reprinted by permission.

CHAPTER 8

Figure 8.3: From Vladimir Zwass, *Introduction to Computer Science*. Copyright © 1981 by Vladimir Zwass. Reprinted by permission of HarperCollins Publishers.

CHAPTER 9

Figure 9.1: Adapted from William W. Cotterman and Kuldup Kumar, "User Cube: A Taxonomy of End Users" in *Communications for the ACM*, 32, 11, Nov. 1989, pp. 1313–20. Copyright © 1989 Association for Computing Machinery, Inc., New York; **Figure 9.3:** From Raymond Panko, *End User Computing: Management, Applications and Technology*. Copyright © 1988 John Wiley & Sons, Inc., New York. Reprinted by permission of John Wiley & Sons, Inc.; **Figure 9.12:** From John G. Burch and Gary Grudnitski, *Information Systems: Theory and Practice*. Copyright © 1989 John Wiley & Sons, Inc., New York. Reprinted by permission of John Wiley & Sons, Inc.; **Figure 9.13:** From Maryann Alavi, R. Ryan Nelson, and Ira R. Weiss, "Strategies for End-User Computing: An Integrative Framework" in *Journal of Management Information Systems*, 4, 3, Winter 1987–88. Copyright © M. E. Sharpe, Inc., Armonk, New York. Reprinted by permission.

CHAPTER 11

Figure 11.1: Adapted with permission from a figure in "The Job(s) of Management" by Thomas A. Mahoney, Thomas H. Jerdee, and Stephen J. Carroll, *Industrial Relations*, 4(2) (1965):97–110; **Figure 11.7:** From Barry E. Cushing and Marshall B. Romney, *Accounting Information Systems and Business Organization*, 4th ed. Copyright © 1987 Addison-Wesley Publishing Co., Inc. Reprinted by permission of Addison-Wesley Publishing Co., Inc., Reading, MA; **Figure 11.10:** Copyright © Channel Computing, Inc., Newmarket, NH, USA. Reprinted by permission.

CHAPTER 12

Figure 12.1: Reprinted by permission of Macmillan Publishing Company from *Management Information Systems* by Kenneth C. Laudon and Jane Price Laudon. Copyright © 1988 by Macmillan Publishing Company; **Figure 12.2:** Adapted with permission from John H. Schermerhorn, Jr., *Management For Productivity*, 2d ed. Copyright 1986 John Wiley & Sons, Inc., New York; **Figure 12.10:** From Clinton Wilder and Nell Margolis, "Information on a Global Scale" in *Computerworld*, May 23, 1988. Copyright © 1988 by CW Publishing, Inc., Framingham, MA 01701. Reprinted by permission.

CHAPTER 13

Figure 13.1: Figure from *The Nature of Managerial Work* by Henry Mintzberg. Copyright © 1973 by Henry Mintzberg. Reprinted by permission of HarperCollins Publishers; **Figure 13.7:** From Tom Gibb, *Software Metrics*. Copyright © 1977 Winthrop Publishers, Cambridge, Massachusetts; **Figure 13.9:** From Nunamaker, Jr., Weber, and Chen in *Journal of Management Information Systems*, 5, 4, Spring 1989. Copyright © M. E. Sharpe, Inc., Armonk, New York. Reprinted by permission; **Figure 13.10:** From Nunamaker, Jr., Weber, and Chen in *Journal of Management Information Systems*, 5, 4, Spring 1989. Copyright © M. E. Sharpe, Inc., Armonk, New York. Reprinted by permission.

CHAPTER 14

Figure 14.5 From Steven L. Alter, *Decision Support Systems: Current Practice and Continuing Challenges*. Copyright © 1979 Addison-Wesley Publishing Co., Inc. Reprinted by permission of Addison-Wesley Publishing Co., Inc., Reading, MA.

CHAPTER 16

Figure 16.6: From Kum-Yew Lai, Thomas W. Malone, and Keh-Chang Yu, "Object Lens: A 'Spreadsheet' for Cooperative Work" in *ACM Transactions on Office Information Systems,* 6, 4, October 1988. Copyright © 1988 Association for Computing Machinery, Inc. By permission; **Figure 16.10:** Reprinted from *Journal of Management Information Systems,* Vol. 6, No. 3, 1989–90, pp. 25–43, by permission of M. E. Sharpe, Inc., Armonk, New York; **Figure 16.12:** Source: BNN Systems and Technologies Corporation, Cambridge, Massachusetts; **Figure 16.15:** From Ronald P. Uhlig, David Farber, and James H. Bair, *Office of the Future.* Copyright © Elsevier Science Publishers, B.V., Amsterdam. Reprinted by permission; **Figure IV.1:** From Dennis O'Connor and Virginia Barker, "Expert Systems for Configuration at Digital: XCON and Beyond" in *Communications of the ACM,* 32.3, 1989. Copyright © 1989 Association of Computing Machinery, New York. Reprinted with permission; **Figure IV.2:** From Dennis O'Connor and Virginia Barker, "Expert Systems for Configuration at Digital: XCON and Beyond" in *Communications of the ACM,* 32.3, 1989. Copyright © 1989 Association of Computing Machinery, New York. Reprinted by permission; **Figure IV.3:** From Dennis O'Connor and Virginia Barker, "Expert Systems for Configuration at Digital: XCON and Beyond" in *Communications of the ACM,* 32:3, 1989.

CHAPTER 17

Figure 17.5: Source: Christine V. Bullen and John F. Rockart, "A Primer on Critical Success Factors" in *CISR Working Paper No. 69,* Sloan School of Management, MIT, Cambridge, Massachusetts, and Michael E. Shank, Andrew C. Boyd, and Robert W. Zmud, "Critical Success Factor Analysis as a Methodology for MIS Planning" in *MIS Quarterly,* 9, 2, June 1985, pp. 121–130.

CHAPTER 18

Figure 18.7: From *Information Systems in Organizations* by Robert W. Zmud. Copyright © 1983 by Scott, Foresman and Company. Reprinted by permission of HarperCollins Publishers; **Figure 18.9:** From J. M. Carey and J. C. Currey, "The Prototyping Conundrum" in *Datamation,* June 1, 1989. Copyright © 1989 Datamation Magazine. Reprinted by permission.

CHAPTER 19

Figure 19.24: Source: Applitech Software, Cambridge, Massachusetts.

CHAPTER 20

Figure 20.8: From Ron Weber, *EDP Auditing: Conceptual Foundations and Practice,* 2E. Copyright © 1988 McGraw-Hill, Inc., New York. Reprinted by permission.

COLOR PLATES

Plate 1a–c: IBM Corporation; **Plate 3:** Frog Design, Inc.; **Plate 4:** Steven Feiner, Assistant Professor, Dept. of Computer Science, Columbia University, NY; **Plate 5:** CSX Corporation; **Plate 6:** © Jeff Zaruba/The Stock Market; **Plate 7:** Sattelite Transmission Systems, Inc.; **Plate 8:** Volkswagon Corporation; **Plate 9:** AT & T Archives; **Plate 10:** Lotus Development Corporation; **Plate 11a:** Source InfoWorld, January 22, 1990; **Plate 11b–c:** Quattro Pro.; **Plate 13:** Mapinfo Corporation; **Plate 14:** Courtesy of Allen Bradley Co.; **Plate 15:** Pilot EIS; **Plate 16:** Comshare, Inc.; **Plate 17:** Chedd/J. F. Nonamaker, Jr.; **Plate 18 a–c:** © Layne Kennedy; **Plate 19:** Index Technology Corporation

PHOTOS

CHAPTER 1

Page 30: Metapraxis, Inc.

CHAPTER 2

Page 42 Middle: Aetna Life Company; **p. 42 Top:** Grid Systems Corporation; **p. 42 Bottom:** © James L. Shaffer; **p. 43 Top:** Fred R. Conrad/NYT Pictures; **p. 43 Middle:** © Derek Berwin/Image

Bank; **p. 43 Bottom:** © Simon Fraser/Welwyn Microcircuts/Science Photo Library; **p. 44 Top:** © George Haling/Photo Researchers, Inc; **p. 44 Middle:** General Motors Corp./Cadillac Motor Car Division; **p. 44 Bottom:** Karp Associates, Inc.; **p. 45 Bottom:** Courtesy of Easel Corporation; **p. 45 Top:** © Gregory Heisler; **p. 45 Middle:** Pilot Executive Software

CHAPTER 6

Page 196: Courtesy of Hitachi; **p. 199 Top:** Bettmann Archives; **p. 199 Bottom:** Texas Instruments, Inc.; **p. 204:** Eastman-Kodak; **p. 206:** Bull HN Information Systems, Inc.; **p. 214:** © Ray Ellis/Photo Researchers, Inc.; **p. 216:** Printed W/Permission of Digital Equipment Corporation, 1991; **p. 217:** Panasonic Corporation; **p. 219:** Regent Peripherals; **p. 220:** Videx, Inc.; **p. 222 Top:** Intervoice, Inc.; **p. 222 Bottom:** Grid Systems Corporation; **p. 223:** Princeton Graphic Systems

CHAPTER 7

Page 254: O'Neill Communications, Inc.; **p. 264:** Novell, Inc.; **p. 270:** Meridian Data, Inc.

CHAPTER 14

Page 531: Barbara Fedder/NYT Pictures

CHAPTER 16

Page 618: Sigma Imaging Systems, Inc.; **p. 621:** Honeywell Bull, Inc.; **p. 622:** Xerox Corporation; **p. 632:** NEC America, Inc.; **p. 642:** © James L. Shaffer

CHAPTER 17

Page 676: Printed with Permission of Digital Equipment Corp., 1991; **p. 677:** © David Powers

CHAPTER 20

Page 820: IBM Corporation; **p. 835:** William E. Sauro/NYT Pictures